THE NEW
AMERICAN
COMMENTARY

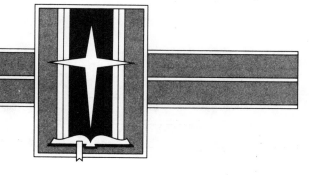

General Editor
E. RAY CLENDENEN

Associate General Editor, OT
KENNETH A. MATHEWS

Associate General Editor, NT
DAVID S. DOCKERY

Consulting Editors

Old Testament
L. RUSS BUSH
DUANE A. GARRETT
LARRY L. WALKER

New Testament
RICHARD R. MELICK, JR.
PAIGE PATTERSON
CURTIS VAUGHAN

Production Editor
LINDA L. SCOTT

THE NEW AMERICAN COMMENTARY

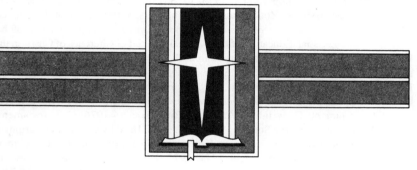

Volume
6

JUDGES, RUTH

Daniel I. Block

BROADMAN
&HOLMAN
PUBLISHERS

Nashville, Tennessee

© 1999 • Broadman & Holman Publishers
All rights reserved
ISBN 0–8054–0106–7
Dewey Decimal Classification: 222.30
Subject Heading: BIBLE. O.T. JUDGES
Library of Congress Catalog Number: 99–11089
Printed in the United States of America
02 01 00 99   4 3 2 1

Library of Congress Cataloging-in-Publication Data

Block, Daniel Isaac, 1943–
    Judges, Ruth / Daniel I. Block.
        p.   cm. — (The new American commentary ; v. 6)
    Includes bibliographical references and indexes.
    ISBN 0–8054–0106–7 (hardcover)
    1. Bible. O.T.   Judges—Criticism, interpretation, etc.   2. Bible. O.T.
Ruth—Criticism, interpretation, etc.   I. Bible. O.T.   Judges. English.
New International. 1999. II. Bible. O.T. Ruth. English.
New International. 1999.   III. Title.   IV. Series.
BS1305.2.B56   1999
222'.3077—dc21

Maps on pages 20 and 766–67 are from the *Holman Bible Atlas,* © 1999 Holman Bible Publishers, Nashville, Tennessee.

To my children,
Jason and Carolyn
and
Jonelle and Douglas

May you be richly blessed
by the LORD
and may you find refuge under his wings
Ruth 2:12

Author Preface

The books of Judges and Ruth present two drastically different pictures of the Israelite people at the end of the second millennium B.C. On the one hand, the book of Judges declares that if God's people ever forget the grace that he has lavished on them in redemption, covenant relationship, and the revelation of his will, the slide into apostasy is inevitable. Flush from the incredible victories over the Canaanites they had won under the leadership of Joshua, the individual tribes should have made quick work of those who remained in the land allotted to the respective tribes. But how different was the reality from the dream! Unable or unwilling to keep the memory of God's grace alive, by the time we reach the end of the book the Israelites about whom we read are scarcely distinguishable from the Canaanites whom they were to replace. The amazing fact is that Israel survives this dark period—but not because of any merit of their own. As I read this book, I am impressed that God is always far more interested in preserving his people—Israel under the old covenant, the church under the new—than his people are in preserving themselves. Repeatedly in the book, by sheer mercy God rescues his people from the dismal fates they, by their own faithlessness and misconduct, have brought upon themselves. The book of Judges teaches its readers in every age that the darker the human heart the more brilliant the light of God's grace.

But then there is the book of Ruth. I am grateful to those who were responsible for arranging the biblical books in the canon we use in the church. By placing this delightful little tractate after the depressing accounts of the judges and their compatriots, we are reminded that God's kingdom is built not by might but by his Spirit. Furthermore, we are instructed that the LORD's work is accomplished not so much by powerful and charismatic leaders but by ordinary people, who in their daily affairs display the transforming work of the Spirit of God—people who not only genuinely seek refuge under the wings of God but who view themselves as his wings where others might find shelter and care. The characters in this book inspire the readers to rejoice in the *hesed* (grace, mercy, kindness, love, faithfulness, etc., all rolled into one beautiful Hebrew word) they experience from God and to embody that same *hesed* in their family and community relationships.

These two commentaries were written that God's people today might, on the one hand, be convicted of the extent to which we have been squeezed into the mold of the world (Rom 12:1, Phillips) and, on the other hand, be inspired to live as salt and light in this dark world (Matt 5:3–16). My commentaries here are less technical than my previous work on Ezekiel, but the questions I ask of the authors of Judges and Ruth are the same: (1) What are you saying? (the text critical issue); (2) Why do you say it like that? (the cultural and literary issues); (3) What do you mean? (the hermeneutical and theological issues); and (4) What is the significance of this message for me today? (the practical issue). While I have been wrestling with these issues, I have also tried to anticipate questions that modern readers actually ask of the text. For all these reasons the reader will find considerable variation in the flow, level, and clarity of my comments. In some passages (most of Ruth, for example), the meaning and significance of the text are fairly near the surface. Others, like Judges 5, are among the most difficult in the Bible. I recognize that my interpretation of the book as a whole and my perception of many, if not most, of the characters in the book runs against the grain of popular perceptions. All I ask of readers is that they check my interpretations against the evidence of the Scriptures themselves rather than against traditions that may be ancient, but may also be misled. As evangelicals we affirm the Scriptures as our only authority in all matters relating to faith and practice. My desire and prayer is that having listened to me speak (via the printed page), all who read the books of Judges and Ruth will discover the relevance and power of God's ancient Word in their own lives. Commentaries are never the final word. And commentaries, the works of sinful mortals, must never replace the pure and living word of God. If our work does not drive our readers back to the biblical texts, we have failed.

This project could not have been completed without the pressure and encouragement of a host of people. The book of Judges had been a special passion of mine for some time when I received the invitation from David Dockery almost a decade ago to participate in the production of a new commentary series for the Southern Baptist Convention. In the meantime the LORD has led us to Kentucky, where we have found a wide open door for our ministry and great encouragement for our work. I owe a special debt of gratitude to Dr. R. Albert Mohler and The Southern Baptist Theological Seminary for providing a joyful and stimulating context in which to pursue my research. I am especially grateful for a one-half year Sabbatical leave I was granted in 1998 so I might complete this project. I also thank my graduate assistants, Kenneth Turner and Michael Roy, not only for their specific help on this project, but especially for taking care of so many other tasks, freeing me to devote my attention to this commentary.

I am especially appreciative of the invaluable aid E. Ray Clendenen and the rest of the editors involved in this series have lent me. With their careful and critical reading they have sharpened my pencil and spared me many an embarrassment. In this context I must also express my thanks to my seminary students at Bethel in St. Paul, Minnesota, here at Southern in Louisville, and in Harrisburg, Pennsylvania, and the students at Providence College in Otterburne, Manitoba, for enduring and responding to the perspectives and interpretations offered here. They, and the churches where I have preached and taught from these books, have provided necessary reminders that in this series we write for the church, more than for the academy.

But special thanks are extended to those closest to me. My wife Ellen has provided daily unwavering support throughout my teaching career. Never has this been more needed than in the past few years as we have wrestled with this project. The publication of this volume also affords me the opportunity to thank my children publicly for the special treasure they are to me. In appreciation for the joy they bring to my life, this book is dedicated to my son Jason, and his wife Carolyn, and my daughter Jonelle, and her husband Douglas. My prayer is that as long as they live they will seek and find refuge under the wings of the LORD and offer themselves as the LORD's wings to those in need.

Above all we bless the LORD, who has not stopped lavishing his *hesed* on us. We offer this commentary to him as our sacrifice of praise. May our work be instructive and inspirational for all who read it, and may it bring glory to God, who through Boaz and Ruth has provided for us a "savior" and "redeemer" in Jesus Christ.

Louisville, Kentucky
May 22, 1999

Editors' Preface

God's Word does not change. God's world, however, changes in every generation. These changes, in addition to new findings by scholars and a new variety of challenges to the gospel message, call for the church in each generation to interpret and apply God's Word for God's people. Thus, THE NEW AMERICAN COMMENTARY is introduced to bridge the twentieth and twenty-first centuries. This new series has been designed primarily to enable pastors, teachers, and students to read the Bible with clarity and proclaim it with power.

In one sense THE NEW AMERICAN COMMENTARY is not new, for it represents the continuation of a heritage rich in biblical and theological exposition. The title of this forty-volume set points to the continuity of this series with an important commentary project published at the end of the nineteenth century called AN AMERICAN COMMENTARY, edited by Alvah Hovey. The older series included, among other significant contributions, the outstanding volume on Matthew by John A. Broadus, from whom the publisher of the new series, Broadman Press, partly derives its name. The former series was authored and edited by scholars committed to the infallibility of Scripture, making it a solid foundation for the present project. In line with this heritage, all NAC authors affirm the divine inspiration, inerrancy, complete truthfulness, and full authority of the Bible. The perspective of the NAC is unapologetically confessional and rooted in the evangelical tradition.

Since a commentary is a fundamental tool for the expositor or teacher who seeks to interpret and apply Scripture in the church or classroom, the NAC focuses on communicating the theological structure and content of each biblical book. The writers seek to illuminate both the historical meaning and contemporary significance of Holy Scripture.

In its attempt to make a unique contribution to the Christian community, the NAC focuses on two concerns. First, the commentary emphasizes how each section of a book fits together so that the reader becomes aware of the theological unity of each book and of Scripture as a whole. The writers, however, remain aware of the Bible's inherently rich variety. Second, the NAC is produced with the conviction that the Bible primarily belongs to the church. We believe that scholarship and the academy provide an indispensable foundation for biblical understanding and the service of Christ, but the editors and authors of this series have attempted to communicate the findings of their research in a manner that will build up the whole body of Christ. Thus, the commentary concentrates on theological exegesis while providing practical, applicable exposition.

THE NEW AMERICAN COMMENTARY's theological focus enables

the reader to see the parts as well as the whole of Scripture. The biblical books vary in content, context, literary type, and style. In addition to this rich variety, the editors and authors recognize that the doctrinal emphasis and use of the biblical books differs in various places, contexts, and cultures among God's people. These factors, as well as other concerns, have led the editors to give freedom to the writers to wrestle with the issues raised by the scholarly community surrounding each book and to determine the appropriate shape and length of the introductory materials. Moreover, each writer has developed the structure of the commentary in a way best suited for expounding the basic structure and the meaning of the biblical books for our day. Generally, discussions relating to contemporary scholarship and technical points of grammar and syntax appear in the footnotes and not in the text of the commentary. This format allows pastors and interested laypersons, scholars and teachers, and serious college and seminary students to profit from the commentary at various levels. This approach has been employed because we believe that all Christians have the privilege and responsibility to read and seek to understand the Bible for themselves.

Consistent with the desire to produce a readable, up-to-date commentary, the editors selected the *New International Version* as the standard translation for the commentary series. The selection was made primarily because of the NIV's faithfulness to the original languages and its beautiful and readable style. The authors, however, have been given the liberty to differ at places from the NIV as they develop their own translations from the Greek and Hebrew texts.

The NAC reflects the vision and leadership of those who provide oversight for Broadman Press, who in 1987 called for a new commentary series that would evidence a commitment to the inerrancy of Scripture and a faithfulness to the classic Christian tradition. While the commentary adopts an "American" name, it should be noted some writers represent countries outside the United States, giving the commentary an international perspective. The diverse group of writers includes scholars, teachers, and administrators from almost twenty different colleges and seminaries, as well as pastors, missionaries, and a layperson.

The editors and writers hope that THE NEW AMERICAN COMMENTARY will be helpful and instructive for pastors and teachers, scholars and students, for men and women in the churches who study and teach God's Word in various settings. We trust that for editors, authors, and readers alike, the commentary will be used to build up the church, encourage obedience, and bring renewal to God's people. Above all, we pray that the NAC will bring glory and honor to our Lord who has graciously redeemed us and faithfully revealed himself to us in his Holy Word.

SOLI DEO GLORIA
The Editors

Contents

Abbreviations

Bible Books

Gen	Isa	Luke
Exod	Jer	John
Lev	Lam	Acts
Num	Ezek	Rom
Deut	Dan	1, 2 Cor
Josh	Hos	Gal
Judg	Joel	Eph
Ruth	Amos	Phil
1, 2 Sam	Obad	Col
1, 2 Kgs	Jonah	1, 2 Thess
1, 2 Chr	Mic	1, 2 Tim
Ezra	Nah	Titus
Neh	Hab	Phlm
Esth	Zeph	Heb
Job	Hag	Jas
Ps (pl. Pss)	Zech	1, 2 Pet
Prov	Mal	1, 2, 3 John
Eccl	Matt	Jude
Song	Mark	Rev

Apocrypha

Add Esth	*The Additions to the Book of Esther*
Bar	*Baruch*
Bel	*Bel and the Dragon*
1,2 Esdr	*1, 2 Esdras*
4 Ezra	*4 Ezra*
Jdt	*Judith*
Ep Jer	*Epistle of Jeremiah*
1,2,3,4 Mac	*1, 2, 3, 4 Maccabees*
Pr Azar	*Prayer of Azariah and the Song of the Three Jews*
Pr Man	*Prayer of Manasseh*
Sir	*Sirach, Ecclesiasticus*
Sus	*Susanna*
Tob	*Tobit*
Wis	*The Wisdom of Solomon*

Commonly Used Sources

AASOR	Annual of the American Schools of Oriental Research
AB	Anchor Bible
ABR	*Australian Biblical Review*
ABD	*Anchor Bible Dictionary,* ed. D. N Freedman
ABW	*Archaeology and the Biblical World*
AC	An American Commentary, ed. A. Hovey
AcOr	*Acta orientalia*
AEL	M. Lichtheim, *Ancient Egyptian Literature*
AHW	W. von Soden, *Akkadisches Handwörterbuch*
AJBI	*Annual of the Japanese Biblical Institute*
AJSL	*American Journal of Semitic Languages and Literature*
Akk.	Akkadian
AnBib	Analecta Biblica
ANET	*Ancient Near Eastern Texts,* ed. J. B. Pritchard
ANETS	*Ancient Near Eastern Texts and Studies*
ANEP	*Ancient Near Eastern Pictures,* ed. J. B. Pritchard
Ant.	*Antiquities*
AOAT	Alter Orient und Altes Testament
AOS	American Oriental Society
AOTS	*Archaeology and Old Testament Study,* ed. D. W. Thomas
ARM	Archives royales de Mari
ArOr	Archiv orientální
AS	Assyriological Studies
ATD	Das Alte Testament Deutsch
ATR	*Anglican Theological Review*
AusBR	*Australian Biblical Review*
AUSS	*Andrews University Seminary Studies*
AV	Authorized Version
BA	*Biblical Archaeologist*
BAGD	W. Bauer, W. F. Arndt, F. W. Gingrich, and F. W. Danker, *Greek-English Lexicon of the New Testament*
BALS	Bible and Literature Series
BARev	*Biblical Archaeology Review*
BASOR	*Bulletin of the American Schools of Oriental Research*
B. Bat	*Baba Batra*
BBR	*Bulletin for Biblical Research*
BDB	F. Brown, S. R. Driver, and C. A. Briggs, *Hebrew and English Lexicon of the Old Testament*
BETL	Bibliotheca ephemeridum theologicarum lovaniensium
BFT	Biblical Foundations in Theology
BHS	*Biblia hebraica stuttgartensia*
Bib	*Biblica*
BibOr	Biblica et orientalia
BibRev	*Bible Review*
BJRL	*Bulletin of the Johns Rylands University Library*
BJS	Brown Judaic Studies
BKAT	Biblischer Kommentar: Altes Testament
BN	*Biblische Notizen*

BO	*Bibliotheca orientalis*
BR	*Biblical Research*
BSac	*Bibliotheca Sacra*
BSC	Bible Student Commentary
BST	Bible Speaks Today
BT	*The Bible Translator*
BurH	*Buried History*
BZ	*Biblische Zeitschrift*
BZAW	Beihefte zur ZAW
CAD	*The Assyrian Dictionary of the Oriental Institute of the University of Chicago*
CAH	*Cambridge Ancient History*
CB	Century Bible
CBSC	Cambridge Bible for Schools and Colleges
CBC	Cambridge Bible Commentary
CBQ	*Catholic Biblical Quarterly*
CBQMS	Catholic Biblical Quarterly Monograph Series
CC	The Communicator's Commentary
CCK	*Chronicles of Chaldean Kings*, D. J. Wiseman
CD	Cairo Damascus Document
CGTC	Cambridge Greek Testament Commentaries
CHAL	*Concise Hebrew and Aramic Lexicon*, ed. W. L. Holladay
Comm.	J. Calvin, *Commentary on the First Book of Moses Called Genesis*, trans., rev. J. King
ConB	Coniectanea biblica
ConBOT	Coniectanea biblica, Old Testament
COT	*Commentary on the Old Testament, C. F. Keil and F. Delitzsch*
CR:BS	*Currents in Research: Biblical Studies*
CSR	*Christian Scholar's Review*
CT	*Christianity Today*
CTM	*Concordia Theological Monthly*
CTR	*Criswell Theological Review*
CurTM	*Currents in Theology and Mission*
DCH	*Dictionary of Classical Hebrew*, ed. D. J. A. Clines
DISO	C.-F. Jean and J. Hoftijzer, *Dictionnaire des inscriptions sémitiques de l'ouest*
DJD	Discoveries in the Judaean Desert
DNWSI	*Dictionary of Northwest Semitic Inscriptions*
DOTT	*Documents from Old Testament Times*, ed. D. W. Thomas
DSS	Dead Sea Scrolls
EAEHL	*Encyclopedia of Archaeological Excavations in the Holy Land*, ed. M. Avi-Yonah
EBC	Expositor's Bible Commentary
Ebib	Etudes bibliques
EDBT	*Evangelical Dictionary of Biblical Theology*, W. A. Elwell, ed.
EE	*Enuma Elish*
EDNT	*Exegetical Dictionary of the New Testament*
EGT	*The Expositor's Greek Testament*

EncJud	*Encyclopaedia Judaica* (1971)
ErIsr	*Eretz Israel*
ETL	*Ephermerides theologicae lovanienses*
EvBC	Everyman's Bible Commentary
EV(s)	English Version(s)
EvQ	*Evangelical Quarterly*
ExpTim	*Expository Times*
FB	Forschung zur Bibel
FOTL	Forms of Old Testament Literature
Gk.	Greek
GBH	P. Joüon, *A Grammar of Biblical Hebrew*, 2 vols., trans. and rev. T. Muraoka
GKC	Gesenius's Hebrew Grammar, ed. E. Kautzsch, trans. A. E. Cowley
GTJ	*Grace Theological Journal*
HAR	*Hebrew Annual Review*
HAT	Handbuch zum Alten Testament
HBD	*Harper's Bible Dictionary,* ed. P. Achtemeier
HBT	*Horizons in Biblical Theology*
HDR	Harvard Dissertations in Religion
Her	Hermeneia
HKAT	Handkommentar zum Alten Testament
HS	*Hebrew Studies*
HSM	Harvard Semitic Monographs
HT	Helps for Translators
HTR	*Harvard Theological Review*
HUCA	*Hebrew Union College Annual*
IB	*Interpreter's Bible*
IBC	International Bible Commentary, ed. F. F. Bruce
IBD	*Illustrated Bible Dictionary,* ed. J. D. Douglas and N. Hillyer
ICC	International Critical Commentary
IBHS	B. K. Waltke and M. O'Connor, *Introduction to Biblical Hebrew Syntax*
IBS	*Irish Biblical Studies*
IDB	*Interpreter's Dictionary of the Bible,* ed. G. A. Buttrick et al.
IDBSup	Supplementary volume to *IDB*
IEJ	*Israel Exploration Journal*
IES	Israel Exploration Society
IJT	*Indian Journal of Theology*
Int	*Interpretation*
INT	Interpretation: A Bible Commentary for Teaching and Preaching
IOS	*Israel Oriental Studies*
ISBE	*International Standard Bible Encyclopedia,* rev. ed., G. W. Bromiley
ITC	International Theological Commentary
ITQ	*Irish Theological Quarterly*
JAAR	*Journal of the American Academy of Religion*
JAARSup	*Journal of the American Academy of Religion,* Supplement

JANES	*Journal of Ancient Near Eastern Society*
JAOS	*Journal of the American Oriental Society*
JBL	*Journal of Biblical Literature*
JBR	*Journal of Bible and Religion*
JCS	*Journal of Cuneiform Studies*
JEA	*Journal of Egyptian Archaeology*
JETS	*Journal of the Evangelical Theological Society*
JJS	*Journal of Jewish Studies*
JNES	*Journal of Near Eastern Studies*
JNSL	*Journal of Northwest Semitic Languages*
JOTT	*Journal of Translation and Textlinguistics*
JPOS	*Journal of Palestine Oriental Society*
JPS	Jewish Publication Society
JPSV	Jewish Publication Society Version
JPST	Jewish Publication Society Torah
JRT	*Journal of Religious Thought*
JSJ	*Journal for the Study of Judaism in the Persian, Hellenistic, and Roman Period*
JSOR	*Journal of the Society for Oriental Research*
JSOT	*Journal for the Study of the Old Testament*
JSOTSup	JSOT—Supplement Series
JSS	*Journal of Semitic Studies*
JTS	*Journal of Theological Studies*
JTSNS	*Journal of Theological Studies, New Series*
JTT	*Journal of Translation and Textlinguistics*
KAT	Kommentar zum Alten Testament
KB	L. Koehler and W. Baumgartner, *Lexicon in Veteris Testamenti libros*
KB^3	L. Koehler and W. Baumgartner, *The Hebrew and Aramaic Lexicon of the Old Testament*, trans. M. E. J. Richardson
KD	*Kerygma und Dogma*
LBBC	Layman's Bible Book Commentary
LBH	Late Biblical Hebrew
LBI	Library of Biblical Interpretation
LCC	Library of Christian Classics
LLAVT	E. Vogt, *Lexicon Linguae Aramaicae Veteris Testamenti*
LSJ	Liddell-Scott-Jones, *Greek-English Lexicon*
LTQ	*Lexington Theological Quarterly*
LW	*Luther's Works. Lecture's on Genesis*, ed. J. Pelikan and D. Poellot, trans. G. Schick
LXX	Septuagint
MT	Masoretic Text
MSS	Manuscripts
NAB	New American Bible
NASB	New American Standard Bible
NAC	New American Commentary, ed. R. Clendenen
NB	*Nebuchadrezzar and Babylon*, D. J. Wiseman
NBD	*New Bible Dictionary*, ed. J. D. Douglas
NCBC	New Century Bible Commentary

NEAEHL	*The New Encyclopedia of Archaeological Excavations in the Holy Land*, ed. E. Stern
NEB	New English Bible
NIB	The New Interpreter's Bible
NICNT	New International Commentary on the New Testament
NICOT	New International Commentary on the Old Testament
NIDOTTE	*The New International Dictionary of Old Testament Theology and Exegesis*, ed. W. A. VanGemeren
NJB	New Jerusalem Bible
NJPS	New Jewish Publication Society Version
NKZ	*Neue kirchliche Zeitschrift*
NovT	*Novum Testamentum*
NRSV	New Revised Standard Version
NRT	*La nouvelle revue the'ologique*
NTS	*New Testament Studies*
NTT	Norsk Teologisk Tidsskrift
OBO	Orbis biblicus et orientalis
OL	Old Latin
Or	*Orientalia*
OTL	Old Testament Library
OTP	*The Old Testament Pseudepigrapha*, ed. J. H. Charlesworth
OTS	*Oudtestamentische Studiën*
OTWSA	*Ou-Testamentiese Werkgemeenskap in Suid-Afrika*
PCB	*Peake's Commentary on the Bible*, ed. M. Black and H. H. Rowley
PEQ	*Palestine Exploration Quarterly*
POTT	*Peoples of Old Testament Times*, ed. D. J. Wiseman
POTW	Peoples of the Old Testament World, ed. A. E. Hoerth, G. L. Mattingly, and E. M. Yamauchi
PTMS	Pittsburgh Theological Monograph Series
PTR	*Princeton Theological Review*
RA	*Revue d'assyriologie et d'archéologie orientale*
RB	*Revue biblique*
REB	Revised English Bible
ResQ	*Restoration Quarterly*
RevExp	*Review and Expositor*
RHPR	*Revue d'histoire et de philosophie religieuses*
RSR	Recherches de science religieuse
RTR	*Reformed Theological Review*
SANE	Sources from the Ancient Near East
SBH	Standard Biblical Hebrew
SBJT	*Southern Baptist Journal of Theology*
SBLDS	Society of Biblical Literature Dissertation Series
SBLMS	Society of Biblical Literature Monograph Series
SBLSP	Society of Biblical Literature Seminar Papers
SBT	Studies in Biblical Theology
SHCANE	Studies in the History and Culture of the Ancient Near East
SJT	*Scottish Journal of Theology*
SJOT	*Scandinavian Journal of the Old Testament*
SJLA	Studies in Judaism in Late Antiquity

SLJA	*Saint Luke's Journal of Theology*
SOTI	*A Survey of Old Testament Introduction*, G. L. Archer
SP	Samaritan Pentateuch
SR	Studies in Religion/Sciences religieuses
SSI	*Syrian Semitic Inscriptions*
ST	*Studia theologica*
STJD	Studies on the Texts of the Desert of Judah
Syr.	Syriac
TBT	*The Bible Today*
TD	*Theology Digest*
TDNT	*Theological Dictionary of the New Testament,* ed. G. Kittel and G. Friedrich
TDOT	*Theological Dictionary of the Old Testament,* ed. G. J. Botterweck and H. Ringgren
Tg(s).	Targum(s)
TJNS	Trinity Journal—New Series
TLOT	*Theological Lexicon of the Old Testament,* ed. E. Jenni and C. Westermann
TLZ	*Theologische Literaturzeitung*
TNTC	Tyndale New Testament Commentaries
TOTC	Tyndale Old Testament Commentaries
TrinJ	*Trinity Journal*
TS	*Theological Studies*
TToday	*Theology Today*
Tur	*Traditionsgeshichtliche Untersuchungen aum Richterbuch*
TWAT	*Theologisches Wörterbuch zum Alten Testament,* ed. G. J. Botterweck and H. Ringgren
TWOT	*Theological Wordbook of the Old Testament*
TynBul	*Tyndale Bulletin*
UF	*Ugarit-Forschungen*
Ug.	Ugaritic
UT	C. H. Gordon, *Ugaritic Textbook*
Vg	Vulgate
VT	*Vetus Testamentum*
VTSup	Vetus Testamentum, Supplements
WBC	Word Biblical Commentaries
WEC	Wycliffe Exegetical Commentary
WHJP	*World History of the Jewish People,* ed. B. Mazer
WO	*Die Welt des Orients*
WTJ	*Westminster Theological Journal*
WMANT	Wissenschaftliche Monographien zum Alten und Neuen Testament
ZAW	*Zeitschrift für die alttestamentliche Wissenschaft*
ZDMG	*Zeitschrift der deutschen morgenländischen Gesellschaft*
ZDPV	*Zeitschrift des deutschen Palästina-Vereins*
ZPEB	*Zondervan Pictorial Encyclopedia of the Bible*
ZTK	*Zeitschrift für katholische Theologie*

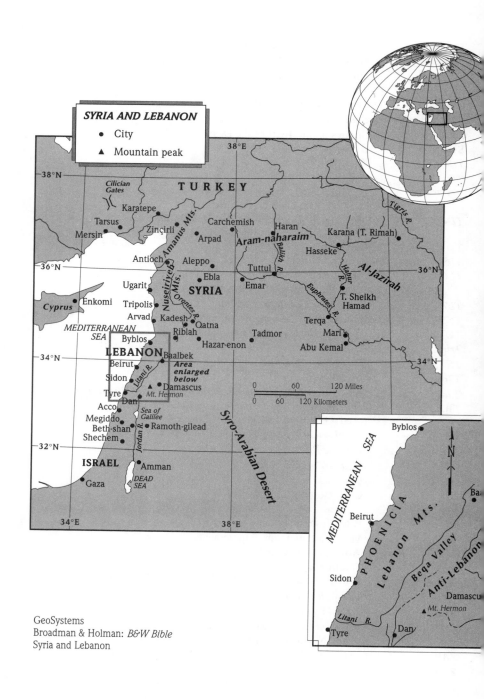

SYRIA AND LEBANON

- City
- ▲ Mountain peak

38°E

38°N

Cilician Gates

TURKEY

Karatepe

Tarsus
Mersin
Zinçirli
Carchemish
Haran
Karana (T. Rimah)

Arpad
Aram-naharaim
Hasseke

Antioch
Aleppo
Tuttul
36°N

36°N

Ebla
Emar
Al-Jazirah

Ugarit
SYRIA

Enkomi
Tripolis
T. Sheikh Hamad

Cyprus
Arvad
Kadesh
Qatna
Terqa
Mari

MEDITERRANEAN SEA
Riblah
Tadmor
Abu Kemal

Byblos
Hazar-enon

34°N

LEBANON Baalbek

Beirut
Area enlarged below

Sidon
Damascus

Tyre
Mt. Hermon

Acco

0   60   120 Miles

Megiddo
Sea of Galilee
0   60   120 Kilometers

Beth-shan
Ramoth-gilead

Shechem

32°N

ISRAEL
Amman

Gaza
DEAD SEA

Syro-Arabian Desert

34°E

38°E

MEDITERRANEAN SEA

Byblos

N

Beirut

PHOENICIA

Lebanon Mts.

Ba

Sidon

Beqa Valley

Anti-Lebanon

Damascu

Mt. Hermon

Litani R.

Tyre
Dan

GeoSystems
Broadman & Holman: *B&W Bible*
Syria and Lebanon

Judges

─────────────── **INTRODUCTION** ───────────────

1. The Title of the Book

The English name for the Book of Judges derives from the Vulgate, which called this biblical composition *Liber Iudicum.* Like *kritai,* the name of the book in the Septuagint (LXX), these designations represent literal translations of the Hebrew name *Šōpĕtîm,* traditionally rendered "judges." In contrast to the Pentateuchal books, which derive their titles from the opening words of the respective books, this title has its origin in the activity of some of the major characters in the book. However, this translation is somewhat misleading for several reasons.

First, none of the individuals we think of as "judges" is specifically identified as a *šōpēṭ*, usually translated as "judge." Indeed the title "the Judge" is only used of a specific individual once, in Jephthah's speech before the Ammonite delegation (11:27), where it applies not to Jephthah but to Yahweh.[1] Before these foreigners, the Israelite leader presents the God of Israel as a universal divine judge who settles disputes between nations (cf. Gen 18:25). The term "judge/judges" *(šōpēṭ/šōpĕṭîm)* is used as a general designation for the leaders of Israel in 2:16–19, from which we may infer that the leaders described in the book may be so designated. The verb *šāpaṭ*, "to judge" (NIV, "to lead") is used to describe the activity of four of the primary[2] judges (Othniel [3:10], Deborah [4:4], Jephthah [12:7], and Samson [15:20; 16:31]) and five of the secondary judges (Tola [10:2], Jair [10:3], Ibzan [12:8,9], Elon [12:11], and Abdon [12:13,14]). Of those usually considered to be "judges," only Deborah is said to have served in what might be understood as a judicial capacity (4:4–5). But even here it is doubtful the verb should be understood in the common judicial sense.[3] Regardless, this function has little to do with the events that made her famous.

Second, the root *špṭ*, "to judge," does not appear in all the book's major sections. It is not found either in 1:1–2:5 or in 17:21–21:25, which provide the framework for the narratives of the "judges'" activity.

Third, the usage of the root *špṭ* in 1 Samuel suggests the title "Book of Judges" could extend beyond the present book. Chronologically, the story of Samuel, particularly the accounts of his activities prior to the appointment of King Saul (1 Samuel 1–7), fits into this period, and the judicial and soteriological roles he plays suggest the designation "Book of Judges" should extend at least this far.[4] This impression is strengthened by the inclusion of Samuel with

---

[1] Although in 3:10 the NIV says that Othniel "became Israel's judge," this is better rendered, "he judged Israel."

[2] The "secondary" judges are so called because they play no active role in the primary narrative. On the designation "primary" and "secondary" judges versus the traditional "major" and "minor" judges see below.

[3] Cp. the similar role of Samuel in 1 Sam 7:15–16. On the questions concerning Deborah's judicial role see comments on that passage as well as D. I. Block, "Deborah among the Judges: The Perspective of the Hebrew Historian," in *Faith, Tradition, and History: Old Testament Historiography in Its Near Eastern Context,* A. R. Millard, et al., eds. (Winona Lake: Eisenbrauns, 1994), 229–53.

[4] This is even more so if Joshua–2 Kings is treated as a literary unit, the Deuteronomistic History (hereafter DH). In his discussion of the Deuteronomist's writing on the period of the judges, M. Noth includes 1 Samuel 1–12 with the Book of Judges. See *The Deuteronomistic History,* trans. D. Orton, JSOTSup 15 (Sheffield: JSOT Press, 1981), 43–52.

Jerubbaal (Gideon), Bedan (Barak), and Jephthah in 1 Sam 12:11 and the narrator's formulaic conclusion to the Eli narrative (1 Sam 4:18), "Thus he judged Israel forty years."

Fourth, the "judges" functioned more as deliverers than as legal functionaries. The problem of the name "judges" surfaces in 2:16–19, the only place in the book where the noun is applied to leaders of the nation. Here the author offers his own definition of the "judges'" role: "Then the LORD raised up judges, who saved [a form of the verb *yāšaᶜ*] them out of the hands of these raiders." This statement announces three important facts. (1) The source of the judges' authority and power was Yahweh.[5] (2) The purpose of their appointment was not judicial but soteriological. Accordingly, the use of the verb *yāšaᶜ* suggests that the main body of the book, if not the book as a whole, should be called the "Book of Saviors/Deliverers."[6] Indeed the designation *môšîaᶜ*, "deliverer, liberator," is specifically applied to several judges,[7] though elsewhere Yahweh is also presented as the deliverer.[8] (3) These individuals were instruments of deliverance from external enemies;[9] their purpose was not the settlement of internal disputes.

In light of this evidence, our English term "judge" obviously fails to capture the nature of the activity and role of Israel's leaders in the Book of Judges. How then can they be called *šōpĕṭîm*, which derives from the verb *šāpaṭ*, usually adequately represented by "to judge"? The problem is best answered by recognizing that the Hebrew root *špṭ* bears a broader sense than simply the notion of acting judicially. In contrast to the semantic cognate *dîn*, which always carries the judicial sense, "to judge," the root *šāpaṭ* means "to govern, administer, exercise leadership,"[10] and its derived usage may be diagrammed as follows:

---

[5] Cf. the use of the verb קוּם (*hiphil*) in 3:9,15. The process of raising a deliverer is described in detail in 4:6–9 (Barak); 6:1–40 (Gideon); 11:1–40 (Jephthah, though the process is presented as an essentially human process; cf. 11:29); 13:1–25 (Samson).

[6] Cf. W. Richter, *Die Bearbeitungen des "Retterbuches" in der deuteronomischen Epoche*, BBB 21 (Bonn: P. Hanstein, 1964).

[7] Othniel (3:9), Ehud (3:15). Cf. the use of the verb יָשַׁע, "to save, rescue" (*hiphil*), of the action of Shamgar (3:31), Gideon (6:15; 8:22), Tola (10:1), Jephthah (12:3), and Samson (13:5).

[8] 3:9; 6:36,37; 7:7; 10:13. On the use of מוֹשִׁיעַ and שֹׁפֵט in Judges see W. Beyerlin ("Gattung und Herkunft des Rahmens im Richterbuch," in *Tradition und Situation: Studien zur alttestamentlichen Prophetie, Festschrift A. Weiser*, ed. E. Würthwein and O. Kaiser [Göttingen: Vandenhoeck & Ruprecht, 1963], 6–7). Beyerlin argues that the term מוֹשִׁיעַ represents the older designation for the charismatic savior figures, and that שֹׁפֵט is secondary, deriving from a later time when a link between the "major" and "minor" was presupposed.

[9] "From the hand of their plunderers" (מִיַּד שֹׁסֵיהֶם) in 2:14; "from the hand of their enemies" (מִיַּד אֹיְבֵיהֶם) in v. 18.

[10] T. L. J. Mafico ("Judge, Judging," *ABD* 3.1104–5) notes that the role of judges was "to restore *shalom*, harmonious relations."

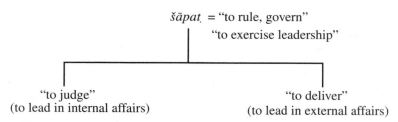

šāpaṭ = "to rule, govern"
"to exercise leadership"

"to judge"
(to lead in internal affairs)

"to deliver"
(to lead in external affairs)

The general, nonjudicial usage found here may also be recognized elsewhere in the Old Testament. Especially telling is 1 Sam 8:5, which occurs in the context of a crisis precipitated by a combination of the Philistine threat and the perversion of Samuel's sons, whom the prophet had appointed to govern Israel (8:1–3). In v. 5 the Israelites explicitly request a king *(melek)* to govern *(šāpaṭ)* them like the nations. Nothing in Samuel's rejoinder suggests a specifically judicial function for this official: (1) Yahweh interprets the request as a rejection of his kingship, not Samuel's judgeship. (2) The expression *mišpaṭ hammelek* in vv. 9–11 has nothing to do with the judicial function of a king.[11] (3) Samuel's warning for the people does not express concern about judicial practice but the exercise of power, the style of government. (4) The people desire a king specifically to lead them in battle and to govern the nation. Accordingly, in v. 5 *šāpaṭ* is best understood as "to govern, to rule as king."[12] This interpretation is supported by the meanings of the cognate expressions in Akkadian,[13] Ugaritic,[14] and Phoenician.[15] When Latin writers deal with the

---

[11] Elsewhere I have argued the expression refers to the oracle of the prophet, given in response to the people's inquiry. See my essay, "Deborah among the Judges," 243.

[12] So also in 2 Kgs 15:5; Isa 40:23 (שֹׁפְטִים//רֹזְנִים), which in Judg 5:3 is paired with מְלָכִים, "kings"; Amos 2:3 (שֹׁפְטִים//שָׂרִים); Pss 2:10 (שֹׁפְטִים//מְלָכִים); 94:2; 96:13; 148:11 (שָׂרִים//מְלָכִים//שֹׁפְטִים).

[13] In the Mari texts *šapāṭum* applied to a judge as well as to a person appointed by the king *(šarrum)* to administer a territory on his behalf. On the root in Akk. see Mafico, "The Term *Šāpiṭum* in Akkadian Documents," *JNSL* 13 (1987): 69–87.

[14] *ṯpṭ*, "to rule," on which see F. C. Fensham, "The Ugaritic Root *ṯpṭ*," *JNSL* 12 (1984): 63–69; H. Cazelles, *"Mṯpṭ a Ugarit,"* *Or* 53 (1984): 177–82; M. Smith, *The Ugaritic Baal Cycle: Introduction with Text, Translation and Commentary of KTU 1.1–1.2*, VTSup 55 (Leiden: Brill, 1994), 1:251–52. Note especially *CTA* 6.6.29:
lyhpk ks mlkk "Surely he will overturn the throne of your kingship;
lyṯbr ḥṭ mṯpṭk "Surely he will break the sceptre of your rule."

[15] Note especially *KAI* 1:2: תחתסף חטר משפטה, "May the sceptre of his rule be torn away; תההפך כסא מלכה, "May the throne of his kingdom be overturned." On this text see J. C. L. Gibson, *Textbook of Syrian Semitic Inscriptions, Vol. III: Phoenician Inscriptions* (Oxford: Clarendon, 1982), 14–16. For further references see R. S. Tomback, *A Comparative Semitic Lexicon of the Phoenician and Punic Languages*, SBLDS 32 (Missoula: Scholars Press, 1974), 329–30. According to the report of S. A. Kaufman to the SBL in November 1997, in the recently discovered but as yet unpublished eighth century B.C. Incirli Trilingual Inscription, *špṭ* identifies the office of the governor of the *dnnym* who were under the overlordship of the Assyrian Tiglath Pileser III.

špṭym, the supreme magistrates in Phoenician and Carthaginian cities, they simply transliterate the term *sūfēs (suffēs)*, plural *sufētis*.[16] Since the judges functioned as princes, rulers, and chieftains over specific territories and clans, the term *šōpĕṭîm* is best understood generally to mean "tribal rulers, leaders, governors" rather than "judges," so the name of the book is better rendered "The Book of Tribal Rulers."[17]

2. Historical and Religious Background to the Book of Judges

(1) The Period of the Judges

The use of phrases like *yĕmê šĕpōṭ haššōpĕṭîm*, "the days when rulers ruled," in the opening line of the Book of Ruth and *yĕmê haššōpĕṭîm ᵓăšer šāpĕṭû ᵓet yiśrāᵓēl*, "the days of the rulers who ruled Israel," in 2 Kgs 23:22 demonstrates that the era of the judges was well defined in Israelite historical thought. The chronological limits of this period are set within the Book of Judges itself. The earliest possible beginning is established by 1:1, "after the death of Joshua," and further defined in 2:6–10. Just as the death of the immediate sons of Jacob had marked the end of the patriarchal era (Exod 1:5–6) and the death of Moses had marked the end of the period of exodus and wanderings (Josh 1:1), so the death of Joshua signaled the transition from the period of conquest to the period of settlement in the land of Canaan.

Scholars are not agreed on the date of commencement for the period of the judges. This question is tightly linked not only with the death of Joshua but also with the date of the exodus of the Israelites from Egypt. But the evidence for the dates of these events is inconclusive. Those who accept the essential historicity of the biblical account of the exodus go in two different directions. Relying on 1 Kgs 6:1[18] and Judg 11:26,[19] American evangelicals have traditionally dated the exodus and the conquest in the latter half of the fifteenth century B.C.[20] But many British evangelicals think the issue is not as clear-cut as it first seems. As we will see, Judg 11:26 should not be used as evidence in the

---

[16] Cf. J. Teixidor, "Les functions de *rab* et de suffégte en Phénicie," *Semitica* 29 (1979): 9–17.

[17] G. W. Ahlström suggests these "judges" should be perceived like all other Canaanite princes and petty kings of the presettlement time (*The History of Ancient Palestine from the Paleolithic Period to Alexander's Conquest*, JSOTSup 146 [Sheffield: Sheffield Academic Press, 1993], 372).

[18] Solomon began constructing the temple 480 years after the exodus.

[19] Jephthah insists that the Israelites have occupied the territory claimed by the Ammonites for three hundred years.

[20] If Solomon began building the temple in 966 B.C. (cf. E. R. Thiele, *The Mysterious Numbers of the Hebrew Kings* [Grand Rapids: Eerdmans, 1965], 28; cf. pp. 29, 55), the date of the exodus would be 1446 B.C. However, the most thorough defense for a fifteenth-century date of the exodus (1470 B.C.!) is provided by a British scholar, J. J. Bimson, *Redating the Exodus and Conquest*, 2d ed., JSOTSup 5 (Sheffield: Almond Press, 1981).

discussion, for Jephthah exaggerates the length of time to attack his enemies' reputation. They also interpret the reference to 480 years in 1 Kgs 6:1 symbolically, perhaps twelve generations of forty years each.[21] Combining these questions with the problematic references to the storage cities of Pithom and Rameses in Exod 1:11, they tend to favor a thirteenth century date.[22] For them the latest possible date for the entry into the promised land would be 1208 B.C., the date of a stela erected by Pharaoh Merneptah (1213–1203 B.C.) to commemorate his campaign in Canaan in his fifth year.[23]

Regardless when one fixes the beginning of the settlement,[24] the latest possible ending for the period is set by the refrain, "In those days Israel had no king," variations of which are repeated in 17:6; 18:1; 19:1; 21:25. As noted earlier, technically this period extends through Eli's and Samuel's tenures, or at least until the coronation of Saul, which occurred in the last half of the eleventh century B.C.[25]

(2) Sources for Recovering the History of the Period of the Judges

The Book of Judges itself is obviously the most helpful source for reconstructing the history of this period. Even scholars who date the book late accept that the stories of the deliverers are rooted in historical reality.[26] Though the Book of Ruth is often wrongly dismissed by critical scholars as a fanciful tale, it provides helpful information on life during this period in a specific community, the town of Bethlehem. References to this period are rare in later historiographic writings. From Samuel's farewell speech in 1 Sam 12:9–11 it is apparent he and the author of this book knew of the oppressions of Sisera, the Philistines, and Moab, as well as the deliverances provided by Jerubbaal

---

[21] For discussion see D. Howard, Jr., *An Introduction to the Old Testament Historical Books* (Chicago: Moody, 1993), 63–64.

[22] Rameses II reigned from 1279–1213 B.C. K. A. Kitchen, "Egypt, History of (Chronology)," *ABD* 2.329.

[23] For the inscription see *ANET*, 376–78. For the dates of Merneptah's reign see Kitchen, ibid.

[24] For a helpful survey of the options see Howard, *Introduction to the Old Testament Historical Books*, 62–65.

[25] In 1 Sam 13:1, which apparently once gave the length of Saul's reign, the number is omitted in the MT. In Acts 13:21 Paul states that Saul reigned forty years. According to this reference, if David began his reign in 1011 B.C. (cf. Thiele, *Mysterious Numbers*, 51–52), Saul would have been crowned in 1051 B.C. But critical scholarship rejects the Pauline statement as too long and sterotypical. D. V. Edelman ("Saul," *ABD* 5.993) proposes a reign of twenty-two years, which yields a date of 1032 for the end of the period of the judges. For discussion of the problems involved see E. H. Merrill, *Kingdom of Priests: A History of Old Testament Israel* (Grand Rapids: Baker, 1987), 192–94.

[26] Although R. Albertz finds little historical value in the Book of Joshua, he relies heavily on Judges to reconstruct the religion and culture of Israel in the premonarchic era (*The History of Israelite Religion in the Old Testament Period*, Vol. I: *From the Beginnings to the End of the Monarchy*, trans. J. Bowden [Louisville: Westminster/John Knox, 1994], 67–103).

(Gideon), Bedan (Barak), and Jephthah, and that Samuel puts himself in this same class of people. In fact, these verses sound so familiar one may suppose that the author was aware at least of the "Book of Deliverers" (Judg 3:7–16:31). In 2 Sam 11:21, Joab warns against the dangers of siege warfare by referring to the death of Abimelech at the hands of the woman who threw the upper millstone on him from on top of the wall (Judg 9:53–54).

Of the prophets, only Isaiah and Hosea allude to this premonarchic period. The former's reference to "the day of Midian" in 9:4[Hb. 3] reflects an awareness of Yahweh's defeat of the Midianites by the hand of Gideon. For Hosea the outrage of the Benjamites of Gibeah (Judges 18–19) represents the ultimate in corruption and depravity (Hos 9:9; 10:9). Earlier (6:7–9) he had alluded to Gilead and Ephraimite Shechem. In keeping with his North Israelite roots, but unlike the author of Judges, this prophet displays a distinctly anti-Gileadite and pro-Ephraimite stance.

Allusions to the period of the judges are also scarce in the Psalter. The references to a theophany and to sheepfolds in Ps 68:7–14[Hb. 8–15] are reminiscent of the Song of Deborah (Judg 5:16). The naming of Zalmon in v. 14[15] recalls the Abimelech account (Judg 9:48). Outside the Book of Judges, Psalm 83 provides the most complete survey of the premonarchic era, as the psalmist lists a series of Israel's oppressors: Edom and the Ishmaelites, Moab and the Hagarites, Gebal (and Sidon), Ammon and the Amalekites, Philistia and Tyre, as well as Assyria. If A. Malamat is correct in dating this psalm during or shortly after the period of the judges, the reference to Assyria probably recalls the appearance in the west of Tiglath Pileser I (1114–1076 B.C.), the first Assyrian emperor to reach the Mediterranean.[27] This psalmist also knows of the defeat of Midian, Sisera and Jabin (even the flooding of the Kishon), Oreb and Zeeb (Judg 7:25), and Zebah and Zalmunnah (Judg 8:21).

Extrabiblical sources for the period of the judges are scarce. The Merneptah Stela, celebrating the victories of Rameses II's successor in Canaan, has yielded the earliest extrabiblical reference to an entity called "Israel." At the end of the document the author breaks out into poetry:

> The princes are prostrate, saying "Mercy!"
> Not one raises his head among the Nine Bows.
> Desolation is for Tehenu; Hatti is pacified;
> Plundered is the Canaan with every evil;
> Carried off is Ashkelon;
> Seized upon is Gezer;
> Yanoʿam is made as that which does not exist;
> Israel is laid waste, his seed is not;

---

[27] A. Malamat, "The Period of the Judges," in *Judges,* vol. 3 of *The World History of the Jewish People,* ed. B. Mazar (Tel-Aviv: Massada, 1971), 134.

Hurru is become a widow because of Egypt!
All lands together are pacified;
Everyone who was restless has been bound
by the King of Upper and Lower Egypt.[28]

In a context in which all the other place names are preceded by the foreign land determinative, Israel is preceded by the foreign people determinative. This change suggests that in the late thirteenth century B.C. the Egyptians either recognized "Israel" primarily as an ethnic rather than geographic designation or that they did not yet link the people who went by this name with a particular territory. Their settlement seemed tenuous at best.

The Amarna Letters provide another source for the cultural and political history of Canaan in the second half of the second millennium B.C.[29] These fourteenth century B.C. documents, written in cuneiform, contain diplomatic correspondence between Canaanite city-kings and their Pharaonic overlords, Amenhotep III and Akhenaten. The Amarna tablets are especially valuable for the social, economic, and political picture they provide of the land of Canaan prior to the Israelite occupation. The territory was divided into a series of small city-states (many with familiar names), whose relationships tended to be turbulent and competitive. Indeed, the account of Abimelech in Judges 9 looks like a page from a Canaanite history textbook.

(3) The Appearance of Israel in Canaan

The reconstruction of the history of premonarchic Israel is extremely difficult. In their understanding of this period scholars divide into several different camps.

THE VIOLENT CONQUEST INTERPRETATION. Traditionally readers of the Old Testament have accepted as essentially historical the accounts of an entire national group escaping the slavery of Egypt, suddenly appearing in Canaan, and displacing the original Canaanite population by violent conquest. Accordingly, Judges 1 reflects the period of consolidation of Israelite control of the territory after the backbone of Canaanite resistance had been broken through the leadership of Joshua. Today many scholars find this reconstruction of Israel's premonarchic history too simplistic and have replaced it with a series of alternative theories of the nation's origins. Space limitations prevent a

---

[28] *ANET,* 378. F. J. Yurco ("Merneptah's Palestinian Campaign," in *The Society for the Study of Egyptian Antiquities Journal* 8 [1982]: 70; id., "Merneptah's Canaanite Campaign," *Journal of the American Research Center in Egypt* 23 [1986], 189–251," id., "3,200-Year-Old Picture of Israelites Found in Egypt," *BAR* 16/5 [1990]: 20–38) correlates this text with the battle scenes on the outer wall of the Cour de la Cachette at Karnak. On the text see Ahlström, *History of Ancient Palestine,* 281–88.

[29] *ANET,* 485–87. For a recent study of these texts and their significance see W. L. Moran, *The Amarna Letters* (Baltimore: Johns Hopkins University Press, 1992), especially xiii–xxxix.

full presentation and evaluation of the options, but three principal alternative proposals deserve mention.[30]

INDEPENDENT MIGRATIONS AND SETTLEMENT BY SEPARATE TRIBAL GROUPS. The occupation of Palestine was supposedly a gradual process, as separate groups of people entered the land, usually from the east, over an extended period of time. Only later, when they joined to form the nation of Israel, were individual conquest traditions combined and telescoped within the lives of Moses and Joshua. Not all, or even most, of the tribal groups constituting the later nation of Israel came out of Egypt, but those that did so came in several waves, mostly during the thirteenth century B.C.[31]

GRADUAL PEACEFUL PENETRATION IN SEARCH OF PASTURAGE. The occupation of Palestine supposedly occurred gradually as nomadic and semi-nomadic tribes moved into unsettled regions in search of pasture. Initially relations between the native population and the newcomers were peaceful, since the latter's search for pasture for their flocks posed no threat to the Canaanite agricultural settlements in the fertile lowlands. Conflicts between the groups arose later, at the end of the period of the judges, as the Israelite tribes gained a foothold in the hill country and began to encroach upon the arable plains and river valleys. These groups were united around the worship of Yahweh at a central shrine, first at Shechem, then at Shiloh.[32]

INTERNAL REVOLT AND CLASS WARFARE. Imposing Marxist ideology on the biblical records, N. Gottwald reinterprets the supposed conquest of Palestine as a revolt of the peasants (known as Israelites) against the overlords (referred to as Canaanites). The revolution may have been initiated by "slave labor captives" who escaped from Egypt and provided in their covenant religion, the worship of Yahweh, the unifying bond for the oppressed lower classes of Palestine.[33]

Those who have developed these theories have contributed greatly to our

---

[30] See the survey by I. Finkelstein, *The Archaeology of the Israelite Settlement* (Jerusalem: Israel Exploration Society, 1988), 295–314.

[31] Thus G. E. Wright, *Biblical Archaeology*, rev. ed. (Philadelphia: Westminster, 1962), 69–85. This was also the earlier view of J. Bright (*A History of Israel*, 1st ed. [Philadelphia: Westminster, 1959], 110–27), but a later edition indicates he changed his mind.

[32] The foremost proponent of this theory was A. Alt, "The Settlement of the Israelites in Palestine," in *Essays on Old Testament History and Religion*, R. A. Wilson, trans. (Garden City: Doubleday, 1968), 173–221. It has been recently revived and modified by Finkelstein, *Archaeology of the Israelite Settlement*, 315–72.

[33] The roots of this theory go back to G. Mendenhall in "The Hebrew Conquest of Canaan," *BAR* 3, ed. E. F. Campbell, Jr., and D. N. Freedman (Garden City: Doubleday, 1970), 100–20. N. K. Gottwald offers his modified and expanded version of the theory in *The Tribes of Yahweh: A Sociology of the Religion of Liberated Israel, 1250–1050 B.C.E.* (Maryknoll: Orbis, 1979). In fact, Gottwald's interpretation is repudiated by Mendenhall. See P. K. McCarter, "A Major New Introduction to the Bible," *BR* 2/2 (1986): 46; B. W. Anderson, "Mendenhall Disavows Paternity," ibid., 46–47.

understanding of the world of Palestine in the premonarchic era, but each proposal depends on a subjective manipulation of the text to suit the theory. The traditional view, that the Israelites who came from Egypt under the leadership of Moses were the descendants of Abraham and that under the command of Joshua they engaged the Canaanite population, is not only reasonable; it lets the Hebrew authors say what they want to say. After all, the ancient writers were much nearer to the original events than we are and in a much better position to know what happened. There is no doubt the Israelite authors who wrote these accounts perceived what they wrote to be factually based and not merely fiction.[34]

(4) Sociopolitical Conditions in Premonarchic Israel

Taking the ancient Greek league of city-states as a model, a previous generation of scholars tended to view premonarchic Israel as united around the worship of Yahweh in a twelve-tribe confederation, or amphictyony.[35] Although scholars today have for the most part abandoned this interpretation, this does not mean that the tribes that constituted the nation lacked a sense of cohesion. The author of the Book of Judges certainly perceived them as one people. This conclusion may be drawn from several stylistic features of the composition: (1) the high frequency of the name "Israel," which exceeds that of any other book in the Hebrew Bible; (2) the frequent use of the pan-Israelite expressions like "all Israel" (8:27), "all the sons of Israel" (2:4; 20:1), "the men of Israel" (7:8,23; 8:22),[36] "the hand of Israel" (3:30; 11:21), "the camp of Israel" (7:15), "the misery of Israel" (10:16), "the daughters of Israel" (11:40), "the border of Israel" (19:29), "the patrimonial possession of Israel" (20:6), and, sixty-one times, "the sons of Israel"; (3) the frequent references to a person judging Israel (3:10; 4:4; 10:2,3; 12:7,8,9,11,13,14; 15:20; 16:31), ruling over Israel (9:22; 14:4 [the Philistines]), saving Israel (3:31; 6:14,15,32,36; 10:1; 13:15),[37] and in the final chapters, "There was no king in Israel" (17:6; 18:1; 19:1; 21:25); (4) the multitude of other expressions involving "Israel" as a collective;[38] (5) the frequent use of the expres-

---

[34] Cf. S. Lasine, "Fiction, Falsehood, and Reality in Hebrew Scripture," *HS* 25 (1984): 24–40.

[35] Alt, "The Origins of Israelite Law," in *Essays on Old Testament History and Religion*, 130–320; Noth, *The History of Israel*, 2d ed. (New York: Harper & Row, 1958), 99–103.

[36] See also 9:55. In 7:14 Gideon is referred to as "the son of Joash, a man of Israel." Note also the way in which the author refers to the forces marshalled against the warriors of Benjamin (20:11,17,20,22,33,36,38–39,41–42,48; 21:1). However, by specifically noting their kinship to the remaining tribes (20:13,23), the narrator emphasizes that the Benjamites were not to be considered less Israelite.

[37] Cf. the deliverer saving "the sons of Israel" in 3:9.

[38] Yahweh's anger burns against Israel (2:14,20; 3:8; 10:7); he tests Israel (2:22; 3:1); ritual mourning becomes a custom in Israel (11:39); disgraceful acts are committed in Israel (20:6); wickedness is removed from Israel (20: 13); events happen in Israel (21:3); a man is a priest to a family and tribe in Israel (18:19).

sion *šibṭê yiśrāʾēl*, "tribes of Israel," in the last two chapters (20:2,10,12; 21:5,8,15; see also 18:1), and the frequent naming of the tribes making up the nation.[39] In fact, to lose Benjamin would render the nation incomplete.[40] In response to those who would perceive these expressions as retrojections of later perceptions, it may be noted that the above expressions appear in all segments of the book, not just the narrator's deuteronomistic comments; the definition of the land of Israel as "from Dan to Beersheba" derives from a time no later than the early monarchy;[41] the archival judge lists (10:1–5; 12:8–15), which appear to be based on early sources, refer to Israel this way;[42] the Song of Deborah, which dates back at least to the eleventh century B.C., uses the national name similarly (5:1,3,5,7,9),[43] even to the extent of listing many of the tribes.[44] It may be safely concluded, therefore, that the Israel that confronts us in the Book of Judges is the Israel mentioned in the Merneptah Stela cited earlier and that this Israel viewed itself as one nation.

Although critical scholarship tends to question the reliability of Israel's traditions, the author of the Book of Judges assumes that common descent from an eponymous ancestor provides the basis for Israel's ethnic unity.[45] This assumption is vaguely hinted at in the ubiquitous references to the nation or portions thereof as *ʿam*, "people," from a root signifying "paternal uncle," which often implies internal blood relationship,[46] but it is given explicit

---

[39] The annalistic summary of the conquest in 1:1–36 lists under "the sons of Israel" Judah, Simeon, Benjamin, Joseph, Manasseh, Ephraim, Zebulun, Asher, Dan, and Naphtali. Ehud, a Benjamite, is raised up for "the sons of Israel" (3:15). The Deborah-Barak narrative (chap. 4) refers to Ephraim, Naphtali, and Zebulun. Gideon's "men of Israel" include men from Manasseh, Asher, Zebulun, and Naphtali (6:35; 7:23), while Ephraim is offended for not having been invited. The objects of Ammonite oppression in 10:9 include Benjamin, Judah, and Ephraim (obviously also Gilead). In 20:1 all "the sons of Israel" are identified geographically as coming "from Dan to Beersheba and the land of Gilead."

[40] Note the references to one tribe "missing in Israel" (21:3), being "cut off" from Israel (21:6), and being "blotted out" from Israel (21:17).

[41] The expression never appears after the division of the kingdom (see 1 Sam 3:20; 2 Sam 3:10; 17:11; 24:2,15; 1 Kgs 5:5; 1 Chr 21:2), except in 2 Chr 30:5, where Hezekiah is apparently attempting to recapture pan-Israelite jurisdiction in his religious reforms, after the pattern of David's and Solomon's realms. On this expression see M. Sæbo, "Grenzbeschreibung und Landideal im Alten Testament mit Besonderer Berücksichtigung der *min-ʿad*-Formel," *ZDPV* 90 (1974): 21–22.

[42] On the authenticity and antiquity of these lists, see R. de Vaux, *The Early History of Israel*, trans. D. Smith (Philadelphia: Westminster, 1978), 759.

[43] Note especially her self-designation as "mother in Israel," v. 7. On the date of Judges 5 see below, p. 213f.

[44] Included are Ephraim, Benjamin, Zebulun, Issachar, Reuben, Gilead, Dan, and Naphtali (5:14–19). These are to be compared with other early tribal lists, the Blessing of Jacob (Gen 49), and the Blessing of Moses (Deut 33), both of which name most of these tribes.

[45] Cf. the references to the ancestors in 2:1,12,17.

[46] See my discussion in *The Foundations of National Identity: A Study in Ancient Northwest Semitic Perspectives* (Ann Arbor: University Microfilms, 1983), 1–83.

expression in Samson's parents' protest over his marriage to the Philistine in 14:3: "Is there no woman among the daughters of your relatives *[ʾāḥêkā]*, or among all our people *[bĕkol ʿammî]*, that you must take a wife from the uncircumcised Philistines?" The Philistine woman, for her part, speaks of her own countrymen as "the sons of my people" (*bĕnê ʿammî*, vv. 16–17). The same ethnic distinction is reflected in the characterization of the inhabitants of Laish as "a people *[ʿam]* quiet and secure" in 18:27. The frequent use of the expression *bĕnê yiśrāʾēl*, "sons of Israel" (sixty-one times in the book) may point in a similar direction.[47] Perhaps the most significant comment comes from the unnamed Levite in 19:12, when his servant proposes that they spend the night in Jebus: "We will not turn aside into the city of foreigners which is not of the sons of Israel." Although the term *ʾāḥ*, "brother," may denote an ally in some contexts,[48] in the opening annalistic summary of the conquest of the land, Judah and Simeon are treated as brothers (1:3,17). Similarly, in the concluding episodes the "sons of Israel" treat the Benjamites as brothers (20:23,28) and vice versa (20:13). In the crisis described in these chapters, the loss of the tribe of Benjamin is treated as the loss of a member of the family (21:6; see also 14:3; 18:14).

The Israelites of the premonarchic era rightly perceived themselves as one large extended kinship group. The hierarchy of the nation's genealogical social structure, reflected in Josh 7:14–18, may be represented diagrammatically as follows:

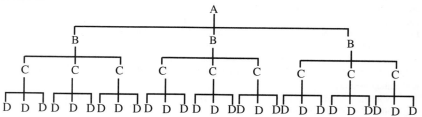

A = *ʿam*, the nation of Israel B = *šēbeṭ*, the twelve tribes
C = *mišpāḥâ*, the clan D = *bêt ʾāb*, "the house of the father"

Strictly speaking the *bêt ʾāb*, "house of the father," which represents the foundational unit of such ethnically based societies, consisted of the patriarch, his wife/wives, and children, all who lived under the same roof. However, the designation could also apply to married children and grandchildren, all living in close proximity to each other. Marriage within this unit is generally forbid-

---

[47] See my discussion " 'Israel' – sons of Israel': A Study in Hebrew Eponymic Usage," in *Studies in Religion* 13 (1984): 301–26.

[48] 1 Kgs 9:13, Hiram and Solomon; 1 Kgs 20:32–33, Ahab and Benhadad. Cf. Gottwald, *The Tribes of Yahweh,* 524.

den. Several large extended families might combine to form clans, established in their own villages and/or settlements and using communal land. Every member of the clan knows everyone else. Unrelated or distantly related clans may be interlocked by exogamous marriage (i.e., marriage outside one's clan). A series of clans combine to form a tribe, though all still claimed descent from a common ancestor many generations removed. The population spreads over a large tract of land, and the members no longer know everyone. Internal endogamous marriage is common. Several tribes combined to form the ethnic group, the ʿam, "people." This social structure determined the shape of Israel's religious, economic, and political life until the time of Solomon (1 Kings 4).

Judges indicates that in premonarchic times tribal and national forces often competed against each other. The absence of political unity is reflected in the fact that the term gôy, "nation,"[49] is applied to Israel only once in this book and never in 1 Samuel. The single occurrence in the former (2:20) occurs in a divine speech in which Yahweh rejects Israel's special status. Since the nation has abandoned her covenant deity, she has become a gôy, "nation," like all the other gôyim, "nations."[50] The nature of government in premonarchic Israel is not entirely clear. Judges 1 suggests that after the death of Joshua political authority passed from the central figure to the separate tribes.[51] But the process of decision making at the tribal level is nowhere defined. Obviously elders (zĕqēnîm), leaders by virtue of seniority and experience, whose presence antedates the exodus (Exod 3:16,18; 4:29), would have been involved. As the tribes settled down, these men constituted the "village council," providing leadership in political, judicial, and religious matters.[52] Naturally, crises precipitated by foreign invasions became the concern of the elders of a community. As the call of Jephthah illustrates, however, such events tended to be dealt with at the tribal level (Judg 11:5–11). The Gileadite elders' impotence in the face of the Ammonite threat is demonstrated by their elevation of Jephthah to the status of "head" (rōʾš, 11:11) and "chief" (qāṣîn, 11:6). Judges 21:16 reports a gathering of elders from all the tribes to determine the appropriate response to the decimation of the Benjamites.[53] Especially instructive is the role of the elders in Samuel's request for a king who would be responsible for military leadership against a foreign enemy and assume their governing roles (1 Sam 8:4–5,19–20).

---

[49] On the significance of גּוֹי and its distinctions from עַם, see Block, *Foundations of National Identity*, 84–127 and 493–521; id., "Nations," *ISBE*, rev. ed., 3:492.

[50] Cf. A. Cody, "When Is the Chosen People Called a *Gôy?*" *VT* (1964): 1–6.

[51] This impression is reinforced by the notice of foreign aggression directed against individual tribes (10:9), the addressing of appeals for military aid to the other tribes (4:10; 6:35; 7:23–24), and the reports of tribal responses to such appeals (5:14–18; 8:1; esp. 12:1–6).

[52] Deut 19:12; 21:1–9,18,21; 22:13–21; 25:1–10; Josh 20:4. Ruth 4:1–12 provides the clearest picture of civil procedures in action. On the role of elders in ancient Israel see H. Reviv, *The Elders in Ancient Israel: A Study of a Biblical Institution*, trans. L. Plitmann (Jerusalem: Magnes, 1989).

[53] Cp. the expression, פִּנּוֹת כָּל הָעָם "chiefs of all the people," in 20:2.

Several other types of functionaries served the political process in ancient Israel. Reference has already been made to Jephthah as a head and chief. The former term, *rōʾš*, is applied to military leaders in this and later contexts,[54] but several important references also assign judicial roles to holders of this office.[55] These men appear to have been appointed on the basis of their special abilities.[56] The Book of Joshua occasionally refers to *šōṭĕrîm*, "clerks" (Josh 8:33), a type of minor judge or subordinate civil officer.[57] This office probably continued into the period of the judges, but it does not figure in the narratives.

The most prominent leaders in the Judges accounts are the *šōpĕṭîm*. The meaning of the term has already been considered, but the role of those who held the office demands further comment. On first sight the Book of Judges appears to deal with two types of judges, often classified by scholars as "minor" and "major" judges. Five of the former are named in two short lists on either side of the Jephthah account (Judg 10:1–5; 12:8–15): Tola, Jair, Ibzan, Elon, and Abdon. Except for Tola, who is also identified as a "deliverer" (10:1), these do not seem to fit the pattern of the main characters in the "Book of Deliverers."[58] Except for the brief account of Shamgar (3:31), the narratives of the major judges are constructed around the recurring cycle of apostasy/oppression/plea for divine aid/deliverance through the judge (see 2:10–3:6).[59] However, the functional distinctions between so-called major and minor judges should not be drawn too sharply. The apparent differences derive either from the sources used by the narrator (family chronicles for the minor judges; folk narratives for the deliverer judges) or the individual's significance for the narrator's literary and theological agenda.[60] In any case they are better characterized as "primary" and "secondary" judges rather than "major" and "minor"

---

[54] E.g., 2 Sam 23:8–39; 1 Chr 11:6,10,11,15,20,42; 12:3,14,18,20,23,32; 27:3. On the expressions see J. R. Bartlett, "The Use of the Word רֹאשׁ as a Title in the Old Testament," *VT* 19 (1969): 1–3.

[55] Deut 33:2–5, 21; cf. Num 25:4–5; Job 29:25. See further Bartlett, "Use of the Word רֹאשׁ," 4–7.

[56] See also Bartlett (ibid.), 10. On the use of the term see further, H. P. Mullet, "רֹאשׁ *rōš* Kopf," *THAT* 2:701–15.

[57] Although שֹׁטְרִים is derived from a root meaning "to write," the place of scribal activity in their work is unclear. For discussion see de Vaux, *Ancient Israel,* 155; Bartlett, "Use of the Word רֹאשׁ," 4, n. 3.

[58] See H. W. Hertzberg, "Die Kleinen Richter," *TLZ* 79 (1954): 285–90 (= *Beiträge zur Traditionsgeschichte and Theologie des Alten Testaments* [Göttingen: Vandenhoeck & Ruprecht, 1962], 118–25); id., *Die Bücher Josua, Richter, Ruth,* ATD 9 (Göttingen: Vandenhoeck & Ruprecht, 1969), 143; de Vaux, *Early History of Israel,* 752–59.

[59] Thus the accounts of Othniel (3:7–11), Ehud (3:12–30), Barak (4:1–24), Gideon (6:1–8:28), and Jephthah (10:6–12:7). Some would include Samuel with the major judges.

[60] The distinction is also questioned by Malamat, "Period of the Judges," 131. Ahlström (*History of Ancient Palestine,* 373, n. 4) notes that these judges are referred to in the same stereotyped form as kings in the succession formulas in the Books of Kings.

respectively.[61] Having jurisdiction over specific tribes and territories, these "judges" functioned as princes *(śārîm)* or petty kings *(mĕlākîm)*, administering justice (1 Sam 7:15–17) and defending the population from external threats.

The human impulses thrusting the "judges" into their office are largely unknown. The occasional references to *gibbôr ḥayil*, which may be translated either "mighty men of valor" or "mighty men of wealth," may suggest they rose from the aristocratic ruling classes,[62] but this interpretation treats the expression too technically. The divine messenger's identification of Gideon as such in Judg 6:12 represents a flattering and/or prospective characterization of the man as a "mighty warrior."[63] The narrator applies the same expression to Jephthah, certainly not because he is a noble man, but as a retrospective characterization (11:1). Since the epochal work of M. Weber,[64] the judges (especially the primary ones) have been commonly characterized as "charismatic leaders."[65] Unfortunately, to modern readers this expression is generally applied to individuals with an engaging personality and endowed with extraordinary talent, who emerge in times of distress to bring relief to a weary people. The Hebrew expression *gibbôr ḥayil*, "mighty man of valor/wealth," could conceivably apply to a person we would characterize as "charismatic," except that prior to the engagement of the persons called to this office, the "judges" tended to represent the antithesis of our "charismatic leader": Othniel is not a native Israelite; as left-handed, Ehud is considered handicapped; Barak is unmanly; Gideon is a skeptic; Jephthah is a brigand. Samson also falls short, even though his extraordinary strength might have qualified him for our definition. Nowhere does the narrative suggest that his strength was the basis of his judgeship; he had no following at all in Israel; he wasted his energy in self-indulgent philandering with foreign women; and in the end he accomplished more in his death than in his life. None of these men would be characterized as a "charismatic leader" as we understand the idiom today.

Even if they had possessed the natural gifts needed for judgeship in exceptional measure, *qualification* for the office must be distinguished from *authori-*

---

[61] Given the lengths of their reigns, it is doubtful the individuals named in 10:1–5 and 12:8–15 would have been considered "minor" by their countrymen: Tola, twenty-three years; Jair, twenty-two years; Ibzan, seven years; Elon, ten years; Abdon, eight years.

[62] Thus R. K. Harrison, *Introduction to the Old Testament* (Grand Rapids: Eerdmans, 1970), 681.

[63] Similarly J. A. Soggin, *Judges: A Commentary,* trans. J. S. Bowden, OTL (Philadelphia: Westminster, 1981), 115; contra R. G. Boling's "aristocrat" *(Judges: A New Translation with Introduction and Commentary,* AB [Garden City: Doubleday, 1975], 131).

[64] M. Weber, *Gesammelte Aufsätze zur Religionstheologie,* vol. III, *Das antike Judentum* (Tübingen: Mohr, 1921), 92–94.

[65] For a critique of Weber see Z. Weisman, "Charismatic Leaders in the Era of the Judges," *ZAW* 89 (1977): 399–411.

zation. In the preface to the "Book of Deliverers" (2:16,18), the author declares emphatically that the authorization to serve as deliverer for each of the primary judges (save Shamgar, who appears not to have been an Israelite) was a divine decision. Yahweh raises up judges/deliverers;[66] Yahweh strengthens *(wayḥazzēq)* Eglon (3:12; cf. 16:28); Yahweh issues the charge to Barak to arm against Sisera (4:6); Yahweh sends his angel *(malʾāk)* to call Gideon (6:11–40); Yahweh plans Gideon's strategy (7:2–23); Yahweh calls Samson before he is born (13:5) and stirs him to action *(wattāḥel,* 13:25); Yahweh's Spirit comes upon the judges (3:10; 11:29; 14:6,19; 15:14) and/or clothes them (6:34). Indeed, apart from the Spirit of Yahweh, Samson has neither the authority nor the power to act (16:20). If the authorization and qualification for judgeship are perceived as supernaturally endowed *charismata,* "gifts of grace," rather than natural gifts, then the characterization of the judges as charismatic leaders applies.[67] But there can be no question that for the narrator, the deliverer/judge, and the citizenry, the official was an agent of God, imbued with and empowered by the divine Spirit to go out and gain the victory over the enemy, always against incredible odds.[68] Later this same "gift" would empower kings (1 Sam 10:10; 11:6; 16:13–14).

In the Book of Judges one may detect tendencies toward the centralization and standardization of political power: judges are described as having jurisdiction over Israel; Gideon is offered the rule over all Israel; they all worship his ephod (8:22–28); and the chiefs of all the people gather at Mizpah to discuss the fate of Benjamin (20:1–2). However, pan-Israelite political aspirations were not achieved until the reign of David. Indeed the final editor of this book associates the deterioration of Israelite society with the absence of centralized authority.[69] It took a severe military crisis to challenge the people to overcome this centrifugal tendency and demand a king for the whole nation (1 Sam 8:4–9). Unlike the convocation of all the elders of Israel before Samuel at Ramah, the meeting at Mizpah to discuss how to deal with the Benjamite outrage described in 20:1–2 was an *ad hoc* gathering whose ultimate aim became military. This convocation could hardly be classified as a typical or customary political assembly of the nation's leaders.

---

[66] וַיָּקֶם יְהוה שֹׁפְטִים/מוֹשִׁיעַ, 2:16,18; 3:9,15.

[67] See the helpful discussion by Malamat, "Charismatic Leadership in the Book of Judges," in *Magnalia Dei: The Mighty Acts of God: Essays on the Bible and Archaeology in Memory of G. Ernest Wright,* ed. F. M. Cross, et al. (Garden City: Doubleday, 1976), 152–68; also Ahlström, *History of Ancient Palestine,* 373–74.

[68] Cp. the later reflection on the divine basis of the judges' rule over the Israelites in 2 Sam 7:11 (= 2 Chr 17:10), "from the day that I commanded judges to be over my people Israel."

[69] Note variations of the expression "In those days Israel had no king; everyone did as he saw fit" (17:6; 18:1; 19:1; 20:25). For discussion see W. J. Dumbrell, " 'In those days there was no king in Israel; every man did that which was right in his own eyes.' The Purpose of the Book of Judges Reconsidered," *JSOT* 25 (1983): 23–33.

The Book of Judges describes a nation in transition and crisis. In spite of the Israelites' consciousness of ethnic and religious unity, the nation seemed determined to destroy itself. Having failed to deal decisively with the Canaanites at the beginning of the settlement period, her men hesitated to assume leadership even when it was thrust upon them. At the tribal level individual tribes and clans hesitated to get involved in national crises (5:17; 21:9). On the other hand, if they were not asked to participate, jealousy tended to precipitate self-destructive responses.[70] When strong leadership did emerge, it patterned itself after the worst aspects of Canaanite city-state despotism,[71] was preoccupied with personal advantage (11:8–11, Jephthah), or treated power as a private plaything, provoking the ire of the nation's enemies and alienating the ruler's countrymen (14:10–15:16, Samson). Israel's drive to self-destruct reached its climax (or nadir) at the end of the book, when the holy war that should have been waged against the Canaanites was directed at one of their own tribes.

(5) Religious Conditions in the Premonarchic Period

In view of Israel's political debacle in the premonarchic era, the narrator's negative evaluation of Israelite society in the absence of kingship, and the circumstances of the demand for a king in 1 Samuel 8, it is not surprising that many scholars, if not most, have understood the Book of Judges as an apology for the monarchy.[72] But even if the books of Samuel and Kings that follow display a pro-Davidic stance, it is doubtful the compiler of the Judges material was concerned chiefly with political structures.[73] And even if the book provides a great deal of information on the political situation in Israel during the period of settlement, it is unwise hermeneutically to use the book primarily for the reconstruction of political structures. Writing from a deuteronomic/prophetic perspective, the narrator was much more concerned about Israel's spiritual state.

The Book of Judges provides an ambivalent picture of Israel's religion in the premonarchic era. Theoretically and officially the term "Israel" denoted more than just the descendants of the twelve sons of Jacob/Israel; "Israel" was

---

[70] 8:1–2; 12:1–6, Ephraim in both instances.

[71] On Abimelech as the antitheses of the charismatic leadership of the judges, see Malamat, "Charismatic Leadership," 163–64.

[72] A. E. Cundall, "Judges—An Apology for the Monarchy?" *ExpTim* 81 (1970): 178–81. See also the comment of Harrison: "The purpose of the work was to show that a centralized hereditary kingship was necessary for the well being of the Covenant theocracy" (*Introduction to the Old Testament,* 692). See more recently the exhaustive study of the book by R. H. O'Connell (*The Rhetoric of the Book of Judges,* VTSup 63 [Leiden: Brill, 1996]), who argues that the book was composed specifically in defense of the Davidic, as opposed to the Saulide, monarchy.

[73] This is not to say that Samuel and Kings are primarily political documents. Like the Book of Judges, in the Jewish canon they are rightly classified with the "former prophets," consisting of the entire Joshua-Kings corpus.

ʿam hāʾĕlōhîm, "the people of God" (20:1).[74] Specifically they were *ʿam YHWH*, "the people of the LORD." Conversely, Yahweh is frequently referred to as *ʾĕlōhê yiśrāʾēl*, "the God of Israel" (4:6; 5:3,5; 6:8; 11:21,23; 21:3) in contrast to "the other gods, from the gods of the surrounding peoples,"[75] and in contrast to Chemosh, whom Jephthah identifies [erroneously] as *ʾĕlōhêkā*, "your God," that is, the God of the Ammonites in 11:23.[76] In the prologue to the "Book of Deliverers" the author of Judges recognizes that Israel's special relationship to Yahweh is based on three important pillars: (1) his status as the God of the patriarchs (*ʾĕlōhê ʾābôt*, 2:12); (2) his role as Israel's deliverer from the bondage of Egypt (2:10,12); and (3) his covenant with Israel at Sinai (2:20). The passion with which Yahweh treasured his relationship with his people is reflected in the narrative itself in a triad of divine visitations in which he and/or his divine agent remind the Israelites of their obligation to exclusive allegiance to himself (2:1–2; 6:10; 10:13–14). It is evident also in his repeated direct involvement in the affairs of the nation, burning with rage over their infidelity, handing them over to the enemy, responding to their cries of pain, raising up deliverers, and providing victory over the enemies.[77]

For their part the Israelites officially acknowledge this relationship repeatedly in the book: (1) by oracular consultation of Yahweh to determine the strategy they are to adopt in their military campaigns (1:1; 20:18,23,27); (2) by responding to Yahweh's messenger, sacrificing to him (2:4–5), and acknowledging their sin (10:15–16); (3) by worshiping Yahweh, at least the generation that had witnessed his saving and warrior acts (2:7); (4) by addressing their cries of pain in the face of their oppressors to Yahweh (3:15; 4:3; 6:6–7,34–35; 10:10); (5) by responding to the call of deliverer judges who went into battle in the name of Yahweh (3:28; 4:10; 5:12–15); (6) by appealing to his prophet for a divine determination on the crisis (4:5); (7) by elevating Yahweh's intervention on their behalf to impressive cosmological dimensions (5:4–5,20); (8) by assembling as "the covenant community" *(hāʿēdâ)* before Yahweh in Mizpah at a time of national crisis (20:1; 21:5); (9) by acknowledging the Ark of the Covenant as a symbol of Yahweh's presence and the descendants of Aaron as Yahweh's official priesthood (20:27–28); (10) by coming before God at Bethel and addressing him as Yahweh (21:2–3); (11) by swearing in the name of Yahweh (21:7);[78] and (12) by cel-

---

[74] The expression occurs only here and in 2 Sam 14:13 (אֱלֹהִים עַם), but cp. עַם אֱלֹהֵי אַבְרָהָם, "the people of the God of Abraham," in Ps 47:10.

[75] אֱלֹהִים אֲחֵרִים מֵאֱלֹהִים הָעַמִּים אֲשֶׁר סְבִיבוֹתֵיהֶם, 2:12.

[76] Elsewhere Israel's special claim to Yahweh is expressed by means of pronominal suffixes: אֱלֹהֶיךָ, "your God" (6:26); אֱלֹהֵינוּ, "our God" (10:10; 16:23–24); אֱלֹהֵיהֶם, "their God" (3:7; 8:34). Cp. the reference to Dagon as "their god," i.e., of the Philistines, in 16:23.

[77] Note esp. 2:14–22 and in each of the six cycles in 3:6–16:31.

[78] Cf. Deut 6:11; 10:20.

ebrating the annual "feast of the LORD" *(ḥag yhwh)* at Shiloh.

Although little is known about the practice of official national religion at this time, these data demonstrate that throughout the period of settlement the Israelite tribes retained a consciousness of their status as the people of Yahweh. But little is known of their formal collective expression of faith in cultic worship. One does indeed encounter occasional references to Bethel, Gilgal, and Shiloh as cultic sites,[79] presumably because they provided successive homes for the Ark of the Covenant, but neither the Book of Judges nor the early chapters of 1 Samuel suggest the Israelites convocated regularly, or even once, to worship Yahweh at a central shrine or that the tribes held any religious festivals in common.[80]

So much for official religion. The practical reality of lay religious expression was something else. The narrator's evaluation of Israel's true spiritual condition is reflected in the sevenfold repetition of variations of the refrain, "The descendants of Israel did evil in the eyes of the LORD; they forgot the LORD and served the Baals and the Asherahs" (2:11; 3:7,12; 4:1; 6:1; 10:6; 13:1). Indeed, according to the prologue (2:1–23), with time the apostasy of the nation intensified. The symptoms of Israel's spiritual progressive degeneracy are recognizable on almost every page: (1) failure to fulfill the divine mandate to rout the Canaanites (1:18–36); (2) failure to transmit the memory of Yahweh's saving acts (2:10); (3) hesitancy/refusal to heed Yahweh's call to arms (5:16–17); (4) the construction of altars for Baal within Israelite villages, and then the villagers' defense of the altar instead of the one who destroyed it; (5) all Israel's harlotrous attention to the "ephod" made by Gideon (8:27); (6) Israel's formal replacement of their God Yahweh with Baal-berith (8:33); (7) the manufacture of sacred images and the establishment of private pagan cults in individuals' homes (17:1–13); (8) tribal sponsorship of pagan cults (18:14–31). This spiritual degeneracy is accompanied by increasingly depraved moral behavior as is evidenced especially by the final episode involving the violence toward the Levite's concubine (19:22–20), and the "daughters of Shiloh" (21:19–24). There the ethical crisis is expressed in the refrain, "In those days Israel had no king; everyone did as he saw fit" (17:6; 21:25) and truncated versions in 18:1 and 19:1.

The involvement of the respective judges in the religious affairs of the

---

[79] On Shiloh in the Book of Judges see D. G. Schley, *Shiloh: A Biblical City in Tradition and History,* JSOTSup 63 (Sheffield: JSOT Press, 1989), 127–38.

[80] 2 Kgs 23:22 suggests the Passover was never celebrated according to the covenantal prescriptions during the period of the judges. For a reconstruction of the evolution of official religion in this period, see Albertz, *History of Israelite Religion,* pp. 76–94. See also K. van der Toorn, *Family Religion in Babylonia, Syria and Israel: Continuity and Change in the Forms of Religious Life,* SHCANE 7 (Leiden: Brill, 1996), esp. chap. 10, "Religion Before the Monarchy: The Gods of the Fathers," 236–65.

nation is telling. Although they all served actively as Yahweh's agents of deliverance from foreign enemies, not one of them had the moral or spiritual constitution to launch a crusade against the enemy within, to denounce the idolatry of the nation, or to call the people back to Yahweh. The only judge who engaged in such tasks was Samuel (1 Sam 7:1–11), who probably disqualified himself for consideration in the Book of Judges on these grounds.[81] Where appeals for religious reform are made in the Book of Judges, the challenge is presented by an envoy *(malʾāk)* of Yahweh (2:1–5), a prophet *(nābîʾ)* of Yahweh (6:7–10), or by Yahweh himself, without reference to an intermediary (10:10–16). Far from being agents of spiritual change, the deliverers demonstrated repeatedly that they were a part of the problem rather than a solution: (1) Ehud's treachery and brutality bear striking resemblance to Canaanite patterns of behavior; (2) Barak is weak-willed and indecisive; (3) Gideon is successively cynical of Yahweh's interest in his people, resistant toward his call, brutal toward his countrymen, and despite his pious comment in 8:23, imperial in his rule; (4) Jephthah, the scion of an immoral man, is ambitious in relation to his countrymen and pagan in his bargaining with Yahweh, not to mention abusive toward his daughter whom he sacrifices; and (5) Samson, whose very name "Little Sun" *(šimšôn)* is suspicious, treats his Nazirite status with contempt and fritters away his high calling with illicit philandering with pagan women. The human materials available to Yahweh for dealing with the foreign oppressors were raw indeed. Far from distinguishing themselves as paragons of virtue and faith, the deliverers tended to be the antithesis. In fact, the judges were the opposite of charismatic leaders, if by the expression we mean those naturally gifted and spiritually qualified for a task. To be sure, Yahweh demonstrated his presence through his Spirit, but even the fact that certain individuals were "clothed"[82] with the Spirit says nothing about their spiritual qualification for the task they were called to perform. To the contrary, this idiom of divine intrusion into human experience describes Yahweh's arresting and empowerment of individuals ill-disposed toward resolving Israel's problems and his equipping of them for the saving task.[83] In other words, the Book of Judges is not so much a written memorial to Israel's heroes in the Early Iron Age as a witness to Yahweh's gracious determination to preserve his people by answering their pleas and providing deliverance.

---

[81] His function as reformer should be associated with his primarily prophetic role rather than his functions as judge (1 Sam 3:19–21).

[82] The expression occurs only with reference to Gideon (6:34), but it functions as a metaphorical variant of "the Spirit coming upon one." See further below.

[83] Note esp. 13:25, according to which Samson did not get involved with the Philistines until the Spirit of Yahweh began to stir him. According to Num 24:3, Balaam son of Beor, a pagan prophet from Mesopotamia, experienced the same phenomenon: "The Spirit of God came upon him," causing him to utter an oracle.

According to the Book of Judges the religious picture of Israel in the centuries preceding the establishment of the monarchy was confused and syncretistic. But how did it come to this? The devolution of Israelite faith appears to have occurred in stages.

First, 2:6–10a suggests that when the Israelites arrived in Canaan under the leadership of Joshua they represented a covenant community, united in their devotion to Yahweh and willing to follow his orders in the divine war of conquest.[84]

Second, once the backbone of Canaanite resistance had been broken and the Israelite clans began to settle down, they established local sanctuaries for the worship of Yahweh. For the average Israelite the cultic services at these regional centers quickly took the place of the great national celebrations at the central shrine. The failure of the religious authorities to establish a permanent home for the tabernacle and the Ark of the Covenant, combined with the necessity of Israelite worshipers to pass through enemy (Canaanite) territory to get to the central place of worship, undoubtedly resulted in a rapid declension in the significance of the central sanctuary in the life of the nation. Without the regular celebration of the tribes' common origin in Yahweh's saving and covenantal acts at the great annual festivals, the nation experienced increasing political and territorial fragmentation. Meanwhile, the worship of Yahweh at the individual sanctuaries degenerated into what H. Donner calls "poly-Yahwism": local differentiation of the Yahweh cult traditions and forms.[85]

Third, the worship of Yahweh at the local shrines was mixed with the worship of Canaanite deities associated with these places. Initially this may have meant merely the identification of Yahweh with other divinities, especially El and Baal. The former name is familiar from authentic Hebrew traditions;[86] but in Canaanite mythology El was the head of the pantheon, the father of the gods and creator of the world. In comparison with Baal, El appeared as a tired old deity.[87] Baal, the storm god, appears to have been the most popular divinity among the Canaanites, being recognized as the power behind the life-giving

---

[84] This image is confirmed by the Book of Joshua.

[85] Analogous to the poly-Baalism reflected in names like Baal-berith of Shechem, Baal-Hermon, Baal-Peor, El-Bethel, and El-ʿOlam in Beersheba. See H. Donner, "'Hier sind deine Götter, Israel!'" in *Wort und Geschichte, FS K. Elliger,* AOAT 18 (Neukirchen: Neukirchener Verlag, 1973), 48–49.

[86] Cf. the compound names El-Shaddai and El-Elyon, descriptive appellations (great God [Deut 7:21], everlasting God [Gen 21:23], compassionate God [Exod 34:6], jealous/impassioned God [Exod 20:5], etc.), numerous personal names involving El (Elijah, Elisha, etc.), and the formal identification of Yahweh and El (Josh 22:22). For numerous additional examples and discussion see F. M. Cross, *TDOT* 1.253–61; R. Rendtorff, "ʾEl als israelitische Gottesbezeichnung," *ZAW* 106 (1994): 4–21. A prominent motif in the anti-idolatry polemic of Isaiah 41–45 is the conviction that only Yahweh is El and no one else.

[87] Cross, ibid., 244–53.

rain that fertilizes the ground and causes the vegetation to grow.[88] Truly committed Yahwists could claim previous Baalistic hymns for Yahweh without compromising their religious beliefs,[89] but for the spiritually weak the distinctions between Yahweh and the gods was blurred.

Fourth, although Yahweh retained the devotion of the people, for many layfolk worshiping at sites previously associated with the god to whom native Canaanites credited their prosperity allowed the religious customs and practices of Baal to become assimilated with the religion of Yahweh.[90] This kind of syncretism is suggested in 17:1–13, in which we find a man with a Yahwistic name (Micah, meaning "Who is like Yahweh?") claiming the support of Yahweh by engaging a Levitical priest; but the manufacture of the image, the cult installation, and the private arrangements for the cult are all pagan features. In chap. 18 the Danites as a tribe succumb to this type of syncretism. In this phase Yahweh, who had previously been worshiped primarily as the gracious divine deliverer and covenant lord, took on more and more of the character of a Baal-type fertility deity (17:13). Concrete evidence of this kind of syncretism is found not only in the bull worship at Sinai (Exodus 32) and Jeroboam's calves at Bethel and Dan (1 Kgs 12:25–33),[91] but also in several inscriptions (from a later time to be sure) that associate Yahweh with a female consort, Asherah.[92]

Fifth, the worship of Yahweh is abandoned entirely and replaced with the

---

[88] M. J. Mulder, *TDOT* 2.181–92.

[89] Cf. Deut 33:26–29, which contains motifs familiar from poetic myths of Baal.

[90] Some such syncretism may underlie the divine designations El-berith ("El of the Covenant") and Baal-berith ("Baal of the Covenant") in Judg 8:33 and 9:4,46.

[91] Attention may here be drawn also to the Iron Age I bronze bull figurine, which Mazar interprets as "a major object of cult, depicting or symbolizing a god," which "expressed the attributes of a particular West Semitic storm god Hadad." "The 'Bull Site'—An Iron Age Open Cult Place," *BASOR* 247 (1982): 32. See also Mazar's less technical treatment of the subject, "Bronze Bull Found in Israelite 'High Place' from the Time of the Judges," *BAR* 9/5 (1983): 34–40. See more recently N. Wyatt, "Of Calves and Kings," *SJOT* 6 (1992): 68–91.

[92] Note the three ninth-century blessings inscribed at Kuntillet ʿAjrud, a caravan stop in northern Sinai:
Pithos 1: I bless you through Yahweh of Samaria and through his Asherah
(ברכת אתכם ליהוה שמרן ולאשרתה).
Pithos 2/3: I bless you through Yahweh of Teman and through his Asherah
(ברכתך ליהוה תמן ולאשרתה).
Cp. the eighth-century blessing in the tomb inscription in Khirbet el-Qom, eight miles west of Hebron: "Blessed be Uriyahu through Yahweh for he has saved him from his enemies through his Ashera [לאשרתה]." For discussion of the pithoi texts see Z. Meshel, *Kuntillet ʿAjrud: A Religious Centre from the Time of the Judaean Monarchy on the Border of Sinai*, Catalogue No. 175 (Jerusalem: Israel Museum, 1978); J. Day, "Asherah in the Hebrew Bible and Northwest Semitic Literature," *JBL* 105 (1986): 391–93; W. A. Maier III, *ʾAšerah: Extrabiblical Evidence*, HSM 37 (Atlanta: Scholars Press, 1986). On the tomb inscription see Day, ibid., 39–95; Maier, ibid.; O. Keel and C. Uehlinger, *Gods, Goddesses and Images of God in Ancient Israel*, trans. T. Trapp (Minneapolis: Fortress, 1998), 225–48.

worship of the Baals and Asherahs/Ashtaroths, local manifestations of the male and female divinities in the fertility religion.[93] The Baal altar and the Asherah on Gideon's father's property represented this final stage in the devolution of Yahwistic faith.

Yahweh's hostility toward any accommodation to pagan religious forms reflects the radical difference between Yahweh's claims on his people and the claims of other gods. Whereas other ancient Near Eastern divinities tolerated the simultaneous worship of other gods, Yahweh demanded exclusive and total devotion from his subjects.[94] Although the root *qn²* never appears in the book, according to the "Deuteronomistic historian" Yahweh's fundamental disposition is reflected in his epithet *²El Qannā²*, "God impassioned."[95] The noun *qin²â* is often rendered "jealousy," but this is both inadequate and misleading. In common parlance jealousy tends to be associated either with envy and covetousness, the desire to own what someone else possesses, or exaggerated possessiveness over what one already owns, that is, an unwillingness to share it with others.[96] In the biblical word *qin²â*, however, one should hear the legitimate, indeed amazing, passion of God for one whom he loves.[97] This love is fueled not by an exploitative need to dominate but ardor for the well-being of the object.[98] In the Old Testament *qin²â* is aroused when a legitimate and wholesome relationship is threatened by interference from a third party. Thus the word expresses an entirely appropriate response by a husband or wife when another "lover" enters the picture (Prov 6:32–35).[99] Since the marriage metaphor provides the basic image for understanding Yahweh's covenant with Israel, the description of his response to infidelity as *qin²â*, "passion, zeal, ardor," is both logical and natural. Indeed, *qannā²*, a variant expression from the same root, is not merely an attribute of God; it is an epithet.[100] Yahweh had

---

[93] Note the use of the verb עָזַב, "to abandon, forsake," with Yahweh as the object in 2:12–13; 10:6,10,13.

[94] Cf. Block, *The Gods of the Nations: Studies in Ancient Near Eastern National Theology,* ETSM 2 (Winona Lake: Eisenbrauns, 1988), 69–71.

[95] The epithet is first introduced in the Decalogue given at Sinai (Exod 20:5) and later reiterated on the plains of Moab (Deut 5:9). Cf. Exod 34:14; Deut 4:24; 6:15; also Josh 24:19; Nah 1:2.

[96] In psychiatric terms jealousy amounts to "vindictiveness born of sexual frustration." See D. J. Halperin, *Seeking Ezekiel: Text and Psychology* (University Park: Pennsylvania State University Press, 1993), 121.

[97] J. Milgrom (*Numbers,* JPS Torah Commentary [Philadelphia, 1990], 303, n. 42) notes that in Arabic and Syriac *qn²* means "become intensely red," a reference to the effects of anger on one's facial complexion.

[98] Song 8:6–7 expresses the security the object of legitimate passion feels.

[99] The "Law of Passions" (תּוֹרַת הַקְּנָאֹת) in Num 5:12–31 seeks to regulate suspicions of such interference.

[100] Cf. the self-introduction formula in Exod 20:5 and Deut 5:9: אָנֹכִי יהוה אֱלֹהֶיךָ אֵל קַנָּא, "I am the LORD your God, El Qanna² (Impassioned God)." Cf. also Exod 34:14; Deut 4:24. In Deut 6:15, Josh 24:19, and Nah 1:2, קַנָּא/קַנּוֹא functions attributively.

committed himself to Israel, a devotion expressed in gracious redemption of the nation from bondage; and he rightfully expected grateful and exclusive loyalty in return. The intensity of his wrath at threats to this relationship arises out of the profundity of his covenant love. Because he feels so deeply, he must respond vigorously. Having been the sole deliverer of his people and having entered into a covenant with them at Sinai, any attention to rivals is denounced as spiritual harlotry.[101]

3. The Composition of the Book of Judges

(1) A Survey of Modern Scholarly Opinion[102]

Like all the historiographic books of the Old Testament, the Book of Judges is anonymous. Traditional Christian interpretation has followed the lead of the Rabbis who recognized Samuel as the author not only of the books by his name but also Judges and Ruth (*B. Bat.* 14b).[103] However, the enlightenment, a philosophical movement in nineteenth century Europe, produced radically different understandings of most biblical texts. Out of this movement arose the classical critical hermeneutic, according to which the same J, E, and D sources supposedly represented in the Hexateuch (Genesis–Joshua) were seen to underlie the Book of Judges as well.[104] This approach has been largely abandoned by scholars today, thanks in large part to the efforts of M. Noth. Noth broke up the Hexateuch and Pentateuch by positing a separate unitary Deuteronomic History (DH), encompassing Joshua–Kings, produced by a Judean historian and conveniently called the Deuteronomist (Dtr). The Book of Deuteronomy, which was originally quite distinct from Genesis–Numbers, was

---

[101] Note the expression אֱלֹהִים אֲחֵרִים אַחֲרֵי זָנוּ, "they committed harlotry [going] after other gods," (NIV "they prostituted themselves to other gods") in 2:17, and variations in 8:27,33.

[102] For a more thorough recent survey see O'Connell, *Rhetoric of the Book of Judges,* 345–68.

[103] For a modern defense of Samuel as the author of Judges see C. J. Goslinga, *Joshua, Judges, Ruth,* trans. R. Togtman; BSC (Grand Rapids: Zondervan, 1986), 217–23.

[104] Among the foremost representatives of this approach are G. F. Moore, *A Critical and Exegetical Commentary on Judges,* 2d ed., ICC (Edinburgh: T & T Clark, 1908); C. F. Burney, *The Book of Judges with Introduction and Notes* (London: Rivingtons, 1918 [reprinted with introduction by W. F. Albright, New York: KTAV, 1970]); C. A. Simpson, *The Composition of the Book of Judges* (Oxford: Basil Blackwell, 1957). To illustrate the results we generalize the conclusions of Burney, who isolated the two basic sources as follows: J = 1:1–2:5; 6:11–24; 13:2–25; the main narrative of 19 and parts of 20. E = 2:6–3:6; 6:7–10; 8:22,23,27aβb, 10:6–16; the main parts of 11:12–28. These narrative strands were brought together shortly after 700 B.C. by a redactor, R^{JE}, who also incorporated the older narratives of the judges themselves. This document was reedited with numerous additions by R^{E2} around 650 B.C. and later touched up by a Deuteronomic hand, D^2 (cf. 2:12,14bβ,15,18,19; 3:1a,3). The book was given its final shape in postexilic times by priestly redactor R^P, who reinserted older narratives (chaps. 9; 17–18; 19–21), the brief notices of the "minor" judges (10:1–5; 12:8–15). The Shamgar note in 3:31 was added later still. See Burney, *Judges,* xxxiv–l.

added later as a paradigmatic prologue to the history work. The purpose of DH was to explain the events of 722 and 586 B.C. These tragedies purportedly occurred as a result of Israel's persistent apostasy and total failure to conform to the terms of the covenant that Yahweh had made with her.[105] Although this theory has undergone numerous refinements and revisions, Noth's work continues to be foundational for most critical investigation of the Book of Judges.[106] Scholarly modifications to the basic thesis tend to revolve around the date of the primary edition of DH[107] and the number and scope of redactions, but the genius of Noth's proposal, the perception of an overall unity of Deuteronomy–Kings, continues to find wide acceptance.[108]

Having sketched the approaches critical scholars take to DH as a whole, we may now focus specifically on reconstructions of the growth of the Book of Judges.[109] Especially significant have been the reconstructions of the book's evolution by W. Richter, U. Becker, and R. Boling. Richter[110] begins by isolating a "Book of Saviors" *(Retterbuch)*, Noth's proposed collection of stories about local heroes. Although this material provides the core of the present book, Richter argues that the stories may have been revised several times before they were incorporated into DH. Ignoring the fundamentally antimonarchic stance of the *Retterbuch*, the first reviser (Rdt1) provided the editorial framework for the individual accounts of the deliverers. In support of his thesis that the worship of Yahweh brings security but the worship of other gods results in defeat, a second redactor (Rdt2) prefaced the stories of the heroes

---

[105] M. Noth, *The Deuteronomistic History*, trans. D. Orton. JSOTSup 15 (Sheffield: JSOT Press, 1981).

[106] Note especially the German works by R. Smend, 'Das Gesetz und die Völker: Ein Beitrag zur deuteronomistischen Redaktionsgeschichte," in *Probleme biblischer Theologie: Gerhard von Rad zum 70. Geburtstag*, ed. H. W. Wolff (München: Chr. Kaiser, 1971), 494–509; and W. Dietrich, *Prophetie und Geschichte: eine redaktionsgeschichtliche Untersuchung zum deuteronomistischen Geschichtswerk*, FRLANT 108 (Göttingen: Vandenhoeck & Ruprecht, 1977).

[107] While Noth assigned DH to the exilic period, some (e.g., F. M. Cross, "The Structure of the Deuteronomic History," in *Perspectives in Jewish Learning* 3 [1968]: 9–24; id., *Canaanite Myth and Hebrew Epic* [Cambridge, Mass.: Yale University Press, 1973], 274–89; R. D. Nelson, *The Double Redaction of the Deuteronomistic History*, JSOTSup 18 [Sheffield: JSOT Press, 1981]) insist the primary edition was completed in the Josianic period, with minor revisions occurring later.

[108] For a convenient survey of critical approaches to DH in general see S. L. McKenzie, "Deuteronomistic History," *ABD* 2.160–68. For a more comprehensive study see McKenzie and M. P. Graham, eds., *The History of Israel's Traditions: The Heritage of Martin Noth*, JSOTSup 182 (Sheffield: JSOT Press, 1994).

[109] For surveys of the study of Judges since Noth see M. A. O'Brien, "Judges and the Deuteronomistic History," in *The Heritage of Martin Noth*, ibid., 235–59; R. Bartelmus, "Forschung am Richterbuch seit Martin Noth," *TRu* 56 (1991): 221–59.

[110] See W. Richter, *Die Bearbeitungen des 'Retterbuches' in der deuteronomischen Epoche*, BBB 21 (Bonn: P. Hanstein, 1964); id., *Traditionsgeschichtliche Untersuchungen zum Richterbuch*, BBB 18 (Bonn: P. Hanstein, 1966). Richter is followed in the main by Soggin, *Judges*, 5–7.

with the paradigmatic account of Othniel (3:7–11) and added numerous amplifications of the people's sins. The influence of Deuteronomy 13 and 17 is recognizable in the sharpened theology of retribution. Richter's third redactor (DtrG) corresponds to Noth's postexilic Deuteronomist. He is responsible for inserting the fragments concerning the "minor" judges and in general integrating the entire work into the broader DH. The book's generally dark tone is the work of this person, who, in reflecting on the tragedy of 587–586, holds the nation accountable by reason of their persistent apostasy. The references to the gods of the Ammonites and Philistines in 10:6 suggest that the Samson stories derive from his hand. Richter does not deal with chap. 1 and the last part of the book, chaps. 17–21. Presumably these were even later additions.

The most thorough examination of the evolution of the Book of Judges since Richter's work is provided by U. Becker.[111] Becker's work is in part a reaction to recent literary approaches, especially in the English speaking world, which have been ever more impressed with the literary qualities of the book as a whole and have eschewed speculative reconstructions of its literary history.[112] Maintaining the strongly analytical direction of German Old Testament scholarship, Becker conducts an exhaustive redactional study of this book, focusing especially on its disposition toward the monarchy. His conclusions, which argue for a three-stage evolution for the book, may be summarized as follows. (1) The major part of 2:11–16:31 is the work of the Deuteronomistic historian (DtrH), who utilized a variety of older, more or less anecdotal and legendary *(sagenhaft)* hero-stories and other traditional fragments to create a coherent picture of the period of the judges.[113] (2) The portrait of the judges was expanded with a multitude of large and small late redactional additions (DtrN), which often contained ancient information but which can no longer be organized, at least not in their relation to each other.[114] (3) A scribe with the style and tone of P, from the same circle as the redactor of the Pentateuch (RP), composed the framework (1:1–18,22–26; 19:121:25) and added several additional sections, influenced by the Book of Joshua. The telltale marks of this literary stage are the priestly style of these sections, as well as concern for Shiloh as a religious center. He concludes that DtrH is fundamentally opposed to the monarchy. DtrN shares this view but places much more stress on the people's guilt in the disasters of the period. The final editor,

---

[111] U. Becker, *Richterzeit und Königtum: Redaktionsgeschichtliche Studien zum Richterbuch,* BZAW 192 (Berlin/New York: de Gruyter, 1990).

[112] See below.

[113] He rejects Richter's notion of a pre-dtr collection of hero-stories.

[114] Segments added in this phase include those which present the judges as preachers of the law (2:12aα,13–14a,16b,17–18aα*,19–21; 3:5–6), the ephod notice (8:24–27), the moral notes in the Abimelech account (9:16b–19a,24,56–57), the list of unconquered sites (1:21,27–36), the divine envoy episode (2:1–5), and the apostate cult of Micah (chaps. 17–18).

on the other hand, looks upon the premonarchic period as a total failure, whose chaos can only be remedied by instituting the monarchy.[115] While Becker claims that his reconstruction of the book's history is simpler than Richter's and his exegetical comments are often insightful, many will question his conclusions because they are obtained only by "piling one speculation upon another."[116]

Boling is much more sensitive to the literary artistry of the book, but his reconstruction of its growth still presupposes Noth's analytical approach.[117] According to Boling, the core of the book is based on historical events, to be sure, but the stories of the heroes have a folkloric rather than objectively historical nature. He proposes that they derive from a guild of professional storytellers in premonarchic Israel. In the interests of both edification and entertainment, they dressed up their accounts, much like the reader witnesses in the stories of Ruth, the framework of the Book of Job, and later Esther. In the eighth century these accounts were supposedly collected and combined to form a more or less unitary literary whole, consisting of the Epic Prologue (2:6–3:6) and history with the judges in two parts: Phase I, 3:7–10:5, minus 6:7–10; Phase II, 10:17–15:20.[118] In the seventh century the Deuteronomic editor revised and adapted this material to the agenda of the broader Deuteronomistic History by inserting three hortatory appeals (by the divine envoy, 2:1–5, by an unnamed prophet, 6:7–10, and by Yahweh himself, 10:11–14) and three negative examples from earlier times (Samson, 16:1–31; Micah, 17:1–2; the Danites, 18:1–31). The turmoil within Israel following the fall of Jerusalem in 586 is reflected in the tragic-comic framework consisting of a new introduction (chap. 1) and a new conclusion (chaps. 19–21). According to Boling the final Deuteronomistic editor counters the disillusionment of the exile with comedy as an escape not from the reality but from the despair the reality evokes (cf. Psalm 137).

While accepting the hypothesis of a Deuteronomistic History, an increasing number of scholars have turned toward a holistic literary approach to the Book of Judges. R. Polzin[119] finds in the present text a complex and subtle dialogue between the "authorian dogmatism" of retributive justice Moses voiced in Deuteronomy and the narrator's own "critical traditionalism." The

---

[115] For a summary of Becker's conclusions see *Richterzeit und Königtum*, 300–306.

[116] The criticism leveled by R. N. Whybray (*The Making of the Pentateuch: A Methodological Study*, JSOTSup 53 [Sheffield: JSOT Press, 1987], 194) at Noth's reconstruction of Pentateuchal traditions.

[117] Boling, *Judges*, 29–38; id., "Judges, Book of," *ABD* 3.1107–17.

[118] Boling conjectures the pre-Deuteronomic work included stories of Eli and Samuel as well (*Judges*, 36).

[119] *Moses and the Deuteronomist: A Literary Study of the Deuteronomic History*, Part I, *Deuteronomy, Joshua, Judges* (New York: Seabury, 1980).

latter is heard especially in the gracious portrayal of Yahweh in the book. Far from destroying Israel, he repeatedly demonstrates his compassion on that nation's behalf. But the stories of the judges present an unpredictable picture in which both authoritarian dogmatism and traditionalism are challenged. Textual ambiguities reflect the growing chaos in Israel, warning the reader against putting too much confidence in any theology. But for Polzin the discordant viewpoints are intentionally preserved in the text as an artistic device within DH.

Apparently dispensing with the hypothesis of DH, L. R. Klein's recognition of the devolution of the Book of Judges in disorder displays affinities with Polzin's conclusions.[120] However, the key to the book is the literary device of irony, which appears in many different guises, then culminates in the rape and murder of the Levite's concubine (chaps. 19–21). In the most detailed examination of the literary structures and devices of Judges to date, B. G. Webb challenges the hypothesis of a unitary Deuteronomistic History, especially Noth's extension of the period of the judges to 1 Samuel 12.[121] Employing a rhetorical analytical method,[122] he argues for a unity of plot and theme by comparing the three main parts of the book to the "Overture" (1:1–3:6), "Variations" (3:7–16:31), and "Coda" (17:1–21:25) of a musical score. The core narrative reaches its climax in the story of Samson, who embodies all that is wrong with Israel. Correctly, in our estimation, instead of adhering to some form of more or less unitary Deuteronomistic History, he posits "an edited series of books" that make up this block of material.[123]

The most recent in-depth attempt to interpret the Book of Judges holistically is provided by R. O'Connell.[124] O'Connell's work is remarkable both for its breadth of view and attention to detail. As the title suggests, he perceives the Book of Judges as an intentional rhetorical product in which plot, structure, characterization, and other literary devices all serve to advance a particular agenda: in general to reorient its readers toward higher religious and political standards and specifically to idealize Judah as the divinely appointed leader of the tribes of Israel. But in advancing the latter, the narrator also pursues an even

---

[120] L. R. Klein, *The Triumph of Irony in the Book of Judges,* JSOTSup 68 (Sheffield: Almond Press, 1987).

[121] B. G. Webb, *The Book of Judges: An Integrated Reading,* JSOTSup 46 (Sheffield: JSOT Press, 1987). For his evaluation of the hypothesis see pp. 19–28.

[122] Paying special attention to the use of alliteration and assonance, inclusion and chiasm, recurring motifs and patterns, semantic shifts and transitions.

[123] For other representatives of the holistic literary approach (in addition to Webb and Polzin) see K. R. R. Gros Louis, "The Book of Judges," *Literary Interpretations of Biblical Narratives,* K. Gros Louis et al., eds. (Nashville: Abingdon, 1974), 141–62; J. P. U. Lilley, "A Literary Appreciation of the Book of Judges," *TynBul* 18 (1976): 94–102; Y. Amit, "The Art of Composition in the Book of Judges" (Ph.D. diss., Tel Aviv University, 1984).

[124] O'Connell, *Rhetoric of the Book of Judges.*

more specific goal—to legitimize the Davidic monarchy and at the same time to vilify the Saulide house. With his anti-Benjamite and pro-Judahite rhetoric, the author attempts to break down the allegiance of northern Israelites to the house of Saul and to convince them to transfer their loyalty to David. Although O'Connell refrains from setting a date for the composition, to make political sense it would need to have been written within the lifetime of David and Ish-bosheth, shortly after Saul's death. Despite fundamental problems with O'Connell's central thesis[125] and methodology,[126] he has presented the stron-gest defense to date of a unifying rhetorical agenda that results in a unitary lit-erary product. Along the way he has provided countless exegetical insights on specific texts.

Although the Book of Judges contains numerous ideological and literary links with the rest of the books in Noth's so-called Deuteronomistic History, the evidence seems convincing that this is an independent literary composi-tion, written in light of the authentically Mosaic theology of Deuteronomy and in light of the written accounts of the conquest as found in the Book of Joshua. The theory of a separate literary work is reinforced by the indepen-dent literary integrity of the Book of Judges itself. While signs of disjunction among the respective parts of the book are obvious, it is apparent to me that a single mind has deliberately selected, arranged, linked, and shaped the sources available to him[127] to achieve a specific ideological agenda, which has yielded a coherent literary work. Few biblical compositions present a plot as tightly knit as that found in the Book of Judges.[128] If this were indeed intended as a segment of a larger unitary DH, one would have expected more

---

[125] The book is essentially a political document.

[126] The compiler/redactor of Judges shaped his materials on the basis of the portrayals of Saul in 1 Samuel. It is more likely that the reverse is the case—the compiler/editor of 1 Samuel shaped his materials on the basis of the portrayals of the judges.

[127] My use of the masculine pronoun is not a vestige of male chauvinism but a reflection of the historico-cultural fact that in the ANE female scribes were extremely rare. See D. W. Baker, "Scribes as Transmitters of Tradition," in *Faith, Tradition, and History,* 65–77.

[128] D. W. Gooding ("The Composition of the Book of Judges," *EI* 16 [1982]: 70–79) recognizes in the book an intentional symmetrical structure, with the Gideon narrative at the center:
Introduction: Part I (1:1–2:5)
    Introduction: Part II (2:6–3:6)
        Othniel (3:7–11)
            Ehud + Shamgar (3:12–21)
                Deborah, Barak, Jael (4:1–5:31)
                    Gideon (6:1–8:32)
                Abimelech + Tola and Jair (8:33–10:5)
            Jephthah + Ibzan, Elon, and Abdon (10:6–12:15)
        Samson (13:1–16:31)
    Epilogue: Part I (17:1–18:31)
Epilogue: Part II (19:1–21:25).

careful integration with the plot structures of preceding narratives in Joshua and the following narratives of Samuel. Surely the story of Samuel, who in the opinion of most functions as a judge, should have been included in this book. But his story is rejected because he is a transitional and primarily prophetic figure, more at home in the monarchic accounts of Samuel than in the narratives of Judges. This is not to deny strong links between the Book of Judges and its canonical literary environment. It is only to doubt a single author for the entire work. The connections that exist between Judges, the preceding Book of Joshua, and the following Samuel–Kings derive not from a single hand but from the common Mosaic theological and literary tradition in which the Yahwistic authors of all of these books were schooled. Any attempt to reconstruct the literary evolution of the Book of Judges must take into account both its links with the rest of DH and its distinctive themes and literary features. We will continue to view the historian responsible for the Book of Judges as a "Deuteronomist," but this characterization says more about his perspective than his identity, which is probably to be distinguished from the authors/editors of the other books in this complex of writings.

(2) The Nature and Design of Judges

GENRE. A discussion of the composition of the Book of Judges is best begun by considering the genre of the work. The individual pieces that make up the book represent a variety of easily identifiable literary genres: conquest annals (1:1–36), paraenetic narrative (2:1–5; 6:7–10; 10:10–16), theological exposition (2:7–3:6), "hero" narratives (most of the accounts of the deliverers), historical notes (3:31), hymnic poetry (5:1–31), short story (6:1–8:35; 13:1–16:31; 17:1–18:31; 19:1–21:25), etiology (6:28–32), fable (9:7–15), battle narrative (9:23–57; 20:1–48), annalistic ruler lists (10:1–5; 12:8–15), political speech (11:15–27), tease/riddle (14:10–20), and poetic fragments (15:16; 16:23–24). But how is the composition as a whole to be classified? It has become fashionable among literary specialists to speak of the Book of Judges, along with many other biblical narratives, as fiction. Many features of the book make this conclusion attractive to some: the artificiality of "twelve" judges who ruled Israel, etiological elements (Gideon's name change, 6:32), legend-like hero-tales, mythological motifs (stars fighting from heaven, 5:20), the ubiquitous intervention of God in human affairs, the dominating theological framework,[129] the formal structure, and the literary

---

[129] With his notion of "imaginary history," Ahlström (*History of Ancient Palestine*, 44) avers that because the biblical texts dealing with the origin of Israel in Palestine proclaim that the divine will is behind the creation of the people Israel these texts do not provide any basic historical information on the emergence of the people or nation of Israel.

artistry of the author.[130] Not surprisingly both literary specialists[131] and historians[132] treat the Book of Judges, along with other biblical narrative texts, as prose fiction, with little or no historical value.[133] Support for this conclusion is often drawn from the fact that few biblical stories are corroborated by extrabiblical or archaeological records.

But is such a negative evaluation of Hebrew narrative necessary? Does the term "fiction" accurately describe what the author of the Book of Judges perceived himself to be writing? The question cannot be answered without first identifying objective criteria by which historical and fictional writing may be distinguished. A. Millard has conveniently pointed out three criteria that could establish a fictional account.[134] First, the account may contain anachronisms [or cultural erratics][135] that betray its origin in a different time or context from what is purported in the text itself. True anachronisms and erratics may appear in the language, dispositions of or actions by the participants, the context of the account, or material artifacts. Second, the account may contain truly imaginary or fantastic elements, such as flying horses or gem-bearing trees, which the author himself would recognize as unreal. Divine interventions do not qualify, since, like other ancient Near Eastern writers, biblical narrators believed God

---

[130] Note the fine rhetorical elements identified in n. 122 and also the skillful literary use of dialogue, characterization, plot development, suspense and surprise, reticence, and other literary conventions. The recognition of these elements has revolutionized the study of Hebrew narrative in recent years. Leading the way have been among others, J. Licht (*Storytelling in the Bible* [Jerusalem: Magnes, 1978]), R. Alter (*The Art of Biblical Narrative* [New York: Basic Books, 1981]), A. Berlin (*Poetics and Interpretation of Biblical Narrative*, Bible and Literature Series 9 [Sheffield: Almond Press, 1983]), and M. Sternberg (*The Poetics of Biblical Narrative: Ideological Literature and the Drama of Reading* [Bloomington, Ind.: Indiana University Press, 1985]). The *JSOT* is devoted largely to publication of articles in this vein. See also *Beyond Form Criticism: Essays in Old Testament Literary Criticism*, ed. P. House, Sources for Biblical and Theological Study 2 (Winona Lake: Eisenbrauns, 1992).

[131] See Alter, *Art of Biblical Narrative*, 23–46.

[132] Note the negative historical assessment of N. P. Lemche (*Early Israel: Anthropological and Historical Studies on the Israelite Society before the Monarchy*, VTSup 37 [Leiden: Brill, 1985], 412): "The OT historical tradition is revealed to be a fiction written around the middle of the first millennium." His fundamental agnosticism regarding the true origins of Israel is reflected in his third axiom: "A saga or legend is ahistorical until the opposite has been proved; it is not historical until its 'historical' contents have been disproved" (p. 416). P. R. Davies (*In Search of 'Ancient Israel,'* JSOTSup 148 [Sheffield: JSOT Press, 1992]) regards the ethnic and religious "ancient Israel" of the OT narratives as a scholarly construct fabricated in the Persian province of Yehud. Elsewhere ("'House of David' Built on Sand: The Sins of Biblical Maximizers," *BAR* 20/4 [1994]: 55) he suspects that "the figure of King David is about as historical as King Arthur."

[133] For an analysis of the contemporary scene see E. Yamauchi, "The Current State of Old Testament Historiography," in A. R. Millard, et al., eds., *Faith, Tradition, and History*, 1–36.

[134] A. R. Millard, "Story, History, and Theology," in A. R. Millard, et al., eds., *Faith, Tradition, and History*, 50.

[135] A geological expression for a boulder that has been picked up by a glacier from an original resting place and deposited in a totally foreign environment.

actually could and did intervene in human affairs. Third, the compositions may contain internal irreconcilable discrepancies or contradictions with other writings familiar to the author that cannot be reconciled. In such cases one may assume the author was aware he was not truly representing historical reality. To these we may add two further considerations. Fourth, the biblical author may signal to the reader he is recounting an unreal event or circumstance. Where a narrative is explicitly identified as a fable, parable, allegory, or metaphor we may assume it is not historical. Fifth, the event described and the genre of the account must both be such that if encountered in extrabiblical literature they would be universally recognized as fictional.[136] One may not *a priori* dismiss biblical narratives as having no historical merit simply because they are biased or theological or stylized if one does not do so consistently with other analogous ancient materials. Without elaborating on these points, it may be generally affirmed that the Book of Judges meets none of these criteria.

But what is the relationship between the historical events experienced by the Israelites in the premonarchic period and the accounts left us by the biblical author? A narrow view of the process of inspiration requires God dictating to the biblical writer everything that happened, even the conversations, exactly as they occurred. Furthermore, the popular designation of the Joshua-Esther material as "the historical writings"[137] tends to value these texts primarily for the aid they provide in reconstructing the history of Israel.

However, a more satisfactory approach to Hebrew narratives like the Book of Judges is suggested by the designation of the Joshua-Kings corpus found in the Jewish canon. These writings constitute the "former prophets," in contrast to the "latter prophets."[138] By classifying Judges as a prophetic work, we acknowledge first, that it addresses a specific historical and religious situation and second, that whatever the genre of individual units, the entire work carries a paraenetic/homiletical agenda. The author's intent is not to produce a cold, rational, and objective record of events; this is literary rhetoric, the language of persuasion, designed to challenge prevailing notions and effect a spiritual and moral transformation in the readers of the composition. The book represents an extended sermon, or a series of sermons, that draws its "texts" from the real historical experiences of the Israelites in the premonarchic period. But like a modern preacher, the biblical author selects, organizes, arranges, shapes, and crafts his material for maximum effect. Recognizing this guards the reader

---

[136] For a helpful comparison of Hebrew historiography with extrabiblical counterparts see Millard, "Story, History, and Theology," in A. R. Millard, et al., eds., *Faith, Tradition, and History,* 37–64.

[137] In contrast to the "Law," the "poetic writings," and the "prophets," which together with the "historical" make up the OT canon.

[138] The Jewish designation for what is usually referred to simply as "the prophets" (minus Daniel) in our canon.

against *the fallacy of misplaced literalism,*[139] by which we force the text to carry freight it was not intended to carry. We recognize that the biblical text must be interpreted within the context of ancient Near Eastern standards of persuasion. At the same time, this approach frees us to appreciate the literary and rhetorical strategies by which the author sought to effect change in the mind and life of the original readers. However, recognizing the sermonic nature of Hebrew narrative also forces us to engage the text as Scripture, or better, to let it engage us, to hear its message, and to respond in accordance with the human and divine author's goal.[140]

Classifying the Book of Judges as prophetic literature does not remove it from the category of authentic historiography.[141] This is religious literature, to be sure, but as a genre "it is not characterized by pretense, and does not suspend the rules which connect serious discourse to reality,"[142] any more than other ancient Near Eastern document that are universally recognized as having a historical base. Those who deny any historical value to Hebrew historiographic writings are guilty of *the fallacy of historical pleading.*[143] Without the event, the biblical writer's "text," the sermon is empty. Even though the author's primary agenda was not to produce a chronology of Israelite history,

---

[139] Defined by D. H. Fischer as misconstruing "a statement in-evidence so that it carries a literal meaning when a symbolic or hyperbolic or figurative meaning was intended" (*Historians' Fallacies: Toward a Logic of Historical Thought* [New York: Harper & Row, 1970], 58).

[140] On the primacy of the authorial intent in determining meaning see E. D. Hirsch, *The Aims of Interpretation* (Chicago: University of Chicago Press, 1976); id., *Validity in Interpretation* (New Haven: Yale University Press, 1967); R. Stein, *Playing by the Rules* (Grand Rapids: Baker, 1994). This approach differs radically from the "reader response" hermeneutic that characterizes many contemporary "metacritical" and feminist readings of Judges, which assume the meaning of a text is never fixed but depends upon the values imposed upon it by the reader. See, e.g., P. Trible, *Texts of Terror: Literary-Feminist Readings of Biblical Narratives* (Philadelphia: Fortress, 1984); M. Bal, *Death and Dissymmetry: The Politics of Coherence in the Book of Judges,* Chicago Studies in the History of Judaism (Chicago: University of Chicago Press, 1988); id., *Murder and Difference: Gender, Genre, and Scholarship on Sisera's Death,* Indiana Studies in Biblical Literature, trans. M. Gumpert (Bloomington: Indiana University Press, 1988); J. C. Exum, *Fragmented Women: Feminist (Sub)versions of Biblical Narratives,* JSOTSup 163 (Sheffield: JSOT Press, 1993); as well as the essays in *A Feminist Companion to Judges,* ed. A. Brenner (Sheffield: JSOT Press, 1993); and G. A. Yee, ed., *Judges and Method: New Approaches in Biblical Studies* (Minneapolis: Fortress, 1995).

[141] For a positive assessment of the historical value of Hebrew historiographic writings see W. W. Hallo, "Biblical History in its Near Eastern Setting: The Contextual Approach," in *Scripture in Context: Essays on the Comparative Method,* ed. C. D. Evans, W. W. Hallo, and J. B. White, PTMS 34 (Pittsburgh: Pickwick, 1980), 1–26; all the essays in *Faith, History, and Tradition,* cited above.

[142] Thus S. Lasine, "Fiction, Falsehood, and Reality in Hebrew Scripture," *HS* 25 (1984): 24.

[143] According to Fischer (*Historical Fallacies,* 110), this occurs "whenever an investigator applies a double standard of inference or interpretation to his evidence—one standard to evidence which sustains his generalizations and another to evidence which contradicts it."

recognizing the factual basis for this genre of literature frees the reader to use these documents, along with extrabiblical evidence of course, as sources for reconstructing the emergence of ancient Israel on the Near Eastern map.

At the same time we admit that we do not know how the author learned of the conversations and even the gestures that he reports. Obviously he did not have the benefit of audio or video recorders; nor was he an eyewitness to all the events described.[144] How then could the narrator produce such detailed accounts of the events, complete with dialogues and speeches? How did he know which gestures accompanied the words? These and similar questions cannot be answered. But a high view of Scripture and the process of inspiration affirms that what is written is an accurate representation of what actually happened. Whether or not the recorded conversations preserve the *ipissima verba* (the exact words) of the characters involved,[145] when we interpret biblical texts as they were intended to be understood, we will discover that they always communicate truth. In the Book of Judges we encounter a form of historiography, which, under the inspiration of God, draws upon a range of authentic sources (oral or written), and creatively stylizes, arranges, and shapes the data they provide in accordance with the author's rhetorical agenda.

SOURCES. The composite nature of the Book of Judges is obvious to any reader. Although a single hand appears to be responsible for the final form and shape of the book,[146] stylistic variations in the subunits often derive from the variety of sources utilized by the author in the composition of the book. From the vast array of potential sources available to him, he has operated selectively, choosing those that might yield data for his thesis. Several types of sources may be identified.

Secondary "Judge" Lists. In 10:1–5 and 12:8–15 we encounter two literary fragments that stand outside the homiletical/theological framework and list five obscure names that play no part in the narrative.[147] These texts tend to be formulaic in nature, constructed around the following basic pattern:[148]

i. *PN* judged Israel after him. (10:1,3; 12:8,11–12)
ii. He judged Israel *X* years. (10:2,3; 12:9,11,14)
iii. Then *PN* died. (10:2,5; 12:10,12,15)

---

[144] Though some of the sources used undoubtedly go back to eyewitnesses.

[145] Insisting on the *ipissima verba* in each recorded conversation creates more difficulties than it resolves. E.g., did Samson actually communicate with the Philistines in Hebrew (chaps. 14–16)? To be more specific, when the Philistines celebrated their capture of Samson, would they have sung their victory songs (16:23–24) in the enemy's language?

[146] See the computerized study using statistical linguistics by Y. T. Radday, G. Leb, D. Wickmann, and S. Talmon, "The Book of Judges Examined by Statistical Linguistics," *Bib* 58 (1977): 469–99.

[147] On these lists see A. J. Hauser, "The 'Minor' Judges—A Reevaluation," *JBL* 94 (1975): 190–200; J. A. Soggin, "Das Amt der 'Kleinen Richter' in Israel," *VT* 30 (1980): 245–48.

[148] In the following, *PN* = Personal Name; *GN* = Geographic Name.

iv. And *PN* was buried in *GN*. (10:2,5; 12:10,12,15)
The information provided about these figures tends to be limited to details of
fact and may be illustrated in tabular form as follows:

The "Judge" Lists

Name	Tola	Jair	Ibzan	Elon	Abdon
Other Data	lineage tribe	gentilic territory	geographic origin	gentilic tribe	lineage gentilic place
Duration of Rule	23	22	7	10	8

To this basic information are added a variety of short narrative notes about
the place of rule, number of children, activity of the children (riding donkeys,
external marriage), and scope of rule. From these observations and the fact that
some of these formulae appear elsewhere (12:7; 15:20; 16:31), it appears the
author had access to official or unofficial lists, analogous to Assyrian
"eponoym lists," Roman "consul lists," or Punic "*špṭm* lists."[149] Presumably
the judges whose affairs are recounted in the book were included in these lists
as well, but because they receive fuller treatment they are not included in these
lists. Other unknown judges may also have been entered in the original source.
These two brief lists are significant for the study of the book not only because
they suggest to the reader that an official source underlay the present text, but
they also show how the author used his sources. He selected five apparently to
complete the symbolic complement of twelve needed for rhetorical reasons,
but he failed to narrate their exploits because they do not contribute materially
to his central thesis.[150] The lengths of some of their rules suggest that historically several of these figures were major. It is best, therefore, to dispense with
a designation like "minor" judges and replace it with "secondary," but they are
such only because they are deemed of secondary significance for the rhetorical
goals of the book.

Primary Hero-Stories. It seems reasonable to suppose that the exploits of
individual judges would have been treasured and even preserved in writing
within the region they governed.[151] It is also reasonable to assume that some-

---

[149] On the last see *KAI* 66:2; 77:3; 80:2–3; 81:6. O'Connell (*Rhetoric of the Book of Judges,*
54) is certainly correct in asserting that formulaic structuring of these lists may derive not from the
sources but from the compiler's consistent application of death and burial formulae of the "primary" judges (cf. 3:11; 8:32–33; 12:7; 16:31) to their "secondary" counterparts.

[150] J. A. Freeman sees in this dodecad feature "presumptive evidence of intelligent control" of
the overall structure of the book ("A Structural Reading of Judges 13–16," in *Literary Interpretations of Biblical Narratives,* vol. 2, ed. K. R. R. Gros Louis [Nashville: Abingdon, 1982], 148).

[151] Boling (*Judges,* 32–33) speculates that the stories of the heroes' actions were preserved and
narrated by a guild of storytellers.

one gathered these and other similar stories from throughout the nation, creating an anthology long before our text was written. The individuals whose activities have significance for the author's rhetorical agenda come from diverse circles: Judah (Othniel), Benjamin (Ehud), Ephraim (Deborah, though Barak is identified as a Naphtalite), Manasseh (Gideon), Dan (Samson), and Gilead (Jephthah). Presumably these stories were treasured both for their entertainment value and for the inspiration they provided for the nation: these judges were looked upon as heroes, embodiments of the Israelite spirit. However, as we will see, the person who wrote the Book of Judges as we have it viewed them quite differently. Like the prophet Ezekiel (chaps. 16; 20; 23), our inspired author offers a divine interpretation of Israel's history that differs radically from prevailing idealistic perspectives.

Conquest Records. The annalistic nature of 1:1–36 suggests dependence upon some official or semiofficial record of tribal achievements (or failures!) after the death of Joshua. It is impossible to know whether the source was oral or written, though the chapter contains a good deal of information found earlier in Joshua, as the following tabulation illustrates:

Judges	Joshua		Judges	Joshua
1:10–15	=	15:13–14	1:21	=	15:63
1:27–28	=	17:12–13	1:29	=	16:10
1:34	=	19:47			

Prophetic Traditions. Three short narrative units are set apart from their literary environment by their style and especially by the divine determination to communicate with his people. That communication occurs in three forms: through an emissary of Yahweh (*malʾāk*, 2:1–5), a prophet (*nābîʾ*, 6:7–10), and Yahweh directly (10:10–16). We may only speculate about the sources behind these accounts, but some origin in prophetic circles, perhaps even Samuel himself, is plausible.

Book of Victory Hymns. Judges 5:1–31 is set apart from the surrounding narrative by its literary style and celebrative tone. This hymn is generally recognized as one of the oldest documents in the Old Testament, preserving archaic grammatical and syntactical forms from the second millennium B.C. The author may have extracted this song, which displays striking links to Exodus 15, from the collection of victory hymns known as *The Book of the Wars of Yahweh* (Num 21:14) or *The Book of Jashar* (Josh 10:13; 2 Sam 1:18). The genre of victory hymns in praise of a deity is common in the ancient Near East.[152]

Other Sources. There is no agreement on the literary home of chaps. 17–21. The negative tone and the critical stance toward the Danites and Benjamites renders a source in the traditions of either of these two tribes unlikely. The

---

[152] Cf. the victory hymns of Thutmose III (*ANET,* 373–75) and Merneptah (*ANET,* 376–78).

interest in cultic matters in chaps. 17–18, and the significance of the ark and of Shiloh in chaps. 19–21 may point to a priestly record, preserved first at Shiloh, where the tabernacle and ark were located, and later in the temple.

We cannot be sure how many of the sources listed above were accessible to the author in written form. Based on archaeological data available to us, however, it is conceivable that written versions of all of these sources were produced shortly after the events, in some instances perhaps even by eyewitnesses.[153] Although the author of the Book of Judges was dependent upon a variety of sources for his information, and for some of his style, he has not left us simply an anthology of raw materials, literary artifacts, from the early Iron Age. Information from these documents was utilized selectively and arranged and shaped in accordance with his rhetorical and theological purposes.

THEME AND PURPOSE OF THE BOOK.   Impressed by the refrain "There was no king in Israel," which appears four times in the last five chapters (17:6; 18:1; 19:1; 21:25), scholars have often interpreted the Book of Judges as an apologetic for the monarchy in Israel. The chaos reflected in the narratives demonstrates the need for a centralized royal constitution. Support for this view may be derived also from the circumstances precipitating the request for a king by the elders of Israel in 1 Samuel 8. The fundamental anti-Ephraimite stance of the book is irrefutable, but M. Brettler's treatment of it as "a political allegory fostering the Davidic monarchy"[154] not only minimizes the significance of several textual units that are critical of the monarchy[155] but also disregards the critical stance toward Judah reflected in the book.[156] Furthermore,

---

[153] A. R. Millard has demonstrated that toward the end of the second millennium B.C. literary activity covering a wide range of texts was widespread in the Levant and that Levantine scribes were clearly capable of producing books ("Books in the Late Bronze Age in the Levant," *IOS* 18 [1998]: 171–81).

[154] M. Brettler, "The Book of Judges: Literature as Politics," *JBL* 108 (1989): 416. This pro-Davidic/Judahite polemical approach is found also in M. A. Sweeney, "Davidic Polemics in the Book of Judges," *VT* 47 (1997): 517–29. See also the promonarchic perspective of Howard (*Introduction,* 101): "The purpose of the book was to show the consequences of disobedience to God and to point the way to a king who, if he were righteous, would lead the people to God." Also Harrison (*Introduction to the Old Testament,* 692): "The purpose of the Book was to show that a centralized hereditary kingship was necessary for the well-being of the Covenant theocracy."

[155] Note Gideon's sham rejection of kingship (8:22–32), Abimelech's kingly style (9:16), and Jotham's fable (9:7–15). On these texts see G. E. Gerbrandt, *Kingship According to the Deuteronomistic History,* SBLDS 87 (Atlanta: Scholars Press, 1986), 123–29. Dumbrell argues for the opposite: the book is an antimonarchic polemic by an exilic author who is calling for a return to direct theocratic reign, freed from the encumbrances of human institutions, especially the bureaucratic monarchy ("'In Those Days There Was No King in Israel,'" 23–33).

[156] Note Judah's Canaanite style brutality toward Adoni-bezek (1:5–7); Judah's absence in the Song of Deborah (5:2–31); Judah's preference for peaceful coexistence with the Philistines and their treacherous handing over of Samson, their own countryman (15:9–13).

it hardly accounts for the overall tenor of the book. This is a prophetic book, not a political tractate. It represents a call to return to the God of the covenant, whom the people have abandoned in favor of the virile and exciting fertility gods of the land. The theme of the book is the *Canaanization of Israelite society during the period of settlement.*[157] The author's goal in exposing this problem is to wake up his own generation. This is an appeal to the covenant people to abandon all forms of paganism and return to Yahweh. In so doing the narrator also offers his readers a profound commentary on the grace of God. Left to their own devices the Israelites would surely have destroyed themselves. Only by the repeated gracious intervention of God do they emerge from the dark premonarchic period as a separate people and nation. In this book God deals with his people only partially in accordance with the formula: obedience brings blessing; disobedience brings the curse. Israel's victories over her enemies say much less about the nation than about their God, who intervenes repeatedly presumably because his long-range goal of using Israel as a light to the nations depends upon the nation's survival of this dark period of her history.

The author's agenda is evident not only in the individual units but in the broad structure of the book as a whole. The Prologue (1:1–3:6) explains the underlying causes of the Canaanization of Israel: the tribes' failure to fulfill the divine mandate in eliminating the native population (Deut 7:1–5). The major part, the "Book of Deliverers" (3:7–16:31), describes the consequences of Israel's Canaanization and Yahweh's response. The collection of "hero-stories" has its own specific prologue (3:1–6) in which the reader is reminded of the problematic historical and spiritual background for the following hero-stories. The sequence of six cycles of "apostasy-punishment-cry of pain-deliverance" not only expresses the persistence of the issue; it demonstrates the increasing intensity of the nation's depravity. The arrangement of the "hero-stories" reflects this process so that in the end we are left with "antiheroes" rather than truly great men of God. In the Epilogue (17:1–21:25), which really is the climax of the presentation, the Danite and Benjamite tribes demonstrate the extent and intensity of the problem in the nation's religious and social dysfunction.[158]

The deliberateness with which the author pursues his course is reflected in

---

[157] I have developed this theme in a series of articles, beginning with "The Period of the Judges: Religious Disintegration under Tribal Rule," in *Israel's Apostasy and Restoration: Essays in Honor of R. K. Harrison,* ed. A. Gileadi (Grand Rapids: Baker, 1988), 39–58. Since then several have picked it up. While I disagree with Sweeney's pro-Davidic polemical interpretation of the book, in his announcement of the theme at the beginning of his outline of the book he gets it right: "Narrative Presentation of Israel's Degeneration/Canaanization in the Premonarchic period" ("Davidic Polemics in the Book of Judges," 529).

[158] For a more detailed discussion of how these parts contribute to the theme see my essay cited in the previous note.

the integration and arrangement of elements of the respective parts. These features will be noted in the commentary. For the moment we draw attention only to the correspondence between the order in which the tribes are named in the Prologue (1:1–36) and the order in which their representatives appear (mostly as deliverers) in the Book of Deliverers: Judah (Othniel), Benjamin (Ehud), Ephraim (Deborah), Manasseh (Gideon), Gilead, (Jephthah), Dan (Samson). Preexistent materials are obviously being adapted and arranged for theological purposes.

Some may object that with the fourfold occurrence of the refrain "In those days Israel had no king" (17:6; 18:1; 19:1; 21:25) the narrator looks to the institution of kingship as the prescription for the chaos of the premonarchic period. However, this is an unlikely interpretation of the refrain for several reasons. First, elsewhere the narrator expresses a decidedly [159] Second, rather than lifting up the kings as an ideal above the confusion of this period, the addition of "everyone did as he saw fit" in 17:6 and 21:25 reduces the population to the moral and spiritual level of Israel's kings in later years.[160] Rebellion against God is democratized. In the mind of the author, during this period Israel did not need a king to lead them into sin; they could all do so on their own. Third, the statement "Israel had no king" is quite ambiguous. A superficial reading suggests that the narrator has an earthly human king in mind. At another level, however, he may be hereby declaring Israel's rejection of the theocracy. Contrary to Gideon's empty confession in 8:23, no one, not even God, rules in Israel.

THE CHRONOLOGICAL PROBLEM OF JUDGES. Related to the issue of theme and purpose of the Book of Judges is the chronological structure of the narrative. Temporal notices appear regularly in the Book of Deliverers, declaring the duration of the external oppressions and the lengths of the respective rulers' terms in office. The internal data may be summarized in tabular form:

Pattern of Chronological Notices in the Book of Judges

Text	Oppressor	Years	Period of Peace	Years	Judgeship	Year	Total Years
3:8	Cushan-Rishathaim	8					8
3:11			After Othniel	40			40[a]

---

[159] Cf. the portrayal of Gideon (8:4–35) and his son Abimelech (9:1–57). Especially significant is the speech of Jotham, whose fable represents the narrator's own view of Israelite kingship as he knows it (9:7–15).

[160] The description of the sins of Manasseh in 2 Kgs 21:1–18 sounds remarkably like the present narrator's portrayal of Israel in the period of the judges.

Pattern of Chronological Notices in the Book of Judges

Text	Oppressor	Years	Period of Peace	Years	Judgeship	Year	Total Years
3:14	Moab	18					18
3:30			After Ehud	80			80
4:3	Jabin	20					20
5:31			After Deborah	40			40
6:1	Midian	7					7
8:28			After/ During Gideon	40			40
9:22					Abimelech	3	3
10:2					Tola	23	23
10:3					Jair	22	22
10:8	Ammonites	18					18
12:7					Jephthah	6	6
12:9					Ibzan	7	7
12:11					Elon	10	10
12:14					Abdon	8	8
13:1	Philistines	40					40
15:20					Samson	20	20
16:31							——
Totals		111		200		99	410

a. The LXX reads fifty years, yielding a total of 420 years.

But if these years unfold in consecutive order, this scheme is difficult to reconcile with 1 Kgs 6:1, which declares that Solomon commenced constructing the temple 480 years after the exodus from Egypt. Simply taken together, the times given in the biblical narrative for the significant events between the exodus and the building of the temple yields the following scheme:

Chronological Notices between the Exodus and the Temple

Text	Event	Ruler	Years
Num 14:33; Deut 2:7	Desert Wandering	Moses	40
Josh 14:7,10[a]	Conquest	Joshua & Elders	7
Judges	Settlement	Judges	410
1 Sam 4:18	Settlement	Eli	40
Josephus, *Ant.* 6.13.5	Settlement	Samuel	12[b]
Acts 13:21; 1 Sam 13:1	Monarchy	Saul	40[c]
1 Kgs 2:11	Monarchy	David	40
1 Kgs 6:1	Monarchy	Solomon	4
TOTALS			593[d]

a. In highlighting his age and vigor at age eighty-five, Caleb uses a round figure of forty years from his being sent as a spy from Kadesh-Barnea to the Israelites' arrival at the Jordan. Deuteronomy 2:14 gives a more precise figure of thirty-eight years, which suggests that the actual duration of the wars under Joshua was seven rather than the five suggested by Caleb's comment. But for another interpretation of Deut 2:14 see Merrill, *Deuteronomy,* 95.
b. The biblical text creates the impression of a long judgeship.
c. The number is taken from Acts 13:21, where Paul offers the only specific biblical statement on the duration of Saul's reign.
d. Josephus contradicts himself on the totals. Cp. *Ant.* 8.3.1, 592 years; *Ant.* 20.10.1, 612 years.

The problem is obvious: 591 years exceeds the 480 cited in 1 Kgs 6:1 by more than a century.[161] The difficulty may be partially resolved by allowing for chronological overlapping among the judges. It is evident that many of the judgeships were tribally based, and the oppressions affected only portions of the Israelite population, as the following chart suggests:

---

[161] The problem is not resolved by positing a shorter reign for Saul, as, e.g., the twenty-two years proposed by D. V. Edelman, "Saul," *ABD* 5.993.

Points of Pressure on Israel

Enemy	Deliverer	Tribal Supporters	Locus of Pressure
Moab	Ehud	Benjamites	Heartland
Philistine	Shamgar		Southwest
Canaanites	Barak	Ephraim, Zebulun, Naphtali, Issachar	North
Midian	Gideon	Manasseh, Ephraim	Heartland
Ammonites	Jephthah	Gileadites	Transjordan
Philistines	Samson	Dan	Southwest

It appears from 10:6 that the Ammonite and Philistine oppressions overlap, which suggests concurrency between Jephthah's and Samson's terms in office, cutting eighteen years from the total. In fact, Samson, Eli, and Samuel, all of whom had to deal with the Philistines, may all have served the nation during the forty years of Philistine oppression, allowing a deduction of seventy-two years from the total given in Table 2. Abimelech's three years should perhaps be deleted from the computation since he was not an actual judge. Perhaps the author intentionally distanced him from the judges proper by having Abimelech function as a *śār*, "officer," over Israel (9:22) rather than judging *(šāpaṭ)*. These deletions total ninety-three years, yielding a figure of 480, the precise figure required to match 1 Kgs 6:1.[162]

Another promising solution is offered by Richter, who works backward from 1 Kgs 6:1.[163] His calculations, arriving at the figure 480, may be summarized as follows:

Monarchic period up to building of the temple	46 years
Times of the "Judges" in the strict sense	136 years
Periods of rest after deliverances	200 years
Periods of oppression before deliverances	53 years
Period of conquest under Joshua	5 years
Period of desert wanderings	40 years
TOTAL	480 years

---

[162] Shamgar's placement between Ehud's victory over the Moabites and Barak's battle with Jabin (3:30,31; 4:1; 5:6) implies some contemporaneity among Moabite, Canaanite, and Philistine oppressions, but how much cannot be determined.

[163] W. Richter, *Retterbuches*, 132–40.

The use of the number 480, however, raises the question of whether this entire scheme is not artificially constructed. The figure, representing twelve generations of forty years, may reflect a theology of history more than a chronology. Even so Richter's scheme is not entirely convincing. Not only does it assume only a two-year reign for Saul, which seems far too short and is based on a textually problematic reading (1 Sam 13:1), but it fails to take into account the fifty-eight years of oppression under the Ammonites and Philistines (more than half the total) and overlooks Abimelech's three years.

The variation in the types of numbers used by the author may suggest that we should not force the calculations into a coherent scheme. Figures included in the formula *"PN* judged Israel *X* years" (9:22; 10:2,3; 12:7,9,11,14) and those identifying lengths of oppressions (3:8,14; 6:1; 10:8) tend to be precise, whereas periods of peace are announced as multiples of forty, presumably because this was considered a generational lifespan. This impression of literary structuring is strengthened by the fact that the number of judges/rulers in/over Israel is exactly twelve, matching the number of tribes.[164] The differences in the types of numbers employed in the book probably derive from the sources used by the author, who was not concerned to synchronize them with external chronological data or make them conform to a predetermined quota.

Further, Jephthah claims in 11:26 that the Israelites have occupied Heshbon for three hundred years. If the Ammonite and Philistine oppressions coincided, this speech must have been delivered within forty to fifty years of David's tenure, ca. 1050 B.C., which fixes the date of conquest at 1350 and the exodus at 1390 B.C. But this does not square with 1 Kgs 6:1 either, according to which, if taken literally, the exodus occurred in 1446 B.C. Furthermore, the reader should note that, unlike the 480 years in 1 Kgs 6:1, this figure is not given by the narrator but by a character in direct speech. Furthermore, since it is a round number uttered in a political speech, it may have been fabricated for polemical reasons.[165] The fact that Jephthah erroneously refers to Chemosh as the god of the Ammonites (11:24)[166] shows that he was not above misrepresenting historical reality in other details. One might also find support for this skeptical interpretation of Jephthah's number from the character of the man himself. Appearing second to last in the narrator's parade of deliverers, only Samson is given a more negative character evaluation than Jephthah.

---

[164] This probably accounts for the Abimelech note in 9:22, which completes the quota.

[165] Contra D. L. Washburn, "The Chronology of Judges: Another Look," *BSac* 147 (1990): 425; Merrill, *Kingdom of Priests*, 68.

[166] The patron deity of Ammon was Milcom (1 Kgs 11:5,33); Chemosh was actually the patron deity of Moab.

(3) Date and Place of Composition

Like most other Old Testament and ancient Near Eastern texts,[167] the Book of Judges is anonymous. Consequently, determining the date and authorship for the book is an extremely difficult task. As already noted, rabbinic tradition ascribes the book to Samuel (*B. Bat.* 14b), a view followed to this day by some conservatives.[168] But most scholars propose a complex scheme of literary evolution, the finished product deriving from the time of the exile in conjunction with the rest of the Deuteronomistic History. But what kinds of clues about the date of writing does the document itself provide?

First, the book contains a series of explanatory parenthetical notes that suggest the final form derives from a time chronologically distant from the events described:

1:11	"Debir (formerly called Kiriath Sepher)."
1:23	"Bethel (formerly called Luz)."
3:1–2	"Israel (all who had not experienced any of the wars of Canaan; only in order that the generations of the sons of Israel might be taught war, those who had not experienced it formerly)."[169]
19:10	"Jebus (that is, Jerusalem)."
20:27–28	"(In those days the ark of the covenant of God was there, with Phinehas son of Eleazar, the son of Aaron, ministering before it)."

The first two geographic synchronisms link the Israelite sites with their Canaanite originals. The Jebus/Jerusalem synchronism goes in the reverse direction, explaining an obscure Canaanite original with a contemporary Israelite name. The note seems to have been added after David's conquest of the city (1 Chr 11:4–9), eliminating Samuel as the author, at least of the note.[170] The third note seems to distinguish the test of Israel settling in the land from the test of those who wandered in the desert. The last note explains that the Israelites made oracular inquiry of Yahweh at Bethel, suggesting that at the time of the addition the memory of such a convocation had been lost. The note probably postdates Jeroboam's establishment of Bethel as a cult center (1 Kings 12). After this event the audience might have found a pan-Israelite congress at this site incongruous.

Second, the Book of Judges contains seven chronological notes that con-

---

[167] On which see W. G. Lambert, "Ancestors, Authors, and Canonicity," *JCS* 11 (1957): 1.

[168] Goslinga, *Joshua, Judges, Ruth*, 217–23.

[169] Author translation. The NIV begins the parenthetical comment at the beginning of v. 2.

[170] The name Jerusalem, however, antedates David's conquest by centuries, appearing in the fourteenth century B.C. El-Amarna correspondence as ^{al}u-ru-sa-lim (EA 287:25,46,61,63; 289:14,29; 290:15) and in eighteenth century B.C. Egyptian execration texts as Rushalimum (*ANET*, 329).

clude with "until this day" (*ʾad hayyôm hazzeh*).[171] These may be grouped into three categories:

Historical notes:

1:21   "To this day the Jebusites live there with the Benjamites."

19:30   "Such a thing has never been seen or done, not since the day the Israelites came up out of Egypt."

Evidential note:

6:24   "To this day it [the altar] stands in Ophrah of the Abiezrites."

Etiological topographic notes:

1:26   "He built a city and called it Luz, which is its name to this day."

10:4   "They controlled thirty towns ... which to this day are called Havvoth Jair."

15:19   "So the spring was called En Hakkore, and it is still there in Lehi."

18:12   "This is why the place west of Kiriath Jearim is called Mahaneh Dan to this day."

Except for 1:21, which apparently antedates David's conquest of the Jebusites and his transformation of the settlement into a Judahite city (2 Sam 5:6–8),[172] these notes are difficult to date. Though some have an etiological character, their primary function is not to justify an existing phenomenon. Rather they function like footnotes, representing the author's personal testimony confirming received traditions.[173] In fact, the note on Gideon's altar at Ophrah in 6:24 invites the readers to check the veracity of the account by visiting the site. These explanatory comments all make the most sense if a preexilic readership in the land of Israel (as opposed to exile) is assumed.[174]

Third, the refrain "In those days Israel had no king," which appears four times in the last five chapters,[175] should not be pressed into promonarchic significance. This is a retrospective time notice, referring to a period prior to the monarchy when people set their own standards of behavior; the nation did not yet have kings who would lead them in doing what was evil in the eyes of Yahweh. These notices could have been composed any time after the

---

[171] The idiom occurs eighty-four times in the OT, mostly in the historiographic writings. See the valuable study by B. S. Childs, "A Study of the Formula, 'Until this day,'" *JBL* 82 (1963): 279–92.

[172] Some, however (e.g., Boling, *Judges,* 59), prefer a late seventh or early sixth century, when Judah and Benjamin were all that was left of the nation of Israel; 2 Sam 24:16 suggests some Jebusites persisted in the city.

[173] Cf. Childs, "Study of the Formula," 292.

[174] Cf. Childs (ibid.), who suggests the formula "until this day" belongs to the earliest traditions of the book, and not to the Deuteronomistic redaction.

[175] 17:6; 18:1; 19:1; 21:25.

coronation of David,[176] specifically the time of peace he inaugurated, hence long after Samuel's death.

Fourth, in 18:30 reference is made to the priestly succession of Jonathan, the son of Gershom, the son of Moses,[177] which managed the apostate cult of the Danites at Dan *ʿad yôm gĕlôt hāʾāreṣ,* literally "until the day of the exile of the land." Although a detailed analysis of this phrase is reserved for the commentary, this is best interpreted as a reference to the conquest of this region by the neo-Assyrians and the removal of the Danite population in 734–732 B.C.[178] This means that the final form of the book could not have been achieved until the end of the eighth century B.C.

These authors also tend to interpret the book as a promonarchic polemic. But this does not square with the general tenor of and specific statements within the Books of Kings. These place responsibility for the exile squarely on the shoulders of kings who led the people into sin. An exilic author would hardly have looked upon the monarchy as an institution to be the solution for the problems reflected in the book. Most scholars attribute the final form of Judges to an exilic or postexilic deuteronomistic redactor. An alternative dating of the book depends upon a correlation of its message with the most likely historical context. If we take seriously that the author of this document was not motivated merely by an antiquarian concern to record the past or to offer a sociopolitical apologetic for the monarchy, but to declare a prophetic word for a particular situation, we must ask when this recitation of the Canaanization of Israelite society would have been most needed. The exilic and/or postexilic contexts are unlikely candidates. Not only had the consequences of persistent apostasy fallen upon Israel/Judah by then; the nation was already being weaned from its pagan past.

The prophetic message of this book would have had the greatest relevance during the long, spiritually ruinous reign of Manasseh. According to 2 Kgs 21:1–18, Manasseh "did evil in the eyes of the LORD, following the detestable practices of the nations the LORD had driven out before the Israelites" (v. 2). Not only does this evaluation echo the oft-repeated refrain of Judges, but the narrative cites numerous specific evils analogous to the abominations pursued by Israelites during the period of the judges. Like Gideon (and his father),

---

[176] The narrator of the Saulide narratives in 1 Samuel seems to suggest that the anarchy of the premonarchic period continued during Saul's tenure.

[177] On this reading see the commentary below.

[178] On which see H. Donner, "The Separate States of Israel and Judah," in *Israelite and Judaean History,* ed. J. H. Hayes and J. M. Miller, OTL (Philadelphia: Westminster, 1977), 427. Less likely is the view of some (e.g., Howard, *Introduction,* 100), who see here a reference to the exile of Judah in 586 B.C., or the supposition of others (e.g., O'Connell, *Rhetoric of the Book of Judges,* 481–82) that the reference is to the Philistine defeat of Israel at Aphek/Ebenezer and the Israelite loss of the ark (1 Samuel 4).

Micah, and the Danites, Manasseh constructs cult installations for Canaanite divinities (vv. 3–5,7). Like Jephthah, he offers his children as sacrifices (v. 6). Like Abimelech in Shechem, Manasseh "shed so much innocent blood" that Jerusalem was filled from one end to the other (v. 16). Like Gideon, Manasseh was a royal sponsor of evil, leading the nation into sin. As in the Book of Judges, the people are reminded of Yahweh's covenant and their requirement to obey the Torah of Moses, but they refused, and the evils intensified (vv. 8–9). As in the days of the judges, Yahweh sends prophets to warn the nation of the consequences of their apostasy, specifically, that if they persist he will "hand them over to their enemies" because they had provoked his ire by doing evil in his eyes "from the day their forefathers came out of Egypt until this day" (vv. 14–15). Like the alarm of those who witnessed the dismemberment of the Levite's concubine, in the face of unprecedented evil this prophetic book serves as a wake-up call: "Think about it! Consider it!" (Judg 19:30).[179]

As already noted, the identity of the author of Judges remains a mystery. If our dating is correct, he must have been a Judahite, which could account for the primacy of place given to this tribe in chap. 1[180] and the presentation of Othniel as the first of the savior judges (3:7–11). This would also account for the pronounced anti-Ephraimite stance evident throughout the book. The phraseology and style of the book suggest an author schooled in the Torah of Moses, particularly in the Book of Deuteronomy.[181] The book's hortatory nature and agenda point to a prophetic figure. Anxious for the revival of pure and orthodox Yahwism, and the spiritual rejuvenation of his people, this preacher draws upon the dark days of the judges to warn his people of the peril of their ways.

4. The History of Interpretation of the Book of Judges

(1) The Old Testament

Although many thematic and stylistic links exist between the Book of Judges and the rest of the deuteronomistic historiographic writings, there is no clear inner Old Testament evidence for the use of this book in the believing community of Israel before the intertestamental period. The opening lines of the Book of Ruth, "In the days when the judges ruled," certainly looks upon the premonarchic period as a clearly self-defined era and probably presupposes

---

[179] A Josianic date is also possible. Thus J. G. McConville, *Grace in the End: A Study in Deuteronomic Theology* (Grand Rapids: Zondervan, 1993), 109. But this would necessitate a shift in the dating of Ruth.

[180] Hebron and Debir were Judean towns.

[181] This view assumes a date for the composition of Deuteronomy much earlier than the late seventh century date commonly accepted by scholars. For a defense of the early date see McConville, *Grace in the End*; E. H. Merrill, *Deuteronomy*, NAC, vol. 4 (Nashville: Broadman & Holman, 1994), 22–23.

some form of the present Book of Judges. The Levitical confession of sin in Neh 9:5–38 offers another possible link. The vocabulary and style of the survey of Israel's spiritual condition during the dark days of the judges in vv. 27–28 suggest strongly that the composers of this poetic piece were familiar with the prologue to the "Book of Deliverers" (Judg 2:1–3:6) and with the narratives that follow in Judg 3:7–16:31.[182] There are several allusions to the period of the judges in the Psalms (Pss 78:56–64; 83:9–12; 106:34–46), but these texts probably provide examples of the adaptation of common traditions rather than of specific literary borrowing. Even so, the period of the judges is consistently viewed negatively, as a time of intense apostasy. But there is also the consistent recognition of Yahweh who, in his grace, raises up saviors to rescue the oppressed from their enemies.

(2) Early Judaism

Allusions to the Book of Judges are frequent in intertestamental writings. In the apocryphal *Book of Ecclesiasticus,* Jesus Ben Sirach provides an early second century B.C. survey of the heroes of Israelite history. Ben Sirach idealizes the deliverers as different from their spiritual and cultural environment:

> The judges also, with their respective names, whose hearts did not fall into idolatry and who did not turn away from the Lord—may their memory be blessed! May their bones send forth new life from where they lie, and may the names of those who have been honored live again in their children! (46:11–12, NRSV)

This idealistic portrayal of the saviors is not based on grammatical historical exegesis of the book.

In the *Testament of the Twelve Patriarchs,* probably written several decades later, the *Testament of Dan* 5:6 reads:

> I read in the Book of Enoch the Righteous that your prince is Satan and that all the spirits of sexual promiscuity and of arrogance devote attention to the sons of Levi in the attempt to observe them closely and cause them to commit sin before the Lord.

The citation is not found in any known *Book of Enoch,* but the Jewish and Patristic linkage of Dan with the Antichrist seems to be based on the Danite idolatry described in Judg 18:11–31 and the prophecies of Danite judgment in Jer 8:16–17.[183] In *Lives of the Prophets* 16:3 (first century A.D.) the period of the judges is referred to as "the days of the anarchy as written in Sphar-

---

[182] Note the identification of the judges as מוֹשִׁיעִים, "saviors," in v. 27.

[183] Thus H. C. Kee, in *The Old Testament Pseudepigrapha,* vol. I, *Apocalyptic Literature and Testaments,* ed. J. H. Charlesworth (Garden City: Doubleday, 1983), 809. Hereafter this volume is referred to as *OTP* 1.

photim,[184] that is, in the Book of Judges." From the same period, in the long section, 25:1–48:5, Pseudo-Philo demonstrates clear dependence upon the biblical book, with numerous midrashic expansions on phrases and formulas found in Judges.[185]

Josephus is obviously aware of the canonical Book of Judges, though he rearranges some of the material[186] and appears to attach the Book of Ruth to Judges.[187] He displays the same idealizing tendency found in Ben Sirach. Gideon is whitewashed as "a man of moderation" and "excelling in every virtue."

> [He] would have laid down the government but was over persuaded to take it, which he enjoyed forty years, and distributed justice to them, as the people came to him with their differences; and what he determined was esteemed valid by all; and when he died he was buried in his own country Ophrah.

Not a word is said of his brutality toward his countrymen (8:4–17) nor his latter-day apostasy.[188] Jephthah is admired as a potent man, on account of his father's virtue and the army he maintained at his own expense, though Josephus does concede that the sacrifice of his daughter was not conformable to law nor acceptable to God.[189] While some of Samson's failures are recognized, in the end Josephus concludes:

> Such was the end of this man ... and indeed, this man deserves to be admired for his courage and strength, and magnanimity at his death, and that his wrath against his enemies went so far as to die himself with them. But as for his being ensnared by a woman, that is to be ascribed to human nature which is too weak to resist the temptation of that sin; but we ought to bear him witness, that in all other respects he was one of extraordinary virtue.[190]

(3) The New Testament

References to the Book of Judges are rare in the New Testament. Usually the allusions are to persons or events analogous to New Testament counterparts. In Luke 1:15 John the Baptist is presented as a Samson-like Nazirite

---

[184] According to D. R. A. Hare, this is a garbled form of Hb. שֹׁפְטִים סֵפֶר (*The Old Testament Pseudepigrapha*, vol. II, *Expansions of the "Old Testament" and Legends, Wisdom and Philosophical Literature, Prayers, Psalms, and Odes, Fragments of Lost Judeo-Hellenistic Works* [Garden City: Doubleday, 1985], 395, note c). Hereafter this volume is cited as *OTP* 2.

[185] *OTP* 2.339–63. Five chapters are devoted to Kenaz, Othniel's father.

[186] Chaps. 19–21 are placed at the beginning after chap. 1. *Ant.* 5.2.1–12.

[187] *Contra Apionem* 1.8.

[188] *Ant.* 5.6.1–7.

[189] *Ant.* 5.7.8–11.

[190] *Ant.* 5.8.12.

(Judg 13:4), a picture alluded to also in Matthew's account of the birth of Jesus (Matt 2:23). Luke 1:31 compares Mary to Samson's mother, who also received an angelic visitation announcing her pregnancy. Luke 1:42 compares the blessedness of Mary with that of Jael, the woman who killed Sisera (Judg 5:24). Elsewhere one finds only scattered references, such as the allusion to Samson's heroic killing of the lion (Heb 11:33; cf. Judg 14:5). Paul knew that God gave Israel judges until Samuel the prophet (Acts 13:20).

The best known reference to the period of the judges occurs in Heb 11:32, where Gideon, Barak, Samson, and Jephthah are listed as heroes of the faith, along with Enoch, Noah, Abraham, Isaac, Jacob, Moses, Rahab, David, Samuel, and the prophets. But this picture differs sharply from the portraits of these men painted in the Old Testament book. How is this extraordinary interpretation to be explained?

The most helpful clue to the treatment by the author of Hebrews is found in the idealizing tendency we have witnessed in other Jewish writings of the time, particularly in Ben Sirach and Josephus. Their laudatory aims accord perfectly with the homiletical aims of Hebrews 11. This chapter is not an exegetical lecture on Old Testament texts but a sermon on faith, which is the key to accomplishing anything for God. The author is convinced, and rightly so, that divine resources are applied to human needs by faith. The message is that if anything positive was accomplished during the dark days of the judges, it was the work of God. The human tools available within Israel were raw, and their characters reveal many flaws. But God's work had to be done; again and again the nation needed deliverance from external enemies. Despite defects of personality and lack of nerve, the deliverers stepped out against overwhelming odds. This was either the mark of folly or of faith. The author of Hebrews is correct in casting his vote with the latter. Empowered by the Spirit of God, the deliverers charged into battle. For the moment, if not for their entire lives, by faith they cast themselves on God, counting on him to fight for them as he had fought against the Egyptians, the Amalekites, Sihon and Og, Jericho, and the rest of the Canaanites, as recounted in the Book of Joshua. But the author of Hebrews was not the first biblical writer to use ancient texts in this selective way. The approach is already evident in the Old Testament, as in the books of Chronicles, which recount only the positive elements of David's reign. Convinced that the power of God is behind every advance of the gospel and that that power is unleashed in human experience through faith, the author of Hebrews 11 hails Gideon, Barak, Samson, and Jephthah as agents of God through whom remarkable victories were achieved. Although the view of the persons named is uncompromisingly favorable, strictly speaking the author of Hebrews makes no comment on their character. For that we must consult the book itself.

(4) The Relevance of the Book of Judges Today

Hebrews 11:32 has exercised a profound and pervasive influence on the history of Christian interpretation of the Book of Judges. With a hermeneutic that tends to read the Old Testament in light of the New, to this day many readers understand the book as a collection of stirring tales of the exploits of genuinely virtuous heroes, mighty men of God.[191] These personalities are held up as models after whom Christians should pattern their lives. It is indeed true that all believers are called to a life of faith and that without faith nothing can be accomplished for God, but this evaluation of the primary judges at least is much too positive, especially when we allow the author of Judges to speak for himself. The primary significance of the book for the modern reader, especially Western Christians lies in quite a different direction.

Earlier it was mentioned that the central theme of the Book of Judges is the Canaanization of Israel. Herein lies the key to the relevance of this ancient composition for North American Christianity, for like the Israelites of the settlement period, we have largely forgotten the covenant Lord and have come to take for granted his gracious redemptive work on our behalf. Like the ancient Israelites we too are being squeezed into the mold of the pagan world around us.[192] Evidences of the "Canaanization" of the church are everywhere: our preoccupation with material prosperity, which turns Christianity into a fertility religion;[193] our syncretistic and aberrant forms of worship; our refusal to obey the Lord's call to separation from the world; our divisiveness and competitiveness; our moral compromises, as a result of which Christians and non-Christians are often indistinguishable; our [male] exploitation and abuse of women and children; our reluctance to answer the Lord's call to service, and when we finally go, our propensity to displace "Thy kingdom come" with "My kingdom come"; our eagerness to fight the Lord's battles with the world's resources and strategies; our willingness to stand up and defend perpetrators of evil instead of justice. These and many other lessons will be drawn from the leaves of this fascinating book as we proceed.

But the book teaches important positive lessons as well, especially about God. First, God graciously calls his people to covenant relationship with himself. This relationship is the highest privilege imaginable, and when the recipients of grace hold their divine Benefactor in contempt, abandoning him for other allegiances, the God of grace is rightfully angry. Second, the impassioned God *(ʾEl Qannāʾ)* tolerates no rivals. The believer cannot serve him and other gods. To do so is to trample his grace underfoot. Third, God is gracious still, often treating his people not according to what they deserve but out of his boundlessly merciful heart. Fourth, if anything positive is ever accomplished in

---

[191] For a summary of Christian interpretation see Moore, *Judges*, xlvii–l.

[192] Cf. J. B. Phillips' rendering of Rom 12:1.

[193] Fertility religion was concerned to secure for the worshiper a large family, large flocks and herds, and abundant crops, the ancient equivalent to the modern health-and-wealth gospel.

the church, it is the work of God. Human leaders have a profound propensity to disappoint and to exploit the church for their own purposes. Fifth, in the words of Jesus, God will build his church, and the gates of hell will not prevail against it (Matt 16:18). The Book of Judges presents the picture of a nation called the people of Yahweh but seemingly determined to negate that appellation if not destroy itself. But the Lord will not let this happen. He has chosen them to be his agents of light and life to the world; he has rescued them from Egypt; he has entered into an eternal covenant with them; and he has delivered the land of Canaan into their hands as an eternal possession. In the final analysis, God cannot let his program abort. The mission of grace to the world depends upon the preservation of his people. So against all odds, and certainly against Israel's deserts, the nation survives the dark days of the judges. The true hero in the book is God and God alone.

5. The Text of Judges

Compared to the rest of the historiographic writings of the Old Testament, the Hebrew text of Judges preserved in the Leningrad Codex of A.D. 1008 (upon which *BHS* is based) and the Aleppo Codex from the early tenth century A.D. is relatively pure.[194] However, a series of fragments discovered in the first and fourth caves of Qumran indicate an inconsistent early Hebrew textual tradition.[195] The omission of vv. 7–10 from 6:2–13 on 4QJud[a] suggests a shorter text, perhaps by accidental omission, an alternative text tradition, or, as some scholars argue, an earlier edition of the book in which the deuteronomistic framework was still missing.[196] Although the Aramaic Targum, Syriac Peshitta, and Latin Vulgate generally follow the MT, the Septuagint presents several traditions so divergent qualitatively and substantively that A. Rahlfs' critical edition of the Septuagint produces both versions on the same page, as if the LXX[A] and LXX[B] represent two independent translations. However, most scholars today prefer a theory of successive revisions of traditions, with LXX[A] representing a superior and older version.[197] In any case, the instances in which the MT can be improved upon by appealing to the LXX are relatively few.

---

[194] Note the relative paucity of textual notes in *BHS*.

[195] These are listed by U. Glessmer, "Liste der biblischen Texte aus Qumran," *RevQ* 62 (1993): 170. Fragments from Cave 1 contain the following texts: 6:20–22; 8:1(?); 9:1–4; 9:4–6; 9:28–31; 9:40–42; 9:40–43; 9:48–49; on which see D. Barthélemy and J. T. Milik, *Qumran Cave I*, DJD 1 (Oxford: Clarendon, 1955), 62–63 and pl. XI. Parchment bits from Cave 4 contain fragments of 6:2–6 and 6:11–13 (4QJud[a]), as well as 19:5–7 and 21:12–25 (4QJud[b]). For photographs of these see R. H. Eisenman and J. M. Robinson, *A Facsimile Edition of the Dead Sea Scrolls: Prepared with Introduction and Index* (Washington: Biblical Archaeology Society, 1991), 1143.

[196] See E. Tov, *Textual Criticism of the Hebrew Bible* (Minneapolis: Fortress, 1992), 344–45; J. T. Barrera, "Textual Variants in *4QJudg[a]* and the Textual and Editorial History of the Book of Judges (1)," *RevQ* 14 (1989): 229–45. See further the commentary on these verses.

[197] For a detailed analysis of the Greek recensions see W. R. Bodine, *The Greek Text of Judges: Recensionsal Developments,* HSM 23 (Chico: Scholars Press, 1980).

———————————— *OUTLINE OF JUDGES* ————————————

Theme: The Canaanization of the Nation of Israel in the Premonarchic Period
  I. Introduction: The Background to the Canaanization of Israel: Israel's
     Failure in the Holy War (1:1–3:6)
    1. The Report of Israel's Performance (1:1–36)
    2. The Theological Significance of Israel's Performance (2:1–23)
    3. The Domestic Consequences of Israel's Performance (3:1–6)
 II. Body: Yahweh's Response to the Canaanization of Israel: The Cycles
    of Apostasy and Deliverance (3:7–16:31)
    1. The Aram-Naharaim and Othniel Cycle (3:7–11)
    2. The Moab and Ehud Cycle (3:12–30)
    3. Parenthesis 1: The Governorship of Shamgar (3:31)
    4. The Canaanite and Barak Cycle (4:1–5:31)
    5. The Midianite and Gideon Cycle (6:1–9:57)
    6. Parenthesis 2: The Governorships of Tola and Jair (10:1–5)
    7. The Ammonite and Jephthah Cycle (10:6–12:7)
    8. Parenthesis 3: The Governorships of Ibzan, Elon, Abdon (12:8–15)
    9. The Philistine and Samson Cycle (13:1–16:31)
III. Climax: The Depths of the Canaanization of Israel (17:1–21:25)
    1. The Religious Degeneration of Israel (17:1–18:31)
    2. The Moral Degeneration of Israel (19:1–21:25)

THEME: THE CANAANIZATION OF ISRAEL IN THE PREMONARCHIC
PERIOD

I. THE BACKGROUND TO THE CANAANIZATION OF ISRAEL:
ISRAEL'S FAILURE IN THE HOLY WAR (1:1–3:6)
1. The Report of Israel's Performance (1:1–36)
  (1) Introduction (1:1–2)
  (2) The Successes and Failures of Judah (1:3–20)
    The Fraternal Alliance (1:3)
    The Upland Campaign (1:4–8)
    The Lowland Campaign (1:9–20)
     Introduction (1:9)
     The Conquest of Hebron (1:10)
     The Conquest of Debir (1:11–15)
     The Settlement of Arad (1:16)
     The Sacking of Zephath/Hormah (1:17)
     The Conquest of the Southwest Coastal Lowland (1:18)
     Conclusion (1:19–20)
  (3) The Failures of the Remaining Tribes (1:21–36)
    The Fortunes of Benjamin (1:21)
    The Fortunes of Ephraim (1:22–26)
    The Fortunes of the Northern Tribes (1:27–36)
     Manasseh (1:27–28)
     Ephraim (1:29)
     Zebulun (1:30)
     Asher (1:31–32)
     Naphtali (1:33)
     Dan (1:34–36)
2. The Theological Significance of Israel's Performance (2:1–23)
  (1) The Divine Messenger's Interpretation (2:1–5)
    The Divine Messenger (2:1a)
    The Divine Message (2:1b–3)
     God's Past Favors (2:1b)
     God's Past Commands (2:2a)
     Israel's Response to God's Grace (2:2b)
     God's Past Warning (2:3)
    The People's Response (2:4–5)
  (2) The Narrator's Interpretation (2:6–20a)

——— I. THE BACKGROUND TO THE CANAANIZATION OF ——— ISRAEL: ISRAEL'S FAILURE IN THE HOLY WAR (1:1–3:6)

The limits of the first literary unit of Judges are not universally agreed upon. Although some see the introduction to the book as a whole extending to 3:6,[1] most recognize the break after 2:5, and with good reason. (1) Whereas 1:1–2:5 narrates events, 2:6–3:6 is overtly theological and sermonic. (2) The notice of Joshua's death in 2:6–9 seems redundant after 1:1 if these are part of one unit. (3) Stylistically and theologically 2:6–3:6 appears to fit better with the "Book of Deliverers" (3:7–16:31) than with the preceding material. (4) Since the notice of Joshua's dismissal of the people in 2:6 chronologically precedes the notice of his death in 1:1, 1:1–2:5 looks like a later addition to the primary narrative. These arguments are not as convincing, however, as they first appear.

First, although chap. 1 seems relatively nontheological, the same cannot be said for 2:1–5. On the contrary, the tone and content of 2:1–5 bear closer resemblance to 2:6–3:6 than to the preceding.

Second, by dividing the text between 2:5 and 2:6, the interpreter has broken an uninterrupted sequence of narrative verb forms (*waw*-consecutive) that runs from 2:1–23. Apparently the narrator intends for the reader to interpret vv. 6–23 in light of and as a continuation of vv. 1–5.[2]

---

[1] B. G. Webb (*The Book of Judges: An Integrated Reading*, JSOTSup 46 [Sheffield, JSOT, 1987], 81–122) interprets 1:1–3:6 as the "overture" to the book.

[2] So also M. A. Sweeney, "Davidic Polemics in the Book of Judges," *VT* 47 (1997): 521. The sequence of *waw*-consecutive verbs actually carries on from chap. 1.

Third, to view 2:6–10 as a redundant variation of 1:1a is to overlook the differences in both form and function of these references to Joshua's death. The notice in 1:1 is necessarily brief, not only because it echoes the opening of the Book of Joshua[3] but especially because its purpose is quickly to set the chronological context for the events that follow. Judges 2:6–10 offers an exposition of the opening announcement, elaborating on the details of Joshua's death and burial and explaining the theological/spiritual significance of his death.

Fourth, the recognition of the significance of the stylistic links between 2:6–3:6 and the following "Book of Deliverers" does not depend upon separating this section from 1:1–2:5. On the contrary, by linking 2:6–23 with the first chapter, the significance of the first chapter for the interpretation of the "Book of Deliverers" is heightened.

Fifth, it makes more sense to divide these literary units according to the current chapter divisions than to break the text after 2:5a and then again after 3:6, for several reasons. (1) The reference to Joshua in 2:23 creates an effective inclusio with the opening statement in 1:1.[4] (2) Despite the shift in vocabulary, the divine speech in 2:20–22 is linked thematically and linguistically with the envoy's speech in 2:1–3.[5] (3) The opening line of chap. 3 not only disrupts the sequence of narrative verb forms that have run through chap. 2 but also is cast formally as a title to a new section: "These are the nations ..." *(wĕʾēlleh haggôyim).*[6] In so doing the narrator has separated 3:1–6 from 2:6–23.

Sixth, 3:1–6 is composed as a separate literary unit, which picks up the theme of "testing" from 2:22 but domesticates the test by declaring the links among coresidency with Canaanites, intermarriage with them, and the adoption of their gods. In so doing it concretizes the abstract notions expressed in chap. 2.

In light of these considerations, it is best to treat 1:1–3:6 as a literary unit whose purpose is to provide a military and theological context to the "Book of Deliverers" that follows. Even so, as already indicated, these opening chapters are complex, being divided on the basis of style and content into two discreet panels. The first (1:1–36) summarizes Israel's military response to the divine mandate concerning the Canaanites; the second offers a theological statement of the significance and implications of the Israelites' response. Chapter 1 consists to a large extent of an analytical, if

---

[3] On which see the commentary below.

[4] Incidentally, this is the last time Joshua is mentioned in the book.

[5] Note the references to "my covenant," disobeying/not listening to Yahweh's voice: לֹא שָׁמַע בְּקוֹלִי/לְ, and Yahweh not driving the enemy out before Israel.

[6] Cp. the form with similar titles elsewhere: Gen 10:1; 11:27;25:7; Exod 1:1; 6:16; 21:1; 28:4; Num 1:5; Josh 12:1,7; etc.

not cold, rehearsal of the fortunes of the tribes of Israel after the death of Joshua; chap. 2 represents a passionate threefold indictment of the nation, first by Yahweh's envoy (2:1–5), then by the narrator (2:6–20a), and finally by Yahweh himself (2:20b–22). Verse 23 functions as an interpretive conclusion, answering to the opening declaration in 1:1. While the variation in style and content, especially in 1:1–26 and 2:1–5, undoubtedly goes back to the sources used by the author, the two parts are intentionally integrated by means of the narrative verb forms that run from beginning to end, as well as the repetition of one of the key words, *ʿālâ*, "to go up," which occurs six times in chap. 1 and at the beginning of chap. 2, albeit with a different subject.[7]

The author of the book has conjoined these two parts to send his readers an early signal of his agenda. Chapter 1 is much more than a summary of military accomplishments or lack thereof. The narrator moves from chap. 1 to chap. 2 like a modern preacher moves from text to exposition. The differences here are that the text of the author's sermon derives from events of history, not a printed page, and the interpretation comes from God himself or from his messengers, be they the envoy of Yahweh or the author of the book. In the combination of these two parts, the reader encounters the typical Hebrew view of history. Historical events always have two dimensions: the earthly, where humans act with genuine freedom, and the heavenly, where the sovereign Lord exercises full control. When human beings fail to take the theological dimension into account, disaster is inevitable.

1. The Report of Israel's Performance (1:1–36)

Sandwiched between the last chapter of Joshua and the following narratives in Judges, the tone of chap. 1 seems remarkably secular and the style repetitive, if not pedantic. Here the narrator offers no evaluative comments, only a matter-of-fact reporting of tribal military adventures, which contrasts with the overt preaching and theologizing evident in the rest of the book. Actually the chapter contains two types of materials: annalistic chronicles focusing on the military achievements (or lack thereof) of the tribes of Israel and anecdotal reports of personal affairs at three literarily critical junctures (vv. 5–7,11–15,23–26). Most scholars recognize the former to be derived

---

[7] The NIV obscures this intentional play on עָלָה by translating the word variously as "go up" (1:1,16; 2:1), "go" (1:2), "come" (1:3), and "attack" (1:4,22). The *hiphil* form in 2:1 is rendered "bring up." On the place of 3:1–6 in the scheme of things see the previous page.

from ancient sources.[8] Whereas Joshua presents a holistic and "pan-Israelite" view of the conquest, the present account is piecemeal, incomplete, and tribal in perspective, leading some to conclude that this account preserves a more genuine memory of the period.[9]

Recent scholars have expressed skepticism about the value of chap. 1 in reconstructing the history of premonarchic Israel, maintaining the information it contains reflects the Davidic and/or Solomonic era rather than the period of Israel's settlement in Canaan.[10] However, as noted earlier, many view this prefatory chapter (along with chaps. 19–21) to have been added to the Book of Judges during the exile,[11] if not later, when the present long Deuteronomistic

---

[8] B. Lindars speaks of "genuinely ancient, if legendary, scraps of tradition" (*Judges 1–5: A New Translation and Commentary*, ed. A. D. H. Mayes [Edinburgh: T & T Clark, 1995], 4–5). Evidences of antiquity include: (1) the absence of any hint of Philistine presence; Judah wrests the Shephelah (v. 9) and Gaza, Ashkelon, and Ekron (v. 18) from Canaanites, and the Danites are hard pressed by Amorites (vv. 34–36) rather than Philistines as in the Samson stories. (2) Dan is still in the southwest (v. 34); there is no hint of the later migration to Laish. (3) Simeon is still relatively independent (vv. 3,17), whereas by the time of Saul they have been absorbed into Judah (1 Sam 30:26–30). (4) Iron war chariots feature as a decisive factor (v. 19), a reality that had changed by the time of Sisera (4:3,13,15; 5:28). (5) The tribes are still fighting for themselves rather than on behalf of the kingdom of Israel. (6) The Canaanite city-states are autonomous. On the basis of these considerations Y. Kaufmann (*The Biblical Account of the Conquest of Canaan*, 2d ed., with preface by M. Greenberg [Jerusalem: Magnes, 1985], 127–28) concludes that the chapter is older than both the Song of Deborah (cf. the position of Dan in 5:17) and the Samson stories.

[9] Cf. the comment by S. R. Driver (*An Introduction to the Literature of the Old Testament*, ICC, 7th ed. [Edinburgh: T & T Clark, 1898], 162): "This section of the book consists of fragments of an old account of the conquest of Canaan—not by united Israel under the leadership of Joshua, but—by the individual efforts of the separate tribes."

[10] Thus Lindars, *Judges 1–5*, 7. N. Naʾaman (*Borders and Districts in Biblical Historiography*, Jerusalem Biblical Studies 4 [Jerusalem: Simor, 1986], 55, 65, 95–98, 198–99) argues that Judges 1:21,27–35 is a "historical" document, formulated at the time of the United Monarchy, recording David's conquest of previously unconquered Canaanite towns. The negative formulation of the "register" and the exclusion of Judah from the list represent deliberate distortions to legitimize this tribe's hold on the territory ascribed to it and to highlight David's achievements. This compares with earlier Pentateuchal source critics, who generally attributed this chapter to the ninth century B.C. Yahwist stratum. Cf. Cf. F. Burney, *The Book of Judges with Introduction and Notes* (London: Rivingtons, 1918 [reprinted with introduction by W. F. Albright [New York: Ktav, 1970]), 1–2; G. F. Moore, *A Critical and Exegetical Commentary on Judges*, ICC, 2d ed. (Edinburgh: T & T Clark, 1908), xxxii–iii; S. Mowinckel, *Tetrateuch–Pentateuch–Hexateuch: Die Berichte über die Landnahme in den drei altisraelitischen Geschichtswerken*, BZAW 90 (Berlin: de Gruyter, 1964), 17–33.

[11] Whereas earlier scholars attributed this editorial work to the priestly school of thought (Burney, *Judges*, 1), recently it has been credited to a Deuteronomistic redactor. Cf. R. G. Boling, *Judges: A New Translation with Introduction and Commentary*, AB (Garden City: Doubleday, 1975), 36; E. T. Mullen, Jr., "Judges 1:1–36: The Deuteronomistic Reintroduction of the Book of Judges," *HTR* 77 (1984): 33–54; J. A. Soggin, *Judges: A Commentary*, trans. J. S. Bowden, OTL (Philadelphia: Westminster, 1981), 4.

History (Joshua–Kings) was divided into the present separate books.[12] The links between the present chapter and the Book of Joshua[13] suggest the author of Judges had some form of Joshua before him, but the differences in expression from the preceding book indicate he also had access to another source, probably an early account of the conquest.[14]

Before commenting on the text in detail, several additional general observations on chap. 1 may be made. First, although it is generally recognized that Judges 1 is dependent upon the narrative account of the conquest of Canaan found in Joshua 13–19, our text summarizes, recasts, and continues the story of the process of Israel's taking possession of the land of Canaan." In so doing the form adopted resembles that of Assyrian summary inscriptions of military campaigns.[15] In such documents events are not arranged chronologically but according to geography. The descriptions are also much shorter, and relatively long periods of time are telescoped into brief spans of reading time. Summary inscriptions tend to describe a static world in general terms rather than dynamic scenes of action developing a narrative plot.[16] This description fits the present text precisely. It does indeed begin with a chronological note, highlighting the fact that after the death of Joshua, Judah was the first tribe to attack the Canaanites. However, it is impossible to construct a chronology of the conquest from this chapter. Except for the anecdotal notes (which represent insertions from other sources interested less in tribal achievements than personal

---

[12] A. G. Auld, "Judges I and History: A Reconsideration," *VT* 25 (1975): 285. Based on the *Wiederaufnahme* (resumption) of Josh 24:28–31 in Judg 2:6–9 and the content of Judg 1:1–35, M. Z. Brettler argues that Judg 1:1–2:10 originally functioned as an appendix to Joshua ("Jud 1,1–2,10: From Appendix to Prologue," *ZAW* 101 [1989]: 433–35).

[13] Note the opening phrase, which deliberately echoes Josh 1:1 and the correlation between Judg 1:10–15 and Josh 15:13–14; Judg 1:21 and Josh 15:63; Judg 1:27–28 and Josh 17:12–13; Judg 1:29 and Josh 16:10; Judg 1:34 and 19:47. See further R. H. O'Connell, *The Rhetoric of the Book of Judges*, VTSup 63 [Leiden: Brill, 1996), 66.

[14] K. L. Younger ("The Configuration of Judicial Preliminaries: Judges 1.1–2.5 and Its Dependence on the Book of Joshua," *JSOT* 68 [1995]: 75–92) argues that Judges 1 utilizes many of the macro-structures found in Joshua 13–19, making explicit what is only implied in Joshua: the success of Judah and the failures of the other tribes, particularly Dan. This is accomplished by paralleling the roles of Judah and Joseph with a concentric design and arranging the narration so that geographical sequence delineates Israel's moral declension. For a recent study of the allotments according to the Joshua account see J. Svensson, *Towns and Toponyms in the Old Testament with Special Emphasis on Joshua 14–21*, ConBOT 36 (Stockholm, Almqvist & Wiksell, 1994).

[15] See the convincing argument of Younger, "Judges 1 in Its Near Eastern Literary Context," in *Faith, Tradition and History: Essays on Old Testament Historiography in Its Near Eastern Context*, eds. J. K. Hoffmeier, et al (Winona Lake: Eisenbrauns, 1994,) 207–27. On the use of ʿālâ, "to go up" (vv. 1–4,16,22), as a technical military expression denoting "to attack," see the commentary on v. 1 below.

[16] According to Younger's comparison ("Judges 1," 208–12), Assyrian annalistic texts narrate events chronologically, employing stereotyped expressions to build an iterative scheme and regularly resort to hyperbole and other forms of rhetorical flourish.

fates/fortunes), the accounts of individual campaigns are brief, static, and without characterization or plot. Rhetorical flourishes are absent completely. One may conclude, therefore, that the present document is not intended as a corrective to the normative narrative found in Joshua but as a summary of Israel's fortunes after the death of Joshua, without which the theological narratives that follow lack historical context. The author is hereby sending an early signal to his readers that the Canaanization of Israel did not occur in a vacuum.[17]

Second, the order in which the fortunes of individual tribes are presented is deliberately geographical.[18] The author devotes the most time and space to Judah (and Simeon) in the south (vv. 3–20) and Joseph (Ephraim) (vv. 22–26); but, reflective of Benjamin's geographic position, this tribe is sandwiched between these two (v. 21). Thereafter the narration mentions successively the northern tribes (Manasseh, Zebulun, Asher, and Naphtali), ending with Dan in the far north. The tribal list is obviously incomplete. The omission of Issachar probably is random,[19] but Reuben and Gad would have been superfluous in this roster since, strictly speaking, they lived outside the original promised land, and their native Amorite population had been totally defeated by Moses (Numbers 21). Levi's name is dropped because this priestly tribe lacked any specific territorial allotment. Beyond this south-north orientation the author is particularly interested in the most important cities of the nation (at least prior to Omride rule in the north): Jerusalem in Judah (despite the questionable legality of the association) and Bethel in Ephraim.

Third, although the document reports the fortunes of individual tribes, as in the rest of the book, the author is concerned about the nation of Israel as a whole. This is not only suggested by the number of tribes he names; it is explicitly declared in the opening line, "After the death of Joshua, the Israelites [*běnê yiśrāʾēl*, "descendants of Israel"][20] asked Yahweh, 'Who will be the first to go up and fight for us against the Canaanites?'" The Israel that addressed Yahweh here is the same Israel that will appear in the Song of Deborah.[21]

---

[17] Younger ("Configuration of Judicial Preliminaries," 80–84) observes in the conquest account a simultaneous geographical axis from south to north, climaxing in the Danite experience (1:34–36), and a theological axis that sinks to its nadir in the same text.

[18] See further Younger, ibid.

[19] Contra Naʾaman, who argues that Issachar was excluded because at the time of the United Monarchy there were no unconquered towns in this tribe's allotment that could be included as points of reference (*Borders and Districts*, 97).

[20] Though some view the presentation of Israel as a retrojection of a later perception into an earlier time, it is clear that for the narrator the Israel of this period represented one nation. See further D. I. Block, "The Period of the Judges: Religious Disintegration under Tribal Rule," in *Israel's Apostasy and Restoration: Essays in Honor of Roland K. Harrison,* ed. A. Gileadi (Grand Rapids: Baker, 1988), 41–45. On the collective significance of the expression יִשְׂרָאֵל בְּנֵי, see id., "'Israel'—'Sons of Israel': A Study in Hebrew Eponymic Usage," *SR* 13 (1984): 301–26.

[21] "Israel" is named seven times in Judges 5.

Fourth, although the author is concerned about all Israel, he expresses special interest in the Judahite experience. Not only does he highlight the pride of place given to Judah in the tribal conquests after the death of Joshua but fully one-half of this chapter (vv. 3–20) is devoted to the accomplishments of this tribe.[22] Furthermore, two of the three anecdotes (vv. 5–7,12–15) add interesting details concerning the conquest of two significant cities, Jerusalem and Hebron, respectively. The narrator's emphasis on the positive achievements of Judah, which contrast with the reports of the failures of most of the other tribes, is often interpreted as a tendentious effort to glorify Judah and to lessen the stature of the northern tribes.[23] However, this interpretation fails to take seriously enough the implicit criticism of Judah for (1) sparing Adoni-bezeq (vv. 5–7), allowing the Kenites first to accompany them and then to settle down among the Canaanites (v. 16), and (2) most seriously, for failing to take the lowlands because of the Canaanites' technological superiority (v. 19). The same presence of Yahweh that had provided victory in the highlands (v. 15a) should have gone before Judah into the lowlands. After the conquest of a major city like Jericho, accompanied by Yahweh (v. 15a) Israel should have found no enemy too great (Deut 7:1–5). Accordingly, the attention and space devoted to Judah probably suggests no more than the author's Judahite citizenship and may, together with his ascription of primary role to Ephraim among the northern tribes, point to a date of composition after the division of the kingdom. To see here a deliberate polemicizing on behalf of Judah is to overstate the case.

Fifth, the account displays several ironical features. Tribal identities aside, the first half of the chapter depicts Israel as the agent of Yahweh's justice against Canaanites (cf. the punishment of the "lord of Bezeq," vv. 4–8) and the object of Yahweh's *ḥesed,* "covenant faithfulness" (cf. vv. 19–20). Ironically, the second depicts the Canaanites as the objects of Israelite *ḥesed* (cf. the Luzite in vv. 22–26) and as agents of divine judgment against the Israelites (vv. 27–36). One also observes an ironically contrastive relationship between the preamble (1:1–2) and the epilogue (2:1–5) inasmuch as the first has the Israelites taking the initiative in communicating with Yahweh, but the second has Yahweh taking the initiative in communicating with Israel. The differences in purpose reflect graphically the spiritual degradation that occurs within the chapter

---

[22] Cf. the graphic representation of the relative textual verbiage for each tribe by Younger, "Judges 1," 217–18.

[23] M. Weinfeld argues this polemic derives from circles from the Davidic house, who tried to show that Judah, David's tribe, not the northern tribes (Israel), are to be credited with the conquest of the land ("Judges 1:1–2:5: The Conquest under the Leadership of the House of Judah," in *Understanding Poets and Prophets: Essays in Honour of Georg Wishart Anderson,* ed. A. G. Auld, JSOT-Sup 152 [Sheffield: JSOT Press, 1993], 388–400). Similarly B. Halpern, *The Emergence of Israel in Canaan,* SBLMS 29 (Chico: Scholars Press, 1983), 181–82; O'Connell, *Rhetoric of the Book of Judges,* 59–70.

and within the book as a whole.

Sixth, although the narrator is aware of specific ethnic groups,[24] the adversary against whom the Israelite tribes campaign is generally (fifteen times) identified by the collective gentilic expression "the Canaanite" *(hakkĕnaʿănî)*. It has become fashionable in some circles recently to deny ancient scribes in general and Israelites in particular any precise social, political, or geographic meaning for this term.[25] As A. F. Rainey and others have demonstrated, however, it is only such scholars' comprehension of the evidence that is imprecise.[26] The cumulative evidence of second millennium B.C. references in extrabiblical texts from Alalakh, Ugarit, Mitanni, Babylon, Egypt, Alashia (Cyprus) suggests that although no specific boundaries are given, they had a clear geographic and social understanding of the term "Canaan" and that the biblically described boundaries accord with Late Bronze Age boundaries. The word probably derives from the root *kānaʿ*, "to bend, to bow low." Specifically the name seems to have identified the coastal and river valley lowlands, in contrast to the hill country.[27] However, the term was generalized to encompass most of Palestine west of the Jordan, the modern Lebanon, and parts of southwestern Syria, as far east as Damascus and northward almost to Hamath.[28]

Seventh, the author has deliberately arranged and shaped the conquest summary to reflect the moral and spiritual decline evident in the rest of the book. The catalog of tribes begins with the most positive examples (Judah) and ends with the most negative (Dan). The fact that between these poles tribal names appear more or less in the same order as in the "Book of Deliverers," where this declension is explicitly described,[29] suggests an intentional effort to portray the recidivism, the spiritual declension in Israel. At the same time, as the table on the next page illustrates, the author has carefully chosen and arranged the key verbs in this chapter to reflect this degeneration.

Accordingly, while the preface to the book is crafted in the form of a summary inscription, the genre of this chapter is transformed ironically into an anticonquest account. Unlike most ancient military reports, the aim of this document is not to celebrate the achievements of the generation of Israelites

[24] Perizzites, v. 5; Jebusites, v. 21; Hittites, v. 26; Amorites, vv. 34–36. Cf. below on 3:3–5.

[25] See especially N. P. Lemche, *The Canaanites and Their Land: The Tradition of the Canaanites*, JSOTSup 110 (Sheffield: JSOT Press, 1991), 48–51.

[26] A. F. Rainey, "Who is a Canaanite? A Review of the Textual Evidence," *BASOR* 304 (1996): 1–15. See also R. S. Hess, "Occurrences of 'Canaan' in Late Bronze Age Archives of the West Semitic World," forthcoming in the Anson Rainey Festschrift.

[27] Cf. Num 13:29; Josh 5:1; 11:3; Judg 1:19,27–29.

[28] For discussions of the land and the people see A. R. Millard, "The Canaanites," *POTT*, 29–52; K. N. Schoville, "Canaanites and Amorites," *Peoples of the Old Testament World*, ed. A. Hoerth et al. (Grand Rapids: Baker, 1994), 157–82; P. C. Schmitz, "Canaan (Place)," *ABD* 1.828–31.

[29] Judah (Othniel), Benjamin (Ehud), Ephraim (Deborah), Manasseh (Gideon), Gilead, (Jephthah), Dan (Samson). Cf. 2:11–23, esp. v. 19.

that survived Joshua but to lament their sorry response to the divine mandate to occupy the land and to eliminate the Canaanites. Although the author delays sermonizing on the subject (cf. 2:1–5; 2:6–3:6), the structure of the chapter declares that this military failure accounts for the disastrous history of the nation in the next two or three centuries, as it is reported in the remainder of the book.

The Retrogression of Israelite Fortunes in Judges

	Primary Action	Result
1:3–21	Israelites defeat *(nākâ)* Canaanites Jerusalem (v. 8) Hebron (v. 10) Hormah (v. 17) Israelites capture *(lāqad)* Gaza, Ashkelon, Ekron (v. 18) Israelites dispossess *(hôrîš)* Canaanites in the hill country *but* They do not dispossess *(lōʾ hôrîš)* the inhabitants of the valleys because of …	*and* Canaanites are destroyed *but* Their Kenite allies live with *yāšab ʾet* the people *and* the law of *ḥerem* is applied (v. 17)
1:21–30	Israelites defeat *(nākâ)* Canaanites Bethel Israelites do not dispossess *(lōʾ hôrîš)* the Canaanites Benjamin[a] Manasseh Ephraim Zebulun	*but* Some Canaanites are allowed to live at a distance *and* Canaanites live among *(bĕ/ bĕqereb)* the Israelites
1:31–33	Israelites do not dispossess *(lōʾ hôrîš)* the Canaanites	*and* Canaanites live among *(bĕ/ bĕqereb)* the Israelites
1:34–36	Canaanites press *(lāḥaṣ)* Israelites Dan	*and* Israelites are permitted to live at a distance

a. Benjamin is sandwiched between Judah and Joseph for geographical reasons (v. 21).

Eighth, the author is careful to give credit for successes where credit is due. This otherwise secular text is punctuated with two theological notes: "the LORD gave *X* into *Y*'s hands" (v. 4); "the LORD was with *TN*" (= tribal name; vv. 19,22). In fact, both Judah and Joseph achieve victory in spite of minor lapses in carrying out the divine mandate to destroy the Canaanites.[30] This observation forces a modification of a common mechanistic view of the Deuteronomistic formula: obedience results in blessing; disobedience brings the curse. On the contrary, as the author will demonstrate throughout the book, Yahweh typically operates on Israel's behalf in mercy and grace, not in response to the people's manifest spirituality or merit.[31]

Ninth, the summary narrative of tribal conquests is interrupted at three critical junctures by anecdotal insertions (vv. 5–7,12–15,23–26). These anecdotes share several characteristics: all shift the attention from tribal to achievements to personal experiences; all are associated with the conquest of significant cities (Jerusalem, Hebron,[32] Bethel); all are cast in typical Hebrew narrative style (complete with characterization, plot, dialogue) rather than iterative summary form; all introduce a character with remarkable and unexpected initiative (a Canaanite who escapes Judah's attack; a woman more assertive than her hero husband; a Canaanite who builds a city within Israelite territory).

(1) Introduction (1:1–2)

¹After the death of Joshua, the Israelites asked the LORD, "Who will be the first to go up and fight for us against the Canaanites?"

²The LORD answered, "Judah is to go; I have given the land into their hands."

1:1–2   The Book of Judges opens with a temporal notice: "After the death of Joshua …"[33] Except for the change of name from Moses to Joshua, this phrase repeats verbatim the opening to the Book of Joshua.[34] The form of the expression invites the reader to treat the centuries *after* the death of Joshua as a distinct era,[35] just as the author of the previous book had considered the period immediately following the death of Moses. It also suggests that the Book of Judges is to be interpreted not as a continuation of the Book of Joshua but as its companion volume. Strictly speaking, according to Josh 24:29–31 (which reports Joshua's death) and Judg 2:6–10, the transition from one era to

---

[30] Judah spares Adoni-bezeq (vv. 5–7); Joseph spares and fraternizes with a Canaanite spy (vv. 23–25).

[31] A point convincingly argued by R. Polzin, *Moses and the Deuteronomist: A Literary Study of the Deuteronomic History,* Part I: *Deuteronomy, Joshua, Judges* (New York: Seabury, 1980), 146–204.

[32] Debir (Kiriath-arba) lay just south of Hebron.

[33] Hebrew narrative often begins a literary unit with *wayĕhî,* followed by a temporal clause or phrase (Josh 1:1; 1 Sam 1:1; 2 Sam 1:1; Ruth 1:1; Esth 1:1; Neh 1:1; cf. also Ezek 1:1; Jonah 1:1). Cf. GKC §111g.

[34] Contra Soggin (*Judges,* 20), there is no need to treat this opening as a sign of a late addition; nor is there any need to emend "Joshua" to "Moses" (*BHS*), as if chap. 1 represented an alternative account of the conquest (so also Lindars, *Judges 1–5,* p. 11).

[35] The author of the Book of Ruth perceived this period similarly. Cf. the opening to that book, וַיְהִי בִּימֵי שְׁפֹט הַשֹּׁפְטִים, "In the days when tribal chieftains ruled."

the other occurred with the passing of the generation that participated in the crossing of the Jordan and the conquest of the land under Joshua's leadership. As is common, the passing of a leader precipitates a political crisis. Who will take charge now?[36] Whereas Moses had formally and publicly made arrangements for a successor (Num 27:15–23; Deuteronomy 31; 34), apparently Joshua had made no such provisions. Not that he should be faulted for this. Joshua's military campaigns had succeeded in breaking the backbone of Canaanite resistance and cleared the way for the tribes to take charge of their own futures. Receiving a message from Yahweh that his time to die was at hand (Josh 13:1–7), Joshua had supervised the apportionment of the tribal land grants, as a general oversees the distribution of the spoils of war (Joshua 13–19). But while Yahweh's instructions regarding Joshua's arrangements for the future said nothing about a successor, the descendants of Israel as a group were to accept the challenge of continuing the holy war against the enemies occupying the land that remained. In his valedictory address Joshua reminded his countrymen that the same conditions that had predicated his work continued in effect for them. They were to fear God, remain true to the Torah of Moses, and, led by the Divine Warrior, drive out the enemy (23:1–13). After he had presided over a covenant renewal ceremony at Shechem, Joshua dismissed the people to their respective tribal allotments and died (24:1–29).

Verses 1–2 presuppose Joshua's reference to the nations that remain (Josh 23:4–5). In the absence of a human commander, but eager to fulfill the challenge of their great military leader, the Israelites seek guidance directly from Yahweh, their divine commander-in-chief. The issue uppermost in their minds was which tribe should lead the way in taking control of its tribal allotment. Although the author does not reveal exactly how the Israelites consulted Yahweh, the expression *šāʾal bĕ,* "to ask of," suggests some sort of oracular consultation. Presumably the divine will on the matter was to be ascertained by the high priest's manipulation of the Urim and Thummim, as prescribed for Joshua in Num 27:21. This procedure seems to have been followed in Joshua 7 (to expose Achan) and in Joshua 18–19 in the apportionment of the tribal land grants.[37] The present action is illuminated by Judges 20, which describes "the sons of Israel" going up *(ʿālâ)* to Bethel three times to inquire of God concerning the conduct of their war against Benjamin (vv. 18,23,27). In vv. 27–28 the narrator explains why they went to Bethel: "In those days the ark of the covenant of God was there, with Phinehas son of Eleazar, the son of Aaron, ministering before it." One may assume accordingly that in 1:1 representatives of the tribes appear before the priest, who

---

[36] Such a crisis seems to be reflected in Isa 6:1.

[37] In the case of the Gibeonites, Josh 9:14 explicitly notes that Israel did not "inquire [lit., "consult the mouth"] of the LORD."

should be able to determine the will of God in a given situation.[38] The fact that the tribes seek the mind of God speaks not only of their early dedication to the divine mission—after the death of Joshua God is still recognized as commander-in-chief for the nation—but it also speaks of the freedom of the tribes to operate independently.

The issue is framed formally by the narrator as a direct question presented to God: "Who will be the first to go up[39] and fight for us against the Canaanites?" Like the question, the answer is presented in direct quotation form: "Judah is to go." With this answer Yahweh offers a promise—the same promise he had given to Joshua earlier: He has delivered the territory allotted to Judah into the tribe's hands. In this idealized form, for the people it becomes simply a matter of claiming what God has reserved for them.

The opening scene of the book offers so much promise. The theocratic system is still in place. Israel is sensitive to the will of God, and God responds to the overtures of his people. In its present canonical position, after the Book of Joshua, the reader expects a continuation of the triumphant narrative encountered in the previous book. But how different will be the reality from the ideal, the history from the dream! By raising the reader's expectations this way the narrator invites us to share the intensity of his own and God's disappointment with his people in the period of settlement. Verses 1–2 throw the remainder of the chapter and the book into sharpest relief.

(2) The Successes and Failures of Judah (1:3–20)

3Then the men of Judah said to the Simeonites their brothers, "Come up with us into the territory allotted to us, to fight against the Canaanites. We in turn will go with you into yours." So the Simeonites went with them.

4When Judah attacked, the LORD gave the Canaanites and Perizzites into their hands and they struck down ten thousand men at Bezek. 5It was there that they found Adoni-Bezek and fought against him, putting to rout the Canaanites and Perizzites. 6Adoni-Bezek fled, but they chased him and caught him, and cut off his thumbs and big toes.

7Then Adoni-Bezek said, "Seventy kings with their thumbs and big toes cut off have picked up scraps under my table. Now God has paid me back for what I did to them." They brought him to Jerusalem, and he died there.

8The men of Judah attacked Jerusalem also and took it. They put the city to the sword and set it on fire.

9After that, the men of Judah went down to fight against the Canaanites living in the hill country, the Negev and the western foothills. 10They advanced against

---

[38] Cf. the explicit reference to the Urim as the means of Saul's consultation in 1 Sam 28:6.

[39] The use of the verb עָלָה, lit., "to go up, ascend," as a quasi-technical term for "to invade, attack," reflects not only the ascent of the armies into the central highlands but also the fact that most fortresses in Palestine were located either on natural elevations or on artificial tells, "mounds, ruin heaps."

the Canaanites living in Hebron (formerly called Kiriath Arba) and defeated Sheshai, Ahiman and Talmai. [11]From there they advanced against the people living in Debir (formerly called Kiriath Sepher). [12]And Caleb said, "I will give my daughter Acsah in marriage to the man who attacks and captures Kiriath Sepher." [13]Othniel son of Kenaz, Caleb's younger brother, took it; so Caleb gave his daughter Acsah to him in marriage.

[14]One day when she came to Othniel, she urged him to ask her father for a field. When she got off her donkey, Caleb asked her, "What can I do for you?"

[15]She replied, "Do me a special favor. Since you have given me land in the Negev, give me also springs of water." Then Caleb gave her the upper and lower springs.

[16]The descendants of Moses' father-in-law, the Kenite, went up from the City of Palms with the men of Judah to live among the people of the Desert of Judah in the Negev near Arad.

[17]Then the men of Judah went with the Simeonites their brothers and attacked the Canaanites living in Zephath, and they totally destroyed the city. Therefore it was called Hormah. [18]The men of Judah also took Gaza, Ashkelon and Ekron— each city with its territory.

[19]The LORD was with the men of Judah. They took possession of the hill country, but they were unable to drive the people from the plains, because they had iron chariots. [20]As Moses had promised, Hebron was given to Caleb, who drove from it the three sons of Anak.

As noted above, fully one-half of the summary of Israelite military fortunes after the death of Joshua is devoted to Judah. This section consists of a series of pieces, each of which contributes something unique to the summary.

THE FRATERNAL ALLIANCE (1:3).   **1:3** Having received the divine mandate to attack the Canaanites, the tribe of Judah immediately accepts its leadership role.[40] However, instead of priding itself in its superior position, this tribe invites Simeon to share the campaign and promises to assist the smaller tribe in conquering its allotted territory.[41] Simeon willingly agrees. Judah's alliance with Simeon is natural for two reasons. First, as the narrator recognizes, the eponymous ancestors of these tribes, Judah and Simeon, were full brothers, the sons of Jacob and his first wife Leah (Gen 29:33,35).[42] Second, this alliance respects and/or reflects the allotment of Simeon's territory within the grant of Judah as described in Josh 19:1–9. According to this text

---

[40]This contrasts with the role of Judah in the rest of the book. Except for the brief Othniel story (3:7–11), Judah never appears in a leadership role again and is missing in the roll call of tribes in the Song of Deborah (5:14–23).

[41]The word for "territorial allotment," גּוֹרָל literally "lot," recalls the process of apportionment in Josh 14:2. Cf. Num 26:53–56; 33:54; 35:13.

[42]This kinship is also reflected in the mode of address; Judah and Simeon communicate as individuals, the tribes being represented by their eponymous ancestors.

this curious allotment redresses Judah's problem of having received a dispro-portionately large grant. However, one suspects this arrangement was also influenced by the size of Simeon's population at the end of the desert wan-derings. According to the census in Numbers 26, Simeon was the smallest tribe by far. This tribe's twenty-two thousand men of military age (v. 14) was less than half the average of the other eleven tribes, so it was probably too small to receive an independent territorial grant.[43] Within a century or two Simeon ceased to exist as a separate tribe.[44]

THE UPLAND CAMPAIGN (1:4–8). The account of Judah's campaigns divides into two parts on the basis of (a) the verbs: $ʿālâ$, "to go up" (v. 4),[45] and $yārad$, "to go down" (v. 9); (b) the naming of two opposition groups: Canaan-ites and Perizzites; and (c) the announcement of the results in v. 19: the upland campaign was successful; the lowland effort failed.

Victory at Bezek (1:4). **1:4** According to the account Judah's initial charge was directed generally at the Canaanites and Perizzites. As noted above, the former name often functions generally for the population of Pales-tine as a whole, though strictly speaking it refers to the inhabitants of the lowlands of the southwest. The Perizzites were a minor segment of the pre-Israelite population of Canaan, also frequently named among the tribes iden-tified as targets of Israel's holy war, hence under the *ḥerem* law.[46] The suc-cess of Judah is credited to Yahweh and concretized by mentioning the battle at Bezek in which they struck down *(nākâ)* ten thousand of their troops. Although the location of Bezek is unknown, the present context suggests it cannot have been far from Jerusalem.[47] The number ten thousand is obvi-ously a rounded figure, perhaps a conventional generic number for "innumer-able." It seems inordinately high, but it correlates well with the census figures for Israel in Numbers 2 and 26 and with the song composed to cele-

---

[43] This arrangement is also anticipated in Jacob's blessing of his sons, which foresees the dis-tribution of both Simeon and Levi among the rest of the tribes (Gen 49:5–7). The drastic reduction in the size of Simeon from the first census (59,300, Num 2:23) probably represents punishment for this tribe's sins of idolatry and fornication in Moab (Num 25:1–14).

[44] Simeon is missing in Moses' blessing of the tribes (Deuteronomy 33) and in the Song of Deborah (Judges 5).

[45] The structural significance of the occurrence of the root at critical junctures in the narrative (1:1, "Who will … go up?"; 1:4 (lit.), "Judah went up"; 1:22 (lit.), "The household of Joseph went up"; 2:1, "The angel of the LORD went up") is widely recognized. See Webb, *Book of Judges*, 102–3, and Younger, "Judges 1," 215–16.

[46] Gen 15:20; Deut 7:1; Josh 3:10; 7:1; etc. The etymology of Perizzite is uncertain, but many associate it with יִפְרָז (Deut 3:5; 1 Sam 6:18), פְּרָזוֹן (Judg 5:7,11), and פְּרָזוֹת, "unwalled cities" (Ezek 38:11; Zech 2:8), hence "inhabitants of unwalled settlements." Cf. S. A. Reed, "Perizzite," *ABD* 5.231.

[47] Boling suggests an identification with Khirbet Bizqa, near Gezer (*Judges*, 55). Contra A. Zertal ("Bezek," *ABD* 1.717–18), the Bezek near Shechem mentioned in 1 Sam 11:8 is too far north for the present context.

brate David's victory over Goliath (1 Sam 18:7).[48]

The Death of Adoni-Bezek (1:5–7). Breaking with the formal style of the chapter as a whole, the narrator devotes three verses to the capture, mutilation, and death of the lord of Bezek. The NIV follows an ancient tradition in interpreting *ʾădōnî bezeq* as a personal name,[49] but this probably is intended as a title, "Lord of Bezek," a reference to the governor or mayor of the city.[50] Obviously the governor's attempt to hide when the city was attacked failed. When he was discovered, he fled, but he soon was captured and tortured by the Judahite troops, who cut off his toes and fingers. The mutilation is described without comment. The narrator restrains himself and permits the governor to offer his own commentary. The aim of such cruel and unusual treatment of a prisoner, which was common in the ancient world,[51] was to incapacitate and humiliate him. But this governor of Bezek interprets his fate theologically: God is repaying him for his own similar cruelty to seventy kings, whom he reduced to scavenging [scraps][52] under his table, that is, he treated them like dogs. Adoni-Bezek's reference to God is ambiguous. As a Canaanite it would have been unusual for him to have named Yahweh, the God of Israel. Accordingly, he ascribes responsibility for his punishment to *ʾelōhîm*, which could refer either to Yahweh by the generic title or his own pagan god. The reference to "seventy" kings probably is intended as a round and/or hyperbolic number meaning "all the chieftains in the area."

Adoni-Bezek's comment is loaded with irony. On the one hand, it reminds the reader that in the ancient world everyone, even pagans, perceived life theologically. On the other hand, the author hereby employs a Canaanite to announce that human beings will account to God/the gods for their action. Furthermore, by quoting the governor the author offers the first hint of the Canaanization of Israelite society in this period. The Judahite treatment of Adoni-Bezek is often perceived as an application of the law of *lex talionis*, "an

---

[48] Boling (*Judges*, 54–55) rationalizes the number by reading אֶלֶף as "head of a clan," hence "contingent." For a recent study of the large numbers in the Book of Judges and elsewhere in the OT see D. M. Fouts, "A Defense of the Hyperbolic Interpretation of Large Numbers in the Old Testament," *JETS* 40 (1997): 377–88.

[49] Like Adoni-Zedek, king of Jerusalem, in Josh 10:1–3; but this is improbable since, unlike בֶּזֶק, צֶדֶק never appears as a name of a divinity.

[50] So also S. Layton, *Archaic Features of Canaanite Personal Names in the Hebrew Bible*, HSM 47 (Atlanta: Scholars Press, 1990), 117. Some emend אֲדֹנִי־בֶזֶק to אֲדֹנִי־עֶדֶק on the assumption the present text represents a garbled version of the same tradition that underlies the Joshua text (cf. *Jerusalem Bible*). Interestingly, the Greek translators of the LXX reverse the operation, reading Ἀδωνιβέζεκ in Josh 10:1,3. For further discussion and citations see Lindars, *Judges 1–5*, 15–16.

[51] For references see Moore, *Judges*, 17–18.

[52] Tg. fills in the ellipsis by adding לַחְמָא, "bread." Hb. reads simply מְלַקְּטִים, "to pick up, scavenge."

eye for an eye and a tooth for a tooth," which represents an acceptable ethic in the Old Testament but was set aside by Christ (Matt 5:38–39).[53] However, not only does this interpretation fail to understand this law as an intentional effort to curb the escalation of violence (by proscribing a reaction greater than the action), but it fails to recognize here the irony of the present situation. The author hereby declares obliquely that the newly arrived Israelites (including the tribe of Judah) have quickly adopted a Canaanite ethic. Apart from the issue of having spared a man who clearly came under the sentence of death with the rest of the people, instead of looking to Yahweh for ethical guidance, the Israelites use the Canaanites as models when deciding how to treat captives.[54]

The last statement in v. 7, which notes that the governor of Bezek was brought to Jerusalem where he died, is tantalizingly ambiguous. First, it raises the question, Who brought him there, his captors or his own people? If it was the latter, his followers must have rescued him and transported him to the security of the Jebusite fortress of Jerusalem. Alternatively, in context it is more natural to treat Judah as the antecedent of the verb, "They brought him ..." If this is correct, the troops of Judah must have moved quickly from Bezek to Jerusalem and conquered the city (v. 8).

Second, how did Adoni-Bezek die? By natural causes or by human hands? After his mutilation it is conceivable that he bled to death or died as a result of infection. In any case, Judah's treatment of their captive is problematic. Why did they let him live in the first place? According to Yahweh's instructions they were to leave no survivors, neither men, women, nor children (Deut 7:1–2; 20:16–17). This Judahite sparing of the governor of Bezek serves as a premonition of things to come and punctures any idealized view of this tribe.

The Conquest of Jerusalem (1:8).   **1:8**   Jerusalem was an old city even by the time the Israelites arrived, having been in existence at least since 3000 B.C. Forms of the name, which means something like "establishment of [the god] Shalem," are attested as early as the nineteenth–eighteenth century B.C. Execration Texts from Egypt. According to the Amarna correspondence, in the fourteenth century the city (spelled *Urusalim*) was ruled by Abdi-Ḫiba, a vassal of the Egyptian Pharaoh Amenophis IV (Akhenaten). The common biblical name for this place, Jebus (cf. v. 21), is unattested outside the Old Testament.

The chronological relation between vv. 5–7 and 8 is not clear. The present arrangement suggests the attack on Jerusalem followed soon after the conquest of Bezek. In contrast to their treatment of Adoni-Bezek, the author observes complete Judahite compliance with the law of *ḥerem*, the total slaughter of Jerusalem's population and the destruction of the city.[55] The association of

---

[53] A. E. Cundall, *Judges and Ruth: An Introduction and Commentary*, TOTC (Downers Grove: InterVarsity, 1968), 53.

[54] Cf. Samson's comment in 15:11.

[55] With this burning of a conquered city cp. Josh 6:24; 8:8; 11:11; also Judg 9:49.

Judah with Jerusalem at this early date is problematic. Not only does 2 Sam 5:6–9 note that David wrested Jerusalem out of Jebusite hands but according to v. 21 and Josh 15:8 Jerusalem was occupied by Jebusites (rather than Canaanites and Perizzites), and according to Josh 18:16,28, the city falls within the territory allotted to Benjamin. The most likely explanation recognizes that Jerusalem was a border city, located on the boundary between Judah and Benjamin. The city that was burned in v. 8 probably identifies the Jebusite fortress on the southern hill of the city, between the Kidron and Hinnom Valleys, and which David eventually captured and made his capital. Accordingly, the unsuccessful Benjamite effort in v. 21 must have been directed against the citadel farther north. The fact that David had to reconquer Jerusalem suggests the Judahite hold on the city was weak and short-lived. It seems that shortly after they had sacked it the Jebusites moved in from the north and took control, which they then held for several centuries.

THE LOWLAND CAMPAIGN (1:9–20). *Introduction (1:9).* **1:9** Verse 9 is transitional, functioning as a general introduction to the new phase of Judah's campaign described in vv. 10–20.[56] The timing is fixed by the adverb *ʾaḥar*, "afterwards," and the direction by the verb *yārĕdû*, "they went down." The Canaanites targeted by this campaign are identified generally according to three topographic areas: "the hill country" *(hāhār)* denotes the Judahite uplands south of Jerusalem; the Negev refers to the southern part of Judah, which is largely desert; the "lowlands" *(šĕpēlâ*; NIV, "western foothills") identifies the transitional region of Judah between "the hill country" and the coastal plain.[57] The specific conquests in each of these three areas are described in the following verses.

The Conquest of Hebron (1:10). **1:10** The campaign in "the hill country" is described in two phases. First, the narrator summarizes the conquest of Hebron, giving the barest of details, generalizing to Judah actions that Josh 15:13–14 had credited to Caleb. As in the earlier text, this author gives the contemporary and ancient name of the city attacked and the names of three of her rulers. Like Jerusalem nineteen miles to the north, Hebron was an ancient city. Though knowledge of the old name Kiriath Arba[58] persisted until the Persian period (Neh 11:25), the switch to Hebron reflects the shift in

---

[56] So also R. de Vaux, *The Early History of Israel, to the Period of the Judges*, trans. D. Smith, (Philadelphia: Westminster, 1978), 541.

[57] שְׁפֵלָה derives from a root meaning "to be low." The NIV's "western foothills" identifies the region, but instead of looking down from the Judean hills, the perspective is up from the coastal plain. On this region see H. Brodsky, "Shephelah," *ABD* 5.1204.

[58] The significance of קִרְיַת עַרְבָּה, "City of Four," remains a mystery. According to Josh 15:13 and 21:11, Arba was the father of Anak, the ancestor of the Anakites. H. Wolf ("Judges," *EBC*, ed F. E. Gaebelein [Grand Rapids: Zondervan, 1992], 3.387) and Cundall (*Judges and Ruth*, 54) suggest the name points to federation of four cities.

its population. Many years earlier Abraham had purchased the nearby cave at Machpelah as a family burial place (Genesis 24), but at the time of the conquest its population consisted of Anakites, descendants of Anak. Later, until he had conquered Jerusalem, David would make Hebron his capital, from which he ruled Judah for seven years (2 Sam 5:1–5).[59] The narrator concretizes the report of the conquest of the city by naming three of the Anakite leaders of Hebron: Sheshai, Ahiman, and Talmai.[60] To the Israelites the name Anakim became proverbial for great and fearsome foes (Deut 9:2).

The Conquest of Debir (1:11–15). **1:11–15** The second phase in the conquest of the "hill country" is directed at Debir, which is also identified by its ancient name, Kiriath Sepher.[61] The name translates literally "city of the letter/document,"[62] which suggests this site may have originally housed an official library or archive.[63] *Kariassōpar*, however, read by one major LXX manuscript (LXX[B]), may point to an original Kiriat Sopher, "city of the [muster-]officer,"[64] in which case Debir may have been an important army or government post. The location of ancient Debir is still uncertain, but the most likely identification links this site with Khirbet Rabud, southwest of Hebron.[65]

Following the formal summary announcement in v. 11, the narrator digresses with an anecdote concerning the manner in which Debir was taken from the Canaanites. Caleb, who had been allotted the territory around Hebron by Joshua (Josh 14:6–15), puts forth a challenge: he will give his daughter Achsah as a reward to anyone who captures neighboring Kiriath Sepher. His close relative Othniel accepts the challenge and captures the city. His exact relationship to Caleb is uncertain. The antecedent of "his younger brother" could be either Caleb or Kenaz, in which case he would be Caleb's nephew.[66] The clarifying comment, which is missing in the Joshua parallel,

---

[59] For an archaeological history of Hebron see A. Ofer, "Hebron," *NEAEHL* 2.606–9.

[60] The LXX harmonizes the identification of these men with Num 13:22 and Josh 15:14 by reading יְלִידֵי הָעֲנָק, "descendants of the Anak," after the names.

[61] Vv. 11–15 represent a verbatim echo of Josh 15:15–19, with the following minor exceptions: (1) The opening verb in Judges is וַיֵּלֶךְ, "and he went"; in Joshua וַיַּעַל, "and he went up" (on which see O'Connell, *Rhetoric of the Book of Judges*, 438); (2) Judg 1:13 inserts "his younger brother" after Caleb; (3) Judg 1:14 has the article on הַשָּׂדֶה; (4) Judg 1:15 adds the indirect object, "And she said *to him*" (לוֹ); (5) The following verb for "to give" is הָבָה, from Aramaic יְהַב, rather than תְּנָה from נָתַן; (6) Judg 1:15 employs shorter forms of the adjectives: עֲלִית for עֶלְיוֹת, and תַּחְתִּית for תַּחְתִּיוֹת.

[62] So also LXX πόλις γραμμάτων.

[63] Wolf, "Judges," EBC 3:388. Boling (*Judges*, 56) proposes "Town of the treaty-stele."

[64] Similarly Tg.'s קִרְיַת אַרְכִּי, "city of the officer."

[65] See M. Kochavi, "Rabud, Khirbet," in *NEAEHL* 4.1252; id., "Khirbet Rabud = Debir," *TA* 1 (1974) 2–33; Rainey, "Debir," *ISBE* I (Grand Rapids: Eerdmans, 1979), 901–4.

[66] The LXX[A] adopts the first reading; the LXX[B], the second.

is added here to emphasize that Othniel represented the next generation.[67]

Modern readers may find Caleb's treatment of his daughter offensive, as if she is mere property, an object to be awarded by one man to another for a job well done. However, we must not impose modern notions of romance or gender relations upon ancient texts. Nor should we expect ancient writers in a patricentric[68] culture like this to reflect, let alone support, contemporary egalitarian preferences. Curiously, while Achsah offers a mild protest to her father over the way he has treated her, her grievance has nothing to do with feeling devalued as a person. Nor would we expect her to. In that context she probably felt honored to be given in marriage to a military hero like Othniel. What she protests is the inadequacy of the land her father gave to her husband. She refers to the area associated with Kiriath Sepher as "Negev land"[69] not because it was located in the Negev[70] but because it had Negev-like characteristics: it was desert land. So she requests of him "reservoirs of water,"[71] and Caleb responds generously by granting her both the upper and lower reservoirs.

The purpose of this short anecdote has long puzzled readers. Why should the author have lifted this note from the Book of Joshua[72] and inserted it in this otherwise cold and formal military conquest summary? Three possibilities may be offered. First, the story reflects the author's interest in the past. Caleb provides a link with Joshua. He represents the generation that knew Yahweh and his work (cf. 2:6–10) and who faithfully fulfilled Yahweh's/Joshua's charge.

Second, the note reflects the author's interest in the present. It provides a delightful picture of normal and positive social relationships as they functioned in this early phase of the conquest. This is one of the few accounts in the book where all the characters are cast in a favorable light. Caleb is an old man now. Decades earlier he had represented the tribe of Judah among the twelve spies (Num 13:6) and had (together with Joshua) silenced the naysay-

---

[67] U. Becker also argues for the priority of the Joshua account (*Richterzeit und Königtum: Redaktionsgeschichtliche Studien zum Richterbuch,* BZAW 192 [Berlin/New York: de Gruyter, 1990] 40–41).

[68] We avoid the term "patriarchy," "the rule of the father," because of modern connotations of abuse and exploitation inherent in the element "archy." "Patricentric" corresponds more closely to the Israelite model reflected in the expression, אָב בֵּית, "house of the father," and allows for the biblical ideal, which emphasizes the responsibility of the father for the welfare of the household rather than his power over its members.

[69] The NIV's "land in the Negev" is somewhat misleading for אֶרֶץ הַנֶּגֶב, lit. "land of the Negev."

[70] Cf. the three stages of the lowland campaign mentioned in v. 9.

[71] גֻּלֹת מָיִם, inadequately rendered "springs of water" in the NIV. The expression גֻּלָּה is rare. Elsewhere it means "bowl" (Zech 4:2–3; Eccles 12:6) or "bowl shaped" object (2 Kgs 7:41–42 = 2 Chr 4:12–13). Lindars (*Judges 1–5,* 32) prefers to read singular with the LXX.

[72] Or the source available to the authors of both books.

ers with his minority report, confident in Yahweh's power to deliver the Canaanites into their hand (Num 13:30; 14:5–10). Moses and Joshua had rewarded him by assigning the major allotment of Hebron within Judah (Josh 15:13). Having taken his own city, Caleb's challenge to anyone to capture nearby Debir (presumably within his own allotment) reflects his eagerness to see the conquest move forward. By offering his daughter as a reward, he not only expresses his commitment to the agenda but also ensures a noble husband for her. His sensitivity is reflected in the way he treats his daughter. When she arrives, he takes the initiative by asking her what is on her mind (1:14),[73] and when she asks for a field with accessible water resources, he lavishes her with the upper and lower reservoirs.[74]

Othniel, also a proselyte, is presented as a brave warrior, who fearlessly defeats the enemy and wins a bride in a single move.

The portrait of Achsah is the most intriguing of all. L. R. Klein correctly views her as a role model of womanly propriety in this patricentric environment.[75] She demonstrates resourcefulness in the way she analyzes the problem and induces[76] her father[77] by asking him to give her a blessing as well. The meaning of *wattĕsîtēhû lišʾôl*, "she induced him [her father] by asking," may be recovered by referring to 2 Sam 24:1: "he [Yahweh] incited David."[78] Accordingly, she convinces her father to give her a field *(śādeh),*

---

[73] מַה־לָּךְ, "What [can I do] for you?" On מַה + *lamed* of interest see *WO* 18.3b.

[74] גֻּלֹּת עִלִּית וְגֻלֹּת תַּחְתִּית, "upper and lower reservoirs," may be interpreted as a merism granting full rights to all the water in the area.

[75] L. R. Klein, "A Spectrum of Female Characters in the Book of Judges," in *A Feminist Companion to Judges*, A Feminist Companion to the Bible 4; ed. A. Brenner (Sheffield: Academic Press, 1993), 25. For her fuller discussion of Achsah see "The Book of Judges: Paradigm and Deviation in Images of Women," ibid., 55–60. "Patricentric" is my term.

[76] The verb וַתְּסִיתֵהוּ (v. 14), which derives from a root סוּת, "to instigate, prompt," is a crux in this context.

[77] The NIV's "she urged him [Othniel]" to ask her father for a field follows traditional scholarly consensus. However, the reading is difficult for several reasons: (1) The suffix on the verb is ambiguous (many scholars follow the LXX, reading the verb as masculine and the suffix as feminine, i.e., he [greedy Othniel] importuned her) and could just as well apply to Caleb as to Othniel, in which case she approaches her father herself, an observation confirmed by the following sentences (see O'Connell, *Rhetoric of the Book of Judges*, 440, for discussion). (2) More seriously, in the Hb. text, Othniel drops out of the story after v. 13. The remainder of vv. 14–15, involving only Achsah and her father, describe how this transpired. (3) If Othniel is inserted here, the sequence of events becomes problematic.

[78] Where the same verb is followed by *lamed* + infinitive construct (functioning as a gerund) of a verb of speech. Similarly Deut 13:7; 2 Kgs 18:32; Isa 36:18. The commonly assumed purpose meaning of the present construction occurs only in Job 2:3 and Jer 43:3. 2 Chr 32:11 conflates both, expressing intention with *lamed* + infinitive but following this up with לֵאמֹר, "by saying." For a fuller discussion of this interpretation see P. G. Mosca, "Who Seduced Whom? A Note on Joshua 15:18 // Judges 1:14," *CBQ* 46 (1984): 18–22. Cf. also D. N. Fewell, "Deconstructive Criticism: Achsah and the (E)razed City of Writing," in *Judges and Method: New Approaches in Biblical Studies*, ed. G. A. Yee (Minneapolis: Fortress, 1995), 135–37.

in addition to the territory her husband had received as his reward. However, her physical posture[79] before her father expresses deep parental respect. The NIV's "Do me a special favor" dilutes the sense of *hābâ lî běrākâ,* "Give me[80] a blessing please," and obscures the allusion to the common custom of a father and/or the paternal household blessing of a daughter when she is given away in marriage or leaves home.[81] This is not a request for a dowry for Othniel (Debir was it) but a "blessing,"[82] which she recognizes as the key to her own and probably her husband's future.[83] She recognizes that the desert (Negev) land she and her husband have received offers little promise. Accordingly she concretizes her need for a blessing with a request for a field with springs of water, without which she will be unable to grow the garden she needs to feed her family. Although she remains gracious and respectful, she will not be simply a passive object of men's deals. Instead she seizes the opportunity to achieve something neither her father nor husband contemplated. But she does so without overstepping the bounds of female propriety.

This is an episode in which everyone (fathers and daughters, husbands and sons-in-law) functions with boldness and creativity but always respectful of the dignity and role of the other person in that socioeconomic environment—which may suggest the real reason for the inclusion of this note in the account. Although the author makes no reference to Yahweh, as in the Book of Ruth, here we see covenant faith in action in everyday life. The treatment of Achsah by these men serves as a backdrop against which to view the abuse and violence perpetrated by men against the Levite's concubine in chap. 19 and the daughters of Shiloh in chap. 21.[84] The author exploits the

---

[79] She gets off her donkey (NIV) at the sight of her father as an act of deference. The verb וַתִּצְנַח derives from a root צָנַח, whose meaning is still unclear. Soggin (*Judges,* 22) speculates it could also mean "she clapped her hands," but this creates problems for interpreting מֵעַל הַחֲמוֹר, "from the donkey." The verb appears elsewhere only in 4:21, where it describes the downward motion of the tent-peg going down through Sisera's temple. For defenses of the traditional interpretation of the expression see A. Gibson, "SNH in Judges I 14: *NEB* and *AV* Translations," *VT* 26 (1976): 275–83; E. W. Nicholson, "The Problem of צנח," *ZAW* 89 (1977): 258–66.

[80] הָבָה, "give," derives from the root יהב, which is commonly used in Aramaic. Josh 15:19 employs the more common Hb. verb נָתַן.

[81] Cf. Gen 24:60, on which see C. Westermann, *Genesis 12–36,* trans. J. J. Scullion (Minneapolis: Augsburg, 1985), 390.

[82] For a long time ברך was thought to derive from a root meaning "to bend the knee" (cf. 2 Chr 6:13), but this connection between בֶּרֶך, "knee," and בָּרַך, "to bless," is now considered dubious. See W. C. Williams, "ברך," *NIDOTTE* 1.755–57.

[83] The blessing of Rebekah in Gen 24:60 involves extraordinary fecundity and security, suggesting perhaps that the present request for a land with springs of water is a veiled request for a blessing involving fertility. On the well/springs at an oasis as a symbol of fertility see R. Alter, *The Art of Biblical Narrative* (New York: Basic Books, 1981), 52–55.

[84] Cf. Klein, *Triumph of Irony,* 172–74; E. T. A. Davidson, "Intricacy, Design, and Cunning in the Book of Judges," in an unpublished paper cited by P. Trible, *Texts of Terror: Literary-Feminist Readings of Biblical Narratives,* OBT (Philadelphia: Fortress, 1984), 90, n. 52.

behavior of men toward women and the conduct of women themselves to expound his general theme of the progressive Canaanization of Israelite society in the course of the book. Ironically, none of the characters in this note is a native Israelite. They are Kenizzite proselytes,[85] who have been so thoroughly integrated into the faith and culture of the nation that Caleb could represent the tribe of Judah in reconnaissance missions, and all model the life of Yahwistic faith in the face of the Canaanite enemy.

Third, the note reflects the author's interest in the future. Othniel will reappear as the first and paradigmatic governor in 3:7–11. Not only is he an energetic person but he is typical of the generation that entered the land with Joshua. He knew Yahweh and the great acts of deliverance, revelation, and conquest that he had performed on Israel's behalf.

The Settlement of Arad (1:16).   **1:16**   Verses 16–17 describe two events in the conquest of the Negev during the second phase of Judah's campaign. The narrator follows the tribe's progress southward by noting that the important site of Arad was not actually conquered by Judahite forces but by relatives of Moses' wife from Midian. According to the MT the author assumes the reader knows the Mosaic connection and does not bother to give the name of his father-in-law; he identifies him only by clan—"the Kenite."[86] The verse begins literally, however, "Now (the) sons of Kenite *(bĕnê qênî)*, the father-in-law of Moses." The absence of the definite article before "Kenite" raises suspicions that the text has suffered some mutilation. The name of Moses' father-in-law and the article seem to have inadvertently dropped out of the text in the course of transmission.[87] A further difficulty with this notice arises from its seeming contradiction of Pentateuchal reports that identify Moses' father-in-law as a Midianite priest. Either Moses had more than one wife or the Israelites were imprecise in their identification of the nomadic groups that migrated back and forth in the desert regions south of Judah. It seems best to interpret Kenite

---

[85] In v. 13 Othniel is referred to as "the son of Kenaz." Cf. Num 32:12 and Josh 14:6,14, which identify Caleb as "the son of Jephunneh the Kenizzite." According to Gen 36:11,15,42, Kenaz was an Edomite chieftain, a descendant of Esau. Gen 15:19 includes the Kenizzites among the peoples occupying a portion of the land promised to Abraham, presumably in the Negev adjacent to Edom proper. On Caleb see J. Milgrom, *Numbers*, JPS Torah (New York: Jewish Publication Society, 1990), 391–92; T. R. Ashley, *The Book of Numbers*, NICOT (Grand Rapids: Eerdmans, 1993), 233.

[86] Cf. 4:11. Judging from the name קֵינִי, "smith," the Kenites may at an early stage have represented an itinerant band of coppersmiths. The area south of the Dead Sea and north of the Gulf of Aqaba around Timnah was an important source of copper in ancient times. See D. W. Manor, "Timnah," *ABD* 6.553–54.

[87] The LXX[B] clarifies the text by reading "The sons of Jethro the Kenite." The LXX[A] reads Hobab, probably under the influence of Num 10:29. In Exodus he is referred to as Jethro (3:1; 18:1) or Reuel (2:18). Cf. the fuller discussion by Becker, *Richterzeit*, 41–42.

as a Midianite clan or subgroup.[88] Specifically these "descendants of the Kenite" may be linked to the Midianite group whom Moses invited to accompany the Israelites to the promised land in Num 10:29–32. According to this note they leave the "City of Palms," which in 3:13 refers to Jericho.[89] However, here the expression functions as a generic designation for a fortified oasis settlement, most likely Tamar on the western edge of the Arabah south of the Dead Sea.[90] Observing the Judahite advance from the north into the highlands, this group, which had earlier been invited by Moses to accompany the Israelites, opportunistically moved northward to Arad in the desert of Judah.[91] The final comment in v. 16 is the key to the significance of this note in context. Like their Judahite hosts in vv. 5–7, these alien allies compromise Israel's mandate to eliminate the Canaanites. Instead of destroying the city and its population they settle down among them, thereby sowing the seeds of Canaanization that sprout and flourish in the following chapters.[92]

The Sacking of Zephath/Hormah (1:17). **1:17** This verse creates the impression that the Simeonite forces were more scrupulous in the fulfillment of the mandate. Accompanied by their Judahite colleagues, they defeat the Canaanites in Zephath, raze the city, and rename it Hormah to commemorate the event. The new name, which means "destruction," plays on the term *ḥerem,* "devoted [to God] for destruction," the technical expression for Israel's mandate to destroy the Canaanites utterly.[93]

The Conquest of the Southwest Coastal Lowland (1:18). **1:18** In v. 18 the narrator cites a significant moment in the third phase of Judah's campaign: the conquest of the lowland (cf. v. 9). With the greatest of economy, he reports that the Judahites overran the major cities of Gaza, Ashkelon, and Ekron, along with their respective territories. His silence on how they treated these places should probably be interpreted positively—the cities and their populations

---

[88] Both Midianites and Kenites are associated with the Amalekites, another migratory southern tribe (Judg 6:3–5,33; 1 Sam 15:4–9). In Gen 15:19 the Kenites are associated with Kenizzites, Caleb's clan. Another Kenite, Heber, will appear in Judg 4:17.

[89] So also Deut 34:3 and 2 Chr 28:15.

[90] See further S. Mittmann ("Ri. 1,16f und das Siedlungsgebiet der kenitischen Sippe Hobab," *ZDPV* 93 [1977]: 213–35), who identifies עִיר הַתְּמָרִים with ʿAin el-ʿAruš.

[91] The expression נֶגֶב עֲרָד, "Negev of Arad," compares with נֶגֶב הַקֵּנִי, "Negev of the Kenite," in 1 Sam 27:10. Arad has been extensively excavated by archaeologists in recent decades. For a survey of its history and bibliography on this site see D. W. Manor and G. A. Herions, "Arad," *ABD* 1.331–36; M. Aharoni, *NEAEHL* 1.75–87.

[92] Contra Becker (*Richterzeit,* 44) and Auld ("Judges I," 272) and many others, rather than supporting a pro-Judahite polemic, this episode reflects negatively on the tribe.

[93] Greenberg (*EncJud,* s.v. "*Ḥerem*") defines the term חֵרֶם as "the status of that which is separated from common use or contact either because it is proscribed as an abomination to God or because it is consecrated to Him." For a study of the term see Milgrom (*Numbers,* 428–30), who rightly asserts, "In effect, it is the ultimate in dedication" (p. 428).

were destroyed. Since the text seems unaware of the takeover of this region in the thirteenth–twelfth centuries by the Sea Peoples (including the Philistines), these events must have transpired soon after the arrival of the Israelites.

Conclusion (1:19–20). **1:19–20** The author ends his survey of Judahite fortunes in the fulfillment of the divine mandate to take the land by offering a summary evaluation. Positively, they were able to wrest control of the hill country. Negatively, they were unable to take the river valleys[94] because of the Canaanites' technological superiority. The infantry of Judah were unable to devise an effective strategy against these state-of-the-art military resources.[95] Chariots were useless in the highlands of Judah, but in the valleys and the river plains they proved a great advantage. The author's note that these were "iron" chariots is extremely significant not only because it expresses the impressive nature of the Canaanites' military hardware but also because it announces the beginning of the iron age in Palestine. Textual and archaeological evidence shows that iron was known in the ancient Near East prior to what is known as the Iron Age (ca. 1200–586 B.C.), but the metal was rare and precious. However, the discovery of the process of carburization at the beginning of this period ushered in a new technological age,[96] which the Canaanites exploited to full advantage. The present reference to iron chariots is often dismissed as an anachronistic retrojection of a later age when iron was abundant and reflective of eighth-century B.C. Assyrian or even later Persian models.[97] However, this interpretation is quite unnecessary in light of the widespread use of iron by the Hittites and the extension of their power as far south as northern Lebanon and Damascus in the thirteenth century. Their new technology could easily have found its way into the Egyptian province of Canaan. How much iron was used in the chariots is an open question. Obviously the chariots were not made entirely of iron, but

---

[94] לֹא לְהוֹרִישׁ is textually problematic. Either the *lamed* on הוֹרִישׁ is a dittographic error or we follow the versions and insert יָכְלוּ, i.e., "they *were not able* to dispossess" (cf. 1:21; Josh 15:63). M. Dahood's proposal has found little acceptance ("Scriptio defectiva in Judges 1,19," *Bib* 60 [1979]: 570). Cf. Soggin, *Judges*, 23–24; Lindars, *Judges 1–5*, 45.

[95] According to Josh 17:16,18, Joshua had faced the same problem.

[96] It used to be thought that the Philistines were responsible for the introduction of iron to Palestine, but recent research has repudiated this view. (For an exhaustive study of the subject see P. M. McNutt, *The Forging of Israel: Iron Technology, Symbolism, and Tradition in Ancient Society*, JSOTSup 108 [Sheffield: Almond, 1990]). However, this does not rule out the possibility of Philistine monopoly of the iron industry in the early centuries of the Iron Age (cf. 1 Sam 13:19–23). So also T. Dothan, *The Philistines and Their Material Culture* (New Haven: Yale University Press, 1982), 91.

[97] Thus R. Drews, "The 'Chariots of Iron' of Joshua and Judges," *JSOT* 45 (1989): 15–23; McNutt, *The Forging of Israel*, 224–25; Lindars, *Judges 1–5*, 45–46.

they could certainly have been reinforced with iron plates or lesser reinforcements.[98]

However, the significance of the author's reference to the Canaanites' iron chariots lies in the theological implications of Judah's inability to overcome superior technology. In light of Deut 7:1–3 and after the miraculous conquest of Jericho (Joshua 6), no one, no matter how technologically superior to the Israelites, should have been able to withstand Judah's attack. This verse must be read in light of Josh 17:16–18, according to which Joshua had encouraged Ephraim and Manasseh by specifically declaring that the Canaanites' superior strength and their possession of iron chariots would be no hindrance to the Josephite tribes' conquest of the river valleys and plains. In our text (v. 18a) the narrator explicitly attributes Judah's successes in the hill country not to equivalent military power but to the presence of Yahweh. Then why could they not take the lowland? Why is Yahweh's presence canceled by superior military technology? The narrator does not say, but presumably the Judahites experienced a failure of nerve at this point, or they were satisfied with their past achievements.

The account of Judah's military fortunes concludes with a final reminder of their treatment of Caleb. Honoring Moses' promise (cf. Josh 14:9 and Deut 1:36), they give him Hebron, which he summarily conquers. This verse corrects the false impression that could have been gained from v. 10, which had generalized credit for the slaughter of the three sons of Anak, Sheshai, Shiman, and Talmai, to the tribe of Judah.

(3) The Failures of the Remaining Tribes (1:21–36)

[21]**The Benjamites, however, failed to dislodge the Jebusites, who were living in Jerusalem; to this day the Jebusites live there with the Benjamites.** [22]**Now the house of Joseph attacked Bethel, and the LORD was with them.** [23]**When they sent men to spy out Bethel (formerly called Luz),** [24]**the spies saw a man coming out of the city and they said to him, "Show us how to get into the city and we will see that you are treated well."** [25]**So he showed them, and they put the city to the sword but spared the man and his whole family.** [26]**He then went to the land of the Hittites, where he built a city and called it Luz, which is its name to this day.**

[27]**But Manasseh did not drive out the people of Beth Shan or Taanach or Dor or Ibleam or Megiddo and their surrounding settlements, for the Canaanites were determined to live in that land.** [28]**When Israel became strong, they pressed the Canaanites into forced labor but never drove them out completely.** [29]**Nor did Ephraim drive out the Canaanites living in Gezer, but the Canaanites continued**

---

[98] For fuller discussion of the evidence see A. R. Millard, "Back to the Iron Bed: Og's or Procrustes'?" *Congress Volume, Paris* 1992, VTSup 61 (Leiden: Brill, 1995): 194–95. It is unlikely the ironwork consisted of scythed wheels. Drews ("'Chariots of Iron,'" 15–23) prefers iron rims as tires.

to live there among them. [30]Neither did Zebulun drive out the Canaanites living in Kitron or Nahalol, who remained among them; but they did subject them to forced labor. [31]Nor did Asher drive out those living in Acco or Sidon or Ahlab or Aczib or Helbah or Aphek or Rehob, [32]and because of this the people of Asher lived among the Canaanite inhabitants of the land. [33]Neither did Naphtali drive out those living in Beth Shemesh or Beth Anath; but the Naphtalites too lived among the Canaanite inhabitants of the land, and those living in Beth Shemesh and Beth Anath became forced laborers for them. [34]The Amorites confined the Danites to the hill country, not allowing them to come down into the plain. [35]And the Amorites were determined also to hold out in Mount Heres, Aijalon and Shaalbim, but when the power of the house of Joseph increased, they too were pressed into forced labor. [36]The boundary of the Amorites was from Scorpion Pass to Sela and beyond.

In v. 21 the tone changes, becoming increasingly pessimistic as the narrator observes what was to be a triumphant campaign of conquest turn into an expedition of compromise. Throughout he laments the diminishing commitment of the Israelite tribes to the wholesale destruction of all Canaanite things and people and Israel's increasing coresidency with the natives.

THE FORTUNES OF BENJAMIN (1:21). **1:21** The account of the efforts and results of the remaining tribes begins with a summary of the Benjamite failure. This verse is transitional. The opening verb of v. 22, *wayyaʿălû,* "and they [the house of Joseph] went up [NIV, "attacked"]," seems to answer to the same verb in v. 4, suggesting the second panel of this chapter actually begins in v. 22. Furthermore, stylistically v. 21 bears a close resemblance to later notices of tribal fortunes in the chapter and announces the formal beginning to the second half of the chapter. Whether or not the verse appeared after v. 26 in an earlier version of this chapter, the author has several reasons for inserting it here. First, having begun his survey of tribal fortunes with Judah and Simeon in the south, moving northward, the first tribe one encounters is Benjamin. Second, just as the territory of Benjamin was squeezed between the super tribal powers of Judah and Ephraim, so here the author inserts this note between the fuller accounts of Judahite and Josephite fortunes. Third, by thrusting Benjamin forward, the author foreshadows the Benjamites' role in the final disastrous chapters of the book (19–21).[99]

The text offers no details of Benjamin's campaign except to identify the adversaries, the Jebusites living in Jerusalem. The verse echoes almost verbatim Josh 15:63, which attributes to Judah the failure to dislodge the Jebusites from Jerusalem.[100] The inconsistency reflects the geographic location of Jerusalem.

---

[99] Similar foreshadowing is evident in the culmination of this survey with Dan (vv. 34–36), which foreshadows the Danite role in chaps. 17–18.

[100] Joshua highlights the impossibility of the task by inserting יוכלו after לֹא, i.e., "They were not able to dispossess …," the only other difference between these two texts.

Apparently both tribes at different times attempted to take this city, and the conquest mentioned in v. 8 was only partial. Jebus occurs elsewhere as a city name, always with an added comment identifying it with Jerusalem,[101] which suggests this may have been the original name for the city and is the name of choice for biblical authors when they have the pre-Israelite city in mind. The form of this note, complete with the final "until this day," is conventional and stereotypical as a comparison with Josh 13:13 and 16:10 reveals. While some see in the phrase a redactional use of a formula, reflecting the situation when Judah and Benjamin were all that was left of ancient Israel, namely, the seventh or sixth centuries,[102] others recognize here an editor's reference to the end of the period covered by the book.[103] However, the phrase probably is lifted from the source document before the author of the book, a document that was composed prior to David's conquest of the city (2 Sam 5:6–9).[104]

THE FORTUNES OF EPHRAIM (1:22–26). **1:22–26** Following the opening verb, *wayyaᶜălû*, "and they went up," the protagonist of the next vignette is introduced surprisingly as "the house of Joseph." With this name the author may intend a generic reference to the northern tribes as a whole, in contrast to Judah,[105] or a more limited reference to Ephraim and Manasseh, the tribes descended from Joseph's two sons and whose pivotal achievement was the capture of Bethel.[106] The fact that the conquest of Bethel was an exclusively Ephraimite concern makes it more likely that "Joseph" functions here as a substitute for Ephraim. The refusal to name the tribe may reflect an anti-Ephraimite stance on the part of the author, who has nothing positive to write about Ephraim in the rest of the book. The fact that Ephraim is mentioned again later in this chapter (v. 29) is not a serious objection, since vv. 22–26 represent another inserted anecdote, stylistically distinguished from the rest of this survey of tribal fortunes. Verse 29 reflects the reading of the primary source used in this conquest report. The reason for the insertion of this anecdote is surely to be found in Bethel's special place in Israelite tradition[107] and history.[108] As elsewhere, the target of this campaign is identified by its Israelite (Bethel) and Canaanite (Luz) names.[109] The exact location of

---

[101] 19:10–11; 1 Chr 11:4–5. The gentilic "Jebusite" occurs frequently in lists of the Canaanite nations: Gen 15:21; Exod 3:17; Deut 7:1; etc. On Jebus and the Jebusites see S. A. Reed, "Jebus (Place). Jebusite," *ABD* 3.652–53.

[102] Boling, *Judges*, 59.

[103] Lindars, *Judges 1–5*, 48.

[104] The notes in Josh 13:13 and 16:10, which are identical in form, include "until this day" as well and may derive from the same source.

[105] Lindars, *Judges 1–5*, 51.

[106] Boling, *Judges*, 59.

[107] Cf. Gen 28:18–22; 35:1–15; 48:3.

[108] Cf. 1 Kgs 12:25–33; 13:1–19; 2 Kgs 23:15–17.

[109] Cf. Gen 28:19; 35:6; 48:3.

Bethel is disputed. While most identify the city with Tell Beitin, others have suggested el-Bireh, a few kilometers farther west.[110]

As in the case of Judah's conquest of the hill country (v. 19), the author notes that Yahweh accompanied Joseph [Ephraim] in the conquest of Bethel. This not only means they had the same resources and everything should have gone well, but it also exposes the superfluity of the Ephraimite strategy as described in vv. 23–25. Although the modifications are significant, the numerous thematic links with the account of the conquest of Jericho in Joshua 2 and 6 suggest that the tribe wished to repeat the earlier event.[111] (1) They send out a surveillance team.[112] (2) They make contact with an ordinary citizen, in this case a man coming out of the city. (3) They request the person's help. Whereas the Jericho spies needed defensive help from Rahab, these men ask for offensive assistance. Since any passerby could have observed the nature of the walls and the location of the gates, the request to be shown the gate of the city sounds ridiculous, unless there is more to the story. Perhaps this is a ruse; they want to be escorted into the city. (4) They offer the aide a reward. The nature of the reward is not specified, but in the clause *wĕʿāśînû ʿimmĕkā ḥāsed*, (lit.) "We will demonstrate lovingkindness/covenant loyalty with you,"[113] one may hear a deliberate echo of the spies commitment to Rahab in Josh 2:12 (cf. 6:22–25). However, in reality the two commitments differ fundamentally. The promise of the earlier spies followed Rahab's testimony concerning all that Yahweh had done for Israel and her acknowledgment that he alone was God in heaven and on earth. In this instance there is no call for testimony or identification with Israel, nor any demand to recognize Yahweh's claims to this land. The use of the expression *ḥesed*, which is technical covenant terminology, also invites the reader to interpret this event in light of the prohibition in Deut 7:2 and the treaty with the Gibeonites in Joshua 9. (5) The city is conquered. However, unlike Rahab, whose family is fully integrated into Israelite faith and life, the "traitor" (from the Canaanite point of view) is permitted to leave and build his

---

[110] On the city see H. Brodsky, "Bethel," *ABD* 1.710–12; J. L. Kelso, "Bethel," *NEAEHL* 1.192–94.

[111] Cf. Webb, *Book of Judges*, 96–97. Cp. also the Danite adventures in chap. 18.

[112] The NIV's rendering of וַיְתִירוּ, as "they spied out" (v. 23), and הַשֹּׁמְרִים, "spies" (v. 24), is questionable. The context and especially the latter word, which normally means "the guards, watchmen," suggest תּוּר speaks of the the erection of an observation post. So also Lindars, *Judges 1–5*, 53. Furthermore, where spies are intended, as in Josh 2:1 and Judg 18:2, מְרַגְּלִים, "foot scouts," is used. The *hiphil* of תּוּר, occurs elsewhere only in Prov 12:26.

[113] The NIV's "We will see that you are treated well" is a weak paraphrastic rendering.

own city and continue his life as a Hittite.[114] Technically Luz/Bethel was conquered, but in reality the city was simply transferred to a new site. The mandate had been betrayed. The new city functions as a sanctioned symbol of "the Canaanite in their midst."

But the literary links between this text and the Jacob accounts in Genesis[115] suggest the author sees additional significance to the present event. The city Ephraim conquers was claimed long ago by Yahweh and the patriarch. This was where God had appeared to the fleeing Jacob, where Jacob had erected a pillar *(maṣṣēbâ)* to commemorate the encounter, where he had built an altar, which he had named Bethel, "the house of God," and where he had buried his dead (Gen 35:8). In Israelite tradition Luz was already a sacred site. The present event is perceived as a restaking of an ancient claim. However, while the physical Canaanite town is obliterated, the spiritual Canaanite Luz is allowed to continue. The Israelites had no idea what consequences this compromising response would produce.

The style and content of this anecdote also invite comparison with the description of the Judahite treatment of Adoni-Bezek, as the following chart illustrates:

Feature	Judah and Adoni-Bezek	Ephraim and the Unnamed Luzite
Status of the Survivor	An important figure with title (lord of Bezek) ruler over many	A nobody without a name traitor of his people

Actions of Israelite Protagonists	Judah finds
	  fights
	  pursues
	  seizes
	  mutilates
	  deports him
		Ephraim entreats
		  negotiates
		  lets him go free
		  spares his family

---

[114] In these texts the Hittites are presented as one of the Canaanite ethnic groups (presumably the חֵת בְּנֵי, "descendants of Heth," Genesis 23). Their relationship with the major Indo-European people of Asia Minor by the same name (though derived from *ḫatti*) located in the upper Mesopotamian region is obscure. Perhaps the pockets of Hittite settlement in Palestine represented remnants of the Hittites after the decline of the Hittite Empire. For discussion of the issues see G. McMahon, "Hittites in the OT," *ABD* 3.231–33; H. A. Hoffner, "The Hittites and Hurrians," *POTT*, 197–228.

[115] Webb (*Book of Judges*, 95) notes (1) the use of the verb עָלָה, "to go up" (v. 22; cf. Gen 35:1); (2) the explicit identification of Israelite Bethel with Canaanite Luz (v. 23; cf. Gen 28:19; 35:6–7; 48:3); the naming of the new Luz (v. 26), which reverses the naming of Bethel (Gen 28:18–19; 35:6–7).

Feature	Judah and Adoni-Bezek	Ephraim and the Unnamed Luzite
Fate of the Antagonist	Loses his realm Loses his fingers and toes Loses his life	Moves to another site Builds a city

THE FORTUNES OF THE NORTHERN TRIBES (1:27–36). *Manasseh (1:27–28).*[116] **1:27–28** The Manassite failure to fulfill the divine mandate is summarized by listing a series of unconquered cities and their respective dependent territories[117] in a narrow strip of land extending from the Jordan in the east to the Mediterranean in the west: Beth-Shean,[118] Taanach,[119] Dor,[120] Ibleam,[121] and Megiddo.[122] As a result the Canaanites persisted in the land. By referring to "Israel" in v. 28 the author generalizes the Manassite experience to the entire nation. The note implies that occasionally the Israelites were able to assert themselves against and over the Canaanites; but instead of destroying and dispossessing them,[123] as per the divine charge, they enslave them.[124]

Ephraim (1:29). **1:29** Now the narrator provides the formal summary statement we might have expected in v. 22. The fact that this verse abbreviates

---

[116] These verses echo almost verbatim Josh 17:12–13. The major differences are the insertion in Josh 17:12 of יָכְלוּ after לֹא, i.e., "they were not able to dispossess" (cf. on v. 21 above), and the omission of the list of cities (which had been listed in the previous verse in Joshua).

[117] בְּנוֹתֶיהָ, lit. "her [the city's] daughters," a reference to the satellite villages and towns under the control of the ruler of the city named.

[118] An important city at the junction of the Jordan and Jezreel valleys. In the twelfth century the site was under Egyptian control (under Rameses III [1184– 53 B.C.]), though later it was occupied by Philistines (1 Sam 31:10). See further P. E. McGovern, "Beth-Shan," *ABD* 1.693–96; A. Mazar, "Beth-Shean," *NEAEHL* 1.214–23.

[119] A site five miles southeast of Megiddo, with which it is often linked (Josh 12:21; 17:11; Judg 5:19; 1 Kgs 4:12). See further A. E. Glock, "Taanach," *ABD* 6.287–90; id., *NEAEHL* 4.1428–33.

[120] An important coastal town just south of the Carmel ridge. Cf. E. Stern, "Dor," *ABD* 2.223–25; id., "Dor," *NEAEHL* 1.357–68.

[121] Probably to be identified with Khirbet Bel'ameh, guarding the easternmost pass from the Ephraimite highlands into the Valley of Jezreel. Cf. M. Hunt, "Ibleam," *ABD* 3.355.

[122] Megiddo was a major fortress in the valley of Jezreel. The city was occupied by Egyptians until the middle of the twelfth century, when it was destroyed, presumably by the Sea Peoples (Philistines). Its strategic location was recognized by Solomon, who rebuilt the city as a major Israelite military fortress. On the history and archaeology of the site see D. Ussishkin, "Megiddo," *ABD* 4.666–79; G. I. Davies, "Megiddo in the Period of the Judges," in *Crises and Perspectives: Studies in Ancient Near Eastern Polytheism, Biblical Theology, Palestinian Archaeology and Intertestamental Literature*, OTS 24 (Leiden: Brill, 1986), 34–53; Y. Shiloh, "Megiddo," *NEAEHL* 3.1003–24.

[123] וְהוֹרִישׁ לֹא הוֹרִישׁוֹ is emphatic, "They did not drive them out at all."

[124] The meaning of וַיָּשֶׂם לָמַס, "they pressed them into forced labor," is illustrated by the treatment of the Gibeonites in Josh 9:21. Solomon's similar treatment of the remnant of the original population in 1 Kgs 9:20–21 (עֹבֵד מַס, "forced labor") is distinguished from the corvée service (עֶבֶד), imposed on his own people (1 Kgs 9:22).

Josh 16:10 may point to the present author's impatience to get on with the narrative. The target city, Gezer,[125] was located on the southwest corner of the Ephraimite allotment, due west of Jerusalem, on the last of the foothills where the Judahite range meets the Shephelah. It guarded one of the most important crossroads of Palestine, where the east-west and north-south roads intersected. Here the Ephraimites permitted the Canaanites to live in their midst.

Zebulun (1:30). **1:30** The descendants of Zebulun failed similarly to dispose of the Canaanites from their targeted cities, Kitron and Nahalol.[126] Instead they permitted them to live among them, enslaving those elements of the population they were able to subdue.

Asher (1:31–32). **1:31–32** The Asherites failed to conquer the cities in their allotted territory, seven of which are named: Acco,[127] Sidon,[128] Ahlab,[129] Achzib,[130] Helbah,[131] Aphek,[132] Rehob.[133] Verse 28 records a significant shift in the description of tribal fortunes. Instead of the Israelites permitting Canaanites to live in their territories, now the Canaanites remain the default population, at whose will the Israelites settle down. The Asherites could not gain the upper hand.

Naphtali (1:33). **1:33** Similarly, the Naphtalites found themselves living among the Canaanites, having failed to drive out the inhabitants of Beth Shemesh ("House of the Sun [God]")[134] and Beth Anath ("House of

---

[125] On which see W. G. Dever, "Gezer," *ABD* 2.998–1003; id., "Gezer," *NEAEHL* 2.496–506.

[126] Neither of these sites has been positively identified.

[127] Though named only here in the OT, Acco was one of the most important seaports in Canaan, later known as Ptolemais. Cf. M. Dothan, "Acco," *ABD* 1.50–53; id., "Tel Acco," *NEAEHL* 1.17–24.

[128] A major Phoenician city that competed with Tyre to the south for economic hegemony for centuries. The inclusion of Sidon meant that most of Phoenicia was originally included in Asher's allotment (cf. Josh 19:24–31). But the major Phoenician cities were never brought under Israelite control. Cf. P. C. Schmitz, "Sidon," *ABD* 6.17–18.

[129] אַחְלָב is textually suspect. Is this a corruption of מֵחֶלֶב (Josh 19:29), which in turn may be a corruption of חֶלְבָּה, Helbah, which appears as *Maḫalliba* (a site near Sidon) in an Assyrian inscription of Sennacherib? Cf. *ANET*, 287. But Helbah appears later in this verse. Cf. M. J. Fretz, "Ahlab," *ABD* 1.123.

[130] On this coastal town north of Acco see M. W. Prausnitz, "Achzib," *ABD* 1.57–58; id., *NEAEHL* 1.32–35.

[131] See the note on Achlab above.

[132] The Asherite Aphek has been identified with both Tel Kurdana, five plus miles southeast of Acco, and Tel Kabri, a large site east of Nahariya. See R. Frankel, "Aphek," *ADB* 1.276–77; P. Beck and M. Kochavi, "Aphek," *NEAEHL* 1.62–72.

[133] Rehob was a Levitical city in Asher (Josh 21:31; 1 Chr 6:75[Hb. 60], usually identified with Tell el-Bi el-Gharbi. Cf. D. L. Petersen and R. Arav, "Rehob," *ABD* 5.661; F. Vitto, "Rehob," *NEAEHL* 3.1272–74.

[134] Beth-Shemesh was located in the Sorek Valley in the northeastern Shephelah. Cf. F. Brandfon, "Beth-Shemesh," *ABD* 1.696–98; S. Bunimovitz and Z. Lederman, "Beth-Shemesh," *NEAEHL* 1.249–53.

Anath").[135] However, they managed to enslave some segments of the Canaan population.

Dan (1:34–36). **1:34–36**   Anticipating the northward adventures of the Danite tribe later in the book and reflecting the final position of Dan in the territorial allotments in Josh 19:40–48, this anticonquest survey ends with the tribe of Dan. This tribe's assigned grant consisted of a small strip of land along the Aijalon Valley extending from the Mediterranean Sea to the Judahite hills west of Jerusalem, sandwiched between Judah and Ephraim. The present note is aware of the Danite failure to make any inroads into the lowland region, having been rebuffed by the resident Amorites.

This is the first reference to the Amorites in the Book of Judges. The name "Amorite" is related to Akkadian *Amurru,* "the west," which could designate a direction, region, or people. The heartland of the Amorites *(Amurru)* described in Mesopotamian texts was located in northern Syria, between the western Euphrates and the Khabur and Balikh rivers. From here elements of the population migrated to lower Mesopotamia, eventually achieving political control in such major cities as Larsa, Babylon (Hammurabi), and Mari. When the Amurru/Amorites migrated west and south into the region of Palestine is not clear. It seems, however, that by the seventeenth century B.C. the term Amurru was increasingly used to designate central and southern Syria, and by the fifteenth century "the Kingdom of Amurru" denoted a realm in the mountains of northern Lebanon and eventually could be used of the mountainous region farther south as well. However, first millennium B.C. Akkadian texts show that the term *Ḫatti* supplanted *Amurru,* the latter being reduced to an archaic term. These Amurru have left their mark on the biblical texts in the name "Amorite." The expression tends to be applied where "Canaanite" is inappropriate, particularly when speaking of the Transjordanian kingdoms of Sihon and Og and the hill country of Cisjordan. "Canaanite" cities were generally located in the valleys and coastal regions; "Amorite" cities tended to be in the highlands. This generalized use, however, should not blind the reader of the Old Testament to the fact that the designation could apparently also be used in a more limited sense of a specific subgroup of the pre-Israelite populations of Palestine.[136]

Objecting that the Danites would not have encountered Amorites so far

---

[135] In the mythology of the Canaanite fertility religion, Anath, a prominent female goddess, is often portrayed as the consort and lover of Baal. Cf. *ANET,* 129–49. See also the identification of Shamgar as *ben ʿanat,* "son of Anath" in 3:31. For further discussion of Anath, see W. A. Meier III, "Anath," *ADB* I, 225–27; on Canaanite religion see P. D. Miller, Jr., "Aspects of the Religion of Ugarit," in *Ancient Israelite Religion: Essays in Honor of Frank Moore Cross,* eds. P. D. Miller, et al (Philadelphia: Fortress, 1987), 53–66. On the possible locations of the site see M. Lubetski, "Beth-Anath," *ABD* 1.680–81.

[136] Cf. Deut 7:1; etc. On the Amorites and their relation to the Canaanites see Schoville, "Canaanites and Amorites," 164–67; M. Liverani, "The Amorites," *POTT,* 100–33; G. Mendenhall, "Amorites," *ABD* 1.199–202.

south and west and would not have pushed the Danites back into the hill country which they themselves occupied, some propose emending the consonantal text to read *hʾdmy*, "the Edomite," rather than *hʾmry*, "the Amorite," with several ancient versions.[137] However, this is excluded on rhetorical and contextual grounds.[138] Like "Canaanite," "Amorite" often functions as a generalized designation for the pre-Israelite population of Palestine, particularly the uplands, and the Transjordanian territory. A previous generation of critical scholars tended to view "Amorite" as a mark of the Elohist Pentateuchal source, in contrast to the Yahwist's preference for "Canaanite." However, biblical writers do not always distinguish between Amorites and Canaanites, and the present narrator may have used the names interchangeably. On the other hand, the present shift may have a historical base, in which case v. 36 declares the southern extent of Amorite settlement.[139]

According to vv. 34–36, the local Amorites forced the Danites back into the hills, retaining control over Aijalon (identified with Yalo, twenty kilometers west northwest of Jerusalem,[140] a city that guarded the most important trade route through the Shephelah), Shaalbim (probably to be identified with Selbit, three miles northwest of Aijalon),[141] and Mount Heres.[142] But not all was lost for the Israelites. When the house of Joseph, that is, Ephraim, increased in strength, they took advantage of the Danite weakness, apparently taking some of their allotted territory and enslaving the native population. The boundary between Amorite and Ephraimite territory eventually was fixed along a line running from the ascent of Akrabbim (NIV "Scorpions"), the farthest point on the southern border of Judah southwest of the Dead Sea,[143] through Sela (site unknown), and up into the hills.

Theological and Practical Implications

This survey of Israel's fortunes after the death of Joshua begins positively enough, with the Israelites consulting Yahweh, the tribes (Judah and Simeon)

---

[137] LXX^A, Old Latin, and several minor versions. This reading is recommended by *BHS*, Gray (*Joshua, Judges and Ruth*, NCB [London: Thomas Nelson, 1967], 242), Soggin (*Judges*, 25). For a full discussion of the textual issue see O'Connell, *Rhetoric of the Book of Judges*, 449–52.

[138] The Edomites are never mentioned in the book.

[139] O'Connell, *Rhetoric of the Book of Judges*, 452.

[140] Cf. Petersen, "Aijalon," *ABD* 1.131.

[141] Cf. W. J. Toews, "Shaalbim," *ABD* 5.1147; A. Segal and Y. Naor, "Shaalbim," *NEAEHL* 4.1339–40.

[142] The location of הַר חֶרֶס, "Sun Mountain," which occurs only here in the OT, is unknown. The name is often associated with Beth-Shemesh, "House of the Sun" (1 Kgs 4:9), also known as Ir-Shemesh, "City of the Sun" (Josh 19:41). Alternatively, K.-D. Schunk ("Har-Heres," *ABD* 3.56) translates "scurfy mountain" and associates this name with Khirbet Khirsha two miles southeast of Yalo, or Khirbet Kharsis nearby; Z. Kallai ("The Settlement Traditions of Ephraim," *ZDPV* 102 [1986]: 68–74) identifies הַר חֶרֶס with Timnath-Heres, Joshua's town in the Aijalon Valley (2:9).

[143] Cf. M. Görg, "Akrabbim," *ABD* 1.141.

cooperating, and families functioning normally. Even so this chapter is pervaded by unfulfilled commitment, incomplete obedience, and compromising tolerance. Even when the Israelites gain the upper hand over the Canaanites, they refuse to carry out Yahweh's agenda. Instead of reshaping the world after the image of Yahweh's will, they live in and with the world, and before long they have taken on the characteristics of the world. Instead of making this the land of the people of God, they become like the people of the land. This not only explains why the ages of the judges/governors turned out to be so dark but also serves as a permanent reminder of the deadly consequences of compromise and disobedience to all who claim to be the people of God. At the same time, the chapter announces that if anything positive is accomplished by God's people, it is because of his gracious presence and his action on his people's behalf.

2. The Theological Significance of Israel's Performance (2:1–23)

(1) The Divine Messenger's Interpretation (2:1–5)

¹The angel of the LORD went up from Gilgal to Bokim and said, "I brought you up out of Egypt and led you into the land that I swore to give to your forefathers. I said, 'I will never break my covenant with you, ²and you shall not make a covenant with the people of this land, but you shall break down their altars.' Yet you have disobeyed me. Why have you done this? ³Now therefore I tell you that I will not drive them out before you; they will be [thorns] in your sides and their gods will be a snare to you."

⁴When the angel of the LORD had spoken these things to all the Israelites, the people wept aloud, ⁵and they called that place Bokim. There they offered sacrifices to the LORD.

Judges 2:1–5 functions as a hinge between the [anti]conquest summary of chap. 1 and the lengthy literary soliloquy in 2:6–23. The tone and style resemble what follows more than what precedes, but it is linked generally to the preceding by a continuation of *waw*-consecutives and specifically by the verb *wayyaʿal*, "And he [the envoy of Yahweh] went up." Chapters 1 and 2 are two sides of one coin, report and interpretation respectively. As noted earlier, the interpretation occurs in stages. In this the first stage the divine response to Israel's failure to fulfill the holy war mandate is reported by Yahweh's special envoy. Even so the text contains no explicit statement of Yahweh's emotion (cf. 2:14,20); instead the reader must determine the divine mind through narrative and more specifically through the direct speech of his messenger.

This is the first of three confrontations between Yahweh and Israel described in the book (cf. 6:7–10; 10:10–16). The similarity in style and tone among all of these may be attributable to the common source from which they are drawn, perhaps a collection of prophetic documents. In comparing the three episodes, one observes a progression in the identities of the communicators of the divine response to events in Israel's life: an envoy of Yahweh (2:1–5); a prophet of Yahweh (6:7–10); Yahweh himself (19:10–16). The present account, which is cast in the form of a judgment oracle, divides into three parts: (1) the introduction of the speaker (2:1a); (2) the divine speech (2:1b–3); (3) Israel's response to the speech (2:4–5).

Anyone who is familiar with previous books of the Old Testament will recognize most of the expressions and concepts presented here. Indeed the narrator seems to have gone out of his way to link this episode with several in the Book of Exodus, specifically Exod 23:20–33 and 34:11–15, as the following exposition will show.

THE DIVINE MESSENGER (2:1a).   **2:1a**   The person who confronts the Israelites is identified as the *mal'ak YHWH*, which the NIV renders "angel of the LORD." Because of the popular misconception of angels as feathery, winged, even effiminate creatures, the term "angel" is best avoided and replaced with either "messenger" or "envoy," for this is what the term *mal'ak* means. Its basic diplomatic sense is illustrated frequently in Judges, as in 6:35, which describes Gideon sending *mal'ākîm*, "messengers," throughout the northern tribes to muster an army to take on the Midianites (cf. also 7:24; 9:31; 11:12–14,17,19). The expression *mal'ak YHWH* "messenger/envoy of the LORD," occurs nineteen times in this book,[144] and its variant, *mal'ak hā'ĕlōhîm*, "envoy of God," occurs three times (6:20; 13:6,9). In each case the *mal'āk* appears as a divinely appointed and authorized envoy of the heavenly court; he is God's official spokesman. Prophets are also often referred to as Yahweh's *mal'ākîm*,[145] and some have proposed that the present messenger is a human prophetic figure.[146] This accords with the fact that this figure is said to come from Gilgal rather than from heaven. However, since chap. 6 clearly distinguishes between the prophet (v. 8) and the *mal'ak YHWH* (v. 11), the present personage is best understood as a heavenly envoy. This is probably the same figure whom Yahweh had promised in the time of Moses to send ahead of the Israelites in their campaigns against the Canaanites (cf. Exod 23:20–23; 33:2; also 32:34) and who functioned as the alter ego of God.[147] This explains

---

[144] 2:1,4; 5:23; 6:11,12,20,21a,21b,22a,22b; 13:3,13,15,16a,16b,18,20,21a,21b.

[145] 2 Chr 36:15–16; Isa 42:19; 44:26; Hag 1:13; Mal 3:1.

[146] Cf. Tg., *nēbiya' bišlĕliḥut min qŏdam YHWH*, "the prophet by the commission from before the LORD."

[147] Note the authority given to the envoy in Exod 23:20–23, especially Yahweh's declaration, כִּי שְׁמִי בְּקִרְבּוֹ, "for my name is in him."

why, in many contexts, Yahweh/God and mal'ak YHWH are freely interchanged (cf. 6:22–23). Later, for Manoah and his wife to see the mal'ak
YHWH is to see God (13:22; cf. vv. 3–21), and in the present context the
envoy's speech is cast as a divine speech in the first person. What the messenger says, God says, and vice versa.

The author notes that this envoy went up from Gilgal, but he does not
explain why. Although Josh 4:19 locates Gilgal "on the eastern border of Jericho," the precise location of Gilgal is not known.[148] The issue is complicated
by the fact that, except for Josh 5:9, which explains the origin of the name, it
always appears with the article, that is, "the Gilgal." According to Joshua 4–5,
knowledge of which the present author seems to assume, Gilgal was the site of
Israel's first camp after crossing the Jordan. At this site they erected a memorial
of twelve stones,[149] circumcised all the males, and celebrated the Passover.
Gilgal appears to have been the base camp from which Joshua went out on his
campaigns.[150] Although the tabernacle was moved to Shiloh within Joshua's
lifetime,[151] Gilgal remained an important cult center into the eighth century.[152] Why this divine messenger should have come up from Gilgal, rather
than Shiloh, is not indicated. In view of the previously cited association of the
mal'ak YHWH with the conquest of the Canaanite tribes, his point of departure
may be linked to the litany of failed campaigns surveyed in chap. 1. One may
reasonably assume that he is to be identified with the "commander of the army
of the LORD" (śar ṣĕbā yhwh), whom Joshua encountered while Israel was
still camped at Gilgal (Josh 5:13–15). If this is so, one suspects here a deliberate attempt on the part of Yahweh to remind the people how the campaign had
started and to get them back to their original purpose. Although Yahweh had
accompanied Judah in the highland offensive (1:19) and Ephraim in the attack
on Bethel (1:22), presumably by the agency of the envoy, after the compromised conclusion of these campaigns references to his presence in any of the
tribal adventures disappear. Had the envoy retreated to Gilgal, perceived as the
base of military operations so long as Canaanites remain in the land, leaving
the Israelites on their own? Whatever the explanation, his appearance before
Israel at Bokim is ominous.

Since the place is not formally named until v. 5, the reference to Bokim in v. 1
obviously reflects the narrator's own chronology, after the people had responded

---

[148] Tell en-Nitla, 3.5 kilometers east of Jericho, and Khirbet el-Mefjir have been proposed. Cf.
W. R. Kotter, *ABD* 2.1022–23; T. Noy, "Gilgal," *NEAEHL* 2.517–18.

[149] The naming of the site הַגִּלְגָּל, "The Circle," may reflect the arrangement of the stones. The
etymology in 5:9 associates the name with "rolling away [גַּלֹּתִי] the reproach of Egypt," that is circumcision.

[150] Cf. Josh 9:6; 10:6–9,15,43; 14:6.

[151] Josh 18:1; 21:2; Judg 18:31; 21:19; 1 Sam 1:3.

[152] Amos 4:4; 5:5; Hos 4:15; 9:15; 12:11.

to the envoy's message. The name "Bokim" translates literally "weepers." The form *habbōkîm*, with the article, is unusual. This may represent simply a stylistic variant of the form with the article in v. 5, influenced perhaps by the preceding *haggilgāl*, "the Gilgal."[153] Alternatively, *habbōkîm*, "the weeping," may function as an abbreviation for *mĕqôm habbōkîm*, "the place of weeping." Bokim is not an actual place name but an artificial construct, most likely a pseudonym for Bethel. This interpretation finds support in the association of the "oak of weeping" (*ʾallôn bākût*) with Bethel in Gen 35:8 and in appearance of the Israelites before the prophet Deborah near Bethel in Judg 4:5.[154]

THE DIVINE MESSAGE (2:1b–3). The bulk of this short unit is taken up with the envoy's speech, cast in the form of a judgment oracle,[155] with a formal statement of the charges against Israel (vv. 1b–2), followed by an announcement of the sentence (v. 3). The charges are patterned after a conventional structure with four main parts: (1) a reminder of Yahweh's past favors, including his deliverance from Egypt; (2) a reminder of his past commandments; (3) a complaint that Israel has refused to listen to him; (4) a reminder of Yahweh's past warning.

God's Past Favors (2:1b). **2:1b** Yahweh's present displeasure with Israel is cast against the backdrop of his gracious actions on the nation's behalf in the past. First, Yahweh had rescued Israel from Egypt, an obvious reference to the exodus.[156]

Second, Yahweh had led the nation to the land he promised on oath to their ancestors. While the promise of land to Abraham represented an early element in the patriarchal blessing[157] and can be traced back to Gen 12:1–9 and 15:7–21 (note the reference to the Canaanite tribes), strictly speaking the only reference to Yahweh's oath in the Abrahamic narratives (Gen 22:14–18) concerns progeny, not land. The present association of the oath with the promise of the land of Canaan, however, occurs in the reiteration of the Abrahamic promise to Isaac (Gen 26:3), in Yahweh's self-introduction speech to Moses (Exod 6:8), and repeatedly thereafter.[158] Although the desti-

---

[153] Webb, *Book of Judges*, 240, n. 83.

[154] Cf. the LXX, which reads "to Bochim and Bethel and the house of Israel." Some prefer to associate Bokim with Shiloh. Cf. Moore, *Judges*, 58.

[155] T. Booij ("The Background of the Oracle in Psalm 81," *Bib* 65 [1984]: 466–67) has recognized similar structures in 6:8–10; Jer 7:22–25; Ezek 20:5–13,18–21; Ps 81:6–11[Hb. 7–12].

[156] From the MT's opening imperfect, אַעֲלֶה, "I will bring you up," followed by a *waw*-consecutive, it appears that a verb such as אָמַרְתִּי, "I said/promised," has dropped out. The versions all grasp the required sense by translating the imperfect with a past tense. Not understanding the identity of envoy and Yahweh, the LXX reads, "The Lord brought you up."

[157] The expression בִּרְכַּת אַבְרָהָם, "blessing of Abraham," is associated with progeny and land in Gen 28:3–4.

[158] Cf. Exod 13:5; Num 14:30. "The land which I promised on oath" is especially common in Deuteronomy. Cf. Deut 1:8,35; 6:10,18,23; 7:13; 8:1; 11:9,21; 19:8; 26:3,15; 28:11; 30:20; 31:23.

nation is identified differently,[159] the verb *hēbîʾ*, "to bring," recalls its two-fold occurrence with the *malʾāk* as the subject in Exod 23:20,23.

Third, Yahweh had promised never to break his covenant with Israel. The word *bĕrît* is used secularly of a pact of friendship between individuals[160] or a treaty/alliance between rulers (Gen 14:13; 21:2,;32; 1 Kgs 5:26; 20:34) or nations (1 Kgs 15:19 = 2 Chr 16:3; Amos 1:9). Where the treaty is between equals, it is called a parity treaty; where it is imposed by a superior king upon an inferior ruler, it is called a suzerainty treaty.[161] The covenant between Yahweh and Israel obviously belongs in the latter category, a fact reflected in the designation of this as "my covenant" rather than "our covenant." Yahweh, the divine King, had graciously invited Israel to become his covenant partner, declaring, "I ... will be your God, and you will be my people" (Lev 26:12).[162] On first sight it would seem that the covenant in view here is the covenant God made with his people at Sinai,[163] but in this context it refers to a specific aspect of his commitment to Israel, his immutable promise to give them the land of Canaan. Originally this had been a fundamental part of God's covenant with the Patriarchs, but in the covenant curses spelled out in Leviticus 26 it is fully integrated into the Sinai covenant (vv. 42–44).

God's Past Commands (2:2a). **2:2a** In all of Yahweh's past actions on Israel's behalf he had acted graciously. The initiative was all his; the privilege of being benefactors of divine kindness, all theirs. Accordingly, any demands he made on the people should have been received with joy. The envoy cites only two commandments, though these probably should be interpreted as shorthand for longer statements found elsewhere.[164] In these two citations the hinge function of this divine speech also becomes apparent.

First, the messenger reminds the Israelites of Yahweh's past prohibition on any alliances or agreements *(bĕrît)* with the inhabitants of the land. The narrator and the envoy undoubtedly look back to Joshua's league with the Gibeonites as a concrete illustration of the breach of this command,[165] and perhaps also the Ephraimites' covenant kindness *(ḥesed)* with the man from Bethel (Judg 1:24), not to mention the general willingness of the Israelite tribes to

---

[159] Here the messenger speaks of "the land sworn to the ancestors." In Exod 23:20,23 the destination is referred to respectively as "the place which I have prepared" (הֲכִנֹתִי אֲשֶׁר הַמָּקוֹם) and "the land of the Amorites, the Hittites, etc."

[160] David and Jonathan, 1 Sam 18:3; 20:8; 23:18.

[161] E.g., Nebuchadnezzar and Zedekiah, Ezek 17:13–19; Egypt and the nations, Ezek 30:5; Assyria and Ephraim, Hos 12:2.

[162] Cf. Ezek 37:27–28. This is known as the covenant formula.

[163] Exodus 20–24, the implications of which are spelled out in detail in Deuteronomy.

[164] See especially Moses' injunctions in Exod 34:12–17 and Deut 7:1–5, as well as Joshua's farewell charge in Josh 23:3–8.

[165] The word בְּרִית occurs repeatedly in Joshua 9 (vv. 6,7,11,15,16). Cf. the discussion by A. Marx, "Form et fonction de Juges 2, 1–5," *RHPR* 59 (1979): 341–50.

come to terms with the Canaanites as described in chap. 1. Since it comes from the mouth of this messenger, however, the command must again be interpreted primarily in light of Exod 23:20–33; 34:11–15. After a series of prohibitions, at the end of the former text, Yahweh explicitly forbids making a covenant with the Canaanites or their gods.[166] This prohibition is expressed even more emphatically with "Guard yourselves that you make no covenants with the inhabitants of the land" in Exod 34:12 and reiterated in 34:15.[167]

The second injunction, which looks forward to 2:6–23, commands the destruction of the Canaanites' altars. This command represents more extensive commands in previous texts to destroy all pagan cult installations. The language is more than Deuteronomic, recalling Deut 7:1–5 and 12:1–3; it echoes particularly Exod 34:13, in which Yahweh commands Israel to "break down their altars,[168] smash their sacred stones, and cut down their Asherah poles." The present text mentions only the first element, which functions as shorthand for all three.[169]

Together these two commands highlight the dangers inherent in the tolerant policies toward the Canaanites adopted by all the northern Israelite tribes, as reflected in the author's summary of their military fortunes in chap. 1. Making covenants with the people of the land and leaving Canaanite institutions in place will lead to covenants with their gods (Exod 34:10–17).

Israel's Response to God's Grace (2:2b). **2:2b** The messenger's review of Yahweh's past actions and past warnings is interrupted in the second half of v. 2 with a sharp denunciation: Israel has not obeyed Yahweh; they have not listened to the voice of the divine suzerain. In this accusation the Israelites and we the readers hear another echo from Exodus 23, specifically vv. 21–22, which had twice charged the Israelites to obey the voice of the divine envoy.[170] Herein lies one of the distinctive features of Israelite faith and life. Unlike other

---

[166] Note the similarity of Exod 23:32 and Judg 2:2a:

Exod 23:32, לֹא־תִכְרֹת לָהֶם וְלֵאלֹהֵיהֶם בְּרִית, "You shall not make a covenant with them or with their gods,"

Judg 2:2a, לֹא תִכְרְתוּ בְרִית לְיוֹשְׁבֵי הָאָרֶץ הַזֹּאת, "You shall not make a covenant with the people of this land."

[167] Note the echo in the way the other party to possible covenants is identified:

Exod 34:12 הִשָּׁמֶר לְךָ פֶּן־תִּכְרֹת בְּרִית לְיוֹשֵׁב הָאָרֶץ

Exod 34:15 פֶּן־תִּכְרֹת בְּרִית לְיוֹשֵׁב הָאָרֶץ

Judg 2:2 לֹא־תִכְרְתוּ בְרִית לְיוֹשְׁבֵי הָאָרֶץ.

[168] Note the similarity of expression:

Exod 34:13 כִּי אֶת־מִזְבְּחֹתָם תִּתֹּצוּן, "Break down their altars,"

Judg 2:2 מִזְבְּחוֹתֵיהֶם תִּתֹּצוּן, "You shall break down their altars."

The command is expressed differently in Exod 23:24 and Num 33:52.

[169] Cp. Gideon's action in Judg 6:25–28.

[170] Cp. וְלֹא שְׁמַעְתֶּם בְּקוֹלִי, "but you have not listened to my voice," in Judg 2:2b, with שְׁמַע בְּקֹלוֹ, "listen to his voice," in Exod 23:21, and כִּי אִם שָׁמוֹעַ תִּשְׁמַע בְּקֹלוֹ, "But if you truly listen to his voice …" in v. 22.

nations, whose gods neither see nor hear nor speak, Israel's God has spoken. The Israelites were never left guessing the will of their God (cf. Deut 4:1–8). In his grace Yahweh had entered into covenant relationship with them, and in his grace he had revealed his will. The injunction to resist all alliances with Canaanites or to tolerate their religious practices was not Moses' or Joshua's idea. In violating these commands they were not defying human will but the revealed will of their God. The question *mah zzōʾt ʿáśîtem,* "What is this you have done?" is an effective rhetorical ploy, forcing the Israelites to reflect on their actions and their implications for their ongoing relationship with Yahweh and their personal futures.[171]

God's Past Warning (2:3). **2:3** In v. 3 Yahweh explains his response to Israel. The NIV and many other translations[172] interpret v. 3 as Yahweh's punitive response to Israel's failure to deal with the Canaanites in chap. 1 as Yahweh had prescribed. This is unlikely, however, on lexical,[173] grammatical,[174] and contextual[175] grounds.[176] *wĕgam ʾāmartî* is better translated simply, "And I also said," linking the remainder of v. 3 with vv. 1b–2a. The phrase is necessitated by the interruption of the survey of Yahweh's past instructions with the rebuke in v. 2b. Resuming the survey, this verse is not intended as an announcement of future judgment for failing to keep the covenant but as a warning reminder of a past declaration of the consequences of making such covenants. The reminder consists of two parts: first, that Yahweh has ceased acting on the Israelites' behalf to drive the Canaanites out of the land, and, second, that he is allowing the Canaanites and their gods to have their way with his people.

This reaction on God's part is neither impulsive nor arbitrary nor capricious; it reflects his own fidelity to past pronouncements, the most recent being Joshua's warning in 23:13. But again the clearest echoes come from Exod 23:20–33; 34:11–15, and they are heard in both segments of this reminder. First, Yahweh had warned the Israelites that if they would not obey him, he would not drive the Canaanites out before them. The use of the verb *gāraš (piel),* "to drive out," is borrowed from Exod 23:28–31, where it appears four

---

[171] Cf. NIV's "Why have you done this?"

[172] Thus NRSV, NAB, NJB, and apparently JPSV, as well as many commentators: Goslinga, *Joshua, Judges, and Ruth,* 263; Auld, *Joshua, Judges, and Ruth,* 139.

[173] The particle גַּם normally means "also, too, as well, likewise" (*DCH* 1.357).

[174] The Hb. reads וְגַם אָמַרְתִּי, which translates naturally, "and I also said." The NIV's "Now therefore I tell you" would have required an introductory לָכֵן, "Therefore," or וְעַתָּה "And now," followed by an imperfect verb, אֹמַר, "I say," or, more likely, the verb dropped all together.

[175] Vv. 1–5 look back on chap. 1, not forward to the remainder of the book in which, except for chaps. 4–5, the problems on the surface at least are not the Canaanites but other outside oppressors.

[176] So also Lindars, *Judges 1–5,* 78; Moore, *Judges,* 59; Soggin, *Judges,* 20; Boling, *Judges,* 53. But for a detailed discussion of the issue see A. van der Kooij, "'And I Also Said': A New Interpretation of Judges ii 3," *VT* 45 (1995): 294–306.

times, and Exod 34:11, where it appears once.[177]

Second, Yahweh had warned the Israelites that they would face an increasingly hostile Canaanite population. Two dimensions of this hostility are cited. Because the first is textually problematic, we will deal with the second dimension first: "Their gods will be a snare[178] to you." Although the construction differs slightly, this clause seems to be borrowed from Exod 23:33b.[179] The simple form in both these texts compares with Joshua's more complex statement in his farewell address (lit.): "They [these nations] will become a trap *[pah]* and a snare *[môqēš]*, and a whip *[šōṭēṭ]*, on your sides *[ṣiddêkem]*, and thorns *[šĕninîm]* in your eyes" (Josh 23:13).

The second dimension is more difficult to interpret. The NIV (as well as the NASB and AV) reads "they will be thorns in your sides." Based on Num 33:55, this interpretation assumes that consonantal Hebrew *lṣdym* is a defective spelling for *lṣnynym bṣdykm*. The NRSV's "adversaries" and the JPSV's "oppressors" are based on ancient versions (LXX, Vg., Tg.), which seem to have read *lṣrym* instead of *lṣdym* in the text from which they were translated.[180] Contextual considerations, however, call for a word semantically parallel to *mwqš*, "snare." This requirement is best met by interpreting *ṣiddîm* as "traps," assuming a derivation from *ṣûd*, a common Hebrew expression for "to chase, hunt,"[181] which has cognates in several other Semitic languages.[182]

Taken together this statement is delightfully ironic. When the Israelites observed the prosperity of the Canaanites, the latters' gods seemed to offer so much: fertility, prosperity, security. But Yahweh hereby turns their twisted theological thinking against them. Rather than finding new freedom in the religious structures of the Canaanites, the Israelites would be caught in the trap of their gods, like a fly in a spider's web.

THE PEOPLE'S RESPONSE (2:4–5). **2:4–5** The people's response to the speech of the divine messenger is dramatic and impressive. They weep over his

---

[177] Cp. especially Exod 23:29, לֹא אֲגָרְשֶׁנּוּ מִפָּנֶיךָ, "I will not drive them out before you," and Judg 2:3, לֹא אֲגָרֵשׁ אוֹתָם מִפְּנֵיכֶם, "I will not drive them out before you." Elsewhere Yahweh's promises to drive out the Canaanites before the Israelites use יָרֵשׁ *(hiphil)*. See Num 33; Josh 23:13; also Judg 2:21.

[178] The word מוֹקֵשׁ, also in Deut 7:16; Josh 23:13, derives from יָקֵשׁ, "to lay bait."

[179] Cp. the texts (following the versions in Exod 23:23 with the NIV):
Exod 23:33 כִּי יִהְיֶה לְךָ לְמוֹקֵשׁ, "for they [their gods] will become a snare to you."
Judg 2:3 וֵאלֹהֵיהֶם יִהְיוּ לָכֶם לְמוֹקֵשׁ, "and their gods will become a snare to you."
A variation of the statement occurs also Exod 34:12.

[180] Confusion of ד/ר for ר/ד (and vice versa) is a common problem in the OT.

[181] Gen 27:3,5,33; Lev 17:13; Jer 16:16; Ezek 13:18,20; Mic 7:2; Ps 140:12; Job 10:16; 38:39; Prov 6:26; Lam 3:25; 4:18.

[182] For Akk. *ṣâdu*, see *AHW*, 1073 and *CAD* 16, 57; Aramaic and Punic ציד, *DISO*, 244; *DNSWI*, 966; Ug., *UT*, Glossary, 473. A. Spreafic interprets the present form as an active participle, "hunters" ("Giud 2,3: *lṣdym*," *Bib* 65 [1984]: 390–92). A derivation from Hb. צָדָה, "to lie in wait" (cf. Exod 21:13; 1 Sam 24:11) seems less likely.

words;[183] memorialize their response by naming the place "Bokim," which means "[place of] weeping"; and offer sacrifices to Yahweh. From these actions it appears their repentance is genuine. They seem to acknowledge that they have fallen short of the covenant obligations and declare their devotion to Yahweh by cultic actions. But the reader will be disappointed to learn that this will be the last time in the book they respond this way. Subsequent events will prove how short-lived this revival was.

Theological and Practical Implications

Through the mouth of the divine envoy and the response of the nation, the author describes a nation in tension. At the beginning of their national history within the land of Canaan the Israelites are torn between two poles: will they remain true to Yahweh, or will they permit themselves, through compromise and toleration, to be drawn into the mind-set and spiritual culture of the Canaanites? The remainder of the book will reveal how shallow the present commitment was and how illusory the solution.

At the same time, this text reveals the tension within Yahweh's own heart. He who swore never to break his covenant now announces that his past warning is about to be fulfilled: he will stop driving out the Canaanites before Israel. Instead of delivering the Canaanites into the hands of Israel, repeatedly this book will describe Yahweh selling the Israelites into the hands of their hunters. With ever-increasing intensity, the reader will learn that if anything positive ever happens in Israel, it arises from the gracious heart of Yahweh. There is nothing in this people to commend them before their divine patron. For the moment, however, the tension evident in 1:3–2:4 seems to have been relieved, and the calm of 1:1–2 seems to have returned in 2:4–5.

(2) The Narrator's Interpretation (2:6–20a)

⁶After Joshua had dismissed the Israelites, they went to take possession of the land, each to his own inheritance. ⁷The people served the LORD throughout the lifetime of Joshua and of the elders who outlived him and who had seen all the great things the LORD had done for Israel.

⁸Joshua son of Nun, the servant of the LORD, died at the age of a hundred and ten. ⁹And they buried him in the land of his inheritance, at Timnath Heres in the hill country of Ephraim, north of Mount Gaash.

¹⁰After that whole generation had been gathered to their fathers, another generation grew up, who knew neither the LORD nor what he had done for Israel. ¹¹Then the Israelites did evil in the eyes of the LORD and served the Baals. ¹²They forsook the LORD, the God of their fathers, who had brought them out of Egypt. They followed and worshiped various gods of the peoples around them. They pro-

---

[183] As they will do in 21:2 and 1 Sam 11:4.

voked the LORD to anger [13]because they forsook him and served Baal and the Ashtoreths. [14]In his anger against Israel the LORD handed them over to raiders who plundered them. He sold them to their enemies all around, whom they were no longer able to resist. [15]Whenever Israel went out to fight, the hand of the LORD was against them to defeat them, just as he had sworn to them. They were in great distress.

[16]Then the LORD raised up judges, who saved them out of the hands of these raiders. [17]Yet they would not listen to their judges but prostituted themselves to other gods and worshiped them. Unlike their fathers, they quickly turned from the way in which their fathers had walked, the way of obedience to the LORD's commands. [18]Whenever the LORD raised up a judge for them, he was with the judge and saved them out of the hands of their enemies as long as the judge lived; for the LORD had compassion on them as they groaned under those who oppressed and afflicted them. [19]But when the judge died, the people returned to ways even more corrupt than those of their fathers, following other gods and serving and worshiping them. They refused to give up their evil practices and stubborn ways.

[20]Therefore the LORD was very angry with Israel

The rest of the book proves how short-lived the repentance reported in 2:4–5 really was. Indeed, if their remorse over their sin had been genuine, Israelite history would have taken a completely different course, the events described in the rest of the book would never have happened, and the Book of Judges would never been written. There is no doubt that 3:7–16:31, "The Book of Deliverers," represents the core of the book. But such a title deflects from the author's real concerns: Israel's apostasy and Yahweh's grace. The farther one reads in the book, the more one realizes that far from being the solution to Israel's problems, the judges are increasingly part of the obstacle. At the same time one becomes increasingly aware that far from responding to his people's conduct on the basis of some mechanical deuteronomistic formula (obedience brings blessing; disobedience yields the curse), Yahweh deals in grace. It may be argued that the remainder of chap. 2 should be treated as a unit, but for the sake of convenience we recognize the shift from narrator's exposition in 2:6–20a to direct divine speech in 2:20b–22. Verse 24 is epilogic. These three sections combine, however, to declare the author's fundamental thesis: the nation of Israel has been thoroughly Canaanized; this accounts for and is fundamental to the darkness demonstrated in the rest of the book. Given the Israelites' increasing depravity, God's merciful interventions on their behalf also become increasingly remarkable.

As already intimated, in vv. 6–20a the reader needs to hear the narrator offer his divinely inspired analysis of Israel's problem during the dark days of the Judges and to learn its lesson for his or her own day. Like the divine envoy in 2:1–3, the narrator is a preacher, appealing to his contemporaries with the question, "What is this you have done?" The narrator's exposition divides into three parts dealing successively with the roots of Israel's problem (vv. 6–10), the expression of Israel's problem (vv. 11–13), and Yahweh's reaction to Israel's problem (vv. 14–20a). Whereas chap. 1 had explored the period of Israel's settlement from the earthly, Israelite, perspective, in 2:6–23 the narrator looks at this era through Yahweh's eyes. Like the analyst of the fall of the Northern Kingdom of Israel centuries later (2 Kgs 17:7–23), our author shows little interest in the political and economic factors underlying Israel's problems in the settlement period; his interest is exclusively spiritual.

Similarly, except for the note on Joshua's death in vv. 6–10, the author offers no specific historical information. By referring to the protagonists as *běnê yiśrāʾēl*, "the descendants of Israel," the author abstracts the experiences of individual tribes. Instead of identifying Israel's specific opponents by name, the author speaks vaguely of "the surrounding peoples" (v. 12), "raiders who plundered them" (v. 14), and "their enemies" (v. 14), or he borrows from earlier stereotypical lists (3:5). Instead of describing the specific offenses, the author generalizes Israel's religious crimes as forsaking Yahweh, "serving," "worshiping," and "following" the Baals and the Ashtartes, and "prostituting themselves." Instead of naming individual governors, he refers generically to "judges who saved them [Israel]" (v. 16). Instead of describing how they emerged as leaders, he observes simply that "the LORD raised up judges" (v. 16). In so doing the author declares his bias and hands the reader the key to the remainder of the book. Any interpretation of the following chapters that loses sight of the agenda set here is off track. Here he offers his answer to the question "What was wrong with Israel during the period of settlement?" The narrator has no intention of offering either an objective social-scientific or political analysis of the period nor of idealizing the nation's history. If we do not get his theological point here, we will miss it all along.[184]

THE ROOTS OF ISRAEL'S APOSTASY (2:6–10). **2:6** The syntax of v. 6 suggests the author intends for the reader to interpret the account of Joshua's death as a natural sequel to v. 5, that is, in light of the assembly of Israel at Bokim. But this creates serious chronological problems, particularly if one interprets chaps. 1; 2:1–5,6–10 as temporally sequential.[185] If the military efforts described in chap. 1 followed the death of Joshua (1:1) and the Bokim episode happened in the wake of and in response to Israel's military failures, how then can Joshua dismiss the people and send them to their patrimonial estates?

One solution is to interpret the verbs in vv. 6–10 as pluperfects, "Now

---

[184] Which is the case with approaches to the book that treat it primarily as a political pro-Judahite and pro-Davidic document.

[185] Which seems to be required by the unbroken sequence of *waw*-consecutive verbs: "And they called … and they sacrificed … and Joshua dismissed … and they went."

Joshua had dismissed the people, and the Israelites had all returned to possess their lands," et cetera, but this forces an unnatural sense upon the narrative (*waw*-consecutive) verbs. It is preferable to answer the question rhetorically rather than chronologically. In addition to the strong thematic and lexical links between vv. 6–23 and the divine envoy's speech, scholars have also recognized numerous echoes of Joshua 24, which reports Joshua's assembly of and speech to the Israelites at Shechem, in the context of a covenant renewal ceremony. On the one hand, the announcement of Joshua's dismissal of the people and his death in Judg 2:6 repeats almost verbatim Josh 24:28. On the other hand, many of the themes in 2:10–20 echo similar statements in Joshua's covenant renewal speech.[186] It seems that the narrator had the Book of Joshua in front of him, and he intentionally extracted and adapted notions from the earlier document for his own rhetorical reasons. Just as the divine messenger had reminded the Israelites of Yahweh's past covenantal grace and Israel's failure to keep the covenant,[187] so the narrator offers a retrospective look at Israel's past commitments in light of which the pattern of apostasy and infidelity described in this book are to be interpreted.

Even if the echoes of Josh 24:28–31 in particular are obvious even to a casual reader, the present narrator's dependence on the Shechem event is not slavish. In fact, he gives them his own stamp with several stylistic[188] and significant syntactical alterations. First, and most obviously, the sequence of statements is rearranged so that the notice of the response of the Israelites to Yahweh appears more logically immediately after the statement that Joshua had released the Israelites to go and claim their respective territorial grants.[189] Second, the addition of "they [the descendants of Israel, *běnê yiśrāʾēl*] went to take possession of the land" in v. 6 thrusts into sharp relief the litany of failures in chap. 1. Third, the present author naturally drops the chronological note, "After these events," which in Josh 24:29a had referred

---

[186] For an analysis of the relationship between these texts see Becker, *Richterzeit*, 64–72.

[187] Note also the links between the divine envoy's speech and Joshua's farewell address, particularly the references to the "snares" in Josh 23:13.

[188] These include dropping the conjunction "and" before "who had known" and replacing the verb יָדַע, "to know" (Josh 24:31), with רָאָה, "to see" (v. 7). Both verbs carry an experiential sense of perceiving and recognizing the significance of the events. Cf. v. 10, where יָדַע is reintroduced. Judg 2:9 drops the subordinating conjunction אֲשֶׁר, "which [is]," before "on the mountain of Ephraim" (v. 9).

[189] This is the first occurrence of נַחֲלָה in the book. The NIV follows tradition in translating the word with inheritance terminology, but this is misleading, inasmuch as "inheritance" is usually perceived as property passed on by a parent to a child, usually at the death of the former. In Deuteronomy and the conquest narratives the word should be interpreted as technical feudal language: a property or privilege received by a subject from his lord in exchange for services (usually military) rendered or anticipated. Cf. Block, *The Gods of the Nations: Studies in Ancient Near Eastern National Theology*, ETSMS 2 (Winona Lake: Eisenbrauns, 1988), 76–79.

to the renewal of the covenant. Fourth, the present author heightens the folly of the Israelite's forgetfulness by describing all the works of Yahweh as "great" (*gādôl,* v. 7). Fifth, and most significantly (for herein lies the key to the author's agenda) following the notice of Joshua's burial, he adds the observation that after Joshua and his contemporaries had died, they were succeeded by a generation of Israelites who knew nothing of the past works of Yahweh on Israel's behalf. We may examine this paragraph further by noting first how Joshua exits from the stage and then how the Israelites respond to Yahweh after this fearless leader has departed.

2:6a,8–9 The author sets the stage for his evaluation of Israel's conduct during the period of the governors by summarizing the circumstances of Joshua's death. Verses 6a and 8–9 represent a virtual quotation of the account of Joshua's death in Josh 24:28–30. According to this report, Joshua's last significant act was to commission[190] his countrymen to go and claim the land that he had apportioned to each of the tribes.[191] Having completed his part in the divine program, this "servant of the LORD" (Josh 24:29)[192] dies and is buried in his personal allotment in Timnath Serah, the "portion of the sun" (Heliopolis!) Joshua had personally built in the territory of Ephraim, the tribe to which he belonged.[193] The site probably is to be identified with Khirbet Tibnah, ten miles northwest of Bethel. In later times the tomb of Joshua became a favorite place for pilgrims to visit.[194]

2:6b–7,10 Verses 6b–7,10 need to be interpreted against this backdrop. In these notes one may recognize the narrator's division of the early history of Israel in the land into three eras, as illustrated in the following chart:

---

[190] The NIV "dismissed" is too passive. Elsewhere שׁלח in *piel* is used of commissioning prophets and sending them out on their mission. Cf. 6:14.

[191] In light of chap. 1 and Joshua's distribution of the territories in Joshua 13–19, it is more natural to interpret אִישׁ לְנַחֲלָתוֹ, "each to his grant," as a reference to tribal rather than individual allotments.

[192] The expression is not used of anyone else in the Book of Judges, but compare the similar characterization of Moses as Yahweh's servant (עֶבֶד) in Josh 1–2. The next person who will bear this honorific title will be David, 2 Sam 3:18 + thirty times. See *HALOT,* 774 and BDB, 714 for definitions and references. For fuller discussion of the term and further bibliography see E. Carpenter, "עבד," *NIDOTTE* 3.304–9.

[193] Josh 19:49–50. The present spelling, תִּמְנַת־חֶרֶס, represents a correction of תִּמְנַת־סֶרַח, which occurs in Josh 19:50; 24:30.

[194] For a full study see E. Noort, "Josua 24,28–31, Richter 2,6–9 und das Josuagrab. Gedanken zu einem Strassenbild," in *Biblische Welten: Festschrift für Metin Metzger zu seinem 65. Geburtstag,* ed. W. Zwickel, OBO 123 (Fribourg: Edition universitaires/Göttingen: Vandenhoeck & Ruprecht, 1993), 109–3; cf. more briefly H. R. Weeks, "Timnath-heres," *ABD* 6.557–58.

Era	Characteristic	Israel's Response
The days of Joshua	The time of Yahweh's great work.[a]	They served[b] Yahweh.
The days of the elders who survived Joshua	The memory of Yahweh's great work	They served Yahweh.
The days after the surviving witnesses	They did not know the great work of Yahweh.	They did not serve Yahweh.

a. For an elaboration of הַגָּדוֹל יהוה מַעֲשֵׂה כָּל, "all the great work of the LORD," and the theological and practical implications see Deut 4:32–40.

b. The verb עָבַד, "to serve," which reflects Israel's subordination to Yahweh, speaks of functioning as Yahweh's agents in general and serving him in cultic worship in particular.

The transition between the first two periods is marked both by the death of Joshua and by the departure of the people to their tribal allotments. It is impossible to tell how long stage two lasted. Judges 1:1 leaves the impression that the Israelites launched their attacks on the Canaanite settlements soon after Joshua died, but most of these charges into enemy territory proved less than successful. One may assume the reason for this was the quick departure of the nation from their fidelity to the covenant, a departure expressed in chap. 1 by a tolerant disposition toward the enemy. For all their good intentions (v. 6b), the respective tribes' efforts were futile, as chap. 1 attests. The present juxtapositioning of the previous summary account and the present theological reflections on the period invite the reader to correlate the military loss of nerve in chap. 1 with the present notice. Because the memory of Yahweh's salvific and providential acts on Israel's behalf died with Joshua and the survivors of his generation were gone,[195] the Israelites stopped "serving" Yahweh, which in this context should have been expressed by driving out the Canaanites.

This text is a witness to the apparent failure of the community to keep alive its memory of Yahweh's gracious saving acts. The priests had failed in their instructional duties (Lev 10:11); and the elaborate system of festivals, memorials, and other customs, designed to pass on the rich spiritual tradition (Deut 6:20) had either lapsed or been reduced to formality. If the Shemaᶜ (Deut 6:4) was being recited at all, the following injunctions to the community (6:5–6) to

---

[195] The expression "they were gathered to their fathers" reflects the Israelite custom of burying the deceased in family/ancestral tombs. Cf. E. Bloch-Smith, *Judahite Burial Practices and Beliefs about the Dead*, JSOTSup 123 (Sheffield: JSOT Press, 1992), 87–88.

instruct the children in the fundamentals of covenant faith were obviously regarded more in the breach than in the observance.[196] When people lose sight of God's grace, they lose sight of God and the sense of any obligation to him. All that follows in the book is a consequence of Israel's loss of memory.

THE NATURE OF ISRAEL'S APOSTASY (2:11–13). Having exposed the roots of Israel's apostasy, the narrator turns to an examination of its character. Verses 11–13 summarize the problem theologically, beginning with a thesis statement (v. 11a) and then elaborating on the same (vv. 11b–13).

2:11a The fundamental problem in Israel is reduced to "The Israelites did evil in the eyes of the LORD and served the Baals." This phrase, which is borrowed from Deuteronomy,[197] provides a formal link between this preamble (2:1–23) and the narratives that follow.[198] *hāraʿ*, "the evil," may be used in an amoral sense of "disagreeable, bad, malignant, ill" as in Deut 30:15, where it is juxtaposed with *ṭôb*, "good, fortunate": "See, I set before you today life and prosperity *[haṭṭôb]*, death and destruction *[hārāʿ]*."[199] In most instances in the Old Testament the word denotes moral and/or spiritual malignancy. When a person "does" *raʿ*, it usually carries a moral/theological sense, "evil," defined as such not only for the negative physical and social effects of the action but for its violation of the will of God. Accordingly the present author adds "in the eyes of the LORD," a reference to the divine Redeemer who, having rescued Israel from slavery and entered into covenant relationship with them, established Israel's definitions of right and wrong.[200] This raises an important question regarding the author's awareness of Yahweh's disposition in this matter. How did he know their actions were evil in the sight of Yahweh? On the one hand, he may have drawn this conclusion by comparing Israel's behavior with the patterns of normative righteous conduct established in the covenant, especially the first two principles of covenant relationship outlined in Exod 20:1–17 and expounded upon by Moses in Deuteronomy 5–11. On the other hand, this comment reflects the author's apparent omniscience. Like the professional prophets he knows the mind of God. While literary critics may attribute this omniscient quality to the independence of the narrator (the author creates his characters),[201] an evangelical response would attribute this to revelation. As a divinely authorized interpreter of historical events, through the agency of the

---

[196] On the importance of memory in the theology of the prophets see Isa 1:14; Hos 4:1–6; Jer 8:4–12; 9:23–24.

[197] עָשָׂה הָרַע בְּעֵינֵי יהוה occurs more than fifty times in the OT. See Num 32:13; Deut 4:25; 9:18; 17:2; 31:29; etc.

[198] Cf. 3:7,12; 4:1; 6:1; 10:6; 13:1.

[199] Cf. also Gen 2:9,17; 2 Sam 14:17; 19:35[36]; 1 Kgs 3:9; Isa 7:15–16.

[200] The article on הָרַע, "the evil," suggests both a specific evil and the supreme evil, the violation of the first Decalogic principle, Exod 20:3.

[201] Cf. Alter, *Art of Biblical Narrative*, 156–58.

Spirit of God, the author is informed by God and therefore is able to describe Yahweh's evaluation of the Israelites' conduct.

2:11b–13　These verses expand on the "evil" perpetrated by the Israelites. The literary skill of the author is reflected in the chiastic structure of the exposition, which may be highlighted by formatting the individual statements as follows:

A　They served the Baals (v. 11b)
　　B　They abandoned Yahweh (v. 12a)
　　　　C　They pursued other gods (v. 12b)
　　　　C′　They worshiped them (v. 12c)[202]
　　B′　They abandoned Yahweh (v. 13a)
A′　They served the Baals and the Astartes (v. 13b)

Israel's apostasy may be explored first by examining the new objects of devotion and then the actions of devotion.

The generation of Israelites that forgot Yahweh and his miraculous actions on their behalf not only abandoned (*ʿāzab*) Yahweh; they committed themselves to other gods, here referred to as the *baʿălîm* and the *ʾaštārôt*. The first expression derives from the word *baʿal*, which in its basic sense is a secular term meaning simply "lord, master, owner,"[203] and in a first level of derived sense, "husband."[204] When applied to a god, it functions as a title, "divine lord, master" rather than a personal name and is used as an appellative for many gods in the ancient world.[205] Baal occurs as a divine title more than seventy times in the Old Testament. Usually it refers to the storm/weather god, who in the Canaanite mythological literature goes by the name Hadad and several other titles: *ʾalʾiyn bʿl*, "the victor Baal"; *rkb ʿrpt*, "Rider of the Clouds"; *bn dgn*, "son of Dagan"; *zbl bʿl ʾrṣ*, "the prince lord of the earth"; *bʿl ṣpn*, "Baal of Zaphon."[206] In Canaanite mythology Baal was one of the seventy offspring of El and Asherah, along with his opposite, Mot, the god of death and the netherworld, and Yam,

---

[202] C′ and B′ are separated by "They provoked Yahweh to anger," which signals the theme of the following section, vv. 14–19. Becker's attribution of this clause to a later redactor (*Richterzeit*, 75) is based on subjective modern definitions of literary style and consistency.

[203] E.g., the owner of an ox, Exod 21:28–29; a pit, Exod 21:34,36; a house, Exod 22:7; Judg 19:22–23; a debt, Deut 15:2.

[204] Gen 20:3; Exod 21:3,22; Deut 22:22; 24:4; Hos 2:18; etc. Cp. the use of the verb בָּעַל, "to rule over" (1 Chr 4:22; Isa 26:13), "to marry" (Gen 20:3; Deut 21:13; 22:22; 24:1; Isa 54:1,5; 62:4–5; Mal 2:11; etc.).

[205] E.g., the Babylonian god Marduk, also known as Bel (the Akk. form of בָּעַל). Note also בַּעַל שָׁמַם, "lord of the heavens"; בַּעַל חָרָן, "lord of Haran"; בַּעַל צֹר, "lord of Tyre." The feminine counterpart is בַּעֲלָת, "mistress," as in בַּעֲלַת גְּבַל, "mistress of Gebal (=Byblos)." For references and discussion see Block, *Gods of the Nations*, 44–46.

[206] Zaphon, "North," was the mythical mountain on which Baal resided, the counterpart to Greek Olympus.

the god of the sea.[207] When the plural form *baʿālîm* occurs, the reference is not to a multiplicity of gods but to numerous manifestations of the one weather god, on whose blessing the fertility of the land was thought to depend.[208]

Hebrew *ʿaštārôt*[209] represents a plural form of *ʿaštart*,[210] commonly known as Astarte, who was worshiped widely as the goddess of love and war.[211] In the Canaanite literature Anath usually functions as Baal's consort.[212] Astarte also appears as Baal's spouse, however, which agrees with the broader ancient Near Eastern world reflected in the Old Testament. Like *baʿālîm*, the present plural form refers to the local manifestations of the deity. In the fertility cult of Canaan, Baal was represented by an upright stone *(maṣṣēbâ);* Astarte was portrayed by carved female figurines, with exaggerated breasts and prominent genitals.[213] Together these two gods formed a powerful force in ancient Near Eastern spirituality. Israel's abandonment of Yahweh may be attributable to an inability to conceive of Yahweh as the God of this land where Baal and Astarte ruled with apparent effectiveness. The newcomers had experienced Yahweh's power in Egypt, at Mount Sinai, and in the desert; but once they crossed the Jordan, they found it easier to change allegiance to the gods of this land than to transfer to Yahweh the fertility functions of a territorial god.

The verbs used to describe their commitment to the gods of this land are instructive. First, whereas during the tenure of Joshua they had served *(ʿābad)* Yahweh (v. 7), now they directed the same activity toward the Baals and the Astartes. Second, if the negative aspect of their change of allegiance is described as abandoning Yahweh, the counterpart is "walking after other gods." The expression *hālak ʾaḥărê ʾĕlōhîm ʾăḥērîm,* "walking after other gods," derives fundamentally from the context of cultic processions in which the devotees of a divinity would follow the image of a deity carried by priests to and from places of religious celebration. Here it is used more generally of any expression of spiritual commitment. Third, they paid homage to the other

---

[207] These myths are conveniently translated in *ANET,* 129–42. For further discussion of this Canaanite divinity see J. Day, "Baal," *ABD* 1.545–49; W. Herrmann, "Baal," *Dictionary of Deities and Demons in the Bible,* 249–65.

[208] These manifestations are reflected in the biblical place names bearing Baal as an element: Baal-Peor; Baal-Hazor, Baal-Gad, Baal-Hermon, Baal-Shalisha, Baal-Tamar. See Even-Shoshan, *A New Concordance of the Bible* (Jerusalem: Kiryat Sepher, 1981), 196, for references.

[209] Mistransliterated in the NIV as Ashtoreths, under the influence of 1 Kgs 11:5,33 and 2 Kgs 23:13, where the form appears to represent a deliberate distortion of עַשְׁתָּרוֹת, *ʿaštārôt,* vocalizing the name with the vowels of בֹּשֶׁת, *bōšet,* "shame." Cp. Ish-bosheth in 2 Sam 2:10, for Ish-baal, 1 Chr 8:33.

[210] Known in Ebla as Ashtar and in Mesopotamia as Ishtar, from which is derived the name Esther.

[211] In classical times Astarte was identified with Aphrodite and Venus.

[212] See below on 3:31.

[213] On Astarte see Day, "Ashtoreth," *ABD* 1.491–94; N. Wyatt, "Astarte," *DDD,* 203–13.

gods. In popular thinking and practice today worship is often (if not generally) confused with exaltation, as in standing before God with hands raised in praise. However, the biblical notion of "worship" is quite the opposite. The verb *hištaḥăwâ*, from the root *ḥwh/ḥyh*,[214] represents court language, denoting fundamentally the physical gesture of prostration before a superior. The gesture has been interpreted as a nonverbal equivalent to the declaration "May X live!"[215] In this instance the posture of the Israelites, bowing down before foreign gods, expresses their subjection to them. Instead of being servants of Yahweh, like Joshua had been, they have become servants of these gods.

It is no wonder that Yahweh is outraged.[216] In direct opposition to Joshua's charge and in betrayal of their covenant renewal commitment at Shechem (Josh 24:14–24), Israel had switched its spiritual allegiance. The unimaginable described in Jer 2:9–13 had happened: this nation had exchanged Yahweh, its patron God, for worthless idols—gods that were not gods at all. In the mind of the author this is the essence of Israel's Canaanization. For the moment "the gods of the peoples around them"[217] appear to have won in the contest with "the God of the fathers." According to the covenant (Leviticus 26; Deuteronomy 28), this abandonment of Yahweh not only absolves him of responsibility for them; it also renders them his enemy.

GOD'S REACTION TO ISRAEL'S APOSTASY (2:14–20a). Yahweh's outraged reaction to Israel's Canaanization was announced in passing in v. 12b. In vv. 14–20a the author describes his reaction in detail. While many dismiss this text as repetitious and clumsy, it is carefully constructed, being framed by identical declarations of divine anger: *wayyiḥar ʾap yhwh bĕyiśrāʾēl*, "the fury of Yahweh burned against Israel."[218] Significantly the subject of this entire subunit is Yahweh. The narrator hereby invites the reader to agonize with the betrayed covenant Lord over what to do with this faithless people.

The Kindling of Divine Anger (2:14–15). **2:14–15** Like the previous segment, this section is introduced with a thesis statement: "The anger of the LORD burned against Israel." Although modern readers may protest this image of God literally "and his nose burned" *(wayyiḥar ʾappô)*, the expression of divine fury must be interpreted against the background of extravagant demonstrations of grace in the past. Yahweh is a passionate God;[219] he cannot stand

---

[214] Although the verb occurs more than 170 times, this is the only verb that appears in the *Hištaphel* stem in the OT.

[215] Directed toward Yahweh the gesture is related semantically to the oath formula, יְהוָה חַי, "As the LORD lives." For studies of the expression see S. Kreuzer, "Zur Bedeutung und Etymologie von *hištaḥăwāh/yštḥwy*," *VT* 35 (1985): 39–60; H. D. Preuss, *TDOT* 4.248–56.

[216] כָּעַס denotes fundamentally "to be vexed, provoked, angered."

[217] אֱלֹהֵי הָעַמִּים סְבִיבוֹתֵיהֶם, the definition of "the other gods" given in v. 12.

[218] The NIV's renderings obscure the inclusio.

[219] This is the sense of קַנָּא, usually inadequately rendered "jealous."

idly by while other divine competitors snatch his people from him. Nor can he passively accept his own people's adulterous affairs with other gods. Yahweh's expression of anger against his people is described in the form of two roughly parallel statements:

He gave them into the power of plunderers;[220]
He sold them into the power of their enemies.[221]

Who these plunderers/enemies were is not yet indicated, but the effect of their hostility is clear. In the first instance the plunderers did indeed fulfill the divine mission; in the second, Israel was no match for them—they could not stand.[222] Verse 15 clarifies the meaning of the last phrase of v. 14. The shocking reality for Israel was that their real enemy was God. Whenever they went out[223] they were confronted with his hostile hand, determined to make life miserable for them.[224] In accordance with his previous warnings *(dibbēr)* and his oath *(nišbaʿ)*, he inflicted them with severe distress.[225] Since neither of these two clauses, introduced by *kaʾăšer*, "just as,"[226] occurs in this book, the antecedent must be found elsewhere, presumably in Deuteronomy. Some point to Deut 6:14–15,[227] but the substantive and verbal links between this passage and Deut 31:16–21 render the latter a better candidate. This text speaks of the Israelites experiencing many *rāʿôt wĕṣārôt*, "disasters and difficulties," because they prostitute themselves to foreign gods, forsake Yahweh, and break the covenant, thereby fueling the ire of Yahweh.

The Kindling of Divine Compassion (2:16–19). These verses divide further into two parts, vv. 16–17 and 18–19, arranged in an *abab* pattern. Each of

---

[220] Although the verb שָׁסַס, "to spoil, plunder," occurs only five times in the OT (+ 1 Sam 17:53; Isa 13:16; Zech 14:2; Ps 89:42), its meaning is confirmed by the more common bi-form שָׁסָה, which also occurs here. See BDB, 1042. The actions of "plunderers" are illustrated by the Midianites in 6:1–6. On the term see further W. R. Domeris, "שׁסה (šsh)," *NIDOTTE* 4.198–99.

[221] וַיִּתְּנֵם בְּיַד־ and וַיִּמְכְּרֵם בְּיַד־ represents two versions of what scholars identify as the committal formula, on which see below.

[222] The NIV renders עָמַד "resist."

[223] Here יָצָא, "to go out," functions as a technical term for marching out into battle. See 5:4; 2 Kgs 18:27; etc.

[224] רָעָה, "distress, harm, calamity," is an abstract feminine form of רַע, "evil," in v. 11. The NIV's "to defeat them" misses the point.

[225] Strictly speaking וַיֵּצֶר should be interpreted impersonally and intransitively, "they were distressed, hard pressed" (cf. Gen 32:8; 2 Sam 13:2; Job 20:22, as well as Judg 10:9 and 1 Sam 30:6; both feminine), rather than as a transitive *hiphil* (as in the LXX). However, this does not absolve Yahweh of a direct hand in their calamity. See the active role of Yahweh in the covenant curses of Leviticus 26 and Deuteronomy 28. Lindars (*Judges 1–5*, 104–5) follows *BHS* in harmonizing this verse with 3:9,15; 6:6; 10:10 by inserting וַיִּזְעֲקוּ אֶל־יהוה, "And they cried out to Yahweh," before וַיֵּצֶר, "and they were distressed," on the assumption it may have been dropped inadvertently by haplography.

[226] The NIV obscures the Hb. by dropping the first clause.

[227] Lindars, *Judges 1–5*, 104.

these segments begins with the notice that Yahweh raised up governors for the Israelites and concludes with an observation on their response.

2:16 Verse 16 summarizes Yahweh's reaction to the faithless conduct of his people: he provided them with tribal rulers *(šōpĕṭîm)*[228] to rescue *(hôšîaʿ)*[229] them from the hands of the plunderers. The fact that this statement follows immediately after the notice of Israel's dire straits suggests Yahweh's raising up of rulers represented a series of emergency measures to relieve the people of pain, which is rather remarkable. The narrator begins to speak of divine mercy without any hint of prior repentance. In this book Yahweh's actions will not typically be bound to any mechanical formula of blessing and or retribution, based upon what human beings earn by their actions. Rather he intervenes on Israel's behalf solely on the basis of his compassion; the scene of Israelite distress moves the divine patron to action.

2:17 Israel's response to Yahweh's agents is described in v. 17. But this verse is difficult because it interrupts the flow of thought and casts the rulers in the roles of spiritual reformers, preachers of the way in which their fathers walked in the commandments of Yahweh *(miṣwôt yhwh)*. Since there is no evidence of any of them functioning this way in the book, many delete this verse as a late insertion.[230] However, this resolves nothing, since a late editor would surely have recognized the dissonance the addition creates. It seems the author is looking back at the period of the governors/judges through the filter of the last governor, Samuel, who clearly functioned in this capacity.[231] The narrator is so exercised by Israel's response to Yahweh's overtures that he interrupts his own train of thought.

The response of the people to the rulers raised up by Yahweh is summarized in one simple sentence: "To rulers they refused to listen."[232] The following clause declares the grounds for this defiant disposition: "because they acted like a prostitute[233] [running] after other gods." This metaphor is

---

[228] On the meaning of this expression see the Introduction, pp. 21–24.

[229] The verb יָשַׁע, "to deliver, save," is adapted in 3:9,15 to describe the office of the שֹׁפֵט. He is מוֹשִׁיעַ, "a savior."

[230] W. Richter, *Die Bearbeitungen des "Retterbuches" in der deuteronomischen Epoche,* BBB 21 (Bonn: P. Hanstein, 1964). 34; Lindars, *Judges 1–5,* 98. But Boling (*Judges,* 76) treats the verse as the conclusion to the original form and vv. 18–19 as additions.

[231] See especially 1 Sam 7:2–6 but also 8:11–18; 10:18–19; 12:6–25; 13:13–14; 15:17–23.

[232] The word order and syntax v. 17a is emphatic: וְגַם אֶל־שֹׁפְטֵיהֶם לֹא שָׁמֵעוּ, "But to the rulers they would not listen." The use of the relatively rare stative form of the verb highlights the psychological state of the subject. Cf. *IBHS* §22.4.b.

[233] On the meaning of Hb. זָנָה see E. A. Goodfriend ("Prostitution [OT]," *ADB* 5.505–10), who suggests several reasons why Israel's spiritual infidelity is characterized as prostitution rather than adultery (נָאַף): (1) זנה implies iterative or habitual illicit behavior; (2) the motive is personal gain, not casual sex; (3) זנה implies a multiplicity of sex partners; (4) the participle זוֹנָה suggests a treacherous and hardened woman; (5) זנה refers only to illicit sex by a female partner.

employed with great rhetorical force by the prophets Hosea, Jeremiah, and Ezekiel, but it is inspired ultimately by Yahweh's warning to his people after the golden calf affair in Exod 34:15–16. There they were told to guard themselves against any covenants with the Canaanites or any tolerance of their gods once they arrive in the promised land, for Yahweh is a passionate *(qinʾâ)* God.[234] This is an appropriate figure of speech to describe Israel's behavior for two reasons. First, Yahweh's covenant relationship with Israel is commonly portrayed in marital terms. His jealousy/passion is kindled whenever his people flirt with other gods.[235] How much more so when they turn their backs on him and commit spiritual harlotry by attaching themselves to the gods of this land. Second, the gods competing with Yahweh for the allegiance of his people are lusty young fertility gods, who seduce the Israelites with promises of prosperity and security. Furthermore, in contrast to the lofty theology and the austere morality of Yahwism, the Canaanite religious system offered exciting and often erotic cult rituals.

Israel's enthusiasm in paying homage *(hištaḥăwâ)* to these forbidden deities is reflected in the haste with which they turn aside from the course *(derek)* traveled by their forebears. The fact that the expression *sārû mahēr,* "they turned aside quickly," occurs elsewhere only in connection with the classic example of apostasy (the golden calf affair in Exod 32:8 and Deut 9:12,16) reinforces our conclusion that this verse is inspired by Exodus 34. The proper course is described as "the way the fathers walked" and "obeying the commandments of the LORD." But like the previous generation, which fell into idolatrous sin within forty days of having accepted the privileges and obligations of Yahweh's covenant, this generation has been unable to resist the attractions of the prevailing religious system, even for a little while. It is as if they could hardly wait to get into the land so they could attach themselves to these exciting gods.

2:18–19 In vv. 18–19 the narrator elaborates on the gracious actions of Yahweh on behalf of his people and the people's ungrateful and treacherous response. The first clause of v. 18 is resumptive, necessitated by the interruption of the train of thought in v. 17.[236] The remainder of the verse describes the secret to the rulers' successes. They represented agents of the divine presence. Through them Yahweh delivered[237] his people from the enemies, into whose hands he himself had given/sold them, as long as the governor lived. The

---

[234] See also Deut 31:16.

[235] See especially Hos 4:12–14. For a study of the metaphor see P. Bird, "'To Play the Harlot': An Inquiry into an Old Testament Metaphor," in *Gender and Difference in Ancient Israel,* ed. P. L. Day (Minneapolis: Fortress, 1989), 75–94.

[236] On כִּי followed by frequentive perfects see *GBH* §166oN.

[237] The subject of וְהוֹשִׁיעָם is not clear: is it Yahweh or the judge? The overall tenor of the text, which highlights the initiative of Yahweh, supports the former.

motive clause that takes up the remainder of the verse offers the reason for Yahweh's response: He was moved to pity by the groaning of his people under the burden of the oppressors.

The people's experience at the hands of the enemies is described with two words, virtual synonyms. *lāḥaṣ,* which has been encountered earlier in 1:34, denotes fundamentally "to squeeze, to pressure"[238] but is frequently used in this book in a metaphorical sense of "to oppress, to put the pressure on,"[239] illustrated in 6:9 by the treatment of this people by the Egyptians. *dāḥaq* is a rare synonym, appearing elsewhere only in Joel 2:8, where it describes a crowd jostling for space.[240] Because of the pressure of the oppressors, the Israelites "groaned." The root *nʾq* is also rare in the Old Testament. Its sense is best reflected in Ezek 30:24, where the verb *nāʾaq* and its cognate noun *nĕʾāqâ* describe the paralinguistic utterances of a wounded man, in this instance Pharaoh, whose arms have been broken. The use of the word here provides a direct link with Exod 2:24, which identifies the groaning of the Israelite slaves in Egypt as the motivation for Yahweh's rescue.[241] As in that earlier context, there is nothing particularly spiritual about the Israelites' expressions of pain. The absence of any hint of repentance or any reference to the people's crying out to Yahweh[242] throws his compassion into even sharper relief.

Yahweh's response to the peoples' expressions of pain is described in a single word, *yinnāḥēm,* which represents the key to the entire book. Etymologically the word is related to Arabic *nahama,* "to breathe deeply," a sense which is still occasionally recognizable in the Old Testament.[243] In several instances the *niphal* denotes "to perform mourning rites"[244] or "to take comfort, to be encouraged."[245] It also often means "to regret" past actions,[246] or "to grieve, feel sorry for," as supposedly in the present context, which identifies the immediate cause of Yahweh's *niḥam* as the people's groaning.[247] However, the

---

[238] E.g., Num 22:25, of Balaam's donkey squeezing against the wall.

[239] 1:34; 4:3; 6:9; 10:12. Cf. also 1 Sam 10:18; etc.

[240] Many interpret this word as an Aramaism, but it is better understood as derived from a common Semitic root.

[241] Cf. also Exod 6:5 and Job 24:12.

[242] Unless one inserts "They cried out to the LORD" in v. 15, which many scholars do but for which there is no textual support.

[243] J. Scharbert (*Der Schmerz im Alten Testament,* BBB 8 [Bonn: P. Hanstein, 1955], 62–63) cites Ezek 14:22; 31:16; 32:31 (all *niphal*); Ezek 5:13; Isa 1:24; Gen 27:42; Ps 119:51 (all *hithpael*); Ezek 14:23; Gen 5:29; Isa 12:1; Pss 23:4; 86:17; Job 7:13 (all *piel*). On the word see further H. J. Stoebe, *THAT* 2.59–66; M. Butterworth, "נחם (*nḥm*)," *NIDOTTE* 3.81–83.

[244] Gen 38:12. L. Boadt (*Ezekiel's Oracles against Egypt: A Literary and Philological Study of Ezekiel 29–32,* BibOr 37 [Rome: Biblical Institute, 1980], 168) cites also Ps 23:4; Job 2:11.

[245] Ezek 14:22; 31:16; 32:31.

[246] As a virtual synonym of שׁוב, "to repent, turn around," as in Jer 4:28; 31:19; Jonah 3:9. In several instances God is the subject: Gen 6:6–7, God regrets he has made humankind; 1 Sam 15:11,35, he regrets he has made Saul king.

[247] מִנַּאֲקָתָם. On the use of מן to indicate the cause whence an effect derives see *GBH* §170i.

present text is sufficiently ambiguous to leave open the possibility that *yinnāḥĕm* should be rendered "he changed his mind." This interpretation becomes especially attractive when the present passage is compared with others in which Yahweh threatened a people with harm *(rāʿâ)*, but then, because of some alteration in the circumstances, he changed his mind *(niḥam)*.[248] Indeed, several texts suggest that "to repent concerning [threatened/real] calamity" *(niḥam ʿal/ʾel hārāʿâ)* is as fundamental to the divine nature as his grace *(ḥannûn)*, compassion *(raḥûm)*, slowness to anger *(ʾerek appayim)*, and abundant covenant love *(ḥesed)*.[249] Unlike humans and other gods, Yahweh is not capricious or whimsical. About certain things Yahweh will not change his mind (see Jer 4:28), but more importantly, his character is immutably consistent and absolutely trustworthy (Num 23:19; 1 Sam 15:29). But this does not mean his mind is fossilized or that he is incapable of changing the way in which he deals with human beings. From the texts cited Yahweh seems especially sensitive to the human experience of calamity *(rāʿâ)*, which is precisely what the present case involves. To be sure Yahweh is moved by the groaning of his people, but the verb *yinnāḥēm* looks back to v. 15, specifically the statement that "the hand of the LORD was upon them [Israel] for calamity *[rāʿâ]*," which is defined in v. 18 as the work of "those who oppressed and afflicted them." Accordingly this verse should be translated "the LORD was with the ruler and he [the LORD] rescued them from the hand of their enemies as long as the ruler lived, for he changed his mind [concerning the calamity] on account of their groaning because of those who oppressed and afflicted them."

Yahweh's provision of rulers who would throw off the yoke of the oppressors should have produced in the Israelites an overwhelming sense of gratitude for his grace. Even though the rulers functioned as agents of the divine presence, their accomplishments in the divine agenda were short-lived. As soon as these rulers would die, the Israelites would revert *(šûb)* to their old ways (v. 19). Indeed, the successive generations became increasingly degenerate,[250] expressing their depravity by pursuing other gods, serving them, and paying homage to them.[251] All three of these expressions are borrowed from v. 12. However, to express the downward spiralling of Israelite faith and conduct, the narrator adds a significant clause: they refused to drop[252] any of[253] their impi-

---

[248] Several different circumstances are attested: (1) when the threatened persons repent (Jer 18:8; 26:3,13,19; Jonah 3:9–10); (2) when an intercessor prays (Exod 32:12,14; Amos 7:3,6); (3) when Yahweh deems the extent of punishment sufficient (2 Sam 24:16); (4) when his people agree to the will of God (Jer 42:10).

[249] Joel 2:13; Jonah 4:2;

[250] הַשְׁחִית derives from a verb meaning "to go to ruin."

[251] On the use of *lamed* + infinitive construct to explain the nature of a preceding action see *IBHS* §36.2.3e.

[252] הִפִּילוּ is a *hiphil* form of נָפַל, "to fall."

[253] The מִן on מֵעַלְלֵיהֶם and וּמִדַּרְכָּם is partitive.

ous actions,[254] or their stubborn[255] ways.[256]

This verse is crucial for interpreting the following narratives. Israel is depicted as increasingly Canaanized, spiralling downward into worse and worse apostasy. Accordingly, while the author recognizes a cyclical pattern in Israel's premonarchic history, the common repetitive view of this period must be modified. Not only do the patterns of evil repeat themselves; the treacherous behavior of the Israelites intensifies, as illustrated in the following diagram:

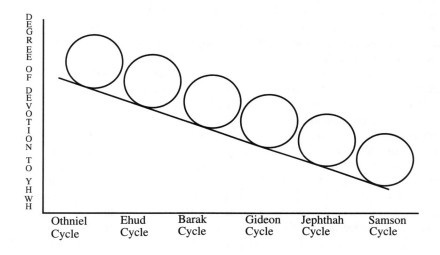

| Othniel Cycle | Ehud Cycle | Barak Cycle | Gideon Cycle | Jephthah Cycle | Samson Cycle |

The rulers raised by God represented stop-gap measures in an apparently irresistible, irreversible, and inevitable process of Canaanization. Instead of effecting fundamental repairs on this deteriorating dike, they plugged the holes with their fingers. As soon as the finger was removed, the water gushed through with increasing force.

The Kindling of the Divine Anger (2:20a). **2:20a** The first half of v. 20 brings the reader full circle by repeating v. 14 verbatim: the fury of Yahweh burned against Israel.

---

[254] מַעֲלָלִים, from a root עָלַל, "to act arbitrarily, independently, without restraint." The word occurs only here in Judges. For additional references see *HALOT,* 834; BDB, 760.

[255] The expression קָשָׁה, "stubborn" (Isa 48:4), is more familiar in the idiom עַם קְשֵׁה עֹרֶף, "a people stiff of neck." Exod 32:9; 33:3,5; 34:9; Deut 9:6,13. Cp. also קְשֵׁי פָנִים, "stiff of face" (Ezek 2:4), and קְשֵׁי לֵב, "Stiff of heart/mind" (Ezek 3:7).

[256] מַעֲלָל and דֶּרֶךְ are also paired in Jer 32:9. Cp. Ezekiel, who prefers the cognate form, עֲלִילָה, "unrestrained action," which he often pairs with דֶּרֶךְ: 14:22,23; 20:43; 24:14; 36:17,19.

(3) God's Interpretation (2:20b–22)

and said, "Because this nation has violated the covenant that I laid down for
their forefathers and has not listened to me, [21]I will no longer drive out before
them any of the nations Joshua left when he died. [22]I will use them to test Israel
and see whether they will keep the way of the LORD and walk in it as their forefathers did."

The narrator's exposition is interrupted briefly by a verbatim quotation of a
divine speech, which as already noted has significant links with the divine messenger's speech in vv. 1b–3. Like the earlier address, this too is a judgment
speech, but this one divides into three parts: the accusation (v. 20b),[257] the
divine reaction (v. 21), and the divine motive (v. 23).

GOD'S ACCUSATION (2:20B).   **2:20b**   Yahweh's complaint against his
people is summarized in two short statements. First, "this nation" has broken
his covenant *(hēpîr běrîtî)*, something Yahweh had said earlier he himself
would never do (v. 1). The reference to Israel as *haggôy hazzeh,* "this nation,"
expresses Yahweh's sense of alienation from his people. Occasions when the
expression *gôy,* "nation," applied to Israel are extremely rare in the Old Testament. When this occurs, it often (though not always) bears overtones of reprimand for the nation's infidelity to Yahweh and its characteristically negative
moral qualities.[258] In this context Yahweh expressly places his own people in a
category with the Canaanite nations, who are twice identified as *gôyim* in vv.
21 and 23 and specifically listed in 3:1–5. Second, they have not listened to
Yahweh's voice, which echoes a similar charge in v. 2.

GOD'S REACTION (2:21).   **2:21**   Yahweh's declaration of his disposition
toward Israel's perfidy opens emphatically: "Now I myself will no longer dispossess any of the nations Joshua left at the time of his death" (cf. v. 3). Instead
going before Israel to sweep away their enemies Yahweh places a moratorium
on his own involvement in the execution of the holy war against the Canaanites. As one examines the battles described in the book, this declaration is confirmed. None of the conflicts, not even the battle against the Canaanite king
(Jabin of Hazor in chaps. 4–5) involve conquest of new territory. Each battle is
concerned with throwing off the yoke of an oppressor.

GOD'S MOTIVE (2:22).   **2:22**   Unlike v. 3, where the messenger had
declared that the purpose/effect of the nations' continued presence in the land
would be to trap/snare the Israelites, here Yahweh's purpose is expressed as
probationary: to test the fidelity of his covenant people. The use of the verb
nāsâ recalls Gen 22:1, where God tests the faith of Abraham by asking him to
sacrifice his son, his only son, Isaac, whom he loved. The purpose of this test

---

[257] Beginning with יַעַן אֲשֶׁר, "Because."

[258] In contrast to עַם, "people," a warm, relational term, גּוֹי is cold, formal, and political. See
further Block, "Nations," *ISBE* 3.492–96.

is announced with equal clarity: Will Israel keep the way of Yahweh by following the course of his revealed will, like their forefathers had, or will they not?

(4) Conclusion (2:23)

[23]The LORD had allowed those nations to remain; he did not drive them out at once by giving them into the hands of Joshua.

2:23 In v. 23 the narrator's voice returns as he summarizes in prose the effect of Yahweh's response. His determination to test Israel was fulfilled. He did not passively permit the nations to remain in the land. The very same rest he had achieved for Israel under the leadership of Joshua he now granted to the Canaanites,[259] and other nations,[260] by not driving them out quickly.[261] The final statement in v. 23 reminds the reader that Yahweh is in complete control of Israel's destiny. If Joshua had not finished the task of driving out the enemy nations, it was because God had not delivered them into his hands. The reason was given in v. 22. Subsequent generations would not simply inherit the blessings, the rewards of a previous generation's faith. They needed to demonstrate their commitment to Yahweh themselves.

Theological and Practical Implications

By way of reflection, from this text the reader has learned the Israelite [Yahwist] definition of apostasy. Apostasy means abandoning Yahweh in favor of other gods; it means claiming to be the people of Yahweh while acting as if one belongs to Baal. This perfidy is expressed in transgressing Yahweh's covenant, not walking in his way, not listening to his voice, not heeding his commandments, especially his call for exclusive allegiance. Unlike the gods of the surrounding nations, Yahweh would tolerate no rivals. There is no room in Yahwistic faith for accommodation to pagan notions or customs. At the same time the reader is reminded of the patience and grace of Yahweh.

This chapter contains no hint of repentance. The word *šûb* occurs only once (v. 19), where it denotes turning from the way of Yahweh to paganism. On the contrary, Israel gets caught in a rut of apostasy that gets deeper with every turn. The patterns of Israel's and Yahweh's experiences may be juxtaposed and compared as follows:

---

[259] וַיָּנַח יְהוָה אֶת־הַגּוֹיִם הָאֵלֶּה, "And he gave these nations rest," echoes Joshua 21:44, וַיָּנַח יְהוָה לָהֶם מִסָּבִיב, "And he gave them rest on every side." Cf. also 23:1. The NIV's "The LORD did not allow those nations to remain" is too passive.

[260] See below on 3:1–3.

[261] As in v. 19 the *lamed* + infinitive construct construction is explanatory.

The Pattern of Israel's
Experience during the
Premonarchic Period

The Pattern of Yahweh's
Reaction during the
Premonarchic Period

Apostasy

Deliverance   Oppression

Groaning

Anger

Deliverance   Punishment

Change of Mind

3. The Domestic Consequences of Israel's Performance (3:1–6)

Because of the complex nature of this segment, scholars have developed elaborate, if speculative, reconstructions of the history/evolution of the text.[262] In the process the relationship of this passage to the preceding is often missed.[263] Structurally the text is dominated by two circumstantial clauses, vv. 1–3 and 5–6, which frame the purpose statement in v. 4. Because of the length and weight of the frame statements, the significance of v. 4 may be overlooked. Beginning with the *waw*-consecutive imperfect verb plus purpose infinitive construct *(wayyihyû lĕnassôt . . . lādaʿat . . .* , lit., "and they became tests ... to know ..."), this verse indicates that this paragraph is intended as an exposition of 2:23. The verse may at one point have followed immediately after 2:23, but it has been separated from that context and wrapped with two circumstantial clauses that transform and expand its significance.[264]

Thematically this paragraph ties together a series of ends that have been raised in the preceding chapters: (1) the notion of testing *(nāsâ,* vv. 1,4) picks up an element from 2:22; (2) with the exception of the Hivites, the list of Canaanite nations in v. 5 echoes nations named in chap. 1; (3) the reference to Israel "living among" *(yāšab bĕqereb)* the Canaanites (v. 5) recalls 1:32,33; (4) the reference to "obeying" *(šāmaʿ)* the commands of Yahweh recall the accusations of 2:3b,17); (5) the mention of the commandments of Yahweh *(miṣwōt yhwh)* in v. 4 links with 2:17b; (6) the reference to commandments given by Yahweh to the fathers *(ʾābôt)* in v. 4 recalls "the covenant which I commanded the fathers" in 2:20b, as well as the promise sworn to the fathers

---

[262] See Lindars, *Judges 1–5,* 112–13; Richter, *Bearbeitung des 'Retterbuches',* 38–40.

[263] So also Sweeney, "Davidic Polemics in the Book of Judges," 522–24.

[264] 3:4 is to 2:23 as fulfillment is to promise. Similar patterns are evident in 2:14a (Yahweh gave them over to plunderers; so they plundered them), 2:14b (He sold them to their enemies; so they could not stand), and 2:23 (He gave the nations rest; so he did not give them over to Joshua).

in 2:1, and the notice of the fathers' fidelity in 2:22; (7) the charge of "serving their gods" in v. 6 offers an abbreviated version of 2:11–13. Despite these connections, however, the addition of new ideas and the structure of this paragraph have resulted in a distinctive literary piece.

Obviously the principal function of this paragraph is to elaborate on the test announced in 2:22. In describing the test and announcing Israel's dismal failure the narrator explores the depth of Israelite depravity. The consequences of their failure to pursue the holy war have extended into the very homes and the faith of the people. In making this statement the narrator reiterates the justice of God in sending in enemy nations against the Israelites, and sets a backdrop for his gracious acts of deliverance from the enemies as described in succeeding chapters.

(1) The Nature of the Test (3:1–3)

[1]These are the nations the LORD left to test all those Israelites who had not experienced any of the wars in Canaan [2](he did this only to teach warfare to the descendants of the Israelites who had not had previous battle experience): [3]the five rulers of the Philistines, all the Canaanites, the Sidonians, and the Hivites living in the Lebanon mountains from Mount Baal Hermon to Lebo Hamath.

As already noted, the opening sentence of this paragraph finally breaks the sequence of *waw*-consecutives that had extended through chaps. 1 and 2. *wĕʾēlleh haggôyim*, "and these are the nations …" is constructed as[265] a formal title, inviting the reader to expect a listing of the agents appointed by God to test his people. The text does not disappoint, but before it gets to the issue, the reader is led on a long detour intended to fix more precisely the context in which the test was administered.

3:1–2 Whereas 2:20–22 has identified the subjects being tested in general terms as "this nation" and "Israel," vv. 1b–2 offer a lengthy parenthetical qualification beginning with "all who had not experienced the battles of Canaan." The expression *milḥămôt kĕnāʿan*, "the battles of Canaan," occurs only here in the Old Testament[266] and functions as a technical term for Israel's holy war in and for the land of Canaan. This comment reinforces earlier statements that Israel's spiritual problems began after the death of Joshua and the generation that had witnessed the mighty works of Yahweh (2:7,10). Verse 2 offers an emphatic elaboration on this issue.[267] When Yahweh expresses his determina-

---

[265] Cp. the form with similar titles elsewhere: Gen 10:1; 11:27; 25:7; Exod 1:1; 6:16; 21:1; 28:4; Num 1:5; Josh 12:1,7; etc.

[266] The nearest equivalent is מִלְחֲמֹת יְהוה, "the battles of the LORD," which refers to the battles Yahweh fights (Num 21:14) or which one fights in Yahweh's name (1 Sam 18:17; 25:28).

[267] The verse consists of two main clauses, each introduced by the emphatic restrictive particle רַק, "only," on which see *IBHS* §38.3.5; T. Muraoka, *Emphatic Words and Structures in Biblical Hebrew* (Leiden: Brill, 1985), 130–32. לְמַעַן is followed by the infinitive construct, דַּעַת. It is omitted in the LXX and looks like a dittographic scribal error before דֹּרוֹת.

tion that the present generation of Israelites should learn[268] war, his concern is not primarily that they learn how to conduct war[269] but that they learn the nature and significance of this war. They have entered the land as Yahweh's covenant people with the mandate to drive out the Canaanites and to claim it as his gift to them. The continued presence of the Canaanites represents a test whether or not they will accept Yahweh as their sovereign and their responsibilities in fulfilling his agenda. In accordance with earlier pronouncements (Deut 7:1–5), Yahweh will not do for Israel what they are not willing to do for themselves. The Canaanite nations represent not only a challenge to him and his historical program, but they also remain as a test, proving whether or not Israel will accept her status as his covenant people, with all the privileges and obligations attached thereto. This generation needs to learn that they have been called to a holy war, that Yahweh is the commander-in-chief, and that the enemy is to be totally exterminated.

3:3 Following the lengthy interruption created by vv. 1b– 2, v. 3 fulfills the promise created by the opening title: "These are the nations the LORD left, by which to test Israel."[270] Four agents of testing are listed: the five Philistine lords, all the Canaanites, the Sidonians, and the Hivites. This list is surprising for several reasons.

First, it differs markedly from the nations listed in chap. 1 and other stereotypical lists of Canaanite tribes in the Old Testament.[271]

Second, it includes the Philistines, who were not native to Canaan. The name *pĕlištîm*[272] identifies one of several groups of Sea Peoples who swept into Palestine from Anatolia and the Mediterranean in the twelfth to eleventh centuries B.C., leaving in their wake a trail of ruins. Biblical tradition traces their origins to Crete.[273] It seems their original goal was to settle in Egypt, but

---

[268] The notion is expressed by two verbs. The first, לְלַמְּדָם, "to teach them," looks at the issue from the perspective of the divine Instructor; the second, לֹא יָדְעוּם, "they have not learned [them]," assumes the point of view of the learner. The final *mem* on the verb may be explained either as an enclitic *mem* (so *BHS*) or a masculine plural suffix, the antecedent being the "battles of Canaan" in v. 1. The inconsistency of gender is obvious (מִלְחֲמוֹת is feminine), but we should be cautious about imposing modern standards of consistency upon an ancient text. On the weakening of gender distinctions, especially the use of masculine plural suffixes with feminine antecedents, see GKC §135.

[269] Cf. Isa 2:4; Mic 4:3.

[270] The NIV's rendering of וְאֵלֶּה הַגּוֹיִם אֲשֶׁר הִנִּיחַ יְהוָה לְנַסּוֹת בָּם אֶת־יִשְׂרָאֵל is paraphrastic.

[271] The supplementary list in v. 5 is more familiar, variations of which occur eighteen times. See especially Deut 7:1.

[272] Cf. Egyptian *P-r-š-t-w*. The modern geographic designation of the ancient land of Canaan, Palestine, derives from this group that occupied the southwestern coastal and Shephelah region rather than either the original inhabitants or the Israelites.

[273] Biblical Caphtor. See Gen 10:13–14; Amos 9:7; Jer 47:4. Num 24:24 may allude to the first waves of Sea Peoples arriving from Kittim (Cyprus).

Rameses III was able to defeat them in about 1190 B.C. He settled the vanquished forces in the coastal towns of southern Canaan, but in the mid-twelfth century the Philistines succeeded in driving out their Egyptian overlords, forming the Philistine Pentapolis, a federation of five major city-states: Ashdod, Ashkelon, Ekron, Gath, Gaza. The identification of their rulers here and elsewhere as *sĕrānîm* suggests these cities had distinctively Philistine political structures, different from both the tribal structures of Israel and the city-states of the Canaanites.[274] In contrast to the latter, faced with a numerically overwhelming native population, the ethnically distinct Philistines appear to have valued cooperation over competition.[275] The presence of the Philistines in this list accords chronologically with earlier statements that Israel's problems with apostasy set in after the death of Joshua. In so doing it also reflects a period later than 1:17–18 and 34–36, which still have Canaanites in the cities that eventually made up the Philistine Pentapolis and the Amorites in the land allotted to Dan.

Third, the reference to "all the Canaanites" suggests that this term applies to all the inhabitants of Palestine in general, inclusive of some of the tribes mentioned in other lists.

Fourth, like the Philistines, the Sidonians, who were mentioned earlier in 1:31, do not figure in the stereotypical lists. The name probably functions generally for the Phoenicians, who in still later times represented the remnant of the original Canaanite population.

Fifth, the author locates the Hivites in the regions north of the Sea of Galilee, in the Lebanon mountains, west of a line running from Mount Baal Hermon to Lebo-Hamath. The former name abbreviates "Baal-gad in the valley of Lebanon at the foot of Mount Hermon" in Josh 11:17.[276] Some render the latter *lĕbôʾ ḥămat*, "the Pass of Hamath,"[277] but it is more likely to be identified with a specific place, modern Lebweh, near the spring of Nabaʿ Labweh, one of the principal sources of the Orontes River in the Beqaʿ,[278] some forty-five miles north of Damascus. The name appears as Lab'u in the Egyptian texts and

---

[274] Cf. Josh 13:3. The etymology of סְרָנִים, which always appears in the plural, remains uncertain. M. Ellenbogen (*Foreign Words in the Old Testament: Their Origin and Etymology* [London: Luzac, 1962], 126–27) proposes a derivation from a root *ser*. Others relate it to Gk. τύραννος (cf. "tyrants," though the LXX reads σατράπείας, "divisions") or *tarwanas*, a designation for neo-Hittite rulers of Asia Minor. See further K. Kitchen, "The Philistines," *POTT* 67, and n. 110; G. H. Johnstone, "סֶרֶן (*seren*)," *NIDOTTE* 3.295–98. Only one Philistine ruler, Achish, is named in the OT, but he is identified as מֶלֶךְ, "king," of Gath.

[275] In addition to Kitchen's article on the Philistines, see T. Dothan, *The Philistines and Their Material Culture* (New Haven: Yale University Press, 1982); T. Dothan and M. Dothan, *People of the Sea: The Search for the Philistines* (New York: Macmillan, 1992).

[276] בַּעַל־גָּד בְּבִקְעַת הַלְּבָנוֹן תַּחַת הַר־חֶרְמוֹן.

[277] JB; cf. J. Gray, *I and II Kings*, rev. ed., OTL (Philadelphia: Westminster, 1970), 615.

[278] Cf. B. Mazar, *Cities and Districts in Eretz Israel* (Jerusalem: Mosad Bialik, 1975), 167–81.

Laba'ûc in Assyrian inscriptions.[279] In later times Lebo-Hamath constituted the northern border of Solomon's kingdom (1 Kgs 8:65) and of Jeroboam II's Northern Kingdom of Israel (2 Kgs 14:25).

In reflecting on the significance of the names in this list, several observations may be made. First, as already intimated, this list of "nations" that Yahweh gives rest in the land obviously goes beyond Deut 7:1–5 and other standard lists of the inhabitants of Canaan. Second, the inclusion of the Philistines reflects the author's theology of history. Like the prophet Amos (9:7) he recognizes that their migration and arrival in this land have been directed by Yahweh. Yahweh has given them rest *(hinnîah)* in the land set aside for his own people. Third, viewed as a whole, this list demonstrates the author's geographic sense. As the following schematized map of the land of Canaan illustrates, these four names have the entire land of Canaan covered: southwest (Philistines), northwest (Sidonians), northeast (Hivites), southeast (Canaanites). Since the spiritual crisis in Israel encompasses the entire nation, it is appropriate that all of the tribal territories be included in Yahweh's test.

(2) The Purpose of the Test (3:4)

⁴They were left to test the Israelites to see whether they would obey the LORD's commands, which he had given their forefathers through Moses.

3:4 In addition to the didactic function specified in v. 2, v. 4 reiterates that Yahweh's aim in not clearing the land of Canaan of its inhabitants is probationary. His purpose is reflected in two infinitives: "to test *(lenassôt)* Israel through them"[280] and "to determine" *(ladaʿat)* whether or not they would express allegiance to Yahweh by obedience to the Mosaic revelation. Of course this test is not for the benefit of Yahweh so he can tell whether or not Israel is faithful. He sees all things. The test is for Israel, to give them an objective instrument that would declare to them the depths of their infidelity and the justice of God. The content of the latter is expressed in the form of a question, literally, "Will they obey the LORD's commands which he gave their ancestors by the hand of Moses?" This question assumes not only the existence of the historical person Moses but also familiarity with the divine revelation transmitted by this man. We have no clear indication of the form in which that revelation was preserved, either at the time of these events or at the time of writing, but one may assume some version of the present Pentateuch, particularly the Sinai ordinances and the Book of Deuteronomy, which contain respectively the terms of the covenant and the exposition of

---

[279] Cf. S. Ahituv, *Canaanite Toponyms in Ancient Egyptian Documents* (Jerusalem: Magnes, 1984), 131; Aharoni, *Land of the Bible*, 72–73.
[280] Hb. בָּם. On the agentive use of *beth* see *IBHS* §11.2.5d.

the same. Here the test is broadened beyond the mandate to drive out the Canaanites to obedience to all the commandments Yahweh gave the ancestors through Moses.

(3) The Results of the Test (3:5–6)

⁵The Israelites lived among the Canaanites, Hittites, Amorites, Perizzites, Hivites and Jebusites. ⁶They took their daughters in marriage and gave their own daughters to their sons, and served their gods.

3:5–6 Verses 5–6 function as a report card, expressing the narrator's (and Yahweh's) evaluation of Israel's performance in this divinely administered examination. The verdict is clear: Israel has failed! In keeping with traditional Israelite laws of evidence, her failure is attested on three counts, each of which reflects a dimension of accommodation to the Canaanites.

First, the descendants of Israel have settled down in the midst of *(yašab beqereb)* the native population. The expression is familiar from chap. 1, but to demonstrate the scope of this failure, the author lists six of the Canaanite tribes among whom they had taken up residence. Of the nations listed in Deut 7:1 only the Girgashites are missing. In other words, wherever the Israelites went, they failed the test. In general, the remainder of the book reveals a people in tension with outsiders, but these outsiders for the most part (chap. 4 is an exception) are not Canaanites, who would have chafed under their domination as well. These enemies are external agents of divine discipline upon Israel. The most telling illustration of accommodation and comfort in coresidency with non-Israelites is provided by the Judahites. In chap. 15, annoyed with Samson because he has disturbed the status quo with the Philistines, they are willing to sacrifice their own countryman to maintain their peaceful coexistence.

Second, they intermarried with the Canaanites, in direct violation of Deut 7:3–4.[281] The purpose and effects of intermarriage are clearly described in Gen 34:16: through intermarriage distinct peoples become one people *(ʿam)*. In general interpreters have underestimated the significance of this comment for the remainder of the book. As a reader proceeds through the book, however, the evidences of this problem increase. Gideon, who has a Shechemite concubine, has a son, Abimelech, who is as Canaanized as can be imagined (8:29–9:57). Gilead's cohabitation with a prostitute (11:1) produces Jephthah, who, in typical Canaanite fashion offers his daughter as a sacrifice. Samson represents the ultimate embodiment of this problem. He marries a Philistine, and when this fails, he resorts to Philistine prostitutes (chaps. 14–16). In the narrator's mind

---

[281] The Hb. idiom for marriage is לָקַח בַּת לוֹ לְאִשָּׁה, "to take a daughter for himself for a wife."

this domestic pattern represents further evidence of Israel's failure. Third, in clear violation of the first principle of the covenant, they served other gods. Moses' warning in Deut 7:4–5 had proved true. This idolatry is often referred to in general terms in the preambles to the deliverer cycles, but Joash's cult installation (6:25–32), Gideon's ephod (8:27), and the affairs of Micah and the Danites (chaps. 17–18) are presented as concrete examples.

Theological and Practical Implications

In these two verses the narrator announces the theme of the book: the Canaanization of Israelite society. Territorial accommodation had resulted in ethnic integration, which has yielded spiritual integration. In the mind of the author, the newcomers, who entered the land as a distinct people, vassals of Yahweh, have sold out. The subsequent narratives must all be interpreted in this light. Israel has failed; she rightfully stands under the judgment of God. When the narrator begins to recount the sociopolitical crises the nation experiences, the reader should not feel sorry for this people. They have it coming, and more. And in the pattern of Israelite behavior expressed by the three verbs of vv. 5–6, the modern reader should hear a warning for his or her own life: residing with, marrying, serving. Peaceful coexistence with the world leads to cohabitation and alliance with the world, which in turn leads to taking on the religious notions of the world. This is the rule; occasions when the influence is in the reverse direction are the exception.

To return to the text, for this reason the reader may justifiably be surprised when Yahweh intervenes on Israel's behalf. If this nation emerges at the end of this period with any sort of national self-consciousness and any sense of significance in history, it is due to no credit of their own. It is attributable entirely to the gracious heart of their covenant Sovereign. He deals mercifully with them, not because they deserve it in any way but because of his long-range mission of mercy for the world. He has chosen this nation to be the instrument of blessing, and he cannot let her die or disappear among the conglomerate populations of the ancient Near East. At times the nation appears determined to destroy itself, but each time he rescues her.

II. GOD'S RESPONSE TO THE CANAANIZATION OF ISRAEL:
THE CYCLES OF APOSTASY AND DELIVERANCE (3:7–16:31)
1. The Aram-Naharaim and Othniel Cycle (3:7–11)
   (1) The Marks of Israel's Canaanization (3:7)
   (2) God's Agent of Punishment (3:8)
   (3) Israel's Response to the Oppression (3:9a)
   (4) God's Agent of Deliverance (3:9b–10a)
   (5) God's Gift of Deliverance (3:10b)
   (6) God's Gift of Security (3:11)
2. The Moab and Ehud Cycle (3:12–30)
   (1) The Marks of Israel's Canaanization (3:12a)
   (2) God's Agent of Punishment (3:12b–14)
   (3) Israel's Response to the Oppression (3:15a)
   (4) God's Agent of Deliverance (3:15b)
   (5) God's Gift of Deliverance (3:16–29)
   (6) God's Gift of Security (3:30)
3. Parenthesis 1: The Governorship of Shamgar (3:31)]
4. The Canaanite and Barak Cycle (4:1–5:31)
   (1) The Narrative Description (4:1–24)
      The Marks of Israel's Canaanization (4:1)
      God's Agent of Punishment (4:2)
      Israel's Response to the Oppression (4:3)
      God's Agent of Deliverance (4:4–10)
      God's Gift of Deliverance (4:11–22)
      God's Gift of Security (4:23–24)
   (2) The Poetic Celebration (5:1–31)
5. The Midianite and Gideon Cycle (6:1–9:57)
   (1) God's Punishment and Deliverance of Israel (6:1–8:3)
      The Marks of Israel's Canaanization (6:1a)
      God's Agent of Punishment (6:1b–6a)
      Israel's Response to the Oppression (6:6b)
      God's Agent of Deliverance (6:7–32)
      God's Gift of Deliverance (6:33–8:3)
   (2) Gideon's Punishment and Subjugation of Israel (8:4–28)
      Gideon's Capture of Zebah and Zalmunna (8:4–21)
      Gideon's Sham Rejection of Kingship (8:22–27)
      God's Gift of Security (8:28)
   (3) The Legacy of Gideon (8:29–9:57)

143

II. GOD'S RESPONSE TO THE CANAANIZATION OF ISRAEL (3:7–16:31)

As mentioned earlier, the main body of the book, the "Book of Deliverers," develops the themes announced in 2:6–3:6. The selection of materials, the organization of the accounts, and the shaping of the narratives combine to reveal an intentional authorial design and goal. Before we consider the accounts in order, several synthetic observations may be made.

First, although the author is aware of other events that happened during this period,[1] he has selected historical memories that develop the thesis announced in 2:6–3:6, namely, the Canaanization of Israelite spirituality and morality during the period of the governors.

Second, the author deliberately notes seven examples of oppression and deliverance.[2] This sevenfold scheme contributes to the impression of totality in the nation's degeneration and suggests that the author viewed the disasters of this period as literal fulfillments of the covenant curses in Leviticus 26.[3]

Third, the order in which the narratives are arranged is not chronological but rhetorical and logical, reflecting the downward spiraling of the Israelite condition during this period. This is evident not only in the author's characterization of the people but especially in the portraits he paints of the respective rulers.

Fourth, rather than being randomly arranged or inserted, the "secondary" rulers appear to be strategically cited so that the entire picture of twelve rulers and their respective tribes corresponds to the cycle of the solar year, beginning with Othniel (Judah) in early winter and ending with Samson in late autumn.[4]

---

[1] Cf. the brief notes on the secondary (in relation to his agenda) judges in 10:1–5 and 12:8–15.

[2] The quota is achieved artificially by adding the Shamgar note, which does not otherwise follow the pattern of narratives noted below.

[3] The number seven occurs four times in Leviticus 26: (1) "I will punish you for your sins seven times" (v. 18); (2) "I will multiply your afflictions seven times over, as your sins deserve" (v. 21); (3) I myself will be hostile toward you and will afflict you for your sins seven times over" (v. 24); (4) "I myself will punish you for your sins seven times over" (v. 28). Cp. Deut 28:25.

[4] For a detailed development of this scheme see J. G. Williams, "The Structure of Judges 2:6–16:31," *JSOT* 49 (1991): 77–85. Williams finds the calendrical anchors in the Deborah-Barak cycle, which has links with Passover and the exodus (i.e., early spring); the Gideon cycle, which bears many allusions to the Sinai experiences; the Jephthah cycle, which relates to the desert wanderings and the early phases of the conquest. Once these are in place, the names of the rulers and their tribes fall into place according to the four seasonal quadrants; winter: Othniel (Judah), Ehud (Benjamin), Shamgar (Simeon); spring: Barak (Naphtali), Gideon (Manasseh), Tola (Issachar); summer: Jair (Gad), Jephthah (Reuben), Ibzan (Asher); autumn: Elon (Zebulun), Abdon (Ephraim), Samson (Dan). Williams cites numerous other features that create the impression of intentional unitary design. Although some of his observations are forced, the overall thesis of a "subtly and ingeniously coherent work" (p. 85) is preferable to those analytical approaches that involve and/or result in the fragmentation of these texts.

Fifth, the structures of the narratives follow a basic paradigm, the essential features of which have already been introduced in 2:11–23.[5] The nature of these elements and their occurrences in the respective accounts may be graphically portrayed as in the following table. Although the basic pattern is discernible in most of the accounts (the Shamgar cycle is a notable exception), the formulaic elements are most faithfully represented in the earlier cycles.

Structural and Formulaic Elements in the "Book of Deliverers"

Formulaic Element[a]	Othniel	Ehud	Shamgar	Barak	Gideon	Jephthah	Samson
"The sons of Israel did evil in the sight of the LORD." (2:11–13)	✔	✔		✔	✔	✔	✔
"The LORD gave/sold them into the hands of [ON]."[b] (2:14)	✔	✔		✔	✔	✔	✔
"The sons of Israel cried out to the LORD." (2:15b,18b)	✔	✔		✔	✔	✔	
"The LORD raised up a deliverer." (2:16,18a)	✔	✔					
"The LORD gave [ON] into the hands of the deliverer." (2:18a)	✔	✔					

---

[5] See the detailed discussion by R. H. O'Connell, *The Rhetoric of the Book of Judges*, VTSup 63 (Leiden: Brill, 1996), 19–57.

Structural and Formulaic Elements in the "Book of Deliverers"

Formulaic Element[a]	Othniel	Ehud	Shamgar	Barak	Gideon	Jephthah	Samson
"The land had rest for *[X]* years."	✔	✔		✔	✔		

a. The formulae vary in length and complexity.
b. ON = oppressor's name.

The breakdown of the structures of the accounts is a rhetorical device, paralleling the general moral and spiritual disintegration of the nation.[6]

Sixth, the narratives are dominated by a series of formulae, which contribute to the stylistic cohesiveness of the entire section. Each of these deserves a brief comment.[7]

The Negative Evaluation Formula: "The Israelites did evil in the eyes of the LORD" (2:11). This formula, which reflects the profound influence of Deuteronomy on the author,[8] occurs six times at the beginning of narrative cycles (3:7,12; 4:1; 6:1; 10:6; 13:1). Indeed, as has been suggested earlier, the author interprets all of Israel's premonarchic experiences through the theological lens created by Moses in Deuteronomy.

The Divine Committal Formula: "The LORD gave/sold the Israelites into the hands of the enemy" (2:14). This formula also occurs six times in the narratives and is generally expressive of Yahweh's wrath given by the formula above.[9] The verbs "to give" *(nātan)* and "to sell" *(mākar)* are both commercial expressions used of transferring ownership of property, including cattle and slaves, which makes this expression, with Yahweh as the subject, all the more remarkable. Yahweh does to Israel what they are forbidden from doing to each other (Lev 25:42,55). Accordingly, this action fulfills Yahweh's warning

---

[6] Cf. J. C. Exum, "The Centre Cannot Hold: Thematic and Textual Instabilities in the Book of Judges," *CBQ* 52 (1990): 410–31; T. Butler, "Daily Meditations in the Book or In One's Own Eyes: Reverse Structures in Joshua and Judges," unpublished paper presented to the Evangelical Theological Society, November 1996.

[7] Cf. the discussion by U. Becker, *Richterzeit und Königtum: Redaktionsgeschichtliche Studien zum Richterbuch*, BZAW 192 (Berlin/New York: de Gruyter, 1990), 86–88, and Lindars, *Judges 1– 5*, 100–101.

[8] Cf. Deut 4:25; 9:18; 17:2; 31:29 (though the formula does appear earlier in Num 32:13). The same influence is evident in the later books of 1, 2 Kings, where the phrase occurs more than forty times.

[9] The milder form, בְּיַד נָתַן, "to give into the hands of," occurs in 1:2; 2:14a,23; 3:10,28; 4:7,14; 6:1; 7:7,9,15; 8:3,7; 9:29; 11:30,32; 12:3; 13:1; 15:12; 18:10; 20:28; the more intense form, בְּיַד מָכַר, "to sell into the hands of," in 2:14b; 3:8; 4:2,9; 10:7. Cf. also בְּיַד נָפַל, "to fall into the hands of," a more passive expression (15:18).

expressed in Israel's "national anthem," in Deut 32:30.

The Cry of Distress Formula: "The Israelites cried out to the LORD." The formula occurs five times (3:9,15; 4:3; 6:6; 10:10), in each instance describing the Israelite response to the heavy hand of the enemy into whose hand Yahweh had sold them. Fundamentally the verb *zāʿaq* or its alternate spelling *ṣāʿaq* expresses not repentance for sin but the anguish of a person in a distressing situation in need of deliverance. Sometimes it is simply a cry of pain,[10] but usually it is expressly directed to one who it is hoped will rescue the person,[11] especially God. In Judges the latter is always the case. In fact, in 10:14, when the descendants of Israel "cried out" to Yahweh, he retorted sarcastically, "Go and cry out *(zāʿaq)* to the gods you have chosen. Let them save *(hôšîaʿ)* you when you are in trouble *(ṣārâ)*."[12]

The Divine Provision of Leadership Formula: "The LORD raised up a deliverer for Israel to save them" (2:16,18). This formula, which occurs only twice in the narratives (3:9,15), highlights God's activity in resolving the crises. Elsewhere, with the *lamed*, "for," it is used of Yahweh's raising up the Davidic king (Jer 30:9; cf. 23:5), prophets (Deut 18:15,18), and the priest (1 Sam 2:35). The formula reflects the theocratic nature of Israel's constitution. As patron deity, it is Yahweh's responsibility/prerogative to provide the nation with leaders.

The Subjugation Formula: "And [oppressing nation] was made subject to Israel." In 4:23 God is explicitly credited with the action; in 3:30 and 8:28 this is implied by the [divine] passives. In either case the credit is deflected from Israel or her ruler.

The Tranquility Formula: "Then the land had peace for *X* years." The meaning of the verb *šāqaṭ* is illustrated in 18:7,27, which describes Laish as a city *šōqēṭ ûbōṭēaḥ*, "tranquil and secure."[13]

The Death Formula: "And [the ruler] died" (2:19).[14] Although in the preamble (2:19) the formula highlights the tenuous nature of Israel's fidelity to Yahweh during a ruler's tenure, the four occurrences of variations of the formula in the narratives (3:11; 4:1b; 8:28; 12:7) emphasize the tenuous nature of Israel's tranquility.

These features and/or formulae are not present in every narrative cycle. The Shamgar cycle (3:31) is in a category of its own, not conforming in any respects to the paradigm set forth in the preamble nor followed in the rest of

---

[10] Cf. Gen 18:20; Exod 2:28; 1 Sam 9:16, which Yahweh happens to hear.

[11] A king, e.g., as in 1 Kgs 20:39 and 2 Kgs 6:26.

[12] Although the preamble omits any reference to the "cry" of distress, it does note the intensity of the distress the Israelites experienced (2:15,18b).

[13] Cf. Ezek 38:11, of the land of Israel prior to Gog's attack.

[14] The iterative nature of 2:19 calls for a temporal clause. Elsewhere the simpler וַיָּמָת + PN (personal name of the ruler) occurs.

the narrative accounts. As we will see, this is deliberate. As for the remaining six, remarkably the first (3:7–11), which is described with the greatest economy of words, is the most complete. Thereafter the structure gradually disintegrates, so that by the time the reader reaches the Samson account, the skeletal elements are barely visible. This too must be regarded as intentional. The progressive disintegration of the literary form reflects what is happening in Israel as a whole. Ironically, as we witness the deterioration in the nation's condition, we also witness an increase in the divine involvement in the individuals' lives.

In short, with the exception of the first, in each cycle the author will select some aspect of the paradigm for fuller elaboration: the nature of the oppression, the manner in which the deliverer is raised up, the way in which the deliverance is achieved, the ruler's subsequent activity, the legacy of the ruler. In this way the narrator enhances the literary quality of the overall work by giving depth and texture to the plots and also heightens reader interest with numerous surprising turns. With these preliminary general comments made, we may now assess the separate accounts in turn, attempting in each case to follow the same outline. In keeping with the narrator's aims to expose the Canaanization of Israel on the one hand and to bring glory to God on the other, our outlines look at the crises in Israel's experience in general and the cycles of oppression and deliverance from Yahweh's point of view.

1. The Aram-Naharaim and Othniel Cycle (3:7–11)

The series of oppression and deliverance accounts opens with the simplest case of all. Indeed, this account is so skeletal as to be almost banal, leaving in the mind of the reader several unanswered questions: Which tribe[s] was[were] involved in the apostasy and therefore affected by the oppression? Where are the altars and images of the Baals and the Asheroth located? From where does this mysterious Cushan-Rishathaim come? How does he oppress Israel? Where/how do the Israelites cry out to Yahweh? How/why does God raise up Othniel? What effect does the Spirit of Yahweh have on him? How does Othniel win the victory? Only one thing is clear—the identity of the deliverer, but even this knowledge is dependent on earlier information (1:11–15). Obviously the narrator's intention here is not to enable the reader to reconstruct in his/her mind the historical events. This brief account functions as a paradigmatic model against which the rest must be interpreted. Similarly, Othniel is presented as a paradigmatic leader. Many have noted that the narrator writes nothing negative about this man. This is intentional. The prologue has prepared the reader to expect a progressive degeneration in the moral and spiritual fiber of the nation. As the embodiment of the people, the leaders whom Yahweh raises in the nation's defense exhibit the same pattern.[15]

Although many issues are left hanging, the narrator modifies several notions that had been introduced in the prologue with new vocabulary or detail: the Israelites "forgot the LORD their God"; they served the Baals and the Asherahs; Othniel is identified as a *môšîaᶜ,* "deliverer," rather than a *šōpēṭ,* "ruler"; Othniel is said to have "governed" *(šāpaṭ)* Israel; the Spirit of Yahweh came upon the deliverer. Also missing from the preamble are the cry of distress formula and any references to how long the land had rest after any of the successive rulers' tenures. Obviously the author did not intend for the prologue, particularly 2:11–23, to serve as an exhaustive introduction to the formulae he will use in the narratives. Nor did he feel bound by the preamble in the development of the narratives. On the contrary, in each of the six major narrative cycles[16] he will introduce fresh ideas and formulae. In 3:7–11, which functions as the paradigmatic (as opposed to theoretical, cf. 2:6–3:6) introduction, these details are kept to a minimum.

Even so the reader may recognize the logic in the author's commencement of the series with this cycle. Chronologically Othniel represents the generation that replaced those Israelites who had first entered the land of Canaan. Accordingly, at this early stage his response to Yahweh's call gives no evidence of personal Canaanization. Ethnically, Othniel is a foreigner, a Kenizzite, but in the parade of deliverers he represents Judah. By beginning with him the narrative reflects the early primacy of Judah, repeating the pattern in chap. 1 and 20:18. The order compensates for Judah's absence elsewhere in the book.

Personally, Othniel is a genuinely noble figure, having demonstrated his faith and military skills in the conquest of Debir (1:11–15). Theocratically, by beginning here, the author announces that if Yahweh can deliver Israel from this emperor he can rescue them from any foe. For in the end the real hero of this story is not Othniel but Yahweh. Yahweh hears the groans of his people, he feels pity toward them, he provides the deliverer, and he achieves the deliverance. This will be the pattern throughout the next twelve chapters.

---

[15] The exemplary image of Othniel and the fact that he is given pride of place in this parade of deliverers suggests to many a general pro-Judahite polemic even in the structure of the book. See O'Connell, *Rhetoric of the Book of Judges,* 81–84, and more recently, B. Oded, "Cushan-Rishathaim (Judges 3:8–11): An Implicit Polemic," in *Texts, Temples, and Traditions: A Tribute to Menahem Haran,* ed. M. V. Fox et al. (Winona Lake: Eisenbrauns, 1996), 89–94 [Hb.]. In response, the narrator makes nothing of Othniel's Judahite status. On the contrary, both here and in 1:11–15 his Kenizzite heritage is highlighted. If anything, this speaks negatively of Judah, a tribe bereft of native leadership. The deliverer who is supposedly presented as their representative is a proselyte.

[16] The Shamgar note presents a seventh historical cycle, but it is not crafted as one of the narrative cycles.

(1) The Marks of Israel's Canaanization (3:7)

⁷The Israelites did evil in the eyes of the LORD; they forgot the LORD their God and served the Baals and the Asherahs.

3:7 The account begins with the negative evaluation formula, but then elaborates on the evil in Israel with two clarifying comments. First, the Israelites forgot Yahweh their God. This is the only occurrence in the book of the verb *šākaḥ*, which is generally understood as "to forget." However in this context it is too passive, suggesting that Israel is simply suffering a case of amnesia, as if, if they really were alert, they would acknowledge and submit to Yahweh, here identified more closely as "their God." However, the verbal links with 2:11–13, which speaks of forsaking (*ʿāzab*) Yahweh demand a more intentional and active interpretation. Here, as frequently elsewhere, *šākaḥ* denotes "to disregard, not to take into account." Instead of taking note/ account[17] of Yahweh, they served (*ʿābad*) the Baals and the Asherahs.

Since the Asherahs are known from other biblical contexts to have been made of wood and their demolition involved chopping down (*giddaʿ*),[18] the AV rendering of *hāʾăšērôt* as "groves," that is, sacred cult trees, is understandable.[19] However, in light of the Ugaritic evidence that has surfaced in this century, Asherah is now known to have been a prominent goddess in Canaanite mythology, the wife of the high god El (*ʾil*) and mother of seventy gods.[20] The seductive power of the Canaanite Asherah cult to the Israelites is attested by several Hebrew inscriptions from the period of the monarchy that speak of "the LORD and his Asherah," presumably his consort.[21] Even with this new information the mention of Asherah alongside Baal (presumably as his consort) is surprising, especially since 2:13 had associated the Baals with the Ashtartes. Either the author confuses the two deities or he recognizes both as consorts of Baal in this fertility religion. In either case the Israelites had exchanged the worship of the living God for the service of wood and stone—mere figments of

---

[17] This is the basic meaning of זְכֹר, usually translated "to remember." Cf. Gen 8:1.

[18] Deut 7:5. Cp. the demolition of altars (מִזְבְּחֹת) by "tearing down" (נָתַץ), Baalistic pillars (מַצֵּבוֹת) by "smashing" (שָׁבֵר), and images (פְּסִילִים) by "burning" (שָׂרַף בָּאֵשׁ).

[19] See C. I. Scofield's note on this passage in the *Scofield Reference Bible*.

[20] Her title is *qnyt ʾlm*, "the procreatress of the gods," who are elsewhere referred to as "the seventy sons of Athirat" (*šbʿm. bn, ʾṯrt, KTU* 1.4.VI.46 = *CTA* 4.VI.46). For a convenient discussion and sources see J. Day, "Asherah," *ABD* 1.483–87; id., "Asherah in the Hebrew Bible and Northwest Semitic Literature," *JBL* 31 (1980): 385–408; N. Wyatt, "Asherah," *DDD*, 183–95.

[21] Cf. esp. the Kuntillet ʿAjrud pithos inscription: *brkt. ʾtkm. lyhwh. šmrn. wlʾšrth*, "I have blessed you by the LORD of Samaria and his Asherah," and the longer Khirbet el-Qom (near Hebron) inscriptions: *ʾryhw. hʾšr. ktbh / brk. ʾryhw. lyhwh / wmṣryh lʾšrth hwšʿlh / lʾnyhw / wlʾšrth / ???rth*, "Uriyahu the rich wrote it. / Blessed be Uriyahu by Yahweh. / For from his enemies by his Asherah he has saved him. / by Oniyahu / and by his Asherah / his A(she)rah." Thus translated by Day, *ABD* 1.484–85.

the depraved human imagination. The lofty theology, austere morality, and abstract cult of Yahwism is replaced with the exciting fertility religion.

(2) God's Agent of Punishment (3:8)

8The anger of the LORD burned against Israel so that he sold them into the hands of Cushan-Rishathaim king of Aram Naharaim, to whom the Israelites were subject for eight years.

3:8 In his passionate anger Yahweh sold his own people into the hands of Cushan-Rishathaim, king of Aram Naharaim. The title of this man appears straightforward. Aram, rendered *Syria* in the LXX, is the name given to the area populated primarily by Arameans, one of the most important ethnic groups in the late second and early first millennia. The territory extended from northeast of the Sea of Galilee to the Taurus mountains in the north and eastward beyond the Habur tributary of the upper Euphrates River. Although his capital is not identified, the addition of Naharaim, "of the two rivers" (cf. English Mesopotamia, "between the rivers") fixes his home somewhere east of the Euphrates—unless, of course, the present name is a corruption of Edom, as some have proposed.[22] While this seems to make sense in the present context, in the company of other nearer neighbors of Israel it is difficult to imagine scribes tolerating a change to the present reading. On the basis of *lectio difficilior,* "the more difficult reading," therefore, the Hebrew must be allowed to stand, which heightens the significance of this first cycle.[23] This means that the first oppressor of Israel sent in by Yahweh was not simply the leader of an alliance of Canaanite city-states (Jabin, 4:2), the recently arrived Philistines (cf. 3:31; 10:67), the migratory Midianites (6:2–3), or the emerging nations of Moab (Eglon, 3:12) and Ammon (10:6–7,17; 11:1–33), beyond the Dead Sea and the Jordan River. He was the most powerful of all the enemies of Israel named in the book. For him to have extended his tentacles as far as Judah in southern Canaan meant he was a world-class emperor, who held Canaan in his grip for at least eight years.[24]

---

[22] J. Gray (*Joshua, Judges and Ruth,* NCB [London: Thomas Nelson, 1967], 260–61) suggests Naharaim was added to clarify Aram, once the error had entered the text. The names Aram (אֲרָם) and Edom (אֱדֹם) are confused elsewhere in 2 Sam 8:12–13; 1 Chr 18:11; 2 Chr 20:2.

[23] Equally unlikely is R. G. Boling's suggestion (*Judges: A New Translation with Introduction and Commentary,* AB [Garden City: Doubleday, 1975], 81) that אֲרָם נַהֲרַיִם is a corruption of אֲרָם מִן הָרִים, "Fortress of the Mountains."

[24] A. Malamat suggests Cushan-Rishathaim's activities in southern Canaan were not undertaken simply to subjugate a small tribe (Judah), but were directed at Egypt ("The Egyptian Decline in Canaan and the Sea Peoples," in *Judges,* WHJP First Series: Ancient Times; ed. B. Mazar [Tel-Aviv: Massada, 1971], 26–27). He links Othniel's deliverance of Israel with the general defeat of this foreign invader of Egypt by Setnakht, the founder of the Twentieth Dynasty, at the end of the thirteenth century B.C.

But who was he? The man's name is even more problematic than his title. Formally it looks like "Cushan of Double Wickedness," in which case it probably functions as a mocking and parodic pseudonym. Some who follow the Edomite interpretation see the name as a scribal corruption of an original Cushan *rō'š hattêmānî,* "the chief of the Temanites."[25] Although most scholars reject this explanation, there is no consensus on who Cushan-Rishathaim might be. A variety of identifications have been proposed: a leader of the Kassite, who controlled Babylonia from 1600–1150 B.C. (cf. Gen 10:8); a Nubian;[26] an Asiatic usurper in Egypt, known in Egyptian sources as Arsu or Irsu;[27] a Midianite chieftain (cf. Num 12:1; Hab 3:7), a surviving chieftain of southern Judah.[28] Josephus (*Ant.* 5.180) proposes an identification with Chusarsathus, king of the Assyrians, which might suggest Tiglath Pileser I of Assyria (1114–1076 B.C.), but this is too late for Othniel. We are forced to concede that it is impossible to link Cushan-Rishathaim with any known historical figure. This does not mean, however, that this first episode is to be dismissed as fictionally contrived, to fill the narrator's quota of twelve rulers, analogous to the twelve tribes of Israel,[29] or to idealize the tribe of Judah, represented by Othniel. It simply means that more evidence is needed to come to a full understanding of this text.

(3) Israel's Response to the Oppression (3:9a)

⁹**But when they cried out to the LORD,**

3:9a According to v. 8b, the Israelites were subservient to Cushan-Rishathaim for eight years. Their response to this servitude is described in the briefest of terms: they cried out *(zā'aq).* This outcry is not to be interpreted as a penitential plea; it is simply a cry of pain, a cry for help.

(4) God's Agent of Deliverance (3:9b–10a)

he raised up for them a deliverer, Othniel son of Kenaz, Caleb's younger brother, who saved them. ¹⁰The Spirit of the LORD came upon him,

3:9b–10a The emergence of a deliverer from this crisis is described in terse but theological terms: Yahweh raised up *(wayyāqem)* a "deliverer, savior" *(môšîa')* who "saved" *(hôšîa')* Israel. The author identifies him only by

---

[25] Gray, *Judges,* 261.

[26] Cush = Nubia.

[27] Papyrus Harris 1/75 (*ANET* 260). Thus Malamat, "Cushan Rishathaim and the Decline of the Near East around 1200 B.C.," *JNES* 13 (1954): 231–42.

[28] On these and other suggestions see B. G. Webb, *The Book of Judges: An Integrated Reading,* JSOTSup 46 (Sheffield: JSOT Press, 1987), 243, n. 5; Lindars, *Judges 1–5,* 131–34.

[29] Thus Becker, *Richterzeit,* 106.

patronymic and clan affiliation: "He is the son of Kenaz, Caleb's younger brother."[30] As the first in the series of rulers raised up by God, however, Othniel plays a paradigmatic role. He is a Judean hero (the last one in the book) of noble, if alien, stock (the Caleb connection), one already distinguished for his courage and prowess (1:11–15). But none of these features is said to have qualified him to take on this foreign emperor. Indeed he had only two, but the prerequisite two, qualifications for the "deliverer" role: he was raised by Yahweh and empowered by Yahweh's Spirit.

The expression *wattĕhî ʿālāyw ruaḥ yhwh*, "the Spirit of the LORD came upon him," is critical for understanding the role of the divinely called deliverers in the Book of Judges and the manner in which Yahweh exercised his power in the Old Testament in general. Variations of this expression occur in four other places in this book (6:34; 11:29; 14:19; 15:14) and three times in 1 Samuel (11:6; 16:13–14). The view persists among many laypeople and ministers that this formula describes the typical operation of the Spirit of God in the Old Testament, in contrast to his modus operandi in the New Testament. Supposedly, whereas the New Testament teaches that the Holy Spirit *dwells in* the believer, in ancient Israel the Holy Spirit *came upon* believers.[31] However, this view not only fails to appreciate the continuity in the operations of the Spirit between the Testaments but it misinterprets this formula.[32] The present expression represents a "spiritual" variation of the more physical version, "the hand of the LORD came upon *X*," which functions as a metaphor of the urgent, compulsive, often overwhelming force with which God operates in an individual's or a group's experience.[33] Similarly, the Spirit of God is the agency/agent through which God's will is exercised, whether it be in creation, his dispensing of life, his guidance and providential care, the revelation of his will, his renewal of unregenerate hearts, or his sealing of his covenant people as his own. The Spirit of God is not a self-existent agent operating independently but "an extension of the LORD's personality," the third member of the Trinity, by which God exercises influence over the

---

[30] The form of identification is identical to 1:13.

[31] Cf. J. H. Walvoord, *The Holy Spirit* (Grand Rapids: Zondervan, 1965), 152.

[32] The Pentecostal experience described in Acts 2 is neither about regeneration nor empowerment for service, but a divine sign of God's covenantal seal on Christian Jews gathered in Jerusalem. This phenomenon occurs three more times in Acts. In each instance the pouring out of thee Spirit signals an extension of the boundaries of the new covenantal body: to Samaritans (Acts 7:14–21); to Gentile God-fearers in the land of Palestine (Acts 10:44–48); to Gentiles outside Palestine (Acts 19:1–7). For further discussion see D. I. Block, *The Book of Ezekiel Chapters 25–48*, NICOT (Grand Rapids: Eerdmans, 1998), 488–493.

[33] See D. I. Block, "The Prophet of the Spirit: The Use of *rwḥ* in the Book of Ezekiel," *JETS* 32 (1989): 33–34.

world.[34] In the Book of Judges when the *rûaḥ yhwh*, "Spirit of the LORD," comes upon individuals, it signals the arresting presence and power of God, often of individuals who are unqualified for or indisposed to service for him. In the present instance the empowering presence of the Spirit of God transforms this minor Israelite officer from Debir into the ruler *(šôpēṭ)* of Israel and the conqueror of a world-class enemy.

(5) God's Gift of Deliverance (3:10b)

so that he became Israel's judge and went to war. The LORD gave Cushan-Rishathaim king of Aram into the hands of Othniel, who overpowered him.

3:10b Othniel's victory over Cushan-Rishathaim is summarized theologically, with a variation of the same committal formula that had described Israel's fall into bondage in v. 8: Yahweh gave him into Othniel's hand. The reader is left to speculate about the occasion, circumstances, and nature of the battle.

(6) God's Gift of Security (3:11)

[11]So the land had peace for forty years, until Othniel son of Kenaz died.

3:11 The unit closes with a declaration of the effects of Othniel's (i.e., Yahweh's) work—a forty-year period of calm *(šqṭ)*. Forty probably is a round number, here presumably signifying the lifespan of an entire generation. Significantly, the narrator notes that it is the land, rather than the people, that enjoyed the rest.[35]

Theological and Practical Implications

This unit sets the literary pattern for the series of six accounts of divine punishment and deliverance by the hands of a specially chosen human agent. In so doing it also serves as a paradigm for us. When people abandon Yahweh in favor of any other allegiance, they absolve him of any obligation to them. In fact, they render him their enemy and may expect his judgment. On the other hand, when an individual who has been called by God into his service challenges the forces of evil and darkness in his [God's] power, the hosts of heaven and earth are dethroned. Herein lies the hope for the moribund church today. In

---

[34] A. R. Johnson, *The One and the Many in the Israelite Conception of God*, 2d ed. (Cardiff: University of Wales, 1961), 61. For a study of the operation of the Holy Spirit in the historiographic writings of the OT see Block, "Empowered by the Spirit of God: The Holy Spirit in the Historiographic Writings of the Old Testament," *SBJT* 1 (1997): 42–61, esp. pp. 44–45 for a discussion of the present empowering type of operation.

[35] Contrast this with 18:7,27, which explicitly ascribes the tranquil state to the people (הָעָם).

the words of Yahweh himself, through his prophet Zechariah, victories are won "not by might or by power, but by my Spirit" (Zech 4:6).

2. The Moab and Ehud Cycle (3:12–30)

After the sober presentation of the Othniel and Cushan-Rishathaim cycle, the author presents a colorful and humoresque[36] account of the confrontation between Israel and the oppressing Moabites, more specifically an Israelite hero's assassination of the oppressor. Apart from the schematic Cushan-Rishathaim and Othniel cycle, the plot of 3:7–11 is the simplest in the book. The narrative contains all the structural formulae of the previous pericope. The major complication occurs in the manner in which deliverance from the oppressor is won. The basic plot may be summarized briefly as follows:

1. With the assistance of Ammonites and Amalekites, Eglon of Moab subjugates a portion of Israel, taking possession of Jericho.

2. In keeping with their status as subjects, the Israelites send Ehud to deliver their tribute payments to Eglon.

3. After the tribute has been delivered, Ehud returns alone, and, getting Eglon into a one-on-one situation in his own house in Jericho, he assassinates him.

4. Meanwhile the king's bodyguards wait outside for their master. When he fails to come out, they enter the throne room and find him dead on the floor.

5. Ehud returns to his people and marshals the Ephraimites to battle.

6. The Moabite army is soundly defeated.

7. The land of Israel is undisturbed for eighty years.

While the sequence of episodes is clear, the narrator is obviously not interested merely in chronicling historical events. With effective employment of ambiguity, irony, satire, hyperbole, and caricature, he sketches a literary cartoon that pokes fun at the Moabites and brings glory to God.[37] In fact, the account is so polemical and coarse that many scholars deny any historical basis to it.[38] On the other hand, although we lack any external archaeological or independent literary attestation of Eglon and Ehud as individuals, as

---

[36] J. A. Soggin ("»Ehud und ʿEglon: Bemerkingen zu Richter III 11b–31," *VT* 29 [1989]: 95) characterizes the humor of the account as "coarse, macabre, and phakalic" *(derbe, makaber und phäkal)*.

[37] For a discussion of the literary artistry of this narrative see especially Y. Amit, "The Story of Ehud (Judges 3:12–30): The Form and the Message," in *Signs and Wonders: Biblical Texts in Literary Focus*, ed. C. Exum, Semeia Studies (Chico: Scholars Press, 1989), 97–124; L. Alonso-Schökel, "Erzählkunst im Buche der Richter," *Bib* 42 (1961): 148–58.

[38] See Soggin, *Judges*, 55; N. P. Lemche, *Early Israel: Anthropological and Historical Studies on the Israelite Society before the Monarchy*, VTSup 37 (Leiden: Brill, 1985), 383; E. A. Knauf, "Eglon and Ophrah: Two Toponymic Notes on the Book of Judges," *JSOT* 51 (1991): 25–34.

B. Halpern has demonstrated,[39] the cultural details in the text certainly reflect what we know of the historical context. This is more than "historicized prose fiction."[40] At the same time, an essentially positivist posture toward this account does not blind one to the polemical agenda of the author. Biblical historians seldom, if ever, wrote their pieces primarily so later readers could reconstruct historical events. Their agendas were generally theological and polemical, and few texts are as overt in the latter respect as ours. Indeed, while assuming the historicity of the Ehud-Eglon narrative, we must recognize that the author has carefully crafted it as an anti-Moabite (as well as anti-Canaanizing Israelite) satire.[41] While keeping our eyes on the literary features that contribute to effectiveness in this regard, our exposition will follow the pattern set in the previous pericope.

(1) The Marks of Israel's Canaanization (3:12a)

12Once again the Israelites did evil in the eyes of the LORD,

3:12a Other aspects of the basic paradigm are developed in considerable detail in the story of Ehud, but the announcement of Israel's spiritual problem is limited to the barest form of the negative evaluation formula. The author seems eager to get on with the story.

(2) God's Agent of Punishment (3:12b–14)

and because they did this evil the LORD gave Eglon king of Moab power over Israel. 13Getting the Ammonites and Amalekites to join him, Eglon came and attacked Israel, and they took possession of the City of Palms. 14The Israelites were subject to Eglon king of Moab for eighteen years.

3:12b–14 Yahweh's response to Israel's apostasy this time is to strengthen *(ḥizzēq)* Eglon, king of Moab. The conscription of the Moabites as Yahweh's agents is remarkable. Not only were the Moabites not included among the peoples of the land whom Yahweh had left to test Israel (3:3–6); they were relatives of the Israelites, having descended from Abraham's nephew Lot (Gen 19:36–37). Furthermore, Eglon's success against Israel contrasts with Balak's earlier attempts to oppose their ancestors when they came from Egypt (Numbers 22–24). Whereas Yahweh had earlier forbidden the Israelites from encroaching upon Moabite territory, which he had given to them (Deut

---

[39] B. Halpern, "A Message for Eglon: The Case of Ehud ben-Gera," in *The First Historians: The Hebrew Bible and History* (San Francisco: Harper & Row, 1988), 39–75; id., "The Assassination of Eglon—The First Locked-Room Murder Mystery," *BibRev* 4/6 (1988): 32–41, 44.

[40] Cf. R. Alter, *The Art of Biblical Narrative* (New York: Basic Books, 1981), 37–41.

[41] On the passage as political satire see M. Brettler, "Never the Twain Shall Meet? The Ehud Story as History and Literature," *HUCA* 62 (1991): 285–304.

2:8–9), now he brings them into the land allotted to the Israelites because the latter had violated the will of their divine Lord with their evil actions (v. 12b).

Although the narrator attributes Eglon's rise to Yahweh, the Moabite king seems to have been unaware of his role as the agent of the God of Israel. On the contrary, he appears to operate quite independently,[42] forging an alliance with the Ammonites[43] and Amalekites, marching out against Israel, defeating them, and occupying the "City of Palms." The latter reference is undoubtedly to Jericho, which Eglon apparently selects as his Palestinian base of operations and/ or rule. The city probably was chosen because of its desirable location at an oasis in the Jordan Valley and because of its long-standing history as a major Canaanite city. Either Eglon was oblivious to the curse that Joshua had invoked upon the city in Josh 6:26 or his occupation of this site represented a deliberate act of defiance against Israel and their God. The former seems more likely.

For all Eglon's achievements, the narrator characterizes him as a comic figure, a buffoon. No Israelite would have missed the caricaturing play on his name, *ʿeglôn,* a diminutive form of *ʿēgel,* "bull, calf," but which also recalls the term *ʿāgôl,* "round, rotund."[44] Every time his name occurs in vv. 12–17, he is also identified by title, *melek môāb,* "King of Moab." Even Ehud addresses him as "O King," in v. 19. However, after v. 20 the author deliberately avoids his name; the man who was "somebody" for eighteen years is reduced to a nameless "nobody"! Contributing to the caricatured picture of Eglon is the emphasis on his corpulence. In fact, the motif of fatness permeates the entire account. In v. 17 the author inserts the circumstantial comment (whose force is diminished in the NIV), "Now Eglon was an extremely fat man." The term *bārî*ʾ is used elsewhere of fattened cattle or sheep.[45] Eglon is portrayed as a fattened calf going to the slaughter. This image of physical obesity is rendered even more vivid in vv. 20–22, with the comment that when Ehud stabbed him, his sword was smothered in the fat *(ḥēleb).*[46] But any native Israelite reader

---

[42] Eglon is the subject of all the verbs in v. 13.

[43] As almost everywhere else in the OT, the Ammonites are referred to as עַמּוֹן בְּנֵי, "the sons of Ammon," rather than עַמּוֹנִים, "Ammonites." The preferred form recalls their descent from Lot's younger daughter (Gen 19:36–37). For a study of the form and its significance see Block, "*Bny ʿmmwn*: The Sons of Ammon," *AUSS* 22 (1984): 197–212.

[44] 1 Kgs 7:31; 10:19. Knauf's argument ("Eglon and Ophrah," 25–34) that Eglon is a Gileadite place name (modern ʿAjlûn) rather than a personal name is speculative and overlooks the fact that Israelite personal names often ended with the diminutive *-ôn* (e.g., Hezron, Samson, etc.). On the mocking character of the name "Eglon" see M. Garsiel, *Biblical Names: A Literary Study of Midrashic Derivations and Puns,* trans. P. Hackett (Ramat-Gan: Bar-Ilan University, 1991), 215.

[45] Of cattle, Gen 41:2,4,18,20; 1 Kgs 5:3; of sheep, Ezek 34:3,26; Zech 11:16; of ears of grain, Gen 41:5,7; of food in general, Hab 1:16. Of healthy human beings, Dan 1:15; a fat body, Ps 73:4.

[46] חֵלֶב is used most frequently of animals, especially the fat of sacrificial animals (Exod 23:18 and many more) and the choice parts to be eaten (Ezek 34:3; 39:19; etc.). See further G. Münderlein, "חֵלֶב *ḥēleb,*" *TDOT* 5.391–97.

would have recognized a double entendre in the motif. The events of this chapter demonstrate that Eglon's bodily corpulence is matched by his mental obtuseness.[47] Eglon loves his luxury. Instead of sitting on his throne in Moab he is in "the City of Palms," that is, Jericho,[48] perhaps his summer residence. He is also stupid. He succumbs to Ehud's flattery and dismisses his bodyguard, leaving this defenseless fat man alone in the room with the enemy (v. 19), and when Ehud says he has a message from God for him, he rises, exposing his fat paunch.

But Eglon is not the only fat/dull person in this text. The characteristic is explicitly democratized in v. 29, which describes all the Moabite soldiers as "stout" men. The word *šemen* usually denotes "olive oil," but the adjective *šāmēn* is used of rich food (Gen 49:20; Isa 30:23; Hab 1:16) and fertile land/lush pasturage (Num 13:20; Ezek 34:14; Neh 9:25,35). Here and in Ezek 34:16 it describes robust, healthy men. Since the verb form of this root, *hišmîn*, "to make fat," is used elsewhere of "dulling the heart/mind,"[49] the Israelites would surely have attributed this quality to the Moabites as well. This was certainly true of the bodyguards, who should never have left their master alone in a room with the enemy (v. 19). Taken as a whole, this literary cartoon of Eglon and his countrymen is not only aimed at the Moabites[50] but is ironical as well. The man whom God had strengthened *(ḥizzēq)* will eventually be reduced to a heap of fat and excrement. The author's deliberate satirizing of Eglon in particular and the Moabites in general should not blind the reader to the ridicule he is casting upon his own people. After all, the Book of Judges was not written primarily to mock foreigners; it challenges the Israelites to reflect on their own condition. Far from being the noble people they claim to be, in their Canaanized state they have been reduced to less than the Moabites.

(3) Israel's Response to the Oppression (3:15a)

15Again the Israelites cried out to the LORD, and he gave them a deliverer— Ehud, a left-handed man, the son of Gera the Benjamite.

3:15a As in the previous episode, the Israelites cry out to Yahweh for help. But again this is not a cry of repentance or a plea for forgiveness; it is simply a cry of pain, a plea for divine aid.

---

[47] Cp. the use of the expressions לֵב חֲלַב, "fat of heart/mind," in Ps 119:70 (cf. 17:10). Note also Ps 73:7, which speaks of the eyes of the wicked "bulging out with fat."

[48] Thus Tg. See also Deut 34:3; 2 Chr 28:15.

[49] Isa 6:10 speaks of "fattening the heart/mind."

[50] On the ethnic humor of the account see L. K. Handy, "Uneasy Laughter: Ehud and Eglon as Ethnic Humor," *SJOT* 6 (1992): 233–46.

(4) God's Agent of Deliverance (3:15b)

The Israelites sent him with tribute to Eglon king of Moab.

3:15b The divine response to the human cry is summarized in v. 15b: "The LORD raised up [NIV 'gave them'] a deliverer *[môšîaʿ]*." Although the author is clear that Ehud is God's gracious gift to the nation, the silence of Yahweh and the focus on the tactics of the deliverer raise doubts concerning Ehud's own sense of place in the divine scheme. In fact, the bulk of the narrative is devoted not to describing God's actions but to narrating the achievements of the agent whom God had called to rescue the Israelites from the Moabite oppression. The character of Ehud is evidently of great interest to the author.

The deliverer is identified by name and patronymic. Ehud *(ʾēhûd)* consists of two elements, *ʾēy* and *hûd,* which together denote "Where is the splendor, majesty?" Like Ichabod *(ʾîkābôd,* "Where is the glory?") in 1 Sam 4:21, this name reflects the despondency of the times.[51] However, not only did Ehud bring a brief ray of hope to his own generation but also his signature appears to be preserved in a Benjamite clan named after him in 1 Chr 7:10. This clan probably was most responsible for keeping alive the memory of his exploits. The authenticity of the name of Ehud's father, Gera, is supported by its appearance as a clan patronymic in the genealogy of Benjamin in 1 Chr 8:3,5,7.

The narrator's identification of Ehud as a Benjamite may seem inconsequential at first, but it is ironic in two respects. First, if the events of chaps. 19–21 belong to the time of the prologue or shortly thereafter,[52] we do not expect much from the Benjamites. The tribe has been decimated by intra-Israelite warfare. Second, the name "Benjamin" means "son of the right hand," that is, "right-handed." But the odd form of the gentilic *ben-hayĕmînî,*[53] rather than the anticipated *ben-yĕmînî* ("son of my right hand"; cf. 1 Sam 9:21) suggests that the irony of the situation was not missed by the author. Ehud is not merely a Benjamite; he is "the son of the right hand" par excellence. But he is left-handed! The author describes him as *ʾîš ʾiṭṭēr yad-yĕmînô* (NIV, "a left-handed man").

Scholars are not agreed on the meaning of *ʾiṭṭēr yad-yĕmînô.* The word *ʾiṭṭēr* occurs elsewhere only in Judg 20:16, where Ehud's condition is generalized to an entire contingent of exceptionally skilled Benjamite warriors. The verb *ʾāṭar* is found only in Ps 69:15[Hb. 16], where it means "to shut" [the

---

[51] The element הוד occurs in another Benjamite name, Abihud, in 1 Chr 8:3. Knauf's suggestion ("Eglon and Ophrah," 29–34) that Ehud is primarily a Benjamite clan name is as unconvincing as his dismissal of Eglon as a personal name.

[52] According to 20:28 Phinehas, the grandson of Aaron was priest at the time of the events recounted in chaps. 19–20.

[53] This form occurs elsewhere in 2 Sam 16:11; 19:17; 1 Kgs 2:8; 1 Chr 27:12.

mouth].[54] The root appears elsewhere only in the postexilic personal name Ater *(ʾāṭēr)*.[55] If the present *ʾiṭṭēr* is to be associated with Ps 69:15[Hb. 16], *ʾiṭṭēr yad-yĕmînî* means something like "shut/restricted with reference to the right hand," which suggests some type of deformity or handicap, hence "left-handed."[56] However, this meaning is excluded in 20:16, which describes an entire contingent of Benjamite soldiers "who could sling a stone at a hair and not miss." Slings require great skill and the efficient use of two hands. Furthermore, 1 Chr 12:2 attests to a different normal expression for "left-handed," *maśmîl*, "to use the left hand." It seems best to follow the lead of the LXX's *amphoterodexios* and interpret Ehud's condition and that of the Benjamites in 20:16 as "ambidextrous," that is, skilled in the use of both hands. The meaning is fleshed out in 1 Chr 12:2, which describes a group of Benjamites, relatives of Saul, who defected to David as "armed with bows" and "able to shoot arrows or to sling stones right-handed or left-handed." But the adjective *ʾiṭṭēr*, "shut, restricted," suggests Ehud and his fellow Benjamites in 20:16 were not naturally left-handed. On the contrary, they were a specially trained group for whom dexterity with the left hand was inculcated by binding up the right hand.[57] In line combat, trained left-handers have a decided advantage over right-handers who are taught to fight sword against shield.[58]

But the narrator is not interested only in Ehud's left-handed skills. He presents him as an exceptionally clever and resourceful man, a master of deceit,[59] and the antithesis to Moabite dull-wittedness. The opportunity for decisive action is provided when the Israelites commission him to deliver their tribute to the Moabite overlord. The expression *minḥâ* may denote either a stipulated amount demanded by the king[60] or voluntarily offered to a recognized superior to maintain the peace (Gen 32:14). The former seems to be the case here. The fact that Ehud headed a team of men to deliver the tribute suggests payment in

---

[54] It is unclear whether the Hb. root is cognate with Arabic *ʾaṭara*, "to bow, to fence around," or *ʾaṭîr*, "mistake." Cf. *HALOT*, 37.

[55] Of a returning exile and signatory of Nehemiah's pledge (Ezra 2:16 = Neh 7:21; 10:18); of the ancestor of returning gatekeepers (Ezra 2:42 = Neh 7:45).

[56] Thus Soggin, *Judges*, 50, and most modern commentators. Cf. Tg., *gĕmîd*, "withered"; Peshitta, *pĕšigaʾ*, "crippled."

[57] W. Kornfeld's derivation of *ʾiṭṭēr* from a cognate of Akk. *eṭēru*, "to deliver," is neither necessary nor convincing ("Onomastica aramaica und das alte Testament," *ZAW* 88 [1976]: 105–7). So also F. Dexinger, "Ein Plädoyer für die Linkshänder im Richterbuch," *ZAW* 89 (1977): 268–69; Lindars, *Judges 1–5*, 141.

[58] See more fully Halpern, *The First Historians,* 40–43.

[59] On the place of deception in Ehud's strategy see H. N. Rösel, "Zur Ehud- Erzählung," *ZAW* 89 (1977): 270–72; M. Wilcock, *The Message of Judges*, BST (Downers Grove: InterVarsity, 1992), 43–44; D. F. Chalcraft, "Deviance and Legitimate Action in the Book of Judges," in *The Bible in Three Dimensions: Essays in Celebration of Forty Years of Biblical Studies in the University of Sheffield*, ed. D. J. A. Clines et al., JSOTSup 87 (Sheffield: Academic Press, 1990), 183–85.

[60] Cp. the reversal of roles in 2 Sam 8:2, where David demands מִדָּה of the Moabites.

kind, as in Mesha of Moab's tribute to Ahab in 2 Kgs 3:4. In v. 15 the narrator explains Ehud's appointment theologically (he was raised by Yahweh) and terrestrially (the Israelites sent the tribute in his hand). Why Ehud was selected is not indicated, but his ambidexterity may have been recognized as a special asset in guarding the tribute against bandits along the way to Eglon.

(5) God's Gift of Deliverance (3:16–29)

[16]Now Ehud had made a double-edged sword about a foot and a half long, which he strapped to his right thigh under his clothing. [17]He presented the tribute to Eglon king of Moab, who was a very fat man. [18]After Ehud had presented the tribute, he sent on their way the men who had carried it. [19]At the idols near Gilgal he himself turned back and said, "I have a secret message for you, O king."

The king said, "Quiet!" And all his attendants left him.

[20]Ehud then approached him while he was sitting alone in the upper room of his summer palace and said, "I have a message from God for you." As the king rose from his seat, [21]Ehud reached with his left hand, drew the sword from his right thigh and plunged it into the king's belly. [22]Even the handle sank in after the blade, which came out his back. Ehud did not pull the sword out, and the fat closed in over it. [23]Then Ehud went out to the porch; he shut the doors of the upper room behind him and locked them.

[24]After he had gone, the servants came and found the doors of the upper room locked. They said, "He must be relieving himself in the inner room of the house." [25]They waited to the point of embarrassment, but when he did not open the doors of the room, they took a key and unlocked them. There they saw their lord fallen to the floor, dead.

[26]While they waited, Ehud got away. He passed by the idols and escaped to Seirah. [27]When he arrived there, he blew a trumpet in the hill country of Ephraim, and the Israelites went down with him from the hills, with him leading them.

[28]"Follow me," he ordered, "for the LORD has given Moab, your enemy, into your hands." So they followed him down and, taking possession of the fords of the Jordan that led to Moab, they allowed no one to cross over. [29]At that time they struck down about ten thousand Moabites, all vigorous and strong; not a man escaped.

Verse 15 has left the reader wondering how Ehud, raised up by God to deliver his people and appointed by the Israelites to deliver the tribute to Eglon, would carry out the divine plan. One might have expected the notice that Ehud was Israel's designated tribute-bearer in v. 15 to be followed immediately by "He blew a trumpet ..." (v. 27). The reader will not learn the answer until vv. 27–29. But the resolution of the question is delayed as the narrator deliberately slows down the narrative, focusing on the actions of the deliverer and paying special attention to the significance of his left-handedness. The narrator's point is that the leader of the enemies must be disposed of before the occupying army can be routed.

THE ASSASSINATION OF THE ENEMY LEADER (3:16–26). Having been appointed by his countrymen to deliver tribute to Eglon, Ehud anticipates an opportunity to assassinate the enemy. Every stage in his strategy is meticulously planned and executed.

3:16 First, he has a special dagger crafted for the occasion.[61] It was about eighteen inches long,[62] so it could be carried easily and unobtrusively,[63] and double-edged *(šĕnê pênôt)*, to facilitate a straight stab rather than a hacking stroke and to slice cleanly into the king's flesh. Being ambidextrous, Ehud fastened the dagger under his garment to his right hip, where no one would suspect it.

3:17–19a Second, after dutifully delivering the tribute to Eglon and returning from the mission with his colleagues who carried it, at the "idols" near Gilgal, Ehud dismisses them and returns alone to Eglon's temporary court. It is difficult to know what to make of these "idols." Elsewhere in the Old Testament the term *pĕsîlîm* always denotes sculpted pagan cult images. These may have been boundary stones analogous to the inscribed Babylonian *kudurru* stones,[64] signifying the border of the territory claimed by Eglon. Verse 26 implies that after the assassination, once Ehud had fled past these objects he was safe, presumably because he was on soil held by the Israelites. If these landmarks were carved with images of Chemosh, the patron god of the Moabites and guarantor of these territorial claims, they could legitimately be designated *pĕsîlîm*. However, this interpretation seems too facile and overly dependent upon Babylonian *kudurru* practices.

Some suggest the term designates the stones erected by Joshua at Gilgal after he had led the Israelites across the Jordan (Josh 4:20). Surely, during the early period of the nation's settlement in the land of Canaan every Israelite who passed by these stones would have reflected on the historical significance of this place. The function of these stones was to memorialize the place where Yahweh had dried up the waters of the Jordan so the people could cross, the Israelites had circumcised all the males who had been born during the desert wanderings, and they had celebrated the Passover in the promised land for the

---

[61] Whether he made it himself or had a craftsman make it is not important. לֹו וַיַּעַשׂ may be rendered either "And he made for himself" or impersonally, "And one made for him."

[62] Hb. גֹּמֶד occurs only here in the OT, but it is generally recognized as equivalent to the אַמָּה, "cubit," presumably the common short cubit, which measured 17.49 inches, rather than the long cubit of 20.405 inches used in Ezekiel. Some interpret a גֹּמֶד as a subdivision (perhaps 2/3) of a cubit. See D. J. Wiseman, "Weights and Measures," *IBD* 3.1636.

[63] The term חֶרֶב, usually translated "sword," is capable of a wide range of meanings, from a razor (Ezek 5:1) to a long curved sword. On the manufacture and use of these weapons see Y. Yadin, *The Art of Warfare in Biblical Lands in the Light of Archaeological Study*, 2 vols.; trans. M. Pearlman (New York: McGraw-Hill, 1963), 2.254–55.

[64] For illustrations see *ANEP*, ##519–22; *IBD* 2.873.

A MOCK-UP OF EGLON'S PALACE IN JERICHO

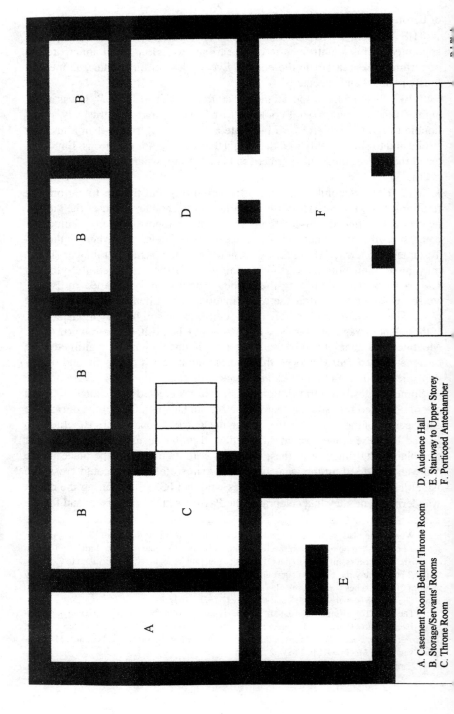

A. Casement Room Behind Throne Room
B. Storage/Servants' Rooms
C. Throne Room
D. Audience Hall
E. Stairway to Upper Storey
F. Porticoed Antechamber

first time (Josh 5:2–11). However, it is unlikely the author would have referred
to stones commemorating so sacred a moment in history by identifying them
with a term as pejorative as *pĕsîlîm*.

It seems best, therefore, to interpret these objects in the normal sense of the
term, that is, as concrete examples of the problem cited in general in v. 2 and
more specifically in 2:11–13. Accordingly these probably were sculpted
images of the Canaanite gods the Israelites were openly worshiping or, like Jeroboam's calves at Bethel and Dan (1 Kgs 12:25–33), evidences of religious
syncretism. The theology associated with Gilgal may have remained orthodox,
but the cultic forms associated with the site had been paganized. The author's
refusal to make any moralistic comment on these images seems intentional; the
Israelites had come to accept such pagan symbols as a part of their own religious landscape.

3:19b–20a   Third, Ehud arranges for a private audience with Eglon in his
throne room. Undoubtedly his success in this was aided by his earlier contact
with the king. Because only a short time had elapsed since he had delivered the
Israelites' tribute, he was familiar to Eglon. Capitalizing on the measure of trust
he might have won and appealing to his vanity, Ehud announces that he has a
secret message for the monarch. The expression *dĕbar sēter* is delightfully
ambiguous. Hebrew *dābār* could mean "word" or "message," but it could also
mean "thing," "object," even "experience." The reader knows he is referring to
the dagger hidden on his right thigh beneath his garment, but stupid Eglon
naively interprets the word in its most common sense. Perhaps he expects an
announcement of additional gifts from Israel or a report of rebellion in his subject territories. In any case he orders his attendants[65] to hush, be quiet,[66] which
they interpret as a signal to leave the room. Meanwhile the king achieves additional privacy by retreating to his throne room, and Ehud follows him.

Our interpretation of *ʿăliyyat hammiqērâ* as "throne room" requires further
comment. The meaning of the first word, "upper, upper chamber," is not in
doubt. The NIV's "cool roof chamber" follows prevailing opinion, which
derives the latter expression from the root *qrr*, "to be cold."[67] Lindars observes
correctly that among the wealthy houses with upper stories were common in
Israel.[68] However, Halpern has rightly noted that not only is "cool" not an archi-

---

[65] הָעֹמְדִים עָלָיו, "those who stand over," is a technical expression for courtiers of the king,
those who have official access to his presence.

[66] Elsewhere the expression הָס, "keep silent," describes the silence before Yahweh (Hab 2:20;
Zeph 1:7; Zech 2:17) and sacred silence in general (Neh 8:11; Amos 6:10). The Arabic cognate *hus*,
"hush," is still used today. Cf. *HALOT*, 253.

[67] The *hithpael* form of the verb occurs in Jer 6:7; the adjective קַר, "cool," in Prov 17:27;
25:25; Jer 18:14; the noun קֹר, "cold," in Gen 8:22; and the feminine counterpart, קָרָה, in Job
24:7; 37:9; Ps 147:17; Prov 25:20; Nah 3:17; Zech 14:6.

[68] Judges 1–5, 144. So also Halpern, *The First Historians,* 45. Cf. 2 Sam 9:25; 1 Kgs 17:19;
2 Kgs 1:2; 4:10.

tectural term; to escape the heat in the southern Jordan Valley near the Dead Sea one does not build upward but burrows down into the ground. Appealing to Ps 104:3, which conjoins ʿăliyyôt, "upper chambers" (plural of ʿăliyyâ), with hamqāreh, a participle form of a denominative verb derived from qôrâ, "rafter, beam" (rather than from qrr, "to be cold"), he suggests plausibly that the present phrase means "the room over the beams,"[69] that is, the raised throne room (Figure 2). Accordingly, one may reconstruct the sequence of events to this point as follows. Originally (v. 17) Ehud presented the tribute to Eglon at the bottom of the stairs in the audience hall (D) while the king was seated on his throne in the "room over the beams" (C) and his courtiers looked on from their posts in the hall (D). The arrangement of the court personnel probably had not changed much when Ehud entered the second time, now with his secret message for the king.[70] Intrigued by this announcement but seeing no reason to be suspicious of the Israelite, the king calls for silence in the court, which the equally obtuse courtiers interpreted as a signal to exit to the Portico (F).

3:20b–22a Fourth, Ehud cleverly gets the king into a vulnerable posture and delivers his fatal stab. Once the retinue had left, Ehud repeated his announcement but rendered it even more tantalizing with a clever adjustment of a single word. "I have a secret message for you" is now "I have a divine message for you."[71] Though Eglon seems not to have had any prior confirmation of Ehud's prophetic status, gullibly he rises, anticipating an oracle from God. Capitalizing on the portliness of the monarch, which would have inhibited his ability to move to defend himself, Ehud rushed up the stairs into the throne room, pulled out his dagger from his right thigh with his left hand, and stabbed[72] the king in the belly. The thrust of Ehud's weapon was so forceful that part of the handle (hanniṣṣāb) was submerged in the fat of the king's abdomen. Apparently the dagger had been crafted without a hilt.

3:22b–26 Fifth, taking precautions to give himself ample time to get away without being suspected by the courtiers, Ehud escapes, leaving the courtiers (and the reader) to contemplate their stupidity. One can sense the narrator's delight in the story as he recounts the assassination in all its gore and the assassin's clever escape. Since time was of the essence, Ehud leaves the king lying

---

[69] Ibid., 45–46; for a popular version of this discussion see id., "The Assassination of Eglon—The First Locked-Room Murder Mystery," *BR* 4 (1988): 32–41, 44, esp. 38. This interpretation finds support in v. 26, which uses חֲדַר הַמִּקְרָה, "upper dark inner room" (*HALOT*, 293) as a variant of the present expression.

[70] The circumstantial clause in v. 20, וְהוּא־יֹשֵׁב בַּעֲלִיַּת הַמְּקֵרָה אֲשֶׁר לוֹ לְבַדּוֹ, "Now he was sitting in the 'throne room' which belonged to him all alone," functions retrospectively and is inserted here to clarify the present spatial arrangements for the reader. The previous clause should be interpreted as a pluperfect, "Now Ehud had come to him ..."

[71] Cp. the constructions in the Hb.: דְּבַר־אֱלֹהִים לִי אֵלֶיךָ. and דְּבַר־סֵתֶר לִי אֵלֶיךָ

[72] The verb תָּקַע, "to plunge," next occurs in 4:21, where it describes the penetration of Jael's tent peg into Sisera's skull.

on the floor of the throne room, the dagger still buried in his belly. The reader might have expected him to withdraw this specially crafted weapon and take it with him, but he had no time to lose, to clean it and try to hide it under his garment, and could not risk staining his garments or hands with blood should he remove the weapon. The following sequence of motions is not quite clear. It seems that, having accomplished his mission, quick-wittedly Ehud turned around and locked the door from the inside, which would later serve two purposes. On the one hand, it would create in the minds of the attendants the impression that the king was demanding a private moment (v. 24). On the other, it would buy Ehud a little extra time. Once the courtiers realized their lord was in trouble, they had to fetch the key and unlock the door.

However, this interpretation creates logistical problems. How would Ehud escape the throne room if the door was locked from the inside? The answer apparently lies in the enigmatic technical hapax expression *hammisdĕrōnâ* in v. 23a, which undoubtedly identifies some architectural feature of the building, but the exact referent remains a mystery. "Porch" (NIV) and "vestibule" (NASB, NRSV, JPSV), which follow Targum's ʾeksedra, seem to suggest Ehud locked the door from the outside once he had left the throne room and exited normally through the porticoed antechamber. Another possibility is a derivation from the root *sdr*, which in Mishnaic Hebrew, Aramaic, and Syriac denotes a row or rank, which may suggest a colonnade or veranda.[73]

On the other hand, if the king is assassinated in his elevated throne room rather than on the cool roof chamber, *hammisdĕrōnâ* probably identifies another opening to the throne room, perhaps in the floor or at the rear. Linking the word with Arabic *sadira*, "to be blinded, puzzled," Halpern proposes a euphemistic expression, "place of concealment," that is, the toilet, perhaps in the back corner of the room. The use of this obscure word for the place of excretion was governed by the same principles of modesty that produced the euphemism "to cover one's feet" for "to relieve oneself."[74] This interpretation seems far-fetched, but it finds support in the previous observation that the king's bowels emptied[75] and the attendant's casual impression that the king had locked the door for the sake of privacy as he relieved himself. Apparently, the throne room contained architectural provision for this comfort for the king. Accordingly Ehud appears to have slid down the *misdārōn*, the opening in the floor, to the cellar below the throne room, from where he emerged through a

---

[73] Cf. Lindars, *Judges 1–5*, 148. Soggin (*Judges*, 51–52) suggests the two hapaxes, הַפַּרְשְׁדֹנָה at the end of v. 22 and הַמִּסְדְּרוֹנָה at the beginning of v. 23, represent alternative expressions. Boling (*Judges*, 87) proposes "a platform with pillars," which means that instead of exiting the way he had entered, after bolting the door from the inside, Ehud escaped from the "roof garden" over the side after locking the door from the inside.

[74] Halpern, *The First Historians*, 58; id., "Eglon's Murder," 40.

[75] On the meaning of וַיֵּצֵא הַפַּרְשְׁדֹנָה in v. 22 see below.

doorway into the Audience Hall and casually made his way past the guards in the porticoed antechamber. Nothing about his visage or his appearance betrayed his treacherous deed or raised the suspicions of the courtiers.

In addition to his own ingenuity and initiative and the obtuseness of the Moabite courtiers, Ehud appears to have been aided by the natural course of events. When Eglon fell to the ground and expired, his bowels relaxed and discharged their contents. This seems the most likely interpretation of the enigmatic expression *wayyēṣēʾ happaršĕdōnâ* at the end of v. 22. Appealing to the omission of these words in the LXX, many delete the clause as a misplaced gloss on the equally unusual *hammisdĕrōnâ* at the beginning of v. 23.[76] By this interpretation, if it is authentic, it also refers to an architectural feature of the building through which the assassin exited.[77] The rendering of the NIV assumes the dagger is the subject of the verb, but this is unlikely because throughout this context *ḥereb* is consistently construed as feminine. It seems best therefore to follow Targum and interpret *paršdōnâ* as a term for excrement, an interpretation which finds support in an Akkadian cognate, *naparšudu*, "to escape."[78]

This interpretation finds additional support in the sequel. According to v. 24, after Ehud had made his exit past them and the attendants reentered the audience hall, to their surprise[79] they observed that the door to the throne room was closed. When they examined it more closely, they discovered it to be locked and concluded that their ruler was relieving himself.[80] Presumably they smelled the odor of the excrement when they came to investigate the closed door. The irony and humor of the situation would not have escaped early Israelite leaders. All that remained of Eglon, the fattened calf, the mighty ruler of Moab, was a corpse and a pile of feces.

In any case they waited[81] for a long time[82] for Eglon to open the door

---

[76] Lindars, *Judges 1–5*, 146; Boling, *Judges*, 86–87.

[77] Comparison is drawn to Akk. *parašdinnu*, "hole." Cf. , 832; KB, s.v.

[78] Thus M. L. Barré ("The Meaning of *pršdn* in Judges iii 22," *VT* 41 [1991]: 1– 11), who argues the form of the present word was influenced by the following הַמְּסְדְּרוֹנָה. Barré suggests one of the *hē*'s on הַפַּרְשְׁדֹנָה is superfluous. One should read either "the excrement" or "his excrement."

[79] This is the force of וְהִנֵּה, "and behold," in v. 24.

[80] On the particle אַךְ meaning "surely, without doubt," see Muraoka, *Emphatic Particles*, 129–30. מֵסִיךְ הוּא אֶת רַגְלָיו, lit., "he was pouring out his feet," is a euphemism for "he was discharging his bowels." On רַגְלַיִם, "feet," used for the private parts see Deut 28:57; Isa 7:20; Ezek 16:25; perhaps also Ruth 3:4,7.

[81] This translation assumes וַיָּחִילוּ represents a corruption of וַיְיַחֲלוּ, from יחל *(piel),* "to await." Cf. *BHS*; BDB, 403–4. If the MT is correct, the word derives from חִיל, "to writhe [in pain]," (cf. *HALOT*, 310–11), which speaks of the attendants' internal struggle.

[82] The NIV's "to the point of embarrassment" follows the common interpretation of עַד־בּוֹשׁ. However, Hb. also knows of a homonymous root, בּוּשׁ, "to tarry, dilly-dally" (cf. 5:28; Exod 32:1; Ezra 8:22), which is what the Tg. *ʿad saggi* seems to have read. This Hb. root finds a Ug. cognate in *bš*, "to remain, be delayed," which is distinguished from *bt*, "to be ashamed." Cf. *HALOT*, 117a.

(v. 25). Finally, when he failed to emerge, they decided to act. They retrieved a key[83] for the door, and when they opened it, they were shocked[84] to find their ruler on the floor, dead. The narrator's statement will be echoed in 4:22, where he reports the death of Sisera at the hands of Jael.[85] Meanwhile, while the murdered king's attendants "dallied,"[86] Ehud escaped past the cult images at Gilgal and arrived at Seirah.[87] His plan had been executed perfectly. The enemy was dead, the Moabites had been totally discredited, and the left-handed right-hander had emerged as a hero in Israel.

THE DEFEAT OF THE ENEMY ARMY (3:27–29). **3:27** Although vv. 27–29 are anticlimactic from a literary perspective, they describe the historical crescendo toward which the personal achievements of Ehud have been providentially directed. In fact, if *wayĕhî bĕbô'ô*, "and when he came," were deleted, v. 27 could follow immediately after "Ehud the son of Gera" in v. 15. Nothing more is said of his left-handedness, which had been the key to the intervening episodes; Ehud functions like a typical military commander. Undoubtedly the story of his assassination of Eglon spread like a brush fire throughout the hills of Ephraim, so that when he summoned the Israelites[88] to battle with his ram's horn *(šôpār)*, they immediately responded by coming down with him. However, the circumstantial clause at the end of v. 27 (lit., "Now he was before them") highlights the narrator's (and the people's) recognition of him as their leader.

3:28a As they launch the attack, Ehud shouts, "Charge *[ridĕpû]*,[89] for the LORD has delivered your enemies, Moab, into your hands." For the first time since v. 15 Yahweh is the subject of a verb, albeit in the speech of Ehud rather than from the narrator's pen. This version of the divine committal formula (cf. comment on v. 8) not only constitutes a reversal of Yahweh's strengthening of Eglon announced in v. 12 but it also represents the theme of the entire unit: the gracious deliverance of God. For the first time Ehud expresses a theological

---

[83] מַפְתֵּחַ, "opener," from פָּתַח, "to open," presumably a flat wooden object that was slipped through a hole in the door and turned to release the bolt. Naturally the door could be bolted from the inside without a key.

[84] As in v. 24, וְהִנֵּה expresses surprise.

[85] Cp. the present מֵת אַרְצָה נֹפֵל אֲדֹנֵיהֶם וְהִנֵּה with מֵת נֹפֵל סִיסְרָא וְהִנֵּה in 4:22.

[86] הִתְמַהְמְהָם, in v. 26, is a *hithpalpel* form of מהה, cognate to Arabic *mahaha*, "to delay" (so also Lindars, *Judges 1–5*, 152). It recurs in 19:8, also with the sense "to linger in indecision" and recalls Lot's dawdling in Gen 19:16.

[87] The location of Seirah is unknown, but apparently it was in the vicinity of Gilgal. According to Knauf ("Eglon and Ophrah," 29, n. 1) the designation שְׂעִירָה, "Seirah," could apply to any slope covered with macchia.

[88] This victory appears to have been achieved primarily by Ephraimites, apparently Ehud's own tribe.

[89] Many (e.g., Lindars, *Judges 1–5*, 153–54) read רְדוּ, "Go down!" with the LXX (καταβαίνετε/κατάβητε).

perspective on his activities. Heretofore his assassination of Eglon has been portrayed as a typical ancient Near Eastern coup—the result of a carefully designed and meticulously executed human scheme, like a leaf from a Canaanite textbook. How genuine his declaration was we may only speculate. The role of the cult images at Gilgal in this story raises questions about the singularity of his spiritual devotion.

3:28b–29   The strategy of the Ephraimite warriors is described in vv. 28b–29. Seizing the fords of the Jordan near the river's entrance to the Dead Sea, they prevented the enemy forces from retreating to the sanctuary of their own land.[90] It also drove a wedge through the Moabite forces; now no reinforcements from the Transjordan could come to the aid of the beleaguered army. In v. 29 the narrator highlights the magnitude of the Israelite victory with three significant statements.

First, the number of Moabite casualties is said to have totaled about ten thousand. Like the census figures in the Book of Numbers, this figure seems inordinately high if interpreted literally. To skirt the problem some would reinterpret the Hebrew term *ʾlp*. Since *ʾelep*, "thousand," can also mean "clan," the numbers may refer to the military force one clan could muster, hence of the clan,[91] in which case Israel's present victory was over ten large Moabite military units. It seems preferable, however, to treat "ten thousand" as a literary figure, which means that ten thousand indicates something like "Israel achieved total victory."[92]

Second, he emphasizes the health of the Moabite warriors. They were not the emaciated remnants of some defeated force but *ʾîš kol šāmēn wĕkol ʾîš ḥayil*, "all vigorous and strong [men]." In contrast to earlier comic references to Eglon as extremely fat (*bārîʾ mĕʾōd*, v. 17), the fat (*ḥeleb*) of whose belly enveloped Ehud's sword (v. 22), the first modifier, *šāmēn*, literally "fat, oil," carries a positive sense. These were robust and healthy warriors, the nobility of Moab.[93]

Third, the narrator notes that not one Moabite soldier escaped. When Yahweh delivers, he delivers!

---

[90] This strategy will be observed again in 7:24 and 12:5.

[91] Cf. J. W. Wenham, "Large Numbers in the Old Testament," *TynBul* 18 (1967): 19–53; R. E. D. Clark, "The Large Numbers of the Old Testament," *JTVI* 87 (1955): 82–90; more recently D. M. Fouts, "A Defense of the Hyperbolic Interpretation of Large Numbers in the Old Testament," *JETS* 40 (1997): 377–88.

[92] Milgrom (*Numbers,* 339) observes that the tendency to inflate numbers was characteristic of ancient epic literature. With the present figure we may compare the legendary Canaanite account of King Keret, who calls for a mighty army, "three hundred myriads, peasant levies without number, regular levies beyond counting, marching in thousands like storm clouds, and in myriads as autumn rains" (*ANET*, 143). Cp. the numbers in Judg 4:6,10; 20:2 and the hyperbolic figures of speech in 6:5.

[93] Cf. the divine envoy's characterization of Gideon as a גִּבּוֹר הֶחָיִל, "mighty warrior," in 6:12.

(6) God's Gift of Security (3:30)

[30]That day Moab was made subject to Israel, and the land had peace for eighty years.

3:30 The unit closes with the tranquility formula. It offers a summary announcement of the subjugation of Moab and notices that the land of Israel was undisturbed for eighty years, a round figure for two generations.

Theological and Practical Implications

Because of the paucity of evidence, the historical significance of the events recounted here is difficult to assess. Minimally, Yahweh's defeat of Moab under Ehud's leadership resulted in peace for Israel for almost a century. This enabled the nation to consolidate its hold on the land of Canaan, but it also offered them another opportunity to turn to Yahweh with undivided attention. But subsequent narratives will demonstrate how miserably they failed in this. In the Transjordan the demise of Moab relieved the pressure from the south on the two and one-half Israelite tribes. At the same time, however, it also relieved the pressure on the Ammonites, who will replace Moab as a major irritation in chaps. 11–12.

At the personal level, in spite of his accomplishments, the figure of Ehud is problematic. Is he a hero or a villain? The answer depends upon one's point of view.[94] To the Moabites he was a traitor, violating the obligations of a vassal. But to the Israelites, from whose perspective the author writes, he was a divinely sent deliverer. To the moralist Ehud is clever, but he is brutal. The Book of Judges is not a catalog of exemplary characters. One may be amused by Ehud's wit and his deception, but one may hardly condone his treachery. Nor should we dismiss his actions simply as symptoms of a primitive ethic, acceptable in Israel's early history but to be superseded by further revelation and enlightenment. The narrator's silence on the role of God in the assassination of Eglon is deafening. Prior to v. 28 there is no hint of any spiritual sensitivity in Ehud's heart nor any sense of divine calling. On the contrary, Ehud operates like a typical Canaanite of his time—cleverly, opportunistically, and violently, apparently for his own glory. But the narrator appears not to be concerned at all about the morality of the affair. He simply describes what happened from his point of view, and in so doing reminds the readers that in the dark days of the governors the tools available to God are crude.

On the other hand, when the story is finished the reader is left with no doubt about the real hero in this story. The narrator knows Ehud is God's

---

[94] Like the participants in the American Revolutionary War. To the British, George Washington is no hero, and in Canada, those who resisted the revolution and stood by the British bear the honorific title "United Empire Loyalists."

appointed agent. If Israel is delivered from the oppression of the Moabites, the credit must go entirely to Yahweh. He raised up the deliverer (v. 15), and he delivered the enemy into the hands of Ehud. He has been gracious again to an undeserving people.

3. Parenthesis 1: The Governorship of Shamgar (3:31)

[31] **After Ehud came Shamgar son of Anath, who struck down six hundred Philistines with an oxgoad. He too saved Israel.**

3:31   The brevity of the Shamgar note and its unconventional literary nature within the context of the narrative cycles of oppression and deliverance have led critical scholarship generally to dismiss this verse as a late insertion.[95] In the absence of all the formulaic[96] and structural[97] features that determine the shapes of the surrounding narratives, one may surmise that the addition was artificially determined by a desire to bring the total number of rulers named in the book to twelve or to bring the number of "deliverers" to seven.[98] The name itself may have been suggested by the reference to Shamgar in the Song of Deborah (5:6). Alternatively, this supposedly "fictitious episode" may have been inspired by Samson's adventures with the Philistines (15:15–16) or the heroic achievements of David's mighty warriors.[99] However, later editors should smooth out readings rather than complicate them. Therefore it is preferable to assume that while this insertion breaks the narrative flow, it represents an intentional addition, driven by important literary and theological considerations, which will be considered after the details of the note have been clarified.

This brief note raises more questions about the person and work of Shamgar than it answers. How and where was the Philistine pressure felt in Israel? Who is this man Shamgar? How did he emerge as the champion of Israel? How could he have slaughtered six hundred Philistines, known for their military might and ruthlessness, with an ox prod? What effect did his heroic deeds have on Israel? The verse is a riddle. For the answer we are dependent upon the scant details it offers and external evidence that is suggestive at best. The informa-

---

[95] Becker (*Richterzeit und Königtum*, 139, n. 58) observes that it disrupts the natural link between 3:30 and 4:1.

[96] The following are all missing: The negative evaluation formula: "The Israelites did evil in the eyes of the LORD." The divine committal formula: "The LORD gave/sold the Israelites into the hands of the enemy." The cry of distress formula: "The Israelites cried out to the LORD." The divine provision of leadership formula: "The LORD raised up a deliverer for Israel to save them." The subjugation formula: "And NN was made subject to Israel." The tranquility formula: "Then the land had peace for X years." The death formula: "And X [the ruler] died."

[97] See the discussion on the Othniel account above.

[98] Note also that Shamgar is said to have "saved" (יָשַׁע) rather than "governed" (שָׁפַט) Israel.

[99] For bibliography see N. Shupak, "New Light on Shamgar ben ʿAnath," *Bib* 70 (1980): 517, n. 2.

tion provided may be reduced to four or five points.

First, Shamgar appeared on the scene "after" Ehud's assassination of Eglon and his military victory over the Moabite army.[100] How soon after we may only speculate. The Song of Deborah (5:6) suggests that the new hero was a contemporary of Deborah, Barak, and Jael, but the historical context of these figures is also difficult to fix. One may surmise preliminarily that, since Shamgar is associated with Ehud rather than Samson (Judges 13–16) and Samuel (1 Samuel 4–7), he appeared relatively early in the settlement period, perhaps when the first waves of Sea Peoples began to encroach upon regions occupied by the Israelites.[101]

Second, the narrator identifies the deliverer by name and patronymic: Shamgar ben Anath. But the name itself is a riddle. Students of Hebrew, who know that this language is based on triliteral roots, will observe that the name has four strong consonants: *š-m-g-r*.[102] The presence of analogous forms of the name in Nuzi texts suggests he may have been a Hurrian[103] operating in Palestine.[104] Equally puzzling is his characterization as *ben ʿAnat*, "son of Anath."[105] In the past this has been interpreted to mean he was a resident of Beth-Anath in Galilee.[106] Now it seems more likely this is intended as a dedicatory expression: Shamgar was devoted to the service of Anath.[107] What this means may be learned from extrabiblical sources.

In Canaanite mythology Anath was at the same time the consort of Baal and Canaanite goddess of war.[108] But Anath's fame extended far beyond Palestine. At the beginning of the nineteenth dynasty she was accepted into the Egyptian pantheon, functioning particularly as the goddess of war and

---

[100] The opening clause, שַׁמְגָּר הָיָה וְאַחֲרָיו, "and after him came Shamgar," correlates Shamgar's appearance with the exploits of Ehud rather than the Moabite oppression. The NIV's "Ehud" correctly finds the antecedent to the pronoun in the previous narrative.

[101] For a more precise dating see below.

[102] Soggin (*Judges*, 57) argues the name could be West Semitic, based on the *šapel* stem of the root מגר, "to submit."

[103] See B. Maisler (Mazar), "Shamgar ben 'Anat'," *PEQ* 66 (1934): 192–94; W. Feiler, "Hurritische Namen im Alten Testament," *ZA* 45 (1939): 219. This Hurrian solution is preferable to a proposed conflation of the transliterated and translated Hebrew forms of Egyptian *sᵓm*, meaning "wanderer, stranger," viz., גֵּר + שָׁם = Sham-gēr. Cf. Shupak, "New Light," 518; E. Danelius, "Judge Shamgar," *JNES* 22 (1963): 191–93.

[104] P. C. Craigie ("A Reconsideration of Shamgar ben Anath (Judg 3:31 and 5:6)," *JBL* 91 [1972]: 239–80) adduces further Ug., Mari, and Egyptian evidence for such foreign mercenaries.

[105] Cp. the name of Jeremiah's hometown, "Anathoth," Jer 1:1.

[106] Cf. 1:33; Josh 19:32–39. Thus Gray, *Joshua, Judges, and Ruth*, 216.

[107] Cp. Mal 2:11, which refers to non-Israelite women as "daughters of a foreign God." Note also names like Ben-Hadad, "Son of Hadad."

[108] On Anath see W. A. Meier III, "Anath (Deity)," *ABD* I:225–26; P. L. Day, "Anat," *DDD*, 62–77.

personal protectress of the Pharaoh.[109] But of special interest is an inscription from the Wadi Hammâmât dated in the third year of Rameses IV (1166–1160 B.C.), which reads "*prw* of the troop of ᶜAn[ath] eight hundred men."[110] On the assumption that the same troop had fought against the Sea Peoples during the reign of Rameses III (1198–1166 B.C.), Shupak suggests that Shamgar may have been one of these *ᶜprw* (Habiru), among whom were found a variety of ethnic elements, including Hurrians. As a member of an ᶜApiru troop of mercenaries in Pharaoh's army named after the Canaanite goddess of war, and a man of valor, he bore the widely used military cognomen, Ben ᶜAnath.[111] Since at first the Sea Peoples' base of land operations in Palestine was located in northern Lebanon and the Song of Deborah associates Shamgar with problems in northern Israel, the latter's confrontation with the Philistines probably occurred in the north at the beginning of the twelfth century B.C.[112] As an officer under the command of the Egyptian Pharaoh, Shamgar ben ᶜAnath was not intentionally serving Israelite interests.[113] In this event, however, his personal heroics benefited the Israelites directly by relieving them of the Philistine pressure for some time.[114]

Third, the narrator describes the manner of victory: he slaughtered six hundred Philistines with an ox goad. *malmed* (from *lāmad*, "to learn") is an Old Testament hapax, but in postbiblical Hebrew the word identifies a guiding instrument, a pointer.[115] The present instrument, normally used to train and control livestock, was made of hardwood and probably tipped with iron. Though the narrator is silent on the role of God, he may well have interpreted Shamgar's feat as a sign of divine intervention.

Fourth, the author identifies Shamgar as a "deliverer," rather than "ruler"

---

[109] For the evidence see Shupak, "New Light," 518–19.

[110] As read by W. Helck, *Die Beziehungen Äegyptens zu Vorderasien im 3. und 2. Jahr. V. Chr.* (Wiesbaden: Harrassowitz, 1971), 487.

[111] Further evidence of the use of *bn ᶜnt* as a military cognomen appears on an El-Khadr arrowhead dated ca. 1100 B.C., bearing the incised inscription *ᶜbdlbʾt bn ᶜnt,* on which see F. M. Cross, "Newly Found Inscriptions in Old Canaanite and Early Phoenician Scripts," *BASOR* 238 (1980): 4, 6–7. Cp. also an eleventh or tenth century bronze arrowhead inscribed *ḥṣ zkrbᶜl / bn bn-ᶜn[t].* Cf. J. T. Milik and F. M. Cross, "Inscribed Javelin-Heads from the Period of the Judges: A Recent Discovery in Palestine," *BASOR* 134 (1954): 5–15.

[112] Although the OT employs the designation פְּלִשְׁתִּים, "Philistines," indiscriminately for the Sea Peoples as a whole, the Philistines (Egyptian *plšt*) emerged as a distinct group among the Sea Peoples during Rameses III's reign.

[113] So also Shupak, "New Light," 524. This may explain the brevity of the note in Judges.

[114] This explanation is preferable to Soggin's suggestion (*Judges,* 59), based on 5:9, that Shamgar was actually one of the oppressors of Israel prior to Barak's decisive victory over the Canaanites at the Kishon and Lindar's contention (*Judges 1–5,* 157–58) that he subjected the northern Israelite tribes to intense harassment.

[115] *Sanh.* 10:28a.

(šōpēṭ), of Israel. By using the verb *hôšîaʿ* he places him in the same category as the other "saviors" *(môšîʿîm)* of the nation.

As intimated earlier, the brevity of the note on Shamgar and the author's eschewal of the conventional formulae and structure found in the rest of his narratives may reflect the fact that he was formally employed by the Egyptian Pharaoh. Since he was not an Israelite, he may have had no more information on this man, who appears out of nowhere, accomplishes his task, and immediately disappears from view. On the other hand, the lack of detail and the primitive plot development may also reflect the author's embarrassment over Israel's dependence on a foreigner for their deliverance. The dearth of native leadership in Israel represented one more symptom of the Canaanization of Israel.

Theological and Practical Implications

The dilemma faced by the Israelites in the dark days of the governors is not without parallel in the contemporary church, which is often at the mercy of the world. Dependence on secular business procedures and the methodologies of the social sciences increases in the church as godliness and genuine spirituality among the leaders decrease. But a church that has permitted itself to be squeezed into the mold of the world should not be surprised to find itself hostage to its enemies. The Lord is under no obligation to those who bear his name in vain, those who claim to be the people of God but act like Canaanites. However, he remains sensitive to the groaning of his people and waits to demonstrate his power and his grace in freeing them from the tyranny of evil and their own foolishness. God is resourceful and often rescues his work through outside agents in spite of his people and their leaders.

4. The Canaanite and Barak Cycle (4:1–5:31)

Judges 4–5 offers a rare presentation of a single event in two versions, one prose (chap. 4), the other poetic (chap. 5). Indeed these chapters offer students of Old Testament literature an invaluable resource for examining the differences between ancient Hebrew poetry and prose. Although the distinctions are not absolute, the typical features of the two major categories of Hebrew literature may be summarized as follows:[116]

---

[116] For helpful studies of Hebrew prose and poetry respectively see Alter, *The Art of Biblical Narrative;* id., *The Art of Biblical Poetry* (New York: Basic Books, 1985).

Feature	Prose	Poetry
Diction	Common diction, employing words and spellings used in everyday speech and commerce	Elevated literary diction, archaic expressions, and rare words
Grammar	Common grammar and syntax, with distinctive prosaic elements[a]	Creative grammatical and syntactical forms, often lacking the prosaic elements.
Style	Logical and chronological description, heavily dependent upon coordinating and subordinating clauses, dialogue, plot development, etc.	Impressionistic and often abstract description, heavily dependent upon the heightened use of parallelism
Tone	Controlled and relatively realistic, though deliberately and artistically composed	Emotionally charged, with heavy reliance on hyperbole and other figures of speech
Aim	To inform, educate, entertain, indoctrinate	To celebrate, commemorate, inspire

a. The *waw* consecutive verb form, אֵת, as the marker of a definite direct object, the subordinate conjunction אֲשֶׁר, etc.

The only parallel to this juxtapositioning of prose and poetic accounts of the same event in the entire Old Testament is found in Exodus 14–15, which recounts and celebrates the Israelite crossing of the Reed Sea.[117] Scholars have expended a great deal of effort and spent a lot of ink discussing the chronological relationship between these two chapters. Although a complete survey of explanations is impossible here, opinion divides among five principal possibilities.

First, the poem is original, and the narrative is derivative. The former's archaic grammatical, lexical, and orthographic features suggest an origin much older than the prose account in which it is embedded. Accordingly, the narrative account is expository, recasting the [often vague and enigmatic] hymnic version of the defeat of the Canaanites under the leadership of Deborah in more realistic narrative form, and completing the picture by filling in missing details from other recollections of these early times.[118]

---

[117] But this phenomenon is attested in extrabiblical writings. See especially the Egyptian prose and poetic accounts of the Battle of Kadesh, in A. H. Gardiner, *The Kadesh Inscriptions of Rameses II* (Oxford: Oxford University, 1960).

[118] See especially Halpern, "Sisera and Old Lace: The Case of Deborah and Yael," in *The First Historians*, 76–103; id., "The Resourceful Israelite Historian: The Song of Deborah and Israelite Historiography," *HTR* 76 (1983): 379–401. See also H.-D. Neef, "Deboraerzählung und Deboralied: Beobachtungen zum Verhältnis von Jdc. iv und v," *VT* 44 (1994): 47–59.

Second, a minority opinion holds the prose account to be original, and the poetic version as a creative distortion of history.[119]

Third, the two accounts represent independent literary versions of a treasured story.[120] The poem may indeed be early, but the texts derive from different oral traditions.[121]

Fourth, both poet and narrator had access to the same basic data, though not necessarily in written form. The differences in the accounts are the result of different genres.[122]

Fifth, recognizing that any reconstruction of the chronological relationship between chaps. 4 and 5 is speculative, in their present literary context the prose and poetic accounts function as complementary versions of the same event.[123] This last approach seems most appropriate if one is to understand the rhetorical function of these variant versions in the context of the book.[124] The reader must recognize at the outset that we know of the poetic version of the battle between Deborah-Barak and Jabin-Sisera only because a prose narrator has embedded it within his larger composition. This means that its present literary purpose cannot be understood without reference to the overall agenda of the book. An understanding of their relationship in context is best achieved by placing the texts side by side, as we have done in the following synopsis:[125]

---

[119] E.g., A. Caquot, "Les tribus d'Israel dans le cantique de Dbora (Juges 5, 13–17)," *Semitica* 36 (1986): 47–70.

[120] See Lindars (*Judges 1–5*, 164–65) and Richter (*Traditionsgeschichtliche Untersuchungen*, 111–12).

[121] Lindars, "Deborah's Song: Women in the Old Testament," *BJRL* 65 (1983): 159; id., *Judges 1–5*, 164–65; M. Bal, *Murder and Difference: Gender, Genre, and Scholarship on Sisera's Death*, Indiana Studies in Biblical Literature, trans. M. Gumpert (Bloomington: Indiana University Press, 1988), 66–67.

[122] M. Sternberg, *The Poetics of Biblical Narrative: Ideological Literature and the Drama of Reading* (Bloomington: Indiana University Press, 1985), 247; Alter, "From Line to Story in Biblical Verse," *Poetics Today* 4 (1983): 634. Malamat ("Period of the Judges," 137) opines that the discrepancies represent "depictions of different stages of one and the same battle."

[123] Thus A. Brenner, "A Triangle and a Rhombus in Narrative Structure: A Proposed Integrative Reading of Judges IV and V," *VT* 40 (1990): 129–38; reprinted in *A Feminist Companion to Judges*, ed. A. Brenner (Sheffield: JSOT Press, 1993), 98–114; D. N. Fewell and D. M. Gunn, "Women, Men, and the Authority of Violence in Judges 4 and 5," *JAAR* 58/3 (1990): 389–411; J. W. Watts, *Psalm and Story: Inset Hymns in Hebrew Narrative*, JSOTSup 139 (Sheffield: JSOT Press, 1992), 82–98; K. L. Younger, "Heads! Tails! Or the Whole Coin! Contextual Method and Intertextual Analysis: Judges 4 and 5," in *The Biblical Canon in Comparative Perspective: Scripture in Context IV; ANETS* 11; ed. K. L. Younger et al. (Lewiston: Edwin Mellen, 1991), 109–35.

[124] For a superb rhetorical analysis see O'Connell, *Rhetoric of the Book of Judges*, 101–39.

[125] Ideally the synopsis should be based on the Hb. text and, failing that, on a literal translation. In keeping with the textual base of this commentary series, the following synopsis employs the NIV in the main, with several modifications based on our understanding of the text.

Israel and the Canaanites: A Synopsis of the Prose and Poetic Accounts (Judges 4–5)

The Prose Account	The Poetic Account
	[1]On that day Deborah and Barak son of Abinoam sang this song: [2]Because of total commitment in Israel Because the people willingly offer themselves— Praise the LORD! [3]Hear this, you kings! Listen you rulers! I to the LORD, I will sing; I will make music to the LORD, the God of Israel. [4]O LORD, when you went out from Seir, when you marched from the land of Edom, the earth shook, the heavens gushed; the clouds gushed down water, [5]the mountains quaked before the LORD, the One of Sinai before the LORD, the God of Israel.
[1]After Ehud died, the Israelites once again did evil in the eyes of the LORD. [2]So the LORD sold them into the hands of Jabin, a king of Canaan, who reigned in Hazor. The commander of his army was Sisera, who lived in Harosheth Haggoyim. [3]Because he had nine hundred iron chariots and had cruelly oppressed the Israelites for twenty years, they cried to the LORD for help.	[6]In the days of Shamgar son of Anath, in the days of Jael, the roads were abandoned; travelers took to winding paths. [7]Village life ceased; in Israel it ceased—
[4]Deborah, a prophetess, the wife of Lappidoth, was leading Israel at that time. [5]She held court under the Palm of Deborah between Ramah and Bethel in the hill country of Ephraim, and the Israelites came to her [for a decision from God].	Until I arose, Deborah, I arose, a mother in Israel. [8]God chose new [leaders], war came to the city gates, and not a shield or spear was seen among forty thousand in Israel.
	[9]My heart is with Israel's princes, with the willing volunteers among the people Praise the LORD! [10]You who ride on tawny donkey, You who sit on saddle blankets, and you who walk along the road, consider [11]Amid the sound of shepherds at the watering places They recite the righteous acts of the LORD, the righteous acts of his villagers in Israel. Then the people of the LORD went down to the city gates.

⁶She sent for Barak son of Abinoam from
Kedesh in Naphtali and said to him, "The
LORD, the God of Israel, commands you:
"Go, take with you ten thousand men of
Naphtali and Zebulun and lead the way to
Mount Tabor. ⁷I will lure Sisera, the commander of Jabin's army, with his chariots
and his troops to the Kishon River and give
him into your hands.""
⁸Barak said to her, "If you go with me, I will
go; but if you don't go with me, I won't go."
⁹Very well," Deborah said, "I will go with you.
But because of the way you are going about this,
the honor will not be yours, for the LORD will
hand Sisera over to a woman."

So Deborah went with Barak to Kedesh,
¹⁰where he summoned Zebulun and Naphtali.
Ten thousand men followed him, and Deborah
also went with him.

¹¹Now Heber the Kenite had left the other
Kenites, the descendants of Hobab, Moses'
brother-in-law, and pitched his tent by the
great tree in Zaanannim near Kedesh.

¹²Wake up, wake up, Deborah!
Wake up, wake up, break out in song!
    Arise, O Barak!
Take captive your captives, O son of Abinoam.
¹³Then the survivors went down
        against the nobles;
the people of the LORD went down with me
        against the mighty.
¹⁴Some came from Ephraim,
        whose roots were in Amalek;
Benjamin was with the people who followed you.
From Makir captains came down,
from Zebulun those who bear
        a commander's staff.
¹⁵The princes of Issachar were with Deborah;
Yes, Issachar was with Barak,
rushing after him into the valley.
In the districts of Reuben
there was much searching of heart.
¹⁶Why did you stay among the campfires
to hear the whistling for the flocks?
In the districts of Reuben
        there was much searching of heart.
¹⁷Gilead stayed beyond the Jordan.
And Dan, why did he linger by the ships?
Asher remained on the seacoast
and stayed in his coves.
¹⁸The people of Zebulun risked their very lives
so did Naphtali on the heights of the field

¹²When they told Sisera that Barak son of Abinoam had gone up to Mount Tabor, ¹³Sisera gathered together his nine hundred iron chariots and all the men with him, from Harosheth Haggoyim to the Kishon River.

¹⁴Then Deborah said to Barak, "Go! This is the day the LORD has given Sisera into your hands. Has not the LORD gone ahead of you?" So Barak went down Mount Tabor, followed by ten thousand men.

¹⁵At Barak's advance, the LORD routed Sisera and all his chariots and army by the sword, and Sisera abandoned his chariot and fled on foot.

¹⁶But Barak pursued the chariots and army as far as Haroshet Haggoyim. All the troops of Sisera fell by the sword; not a man was left.

¹⁷Sisera, however, fled on foot to the tent of Jael, the wife of Heber the Kenite, because there there were friendly relations between Jabin king of Hazor and the clan of Heber the Kenite.

¹⁸Jael went out to meet Sisera and said to him, "Come, my lord, come right in. Don't be afraid." So he entered her tent, and she put a covering over him.
¹⁹"I'm thirsty," he said. "Please give me some water." She opened a skin of milk, gave him a drink, and covered him up.

²⁰"Stand in the doorway of the tent," he told her. "If someone comes by and asks you, 'Is anyone here?' say 'No.'"

²¹But Jael, Heber's wife, picked up a tent peg and a hammer and went quietly to him while he lay fast asleep, exhausted. She drove the

¹⁹"Kings came, they fought;
the kings of Canaan fought;
At Taanach by the waters of Megiddo,
they carried off no silver, no plunder.

²⁰From the heavens the stars fought,
from their courses they fought against Sisera.
²¹The river Kishon swept them away,
the age-old river, the river Kishon.
March on, my soul; be strong!
²²Then pounded the horses' hoofs—
Rearing wildly his mighty steeds.

²³Curse Meroz, said the angel of the LORD.
'Curse its people bitterly,
because they did not come to help the LORD,
to help the LORD against the mighty.'

²⁴Most blessed of women be Jael,
the wife of Heber the Kenite,
most blessed of tent-dwelling women.

²⁵He asked for water,
    and she gave him milk;
in a bowl fit for nobles
    she brought him curdled milk.

²⁶Her hand reached for the tent peg,
her right hand for the workman's hammer.
She struck Sisera, she crushed his head,

peg through his temple into the ground, and he died.

²²Barak came by in pursuit of Sisera, and Jael went out to meet him. "Come," she said, "I will show you the man you're looking for." So he went in with her, and there lay Sisera with the tent peg through his temple—dead.

²³On that day God subdued Jabin, the Canaanite king, before the Israelites. ²⁴And the hand of the Israelites grew stronger and stronger against Jabin, the Canaanite king, until they destroyed him.

⁵:³¹ᶜThen the land had peace for forty years.

she shattered and pierced his temple.
²⁷At her feet he sank, he fell, he lay;
Where he sank, there he fell—plundered.

²⁸"Through the window peered Sisera's mother;
behind the lattice she cried out,
'Why is his chariot so long in coming?
Why is the clatter of his chariots delayed?'"
²⁹The wisest of her ladies answers her;
But she answers herself,
³⁰'Are they not finding and dividing the spoils:
A girl or two for each man,
colorful garments as plunder for Sisera,
colorful garments embroidered,
highly embroidered garments
for the neck of the spoiler?'

³¹"So may all your enemies perish, O LORD!
But may they who love you be like the sun
when it rises in its strength."

Juxtaposed like this, the peculiarities of the prose and poetic accounts of Israel's victory over Sisera and the Canaanites are obvious. In addition to the differences in vocabulary, tone, and poetic style, the following differences may be noted. First, and most obviously, although the sequence of events described/reflected in the two versions is parallel, the versions highlight different aspects. Without belaboring variations in detail, the prose version lacks any reference/allusion to: (1) Israel's celebrative response (5:1–3); (2) Yahweh's approach from Sinai to aid the Israelites (5:4–5); (3) praise for Israel's warriors (5:9–11); (4) a roll call and evaluation of tribal participation (5:13–18);[126] (5) cosmic involvement in the victory over Sisera's army (5:20–21);[127] (6) the curse of Meroz for noninvolvement (5:23), or anyone else for that matter; (7) interest in

---

[126] From 4:10 it appears only Naphtalites and Zebulunites were summoned and responded.
[127] 4:15 notes that the victory was achieved by the sword.

the secondary victims of the slaughter on the battlefield, the families of the warriors (5:28–30).

On the other hand, the poetic account lacks any reference/allusion to: (1) the role of Jabin, king of Canaan (4:2); (2) the personal background and professional activity of Deborah prior to the battle (4:4–5); (3) her role in calling up Barak (4:6–9); (4) the relationship between Heber, the husband of Jael, and the Canaanites (4:11); (5) Sisera's mustering of his forces (4:12); (6) Deborah's specific involvement in the battle (4:14); (7) Barak's pursuit and defeat of Sisera's army (4:16); (8) Sisera's flight to Jael (4:15,17); (9) Barak's pursuit of Sisera, his encounter with Jael, and discovery of the slain enemy (4:22).

Second, whereas the prose version provides a self-contained logical and chronological account leading up to a climax (4:23–24), the poetic version consists of a collage of more or less independent scenes, with little or no effort on the part of the composer to create a coherent plot line.[128] Indeed, if the narrative account were not available, it would be difficult to reconstruct the course of the battle from the ode alone.

Third, God's participation and Israel's participation in the victory are portrayed quite differently. The prose account highlights the role of Yahweh with overt references to his activity.[129] Although the poet calls for praise to God for the victory (5:2,9) and the reader of the poem cannot imagine this victory without him, he/she alludes to his involvement only obliquely.[130] On the other hand, quite ironically, the narrator's lens focuses on Barak, even though his role is deliberately diminished. He pursues the enemy army, but Yahweh routs them (4:15–16); he pursues Sisera, but Jael claims the prize (4:17–22).[131]

Fourth, these portrayals of Yahweh are matched by the portrayals of women in the respective texts. Although both accounts highlight the involvement of women in the pursuit and outcome of the battle, only the prose

---

[128] On which see A. J. Hauser, "Judges 5: Parataxis in Hebrew Poetry," *JBL* 99 (1980): 23–41.

[129] He summons Barak [through his prophet] (4:6), promises to lure Sisera into battle and deliver him into Barak's hands (4:7), announces through his prophet the day of victory (4:14), routs the enemy (4:15), and effects the subjugation of Jabin (4:23).

[130] The poet announces his epiphany from the south (5:4–5), notes his choice of new leader (5:8; see our commentary on this verse below), speaks of "his righteous acts" (5:11), and observes the involvement of cosmic elements in the victory (5:20–21). Note also the oblique allusions to his involvement by identifying the human warriors as "the people of the LORD" (יהוה עַם, 5:11,13) and the one who curses Meroz as "the envoy/messenger of the LORD" (יהוה מַלְאַךְ, 5:23), as well as the rebuke of Meroz for not coming to the aid of Yahweh, as if he were in dire straights (5:23), and the reference to the enemies of Israel as the enemies of Yahweh (5:30).

[131] Y. Amit has correctly noted that the theological emphasis is present in both; the differences lie in the modes of presentation ("Judges 4: Its Content and Form," *JSOT* 39 [1987]: 103).

account explicitly raises gender as an issue (4:9).[132] Indeed, the narrator deliberately highlights the initiative and power of female participants while humiliating the male characters. The song, on the other hand, minimizes the role of Barak, but it does not humiliate him. Whereas the prose narrative portrays him as subservient to Deborah, the ode itself and the prose preamble perceive them in a complementary relationship (5:1,12). Gender issues are not a primary concern of chap. 5, but the chapter's womanly outlook gives this text its distinctive flavor.[133] One may propose that whereas the narrator expresses the way the world views women, the poet expresses how women view the world.

These differences should not blind the reader to the onomastic,[134] lexical,[135] and thematic[136] links that prove that the narrative and the song have in mind the same crisis, the same characters, and the same events.[137] But the ode also fits the picture of Israel painted in the rest of the book. Not only do the varied responses of the tribes to the crisis reflect the same fractured sociopolitical realities portrayed elsewhere, but the tribes listed in the roll (5:14–18) are also reminiscent of the "anticonquest" survey in chap. 1; the references to Taanach and Megiddo in 5:19 recall 1:27–28; Amalek (5:14) will resurface in chaps. 6–7 and 10; Issachar (5:15) and Gilead (5:17) reappear in chaps. 10–12 and 21.[138] The chronological note in 5:6 links the time of the crisis and the ensuing battle to events known from elsewhere in the book (3:31), but the preamble fixes the composition of the song in the aftermath of the present defeat of the Canaanites.[139]

These similarities reflect the complementarity of Judges 4 and 5. Whatever the origin of the Song of Deborah, by juxtaposing these two texts the author has presented the reader with two lenses with which to view a single event. The texts do indeed display obvious dissimilarities in style, tone, texture, and emphases, but the versions do not contain any significant differences that cannot be attrib-

---

[132] Cf. K. R. R. Gros Louis, "The Book of Judges," *Literary Interpretations of Biblical Narratives*, ed. K. R. R. Gros Louis et al. (Nashville: Abingdon, 1974), 148; Lindars, "Deborah's Song," 158–175, esp. 172–75; J. A. Hackett, "Women's Studies and the Hebrew Bible," in *The Future of Biblical Studies: The Hebrew Scriptures*, ed. R. E. Friedman and H. G. M. Williamson (Atlanta: Scholars Press, 1989), 154–55.

[133] So also Watts, *Psalm and Story*, 88.

[134] Note the names of the main characters (Yahweh, Deborah, Barak ben Abinoam, Sisera, Jael), the reference to Shamgar ben Anat (3:31; 5:12), the tribal names (Ephraim, Zebulun, Naphtali), the Kishon River (4:7,13; 5:21).

[135] The versions use the same word for "to muster," מָשַׁךְ (4:6, 5:14); Yahweh's advance, "to go out," יָצָא (4:14; 5:14); the Israelite's downhill charge, יָרַד, "to go down" (4:14; 5:13).

[136] The battle and the death of Sisera relieve the Israelite suffering; Deborah and Barak lead Israel; Sisera is the primary enemy; Jael is the final [treacherous] hero.

[137] So also Watts, *Praise and Story*, 84–85.

[138] Cf. ibid., 86.

[139] הַהוּא בַּיּוֹם in 5:1 echoes the same expression in 4:23.

uted to differences in genre and function. Both versions of the story go back to a common source, the historical victory of the Israelites under the prophetic inspiration of Deborah and the military leadership of Barak over the Canaanites.

It is evident from Judges 4 and 5 (and Exodus 14–15) that Israelite scribes could compose different accounts of the same events. In this they followed a common ancient Near Eastern pattern. The numerous prose and poetic accounts of the same battles that have been preserved in ancient Assyrian and Egyptian writings demonstrate that differences in form, style, and detail reflect differences in purpose. Texts that aimed to inform tended to be written in prose; those intended to praise the victorious king of gods tended to be composed in poetry or at least an embellished rhetorical style.[140] Unlike most of the extrabiblical variant versions, which are known from independent sources,[141] in Judges 4–5 we observe a narrator deliberately juxtaposing these accounts for heightened rhetorical effect.

The placement of the victory hymn *after* the prose account of the battle intentionally mirrors the celebration of victors *after* the historical event. The poetic mode is deliberately employed because it captures the emotion of the original participants and inspires the reader to rejoice with them. The poem was deemed useful to the author of the book because it draws the reader into the ancient celebrants' praise to God for his gracious intervention in the affairs of his people when they had nowhere else to turn. Through the mouth of Deborah (and Barak) the writer was able to express his feelings of joy and delight in God (and ridicule of the enemy) with an intensity denied him in the conventions of narrative discourse.[142]

Concerning the origins of these prose and poetic reminiscences we may only speculate. Since Deborah's base of operations was "under the palm tree of Deborah" (4:5) between Bethel and Ramah, it is conceivable the Ephraimite inhabitants of these towns treasured these traditions and passed them on orally from generation to generation. On the other hand, since Deborah was a prophet, the accounts of her activity may have been preserved by the guild of prophets along with other stories involving this profession.[143] If Deborah was indeed the composer of the song,[144] both

---

[140] For a study of several significant, analogous, complementary pairs of accounts in prose and poetry see Younger, "Judges 4 and 5," 110–27.

[141] Watts (*Psalm and Story*, 97–98) cites several extrabiblical examples of poetic victory accounts inserted in prose contexts.

[142] Which raises the question of why this is the only celebrative poem preserved in the book. Presumably this was the only such document available to the author (so also Watts, *Psalm and Story*, 97), though a similar rhetorical effect is achieved in 19:30 by quoting the saying that spread throughout the land in the wake of the Levite's dismemberment of his concubine.

[143] Cf. 2:1–5; 6:7–10; 10:10–16; 1 Chr 29:29 recognizes that the keeping of such records dates back at least to Samuel. Cp. 2 Chr 9:29; 12:15; 13:22; 20:34; 26:22; 32:32; 33:19.

[144] See below.

versions may derive ultimately from the same circles.

No unit in the Book of Judges has engaged more scholarly discussion than Judges 4–5. In addition to the problem of the relationship between these chapters, critical scholarship has often been concerned with reconstructing the evolution of the text and/or the historical events described here.[145] Some have suggested that these chapters represent a variant tradition of the events recorded in Josh 11:1–11.[146] Others have argued for the fusion of two separate traditions, the defeat of Jabin of Hazor at Kadesh in upper Galilee and Barak's battle against Sisera in the central plain.[147] More recent source and tradition critical analysts prefer to speak in terms of the growth of the text from an original core, by a series of additions to the present form.[148] But the majority of contemporary studies eschew speculation about the evolution of the text in favor of a holistic literary or a feminist ideological interpretation. The heroic roles played by women and the negative light in which men are cast in this chapter offers investigators fertile ground for feminist commentary.[149]

---

[145] N. Naᶜaman ("Literary and Topographical Notes on the Battle of Kishon (Judges IV–V)," *VT* 4 [1990]: 427) observes that the battle at the wadi Kishon is the only geographically detailed story we have from northern Israel. He suggests the [apparent] topographical confusion is the result of a Judean redactor who lacked knowledge of certain details of the old story and had no real knowledge of the topography of the north. See also the essay by A. D. H. Mayes, "The Historical Context of the Battle Against Sisera," *VT* 19 (1969): 353–60.

[146] H. W. Hertzberg, *Die Bücher Josua, Richter, Ruth*, ATD 9; 2d ed. (Göttingen: Vandenhoeck & Ruprecht, 1953). But see the critique by Gray, *Joshua, Judges, and Ruth*, 217.

[147] Gray, *Joshua, Judges, and Ruth*, 217–19.

[148] H.-D. Neef identifies vv. 10,12–16 and 17a,18–21 as the oldest sections, to which were added vv. 4a,6–9 to form the center of the chapter ("Der Sieg Deboras und Baraks über Sisera: Exegetische Beobachtungen zum Aufbau und Werden von Jdc 4,1–24," *ZAW* 101 [1989]: 28–49). Verses 4b,5,11,17b represent later additions to the story; vv. 1–3 provide the editorial framework. Cf. Becker's conclusions, *Richterzeit und Königtum*, 138–39.

[149] Following the lead of Y. Zakovitch ("Siseras Tod," *ZAW* 93 [1981]: 364–74), the foremost representative of this approach, M. Bal, pays special attention to the reversal of sexual roles, the evocative symbolism of intercourse, childbirth, and murder as keys to understanding the accounts of Sisera's death (*Murder and Difference: Gender, Genre, and Scholarship on Sisera's Death*, ISBL [Bloomington/Indianapolis: Indiana University, 1988]). See also R. Rasmussen ("Deborah the Woman Warrior," *Anti-Covenant: Counter Reading Women's Lives in the Hebrew Bible*, ed. M. Bal JSOTSup 81, Bible and Literature 22 [Sheffield: Almond, 1989], 79–94), who suggests that Deborah's story was originally told as a rite within women's cults but that the author and readers deliberately obscure Deborah's achievements by highlighting Yahweh's direct involvement in the battle, and S. Hanselman ("Narrative Theory, Ideology, and Transformation in Judges 4," ibid., 95–112), who concludes that chap. 4 celebrates Deborah's and Jael's subversion of the patriarchal order; and Fewell and Gunn, "Controlling Perspectives," 389–411. Exum ("Feminist Criticism: Whose Interests Are Being Served?" in *Judges and Method: New Approaches in Biblical Studies*, ed. G. A. Yee [Minneapolis: Fortress, 1995], 71–75) sees in Deborah's song about another woman, Sisera's mother, and about the rape of women (5:12) the voice of a good mother being appropriated to male ideology. Cp. the more moderate analysis by B. Lindars, "Deborah's Song: Women in the Old Testament," *BJRL* 65 (1983): 158–75.

While feminist approaches offer many fresh insights into the biblical text, too often modern agendas are imposed upon these ancient documents, overriding and obscuring the original intention of the narrator/song writer. In their enthusiasm to celebrate the subversion of patriarchy, such interpretations subvert the authority of God and obscure the message he seeks to communicate through this text. The biblical author was obviously interested in women's affairs and achievements, but in the final analysis Deborah and Jael are not heroic figures because of their revisionist challenges to prevailing social structures; they are heroines because of what they accomplish as agents of the divine agenda, which in this instance has less to do with overthrowing oppressive patriarchy than the role they play in Yahweh's overthrowing oppressive Canaanites.[150] The entire account is deliberately crafted to highlight the salvation provided by God. He is the chief Operator, pulling the strings, raising generals, deploying armies, dictating strategy, and effecting victory. In the end both narrative and song celebrate the saving work of Yahweh.[151]

The basic structure of this account is determined by the paradigm that governs all six deliverance narratives. While the shapes of the opening (vv. 1–3) and closing (vv. 23–24) verses are determined largely by the anticipated formulae, the actual story of salvation that falls between this formulaic framework is recounted with great skill, making ample use of repetition, irony, dialogue, characterization, ambiguity, and surprise.[152] This central core breaks into four discreet acts, each signaled by a circumstantial clause that functions as an episode marker: the call of Barak (vv. 4–10); the defeat of Sisera's forces (vv. 11–16); the slaying of Sisera (vv. 17–21); the arrival of Barak (v. 22).

(1) The Narrative Description (4:1–24)

[1]After Ehud died, the Israelites once again did evil in the eyes of the LORD. [2]So the LORD sold them into the hands of Jabin, a king of Canaan, who reigned in Hazor. The commander of his army was Sisera, who lived in Harosheth Haggoyim. [3]Because he had nine hundred iron chariots and had cruelly oppressed the Israelites for twenty years, they cried to the LORD for help.

[4]Deborah, a prophetess, the wife of Lappidoth, was leading Israel at that time.

---

[150] A point missed completely by Yee, "By the Hand of a Woman: The Metaphor of the Woman Warrior in Judges 4," *Semeia* 61 (1993): 99–132. Although both Deborah and Jael are involved in this battle, this does not make either a warrior figure. Deborah is a female prophet announcing the word of God to the warrior; Jael is a treacherous woman acting on her own.

[151] See the superb discussion on this theme by Amit, "Judges 4: Its Content and Form," *JSOT* 39 (1987): 89–111. Accordingly, Exum's overstatement "Deborah provides the only unsullied hero of the book" not only demeans Othniel unnecessarily; more seriously, it has lost sight of Yahweh, the gracious redeemer and liberator of Israel ("The Center Cannot Hold: Thematic and Textual Instabilities in Judges," *CBQ* 52 [1990]: 415).

[152] See the superb literary study of this text by Sternberg, *Poetics of Biblical Narrative*, 270–83.

⁵She held court under the Palm of Deborah between Ramah and Bethel in the hill country of Ephraim, and the Israelites came to her to have their disputes decided. ⁶She sent for Barak son of Abinoam from Kedesh in Naphtali and said to him, "The LORD, the God of Israel, commands you: 'Go, take with you ten thousand men of Naphtali and Zebulun and lead the way to Mount Tabor. ⁷I will lure Sisera, the commander of Jabin's army, with his chariots and his troops to the Kishon River and give him into your hands.'"

⁸Barak said to her, "If you go with me, I will go; but if you don't go with me, I won't go."

⁹"Very well," Deborah said, "I will go with you. But because of the way you are going about this, the honor will not be yours, for the LORD will hand Sisera over to a woman." So Deborah went with Barak to Kedesh, ¹⁰where he summoned Zebulun and Naphtali. Ten thousand men followed him, and Deborah also went with him.

¹¹Now Heber the Kenite had left the other Kenites, the descendants of Hobab, Moses' brother-in-law, and pitched his tent by the great tree in Zaanannim near Kedesh.

¹²When they told Sisera that Barak son of Abinoam had gone up to Mount Tabor, ¹³Sisera gathered together his nine hundred iron chariots and all the men with him, from Harosheth Haggoyim to the Kishon River.

¹⁴Then Deborah said to Barak, "Go! This is the day the LORD has given Sisera into your hands. Has not the LORD gone ahead of you?" So Barak went down Mount Tabor, followed by ten thousand men. ¹⁵At Barak's advance, the LORD routed Sisera and all his chariots and army by the sword, and Sisera abandoned his chariot and fled on foot. ¹⁶But Barak pursued the chariots and army as far as Harosheth Haggoyim. All the troops of Sisera fell by the sword; not a man was left.

¹⁷Sisera, however, fled on foot to the tent of Jael, the wife of Heber the Kenite, because there were friendly relations between Jabin king of Hazor and the clan of Heber the Kenite.

¹⁸Jael went out to meet Sisera and said to him, "Come, my lord, come right in. Don't be afraid." So he entered her tent, and she put a covering over him.

¹⁹"I'm thirsty," he said. "Please give me some water." She opened a skin of milk, gave him a drink, and covered him up.

²⁰"Stand in the doorway of the tent," he told her. "If someone comes by and asks you, 'Is anyone here?' say 'No.'"

²¹But Jael, Heber's wife, picked up a tent peg and a hammer and went quietly to him while he lay fast asleep, exhausted. She drove the peg through his temple into the ground, and he died.

²²Barak came by in pursuit of Sisera, and Jael went out to meet him. "Come," she said, "I will show you the man you're looking for." So he went in with her, and there lay Sisera with the tent peg through his temple—dead.

²³On that day God subdued Jabin, the Canaanite king, before the Israelites. ²⁴And the hand of the Israelites grew stronger and stronger against Jabin, the Canaanite king, until they destroyed him.

THE MARKS OF ISRAEL'S CANAANIZATION (4:1). **4:1** The negative evaluation formula with which this cycle opens is virtually identical in form to the opening of the Moab and Ehud cycle. As in 3:12, the expression *wayyōsipû ... laʿăśôt*, literally "and they added ... to do," in context means "and they relapsed into a pattern of behavior." This beginning highlights the fundamentally unresolved spiritual issue in Israel. The divine victory had not altered their deeply rooted bent toward paganism, expressed in actions found evil in the eyes of Yahweh. The formula is modified only by the awkward addition of a circumstantial clause, *wĕʾēhûd mēt*, "And Ehud died," which most translations interpret as a pluperfect. This comment suggests the Deborah-Barak story originally followed immediately after the account of Ehud's life and that the Shamgar note represents a later, though intentional insertion.

GOD'S AGENT OF PUNISHMENT (4:2). **4:2** Yahweh's response to Israel's apostasy is expressed in the stronger version of the divine committal formula.[153] The benefactor/oppressor is identified as "Jabin, king of Canaan, who reigned in Hazor." Since Josh 11:1–15 describes Joshua's victory over Jabin and his total razing of his capital, Hazor, the present account is often interpreted as a garbled version of the same event. The name Jabin is not the problem,[154] since this probably represents a sort of dynastic name at Hazor rather than a personal name.[155]

The reference to Hazor presents a more serious problem. This city, appropriately referred to in Josh 11:10 as "the head of all these kingdoms," dominated the valley north of the Sea of Galilee for five centuries until its utter destruction under Joshua.[156] It was not to be rebuilt until the time of Solomon, for whom it represented the major northern fortification. How then could the king of this city hold Israel hostage for twenty years prior to the victory achieved under Barak? Some argue that since Jabin's name and the reference to Hazor appear only incidentally in the account (vv. 2,17) and Hazor does not

---

[153] See p. 147f.

[154] The authenticity of the name is supported by (a) the reference to Qishon of Jabin *(ybn)* in a topographical list of Rameses II at Karnak [see C. H. Krahmalkov, "Exodus Itinerary Confirmed by Egyptian Evidence," *BAR* 20/5 (1994]: 61); (b) references to King Ibni-Addu (Akk. for Yabin-Adad) of Hazor in the Mari texts (see the following note); (c) a fragment of a royal letter found at Hazor from the eighteenth to seventeenth centuries addressed to Ibni (=Yabin). See W. Horowitz and A. Schaffer, "A Fragment of a Letter from Hazor," *IEJ* 42 (1992): 165–67.

[155] So Malamat, "The Period of the Judges," 135. Jabin is probably a hypocoristic form of the full theophoric name, Yabni-Addu, the Akk. form of which (Ibni-Addu) identifies the king of Hazor in the texts from Mari. Cf. id., "Hazor, 'the head of all those kingdoms,'" *JBL* 79 (1960): 12–19; id., "Northern Canaan and the Mari Texts," in *Near Eastern Archaeology in the Twentieth Century*, J. A. Sanders, ed. (New York: 1970), 168, 175 n. 22.

[156] According to Josh 11:10–15, Hazor received more severe treatment at the hands of the Israelites than any other northern city. According to the archaeological record, the city's destruction is dated in the thirteenth century B.C. See further Yadin, "Hazor," *NEAEHL* 2.594–603.

fit the topographical picture in the accounts that follow, these must be seen as a later interpolation inspired by Joshua 11.[157] Such solutions, however, are based on silence. It is conceivable that elements of the Hazor dynasty escaped the destruction of Joshua and that, with the Israelite failure to consolidate control over all the conquered territory in the wake of the Conquest, a member of the royal house returned to the ruins and reasserted his rule. Because of his connections as the head of the Canaanite city states,[158] within decades he may have managed to rearm and reassert his authority over the Israelites. But since his rule was short-lived, he left no lasting mark on the archaeological record. The absence of Jabin from the events described in this chapter reflects the author's primary interest in his general, whose defeat was decisive in the Israelites' salvation from the Canaanites. The loss of Jabin's army at Kishon marked the decline of Hazor's power in the region. Later reminiscences of these events recognize the roles of Hazor and its king (1 Sam 12:9; Ps 83:9 [Hb. 10]), confirming that their insignificance in the present narrative is more apparent than real. In fact, contrary to prevailing opinion, the main character in vv. 1–3 is Jabin. Sisera is introduced by means of two circumstantial clauses,[159] almost as an afterthought because of the role he will play in the narrative that follows.[160]

The brunt of the Israelite challenge to Jabin's authority will be felt by his surrogate, Sisera. Sisera is unknown as a Canaanite name. The form *sîsĕrāʾ* suggests he may have been a Hittite or Hurrian mercenary like Shamgar in 3:31 or a member of the Sea Peoples.[161] This need not mean that the Canaanites and Sea Peoples (Philistines) were allied against Israel. Mercenaries were opportunists, offering their services to anyone who would hire them. This identification offers further evidence for the power and influence of Jabin, who apparently was able to attract an enemy general to lead his own forces. His title is given as *śar ṣĕbāʾô*, "commander of his army."[162] The circumstantial clause at the end of v. 2 identifies his base of operation (v. 16). Some interpret the participle *yôšēb*, from *yāšab*, "to sit," as equivalent to "to sit as king, to rule."[163] However, this need not mean that his power rivaled that of Jabin. In

---

[157] Malamat, "Period of the Judges," 136; R. de Vaux, *The Early History of Israel,* trans. D. Smith (Philadelphia: Westminster, 1978), 791.

[158] His hegemonic/suzerain status is reflected in the title כְּנַעַן מֶלֶךְ, "king of Canaan."

[159] Accordingly the primary narrative in vv. 2–3 flows as follows: "So the LORD sold them into the hands of Jabin, king of Canaan, who reigned in Hazor. And the sons of Israel cried out to the LORD because he possessed nine hundred chariots, and he cruelly oppressed the sons of Israel for twenty years."

[160] Precisely the same considerations evoked the inserted reference to Heber the Kenite in v. 11.

[161] Soggin (*Judges,* 63) follows W. F. Albright ("Prolegomenon" to Burney, *Book of Judges,* 15) in accepting Sisera as a Luvian name. See also de Vaux, *Early History of Israel,* 792.

[162] Cp. the title שַׂר חָצוֹר צְבָא, "commander of the army of Hazor," in 1 Sam 12:9.

[163] Cf. Lindars, *Judges 1–5,* 177.

the ancient world a suzerain would often reward a vassal for services rendered by granting him his own territory *(naḥălâ)*. Harosheth-Haggoyim may have been Sisera's grant from Jabin.[164] The location of Harosheth-Haggoyim is frustrated by the absence of this name anywhere else. Attempts to link it with *Muḥrashti* named in the Amarna archives[165] seem forced. The form of the name resembles *gĕlîl haggôyim*, "district of the nations/Gentiles," in Isa 9:1 [Hb. 8:23]. But what is to be made of *ḥărōšet?* Prevailing opinion understands the word to mean "forested area."[166] However, the fact that Sisera's forces included nine hundred chariots, which could be deployed only in coastal and alluvial plains (1:19), renders this interpretation problematic.[167] A more logical solution relates the expression to an Akkadian cognate, *erištu*, "cultivated land,"[168] and explains the vocalization as another example of "pejorative pointing," presumably because of some pagan association.[169] Accordingly, Haroshet-Haggoyim probably means "cultivated field of the Gentiles," an explanation that not only suits the fertile alluvial plain between Taanach and Megiddo but also accords with the present linkage with chariots, the reference to the Canaanite chariot bases in the river plains *(ʿēmeq)* in 1:19,[170] and the location of the battle in 5:19.

ISRAEL'S RESPONSE TO THE OPPRESSION (4:3). **4:3** As in the previous episodes, the pain of oppression causes the Israelites to cry out to Yahweh for help. However, this time the narrator adds two significant causal clauses. First, they felt the pressure of a military force that included nine hundred chariots of iron.[171] Whether the number is interpreted literally or as epic exaggera-

---

[164] This conclusion is not negated by 5:19–20, where Sisera appears to head a coalition of kings. His role is military, not monarchic.

[165] Cf. Boling, *Judges*, 94.

[166] *HALOT* 1.358.

[167] As does an association with the supposed Akk. cognate, *ḫuršānu*, "mountain." So also A. F. Rainey ("Toponymic Problems," *TA* 10 [1983]: 46), who notes that the association of הרשׁ with forests is based exclusively on the LXX[A], which translates the word ὀρυμον in v. 16.

[168] *CAD* E, 300b.

[169] By pejorative pointing I mean revocalizing a word or name in a way that evokes negative feelings in the hearer/reader because of the author's negative disposition toward the object or person. The classic illustrations are provided by the names of Saul's son Ishbaal (Hb. אִישׁ־בַּעַל, 1 Chr 8:33; 9:39), which means "man of Baal," to Ishbosheth (Hb. אִישׁ־בֹּשֶׁת, 2 Sam 2:8–19; etc.), which means "man of shame," and grandson (by Jonathan) Meribaal (Hb. מְרִיב־בַּעַל, 1 Chr 8:34; 9:40), which means "Baal defends [my] cause," to Mephibosheth (Hb. מְפִיבֹשֶׁת, 2 Sam 4:4; 9:6–13), a corrupted version of a form meaning "Shame defends my cause." The suggestion is that the *-osheth* ending of Harosheth derives from בֹּשֶׁת *(bōšet)*, the Hb. word for shame. Cp. also the *o-e* sequence of vowels on תֹּמֶר *(tōmer)*, the odd spelling of "palm" in 4:4. See further below, p. 195.

[170] See further Rainey, "Toponymic Problems," 46–48; id., "The Military Camp Ground at Taanach by the Waters of Megiddo," *EI* 15 (1981): 61*–66*.

[171] Although the nearer antecedent of the pronominal form לוֹ, "to him," is Sisera, this name occurs in a parenthetical clause. The more natural and logical antecedent is Jabin in v. 2.

tion,[172] in light of 1:19 this superior technology had rendered the Canaanites invincible to Israelite armies marching out in their own strength.[173] In view of the note in 1:19, this observation prepares the reader for a later encounter in the plains. Second, Jabin is said to have oppressed[174] Israel severely for twenty years. While the pressure was undoubtedly felt most by the northern tribes, the author generalizes the problem and the response with the inclusive reference to "the descendants of Israel."

GOD'S AGENT OF DELIVERANCE (4:4–10). In contrast to the preceding episodes, the present narrative places great emphasis on the manner in which a deliverer is raised up for Israel. Although the narrator's comments omit any explicit reference to Yahweh's intervention on Israel's behalf and the account lacks the divine provision of leadership formula,[175] vv. 4–10 represent an exposition of the formula, "And the LORD raised up a deliverer for them." This is also his response to their cry in v. 3, a response communicated from start to finish through his spokesperson, Deborah. Indeed from a form critical perspective, vv. 4–10 function as a call narrative, more particularly a "protested call" account,[176] in which the challenge to enter divine service is resisted by the person called.[177] The narrative breaks down into four discreet segments.

The Prophetic Agent of the Call (4:4–5). **4:4** The account of the call of

---

[172] Cp. Thutmose III's fifteenth-century claim to have captured 924 chariots at Megiddo, including the ruler of Megiddo's chariot decorated with gold (*ANET*, 237). On epic exaggeration see Milgrom, *Numbers*, 336–39.

[173] On the nature and significance of iron chariots see above on 1:19.

[174] The verb *lāḥaṣ*, "to oppress," is familiar from 2:16.

[175] See above on 2:16,18; also 3:9,15.

[176] To be distinguished from the "overwhelming call" narrative (cf. Isa 6). The following have been identified as typical features of a protested call: (1) The person called experiences a personal encounter with Yahweh or his messenger. (2) The person receives word of the task to which he is being called. (3) The person expresses resistance and objects to the divine call. (4) The person is reassured by special authenticating signs and/or promises of Yahweh's presence. Other examples include the calls of Moses (Exodus 3–4), Gideon (Judg 6:11–18), and Jeremiah (Jer 1:1–10). On the nature and forms of call narratives in general see also N. C. Habel, "The Form and Significance of the Call Narratives," *ZAW* 77 (1965): 297–323; R. Kilian, "Die prophetische Berufungsberichte," in *Theologie im Wandel: Festschrift zum 150 jährigen Bestehen der Katholisch-Theologischen Fakultät an der Universität Tübingen 1817–1967*, Tübinger Theologische Reihe 1 (Munich & Freiburg: Wewel, 1967), 356–76; W. Zimmerli, *Ezekiel 1*, Her (Philadelphia: Fortress, 1979), 97–101.

[177] J. S. Ackerman ("Prophecy and Warfare in Early Israel: A Study of the Deborah-Barak Story," *BASOR* 220 [1975]: 5–13) demonstrates that this passage incorporates the basic features which W. Richter (*Die sogenannten vorprophetischen Berufungsberichte*, FRLANT 101 [Göttingen: Vandenhoeck & Ruprecht, 1970]) identified in a call account: (1) allusion to distress, (2) commission, (3) objection, (4) assurance, (5) sign. For a fuller discussion of this as a call narrative see D. I. Block, "Deborah Among the Judges: The Perspective of the Hebrew Historian," in *Faith, Tradition, and History: Old Testament Historiography in Its Near Eastern Context*, ed. A. R. Millard, et al. (Winona Lake: Eisenbrauns, 1994), 247–49.

the deliverer opens formally with the identification of the principal character, Deborah, and a description of her activity by means of two circumstantial clauses. The name Deborah, which means "bee," has been encountered once before, in Gen 35:8, where it identifies Rachel's nurse. The expression *ʾiššâ nĕbîʾâ*[178] classifies her professionally: she is a prophet. Although the etymology of *nābîʾ* remains uncertain,[179] the role of the prophet is clearly defined in texts like Exod 4:15–16 and 7:1–2. A prophet serves as a spokesperson for deity to the people. The designation here deliberately places Deborah in the succession of Moses (cf. Deut 18:15–22) and in the company of other female bearers of this title.[180] Whatever else the narrative will say about Deborah, the reader must remember that she is first and foremost, if not exclusively, a prophet.

In keeping with the patricentric nature of ancient Israelite society and the pattern of biblical narrative generally, Deborah is identified further with reference to the significant man in her life; she is the wife of Lappidoth.[181] The use of a feminine plural form for a man's name seems odd at first, but *lappîdôt,* literally "torches, flashes," probably should be interpreted as an abstract plural.[182] The association of the wife of "Lappidoth" with Barak, which means "lightning," makes it tempting to identify the two, especially since the name does not appear again.[183] However, not only is this an Ephraimite family, against Barak, who comes from Kadesh in Naphtali, but the parallels with the way other female prophets are introduced also eliminates the need for him to play a role in the story. These same parallels also show how equally misguided are more recent attempts to rob Deborah of a husband by interpreting *ʾēšet lappîdot* as an adjective, that is, "fiery woman."[184] If any significance is to be attached to the name, it probably points to Deborah as a brilliant light in the

---

[178] The compound expression אִשָּׁה נְבִיאָה, "a woman, a prophet," an apposition of genus (GKC §131b), thrusts Deborah's gender into sharper relief. This form of the expression occurs nowhere else, though it compares with אִישׁ נָבִיא, "a man, a prophet," in 6:8.

[179] The most plausible explanation is provided by D. E. Fleming ("The Etymological Origins of the Hebrew *nābîʾ*: The One Who Invokes God," *CBQ* 55 [1993]: 217–24) who relates Hb. נָבִיא to Syrian *nābû*, which is best understood as "one who invokes the gods," the noun being an active participle of *nabû*, "to name." Cf. J. Jeremias, "נָבִיא, Prophet," *THAT* 2.7–26.

[180] Those named in the OT include Miriam, Exod 15:20; Huldah, 2 Kgs 22:14; and Noadiah, Neh 6:14. Cf. also Anna in Luke 2:36. Isaiah's wife is unnamed (Isa 8:3).

[181] Cp. Miriam, who is introduced as "Miriam, the prophetess, the sister of Aaron" (Exod 15:20); Huldah, who is "Huldah, the prophetess, the wife of Shallum ben Tikvah" (2 Kgs 22:14). The exception is Noadiah, a false prophetess, who is introduced in conjunction with "the rest of the prophets who are trying to intimidate me" (Neh 6:14). Cp. also the elderly widow Anna, the only woman in the NT called a prophetess (προφῆτις), who is identified as "Anna, the prophetess, the daughter of Phanuel" (Luke 2:36).

[182] On biblical names with fiery connotations see Garsiel, *Biblical Names*, 115, 185.

[183] Thus Boling, *Judges*, 95.

[184] Cf. F. Gottlieb, "Three Mothers," *Judaism* 30 (1981) 195; Rasmussen, "Deborah the Woman Warrior," 93, n. 3; Bal, *Murder and Difference*, 57–58.

dark days of the governors.

4:5 After identifying Deborah as a professional prophet, the description of her professional activity as "judging Israel" catches the reader off guard. The participle form šōpĕṭâ invites one to view her as a female version of the other deliverers identified as šōpĕṭîm, "governors, rulers."[185] Deleting v. 5 as secondary, G. F. Moore found the weight of this evidence so convincing that he argued for translating hî' šōpĕṭâ 'et yiśrā'ēl in v. 4 (NIV, "she was leading Israel") as "she delivered Israel."[186] He finds parallels to Deborah in the German Veleda, who supported Civilis in his efforts to throw off the Roman yoke, and Joan of Arc, the devout maid from Domrémy, Champagne, who led the French forces in delivering her land from England.[187] Accordingly, Cundall introduces Deborah as "the savior of her people and the only woman in the distinguished company of the Judges."[188] Commenting on 5:6–8, he notes that "this desperate situation obtained until Deborah arose to effect the deliverance of the nation."[189]

Support for this interpretation is found in 5:6–8, which associates Deborah's appearance in Israel with the return of security in the countryside. Indeed, despite their difficulty, the verses that follow create the impression that Deborah was involved in marshalling the troops. Furthermore, the placement of her name ahead of Barak's in 5:1 suggests primary credit for the victory is hers. Finally, the striking parallel between Sisera, Jabin's army commander, who "sits/rules" (yāšab) in Harosheth-Haggoyim, and Deborah, who "sits/rules" under her own palm tree, suggests that this woman represents the Israelite counterpart to Sisera.

However, upon closer reading, the presentation of Deborah as a savior of her people is more apparent than real,[190] and the participle šōpĕṭâ may call for different interpretation.[191] The "altogether enigmatic"[192] nature of the narrative raises numerous questions. If the author looked upon Deborah as one of the deliverers of Israel:

1. Why is she not introduced as one whom Yahweh had raised up?

---

[185] Cf. 3:16,18.

[186] Moore, *Judges*, 114; cf. Lindars (*Judges 1–5*, 182–83), whose deletion of "she was judging Israel at that time" as an editorial gloss giving her the ruling function of the deliverers, also misses the point.

[187] Ibid., 112–13.

[188] Cundall, *Judges and Ruth*, 82.

[189] Ibid., 95.

[190] Cf. R. Polzin's comment "that the story is all about how things are not what they seem" (*Moses and the Deuteronomist: A Literary Study of the Deuteronomic History,* Part I, *Deuteronomy, Joshua, Judges* [New York: Seabury, 1980], 163).

[191] See below on מִשְׁפָּט in v. 5.

[192] So also L. R. Klein, *The Triumph of Irony in the Book of Judges,* JSOTSup 68 (Sheffield: Almond Press, 1987), 42.

2. Why is there no reference to her inspiration and empowerment by Yahweh's Spirit *(rûaḥ yhwh)?*[193]
3. Why does she need Barak to accomplish the deliverance?
4. Why is the verb *yāšaʿ*, "to save," never applied to her?
5. Why does she say, "The LORD will sell Sisera into the hands of a woman" instead of "into my hands"?
6. Why does the author observe that "she went up with Barak" (4:10) but avoid placing her at the head of the troops?
7. Why does Deborah announce to Barak, "This day the LORD has given Sisera into *your* hands" rather than "my hands" (4:14)?
8. Why is she absent from the description of the actual battle (4:15–17), and why does she never meet Jabin or Sisera?
9. Why did the poet prefer the title "mother in Israel" over "savior of Israel" (5:7)?
10. Why does the poet avoid the root *qûm*, "to rise," let alone referring to Yahweh as the causative subject, when he speaks of Deborah's rise?[194]
11. What is this woman doing in what everyone acknowledges traditionally as a man's world—leading soldiers into battle?[195]
12. Perhaps most intriguing, why does the narrator portray her character so different qualitatively from most of the other deliverers?

Admittedly, the narrative says nothing negative about the paradigmatic Othniel. Ehud's personality is not criticized overtly, but his tactics, which look for all the world like typical Canaanite behavior, leave the reader wondering whether he is to be viewed as a hero or as a villain. The moral and spiritual characters of the governors who follow Deborah display a rapid downward spiral. Far from being solutions to the Canaanization of Israelite thought and ethic, Gideon, Jephthah, and Samson were themselves all parts of the problem. These are not noblemen; they are "antiheroes."[196] But as the only unequivo-

---

[193] Cp. the empowerment of Othniel (3:10), Gideon (6:34), Jephthah (11:29), and Samson (14:19; 15:14).

[194] In 5:7 םקשׁ *(piel)* occurs twice. On the verb see further p. 226 and notes there.

[195] On her presence in a man's world see Gros Louis, "The Book of Judges," in *Literary Interpretations of Biblical Narratives*, ed. K. R. R. Gros Louis et al. (Nashville: Abingdon, 1974), 148; Lindars, "Deborah's Song: Women in the Old Testament," *BJRL* 65 (1983): 158–75, esp. 172–75; J. Hackett, "Women's Studies and the Hebrew Bible," in *The Future of Biblical Studies: The Hebrew Scriptures*, ed. R. E. Friedman and H. G. M. Williamson (Atlanta: Scholars Press, 1989), 154–55. While a female general leading troops into battle would have been quite exceptional in the ancient world, female prophets were not uncommon. Malamat has recognized an unusually high proportion of women among the lay prophets at Mari; see "A Forerunner of Biblical Prophecy: The Mari Documents," in *Ancient Israelite Religion*, ed. P. D. Miller, P. D. Hanson, and S. D. McBride (Philadelphia: Fortress, 1987), 43–44.

[196] An expression used by Brettler, "The Book of Judges: Literature as Politics," *JBL* 108 (1989): 407. Deborah's Ephraimite nativity casts doubts, however, on Brettler's political interpretation of the book.

cally positive major personality and as the only one involved in the service of God prior to her engagement in deliverance activities, she stands out as a lonely figure indeed.[197] Significantly, in later lists of the deliverers, Barak's name may appear, but never Deborah's,[198] presumably because this was not her role.[199] She communicates Yahweh's response to the people's cry, but she is not the answer.[200]

Verse 5 describes the manner in which Deborah performed her professional duties and sets the stage in the reader's mind for the call of the deliverer. Her posture is described as "sitting" under the Palm Tree of Deborah. The verb *yāšab* certainly implies exercising official function, but the NIV's "she held court" represents too legal an interpretation, as we shall see. The reference to the Palm of Deborah suggests some association with the "oak of weeping" *(ʾallôn bākût)*, under which her namesake, Rebekah's nurse, was buried.[201] The present vocalization of "palm" *(tōmer)*, which occurs elsewhere only in Jer 10:5, where it denotes a post or scarecrow in a field, either represents a dialectical variation of the more common *tāmār* (3:13) or another case of "pejorative pointing," reflecting the narrator's disposition toward trees treated as sacred in paganized contexts.[202] More significant than the tree itself is its location between Ramah and Bethel in the hills of Ephraim. Accordingly she sits not at Bethel or at Shiloh, where the ark is, but outside the town. But there is more. With her seat centrally located in the hill country of Ephraim, Deborah was accessible to the entire nation of Israel, and so they came up to her for "judgment."

Every word in the last clause of v. 5 is carefully chosen. First, those who come to Deborah are identified as *běnê yiśrāʾēl*, "the sons of Israel." Although many interpret the expression individually, as if the citizens were approaching her to settle their private disputes, in the book it always functions as a collective

---

[197] Boling (*Judges*, 94) describes Deborah as an "honorable honorary judge" in contrast to the "dishonorable divinely appointed judge Samson."

[198] Cf. 1 Sam 12:9–11; Heb 11:32.

[199] J. Nunnally-Cox's complaint of the bias of the author of Hebrews in omitting her name but including that of the "weak-kneed character" Barak (*Foremothers, Women of the Bible* [New York: Seabury, 1981], 49–50) fails to grasp this point. If she had been included, it would have been with Samuel and the prophets, not the deliverers of Israel.

[200] For a full discussion of Deborah's prophetic status see Block, "Deborah Among the Judges," 229–53. O'Connell (*Rhetoric of the Book of Judges*, 107–8) speaks of Deborah's catalytic role in this chapter.

[201] Cp. the reference to the "Oak of Tabor" (תָּבוֹר אֵלוֹן) in the vicinity of Bethel mentioned in 1 Sam 10:3.

[202] On the palm as a sacred symbol in the ancient Near East see U. Magen, *Assyrische Königsdarstellungen—Aspekte der Herrschaft*, Baghdader Forschungen 9 (Mainz am Rhein: Philipp von Zabern, 1986), 79–81.

for the entire nation.[203] In this context "sons of Israel" should be interpreted exactly as it has been in v. 3. Second, the nation "went up" to her. Since Deborah sits "in the hill country of Ephraim," the choice of the verb *ʿālâ* is natural (cf. 1:4). However, the affinities of vv. 4–5 with 20:18,23,27 suggest that the verb functions almost technically for "to go up [to the high place] to inquire [of the deity]." By stationing herself near Bethel, Deborah represents an alternative to the priesthood which had lost its effectiveness as mediator of divine revelation, and her pronouncements function as a substitute for the Urim and Thummim.

But why were the Israelites coming to her? While the answer is implicit in the verb "to go up," it is explicitly expressed in *lammišpāṭ*. The NIV's "to have their disputes decided" reflects the traditional interpretation of the word, perhaps on the model of Moses in Exod 18:16.[204] Accordingly, Deborah holds what Soggin calls a "forensic office."[205] However, not only is it difficult to see a connection between such a judicial function and her role in the rest of the narrative; unlike the surrounding narratives, the conclusion to the account also omits any reference to the duration of her service as judge after the defeat of Jabin.[206] The forty years of rest (5:31) is attributed to God and the Israelite's collective power (4:23–24). By this time Deborah is long out of the picture. In fact, the author seems to have had no interest in any judicial activity at all. It is tempting to interpret this text through the lens of 1 Sam 7:15–17, which describes the service of Samuel in similar terms, but the differences are significant.[207] In any case, nowhere is Deborah (or Samuel for that matter) portrayed as actually holding court and settling disputes among the citizens.

The case for Deborah as a legal functionary rests entirely upon the presence of the root *šāpaṭ* in "she was judging *[šōpĕṭâ]* Israel at that time" (4:4), and "The sons of Israel came to her for the judgment *[lammišpāṭ]*" (4:5). Nowhere else in the book does the term require a judicial interpretation. Where their roles are defined, the "judges" are presented primarily as deliverers. Even in the formulaic notes that an individual "judged" Israel so many

---

[203] See the brief discussion in Block, "The Period of the Judges," as well as the fuller treatment of the expression in id., "'Israel' - 'sons of Israel:' A Study in Hebrew Eponymic Usage," *Studies in Religion/Sciences Religieuses* 13 (1984): 301–26.

[204] According to J. H. Stek, the narrator presents Deborah as "the source of justice where the wronged in Israel can secure redress and the oppressed relief" ("The Bee and the Mountain Goat: A Literary Reading of Judges 4," in *A Tribute to Gleason Archer*, ed. W. C. Kaiser, Jr. and R. F. Youngblood [Chicago: Moody Press, 1986], 62).

[205] Soggin, *Judges*, 72.

[206] Cf. 12:7 (Jephthah); 15:20; 16:31 (Samson). Note also the archival notes regarding Tola (10:1–2), Jair (10:3–5), Ibzan (12:8–10), Elon (12:11–12), Abdon (12:13–15).

[207] (1) The text declares explicitly that Samuel's judgeship was a lifelong occupation; (2) Samuel carried out his duties as a circuit judge, presiding annually at Bethel, Gilgal, and Mizpah; (3) Samuel was also engaged in cultic activity, as his construction of the altar to Yahweh at Ramah indicates.

years,[208] the word carries a more general meaning, "to govern."[209] Indeed one wonders why the narrator would have inserted this parenthetical reference to the settlement of relatively petty civil disputes when the issue in the chapter is a national crisis. This seems to have been the conclusion of the Massoretes, whose vocalization of *lammišpāṭ* translates "for *the* judgment." This reading suggests that a particular issue is in mind, not a series of cases or a routine fulfillment of professional duties. In the present context the issue that concerns the Israelites is their oppression at the hands of Jabin and the Canaanites.

Accordingly, the action described in v. 5 represents an exposition on "the sons of Israel cried out *[ṣāʿaq]* to the LORD" in v. 3a.[210] In the narratives on the united monarchy, when subjects appeal *(ṣāʿaq)* to a king for help in a matter, his pronouncement in response is designated his *mišpāṭ*.[211] In the Book of Judges such cries *(ṣāʿaq/zāʿaq)* for deliverance are always directed to Yahweh by "the sons of Israel."[212] Especially instructive is 10:14, which notes that when "the sons of Israel" made their appeal to him, he retorted sarcastically, "Go and cry out *(zāʿaq)* to the gods whom you have chosen! Let them save *(hôšîaʿ)* you from your distress *(ṣārâ)!*" Accordingly, when "the sons of Israel" come to Deborah for "the judgment," they are not asking her to solve their legal disputes but to give them the divine answer to their cries, which is described in the following verses. The fact that the Israelites come to her instead of the priest reflects the failure of the established priestly institution to maintain contact with God, a spiritual tragedy explicitly described in the early chapters of 1 Samuel.[213]

The Commissioning of Barak (4:6–7). **4:6–7** In vv. 6–7 the focus shifts from Deborah, the medium through whom the divine response to the Israelite distress is sought and received, to Barak, whom God calls to solve the crisis.

---

[208] 10:2,3; 12:7,9,11,14; 15:20;16:31. Cf. also 3:10; 12:8,13.

[209] See the Introduction.

[210] So also Ackerman, "Prophecy and Warfare," 11, following Boling, *Judges*, 81, 95.

[211] Cf. 1 Kgs 3:16–20; 20:39–40; 2 Kgs 6:26; cf. also 2 Sam 15:1–6. This use of מִשְׁפָּט as the response to life-threatening situations is illustrated also in Job 19:7: "Look! I cry out [אֶצְעַק] 'Violence!' But I am not answered [עָנָה]. I shout aloud, but there is no response [מִשְׁפָּט אֵין]" (author's translation).

[212] 3:9,15; 4:3; 6:6; 10:10.

[213] 1 Sam 2:12–13 describes Eli's sons as "scoundrels" (בְּנֵי בְלִיַּעַל), who "did not know the LORD [לֹא יָדְעוּ יְהוָה] nor the 'oracle' of the priests [מִשְׁפַּט הַכֹּהֲנִים] with the people." This accords with 1 Sam 3:1–3, which alludes to the growing darkness: messages from Yahweh were rare in those days, visions were infrequent, Eli was becoming blind(!), and the lamp of God was going out. The Israelites soon learn that if they want a determination from Yahweh, they go to Samuel, not Eli (3:19–21). The implication of a protracted period of divine silence in v. 21 suggests that the events described in Judges 20–21 transpired relatively early in this period of the judges. For fuller discussion of this use of מִשְׁפָּט and extrabiblical parallels to Deborah's role in this context see Block, "Deborah Among the Judges," 242–46.

Deborah answered the Israelites' inquiry by dispatching *(šālaḥ)* her own representative(s) to call *(qārāʾ)* Barak to divine service. The deliverer is identified by name, patronymic, and home. Barak, "lightning,"[214] was the son of Abinoam ("Father is pleasant") of Kedesh in Naphtali. Because Kedesh ("sanctuary") was a common place name, several candidates for this site appear. Assuming this Kedesh must be relatively near to Mount Tabor and that it is the same Kedesh as is mentioned in v. 11, most identify this site with modern Khirbet Qedish, one mile west of the southern end of the Sea of Galilee.[215] However, it is preferable to equate this site with Tell Qadesh in upper Galilee, north of Lake Huleh.[216] Joshua had conquered this city earlier (Josh 12:22) and set it aside as a Levitical city (Josh 21:32) and city of refuge (Josh 20:7).[217] The distance of this city from the sight of the battle with Sisera is no obstacle to this interpretation; the text says only that Barak the son of Abinoam was *from* Kedesh of Naphtali. Why Barak was chosen we may only speculate, but the proximity of his home in Kadesh to Hazor, the seat of Jabin the oppressor, adds a special dimension to his appointment.

Although no details of Deborah's initial meeting with Barak are given, significantly she enters the picture at precisely the same point as does the *malʾāk* ("envoy") of Yahweh in 6:11. The text does not mention that she received any explicit orders from God, but the form of her commissioning speech reflects a clear prophetic self-consciousness. She introduces her speech with a variation of the prophetic citation formula which in context signifies a firm declaration: "Surely the LORD God of Israel has commanded, 'Go!'" *(hălōʾ ṣiwwâ yhwh ʾělōhê yiśrāʾēl lēk).*[218] In addition, as an authorized representative of Yahweh she communicates his charge in the first person.

The commissioning speech itself consists of two parts. First, by means of a

---

[214] On which see Garsiel, *Biblical Names*, 115.

[215] E.g., A. Ovadiah, et al., "Kedesh (In Upper Galilee)," *NEAEHL* 3. 855; Naʿaman, "Literary and Topographical Notes," 429; C. Rasmussen, *NIV Atlas of the Bible* (Grand Rapids: Zondervan, 1989), 241.

[216] D. J. Wiseman, "Kedesh, Kedesh in Naphtali," *IBD* 2.847; Soggin, *Judges*, 64; Halpern, *The First Historians*, 92–93. On this site see A. Ovadiah, et al, "Kedesh (In Upper Galilee)," *NEAEHL* 3.855–59.

[217] This was the first Naphtalite city to fall to Tiglath Pileser III when he invaded northern Israel in 734–732 B.C. (2 Kgs 15:29).

[218] Literally "Has Yahweh the God of Israel not commanded, 'Go'?" On the use of *hălōʾ*, lit., "Is it not," as an emphatic particle, virtually synonymous with "Behold," see M. L. Brown, "'Is it not?' or 'Indeed!': HL in Northwest Semitic," *MAARAV* 4/2 (1987): 201–19; D. Sivan and W. Schneidewind, "Letting Your 'Yes' be 'No' in Ancient Israel: A Study of Asseverative לֹא and הֲלֹא," *JSS* 38 (1993): 209–26. Our text is discussed on p. 217. Cp. this form of the citation formula with the most common form: כֹּה אָמַר אֲדֹנָי יְהוִה, "Thus has the Lord Yahweh declared." For discussion of the citation formula and its function see S. A. Meier, *Speaking of Speaking: Marking Direct Discourse in the Hebrew Bible*, VTSup 46 (Leiden: 1992), 238–39; C. Westermann, *Basic Forms of Prophetic Speech* (Philadelphia: Fortress, 1967), 100–115.

series of imperatives, Barak is charged to go *(lēk)* and deploy *(māšak)*[219] ten thousand troops from Naphtali and Zebulun at Mount Tabor.[220] Mount Tabor rises steeply 1,843 feet above sea level at the northeast corner of the Jezreel Valley, controlling one of the most important crossroads in the region. This command signals that God is not only calling the general; he also determines the strategy.

Second, Barak is promised Yahweh's personal support in the anticipated battle. The divine Commander will deploy *(māšak)*[221] Sisera and all his forces (identified as chariots and infantry) against Barak, but he will deliver them over into his hand.[222] Reminiscent of Yahweh's manipulation of Pharaoh and his armies in Exodus 14 and Gog in Ezekiel 38–39, the enemy is portrayed as a puppet controlled by the hands of God. The One who had sold Israel into the hands of Jabin will also engineer the oppressors' defeat.

The Hesitation of Barak (4:8). **4:8** The narrative should have moved directly from v. 7 to v. 10, but Barak's response provides one of the keys to the rest of the chapter. Despite Yahweh's assurance of victory, Barak resists the call. His protestation is less emphatic than Moses' in Exodus 3–4 and less apologetic than Gideon's in Judg 6:15,[223] but it is clear he is not impressed with Deborah's commissioning speech. On the surface his reaction, "If you go with me I, I will go; but if you don't go with me, I won't go," appears cowardly.[224] He will not enter the fray unless he has this woman beside him holding his hand. And this impression is reinforced by Deborah's response. But at a deeper level the objection reflects a recognition of Deborah's status. The request to be accompanied by the prophet is a plea for the presence of God.[225]

The Promise of Divine Presence (4:9a). **4:9a** At this point in other call narratives Yahweh responds with reassuring promises of his presence and/or authenticating signs. Both elements are found here, albeit in veiled form. The first is evident in Deborah's firm promise of her own presence (lit., "I will certainly go with you").[226] It is easy to trivialize the significance of this declara-

---

[219] On this use of מָשַׁךְ see Boling, *Judges*, 96, and Ackerman, "Prophecy and Warfare," 8.

[220] For a form critical study of charges to attack see R. Back, *Die Aufforderung zur Flucht und zum Kampf in Alttestamentlichen Prophetenspruch* (Neukirchen-Vluyn: Neukirchener Verlag, 1962).

[221] The NIV's "lure" obscures the use of the same term as in the previous verse.

[222] On the form and function of the committal formula see p. 147f. D. F. Murray observes correctly that both Barak and Sisera marshal their forces at the instigation of Yahweh ("Narrative Structure and Technique in the Deborah-Barak Story [Judges IV 4–22]," in *Studies in the Historical Books of the Old Testament*, ed. J. A. Emerton, VTSup 30 [Leiden: Brill, 1979], 169).

[223] Cp. also Saul in 1 Sam 9:21 and Jeremiah in Jer 1:6.

[224] On Barak's motives see O'Connell, *Rhetoric of the Book of Judges*, 108–9.

[225] This interpretation is preferable to that of Fewell and Gunn ("Controlling Perspectives," 398–99), who argue that Barak's question reflects suspicion of Deborah's authority as a woman.

[226] *GBH* §123i treats the construction הָלֹךְ אֵלֵךְ עִמָּךְ as a concession, "I will go with you, but …"

tion by interpreting them simply as the words of a strong woman to a weak-willed man. The timing of Deborah's words is critical, for it occurs precisely at the point where, in other call narratives, Yahweh promises his personal presence to a reluctant agent.[227] The prophet obviously functions as Yahweh's alter ego. Her presence alone is enough to guarantee victory over Sisera.[228] To reinforce Yahweh's commitment to Barak, Deborah also offers him an authenticating, if ironic, sign. Barak will need to step out in faith in the divine promise, for the sign she presents is proleptic in nature: Yahweh will sell Sisera into the hands of a woman, to whom the glory would go.[229] When this happens, Barak will know that he has been called by God and that God has intervened on Israel's behalf. But the sign raises the question whether or not she expected to be that woman. In the end the answer to the question catches Barak and the reader off guard.

The Summons to Arms (4:9b–10). **4:9b–10** The final scene in the call of Barak demonstrates the success of Deborah's mission. True to her words, she rises from her "prophetic chair" and accompanies Barak to Kedesh.[230] From his home he summons *(zāʿaq)* the men of Zebulun and Naphtali to assemble, and they come by the thousands. The narrative offers no explanation for the troops' response, but one may surmise that Deborah's presence in Kedesh was a critical factor. Since all Israel recognized her as a prophet, her presence alongside Barak symbolized the divine imprimatur on his leadership.[231] The ten thousand men who answered Barak's call testify to her standing in Israel[232] and the newfound credibility of Barak as a savior of the nation. Deborah's mission on Yahweh's behalf has been a complete success. The reluctant general has been commissioned, and his troops have gathered.

To clarify the preceding sequence of scenes, we may summarize the move-

---

[227] Cf. Exod 3:12; Judg 6:16; 1 Sam 10:7; Jer 1:8.

[228] Accordingly, not only do speculations about whether or not the Spirit of Yahweh came upon Deborah reflect a fundamental misinterpretation of her role (she is neither the deliverer, nor is her infusion with the divine Spirit the issue) but references to the Spirit's presence with Barak would have been superfluous (cf. 3:10; 6:34; 11:29). Since where the prophet is, there is God, and where the Spirit is, there is God, by the axiom of equality where the prophet is, there is the divine Spirit (רוּחַ). Both represent concretizing expressions of the presence of God. For a preliminary correlation of the involvement of Samuel and the Spirit of Yahweh in the lives of Saul and David see Block, "Deborah Among the Judges," 249–51.

[229] Cp. God's proleptic sign for Moses in Exod 3:12: Moses would know that it is God who sent him when he will have brought his people out of Egypt back to this mountain (Sinai). The present construction, לֹא תִהְיֶה תִּפְאַרְתְּךָ, translates lit. "your glory will not be."

[230] Becker (*Richterzeit und Königtum*, 130) rightly insists that the Kedesh referred to in vv. 9–11 must be the identified with Kedesh of Naphtali, the home of Barak (v. 6).

[231] The final clause in v. 10 reiterates the importance of Deborah's presence.

[232] Their response to Barak, accompanied by Deborah, parallels that of the Gileadites and Manassites to Jephthah, empowered by the Spirit of Yahweh in 11:29. The figure ten thousand is conventional for vast numbers. Cf. 3:29.

ments of the primary participants as follows: (1) The Israelites come to Deborah under her "palm" to seek an answer from Yahweh regarding their oppression at the hands of King Jabin of Hazor. (2) Having received a response from God, Deborah sends messengers to Kadesh-Naphtali, north of Hazor, to fetch Barak. (3) Barak answers their call and comes to Deborah under her "palm." (4) Pursuant to their conversation in vv. 6–9a, Barak returns to his home in Naphtali, accompanied by Deborah. (5) When he summons the men of Zebulun and Naphtali, a huge force of ten thousand troops assembles to him in Kedesh.

GOD'S GIFT OF DELIVERANCE (4:11–22). In light of the patterns set by 3:10 and 3:27–29, the reader expects Barak's victory over Sisera and his army to be swift and decisive, even though, in light of 4:9, somehow the glory will ultimately go to Deborah. But both expectations prove mistaken. The description of the conflict is unusually long and takes some unexpected turns. Verse 11, constructed as a complex circumstantial clause, signals an ominous complication in the plot. The reader does not know yet that the information provided here will be important for the ending of the story. It could have been inserted before v. 17, but that would have detracted from the connection between vv. 12–16 and 17–22. The remainder of the text divides into two parts: vv. 12–16 describe the fulfillment of Deborah's first speech (vv. 6–7); vv. 17–22 describe the fulfillment of the second (v. 9). Together these segments explain the resolution of the ambiguity in the latter. We expect that Deborah will be the hero, but once she has given her speeches, she disappears from the scene.

With respect to plot, cast, and detail of presentation, juxtaposed the two accounts of the victories over the Moabites (3:16–29) and the Canaanites (4:12–22) display an impressive chiastic *A B B A* structure, which may be illustrated as follows:

A	3:16–26	Assassination of Enemy Leader	Individual Activity	Expanded Narrative
B	3:27–29	The Defeat of Enemy Army	Mass Activity	Compressed Narrative
B′	4:12–16	The Defeat of Enemy Army	Mass Activity	Compressed Narrative
A′	4:17–22	Assassination of Enemy Leader	Individual Activity	Expanded Narrative

Additional links in detail will be noted in the commentary.

The Complication in the Plot (4:11). **4:11** From out of nowhere, and for no immediately apparent reason, the narrator introduces a new character,

Heber the Kenite. Some see here an allusion to a clan of Kenites[233] rather than
an individual, but the following narratives, particularly vv. 17–22, require a
personal, individual interpretation.[234] The narrator takes pains to link Heber
with the Kenites whom he had introduced earlier in 1:16, adding the name of
Moses' father-in-law, Hobab, which had been missing in that context. The
actions of Heber reflect both his nomadic spirit and his independence.[235] Not
satisfied with the arid environment of Arad in southern Judah, he picks up
stakes and moves to the more hospitable region of northern Naphtali.

Scholars are not agreed on the place where Heber pitched his tent.[236] The
issue is complicated by the fact that the Hebrew phrase translated "by the great
tree in Zaanannim near Kedesh" (ʿad-ʾēlôn běṣaʿănannîm ʾăšer ʾet-qedeš) is
problematic at every point. Though some force the preposition ʿad (NIV, "by")
to mean "near,"[237] it actually means the opposite, highlighting the distance
between Heber's point of origin (1:16) and his destination. It seems he moved
as far away from his clan as possible. ʾēlôn may denote any large tree, but it
often refers to a specific tree, a terebinth or oak that marks a sacred spot.[238]
Heber may have viewed the tree as a symbol of divine protection and blessing.
The word rendered "Zaanannim" has an inner-Masoretic spelling variant. The
NIV has probably chosen correctly to read with the variant as in Josh 19:33. Its
meaning, however, is uncertain. While most translations treat it as a proper
noun, if the word derives from ṣāʿan, "to pack up,"[239] and is cognate to Arabic
ṣʿn, "to wander about as a nomad, roam," then the reference could be to a place
where caravaneers stop or transfer goods.[240] The proposition ʾet in ʾet qedeš

---

[233] Noting that Heber (חֶבֶר) derives from a root meaning "to unite, be joined," Malamat ("Mari
and the Bible," 146) finds in the name an allusion to a nomadic tribal subdivision that had broken
off from the parent Kenite tribe. Cf. also Soggin, *Judges*, 65–66; id., "'Heber der Qenite,'" *VT* 31
(1981): 89–92.

[234] So also Lindars, *Judges 1–5*, 191; Neef, "Der Sieg Deboras und Baraks," 43, n. 88.

[235] The NIV's rendering of מָעַם דְרַמְנ (lit. "he separated himself from") as "he left" misses the
point. According to Gen 13:9 the phrase suggests a deliberate act of severance. Here the choice of
vocabulary is brilliantly ambiguous; it speaks not only of physical and economic separation but
also of political independence, as the reader will learn in v. 17.

[236] The expression reflects Heber's nomadic past and anticipates vv. 17–22.

[237] Boling, *Judges*, 96.

[238] The expression appears in several compound place names: Elon-muzzab (Judg 9:6, NIV,
"the great tree at the pillar"), Elon-Tabor (1 Sam 10:3, NIV, "the great tree of Tabor"), Elon-Moreh
(Gen 12:6, NIV, "the great tree of Moreh"). Note also the variant Allon-Bacuth in Gen 35:8.

[239] The verb occurs in Isa 33:20.

[240] Thus Soggin (*Judges*, 66), who rightly rejects an identification with the similar sounding
place name referred to in Josh 19:33. B. Margalit ("Observations on the Jael-Sisera Story (Judges
4–5)," in *Pomegranates and Golden Bells: Studies in Biblical, Jewish, and Near Eastern Ritual,
Law, and Literature in Honor of Jacob Milgrom*, ed. D. P. Wright, et al. (Winona Lake: Eisenbrauns, 1995], 630–31) follows B. Mazar in interpreting אֵלוֹן בְּצַעְנִים as an abbreviation for
בֵית־צַעְנִים, "Oak-Home-of-Wanderers."

may bear the sense "near, alongside of,"[241] but this still does not tell us which Kedesh the author has in mind.

Assuming Heber's camp must be located near Mount Tabor, most understand Heber to have pitched his tent at Khirbet Qedish, near the southern end of the Sea of Galilee.[242] While this identification may answer one geographic question, it creates several of its own, and an identification with the northern Kedesh remains the best solution for several reasons.[243] (1) It avoids the need to identify Kedesh with two different locations in a single literary context. (2) It takes seriously the preposition ʿad, which is best understood as an extreme [northerly] location. (3) A seminomad allied with the king of Hazor (v. 17) is better located near Hazor than at the southern end of the Sea of Galilee. (4) Since Sisera is portrayed as Jabin's commander, with his forces in shambles (v. 15), he would naturally seek protection from his superior and head for the vicinity of Hazor. Heber's tent nearby would not be suspected by his pursuers. (5) If Heber's camp was near Barak's Kedesh, he may be the informer who reported to Jabin (and by extension to Sisera) that Barak's troops had left Kedesh and were headed for Mount Tabor (v. 12).[244] Although this identification does not solve all the logistical problems, it heightens the irony of the story. By seeking refuge with Jael, the wife of Jabin's ally, Sisera virtually placed himself in Barak's hands. But in the end the glory eluded Barak!

The Defeat of the Enemy Army (4:12–16).   The chapter is half over by the time we finally get to the battle between the forces of Israel and the enemy. The tempo picks up in vv. 12–16.

4:12–13   Sisera hears that Barak has moved his troops down from Kedesh and has assembled them on Mount Tabor. The identity of the informer is not revealed. One may surmise that Heber passed on the word that Barak had assembled his troops or that Jabin had observed them move from Kedesh to Mount Tabor and had relayed orders to Sisera to mobilize. The general responds immediately, summoning[245] all nine hundred of his iron chariots and

---

[241] *IBHS* §11.2.4.a.

[242] In addition to the sources cited above on v. 6, see Margalit, "Observations on the Jael-Sisera Story," 629–31.

[243] Some identify the site with Tel Kedesh (Tell Abu Qedesh) in the Jezreel valley, midway between Taanach and Megiddo (so E. Stern, "Kedesh, Tel [In Jezreel Valley]," *NEAEHL* 2.860; Soggin, *Judges*, 66); J. Hofbauer, in a review of W. Richter, *Traditionsgeschichtliche Untersuchungen zum Richterbuch*, *ZKT* 87 (1965): 319. However, one wonders why Heber would settle here if he was allied with and counting on the protection of Jabin.

[244] Especially if he was a nomadic mercenary charged by the king of Hazor with policing the area around Kedesh, as Margalit argues ("Observations on the Jael-Sisera Story," 640), though he locates Kedesh southwest of Galilee.

[245] The syntax and vocabulary of Sisera's mobilization echo Barak's:

v. 10   וַיִּזְעַק בָּרָק אֶת־זְבוּלֻן וְאֶת־נַפְתָּלִי קֶדְשָׁה

v. 13   וַיִּזְעַק סִיסְרָא אֶת־כָּל־רִכְבּוֹ אֶל־נַחַל קִישׁוֹן

The verb זָעַק, "to summon, raise a battle cry" (also in 6:34; 12:2; 18:23) is also used in the cry of distress formula for "to cry out [for help]."

the rest of his troops[246] from Harosheth-Haggoyim to the Kishon River, which drains the Jezreel (Esdraelon) Valley, beginning its course in the hills of northern Samaria near Megiddo[247] and flowing northwestward through the plain of Acre, finally emptying into the Mediterranean at the foot of Mount Carmel. The narrative leaves the impression that Sisera is functioning on his own (or Jabin's) initiative, but the reader knows from v. 7 that Yahweh is setting the stage for the showdown.

4:14 Through his prophet Deborah, Yahweh signals the moment of his own action on Israel's behalf by calling the people to action and announcing his victory over the enemy. The call to action, "Arise" (*qûm*, NIV, "Go!") is ambiguous, leaving open the question whether the Israelites are to go on the offensive or simply to stand by and watch the salvation of Yahweh.[248] The narrator records no call to attack, only Deborah's declaration that the day for God to deliver Sisera into Barak's hands has arrived. The form of the committal formula used by Deborah tempts the reader to look upon her as a female version of Ehud,[249] but only for a moment. Not only does she not address the troops; instead of calling Barak to follow her, she declares that Yahweh assuredly goes before him.[250] Barak obeys dutifully, with all his troops behind him.

4:15–16 Verse 15 is the key to the entire chapter: despite the presence of ten thousand Israelite troops, it was Yahweh who caused Sisera's entire fleet of chariots and all his troops to panic before his sword and before Barak. The verb *hāman*, which means "to bring into motion and confusion,"[251] recalls several other texts, most notably God's action against the Egyptians in Exod 14:24, in which natural phenomena are marshalled to effect the rout.[252] The role of Barak is deliberately diminished, not only by retaining Yahweh as the subject of the verb, but also by taking the sword out of Barak's hand[253] and emphasizing that all the action occurs "before" (*lipnê*) him.[254] Yahweh is the divine warrior who goes before his hosts. Sensing the hopelessness of his army's sit-

---

[246] On עַם, "people," used in the military sense of "troops, infantry" see 20:10; 1 Sam 14:17.

[247] Cf. the Song of Deborah (5:19), which calls the Kishon "the waters of Megiddo." For a reconstruction of the events involved in this battle see A. F. Rainey, "The Military Camp Ground at Taanach by the Waters of Megiddo," *Eretz Israel* 17 (1981): 15,61*–66*.

[248] Cp. Ehud's command in 3:28: רִדְפוּ אַחֲרַי, "Pursue after me …" in 3:28. Is the present verb equivalent to הִתְיַצֵּב, "station yourself," in a similar context in Exod 14:13, and is the verb רְאֵה, "See," implied?

[249] There is a verbal echo of 3:28 in 4:14.

[250] The verb קוּם and the pronominal suffixes are singular. On הֲלֹא as an expression of certainty see above on v. 6.

[251] *HALOT* 1.251; *DCH* 2.571.

[252] Cf. also Josh 10:10; 1 Sam 7:10.

[253] לְפִי־חָרֶב, "before the edge [lit. 'mouth'] of the sword" leaves the wielder unidentified; presumably it is Yahweh's sword. So also in v. 16b.

[254] Cp. 3:28–29, where although Ehud announces Yahweh's victory, the narration credits the success entirely to human activity.

uation, Sisera leaps *(yārad)* from his chariot[255] and flees on foot. But Barak, worried primarily about the army, pursues the Canaanite troops as far as Sisera's headquarters in Harosheth-Haggoyim. He does not stop until all have been slaughtered.

The Assassination of the Enemy Leader (4:17–22). **4:17–22** Verse 15 had introduced a complication in the drama: the army was routed, but Sisera had escaped, leaving the reader wondering how God's word through Deborah would be fulfilled. Would the prophet go after him while Barak chased the army? But after her announcement that Yahweh was about to deliver Sisera into Barak's hands, she too had disappeared. And once the army has been destroyed, Yahweh also exits the narrative. In the meantime the plot slows down to a crawl, as the intense action of the masses in vv. 12–16 gives way to the deliberate activity of an individual, a newcomer to the scene, a second woman, Jael.

The stylistic and verbal links between vv. 17–22 and a part of the Ehud narrative in 3:16–26 are obvious: (1) the absence of the divine hand; (2) the focus on individual actions; (3) the use of speech to get the victim into a vulnerable position; (4) the motif of treachery and deception; (5) the sequence of murder and discovery; (6) the use of the verb *tāqaʿ*, "to thrust," at the critical moment (3:21; 4:21); (7) the sequence of entry and discovery.[256]

Verse 15 had ended with the reader's eyes fixed on Sisera, fleeing on foot and disappearing over the horizon. After the summary description of Barak's mopping up operations with respect to Sisera's army (v. 16), the reader's gaze is returned to the fleeing general. How much time has elapsed we may only speculate. While Barak is occupied with the mopping-up operations at Harosheth-Haggoyim, Sisera would logically have headed northeast along the Grand Trunk Highway that ran from Megiddo to Hazor, the seat of his suzerain Jabin.[257] Recognizing that with Jabin's main forces decimated no protection was to be found in the capital (cf. v. 23), the general continued running northward until he came to the tent of Heber the Kenite, a recognized ally of Jabin.

4:17 For its treachery, brutality, and the element of surprise, the description that follows in vv. 17–22 is matched in the book only by Ehud's assassination of Eglon. The episode begins innocently enough. In his flight Sisera heads for the tent of Jael, the wife of Heber the Kenite, who had entered into an alli-

---

[255] On the article on הַמֶּרְכָּבָה functioning as equivalent to the possessive pronoun see *GBH* §137f.

[256] Note the echo of 3:25 in 4:22: נֹפֵל ... וְהִנֵּה. For further reflection on the matching stylistic features see A. Schökel, "Erzählkunst," 166.

[257] The road ran diagonally through the Jezreel valley, between the hills of Nazareth on the west and Mount Tabor on the east, past the "Horns of Hattin," through the Arbel pass, into the plain north of the Sea of Galilee, where Hazor was situated. See B. Beitzel, "Roads and Highways (Pre-Roman)," *ABD* 5.778–79; id., *Moody Atlas*, 67–68. As the crow flies, these cities were less than forty-five miles apart, considerably less than one-half the distance Elijah ran in his flight from Jezebel in 1 Kgs 19:3.

ance with Jabin. The expression šālôm, "friendly relations," denotes much more than the absence of hostilities. In contexts like this it functions as a covenant term. The fact that Sisera thought he would be safe in Heber's camp suggests the alliance had been formalized in some sort of treaty. Accordingly, Heber posed a double threat to Israel. Not only had he separated from the main clan of the Kenites, who were allies of Israel (1:16), but he had also formally bound himself by treaty to their enemy. By all political and ethical standards Sisera should have found security here. But his dream of safety would turn into the worst possible nightmare.

4:18 Without a hint of any connection with Deborah or her pronouncement that Yahweh would sell Sisera into the hands of a woman (v. 9), the narrator introduces us to Jael. It is doubtful her name, yāʿēl, which means "mountain goat,"[258] bears any literary importance. Instead the reader must look to the narrative itself, paying particular attention to the author's skillful characterization through speech and action.

From beginning to end, Jael controls the events described. She goes out to meet Sisera; she initiates the conversation; she, a woman, invites this strange man into her tent; she covers him with a rug—all this before Sisera utters his first word. But this obviously did not strike Sisera as unusual or odd. Even her speech has a soporific effect. The form of her address and invitation, literally, "To me turn aside, my Lord, turn aside to me" (ʾēlayw sûrâ ʾădōnî sûrâ ʾēlay)[259] and her words of reassurance, "Don't be afraid," offers him all the security he needs.[260] Like Eglon in 3:20, he is seduced by her speech. Innocently he enters her tent and lets her put "a covering" (śĕmîkâ) over him. The word occurs only here in the Old Testament, and its meaning remains unsure. The NIV follows the early versions, which appear to have read bimĕkasseh, "with a covering,"[261] which makes sense in the context. One may imagine a thick sheep or goat skin rug, which would have been extremely warm, to be sure,[262] but this is no time to worry about comfort. In addition to Sisera's concern for concealment, Jael may have been taking

---

[258] Variations of the name are found in Jaalah (יַעְלָה) in Ezra 2:56 and Jaala (יַעְלָא) in Neh 7:58. Cognate parallels are found in Ug. yʿl, Amorite ia-ḫi-la and ia-ḫi-la-tum, and Phoenician yʿl, the last of which occurs on a seal accompanied by a representation of a mountain goat. For a discussion and references see S. C. Layton, "Yaʿel in Judges 4: An Onomastic Rejoinder," ZAW 109 (1997): 93–94. Layton refutes an earlier attempt by E. van Wolde ("Yaʿel in Judges 4," ZAW 107 [1995]: 240–46) to explain the name as a third person masculine singular yiqtol form of the root עָלָה, "to go up."

[259] Note the rhythm and the chiastic structure.

[260] W. G. E. Watson ("A Note on Staircase Parallelism," VT 33 [1983]: 310–11) compares the staircase parallelism with Judg 19:23, 2 Sam 13:12, and 2 Kgs 4:16.

[261] LXX^B ἐπιβολαίῳ, Syr. ḥămiltaʾ, and Tg. gunkaʾ. Two MSS read בְּסָמִיכָה, as if from סָמַךְ, "to support."

[262] Cf. Boling, Judges, 97.

intentional steps to stifle the noise involved in her subsequent actions.

4:19 Once inside, Sisera tries to take the initiative, with a polite request for a little water to quench his thirst. Having been on the run for so far and so long, his thirst is understandable. But the significance of Jael's substitution of milk for water is not clear. Some suggest it is part of her seduction; to induce sleep.[263] Others propose the introduction of milk to the narrative intentionally intensifies the "mothering" motif.[264] In any case, by giving Sisera milk rather than water Jael reseizes the initiative, a conclusion supported by the following verbs, which succeed each other in rapid fire: "she opened a skin[265] of milk, and she gave him to drink, and she covered him."

4:20 In v. 20 Sisera attempts to regain control of the situation, without realizing that in the process he is actually prescribing his own dissolution. His command to her to stand[266] at the entrance of the tent to deflect any curious visitor is natural and seemingly innocent, but his instructions to Jael are filled with irony. On the surface the hypothetical question that he anticipates people approaching her tent will ask seems to raise questions about her morality. Which man (ʾîš) would come to her tent and ask her, "Is there a man [ʾîš] inside?" Obviously, this is the question of a husband, who suspects his wife of adulterous behavior, for which an Israelite woman would be subject to the death sentence.[267] But to Sisera it is a matter of his own life and death. Little does he realize that in prescribing her answer to the question, ʾāyin, "There is no one,"[268] he is passing judgment on himself, for in the end this mighty general of Jabin turns out to be a nobody.[269]

4:21 This verse describes this transformation in brutal detail. Jael, intentionally identified as Heber's wife,[270] takes a tent peg *(yĕtad hāʾōhel)* and a

---

[263] Following Burney's suggestion that milk has a soporific effect (*Judges*, 93), Boling (*Judges*, 98) comments, "She doped and duped him."

[264] Cf. Bal, *Death and Dissymmetry: The Politics of Coherence in the Book of Judges*, Chicago Studies in the History of Judaism (Chicago: University of Chicago Press, 1988), 212–13; cf. Exum, "Feminist Criticism," 72.

[265] נאוד, probably an abbreviation for נאוֹד. Skins were particularly suitable for storing milk that was to be churned for curds.

[266] Hb. עֲמֹד, "Stand," is problematic. The consonantal form may represent a scribal error for feminine עִמְדִי (cf. the versions) or a mispointed infinitive absolute functioning as an imperative (cf. Boling, *Judges*, 98). On the other hand, since Sisera was a general, accustomed to ordering men, the form may be habitual, reflecting his persistent illusions of control.

[267] See the procedure for dealing with a suspicious wife prescribed in Num 5:11–31.

[268] On the negative אַיִן used absolutely in this sense see *GBH* §160j.

[269] There is no need to interpret this detail sexually, as if Jael's actions emasculate him. The primary issue is not his gender but his existence.

[270] The insertion of "the wife of Heber" after Jael highlights the treachery of the woman's actions. Sisera may be a nobody, but she is not. She is the wife of the ally of Jabin.

mallet *(maqqebet,* NIV, "hammer"),[271] sneaks up to him,[272] and drives[273] it through his skull *(raqqâ),* pinning his head to the ground.[274] The circumstantial clause at the end of the verse explains how this was possible. Sisera had collapsed[275] and had fallen into a deep sleep;[276] therefore he died.

4:22 The story concludes by returning the reader's attention to Barak, who was last seen pursuing Sisera's beleaguered forces to Harosheth-Haggoyim (v. 16). Although Sisera has feared that someone might be chasing him, the reader has had no hint that Barak might reappear. In fact, Deborah's pronouncement in v. 9 might even have led one to believe that he was out of the picture for good. But suddenly, from out of nowhere, he bursts back into the picture[277] in hot pursuit of Sisera. Though Deborah had predicted that the honor of victory would elude his grasp and be seized by a woman, the narrator portrays him as doing everything in his power to negate the divine word. Flush from [his?] victory of the Kishon, the man who had hesitated to heed the call of God in the beginning succumbs to the call of ambition. Barak is not only running after Sisera; he is running after glory! The final scene bursts his egotistical balloon.

In words echoing her welcome to Sisera in v. 18, Jael again seizes the initiative and goes out to meet Barak.[278] She knows his agenda, but he does not know hers. She is the only one who speaks. She invites him in, promising to show him the person he is seeking. He probably expects to find Sisera cowering in a corner, easy prey for him. She escorts him into the tent, and there, to his shock,[279] is Sisera, pinned to the ground with a tent peg through his skull. His silence is deafening. In a flash,[280] gone is the victory! In a moment, gone is the glory, from Barak, that is! With magnificent irony Deborah's dual prophecy has been fulfilled. Yahweh has committed Sisera into Barak's hands (v. 7),

---

[271] On indeterminate objects constructed as determinate because they are used for a specific goal see *GBH* §137m.

[272] Lit., "went to him secretly."

[273] תָּקַע, the same verb used in 3:21. What Ehud's dagger had been to Eglon, Jael's tent peg was to Sisera.

[274] צָנַח, the same verb used in 1:14 of Achsah getting off her donkey, here means "to penetrate downward."

[275] For the sense of יָעֵף see Isa 40:28,30,31; 44:12. The latter parallels weariness with אֵין כֹּחַ, "no strength," and attributes this exhaustion to strenuous effort and thirst.

[276] The choice of the verb נִרְדָּם (from רָדַם, "to be in a deep sleep") cognate to the noun תַּרְדֵּמָה, "deep sleep," in Gen 2:21, seems deliberate, hinting at divine inducement. In the Hb. the verbs are illogically reversed: "He had fallen asleep and was exhausted."

[277] As in 3:24–25 וְהִנֵּה, "and behold," expresses surprise.

[278] Cp. the construction:

v. 18 וַתֵּצֵא יָעֵל לִקְרַאת סִיסְרָא וַתֹּאמֶר אֵלָיו

v. 22 וַתֵּצֵא יָעֵל לִקְרָאתוֹ וַתֹּאמֶר לוֹ

[279] On וְהִנֵּה expressing surprise see above on 3:24–25. In this scene the Israelite Barak is made to look like a buffoon by being cast in the same role as the Moabite guards after the death of Eglon.

[280] The name Barak means "flash [of lightning]."

but he has also committed him into the hands of a woman. Unfortunately for him, the woman has won the honor (v. 9).

As in the case of Ehud, the events described in vv. 17–22 raise serious questions about Jael. How is the reader to interpret her? Is she to be viewed as a heroine or a villain? The answers obviously depend upon one's point of view.

To the author of the account Jael was obviously an agent of divine deliverance, the fulfillment of Deborah's prediction (v. 9), though he too will have marveled that this role should have been played by one who not only is not a prophet nor an Israelite. She is the wife of one allied against the Israelites! It is understandable that to the Israelites, who benefited from her actions, she became a hero (5:24–27).[281] However, upon closer analysis, her actions and character are patently ambiguous.

In Barak's eyes, Jael had triumphed in a masculine role, and in so doing she had shamed him and robbed him of the glory of victory. Her speech and actions had displayed a deep contempt not only for Sisera but also for him.[282] To the Canaanites, Jael's conduct represented the ultimate in treachery. In assassinating Jabin's five-star general, she had guaranteed the enemy the victory.

One can only imagine how Jael's husband, Heber, felt about her actions. Not only had she broken fundamental social rules of wifely support; she had also violated deeply entrenched customs of ancient Near Eastern hospitality.[283] First she, a woman, usurps his exclusive right as a male to offer hospitality to a male.[284] Then, having lulled her guest into a false sense of security, she premeditates and executes his murder.

If the song in chap. 5 will ascribe to Deborah the honorific title of "Mother in Israel" (5:7), Jael obviously represents a different paradigm of motherhood. Like Ehud's assassination of Eglon in the previous chapter, the account of her behavior seems to have been lifted from a Canaanite notebook. The narration offers no hint of any spiritual motivation on her part or any concern for Israel. She acts entirely on her own and for her own (mysterious) reasons. Her actions

---

[281] Klein (*Triumph of Irony*, 43) concludes that Jael's pro-Israelite actions identify her as an Israelite. For an emphatically contrary position see Webb, *Book of Judges*, 137.

[282] According to Bal (*Murder and Difference*, 116), *"the honor-shame opposition, linked to that between the sexes"* [italics hers] is central to the narrative.

[283] For a full discussion see V. H. Matthews, "Hospitality and Hostility in Judges 4," *BTB* 21 (1991): 13–21.

[284] Matthews (ibid., 15–19) recognizes correctly that Sisera had himself flaunted the customs of hospitality first by seeking hospitality in the tent of a woman rather than the head of the household, accepting Jael's invitation to enter her tent, requesting water from the host, and ordering the host to protect him, the guest. Matthews insists that Jael's actions were not treacherous; she did not consciously betray her husband's alliance with Jabin. On the contrary, she was dealing with a man who by his own speech and action had become a "nobody." However, it is not that simple, and she seems not to be that innocent. It is difficult to conceive of a woman murdering her guest because he had violated the laws of hospitality.

are not only deviant[285] and violent but socially revolutionary, challenging prevailing views of female roles in general and the relationship of husband and wife in particular.[286] However, just because the author records her deeds does not mean he approves of them. It simply adds to the mystery of divine providence, demonstrating implicitly what the following verses explicitly affirm: God is able to incorporate the free activities of human beings into his plan for his own glory and for the salvation of his people.[287]

GOD'S GIFT OF SECURITY (4:23–24). **4:23–24** The story concludes provisionally in vv. 23–24 with an editorial summary of the effects of the defeat of Sisera's army.[288] Remarkably, the protagonists in the drama that has riveted our attention since v. 4 have all disappeared. The reader learns hereby that this story is not primarily about Deborah and Barak, or Barak and Sisera, or Sisera and Jael, or Jael and Barak. The author would be disappointed if our analyses ended with these intriguing characters or the dynamics of power and control that play between them. This is a story about God, who is the real hero,[289] and his people Israel, and their enemies the Canaanites,[290] represented by Jabin their king. The conclusion reminds the reader that the conflict in the Book of Judges is not between patriarchy and egalitarianism, between men and women,[291] or even between Israelite leaders and the rulers of the nations. The conflict is between the divine King and the kingdom of Light on the one hand and the forces of the kingdom of darkness on the other.

---

[285] Cf. Chalcraft, "Deviance and Legitimate Action," 182–83. S. Niditch ("Eroticism and Death in the Tale of Jael," in *Gender and Difference in Ancient Israel*, ed. P. L. Day [Minneapolis: Fortress, 1989], 45) rightly rejects the view of those who claim the picture of Jael derives from ancient Near Eastern goddesses (e.g., J. G. Taylor, "The Song of Deborah and Two Canaanite Goddesses," *JSOT* 23 [1982]: 99–108), though like such characters she is "a warrior and seducer, alluring and dangerous, nurturing and bloodthirsty."

[286] According to Zakovitch ("Sisseras Tod," *ZAW* 93 [1981]: 364–74), although Jael's intentions were erotic and seductive, the prose account of Sisera's death lacks sexual elements, which she attributes to the biblical author's desire to present Jael in an honorable light. But this interpretation is modified by recent essayists who exploit this text for feminist purposes. In the eyes of some the account is filled with sexual symbolism: Jael's invitation to enter the tent, her monopoly of the conversation, the substitution of milk (female symbol) for water (male symbol), the penetration of the tent peg (phallus), the rug as symbol of the feminine domain, the "de-manning" of Sisera. Cf. Brenner, "A Triangle and a Rhombus in Narrative Structure: A Proposed Integrative Reading of Judges 4 and 5," *A Feminist Companion to Judges*, The Feminist Companion to the Bible 4 (Sheffield: Academic Press, 1993), 99–101; Niditch, "Eroticism and Death," 43–57.

[287] The Song of Deborah in the following chapter will explicitly praise Jael as "most blessed of women" (5:25).

[288] The editorial conclusion is interrupted by the insertion of the Song of Deborah. The final ending comes in 5:31b.

[289] Thus also Amit, "Judges 4," 89–111.

[290] The collective significance of Jabin is reflected in the threefold repetition of "Jabin the king of Canaan" in two verses.

[291] Contra Bal, J. W. H. Bos ("Out of the Shadows: Genesis 38; Judges 4:17– 22; Ruth 3," *Semeia* 42 [1988]: 49–57), et al.

The narrator's commentary in vv. 23–24 reflects his perception of the synergy between the divine hand and human effort in historical events. On the one hand, on that day it was God[292] who subdued[293] the Canaanites. The expressions "on that day" and "before Barak" intentionally allude to vv. 14–15. On the other hand, the Israelites maintained their pressure[294] on the Canaanites until they had annihilated[295] Jabin and the Canaanites. The reader will have to wait until the end of the next chapter to learn how long they enjoyed the benefits of this victory.

(2) The Poetic Celebration (5:1–31)

After the dramatic narrative of the victory over the Canaanites, we encounter one of the oldest poems in the Old Testament. Few texts in the historiographic writings of the Old Testament have engaged as much study in the past two or three decades as Judges 5. Intrigued by its textual riddles, emotional intensity, psychological energy, and theological profundity, scholars have found in the "Song of Deborah" grist for a steady stream of publications.[296] The first item on the agenda of many of these is to reconstruct the literary evolution of the piece by isolating the original core and identifying the redactional additions.[297] Recognizing that any reconstructions are speculative, others fol-

---

[292] The use of אֱלֹהִים, "God," instead of יהוה, "the LORD" (vv. 1–3), is striking. It may have struck the narrator incongruous to link "the LORD" with a verb associated with "Canaanites."

[293] The verb כָּנַע (kānaʿ), "to bring low," plays on the name כְּנַעַן, "Canaan." The present hiphil form compares with the niphal in 3:30; 8:28; 11:33.

[294] On the construction הָלֹוךְ וְקָשֶׁה, with the infinitive absolute of הָלַךְ followed by waw plus perfect, to express continuity see GBH §123s.

[295] הִכְרִית, lit. "cut away/off," occurs only here in Judges.

[296] For recent studies reflecting the state of scholarship see J. Gray, "Israel in the Song of Deborah," in Ascribe to the Lord: Biblical and Other Studies in Memory of Peter C. Craigie, ed. L. Eslinger and G. Taylor, JSOTSup 67 (Sheffield: 1988), 421–55; H. Schulte, "Richter 5: Das Debora-Lied: Versuch einer Deutung," in Die Hebräische Bibel und ihre zweifache Nachgeschichte: Festschrift für Rolf Rendtorff zum 65. Geburtstag, ed. E. Blum et al. (Neukirchen-Vluyn: Neukirchener, 1990), 177–91. For textual studies of the relationship between the MT and the LXX see E. Tov, "The Textual History of the Song of Deborah in the Text of the LXX," VT 28 (1988): 224–32; J. Schreiner, "Textformen und Urtext des Deboraliedes in der Septuaginta," Bib 42 (1961): 173–200.

[297] Soggin (Judges, 96) finds an original secular "lay" song in vv. 6–30, which breaks down as follows: (1) Prelude, vv. 6–8; (2) The Assembly of Combatants, vv. 13–18; (3) The Description of the Battle, vv. 19–22[23?]; (4) The Flight and Slaying of Sisera, vv. 24–27; (5) The Waiting Mother, vv. 28–30. The additions, vv. 2–5 and 9–12, transformed this lay song into a theological and cultic hymn in which the heroes are no longer the mighty men of Israel but Yahweh, the coalition of troops becomes "the LORD's troops," an economic/political conflict becomes a "holy war," and conscription replaces volunteerism. Richter (TUR 81–93) includes vv. 9–11. In a more recent study Schulte ("Richter 5: Das Debora-Lied: Versuch einer Deutung") proposes that the three strophes that constitute the Sisera epic (vv. 19–22,24–30) represent the oldest segment. Neither Yahweh nor Israel, neither Deborah nor Barak, appear. To this core were added the expressions of praise to the nine (ten?) tribes (vv. 13–19), the description of the uncertain context (vv. 6–8), and the call to celebration (vv. 9–11), all of which reflect a north-Israelite provenance. The theophanic portrayal (vv. 4–5) and the formulaic liturgical expansions (vv. 1–3,9b, 12,21b) represent later Southern (Judean) expansions. The curse of Meroz (v. 23) is of uncertain derivation.

low a holistic approach,[298] even though the text consists of a series of more or less independent literary fragments, often unconnected thematically or syntactically. But these problems obviously loom larger in the minds of modern Western readers than in the minds of those responsible for composing and transmitting the final form of the poem.

By noting that this literary piece was "sung" *(šîr)*, the preamble to chap. 5 (v. 1) distinguishes it formally from the surrounding narrative. As a song, it bears the marks of typical Hebrew poetry: the parallelistic balancing of lines based on conventional pairs of words, alliteration, paranomasia, chiasmus, and formulaic constructions.[299] Like Hebrew poetry generally, it is divided into a series of stanzas and/or strophes, but in this case each bears its own literary stamp and contributes its own substance to the overall development of the theme.[300] This poem also displays a pronounced meter,[301] though the metric pattern is too inconsistent to provide a reliable basis for surgical textual operations.

The composite nature of the poem complicates its generic classification. In its present context (immediately after a narrative account of Israel's victory over the Canaanites) the song as a unit functions as a victory hymn of praise to Yahweh, analogous to Egyptian victory odes of Thutmose III and Merneptah,[302] Tikulti-Ninurta I's ode of triumph over Kaštiliaš,[303] and especially the Song of

---

[298] See Boling, *Judges*, 105–20; Webb, *Book of Judges*, 138–44; A. Globe, "The Literary Structure and Unity of the Song of Deborah," *JBL* 93 (1974): 493–512; Hauser, "Judges 5: Parataxis in Hebrew Poetry," *JBL* 99 (1980): 23–41; J. P. Fokkelman, "The Song of Deborah and Barak: Its Prosodic Levels and Structure," in *Pomegranates and Golden Bells: Studies in Biblical, Jewish, and Near Eastern Ritual, Law, and Literature in Honor of Jacob Milgrom*, ed. D. P. Wright, et al. (Winona Lake: Eisenbrauns, 1995), 595–628.

[299] See M. D. Coogan, "A Structural and Literary Analysis of the Song of Deborah," *CBQ* 40 (1978): 143–66. For a study of the parallelism in the song see Craigie, "Parallel Word Pairs in the Song of Deborah (Judges 5)," *JETS* 29 (1977): 15–22. Craigie finds eighty-two word pairs in Judges 5, twenty-two of which also occur in Ugaritic.

[300] Scholars are not agreed on the number of stanzas in the poem; our analysis recognizes nine. The most thorough stanzaic analyses are provided by Fokkelman ("The Song of Deborah and Barak," 595–628) and Coogan ("Structural and Literary Analysis," 143–66), but see also Webb, *Book of Judges*, 139–43.

[301] Some scholars base their metrical analyses on syllable count (Coogan, "Song of Deborah," 157–58; D. N. Freedman, "Pottery, Poetry, and Prophecy: An Essay on Biblical Poetry," *JBL* 96 [1977]: 5–26; Boling, *Judges*, 106); others base it on stress beats (Lindars, *Judges 1–5*, 219; Fokkelman, "Song of Deborah and Barak," 595–629, *passim*, though he ends the essay with a tabulation of the syllables in the cola).

[302] *ANET*, 234–41, 377, respectively. For analyses see Younger, "Judges 4 and 5," 117–27.

[303] See especially Younger ("Judges 4 and 5," 110–13) and Craigie ("The Song of Deborah and the Epic of Tikulti-Ninurta," *JBL* 88 [1969]: 253–65). The latter observes in both: (1) divine aid invoked on the basis of a previous relationship and covenant with the deity; (2) the use of a war cry to conjure up the drama of the battle; (3) sarcastic and taunting references to the pathetic flight of the enemy leader; (4) the involvement of females (human or divine) in inspiring the victorious warriors; (5) similar literary characteristics. For additional similarities see Globe, "Literary Structure and Unity of the Song of Deborah," 495–99.

the Sea in Exodus 15.[304] Whereas the extrabiblical odes represent hyperbolic celebrations of superhuman achievements, Exodus 15 and Judges 5 overflow with praise to God. But our text is not exclusively so. The last two stanzas focus on individual human activity: Jael's brutal murder of Sisera and the portrait of Sisera's anxious mother, waiting for her son. Because this seems odd in a victory hymn, some have preferred to identify this poem as a ballad, which "moves quickly from theophany to troubled times, from the appearance of Deborah to the muster of the tribes, and finally to the battle and its climatic sequel."[305] On the other hand, the poet's inclusion of this unrestrained praise of the woman not only assumes her participation in the divine work but also functions as a taunt of Sisera, and with him the Canaanites, who stand in the way of Yahweh's agenda. In form and content the Song represents a mixed genre. Each of the successive segments possesses its own generic integrity and must be analyzed on its own terms. But the final lyric product is immeasurably more brilliant and powerful than the sum of its parts, celebrating in a single ode the victory of God over the enemy and the heroism of the human participants.

Scholars are divided on questions of date and authorship of this ode. Most agree that—along with the Blessing of Jacob (Genesis 49), the Song of the Sea (Exodus 15), the oracles of Balaam (Numbers 23–24), and the Blessing of Moses (Deuteronomy 33)—Judges 5 ranks among the oldest monuments of Hebrew literature.[306] But how close the composition of the song was to the events it describes is not clear. Some, especially those who prefer to classify this text as a cult-liturgical piece rather than a victory psalm,[307] date it a century or two after the events.[308] The preamble declares that Deborah and Barak sang this song, which suggests it was created for the celebrations that occurred

---

[304] The shared features include (1) an introductory statement identifying the action of those who recited the poem with שִׁיר, "to sing"; (2) style: poetry (šîr) following a prose account; (3) the involvement of female singers; (4) motif: the role of waters in the victory; (5) archaic language; (6) similar opening lines; (7) colorful and mythological imagery. For a closer comparison of these poems see Hauser, "Two Songs of Victory: A Comparison of Exodus 15 and Judges 5," in *Directions in Biblical Poetry*, ed. E. R. Follis, JSOTSup 40 (Sheffield: JSOT Press, 1987), 265–84; also O'Connell, *Rhetoric of the Book of Judges*, 133–37.

[305] Thus Coogan, "Structural and Literary Analysis," 165. Coogan's unitary interpretation is preferable to that of J. Blenkinsopp ("Ballad Style and Psalm Style in the Song of Deborah," *Bib* 42 [1961]: 61–76), followed by Lindars ("Deborah's Song: Women in the Old Testament," *BJRL* 65 [1983]: 165–72), who propose that an originally secular ballad has been touched up with liturgical features to create a psalm celebrating the mighty acts of God.

[306] Many would also add the Song of Moses, Deuteronomy 32.

[307] A. Weiser ("Das Deboralied—eine gattungs-und traditionsgeschichtliche Studie," *ZAW* 71 [1959]: 67–97) finds its Sitz im Leben in a covenant renewal festival. He is followed by Gray (*Joshua, Judges and Ruth*, 275) and Boling (*Judges*, 116–17). Schulte ("Richter 5," 190) prefers to characterize it as "liturgical-dramatic."

[308] Boling, *Judges*, 101–20; P. R. Ackroyd, "The Composition of the Song of Deborah," *VT* 2 (1952): 160–62. Soggin (*Judges*, 80–81) proposes a date near the time of the Gezer calendar.

immediately after the victory over Sisera. But this does not yet identify the composer. The fact that Deborah and Barak sang this song does not necessarily mean that either of them composed it.[309]

However, the traditional view that Deborah was responsible for its composition rests on fairly solid ground. First, the composer frequently speaks in the first person, especially the first half.[310] Second, in v. 7, the identity of the first person speaker is explicitly named ("Deborah") and described ("mother in Israel"). Third, in v. 23 the poet quotes a curse attributed to the envoy (NIV, "angel") of Yahweh *(mal'ak yhwh)*. While the identity of this "angel" is uncertain, this may be an evasive self-reference. The expression recalls 2:4, where the same title had been given to another messenger of a divine word. Fourth, though not conclusive, this identification fits with the order of the names, "Deborah and Barak," and the use of the feminine singular verb, *wattāšar,* "And she sang," in the preamble.[311] Fifth, the leadership of Deborah, a woman, in victory celebrations accords with the picture of the role of women in other biblical[312] and extrabiblical texts.[313] This may also account for the sensitive female perspective evident especially in the latter parts of the song in particular. Sixth, the attribution of the song to Deborah agrees with her prophetic status as announced and described in chap. 4.[314] The song itself represses her prophetic standing before God,[315] but in its theological interpretation of the victory over the Canaanites it clearly reflects a prophetic understanding of the event. In this regard too the song complements the narrative account. In chap.

---

[309] Considering the name, "Song of Deborah," "an awful misnomer," Fokkelmann argues that the "I" that occurs frequently in the poem does not refer to Deborah or Barak but to the lyricist as an independent single voice ("The Song of Deborah and Barak," 596).

[310] The pronoun אָנֹכִי, "I," occurs twice in v. 3; the first person singular suffix occurs twice, in v. 9 (לִי, "to me") and v. 21 (נַפְשִׁי, "my soul, person"); first person verbs occur in v. 3 (אָשִׁירָה, "I will sing"; אֲזַמֵּר, "I will make melody") and v. 7 (שַׁקַּמְתִּי, "I will arise," twice). According to Fokkelman ("Song of Deborah and Barak," 596, n. 4) the first person is implied wherever a second person is addressed (vv. 2c,3ab,4ab,7cd,9c,10c,12abcd,14b,16a,31a). The first person verbs in v. 3 reflect the same situation that obtains in the Song of the Sea, Exod 15:1, where, according to N. Sarna אָשִׁירָה, "I will sing," "can refer only to Moses" *(Exodus*, 77).

[311] Fokkelman (ibid., n. 3) correctly notes that the feminine singular form is determined by the author's desire to report an action by female X and male Y with a preceding preterite. See *GBH* §150q, which cites also Num 12:1 (Miriam and Aaron speaking). Exod 15:1 has the singular יָשִׁיר, "He sang," before "Moses and the Israelites."

[312] Note the involvement of Miriam in Exod 15:20–21, which is echoed in the activity of Jephthah's daughter in Judg 11:34, and the women singers after David's defeat of Goliath, 1 Sam 18:6–7. Cf. also Jer 31:4.

[313] On women's involvement in victory celebrations in Neo-Assyria see E. B. Poethig, "The Victory Song Tradition of the Women of Israel" (Ph.D. diss., Union Theological Seminary, New York, 1985), 192.

[314] Cf. the reference to Miriam as a female prophet in Exod 15:20.

[315] "Until I arose, Deborah; until I arose, a mother in Israel," in v. 7 highlights her maternal relationship to Israel rather than her professional involvement as spokeswoman for Yahweh.

4 the focus was not on the battle against Sisera as such[316] but on the course of events as the fulfillment of Deborah's prophecies in vv. 6–7,9,14. Although the Song makes no direct reference to her prophetic involvement,[317] it arises out of Deborah's prophetic self-consciousness. By placing the ode in Deborah's mouth, the author of the book correctly recognizes that her interpretation of the battle is fundamentally a prophetic word.[318]

But the attribution of the psalm to Deborah must be qualified. Not only does the preamble note that Barak sang it with her but the description of the theophany in vv. 4–5 may also have been inspired by conventional images of a divine appearance. More importantly, on the basis of internal evidence, the song itself appears to be multivoiced. Deborah herself is addressed (along with Barak) in the second person in v. 12 and in the third person in v. 15. But the reader must remember that this is not a literary photograph but impressionistic poetry. These extraordinary constructions may be attributable entirely to the text's poetic genre.

The ascription of the Song to Deborah and Barak in the preamble suggests it must have been composed shortly after Israel's victory over Jabin and the Canaanites. The vividness of the description and the energy of the poem, with its rapid succession of vocatives, exclamations, and imperatives, reflect the excitement of the event.

Several additional considerations argue for an early, premonarchic date. First, the absence of Judah from the list of tribes points to a time when Judah had not yet achieved her hegemonic position in Israel. Second, according to v. 6, the poet recognizes the chronological simultaneity of Jael's and Shamgar's times.[319] Third, and most impressively, the language of the poem represents an archaic style of Hebrew.[320] Scarcely a line of this song is without problems; by some estimates in 70 percent of the verses the key words are difficult.[321] Unlike the surrounding narrative, characteristic of classical Judean Hebrew, the ubiquity of archaic and hapax (unique) forms suggests that this

---

[316] The battle is summarized in a single verse (v. 15).

[317] One may recognize an allusion to her prophetic involvement in the call of Barak in vv. 7b–8a, which juxtaposes her rise with God's choice of new leaders. One might also argue that the portrayal of Sisera's mother in vv. 28–30 derives both from a vivid imagination and prophetic insight, analogous to Samuel's prescient awareness of the location of Kish's donkeys (1 Sam 9:6,19–20).

[318] So also Watts, *Psalm and Story*, 90.

[319] Unless of course the omission of Judah is an intentional anti-Judahite polemical feature.

[320] The details will be cited below.

[321] The intensity and extent of the difficulties posed by the text is reflected in the Tg., which in terms of word count is five times as long as the Hb. version. D. J. Harrington ("The Prophecy of Deborah: Interpretive Homiletics in Targum Jonathan of Judges 5," *CBQ* 48 [1986]: 432–42) describes the targumic version as "interpretive homiletics." Cf. id. and A. J. Saldarini, *Targum Jonathan of the Former Prophets: Introduction, Translation and Notes*, The Aramaic Bible 10 (Wilmington: Michael Glazier, 1987), 11.

document is ancient. Like Chaucerian and Shakespearean poetry, this ode was passed on from generation to generation unchanged.[322]

Two introductory questions of intention remain: (1) Why was this song composed in the first place? (2) Why did the author of the Book of Judges insert it here? The answer to the first depends upon the generic classification ascribed to the poem: as history it informs; as a ballad it entertains; as a heroic ode it inspires; as a hymn it calls for celebration. As a poetic recital of historical events, this ode offers the reader/hearer a glimpse into the early history of Israel. Because it offers a nearly contemporary picture of premonarchic Israel, some would argue that the picture it paints of Israel's formative years is more reliable than the surrounding prose narrative. It characterizes these early decades as troubled times. Not only was the nation at the mercy of outsiders with whom they competed for control of the land (control of the Jezreel Valley seems to have been a key element in this conflict), internally the tribes found it difficult to work in concert. To be sure, Israel's sense of a national community consisting of at least nine (or ten) tribes antedated the monarchy, but internal tensions were created by varying levels of tribal loyalty to the confederate ideal. The ode also offers a picture of the economy of the Israelites, who made their living by trading, herding sheep, and supporting the maritime trade of the Phoenicians.

Above and beyond its sociopolitical significance, this poem reflects religious conditions in early Israel.[323] Most obviously, the ideal Israel is portrayed as the people of Yahweh,[324] engaged in his service,[325] committed to him in covenant love,[326] and called upon to bless and praise him (vv. 2–3). Conversely, the twofold occurrence of "The LORD, the God of Israel" in vv. 3 and 5 formally presents him as the patron deity of the nation. But unlike the gods of the nations around, Yahweh is not a territorial deity, hemmed in by the geographical boundaries of the land his people occupy. He is the cosmic Lord, the Commander of all the hosts of heaven (v. 20), who resides in Sinai and marches

---

[322] While conceding that the core of the poem reflects early events, as already intimated, many argue that the present form, with its so-called liturgical features, derives from a much later time. Cf. Lindars, *Judges 1–5*, 213–16; Soggin, *Judges*, 80–81; G. Garbini, "Il cantico di Debora," *La parola del passato* 178 (Naples: 1978), 5–31.

[323] On the significance of this and other early poetic texts for recapturing the religion of early Israel, see Freedman, "'Who Is Like Thee Among the Gods?' The Religion of Early Israel," in *Ancient Israelite Religion: Essays in Honor of Frank Moore Cross*, ed. P. D. Miller et al. (Philadelphia: Fortress, 1987), 315–36.

[324] Note the suffixed expression פְּרָזֹנוֹ בְּיִשְׂרָאֵל, "his peasantry [NIV, "warriors"] in Israel" (5:11).

[325] Note the expression לֹא־בָאוּ לְעֶזְרַת יְהוָה, "They [Meroz] did not come to the aid of the LORD" (v. 23).

[326] Note the expression אֹהֲבָיו, "those who love him," in contrast to אֹיְבֶיךָ, "those who hate you," that is, Yahweh's enemies, in v. 31.

forth from Seir, the mountain of Edom, as the divine Warrior. But this song is also well aware of the fickleness of Israel's devotion to their God. In fact, like the narrator of the Book of Judges as a whole, the composer attributes the turmoil and terror within Israel in this period to the nation's betrayal of their God. "War in the gates" (NIV, "war came to the city gates") is associated directly with the people's choosing *(bāḥar)* "new gods," that is, gods unknown to their ancestors (v. 8).

Although this poem offers a window into the premonarchic social and religious world of Israel, its value in reconstructing specific historical events of this period is limited. This is after all a song, an impressionistic literary portrait, rather than a historical narrative. Driven by emotion, it is pervaded by figurative language. Without the benefit of chap. 4 only the barest of historical details could be extracted. The Israelites were engaged in a battle in the valley of Jezreel with Canaanite forces under the leadership of Sisera. Although the summons to battle appears to have gone out to the entire nation, not all the tribes responded. The Israelites seem to have been galvanized into action by two characters, Deborah and Barak, but their precise roles are not clear. In the end Israel's victory was achieved with the aid of meteorological intervention and the heroic action of an outsider, Jael, who personally killed the enemy general. More than this we cannot extract from this poem. For the context and course of the battle and the specific actions of the protagonists we must consult the preceding prose account.

This piece was also written at least in part to entertain an Israelite audience. The images of Yahweh marching forth from Seir like a conquering warrior, the deserted highways, Deborah the mother in Israel, affluent merchants riding on white donkeys draped with rich carpets, and stars fighting from heaven captivate the reader. Hardly anyone would fail to be amused by the ironic portrayals of Jael and Sisera's mother in the concluding scenes.

But the poem is much more than a ballad. The admiration of the poet for the principal characters is transparent. As a group the warriors of several tribes of Israel, especially the troops of Zebulun and Naphtali, who were willing to sacrifice their lives for the nation, are held up as models of courage. But individually the highest accolades go to two women, Deborah and Jael, whose courage and sagacity won the day for Israel. The feminine motif is obvious and intentional. On the one hand, Barak ("lightning"), the champion of Israel, is totally outshone by Deborah. He takes second place to her in the preamble (v. 1) and plays only a limited role in the ode. Deborah's rise accounts for the turn in Israel's fortunes, she receives the honorific epithet of "Mother in Israel" (v. 7), and she wins the loyalty of the troops (v. 15). On the other hand, Sisera, the champion of Canaan, falls victim to the shrewdness and energy of Jael. For her courage this outsider receives her own honorific epithet, "most blessed among women" (v. 24). Indeed because of her heroics this period in Israel's history is referred to as "the days of Jael" (v. 6).

Although the deeds of these two women awe and inspire the reader, the composer would be disappointed with many contemporary studies that fail to rise beyond the human performances on the earthly stage to the heavenly sphere, where Yahweh sits enthroned above all the hosts of the universe. In the last analysis this is a hymn of celebration to God. He is the divine warrior, who has routed Sisera and his army, for whom the stars have fought from above and for whom the Kishon has fought from below. The warriors of Israel are Yahweh's army (v. 23), and those who refuse to respond to the call to arms betray him. At the same time Sisera and his army are not merely the point men for Jabin and the Canaanites; they are enemies of Yahweh (v. 31). Obviously this ode has more than one aim. However, the opening summons to "bless the LORD" (v. 2; cf. v. 9) and to "sing praises to the God of Israel" (v. 3) and the concluding recognition of those who love determine its primary function: the celebration of Yahweh's triumph over Israel's foes. But in celebrating God's triumph over the Canaanites, the poet also wages a polemical war against the gods of the Canaanites. In this ode, filled with allusions from Canaanite mythology, Yahweh assumes roles that the natives (and compromising Israelites) had ascribed to Baal, then beats the Canaanite deity at his own game.[327]

These observations may clarify the composition of the poem as an independent entity in the first place, but they do not explain its present incorporation in a larger literary composition. The prose conclusion (v. 31b) logically and stylistically follows immediately after 4:24. Why then does the author of the book interrupt the flow of the narrative with this lengthy insertion of an extraneous piece? What contribution does the poem make to the overall thesis of the book? The answer has already been hinted at in the discussion of its religious significance.

First, the poem lends credibility and authority to the author's perception of the premonarchic era as a time of religious syncretism, a problem that underlies the recurring crises in the book. His impressions of the causes of Israel's problems are not figments of his imagination. This poem offers early objective evidence of this fundamental point.

Second, this poem recognizes that Israel was rescued from her enemies by extraordinarily courageous and gifted individuals. But more important, if the nation ever triumphs over her enemies, the glory must go ultimately and primarily to Yahweh, who deals with his people in mercy and grace, not according to what they deserve. God does indeed act for the benefit of his people,

---

[327] So also W. R. Herman, "The Kingship of the LORD in the Hymnic Theophanies of the Old Testament," *SBT* 16 (1988): 174–77. Cf. S. J. Dempster, "Mythology and History in the Song of Deborah," *WTJ* 41 (1978): 33–53. Although helpful for its portrayal of Canaanite religion, J. G. Taylor's argument that the figures of Deborah and Anath derive from ANE goddesses goes too far. "The Song of Deborah and Two Canaanite Goddesses," *JSOT* 23 (1982): 99–108.

but he is driven by his own sovereign power and the determination to preserve a people called by his name. No one can stand against him when he appears.

¹On that day Deborah and Barak son of Abinoam sang this song:

PREAMBLE (5:1).   **5:1**   Verse 1 functions as an editorial introduction to the song, comparable to the introductions to other ancient poems in the Old Testament.[328] Three features of the note are significant. First, the role of Barak continues to be suppressed by naming him after Deborah. Second, as already observed, the genre of the document is suggested by the verb *šîr,* "to sing." Third, the author intentionally links the singing of the song chronologically with the defeat of Sisera. The expression "on that day" *(bayyôm hahû³)* suggests it was composed as a spontaneous and instantaneous response to the triumph.[329]

²"When the princes in Israel take the lead,
 when the people willingly offer themselves—
 praise the LORD!
³"Hear this, you kings! Listen, you rulers!
 I will sing to the LORD, I will sing;
 I will make music to the LORD, the God of Israel.

STANZA I: INTROIT (5:2–3).   **5:2**   The song opens with a rousing call for praise to God. The introit divides into two parts, an exhortation to praise God, expressed in the plural imperative, and the personal response of the lyricist, expressed in the first person.[330] However, the former (v. 2) also divides into two segments, which respectively announce the context/occasion for celebration and charge the hearers/readers to bless Yahweh. The reasons for praise are

---

[328] See the introductions to Jacob's Blessing (Gen 49:1), the Song of the Sea (Exod 15:1), the Song of Moses (Deut 31:30), the Blessing of Moses (Deut 33:1), and David's Song of the Bow (2 Sam 1:17–18).

[329] Fokkelman's contention that the first person represents the voice of an distanced lyricist is not convincing ("Song of Deborah and Barak," 596–97).

[330] The introit is cast in the form of four poetic versets ("a pair or group of words semantically and logically united to complete a thought"). These should really be designated "verses," but this would confuse the entities with the segments of text traditionally recognized in our translations and in the Hb. The following breakdown reveals the 3:2:2 stress-meter in the first verset and the 2:2 parallelistic pattern in the second:

| בָּרְכוּ יְהוָה: | בְּהִתְנַדֵּב עָם | בִּפְרֹעַ פְּרָעוֹת בְּיִשְׂרָאֵל | 2 |

| אָזַמֵּר לַיהוָה | אָנֹכִי לַיהוָה | שִׁמְעוּ מְלָכִים | 3 |
| אֱלֹהֵי יִשְׂרָאֵל: | אָנֹכִי אָשִׁירָה | הַאֲזִינוּ רֹזְנִים | |

expressed by means of two semantically parallel lines[331] (each consisting of the preposition *beth* + infinitive construct + subject): the rulers of Israel took charge, and the people volunteered. Typical of poetry, objects for the verbs are omitted; the poet assumes familiarity with the historical event.

The verse presents three major interpretive issues. First, what is the function of *beth* + infinitive construction? The NIV understands it in the usual sense, that is, as a temporal adverb, "When ..." But this makes little sense before the imperative. In this context the preposition + infinitive is better interpreted "in view of the fact that ...,"[332] a function normally born by ʿal or ʾăšer.[333]

Second, what is the meaning of the root *prʿ*, which occurs twice, in the infinitive *(biprōaʿ)* and its cognate subject *(pĕrāʿôt)*? The NIV's "when princes take the lead" assumes a derivation from a root cognate to Arabic *faraʿa*, "to excel, be eminent." Conjoined with ʿam, "people," Deborah hereby apparently recognizes the involvement of the leadership and the general population. But this interpretation is far from certain. If the present usage is to be related to Num 5:18 and 6:5, where the verb speaks of loosing the hair, then one may imagine either some routine act of preparation for battle or a ritual act of dedication. The context requires a correlative for *hitnaddēb*, "to present oneself, volunteer," in the next line, which suggests a derived meaning something like "to let go, to abandon everything" [for the battle].[334] N. K. Gottwald is on the right track when he opines that the verse praises "the spontaneity and enthusiasm of the citizens in arms in their spirited response to the call to battle."[335] Accordingly, the first line of this pair may be translated "Because of the total commitment in Israel."[336]

Third, what does it mean to "bless the LORD"? When the verb *bērēk (piel)* is used of someone greater "blessing" an inferior, it means "to endue someone with special power, to bestow special benefactions upon." However, when someone lesser "blesses" a superior, it means "to acknowledge that person as the source of special power/benefactions." In such contexts the verb functions

---

[331] Semantically parallel lines exhibit a balance and symmetry of meaning and thought, achieved by employing fixed pairs of words (roughly synonymous or antithetical). The present example must be subclassified as elliptical semantic parallelism, inasmuch as an element בְּיִשְׂרָאֵל, "in Israel") of line 1 is dropped in line 2 without any compensatory addition. The phrase performs double duty, being assumed in line 2.

[332] Cp. the causal use of *beth* + infinitive construct in Gen 19:16; Exod 16:7; Deut 1:27; 1 Kgs 18:18. Cf. *DCH* 2.83–84.

[333] In Deut 8:10 the grounds for praise, blessing (בָּרַךְ) is introduced with ʿal.

[334] As in v. 9, עַם, "people," is used in a military sense, "troops."

[335] *The Tribes of Yahweh: A Sociology of the Religion of Liberated Israel, 1250–1050 B.C.E.* (Maryknoll: Orbis, 1979), 539. For a detailed study of the root see J. G. Janzen, "The Root *prʿ* in Judges V 2 and Deuteronomy XXXII 42," *VT* 39 (1989): 393–406. See also Craigie, "A Note on Judges V 2," *VT* 18 (1968): 397–99.

[336] Thus Gray, "Israel in the Song of Deborah," 423.

as a virtual synonym of "to praise, extol."[337] This is clearly the sense required here. Yahweh is recognized as the worthy object of praise because the people have eagerly volunteered for battle.

5:3 The rhythm of the poem becomes more regular in v. 3, as Deborah summons the kings and commanders[338] of Canaan to listen[339] to him as she sings her praise to Yahweh. Of course the kings are not present to hear her, and even if they were, they would hardly have relished the triumphalist tone of this song. On the contrary, to the defeated Canaanites the sound of the victors expressing their delight in God for having triumphed over them (and by implication over their gods) will have been like salt in the wounds they were still licking. The singers' enthusiasm is reflected in the parallelism of the next lines:

> I to the LORD, I I will sing;
> I will make music to the LORD the God of Israel.

Within the context of the Book of Judges this is a rare and welcome expression of devotion to Yahweh, here explicitly recognized as the God of Israel. These lines represent Deborah's response to her own summons in the previous verse, and the verbs "to sing" and "to make music" represent her definition of the verb to "bless."[340] These verbs not only set the tone for the entire song but also announce the theme. Although Deborah will draw the reader into the scenes of Jael and Sisera's mother toward the end of the ode, the reader must be aware that this is first and foremost a song of praise to God, not to any human hero.

4"O LORD, when you went out from Seir,
when you marched from the land of Edom,
the earth shook, the heavens poured,
the clouds poured down water.
5The mountains quaked before the LORD, the One of Sinai,
before the LORD, the God of Israel.

STANZA II: THE INTRODUCTION OF YAHWEH (5:4–5). **5:4–5** Having declared her purpose in vv. 2–3, Deborah introduces the One who is to receive her praise in four versets of exquisite poetry. In theophanic form she envisions

---

[337] Cf. *HALOT* 1.160; J. Scharbert, "בָּרַךְ, brk; בְּרָכָה, bĕrākâ," *TDOT* 2.279–308.

[338] רֹזְנִים (NIV "rulers") is a rare term, occurring elsewhere only five times, always in poetic texts and always paired with another term: מְלָכִים, "kings," on Hab 1:10; Ps 2:2; Prov 8:15; 31:4; שֹׁפְטֵי אָרֶץ, "judges of earth," in Isa 40:23. Cf. also רֹזֵן, "potentate," paired with מְלָכִים in Prov 14:28.

[339] שָׁמַע, "listen," and הַאֲזִין, "give ear," are often paired in Hb. poetry. For references see BDB, 24.

[340] שִׁיר //זָמַר, "sing//make music," is a common word pair in Hb. (cf. BDB, 274) and is found also in Ug. See Y. Avishur, *Stylistic Studies of Word Pairs in Biblical and Ancient Semitic Literatures*, AOAT 210 (Neukirchen-Vluyn: Neukirchener Verlag, 1984), 404–5.

Yahweh[341] as a divine warrior marching forth from Seir/Edom to the aid of his people.[342] In Gen 36:20–21 and 1 Chr 1:38 Seir is a personal name, identifying the ancestor of an ethnic group associated with the Horites, who lived in the hill country of Seir (Gen 14:6). Deuteronomy 2:12,22 notes that by the time the Israelites came up from Egypt the Edomites, descendants of Esau, Isaac's elder son, had displaced the Horites and taken over their territory south and east of the Dead Sea. In terms reminiscent of his descent on Mount Sinai (Exodus 19), the song celebrates the arrival of Yahweh. When he passes through the heavens, the clouds release their water, and when he touches down on earth,[343] the mountains quake.[344]

Scholars have long been intrigued by the association of Yahweh not only with Sinai but also with Seir/Edom in this text, as well as several other ancient and/or archaizing poems.[345] Many find in these allusions support for what is commonly known as the speculative Kenite/Midianite hypothesis, according to which Yahweh was originally a Kenite or Midianite deity. By this theory the Israelites supposedly first learned of Yahweh when the group that came out of Egypt encountered the Midianites on their journey that eventually led them to

---

[341] For a comparison of this text with other theophanic passages see D. A. Patrick, "Epiphanic Imagery in Second Isaiah's Portrayal of a New Exodus," *HAR* 8 (1984): 125–41, esp. 127–28.

[342] Note the compensatory parallelism:
O LORD! When you went out from Seir, יְהוָה בְּצֵאתְךָ מִשֵּׂעִיר
When you marched forth from the field of Edom. בְּצַעְדְּךָ מִשְּׂדֵה אֱדוֹם

[343] Note the parallelism in the prepositional phrases at the ends of each line of v. 5:
מִפְּנֵי יהוה זֶה סִינַי, At the presence of Yahweh, this One of Sinai,
מִפְּנֵי יהוה אֱלֹהֵי יִשְׂרָאֵל, At the presence of Yahweh, the God of Israel.

[344] Note the chiastic parallelism of noun (earth : heavens : clouds : mountains) and verb forms (quaked : gushed forth : gushed forth : shook):
אֶרֶץ רָעָשָׁה   גַּם־שָׁמַיִם נָטָפוּ
גַּם־עָבִים נָטְפוּ מָיִם: הָרִים נָתְלוּ
The earth quaked,   the heavens gushed forth,
The clouds gushed forth water, the mountains shook.
The last verb, נָזֹלוּ is pointed as if from נָזַל, which normally means "to flow." But the verb should be repointed as a *niphal* of זָלַל, "to shake, quake," as in Isa 63:9; 64:2. Cf. *HALAT* 1.272.

[345] In Deut 33:2, Yahweh comes from Sinai/Seir/Mount Paran; In Hab 3:3 God comes from Teman/Mount Paran; In Ps 7–8 [Hb. 8–9], God came from the wasteland. The last text in particular is heavily dependent upon our text, as the following synopsis illustrates:

Judg 5:4–5	*Ps 68:7–8[MT8–9]*
O LORD, when you went forth from Seir,	O God, when you went forth before your people,
When you marched forth from the field of Edom—	When you marched through the wasteland—
The earth quaked,	The earth quaked,
The heavens gushed forth,	The heavens gushed forth—
The clouds gushed forth water,	
The mountains shook—	
Before the LORD, the One of Sinai;	Before God, the One of Sinai;
Before the LORD, the God of Israel.	Before God, the God of Israel.

Canaan.[346] This passage supposedly alludes to Yahweh's homeland in the south. Although the Israelites did indeed receive their primary revelation of him at Sinai, hypotheses like these are not only too speculative to be taken seriously but they distract from the primary intention of the text. This portrayal of Yahweh marching forth from Sinai/Seir/Edom represents a deliberate polemic against the perspectives cherished by the kings whom the poet has summoned to listen. They were Canaanites, whose god Baal resided in the north, on Mount Zaphon. But the Israelite triumph over Sisera and Jabin represented more than an earthly victory of an oppressed people over the oppressor. Yahweh, the Lord, had triumphed over Baal.

The biblical records consistently portray Sinai in the south as the site where Yahweh had appeared to the nation, gathered at the foot of the mountain, entered into covenant relationship with them, and then revealed the Torah. This was the definitive moment when he established himself as "the God of Israel" and Israel as "the people of the LORD." Accordingly he may be designated *zeh sînai*, "the One of Sinai."[347] Having become their God, he led them from the south through Seir and Edom to the promised land. The present victory is of a piece with the history of his battles on Israel's behalf since that date.

If this introduction to Yahweh announces to the kings of Canaan that Yahweh, not their god, Baal, reigns supreme, it does the same for the Israelites whose fascination with Baal had brought on the present crisis. Like Elijah at Mount Carmel many years later (1 Kings 19), Deborah hereby announces that Yahweh who brought the nation up from Sinai alone is the God of Israel. This agenda is reinforced by the storm imagery, which the Canaanite religion generally associates with Baal. But the poet hereby claims that Yahweh, not Baal, rides the clouds to the aid of his people.[348] At the same time the storm imagery anticipates the cosmic aspects of the victory later in the poem (vv. 19–21).[349]

6 "In the days of Shamgar son of Anath,
   in the days of Jael, the roads were abandoned;

---

[346] Proponents observe (1) Moses first learned the name of Yahweh at Sinai while he was herding sheep for his father-in-law, Jethro (Exod 13–15); (2) Jethro was a "priest of Midian" (Exod 2:16; 3:1; 18:1); (3) Jethro invoked the name of Yahweh (Exod 18:10); (4) Jethro presided at a sacrificial meal for Yahweh (Exod 18:12). Many years later Elijah returned to Sinai/Horeb for a "refresher course" on Yahweh (1 Kgs 19:8–13). For a classical discussion of the hypothesis see de Vaux, *Early History of Israel*, 333–38; for recent surveys of the issue see K. van der Toorn, "Yahweh," *DDD* 1714–17; Halpern, "Kenites," *ABD* 5.20–21.

[347] The expression appears only here and in the derivative Ps 68:8 [Hb. 9] and may be considered an archaic title of Yahweh. זֶה, with genitive meaning "the one of," is cognate to Amorite *zu*, Ugaritic *d*, Old Sinaitic *d*, *dt*, and Arabic *dū*. For bibliography see *HALOT* 1.264. For a contrary opinion see Lindars, *Judges 1–5*, 233–34.

[348] Cf. Deut 33:26–29; Ps 68:33–34 [Hb. 34–35]; 104:3,13.

[349] So also Globe, "The Text and Literary Structure of Judges 5,4–5," *Bib* 55 (1974): 178.

> travelers took to winding paths.
> [7]Village life in Israel ceased,
>   ceased until I, Deborah, arose,
>   arose a mother in Israel.
> [8]When they chose new gods,
>   war came to the city gates,
>   and not a shield or spear was seen
>   among forty thousand in Israel.

STANZA III: THE EMERGENCE OF DEBORAH (5:6–8). **5:6–8** Having introduced the One who is worthy of all praise, Deborah describes her own rise as his agent in six picturesque binary versets. Self-effacingly she does not identify the chronological context as "the days of Deborah" but as "the days of Shamgar" and "the days of Jael." The expressions are significant for several reasons.

First, and most obviously, they express Deborah's admiration for these individuals and their significance in Israel's history.

Second, they reflect the ad hoc nature of the prophetic office. Deborah's prophetic self-consciousness is beyond doubt, but she refuses to claim the right to designate an era after herself.

Third, by naming the period after not one but two foreigners, Deborah laments Israel's own lack of civil leaders by whom the period could be named. Fourth, by identifying Shamgar by patronymic, "son of Anath," she heightens the irony of the situation.[350] Yahweh, who has discredited Baal with this victory over the Canaanites, is not above employing Shamgar, a member of a military guild dedicated to Anath, the consort of Baal in Canaanite mythology.

Verses 6–8 do not reflect a precise chronology, but like the narrator of chap. 4, Deborah presents her own rise against the background of the crisis that gripped Israel in the eleventh century. She does so by describing the symptoms of the emergency in a series of colorful word pictures.

First, the roadways were deserted. The word *ŏrāhôt*, "paths,"[351] from *ārah*, "to be on the road, to wander," refers to the winding caravan routes that criss-crossed the land of Palestine, especially across the Jezreel Valley linking northern Israelites with their countrymen to the south, perhaps in contrast to the main roads. The verb *ḥādal*, meaning "to cease, to hold back, refrain,"[352] occurs three times in vv. 6–7 and functions as a key word.[353] With the present

---

[350] Cf. above on 3:31.

[351] On the basis of the parallelism, many (cf. *BHS*; Lindars, *Judges 105*, 236; O'Connell, *Rhetoric of the Book of Judges*, 462) repoint אֳרָחוֹת as אֹרְחוֹת, "caravans," but this is unnecessary.

[352] See T. Lewis, "The Songs of Hannah and Deborah: *HDL*–ii ("Growing Plump")," *JBL* 104 (1985): 105–14, and J. D. Schloen, "Caravans, Kenites, and Casus belli: Enmity and Alliance in the Song of Deborah," *CBQ* 55 (1993): 22–25, in response to the view that in v. 7 חדל means "to become plump." For bibliography see id., 106.

[353] The NIV renders the word "abandoned" in v. 6; "ceased" in v. 7.

inanimate subject the clause functions as a figure of speech for deserted high-ways. Israelite caravaneers have ceased to travel on their normal trade routes for fear of attack and/or extortionary tolls demanded at crossroads by the Canaanite oppressors.

Second, instead of taking direct routes *(nĕtîbôt)* to their destinations, cara-vaneers and travelers resorted to evasive side roads,[354] presumably through thickets and rough mountain passes to avoid detection by the enemy.[355]

Third, the villagers in Israel held back. There is no agreement on the correct interpretation of the first verset of v. 7. It seems best, however, to understand *pĕrāzôn* ("village life") as a collective designation for residents of rural unwalled settlements, in contrast to *ʿārîm*, "towns," which were by definition fortified with protective walls.[356] Unlike the walled Canaanite towns of the val-leys and plains, Israelite villages in the hill country were unfortified (cf. Ezek 38:11). Instead, defense was based on their elevated hilltop locations and the arrangement of houses on the village perimeters. The psychological paralysis of the villagers is reflected in the twofold use of *ḥādal*, "to refrain, hold back."[357] Afraid of attack from the enemy in the open field, these folks stayed at home—farmers refused to go out to the fields, and trade among the tribes of Israel came to a standstill. In view of the Canaanite stronghold in the Jezreel Valley, the northern tribes seem to have been completely cut off from their southern fellow Israelites.

With (lit.) "Until I, Deborah, arose; Until[358] I arose, a mother in Israel," Deborah announces a break in the crisis. Her amazement at the turn of events

---

[354] עֲקַלְקַל, "crooked," which occurs elsewhere only in Ps 125:5, derives from עָקַל, "to bend, twist."

[355] The sense of v. 6b is caught with a translation something like "the roads stopped [being used]; travelers took to the side trails."

[356] This interpretation is confirmed by the cognate Akk. expression *ālāni pu-ru-zi-ši*, which occurs several times in the Amarna Correspondence. Since it occurs nowhere else in cuneiform texts, it is best understood as a Canaanite loan word. Thus N. Naʿaman, "Amarna *ālāni pu-ru-zi* (EA 137) and Biblical *ʿry hprzy/hprzwt* (Rural Settlements)," in *Zeitschrift für Althebräistik* 4 (1991): 72–75. For discussion of the Hb. expression see L. E. Stager, "Archaeology, Ecology, and Social History: Background Themes to the Song of Deborah," in *Congress Volume: Jerusalem, 1986*, VTSup 40, ed. J. A. Emerton (Leiden: Brill, 1988), 224–25; id., "The Song of Deborah: Why Some Tribes Answered the Call and Others Did Not," *BAR* 15/1 (1989): 55; Lindars, *Judges 1–5*, 237. The REB's "champions" and Boling's (*Judges*, 109) "warriors" are based on an Arabic cog-nate *baraza*, "to go forth into battle." Cf. Craigie, "Some Further Notes on the Song of Deborah," *VT* 22 (1972): 350. G. Garbini's interpretation of פְּרָזוֹן as a dialectical version of בַּרְזֶל, "iron" ("**PARZON* 'Iron' in the Song of Deborah," *JSS* 23 [1978]: 23–24) has found little acceptance. Cf. Ackroyd, "Note to **PARZON* 'Iron' in the Song of Deborah," *JSS* 24 (1979): 19–20.

[357] The NRSV's "prospered" and "grew fat" respectively assume a root חָדַל-II, "to be plump, grow fat." Cf. Boling, *Judges*, 108. On the gemination of the final *lamedh* in the second case see *GBH* §18gN.

[358] עַד in the second line of this verset does double duty.

is highlighted in four ways: (1) the repetitive parallelistic construction; (2) shifting from third to first person;[359] (3) replacing conventional *qamtî,* "I rose," with the awkward form *šaqqamtî,* which, if not a dialectical variant of *šākam,* "to rise early,"[360] certainly sounds like it;[361] (4) interjecting her personal name, Deborah, in the first line and interpreting her role in Israel with "mother in Israel" in the second.

At first sight the expression *'ēm běyiśrā'ēl* ("as mother in Israel") appears to be an honorific title, perhaps reflecting Deborah's acknowledged prophetic status within the nation.[362] However, it probably should be interpreted less technically, anticipating the contrasting reference to Sisera's mother in v. 28 and highlighting Deborah's surprise that a woman should have played the decisive role in turning the tables. At the same time, the expression evokes affectionate maternal images, as if Deborah is the agent through whom Yahweh expresses his protective care over a people in a stressful and bewildering period.[363]

Although v. 8 is notoriously difficult, particularly the first line, it seems to describe resultant and/or concomitant circumstances to the rise of Deborah. First, God chose new leaders for Israel. The NIV follows the traditional interpretation in assuming that the subject of *yibḥar,* "to choose," is Israel. It also assumes that the allusion is to Israel's apostasy, which brought on the economic and political crisis, and the war referred to in the following line, in keeping with the general perspective of the surrounding narratives. However, not only does this interpretation introduce a notion that is otherwise foreign to the Song; it calls for a plural verb in place of the present singular.[364] Furthermore,

---

[359] Many (e.g., Lindars, *Judges 1–5,* 238; Soggin, *Judges,* 86) interpret the final *yodh* on שַׁקַּמְתִּי as an archaic second feminine singular ending, namely, "You arose." Cf. GKC §44h. The use of the first person with the *qal* instead of third person with *hiphil,* "Until she was raised up [by the LORD]," which is common in the book (cf. 2:18), not only sets her apart from the deliverers whom Yahweh raised up but also reflects her confidence in her own role.

[360] Cf. the interchange of *kaph* and *qoph* in קוֹבָע/כּוֹבַע, "helmet," which C. H. Gordon considers a Philistine loanword (*Ugaritic Textbook: Grammar,* AnOr 38 [Rome: Pontifical Biblical Institute, 1967], 35), and Akk. *kaqqadum/qaqqadum,* on which see A. Ungnad, *Akkadian Grammar,* rev. by L. Matouš and trans. by H. A. Hoffner (Atlanta: Scholars Press, 1992), 26–27. The NRSV links עַד, "until," with the previous line and reinterprets it as *ʿad* III "booty."

[361] The prefixed שׁ on שַׁקַּמְתִּי is generally understood as the relative particle, substituting for אֲשֶׁר, with rare vocalization. Cf. GKC §36; *GBH* §39N. Soggin's suggestion (*Judges,* 86) that this represents an ancient causative *šafel* form has found little acceptance.

[362] Lindars (*Judges 1–5,* 239) suggests the original description was "prophetess" (cf. 4:4), a reading reflected in the Tg., "Until I was commissioned to prophesy."

[363] No exact parallels to this expression occur in the OT, but cp. the image of the eagle protecting its young in Deut 32:11 and Jesus' lament over Jerusalem in Matt 23:37. The nearest analogue in the Book of Judges is the use of אָב, "father," as an honorific title in 17:10. For a study of Deborah as "mother in Israel," see C. Exum, "'Mother in Israel': A Familiar Figure Reconsidered," in *Feminist Interpretation of the Bible,* ed. L. Russell (Philadelphia: Westminster, 1985), 73–85.

[364] Cf. חָדְלוּ with the collective noun פְּרָזוֹן at the beginning of v. 7.

it overlooks the chronological sequence of events reflected in vv. 7–8: Deborah arose; then God chose new leaders; then fighting broke out. Thus it seems more natural to treat "God" as the subject of the verb and *ḥădāšîm,* "new ones," that is, "new leaders," as the object. One should see in the sequence of statements an allusion to Deborah's involvement in the choice of Barak. But Barak's role is deliberately downplayed by avoiding his name and by the use of a generalizing plural. In keeping with the theocentric agenda of the song, however, God is credited with the action.

With the rise of Deborah and the choice of new leaders, the time had come for Israel to go on the offensive.[365] The consonantal form of *lḥm šʿrym* looks like "bread *(leḥem)* in the gates," but the Massoretes seem to have recognized that this makes no sense. So to avoid confusion they vocalized the first word *lāḥem,* creating a noun from a root meaning "to fight, engage in battle." Since the Israelites lived in unwalled villages *(pĕrāzôn),* the "gates" must refer to the fortified Canaanite towns in the valleys. In the absence of any references to Israelite aggression toward Canaanite settlements in the previous narrative, this description is best interpreted as a licensed poetic portrayal of Canaanite attacks on Israelite villages as if they were walled towns.[366]

The last line of v. 8 describes Israel's lack of weapons of war. Expending all their energies in eking out a living, the Israelites lacked any shields or spears needed to defend themselves. The number forty thousand represents a round figure for the tally of Israelite troops who responded to the call to arms. The lack of arms is rightfully interpreted as another symptom of the nation's depressed condition, but in this context it represents another way of highlighting the role of Yahweh in the victory over the Canaanites. Like the earlier battle of Jericho, this battle will be won by God in spite of human inadequacy.

[9]**My heart is with Israel's princes,**
   with the willing volunteers among the people.
   Praise the LORD!

[10] **"You who ride on white donkeys,**
   sitting on your saddle blankets,
   and you who walk along the road,
   consider [11]**the voice of the singers at the watering places.**
   They recite the righteous acts of the LORD,
   the righteous acts of his warriors in Israel.

---

[365] The chronological link between the first two lines of v. 7a is highlighted by the particle אָז, "Then."

[366] D. Hillers ("A Note on Judges 5,8a," *CBQ* 27 [1965]: 124–26) rewrites the clause as אָז לָחֲמוּ שְׂעִירִים, "indeed they desired demons," but this is unnecessarily speculative. K. J. Cathcart's reading of לְחֻם as *laḥmu*-demons ("The 'Demons' in Judges 5:8a," *BZ,* n.s. 21 [1977]: 111–12) is no more convincing.

STANZA IV: A CALL FOR PRAISE FOR YAHWEH'S RIGHTEOUS ACTS
(5:9–11c).   **5:9**   Verses 9–11a express Deborah's pride in Israel and praise to
God for their response to the call to arms. The first verset (v. 9) bears several
resemblances to v. 2: the same admiration for the leaders and volunteers among
the troops, and the same summons to the hearer to bless Yahweh. The first word,
libbî, "my heart, my thoughts," expresses Deborah's admiration for her people.
The word for "princes," *ḥōqĕqê*, is new. The participle derives from the root
ḥāqaq, "to engrave, inscribe," from which we also get *ḥōq*, "ordinance, law."
Accordingly, *ḥōqēq* suggests a leader in the community, tribal governor, perhaps one who writes down the names of those who volunteer and/or command
the troops in battle (cf. v. 14).[367]

5:10   This verse fulfills the same function in this stanza as the first verset
of v. 3 does in the first. The three designations for the addressees answer to
the "kings" and "rulers" mentioned in the earlier context. However, instead
of calling upon the Canaanite princes, Deborah now appeals to the rich merchants who smugly continued to ply their trade while the Israelites languished in their deprivation and vulnerability. Tawny[368] female donkeys
were preferred by the rich over the generic gray animals. They advertised
their status by dressing the donkeys with luxurious [saddle] blankets.[369] The
Canaanite merchants' sense of security in these troubled times for Israel is
reflected in their confident traveling up and down the public roads.[370]
Whereas Deborah had earlier called upon the kings to listen to her ode, these
she summons to meditation.[371] Let them reflect and speak about Yahweh's
deeds and the sudden change in the fortunes of her countrymen. As in the
appeal to the kings, one detects here a note of scorn and derision. The losers
are called upon to sing with the victors.

5:11a–c   Every phrase in v. 11 is difficult. The first[372] is best interpreted as
a reference to the excited conversations that engage those who gather at the
water holes, whether these be wells or springs or pools of water. "Singers"
translates a participle form that occurs only here. It should probably be under-

---

[367] In Gen 49:10 a cognate noun form, מְחֹקֵק, denotes a ruler from Judah. The word functions
synonymously with שֵׁבֶט, "ruler," and מֶלֶךְ, "king," in Isa 33:22. חֹקֵק, "notable," occurs also in
Num 21:18, a fragment of another early poem.

[368] צְחֹרוֹת is a hapax in the OT, meaning "tawny," referring to light colored animals, brownish
orange to light brown. "White," as NIV reads, would have been rare.

[369] On the Aramaized plural of מִדִּין see GKC §87e. Schloen ("Song of Deborah," 26) reads
"Midian," but this is not convincing. Boling (*Judges*, 110) derives the word from דִּין, "to judge,"
hence, "on the judgment seat." The traditional derivation from מַדָּד, "to measure," is preferable.

[370] Gray ("Song of Deborah," 431) interprets those who ride on tawny donkeys and those who
walk on the road as gentle and simple folk.

[371] שִׂיחַ means "to muse, contemplate," but in this context it must mean vocal expression rather
than simply interior thought.

[372] Beginning with a circumstantial מִן, "in the midst of." Cf. Ps 104:12.

stood as deriving from *ḥāṣaṣ*, "to divide,"[373] alluding either to the distribution of water[374] or the division of flocks for the purpose of watering (NASB). Like the post office in many small towns of the prairies, the watering holes served as community gathering places, where gossip was exchanged and significant events celebrated. There the Canaanite travelers stop and listen and join in the celebration[375] of Yahweh's victory. The reason for celebration is the "the righteous acts of the LORD" *(ṣidqôt yhwh)* and "the righteous acts of his villagers (NIV, "warriors"[376]) in Israel." However, since the fundamental meaning behind *ṣdq* is vindication rather than moral justice, and since this event in particular vindicates the Israelites as well as Yahweh, many interpret these righteous acts as victories.[377] Deborah will herself recite those righteous actions in reverse order. Verses 11e–18 recount the righteous acts of God's *pirzōn*, "villager[s]" in Israel; vv. 19–23 recite Yahweh's righteous actions.

"Then the people of the LORD
    went down to the city gates.
[12]"Wake up, wake up, Deborah!
    Wake up, wake up, break out in song!
Arise, O Barak!
    Take captive your captives, O son of Abinoam.'

[13]"Then the men who were left
    came down to the nobles;
the people of the LORD
    came to me with the mighty.
[14]Some came from Ephraim, whose roots were in Amalek;
    Benjamin was with the people who followed you.
From Makir captains came down,
    from Zebulun those who bear a commander's staff.
[15]The princes of Issachar were with Deborah;
    yes, Issachar was with Barak,
    rushing after him into the valley.
In the districts of Reuben
    there was much searching of heart.
[16]Why did you stay among the campfires
    to hear the whistling for the flocks?
In the districts of Reuben

---

[373] JPSV's "archers" assumes a derivation from יִ‍חָ, "arrow."

[374] *HALOT* 1.344.

[375] The verb תָּנָה, which occurs only in Judges (cf. 11:40), may be viewed as a dialectical version of Ugaritic *tny*, "to recite, repeat." Cf. Deut 6:7.

[376] NIV inconsistently renders פְּרָזוֹן in v. 7 as "village life" and פְּרָזוֹנ‍וֹ in v. 11 as "warriors."

[377] Lindars, *Judges 1–5,* 247; Boling, *Judges,* 111. Soggin (*Judges,* 87) suggests "glorious achievements."

there was much searching of heart.
^{17}Gilead stayed beyond the Jordan.
And Dan, why did he linger by the ships?
Asher remained on the coast
    and stayed in his coves.
^{18}The people of Zebulun risked their very lives;
    so did Naphtali on the heights of the field.

STANZA V: A RECITATION OF ISRAEL'S RIGHTEOUS ACTIONS (5:11d–18). **5:11d**   The strophe breaks are not easily established in this poem, but the last line in v. 11 is best treated as a thesis statement to vv. 12–18.[378] The opening word *ʾāz*, "then," echoes its earlier appearance in v. 8 and commends the interpretation of "Then the people of the LORD went down to/against the gates"[379] as a clarification of "Then [there was] war in the gates." The verb *yārad* reflects the topography of the land, the Israelites occupying the hill country and having to go down to the cities in the plains. Again the reference to "gates" serves figuratively for the fortified cities of the Canaanites. Remarkably only here in the entire Book of Judges are the Israelites identified as *ʿam yhwh*, "the people of the LORD." The expression reflects the ideal established by Yahweh's covenant with his people at Mount Sinai many years earlier.[380] Yahweh is the patron God of Israel; it is as his people that they volunteer for military service.[381]

5:12   The emotional intensity of the ode picks up in v. 12 as Deborah imaginatively portrays God summoning to action the principal Israelite protagonists in the battle. The parallelism is deliberate, but so are the subtle distinctions drawn between Deborah and Barak. She begins logically with Yahweh's summons to her to prophetic action. The twofold repetition of the imperative *ʿûrî ʿûrî* does not mean to "awake" from slumber but to rouse oneself for action. The prescribed action is identified with *dabběrî šîr*, literally "Speak a song!"[382] It is difficult to know whether Deborah has in mind her own call of Barak (cf. 4:4–10) or her summoning of the army to battle (4:14). In either case by referring to the moment as a "song," Deborah expresses her delight in reflecting on the event. This was the turning point in the struggle with the oppressor.

The summons to Barak is more martial in tone. The verb *qûm*, "Arise," employs the same root as the narrator's declarations that God "raised" a deliv-

---

[378] Boling (*Judges*, 111) observes the inclusio/envelope construction in vv. 11e–13, which begins and ends with variant forms of this statement.

[379] On the adversative force of בְּ/לְ יָרַד in vv. 11 and 13, see Stager, "Song of Deborah," 226.

[380] The phrase עַם יהוה occurs elsewhere only in v. 13; Num 11:29; 16:41[Hb. 17:6]; 1 Sam 2:24; 2 Sam 1:12; 6:21; 2 Kgs 9:6; Ezek 36:20; Zeph 2:10.

[381] The expression compares with עַם כְּמוֹשׁ, "the people of Chemosh," in Num 21:9; Jer 48:46. On the significance of these expressions see Block, *Gods of the Nations*, 28–29.

[382] דַּבְּרִי plays on the name Deborah.

erer for Israel in 3:9 and 15. The avoidance of this term for Deborah is deliberate. She does indeed play the most important role, but not as deliverer; as
prophet she represents the presence and voice of God. Whereas the charge to
Deborah is to "pronounce a song," Barak, the son of Abinoam, is commanded
to "take captive his own captives," reversing the present situation in which
Israel is held hostage by the Canaanites and ironically inverting the expectation
of Sisera's mother in v. 30.

5:13 In v. 13 the recitation of Israel's "righteous" response resumes.[383]
The prophet has been aroused and the general summoned; now let the troops
answer the call. This verse functions as a thematic opening announcement,
describing in general terms the reaction of the Israelites to Yahweh's call to
arms. Although the second line ascribes to the respondents the honorific title of
"people of the LORD," the first line seems to identify them less nobly as *śārîd*,
"escapees, survivors,"[384] an apparent allusion to the oppression under which
they had languished for so long.[385] The endings of these lines are difficult.
Assuming they function relatively synonymously, most interpret both
ʾaddîrîm, "nobles," and *gibbôrîm*, "the mighty," as complimentary character-
izations of the Israelite troops.[386] However, this requires either an unnatural
interpretation of the preposition before the first word or an emendation of the
text. It is preferable to see in the first line a variation of v. 11de, with *śārîd*,
"survivors" (NIV, "the men who were left") substituting for "people of the
LORD" and "the nobles" referring to the Canaanites who live in the "gates."
The use of contrasting expressions "survivors" and "people of the LORD" to
refer to the same group is continued in the next line as "the people of the
LORD" is brought back from v. 11d, and "against the nobles" is replaced by
"against the mighty ones."[387] The motley remnant of Israelite survivors of the
oppression dares to attack the vastly superior might of the Canaanites for Deborah,[388] that is, for Yahweh, since as his prophet she represents him before the
troops.[389]

In vv. 14–18 Deborah recites the roll of Israelite warriors. However, in so
doing she laments the incompleteness of the list. The catalog of troops is
divided into three groups: the volunteers (vv. 14–15a); the resistors (vv. 15b–

---

[383] For a detailed study of vv. 13–17 see Caquot, "Les tribus d'Israël dans le Cantique de
Débora (Judges 5, 13–15)," 47–70.

[384] On שָׂרַד "to escape," and שָׂרִיד, "escapees," see BDB, 974–75; *HALOT*.

[385] Naʾaman ("Literary and Topographical Notes on the Battle of Kishon (Judges IV–V)," *VT*
40 [1990]: 423–26) argues that *śārîd* is a place name here used adverbially, namely, "They
marched down to Sarid." Sarid is a well-known town in southern Zebulun, six miles north of
Megiddo, named in v. 18. Josh 19:10,12.

[386] NRSV, REB, NEB; Gray, "Song of Deborah," 434–35.

[387] On the adversative use of the prepositions *lamedh* and *beth* see above on v. 11d.

[388] The suffix on לִי refers to the primary singer, Deborah.

[389] Cf. our comments on 4:8–9.

17); the award winners (vv. 18).

The Volunteers (5:14–15a). **5:14–15a** Pride of place in the list of gallant troops goes to the Ephraimites,[390] perhaps because this was Deborah's tribe. Whatever the reason, this early impression of the Ephraimites is quite different from the centuries-later view of the narrator, who rarely has anything positive to say about this tribe. The following phrase, "whose roots were in Amaleq," makes little sense in the context unless at this time the Amalekites (who later joined with the Midianites in oppressing Israel; cf. 6:3) had established a foothold in some of the Ephraimite highlands.[391] Next came the Benjamites, with their military companies,[392] followed by the commanders (*měḥōqěqîm*, cf. v. 9) of Makir. Pentateuchal records observe that Makir was the eldest of Manasseh's sons (Gen 50:23) and the father of Gilead.[393] Numbers 32:39–40 reports that Makir captured the land of Gilead and that Moses assigned the land to him.[394] Some suggest that Makir is the name of an originally itinerant mercenary group,[395] but since the name here obviously refers to Manassite territory west of the Jordan, it is less speculative to accept Makir as a "poetic substitute" for Manasseh.[396] According to the last line of v. 14, Zebulun's contribution consisted of military leaders, "those who mustered[397] with the staff of the commander."[398] Judging by the amount of attention given to Issachar in v. 15, Deborah has the highest praise for this tribe. Their officers stood by her, and the tribe was loyal to Barak.[399] Set under his immediate command (NIV "rushing after him"; lit. "sent at his feet"), they charged into the valley [of Jezreel].

---

[390] In each case the introductory מִנִּי is interpreted partitively, i.e., "Some from Ephraim," etc. On the poetic form see *GBH* §103d.

[391] Scholars tend to emend שָׁרְשָׁם בַּעֲמָלֵק to בָּעֵמֶק, "in the valley," following LXX^A, ἐν κοιλάδι. Thus NRSV, REB, NAB. For discussion see Lindars (*Judges 1–5*, 252–53), who follows Craigie's proposal ("Further Notes," 351) that שׁרשׁם, "their roots," derives from an Egyptian loanword, *srs*, "officer (of high rank)." Gray ("Song of Deborah," 436, n. 45) suggests the MT is a scribal corruption of שָׂרִים בָּעָם. "The princes among the people," or an Ephraimite war-cry, שָׁרְשׁוּם כַּעֲמָלֵק, "Eradicate them like Amalek!"

[392] The expression אַחֲרֶיךָ בִנְיָמִין, "after you, Benjamin," is borrowed by Hosea in Hos 5:2. On the triliteral form בַּעֲמָמֶיךָ see GKC §93aa.

[393] Num 26:29; 27:1; 36:1.

[394] So also Josh 13:31; 17:1–3.

[395] Thus Lindars, *Judges 1–5*, 254.

[396] Thus Globe, "The Muster of the Tribes in Judges 5 11e–18," *ZAW* 87 (1975): 173.

[397] On מְשֵׁךְ, "to muster," see above on 4:6.

[398] סֹפֵר may be cognate to Akk. *šapāru*, "to rule" (thus M. Tsevat, "Some Biblical Notes," *HUCA* 24 [1952–53]: 107), but the normal Hb. sense, "scribe," also makes sense if the musterer is viewed as the one who records the names of the enlisted.

[399] Gray ("Song of Deborah," 437) argues that since Issachar has been named in the previous line, since Naphtali is missing in vv. 15–17, and since Barak comes from Naphtali (4:6), the second reference to Issachar is a scribal error for Naphtali.

The Resistors (5:15b–17).   **5:15b**   But not all was well in Israel. Among the clans (NIV "districts")[400] of Reuben there was serious reflection. It is difficult to know what to make of the pair of similar expressions that occur at the ends of vv. 15 and 16 respectively. At first sight the first (lit.), "the resolutions of heart were great/intense,"[401] appears to suggest a loyal Reubenite response to the call up of troops. But the clause is quite ambiguous and could just as well be interpreted negatively: they were resolute in their refusal to go.

5:16   This verse settles the issue, as Deborah asks why the Reubenite clans sat around their campfires/open hearths[402] while musicians entertained them with shepherds' pipes.[403] This is an image of men who cannot be bothered; these pastoralists are indifferent to the wars of their sedentary countrymen on the other side of the Jordan. The last line creates an inclusio with v. 15b, but it also represents a clever play on the earlier version. They appeared to have serious second thoughts,[404] but in the end they refused to get involved.

5:17   Verse 17 adds the names of Gilead, Dan, and Asher to the list of those who could not be bothered to intervene on behalf of their countrymen. Gilead remained on the other side of the Jordan. Gilead is a topographical designation for the region east of the Jordan between the Yarmuk River in the north and the Wadi Hesban in the south. Here the name substitutes for Gad, to whom the southern part of this region was allotted (Josh 13:24–28). In the west Dan was busy in the shipping industry, presumably as clients of the Phoenicians.[405] While the association of Dan with the northern tribe of Asher suggests that the battle with the Canaanites occurred later than the events described in chaps. 17–18, the use of the verb *gûr,* "to sojourn" (NIV "linger"), indicates they had not yet established themselves firmly in their new territory in the Hulah Valley north of the Sea of Galilee. As for the men

---

[400] The meaning of פְּלַגּוֹת is uncertain, but the usage of the term in its two other occurrences, Job 20:17 ("streams, channels") and 2 Chr 35:5 ("family divisions") suggests the branches of the Reubenite tribe.

[401] חִקְקֵי, lit. "decisions, decrees," occurs elsewhere only in Isa 10:1. On the form see GKC §93aa. Many emend to חִקְרֵי, after v. 16c–d, itself deleted as a dittograph of the present line.

[402] מִשְׁפְּתַיִם derives from שָׁפַת, "to set the pot on the fire." The word occurs elsewhere only in Gen 49:14, on which see N. Sarna, *Genesis,* JPS Torah Commentary (Philadelphia: Jewish Publication Society, 1989), 339.

[403] לִשְׁמֹעַ שְׁרִקוֹת עֲדָרִים, lit., "to listen to the whistling/piping of the flock. שְׁרִיקָה occurs elsewhere only in Jer 18:16, where it speaks of derisive hissing. The verb is more common. See BDB, 1056.

[404] חִקְרֵי־לֵב means lit. "searchings of the heart." לֵב occurs with the verb חָקַר, "to search," in Jer 17:10 and Prov 18:17, but the sense is somewhat different.

[405] The word אֳנִיּוֹת, "ships," functions as an adverbial accusative, "with reference to ships." On the Danites as גֵּרִים, "clients" of the coastal Canaanites or the Sea Peoples see Stager, "Song of Deborah," 229–32.

of Asher, they preferred the beaches[406] and harbors[407] of the Mediterranean to the inland battlefields.[408] All of these tribes (Reuben, Gad, Dan, Asher) might have been excused for noninvolvement because of distance or preoccupation with other duties, but the statement contains a strong element of rebuke.

The Award Winners (5:18). **5:18** The roll call of Israelite tribes concludes in v. 18 as Deborah singles out Zebulun and Naphtali for special honor. Both are characterized for their bravery, disdaining[409] their lives *(nepeš)* to the point of death. The final phrase, "on the heights of the field," seems to do double duty, describing the Esdraelon Valley, where the battle occurred, as a region of undulating fields and gentle hills. The latter give way to higher foothills as one moves to the edges of the valley.

It has already been observed that this document preserves one of the earliest extant records of Israel's premonarchic period. Ten names are listed. Two tribes are referred to by secondary names (Makir = Manasseh; Gilead = Gad). The absence of two tribes that received territorial allotments from Joshua (Judah and Simeon)[410] suggests either that this song antedates the ascendancy of Judah under David's reign or that it reflects a subtle anti-Judahite posture. Some tribes refused to join the campaign; Judah and Simeon are out of the picture altogether.[411] Although Deborah expresses a keen sense of nationality and

---

[406] חֹף יַמִּים, "shores of the seas," always refers to the Mediterranean coast. Cf. Gen 49:13; Deut 1:7; Josh 9:1; Jer 47:7; Ezek 25:16.

[407] מִפְרָצָיו, "his harbors," is a hapax legomenon.

[408] For an illuminating portrayal of shipping in the eastern Mediterranean in the second half of the second millennium B.C. based on the underwater archaeological discovery off the coast of Turkey, see G. F. Bass, "Splendors of the Bronze Age," *National Geographic* 172/6 (1987): 692–733.

[409] חָרַף, "to defy, taunt," is cognate to Arabic *ḥarafa,* "to be sharp," hence "to treat badly, with sharpness." Cf. *HALOT* 1.355.

[410] The Levites are also missing, but they did not receive any territorial grant in the first place.

[411] Gray ("Song of Deborah," 440) concludes from this that the twelfth-century sacral community of Israel was a northern entity, exclusive of Judah, Simeon, and Levi. J. C. de Moor ("The Twelve Tribes in the Song of Deborah," *VT* 43 [1993]: 483–93) argues that these were included in the original version of the song, which listed the tribes in the same order as they are found in Genesis 49. This interpretation requires rereading the consonantal text as follows:

אָז יֵרַד [וֹן] שָׂר [יִן] ט [וֹן] דּ [הֵן] לְאַדִּירִים
עִם יהוה יֵרַד לֵוִ [יִן] בְּגִבּוֹרִים
מִנִּי אֶפְרַטֶם שָׂר [יִן] שָׁם
בְּעֵמֶק אַחֲרֶיךָ בִּנְיָמִין בַּעֲמְמִיךָ

Then the princes of Yôdah descended to the dignitaries,
   with YHWH descended Levi with heroes;
   from Ephraim princes of fame,
   in the valley behind you Benjamin with your kinsmen.

Simeon is rehabilitated by identifying this tribe with Makir, while Ephraim in v. 14 represents both tribal descendants of Joseph: Ephraim and Manasseh. But this interpretation is wishfully speculative and driven by external concerns.

clearly recognizes which tribal groups are in and which are out, she also recognizes several fundamental problems in Israel.

First, restricted to the hill country of Palestine, they reside in unwalled settlements without defensive weapons and are vulnerable to outside harassment. This situation undoubtedly derives from the economic and military superiority of the Canaanites living in the fertile valleys, but it may also be a leftover effect of Merneptah's campaign in Palestine in 1207 B.C.[412]

Second, while theoretically united in their worship of Yahweh, the Israelites lack political and military cohesion.[413] Some tribes refused to sacrifice individual interest and well-being for the sake of the nation. These come under sharp rebuke.

On the other hand, Deborah acknowledges the loyalty of Zebulun and Naphtali, two tribes that were relatively insignificant in later history, but at this time they played a vital role in rescuing the nation from oblivion at the hands of aliens' oppressions. Ephraim's rising influence is reflected in this tribe's position at the head of the list in vv. 11–17. In any case, contrary to minimalists who argue that the history of Israel begins with David, or even later, this song attests to a vibrant sacral community of faith united by traditions of common descent from an ancestor Jacob and the worship of Yahweh that existed in Palestine in the twelfth century B.C.

[19]"Kings came, they fought;
the kings of Canaan fought
at Taanach by the waters of Megiddo,
but they carried off no silver, no plunder.
[20]From the heavens the stars fought,
from their courses they fought against Sisera.
[21]The river Kishon swept them away,
the age-old river, the river Kishon.
March on, my soul; be strong!
[22]Then thundered the horses' hoofs—
galloping, galloping go his mighty steeds.

---

[412] Thus Stager, "Merenptah, Israel and Sea Peoples: New Light on an Old Relief," *EI* 18 (1985): 61*, and Freedman, *Pottery, Poetry and Prophecy: Studies in Early Hebrew Poetry* (Winona Lake: Eisenbrauns, 1980), 176.

[413] This accords with Merneptah's "Israel Stela," which contains the earliest extrabiblical reference to Israel but unlike the surrounding Canaanite names is preceded by the "people" rather than land determinative (*ANET*, 378). This form has provoked endless discussion, but F. Yurco provides the most satisfactory explanation: "'Israel is devastated, *his* seed is not,' shows clearly that 'Israel' is understood to be a collective, a distinct people, not named after any particular territory or city. In Egyptian, the names of foreign countries, cities, and provinces are treated syntactically as feminine. But with Israel the masculine pronoun is used. Israel (the people) is a masculine entity, possibly indicating identity with a male deity or eponymous ancestor." Cited by Stager, "Merenptah, Israel and Sea Peoples," 61*.

^{23}'Curse Meroz,' said the angel of the LORD.
'Curse its people bitterly,
because they did not come to help the LORD,
to help the LORD against the mighty.'

STANZA VI: THE BATTLE (5:19–23). Verses 19–23 represent the climax of the Song, telescoping into five short poetic verses the actual battle between the Israelite and Canaanite forces. In the absence of any corresponding reference to kings fighting in the prose account (4:13–16), the opening double reference (in chiastic arrangement) may be explained as poetic hyperbolic flourish. To Deborah, the Israelite triumph over Sisera represented a victory over all the Canaanite kingdoms of the land, a truly remarkable feat in view of the deprivation described in vv. 6–7 and the superiority of Canaanite military technology. Indeed the primary antagonist, Sisera, is not mentioned until the end of v. 20.

5:19 The construction in v. 19 construes the enemies as going on the offensive, rallying their forces "at Taanach, by the waters of Megiddo." Since Megiddo is not located on the Wadi Kishon, the phrase "the waters of Megiddo" anticipates the course of the battle.[414] Waiting until Barak's troops had come down Mount Tabor and entered the Jezreel Valley, Sisera mobilized his forces and crossed the Kishon, which lay between the two armies. For most of the year the Kishon is little more than a brook and would have posed no problem for infantry or chariotry. But the last line of v. 19 hints at how badly the battle went for the Canaanites: they failed to make off with any loot, here referred to in terms of "plunder" (or "plunder," *beṣaʿ*) and "silver" *(kesep)*.

5:20–21 Undoubtedly Sisera expected a swift and easy victory for his vastly superior military forces. There was no way he could have prepared for what actually happened: the intervention of heavenly forces on Israel's behalf, the sudden flooding of the Kishon, and the crippling of the chariotry.[415] The first phenomenon is described in magnificently enigmatic form: the stars left their courses[416] and fought against Sisera from heaven. In this imagery Debo-

---

[414] On Megiddo and Taanach see above on 1:28.

[415] M. Weinfeld ("Divine Intervention in War in Ancient Israel and in the Ancient Near East," in *History, Historiography and Interpretation: Studies in Biblical and Cuneiform Literatures*, ed. H. Tadmor and M. Weinfeld [Jerusalem: Magnes, 1986], 124) notes that all three of these elements also appear in the prose account of Yahweh's victory at the Reed Sea, Exod 14:19–28. For a comparison of Judges 5 and Exodus 15 see Hauser, "Two Songs of Victory: A Comparison of Exodus 15 and Judges 5," in *Directions in Biblical Poetry*, ed. E. R. Follis, JSOTSup 40 (Sheffield: JSOT Press, 1987), 265–84.

[416] Most interpret מִמְּסִלּוֹתָם, "from their courses," to mean that the stars functioned like an army, each in its place, but it is preferable to see here the heavenly bodies leaving their normal orbits to fight against Israel's enemy. Weinfeld ("Divine Intervention," 127) suggests "a comet fell out of its fixed place." J. F. A. Sawyer ("From Heaven Fought the Stars," *VT* 1 [1981]: 87–89) sees here a reference to the total eclipse of the sun in the vicinity of Megiddo and Taanach in 1131 B.C., in which case at least the nucleus of the song is to be dated early, its composer being an eyewitness of the eclipse.

rah draws on a common ancient Near Eastern literary motif, according to which the gods intervene on their devotees' behalf by engaging the heavenly hosts. Note especially the following excerpt from the Gebel Barkal stela of Thutmose III of Egypt (1479–1425 B.C.):

> Hear you, O people of the South who are at the holy mount ... so that you may know the wonderful deed (of Amon-Ra) ... (the guards) were about to take up (their watchposts) in order to meet at night and carry out the watch command. It was in the second hour (=in the second watch) and a star came from the south of them. Never had the like occurred. It flashed against them from its position. Not one withstood before it ... with fire for their faces. No one among them found his hand nor looked back. Their chariotry/horses were not more ...[417]

The second phenomenon, the flooding of the Kishon, echoes what happened to Pharaoh's armies at the Reed Sea. Suddenly, what had previously been an immeasurable advantage becomes a death trap. The heavens opened up, deluging the Jezreel Valley with rain and turning the placid and predictable[418] Kishon into a mighty torrent, softening the ground for horses and chariots and sweeping[419] the chariots away. This association of the stars fighting from heaven and the flooding of the Kishon seems odd to the modern reader, but both may be understood as evidences of the arrival of Yahweh (cf. vv. 4–5), who usurps the signs of theophanic advent which Canaanites had associated with Baal. In some Ugaritic texts the stars are declared to be the source of rain.[420]

The last line of v. 21, which is awkward in context, seems to represent Deborah's spontaneous outburst at the thought of this incredible event.[421] The self-exhortation to "advance with strength"[422] is triumphalist, conjuring up images of a conqueror treading the neck of the vanquished.

5:22 The sense of v. 22 is also obscure, primarily because the roots of the verb *hālam* and the noun *dahărôt* are extremely rare. The first ("thundered"), which elsewhere means "to hammer,"[423] is generally viewed as a reference to

---

[417] The translation of W. Helck, as cited by Weinfeld, "Divine Intervention," 125. For full discussion of the motif see ibid., 124–31.

[418] נַחַל קְדוּמִים, literally "ancient stream," is often emended to נַחַל קְדָמָם קְדָמָם, "the stream overwhelmed them." Cf. *BHS*, Boling, *Judges*, 113. Relating קְדוּמִים to the piel verb, קִדֵּם, "to be in front," G. Ahlström ("Judges 5:20f. and History," *JNES* 36 [1977]: 287) sees here a reference to "the front, outstanding part," that is the swelling flood.

[419] גָּרַף, "to sweep away," occurs only here but is cognate to מִגְרָפָה, "shovel," in Joel 1:17.

[420] *UT* 'nt II 41 (=*KTU* 1.3 II 41).

[421] Lindars (*Judges 1–5*, 271) suggests it may be a liturgical fragment; Boling (*Judges*, 113) proposes the loss of a parallel line. F. M. Cross (*Studies in Ancient Yahwistic Poetry* [Baltimore: Johns Hopkins University Press, 1950], 35–36) emends עֹז נַפְשִׁי תִּדְרְכִי as תִּדְרְכַן פַּרְשֵׁי עֹזּוֹ, "his mighty chargers pounded [the ground]." The *resh* supposedly dropped out by haplography because of the resemblance of *resh* and *pe* in the archaic script.

[422] On דָּרַך, "to march, advance," see *DCH* 2.462–63.

[423] Cf. v. 26; Ps 74:6. Note also the cognate noun הַלְמוּת, "hammer," in v. 26.

the pounding of horses' hooves as they gallop off.[424] The duplication of *dahărôt dahărôt* (NIV, "galloping, galloping")[425] supposedly captures the rhythmic clatter of galloping horses. But the context renders this interpretation unlikely. Both the prose account, which speaks of the total rout of the chariot group by Barak's infantry (4:15–16), and the poetic version, which speaks of the chariots being swept away, leave little room for galloping horses. It is preferable to interpret *dāhărôt* as the wild rearing of the stallions[426] in the frenzy of battle[427] and *hālĕmû* as the frantic flailing of their fore hooves in the tumult of torrent. In any case, v. 22 is best understood as the incapacitation of the horses. This is the last in a triad of supernatural events that conspired against the Canaanites.[428]

5:23 The stanza concludes with a command by a messenger of Yahweh *(maPak yhwh)* to curse Meroz because they did not support Yahweh against the Canaanite heroes (NIV, "mighty," *gibbôrîm*). The verse is awkward for several reasons. In the first place it would have been more appropriate after the complaints about Reuben, Gilead, Dan, and Asher in vv. 16–17.

Second, Meroz, which is mentioned only here in the Old Testament, cannot be located. It must have been located within a triangle whose apexes are marked by Mount Tabor on the east, where Barak assembled his troops (4:6,12,14), the Kishon in the west, and Megiddo or Taanach in the south, perhaps near Sarid,[429] though a closer identification is impossible.[430]

Third, what is the envoy (traditionally rendered "angel") of Yahweh doing here? We have not heard from him or any such figure since 2:4. In view of the similarity of roles between prophets and messengers in this book and elsewhere,[431] this verse could be considered a prophetic utterance, Deborah being the most likely candidate for speaker. Accordingly, she who had announced the arrival of Yahweh to fight for his people (4:14) would hereby invoke a curse on this town at God's command.

On the other hand, Neef has recently associated this angelic figure with the

---

[424] Cf. Lindars, *Judges 1–5*, 271.

[425] The *mem* prefixed to the first probably reflects faulty word division and should be reattached as the plural ending to the preceding עִקְּבֵי־סוּס, viz., "hooves of horses."

[426] אַבִּירָיו, "his stallions." אַבִּיר is cognate to Ug. *ʾibr*, "buffalo," and Egyptian *ibr*, "stallion." The Hb. word denotes "bull" in Isa 34:7; Jer 46:15; "stallion," in Jer 8:16; 47:3; 50:11. Cf. *HALOT* 1.6.

[427] This interpretation also suits Nah 3:2, the only occurrence of the verb דָּהַר.

[428] Weinfeld ("Divine Intervention," 124, n. 17) interprets הָלְמוּ, "they pounded," intransitively: "the heels of his horses were battered by the gallop galloping of his steeds."

[429] Josh 10:10,12. Cf. Naʾaman, "The Battle of Kishon," 426; M. Hunt, "Meroz," *ADB* 4.705–6.

[430] See the discussion by Neef, "Meroz: Jdc 5,23a," *ZAW* 107 (1995): 118–22.

[431] The "messenger" of Yahweh in 2:1–4 plays the same role as the prophet (נָבִיא) in 6:7–10. Prophets are frequently associated with מַלְאָכִים elsewhere: Isa 42:19; 44:26; 2 Chr 36:15–16; Hag 1:13; Mal 3:1.

mal'ak yhwh, "messenger of the LORD," who appears elsewhere in texts involving the conquest of Canaan.[432] In Exod 23:20; 32:34; 33:2 the "angel" is the one sent by God to go before Israel, guide them through the desert, and lead them into the promised land.[433] Since these references occur within contexts where Israel is not to turn away to the gods of the Canaanites (Exod 23:23) and to refuse to enter into any agreements with them,[434] lest they become a snare to Israel (Exod 23:28–33; Judg 2:3), the messenger's involvement may provide the clue to the Meroz problem. The people of Meroz have violated the divine command specifically. They seem to have arrived at agreements with the Canaanites who lived in the vicinity and adopted their gods. By invoking this curse on Meroz, the town is presented as an example for the rest of the nation. This interpretation is rendered all the more plausible in view of the juxtapositioning of the reference to the curse next to Jael. As noted earlier, the verse seems awkwardly placed until one recognizes the contrast. Meroz represents those Israelites who have taken their stand on the side of the Canaanites; Jael represents those non-Israelites who have taken their stand on the side of Israel.[435]

24"Most blessed of women be Jael,
the wife of Heber the Kenite,
most blessed of tent-dwelling women.
25He asked for water, and she gave him milk;
in a bowl fit for nobles she brought him curdled milk.
26Her hand reached for the tent peg,
her right hand for the workman's hammer.
She struck Sisera, she crushed his head,
she shattered and pierced his temple.
27At her feet he sank,
he fell; there he lay.
At her feet he sank, he fell;
where he sank, there he fell—dead.

STANZA VII: IN PRAISE OF JAEL (5:24–27). The Song takes an unexpected turn in vv. 24–27, as Deborah shifts her attention from the public spectacle of armies battling in the Jezreel Valley to the private encounter between two individuals, Jael and Sisera. The events portrayed transpire inside the former's tent. No information on how or why Sisera found himself inside Jael's

---

[432] Neef, "Meroz: Jdc 5,23a," 118–22.

[433] Accordingly the "messenger" exercises both a leadership and a protective function (Exod 14:19; 23:20; 32:34; 33:2; Judg 2:2).

[434] Exod 23:32; 34:12,15.

[435] This interpretation contrasts with the view of some that Meroz was a Canaanite city. But Neef rightly questions why a specific curse should be placed on the place when the Canaanites as a whole were already under the divine curse.

tent is offered; the composer assumes familiarity with the story as told in chap. 4. Although scholars have tended to highlight the discrepancies between this account of Jael's heroic deeds and the prose narrative in 4:17–22, we may begin by noting the points of agreement. (1) The human hero of the story is a woman, Jael by name. (2) Jael is the wife of Heber the Kenite. (3) The critical event occurs inside a tent. (4) Jael responds to Sisera's request for water by giving him milk. (5) Her instruments of death were a hammer[436] and a tent peg *(yātēd)*. (6) She drove the tent peg through Sisera's skull. (7) Sisera ended up dead on the ground.

5:24–25 The killing of Sisera is described with savage pleasure. The stanza opens with an unrestrained praise of Jael, an outsider, the wife of Heber the Kenite (cf. 4:17). Indeed Deborah recognizes her initially as the most blessed of women.[437] Perhaps because of the composer's high esteem for Deborah in particular and Israelite women in general, however, the blessing is qualified by limiting the comparison to women who live in tents. These would include the Kenites and other non-Israelite migratory folk who moved up and down Palestine, in contrast to the Israelites who lived in houses. What draws Deborah's admiration is Jael's resourcefulness and her courage. First, when Sisera, her guest, asked for water, she not only brought him milk but treated him royally by serving the milk in a magnificent bowl,[438] fit for the leader of the Canaanite nobles.[439] Even the verb, *hiqrîbâ*, "she brought/presented," in the second line is formal, as in the presentation of tribute to a king (3:17,18) or offerings to God.[440] The reference to curds or yogurt *(ḥemʾâ)* in the second line does not mean she presented him with two kinds of food. The expression concretizes and/or specifies *ḥālāb* in the first line, which may refer to any milk product. The canons of poetic parallelism require the double reference.[441]

5:26 The narration slows down deliberately in vv. 26–27 as the poem describes with obvious relish the death of the enemy of Israel. Verse 26 con-

---

[436] Though the words differ: מַקֶּבֶת (4:21); הַלְמוּת (5:26).

[437] The preposition on מִנָּשִׁים is a superlative *min*. Cf. 2 Kgs 10:3. The form of Elizabeth's blessing of Mary in Luke 1:42 assumes a *beth* rather than a *min*, as in Song 1:8.

[438] סֵעֶל אַדִּירִים, "a stately dish."

[439] The term אַדִּירִים links the quality of the bowl with the quality of the Canaanite forces in v. 13.

[440] For references see BDB, 898.

[441] There is no need to construe this gift of milk as a sexual invitation; it symbolizes her desire for a lavish expression of hospitality. While not going as far as Y. Zakovitch ("Sisseras Tod," *ZAW* 93 [1981]: 364–74), who views the sexual details as central to the portrayal, Lindars (*Judges 1–5*, 275) concurs with many in recognizing in Jael's performance a parody of a sexual encounter. At first she plays a woman's part by offering Sisera milk, but she takes over the man's role in taking a tent peg and crushing his skull. In the final scene, with Sisera between her legs, the proper roles are resumed. The account is filled with irony, to be sure, but such sexual interpretations say more about the interpreter than the text.

sists of two pairs of semantically parallel lines. In each case the second line offers a more precise definition of the action cited in the first line. The first pair of lines focuses on the murderer, Jael, who grasps the tools of murder—a tent peg and a workman's hammer. The specification occurs in the designations for hand; *yādāh*, "her hand," is replaced with *yĕmînāh*, "her right hand." While the second pair highlights the action of Jael by employing four different but similar sounding words for "striking,"[442] the attention is drawn to Sisera the victim by replacing the general term, "his head," with, "his temple."

5:27   Verse 27 offers one of the most impressive examples of staircase parallelism in the Old Testament.[443] But it is not only the repetition that determines its force. The visual impression is reinforced by beginning the lines with the prepositional phrase "Between her feet …" Though Deborah refuses to take the focus off Jael, what she describes here is the sight Barak would have faced when he entered the tent: Sisera collapsed, fallen, lying dead on the floor.[444] The verbs function as virtual synonyms; their combination creates the image of a totally vanquished foe, an impression reinforced by the replacement of the verb *šākab*, "to lie,"[445] with the passive participle, *šādûd*, "plundered, violently despoiled" (NIV, "dead") of his manly glory.[446]

> [28]"Through the window peered Sisera's mother;
>   behind the lattice she cried out,
> 'Why is his chariot so long in coming?
>   Why is the clatter of his chariots delayed?'
> [29]The wisest of her ladies answer her;
>   indeed, she keeps saying to herself,
> [30]'Are they not finding and dividing the spoils:
>   a girl or two for each man,
>   colorful garments as plunder for Sisera,
>   colorful garments embroidered,
>   highly embroidered garments for my neck—
> all this as plunder?'

---

[442] הָלְמָה, "she hammered"; מָחֲקָה, "she crushed"; מָחֲצָה, "she shattered"; חָלְפָה, "she pierced," transliterated as follows: *hālĕmâ, māḥăqâ, māḥăṣâ, ḥālĕpâ.*

[443] Note the pattern of repetition: ABCD/ABC/EBFCG

[444] The twofold occurrence of נָפַל, "he fell," does not mean he fell as a result of Jael's blow. This is poetic license for "fallen." The MT points בַּאֲשֶׁר as the preposition *beth* + the relative particle, "at where," but אֲשׁוּר should be understood as an archaic noun, "place," cognate to Aramaic אֲתַר. Thus Boling, *Judges*, 115.

[445] Cf. Lindars, *Judges 1–5*, 279–80.

[446] שָׁדַד usually refers to cities and people who have experienced the ravages of war. Isa 15:1; 23:1; Jer 47:4. Recent interpretations of these verses (e.g., Niditch, "Eroticism and Death," 43–57) have ascribed to these verses strong sexual content, but such approaches detract from the author's intention to glorify God whose mysterious but providential hand produces the victory.

STANZA VIII: WAITING IN VAIN FOR THE PRIZE (5:28–30).   The shocking shift in image and emotion from stanza VII to VIII is almost too much for the reader. One moment we are inside Jael's tent, observing Jael, who has cast off her traditional matronly role[447] and now stands triumphantly over the corpse of Sisera, a victim of her violent act. The next moment we are in his mother's house as she gazes out her window and wonders why her son does not return from the battle. If the first scene seems contrived, the pathos of the second is entirely realistic. With extraordinary poignancy Deborah has captured the hope and horror of war as seen through a woman's eyes. The men are engaged in the fury of battle, while the women wait and wonder at home. As we listen, we do not know whether or not to feel sorry for Sisera's mother. We know that Sisera will never return, but she does not. We know that if he did, he would come bearing the spoils of war, but it would be at Israel's expense. Deborah, the literary artist, is an Israelite, and her intent is to draw us into her view of the world. But Sisera's mother is a human being too; she is a mother, worried about her son.

5:28–29   Assuming the posture of an outside observer, the poet describes Sisera's mother gazing out her window[448] and weeping.[449] The image of this noble woman in her palace with royal retainers presents a sharp contrast to Jael, the rustic wife of Heber the Kenite living in her tent. And the poignancy of the scene is heightened by the rare (in poetry) insertion of direct speech. Her feelings are expressed in a pair of parallel questions, each beginning with "Why?" With just cause she worries about the delay[450] of Sisera's chariots. But she waits in vain for the sight of his chariots[451] on the horizon and the sound of horses' hooves.[452] The personal attendants[453] of Sisera's mother try to console her, no doubt by describing the best-case scenario. However, she tries to convince herself that all is well by answering her own question.[454] No doubt based on stories that her own son has told after previous victories, she imagines a scene in the

---

[447] For a study of Jael's and Deborah's reversal of traditional roles see Fewell and Gunn, "Controlling Perspectives: Women, Men, and the Authority of Violence in Judges 4 and 5," *JAAR* 58/3 (1990): 389–411.

[448] שָׁקַף (*niphal or hiphil*), "to look out," occurs with חַלּוֹן. בְּעַד, "through a window," occurs elsewhere in Gen 26:8; 2 Sam 6:16 = 1 Chr 15:29; 2 Kgs 9:30; Prov 7:6. אֶשְׁנָב, "lattice," occurs elsewhere only in Prov 7:6, where it is also paired with חַלּוֹן "window."

[449] The verb יָבַב, "to cry shrilly," occurs only here in the OT.

[450] Two verbs express "delay." With the present use of בֹּשֵׁשׁ, a *polel* of בּוּשׁ, "to be ashamed, embarrassed," cp. Exod 32:1. אָחַר (*piel*), "to stay behind, delay," occurs elsewhere in Deut 7:10; Pss 40:18; 70:6; Prov 23:30; Isa 5:11; 46:13; Dan 9:19; Hab 2:3.

[451] Two different words are used for chariot, רֶכֶב and מַרְכָּבָה, both deriving from the same root, רָכַב, "to ride." The singular form of the first probably refers to Sisera's personal chariot.

[452] פַּעֲמֵי מַרְכְּבוֹתָיו, lit. "the steps of his chariots."

[453] חַכְמוֹת שָׂרוֹתֶיהָ, "the wisest of her princesses." חַכְמוֹת is either a Canaanite feminine singular form (Boling, *Judges*, 115) or a misreading for חַכְמַת.

[454] Contra NIV, אַף־הִיא תָּשִׁיב אֲמָרֶיהָ לָהּ does not mean she kept talking to herself, but that she provided her own answer to her question.

enemy camp after they have been defeated.

5:30 The answer of Sisera's mother is cast in the form of a complex rhetorical question, which, in anticipating a positive answer, reflects the woman's heartlessness. Even as she speaks she imagines her son's soldiers discovering the loot in the enemy camp and dividing it as booty. The items she lists represent the highest prizes of war. For the victors, at the top of the list are the enemy's women, here referred to as *raḥam raḥămātayim,* literally "a womb, a pair of wombs" for each man,[455] that is, "a wench, two wenches." One might have expected a refined woman like Sisera's mother to be more sensitive to the vulnerability of women in the violent world of male warfare. At the very least she could have used a more neutral expression like *naʿărāh,* "girl, damsel," or *ʾāmāh,* "maid, handmaid." Her preference for this overtly sexual expression reflects the realities of war: to victorious soldiers the women of vanquished foes represent primarily objects for their sexual gratification, another realm to conquer. Obviously this woman's loyalties to her son and her own people overshadow her concern with the welfare of her gender as a group. The second treasured prize of war was rich garments plundered from the enemy camp. Two expressions describe these garments. The first is "colorful garments as plunder" (lit., "the plunder of colorful garments").[456] The second is more literally "a garment double embroidered[457] for the neck[458] of the spoiler."[459]

> [31]"So may all your enemies perish, O LORD!
> But may they who love you be like the sun
>   when it rises in its strength."

STANZA IX: CONCLUDING ASPIRATION (5:31a). Having focused on matters of personal human interest for seven verses, in v. 31 the poem returns to the theological plane. This is after all an ode of praise to Yahweh for the victory he has won on Israel's behalf. The conclusion is cast in the form of a double petition addressed to God,[460] reflecting a consciousness of the covenant blessings and curses as spelled out in Leviticus 26 and Deuteronomy 28. First, the composer prays that all Yahweh's enemies would perish, that is, experience the same fate as Sisera and the Canaanites. In keeping with other

---

[455] The distributive expression לְרֹאשׁ גֶּבֶר, "for the head of a man," is unparalleled in the OT.

[456] צֶבַע/זְבָעִים occurs nowhere else in the OT. The meaning of the root is established by reference to the Akk. cognate, *ṣubātum,* "fabric, dyed material" (*AHw,* 1107), and *ṣīp/bu,* "dyed fabric" (*CAD* 16.205).

[457] רִקְמָתַיִם derives from רָקַם, "to embroider."

[458] With Boling (*Judges,* 115) reading לְצַוְּארֵי as a plural construct with a singular meaning.

[459] Repointing MT's שָׁלָל, "booty, plunder," as a participle, שֹׁלֵל, "the plunderer."

[460] Many consider this stanza a liturgical gloss, hence not part of the original song. Cf. Coogan, "Structural and Literary Analysis," 144, n. 4.

early poems in which enmity against God is a common theme,[461] this plea assumes that anyone who opposes Israel opposes Yahweh. Accordingly, the composer of this song must have had in mind any non-Israelite enemies of Yahweh, like Sisera and the Canaanites or Pharaoh in Exodus 15. But the expression is deliberately ambiguous and, within the present literary context of the Book of Judges, the narrator undoubtedly intends a paraenetic challenge to his readers. An enemy of God is anyone whose actions and aims run counter to Yahweh's agenda.[462] If the Israelites persist in their apostasy and continue behaving like Canaanites, this virtual curse applies to them as well.

Second, Deborah prays for the vindication and victory of "those who love him." Her original audience will surely have identified these as the people of Israel, in opposition to the Canaanites. Like "those who are your enemies" in the previous line, however, the expression ʾōhăbāyw (lit., "ones loving him") intentionally opens the possibility of divine vindication to anyone who loves Yahweh. The semantic range of Hebrew ʾāhēb corresponds to the English "love," and its recognized opposite is also "hate" (śānēʾ), as Judg 14:16 indicates. The word occurs only two additional times in Judges, in each case describing the sexual and/or marital love between a man and a woman.[463] But the Hebrew term ʾāhēb is much more than an emotional term; it denotes, fundamentally, "covenant commitment." The theological antecedent to the present reference is found in the second command of the Decalogue and has direct relevance for the problem that plagued Israel during the period of Judges:

> You shall not make for yourself an idol in the form of anything. … You shall not bow down to them or worship them; for I the LORD your God am a jealous God, punishing the children for the sin of the fathers to the third and fourth generation of those who hate [śānēʾ] me, but showing love [ḥesed] to thousands who love [ʾāhēb] me and keep my commandments. Exod 20:5–6[464]

Deborah prays that those who are covenantally committed to Yahweh and who express that commitment with grateful and unreserved obedience may be like the sun when it rises in full force. Although the idiom derives ultimately from the daily emergence of the sun on the eastern horizon, one may recognize in the present usage a polemic against pagan notions. In ancient Near Eastern thought the sun was worshiped as a deity[465] who rode triumphantly across the sky in his chariot each day. The association of the sun with a chariot derives

---

[461] Exod 15:6; Num 10:35; Deut 32:42. The notion also occurs in prose texts, such as Num 32:21.

[462] Cf. Isa 1:24;

[463] Judg 14:16; 16:4,15.

[464] Cf. also the shemaʿ and its commentary in Deut 6:4–5.

[465] Shamash in Mesopotamia; Shemesh in Canaan. Cf. the reference to Beth Shemesh, "the temple of Shemesh," along with Beth Anath, "the temple of Anath," in 1:33.

from the sun's disclike appearance. The ancients perceived it as a chariot wheel turning through the heavens.[466] Indeed the present image may have been suggested to Deborah by the earlier references to Sisera's chariots. If this interpretation is correct, the prayer not only wishes for Yahweh's people continued triumph against their enemies; this military nuance also creates a fitting inclusio with the opening vision of Yahweh coming forth from Sinai ahead of his people (v. 4). No earthly chariots can stand against those who are covenantally committed to God.

Then the land had peace forty years.

GOD'S GIFT OF SECURITY (CONTINUED) (5:31b).   **5:31b** Having interrupted the final note on this narrative concerning Deborah and Barak and the Canaanites with the Song that derives from shortly after the events described in chap. 4, the narrator returns to some unfinished business. Without commentary or interpretation he notes simply that the land had rest for forty years, that is, for one generation, after the defeat of Sisera and Jabin. But the reader is left to wonder whether the internal causes of the previous crises have actually been resolved. Only by reading on does one learn the truth.

Theological and Practical Implications

The Book of Judges portrays a degenerate Israelite society. Little that transpires in the book is normal or normative. The Canaanite oppression was Yahweh's response to the persistent idolatry of his people. It is remarkable that when they cry out and come to Deborah for a word from God concerning their problems, he answers. But the answer he provides catches everyone by surprise. On first sight the call and commissioning of Barak seems natural enough, except that Barak is an unlikely leader. Weak-willed and indecisive, he hesitates to enter the fray. When he engages the enemy in battles at Yahweh's command, Yahweh provides a remarkable victory, but he will not allow Barak the satisfaction of using this event for personal glory. God's battles are not fought with human weapons nor for the sake of human glory. The honor of Yahweh's name is the primary concern.

From another perspective this account paints a remarkable picture of strong and courageous women. Jael dares to break with convention and with her family's loyalties to come to the aid of Yahweh's people. The author draws no moral lessons from her action; he merely presents these as another extraordi-

---

[466] According to the eighth-century Aramaic inscriptions from Zinjirli, which recognize a triad of major deities, El, Shemesh, and Rakib-El ("the charioteer of El"), the chariot appears to have belonged to El the high god, with the Sun-god as his attendant and Rakib-El the charioteer. Cf. E. Lipinski, "Shemesh," *Dictionary of Deities and Demons in the Bible,* ed. K. van der Toorn et al. (Leiden: Brill, 1995), 1445–51.

nary example of God's ability to incorporate the free actions of human beings in the fulfillment of his plan.

As for Deborah, this remarkable woman is without doubt the most honorable human figure in the Book of Judges and one of the most remarkable characters in the entire Old Testament. As the prophet of God in a dark and dismal age she represented a ray of light and hope. Yahweh is the true hero of the account, but the character and achievements of his agent should not be minimized. In an era of weak men God raised a woman to serve as a lightning rod against his wrath. The priesthood's silence in the chapter is deafening. But just because they are in spiritual decline does not mean that Yahweh has abandoned his people totally. He still has his representative. She sits not at Bethel or Shiloh, where the ark is, but outside the town, receiving the pleas of the Israelites on Yahweh's behalf. Her commissioning of Barak represents the divine *mišpāṭ*. In fact, as his representative she goes the second mile. She accompanies him into battle, as a recognized representative and spokesperson for the Commander in Chief.

That is her role; no more and no less. In so doing she is granted full authority to take her place among the continuous line of God's servants the prophets. While they served as agents of God's grace in every age, in none was it more welcome (and undeserved) than in the dark days of the governors. To borrow a note from the first century A.D. author Pseudo-Philo, in Deborah the grace of God has been awakened; through her the works of Yahweh have been praised.[467] That people in our day, especially women, should find inspiration in Deborah is not surprising. She does not displace men in officially established positions of leadership, but her gender does not disqualify her from significant service for God. And so it will be in any age. God's call to service often catches his people by surprise, but when he calls, we must respond to his command, even when it appears to run counter to convention.

---

[467] The generally more sermonic tone of Pseudo-Philo's version of the Song of Deborah and Barak (32:1–18) and a concluding farewell address (33:1–6) lend support to this "prophetic" interpretation of Deborah's role. For a translation of these texts see D. J. Harrington in J. H. Charlesworth, ed., *The Old Testament Pseudepigrapha*, vol. 2 (Garden City: Doubleday, 1985), 345–48.

5. The Midianite and Gideon Cycle (6:1–9:57)

Of all the accounts of deliverance in the Book of Judges, none is more complete nor complex than the story of Gideon. It is evident even from a casual reading that the account divides into two major parts, the actual account of Israel's deliverance from the Midianite oppression under the leadership of Gideon (6:1–8:35) and the story of his son Abimelech (9:1–57). Not only do these parts differ markedly in style and tone, but the latter falls outside the controlling structural paradigm of the deliverance accounts. In fact, it bears the marks of a separate short story, which the narrator has integrated thematically with the preceding account of Gideon/Jerubbaal.[468] However, before we examine more closely the textual, redactional, and literary issues raised by this account, it may be helpful to summarize the events in 6:1–8:35:

1. The Israelites are harassed and oppressed by marauding bands of Midianites and Amalekites.

2. A reluctant leader, Gideon, emerges to lead the Israelites against these bands.

3. His first significant act, however, is to destroy a Baal cult installation in his father's backyard, which raises the ire of the people of Ophrah.

4. With a small band of three hundred men Gideon routs the enemy forces.

5. Two leaders, Oreb and Zeeb, are killed in the course of the pursuit, but Zebah and Zalmunnah along with their armies escape across the Jordan.

6. When Gideon asks the residents of Succoth and Penuel the whereabouts of these kings, they refuse to cooperate.

7. Gideon captures the two Midianite kings.

8. On his return from battle Gideon passes through Succoth and Penuel and razes these towns for their previous intransigence.

9. The two kings are slain and their royal accoutrements retained as booty.

10. The kingship is offered to Gideon, but he formally declines the offer, arguing that God alone is King in Israel.

11. Gideon adopts the manner of a king.

12. The land of Israel enjoys relative peace for a protracted period of time.

13. After Gideon's death one of his sons, Abimelech, seizes the throne in Shechem and consolidates his control by having all potential sibling rivals (save Jotham) killed.

14. Shortly after Abimelech's seizure of the throne, the land is wracked by civil war, which climaxes in the death of Abimelech at the hands of a woman.

Although the plot follows a definite trajectory, the narrative is complex, consisting of a series of episodes that differ in foci and style. For more than a

---

[468] Cf. 9:1–5,16–17,23–24,55–57.

century scholars have exploited the apparent contradictions, discrepancies, and tensions in the text to reconstruct the evolution of the literary account. In the past classical source analyses have tended to find in the Gideon narratives extensions of the hypothetical Pentateuchal sources referred to by scholars as J, E, D, and P.[469] This approach is now largely discounted, being replaced by tradition analysis, which seeks to identify the preliterary traditions that underlie the original narration and to show how subsequent editorial additions have altered the meaning of composition. See especially the recent analysis of Becker,[470] who proposes the following evolution of the text:

1. Underlying chaps. 6–9 are two sets of relatively disparate [preliterary] traditions: (a) local traditions of Gideon and his role in the battle against Midian (6:11–24; 7:11–15,16–22; 8:5–21 [with minor deletions]); (b) the rise and fall of Abimelech ben Jerubbaal (9:1–6,21,24–41,46–54).

2. A Deuteronomistic historian (DtrH) created a coherent Gideon-Abimelech story by linking these traditions with a cleverly devised renaming of Gideon into Jerubbaal (6:25–32). However, his rhetorical agenda is clear. In the wake of the destruction of Jerusalem in 586 B.C. and the failed monarchy, DtrH sought to demonstrate that in Israel's premonarchic period two fundamentally opposed principles were operative: (a) the rule and reign of Yahweh, as represented by Gideon through whom Yahweh works, and (b) the rule of a king, as represented by the brutal Abimelech. Gideon represents an office that offers an alternative to kingship, a perspective that is highlighted by DtrH's narrative framework (6:1–6; 8:28[29–32]), the completeness of the call narrative (6:11–24), the emphasis on divine deliverance (7:11–22), Gideon's speech (8:22–23), and especially the application of the preexistent fable (9:8–15) to Abimelech (9:16a,19b,20–21).

3. The present text incorporates numerous expansions on the basic composition of DtrH. The most significant additions represent the work of DtrN, whose moralistic and anti-idolatrous stance is evident in 8:24–27,33–35; 9:16b–19a,56–57). This editor does not recognize DtrH's sharp contrast between Gideon and Abimelech. (4) The prophetic speech (6:7–10), also from the Deuteronomistic school, the account of the conflict between Ephraim and Abieser (7:24–8:3), which derives from an ancient tradition, and miscellaneous

---

[469] J represents the Yahwist source, E the Elohist, D the Deuteronomist, and P the Priestly source. Note the conclusions of Moore as a representative of this approach (*Judges*, 175–77 and *passim* in 177–270): J = part of the older material incorporated in 6:2–6a,11–24,34; 7:1,9–11,13–15 (with minor editorial traces), 16–21 (the parts involving jars and torches), part of 22b; 8:4–21,24–27a,30–32; 9:26–41 E = part of 6:2–6,7–10,25–32,33,35a,36–40; 7:2–8,16–21 (the parts involving horns) 22a,22b (part), 23(E2?), 24–25; 8:1–3,22–23(E2); 29; 9:1–25,42–57. These E parts do not necessarily derive from a single hand. Judg 6:7–10 in particular appears to be secondary. D = 6:1, 6b, the exaggerated notes in vv. 1–5; 8:33–35 Miscellaneous editorial additions: 6:35b; 7:12,27b; 8:27b,28.

[470] Becker, *Richterzeit und Königtum,* 140–207.

additions (6:33–34; 6:35 + 7:1–7; 6:36–40) represent further expansions.[471] However, because of the speculative nature of all these reconstructions of the evolution of the text, recent literary analysts have adopted a more holistic stance. Recognizing that ancient Near Eastern authors were not governed by the same literary canons that drive modern writers and assuming an intentional literary product, they attempt to make sense of the irregularities and tensions in the text as they appear. Polzin, for example, argues that elements like the variation in divine and human names is intentional, reflecting the vacillation of Gideon and Israel during this period. Accordingly, the story of Abimelech functions as a fitting climax to the Gideon narrative.[472]

More recently O'Connell has identified three subplots in 6:1–9:57, "each with its own exposition, development and resolution."[473] (1) Plot A involves Yahweh's rescue of Israel from the Midianites through Gideon.[474] (2) Plot B involves Yahweh's judgment upon Gideon and his tribe for holding on to foreign cult practices.[475] (3) Plot C involves Yahweh's judgment of Gideon, his sons, and his tribe for covenant (social) injustices.[476] The extreme complexity of O'Connell's analysis raises questions about the details (would ancient writers really have been this sophisticated?); still, he has performed an invaluable service by demonstrating that the entire unit, 6:1–9:57, functions as a single intentional literary unit.[477] Some scholars argue that because the Abimelech story fails to develop the theme announced in 2:11–23 it repre-

---

[471] Others argue that Gideon and Jerubbaal represent two traditions linked by the Deuteronomist. Cf. Richter, *Traditionsgeschichtliche Untersuchungen*, 112–318; T. Veijola, *Das Königtum in der Beurteilung der deuteronomistischen Historiographie: Eine redaktionsgeschichtliche Untersuchung*, Acta/Annales Academiae Fennicae, Series B 193 (Helsinki: Suomalainen Tiedeakatemia, 1977); de Vaux (*Early History of Israel*, 770–71, 801–2). For another treatment see A. G. Auld, "Gideon: Hacking at the Heart of the Old Testament," *VT* 39 (1989): 257–67, in which it is argued that the story of Gideon was added to the Book of Judges in the Persian period. For another complex reconstruction of the events and the traditiohistorical reconstruction of the evolution of the text see H. Rösel, "Studien zur Topographie der Kriege in den Büchern Josua und Richter. Schluss," *ZDPV* 92 (1976): 10–46.

[472] *Moses and the Deuteronomist*, 168–76.

[473] O'Connell, *Rhetoric of the Book of Judges*, 139.

[474] This plot is developed in 6:1–6[7–10],11–24[25–32],33–35[36–40]; 7:1[2–8a],8b–9[10–15a],15b–25; 8:[1–3 4[5–9]10–12[13–17,18–21?,22–23,24– 27],28[29–31],32.

[475] This plot is developed in 6:25–32; 8:24–27,33–34; 9:1–44 [note esp. 9:4,6,27,37],46–49, 56–57.

[476] This plot is developed in 8:5–9,13–23,29–31,35; 9:1–49a,50–57.

[477] J. P. Turner ("The Gideon Narrative as the Focal Point of Judges," *BibSac* 149 [1992]: 146–61) proposes a chiastic pattern with the resolution of Gideon's fear in C being the focal point:

A   6:1–10
B   6:11–32
C   6:33–7:18
B′   7:19–8:21
A′   8:22–32

sents a later independent addition,[478] but chap. 9 is clearly designed to bring resolution to the complications in the plot occurring in chaps. 6–8. Indeed, on closer examination chap. 9 does develop the theme announced in 2:11–23, inasmuch as it demonstrates the symptoms and effects of the escalation of religious compromise announced in 2:19. Further, it illustrates the effects of the covenantal and marital compromises summarized in 3:1–6. The manner in which the crisis is resolved in the end also echoes several important motifs in the Deborah/Barak/Jael narrative.

The Gideon narrative may be divided into three parts: A = 6:1–8:3; B = 8:4–28; C = 8:29–9:57. In A the narrator has generally followed the paradigmatic scheme of the "deliverer accounts." One might have expected the concluding comment found in v. 28 to appear immediately after the resolution of the Midianite crisis (8:3). However, although differing generically from the Song of Deborah, like the Canaanite-Barak account, part B interrupts A with the recounting of a new series of events that echo 7:23–25.[479] Whereas in A the deliverance of Israel from the Midianites is carefully credited to Yahweh, in B God is absent altogether. His name appears only in flippant and falsely pious comments from the lips of Gideon. Part C looks like a leaf from a Canaanite history notebook. Israel poses as her own worst enemy, and Yahweh intervenes (indirectly through his Spirit) against her self-interest. Instead of acting out of mercy and compassion toward his undeserving people, for the first time in the book he acts retributively, and well he must, for here an aspect of Israelite life has been totally Canaanized.

Indeed the Canaanization of Israel represents the key idea in the narrative. After the account of Deborah and Barak in chaps. 4–5, the reader is primed for high expectations.[480] Instead the heroic women of the song give way to an unheroic "man of Israel" (7:14) who not only does all he can to evade the call of Yahweh but in the end abandons God. At the same time, the spiritual state of the nation as a whole is exposed through the skillful framing of the Gideon experience (A + B) by references to Ophrah. In the beginning Ophrah is the scene of clan idolatry (6:25–32); in the end Ophrah is the focus of national idolatry (8:27). In the person of Gideon the narrator recognizes the schizophrenic nature of Israel's spiritual personality. On the one hand she treasures her call to be God's covenant people; on the other she cannot resist the allurements of the prevailing Canaanite culture.

---

[478] S. R. Driver, *An Introduction to the Literature of the Old Testament*, 9th ed. (Edinburgh: T & T Clark, 1913), 166.

[479] Note in particular the capture of two Midianite rulers, followed by Gideon's communication with the people.

[480] So also Klein, *Triumph of Irony*, 50.

(1) God's Punishment and Deliverance of Israel (6:1–8:3)

¹Again the Israelites did evil in the eyes of the LORD, and for seven years he gave them into the hands of the Midianites. ²Because the power of Midian was so oppressive, the Israelites prepared shelters for themselves in mountain clefts, caves and strongholds. ³Whenever the Israelites planted their crops, the Midianites, Amalekites and other eastern peoples invaded the country. ⁴They camped on the land and ruined the crops all the way to Gaza and did not spare a living thing for Israel, neither sheep nor cattle nor donkeys. ⁵They came up with their livestock and their tents like swarms of locusts. It was impossible to count the men and their camels; they invaded the land to ravage it.

THE MARKS OF ISRAEL'S CANAANIZATION (6:1a).   **6:1a**   As in 3:12a and 4:1, the Gideon cycle opens with the negative evaluation formula. But the formula is unadorned with extra detail. The author seems eager to get on with the story.

GOD'S AGENT OF PUNISHMENT (6:1b–5).   **6:1b–5**   The expansive style of the Gideon narrative is evident from the outset, for the author spends five verses to describe Yahweh's response to the new cycle of apostasy. Because God's name is missing in vv. 2–6b, the reader is tempted to interpret the events described as merely human affairs; in a moment of political and military weakness Israel is overrun by opportunistic Midianites. But v. 1b holds the key to this paragraph. Employing the milder form of the divine committal formula,[481] the historian attributes the disasters that befall Israel directly to the hand of God, who is punishing his people for their sin. Undoubtedly he saw in these events the fulfillment of the covenant curses outlined in Leviticus 26 and Deuteronomy 28.[482]

The primary agent of judgment is identified as "the Midianites," but they were accompanied by Amalekites and "Easterners." The Midianites were a seminomadic people of the Sinai peninsula and western Arabia. According to Gen 25:2–4, they were distant relatives of the Israelites, being descended from Abraham by his second wife, Keturah. The Israelites' relations with the Midianites is generally portrayed in the Old Testament as problematic. According to Gen 37:25–36, Midianites were involved in the sale of Joseph to Egypt, but the narrative casts no judgment upon them for this act.[483] On the contrary, in long-range terms Joseph himself viewed them as agents of divine providence.[484]

---

[481] See p. 147f.

[482] In addition to the divine committal formula, which derives from Lev 26:25, cp. the vain sowing of the fields (v. 3) with Lev 26:16 and Deut 28:30,33,38; the produce of the land (יְבוּל הָאָרֶץ, v. 4) with Lev 26:4,20; and the motif of flight and hiding (v. 2) with Lev 26:17,25.

[483] The interchange of "Midianite" and "Ishmaelite" in the Genesis context continues in Judg 8:24, where the term "Ishmaelite" is applied to Midianites. To the Israelites these were overlapping ethnicons.

[484] Gen 45:4–8; 50:19–20.

In the Exodus narratives the Midianites are painted in an extremely posi-
tive light. They provided Moses with a haven when he fled from Pharaoh;
indeed his wife was a daughter of the Midianite priest (Exod 2:15–22).
While in their land, Moses received his call from God (Exod 3:1–4:23).
Then, having led them out of Egypt, he brought his entire nation here. On
Midianite soil the Israelites entered into covenant relationship with Yahweh
and received the revelation of his will, the Torah (Exodus 19–Numbers 7).
Moses' Midianite father-in-law, Jethro, even had a hand in the civil reorgani-
zation of the nation (Exodus 18).

Once the Israelites left Sinai, however, relations with the Midianites deteri-
orated. According to Num 25:6–18, because of Midianite initiative in leading
Israel away from Yahweh, an anti-Midianite stance became official, divinely
sanctioned policy, later expressed in a full-scale war against them (Numbers
31). In more recent times some of their Kenite kinsfolk had allied with the
Canaanites against the Israel.[485] The revival and expansion of Midian and their
present encroachment on Israelite territory may have been occasioned by insta-
bility in the region. In any case the present account portrays them not as cara-
vaneers but as camel-riding warriors, who may have been driven by the need to
supplement the [inadequate] foodstuffs being produced in their own territory.[486]

But this is not the first time their allies the Amalekites have appeared as enemies of Israel in the Book of Judges. In 3:13 these descendants of Esau (Gen
36:12,16)[487] had allied with Eglon of Moab. *Běnê Qedem*, literally "sons of
the east,"[488] could serve as an explanatory designation for Midian and Amalek
since these must have entered across the Jordan, or it could refer to another
desert group. *Běnê Qedem*, is not a proper name, nor a self-designation, but a
vague gentilic label used by Westerners to denote the nomadic groups that
migrated about the Arabian desert,[489] often raiding the settled communities of
the Transjordan and, as opportunity provided, of Cisjordan.[490] In this instance
the Amalekites and other Bedouin tribes opportunistically joined the Midianites in a confederation of desert peoples and crossed the Jordan with them to
pillage and generally wreak havoc on Israelite settlements.

---

[485] Cp. 1:16 and 4:11,17.

[486] G. E. Mendenhall's suggestion that these raids represented regular tax-gathering expedi-
tions seems unlikely in the face of the description of the Midianite tactics ("Midian," *ABD* 4.816).

[487] Cf. Israel's earlier hostile encounter with the Amalekites in Exod 17:8–16 and Balaam's
curse of this people in Num 24:20–21. According to 1 Samuel 15, their last king was slain by Samuel, though remnants of the people remained until David's reign (1 Sam 27:8; 30:1,18; 2 Sam 1:1).

[488] Cf. NIV's "other eastern peoples."

[489] Cp. *amurru*, "west," from which is derived "Amorite," an Akk. designation for the territory
to the [north]west of Mesopotamia.

[490] Cf. Gen 29:1; Job 1:3. The *běnê Qedem* are frequently mentioned in the prophets: Isa 11:14;
Jer 49:28; Ezek 25:1–10.

Although the invaders probably were only loosely organized, the narrator recognizes a clear pattern to their tactics. Just when the freshly seeded crops had begun to sprout, Midianite, Amalekite, and "Qedemite" hordes would irrupt from across the Jordan. Bringing with them their own livestock and camels (v. 5),[491] and even their tents, the raiders would set up camp at strategic locations. From here they would send their herds out in search of pasturage and launch their raiding parties, which extended as far west as Gaza, the southwestern border the Israelites shared with the Philistines.

Seven years of Midianite terror had a devastating effect on the Israelite economy and emotion. Like locusts, their innumerable hosts devoured every green plant in sight, leaving the land devastated, with nothing left over for the Israelite flocks and herds. Fearing the brutality of the invaders, as soon as they appeared on the horizon, the Israelites fled for the hills, transforming natural geological features into defensive strongholds. The narrator highlights the intensity of their fright by citing a triad of refuges: *minhārôt*, "mountain clefts";[492] *měʿarôt*, "caves"; and *měṣādôt*, "strongholds."

⁶Midian so impoverished the Israelites that they cried out to the LORD for help.

ISRAEL'S RESPONSE TO THE OPPRESSION (6:6). **6:6** This verse captures the Israelite disposition toward their calamities in a single word translated "impoverished," or literally, Israel "became small" *(wayyiddal)*, which says as much about her emotional state as about her economic condition. Israel is completely paralyzed before the Midianite menace. Like the opening announcement of Israel's Canaanization (v. 1a), the declaration of the nation's response to the oppression at the hands of Yahweh's agents is cast in the briefest of terms: they cried out to God. As we have come to expect, there is no hint of repentance, only a cry of pain.

GOD'S AGENT OF DELIVERANCE (6:7–32). Like the account of Deborah and Barak, the present narrative places great emphasis on the manner in which a deliverer is raised up for Israel. In fact, the call of Gideon to be the deliverer of Israel represents the longest and most formally constructed call narrative in the book. Although the summary statement, "the LORD raised up a deliverer for the descendants of Israel" *(wayyāqem yhwh môšîaʿ libnê yiśrāʾēl)*[493] is missing, what transpires in vv. 7–32 represents an exposition of this formula. The core of this passage (vv. 11–24) follows the classic paradigm of a call narrative; the introductory prophetic speech (vv. 7–10) and the con-

---

[491] On the domestication and use of camels in the ANE see E. Firmage, "4. Camels," *ABD* 6.1138–40.

[492] The word occurs only here in the OT. Being derived from the same root as נָהָר, "river," suggests "river valleys," "mountain gorges."

[493] Cf. 3:9; also 2:16.

cluding episodes (vv. 25–40) depart from the standard paradigm. With this plot strategy the reader learns more about the author's perception of Israel and the one called to deliver the nation respectively.

⁷When the Israelites cried to the LORD because of Midian, ⁸he sent them a prophet, who said, "This is what the LORD, the God of Israel, says: I brought you up out of Egypt, out of the land of slavery. ⁹I snatched you from the power of Egypt and from the hand of all your oppressors. I drove them from before you and gave you their land. ¹⁰I said to you, 'I am the LORD your God; do not worship the gods of the Amorites, in whose land you live.' But you have not listened to me."

The Prophetic Scolding (6:7–10). **6:7–10** Several features of this segment convince most scholars to delete it as a late insertion by a prophetic redactor. The first clue to its secondary nature is found in the reference to Israel's cry to Yahweh in v. 7, which repeats a similar notice in v. 6 almost verbatim.[494] This conclusion is supported by the unique stylistic features found in vv. 7–10, as well as the fact that these verses may be deleted without any serious loss of meaning.[495] In fact, vv. 11ff. provide a much more logical sequel to vv. 1–6 than the present paragraph.

However, although this segment may derive from a different (prophetic) source than the surrounding narrative, to delete it robs the author of both stylistic flexibility[496] and an important emphasis in the book as a whole. Indeed this segment plays an extremely important rhetorical function. Not only does it remind the reader of the theological implications of Israel's actions and/or experiences but it also highlights the undeserved nature of Yahweh's intervention on her behalf. Furthermore, these verses are not as intrusive as they seem. The unnamed prophet appears in this narrative at precisely the same point as Deborah had been introduced in 4:4, namely, immediately after the notice that Israel had cried out to Yahweh.[497] Indeed, the odd expression ʾîš nābîʾ, lit., "a prophet man" (NIV, "a prophet") represents a perfect counterpart to ʾiššâ

---

[494] On such repetition as a mark of secondariness see C. Kuhl, "Die 'Wiederaufnahme'—ein literarkritisches Prinzip?" *ZAW* 64 (1952): 1–11.

[495] This may explain why 6:7–10 is missing from 4QJudga. For a study of this textual fragment see J. T. Berrera, "La aportacion de 4QJuecesa al estudio de la historia textual y literaria del libro de los Jueces," *MEAH* 40 (1991): 5–20; J. Trebolle, "Light from 4QJudga and 4QKgs on the Text of Judges and Kings," in *The Dead Sea Scrolls: Forty Years of Research*, ed. D. Dimant and U. Rappaport; Studies on the Texts of the Desert of Judah 10 (Leiden: Brill, 1992), 315–24. F. H. Polak ("The Biblical Narrative as Palimpsest: Concerning the Role of Diachrony in Structural Analysis" [Dutch, "Het bijbelverhaal als palimpsest: Over de rol van de diachronie in de structurele analyse"] *Amsterdamse Cahiers voor Exegese en Bijbelse Theologie* 9 [1988]: 23–34) argues for a palimpsest addition to the broader narrative.

[496] Literary style is determined by a variety of considerations: content, data source, authorial intent.

[497] Noted also by Webb, *Book of Judges*, 145.

nĕbî°â, "a prophet woman" (NIV, "a prophetess") in 4:4. To be sure, rather than calling a deliverer for the people,[498] this prophet's function is more like that of the *mal°ak yhwh,* "messenger/angel of the LORD," in 2:1–5; but like Deborah, his appearance represents the divine response to the cry of Israel. Before Yahweh calls his deliverer, he offers him a scolding similar to that expressed through the earlier envoy.

This segment is cast in the classic form of a judgment speech. Following a notice of the occasion of the speech (Israel's cry in response to the Midianite oppression, v. 7), the narrator notes the divine commission of an official spokesman to confront the nation on his behalf. There is no hint yet that God has singled out a man to deliver his people. The divine envoy commences his speech appropriately with the citation formula, "this is what the LORD, the God of Israel, says" *(kōh °āmar yhwh °ĕlōhê yiśrā°ēl).* This statement is critical not only because it authenticates the prophet as an authorized spokesman for Yahweh but also because it reminds the audience of the source of his message.[499] It comes from Yahweh, the divine patron and covenant Lord of Israel, who has heard the cry of his people. In typical prophetic fashion, following the formula, the prophet's speech is cast in the first person, as if God himself were addressing Israel.[500]

The divine message consists of two parts: a survey of Yahweh's past actions on Israel's behalf (vv. 8b–9) and an indictment of Israel for her treacherous response (v. 10). With regard to the former, the NIV's rendering of v. 8b obscures the emphatic construction: "I am the one who brought you up…" The verbs employed in vv. 8b–9 offer Israel (and the reader) an expanded version of the earlier messenger's review (2:1) of Yahweh's gracious past actions for Israel's benefit: he had (1) brought them up from Egypt; (2) brought them out of the slave barracks *(bêt °ăbādîm);* (3) rescued them from all their oppressors;[501] (4) dispossessed the inhabitants of their land; (5) delivered it into Israel's hands; and (6) committed himself to being Israel's God. To prick the memory of the Israelites the last demonstration of grace is expressed by explicitly quoting Yahweh's stereotypical self-introductory formula: "I said to you, 'I am the LORD your God.'" This statement highlights God's actions as expressive of a special relationship that he had by his sovereign grace established with Israel. Since he had demonstrated such grace in delivering them from all their enemies and providing

---

[498] That role will fall to the יהוה מַלְאַךְ, "messenger/angel of the LORD," in the following scene.

[499] The formula is derived from the court. For an example of its use in a secular context see Judg 11:15.

[500] The citation formula is missing in 2:1–3, but the messenger there also employs the same first person, as if Yahweh himself were speaking.

[501] The verb לָחַץ occurs elsewhere in Judges in 1:34; 2:18; 4:3; 6:9; 10:12.

them with their own land, and since he had committed himself to be their covenant Lord, surely his demand for exclusive and undivided allegiance to him was not too much to ask. As Israel's divine covenant partner, he would not tolerate rivals; he would brook no interference from other gods, particularly the gods of the Amorites, who had occupied this land.[502]

Yahweh's disappointment with the response of his people is summarized in a few words: "You have not listened to me [lit., "my voice"]." The issue of 2:1–5 has resurfaced. God had spoken, but they had not listened. The reference to Yahweh's voice refers ultimately to his detailed revelation of his will at Sinai, but it refers also to the exhortations of human spokesmen like Moses (Deuteronomy) and Joshua (Joshua 23–24), as well as specially commissioned envoys (Judg 2:1–5) and prophets.

This brief episode leaves the reader wondering how God will respond to the people's persistent perfidy. We know that the Midianite oppression represents just judgment, but the form of the speech leads us to expect further punitive actions. What happens in vv. 11–24 catches us by surprise. The narrator's purpose in inserting this prophetic scolding at this point is to set the stage for the call of Gideon. If God raises a deliverer for Israel, it is an entirely gracious act. There has been no hint of repentance nor any announcement of divine forgiveness. Yahweh's subsequent intervention on Israel's behalf must be interpreted in light of the people's persistent apostasy.

[11]The angel of the LORD came and sat down under the oak in Ophrah that belonged to Joash the Abiezrite, where his son Gideon was threshing wheat in a winepress to keep it from the Midianites. [12]When the angel of the LORD appeared to Gideon, he said, "The LORD is with you, mighty warrior."

[13]"But sir," Gideon replied, "if the LORD is with us, why has all this happened to us? Where are all his wonders that our fathers told us about when they said, 'Did not the LORD bring us up out of Egypt?' But now the LORD has abandoned us and put us into the hand of Midian."

[14]The LORD turned to him and said, "Go in the strength you have and save Israel out of Midian's hand. Am I not sending you?"

[15]"But Lord," Gideon asked, "how can I save Israel? My clan is the weakest in Manasseh, and I am the least in my family."

[16]The LORD answered, "I will be with you, and you will strike down all the Midianites together."

[17]Gideon replied, "If now I have found favor in your eyes, give me a sign that it is really you talking to me. [18]Please do not go away until I come back and bring my offering and set it before you."

And the LORD said, "I will wait until you return."

[19]Gideon went in, prepared a young goat, and from an ephah of flour he made bread without yeast. Putting the meat in a basket and its broth in a pot, he

---

[502] Cf. Deuteronomy 6–7.

brought them out and offered them to him under the oak. **20**The angel of God said to him, "Take the meat and the unleavened bread, place them on this rock, and pour out the broth." And Gideon did so. **21**With the tip of the staff that was in his hand, the angel of the LORD touched the meat and the unleavened bread. Fire flared from the rock, consuming the meat and the bread. And the angel of the LORD disappeared. **22**When Gideon realized that it was the angel of the LORD, he exclaimed, "Ah, Sovereign LORD! I have seen the angel of the LORD face to face!" **23**But the LORD said to him, "Peace! Do not be afraid. You are not going to die." **24**So Gideon built an altar to the LORD there and called it The LORD is Peace. To this day it stands in Ophrah of the Abiezrites.

The Call and Commissioning of Gideon (6:11–24). Form critical scholars have long recognized in the account of Gideon's rise to the office of deliverer for Israel the form of call narratives as a genre. Such narratives typically consist of (1) a confrontation with God and/or his messenger; (2) an introductory address of the person being called; (3) the divine commission; (4) the raising of objections by the person called; (5) divine words of reassurance; and (6) a sign authenticating the call experience.[503] From the allusion to the exodus narratives in 7:13, and the numerous links this account bears with the call of Moses in Exodus 3–4,[504] the narrator intentionally presents Gideon as sort of a second Moses. In addition to the basic elements of the call narrative, the narrator adds other details which all contribute to the portrait of this man he is trying to paint. The dialogue in particular is revealing.

The Commissioning (6:11–14). **6:11** Verse 11 provides the reader with vital background information for understanding the personality and mission of Gideon. First, it identifies him by name, Gideon, which means "hacker," or "hewer," a function he will soon be called upon to fulfill as he destroys the altar

---

[503] See Habel, "The Form and Significance of the Call Narratives," 297–305; W. Richter, *Die sogenannten vorprophetischen Berufungsberichte*, Forschungen zur Religion und Literatur des Alten und Neuen Testaments 101 (Göttingen: Vandenhoeck & Ruprecht, 1970), 1965; id., *Traditionsgeschichtliche Untersuchungen*, 146–49; E. Kutsch, "Gideons Berufung und Altarbau Jdc 6,11–24," *TLZ* 81 (1956): 75–84.

[504] (1) The precipitating cry for help (6:7; Exod 2:23–24); (2) the timing of the call—while the person called is hiding from the enemy but working for his father [father-in-law], who is patron of a pagan shrine; (3) the commissioning word, שְׁלַחְתִּיךָ, "I have sent you" (6:14; Exod 3:12); (4) human protestations of inadequacy (6:16; Exod 3:11); (5) assurance of divine presence (6:16; Exod 3:12); (6) the sign of reassurance (6:17; Exod 3:12); (7) an accompanying fear-inducing fire theophany (6:22; Exod 3:6). Cf. Webb (*Book of Judges*, 148), who also compares Gideon's seeing the face of Yahweh's angel "face-to-face" with Moses' direct "face-to-face" knowledge of Yahweh (Deut 34:10). To these parallels with the life of Moses we may add Gideon's taking matters into his own hands (8:4–28; cf. Numbers 20) and the production of an idolatrous object (8:27; cf. Numbers 21). Cf. also Klein, *Triumph of Irony*, 51.

of Baal on his father's property (vv. 25–27).[505] In fact, there is considerable support for the view that Gideon was this man's nickname and that his real name was Jerubbaal.[506]

Second, Gideon is identified by patronymic, "son of Joash the Abiezrite." Although Joash, a shortened version of Jehoash, "Yahweh is strong,"[507] was a common Israelite name, all that is known of this man is derived from this account. From Josh 17:2 and 1 Chr 7:18 we learn that the Abiezrites constituted a clan of Manasseh, a tribe which was granted land on both sides of the Jordan.[508] But v. 35 makes clear that the Abiezrite allotment was located west of the Jordan. Joash's estate was located at Ophrah, which many identify tentatively with modern ʿAfulleh in the Jezreel Valley.[509] Despite Gideon's protest that his family was the least significant in the entire tribe of Manasseh, the course of subsequent events suggests Joash must have been a man of considerable wealth and standing in the community. Not only does his son Gideon have at least ten servants (v. 27), but he is the sponsor of a significant Baal cult site that includes altar, Asherah image, and temple fortress (cf. vv. 25–26), the desecration of which raises the ire of the entire community. Only by serious argumentation is he able to convince the elders to abandon their demand for punishment of the perpetrator of the crime.

At the time of his encounter with the divine envoy Gideon was beating out[510] grain in a winepress. This was a sign of the uncertainty of the times. In the absence of modern technology, grain was threshed by first beating the heads of the cut stalks with a flail, discarding the straw, and then tossing the mixture of chaff and grain in the air, allowing the wind to blow away the chaff while the heavier kernels of grain fell to the floor. In the present critical circumstances this obviously would have been unwise. Threshing activity on the hilltops would only have aroused the attention of the marauding Midianites. Therefore Gideon resorts to beating the grain in a sheltered vat used for press-

---

[505] Though in that context the narrator uses כָּרַת, "to cut off," a synonym of גָּדַע. These two words appear as a pair in Isa 22:25 and are alternated elsewhere in Exod 34:13; 2 Kgs 18:4; Deut 7:5; 2 Chr 14:2; 31:1. In 6:19 the word for young goat, גְּדִי, plays on his name as well. On the implicit connection between Gideon's name and his cutting down the Asherah see Garsiel, *Biblical Names*, 106; and on other metaphorical associations of the root גָּדַע see id., "Homiletical Name-Derivations as a Literary Device in the Gideon Narrative: Judges VI–VIII," *VT* 43 (1993): 305.

[506] See below on 7:32. For a consideration of the issues see D. I. Block, "Will the Real Gideon Please Stand Up? Narrative Style and Intention in Judges 6–9," *JETS* 40 (1997): 359–60.

[507] Cf. the alliterative pun on his name in 7:14, יוֹאָשׁ אִישׁ יִשְׂרָאֵל, "Joash a man of Israel."

[508] "The Abiezrite" translates אֲבִי הָעֶזְרִי, lit. "my father the Ezrite," a gentilic modification of אֲבִיעֶזֶר, which means something like "my [divine] Father is help." Cf. Garsiel, who translates the name "the God of my father has or will come to my aid" ("Homiletic Name Derivations," 304).

[509] Cf. J. M. Hamilton, *ABD* 5.28. On ʿAfula see M. Dothan, "ʿAfula," *NEAEHL* 1.37–39.

[510] The word חָבַט occurs elsewhere in Deut 24:20 (of olives), Ruth 2:17 (of grain), Isa 28:27 (of dill), and Isa 27:12 (of the nations).

ing grapes. Generally winepresses involved two excavated depressions in the rock, one above the other. The grapes would be gathered and trampled in the upper, while a conduit would drain the juices to the lower. The present location would have been satisfactory for beating out the grain, but separating the grain from the chaff in these circumstances would have been more difficult. Either he would have had to wait for a very windy day or the grain and chaff mixture would have to be carried quickly to an exposed area, tossed in the air, and the grain quickly whisked away[511] to protect it from the Midianites.

Suddenly, while he is preoccupied with his threshing activity, a messenger of Yahweh appears, seated under the oak tree that apparently provided shade and shelter for the winepress. Contrary to popular opinion, as in 2:1–4, this *malʾak yhwh* is not to be confused with winged angelology. The term *malʾāk* simply means an officially authorized spokesperson for a superior. The narrator highlights the total identification of the envoy with his commissioning authority by having him speak in the first person, thereby representing the voice of Yahweh and identifying the speaker in this exchange alternatingly as Yahweh's "messenger/angel" and as Yahweh himself. Indeed, as in Exodus 23 and 34 this *malʾāk* functions as Yahweh's alter ego. The following sequence of events will demonstrate that this is not a human prophet (*ʾîš nābîʾ*, v. 8) but a heavenly visitor.[512] This person represents/delivers God's answer to the cry of the Israelites (vv. 6–7).[513]

6:12 The narrator offers no clue in v. 11 how long the messenger had been sitting under the oak watching the thresher at work before he allowed himself to be seen[514] by Gideon in v. 12. Suddenly he becomes visible and audible, initiating conversation by announcing the presence of Yahweh with Gideon. "The LORD is with you, mighty warrior!" is a strange way to begin a conversation, but it focuses Gideon's (and the reader's) attention on the central issue in the narrative: Where is Yahweh when you need him?

The opening statement is also strange because of its double incongruity. First, how can Gideon be addressed as a "mighty warrior/hero" *(gibbôr heḥāyil)* when he is threshing his grain in the winepress and hiding under the oak? He looks anything but valiant. Some interpret the messenger's characterization of Gideon as a prophetic/proleptic statement. But it is preferable to

---

[511] לְהָנִיס, thus correctly rendered by Boling, *Judges*, 130.

[512] Though the parallels in construction between "and he sat under the oak which is at Ophrah," and "and she sat under the palm between Ramah and Bethel" (4:5; author translation), suggest this person's role in this narrative corresponds to that of Deborah in chap. 4.

[513] It may be significant that from the time the messenger declares, "The LORD is with you" (v. 12) until the person responds to Gideon's offering in v. 20, the divine being is referred to as the Lord. When the word מַלְאָךְ returns, it is as "the messenger of God" rather than "the messenger of the LORD," which takes over in v. 21.

[514] וַיֵּרָא, NIV "appeared," may be interpreted as a tolerative *niphal*, on which see *IBHS* §23.4g; *GBH* §51c.

understand this simply as a flattering address, designed to win the sympathy of the man to what he is about to tell him. Alternatively, one may interpret the phrase less as an expression of commendation than as a recognition of his standing in the village; he is an "aristocrat."[515] Second, how can the messenger declare that God is with Gideon or any of the Israelites for that matter?

6:13 On the surface Gideon's initial response, "Excuse me, my lord!" sounds polite, but the expression may also be interpreted less positively.[516] In the following comment he disregards the divine envoy's personal flattery and answers with a cheeky and sarcastic focus on the theological incongruity: "If the LORD is with us, then why our present crisis! And where are all his miracles which the ancestors talked about? They told stories[517] about Yahweh bringing them up from Egypt, but where is he now? Why have the miracles stopped?"[518] The change from singlular "you" to plural "us" suggests that Gideon did not even hear the messenger's personal word of assurance. Instead he draws two conclusions that undoubtedly expressed the verdict of many of his countrymen: (1) Yahweh has abandoned Israel. (2) Yahweh has delivered the nation into the Midianites' hands.[519]

Gideon's response to the divine messenger is theologically correct and in agreement with the unnamed prophet's word in vv. 9–10, but his tone of voice is wrong. Instead of acknowledging Israelite responsibility for the present crisis (v. 1), he blames God. Gideon is an example of those who know what God has done in the past,[520] who have memorized the creed, but find it belied by present reality. Stories of past deliverance are irrelevant in light of the Midianite crisis.

6:14 But the divine messenger seems not even to have been listening to Gideon. Verse 14 could have followed logically immediately after v. 12. "Go in this your strength," Yahweh says.[521] The expression *bĕkōḥăkā zeh*, "in this your strength," is quite ambiguous. On the one hand, if the divine messenger is looking at Gideon from the perspective of the end of the story, that is, Gideon's conduct in chap. 8, he may be referring to the man's natural power and courage. On the other hand, he probably is thinking of the power with which God will invest him as he commissions him. Later the enduement with divine power

---

[515] Thus Boling, *Judges*, 131.

[516] This rendering for בִּ֣י אֲדֹנִי is preferable to the NIV's bland "But Sir." Cf. *GBH* §105c.

[517] Hb. סִפְּרוּ, "narrated."

[518] The expression נִפְלְאוֹת, "miracles, extraordinary acts," links this narrative with the call of Moses and the Exodus narratives (Exod 3:20; 34:10).

[519] Gideon's rebuttal represents a sarcastic rejection of the theology expressed by the name of his clan, Abiezer ("the [divine] father is my aid").

[520] It has been handed down by the ancestors. Cf. 2:10.

[521] The LXX "fixes" the text by reading "the angel" in place of "the LORD." The MT, which is preferred as the more difficult reading, highlights the identification of Yahweh's envoy with God himself. Cf. the use of the first person in the following speech.

will be expressed more graphically as "being clothed with the Spirit of the
LORD" (v. 34). Like the other deliverers in the book, Gideon's authority and
power are charismatically bestowed by God. Gideon's specific charge is to
deliver Israel from the grasp of Midian. The commissioning (and investiture)
formula, "Surely I have sent you,"[522] presents Gideon with all the authority he
will need for the task. This fearful and cynical farmer is hereby informed that
God has indeed heard the people's cry of pain, and he has personally chosen
him to solve the problem.[523]

The Objection (6:15). **6:15** As in v. 13, Gideon's opening response to
the envoy's second speech, "Excuse me, my lord!"[524] sounds polite, but his
tone continues to be cynical. He obviously does not yet recognize the person
who has addressed him. Like Moses in an earlier era, Gideon expresses his
sense of incompetence and inadequacy, particularly his lack of social standing
in Israel. Disregarding the envoy's opening address, "mighty warrior/hero," or
"aristocrat," he complains of two strikes that are already against him: his clan
(*eleph*) is the least important[525] in Manasseh, and he is the youngest in his
father's household.[526] Gideon does not realize that in Yahweh's work it does
not matter what one's social position is; the authorization of Yahweh is all he
needs. Having no experience with the divine presence, he cannot imagine
beyond his own human resources (or lack thereof).

The Reassurance (6:16). **6:16** In response to Gideon's objection, Yahweh[527] offers two words of encouragement. First, playing on Exod 3:12–
14,[528] he promises his presence in the undertaking.[529] As in the case of
Moses, the fearful Gideon is to be transformed into the deliverer of his people by the powerful presence of God.[530] This utterance provides the clue to
Gideon's actions later when he finally goes on the offensive against the Midianites. Second, Yahweh predicts an easy victory: Gideon will smite Midian
as if he were engaging a single person. Glancing backward one notices that

---

[522] The NIV treats הֲלֹא שְׁלַחְתִּ֑יךָ as a rhetorical question, but the introductory word is better
treated as an emphatic particle. Cf. Brown, "'Is it not?' or 'Indeed!'" 201–19. The present expression is equivalent to אָנֹכִ֖י שְׁלַחְתִּ֑יךָ, "It is indeed I who send you," in Exod 3:12.

[523] Compare Yahweh's fuller speech to Moses in Exod 3:7–12.

[524] The NIV follows the MT, "but LORD" (אֲדֹנָ֑י), in v. 13 rather than the LXX κύριε μου, "my
Lord," reflecting אֲדֹנִ֑י, "but Sir." The LXX probably preserves the original reading.

[525] דַּל, "poor, thin, weak," is cognate to the verb דָּלַל, "to be low," in v. 6.

[526] On the relative status of "father's house" and clan see p. 32f.

[527] The LXX again reads "angel."

[528] כִּ֥י אֶֽהְיֶ֖ה עִמָּ֑ךְ here is a direct quotation from Exod 3:12. Cp. also אֶהְיֶ֖ה אֲשֶׁ֣ר אֶהְיֶ֑ה, "I
am who I am," in 3:14. Boling (Judges, 132) treats *Ehyeh* as a divine name.

[529] The present use of the future אֶֽהְיֶ֖ה עִמָּ֑ךְ compares with the preference for the present
יהוה עִמְּךָ in v. 12.

[530] Cf. C. D. Isbell, "The Divine Name *ʾhyh* as a Symbol of Presence in Israelite Tradition,"
HAR 2 (1978): 107.

each of Yahweh's/the messenger's speeches has referred to God's presence with him (though the pattern changes) and the strength present/available to Gideon.[531]

The Authenticating Sign (6:17–24). **6:17** Having received the promise of divine presence and perhaps recognizing the connection between Yahweh's speeches here and his words of reassurance to Moses, Gideon goes on the offensive. In Moses' case God's authenticating signs were performed in response to the man's expressed worry that his countrymen would not believe that God had appeared to him or listen to what he said (Exod 4:1). Reflecting Gideon's growing self-confidence, on his own initiative he dares to put the messenger/God to the test by demanding a sign.[532] His demand is driven by two concerns: (a) to confirm Yahweh's favor upon him, expressed in the opening conditional clause; (b) to confirm Yahweh's presence with him in this venture. The first aim reflects Gideon's nagging uncertainty regarding his own relationship to the person speaking, the commissioner. The second relates to his commission: he seeks confirmation that God will in fact be with him and that he will receive the needed strength to defeat Midian as if they were a single man.[533] Gideon's lack of confidence in Yahweh persists until vv. 36–40, where he self-consciously tests God that he may know that God will deliver Israel through him as he has promised.

6:18–19 Gideon does not only demand a sign of Yahweh/the messenger but also dictates the nature of the sign. First, he requests the divine visitor not to move until he comes back with an offering, which he proposes to lay before

---

[531] Note the AB BA AB pattern of motifs:
v. 12   a   "the LORD is with you."
          b   "Mighty hero."
v. 14   b   "Go in this your strength."
          a   "Surely I have sent you."
v. 16   a   "I am with you."
          b   "You shall defeat Midian as if they were one man."

[532] Gideon's demand for a sign also contrasts with Yahweh's invitation to Ahaz to request a sign in Isa 7:11. "Perform a sign for me" is a more accurate rendering for אוֹת לִי וַעֲשִׂיה than the NIV's "Give me a sign."

[533] Although the NIV's "that it is [really] you talking to me" reflects prevailing opinion (cf. Soggin, *Judges*, 116), it is odd that Gideon should ask for a sign that the person who is talking to him is talking to him. If this had been his intention, the text should read either "then I will know who you are, talking to me" (עִמִּי מְדַבֵּר אַתָּה מִי וְיָדַעְתִּי) or "then I will know that the LORD is the one who is talking to me" (עִמִּי הַמְדַבֵּר יהוה כִי יָדַעְתִּי). W. Rudolph solves the problem by inserting the divine name in the clause: עִמִּי מְדַבֵּר יהוה אַתָּה שָׁאַתָּה, "that you are the LORD speaking with me" ("Textkritische Anmerkungen zum Richterbuch," *Festschrift Otto Eissfeldt zum 60. Geburtstag, 1. September dargebracht von Freunden und Verehren*, ed. J. Füch [Halle an der Saale: 1947], 202–3). Not only does the odd construction remain, however, but purposive "that" is an unusual interpretation of the relative conjunction שֶׁ (for שׁ, on which see *GBH* §39N). All the interpretive problems are resolved if this archaic particle (cf. above on 5:7) is rendered "pertaining to what [you are telling me]." Cf. Boling, *Judges*, 132.

him.[534] To this request the messenger agrees: "I will sit [here] until you return" (v. 18). Then Gideon goes home and prepares an offering, apparently based entirely on his own evaluation of what is appropriate. That he is preparing a meal for the gods/a god is evident from the nature and size of the offering: (1) "a young goat," which refers to an animal specially selected, rather than randomly picked;[535] (2) a huge amount of unleavened bread made from an ephah (twenty-two liters) of flour;[536] (3) a pot[537] of broth.[538] Carrying the meat in a tray,[539] he brings the offering to Yahweh/messenger under the oak.

6:20–21 Verses 20–21 describe the commissioner's response to the offering. As Gideon presents[540] the food, the messenger/Yahweh[541] seizes the initiative, commanding Gideon to lay the meat and the bread on the rock next to him[542] and to pour the broth over them. Gideon complies dutifully. When the envoy touches the meat and bread, fire bursts forth from the rock and burns up the entire offering. And the messenger vanishes from Gideon's sight. While the narrative offers no interpretation of the act, its significance is clear: when a deity consumes the meal a worshiper has brought, this is a sign the latter has found favor in the deity's sight. Gideon's first concern (v. 17a) should have been addressed.

6:22 But from Gideon's response in v. 22 he seems to have interpreted the messenger's response precisely the opposite. Recognizing appropriately that "no man can see the LORD's face and live,"[543] when the messenger disappears he bursts out "Alas,[544] my Lord Yahweh (NIV, "Sovereign LORD)!" It makes

---

[534] The word מִנְחָה refers fundamentally to a gift or tribute presented to secure or retain good will. Although the word usually denotes a particular kind of offering (cereal or grain), it may also function as a catchall expression, matching in scope the whole burnt offering (עוֹלָה). This seems to be the case here since in vv. 19–20 the מִנְחָה is seen to consist of the meat of the young goat, unleavened bread, and a broth libation. On the term see further Milgrom, *Leviticus*, 195–202, esp. pp. 196–97.

[535] So also in 13:15,19; 15:1. Cf. Gen 27:9,16; 38:17,20; 1 Sam 16:20.

[536] In 1 Sam 1:24 an ephah of flour accompanies a three-year-old bullock. According to Zech 5:6–10, an ephah container was large enough to hold a person.

[537] פָּרוּר refers to some type of boiling pot, but its precise nature is unknown. Cf. Num 11:11; 1 Sam 2:14. The term is related to Akk. *pūru*, "stone basin," for oil or fat. Cf. *AHw*, 881.

[538] מָרָק, which occurs elsewhere only in Isa 65:4 (*qere*; cf. *kethib* פָּרָק), refers to the liquid that results when meat is boiled in water. Syr *maṣlōl*, "wine," suggests it may have been flavored with wine.

[539] סַל denotes a shallow basket or tray. Cf. Gen 40:16–18; Exod 29:3,23,32; Lev 8:2,26,31; Num 6:15–19.

[540] וַיַּגֵּשׁ, "and he presented," at the end of v. 19 goes best with v. 20.

[541] The versions (LXX^A, Vg, Tg, Syr) harmonize MT's מַלְאַךְ אֱלֹהִים, "messenger of God," by reading מַלְאַךְ יהוה.

[542] חַסֶּלַע הַלָּז, "this here stone."

[543] Exod 33:20; cf. 24:11.

[544] The NIV's "Ah," for the paralinguistic utterance אֲהָהּ is too mild. Elsewhere this exclamation is equivalent to הוֹי or אוֹי, "Woe!" Cf. Joel 1:15. See further *DCH* 1.142.

no difference to Gideon whether this is Yahweh himself or the messenger of Yahweh. To encounter the messenger face-to-face is as lethal potentially as encountering God himself. In Gideon's confession one may hear echoes of Moses' encounters with God,[545] but Gideon does not interpret this as a sign of intimacy. He fears for his life.

6:23   Recognizing Gideon's fright, Yahweh reassures him with three weighty declarations: "Peace [to you]! Do not be afraid. You are not going to die." In the absence of any reference to the messenger, one may ask whether Gideon hears Yahweh's voice from the sky, without any visible sign of his presence. In any case, Gideon is encouraged to interpret this encounter with God in the most positive sense possible. His encounter with Yahweh is a mark of his acceptance with God. He may therefore get on with the mission to which he has been called.

6:24   Gideon demonstrates his acceptance of the intended meaning of the sign by constructing an altar and commemorating this event by naming it *yhwh Šālôm*, "Yahweh Is Peace." For the sake of his immediate readership, the narrator adds that the altar is still to be found in Ophrah,[546] in the territory allotted to the Abiezrite clan. Although critical scholars generally interpret this last comment as a literary mark of an aetiological legend,[547] it is more natural to accept the comment at face value. Like a footnote in a research paper, the author hereby invites his readers to check out the veracity of his story by going and visiting the site.

---

[25]That same night the LORD said to him, "Take the second bull from your father's herd, the one seven years old. Tear down your father's altar to Baal and cut down the Asherah pole beside it. [26]Then build a proper kind of altar to the LORD your God on the top of this height. Using the wood of the Asherah pole that you cut down, offer the second bull as a burnt offering."

[27]So Gideon took ten of his servants and did as the LORD told him. But because he was afraid of his family and the men of the town, he did it at night rather than in the daytime.

[28]In the morning when the men of the town got up, there was Baal's altar, demolished, with the Asherah pole beside it cut down and the second bull sacrificed on the newly built altar!

[29]They asked each other, "Who did this?"

When they carefully investigated, they were told, "Gideon son of Joash did it."

[30]The men of the town demanded of Joash, "Bring out your son. He must die, because he has broken down Baal's altar and cut down the Asherah pole beside it."

---

[545] Cf. Exod 33:11–23; Deut 34:10.

[546] The MT misvocalizes עָפְרָת for עָפְרָת.

[547] So Soggin, *Judges*, 117. Cf. Becker (*Richterzeit und Königtum*, 151), who suggests an ancient tradition of an altar aetiology has been secondarily combined with the tradition of the call of Gideon.

[31]But Joash replied to the hostile crowd around him, "Are you going to plead Baal's cause? Are you trying to save him? Whoever fights for him shall be put to death by morning! If Baal really is a god, he can defend himself when someone breaks down his altar." [32]So that day they called Gideon "Jerub-Baal," saying, "Let Baal contend with him," because he broke down Baal's altar.

The Charge to Clean House (6:25–32). Under normal circumstances the narrative should have proceeded directly from v. 24 to vv. 33–35, and then on to 7:1. But the normal sequence is interrupted twice to deal with a pair of abnormalities. The first is an objective issue, the presence of a pagan cult installation in Gideon's father's own backyard. The second is a subjective problem, Gideon's persistent resistance to the call of God. Gideon's construction of the altar to Yahweh at Ophrah (v. 24) represents a direct challenge to prevailing religious practices and perceptions in the area, symbolized by the altar of Baal at Ophrah. The narrator's reference to this altar catches the reader quite by surprise. On the other hand, it may help to account for Gideon's ignorance of Yahweh and his doubts concerning Yahweh's interest in his people. Like many others in Israel, this village has been paganized, and, while Gideon is aware of the traditions of Yahweh (v. 13), for all practical purposes he and his family are Baalists. Accordingly, just as Moses' son had to be circumcised before Moses could deliver Israel,[548] before he can embark on God's mission of deliverance Gideon must cut out the mark of apostasy at home. Pagan gods may tolerate the simultaneous worship of more than one deity, but Yahweh will brook no rivals. A fundamental tenet of covenant relationship in orthodox Yahwism is "You shall have no other gods besides me."[549] Therefore, for Gideon to serve as an agent of Yahweh in battle while his family was worshiping Baal at home posed a fundamental incongruity. This is one dimension of bearing the name of Yahweh in vain. At the same time, in charging Gideon to demolish the altar of Baal, God is pointing to the real problem in Israel. More serious than the oppression of the Midianites is their bondage to the spiritual forces of the land.[550]

The Divine Command (6:25–26). **6:25–26** The narrator is careful to emphasize that God wastes no time in engaging Gideon to challenge the prevailing religious establishment. That same night he returns to Gideon with

---

[548] Exod 4:24–26.

[549] Exod 20:1–7; cf. Deut 6:4.

[550] A. de Pury ("Le Raid de Gédéon (Juges 6,25–32) et l'histoire de l'exclusivisme Yahwiste," *Lectio Difficilior Probabiblior? Comme expérience de décloisonnement. Mélanges offerts à Françoise Smyth-Florentin,* ed. T. Römer [DBAT Beiheft 12; Heidelberg: Wissenschaftliche Theologie, 1991], 173–205) interprets this paragraph against the background of the Elijah cycle of narratives in which the primary emphasis is the impotence of Baal, vis à vis Yahweh. But he supposes an older tradition involving an earlier conflict between Gideon/Jerubbaal and the tribal deity Baal/Yahweh.

two demands, one negative, the second positive. First, he commands Gideon to destroy the cult installation on his father's property which includes an altar of Baal[551] and an Asherah pole. The text could be taken to suggest that Gideon is to "tear down" *(hāras)* the altar with two bulls. It could be more literally translated "Take the bull of the bullock [or "cattle" if understood collectively as in the NIV] which is your father's and [or "even"] the second [as traditionally understood] bull seven years old." However, not only does the first bull play no role in the narrative after v. 25, but also the narrator's method of identifying them is odd.[552] The problem is best resolved if one recognizes only one bull in this verse. Because the animal is sacrificed to Yahweh after it has been used to tear down the pagan altar, the narrator deemed it necessary to stress its appropriateness for this purpose. He does so by employing a triad of phrases to describe it.

First, the bull is identified as *par haššôr,* literally "the bull of the bullock," a strange expression that occurs only here. One might have expected an appositional form, *happar haššôr,* "the bull, that is the bullock," or *par ben bāqār,* literally "a bull the son of the herd," an expression that is common in sacrificial contexts. It is possible that since this bull belongs to Gideon's father, who is the sponsor of a pagan cult installation, and since it will be used to destroy a pagan altar, the traditional designation is to be avoided. The phrase appears to combine in a construct relation two words that appear elsewhere as a standardized pair, perhaps to express superlative or at least superior quality, "the prime bullock."[553]

Second, here, and twice more in vv. 26,28, the bull is also described as *par haššēnî,* traditionally rendered "the second bull."[554] Scholars have long recognized, however, the reference to a second bull in this context to be pointless. Although many resolve the issue by deleting the reference to a second bull as a later scribal insertion,[555] it is preferable to work with the received text and try to make sense of it. The most likely reading is provided by J. A. Emerton, who derives *haššēnî* from a different root (rather than "second"), meaning "to be exalted, of high rank."[556]

Third, the bull is seven years old,[557] that is, a mature animal. By this inter-

---

[551] The article on Baal and Asherah here and throughout this text reflects the fact that this Baal of Ophrah represents one of many local manifestations of the storm god Baal. Cf. Baal-Peor, Baal Hermon, etc.

[552] The problems with this verse are summarized by J. A. Emerton, "The 'Second Bull' in Judges 6:25–28," *ErIsr* 14 (1978): 52*.

[553] Cf. Ps 69:31 [Hb. 32].

[554] So NIV, NAS, AV, RSV, NRSV, JPSV.

[555] Becker (*Richterzeit und Königtum,* 151–60) suggests that the reference to the second bull along with Yahweh's altar and the Asherah were late insertions inspired by Elijah's contest with the Baal prophets in 1 Kings 18. But later scribes should clarify readings, not complicate them!

[556] Emerton, "The 'Second Bull' in Judges 6:25–28," 55–55*. Cognates have been suggested in Arabic and Syriac (where the root means "to sparkle, catch the eye"), as well as Ethiopic, Akk., and Ug.

pretation only one animal is involved.[558] To tear down the altar it had to be a strong animal, but as a sacrifice to Yahweh it had to be of the highest quality possible, "the prize bull, seven years old."

Yahweh instructs Gideon further to "cut down"[559] the Asherah. As noted earlier, Asherah functioned as the female counterpart to Baal in the fertility religion. This deity was normally represented as a carved wooden image with exaggerated sexual features.[560] After Gideon had destroyed the altar and the Asherah image, he was to construct an altar to Yahweh on top of the stronghold *(māʿôz)*.[561] Canaanite temple sanctuaries were often fortified with walls and towers. By commanding Gideon to build the altar on this pagan site, Yahweh is ordering him to reclaim this paganized land for himself. Then he was to commit the ultimate indignity against the pagan cult by offering to God the bull that he had used to destroy the altar to Baal, and he was to use the wood of the Asherah image as fuel.

Gideon's Obedient Response (6:27). **6:27** The ambiguities in Gideon's character are evident in the narrator's description of his response to the divine charge. On the one hand, his obedience is immediate. Before the night on which Yahweh had visited Gideon is over, he rushes to the place where the household servants sleep, awakens ten of them, and destroys the pagan installation "as the LORD told him." Generally Hebrew narrative invites readers to draw their conclusions regarding a person's character and motivation from his or her speech, gestures, and actions. Accordingly, if the verse had ended at the midpoint, we the readers would be favorably impressed with Gideon. However, the second half of the verse represents a rare literary moment when the narrator offers us access to the internal motivation of a character by explicit reference to an emotion.[562] The reader cannot help but be disappointed that the real motivation for his hasty obedience was not an eagerness to obey God but fear of the consequences from the citizens of Ophrah if he should tear down the altar of Baal in broad daylight.

But the necessity to act at night also leaves us disappointed with Israel because Gideon's fear arises out of an awareness of the true spiritual condition of the nation in premonarchic times. Gideon knows that his own family and his townsfolk will come to the defense of these pagan idols before they defend him, their kinsman, and fellow citizen.

---

[557] Though some prefer to read שֶׁבַע as שָׁבֵב, i.e., "fattened." Cf. Soggin, *Judges*, 124.

[558] So also REB, NAB, NJB.

[559] The verb כָּרַת is appropriate for a wooden image.

[560] On Asherah see J. Day, "Asherah in the Hebrew Bible and Northwest Semitic Literature," *JBL* 105 (1986): 385–408; id., *ABD* 1.483–87; Wyatt, "Asherah," *DDD*, 183–95.

[561] Or "place of refuge" (*HALOT*, 2.610). NIV translates "bluff."

[562] Cf. Alter, *Art of Biblical Narrative*, 163.

The Public Reaction (6:28–30).   **6:28–29a**   Verses 28–31 confirm the correctness of Gideon's assessment of his people. When the men of the city arise early the next day, they observe a shocking sight: the altar of Baal is smashed,[563] the Asherah image is cut down, and the ashes of Joash's bull are on the altar that had been built. Inadvertently they become witnesses to Gideon's compliance with every element in God's command.[564] Through the use of direct speech the narrator highlights their consternation. First, the agenda for their deliberation is set: "Who did this [thing]?" (i.e., "Who committed this crime?"). Significantly, there is no reflection on why their pagan cult installation lies in ruins. They have only one concern: to bring the "criminal" to justice (when they are the real criminals).

6:29b–30   Accordingly, they set up a commission to investigate the outrage. When they have completed their work, they present their report (again in direct speech): "Gideon the son of Joash did this [thing]" (i.e., "committed this crime"). Because Gideon was still living at home[565] and because in this patricentric society the head of a household was held accountable for the conduct of all its members, the men of the city approach Joash and demand that he deliver his son over to them. In typical Hebrew narrative style (cf. v. 27), their demand and motivation are transparent from their speech: they intend to execute Gideon for his crime. Again Gideon's earlier fears prove correct. The sentence that should have been imposed on idolators[566] is pronounced upon the one who destroys the idol! The Canaanization of Israelite society appears complete, leaving the reader amazed that Yahweh was still interested in delivering them!

In their citation of the incriminating evidence against Gideon, the men of Ophrah inadvertently give verbal testimony to the faithfulness of their townsman. In fact, their justification for the death penalty represents an almost verbatim repetition of Yahweh's original command and their earlier

---

[563] Hb. נָתַץ functions as a stylistic variant of הָרַס in v. 25.

[564] The opening particle הִנֵּה, "behold," and the detail with which the narrator describes the sight that greets the townsfolk concretizes the evidence of Gideon's obedience.

[565] He threshes grain in his father's winepress (v. 11); he claims to be the youngest in (not from) his father's house (בְּבֵית אָבִי, v. 15); the bull he uses to tear down the altar and then offer as a burnt offering belongs to his father (v. 25); the altar of Baal he tears down belongs to his father (v. 25); he acts at night because he fears the members of his father's household (v. 27).

[566] See Deut 13:1–18 [Hb. 13:2–19].

observation.[567] Significantly their report to Joash omits any reference to Yahweh's altar that Gideon had built or his own (best) bull, which had gone up in smoke on top of it.

Joash's Defense of His Son (6:31). 6:31 Remarkably Joash shows no interest whatsoever in the prime bull or even the cult installation he has lost. All that matters to him is his son. Recognizing the illogic of the position adopted by his accusers,[568] he begins by posing two rhetorical questions. The NIV rightly captures the legal force of the first, "Are you going to plead Baal's cause?" While the verb *rîb* may carry the simple sense of "strive, contend," in this legal context it denotes "stand up in defense of someone,"[569] as if Baal needs a defense attorney. The second question is even more pointed (lit.): "Will *you* save *him*?" (that is, Baal). The verb *hôšîaʿ* is the same word the narrator has used to define the role of the governors who deliver Israel. The irony is obvious. Instead of people needing deliverance from a hostile god, the god requires deliverance from the people! The words of Joash also express the author's disposition.

As the owner of the site on which these legal proceedings are being conducted and the installation that had been desecrated, Joash answers the sentence of the men of Ophrah upon his son with a sentence of his own. Anyone who stands up to defend Baal will be put to death before the night is over. There is no hint here of any awareness of Moses' pronouncement in Deuteronomy 13. He seems to assume simply that the one who defends Baal will come forward and execute his son on behalf of Baal, in which case, as father, he is authorized to mandate the death penalty for murder. The logic of his final argument is impeccable: "If Baal really is a god, let him defend himself because someone has torn down his altar." In other words, to desecrate a sacred object is to desecrate the one in whose name that object exists.

Joash's response leaves the reader wondering whether he himself has

---

[567] The principal elements in the three statements may be compared by juxtaposing them as follows:

vv. 25–26   Tear down (הֲרֹס) the altar of the Baal,
             And the Asherah which is beside it cut down,
             Take the finest bull and offer it as a whole burnt offering
             with the wood of the Asherah which you cut down.
v. 28   Behold the altar of the Baal was pulled down (נָתַץ),
             And the Asherah which was beside it was cut down,
             And the finest bull was offered as a whole burn offering on the altar on the altar which
                 had been built.
v. 30   Because he has pulled down (נָתַץ) the altar of the Baal,
             And because he has cut down the Asherah which was beside it.
[568] The hostile posture of Gideon's accusers toward him is clear to the narrator: עָמְדוּ עָלָיו,
"They stood against him."
[569] The opposite of their hostile posture toward Joash.

become convinced of the folly of his pagan ways. It sounds as though he has drawn the correct theological conclusions from his son's actions. As in the case of Elijah's contest with the prophets of Baal at Mount Carmel (1 Kings 18), Gideon appears to have won this contest on behalf of Yahweh. But the questions are rhetorical, and the issues are left hanging. Only time will tell.

The Aetiological Epilogue (6:32). **6:32** The call of Gideon had concluded with a confirming sign, an event that is memorialized in the construction and naming of an altar (v. 24). This event also concludes with a [re]naming ceremony: Gideon's father renames him "Jerub-baal" that very day.[570] The form of the name is difficult. Joash's explanation puts a positive spin on it, as if by hacking down Baal's altar and the Asherah Gideon has contended against Baal, and Baal is now challenged to defend himself against Gideon.[571] Traditionally the name *yĕrub-baʿal* has been interpreted as a jussive, "Let Baal contend [against him]." But this understanding is problematic for several reasons. First, *yārûb* never occurs as the jussive of *rîb*, "to strive, contend."[572] Second, by adding *bô*, "against him," the interpretation offered by Joash is in fact the opposite of what this form of theophoric name would have meant to a person not familiar with this story. Jerubbaal is a verbal sentence name following the prevalent predicate-subject order with "Baal" functioning as the subject of the verb, "will contend." Normally names of this sort lauded the deity for action on behalf of the one who gave or bore the name.[573] Accordingly, Joash may hereby be reflecting his fundamentally pro-Baalistic stance. This occurs ironically despite Gideon's apparent discrediting of Baal. Significantly, when later writers refer to Gideon by name, they use this name rather than "Gideon." Because some writers find its Baalistic form offensive, however, they change Jerubbaal to Jerubbesheth.[574]

---

[570] This verse is commonly attributed to a different hand, but see J. A. Emerton, "Gideon and Jerubbaal," *JTS* 27 (1976): 291.

[571] The jussive form יָרֶב בּוֹ הַבַּעַל, translates lit., "Let the Baal contend against him." Note the change of preposition from "Will you plead for [לְ] Baal" in v. 31 to בְּ, "against," in v. 32.

[572] Presumably *rûb* functions as a biform of *rîb*. This is not uncommon in "hollow" verbs (e.g., שִׂים/שׂוּם, "to set, put"). The imperfect form תָּרוּב occurs in Prov 3:30 (*kethib*) and the infinitive construct רוּב occurs in Judg 21:22 (*kethib*). But in both cases the scribes recognized the problem and called for a more conventional *qere* reading. See further *GBH* §81a. An alternative etymology has been proposed by M. Noth (*Die Israelitische Personennamen im Rahmen der Gemeinsemitischen Namengebung* [1928; reprint, Hildesheim: G. Olms, 1966], 206), who derives יָרֵב from רָבַב, "to be great," hence, "Let Baal prove himself to be great." Less likely is the derivation of the verb element from רָבַב, "to hurt, shoot," as proposed by M. Tsevat ("Ishbosheth and Congeners," *HUCA* 46 [1975]: 82).

[573] Cf. J. D. Fowler, *Theophoric Personal Names in Ancient Hebrew: A Comparative Study*, JSOTSup 49 (Sheffield: JSOT Press, 1988), 84–111.

The ambiguity of the name is heightened by a comparison of the immediate event with the long-range character of Gideon's rule. Gideon's action here appears to have exposed the impotence of Baal irrefutably. But this account should be read in light of 8:27, according to which Gideon himself revives and expands the influence of the Baal cult at Ophrah, and 8:33, which seems to have the Israelites entering into some sort of covenant with Baal. Did Baal contend for himself? Apparently yes. In the end he is vindicated. He has risen again in Israel, which makes the coming deliverance that Yahweh provides all the more remarkable. Despite the nation's fundamental Canaanization, God still acts on their behalf.

GOD'S GIFT OF DELIVERANCE (6:33–8:3).   The primary plot resumes in 6:33, which would have followed immediately after v. 24 if the narrator had not chosen to dwell on the circumstances in Israel attendant to Gideon's call.

³³Now all the Midianites, Amalekites and other eastern peoples joined forces and crossed over the Jordan and camped in the Valley of Jezreel. ³⁴Then the Spirit of the LORD came upon Gideon, and he blew a trumpet, summoning the Abiezrites to follow him. ³⁵He sent messengers throughout Manasseh, calling them to arms, and also into Asher, Zebulun and Naphtali, so that they too went up to meet them.

Gideon's Preparation for Battle (6:33–35).   **6:33–35**   Verse 33 brings the reader back to the broader reality, reminding the reader of the crisis that had precipitated the call of Gideon. The Midianites and their allies have crossed the Jordan again and have set up camp in the fertile valley of Jezreel. This incursion into northern tribal territory suggests they were free to roam about the land at will. Remarkably, according to vv. 34–35, when Gideon summons his clansmen, the Abiezrites, to battle against the enemy, the very people who had just called for his death (v. 30) respond to the sound of his ram's horn *(šôpār)* and prepare for battle (cf. on 3:27). Gideon then extends the call to arms, first to the rest of his own tribe, Manasseh, and then to Manasseh's northern tribal neighbors, those who were also feeling the pressure of the enemy camped in the Jezreel Valley: Asher, Zebulun, Naphtali. Remarkably, when his messengers *(malʾākîm)* deliver his summons, they all the people respond.

This raises an extremely important question: Why are Gideon's clansmen, tribesmen, and countrymen so ready to respond to him? Are they impressed with his leadership ability or his courage? Do they recognize him as the "valiant warrior," whom the messenger of Yahweh had addressed in v. 12? Not if one may judge from his expressed perception of his standing within his own

---

⁵⁷⁴ 2 Sam 11:21. The name of Baal is replaced by a form of the Hb. word for "shame." Cp. similar alterations of Ishbaal, "man of Baal" (1 Chr 8:33; 9:39), to Ishbosheth, "man of shame" (2 Sam 2:8), and Meribaal (1 Chr 8:34) to Mephibosheth (2 Sam 11:21). By this reading "Jerubbesheth" means "Let shame contend." For other homiletical implications of the renaming of Gideon as Jerubbaal see Garsiel, "Homiletical Name-Derivations," 306–7; id., *Biblical Names,* 180.

family and his tribe (v. 15) when God calls him to military leadership or from the trepidation with which he destroyed the Baal cult site in the preceding account (v. 31). From the succeeding narrative of the dew and the fleece (vv. 36–40) it seems that nothing has changed internally or personally. Gideon remains hesitant. Juxtaposed with a text that portrays Gideon doing all he can to avoid a leadership role, the answer must lie in the opening clause of v. 34: the Spirit of Yahweh "clothed" Gideon. This idiom expresses in more dramatic form the notion expressed earlier in 3:10: "The Spirit of the LORD came upon X,"[575] that is, the Spirit took possession of the man.[576] As we have noted earlier and will witness repeatedly hereafter, if anything positive happens to Israel in the Book of Judges, the credit must go to God. As in the cases of Jephthah in 11:29, and especially Saul in 1 Sam 11:6–8, the same Spirit which possesses the divinely called deliverer compels the recipients of the summons to respond to his call.

[36]Gideon said to God, "If you will save Israel by my hand as you have promised— [37]look, I will place a wool fleece on the threshing floor. If there is dew only on the fleece and all the ground is dry, then I will know that you will save Israel by my hand, as you said." [38]And that is what happened. Gideon rose early the next day; he squeezed the fleece and wrung out the dew—a bowlful of water.

[39]Then Gideon said to God, "Do not be angry with me. Let me make just one more request. Allow me one more test with the fleece. This time make the fleece dry and the ground covered with dew." [40]That night God did so. Only the fleece was dry; all the ground was covered with dew.

Gideon's Second Thoughts (6:36–40). **6:36–40** These verses catch the reader totally by surprise. Even though Gideon has been empowered by Yahweh and is surrounded by a vast army of troops, he hesitates. He continues to test God with demands for signs, this time specifically for assurance that God will indeed use him to provide deliverance for the nation,[577] "as [he] has promised." The latter expression, which occurs twice (vv. 36,37), is the key to this text. Contrary to popular interpretation, this text has nothing to do with discovering or determining the will of God. The divine will is perfectly clear in his mind (v. 16). Gideon's problem is that with his limited experience with God he cannot believe that God always fulfills his word. The request for signs is not a

---

[575] The present idiom, רוּחַ יהוה לָבְשָׁה, occurs elsewhere only in 1 Chr 12:18 and 2 Chr 24:20. Contra Soggin (*Judges*, 129), the expression occurs too infrequently to be characterized as "late."

[576] N. M. Waldman ("The Imagery of Clothing, Covering, and Overpowering," *JANES* 19 [1989]: 161–70) has demonstrated that the Spirit's clothing of Gideon reflects a well-known ANE idiom describing a person as covered/overwhelmed by divine or demonic forces.

[577] Cp. the form of the conditional clause אִם־יֶשְׁךָ מוֹשִׁיעַ with Gen 24:42,49; 43:4; 1 Sam 23:23. For a discussion of the form see Muraoka, *Emphatic Words*, 77–82.

sign of faith but of unbelief. Despite being clear about the will of God, being empowered by the Spirit of God, and being confirmed as a divinely chosen leader by the overwhelming response of his countrymen to his own summons to battle, he uses every means available to try to get out of the mission to which he has been called. The narrator apparently recognizes the incongruity of the situation by deliberately referring to God by the generic designation Elohim rather than his personal covenant name Yahweh. Apparently Gideon has difficulty distinguishing between Yahweh, the God of the Israelites, and God in a general sense.[578] The remarkable fact is that God responds to his tests. He is more anxious to deliver Israel than to quibble with this man's semipagan notions of deity.[579]

Gideon does not confess his motives at the beginning, but in the end he admits that he has been testing (*nissēh*, v. 39) Yahweh, which places this event in the same category as Israel's testing of Yahweh at Rephidim (Exod 17:2,7). The present sequence of events, in which the test of Yahweh follows a divine word and particularly miraculous signs (*ʾôt*) of his presence, links Gideon's response even more closely with the Israelites' testing of Yahweh during the desert wanderings.[580]

Gideon's test of Yahweh occurs in two stages. First, he proposes to lay a fleece[581] of wool on the threshing floor overnight. If the fleece is wet with dew in the morning but the ground around it is dry, then he will know [and presumably accept] that Yahweh will fulfill his promise to deliver Israel through him. That is precisely what happened. In fact, like Gideon in v. 19 God's demonstration of the veracity of his word exceeds normal expectations. In the morning the fleece is so wet Gideon is able to wring a bowl of water from it. Unlike Yahweh, Gideon is not true to his word. Gideon's refusal to believe and/or accept the divine word and the divine sign leaves the reader suspicious that Gideon is trying to get out of his assignment. In any case, although he initiates his new demand apologetically, this should not blind the reader to the manner

---

[578] Despite the characterization of Yahweh as Gideon's God in v. 26.

[579] M. Dijkstra ("KTU 1.6 [= CTA].III.1FF. and the So-called Zeichenbeweiss [Proof by a Token]," *VT* 35 [1985]: 105–9) notes that in the ANE people often arranged for a test to remove doubt or settle a question by means of a sign or an ordeal. The following represents his translation of a Ug. account of a comparable sign demanded of El in an incubation dream in KTU 1.6.III:

    a. And if Baʿal, the Almighty, is alive and if his Highness, the Lord of the Earth, exists,

    b. in a dream of the Benevolent, El, the Good-Hearted, in a vision of the Progenitor of creation (?)

    c. the skies will rain oil,

    the wadies will run with honey,

    d. and I shall know that Baʿal, the Almighty, is alive,

    that his Highness, the Lord of Earth, exists.

[580] Note the linkage between signs and testing in Num 14:22; Pss 78:17,41, 56; 95:9; 106:14.

[581] The term for fleece, גִּזָּה, which appears only in this context (vv. 37,40), derives from גָּזַז, "to shear." Cf. Gen 31:19; 38:12–13.

in which Gideon is trying to manipulate God. As we have witnessed so often before, the remarkable fact is that Yahweh lets himself be manipulated. Despite the nation's spiritual disaffection, he is obviously more interested in preserving his people than they are in preserving themselves.

¹Early in the morning, Jerub-Baal (that is, Gideon) and all his men camped at the spring of Harod. The camp of Midian was north of them in the valley near the hill of Moreh. ²The LORD said to Gideon, "You have too many men for me to deliver Midian into their hands. In order that Israel may not boast against me that her own strength has saved her, ³announce now to the people, 'Anyone who trembles with fear may turn back and leave Mount Gilead.'" So twenty-two thousand men left, while ten thousand remained.

⁴But the LORD said to Gideon, "There are still too many men. Take them down to the water, and I will sift them for you there. If I say, 'This one shall go with you,' he shall go; but if I say, 'This one shall not go with you,' he shall not go."

⁵So Gideon took the men down to the water. There the LORD told him, "Separate those who lap the water with their tongues like a dog from those who kneel down to drink." ⁶Three hundred men lapped with their hands to their mouths. All the rest got down on their knees to drink.

⁷The LORD said to Gideon, "With the three hundred men that lapped I will save you and give the Midianites into your hands. Let all the other men go, each to his own place." ⁸So Gideon sent the rest of the Israelites to their tents but kept the three hundred, who took over the provisions and trumpets of the others.

Now the camp of Midian lay below him in the valley.

The Reduction of Gideon's Troops (7:1–8). The transition between chaps. 6 and 7 is awkward, for chap. 6 closes with the reader wondering how Gideon might have responded to Yahweh's compliance with his second request concerning the fleece. It is evident from 7:1, however, that Gideon finally accepted God's call to divine service. Within the Gideon story proper (6:1–8:35) the plot reaches its climax in chap. 7 as Yahweh provides a spectacular victory over the dreaded enemy. But the victory is not immediate. One might have expected the narrative to move quickly from v. 1 to v. 19, but it takes several detours, the first instigated by God (vv. 2–8) and the second originating with Gideon (vv. 9–18). The author's inclusion of both episodes is intentional, highlighting in different ways the fact that if the Midianite menace is ever removed it is entirely to Yahweh's credit.

7:1 Chapter 7 opens with Gideon and the troops he has assembled from Manasseh, Asher, Zebulun, and Naphtali (6:35) rising early and setting up camp at the spring of Harod. The narrator surprises the reader once more, however, by identifying the general as Jerubbaal instead of Gideon.[582] In fact, the narrator seems to have caught himself by surprise, for he adds that

---

[582] This will not happen again until 8:29.

Gideon is his familiar name. It seems that even though the author is on to the next phase of the account, the previous episode lingers in his mind. Gideon is inconsistent—in the end he steps out for Yahweh and wins a great victory, but as the reluctant warrior who manipulates God his name is Jerubbaal.[583]

The site where Gideon deploys his forces is significant for several reasons. Most obviously, as v. 1b indicates, the Israelite base is located opposite the Midianite forces camped on the north side of the Harod Valley, against the hill of Moreh.[584] Strategically, by camping at a spring[585] Gideon ensures that a refreshed force may be sent against the enemy. But from a literary point of view, since the name "Harod" derives from a verb, *harad,* "to tremble," this is also "the spring of trembling." Whether or not Gideon still trembles at the sight of the Midianites despite Yahweh's repeated assurances, v. 3 indicates the majority of his troops did.

7:2 In v. 2 Yahweh raises a problem before Gideon, but it is quite the opposite of what we would have expected. From a human perspective we might have anticipated, "The people who are with Midian are too many for me to give them into your hands," but the problem here is the opposite (lit.): "The people who are with you are too many." Obviously the issue is not that God cannot win the victory but Israel's potential response. Given their spiritual independence and waywardness, if the massive forces under Gideon defeat the Midianites, they will claim the credit for themselves rather than crediting Yahweh with delivering the enemy into their hands.[586] So as Commander in Chief, Yahweh prescribes a two-stage process of refinement by which Gideon must reduce his troops (v. 3).

7:3 First, God instructs Gideon to announce to all the troops that any who are frightened[587] at the prospect of battle with the Midianites may turn around

---

[583] For a detailed analysis of the ambivalent characterization of Gideon see Block, "Will the Real Gideon Please Stand Up?" 353–66.

[584] The Hill of Moreh (גִּבְעַת הַמּוֹרֶה), lit. "hill of the teacher" (cf. Boling's "Teacher's Hill," *Judges,* 144) witnessed several other significant events recorded in the Bible: Saul's rendezvous with the witch of Endor (1 Samuel 28); Elisha's raising of the Shunemite woman's son (2 Kings 4); Jesus' raising of the son of the widow of Nain (Luke 7). According to Malamat ("The War of Gideon and Midian—A Military Approach," *PEQ* 84 [1952]: 61–65; id., "Period of the Judges, 143–47), the geographical requirements of this passage are well satisfied by the topography of the Harod Valley.

[585] The spring of Harod is traditionally identified with Ain Jalud, nine miles WNW of Beth Shan. See M. Hunt, "Harod," *ABD* 3.62.

[586] Cf. Deut 8:17; 32:26–27.

[587] מִי יָרֵא וְחָרֵד, "Who is afraid and trembling," is a hendiadys for "who tremble with fright."

and "fly"[588] from the "mount of trembling."[589] For one as fearful as Gideon himself, the sight of more than two-thirds of his troops (twenty-two thousand of thirty-two thousand)[590] abandoning him must have been both shocking and dismaying.

7:4 Second, Yahweh no doubt increases Gideon's anxiety by telling him the troops are still too many. He commands Gideon to take his people down to the spring where God will refine them.[591]

At the spring Yahweh prescribes the refining process. The NIV follows the traditional understanding of vv. 5b–6 in assuming the two conditions specified represent two different groups of men: those who lap water like a dog (clause A) and those who kneel to drink (clause B). This creates serious textual and logistical problems,[592] however, since the responses described in v. 6 do not match the conditions. On the other hand, if the conjunction at the beginning of the second condition is treated as an epexegetical *waw*, that is, if clause B is intended to clarify clause A, then the picture becomes perfectly clear. When these men go down to the spring and try to lap water like a dog, they must get down on their knees. It is impossible to drink otherwise.[593] Whereas the first phase of the troop reduction had eliminated those who were afraid (v. 3); in the

---

[588] וְיִצְפֹּר is a hapax verb form of uncertain meaning. It seems best to associate the verb with צִפּוֹר, "bird," and to link it with Akk. *sabaru*, which in the D stem describes an enemy jumping up from a table in fear. Cf. *AHw*, 1065.

[589] The traditional reading of הַר הַגִּלְעָד, reflected in the NIV's "Mount Gilead," creates impossible problems inasmuch as the only Gilead known in the OT is the mountainous region east of the Jordan. The NRSV's "Gideon sifted them out" follows BHS' suggested emendation to נִדְעוֹן וַיִּצְרְפֵם. So also *HALOT* 1.195. A more likely alteration is to read גִּלְבֹּעַ, "Gilboa," the name of the mountain overlooking the Harod Valley from the south (*DCH* 2.356). But the best solution associates גִּלְעָד with the modern name of the spring, Ain Galud, the latter word of which is cognate to Akk. *galadu/galtu*,, "to be afraid." Cf. *AHw*, 274.

[590] The numbers seem high, but they accord with 4:6.

[591] The NIV's translation of the verb צָרַף, as "to test," misinterprets it as synonymous with נָסָה, used in Gen 22:1 and above in Judg 6:39. But צָרַף is a metallurgical term used of refining ore by removing the impurities. Cf. 17:4, where the participle of the same root denotes a [gold]smith.

[592] Hebrew consists of two uneven clauses (rendered lit.): "Everyone who laps with his tongue from the waters like the dog laps you shall set him by himself; and [or "even"] everyone who bends on his knees to drink [...?]" BHS and many commentators assume a garbled text and add the supposedly missing part to the end from LXX^A: μεταστήσεις αὐτὸν καθ᾿ αὐτόν, "you shall remove him by himself" (cf. also Syr and Vg). With O'Connell (*Rhetoric of the Book of Judges*, 467), it may be argued that the ellipsis is original, the author expecting the reader to fill in the blank. Klein (*Triumph of Irony*, 56–57) resolves the logistical problems by proposing a two-step process, with v. 5 distinguishing "kneelers" from "nonkneelers" and v. 6 "kneelers who lap from their hands" and "kneelers who bow down to drink directly." For a detailed discussion of the issues see O'Connell, *Rhetoric of the Book of Judges*, 467–69, though O'Connell misses the most obvious solution proposed here.

[593] There is no need to follow O. Margalith ("*KELEB:* Homonym or Metaphor," *VT* 33 [1983]: 493), who interprets *keleb* as a synonym for "slave." Cf. G. Brunet, "L'hébreu kèlèb," *VT* 35 (1985): 485–88.

second phase those who tried to drink this way were to be considered slag or dross and sent back to their tents. Some have speculated that if the first phase (v. 3) represented a test of courage, the second was a test of alertness. It is difficult to watch out for the enemy if one kneels down and laps water directly from the spring.[594] But the means by which Yahweh identifies the men through whom he will achieve the victory over Midian may have been purely arbitrary.

7:5–7 The reader can only imagine Gideon's increased dismay when he saw the response of the troops to the refining conditions prescribed by Yahweh. While ninety-seven hundred knelt to drink water [like dogs], only three hundred brought the water up to their mouths with their cupped hands and lapped from them.[595] But this handful of men represents the pure gold which Yahweh desires in his service. His intentions are clarified in v. 7. Promising Gideon that he will indeed rescue Israel with the three hundred who lapped [from their hands] by handing the Midianites into their hands, he orders him to dismiss the rest.

7:8 The NIV rearranges the clauses of v. 8 to smooth the awkward transition from v. 7.[596] However apprehensive Gideon may have been, he dutifully sent those who had lapped like dogs back to their tents.[597] They would not be needed in this battle. However, the provisions[598] and trumpets they had brought with them down to the spring they left in the hands of the three hundred. Then Gideon took charge[599] of this pathetically small band and prepared to face the vast army of Midianites camped below them in the valley.

⁹**During that night the LORD said to Gideon, "Get up, go down against the camp, because I am going to give it into your hands. ¹⁰If you are afraid to attack, go down to the camp with your servant Purah ¹¹and listen to what they are saying. Afterward, you will be encouraged to attack the camp." So he and Purah his servant went down to the outposts of the camp. ¹²The Midianites, the Amalekites and all the other eastern peoples had settled in the valley, thick as locusts. Their camels could no more be counted than the sand on the seashore.**

¹³**Gideon arrived just as a man was telling a friend his dream. "I had a dream," he was saying. "A round loaf of barley bread came tumbling into the**

---

[594] Cf. Boling, *Judges*, 145.

[595] M. A. Zipor ("What Were the *kĕlābîm* in Fact?" *ZAW* 99 [1987]: 426–28) mistakenly reverses the numbers: three hundred lapped like dogs; the rest cupped their hands.

[596] Hb. v. 8 begins with the comment on the appropriation of the provisions of those who went home by those who remained with Gideon.

[597] The reference to "tents" (אָהֳלִים) suggests they did not go home but returned to the base, up the hill from the spring where the purification process had transpired.

[598] צֵדָה denotes the food and other supplies a person would pack for a journey or an army would take on a march. Cf. Judg 20:10; also Gen 42:25, etc.; 1 Sam 22:10. Contra *BHS* there is no need to emend צֵדָה, "provisions," to כַּדֵּי, "jars." However, the relationship with following הָעָם requires the construct form צֵדַת.

[599] הֶחֱזִיק means "to take hold of, to seize."

Midianite camp. It struck the tent with such force that the tent overturned and collapsed."

¹⁴His friend responded, "This can be nothing other than the sword of Gideon son of Joash, the Israelite. God has given the Midianites and the whole camp into his hands."

¹⁵When Gideon heard the dream and its interpretation, he worshiped God. He returned to the camp of Israel and called out, "Get up! The LORD has given the Midianite camp into your hands."

Gideon's Third Thoughts (7:9–15).   **7:9**   With the excess dross eliminated from Gideon's forces, Yahweh seems eager to get on with the battle. That same night, that is, as soon as the divinely elected warriors had been identified, God commanded Gideon to attack the Midianite camp, reassuring him that he had already won the victory for him. After the pattern of 4:14, following Yahweh's announcement, the reader expects Gideon to rally the troops and charge the Midianite camp. In fact, this would be the case if v. 9 were immediately followed by v. 15b. Verses 10–15a seem quite superfluous.[600] But unexpectedly the narrative takes a second detour. Whereas the earlier digression had been precipitated by the potential of smugness on Israel's part should they defeat the enemy in their own strength (v. 2), this one arises from the opposite problem: Gideon's personal lack of faith.

7:10–11   But this time God did not wait for Gideon to protest the reduction of his forces. He raised the issue himself when he addressed Gideon with a conditional clause, "If you are afraid …" The clause is cast as hypothetical, but obviously the problem is real. Yahweh had already designed a cure, however, and Gideon readily took him up on his offer. The fact that Gideon has had no experience with God working for Israel (cf. 6:13) no doubt contributed to his persistent faithlessness. To him the reduction of the forces to three hundred men must have seemed insane.

But Yahweh continued to be patient with Gideon. His prescription for the man's unbelief this time was a nocturnal visit to the enemy camp with Purah, his right hand man.[601] He predicted that Gideon would overhear a conversation among the Midianites that would give him new courage to launch the attack.[602] The open-endedness of the prediction no doubt created anticipation in Gideon's mind, even as it does for the modern reader. Not knowing what to

---

[600] Cp. the verses:

v. 9b קוּם רֵד בַּמַּחֲנֶה כִּי נְתַתִּיו בְּיָדֶךְ, "Get up, go down against the camp, because I am going to give it into your hands."

v. 15b קוּמוּ כִּי־נָתַן יְהוָה בְּיֶדְכֶם אֶת־מַחֲנֵה מִדְיָן, "Get up! The LORD has given the Midianite camp into your hands."

[601] Hb. נַעַר normally means "young man," but in military contexts such as this it refers to Gideon's personal attendant, perhaps his armor/shield bearer. Cf. 9:54. In 2 Sam 2:14–17 it refers to a "champion," in the classic sense of the term.

[602] The Hb. idiom תֶּחֱזַקְנָה יָדֶיךָ translates literally "your hands will be strengthened."

expect, Gideon and his attendant crept down to the edge of the Midianite camp where the sentries were posted.[603] What the two men witnessed there catches the reader by surprise.

7:12 Before describing the scene, the narrator inserts a parenthetical reminder of the gravity of Israel's situation (v. 12). Gideon's three hundred men are faced with an alliance of Midianite and Amalekite forces who blanket the valley like a locust plague[604] and whose camels are as innumerable as the sand on the seashore. Obviously, if Gideon was to find new courage, it would not come through any external alteration in Israel's desperate circumstances (cf. 6:5).

7:13 Yahweh's promise to Gideon that he would overhear a conversation that would give him new courage is fulfilled in v. 13. When Gideon and his attendant approached the Midianite camp, they overheard one of the enemy relating a portentous dream to his friend. The opening comment, "Behold, I had a dream," recalls reports of Joseph's dreams in Genesis.[605] From the advance notice of this conversation (v. 11) it is obvious to the author that Yahweh is exercising his own sovereign control over these historical events and that he has planted this dream in the Midianite's mind, specifically for the purpose of bolstering Gideon's spirit. At the same time, it is appropriate that, if he is to communicate with Gideon through this pagan, the message should come in the form of a dream. Only in exceptional cases (such as Balaam, Numbers 22–24) did he communicate to non-Israelites through visions or oracles. But with outsiders the preferred medium of revelation was the dream.[606] In keeping with common human experience, the content of this dream was quite absurd: a cake[607] of barley bread tumbled into the Midianites' camp, smashing

---

[603] Hb. חֲמֻשִׁים is a passive participle of a denominative verb from חָמֵשׁ, "five." Literally it means "divided in five parts," but in military contexts it means "lined up for war." Cf. *HALOT* 1.331.

[604] On the locust as a metaphor for invading armies see T. Hiebert, "Joel, Book of," *ABD* 3.876–77.

[605] הִנֵּה חֲלוֹם חָלַמְתִּי, "Behold a dream I dreamed," resembles חֲלוֹם חָלַמְתִּי הִנֵּה, "Behold I dreamed a dream" in Gen 37:9. This combination of cognate verb and object noun is regular in Hb. Cf. Gen 37:5,6,9,10; 40:5,8; 41:11a,11b,14; 42:9; Deut 13:2,4,6; Jer 23:25; 29:8; Dan 2:1,3; Joel 3:1. For a study of dream revelations in the OT see A. Jeffers, "Divination by Dreams in Ugaritic Literature and in the Old Testament," *IBS* 12 (1990) 167–83. On the form of biblical dream reports see R. Gnuse, "Dreams in the Night—Scholarly Mirage or Theophanix Formula? The Dream Report as a Motif of the So-called Elohist Tradition," *BZ* n.s. 39 (1995): 28–53.

[606] For other examples of God speaking to non-Israelites this way see the dreams of Abimelech (Gen 20:3,6), Laban (Gen 31:24), Pharaoh and his servants (Genesis 40–41), and Nebuchadnezzar (Dan 2:1–3). Orthodox Israelites seem to have viewed dreams as a lower order of revelation than visions or oracles (cf. Num 12:6), characteristic of false prophets (Deut 13:2,4,6; Jer 23:27,28,32; 27:9; 29:8; Zech 10:2) and resorted to by desperate men (Saul, 1 Sam 28:6,15). On divine communication through dreams in the ANE see A. L. Oppenheim, *The Interpretation of Dreams in the Ancient Near East*, Transactions of the American Philosophical Society 46/3 (Philadelphia: 1956).

into the tent[608] with such force that it overturned and collapsed it.

7:14 Like the dreams with which God providentially visited Pharaoh and Nebuchadnezzar, here he also provided an interpreter, in the form of a second Midianite. According to the construction of his response,[609] the interpreter had no doubts about its significance, but it leaves the reader wondering how this message can be derived from this dream. How can he link the cake of bread with Gideon? How does he know Gideon's name? Why does the tent represent Midian? Why does he interpret the dream negatively from the Midianite point of view? Why could the cake not represent the Midianite forces; and the smashed tent, the Israelite camp? For the narrator and for Gideon the answer is clear: this can be nothing other than the fulfillment of Yahweh's promise in v. 11.

7:15 Immediately upon hearing the dream and its interpretation[610] Gideon prostrated himself in worship before Yahweh.[611] Then he returned to the Israelite camp and summoned his troops to battle. Gideon's newly found confidence (also in fulfillment of God's promise, v. 11) is expressed in his call to action (*qûmû*, "Arise!") and his declaration to his troops that Yahweh has already delivered the Midianite camp into their hands.[612] The problem of Gideon's fearfulness had been resolved.[613] Now he is ready to proceed with Yahweh's agenda.

16Dividing the three hundred men into three companies, he placed trumpets and empty jars in the hands of all of them, with torches inside.
17"Watch me," he told them. "Follow my lead. When I get to the edge of the camp, do exactly as I do. **18**When I and all who are with me blow our trumpets, then from all around the camp blow yours and shout, 'For the LORD and for

---

[607] Hb. צָלִיל (Kethib צְלוּל) probably refers to a specific kind of pastry, perhaps a griddle cake (cf. Ezek 4:12), especially if the word is to be associated with the Hb. verb צָלַל, "to be, grow dark" (cf. Neh 13:19). Some link the word to Arabic *ṣalla*, "to go bad, become dry, stink, be putrid," hence "moldy" (thus Boling, *Judges*, 146). A connection with Akk. *ṣalālu*, "to lie, lay down" (*AHw*, 1075), hence "flat," is also possible.

[608] The singular "tent" functions as a collective for the entire camp.

[609] Hb. reads more literally, "This is nothing but the sword of Gideon the son of Joash, a man of Israel; God has given into his hands Midian and all the camp."

[610] The word for interpretation, שֶׁבֶר, lit. "breaking" [i.e., "solve" a riddle or code?], occurs with this sense only here in the OT. Elsewhere the notion of "solution, explanation" is expressed with פִּתְרוֹן (Gen 40:8,16,22; 41:8,12,13,15) and פֵּשֶׁר (Qoh 8:1; פְּשַׁר in Aramaic—Dan 2:4 + thirty times in Daniel).

[611] This is the only place in the book where the verb הִשְׁתַּחֲוָה, "to bow down, to worship," describes an Israelite's response to Yahweh. In its only two other occurrences (2:12,17) it describes Israel's response to pagan gods.

[612] The committal formula כִּי־נָתַן יְהוָה אֶת־מַחֲנֵה מִדְיָן בְּיֶדְכֶם, "For the LORD has given the camp of Midian into your hands," echoes Yahweh's words in v. 9 and recalls Ehud's and Deborah's similar declarations in 3:28 and 4:14 respectively.

[613] The scope of the noun שֶׁבֶר, "break, interpretation, solution," in v. 15a extends to the dream's effect on Gideon.

Gideon.'"

¹⁹Gideon and the hundred men with him reached the edge of the camp at the beginning of the middle watch, just after they had changed the guard. They blew their trumpets and broke the jars that were in their hands. ²⁰The three companies blew the trumpets and smashed the jars. Grasping the torches in their left hands and holding in their right hands the trumpets they were to blow, they shouted, "A sword for the LORD and for Gideon!" ²¹While each man held his position around the camp, all the Midianites ran, crying out as they fled.

²²When the three hundred trumpets sounded, the LORD caused the men throughout the camp to turn on each other with their swords. The army fled to Beth Shittah toward Zererah as far as the border of Abel Meholah near Tabbath. ²³Israelites from Naphtali, Asher and all Manasseh were called out, and they pursued the Midianites. ²⁴Gideon sent messengers throughout the hill country of Ephraim, saying, "Come down against the Midianites and seize the waters of the Jordan ahead of them as far as Beth Barah."

So all the men of Ephraim were called out and they took the waters of the Jordan as far as Beth Barah. ²⁵They also captured two of the Midianite leaders, Oreb and Zeeb. They killed Oreb at the rock of Oreb, and Zeeb at the winepress of Zeeb. They pursued the Midianites and brought the heads of Oreb and Zeeb to Gideon, who was by the Jordan.

Victory at Last (7:16–25). **7:16–18** Having been assured of victory, Gideon immediately began to prepare for the battle. His actions and instructions in vv. 16–18 demonstrate great concern for detail; but like Yahweh's instructions to Joshua before the storming of Jericho (Josh 6:1–5), the strategy appears totally absurd. Gideon's division of his forces into three companies[614] of one hundred men each follows traditional military custom,[615] to be sure, but to face the vast host of Midianites armed only with trumpets (i.e., rams horns, *šôparôt*)[616] and empty jars *(kaddîm)* with torches *(lappidîm)*[617] hidden inside is ridiculous. Obviously the outcome of this battle will not be determined by conventional standards of warfare.

The narrator's report of Gideon's instructions to his troops makes no reference to specific directives from God,[618] but the confidence exuded in Gideon's words[619] reflects an amazing personal transformation. He instructed his forces to keep their eyes on him and to do as he would do. When he would arrive at the edge of the Midianite camp, he and his group would blow their horns and

---

[614] Lit. "heads" (רָאשִׁים).
[615] Cf. 9:43; 1 Sam 11:11,13,17–18; 2 Sam 18:2.
[616] On which see 3:27.
[617] Cf. the name of Deborah's husband, Lappidoth, in 4:4.
[618] Cp. Yahweh's directives in Josh 6:1–5 with Joshua's instructions in vv. 6–7.
[619] The first person pronoun occurs six times in vv. 17–18.

cry out, "Belonging to the LORD and to Gideon!"[620] This declaration recognized that the battle belonged to Yahweh, the Commander-in-Chief,[621] and that Gideon was his deputy. Gideon's addition of his own name seems innocent enough, but in light of what follows in chap. 8 one wonders if the narrator does not intend some ambiguity here.

7:19–21a The account of the actual battle (vv. 19–22a) divides into two uneven parts: a detailed description of the human actions (vv. 19–21) and a summary theological interpretation (v. 22a). The elements of the former may be summarized briefly: (1) at the darkest hour of night[622] Gideon and the hundred men with him approached the enemy camp; (2) they blew their horns; (3) they smashed their jars; (4) they held high the torches that had been concealed in the jars; (5) they shouted[623] at the tops of their voices, "A sword belonging to the LORD and to Gideon!" Although *hereb*, "sword," stands figuratively for "the battle," at its literal level the declaration expresses a magnificent irony: no one on the offense carried a sword! As it turns out, the only swords were in the enemies' hands, and they were used against each other (v. 22a). No less amazing than Gideon's personal transformation was the response of his troops. Not only did they immediately follow this timid fellow from Ophrah but they obeyed his absurd instructions to the letter. Each one stood in his place around the enemy camp[624] while the enemy troops frantically tried to escape.

7:21b The bedlam in the enemy camp is described in three verbs: *wayyaruṣ*, "and they [all the camp] ran";[625] *wayyariʿû*, "and they cried out [wildly]"; and *wayyanûsû*, "and they fled."[626] This is the natural response of

---

[620] "Belonging to" is a more likely understanding of the preposition לְ than the NIV "for." The significance of the לְ before Yahweh's and Gideon's names is not specified, but several minor manuscripts, Tg, and Syr add "a sword for ..." in conformity to v. 19 (cf. Moore, *Judges,* 210; O'Connell, *Rhetoric of the Book of Judges,* 374 n. 16). In both cases לְ is best interpreted as indicating ownership rather than dedication. The truncated construction expresses the excitement of the moment (GKC §147c). C. R. Krahmalkov ("The Foundation of Carthage, 814 B.C.: The Douïmès Pendant Inscription," *JSS* 26 [1981]: 85–86) interprets this form as the soldier's oath of allegiance to God and ruler.

[621] Cf. David's fuller comment when he faced Goliath in 1 Sam 17:47, "The LORD does not deliver by sword or spear, for the battle belongs to the LORD [כִּי לַיהוָה הַמִּלְחָמָה], and he will deliver you into our hands." Cf. also 2 Chr 20:15.

[622] The beginning of the middle watch, when new sentries had just been posted, is midnight. Traditionally the night was divided into three watches of four hours each: 8:00–12:00, 12:00–4:00, and 4:00–8:00. The "third watch" is called the "morning watch" in Exod 14:24 and 1 Sam 11:11. Mark 13:35 suggests that later Roman military custom divided the night into four watches. Klein (*Triumph of Irony,* 58–59) has perceptively observed the association of night activity with the motif of fear and unbelief. In 6:27 Gideon destroys the altar of Baal because he is afraid; in 6:28–32 Yahweh provided signs at night to dispel his doubt; in 7:9–16 Yahweh provides a dream sign to dispel his fear; in 7:19–23 Yahweh sends fear and panic upon the camp of Midian.

[623] The more dramatic קָרָא, "to cry out," replaces the colorless אָמַר, "to say," in v. 18.

[624] The clause וַיַּעַמְדוּ אִישׁ תַּחְתָּיו expresses loyalty to the commander.

[625] Many emend to *wayyaqeṣ,* "and they woke up" (cf. Moore, *Judges,* 212), which is logical, but not necessary.

those who have been awakened from the deepest of sleep (at midnight) to the sound of horns blowing, jars smashing, people shouting, and the sight of three hundred blazing torches around the camp. This is psychological warfare at its best.

7:22a As if to remind the reader that this battle does indeed belong to Yahweh, the narrator adds an interpretive note of divine causation in v. 22a. The confusion in the entire Midianite camp[627] was God's doing. Only a remnant survives, fleeing toward the desert from which they came.

7:22b–23 The sight of the enemy in flight amplifies the picture of Barak's pursuit of Sisera in 4:17. In place of one individual pursuing another, however, we now witness the remnant of an entire camp fleeing from a force of three hundred Israelites. The pursuit is recounted in two phases. First, the author summarizes the flight of the major enemy force to Beth Shittah toward Zerarah, to the border of Abel Meholah near Tabbath. The location of all these places is uncertain,[628] but the path of flight must have been toward the Jordan, which the Midianites and Amalekites hoped to cross to escape into the desert.

But having achieved the divinely intended goal with the three hundred core troops, Gideon appeared to forget the point of Yahweh's reduction of the troops. Instead of operating by faith and seeking guidance from God, he relied on human strength[629] and mobilized[630] the troops of Naphtali, Asher, and all Manasseh. These, along with the men from Asher who are not listed here, probably consisted of the twenty-two thousand who had been eliminated in v. 3 and those ninety-seven hundred who had been sent back to their tents for lapping water like dogs in v. 8. In the words of L. R. Klein:

---

[626] Reading וינוסו with *qere*, rather than *kethib* וינס, which explicitly ascribes Israelite causation to the response.

[627] The *waw* conjunction before וּבְכָל הַמַּחֲנֶה, "even before the entire camp," is emphatic.

[628] The name Beth Shittah means "house of acacia [woods]." The place has been identified with Shatta, 2.5 miles east of Harod (west of Beth Shan) and Tell Sleihat, east of the Jordan. Zererah (צְרֵרָה) is probably a variant spelling of Zeredah (1 Kgs 11:26) and Zarethan (Josh 3:16; 1 Kgs 4:12). Abel Meholah, in the Jordan Valley west of the river, twelve miles south of Beth Shan, was the hometown of Elisha (1 Kgs 19:16). Tabbath has been linked with Ras Abu Tabat on the Wadi Kufrinje halfway between Succoth and Jabesh-gilead. These places are all discussed by H. O. Thompson, "Tabbath," *ABD* 7.291–92. Cf. id., "Beth-Shittah," *ABD* 1.698; "Zererah," *ABD* 6.1082–83. On Abel Meholah see also D. V. Edelman, "Abel-Meholah," *ABD* 1.11–12.

[629] Which Klein (*Triumph of Irony*, 57) interprets as ironically illogical.

[630] As in 6:34, the verb צָעַק, an alternate form of זָעַק, "to cry out," means "to rally" the troops.

The coward has become confident; he directs far-flung mopping up operations which are effectively carried out. But the voice of the LORD is stilled, not to be heard for the balance of Gideon's narrative. And the spirit of the LORD, which brought the courage to fight a far greater military force, seems to slip from Gideon's shoulders in the process.[631]

7:24–25 In the second phase of the account (vv. 24–25)[632] Gideon is described as sending messengers *(malʾākîm)* throughout the Ephraimite highlands, calling on the men of this tribe to join the rout of the Midianites and seize control of the Jordan River as far as Beth Barah.[633] The Ephraimites responded[634] to the challenge, seized the Jordan crossings, and captured two of the Midianite commanders *(śārîm),* Oreb ("Raven") and Zeeb ("Wolf").[635] The Ephraimites' contribution to the victory over Midian was memorialized in new names given to the sites where they killed the commanders: "the rock of Oreb" and "the winepress of Zeeb," respectively. With the heads of the two Midianite commanders in their possession, the Ephraimites crossed the Jordan to join Gideon in the pursuit of the rest of Midian. When they caught up with him, they presented their trophies to him.

¹Now the Ephraimites asked Gideon, "Why have you treated us like this? Why didn't you call us when you went to fight Midian?" And they criticized him sharply.
²But he answered them, "What have I accomplished compared to you? Aren't the gleanings of Ephraim's grapes better than the full grape harvest of Abiezer? ³God gave Oreb and Zeeb, the Midianite leaders, into your hands. What was I able to do compared to you?" At this, their resentment against him subsided.

Postscript (8:1–3). **8:1** The reader of the Gideon story might have expected the narrative to move quickly to the summary statement in 8:28,[636] but the plot is complicated by two persistent problems: the fractious nature of the Ephraimites (8:1–3) and character flaws in Gideon (8:4–27). After the energetic participation of the latter in 7:24–25, once again the narrator catches the reader by surprise in 8:1–3. Why should the Ephraimites complain when they

---

[631] Klein, *Triumph of Irony,* 57–58.

[632] Becker (*Richterzeit und Königtum,* 172–74) is correct in viewing the primary narrative as moving naturally from 7:23 to 8:4, but to delete the intervening material as extraneous and/or secondary is to miss the rhetorical intention of the book as a whole. Cf. O'Connell, *Rhetoric of the Book of Judges,* 154–56, 314.

[633] Beth Barah is named only here in the OT. The location of the site is unknown, but the name may be a corruption of בֵּית עֲבָרָה, "house of crossing, fording."

[634] If the *niphal* form, וַיִּצָּעֵק, is interpreted as a tolerative *niphal* (viz, "they allowed themselves to be mobilized"; cf. *IBHS* §23.4f.), "every man of Ephraim" is the subject, and there is no need to add אֵת, the sign of a definite object with the LXX, Syr, and Vg.

[635] The names contribute to the image of the enemy's character and conduct in war. So also Garsiel, "Name-Derivations," 308.

[636] Cf. 3:10–11; 3:29–30; 4:23–24 and 5:31b.

have played such a significant role in the victory over the Midianites to this point? The strength of the Ephraimite disaffection is reflected in the pointed nature of their accusation (lit.): "What is this thing you have done to us in not calling us when you went to fight Midian?"[637] And in case the reader fails to catch their tone of voice, the narrator adds his own interpretive comment: "They contended[638] forcefully with him." From the Ephraimites' charge it is difficult to tell whether they are angry with Gideon for failing to invite them along with the Manassite, Asherite, Zebulunite, and Naphtalite tribes or instead of them. In any case, the facts are clear: (1) the Ephraimites had not been summoned initially (6:35); (2) they were not involved in the primary rout of Midian (7:24); (3) they were called upon only at the last minute when it appeared the enemy might escape through their territory. All these are interpreted as more than a snub; it is action directed against the Ephraimites.[639]

8:2–3 The care with which Gideon chooses all his words in vv. 2–3 shows him at his diplomatic best. Taking to heart the adage that "A gentle answer turns away wrath/But a harsh word stirs up anger,"[640] he offers a four-dimensional response. First, with a rhetorical question he minimizes his own role in comparison with theirs.[641] Second, he flatters the tribe of Ephraim with a proverb, also cast as a rhetorical question but expecting a positive answer. The vintage of Abiezer (the clan to which Gideon belongs, 6:11) is insignificant compared to the gleaning[642] of Ephraim. To change the metaphor, the best the Abiezrites can produce is less than the scraps off the Ephraimite's table. The proverb has the ring of a clever political slogan. Third, he acknowledges that God has rewarded their contribution by giving them the real trophies—the Midianite commanders Oreb and Zeeb.[643] Fourth, he minimizes his personal

---

[637] L. B. Kutler ("Features of the Battle Challenge in Biblical Hebrew, Akkadian, and Ugaritic," *UF* 19 [1987]: 95–99) has recognized in this account the fullest expression of the battle challenge, which typologically involves the following elements: (1) an offense is committed; (2) the factions assemble and confront each other; (3) one of the parties declares the challenge; (4) the battle occurs or is avoided.

[638] The NIV's rendering of רִיב as "criticized" is much too mild. This legal term, which appeared earlier in 6:32, means "to contest, to challenge, to conduct a legal case."

[639] Note the directness of the question: מָה־הַדָּבָר הַזֶּה עָשִׂיתָ לָּנוּ, "What is this thing you have done *to us?*" Similar constructions occur frequently, as in Gen 12:18; 20:9; etc. For another example of ... לְ עָשָׂה in the sense of "to do to someone" in a negative sense see 9:56.

[640] Prov 15:1. Cf. Prov 25:15.

[641] The rhetorical question מֶה־עָשִׂיתִי עַתָּה כָּכֶם, "What have I done now compared to you?" anticipates a negative answer, "Nothing."

[642] עֹלְלוֹת, a plural of intensity from a root עָלַל, "to glean," refers to grapes or olives that are picked when one goes over a vineyard or olive grove a second time. When the harvest involves grain, לֶקֶט is used. Cf. Ruth 2:3ff.

[643] The word order highlights the Ephraimites' role by thrusting the indirect object to the front of the sentence: "Into your hands God has given ..."

role a second time, though with greater intensity.[644]

This short episode is significant in the Gideon narrative and the Book of Judges as a whole for several reasons. First, it reveals to the reader something of Gideon's personality. As the narrator's final comment in v. 3 expresses, at his best Gideon is an extremely sensitive and effective diplomat: when he had finished his speech, the passions (*rûah,* lit. "spirit") of the Ephraimites relaxed (*rāpâ).* At the same time, Gideon's answer raises several questions. Why does he refer to God as "Elohim" rather than Yahweh (v. 3)?[645] Does this reflect his own fundamental disaffection from Yahweh, or is he accommodating his response to the spiritual disaffection of the Ephraimites? It is hardly accidental that his use of "Elohim" echoes the comment of the Midianite in 7:14.

Second, in his defense, why does Gideon say nothing about his own call to divine service or his divine empowerment/inspiration by the Spirit of Yahweh? According to 7:34–35 his summoning of the northern tribes and their response to his call[646] were both expressive of his being "clothed" by Yahweh's Spirit. Nor does he say anything about God's desire to defeat the Midianites with a minimal human force (7:1–8). Instead, his arguments are all psychologically rather than theologically based.

Second, this series of episodes reveals some fundamental flaws in Israel as a nation. On the one hand, many are fearful of the enemy (7:3) and apparently would rather not fight. On the other hand, some are offended when they are not called. The tribal cohesion is crumbling. Unlike the period of conquests under Joshua, it is impossible for the nation to operate in concert. More specifically this episode exposes a fundamental problem with the Ephraimites that will resurface in 12:1–6. They are a self-centered and fractious lot, easily offended, and with an inflated estimation of their significance within the nation.[647] Even in victory Israel remains her own worst enemy.

(2) Gideon's Punishment and Subjugation of Israel (8:4–28)

On the surface 8:4 seems to follow naturally after 7:23. Judges 7:1–8 and 7:19–22 had created the impression that God had placed the outcome of the

---

[644] Cp. "What have I done now compared to you?" (v. 2) with "And what am I able to do compared to you" (v. 3).

[645] The rhetorical force of this small detail is eliminated by several MSS, the LXX, and the Vg, which read יהוה, not אֱלֹהִים. So also Boling, *Judges,* 151, who treats Elohim as a secondary northernism, accommodating the Ephraimites.

[646] From 7:3 it is evident that two-thirds of the men who had responded to Gideon's summons in 6:35 came despite fundamental fears. No doubt they were driven by the same Spirit that clothed Gideon so Yahweh could make his point even more effectively that this battle is his, not Israel's.

[647] This episode illustrates the fundamentally anti-Ephraimite stance of the author. O'Connell's argument (*Rhetoric of the Book of Judges,* 314), however, that the original readership for whom the Book of Judges was written consisted of members of the Ephraimite league who supported the Saulide dynasty against David, interprets the book too politically.

battle with the Midianites entirely in the hands of Gideon and his band of three hundred men. So the summoning of the rest of the troops who had come down to the spring of Harod with Gideon (7:23) and the two episodes involving the Ephraimites (7:24–25; 8:1–3) are unforeseen. But far from dismissing unexpected segments like this as inauthentic or secondary, in Hebrew narrative they are often the key to discovering the author's rhetorical goals. The main plot of the Gideon story resumes in 8:4.

Although the plot takes an unexpected turn, vv. 4–27 parallel the preceding account in several significant respects. Again Gideon and his band of three hundred men play key roles. Again they take the enemy camp by surprise. Again two Midianite leaders are captured and executed. But the differences between this chapter and the preceding are even more striking than the links. The following is a list of some of the similarities:

1. Yahweh is not involved in this phase of the plot at all (except in Gideon's own glib comments).

2. The two captured Midianite leaders have strange names and are called "kings" *(mĕlākîm)* rather than "commanders" *(śārîm).*

3. The campaign takes Gideon and his men far afield to Karkor east of the Dead Sea.

4. Gideon runs into serious conflict with his Transjordanian countrymen.

5. Gideon is personally involved in the capture and execution of the enemy kings.

6. Personal blood vengeance replaces national deliverance as a motive for Gideon's action.

7. Gideon, the fearful young man, has become a brutal aggressor.

Indeed the last feature represents the most striking element in the narrative. When the plot resumes, something seems to have happened to the character of the hero. In chaps. 6–7 we have witnessed his transformation from a fearful private citizen to a fearless agent of God, willing to take on the enemy against all odds, not to mention a sensitive diplomat. But the portrait of the man the author paints in this chapter creates a radically different impression in the reader's mind. If 8:1–32 had been handed down without the literary context in which it is embedded, modern readers would reject Gideon as a tyrant, arbitrary in his treatment of the enemy and ruthless in his handling of his own countrymen. Instead of "hacking" and "contending" with the enemy, Gideon/Jerubbaal "contends" and "hacks" his own people.[648] All of this raises the question of why the narrator spoils the reader's assessment of this one who accomplished so much for God? Does he see in Gideon's addition of his own name to the battle cry "[The sword] belonging to the LORD and to Gideon" (7:18,20) a premonition of a future problem? Is he deliberately

---

[648] Cf. Klein, *Triumph of Irony,* 62.

painting a picture of a human deliverer who is the antithesis of the divine Savior? In contrast to Yahweh's remarkable patience and grace with his people, Gideon turns out to be an impatient and ruthless ruler.

Like the previous chapter, this account is complex, consisting of several easily identified segments, each of which will be examined in turn.

GIDEON'S CAPTURE AND EXECUTION OF THE KINGS OF MIDIAN (8:4–21). The chronological connection between vv. 4–21 and the preceding narrative is uncertain. The previous text had left no hint that any of the Midianite host had escaped. But it is evident from 8:10 that two Midianite kings, Zebah and Zalmunna, and fifteen thousand men had made it across the Jordan and were fleeing into the desert. Having recognized that v. 4 follows logically from 7:22, the reader expects a quick and final solution to the Midianite menace. We are surprised to learn, however, that not only are Gideon's mopping-up operations more complicated than anticipated, but this theme also is interwoven with another: Gideon's disposition toward his fellow Israelites. In fact, these two themes alternate in the narrative in an A B A′ B′ pattern, with A (8:4–9) and A′ (8:13–17) involving the latter issue and B (8:10–12) and B′ (8:18–21) concerning the former.

⁴Gideon and his three hundred men, exhausted yet keeping up the pursuit, came to the Jordan and crossed it. ⁵He said to the men of Succoth, "Give my troops some bread; they are worn out, and I am still pursuing Zebah and Zalmunna, the kings of Midian."

⁶But the officials of Succoth said, "Do you already have the hands of Zebah and Zalmunna in your possession? Why should we give bread to your troops?"

⁷Then Gideon replied, "Just for that, when the LORD has given Zebah and Zalmunna into my hand, I will tear your flesh with desert thorns and briers."

⁸From there he went up to Peniel and made the same request of them, but they answered as the men of Succoth had. ⁹So he said to the men of Peniel, "When I return in triumph, I will tear down this tower."

Gideon's Demand for Support from His Countrymen (8:4–9). **8:4–5** The new movement in the narrative is signalled by the arrival of Gideon and his band of three hundred at the Jordan and their crossing over the river (v. 4). The men's physical condition and determination are expressed in two expressions, ʿāyēpîm, "exhausted," and rōdĕpîm, "pursuing" (NIV, "keeping up the pursuit"), which together may be understood as a hendiadys: "wearily giving chase." The phrase sets the stage for the next scene.

Apparently having crossed the Jordan just north of where the Wadi Jabbok enters the main river, Gideon's band followed the wadi as far as Succoth (meaning "Booths"), generally identified with Tell Deir ʿAllah in the Transjordan.[649] At this time Succoth was under Israelite control, having been taken from Sihon, king of Heshbon, and allotted by Moses to the tribe of Gad (Josh 13:27). But the ensuing dialogue indicates that the residents of this town were obviously suspicious of Gideon.

When he arrived in Succoth, Gideon requested of its citizens food to nourish his men in their pursuit of the Midianite kings, Zebah and Zalmunna. The meaning of the first name ("Sacrifice") is clear, but the second may be interpreted either as "Shade withheld/shelter refused"[650] or "May [the god] Salm protect."[651] The pair of names obviously answers to Oreb and Zeeb in 7:24–25. Whereas the former had been identified as *śārîm*, "commanders," however, these are *mĕlākîm*, "kings," the senior rulers of these marauding bands.[652] Gideon's request seems reasonable enough. On the one hand, he naturally assumes that even if they were Transjordanians, these fellow Israelites would be eager to assist in the capture of a common enemy. On the other hand, by common custom, as the commander of a group of soldiers passing through the land, he could simply have confiscated the needed provisions. But the narrator has Gideon continuing with the sensitive diplomatic style evident in vv. 1–3. He is respectful in framing the solicitation[653] and careful to explain the reason: his men are exhausted from pursuing the Midianite kings.

8:6 But the officials[654] of Succoth answer his tactful request with brusque rejection (lit.): "Is the palm *[kap]* of Zebah and Zalmunna in your hand *[yād]* now?" The rhetorical question is ambiguous. Do they mean this literally? If so, they expect Gideon to mutilate the kings (like Judah had done to Adoni-Bezek in 2:6–7) and bring their hands in as evidence of their heroism/achievements (like the heads of Oreb and Zeeb in 7:24–25). Or do they mean it figuratively? Do they simply expect to have the kings in tow as proof of his authority? The reaction of the Succothites contrasts sharply with their Cisjordanian countrymen's immediate response to Gideon's summons to battle in 7:23. This raises an intriguing question: Has the Spirit of Yahweh, so evident in the earlier context, left him?

8:7–9 Judging by the narrator's silence on the role of Yahweh in the fol-

---

[649] Not to be confused with the first stopping place of the Israelites when they came out of Egypt (Exod 12:37; Num 33:5). Jacob had stopped and built "booths" here for his cattle when he returned from Paddan-Aram (Josh 13:27). See further J. A. H. Seely, "Succoth," *ABD* 6.217–18; G. van der Kooij, "Deir ʿAlla, Tell," *NEAEHL* 1.338–42.

[650] Soggin, *Judges*, 149.

[651] Mendenhall, "Zebah and Zalmunna," ABD 6.1055. Garsiel ("Homiletic Name-Derivations," 308) prefers an association with צֶלֶם, "image, shape."

[652] One may speculate that one was king of the Midianites and the other of the Amalekite allies.

[653] Note the construction of the Hb., תְּנוּ־נָא כִּכְּרוֹת לֶחֶם לָעָם אֲשֶׁר בְּרַגְלִי, "Please give loaves of bread for the people at my feet."

[654] Hb. שָׂרֵי. Since the word was used in 7:25 to identify the position of Oreb and Zeeb in the Midianite camp, it is possible that Succoth was a military outpost.

lowing sequence of events and Gideon's reaction to the Succothites' imperti-
nence, the question may be answered in the affirmative. Instead of answering
impudence with a gentle word (cf. v. 2), he throws diplomacy to the wind and
responds in kind. Glibly invoking the name of Yahweh, he threatens to take the
law into his own hands and beat (rather than NIV, "tear") their bodies with a
switch of desert thorns *(qôṣîm)* and briars *(barqānîm)*,[655] like a man beats
grain on the threshing floor.[656] Fuming at his rejection by the people of Succoth, Gideon moves on up the Wadi Jabbok to Penuel, modern Tell edh-Dha-
hab.[657] The narrator summarizes this visit by noting simply in the third person
that Gideon approached the residents of Penuel just as he had the people of
Succoth and that the people here responded the same. But his reaction to their
rejection is couched in different terms: when he returns victorious,[658] he will
tear down their defensive tower.[659]

The inclusion of these two episodes in Gideon's Transjordanian adventures
raises questions concerning their rhetorical function in the broader narrative.
On the one hand, it exposes the fractures in Israel's tribal constitution. There is
reluctance to treat the enemies of another tribe as a threat to oneself. But there
probably is more to it than this. By citing these two examples the narrator demonstrates that the reaction of Succoth was not an isolated event but reflective of
the general Transjordanian disposition toward Gideon. At the same time the
reader cannot help but notice the contrast between the willingness of the northern Cisjordanian tribes to answer Gideon's call to rid them of the Midianite
yoke and the cynical response to Gideon's campaign in the east. This is the
narrator's way of distinguishing between Gideon's wars of liberation and his
personal crusades (cf. vv. 18–21). So long as the former was clear, they were
ready to help, but now the agenda has changed. Gideon and his band of three
hundred men were off on a private campaign. The divinely chosen force has
become his private army.

**¹⁰Now Zebah and Zalmunna were in Karkor with a force of about fifteen thou-
sand men, all that were left of the armies of the eastern peoples; a hundred and**

---

[655] On בַּרְקָנִים, which occurs only here and in v. 16, see M. Zohary, *Plants of the Bible* (London: Cambridge University Press, 1982), 158–59.

[656] The verb דּוּשׁ, "to beat," is used of Ornan (Araunah) beating grain on a threshing floor in
1 Chr 21:20. Elsewhere it denotes "thresh" in general (Deut 25:4; Jer 50:11; Amos 1:3; Mic 4:13).
The threshing was done with sledges or carts fitted with metal spikes pulled by draft animals.

[657] Penuel/Peniel is renowned especially as the site where Jacob wrestled with the divine "man"
(Gen 32:22–32). On this place see W. Thiel, "Pnuël Im Alten Testament," in *Prophetie und
Geschichtliche Wirklichkeit Im Alten Israel,* Siegfried Herrmann Festschrift, ed. R. Liwak and
S. Wagner (Stuttgart: W. Kohlhammer, 1991), 398–414.

[658] Hb. בְּשָׁלוֹם, "in peace."

[659] The reference to the מִגְדָּל supports our suggestion that the שָׂרִים in v. 6 were military commanders.

twenty thousand swordsmen had fallen. [11]Gideon went up by the route of the nomads east of Nobah and Jogbehah and fell upon the unsuspecting army. [12]Zebah and Zalmunna, the two kings of Midian, fled, but he pursued them and captured them, routing their entire army.

Gideon's Capture of Zebah and Zalmunna (8:10–12). **8:10** The circumstantial clause at the beginning of v. 10 functions as an episode marker.[660] Zebah and Zalmunna had managed to escape to Karkor. Although the site cannot be located with certainty, the most likely identification places Karkor *(qarqōr)* on the Wadi Sirḥān, one hundred miles east of the Dead Sea, approaching the Midianite homeland.[661] The narrator notes that fifteen thousand men had escaped with these two kings. This number seems to accord with other large figures in the book[662] until we learn that these represented the remnant of a force that had consisted of 135,000 swordsmen, "all that were left of the armies of the eastern peoples ["the sons of the east"]."[663] Unless *ʾelep* is to be interpreted as "contingents, units,"[664] the number of 120,000[665] may be intended as a symbolic figure, quantifying not only the forces that were earlier described as numerous as locusts (6:5; 7:12) but also the extent of the slaughter when Yahweh had caused the Midianites to take out their swords against each other. The vagueness of the statement in 7:22 had led the reader to imagine the consequences of God's actions (the verse does not indicate that there were any Israelite casualties at all), but now, with delightful irony the narrator describes the victims as 120,000 "swordsmen" (lit., "men who draw the sword [from the sheath])," in this case against each other rather than the enemy.

8:11–12 Verse 11 is somewhat uncertain textually, but one can extract from it Gideon's strategy. Following the caravan route (lit., "the way of those who live in tents"), Gideon seems to have caught up with the Midianite kings east of Nobah and Jogbehah. The exact location of Nobah is unknown,[666] but Jogbehah is commonly identified with Ruǧm ʾal-Gubēḥah, on an ancient caravan route northwest of Amman. Gideon came upon them suddenly, when the camp was relaxing.[667] He routed[668] the entire army and eventually cap-

---

[660] Cf. F. I. Andersen, *The Sentence in Biblical Hebrew* (The Hague: Mouton, 1974), 79.

[661] Cf. H. O. Thompson, "Karkor," *ABD* 4.6.

[662] Cf. 4:6 and 7:3.

[663] Here בְּנֵי קֶדֶם functions as a generic designation for the seminomadic desert peoples represented by the Midianites and Amalekites. Cf. 6:3.

[664] Boling, *Judges*, 156.

[665] The high number matches the census figures found in Numbers 1 and 26, on which see J. W. Wenham, "Large Numbers in the Old Testament," *TynBul* 18 (1967): 19–53.

[666] An identification with Kenath, which the Manassite Nobah renamed after himself (Num 32:42) is possible.

[667] In 18:7 the word בֶּטַח, "unsuspecting, tranquil," describes the state of Laish before the Danites attack.

[668] Hb. הֶחֱרִיד, "he routed," lit. "he frightened," builds on the same root as חֲרֹד, "Harod," and חָרֵד, "trembling," in 7:3.

tured the prize he was after—Zebah and Zalmunna, the kings of Midian.

13Gideon son of Joash then returned from the battle by the Pass of Heres. 14He caught a young man of Succoth and questioned him, and the young man wrote down for him the names of the seventy-seven officials of Succoth, the elders of the town. 15Then Gideon came and said to the men of Succoth, "Here are Zebah and Zalmunna, about whom you taunted me by saying, 'Do you already have the hands of Zebah and Zalmunna in your possession? Why should we give bread to your exhausted men?'" 16He took the elders of the town and taught the men of Succoth a lesson by punishing them with desert thorns and briers. 17He also pulled down the tower of Peniel and killed the men of the town.

Gideon's Vengeance on Succoth and Penuel (8:13–17). **8:13–14** Gideon's high-handed behavior continues in vv. 13–17. Identified by patronymic for the first time since 7:13, Gideon the son of Joash, the conqueror, returns to Succoth via the Heres Pass.[669] Seizing[670] a young official of the town council[671] and questioning him, he forced him to write down for him the names of the seventy-seven elders of the town. This is the first time elders are mentioned in the book. In the absence of a king, towns were governed by a body of senior members of the community, usually heads of the clans, who conducted the community's business in the city gate.[672] The narrator does not inform us on what he recorded the names, but one may assume he used either ostraca (pieces of broken pottery) or tanned skins. He probably wrote in the "Canaanite" alphabetic linear script, which had been developed and diffused in the Levant during the previous four or five centuries.[673]

8:15–17 Presumably when the elders had gathered before him, Gideon presented Zebah and Zalmunna to them, and he reminded them of their earlier

---

[669] Not to be confused with הַר־חֶרֶס, "Mount Heres," named in 1:35 and תִּמְנַת־חֶרֶס, "Timnath Heres," in 2:9. The location of this pass is unknown.

[670] In v. 12 the same verb, לָכַד, had described Gideon's capture of the Midianite kings.

[671] The term נַעַר, which means fundamentally "young man," had referred to Gideon's personal attendant, perhaps his armor/shield bearer, in 7:10. Here it probably identifies an attendant of one of the elders or a young member of the council, perhaps the scribe.

[672] On the institution of eldership in Israel see J. Liver, "The Israelite Tribes," in *The World History of the Jewish People*, vol. III: *Judges* (Tel Aviv: Masada, 1971), 190–91; H. Reviv, *The Elders in Ancient Israel: A Study of a Biblical Institution*, trans. L. Plitmann (Jerusalem: Magnes, 1989).

[673] On the history of the alphabet and the diffusion of writing in ancient Israel see A. R. Millard, "The Practice of Writing in Ancient Israel," *BA* 35 (1972): 98–111; id., "An Assessment of the Evidence for Writing in Ancient Israel," in *Biblical Archaeology Today: Proceedings of the International Congress on Biblical Archaeology, Jerusalem, April 1984*, ed. A. Biran (Jerusalem: Israel Exploration Society and the Israel Academy of Sciences and Humanities, 1985), 301–12. For an example of an ostracon inscribed with Proto-Canaanite characters from this very period from ʿIzbet Ṣarṭa (two miles east of Tel Aphek) see M. Kochavi, "An Ostracon of the Period of the Judges from ʿIzbet Ṣarṭa," *TA* 4 (1977): 1–13; F. M. Cross, "Newly Found Inscriptions in Old Canaanite and Early Phoenician Scripts," *BASOR* 238 (1980): 8–15.

taunting challenge to produce the palms of these kings before they would offer any food to his exhausted band of men (cf. v. 6). Then he took the elders and "threshed" (rather than NIV, "taught … a lesson)[674] them with switches made of desert thorns and briars. Then he moved on to Penuel/Peniel, whose fate at his hands turns out to be much more tragic than that of Succoth. Making good on his threat in v. 9, he destroyed their defensive tower. But in his rage he went beyond the threat and slaughtered all the men of the city. Gideon's behavior could be justified if Penuel were a Canaanite city, but these were fellow Israelites! His character has been transformed again—he acted like a general out of control, no longer bound by rules of civility, let alone national loyalty.

[18]Then he asked Zebah and Zalmunna, "What kind of men did you kill at Tabor?"

"Men like you," they answered, "each one with the bearing of a prince."

[19]Gideon replied, "Those were my brothers, the sons of my own mother. As surely as the LORD lives, if you had spared their lives, I would not kill you." [20]Turning to Jether, his oldest son, he said, "Kill them!" But Jether did not draw his sword, because he was only a boy and was afraid.

[21]Zebah and Zalmunna said, "Come, do it yourself. 'As is the man, so is his strength.'" So Gideon stepped forward and killed them, and took the ornaments off their camels' necks.

Gideon's Vendetta against the Kings of Midian (8:18–21). In vv. 18–21 the story of Gideon's victory over the Midianites finally comes to a conclusion. But the ending is unexpected. Having taken care of his Israelite cynics, Gideon turned his attention to his captives, Zebah and Zalmunna. Ironically, although the kings' fate seems sealed from the beginning and although Gideon's disposition toward them was devoid of any sentimentality, his treatment of these enemies was tempered by a modicum of decency. The dialogue in vv. 18–19 follows the conventions of epic chivalry—question, answer, action. Although each component contains its own element of surprise, the greatest surprise of all is that in the end the reader's sympathies may have shifted completely from Gideon to the other participants in the scene, first the two kings, then his hapless son.

8:18 The question with which Gideon interrogates his captives ("Where are the men you killed at Tabor?"[675]) is strange for several reasons: First,

---

[674] The NIV's "taught a lesson" follows the MT's וַיֹּדַע, "and he caused to know." But the precedent of v. 7 and the consistent reading of all the versions suggest a misspelling of וַיָּדָשׁ, "and he beat/threshed." For discussion and bibliography on this text see O'Connell, *Rhetoric of the Book of Judges*, 156, 469.\

[675] The introductory particle אֵיפֹה is difficult. Consisting of two elements, אֵי, "where?" + פֹה, "here," elsewhere it always means "Where?" Cf. *HALOT* 1.43; *DCH* 1.221. The NIV's "What kind of …?" is mistakenly driven by the answer. So also Moore, *Judges*, 226.

Gideon seems to be mocking his captives by asking for the whereabouts of men who are dead, as if these kings could spare their own lives by delivering them to him alive. Second, we now learn that in addition to harassing the Israelites and ravaging the countryside (6:4–5), the Midianites had committed murderous acts against the population. It is no wonder that Gideon was afraid of these folk (6:11). Third, some of these atrocities had been committed at Tabor, a major mountain north of the Valley of Jezreel. Because Tabor has been totally out of the picture in the preceding narrative and because of its distance from Ophrah, the seat of the Abiezrite clan, some doubt the authenticity of this statement. However, since Tabor was not far removed from the Midianites' camp on the northern side of the Valley of Harod (7:1), forays by their leaders to Tabor are not out of the question. Indeed, given its location, where the borders of Naphtali, Zebulun, and Issachar meet, atrocities like this may have galvanized these tribes behind Gideon (cf. 6:35).

The response of the kings is equally surprising and highly significant because it introduces the motif of Israelite kingship for the first time in the book. Instead of answering Gideon's question, they flatter him by describing their impression of Gideon and the men they had killed:[676] just like Gideon, they had the appearance and bearing[677] of "the sons of the king" (NIV "a prince"). This response is both evasive and ambiguous. The use of the definite article with "the king," suggests Zebah and Zalmunna had a specific person in mind, perhaps Joash of Ophrah, whom they knew to be the father of Gideon and their victims. Their evaluation of Joash may have been based on the knowledge that he was the host and sponsor of the local cult site (6:25–32) and may be reflected in the dream interpreter's honorific reference to Gideon by patronymic, "son of Joash, a man of Israel" in 7:14. At the same time, by referring to Gideon and their victims as "sons of the king" rather than "kings," they were putting Gideon in his place. Interpreted sociopolitically, "sons of kings" were inferior to "kings." Gideon could draw his own conclusions.

8:19 In Gideon's reaction to their answer the reader is offered another surprise: the victims of the Midianite kings' brutality were his own full brothers, the sons of his mother.[678] Thereupon he informed Zebah and Zalmunna that he would have let them live had they spared his brothers' lives, but we cannot be sure that he meant what he said. The fact that Gideon strengthens this declaration with an oath, *ḥay yhwh*, "as the LORD lives," or preferably, "by the life of

---

[676] The construction כְּמוֹךָ כְמוֹהֶם, "like you like them," does not signify "You are like them" nor "They are like you," but in context, "You and they are the same; each has the appearance/form of king's sons." Cf. *GBH* §174i.

[677] Hb. תֹּאַר means "outline, form." For references see BDB, 1061.

[678] The legitimacy of Gideon and his brothers contrasts with his own son Abimelech (8:31; 9:1) and Jephthah in the following cycle (11:1).

the LORD,"[679] sounds pious but does little to allay suspicions. The oath was undoubtedly intended to impress his captives, but it is an empty exploitation of the divine name in violation of the Third Commandment (Exod 20:7; Deut 5:11). It was a glib reference to Yahweh to sanctify his personal vendetta.

Gideon's reference to his brothers introduces a new theme to the narrative. It is possible that the misfortunes of his family had played into Yahweh's choice of Gideon as a deliverer, but his earlier hesitation leaves no trace of this motivation. Inserted here, this new element transforms our understanding of the man, particularly his motivation in his pursuit of the Midianite kings. If in the past he was ever driven by theological and/or nationalistic concerns, in the present adventure he is simply executing blood vengeance.[680] In fact, so glaring is the switch from national to personal concerns that the reader is driven to go back and reread the preceding episodes.[681]

8:20 The narrator's negative impression of Gideon's character becomes even more transparent in v. 20 when he tells his son Jether[682] to do his dirty work and kill the Midianite kings. In so doing Gideon places his son in an awkward position. He may demonstrate his own maturity and nobility [by Canaanite standards] in defense of the [royal?] house and become an accomplice in his father's personal vendetta, or he may disobey his father and prove himself unmanly. In a second rare moment in the Gideon story (cf. 6:27),[683] the narrator offers us access to the motivation of his character, and in so doing he drives us to sympathize with Jether rather then the so-called "hero" of the story. The boy chooses to defy his father, not because his own sympathies were with the Midianite kings, but because he was afraid *(yārēʾ)*, "for he was still a young boy."[684] Portraying Jether as an alter ego of Gideon's former (preferred) self, the lad had not yet grown up and developed a stomach for violence.

Unlike Bezek in 1:5–7, Zebah and Zalmunna were defiant to the end. They rebuked Gideon and told him to kill them himself and prove himself a man.[685] But the narrator is not amused. He tersely recounts Gideon's execution of the Midianite kings and then closes the scene with an image of a conqueror claim-

---

[679] On the idiom see M. Greenberg, "The Hebrew Oath Particle *ḥay/ḥē*," *JBL* 76 (1957): 34–39.

[680] Cf. Exod 21:23; Deut 19:21; Lev 24:17.

[681] Cf. Sternberg, *Poetics of Biblical Narrative*, 312.

[682] One may surmise that Jether, whose name means "Remainder, Excess," was Gideon's eldest son (in contrast to Gideon [6:1–11] and Jotham [9:7–21], both of whom were the youngest), presumably his heir. The name recalls that of Jethro, Moses' Midianite father-in-law (Exod 4:18).

[683] Whereas in the earlier episode Gideon was driven by fear for his father's house, this boy refuses to defend his father's house.

[684] This is obviously the sense of נַעַר required here, in contrast to the significance of the word in 7:10 and 8:14.

[685] כִּי כָאִישׁ גְּבוּרָתוֹ, "for as a man [so] is his strength," sounds like a popular proverb. Cf. Richter, *Traditionsgeschichtliche Untersuchungen*, 227. This comment is provocative in light of 6:12, where the messenger of Yahweh has characterized Gideon as a גִּבּוֹר הֶחָיִל, "strong hero."

ing the customary trophies of victory—the crescent ornaments[686] worn on the necks of "royal" camels. The Midianite crisis is over, but the picture of Gideon, "Hacker," who is finally living up to his name, is far from attractive.

[22]The Israelites said to Gideon, "Rule over us—you, your son and your grandson—because you have saved us out of the hand of Midian."
[23]But Gideon told them, "I will not rule over you, nor will my son rule over you. The LORD will rule over you." [24]And he said, "I do have one request, that each of you give me an earring from your share of the plunder." (It was the custom of the Ishmaelites to wear gold earrings.)
[25]They answered, "We'll be glad to give them." So they spread out a garment, and each man threw a ring from his plunder onto it. [26]The weight of the gold rings he asked for came to seventeen hundred shekels, not counting the ornaments, the pendants and the purple garments worn by the kings of Midian or the chains that were on their camels' necks. [27]Gideon made the gold into an ephod, which he placed in Ophrah, his town. All Israel prostituted themselves by worshiping it there, and it became a snare to Gideon and his family.

GIDEON'S SHAM REJECTION OF KINGSHIP (8:22–27).
8:22 Although the narrator is not attracted to the character of Gideon, the latter's countrymen were extremely impressed with his achievement. They responded to his resolution of the Midianite crisis by offering him and his descendants dynastic rule over the nation. The offer, as presented in v. 22, deserves several comments.[687]

First, while we can only speculate about how many men were in the delegation that approached Gideon, the narrator sees them as representing the entire nation. The close links between this event and the preceding narrative suggest the people who come before the hero consisted minimally of the three hundred men who had accompanied Gideon in the pursuit of the Midianites (v. 4) and had witnessed his killing of Zebah and Zalmunna (v. 21) and maximally of the tribes who had been involved in the battles with the Midianites and their allies (Manasseh, Asher, Zebulun, Naphtali, Ephraim). The former particularly would certainly have had a lot to gain by their proposal. Perhaps they envisaged themselves as the king's select military core, like David's six hundred men some time later.[688] Regardless of the consistency of the delegation, the author deliberately characterizes them as (lit.) "the men of Israel" (*ʾîš yiśrāʾēl*), making this look like a pan-Israelite assembly offering

---

[686] The word שַׂהֲרֹנִים, from שַׂהַר, "moon," occurs elsewhere only in Isa 3:18.
[687] Lindars ("Gideon and Kingship," *JTS*, n.s. 16 [1965]: 315–26) argues on tradition critical grounds that Gideon had nothing to do with the offer of kingship; it belongs exclusively to the local history of Jerubbaal.
[688] 1 Sam 25:13; 27:2; 30:9.

rule over the entire nation.[689] Their offer is symptomatic of a nationwide problem. On the surface it appears laudable that the tribes have finally united, but as the sequel demonstrates, it was for the wrong agenda.

Second, although it is clear that the issue is kingship,[690] the word "king" *(melek)* and the related verb "to reign as king" *(mālak)* are studiously avoided in the offer, presumably because this represents an illegitimate attempt to establish the monarchy (cf. 9:22). On the one hand, coming immediately after v. 21b, it appears that the idea to offer Gideon the rule over all Israel was triggered by his claiming the [royal] crescent ornaments of the Midianite kings' camels. On the other hand, while the verb *māšal* means "to rule" in a general sense, it is often used of royal[691] and divine dominion.[692] Furthermore, both the fact that Gideon is offered a hereditary office[693] and the nature of his refusal point to the offer of a royal office. This interpretation finds support in the reminiscences of this text in 1 Samuel 8, where the account of the Israelite's request to Samuel for a king is recounted.[694] The narrator may have avoided the term *melek* because the issue in Gideon's statement is not a title or an office but performance, which from beginning to end belongs to God.

Third, this offer flies in the face of the Mosaic charter for kingship in Deut 17:14–20 in several important respects. On the one hand, there is no hint here that Gideon had been divinely chosen to be king or that the Israelites were concerned about this issue in the least. On the other hand, at this, the first experiment in kingship in Israel, there is immediate talk of hereditary civil rule. One may assume therefore that, as in 1 Samuel 8 (vv. 5,19–20), Israel's paradigm for kingship was derived from the surrounding nations.

Fourth, the people of Israel present this offer to Gideon as a reward

---

[689] W. Beyerlin ("Geschichte und Heilsgeschichte Traditionsbildung im Alten Testament," *VT* 13 [1963]: 4–5) argued that "the men of Israel" denotes the militia of the sacral tribal union that finds its unity in the Lord cult.

[690] So also G. E. Gerbrandt, *Kingship According to the Deuteronomistic History*, SBLDS 87 (Atlanta: Scholars Press, 1986), 123.

[691] מָשַׁל is used of royal dominion when the verb occurs with מֶלֶךְ, "king" (Josh 12:2,5; Isa 19:4), or מַלְכוּת, "kingship" (Ps 103:19), as subject; when it is associated with sitting on a throne (Zech 6:13); or when the participle is juxtaposed with מֶלֶךְ, "king," or כִּסֵּא מַלְכוּתֶךָ, "the throne of your kingship" (2 Chr 7:18).

[692] Yahweh is the subject in 1 Chr 29:12; 2 Chr 20:6; Isa 40:10; 63:19; Pss 22:28[Hb. 29]; 59:13[Hb. 14]; 66:7; 89:9[Hb. 10]; 103:19. Yahweh is the subject in 1 Chr 29:12; 2 Chr 20:6; Isa 40:10; 63:19; Pss 22:28[Hb. 29]; 59:13[Hb. 14]; 66:7; 89:9[Hb. 10]; 103:19.

[693] Note the emphatic construction of מְשָׁל־בָּנוּ גַּם־אַתָּה גַּם־בִּנְךָ גַּם בֶּן־בְּנֶךָ, "Rule over us, yes you, and yes your son, yes your son's son."

[694] O'Connell (*Rhetoric of the Book of Judges*, 291) argues that the narrator interprets the present event in light of the later selection of Saul. It is more likely that the reverse is the case; the Saul narrative was composed against the backdrop of the Book of Judges. Cf. S. Dragga, "In the Shadow of the Judges: The Failure of Saul," *JSOT* 38 (1987): 39–46.

for his heroism in ridding the land of the Midianite menace. The causal clause with which v. 22 ends leaves no doubt about the people's interpretation of the preceding series of events. But in this comment the reader also recognizes a fundamental problem: they have misinterpreted the nature and the agent of their own deliverance. The key word, *hôšaʿtānû*, "you have saved/delivered us," must be interpreted in light of the previous six occurrences of the root *yāšaʿ*, "to save," in the Gideon narrative. While each of these is significant for setting the stage for the present comment, the most telling statement is found in 7:2, where Yahweh declares his rationale for reducing Gideon's men to three hundred: if the full force defeats the Midianites, Israel will claim the credit for the victory herself.[695] Inasmuch as there is no hint of self-laudation on Gideon's part in 8:22, Yahweh appears to have achieved his goal. But their attribution of the victory is certainly misplaced. Although the narrator has emphasized repeatedly that God, not Gideon, nor Israel, is the one who saves, the people have either failed to recognize the hand of God at all or the image of the latter heroism of Gideon has eclipsed the memory of Yahweh's involvement. Gideon himself had prepared the way for this conclusion when he had shouted, "A sword [belonging] to the LORD and to Gideon" (7:18,20). In the end, despite the miraculous nature of the victory over the Midianite camp (7:22), they forgot the first part of the challenge and attributed the outcome of the conflict entirely to the human agent.

8:23 Gideon's response in vv. 23–27 divides into two parts: a verbal answer to the offer (v. 23) and a nonverbal response (vv. 24–27). The former looks like a straightforward rejection of the Israelites' proposal. Choosing his words carefully and casting his answer as a solemn triple assertion,[696] he categorically rejected the opportunity to be the founder of the first dynasty in Israel. His rationale is theologically correct[697] and appears to be perfectly noble. Far be it from him or his sons to usurp the role of Yahweh, the only true ruler over Israel. But scholars are sharply divided in their understanding of the significance of this statement. Some interpret it as a late antimonarchic insertion, reflecting the view of certain groups opposed to the royal ideology centered in Jerusalem, especially the temple and the palace.[698] Others inter-

---

[695] Cf. 6:14–15 (Gideon responds to the divine messenger's charge to deliver Israel with "How can I rescue Israel?"); 6:36–37 (Gideon twice raises the issue of Yahweh saving Israel through him); 7:7 (Yahweh promises to deliver Israel with three hundred men).

[696] Note the repetition of "X will ... rule over you."

[697] Cf. 1 Sam 8:7b.

[698] Cf. Soggin, *Judges*, 160; F. Crüsemann, *Der Widerstand gegen das Königtum. Die antiköniglichen Texte des Alten Testaments und der Kampf um den frühen israelitischen Staat*, WMANT 49 (Neukirchen: Neukirchener Verlag, 1978), 42–54.

pret it more positively, not as a rejection of the monarchy as an institution per se but as Gideon's responsible rejection of an ill-motivated offer.[699] This is a desirable conclusion and maybe even natural, especially if vv. 22–23 are interpreted in isolation from the description of both his previous and subsequent behavior.

However, the issue is not that simple. To be sure, Gideon appears to have deferred to Yahweh, but it is curious that he did not correct the people's mistaken interpretation of the victory over the Midianites. Why did he not say, "I will not be king over you because I am not the one who rescued you from the Midianites. It was the LORD!"? As recorded, his answer contrasts sharply with his earlier self-deprecation in the face of the Ephraimite challenge (vv. 2–3). Instead of giving the credit for the victory to God, he merely alluded to a vague and platitudinal ideal of divine rule over Israel. While verbally appearing to acknowledge the sovereignty of God, the answer belies his previous actions. Since Gideon launched his pursuit of Zebah and Zalmunna in 8:4, his behavior has followed the typical pattern of oriental kings: (1) he treated his subjects/countrymen ruthlessly (vv. 5–9,13–17); (2) his actions were driven by a personal agenda rather than theological or national ideals; (3) he reacted to the death of his brothers as if they were royal assassinations requiring blood vengeance; (4) he made ridiculous demands on his people (v. 20); (5) he claimed for himself the symbols of royalty taken from the enemy. As already suggested, coming after this series of events, it appears the Israelite offer of kingship to Gideon simply seeks to formalize *de jure* what is already *de facto*.

8:24–26 This interpretation is confirmed by Gideon's subsequent conduct. First, he requested that each of his men give him a gold earring from their share of the spoils of war.[700] This action is doubly significant. On the one hand, by requesting gifts from each of his men, Gideon demanded a symbolic gesture of submission. Gladly surrendering a share of their loot, they confirmed their status as his vassals. On the other hand, the amount of gold Gideon received takes on the character of a royal treasure. Seventeen hundred shekels of gold

---

[699] According to Deut 17:14–20, Yahweh would choose Israel's king. See further D. M. Howard, Jr., *Introduction to the Old Testament Historical Books* (Chicago: Moody, 1993), 121; id., "The Case for Kingship in Deuteronomy and the Former Prophets," *WTJ* 52 (1990): 107–11. Boling (*Judges*, 160) sees in Gideon's comment an unwitting anticipation of the fate of his son in chap. 9.

[700] The comment in v. 24 is clarified with a parenthetical comment, "for they had gold earrings, for they were Ishmaelites." Strictly speaking Ishmael was the [elder] son of Abraham by Hagar (Gen 25;12). But the present identification of Midianites as Ishmaelites (cf. also Gen 37:27–28,36) suggests that either the latter gentilic could also be used of desert people [bedouins?] in general or the Midianite alliance extended beyond the Amalekites and the "sons of the east" mentioned earlier. In the latter case Zebah and Zalmunna may actually have belonged to the Ishmaelites' branch of this alliance.

amounts to 43 pounds.[701] This is indeed a treasure fit for a king!

Second, Gideon retained the king's symbols of royalty: the crescent amulets worn by the camels (cf. v. 21), the pendants,[702] the purple robes formerly worn by the Midianite kings, and the neck bands worn by the camels.

8:27 Third, Gideon assumed a king's role as sponsor of the cult by crafting an ephod and erecting it in his city, Ophrah. The nature of this object is not clear. Elsewhere in the Old Testament "ephod" *('ēpôd)* denotes the priest's special breast piece.[703] Because this object was "placed" *(yāṣag)* in Gideon's city and became an object of pagan worship, this meaning seems unlikely here. The solution to the present problem may be suggested by the Akkadian cognate *epattu,* which, in several old Assyrian texts apparently refers to the costly garments worn by high officials and/or draped over images of the gods.[704] The present usage suggests a figure of speech in which the part stands for the whole. Accordingly, the word "ephod" here represents not only the garment that clothed a sacred image but also the image over which the garment was draped and which became the object of worship for the Israelites. The narrator does not reveal the nature of the image, but it seems most likely that he has reconstructed the shrine to Baal he earlier had torn down at Yahweh's command (6:25–32). This fits the response of the Israelites, who "played the harlot" *(zānâ,* NIV "prostituted themselves") with it and for whom it became a "snare."[705] But the irony and twistedness of his actions should not be missed. Instead of himself, an image of God, clothed with the Spirit of Yahweh (6:34), Gideon created his own image and clothed it with pagan materials.

Fourth, in attracting Israelites from all over to the cult of the "ephod" in Ophrah, Gideon established this town as his capital. This conclusion seems to be supported by v. 29, which declares that Gideon ben Joash (note the dynastic form of the name) went and lived in his own house. The statement is superfluously tautological unless the verb *yāšab,* "to live," means more than "to reside."[706] Naturally people reside in their own houses. But if the verb is

---

[701] Calculated at .4046 ounces (11.33 grams) per shekel. On the weight of a shekel see Y. Ronen, "The Enigma of the Shekel Weights of the Judean Kingdom," *BA* 59/2 (1996): 122–26.

[702] נְטִפוֹת, from נָטַף, "to drip." Cf. נָטָף, "raindrop," in Job 36:27.

[703] Exod 28:15–30. In Judg 17:5; 18:14–20 the same word refers to Micah's priestly vestments.

[704] *CAD* E.183. Cf. C. Meyers, "Ephod," ABD 2.550. Recently H. A. Hoffner ("Hittite Equivalents of Old Assyrian *kumrum* and *epattum,* " *WZKM* 86 [1996]: 154–56) has suggested an association between the Old Assyrian word *epattu* (cognate to Hb. אֵפוֹד) and Hittite *ipantu,* the latter of which in at least one instance is construed with the preceding genitive of silver. This suggests minimally that precious metals were used for the ephod's ornamentation and maximally that the garment itself was made of precious metal fiber.

[705] The former expression represents one of the key words in the book describing Israel's conduct with pagan gods (2:17; etc.); the latter is used in 2:3 of the effect pagan gods had on Israel.

[706] Contra Webb (*Book of Judges,* 154), who maintains that Gideon retired to private life, in accordance with his rejection of the kingship. He admits, however, that in vv. 30–31 Gideon's house looks much more like that of a ruler than a private citizen.

understood mansively, "to sit [on a throne]," that is, "to be king, to reign," then the comment is sensible.[707]

Fifth, the ephod is said to have become a snare to Gideon "and his household." The expression "his household" *(bêtô)* is ambiguous, but in the context it also carries dynastic overtones.

Taking all these features of the narrative into account, the conclusion seems inescapable that despite his protestation, Gideon actually assumed the role of king "over Israel." But his is an aberrant and illicit kingship from the beginning. In the first instance the procedure by which they select their king is wrong. As noted above, he was not chosen by Yahweh to be king, as the Mosaic charter for kingship" (Deut 17:14–20) had explicitly demanded. Yahweh had indeed called Gideon to be his agent of deliverance from the Midianites, but there is no evidence that he envisaged him as king. In the second instance Gideon's conduct as king is aberrant from the beginning. The Mosaic charter had explicitly forbidden Israelite kings from using their position of power to multiply gold for themselves (v. 17). In his first act as king, this was precisely what he demanded.[708] But it was not his last nor his worst. None of the governors received as much from Yahweh as Gideon (except perhaps Samson); only he was "clothed" with the Spirit. But none of the governors does more harm to Israel. For the first time idolatry is officially sponsored by a leader of the nation. Israel need not wait for an officially anointed king to steepen the slope of their spiritual declension.[709] Gideon, as representative and leader of the people, will do what is right in his own eyes[710] and invite the people to follow him. Isaiah may remember the defeat of the Midianites as "the day of [the LORD's victory over] Midian" (Isa 9:4–7), but to the narrator, this is the day of Gideon.

28Thus Midian was subdued before the Israelites and did not raise its head again. During Gideon's lifetime, the land enjoyed peace forty years.

GOD'S GIFT OF SECURITY (8:28).   **8:28**   As in 3:11,30, and 4:23–24 together with 5:31b, the Gideon narrative concludes with a formal editorial reflection on the significance of Gideon's work for Israel in the dark days of the governors. Verse 28 announces that the Midianite problem was fully resolved and the land enjoyed forty years of quiet during Gideon's life. Two observa-

---

[707] For this usage of יָשַׁב see Exod 18:13 (and Joel 3:12 [Hb. 4:12], "sit to judge"); Exod 18:14; Pss 2:4; 9:7 [Hb. 8]; 29:10; 55:19 [Hb. 20]; 61:7 [Hb. 8]; 102:12 [Hb. 13]; Lam 5:19; Zech 9:5–6; Mal 3:3 For discussion of this use of יָשַׁב see M. Görg, "יָשַׁב, *yāšab*," *TDNT* 6.430–38.

[708] This interpretation of Gideon's response contrasts with that of G. I. Davies ("Judges VIII 22–23," *VT* 13 [1963]: 151–57), who argues that Gideon has not hereby refused the kingship. Rather, he has protested a kind of kingship and avowed that the kingship of him and his family would eliminate any personal and tyrannical element in their kingly rule.

[709] Cf. Solomon's court-sponsored apostasy in 1 Kgs 11:1–8.

[710] Cf. 17:6; 21:25.

tions may be made on the verse. First, the passive form of the verb, "and [Midian] was subdued," is ambiguous, leaving unspecified the agent of the subjugation. Although Gideon's countrymen credited the man with this benefit, the narrator intends this as a divine passive. Second, unlike his successor, Jephthah (12:7), and the "minor" governors (10:1–5; 12:8–15), Gideon is nowhere said "to have governed Israel." To the narrator he reigns *(mālak)*; he does not govern *(šāpaṭ)*. Unlike the victory over the Canaanites under the leadership of Deborah and Barak, there is no celebration of divine salvation. Only the narrator's note of quiet. The silence of Yahweh in this chapter and the silence of human lips that should have praised him are profound.

(3) The Legacy of Gideon (8:29–9:57)

If the foregoing narrative has left any doubts in the reader's mind about the author's disposition toward Gideon, these are put to rest in vv. 29–35. Whereas the paradigm followed in the other accounts would have this Midianite-Gideon cycle end with v. 28, here the narrator adds a seven-verse epilogue. The ambivalent character of the man is reflected in the alternation of names for the man in the remainder of this chapter. The name Gideon occurs in vv. 30,32, and 33, but these verses are framed by references to Jerubbaal (vv. 29,35).[711] In chap. 9 only Jerubbaal is used (9:1,16,24,57). Gideon's legacy is presented in the form of two short epilogic notes (vv. 29–32 and 33– 35 respectively) and a lengthy account of the adventures of his son (9:1–57).

[29]**Jerub-Baal son of Joash went back home to live.** [30]**He had seventy sons of his own, for he had many wives.** [31]**His concubine, who lived in Shechem, also bore him a son, whom he named Abimelech.** [32]**Gideon son of Joash died at a good old age and was buried in the tomb of his father Joash in Ophrah of the Abiezrites.**

GIDEON'S POSTDELIVERANCE REIGN (8:29–32). **8:29–32** Whereas vv. 22–27 had described Gideon's actions in the immediate aftermath of the victory over the Midianites, vv. 29–32 summarize his conduct during the forty years of peace that followed this victory. The description demonstrates that the behavior displayed in the final phases of the Midianite campaign set the pattern for the rest of his life. Despite Gideon's apparent rejection of dynastic rule over Israel (v. 23), the features noted bear all the marks of a monarchic administration.

First, as noted above, Gideon ruled as Jerubbaal ben Joash from his own house. Not only has he obviously separated from his father (cf. 6:25–32) and established his own household, but he "sits [as king?]" in his house. The narrator's preference for the name Jerubbaal at this point suggests this action

---

[711] Cf. above on 6:32 and 7:1.

reflected the Canaanite in him.

Second, Gideon established a large harem and fathered numerous progeny (v. 30). The number of his wives is not indicated, but this must be interpreted as one more violation of the Mosaic paradigm for kingship outlined in Deut 17:14–20.[712] The number of his sons, seventy, sounds like an idealized number, perhaps the number of a complete royal household.[713] In any case, such families were rare among private citizens. But the author may also have seen Gideon's family as a reflection of the Canaanite pantheon. According to the mythological texts discovered at Ras Shamra/Ugarit, the high god El and his wife Asherah had seventy sons.[714]

Third, Gideon regarded himself above the Deuteronomic proscriptions and married a concubine from Canaanite Shechem. The etymology of *pîlegeš* (NIV, "concubine") is obscure,[715] but the word always identifies female persons, whose primary function appears to have been to gratify the sexual desires of the man/husband. In most contexts in the Old Testament the concubine was considered a legal if second-ranked wife. The problem with this woman is not only that she is an addition to an already large harem; she is a Shechemite, that is, a Canaanite woman. Gideon's marriage to her represents a specific violation of Moses' absolute ban on all such marriages for all Israelites[716] and a general elevation of himself above the Torah, in violation of the Mosaic Charter for Kingship (Deut 17:18–19).

Fourth, Gideon names his son Abimelech. Like many Hebrew names, Abimelech is a sentence name, but Gideon's intention in naming his son is not clear. Several interpretations of the name are possible.

1. "Melek is my father." By this interpretation *mlk* is a proper divine name, related to Malik, a deity worshiped at Ebla (third millennium B.C.), Ugarit (second millennium B.C.), Phoenicia (first millennium B.C.),[717] and

---

[712] The added clause "for he had many wives" Deut 17:17.

[713] Cp. the seventy kings subject to Adoni-bezeq in 1:7 and Abdon's seventy sons in 12:14. Elsewhere we read of seventy sons of Jacob (Gen 46:27), seventy elders in Israel (Exod 24:1), and the seventy sons of Ahab (2 Kgs 10:1–7). The "Table of Nations" in Genesis 10 lists seventy descendants of Noah's three sons (not counting the names in the parenthetical comments). See also the reference to the seventy kinfolks (אחיו) of Panammu, king of YᵓDY (*KAI* 215:3; *SSI* I.14:3).

[714] *ANET*, 134. See F. C. Fensham, "The Numeral Seventy in the Old Testament and the Family of Jerubbaal, Ahab, Panammuwa and Athirat," *PEQ* 109 (1977): 113–15. The city of Ugarit was destroyed circa 1180 B.C., apparently at the hands of the Sea Peoples (of whom the Philistines represented one group), precisely during the period of the judges.

[715] The quadrilitaral structure points to a non-Semitic origin, perhaps Philistine. So C. Rabin, "The Origin of the Hebrew Word *Pīlegeš*," *JJS* 25 (1974): 353–64. Cf. Görg, "*Piggul* und *pilaegaeš* - Experimente zur Etymologie," *BN* 10 (1979): 10–11.

[716] Exod 34:15–16; Deut 7:3–4.

[717] The chief deity of Tyre was Melqart, a conflated form of *mlk* + *qrt*, "MLK/King of the City."

among the Ammonites (first millennium B.C.).[718] Three other characters in the Old Testament bear the name Abimelech. The fact that all of these were non-Israelites[719] heightens the suspicion that Gideon has given his son a syncretistic foreign name.[720]

2. "The [divine] king is my father."[721] By this interpretation the divine king could be Yahweh, which accords well with Gideon's statement in v. 23, but it flies in the face of Gideon's conduct. By this interpretation it is ironic that the son whose parentage represents a rejection of Yahweh's kingship is given this pious name.

3. "The king [Gideon] is my father." Under normal circumstances a name like Abimelech would have reflected the faith of the person giving the name, in this case Gideon. Regardless how sanctimonious the name sounds, however, the self-service we have witnessed in Gideon's behavior makes it difficult to resist the conclusion that the name Abimelech reflects the human father's perception of his own status in Israel. Many an Israelite who heard the name and who knew Gideon would have seen in "Abimelech" further evidence of his egotism. Whether or not this last interpretation reflects Gideon's own intention, the next chapter describes the conduct of a person who is driven by a ruthless passion to prove himself the heir of the human monarch Gideon.

Fifth, Gideon was buried in the dynastic tomb. The notice of Gideon's death in v. 32 is brief and to the point. Like Samson (16:31), Gideon was buried in the family tomb in his hometown. Unlike Samson, however, the narrator again refers to Gideon by patronymic, "son of Joash," the founder of the line from which this man came.

[33]No sooner had Gideon died than the Israelites again prostituted themselves to the Baals. They set up Baal-Berith as their god and [34]did not remember the LORD their God, who had rescued them from the hands of all their enemies on every side. [35]They also failed to show kindness to the family of Jerub-Baal (that is, Gideon) for all the good things he had done for them.

ISRAEL'S POST-GIDEON CONDUCT (8:33–35). **8:33–35** Despite Gideon's establishment of the aberrant "ephod" cult in his hometown, the final verses of the chapter seem to suggest that Gideon actually inhibited

---

[718] The national deity of the Ammonites was Milkom. Cf. 1 Kgs 11:5,33; 2 Kgs 23:13. For discussion of the deity Malik see H.-P. Müller, "Malik," *DDD*, 1005–12. On Milkom see E. Puech, "Milkom," *DDD*, 1076–80.

[719] They were all Philistines: Gen 20; 26:1–33; Psalm 34, superscription. In the last case the name replaces Achish (cf. 1 Sam 21:10–15), the name of the king of Gath, lending support to the view that Abimelech functioned as a dynastic title for Philistine kings. Cf. V. H. Matthews, "Abimelech," *ABD* 1.21.

[720] This will occur again Judg 13:24, where Samson is apparently named after the sun deity. See further below.

[721] Cf. Fowler, *Theophoric Personal Names*, 50–52; Layton, *Archaic Features of Canaanite Personal Names*, 116–17, 145–50; Halpern, "Abimelech," *ABD* 1.21.

Israel's spiritual and moral declension. As soon as he died, all restraint was cast to the wind, and the nation rushed headlong into apostasy. The narrator notes three dimensions to their evil.

First, the Israelites played the harlot with the Baals, committing themselves specifically to Baal-Berith. The name, which occurs only here and in 9:4, translates literally as "Lord/Baal of the Covenant." But who is this divinity? To answer the question we must resolve two issues: the identity of Baal and the nature of the covenant.

In view of the prominence of Baal in the book and especially in the Judges narratives, one's immediate response is to equate this Baal with the Canaanite storm and warrior deity.[722] The issue is complicated, however, by the reference to the Shechemite temple of El-Berith in 9:46. It is possible that Baal-Berith and El-Berith represent two separate deities, both of whom were worshiped in Shechem, but it is more likely that Baal and El were interchangeable designations for the same god. As I noted earlier, in Canaanite mythology El was the name of the supreme god, the husband of Asherah and father of seventy offspring, including Baal.[723] The word *baʿal* is not primarily a proper name, however, but a title meaning "lord, master," and the phrase *baʿal bĕrît*, "lord of the covenant."

Many understand El to have been the patron deity of Canaanite Shechem. This theory may be supported by the second part of the phrase, *bĕrît*, "covenant, treaty." It is the view of some that behind the word lies a political treaty between Shechem and some other Canaanite state, perhaps even Israel, in which El\Baal-Berith was invoked as the divine guardian and guarantor.[724] It is preferable to see in El/Baal-Berith an allusion to a treaty between Shechem and El which knit the deity and the population of the city in a special relationship, analogous to, but certainly different in many ways from, Yahweh's covenant with Israel.[725] This probably explains why the resi-

---

[722] Portrayed in iconographic images as a striding male figure brandishing a club and/or holding the lightning bolt in his hand. See *IBD* 1.153. Cf. Ora Negbi's Type III warrior deities in *Canaanite Gods in Metal* (Tel Aviv: University Institute of Archaeology, 1976), 29–41.

[723] Cf. *ANET*, 134. The name El is prominent in the patriarchal narratives, often appearing in conjunction with other names: El Elyon, El Shaddai, El Roi, etc.

[724] See the review of this position by T. J. Lewis, "The Identity and Function of El/Baal Berith," *JBL* 115 (1996): 403–4.

[725] So also Lewis, "El/Baal Berith," 415. Cf. pp. 404–14 for a discussion of possible analogues to Yahweh's covenant with Israel, though none of these is unequivocal. For variations of Lewis's theory see R. E. Clements ("Baal-Berith of Shechem," *JSS* 13 [1968]: 21–32), who interprets the "men/sons of Hamor" as "men/sons of the ass," the donkey being commonly slaughtered ritually in covenant ceremonies, and Y. Kaufmann (*The Religion of Israel*, trans. and abr. M. Greenberg [London: 1961], 138–39), who suggests that Israel drew its own understanding of Yahweh's covenant with them from Baal's relationship with Shechem. This interpretation is preferable to that of M. J. Mulder (*TDOT* 2.278; id., *DDD*, 272), who, appealing to 9:24, sees a connection between Baal-Berith and wine festivals and concludes that this god must have been a god of vegetation, the local manifestation of Baal par excellence.

dents of Shechem retreated to the temple of El-Berith for protection when they were in mortal danger (9:46).

Accordingly the Israelites added the sin of worshiping the patron deity of Shechem to the veneration of Baal in Ophrah, once again confirming the thesis announced in 2:18–19. In making El/Baal-Berith their god Israel went beyond mere harlotry with the local Baals. They have displaced Yahweh, their own covenant God, with this "Baal of the Covenant," and reversed the order of divine human relations. The exodus and Sinai narratives highlight Yahweh's initiative in calling Israel out of the nations to be his people (Exod 19:4), but now Israel has installed[726] as her god a pagan divinity of her own choosing.

Second, Israel forgot Yahweh their God, the one who had rescued them from all their enemies on every side. Like *šākaḥ*, "to forget," in 3:7, the expression *lōʾ zākĕrû*, "they did not remember," does not signify merely "to suffer amnesia." Surely the memory of the Midianite victory survived in their minds. Their problem was that they failed to take into account Yahweh's past saving acts on their behalf and to respond in accordance with his gracious salvation. How true this was will be demonstrated in the following chapter, which exhibits no knowledge of or allegiance to Yahweh whatsoever.[727]

Third, they acted treacherously toward Jerubbaal (Gideon) and his household. In this concluding comment the narrator tries to salvage something of Gideon. After all, he was called by God, and he was indeed the deliverer of Israel. Israel should have shown respect to the man and his household out of profound gratitude for what he had done. But the verse also contains several troubling elements concerning Gideon and his position in Israel, which support our interpretation of him as king over the nation. Significantly to the narrator the human hero of this cycle is primarily Jerubbaal and only secondarily Gideon. Furthermore, the narrator notes that the Israelites failed to demonstrate covenant commitment toward his house. The phrase *ʿāśâ ḥesed*, "to show kindness," refers to conduct in support of or in accordance with relational norms, whether they be between relatives, friends, host and guest, or master and servant.[728] Indeed the fact that *ḥesed*,[729] "kindness," is often associated with *bĕrît*, "covenant,"[730] raises questions concerning the nature of Gideon's relationship with Israel. It seems that despite his formal rejection

---

[726] The verb שִׂים means "to appoint, set in place."

[727] Cf. Polzin, *Moses and the Deuteronomist*, 174.

[728] Cf. *HALOT*, 336.

[729] The word occurs elsewhere in Judges only in 1:24, where עָשָׂה חֶסֶד, "to show loyalty," denotes the faithful fulfillment of an agreement with a Canaanite!

[730] See especially David's plea with Jonathan in 1 Sam 20:8: "Show kindness (וְעָשִׂיתָ חֶסֶד) to your servant, for you have brought your servant into a covenant of Yahweh (בְּרִית יהוה) with you." For discussion of the term see H.-J. Zobel, "חֶסֶד," *TDOT* 5.44–64, though Zobel downplays the covenantal implications of the term.

of the kingship, they had formalized some kind of official relationship with him. Finally, that relationship appears to have extended to Gideon's house, suggesting again that Gideon had indeed been offered and had accepted the dynastic rule over Israel.

Theological and Practical Implications

Four major truths flow from this account. First, like the rest of the stories of the deliverer governors, this account declares that if anything positive happens in the lives of the people of God it is by his grace, and not on account of merit. Evidence of any positive disposition toward Yahweh on the part of the Israelites as a whole or even Gideon in particular is scant. Nonetheless, moved to pity by the cries of his people over the distress caused by the enemy, God intervenes, calling forth his agent of deliverance and effecting the victory over the enemy. Yahweh is the only hero in the account.

Second, with God on one's side no enemy is invincible, and the victory is sure. The fact that three hundred men were able to defeat 135,000 Midianites without conventional weapons or conventional military strategy attests to the power of God. Indeed, God often deliberately selects ridiculous means to achieve his ends that we might learn that his kingdom is built "not by might, nor by power, but by my Spirit" (Zech 4:6).

Third, the greatest obstacle to the work of God among his people and in the world at large is the faithlessness of his people. Gideon was one of these faithless persons. He refused at first to follow the call of God. Only after he had [presumptuously] subjected Yahweh to a series of tests and after he had witnessed Yahweh's gracious answer did he finally accept the call to deliver his people. But Gideon's fleece was not about discovering the will of God, and his actions are not to be taken as a normative paradigm for discovering the will of God. It was about stubborn resistance to what one knows clearly to be God's will. In such cases God is not obligated to respond, and if he does, it is only by grace.

Fourth, those who are called to leadership in the kingdom of God face constant temptation to exchange the divine agenda for personal ambition. Ironically, the more impressive one's achievements for God, the greater the temptation. Having won deliverance for his people with a spectacular victory over the Midianites, Gideon began to act like it had been achieved with the "sword of Gideon" rather than the "sword of the LORD." Before long "Thy kingdom come" was replaced with "My kingdom come." Heedless of Deut 17:14–20, the servant of the people had become their despot. Unfortunately, the old adage "Power corrupts; absolute power corrupts absolutely" often holds true even in the church.

THE CANAANITE KINGSHIP OF GIDEON'S SON ABIMELECH (9:1–57). Given the change in tone and style and the relatively self-contained plot of chap. 9, it is not surprising that popular and scholarly treatment have tended to deal with the story of Abimelech as a separate literary unit. Following the pattern of previous cycles, the story should have ended at 8:28, to be followed by the next cycle beginning with the narrator's formulaic introduction to a new cycle: "The Israelites did evil in the eyes of the LORD."[731] But the story is far from finished. The ethical and spiritual seed sown by Gideon/Jerubbaal came to full bloom and fruition in the life of his son Abimelech. Chapter 9 may derive from a separate source, perhaps a Shechem tradition.[732] But the narrator invites the reader to recognize its organic coherence with the foregoing with a series of deliberate links: (1) references to the good that Jerubbaal had done for Israel (9:16–21,57; cf. 8:35); (2) Jerubbaal's connection with Shechem through his concubine (9:1; cf. 8:31); (3) references to El/Baal-Berith (9:4,46; cf. 8:33); (4) the identification of Abimelech's father as Jerubbaal (9:1–2,5,16,24,57; cf. 6:25–32; 7:1; 8:29,35); (5) references to the seventy sons of Jerubbaal (9:2,24; cf. 8:30); (6) references to Ophrah as the home of Jerubbaal (9:5; cf. 8:27); (7) the role of blood vengeance (9:24; cf. 8:19). Clearly the narrator views chap. 9 as a necessary sequel to and indeed the climax of the Gideon story. Despite these obvious connections, however, the story of Abimelech goes its own way in several extremely significant features.

First, from a stylistic perspective, in this the longest single pericope in the "Book of Deliverers" (2:6–16:31) the pace of the narrative is deliberately retarded with extraordinary emphasis on detail.

Second, in the use of names, Jerubbaal is used throughout for Gideon, and Yahweh is referred to only by the generic Elohim. These features reflect the author's unambiguous stance toward the nation and the characters:[733] Israel has been totally Canaanized; Baal has contended for himself and prevailed.

Third, with its preoccupation with the machinations and violence of Abimelech and the Shechemites, this chapter reads like a page out of a

---

[731] Cf. 3:7; 3:12; 4:1; 6:1; 10:6; 13:1.

[732] V. Fritz ("Abimelech und Sichem in Jdc. ix," *VT* 32 [1982]: 129–44) offers a complex five-stage history of the text of chap. 9, which begins with the Gaʿal episode (vv. 26–41) and ends with applicational commentary on Jotham's fable (vv. 16b–19a,24,57). Even if in its earliest phases the account affirmed kingship and the insertion of the Jotham fable yielded a more realistic picture, Fritz judges the account to be without any historical value. For a response and a more positive historical evaluation see H. N. Rösel, "Überlegungen Zu Abimelech und Sichem in Jdc. ix," *VT* 33 (1983): 500–503, who sees in the recollection of Abimelech's death at Thebez in 2 Sam 11:21 evidence of the historicity of the story.

[733] Cf. Polzin, *Moses and the Deuteronomist*, 174.

Canaanite history notebook.[734]

Fourth, unlike the surrounding narratives of the deliverer governors, this account is not concerned with an external threat but a problem of internal politics.

Fifth, this story concentrates on one small part of the country, Shechem. Apart from the editorial observation in v. 22, the only place Israel is named (v. 55), the reference is awkward. On the other hand, in apparent contradiction to 18:1; 19:1; and 21:25, which observe there was no king in Israel in those days, the narrator leaves the impression that Abimelech's rule extended beyond the Canaanite city of Shechem to the surrounding Israelite countryside (vv. 22,55).[735]

Sixth, in contrast to chaps. 6–7, but continuing the trend set in chap. 8, the reader observes the complete silence of Yahweh. God is mentioned only three times (as Elohim) in vv. 22,56–57, where the author breaks his pattern to provide a theological interpretation of events. Although ultimately Yahweh was behind the demise of Abimelech and Shechem, to a large extent he lets Israel destroy herself. There is no place here for divine soteriological intervention.

Structurally chap. 9 is complex,[736] but it may be divided into four principal segments, which together deliberately carry the plot to its [divinely] determined conclusion: Abimelech's seizure of the throne of Shechem (vv. 1–6); Jotham's response to Abimelech's usurpation of rule (vv. 7–21); the demise of Abimelech (vv. 22–55); epilogic conclusion (vv. 56–57). The striking feature of this structure is the extraordinary amount of space devoted to Abimelech's demise, which contrasts with the extremely small amount of interpretive narratorial comment (vv. 22–23,56–57). We will deal with each segment in turn.

¹Abimelech son of Jerub-Baal went to his mother's brothers in Shechem and said to them and to all his mother's clan, ²"Ask all the citizens of Shechem, 'Which is better for you: to have all seventy of Jerub-Baal's sons rule over you, or just one man?' Remember, I am your flesh and blood."

---

[734] Cf. the complaints of the petty kings of city-states in Canaan to their Egyptian overlord in the Amarna letters, *ANET*, 483–90. For a study of the political situation in Canaan during the period of Israel's conquest and settlement see J. P. van der Westhuizen, "The Situation in Syro-Palestine Prior to the Exodus/Conquest/Settlement as Reflected in the Amarna Letters," *Journal for Semitics* 7 (1995): 196–231. Would Abimelech have been considered a representative of the SA.GAZ/ʿApiru, a designation in the Amarna letters for troublesome segments of society accused of disloyalty, taking over cities, looting, and robbery? For a discussion of these elements see A. F. Rainey, "Unruly Elements in Late Bronze Canaanite Society," in *Pomegranates and Golden Bells: Studies in Biblical, Jewish, and Near Eastern Ritual, Law, and Literature in Honor of Jacob Milgrom*, ed. D. P. Wright et al. (Winona Lake: Eisenbrauns, 1995), 481–96.

[735] Cf. the survey of distinctive features of this chapter within its broader literary environment by Halpern, "The Rise of Abimelech Ben-Jerubbaal," *HAR* 2 (1978): 79–81.

[736] But not so complex as to be fragmented into a series of independent and secondary elements as we find in Richter, *Traditionsgeschichtliche Untersuchungen*, 246–61.

³When the brothers repeated all this to the citizens of Shechem, they were inclined to follow Abimelech, for they said, "He is our brother." ⁴They gave him seventy shekels of silver from the temple of Baal-Berith, and Abimelech used it to hire reckless adventurers, who became his followers. ⁵He went to his father's home in Ophrah and on one stone murdered his seventy brothers, the sons of Jerub-Baal. But Jotham, the youngest son of Jerub-Baal, escaped by hiding. ⁶Then all the citizens of Shechem and Beth Millo gathered beside the great tree at the pillar in Shechem to crown Abimelech king.

Abimelech's Seizure of the Throne of Shechem (9:1–6). **9:1** By naming one of Gideon/Jerubbaal's seventy sons and by commenting on his irregular parentage in 8:31, the narrator has created a sense of anticipation. This expectation is met in 9:1–6 as he describes in detail Abimelech's conduct after the death of his father.[737] Perhaps inspired by his own name ["my father is king"], Abimelech moved to Shechem, the home of his mother, determined to carve out his own kingdom. His strategy was carefully planned.

First, he secured the support of all his mother's relatives,[738] which included the entire extended family of his mother's father.[739] Actually, he dismembered his extended family into two irreconcilable factions: he sought the support of his maternal kin to elevate him to the throne, but to do so he put to death all his relatives on his father's side.[740]

9:2 Second, he enlisted his relatives to secure the support of the Shechemite aristocracy. The latter are referred to here and throughout this chapter as *ba῾ălê šĕkem*, "the lords/masters of Shechem" (not "citizens of Shechem" as NIV). Whereas previously in the book *ba῾ălîm* has always referred to "the baals," or local manifestations of the Canaanite deity,[741] here *ba῾ălê šĕkem* bears a nontheological sense.[742] But the choice of this word seems deliberate, keeping alive in the reader's mind the fundamental problem of Baalism on the one hand and providing a link with "Baal-Berith" (v. 4) and "Jerubbaal" on the other. If a *ba῾al bĕrît*, "one who owns a treaty," is a technical term for one who enters into a covenant relationship with another,[743] then a plurality of treaty partners would be designated *ba῾ălê bĕrît*, "owners of a

---

[737] By identifying Abimelech by patronym, "son of Jerubbaal," the narrator thrusts forward the Canaanite element in the event.

[738] Hb. אֲחֵי אִמּוֹ, lit., "brothers of his mother."

[739] Hb. כָּל־מִשְׁפַּחַת בֵּית־אֲבִי אִמּוֹ, lit., "the whole clan of the house of the father of his mother."

[740] Cf. Fokkelman, "Structural Remarks on Judges 9 and 19," *Sha῾arei Talmon*, ed. M. Fishbane et al. (Winona Lake: Eisenbrauns, 1991), 35.

[741] Cf. 2:13; 3:7; 8:33.

[742] So throughout this chapter: vv. 2,3,6,7,18,20,23a,23b,24,25,26,39. Cf. בַּעֲלֵי הָעִיר, "lords of the city," in v. 51. This usage occurs elsewhere in Josh 24:11; Judg 20:5; 1 Sam 23:11,12; 2 Sam 21:12, as well as in Aramaic (KAI 222 A:4; B:4–5; 224:23–24). Cf. *DNWSI* 1.184.

[743] Cf. Lewis, "El/Baal Berith," 413.

treaty." Indeed this usage of *ba‘ălîm* is attested in Gen 14:13, where Abraham's allies are referred to as *ba‘ălê bĕrît*. Accordingly, the aristocrats in this text may represent the human signatories to the covenant with El/Baal-Berith. Support for this interpretation may be drawn from v. 4a, which has Abimelech's allies financing his campaign of violence with seventy pieces of silver from the temple of Baal-Berith. Further support is found in vv. 46–47, where the nobles, identified as "lords of [NIV, "citizens in"] the tower of Shechem," seek asylum in the temple of El-Berith, their divine covenant partner and patron.

Abimelech dictated to his maternal relatives the speech they were to give to the nobility of the city. Appealing to the nobles' self-interest, they were to open with a rhetorical question (v. 2): *mah ṭôb lākem*, "Which is better [lit., "what is good"] for you?" Here the word *ṭôb* encompasses all that is necessary for their social, political, and economic well-being, but the word may also imply covenantal amity.[744] Continuing the interrogative method, this general question was to be followed up with two subarguments that appeal to the intelligence and pride of the city aristocracy: (1) the rule[745] of one man is preferable to the rule of seventy; (2) the rule of a relative is preferable to the rule of outsiders. Abimelech highlighted his own qualification for the latter by characterizing himself as being of their own bone and flesh.[746]

9:3–4 Abimelech's effectiveness as a politician is reflected in vv. 3–4. His relatives accepted his invitation to serve as his spokesmen and relay his message to the city fathers just as he had requested. The argument based on blood works and their sympathies quickly turn toward Abimelech.[747] Whereas the rest of Gideon's sons have no ethnic links with the people of Shechem, Abimelech is a relative through his mother. They agreed to finance his campaign to get rid of the existing rulership, providing him with seventy [shekels][748] from the temple [of El/Baal-Berith] treasury to hire hit men, one shekel for each targeted victim.[749] Abimelech's half-brothers may have been princes, sons of Gideon, but in the face of his inordinate hubris, their lives were incredibly cheap.[750] As in other ancient Near Eastern cities, the temple was the center of economic life, being the recipient of income of many kinds: vows, sacrificial

---

[744] See comments at v. 16. Cf. Boling, *Judges*, 171.

[745] The word for "rule," מָשַׁל, occurs twice, echoing its three occurrences in Gideon's sham rejection of the kingship in 8:22–23.

[746] The clause (lit.) "your bone and flesh am I" recalls Gen 2:23a, "This one is bone of my bone and flesh of my flesh," a covenantal idiom of kinship.

[747] NIV "they were inclined to follow Abimelech" is lit., "their hearts reached out toward Abimelech."

[748] No amount is specified in the Hebrew, but money was generally measured in shekels.

[749] Cf. 8:30; 9:2.

[750] Although the prices for slaves varied in different centuries, according to Lev 27:3–7 an adult male slave was worth fifty shekels; a female, thirty shekels.

offerings, gifts, penalties, et cetera. As the city aristocracy [and as heirs of the original makers of the covenant with El/Baal- Berith?] the *baʿālîm* of Shechem had access to the temple coffers. The men hired to perform the murderous acts are characterized as "reckless adventurers."[751]

9:5 Third, Abimelech led his hirelings in slaughtering sixty-nine of Jerubbaal's seventy sons. With his team of assassins at his heel, Abimelech traveled thirty miles from Shechem north to Ophrah, Jerubbaal's capital,[752] where they found his half-brothers. The narrator describes the actual location of the crime as "on one stone," an expression whose meaning and significance are uncertain. Some have seen in Abimelech's action a deliberate perversion of the Yahwistic cultic system,[753] but the event takes place at Ophrah, a pagan cult center (8:27). The most helpful clue comes from 1 Sam 14:33–34, where Saul calls for an abattoir's (=slaughterhouse) stone on which he slaughters all the oxen and sheep his forces had kept after the defeat of the Amalekites. Assuming a similar use of the stone, all of Gideon's sons could have been killed "on one stone" only by murdering them serially, one after the other. This was a calculated, brutal act of murder, not a quick slaughter of unsuspecting victims.[754]

In trying to establish the significance of these events one might compare this account with the description of Jehu's slaughter of Ahab's sons in 2 Kings 10. The parallels between the two events as reported are remarkable.[755] In both cases (1) the fathers, Gideon and Ahab, ruled with a high hand, murdering their own countrymen[756] and officially sponsoring pagan cults;[757] (2) the number of sons is explicitly declared to be seventy;[758] (3) the conspiracy against the sons is led by an ambitious individual (Abimelech, Jehu); (4) the leader is an outsider who secures the support of the aristocracy of the city through negotiation;[759] (5) the seventy sons of the king are brutally murdered;[760] (6) the leader of the conspiracy is an outsider who is publicly acclaimed king.[761]

---

[751] Hb. אֲנָשִׁים רֵקִים וּפֹחֲזִים, lit., "empty and reckless men."

[752] As absentee rulers the seventy sons of Jerubbaal probably did not affect the everyday life of Shechem significantly, but they would certainly have required tribute and taxes from the Canaanite city.

[753] According to Boling (*Judges,* 171), Abimelech demonstrates his contempt for Yahweh by slaughtering his half-brothers as sacrificial victims at the establishment of his new covenantal relationship with Shechem.

[754] This interpretation is less forced than that of Boling (*Judges,* 171), who sees here a "disastrous perversion of Yahwist sacrificial cultus."

[755] Cf. the similarities noted by Halpern, "The Rise of Abimelech Ben-Jerubbaal," *HAR* 2 (1978): 88–89.

[756] Judg 8:17; 1 Kgs 21:1–26; 2 Kgs 9:25–26.

[757] Judg 8:27–28; 1 Kgs 16:29–34; 2 Kgs 10:18.

[758] Judg 9:2,5; 2 Kgs 10:1,7.

[759] Judg 9:1–2; 2 Kgs 10:1–6a. In the former the nobility is identified as בַּעֲלֵי שְׁכֶם, "lords of Shechem"; in the latter, as גְּדֹלֵי הָעִיר, "great men of the city."

[760] Judg 9:4; 2 Kgs 10:1–11, esp. vv. 7–8.

[761] Judg 9:6; 2 Kgs 10:13.

Although these parallels are impressive, the differences are striking, particularly in the driving forces behind the two slaughters. The narrator of the Book of Kings is careful to characterize Jehu as the specially anointed agent of Yahweh's judgment upon Ahab,[762] but Abimelech appears to act on his own and to be driven by raw personal ambition. The narrator of Judges expresses obvious repulsion at the way Jerubbaal and his family were treated (8:34–35; 9:24). Nevertheless, in view of the links between the two accounts one suspects that in his mind Abimelech unconsciously also functions as Yahweh's agent of judgment upon the house of Gideon.

9:6 Fourth, Abimelech achieved his goal and was officially proclaimed king by the aristocracy of Shechem. Those who assembled to honor him are identified by two expressions, the familiar *kol baʿălê šĕkem*, "all the lords [NIV, "citizens"] of Shechem," and *kol bêt millôʾ*, "the entire house of Milloʾ." The meaning of the latter phrase remains uncertain. Some propose a massive earthen platform made of earthen fill for large urban structures such as the temple;[763] others, an artificially constructed acropolis, perhaps associated with the tower *(migdāl)* and functioning as part of the defensive system.[764] Since the phrase is appositional to "all the lords of Shechem," it is best interpreted as another designation for the nobility, those who had authority to participate in Abimelech's installation as king, perhaps the official administrators of the city.[765] The installation ceremony is conducted by the "Oak of the Pillar."[766] The nature and significance of this tree is unclear, but the association with the "pillar," a propped up stone representing Baal in Canaanite cult installations,[767] suggests a sacred tree in the sanctuary area.[768] The location heightens the religious significance of the event.

In reflecting on the process by which Abimelech achieved the kingship of Shechem, several observations on the political realities of the region may be made. First, whether or not Gideon exercised kingship, his sons exercised de facto power in a subject city-state and by their rule provoked the unrest of the citizens. Second, prior to Abimelech's rise, Shechem appears to have been governed by an assembly of notables, who apparently had the authority

---

[762] 1 Kgs 19:16; 2 Kgs 9:1–10; 10:9–11.

[763] Boling, *Judges,* 171; Gray, *Joshua, Judges and Ruth,* 318.

[764] Soggin (*Judges,* 168) suggests it was inhabited by soldiers and priests.

[765] Thus Görg ("Beth-Millo," *ABD* 1.690), who suggests a derivation from Egyptian *m rw,* which refers to a part of the king's court.

[766] The NIV renders מֻצָּב אֵלוֹן "the great tree at the pillar."

[767] Cf. 2 Kgs 3:10; 10:26,27. מֻצָּב is a variant spelling of the more common מַצֵּבָה.

[768] L. Wachter ("Zur Lokalisierung des sichemitischen Baumheiligtums," *ZDPV* 103 [1987]: 1–12) argues that the shrine probably was located at a spring, perhaps the spring of Askar, just northeast of Tel Balata.

to name the king.[769] Third, although Abimelech had no natural rights to the crown and had to win the support of the citizens, his success was undoubtedly due to his father Gideon's ties to Shechem.[770] But in so doing he was driven by extreme hubris. His insatiable lust for power probably contributed to the Shechemites' hasty shift in allegiance to Gaal, son of Ebed, the warrior kinsman, whose ethnic affiliation with them was undiluted.[771]

[7]When Jotham was told about this, he climbed up on the top of Mount Gerizim and shouted to them, "Listen to me, citizens of Shechem, so that God may listen to you. [8]One day the trees went out to anoint a king for themselves. They said to the olive tree, 'Be our king.'

[9]"But the olive tree answered, 'Should I give up my oil, by which both gods and men are honored, to hold sway over the trees?'

[10]"Next, the trees said to the fig tree, 'Come and be our king.'

[11]"But the fig tree replied, 'Should I give up my fruit, so good and sweet, to hold sway over the trees?'

[12]"Then the trees said to the vine, 'Come and be our king.'

[13]"But the vine answered, 'Should I give up my wine, which cheers both gods and men, to hold sway over the trees?'

[14]"Finally all the trees said to the thornbush, 'Come and be our king.'

[15]"The thornbush said to the trees, 'If you really want to anoint me king over you, come and take refuge in my shade; but if not, then let fire come out of the thornbush and consume the cedars of Lebanon!'

[16]"Now if you have acted honorably and in good faith when you made Abimelech king, and if you have been fair to Jerub-Baal and his family, and if you have treated him as he deserves— [17]and to think that my father fought for you, risked his life to rescue you from the hand of Midian [18](but today you have revolted against my father's family, murdered his seventy sons on a single stone, and made Abimelech, the son of his slave girl, king over the citizens of Shechem because he is your brother)— [19]if then you have acted honorably and in good faith toward Jerub-Baal and his family today, may Abimelech be your joy, and may you be his, too! [20]But if you have not, let fire come out from Abimelech and consume you, citizens of Shechem and Beth Millo, and let fire come out from you, citizens of Shechem and Beth Millo, and consume Abimelech!"

[21]Then Jotham fled, escaping to Beer, and he lived there because he was afraid of his brother Abimelech.

---

[769] Soggin ("Il regno di'Abimelek in Sichem [Giudici 9] e leistituzioni della città-stato siro-palestinese nei secoli XV–XI avanit Cristo," in *Studi in onore di Eduoardo Volterra* 6 [1973]: 161–89) notes that the Shechemites' retention of rule after they have installed Abimelech represents the reverse of what normally obtained in late second millennium Palestine.

[770] So also Reviv, "Early Elements and Late Terminology in the Descriptions of Non-Israelite Cities in the Bible," *IEJ* 27 (1977): 192–93. In this article (pp. 189–96) and his earlier essay ("The Government of Shechem in the El-Amarna Period and in the Days of Abimelech," *IEJ* 16 [1966]: 252–57) Reviv offers detailed discussions of the government of pre-Israelite Shechem.

[771] Thus also Reviv, ibid., 257.

Jotham's Response to Abimelech's Crimes (9:7–21).   So far Abimelech's plot seemed to be proceeding according to plan, except for one small problem. As noted at the end of v. 5, one of Jerubbaal's sons, Jotham, the youngest, had hidden from Abimelech and managed to escape his sword. The narrator had mentioned this small detail only in passing and had immediately resumed the main plot line concerning Abimelech, as if the usurper would have it all his way. But the early reference to Jotham has created an expectation for a complication in the plot. We are not disappointed. In vv. 7–21 the focus shifts to this young lad, who is presented as a positive character unlike his half-brother. In contrast to Abimelech, whose name reflects his ambition, Jotham's name is an expression of true Yahwistic faith: "the LORD is perfect/honest."[772] This will be confirmed by the manner in which God resolves the problems raised by Abimelech's conduct. In contrast to Abimelech, who seeks to rule by sheer power, Jotham is impotent. Since he is the only survivor of a family murdered by his half-brother, he cannot enter Shechem to make his point. Therefore he must speak from the mountain outside the city, and he must flee for his life as soon as he is through with his speech. Precisely because he has no power politically, he chooses a powerful rhetorical device—the fable.[773]

The text of vv. 7–21 is carefully constructed in standard Hebrew narrative style, but it is dominated by a lengthy speech by the lone escapee of Abimelech's purge. These verses are intentionally integrated with the surrounding narrative by the introductory comment in v. 7 and an epilogic statement in v. 21. The material between these borders, however, may be read as a semi-independent unit consisting of two major sections, Jotham's fable (vv. 8–15) and its interpretation (vv. 16–20). In function and content Jotham's speech parallels that of the prophet in 6:7–10.[774] In the former the prophet had brought a lawsuit against the people of Israel in the name of Yahweh. Here Jotham brings a lawsuit against the lords of Shechem in the name of his father Jerubbaal. Covenant language flavors both.

The Preamble to Jotham's Speech (9:7).   **9:7** Having heard of Abimelech's achievement of the throne in Shechem, the young Jotham came out of hiding [in Ophrah?] and headed for Mount Gerizim (modern Jebel et-Tor on the south side of the Nablus Valley), which overlooked the city of Shechem from the south.[775] From the acoustically advantageous top of the

---

[772] יוֹתָם is an abbreviated sentence name from יהוה + תָּמַם (cf. Fowler, *Theophoric Personal Names*, 80, 112) bearing assonantal links with אֱמֶת, "truth, integrity," the Leitmotif of Jotham's interpretation of his fable (vv. 16,19). Garsiel (*Biblical Names*, 224–25) rightly rejects an association of the name with יַתְמוּת, "orphanhood."

[773] Cf. G. Savran, "The Character as Narrator in Biblical Narrative," *Proof* 5 (1985): 12.

[774] So also Webb, *The Book of Judges*, 155–56.

[775] Opposite Mount Ebal north of the city.

mountain[776] he raised his voice and called the aristocracy of Shechem to attention. Like a herald announcing an official proclamation, Jotham begins formally with a carefully constructed sentence: "Listen to me, lords [NIV "citizens"] of Shechem, so that God may listen to you." Unlike Abimelech, who is driven entirely by self-interest, Jotham seems to have the best interests of the Shechemites at heart, holding out the possibility that they may receive a hearing with God. The opening clause, however, suggests that a favorable response from God is contingent upon their listening to him instead of to the seductive promises of Abimelech. The implication is that Jotham posed as a true spokesman for God. Only time will tell whether the narrator confirms this role for him. Additionally, Jotham does not attack Abimelech directly; this address is for the citizens of the city.

The Report of Jotham's Speech (9:8–15). Jotham proceeded to lecture the lords of Shechem with a story that has become a classic in world literature. In terms of genre vv. 8–15 contain the finest example in Scripture of a fable, which by definition typically involves a short narrative in poetry or prose that teaches a moral lesson and involves creatures, plants, and/or inanimate objects speaking or behaving like human characters.[777] Most scholars assume that the narrator has taken over a preexistent story and adapted it to its present literary context because it suited the narrator's antimonarchic stance. The tensions between the fable and the surrounding text are obvious: (1) Whereas this *apologia* is composed in poetry, the surrounding narrative is prose. (2) Whereas this *apologia* has the trees approaching candidates when looking for a king, in the narrative Abimelech approaches the people and actively seeks their support. (3) Whereas this *apologia* considers three candidates before settling on the fourth, the narrative knows of only one candidate, Abimelech. (4) Whereas this *apologia* appears to critique kingship in general, the narrative is concerned only with the style of kingship represented by Abimelech. (5) Whereas this *apologia* speaks only of "the trees," v. 15b, which most consider an editorial addition, refers to "the cedars of Lebanon" in v. 15b.[778] (6) Whereas this *apologia* is overtly political in character, the narrative is theologically neutral. (7)

---

[776] Cf. Deut 11:29 and 27:12–13, where Moses selects the slopes of Gerizim and Ebal as the place where Israel was to recite antiphonally the covenant blessings and curses of the covenant once the Israelites have crossed into the promised land. For a study of the acoustical qualities of this site see B. C. Crisler, "The Acoustics and Crowd Capacity of Natural Theaters in Palestine," *BA* 39/4 (1976): 138–39.

[777] See J. A. Cuddon, *A Dictionary of Literary Terms and Literary Theory*, 3d ed. (Oxford: Basil Blackwell, 1991), 322. On OT fables see O. Eissfeldt, *The Old Testament: An Introduction: The History of the Formation of the Old Testament*, trans. P. R. Ackroyd (New York: Harper & Row, 1965), 37–38. For a comparable fable from ancient Babylon see "The Dispute Between the Tamarisk and the Date Palm," *ANET*, 592–93.

[778] Not to mention the shift from second to third person between 15a and 15b. But the shift from second to third person in v. 15 is matched by the same shift in the interpretation, vv. 19–20.

Whereas the narrative (v. 57) interprets Jotham's words as a "curse," this notion is foreign to the *apologia*.[779] The points of disjunction are unmistakable. Nevertheless, to argue on these grounds that the fable has been artificially inserted into the narrative is to impose modern Western standards of literary consistency upon an ancient historiographic treatise with a distinct theological and rhetorical agenda.[780] When rhetoricians employ illustrative stories, they do not generally insist that every element of the story be consistent with every element of the rest of the speech. Admittedly, there the fable could have been inserted into the account, but there is no reason a person as clever as Jotham could not have composed the speech for this particular occasion. For all its distinctive features, it suits the original rhetorical context and fits in perfectly with its present literary environment. Whether or not these verses are formatted as poetry,[781] stylistically the repetitive pattern certainly gives it the feel of elevated prose.

Structurally the *apologia* divides into two uneven parts, a preamble setting forth the agenda (v. 8a), followed by four overtures[782] in which the agenda is developed (vv. 8b–15). The former sets the stage for the fable with a terse announcement that the trees went out to anoint a king over themselves. Performed at the time of coronation, the rite of anointing *(māšaḥ)* involved an authorized official pouring sacred oil over the head of the person selected for public office.[783] The course of the tree's search is sketched in four stages, as they went from plant to plant requesting them to come and "reign" *(mālak)* over them (NIV, "be our king"), the Shechemites (vv. 8b,10,12). The first three candidates represent the three most prized species of domestic plants in ancient Palestine: the olive tree, the fig tree, and the grape vine. When approached, each plant declined the offer of kingship because it was too busy with productive service to be bothered with the worthless office of king-

---

[779] Similarly Soggin, *Judges*, 174–75. See also Becker *Richterzeit und Königtum*, 190–93. For a contrary view see R. Bartelmus, "Die sogenannte Jothamfabel-eine politisch-religiöse Parabeldichtung. Anmerkungen zu einem Teilaspekt der vordeuteronomischen israelitischen Literaturgeschichte," *ThZ* 41 (1985): 101. Bartelmus argues that the fable derives from an ancient Israelite tradition from the period of the settlement, but the composition is the work of the author of the book, a north Israelite with a rigorous antimonarchic Yahwistic agenda.

[780] This is true of the Book of Judges as a whole and the Gideon narrative in particular.

[781] See *BHS*, followed by Soggin (*Judges*, 171) and Boling (*Judges*, 166). For an analysis of the lines and their syllable counts see Boling (pp. 172–73).

[782] Vv. 8b–9,10–11,12–13,14–15a.

[783] On the rite see Z. Weizman, "Anointing as a Motif in the Making of the Charismatic King," *Bib* 57 (1976): 378–98; E. Kutsch, *Salbung als Rechtsakt im Alten Testament und im Alten Orient* (Berlin: A. Töpelmann, 1963); R. de Vaux, "The King of Israel, Vassal of the LORD," in *The Bible and the Ancient Near East*, trans. D. McHugh (London: Darton, Longman & Todd, 1972), 152–80; T. N. D. Mettinger, *King and Messiah: The Civil and Sacral Legitimation of the Israelite Kings* (Lund: CWK Gleerup, 1976), 185–232.

ship—waving (*nûaᶜ*, NIV "hold sway") over the trees.[784] If this is not an evaluation of kingship in general, this story is at least a derisive repudiation by the narrator of the style of kingship represented by Abimelech. Such kings have no nobility or value for their subjects.

Unlike Abimelech, whose seizure of the throne was driven by sheer self-interest, each of these trees acknowledged its value to society as a whole and expressed its refusal to abandon what all would recognize as true public service.

9:8–9   First, the olive tree *(zayit)* declared its unwillingness to continue to provide oil with which gods and humans are honored. The product of the olive is identified as *dešen*, literally "fatness," which serves as a synonym for *šemen*, the more common term for olive "oil." Olive oil probably was the most valuable agricultural product in the ancient world, being used every day as cooking oil, medicine, laxative, lubricant, leather softener, fuel in lamps, an ingredient in perfumes, and as in sacred rituals as a sacrificial offering and in anointing ceremonies. In a context involving an invitation to kingship, the olive appropriately cites its ceremonial value. The olive would rather honor others than be narcissistically anointed with its own oil.

9:10–11   Second, the fig *(tĕ'ēnâ)* refused to stop producing sweetness and fruit for others. The fruit of the fig could be eaten fresh, made into cakes or fig wine, and used as a sweetener.

9:12–13   Third, the vine *(gepen)* declined the honor of kingship so it may continue to cheer gods and humans with its wine. The vine highlighted the value of its product by using the term for fresh wine *(tîrôš)* rather than the generic word *yayin*.[785]

9:14–15   The fable reaches its climax in the fourth overture (vv. 14–15) when the trees approach the bramble *('āṭād)*[786] with the identical offer of kingship. Ironically it was the plant with absolutely nothing positive to contribute to human or divine life who accepted the proposal. His acceptance speech consists of three parts. First, repeating the three key expressions from v. 8 ("anoint," "king," "over us/you"), it appeared to question their good faith (*be'ĕmet*, lit., "in truth"; NIV, "really"),[787] but he was a flippant formality. Second, he invited the trees to take refuge in his shade. The image of trees "seeking cover" beneath a bramble is absurd, not only for reasons of size, but also because buckthorn offer neither shade nor cover; they have thorns!

---

[784] According to J. Joosten, "הֶחָדֵלְתִּי *forma mixta?*" *ZAW* 102 (1990): 96–97, the first word in each line, הֶחָדֵלְתִּי is a mixed form, the vowel under the *ḥêth* being a combination of *šĕwâ* and *qameṣ*, rather than a *ḥatep-qameṣ*.

[785] On wine (either תִּירוֹשׁ or יַיִן) gladdening (שָׂמַח, in *piel*) see elsewhere Pss 46:5; 104:15; Eccl 10:19; cf. "the heart will be gladdened as with wine" in Zech 10:7.

[786] A species of buckthorn, usually equated with *lycium europaeum. HALOT* 1.37; *DCH* 1.202.

[787] אֱמֶת involves covenant commitment. Cp. the performance of Abimelech's anointing under the sacred oak in v. 6.

Third, in case the trees were playing games with him, he invoked a curse upon the trees, that fire may come and consume them in one great conflagration. The bramble's excessively high self-esteem is reflected in his claiming his own person as the source of the fire (the king himself would punish faithless subjects), as well as in his specific designation of the trees as the "cedars of Lebanon." He will not be king over just any trees; the most majestic trees on earth are subject to him.

The Interpretation of Jotham's Speech (vv. 16–20).   Abandoning the third person style of a storyteller, Jotham addressed the people of Shechem directly in v. 16. The interpretation divides into two uneven parts, the first (vv. 16–19) challenging the integrity of those who have made Abimelech king (matching the bramble's questioning of the trees' integrity in v. 15a); the second (v. 20) invoking a curse upon them if they have indeed acted in bad faith (matching the bramble's curse in v. 15b).

9:16   By beginning and ending the interpretation with the identical clause in vv. 16 and 19, "If you have acted honorably and in good faith," that is, "with complete integrity" (a hendiadys),[788] The clause is literally, "and now if with truth [*ʾĕmet*, which can be translated "good faith"] and with perfection [*tāmîm*] you act..." Jotham identifies the critical issue in their anointing of Abimelech. Like the term for "good faith" *(ʾĕmet)*, in contexts like this *tāmîm*, "perfection," conveys the notion of absolute and total fidelity.[789] The rest of the chapter will demonstrate how sincere they were in making him king. But there is another dimension to this matter of integrity that Jotham must probe. In view of Abimelech's brutality against his own family he might have encouraged the people of Shechem to renege on their covenant with their newly anointed king. But they have been accomplices in Abimelech's crimes. Therefore he lifts the issue of integrity to another level: have they treated Jerubbaal rightly,[790] in accordance with the merits of his actions?[791]

9:17–18   Initially (v. 16) it appears that Jotham will deal objectively with the issue of the Shechemites' treatment of Jerubbaal, but in v. 17 he breaks off in a eulogy of his father that reveals his own personal pain.[792] After Jerubbaal had risked his life,[793] fighting on Shechem's behalf and rescuing them from the

---

[788] Because the material between these clauses is deemed to interrupt the context, M. Anbar ("La 'Reprise'," *VT* 38 [1988]: 391) treats the repeated words and the intervening material as a secondary interpolation.

[789] Cf. M. Weinfeld, "The Covenant of Grant in the Old Testament and in the Ancient Near East," *JAOS* 90 (1970): 186.

[790] On the contextual meaning of טוֹב, "good," see above on v. 2.

[791] Hb. כִּגְמוּל יָדָיו, lit. "according to the accomplishment of his hands." The expression occurs elsewhere only in Prov 12:14; Isa 3:11.

[792] Note the first person pronominal suffixes on אָבִי, "my father" (v. 17), and בֵּית אָבִי, "house of my father" (v. 18).

[793] Hb. וַיַּשְׁלֵךְ אֶת־נַפְשׁוֹ מִנֶּגֶד, lit. "he threw his own life forward."

Midianites, they have committed treachery against him by attacking his (Jotham's) father's house, killing his seventy sons one by one[794] and making Abimelech the son of his slave girl[795] king over themselves because he was their relative.

9:19–20 In v. 19 Jotham returns to the train of thought suspended at the end of v. 16. If the people of Shechem have acted with complete integrity toward Jerubbaal and his family, then let them celebrate with Abimelech, and let him celebrate with them. But if not—then let the two parties to this treacherous alliance destroy each other. Like the fable in v. 15a, in v. 20 the dialogue shifts from the second person of direct address to the third person. Except for the appropriate substitution of "Abimelech" for "the bramble," and "the lords [NIV, "citizens"] of Shechem" for "the cedars of Lebanon," the construction of the first part of the verse echoes the bramble's words in v. 15b verbatim. However, in keeping with Jotham's own bitterness toward his half-brother for his treachery against Jerubbaal and his family, to the threat from Abimelech upon the citizens of the city he adds a threat from the residents[796] upon Abimelech. Although the word "curse," does not appear in this context, the narrator is certainly correct in v. 57 to interpret v. 20 as a curse.

Jotham's Flight (9:21).   **9:21**   The episode involving Jotham concludes with a note on the youngest son of Jerubbaal. Knowing that his brother Abimelech would not let up on his crusade against the family until every member had been killed, and having invoked the curse upon Shechem and Abimelech, Jotham fled for his life to Beer. The site cannot be identified, and the word *bĕʾēr*, "well," may in fact be intended as a generic designation for an empty well where he hid out for a long time, presumably until after Abimelech's death.[797]

Theological and Practical Implications

Jotham's speech giving his view on kingship is rendered all the more significant since he functions here as the *alter ego* of the narrator. As it turns out, his speech is a literary cartoon whose message is remarkably relevant even in the modern world.

---

[794] On the expression "on one stone" see above on v. 5.

[795] The disparaging expression בֶּן אֲמָתוֹ, "son of a slave girl," also occurs in Gen 21:10 and Exod 23:12. The choice of word reflects an intentional degradation of Abimelech from the son of a concubine (פִּילֶגֶשׁ, 8:31). Cf. A. D. Crown, "Judges IX in the Light of Its Humour," *Abr Nahrain* 3 (1961/62): 96.

[796] As in v. 6 בַּעֲלֵי שְׁכֶם, "the lords of Shechem," is paired with בֵּית מִלּוֹא, "house of Millo," which apparently represents another designation for the nobility of the town.

[797] Cf. 2 Sam 17:18–21, which describes David's advisors Jonathan and Ahimaaz hiding in a well.

First, whereas in the ancient Near East kingship was viewed as positive, desirable, necessary, and coveted by all, Jotham perceives it as fundamentally negative. It is self-destructive and destructive of the very ones it is intended to protect.[798]

Second, persons of honor engaged in constructive activity have no time for political agendas. They are too caught up in serving humanity, and so the rule often falls to the despicable elements of society.

Third, rulers have a tendency to desire power for the worst reasons—their own narcissistic self-interest. In order to gain power they are often forced to offer promises they cannot fulfill.

Fourth, in the words of a modern sage, people tend to get the leaders they deserve. Jotham's fable is not only a polemic against a certain kind of kingship; it is actually directed primarily at those who are foolish enough to anoint a worthless man to be their king.[799] But this is not to be confused with the ancient Israelite ideal by which the ideal monarch was the least member of the least family of the least clan of the least tribe. Abimelech, the worthless man, who was significant in his own eyes, contrasts with the early Saul and David.

Although Jotham's fable can be interpreted as a general critique of kingship, as a whole and in context his speech represents the rejection of Abimelech's style of kingship in particular. As Webb has observed,[800] Abimelech's crime is not that he became king, nor is the Shechemites' crime that they made him king. The issue is their treacherous acts against Gideon, the person God had chosen to be his agent of deliverance from the Midianites. As in 8:22, Israel's well-being and her future are not to be found in new constitutional forms and political institutions but in a wholehearted return to Yahweh. In the Book of Judges the issue is primarily religious and spiritual, not political.

The Demise of Abimelech (9:22–55). The bulk of the remainder of the chapter is concerned with the fulfillment of Jotham's words. Since the author nowhere explicitly characterizes Jotham's speech as a message received from Yahweh,[801] the reader may assume that Jotham's story and its interpretation are concoctions of his own mind. Nowhere does the young man claim divine inspiration, not even in the interpretive lessons he draws from it. However, the reader has been alerted to consider the possibility of his divine inspiration by his opening words in v. 7b: "Listen to me, lords of Shechem, that God may listen to you." At the very least he speaks from a theological base. In any case, the rest of the chapter is concerned with proving his words true. In fact, in a

---

[798] Cf. Samuel's speech in 1 Sam 8:10–18.

[799] So also E. H. Maly, "The Jotham Fable—Anti-Monarchical," *CBQ* 22 (1960): 299–305. Halpern ("The Rise of Abimelech," 93) observes that the fable does not impugn any political institution as the conduct of the Shechemites.

[800] Webb, *Book of the Judges,* 159.

[801] Cf. 2:1–4; 6:7–10; 10:11–15.

rare moment in an otherwise totally secular chapter, in v. 23 God intervenes in human affairs so that the sequence of events culminating in the death of Abimelech and the decimation of the Shechemite lords confirms the accuracy and vitality of both the first and second elements of Jotham's curse.

²²After Abimelech had governed Israel three years, ²³God sent an evil spirit between Abimelech and the citizens of Shechem, who acted treacherously against Abimelech. ²⁴God did this in order that the crime against Jerub-Baal's seventy sons, the shedding of their blood, might be avenged on their brother Abimelech and on the citizens of Shechem, who had helped him murder his brothers. ²⁵In opposition to him these citizens of Shechem set men on the hilltops to ambush and rob everyone who passed by, and this was reported to Abimelech.

The Roots of Abimelech's Demise (9:22–25).   The following narrative is carefully crafted, follows an easily recognized structure, and begins on an extremely significant note. Although the course of events seems to be determined by the free decisions and machinations of the actors in the drama, the narrator serves early notice that this is not really the case. If in the end Shechem was torn by civil war and Abimelech himself was slain, this is to be attributed to the work of God, whose hand may be hidden to the personalities involved but is obvious to the eyes of faith.

9:22   A hint of things to come is given by the opening time notice: Abimelech governed Israel three years. Three elements of the statement are significant. First, the verb for "govern" *(śārar)*⁸⁰² is derived from the word for "captain, official" *(śār)*. Although the lords of Shechem have anointed him as *melek,* "king," the narrator refuses to dignify him with the title. Second, the narrator appears to expand the scope of his authority beyond the walls of Shechem to Israel as a whole. As elsewhere in the book, however, "Israel" does not necessarily mean the entire nation but may be restricted to a local area the narrator recognizes as representative of the country as a whole. His bias is reflected in the fact that a Canaanite city is identified as a part of Israel.⁸⁰³ Third, unlike the other narratives in the book, the length of Abimelech's reign is announced at the beginning, sending an early signal to the reader that Abimelech will not enjoy for long the power he seized through his treacherous and criminal actions against the family of his father.

9:23–24   In v. 23 the narrator announces the plan for Abimelech's quick demise: God has personally intervened in the affairs of Shechem to avenge the violence committed by Abimelech and the lords of Shechem against the members of Jerubbaal's family. Reflective of the pervasively Canaanite tone of this chapter, the narrator prefers the generic designation for God, *ʾĕlōhîm,*

---

⁸⁰² The verb is שָׂרַר, vocalized as if from סוּר.
⁸⁰³ Cf. 1:27–30.

to the personal name of Israel's covenant Lord, *yhwh*. The agent/agency through which Yahweh achieves this end is identified as a *rûaḥ rāᶜâ*, translated in the NIV as "an evil spirit." But this translation is unfortunate because it raises unnecessary questions concerning the morality of God's character and actions.

To understand the meaning of the phrase *rûaḥ rāᶜâ*, two considerations must be borne in mind. First, the Hebrew word *rāᶜâ* can have two meanings: moral malignancy or experiential misfortune, analogous to English "ill," which refers primarily to moral evil[804] and secondarily to unpropitious conditions.[805] In contexts like this the word is not to be interpreted in a moral sense, as if the Spirit of God is morally defective, but in the normal profane sense, "bad" as opposed to "good."[806] Second, in each of the four contexts in which some variation of the phrase *rûaḥ rāᶜâ* occurs, this spirit produces negative and destructive effects upon the object, that is, unpropitious conditions.[807]

This activity of the *rûaḥ* comes dangerously close to the role played by demons in ancient Near Eastern thought. In general demons were perceived as agents of the gods, whose role was to execute divinely decreed blessings and punishments for sin, the latter usually by inflicting their victims with illnesses. In the first millennium B.C., however, a revolution in conception occurred as demons came to be increasingly associated with the netherworld, which was thought to be populated by them.[808] This extrabiblical preoccupation with demons contrasts with the picture in the Old Testament, which fails to develop a sophisticated demonology. Although in later Jewish magical

---

[804] Note expressions like "ill will," "ill repute," "ill feelings toward someone."

[805] Cf. *The Compact Edition of the Oxford English Dictionary* (Oxford: Oxford University Press, 1971), 37–38.

[806] Cf. Neh 9:20. Note the merism in "the tree of the knowledge of good and bad" in Gen 2:9.

[807] In 1 Sam 16:14–23 the phrase רוּחַ אֱלֹהִים רָעָה, "bad spirit of God," appears five times. Here the "bad spirit" that torments (בעת) Saul with some sort of mental derangement finds its positive counterpart in David, whose inspired musicianship brings healing to the king (טוֹב לוֹ, "it was good to him" [vv. 16,23], answers to רָעָה, "bad," in רוּחַ רָעָה). In 1 Sam 18:10–12a רוּחַ אֱלֹהִים רָעָה, "bad spirit of God," rushes upon Saul *while* David is playing his harp, inspiring prophetic behavior in Saul and driving him to hurl his spear at David. A similar event happens in 1 Sam 19:9, though without the prophetic response. 2 Kgs 19:7 does not identify the רוּחַ either as אֱלֹהִים רוּחַ or יהוה רוּחַ, but the grammatical construction, "I will put [נָתַן] a רוּחַ in him" and the effects of the רוּחַ suggest a phenomenon similar to 1 Sam 16:14–23. Through this רוּחַ Yahweh causes derangement in mind of the Assyrian king so he hears rumors, lifts the siege of Jerusalem, and returns home, where he dies. For further discussion of this issue see D. I. Block, "Empowered by the Spirit of God: The Work of the Holy Spirit in the Historiographic Writings of the Old Testament," *SBJT* 1 (1997): 50–52.

[808] For summaries of ANE conceptions see J. Black and A. Green, *Gods, Demons and Symbols of Ancient Mesopotamia: An Illustrated Dictionary* (London: British Museum Press, 1992), 63–65; G. J. Riley, "Demon," *DDD*, 447–49; J. K. Kuemmerlin-McLean, "Demons," *ABD* 2.138–40.

texts *rûaḥ* may denote "demon,"[809] in our passages the identity of the *rûaḥ* remains vague, and its role is clearly subservient to Yahweh. According to vv. 23–24, God's intention in sending the bad *rûaḥ* is twofold. On the one hand, by sending the "calamitous spirit" between Abimelech and the nobles of Shechem he dissolves the amity that existed between king and subjects. This disturbance in the relationship of former allies causes the nobles to renege on their covenant with Abimelech (v. 23b). The verb *bāgad* denotes fundamentally "to break faith, to deal treacherously," especially with someone with whom one is in covenant relationship.[810] The narrator's word choice is deliberate, representing the polar opposite to the "absolute fidelity" called for by *ʾĕmet* and *tāmîm* with which Jotham had been so preoccupied in vv. 16 and 19. The use of the verb *šālaḥ*, "to send," puts this *rûaḥ* in a category with other calamitous agents sent out by Yahweh: fire, plague, bloodshed, wild beasts, the sword, and famine.[811] Because of this *rûaḥ* former allies become mortal enemies. Although the immediate cause of Abimelech's death was a resourceful woman of Thebez (v. 53), ultimately the circumstances that led to his ignominious end were caused by the *rûaḥ* sent by God.

On the other hand, God sends his "calamitous spirit" to punish both Abimelech and the lords of Shechem. Through the activity of the spirit God will avenge Abimelech's crime[812] against Jerubbaal's seventy sons and bring their blood on Abimelech's head.[813] At the same time through the Spirit's work God will punish the aristocrats of the city because they supported Abimelech[814] in the murder of his brothers.

9:25 Verse 25 describes how the divine intention announced in v. 23 was

---

[809] The expression רוּחַ רָעָה, "bad spirit," represents an exact equivalent to *rwḥh bšth*, "the evil spirit," mentioned in numerous Aramaic amulets from the early Christian period. For a study of these and other magical texts see J. Naveh and S. Shaked, *Amulets and Magic Bowls: Aramaic Incantations of Late Antiquity* (Jerusalem: Magnes, 1985). See especially text 7:6 but also 3:4 and 7:12. These demons could be either male or female *(zkr wnqbn)*. One, whom the author of the amulet inscription is trying to exorcise, is called "Fever [and] Shivering" *(rwḥh dmtqrʾ ʾšth ʾwryth*, 9:1; cf. Naveh and Shaked, pp. 82– 83); another is called *rwḥ grmyh*, "demon [that causes sickness] of the bones" (1:20–21, on which see Naveh and Shaked, p. 45). But this late Jewish usage was anticipated by the Nabateans, who also employed *rḥ* with this sense. A second century B.C. incantation text opens with an address to *rwḥʾ*, "O Spirit," which is paired with *ʾʿtryʾ*, "O Aʿattars," which Naveh understands as "gods, spirits, or demons" ("A Nabatean Incantation Text," *IEJ* 29 [1979]: 116).

[810] Cf. *HALOT*, 108.

[811] In the Book of Ezekiel we find a remarkably complete series of punitive agents: fire (אֵשׁ, 39:6), plague (דֶּבֶר, 14:19,21; 28:23), bloodshed (דָּם, 23:3), famine (רָעָב, 5:16; 14:13,21), wild beasts (חַיָּה רָעָה, 5:17; 14:21), the sword (חֶרֶב, 14:21).

[812] Hb. חָמָס לָבוֹא, "that the violence [of the seventy sons of Jerubbaal] might come," on Abimelech.

[813] שׂוּם דָּם עַל, lit. "to place the blood upon," is a figure of speech for holding a murderer responsible for taking the life of another and imposing on him the death sentence.

[814] The idiom חִזְּקוּ אֶת־יָדָיו translates lit. "they strengthened his hands" to kill his brothers.

fulfilled. Expressing a complete reversal in their disposition toward Abimelech, the lords of Shechem adopted the strategy of highway robbers setting ambushes[815] against Abimelech on the hilltops and robbing all who went up and down the roads in the vicinity of Shechem. The *ṭôb,* "good, well-being," which Abimelech had promised the Shechemites in v. 2 will be denied him and his subjects. Eventually word of the noblemen's terrorist activities reached the king.

²⁶Now Gaal son of Ebed moved with his brothers into Shechem, and its citizens put their confidence in him. ²⁷After they had gone out into the fields and gathered the grapes and trodden them, they held a festival in the temple of their god. While they were eating and drinking, they cursed Abimelech. ²⁸Then Gaal son of Ebed said, "Who is Abimelech, and who is Shechem, that we should be subject to him? Isn't he Jerub-Baal's son, and isn't Zebul his deputy? Serve the men of Hamor, Shechem's father! Why should we serve Abimelech? ²⁹If only this people were under my command! Then I would get rid of him. I would say to Abimelech, 'Call out your whole army!'"

The Conspiracy of Gaal (9:26–29). **9:26** In v. 26 the narrative takes a surprising turn. Instead of describing Abimelech's response to the report of the Shechemite treachery, which the concluding clause in v. 25 had led the reader to expect, a new but enigmatic figure, Gaal, appears out of nowhere to champion the cause of the rebels. Information on Gaal is sketchy. The name, from *ga⁽al,* "to loathe," looks suspiciously like a nickname, but it bears a striking assonantal resemblance to *gō⁾ēl,* "kinsman redeemer."[816] His patronymic, "son of Ebed," is an abbreviation for a common type of name, ⁽*ebed*-DN, "servant of god X."[817] Gaal's origin is unknown, but like Abimelech he appears with his relatives. From v. 28 he seems to be a native and true Shechemite, claiming descent from Hamor, the founder of the city.[818] He may have been one of the "lords of Shechem," but unlike the rest of his aristocratic peers, he and his clan refused to support Abimelech's purge and were forced to flee into exile, from where they waited patiently for an opportunity to return. Compelled by the hidden hand of God (from the narrator's point of view) he and his clansmen returned to Shechem, and immediately the "lords of Shechem" accept him as their champion.[819]

---

[815] The form מְאָרְבִים is a *piel* participle of אָרַב, "to lie in wait," whose basic meaning is illustrated in 16:2.

[816] Cf. Garsiel, *Biblical Names,* 55–57. Josephus (*Ant* 5.7.35–36) reads Γυάλης, which suggests an original גֻעַל or גַעַל. The LXX reads Γαλααδ.

[817] Cf. Obadiah, Obed⁾el, Obedbaal, etc. The LXX^B reads Ιωβηλ, presumably a mistake for an original Ιωβνδ, the uncial Λ replacing an original Δ. So also Soggin, *Judges,* 183–84.

[818] In Gen 33:19 Hamor is identified as the father of Shechem.

[819] The verb בָּטַח means "to put one's trust in."

9:27　　But the Shechemites' response to Gaal goes far beyond passive acceptance of his leadership; they celebrate his return by throwing a wild party. The excitement of the revelers is reflected in the concentration of seven active verbs: (1) they went out to the fields; (2) they gathered [the grapes]; (3) they trod [them]; (4) they made praise;[820] (5) they crashed the temple of their god [El/Baal-Berith];[821] (6) they ate; (7) they drank. But the climax is reached with an eighth verb: They cursed Abimelech. The scene of Shechem taken over by a mob of drunken men contrasts sharply with the picture of well-being Abimelech had promised the city.

9:28–29　　At the height of the celebration Gaal addressed the crowd (v. 28) with an effective harangue. He began with a series of rhetorical questions intended to rekindle the Shechemites' ethnic pride and challenge them to recognize the absurdity of their servitude[822] to Abimelech. They were Shechemites![823] How ridiculous it was for them to cower to this outsider, this son of Jerubbaal, and his deputy[824] Zebul![825] So let them be true to their noble Shechemite identity—serve the men of Hamor, the father [founder] of Shechem (Gen 33:19).[826] Let them cease their servitude to this foreigner. Claiming to represent the true Shechem, in v. 29 Gaal boastfully declares that if all of the people[827] were under his authority,[828] he would get rid of Abimelech. Typical of modern political speeches, Gaal concludes with a challenge to Abimelech to beef up[829] his forces and come out [to meet him].

Like Abimelech's speech in v. 2, Gaal skillfully plays the ethnicity card in gaining the support of the lords of Shechem. If blood is the issue, then let it be kept pure, and let the kingship be brought home. Abimelech may claim kinship with the Shechemites through his mother, but his identity and nationality are determined by his father, Jerubbaal. Therefore, let the yoke of this foreigner be cast off.

---

[820] The Hb. phrase הִלּוּלִים וַיַּעֲשׂוּ, which translates lit. "they made praises," echoes Lev 19:24, where the same expression describes a harvest celebration.

[821] Presumably to formalize their acceptance of Gaal as their leader. Cf. v. 6, which had the "lords of Shechem" making Abimelech king at the pillar of the oak of Shechem.

[822] The root עבד occurs four times in this verse.

[823] The LXX grasps the import of the second question, שְׁכֶם מִי, "Who is Shechem?" by translating "Who is a/the son of Shechem?" The LXX[A] includes the article; the LXX[B] omits it. See further Boling, "'And who is Š-K-M?' (Judges IX 28)," *VT* 13 (1963): 479–82.

[824] Hb. פָּקִיד denotes "musterer, recruiter," the one who calls up the troops, in modern parlance the party whip.

[825] The name זְבֻל, which means "prince," recalls *zbl b*ʿ*l arṣ*, "prince, lord of the netherworld," an epithet of Baal in the Ug. mythological texts. Cf. Herrmann, *DDD*, 294–96.

[826] The name Hamor, which means "ass," calls to mind the custom of sacrificing an ass to ratify a treaty by the second millennium B.C. Amorites of Mari. On Hamor see further E. C. Hostetter, "Hamor," *ABD* 3.42–43.

[827] The word עַם in this context is ambiguous, referring to either or both the lords of Shechem and the population of the city in general.

[828] Lit., "O that someone would give this people into my hands."

[829] The NIV's "prepare," is inadequate for the Hb.'s רַבֶּה, "multiply, increase."

Although the narration makes no allusion to God's involvement in the emergence of Gaal, it is difficult to resist the conclusion that in the narrataor's mind this man represents the hidden hand of God, the catalyst through whom Jotham's curse will be fulfilled.

³⁰**When Zebul the governor of the city heard what Gaal son of Ebed said, he was very angry. ³¹Under cover he sent messengers to Abimelech, saying, "Gaal son of Ebed and his brothers have come to Shechem and are stirring up the city against you. ³²Now then, during the night you and your men should come and lie in wait in the fields. ³³In the morning at sunrise, advance against the city. When Gaal and his men come out against you, do whatever your hand finds to do."**

³⁴**So Abimelech and all his troops set out by night and took up concealed positions near Shechem in four companies. ³⁵Now Gaal son of Ebed had gone out and was standing at the entrance to the city gate just as Abimelech and his soldiers came out from their hiding place.**

³⁶**When Gaal saw them, he said to Zebul, "Look, people are coming down from the tops of the mountains!"**

Zebul replied, "You mistake the shadows of the mountains for men."

³⁷**But Gaal spoke up again: "Look, people are coming down from the center of the land, and a company is coming from the direction of the soothsayers' tree."**

³⁸**Then Zebul said to him, "Where is your big talk now, you who said, 'Who is Abimelech that we should be subject to him?' Aren't these the men you ridiculed? Go out and fight them!"**

³⁹**So Gaal led out the citizens of Shechem and fought Abimelech. ⁴⁰Abimelech chased him, and many fell wounded in the flight—all the way to the entrance to the gate. ⁴¹Abimelech stayed in Arumah, and Zebul drove Gaal and his brothers out of Shechem.**

Abimelech's Victory over the Lords of Shechem (9:30–41). **9:30–33** As in v. 26, where Abimelech had been expected to respond to the report he heard in v. 25, so in v. 30 he does not appear. From the following verse it appears he was out of town, perhaps holding court in Ophrah, having claimed Jerubbaal's throne after he had slaughtered all his half-brothers, or perhaps in Arumah, which v. 41 suggests served as his capital. Instead of responding personally to Gaal's challenge, Abimelech's deputy, Zebul, now characterized as "commander [NIV "governor"] of the city" *(śar hāʿîr)*, appeared, fuming with rage over Gaal's insults. He covertly[830] sent messengers to Abimelech, reporting to his superior that Gaal and his clan had returned and were stirring up[831] the city against him (v. 31). Answering to the tactics of the Shechemites against

---

[830] On the basis of v. 41 *BHS* (also O'Connell, *Rhetoric of the Book of Judges*, 469) suggests that MT's בְּתָרְמָה is a corruption of an original בָּארוּמָה, "in Arumah." But the MT is supported by all the versions and is comprehensible if the hapax בְּתָרְמָה, from רָמָה, "to deceive," is interpreted "by a ruse," hence "surreptitiously, secretly." Cf. Boling, *Judges*, 178; Soggin, *Judges*, 187.

[831] Hb. צָרִים is a masculine participle from צוּר, "to alienate." This rare transitive usage of the verb occurs elsewhere in Deut 2:2,19 and Est 8:11.

Abimelech in v. 2, he advised Abimelech to take his supporters[832] and lie in wait in the field at night (v. 32). Then in the morning, as the sun rose, they should make their move against their foes. The last clause of v. 33 suggests that when Gaal and his troops would come out against Abimelech, the victory would be easily achieved.

9:34–37 Abimelech accepted his commander's advice and prepared for action by dividing his forces into four companies (v. 34).[833] The narrator never states specifically who Abimelech's supporters were, but one may surmise that they consisted of those relatives to whom he had appealed in the first instance (v. 1), as well as the retainers who had come with him from Ophrah. In the morning, when they saw Gaal and his troops emerge from inside the city in the city gate, Abimelech's forces rose from their ambush. Apparently the contingent led by Zebul was nearest the gate, for when Gaal saw him he tried to distract him by telling him to look to the surrounding mountains where he would see the allies of the Shechemites coming down to their aid. But Zebul dismissed this comment as a ruse. Then Gaal concretized the threat by telling his opponent to look up and see companies of his allies coming from the height of the land (NIV, "the center of the land") and "the soothsayer's tree." Both of these expressions call for explanation.

The first expression, *ṭabbôr hāʾāreṣ*, which occurs elsewhere in the Bible only in Ezek 38:12, has traditionally been interpreted as "navel of the earth."[834] The NIV's "center of the land" reflects a common modern interpretation. By this understanding the reference must be to Mount Gerizim overlooking Shechem, which some contend was considered by the Canaanites as the navel, viz., center of the land of Canaan.[835] Support for this understanding is also drawn from extra-Israelite attestation to the notion of a navel or center of the earth.[836] But this interpretation probably should be aban-

---

[832] Hb. אֲשֶׁר־אִתָּךְ הָעָם, "the people who are with you," bears a military sense here and in the following verses.

[833] Hb. רָאשִׁים, "heads."

[834] The Eng. rendering derives from the LXX's ὀμφαλὸν via the Vg's *umbilici terrae*. Based on Ezek 38:12, the pseudepigraphic *Book of Jubilees* (8:19), Josephus (*Wars* 3.3.5), and rabbinic writings (*b. Yoma* 54b, *Midrash Tanhuma Qedoshim* 10, Sanhedrin 37a.) treat Zion as the navel of the earth. G. R. H. Wright ("The Mythology of Pre-Israelite Shechem," *VT* 20 [1970]: 79) suggests the תַּבּוּר identified some physical (stone?) object, which, as at Delphi, symbolized the cosmic omphalos. This perception is reflected in several renowned medieval maps, particularly the map from the thirteenth century Latin manuscript of the Book of Psalms and the sixteenth century "clover leaf" map, reproduced and discussed by Beitzel, *Moody Atlas*, 201–3.

[835] B. W. Anderson, "The Place of Shechem in the Bible," *BA* 20 (1957): 10–11. H. Eshel and Z. Erlich ("Abimelech's First Battle with the Lords of Shechem and the Question of the Navel of the Land," *Tarbiz* 58 [1988–89]: 111–16) identify תַּבּוּר הָאָרֶץ with Ras e-Tagur, on the southwestern corridor of Jebel el-Kabir, northeast of Shechem; similarly Z. Ilan, "The Location of the Navel of the Land," *Beth Mikra* 27 (1981/82): 122–26 (Hb.).

[836] For discussion and bibliography see S. Terrien, "The Omphalos Myth and Hebrew Religion," *VT* 20 (1970): 315–38; cf. Zimmerli, *Ezekiel 2*, 311.

doned.[837] Although *ṭabbûr* is used of the umbilical cord in Mishnaic Hebrew and later Aramaic, biblical Hebrew refers to the "navel" or "umbilical cord" with *šōr*.[838] Second, in light of the previous verse, the needs of the present context are met perfectly if *ṭabbûr* is interpreted simply as "elevated ground."[839] Third, this interpretation also suits the only other occurrence of the phrase, Ezek 38:12, where its juxtaposition with "unwalled villages" points to some safe and secure location. Accordingly the phrase is best interpreted as an elevated plateau without external fortifications.[840]

The second expression, *ʾēlôn měʿônĕnîm*, "soothsayer's tree" (or "diviner's oak") is equally enigmatic. There is no problem with the words themselves. As in 4:11, *ʾēlôn* refers to a terebinth or oak tree, and *měʿônĕnîm* is a participle from *ʿānan*, "to practice divination." Accordingly this tree seems to have marked a sacred spot, perhaps to which the Canaanites of the region resorted for a decision from the gods.[841] But its precise location cannot be determined.

9:38–41 Zebul, however, did not fall for Gaal's distractions. Abimelech's commander challenged his opponent to make good on his boasting[842] and his derisive comments concerning Abimelech (v. 38). If Abimelech is a nobody, as Gaal has claimed, and if his supporters are of so little consequence,[843] then let him and his men fight them! Gaal accepted the challenge and, with the lords of Shechem behind him, he attacked Abimelech (v. 39). But his forces were routed by the king, many of them falling at the gate of the city. Instead of occupying the city himself, however, Abimelech left it in the hands of his commander, who drove out Gaal and his relatives. Meanwhile Abimelech returned to Arumah,[844] the place where he continued to hold court.[845]

⁴²The next day the people of Shechem went out to the fields, and this was reported to Abimelech. ⁴³So he took his men, divided them into three companies and set an ambush in the fields. When he saw the people coming out of the city, he rose to attack them. ⁴⁴Abimelech and the companies with him rushed forward

---

[837] So also S. Talmon, *TDOT* 3.437–38.

[838] Ezek 16:4; *Cant.* 7:3[2]; Prov 3:8.

[839] So also D. W. Thomas, "Mount Tabor: The Meaning of the Name," *VT* 1 (1951): 230.

[840] Tg interprets the phrase as "the strength of the land." See further Block, *Ezekiel 25–48*.

[841] Cf. the "oak of the pillar" inside the city referred to in v. 6.

[842] The NIV's "big talk" translates Hb. פִּיךָ, "your mouth."

[843] The NIV's "the men you ridiculed" translates אֲשֶׁר מָאַסְתָּה בּוֹ, "whom you rejected."

[844] Generally located at Khirbet el-ʿOrmah, five miles southeast of Shechem. Cf. Thompson, "Arumah," *ABD* 1.467–68; Boling, *Judges*, 121.

[845] On יָשַׁב, "to sit, to rule," see above on 8:29.

to a position at the entrance to the city gate. Then two companies rushed upon those in the fields and struck them down. [45]All that day Abimelech pressed his attack against the city until he had captured it and killed its people. Then he destroyed the city and scattered salt over it.

Abimelech's Victory over the People of Shechem (9:42–45). **9:42–45** Here Gaal and the lords of Shechem seem to be out of the picture, having been routed by Zebul the day before. Meanwhile the common folk of Shechem[846] tried to resume their normal lives, going out of the city the next day to work in the fields. But the man who had earlier victimized his own family members now turned on the innocent residents of Shechem. When he heard that the people were leaving the city, he divided his forces into three companies[847] and set ambushes for the unsuspecting residents of the town. Once they were out in the fields, Abimelech made his move against them and struck those who approached the place where his own company was hiding (v. 43). The other two companies did the same (v. 44b).

Encouraged by his successes, Abimelech and the troops with him made their move against the city of Shechem itself, taking up their positions outside the city gate.[848] They must have overpowered the guards in the gateway, for the narrator reports that after fighting all day they captured the city, slaughtered its inhabitants, razed it to the ground, and spread salt over it. This sequence of actions against a conquered site seems to have been typical of ancient Near Eastern victors. Nevertheless, the significance of the last act remains uncertain. Since salt renders a land infertile, by spreading salt on a city a conqueror may have sought to guarantee that it would never rise again. But more likely is the suggestion that this was a ritual act invoking an irrevocable curse on the site.[849]

---

[846] Whereas earlier הָעָם had been used of military forces, now it is used in its common sense of the population in general.

[847] Hb. רָאשִׁים, "heads" as in v. 34.

[848] Hb. וַיַּעַמְדוּ פֶּתַח שַׁעַר הָעִיר, "and they stood at the entrance of the gate of the city. For a mock-up of an ancient Canaanite city gate see graphic on next page.

[849] On salt as a symbol of barrenness and desolation see Deut 29:23; Ps 107:34; Jer 17:6; Zeph 2:9. See further Gray, *Joshua, Judges, and Ruth*, 325.

Mock-up of a Canaanite/Israelite City Gate

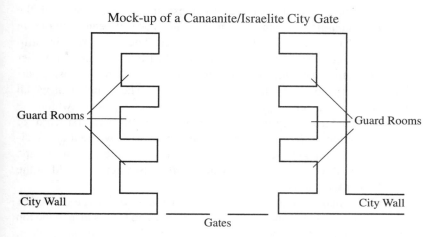

⁴⁶**On hearing this, the citizens in the tower of Shechem went into the stronghold of the temple of El-Berith. ⁴⁷When Abimelech heard that they had assembled there, ⁴⁸he and all his men went up Mount Zalmon. He took an ax and cut off some branches, which he lifted to his shoulders. He ordered the men with him, "Quick! Do what you have seen me do!" ⁴⁹So all the men cut branches and followed Abimelech. They piled them against the stronghold and set it on fire over the people inside. So all the people in the tower of Shechem, about a thousand men and women, also died.**

Abimelech's Capture of the Citadel of Shechem (9:46–49). **9:46** Whereas vv. 42–45 portrayed Abimelech as having won a resounding victory over Shechem, it is evident from this paragraph that not every corner of the city had fallen to him. The previous verses seem to have involved his destruction of the lower part of the city, as opposed to the acropolis on which the temple fortress stood. The former, which represented the areas where people lived and carried on their daily activities, took up the larger portion of the city, to be sure, but the last line of defensive personnel and structures still remained. Situated at the top of the acropolis, the citadel and the temple of El-Berith had so far escaped the destructive terror of Abimelech, and the lords of Shechem who were responsible for its defense were holed up in one of the inner rooms.[850]

The notables who managed to find refuge in the citadel are designated *ba'ălê migdol-šĕkem*, "the lords [NIV, "citizens"] of the Tower of Shechem." Presumably the men so designated represented a subset of "the lords of Shechem," most of whom had by now been eliminated. However,

---

[850] Soggin (*Judges*, 192–93) argues that the Tower of El-Berith was located outside the city of Shechem, perhaps at Tell Ṣôfar, on the western side of the valley of Nablus, but it is preferable to associate this tower with the Beth Millo mentioned in vv. 6,20. Thus Malamat, *WHJP* 3.150.

because they represented the last line of defense and were charged with the sacred duty of guarding the temple complex, they had not been called up in Gaal's general mobilization of the aristocracy. The exact relationship between the Tower of Shechem and the temple of El-Berith is unclear. Either the tower was a free-standing structure designed especially for defensive purposes or it was integrated with the temple itself.[851] The chamber in which these officials sought refuge is designated *ṣĕrîaḥ bêt ʾel bĕrît*, which the NIV renders "the stronghold of the temple of El-Berith." The first word, of unknown derivation, occurs elsewhere only in 1 Sam 13:6, where it is associated with "caves, thickets, cliffs, and pits," where people hide to escape invading armies. Accordingly, the present *ṣĕrîaḥ* must refer to a hold in the tower portion of the temple.[852]

9:47–49 When Abimelech heard that all the lords of the Tower of Shechem had assembled in one place, he took his axe and led his men to the top of Mount Zalmon,[853] where he cut a limb off a tree, placed it on his shoulder, and ordered his followers to do likewise. Then he led them back down, into the city to the structure where the "lords of the Tower" were barricaded. They piled the branches next to the building, lit them, and watched as the flames engulfed the structure and the one thousand men and women who had sought asylum inside. Ironically, the building Gaal's men had crashed in their revelry in v. 27 had become their death trap. As the bramble in Jotham's fable had predicted (v. 15), fire had burst forth from the king and consumed the cedars of Lebanon. Abimelech's triumph was complete. All his rivals, sibling and Shechemite, had been eliminated.

[50]Next Abimelech went to Thebez and besieged it and captured it. [51]Inside the city, however, was a strong tower, to which all the men and women—all the people of the city—fled. They locked themselves in and climbed up on the tower roof. [52]Abimelech went to the tower and stormed it. But as he approached the entrance to the tower to set it on fire, [53]a woman dropped an upper millstone on his head and cracked his skull.

---

[851] For a discussion of these kinds of defensive temple towers see A. Mazar, *Archaeology of the Land of the Bible 10,000–586 B.C.E.* (New York: Doubleday, 1990), 248–57. For discussions of the archaeological evidence for this temple see G. E. Wright, *Shechem: The Biography of a Biblical City* (New York: McGraw-Hill, 1965), 134–36; M. Fowler, "A Closer Look at the Temple of El-Berith at Shechem," *PEQ* 115 (1983) 49–53; E. F. Campbell, "Judges 9 and Archaeology," in *The Word of the Lord Shall Go Forth* (D. N. Freedman Festschrift) ed. C. L. Meyers and M. O'Connor (Winona Lake: Eisenbrauns, 1983), 263–7. For a survey of the archaeological exploration of Shechem (modern Tell Balatah) see id., "Shechem," *NEAEHL* 4:1345–54.

[852] K. Jaros ("Zur Bedeutung von צְרִיחַ in Ri 9,46.49," *AUSS* 15 [1977]: 57–58) interprets the word to mean "an enclosed space," referring here to the inner room of the temple of El-Berith.

[853] The identity and location of this "mountain of deep darkness" remains a mystery. Is this another designation for Ebal, or Gerizim?

[54]Hurriedly he called to his armor-bearer, "Draw your sword and kill me, so that they can't say, 'A woman killed him.'" So his servant ran him through, and he died. [55]When the Israelites saw that Abimelech was dead, they went home.

The Death of Abimelech (9:50–55). **9:50–52** The previous episode had left the reader wondering whether Abimelech has escaped the second part of Jotham's curse (v. 20b). But not for long. Flush from his total victory over Shechem and determined to enhance his position within Israel and Canaan, Abimelech took steps to extend the borders of his realm. He set his sights on Thebez, probably a satellite town,[854] where he set up his military camp. Judging by the brevity of the description, the defenses at the gates seem to have been overcome without great difficulty (v. 50), forcing all the common residents[855] and the aristocracy *(baʿălê hāʿîr)* to seek refuge in the "strong tower" *(migdol ʿōz)* in the center of the city. They locked the door and climbed to the roof of the tower (v. 51). Seeking to duplicate his achievement in Shechem, Abimelech attacked the tower and tried to burn it down, beginning at the doorway, which would have been made of wood (v. 52).

9:53–54 Just when the reader expects the tower to be ignited and collapse, however, the narrative takes a surprising turn. A nameless woman,[856] perhaps possessing extraordinary strength,[857] picked up an upper millstone and threw[858] it from the roof of the tower down on Abimelech's head, crushing his skull (v. 53). The king retained consciousness long enough to command his personal attendant, his armor bearer, to stab him with his sword to spare him an ignominious death at the hands of a woman. More disgraceful than being killed by an uncircumcised Philistine,[859] to be slain by a woman struck at the heart of his manly pride.[860] To the end Abimelech remained belligerent, defiant, arrogant. The young man obeyed dutifully, but this does not neutralize the irony of the scene. The man who had accomplished so much so quickly—gaining the kingship of the significant city of Shechem, murdering sixty-nine of his sibling rivals, staving off a revolt and destroying all the rebels, conquering the city of Thebez—falls victim to a woman. The man who had shamelessly played the

---

[854] Cf. below on v. 57. The location of Thebez (תֵּבֵץ) is uncertain, though many (eg., E. H. Dyck, "Thebes," *ABD* 6.443) identify it with modern Tubas, thirteen miles northeast of Shechem. A. Malamat (*WHJP* 3.320, n. 61) follows Y. Aharoni in treating תֵּבֵץ as a corruption of תִּרְצָה, "Tirzah" (Tell el-Farʿah), six miles northeast of Shechem. Thebez is mentioned elsewhere only in 2 Sam 11:21.

[855] "All the men and women" refers to the common citizens.

[856] Hb. אִשָּׁה אַחַת, lit. "one woman," but the word "one" functions as the indefinite article.

[857] Though it is not excluded that she did have help.

[858] Hb. וַתַּשְׁלֵךְ may be hyperbolic for וַתַּפֵּל, "and she dropped." פֶּלַח רֶכֶב, "rider stone," refers to the upper stone that rotates over a fixed stone.

[859] Cf. Saul's appeal to his armor bearer in 1 Sam 31:4.

[860] The issue of manly pride recalls Deborah's comment to Barak in 4:9 that he would lose the glory for the victory over the Canaanites to a woman.

female card to seize the throne (vv. 1–2) now shamefully falls victim to a representative of this gender. Indeed the story of Abimelech the macho man is framed by two women: the first, who gave him life (8:31), and the second, who took it (9:53).

9:55 Seeing their leader slain, Abimelech's men abandoned the siege of the tower and returned to their homes. Reflecting the pan-Israelite concern of the narrator, in a surprising turn he identifies these warriors as "the men of Israel" (v. 55). It seems that with Abimelech's decisive victory over the Canaanite city of Shechem he had won the allegiance of many Israelites. But with the death of their leader not only had this military adventure ended, but the Israelite experiment in Canaanite kingship also had fittingly aborted.

⁵⁶Thus God repaid the wickedness that Abimelech had done to his father by murdering his seventy brothers. ⁵⁷God also made the men of Shechem pay for all their wickedness. The curse of Jotham son of Jerub-Baal came on them.

Epilogue (9:56–57). **9:56–57** The chapter concludes with the narrator's editorial comment on the death of Abimelech. The author observes that both elements of Jotham's curse have been fulfilled and that God has been the agent behind the remarkable turn of events. Reversing the order of v. 20, he notes first that God has paid Abimelech back for his murderous crimes against his father and brothers. By attributing his death to God (Elohim, not Yahweh) he interprets the nameless woman of Thebez both as a divine agent by which the curse is fulfilled and (along with the people of Thebez) as a surrogate for the Shechemites whom the curse had identified as the source of Abimelech's demise. The question that had remained after v. 49 had been answered. Second, the narrator notes that with this sequence of events God has also carried out Jotham's curse upon the Shechemites for their complicity in the crimes against Jerubbaal. As Fokkelmann has so aptly observed,[861] Abimelech has craved desperately to prove himself a worthy successor to his father by living up to one interpretation of his name ("The king [Gideon] is my father"), only to experience the original intention of the name ("The king [divine] is my father"). Neither human pretension (8:22–32) nor human ferocity (9:1–55) could dislodge Yahweh from his throne. In the end Abimelech's egomaniacal ambition must yield to the kingship of God, and with this the story of Gideon is complete.

Theological and Practical Implications

While many isolate this chapter as extraneous to the overall theme and flow of the book, the author has taken great pains to integrate it with its broader literary context. In so doing he drives the reader to recognize the contributions

---

[861] Fokkelman, "Structural Remarks on Judges 9 and 19," 34.

the story of Abimelech makes to his overall agenda. Several lessons may be highlighted.

First, from a theological perspective, God is in firm control of Israelite affairs whether or not they like it or acknowledge it. Although he is referred to only twice in this chapter (vv. 23,56), all the events move inexorably toward his intended outcome. Between these references the hand of God may be hidden, but we must recognize his involvement in (a) the emergence of Gaal out of nowhere; (2) Abimelech's initial victory over Gaal, emboldening him to attempt greater exploits; (3) the ease with which Abimelech conquers Thebez; (4) the inspiration and empowerment of the woman to drop the millstone from the tower of Thebes; (5) the guidance of the millstone to Abimelech's head.

Second, for the first time in the book we observe God operating on the basis of "fairness and honesty *[bĕʾĕmet ûbĕtāîm]*," doing what is right and giving people what they have earned. This time God does not act in mercy. He gives people the king they deserve, and he gives the king subjects he deserves. As dramatically as anywhere in Scripture, we observe a rigorous divine application of the principle of retribution. Fratricide has been answered with fratricide. He who had slaughtered his brothers "upon one stone" has his skull crushed beneath one stone.[862] Ironically, when the enemy is within, rather than without, God withdraws his gracious hand. By making Baal-Berith their god, the Israelites had formally declared themselves spiritual Canaanites, absolving Yahweh of responsibility for their well-being and bringing them under the fury of his covenant curse. Correspondingly, in the absence of a heart after God, Israel's future could not be secured simply by changing the political constitution in accordance with prevailing and apparently effective patterns. Only radical repentance would reverse the fate of the nation.

The structure of the book and the timing of this episode suggest that in the mind of the narrator, Israel's Canaanite character has set. From here on it will all be downhill. At the same time, however, with an eye to the welfare of the nation as a whole, the elimination of Abimelech, the bramble king, has the effect of surgical amputation. In the removal of this cancer only three years into Abimelech's reign (v. 22) the nation has been saved. But this awareness does not cancel the chilling change in the operation of the "Spirit of the LORD." Heretofore the Spirit had been the divine agent of deliverance, but now he functions as the "Spirit of Disaster," the agent of divine retribution. In the end Israel wins the war over Shechem, but Yahweh wins the war over his people.

Third, the seeds of apostasy in Gideon's "reign" come to full blossom in the life of his son. The flaws in Abimelech's character have not been inherited only

---

[862] For discussions of the theme of retribution see T. A. Bogaart, "Stone for Stone: Retribution in the Story of Abimelech and Shechem," *JSOT* 32 (1985): 45– 5; Janzen, "A Certain Woman in the Rhetoric of Judges 9," *JSOT* 38 (1987): 33–37.

from his Shechemite mother. Carrying to an extreme the tendencies already evident in Gideon, Abimelech has proved his true parentage. This apple has not fallen far from either parental tree By assuming the prerogatives of God, Abimelech exchanges the pattern of servant leadership espoused by Moses (Deut 17:14–20) for crass Canaanite rule that is truly the politics of power. In so doing he guarantees both his own and his people's ruin.

Although the issue of kingship is prominent in this chapter, however, retribution, not kingship as an institution, drives the narrative. Abimelech is not condemned for desiring the throne, nor are the lords of Shechem denounced for granting his request. The crime in this chapter is that they have committed treachery against Gideon by murdering his sons.[863]

Fourth, this account offers another fascinating study in issues of gender. In the beginning (v. 1) Abimelech roots his political ambition in the identity of the woman who gave him life; in the end (v. 52) it is a woman who takes his life.[864]

6. Parenthesis 2: The Governorships of Tola and Jair (10:1–5)

As noted repeatedly, the primary narratives in the "Book of Deliverers" are constructed around the recurring cycle of apostasy-oppression-plea for divine aid-deliverance through the judge (see 2:10–3:6).[865] Three times, however, these narratives are interrupted by brief notices of six additional men who exercised leadership in Israel during the period of Israel's settlement in the land of Canaan. The exploits of Shamgar, the first of these (3:31), have already been discussed. The remaining five (Tola, Jair, Ibzan, Elon, Abdon) are named in two summary notes framing the Jephthah narratives (10:6–12:7) in 10:1–5 and 12:8–15. Except for Tola, who is also credited with saving Israel, these do not seem to fit the pattern of the main characters in the "Book of Deliverers."[866]

But this does not mean that these governors played a less important role than the rest or that they should be dismissed as "minor judges." The differences in presentation probably derive either from the sources used by the narrator (family/tribal chronicles for these judges; folk narratives for the deliverer judges) or the individuals' significance for the narrator's literary and theologi-

---

[863] Cf. Webb, *The Book of Judges*, 159.

[864] See further the theological reflection of M. Wilcock, *The Message of Judges*, BST (Downers Grove: InterVarsity, 1992), 100–102.

[865] Thus the accounts of Othniel (3:7–11), Ehud (3:12–30), Barak (4:1–24), Gideon (6:1–8:28), Jephthah (10:6–12:7), Samson (13:1–16:31).

[866] See H. W. Hertzberg, "Die Kleinen Richter," *TLZ* 79 (1954): 285–90 (= *Beiträge zur Traditionsgeschichte and Theologie des Alten Testaments* [Göttingen: Vandenhoeck & Ruprecht, 1962], 118–25); id., *Die Bücher Josua, Richter, Ruth*, ATD 9 (Göttingen: Vandenhoeck & Ruprecht, 1969), 143; de Vaux, *Early History of Israel*, 752–59.

cal agenda.[867] Indeed, the form and style of 12:7 suggest that the source document, which included a note on Jephthah, consisted of 10:1–5; 12:7,8–15. Because of its value in developing the overall thesis of the book, the Jephthah story has been filled out and has become a part of the "Book of Deliverers."[868] But the story of Jephthah is linked to these "secondary" governors also by the fact that he, like they, emerges a leader in Israel without the apparent involvement of God.[869] The primary difference is we know how Jephthah rose—by manipulating the will of his compatriots. Although the brief notes on the minor governors appear to come from a different source and do not appear to carry the plot of the book as a whole forward, by inserting them at critical points the narrator has given the reader brief if nostalgic glimpses of what normal life and rule in Israel could look like. Between the major narratives of oppression and deliverance there were short periods of peace that offered Israel hope for the future. Unfortunately these periods were short-lived and localized, and long range national dreams were repeatedly shattered by external interference, caused ultimately by Israel's own chaotic spiritual state. Significantly, against those who view the book as a polemic in favor of kingship, these periods of peace have no relation to kingship.[870] If anything, these local rulers offer an alternative to kingship, as exemplified in the preceding chapters by Gideon and Abimelech, who turn out to be unmitigated disasters for the nation. Although the notes are all thoroughly secular, they portray a tranquil and ordered communal life.

The present arrangement exploits the five minor governors as a foil against which to present the story of Jephthah. With only one child, a daughter at that, the latter is painted as a pathetic figure, sandwiched between Jair and Ibzan, two natural rulers if not regal figures, each with thirty sons. The well-being, wealth, and tranquility of the former's reign are measured by his thirty sons riding on thirty donkeys; of the latter's, by the thirty clans subordinated to him by marriage. By contrast, Jephthah's ascent is highly irregular. Marginalized by birth and an outcast by clan decision, he must scratch and negotiate his way to the top.

These notes seem to have been added to bring the total number of gover-

---

[867] On the relationship of the two types of judges see E. T. Mullen, "The 'Minor Judges': Some Literary and Historical Considerations," *CBQ* 44 (1982): 185–201; Malamat, "The Period of the Judges," 131; Hauser, "The 'Minor Judges'—A Re-Evaluation," *JBL* 94 (1975): 190–200; Rösel, "Die 'Richter Israels.' Rückblick und neuer Ansatz," *BZ* 25(1981): 180–203.

[868] Cf Rösel, "Jephtah und das Problem der Richter," *Bib* 61 (1980): 251–55.

[869] When Wilcock speaks of Jephthah as "God's chosen savior" (*The Message of Judges*, BST [Downers Grove: InterVarsity, 1992], 124), he makes explicit what is only implicit in the biblical text.

[870] Contra B. Beem, "The Minor Judges: A Literary Reading of Some Very Short Stories," in *The Biblical Canon in Comparative Perspective*, Scripture in Context 4, ed. K. L. Younger, Jr. et al. (Lewiston: Edwin Mellen, 1991), 165.

nors named in the book to twelve. Although the governors do not represent each of the twelve tribes, with this quota of twelve the narrator declares that all Israel was affected by the events described in the book. At the same time, he signals to the reader his awareness of persons and events other than those he recounts in detail, as well as providing a foil for the stories of the "deliverers." The "deliverers" whose exploits he has described in detail have been selected because their experiences illustrate the thesis spelled out in 2:10–3:6. Rather than describing the personal achievements of these five secondary rulers, the author simply summarizes their roles: these governors functioned as local rulers *(śārîm)* who, by a very loose understanding of the term, may be considered kings *(mĕlākîm)*, inasmuch as they administered justice and/or defended the population from external threats. But the narrator eschews the designation "kings," perhaps reacting against the preceding accounts.

(1) Tola (10:1–2)

[1]After the time of Abimelech a man of Issachar, Tola son of Puah, the son of Dodo, rose to save Israel. He lived in Shamir, in the hill country of Ephraim. [2]He led Israel twenty-three years; then he died, and was buried in Shamir.

10:1–2 The name of the first "secondary" governor, Tola, means "worm." The narrator's note that he led Israel "after Abimelech" invites the reader to interpret this "lowly person" against the backdrop of the ambitious and pretentious son of Jerubbaal.[871] Tola is identified more closely by lineage as the son of Puah and grandson of Dodo,[872] both of whom are otherwise unknown. He is also labelled "a man of Issachar." The fact that the name Tola identifies only one other individual in the Old Testament, the first of four sons of Issachar (Gen 46:13; Num 26:23; 1 Chr 7:1–2) suggests this was an authentic Issacharite name.

Tola's achievements are described with three verbal expressions. First, he arose to save Israel. The combination of "to arise" and "to save" suggests a role similar to Othniel, Ehud, Barak, and Gideon; but unlike the earlier accounts, there is no reference to Yahweh having raised the deliverer, and the enemy whom he apparently defeated is not named. It is curious, however, that the nation is in need of deliverance after the death of Abimelech. This probably reflects the seriousness of the chaos produced in the wake of Abimelech's

---

[871] The phrase "after Abimelech" is generally interpreted as a chronological marker, i.e, Tola ruled after Abimelech's death; but it also functions as a literary device, signaling narratorial rather than strict historical sequence.

[872] Dodo, which occurs elsewhere as a personal name in the OT (2 Sam 23:9 [Qere; Kethib reads Dodî] = 2 Chr 11:12; 2 Sam 23:24 = 2 Chr 11:26) and in the Amarna correspondence (*EA* 158, 164: *Dudu*), is related etymologically to "David." Hb. דּוֹד, "paternal uncle," derives from a root meaning "beloved." Cf . *HALOT*, 215.

rampages.[873] Second, he ruled *(yāšab)*[874] from his capital in Shamir in Ephraim. The location of Shamir is unknown,[875] but wherever it was, it seems significant that the first successor to Abimelech named by the narrator comes from the tribe just across the border from Shechem where Abimelech tried to assert himself. Third, he governed *(šāpaṭ)* Israel for twenty-three years. The exactness of the number suggests strict adherence to a source rather than an approximation or schematized number with symbolic significance.[876] After his tenure was over, Tola was buried in his capital city. The simple details "he lived, he governed, he died, he was buried" suggest an orderly and stable tenure.

(2) Jair (10:3–5)

³He was followed by Jair of Gilead, who led Israel twenty-two years. ⁴He had thirty sons, who rode thirty donkeys. They controlled thirty towns in Gilead, which to this day are called Havvoth Jair. ⁵When Jair died, he was buried in Kamon.

10:3–5 The narrator prepares the way for the following Jephthah narrative by characterizing Jair, the second "secondary" judge, by geography rather than by lineage. Like Jephthah he is a Gileadite (cf. 11:1). His name, *yāʾîr*, which means "may [God] enlighten," was also borne by one of Manasseh's sons, a man whose descendants gained control of a number of Gileadite villages ("tent cities"), which they called Havvoth-jair, "the towns of Jair" (Num 32:41).[877] That this judge should also be called Jair suggests that the name was popular among the Gileadite Manassites and/or that Gileadite leaders tended to be named honorifically after their eponymous ancestors.[878] This Jair governed the Transjordanian Israelites of Gilead for twenty-two years before he died and was buried in Kamon.[879]

In the mind of the narrator, Jair's significance derived not from his own

---

[873] Cf. Beem, "The Minor Judges," 149.

[874] On the mansive use of the verb see above on 8:29.

[875] An identification with Samaria is unlikely since Omri, who established this site as the capital of the Northern Kingdom, is said to have named it after Shemer, from whom he purchased it (1 Kgs 16:24). So also W. R. Kotter, "Shamir," *ABD* 5.1157.

[876] Like "forty" and "twenty" elsewhere in the book. The attempt by J. Hughes (*Secrets of the Times: Myth and History in Biblical Chronology*, JSOTSup 66 [Sheffield: JSOT Press, 1990], 74–77) to find a schematic significance in the number of years ascribed to Tola and the other "secondary" judges is forced.

[877] Deut 3:14 is even more specific, for it asserts that Jair took the entire region of Argob, i.e., Bashan, as far as the border of the Geshurites and Maacathites.

[878] Est 2:5, a much later text, ascribes the name to a Benjamite.

[879] Kamon probably is to be identified with Qamm/Qumeim, halfway between the Sea of Galilee and Ramoth Gilead. Cf. Thompson, "Kamon," *ABD* 4.5.

heritage and lineage (unlike Tola) but from his progeny (thirty sons) and the inheritance he left them (a Gileadite town and donkey for each). It is difficult to know the narrator's intent in this highly schematic picture. In contrast to the specificity of the duration of Jair's rule (twenty-two years), the number thirty could be symbolic of an ideal royal family,[880] but the narrator does not make this connection. The fact that each is said to have owned one of the thirty cities that made up the "towns of Jair" (Havvoth-jair) suggests that Jair divided his territory among his sons. On the other hand, this note may also be interpreted sociopolitically, that is, the territory governed by Jair consisted of a confederacy of thirty cities. The significance of the donkeys is not clear, though the narrator's designation of these as ʿayîr rather than ḥămôr highlights their function as riding rather than pack animals.[881] The most likely interpretation is that the image of thirty sons riding on thirty donkeys conveys a picture of peace and prosperity, in contrast to the insecurity and danger that characterized the days of Shamgar and Jael (5:6–10).[882]

It is hardly coincidental that this notice of Jair's rule in Gilead is placed immediately prior to the Jephthah narrative, which also unfolds in the Transjordan. The turmoil and distress that precipitates the rise of Jephthah contrasts with the order and tranquility of Jair's rule. Apparently the Gileadites were unprepared for the coming emergency. When Jephthah appears, he must earn the authority to rule; it is neither an inherited nor a natural right.

---

[880] Like the seventy sons of Gideon in 8:30. The LXX reads thirty-two; 1 Chr 2:22 reads twenty-two. Thirty sons suggests also a multiplicity of wives.

[881] The prestige associated with owning donkeys is reflected not only in the Song of Deborah (5:10) but in extrabiblical writings as well. Several centuries earlier a palace official had written King Zimri-Lim of Mari:

> [If] you are the king of the Haneans, you are, moreover, a 'king of the Akkadians.' [My lord] should not ride horses (that is, in tribal fashion). May my lord drive in a wagon and mules (that is, in a "civilized manner"), and may he (thus) honor his royalty (ARM 6.76:20–25).

Thus Malamat, "Mari," *BA* 34 (1971): 18; id., *Mari and the Early Israelite Experience* (Oxford: Oxford University Press, 1989), 2–4, 80.

[882] Beem ("The Minor Judges," 152) suggests that to describe each son as riding on his own donkey is like saying each son was given his own Porsche.

7. The Ammonite and Jephthah Cycle (10:6–12:7)
   (1) The Marks of Israel's Canaanization (10:6)
   (2) God's Agent of Punishment (10:7–9)
   (3) Israel's Response to the Oppression (10:10–16)
       The Confession (10:10)
       God's Rejoinder (10:11–14)
       The People's Surrender (10:15–16a)
       God's Rebuff (10:16b)
   (4) Israel's Agent of Deliverance (10:17–11:11)
       The Need for a Deliverer (10:17–18)
       The Emergence of a Candidate (11:1–3)
       The Engagement of the Leader (11:4–11)
   (5) God's Gift of Deliverance (11:12–40)
       Jephthah's Negotiations with the Ammonites (11:12–28)
       Jephthah's Tarnished Victory (11:29–40)
   (6) The Legacy of Jephthah (12:1–7)
       Jephthah's Conflict with Ephraim (12:1–6)
       Epilogue (12:7)
8. Parenthesis 3: The Governorships of Ibzan, Elon, Abdon (12:8–15)
   (1) Ibzan (12:8–10)
   (2) Elon (12:11–12)
   (3) Abdon (12:13–15)
9. The Philistine and Samson Cycle (13:1–16:31)
   (1) The Marks of Israel's Canaanization (13:1a)
   (2) God's Agent of Punishment (13:1b)
   (3) God's Agent of Deliverance (13:2–24)
       The Promise of a Deliverer (13:2–7)
       The Reiteration of the Promise of a Deliverer (13:8–14)
       Manoah's Response to the Messenger of Deliverance
       (13:15–23)
       The Birth of the Deliverer (13:24)
   (4) God's Gift of [Partial] Deliverance (13:25–16:31a)
       Samson's Timnite Affairs (13:25–15:20)
       Samson's Gazite Affairs (16:1–31a)
   (5) Epilogue (16:31b)

7. The Ammonite and Jephthah Cycle (10:6–12:7)

The style and form of the conclusion to the Jephthah narrative (12:7) link this judge with Tola and Jair before and Ibzan, Elon, and Abdon who follow. However, knowledge of several stories from this man's life renders his career a valuable piece of evidence for the narrator's broader thesis, hence the integration of the Jephthah narrative into the sequence of deliverer cycles. Sandwiched between 10:1–5 and 12:8–15 the Jephthah narrative is best interpreted in comparison with and in contrast to the notes on the "secondary" governors. With some modifications, the first part of this account follows the pattern of previous accounts, particularly the notices of apostasy, punishment, and cry for relief; but after that the structure breaks down. First, the account is silent on Yahweh's raising up a deliverer. On the contrary, the rise of Jephthah is portrayed as a purely human event. Second, the narrator does indeed note that the Spirit of God empowers Jephthah and Yahweh gave the Ammonites into his hands, but these elements are overshadowed by Jephthah's vow. Third, the account says nothing about a period of peace and security after Jephthah's soteriological actions. Like the short notes on the secondary governors, this cycle ends simply with a notice of the length of his tenure (a short six years), his death, and his burial somewhere in Gilead.

In addition to these structural features, as in the previous cycles the deviations from the basic paradigm reflect the author's special interest in this cycle. Scholars have recognized that the text divides into five dialogic episodes, each of which involves a confrontation and a resolution:[1]

Episode 1	Yahweh versus Israel (10:6–16)
Episode 2	Jephthah versus Gilead (10:17–11:11)
Episode 3	Jephthah versus Ammon (11:12–28)
Episode 4	Jephthah versus His Daughter (11:29–40)
Episode 5	Jephthah versus Ephraim (12:1–6)[2]

In each episode the power of the spoken word is a key motif. At the same time the narrator plays with the verb ʿābar, which occurs sixteen times but with a range of meanings from the literal "to cross over" to the theological "to transgress."[3]

The links between the Jephthah cycle and the Gideon narrative have often been noted. Both open with a confrontation between God and Israel (6:7–10;

---

[1] Cf. the breakdown by Webb, *Book of Judges*, 41–78; Polzin, *Moses and the Deuteronomist*, 176–81. These holistic analyses may be compared with the traditional source-critical approach of W. Richter, "Die Überlieferungen um Jephtah: Ri 10,17–12,6," *Bib* 47 (1966): 485–586.

[2] For a more complex analysis of the plot see O'Connell, *Rhetoric of the Book of Judges*, 171–203.

[3] 10:8,9; 11:17,18,19,20; 11:29(3x),32; 12:1(2x),3,5(2x),6.

10:6–16). Both men begin as nobodies and become tyrants in Israel. Both are
empowered by the Spirit of God, an event that is immediately recognized by
the rallying of the troops (6:34–35; 11:29). Both follow up the divine empowerment with expressions of doubt (6:36–40; 11:30–31). Both win a spectacular
victory over the enemy (7:19–25; 11:32–33). Both engage in confrontations
with jealous Ephraimites after the battle has been won (8:1–3; 12:1–6). Both
brutalize their countrymen (8:4–17; 12:4–6).

But Jephthah is no carbon copy of Gideon. Indeed in several significant
respects he parallels the character of Abimelech, Gideon's son. Both he and
Abimelech are born of secondary [probably foreign] wives (8:31; 11:1) and
surround themselves with brigands and good-for-nothings (9:4; 11:3). Both are
opportunists who negotiate their way into leadership positions (9:1–6; 11:4–
11). Both seal the agreement with their subjects in a formal ceremony at a
sacred shrine (9:6; 11:11). Both turn out to be brutal rulers, slaughtering their
own relatives (9:5; 11:34–40) and engaging their countrymen in battle (9:26–
57; 12:1–6). Both end up as tragic figures without a future (9:50–57; 11:34–
35). Despite these similarities, however, Jephthah and Abimelech are separated
by one major difference: Abimelech is nothing more than a destroyer; Jephthah
is a deliverer.

Of special interest in the Jephthah cycle is the narrator's portrayal of the role
of God. In the Gideon cycle Yahweh had been active in the first phase (6:1–
7:22), but as the narrative proceeds, his involvement is increasingly repressed,
to the point where he is completely eclipsed in the Abimelech phase of the
cycle. His marginalization by the Israelites is mirrored in his decreasing
involvement in the narrative. To be sure Yahweh is central in the first episode
of the Jephthah cycle but only to provide the reader with a theological rationale
for his increasing absence. In fact, the conclusion to his confrontation with
Israel leads the reader to anticipate total silence in the subsequent episodes. But
he does reappear surprisingly—by grace alone—in the stereotypical announcements of Jephthah's spiritual empowerment in 11:29 and the divine committal
formula in 12:32. But thereafter the narrator makes no further reference to him.
To be sure, as in the Gideon narrative Yahweh's name does indeed surface several additional times, particularly in the speeches of Jephthah and his daughter,
creating the impression of genuine devotion. The image is illusory, however,
for it is belied by the fundamentally corrupted character of the man.[4]

(1) The Marks of Israel's Canaanization (10:6)

**⁶Again the Israelites did evil in the eyes of the LORD. They served the Baals
and the Ashtoreths, and the gods of Aram, the gods of Sidon, the gods of Moab,**

---

[4] Israel's tenuous existence is highlighted by the absence of the tranquility formula ("The land
had peace for X years") at the conclusion of the narrative. Cf. 3:11; 3:30; 5:31; 8:28. The formula
is also missing after the Samson cycle (16:31).

the gods of the Ammonites and the gods of the Philistines. And because the Israelites forsook the LORD and no longer served him,

10:6 The Jephthah cycle opens with the most elaborate description of Israelite apostasy in the book and thus signals the nadir of Israel's degradation and the climax of the process of her Canaanization.[5] The intensity of the evil committed by the nation in Yahweh's sight is expressed by a sevenfold catalogue of foreign divinities the people were serving: the Baals *(ba'ălîm)*, the Astartes *('aštārôt)*, the gods of Aram *('ĕlōhê 'ărām)*, the gods of Sidon *('ĕlōhê ṣîdôn)*, the gods of Moab *('ĕlōhê mô'āb)*, the gods of Ammon *('ĕlōhê bĕnê 'ammôn)*,[6] and the gods of the Philistines *('ĕlōhê pĕlištîm)*.[7] The first two entries in the list may be viewed as a general heading for the list, equivalent to Akkadian *ilāni u ištarāti*, "gods and goddesses." On the other hand, in the absence of a specific reference to the gods of the Canaanites,[8] the pair is better interpreted as designations for the local manifestations of the male and female fertility divinities. In any case, the seven-member list corresponds to the list of Canaanite nations in Deut 7:1 and in so doing highlights the total spiritual corruption of the nation. This is reiterated by the verbs employed: they "did not serve" *(lō' 'ābad*; NIV "no longer served") Yahweh but rather "forsook/abandoned" *('āzab)* him and "served" *('ābad)* the Baals, exchanging devotion to the living God of Israel for the lifeless gods of the nations.

(2) God's Agent of Punishment (10:7–9)

[7]**he became angry with them. He sold them into the hands of the Philistines and the Ammonites,** [8]**who that year shattered and crushed them. For eighteen years they oppressed all the Israelites on the east side of the Jordan in Gilead, the land of the Amorites.** [9]**The Ammonites also crossed the Jordan to fight against Judah, Benjamin and the house of Ephraim; and Israel was in great distress.**

10:7–8a The description of Yahweh's response to Israel's spiritual defection confirms our suggestion that in the narrator's mind the nation's Canaanization is coming to a climax. First, for the first time since 3:8 the text mentions God's anger as the emotion behind his selling[9] the Israelites into the hands of the enemies.[10] Second, for the first time the narrator notes that Yahweh has handed his people into the power of two different nations—the

---

[5] The last such notice in 13:1 is much briefer, probably because these two cycles are perceived to have occurred simultaneously.

[6] As in 3:18 and most other places in the OT the compound form of the name is used for the Ammonites. See above on 3:18.

[7] The reference to the Philistines also prepares the reader for the Samson cycle.

[8] Though Sidon may represent the Canaanites here and in v. 12.

[9] On the "committal formula" see above, p. 147f.

[10] Except for the names of the enemies, v. 7 quotes 3:8 verbatim.

Philistines and the sons of Ammon. This bifurcation of stress points indicates that vv. 6–7 function as the prelude not only to the Jephthah cycle but to the Samson narratives as well (13:1–16:31). When the geographic relationship to Israel of these two nations is observed, one may recognize God's strategic wisdom. Like a military general, he divides his forces so they may afflict his people pincerlike from two sides.

Third, the narrator describes the action of the enemies with a pair of new verbs that appear to have been selected for assonantal reasons: "shattered" *(wayyir'āṣû)* and "crushed" *(wayyirṣĕṣû)*. The first occurs elsewhere only in Exod 15:6. The second is slightly more common, but it appears in Judges elsewhere only in 9:53, where the causative verb form *(hiphil)* form described the "crushing" effect on Abimelech's head of the millstone the unnamed woman dropped from the tower.[11]

10:8b–9   Verses 8b–9 focus the reader's attention on the Ammonite oppression. For eighteen years[12] the Ammonites harassed all the Israelites living east of the Jordan in the hill country of Gilead, which was occupied by Amorites until the Israelites had arrived from Egypt. But the divine general's eastern force crossed the Jordan and attacked Judah, Benjamin, and Ephraim, thus creating extreme "distress" in Israel's heartland.

(3) Israel's Response to the Oppression (10:10–16)

10Then the Israelites cried out to the LORD, "We have sinned against you, forsaking our God and serving the Baals."

11The LORD replied, "When the Egyptians, the Amorites, the Ammonites, the Philistines, **12**the Sidonians, the Amalekites and the Maonites oppressed you and you cried to me for help, did I not save you from their hands? **13**But you have forsaken me and served other gods, so I will no longer save you. **14**Go and cry out to the gods you have chosen. Let them save you when you are in trouble!"

15But the Israelites said to the LORD, "We have sinned. Do with us whatever you think best, but please rescue us now." **16**Then they got rid of the foreign gods among them and served the LORD. And he could bear Israel's misery no longer.

If in the Gideon cycle the narrator provides the most detailed description of the oppression of Israel (6:1b–6b), here he offers the most detailed account of Israel's response. This phase of the cycle is cast in the form of a confrontational

---

[11] Elsewhere לָחַץ, "to oppress" (2:18; 4:3; 6:9; 10:12 [cf. 1:34]), and צָרַר, "to be distressed" (2:15; 10:9,14; 11:7), are used.

[12] The Hb. בַּשָּׁנָה הַהִיא שְׁמֹנֶה עֶשְׂרֵה שָׁנָה, "in that year, for eighteen years," is awkward. It seems that the first number refers to the initial simultaneous oppression and the second to the duration of the Ammonite harassment of the transjordanian Israelites. Many delete the reference to "eighteen years" as a clarifying gloss after the enigmatic "in that year." Cf. Becker, *Richterzeit,* 211; Richter, *Bearbeitungen des "Retterbuches,"* 17–18; Hughes, *Secrets of the Times,* 71, though his following discussion on the chronological scheme of the book assumes its integrity.

dialogue between Yahweh and his people, framed on either side by the latter's confession of sin. Stylistically this section displays obvious connections with 2:1–5 and 6:7–10. Whereas in the previous accounts Yahweh had communicated his displeasure with Israel through mediators, viz., a "messenger/angel" *(malʾāk)* and a "prophet" *(nābîʾ)* respectively, here he deals with Israel directly.

THE CONFESSION (10:10). **10:10** For the first and only time in the book the narrator expands on Israel's cry of distress. And for the first time in the book a confession of sin is heard from the Israelites.[13] The confession takes the form of a general statement, "We have sinned against you," and a specific explication, "We have forsaken our God and served the Baals." The possessive pronoun "our" is significant, for by it the people recognize their special affiliation with Yahweh. In direct violation of the first principle of covenant relationship (Exod 20:3; Deut 5:7), however, they have succumbed to the seductive attraction of the fertility gods of Canaan and allowed these rivals to take Yahweh's place. On the surface the confession appears genuine, and the reader welcomes this acknowledgment of responsibility for their fate. But the reader also notes the absence of any appeal for forgiveness or plea for grace. We must read on to find out whether or not this is more than a utilitarian manipulation of deity to be delivered from a painful situation or authentic heartfelt repentance.

GOD'S REJOINDER (10:11–14). Although the opening statements in Yahweh's response appear hopeful, the reader quickly learns that Yahweh does not take the confession seriously. Indeed, his verbal reaction is essentially negative, being cast in the form of a modified judgment speech, curt and angry in tone. Yahweh's address divides into three readily identifiable parts.

10:11–14 First, as in the earlier sermons by the "messenger" (2:1) and the "prophet" (6:8–9), Yahweh reminds the Israelites of his past favors, cataloguing the enemy nations from whose hands he had delivered them (vv. 11–12). Like the list of pagan deities in v. 6, this list consists of seven names, presumably to highlight the fact that he has always saved his people from all their enemies. The list begins logically with Egypt, and then moves to the Amorites,[14] Ammonites, Philistines, Sidonians, Amalekites, and Maonites.[15] One may assume that the reference to the victory over the Amorites recalls the days of Moses when Sihon of Heshbon and Og of Bashan were defeated (Num 21:21–35). The reference to the Ammonites alludes to Ehud's victory over Moab, with

---

[13] This contrasts with 2:4, which has them weeping in response to the divine messenger's announcement of the withdrawal of Yahweh's support, and 6:10, which describes no response at all to God's scolding.

[14] The NIV's plural follows the versions in reading הָאֱמֹרִי, "the Amorite," as a collective.

[15] The Hb. construction of vv. 11–12 is difficult. A phrase (הוֹשַׁעְתִּי אֶתְכֶם, "I delivered you") has either dropped out after הֲלֹא, "Have not …" in v. 11, by haplography, or has been suppressed by anacoluthon. Cf. O'Connell, *Rhetoric of the Book of Judges*, 467–68.

whom the Ammonites were allied (Judg 3:15–30).[16] Yahweh's naming of the
Philistines is apparently based on Shamgar's victory, briefly noted in 3:31. As
in v. 6 "Sidon" seems to represent the Canaanites, over whom Barak had won
the victory in chap. 4. The Amalekites have appeared twice before, as allies of
Moab (3:13) and Midian (6:3,33; 7:12). The last name, Maon, is new and surprising. Where one would have expected the name "Midian" (in light of chaps.
6–8), one encounters a nation never heard of before, let alone remembered in
lists/accounts of enemies defeated by Israel.[17] The translators of the LXX
wrote *Midian,* which is exactly what they expected to find.[18] It seems best to
associate the name with the Meunites, who were at home in the same region as
the Midianites and may even have been a confederate or dependent group.[19]

Second, Yahweh scolds Israel for the nation's ungrateful and treasonous
response (v. 13a). Instead of answering his repeated demonstrations of grace
and goodness with increased commitment, the nation abandoned their covenant Lord and Protector in favor of the service of other gods.

Third, Yahweh rejects the confession of the people and closes his ears to
their cry for help. Since in the past Yahweh had always rescued his people from
the oppression *(ṣārar)* of the nations when they cried out *(ṣāʿaq)* to him, the
present audience probably expected the catalogue of victories in vv. 11–12 to
be followed by a promise of another act of deliverance, or, as in earlier cases,
the call of a deliverer. But Yahweh declares that because of their persistent infidelity he is absolved of all responsibility to them. He will rescue them no more.

With intense sarcasm and irony he challenges Israel to go and cry out
(zāʿaq) to the gods they have chosen. Let them deliver *(hôšîaʿ)* them in their
time of distress *(ṣārâ)*! The words are carefully selected to echo the people's
pleas and to highlight the fundamental perversion in Israel's behavior. In reality God in his grace had chosen them (cf. Ps 135:5; Deut 32:8), but they had
done the unthinkable: they had transferred their allegiance to other gods, whom
they had selected for themselves (cf. Jer 2:9–13). In effect he says: "Show
some consistency. You made your bed, now sleep in it!"

In his response to the people's expression of distress Yahweh recognizes and
exposes the purely utilitarian and manipulative nature of their cry. The people
have used him repeatedly simply to get them out of difficult circumstances. In
the past he has responded to their pleas, but no more. Their confession sounds
like true repentance, but God sees past their pious words to their treacherous
and parasitic hearts.

THE PEOPLE'S SURRENDER (10:15–16a).   **10:15–16a**   The Israelites'

---

[16] Which probably explains the substitution of "Moab" for "the Amorite" in the Syr Peshitta.

[17] Maon occurs as the name of a town in the Judean hills (Josh 15:55; cf. 1 Sam 23:24–25), but
this is obviously a different place.

[18] So also REB, NAB, NJB.

[19] Cf. E. A. Knauf, "Meunim," *ABD* 4.802.

reaction to Yahweh's speech is expressed in both verbal and nonverbal forms. In the former (v. 15) they intensify their earlier confession. After acknowledging again that they have sinned, they call on Yahweh to do to them what is right (or good/best, *haṭṭôb*) in his eyes. The response appears to be completely submissive, an appropriate response to their own habit of "doing what is evil *[hārāʿ]* in the eyes of the LORD," but their surrender is belied by the following demand to rescue/deliver them immediately (lit., "this day"). The people's verbal response to Yahweh's rejection betrays a blindness not only to the fundamental contradiction in their demand, but also to the manner in which Yahweh has consistently worked heretofore in the book. Given their bent for doing what is evil in the sight of Yahweh, Yahweh has done what is right in his eyes by sending foreign enemies as his agents of judgment. They do not realize that by providing deliverers and deliverances in the past, what is right had been suspended in favor of what is gracious. In their nonverbal response to God's rebuttal the people demonstrate with actions what their lips had confessed: they dispose of the foreign gods and served Yahweh. We are not told what form that service took, but presumably it involved the presentation of sacrifices and other cultic expressions of devotion.

GOD'S REBUFF (10:16b). **10:16b** Scholars are not agreed either on the sincerity of the people's second confession or on the nature of Yahweh's answer in v. 16b. The NIV's rendering, "He could bear Israel's misery no longer," reflects the traditional consensus.[20] According to this consensus, Yahweh recognized the genuineness of their confession and, as in numerous other instances, "repented of the calamity he said he would do to them."[21] But several scholars have recently rightly challenged this interpretation.[22] Regardless of how one interprets v. 16b, the subsequent episodes raise several serious questions about Yahweh's response. Why is the word "repent" absent from this text? Why is there no promise of deliverance to negate the statement in v. 13? Why is God silent after v. 16a? Why is Jephthah never described as having been "raised up" (*hēqîm*, 3:9) or "strengthened" (*ḥizzēq*, 3:12) by Yahweh? Why is God totally absent in the account of the rise of Jephthah to leadership in Israel (cf. 4:4–10; 6:11–24)?

Apart from these questions arising from the following narrative, v. 16b itself remains a crux. A literal translation would be "and his soul/person was short because of the efforts of Israel." The meaning of the sentence may go different directions, however, depending upon how individual words are understood. In

---

[20] Similarly the early versions and all modern translations: NLT, NAS, NRSV, REB, NAB, NJB, JPSV. So also Boling, *Judges*, 190; Soggin, *Judges*, 202; Goslinga, *Joshua, Judges, Ruth*, 379.

[21] Cf. Exod 32:14; Amos 7:3–6; Joel 2:13–14; Jer 26:10; Jonah 3:10.

[22] Cf. Webb, *Judges*, 42–46; O'Connell, *Rhetoric of the Book of Judges*, 187–88; cf. Polzin, *Moses and the Deuteronomist*, 178.

this context the idiom *tiqṣar nepeš*, "the soul is short,"[23] expresses frustration, exasperation, and anger in the face of an intolerable situation.[24] But what is so intolerable? The answer is expressed by the word *ʿāmāl*, which may be interpreted either as their "pain, trouble"[25] or their "hard work, effort,"[26] which refers to their confessional and sacrificial attempts to win divine favor. If the first sense had been intended, one would have expected the narrator to use *ṣārâ*, "distress," as in v. 14. In view of the frequent pairing of *ʿāmāl* with the overtly ethical term *ʾāwen*, "iniquity, evil, disaster,"[27] Yahweh may be dismissing the Israelite actions as further evidence of their iniquitous condition. The words themselves are ambiguous, but there is rejection in Yahweh's voice. The Israelites' present efforts are intolerable, and the attempts to wrest deliverance from him are an affront. The repentance is external only; theirs is a conversion of convenience. The covenant God who has been slighted despite his repeated gracious interventions on the nation's behalf and abandoned in favor of the more exciting and physical deities of Canaan has grown tired of their calls for help. He sees through their empty cry.[28] These people are interested only in relief from their oppressions. Because their confession lacks sincerity, Yahweh will withdraw and be used by this parasitic people no longer.

(4) Israel's Agent of Deliverance (10:17–11:11)

[17]When the Ammonites were called to arms and camped in Gilead, the Israelites assembled and camped at Mizpah. [18]The leaders of the people of Gilead said to each other, "Whoever will launch the attack against the Ammonites will be the head of all those living in Gilead."

[1]Jephthah the Gileadite was a mighty warrior. His father was Gilead; his mother was a prostitute. [2]Gilead's wife also bore him sons, and when they were grown up, they drove Jephthah away. "You are not going to get any inheritance in our family," they said, "because you are the son of another woman." [3]So Jephthah fled from his brothers and settled in the land of Tob, where a group of adventurers gathered around him and followed him.

[4]Some time later, when the Ammonites made war on Israel, [5]the elders of Gilead went to get Jephthah from the land of Tob. [6]"Come," they said, "be our

---

[23] The idiom occurs elsewhere four times: "Num 21:4; Judg 16:16; Job 21:4; Zech 11:8. Cf. the related expression קָצַר רוּחַ יְהוה, "the Spirit of the LORD was short/impatient," Mic 2:7; also the phrases קְצַר אַפַּיִם, "long of nose, impatient" (Prov 14:17); קְצַר רוּחַ, "Short spirited, impatient" (Prov 14:29). More concretely קְצַר יָמִים, "short-lived" (Job 14:1); קְצָרֵי יָד, "short-handed, feeble" (2 Kgs 19:26; Isa 37:37). For a study of these texts see R. D. Haak, "A Study and New Interpretation of *QṢR NPŠ*," *JBL* 101/2 (1982): 161–67.

[24] Webb, *The Book of Judges*, 46–7.

[25] Cf. BDB, 765.

[26] Cf. Ps 127:1; Prov 16:26.

[27] See Avishur, *Word-Pairs*, 58; *DCH* 1.154–55.

[28] Cf. Job 35:9–16.

commander, so we can fight the Ammonites."

⁷Jephthah said to them, "Didn't you hate me and drive me from my father's house? Why do you come to me now, when you're in trouble?"

⁸The elders of Gilead said to him, "Nevertheless, we are turning to you now; come with us to fight the Ammonites, and you will be our head over all who live in Gilead."

⁹Jephthah answered, "Suppose you take me back to fight the Ammonites and the LORD gives them to me—will I really be your head?"

¹⁰The elders of Gilead replied, "The LORD is our witness; we will certainly do as you say." ¹¹So Jephthah went with the elders of Gilead, and the people made him head and commander over them. And he repeated all his words before the LORD in Mizpah.

Although Yahweh will empower Jephthah with his Spirit (11:29) and be credited by the narrator with his victory over the Ammonites, he is totally out of the picture in the account of Jephthah's rise as leader and deliverer of Israel. Whereas in every other narrative cycle Yahweh had played the decisive role in the emergence of a deliverer,[29] Jephthah's emergence is treated as a purely human development. Yahweh is indeed invoked as a witness to the covenant between Jephthah and Israel, but this is a far cry from earlier episodes.

THE NEED FOR A DELIVERER (10:17–18). **10:17–18** The need for deliverance crystallizes as the Ammonite army was summoned[30] to battle and took up its military position in Gilead. The Israelite troops responded by setting up their own camp at Mizpah. This Mizpah, located in Gilead, is not to be confused with the Benjamite town of the same name in chaps. 19–21. It is possible the place is to be identified with the Mizpah/Galeed where Jacob and Laban signed their treaty of nonaggression in Gen 31:43–55, but this cannot be confirmed.[31]

The mobilization of the Ammonite army in the heart of Transjordanian Israel raises the specter of the latter's dearth of leadership. The Israel's response to the Ammonite challenge was initially presented as a pan-Israelite reaction, but it will soon become evident that at this stage the crisis affected the Gileadites primarily. Accordingly, the leaders/captains (*śārîm*) of Gilead took the initiative to seek out a man to lead them against the enemy. Their dilemma is framed in direct speech and expresses the consensus of the leaders that anyone who will volunteer to lead the forces of Gilead against the Ammonites would be rewarded with the presidency (*rō'š*) over all the inhabitants of Gilead.

The call for someone to begin the fight against the sons of Ammon, particu-

---

[29] 3:9, 15; 4:4–10; 6:11–24; 13:3–25.

[30] The present use of the verb פעק, "to cry out, summon," finds a precedent in 7:23–24, but usually in this book the word describes the Israelites' cry of distress to Yahweh.

[31] Cf. P. M. Arnold, "Mizpah," *ABD* 4.880–81.

larly the phrase "[who] will launch the attack" *(yāḥēl lĕhillāḥēm)* invites the reader to compare this event with 1:1, where a similar phrase occurs. However, the circumstances and motivations have changed drastically. Whereas in the earlier context the people's actions had a theological base and theological focus, this appears to be an ad hoc decision. There is no reference to an orderly assembly, no presiding individual, no sign of unity with Israel (they want a leader for Gilead), no strategy or plan, and no determination to carry through to victory. Appealing to the worst of human motives, the leaders of Gilead simply call for a volunteer and then offer him the carrot of leadership over the entire region. But in the Book of Judges there are no volunteers, except for the rogue Abimelech in chap. 9. The reader has already learned from his life and rule the lethal effect of any approach to leadership that is based on and caters to personal ambition rather than the care and needs of those to be led. Nevertheless, as in the story of Abimelech, in the leadership style of Jephthah the reader will again be confronted with the tragic effects that arise from treating leadership as a matter of power rather than a call to service on behalf of those led.

Even more seriously, unlike the situation in 1:1, the narrative leaves no hint of any spiritual sensitivity on the part of the Gileadites. There was no consciousness of being the people of Yahweh, no appeal to God to solve the crisis in leadership, and subsequently no reference to Yahweh raising a man. This was a purely secular moment; as a Canaanized people the Gileadites were left to their own wits and resources, and, as in the case of Abimelech, a bramble would not be long in sprouting. Through this entire episode Yahweh's silence is deafening.

THE EMERGENCE OF A CANDIDATE (11:1–3). **11:1–3** A new episode in the narrative is signalled by the circumstantial clause in 11:1.[32] The narrator interrupts the main plot by introducing the figure who will dominate the following events. In effect, the narrator raises the leader, a bramble in the tradition of Abimelech. But who is this man?

His name is *yiptāḥ*, which means "He [the deity] has opened."[33] In a cultural context in which fertility is a paramount concern and the bearing of children by a woman the highest goal, the name presumably reflects the gratitude of Jephthah's mother for having been enabled to bear a son. But as an abbreviated form, the name is ambiguous. Who/which deity is being credited with his birth? From an orthodox point of view, the most optimistic interpretation would reconstruct the full name as *yiptaḥ-yhwh*, "the LORD has opened [the womb]." But the sequel will expose how unlikely this was. Less optimistically the full name could be reconstructed as *yiptaḥ-ʾēl*, "El has opened [the womb],"[34] which carries an

---

[32] Webb *(Book of Judges*, 50) characterizes vv. 1–3 as a flashback.

[33] In the tragic meeting between Jephthah and his daughter in 11:35–36, Jephthah offers an evasive play on his name by using a synonym, "I have opened [פָּצָה] my mouth." For the synonyms פָּצָה/פָּתַח see Num 16:30,32; 26:10; Deut 11:6; Ezek 2:8; 3:2.

[34] This form occurs as a place name in Josh 19:14,27.

ambiguous sense, since a deity named El was worshiped by both Israelites and Canaanites. As a third possibility we must also consider *yiptaḥ-baʿal,* "Baal has opened [the womb]." As we will see, the mother's profession, the father's actions, the character of Jephthah's half-brothers, and Jephthah's own lifestyle all point to a thoroughly Canaanized environment.

Jephthah is identified as a bona fide Gileadite, having been fathered by a man who bore the same name. Gilead is technically a geographic designation (Gen 31:48), but it is also used as a tribal/clan/family eponym.[35] Although Jephthah's father bore a name of nobility, his mother was a harlot. Whether she was an Israelite or a Canaanite we are not told, but the latter is as likely as the former. But there were other members of this family. According to v. 2, Gilead's true wife bore him sons as well.

Echoing the divine messenger's characterization of Gideon in 6:12, the narrator describes Jephthah as a *gibbôr ḥayil.* By itself the expression may be interpreted either as "a noble/rich man" or "valiant warrior," but given this man's parentage and the manner in which his brothers treated him, the former definition seems unlikely. On the other hand, the latter is most appropriate when one observes the manner in which he conducted himself. The narrative will portray him as a person who, expelled from his own family, distinguished himself as a resourceful warrior, one without any hint of timidity. Expelled from his home, he fled to the land of Tob, where he lived a life of brigandry and banditry.[36] Gathering around himself a group of "worthless men,"[37] Jephthah led raiding parties[38] into the towns and villages of Gilead. With this characterization the narrator invites the reader to compare Jephthah with Abimelech.[39] But this man's lot was considerably worse. Even if Abimelech's mother was a concubine, at least she was recognized as a legitimate [if secondary] wife of Jerubbaal/Gideon. As the rejected son of a prostitute Jephthah was a man with-

---

[35] Josh 17:1,3; Judg 5:17; etc.

[36] Note the irony in אֶרֶץ טוֹב, "the land of Tob" or "land of goodness," which is anything but good for him. The location of Tob is uncertain. A place by the same name is mentioned several times in the David narrative (1 Sam 22:2; 27:8; 2 Sam 10:6,8), but it is not clear that these refer to the same place. Tob has not been definitively located. In context the narrator seems to be referring to the sparsely populated district north of the Jabbok. Note that Jephthah does not go to the city of Tob but the region of Tob. Cf. de Vaux, *Early History of Israel,* 820.

[37] The NIV's rendering of אֲנָשִׁים רֵקִים as "adventurers" misses the narrator's intentionally negative evaluation of these men. The same expression had been used in 9:4 of the hit men hired by Abimelech.

[38] Hb. וַיֵּצְאוּ עִמּוֹ, "and they went out with him," is cryptic, but one may assume it refers to their raiding parties from their base.

[39] Soggin (*Judges,* 208; following Hertzberg (*Die Bücher Josua, Richter, Ruth,* 5th ed., ATD 9 [1973]: s.v.) perceives Jephthah too favorably in interpreting him as "the positive antithesis to Abimelech." As in the case of Abimelech, the characterization invites comparison with the SA.GAZ/ʿApiru mentioned frequently in the Amarna letters. Cf. Rainey, "Unruly Elements in Late Bronze Canaanite Society," 481–97.

out a physical or social home, and without a future.

The background of Jephthah provides another illustration of the moral degeneration, the Canaanization of Israelite society. First, his origin raises the question of why his father Gilead visits prostitutes. The God of Israel was highly intolerant of any sexual relations outside the bonds of marriage, including those with professional prostitutes. It is widely recognized that in the ancient world women would often be driven to a life of prostitution if they had no other means of economic support, especially if they were widows or orphans.[40] But according to official Israelite standards, for men to treat a girl as a prostitute was both an offense to family honor[41] and a violation of the marriage covenant with one's wife. This raises a second question: Who was this woman? Since she remains nameless, the text leaves open the question of her nationality. Was she an Israelite or a Canaanite woman? If she was an Israelite, we witness a direct violation of Yahweh's taboos on extramarital sexual relations, as well as laws prohibiting a father from selling his daughter into prostitution (Lev 19:29). If she was a Canaanite, we see the violation of the proscription on all intercourse with Canaanites (Exod 34:15–16; Deut 7:1–5). If she was a prostitute working in the service of a Canaanite cult center, the crime is worse still, for then Gilead has become a patron and contributor to the Canaanite religious establishment.[42] Even if the question cannot be answered finally, Jephthah's later conduct certainly follows Canaanite patterns.

Contributing to the negative picture of Israel's spiritual condition suggested by this paragraph is the manner in which Jephthah's brothers treat him. Their expulsion of their half-brother was motivated by greed—they did not want him to share in the inheritance—and grounded in his putative social inferiority—he was the son of another woman. But with this act they betray their half-brother and in so doing violate Israelite laws enjoining care and compassion for the outcast (e.g., Deut 10:12–22), particularly injunctions commanding one to love one's neighbor [let alone one's brother] as oneself (Lev 19:33–34). But by this act they also violate Israelite inheritance law, which depended not on the mother but on the father.[43] Jephthah's birth from a prostitute mother offers them an excuse for expelling him, but this aim required a legal decision of the court.[44]

---

[40] On prostitution in the ANE and in Israel see E. A. Goodfriend, "Prostitution," *ABD* 5.505–10.

[41] Gen 34:31; 38:23; Amos 7:17; 1 Kgs 22:38.

[42] On the possibility/problem of cult prostitution see Goodfriend, *ABD* 5.507–9; for a different interpretation see van der Toorn, "Cultic Prostitution," *ABD* 5.510–13; ibid., "Female Prostitution in Payment of Vows in Ancient Israel," *JBL* 108 (1989): 193–205.

[43] Thus D. Marcus, "The Legal Dispute Between Jephthah and the Elders," *HAR* 12 (1990): 107–8. This renders untenable the thesis of H. Schulte ("Beobachtungen zum Begriff der Zônâ im Alten Testament, "*ZAW* 104 [1992]: 255–62) that in this context the expression אִשָּׁה זוֹנָה refers to a woman member of a matrilinear family living independently, and that the brothers were justified in expelling Jephthah, since he was a full member of the house of his mother, and heir to the property attached thereto.

[44] Ibid., 107–11.

THE ENGAGEMENT OF THE LEADER (11:4–11). The primary plot resumes in v. 4. As in 10:10–16, this episode is dominated by dialogue. In fact, the conversation echoes the earlier dialogue between Yahweh and Israel, as the following synopsis of motifs shows:

1. The Ammonite oppression (10:7–9)	1. The Ammonite oppression (11:4)
2. Israel appeals to Yahweh (10:10)	2. Gilead appeals to Jephthah (11:5–6)
3. Yahweh retorts sarcastically (10:11–14)	3. Jephthah retorts sarcastically (11:7)
4. Israel repeats the appeal (10:15–16a)	4. Gilead repeats the appeal[45] (11:8)
5. Yahweh refuses to be used (10:16b)	5. Jephthah seizes the moment opportunistically (11:9–11)

11:4–6 The context for the engagement of Jephthah is summarized in vv. 4–5. The opening chronological note, "Some time later" (lit., "from days"), is idiomatic for "after some time, some days thereafter," reflecting the time it would have taken for the call for a volunteer by the leaders of Gilead (10:18) to circulate throughout the villages and towns of Gilead. In any case, after several days it became obvious that no one would come forward to take up the challenge. Meanwhile the Ammonites continued to put military pressure on Israel. Finally, in desperation the Gileadites sent a delegation of elders[46] to look for Jephthah, authorized to offer him rule over all Gilead. Undoubtedly the approach was based on the reputation Jephthah had established in Gilead as the fearless and crafty leader of his band of brigands.

The negotiations between the elders and Jephthah were hard-nosed and businesslike. There was no appeal to tribal or national loyalty, or to the critical role Jephthah could play in rescuing the people of Yahweh from this critical hour. The elders were careful not to offer Jephthah too much; they invited him to come and be their "commander in chief" in this battle against the Ammonites. Whereas in 10:18 the leaders had promised headship *(rōʾš)* over all the inhabitants of Gilead to anyone who would volunteer to lead them in battle, what they offered Jephthah is chieftainship *(qāṣîn)* for them in battle. The word *qāṣîn* is relatively rare, occurring elsewhere only eight times. In contexts where it bears a sense more specific than "leader, man in authority,"[47] it serves as a precise title for military leader.[48] In this context the Gileadites were desperate for a military leader. In presenting their case they were careful to offer him a lesser role than they had made available to full citizens of Gilead. It was enough that they had to beg one whom they had rejected now to come and lead them in battle. They could entrust themselves into his hands on a broader and more permanent basis.

---

[45] Both using the language of repentance. In the 10:15, the Israelites confess their sin. In 11:8 the Gileadites say they have returned to (שׁוּב לְ) Jephthah.

[46] The term זְקֵנִים functions as a stylistic variant of שָׂרִים, "leaders," in 10:18.

[47] Isa 1:10; 22:3; Mic 3:1,9; Prov 6:7.

[48] Josh 10:24; Isa 22:3 (dictator in a battle context); Dan 11:18.

11:7 Jephthah recognized immediately that he held the trump card and deliberately played hard to get. He responded by noting how the Gileadites had rejected him and driven him from his father's house. According to v. 2 it was his half-brothers, the sons of his father's wife, who had driven him away.[49] Then he generalized this inhumane treatment to all Gilead. Seizing on the irony of the situation, he asked them why, having sentenced him to a life of perpetual distress, they should come to him now that they were in trouble *(ṣar)*.[50] Why should he be a mere tool to be used by them?[51] According to the following narrative, Jephthah demanded that he be legally reinstated as a full citizen of Gilead with all the rights and privileges attached thereto.[52]

11:8 The irony continues in the elders' reply. Reinterpreting the original hostile act against Jephthah, they declared that they have returned to him. To be precise, they had never left him; they had forced him to leave them. But now they realized that they had run out of options in meeting the Ammonite threat. Condescendingly, they appealed to him to go with them[53] to engage the Ammonites in battle. Increasing the stakes for Jephthah, they repeated the offer made originally to any volunteer from full citizens of Gilead.[54] This time they offered Jephthah the presidency over all the residents of Gilead.

11:9 In v. 9 Jephthah's calculating opportunism becomes evident. It is possible to interpret Jephthah's response positively, as if no leader worth his salt would accept the Gileadite appeal without clear guarantees that he would have command. But Jephthah knew the elders were were desperate and was determined to get as much as he could out of this contract. At the same time he did not trust them and demanded firmer guarantees that they would keep their word if he returned with them and was victorious over the Ammonites. His sense of alienation is reflected in the way the beginning of his response reinterprets their opening statement in v. 8: "Suppose [lit., "if"] you take me back …"[55] His appeal to Yahweh sounds pious—a tacit recognition of Yahweh as the national deity[56]—but like Abimelech he was driven only by self-interest. So he asked again if they would really recognize him as their head if he would resolve the Ammonite problem.

---

[49] After the reference to expulsion from his father's house, the LXX adds "and sent me away from you."

[50] The language of v. 7 suggests they were the very ones responsible for his expulsion from his home, which suggests that his banishment was the result of legal procedure by which he was formally disinherited in a court setting. So also Marcus, "Legal Dispute between Jephthah and the Elders," 106.

[51] Cp. the sarcasm in Yahweh's response in 10:11–14.

[52] See Marcus, "Legal Dispute between Jephthah and the Elders," 110–11.

[53] The phrase had been missing in the first overture (v. 6).

[54] The only deviation from the original is an added לָּנוּ, "for us" (NIV, "our"), with "head." The addition highlights the need for the delegation to let Jephthah identify with them.

[55] מְשִׁיבִים is the *hiphil* participle of שׁוּב, which they had used in v. 8.

[56] This will become more evident in his negotiations with the Ammonites.

11:10–11 Left with no options, the elders of Gilead appealed to Yahweh as a witness to their good faith in promising to make him their head. Finally Jephthah agreed, and they all went to the sanctuary at Mizpah to ratify their contract "before the LORD" and presumably before the Israelite military forces (cf. 10:17). There with the "oath of office" Jephthah was sworn in and officially made head *(rōʾš)* and "commander in chief" *(qāṣîn)* of Gileadite Israel.

The manner in which Jephthah was engaged as military commander raises several questions. First, how could Jephthah be sworn in "before the LORD" at Mizpah? We have had no hint prior to this that a sacred shrine was located in Transjordanian Mizpah. It is difficult not to conclude that, like Jephthah's reference to Yahweh in v. 9 and the elder's appeal to him in v. 10, the entire ceremony represents a glib and calculated effort to manipulate Yahweh. In reality the witness Jephthah is concerned about is not Yahweh, but the army of Gilead, camped at Mizpah.

Second, where is God in this complex process of engaging Jephthah? Far from playing the decisive role, as he had in the provision of all the other judges, God is relegated to the role of silent witness to a purely human contract between a desperate people and an ambitious candidate. The entire narrative leaves the reader wondering how Yahweh will respond hereafter. In 10:10–16 God had refused to let himself be used by Israel. Nevertheless, Jephthah and the Gileadites have no hesitation in using him to seal their agreements.

Third, what is Jephthah's own relationship with Yahweh? Will he appeal to God for help? Will he recognize the hand of God upon him? Will his leadership bring the desired results? Or is Jephthah really a Canaanite at heart? Only time will tell.

(5) God's Gift of Deliverance (11:12–40)

The narrator does not answer these questions immediately. However, it is clear from vv. 29 and 32 that, regardless of Jephthah's and the Gileadites' views of the role of God, the author credits Yahweh with the decisive role in Israel's deliverance from the Ammonite oppression. Once again he graciously conceded to work on Israel's behalf. But the process by which deliverance was achieved took several surprising turns.

[12]**Then Jephthah sent messengers to the Ammonite king with the question: "What do you have against us that you have attacked our country?"**
[13]**The king of the Ammonites answered Jephthah's messengers, "When Israel came up out of Egypt, they took away my land from the Arnon to the Jabbok, all the way to the Jordan. Now give it back peaceably."**
[14]**Jephthah sent back messengers to the Ammonite king,** [15]**saying:**

"This is what Jephthah says: Israel did not take the land of Moab or the land of the Ammonites. [16]**But when they came up out of Egypt, Israel went through the**

desert to the Red Sea and on to Kadesh. [17]Then Israel sent messengers to the king of Edom, saying, 'Give us permission to go through your country,' but the king of Edom would not listen. They sent also to the king of Moab, and he refused. So Israel stayed at Kadesh.

[18]"Next they traveled through the desert, skirted the lands of Edom and Moab, passed along the eastern side of the country of Moab, and camped on the other side of the Arnon. They did not enter the territory of Moab, for the Arnon was its border.

[19]"Then Israel sent messengers to Sihon king of the Amorites, who ruled in Heshbon, and said to him, 'Let us pass through your country to our own place.' [20]Sihon, however, did not trust Israel to pass through his territory. He mustered all his men and encamped at Jahaz and fought with Israel.

[21]"Then the LORD, the God of Israel, gave Sihon and all his men into Israel's hands, and they defeated them. Israel took over all the land of the Amorites who lived in that country, [22]capturing all of it from the Arnon to the Jabbok and from the desert to the Jordan.

[23]"Now since the LORD, the God of Israel, has driven the Amorites out before his people Israel, what right have you to take it over? [24]Will you not take what your god Chemosh gives you? Likewise, whatever the LORD our God has given us, we will possess. [25]Are you better than Balak son of Zippor, king of Moab? Did he ever quarrel with Israel or fight with them? [26]For three hundred years Israel occupied Heshbon, Aroer, the surrounding settlements and all the towns along the Arnon. Why didn't you retake them during that time? [27]I have not wronged you, but you are doing me wrong by waging war against me. Let the LORD, the Judge, decide the dispute this day between the Israelites and the Ammonites."

[28]The king of Ammon, however, paid no attention to the message Jephthah sent him.

JEPHTHAH'S NEGOTIATIONS WITH THE AMMONITES (11:12–28).   As if to highlight the human dimension in the Jephthah cycle, the narrator devotes a remarkable amount of space to a new element in his recounting of the respective cycles—Jephthah's negotiations with the Ammonites.[57] It appears this man got down to business as soon as his leadership had been publicly and officially established. It also appears that, unlike Abimelech, Jephthah was determined at all cost to settle the Ammonite crisis peacefully by negotiating with them concerning Israel's and the Ammonites' conflicting land claims. In the

---

[57] By word count this segment takes up more than one-third of the Jephthah narrative as a whole: about 345 out of 1,000 words in the Hb. text. Critical scholars generally isolate this speech as a late [postexilic] cultured scribal composition. Becker (*Richterzeit und Königtum*, 217–19), who speaks of a "schriftgelierter Traktat" based on Deuteronomy 1–2, follows Richter ("Die Überlieferungen um Jephtah. Ri 10:17–12:6," *Bib* 47 [1966]: 524–25) in identifying an older argumentation (vv. 15abα,16–26) clearly directed against Moab (not Ammon!) and a more recent framework (vv. vv. 12– 14,15bβ,27–28) through which the originally anti-Moab address was adapted to the present anti-Ammonite context. Cf. M. Wuust, "Die Einschaltung in die Jiftachgeschichte. Ri 11,13–26," *Bib* 56/4 (1975): 464–79.

358

process he demonstrates great skill as a statesman and a firm negotiator. The dialogue between him and the Ammonites is just as hard-nosed as his previous conversations with the elders of Gilead had been. There is little room for movement on either side. Consequently, although Jephthah's intentions in seeking a diplomatic solution were honorable, his tone was far from conciliatory. With reference to literary style and form, Jephthah's speech is formal and conventional. Specifically, O'Connell has shown that this address contains many features of the ancient Near Eastern *rîb* or lawsuit genre.[58]

Jephthah's Overture (11:12–13). **11:12** From the opening summary of the first overture in v. 12, it is evident that Jephthah views himself as the one in charge. Indeed, he acts remarkably kinglike, dispatching envoys *(maPākîm),*[59] negotiating directly with the king of Ammon, dealing with the conflicting issues as if they were personal between him and the Ammonite king, and claiming the land as his own. The opening rhetorical question his ambassadors ask of the enemy, "What do you have against us?" (lit., "what is [the issue] between me and you?")[60] certainly creates the impression that he perceives himself as an equal. The following clause declares the issue that has precipitated the crisis: Jephthah accused the Ammonites of unmitigated military aggression against his territory.

11:13 The response of the king of the sons Ammon to Jephthah's first approach is curt and to the point.[61] By invading the land of Gilead he has reclaimed land the Israelites had taken away from him. The king's historical sense is both remarkable and skewed. On the one hand, he was aware of Israel's origins in Egypt and their earlier migration to the land of Canaan. On the other hand, he accused them of injustice against him, inasmuch as they had robbed him of the territory between the Arnon and Jabbok tributaries of the Jordan (modern Wadi Mugîb and Wadi Ez-Zarqa respectively). But this is patently false. The Ammonites had never occupied this land. Even so, the new

---

[58] He identifies the following elements: (1) declaration of obligations/rhetorical interrogation (by Jepththah, vv. 12b,23,25–26); (2) declaration of violations (by the Ammonite king, v. 13a); (3) declaration of culpability (by Jephthah, v. 27a); (4) declaration of covenant innocence by Jephthah in two parts: (a) initiation of the covenant/status quo (vv. 15b–16a,21); (b) loyalty to the covenant/status quo (vv. 16b–21a); (5) declaration of the right to vindication (by Jephthah, v. 24); (6) ultimatum consisting of a summons to trial by combat (by Jephthah, v. 27b); (7) appeal, declaring the terms of reinstatement/reparations (by the Ammonite king, v. 13b). See O'Connell, *Rhetoric of the Book of Judges*, 195.

[59] The same word had been used in 2:1,5; 6:11–24 of the messenger of the Lord. So also 13:3–23.

[60] The *lamed* before the two pronouns is a *lamed* of interest. Cf. *IBHS* 18.3b. For similar constructions see 2 Sam 16:10; 19:23; 1 Kgs 17:18; 2 Kgs 3:13; 2 Chr 35:21.

[61] The identity of the king is unknown. The first Ammonite king known by name is Nahash (ca. 1030–1000 B.C.), who appears in 1 Sam 11:1–12; 12:12; 2 Sam 10:2. On the history of the Ammonite monarchy see J.-M. de Tarragon, "Ammon," *ABD* 1.195 (trans. G. J. Norton).

territorial claims are understandable because the Ammonite heartland consisted of an amorphous region without distinct geographic boundaries between the desert to the east and the hills of Gilead in the west.[62] The present claims arise not only from a desire for more land but also out of a need for fixed and definable borders, such as these rivers would provide. But the Ammonite's claim is based more on wishful thinking than on historical reality. According to the biblical record the Arnon served as the border between Moab and the Amorites (not the Ammonites), and the Israelites had gained title to the land between this river and the Jabbok by defeating the Amorite king Sihon, who ruled in Heshbon.[63] But the Ammonite king's reply to Jephthah is a typical political speech, claiming land that his people have never owned but basing his claim on history.

Jephthah's Speech (11:14–27). The Preamble (11:14–15). **11:14–15** Jephthah responded to the king of Ammon's rebuff with a second delegation of envoys, sent with a specific message dictated by the Gileadite leader (vv. 14–27). This speech is remarkable not only for its length but also the formality and sophistication of Jephthah's argumentation. The address proper begins formally with the "citation formula": *kōh ʾāmar PN,* "Thus has *PN* declared," in which *PN* identifies the source of the speech (v. 15a). This formula highlights the speaker's heraldic role and the speech that follows as the very words of the one who sent him. Accordingly, the speech will be cast in the first person, with the messenger's own voice functioning in place of the king's.[64] Jephthah's address is a masterpiece in argumentation. He launches the speech with a thesis statement (v. 15): Israel has never claimed title to any land belonging either to Moab or Ammon. Thereafter he asserts Israel's occupation of the territory the Ammonites are claiming with successive historical (vv. 16–22), theological (vv. 23–24), personal (v. 25), and chronological (v. 26) arguments, to a large extent expressed through effective rhetorical questions. His concluding statement (v. 27) brings the address begun with the thesis statement in v. 15 to a fitting close.

The Historical Argument (11:16–22). In his speech Jephthah spent most of his time defending Israel's historical stake in the land between the Arnon and Jabbok rivers. Superciliously he contrasted the righteousness of his own nation with the aggressiveness of the Ammonites by adding the name of Moab and placing this name first. Drawing heavily on Numbers 20–21 and

---

[62] See further R. W. Yonker, "Ammonites," in *Peoples of the Old Testament World,* ed. A. J. Hoerth et al. (Grand Rapids: Eerdmans, 1994), 296–97.

[63] Num 21:10–35; Deut 2:16–37; 3:1–17.

[64] On the style and function of this formula (often referred to as "the messenger formula") see S. A. Meier, *Speaking of Speaking: Marking Direct Discourse in the Hebrew Bible,* VTSup 46 (Leiden: Brill, 1992), 179–90.

Deuteronomy 2,[65] Jephthah lectured the king of Ammon on the historical circumstances that led to the Israelites' occupation of Gilead. Like many modern politicians, in his argumentation he mixes up the facts and conflates Israel's encounters with Moabites, Ammonites, and Amorites; but he makes three key points.

11:16–18 First, when Israel came up from the land of Egypt, they showed the utmost respect for the territorial integrity of Moab and Edom. Having arrived at Kadesh via the desert and the Red Sea, they knew that they were to enter the land of Canaan from the east. However, this meant they would have to pass through the territories of Edom and Moab, two nations that were at this very moment trying to establish themselves south and east of the Dead Sea respectively. As if to answer the Ammonites' charge of aggressiveness and to paint a picture of his own people in the most positive light, Jephthah highlighted the diplomatic steps his own people took to secure permission to pass through the lands of Edom and Moab. And when that permission was refused, rather than forcing their way, the Israelites had marched through the desert around these two nations until they arrived from the east at the Arnon River. Not once did they enter Moabite territory. Because of the emphasis on Moab and the absence of the name of Ammon in vv. 15–18, some argue that this address was originally an independent text directed at Moabite aggression. The omission is indeed remarkable, especially since the antecedent text, Deut 2:16–22, describes the Israelites treating Ammon the same way they had treated Edom and Moab. It is preferable, however, to see in the omission of a reference to Ammon an intentional counter to the Ammonite charge. Far from robbing the territory of Gilead from the Ammonites, the latter were completely out of the picture when the Israelites had first arrived on the scene. The Ammonites' present claim is a fabrication based on a revisionist understanding of history.

11:19–21 Second, originally Israel had no interest in the territory Ammon is claiming—they just wanted to pass through (vv. 19–21). It fell into their hands only because the Amorite ruler of the region, Sihon, King of Heshbon,[66] had rejected their request to pass through the land. But in making this point Jephthah highlights the fundamentally peace-loving character of the Israelites. The Israelites had tried to deal with Sihon diplomatically, but,

---

[65] Contra J. Van Seters, "The Conquest of Sihon's Kingdom: A Literary Examination," *JBL* 91 [1972]: 182–97), who argues that Num 21:21–35 conflates data found in Deut 2:24–3:11 and Judg 11:19–26. For defense of the chronological priority of Num 21:21–35 see J. R. Bartlett, "The Conquest of Sihon's Kingdom: A Literary Re-Examination," *JBL* 97/3 (1978): 347–51.

[66] Modern Tell Hesban in Jordan, circa twenty km southwest of Amman. On this site see L. T. Geraty, "Heshbon," *ABD* 3.181–84; id., "Heshbon," *NEAEHL* 2.626–30.

having no confidence[67] in the word of the Israelites, the Amorite king had called up his troops and engaged the Israelites in battle. Yahweh, the God of Israel, however, had delivered the Amorites into the newcomers' hands.

11:22 Third, Ammon has no historical claim to this land (v. 22). The land between the Arnon and the Jabbok, the desert and the Jordan, had previously belonged to the Amorites, not Ammon. When the battle was over, this territory passed directly into the hands of the Israelites. Accordingly, Israel has never claimed any land belonging Edom, Moab, or Ammon. The Ammonites have no historical claim to this land.

The Theological Argument (11:23–24). **11:23–24** In v. 21 Jephthah mentioned in passing that Yahweh, the God of Israel, had delivered Sihon and the Amorites into the hands of the Israelites.[68] Now he expands on this theme by using two rhetorical questions, with which he presents two theological arguments. First, since Yahweh had driven the Amorites from the land, it naturally fell to Israel; the Ammonites are out of the picture once more. Jephthah highlighted the special relationship between Yahweh and Israel by referring to this association from both sides: Yahweh is the God of Israel; Israel is the ʿpeople of Yahweh. Second, Israel possesses whatever Yahweh gives them, and so the Ammonites must be satisfied with whatever they have received from their god Chemosh. These arguments would have been understood by all ancient Near Easterners who accepted that each nation had a patron deity whose duty and passion was to care for his people, which included providing them with a homeland.[69]

Jephthah's theology contains at least one serious flaw: Chemosh was not the patron deity of the Ammonites but of Moab.[70] The divine patron of Ammon was Milkom.[71] This discrepancy has been explained in several ways. First, Jephthah was actually involved in a war with Moab, not Ammon. The sequence of this war with Moab has been lost.[72] Second, the tradition does indeed have Jephthah involved in a conflict with Ammon, but this speech originally con-

---

[67] The Hb. וְלֹא־הֶאֱמִין סִיחוֹן, "but Sihon did not trust," in v. 20 is awkward and looks suspicious textually. On the basis of Num 20:21 (וַיְמָאֵן אֱדוֹם, "and Edom refused") *BHS* suggests reading וְלֹא־אָבָה וַיְמָאֵן תֵּת, "But he was not willing and refused to give …," which makes better sense in the context and accords better with v. 17 and Num 20:21.

[68] On the committal formula see above, p. 147f.

[69] Cp. the Mesha Inscription from Moab (mid-ninth century B.C.), which describes King Mesha attacking the Transjordanian Israelites at the command of their god Chemosh, and then Chemosh defeating the Israelites before Mesha (*ANET*, 320–21).

[70] See the Mesha Inscription referred to in the previous note. On this deity see G. L. Mattingly, "Chemosh," *ABD* 1.895–87; H.-P. Müller, "Chemosh," *DDD*, 356–62.

[71] Cf. 1 Kgs 11:5,7,33; Zeph 1:4–6. Also the recently discovered seal from Tell El ʿUmeiri with the inscription *lmlkm-ʾwr ʿbd bʿl-yšʿ*, "belonging to Milkom-ʾur, servant of Baal-yashaʿ." See Geraty, "Baalis," *ABD* 1.556–57 for discussion and bibliography.

[72] Moore, *Judges*, 283, 295; Burney, *Judges*, 298–99.

362

cerned a conflict with the Moabites and was secondarily attached to the Jephthah story.[73] Third, the territory in question was originally Moabite, hence
under the jurisdiction of Chemosh. Because Chemosh was angry with his land,
however, the power of Moab declined, and he entrusted it to the sons of
Ammon.[74]

The problem with all these explanations is they take Jephthah too seriously,
as if he was giving a historical and/or theological lecture. But this is a political
speech. Jephthah is either engaging in propaganda for purposes of his own or
is simply incorrect. As an Israelite, an inadvertent faux pas mismatching deity
and nation would be excusable. On the other hand, it seems more likely that the
error is intentional. The substitution of Chemosh for Milkom is of a piece with
his earlier omission of Ammon in his historical survey of Israel's association
with this territory (v. 17). Jephthah's obvious contempt for his antagonists
undoubtedly contributed to the hostile response his speech received. But in this
comment Jephthah also displayed contempt for his own theological traditions.
Orthodox Yahwism acknowledges only one God, who is also Israel's covenant
Lord. Yahweh alone determines the boundaries of the nations.[75] More specifically, the same tradition that recalls how the Israelites negotiated their way
around Edom and Moab to the promised land also explicitly credits Yahweh
with giving the Edomites, Moabites, and Ammonites the land they now
occupy.[76] But, as the next episode indicates, despite Jephthah's pious reference
to "the LORD our God" in v. 24, his theology is fundamentally syncretistic, so
ideological compromises like this are not surprising.

The Personal Argument (11:25). **11:25** Having scored his historical and
theological points, Jephthah resorted to *ad hominem* argumentation. The opening question in v. 25 should be translated, "Are you indeed superior to Balak,
son of Zippor, the king of Moab?" In other words, "Who does the king of
Ammon think he is?" The precise identification of the king of Moab contrasts
sharply with the namelessness of the Ammonite king, contributing to the image
of contempt. Appealing to precedent, Jephthah presented the Ammonite with
two more rhetorical questions: Did Balak ever contest[77] Israel's claim to this
land in a court of law? Or did Balak ever try to gain control of this territory by
military force? Assuming a negative answer to both questions, Jephthah in
effect informed the Ammonite king that he had no business doing so either. In
reality Balak did indeed resist Israel (Numbers 22–24), but not over land

---

[73] Becker, *Richterzeit und Königtum*, 218.

[74] Cf. 3:15–30. Thus Boling (*Judges*, 203–4), who compares this text with the Cylinder Inscription of Cyrus the Persian, which has Marduk, the patron god of Babylon, giving his own city into
the hands of this foreigner (*ANET*, 315–16).

[75] Cf. Deut 32:8–9; Amos 9:7.

[76] Deut 2:3–25, especially vv. 5,9,19.

[77] The root רִיב is the same as had been used in 6:31–32.

claims. After the Israelite defeat of the Amorite kings, Sihon and Og, the Moabites simply feared the power and presence of this newly arrived people. The Chronological Argument (11:26–27). Jephthah offered one final rhetorical question: If there is any justice to the Ammonite claims to the land of Gilead, why have they waited three hundred years to act on the claim? He concretizes the issue by referring to the villages of Heshbon and Aroer and the cities along the Arnon. Scholars' evaluation of Jephthah's figure range from a fundamental acceptance[78] to the dismissal of the number as a late editorial insertion.[79] Even if the first interpretation is desirable, it may be questioned on several counts: (1) The roundness of the number allows either an approximation or a symbolic sense. (2) Since Jephthah is either incorrectly or purposefully mistaken in other details (Chemosh for Milkom), one should perhaps not make this speech the final word on this point. (3) Since this is a political speech, Jephthah crafts his comments deliberately for propaganda purposes rather than factual reconstruction. On the other hand, as Soggin observes, Jephthah's statement finds an approximate analogue in the Mesha Inscription referred to earlier.[80] Line 10 asserts, "Now the men of Gad had dwelt in the region of Ataroth since time immemorial [*m'lm*]."[81] Surely Jephthah knew that the Israelites had lived in this area for generations. A figure like three hundred years was intended to make an impression on the Ammonites.

11:27 Jephthah concluded his speech (v. 27) with a declaration of his personal innocence and a direct accusation of wrongdoing on the part of the Ammonites for their military aggression against Israel. He also announced his resignation of the case to Yahweh, the divine Judge. He obviously had no intention of peacefully *(běšālôm)* turning this region of Gilead over to the Ammonites, as the latter had requested (v. 13).

The King of Ammon's Response (11:28). **11:28** But the king of Ammon was equally stubborn and refused to listen to the message delivered by the delegation from Jephthah. These were uncertain times in the eastern Mediterranean region. New nations were emerging in the region, and conflict

---

[78] Scholars who defend an early (fifteenth century B.C.) date for the exodus treat the number literally, claiming this figure and 1 Kgs 6:1 as the primary evidence for their position. See Howard, *Old Testament Historical Books*, 63– 65; W. H. Shea, "Exodus, Date of the," *ISBE* 2.233; J. J. Bimson and D. Livingston, "Redating the Exodus," *BAR* 13/5 (1987): 42; D. L. Washburn, "The Chronology of Judges: Another Look," *BSac* 147 (1990): 414–25.

[79] Hughes (*Secrets of the Times*, 74) insists the number is intended *as an exact figure* [italics his], but the figure is a secondary insertion that can easily be detached from the context. In fact, he argues that Jephthah's rhetorical question makes better sense without the number. Similarly Boling (*Judges*, 204), who notes that the years of oppression and the successive judges to this point in the book total 301 years. Therefore the number must be a gloss.

[80] Soggin, *Judges*, 211.

[81] Cf. *ANET*, 320; for the Hb. text, J. C. L. Gibson, *Textbook of Syrian Semitic Inscriptions*, vol. I, *Hebrew and Moabite Inscriptions* (Oxford: Clarendon, 1971), 75.

was inevitable. Not until the reign of David would political order be established. The Ammonite king was eager to flex his muscles and establish his place in the region.

The image this episode creates of Jephthah is filled with ambiguity. On the one hand, he sounds orthodox, particularly in his recognition of Yahweh's role in defeating the Amorites (v. 21) and in his final commitment of the entire affair to Yahweh. On the other hand, his recognition of Chemosh's role *[sic])* in Ammonite history exposes obvious flaws in his theology. As in the previous scene, the Gileadite leader's negotiations with the Ammonites betray a practical Yahwist. He is the sort of man whom we wonder if God will use but who has no reservations about manipulating God for his own use.

²⁹**Then the Spirit of the LORD came upon Jephthah. He crossed Gilead and Manasseh, passed through Mizpah of Gilead, and from there he advanced against the Ammonites. ³⁰And Jephthah made a vow to the LORD: "If you give the Ammonites into my hands, ³¹whatever comes out of the door of my house to meet me when I return in triumph from the Ammonites will be the LORD's, and I will sacrifice it as a burnt offering."**

³²**Then Jephthah went over to fight the Ammonites, and the LORD gave them into his hands. ³³He devastated twenty towns from Aroer to the vicinity of Minnith, as far as Abel Keramim. Thus Israel subdued Ammon.**

³⁴**When Jephthah returned to his home in Mizpah, who should come out to meet him but his daughter, dancing to the sound of tambourines! She was an only child. Except for her he had neither son nor daughter. ³⁵When he saw her, he tore his clothes and cried, "Oh! My daughter! You have made me miserable and wretched, because I have made a vow to the LORD that I cannot break."**

³⁶**"My father," she replied, "you have given your word to the LORD. Do to me just as you promised, now that the LORD has avenged you of your enemies, the Ammonites. ³⁷But grant me this one request," she said. "Give me two months to roam the hills and weep with my friends, because I will never marry."**

³⁸**"You may go," he said. And he let her go for two months. She and the girls went into the hills and wept because she would never marry. ³⁹After the two months, she returned to her father and he did to her as he had vowed. And she was a virgin.**

From this comes the Israelite custom ⁴⁰that each year the young women of Israel go out for four days to commemorate the daughter of Jephthah the Gileadite.

JEPHTHAH'S TARNISHED VICTORY (11:29–40). *Jephthah's Rout of the Sons of Ammon (11:29,32–33).* **11:29** If the engagement of Jephthah as the leader of the Transjordanian Israelites had left the reader wondering if and how God would respond, the same is true of his termination of negotiation with the Ammonites. Remarkably, it appears that as soon as the discussion had broken off, Jephthah experienced the same kind of divine empowerment that earlier judges, specifically Othniel (3:10) and Gideon (6:34) had experienced: the

Spirit of Yahweh came upon him. For the first time in the narrative Yahweh ceases to be a passive witness and becomes actively involved in his life.[82] The question raised by the divine scolding in 10:11–16 had been answered. Once again God reached out in mercy and empowered this self-made leader for his own (Yahweh's) agenda. Whether or not Jephthah was aware of his divine empowerment is not clear, but the Spirit seems to have prompted him to tour the Transjordanian regions to recruit troops for the coming battle. The narrator only summarizes his itinerary: leaving the Israelite military base at Mizpah of Gilead (10:17), he traveled through Gilead (across the Jabbok River), into the territory of Manasseh, and then back home to Mizpah of Gilead. From here he went on to the area where the Ammonites were camped and engaged them in battle.

The narrator does not say what Jephthah did on this tour, but on the analogy of the Gideon narrative (6:34–35) we may assume that he blew the trumpet throughout the land, summoning all able-bodied men to arms. Unlike the report of the spontaneous and overwhelming response of Gideon's countrymen, however, the narrator provides no information on how many Transjordanians answered Jephthah's call to arms. Nor is there any reference to a reduction of his forces for Yahweh's sake. The narrator is concerned only with the movements of Jephthah.

11:30–31 Jephthah's vow is without parallel in the book or the Bible and is unique within the Jephthah narrative itself. Verse 30 records the first and only time in which the man speaks directly to God himself. Having successfully negotiated favorable terms for his leadership over Gilead, but having unsuccessfully avoided confrontation with the Ammonites through negotiation, he sought to secure victory from God with words. But he was still negotiating— manipulating God and seeking to wrest concessions and favors from him like he had from the Gileadites and Ammonites. But in this three-linked chain of haggling one may recognize an obvious and intentional decline in his effectiveness. With the Gileadites he achieved all that he wanted (vv. 4–11); with the Ammonites he received a verbal if negative response (vv. 12–28); with Yahweh there would be only silence. Not only does the narrator fail to cite an answer, but he does not even note that God disregarded Jephthah's vow.[83] Ironically, although the vow was intended to win security for Jephthah, it became a trap for him. Despite his confident final declaration to the Ammonites, "Let the LORD, the Judge decide!" (v. 27), and despite his divine endowment with the Spirit, a fact apparently recognized by his troops, he remained insecure about

---

[82] The fourfold repetition of the verb עָבַר in vv. 29,32a links the divine endowment of the Spirit with the divine victory. Jephthah's "crossing," "passing," "advancing," and "going over" are driven by the Spirit. Cf. Webb, *Book of Judges*, 62.

[83] This contrasts not only with the description of the Ammonite response in v. 28, but also with Num 21:1–3, which contains the closest grammatical and syntactical parallel to Jephthah's vow.

the way in which Yahweh would adjudicate. At the same time it becomes apparent that his personal agenda superseded any concern for the plight of the Israelites.[84]

Jephthah's vow conforms structurally to four other vows in the Old Testament: Jacob's vow in Gen 28:20–22; Israel's vow in Num 21:2; Hannah's vow in 1 Sam 1:11; and Absalom's vow in 2 Sam 15:7–8.[85] Jephthah's fundamental doubts are reflected in the shape of the condition: "If you will only deliver the Ammonites into my hand …"[86] Jephthah had everything to lose if God should fail him; all that he had gained politically would slip from his fingers. If God should abandon him, so would the people.

Neither part of Jephthah's bargain leaves any doubts about his expectations from Yahweh. He demanded that Ammon be delivered into his hands and that he return from battle "safe and sound."[87] But the promise he made to God in return raises several questions. First, what did Jephthah vow to present to Yahweh? The NIV's rendering, "whatever comes out of the door[s] of my house to meet me," captures the ambiguity of the Hebrew.[88] Did he expect an animal or a person? Several considerations argue for the former. First, in the Old Testament the phrase "to present as a whole burnt offering," normally refers to a nonhuman sacrifice.[89] Second, the Old Testament displays an intense abhor-

---

[84] Note the first person singular pronouns in the protasis of the vow: "If you indeed deliver Bene Ammon into *my* hand, whatever comes out of the door of *my* house to meet *me* when *I* return from Bene Ammon."

[85] The four parallel structural elements are (a) an opening verb וַיִּדַּר and its cognate accusative נֶדֶר, "And X vowed a vow"; (b) the naming of the divine addressee ("to the LORD"); (c) the verb וַיֹּאמַר introducing the actual words of the vow ("and X said"); (d) a protasis introduced by אִם and followed by an infinitive absolute plus the same verb in the imperfect; (e) an apodosis expressed by the perfect consecutive. For discussion see D. Marcus, *Jephthah and His Vow* (Lubbock: Texas Tech Press, 1986), 18–19. In a study comparing Israelite and Ugaritic vows, S. B. Parker ("The Vow in Ugaritic and Israelite Narrative Literature," *UF* 11 [1979]: 693–700) observes that vows in Israel were concerned with (1) a safe return from abroad (Gen 28:20–22; 2 Sam 15:7–8), (2) military victory (Num 21:2; Judg 11:30–31), and (3) the birth of children (1 Sam 1:11).

[86] The construction is virtually identical to the protasis in Israel's vow in Num 21:2 as the following synopsis reveals:

Judg 11:30   אִם־נָתוֹן תִּתֵּן אֶת־בְּנֵי עַמּוֹן בְּיָדִי:
Num 21:2   אִם־נָתֹן תִּתֵּן אֶת־הָעָם הַזֶּה בְּיָדִי:

On the use of the infinitive absolute in a conditional clause to express doubt see *IBHS* §35,3,1g; *GBH* §123fg.

[87] Soggin's rendering of שָׁלוֹם, "peace" (*Judges*, 213; similarly JPSV, REB) is preferable to the militaristic rendering of the NIV ("in triumph") and most other translations.

[88] Contributing to the ambiguity is the use of masculine verb forms and suffixes throughout. Only later does the reader learn that Jephthah had only a daughter. *BHS* and many commentators follow the LXX and the Vg and plausibly delete one of the verbs in the first part as a dittographic gloss.

[89] God's command to Abraham to sacrifice Isaac in Gen 22:2 is obviously exceptional; Mesha's sacrifice of his son in 2 Kgs 3:27 is pagan.

rence of human sacrifices.[90] Accordingly, "whatever comes out of the door[s] of my house" should be interpreted broadly to mean anything in Jephthah's possession that comes out to meet him. By this interpretation Jephthah's vow may be interpreted like many others: a pious expression adding force to a prayer by making a contract with God.[91]

But this interpretation not only leaves unexplained Jephthah's extreme grief at being greeted by his daughter (v. 34) but also contradicts custom[92] and, more seriously, overestimates the virtue of Jephthah.[93] Although some may interpret the vow as rash and hastily worded,[94] it is preferable to see here another demonstration of his shrewd and calculating nature, another attempt to manipulate circumstances to his own advantage.[95] In this instance Jephthah was neither rash nor pious (in the orthodox Yahwistic sense)—he was outrightly pagan. Rather than a sign of spiritual immaturity and folly, like Gideon's ephod, his vow arose from a syncretistic religious environment. In 10:10 the narrator testifies to the fact that at this time the Israelites worshiped Milkom, the Ammonite god, and Chemosh, the god of the Moabites, whose leaders are known to have sacrificed children (2 Kgs 3:27). One should not expect too much from this man, who made a name for himself as a brigand in the hills of Gilead. It is conceivable that in his travels he had many contacts and had learned much from the neighboring/oppressing Ammonites. Indeed his motives and the form

---

[90] Usually human sacrifice in Israel is associated with the words, "to cause one's son or daughter to pass over by fire to Molech." Variations of the expression occur in Lev 18:21; 20:1–5; 1 Kgs 11:7; 2 Kgs 23:10; Jer 32:35. Cf. also Jer 7:31–32; 19:5–6,11; Ezek 16:20–21; 20:25–26,30–31; 23:36–39. But scholars are not united in their interpretation of the idiom or the history of child sacrifice in Israel. For a full discussion see G. C. Heider, *The Cult of Molech: A Reassessment,* JSOT-Sup 43 (Sheffield: JSOT Press, 1985; P. G. Mosca, "Child Sacrifice in Canaanite and Israelite Religion: A Study in *Mulk* and *mlk*" (Ph.D. diss., Harvard University, 1975); J. Day, *Molech: A God of Human Sacrifice in the Old Testament* (Cambridge: Cambridge University Press, 1989).

[91] The amount of attention given to vows in the OT suggests that they were common if simple expressions of zeal or devotion to Yahweh (Ps 22:25 [Hb. 26]). Once expressed a vow was as binding as an oath (Num 30:3; Deut 23:21–23), and unfulfilled vows bring on a curse (Mal 1:14). Vows should not be made hastily or rashly Prov 20:25; Qoh 5:3–5). Like sacrifices, in and of themselves they have no virtue (Ps 51:16–17) and may be only pretentious expressions of piety from a treacherous (2 Sam 15:7–8) or immoral person (Prov 7:14).

[92] M. Bal (*Death and Dissymmetry: The Politics of Coherence in the Book of Judges* [Chicago: University Press, 1988], 45) is correct in reminding us that in the ancient world animals did not go out to meet returning conquerors.

[93] Recently S. Landers ("Did Jephthah Kill His Daughter?" *BR* 7/4 [1991]: 27–31, 42) has revived the rabbinic view that because Jephthah's child was female she would have been unacceptable as a sacrifice (cf. Lev 1:3–10) and that לְתַנּוֹת in v. 40 should be translated "to console" rather than "to lament." Accordingly Jephthah must have modified his vow and "consigned her to an isolated life as a virgin" (p. 42).

[94] Klein, *Triumph of Irony,* 95; Boling, *Judges,* 215–16; Marcus, *Jephthah and His Vow,* 54–55.

[95] So also O'Connell, *The Rhetoric of the Book of Judges,* 180–81; Webb, *The Book of Judges* 64, 227 n. 54; Soggin, *Judges,* 215–16.

of his vow bear a striking resemblance to many vows inscribed in funerary monuments in Carthage by Punic descendants of the Canaanites/Phoenicians in northern Africa. The following votive inscription is typical:

> To our lady, to Tanit, the face of Baʿal and to our lord, to Baʿal Hammon that which was vowed (by) PN son of PN, son of PN because he [the deity] heard his [the dedicant's] voice and blessed him.[96]

For these people vows to sacrifice children were not rash or impulsive but deadly serious expressions of devotion.[97] Jephthah was so determined to achieve victory over the Ammonites that he was willing to sacrifice his own child to gain a divine guarantee. The clause "whatever comes out of the doors of my house to meet me" envisages the exuberant welcome by children of a father who has been away on a military campaign. For the moment the reader does not know that Jephthah has only one child, that in putting her at risk he also jeopardizes himself, and that, ironically, in securing his own victory he sentences his lineage to death.

If Jephthah's vow follows the stereotypical form of Israelite vows in general, then the relationship between condition and consequence is quite extraordinary. Whereas other vows exhibit a close link between what is requested and what is vowed,[98] Jephthah's promise to sacrifice whatever would come out of the house to meet him has no connection with the battle against the Ammonites at all. On the analogy of Num 21:2 he should have offered the inhabitants of the cities he would conquer. Instead he would offer the one who should have helped him celebrate a safe return from battle.

The treatment Jephthah promises for the victim of his vow is described by two clauses in the last part of the consequence: "It [He] will belong to the LORD, and I will offer it [him] as a burnt offering." But the syntactical construction is unusual.[99] In place of the compound clause one might have expected "and I will offer it [him] up as a whole burnt offering to the LORD."

---

[96] See the popular presentation of the archaeological evidence from Carthage by L. E. Stager and S. R. Wolff, "Child Sacrifice at Carthage—Religious Rite or Population Control," *BARev* 10/1 (1984): 30–51. This quotation is cited from p. 45.

[97] Cf. 2 Kgs 3:27. For a comparison of Ug. and Israelite vows see S. B. Parker, *UF* 11 (1979): 693–700.

[98] Accordingly Jacob vowed to be God's devotee if God would be with him (Gen 28:20–22); the Israelites promised to return to Yahweh the Canaanite cities if he would deliver them into their hands (Num 21:2); Hannah vowed that if God would give her a male child she would return him by consecrating him to God (1 Sam 1:11); Absalom vowed to worship Yahweh if he would bring him back to Jerusalem from exile in Geshur (2 Sam 15:7–8). For a discussion see Marcus, *Jephthah and His Vow*, 19.

[99] First, the introductory וְהָיָה cries for a subject corresponding to the suffix on the following verb. On the analogy of Gen 28:20–22 something like הוּא לַיהוָה וְהָיָה, or הוּא יְהְיֶה לַיהוָה, "It shall belong to the LORD," is expected. Second, without an indirect object after the second, the regular form of the idiom calls for the preposition *lamedh* before the עוֹלָה. Cf. Gen 22:13.

This raises the question whether the narrator has deliberately reconstructed the consequence to soften the suggestion (intolerable in the narrator's mind) that Jephthah might have contemplated a human sacrifice to Yahweh.[100] The word *ʿōlâ* derives from a root meaning "to go up" and denotes a sacrifice that was entirely burnt on an altar, its scent and smoke ascending to God.[101]

11:32–33 Following the pattern of earlier accounts, after learning of Jephthah's divine empowerment and the marshalling of the troops, the reader expects the narrative to move quickly to its denouement. It does indeed do so if we eliminate vv. 30–31. The narrative flows smoothly from v. 29 to v. 32 without the intervening material. In fact the account follows a pattern common in biblical victory accounts:

Element	Othniel	Gideon	Jephthah	Saul
The Spirit of Yahweh comes upon a deliverer	3:10	6:33	11:29	1 Sam 11:6
The deliverer marshals the troops		6:34–35	11:29	1 Sam 11:7–11
The Israelites go out to battle	3:10		11:32	
Yahweh gives the enemy into the deliverer's hands	3:10		11:32	1 Sam 11:13?

The account leaves the impression that, having returned with his recruits, Jephthah immediately went on the offensive against the sons of Ammon (v. 32a). However, employing the stereotypical committal formula, the narrator is quick to give credit where credit is due: Yahweh gave the enemy into Jephthah's hands. There is an element of ambiguity in v. 33 to be sure, but the construction suggests that Yahweh continues to be the subject.[102] It was he who struck twenty enemy fortifications[103] with (lit.) "an extremely great striking/slaughter"[104] and caused the Ammonites to be subdued before the Israelites.

---

[100] Similarly Marcus, *Jephthah and His Vow*, 24.

[101] In Jer 19:5 the prophet speaks of "burning children with fire (בָּאֵשׁ שָׂרַף) as whole burnt offerings (עֹלוֹת) to Baal." On whole burnt offerings see G. A. Anderson, "Sacrifice and Sacrificial Offerings (OT)," *ABD* 5.877–78; Milgrom, *Leviticus*, 172–77.

[102] Since Yahweh is the nearest named antecedent, the sequence of verbs is best translated, "And the LORD gave them into his hands and he struck them." Furthermore, the verb form וַיִּכָּנְעוּ, "and they were subdued," is best interpreted as a divine passive. Cf. 4:23, the only occurrence of the active stem of this verb *(hiphil)*, where the subject is explicitly identified as God. The present idiom, "to be subdued before the sons of Israel," was encountered earlier in 8:28. Cf. 3:30, which reads "under the hand of Israel."

[103] The term עִיר (NIV "towns") refers fundamentally to a walled settlement.

[104] The NIV renders this entire phrase with "devastated."

The narrator concretizes the scope of the victory by defining the rout in geographic terms: from Aroer to the entrance to Minnith and as far as Abel-keramim. Although some identify Aroer with the well-known city on the Arnon,[105] it is preferable to link this site with "Aroer that is before Rabbah" (Josh 13:25), that is, southwest of modern Amman.[106] Minnith has not been identified with certainty, but a location between Amman and Heshbon is reasonable.[107] Abel-keramim, "pasture of vineyards," probably is to be equated with Abila, located by Eusebius[108] six Roman leagues from Amman.[109] Since the territory of the sons of Ammon lacked clear geographical boundaries, these three sites, together with the rest of the twenty "towns," performed an important function in defining the border between Israelite and Ammonite land. Unlike Gideon, Jephthah appears not to have pursued the Ammonites into their own heartland. But by destroying their border fortifications he eliminated the pressure they were applying to his people.

11:34 Interrupted by the notice of Yahweh's victory over Ammon the narrative of Jephthah's vow resumes in v. 34. Whereas in Jephthah's mind at least vv. 30–31 had concerned his negotiations with Yahweh, in vv. 34–39 the focus is on his relationship with his daughter. The narrator creates suspense by opening with the scene of the conquering hero returning from battle to his house at Mizpah. However, the author immediately shifts the reader's attention[110] from the returning conqueror to the one coming out the door of his house to meet him. In his portrayal of these two personalities the narrator is at his literary best.

The portrait of the young girl is painted in most sympathetic and attractive colors. Though the narrator leaves her nameless,[111] in his mind she was obviously a special child, a perfect foil for her ambitious and calculating father. Unlike Gideon and Jephthah, but like Zebah and Zalmunnah (8:21), this girl knew the code of honor.[112] When she saw her father approaching, with natural

---

[105] Rasmussen (*NIV Atlas of the Bible*, 227) identifies the site with modern Arair, fourteen miles east of the Dead Sea.

[106] So also Malamat, "Period of the Judges," 157; G. L. Mattingly, "Aroer," *ABD* 1.399.

[107] Cf. R. W. Younker, "Minnith," *ABD* 4.842.

[108] *Onomastica* 32.14–25.

[109] Some identify the site with Naur, eight miles southwest of Amman. Cf. Malamat, "Period of the Judges," 157; Rasmussen, *NIV Atlas of the Bible*, 224. For a discussion of these names see S. Mittmann, "Aroer, Minnith und Abel Keramim," *ZDPV* 85 (1969): 63–75; E. A. Knauf, "Abel Keramim," *ZDPV* 100 (1984): 119–21; id., "Abel-Keramim," *ABD* 1.10–11.

[110] The transition is marked by the focusing particle, וְהִנֵּה, "and behold."

[111] It has become fashionable in recent times for interpreters to attempt to rectify the patricentrism of biblical authors by giving anonymous female characters names. See, e.g., B. Gerstein ("A Ritual Processed: A Look at Judges 11:40," in *Anticovenant: Counter-Reading Women's Lives in the Hebrew Bible*, ed. M. Bal, JSOTSup 81 [Sheffield: Almond Press, 1989], 175–93), who attempts to refocus the story and make Jephthah's daughter the primary actor by naming her Bat, the Hb. equivalent of "daughter." Similarly M. Bal, "Between Altar and Wondering Rock: Toward a Feminist Philology," ibid., 212–31.

[112] Thus Auld, *Joshua, Judges, and Ruth*, 202.

childlike exuberance she picked up her timbrels and danced out to greet him. The victory over the Ammonites may have made him a military hero to the Transjordanian Israelites, but to this young girl he was a hero simply because he was her father.[113] But the intentionally redundant circumstantial clause in v. 34b emphasizes that she was no ordinary child to Jephthah either. On the contrary, she was all he had; there were no other children.[114] In fact, with the expression *yĕḥîdâ*, "only child," the narrator intentionally links this account with the account of Abraham's sacrifice of Isaac as a whole burnt offering in Genesis 22, where Isaac is identified as Abraham's son, his *yāḥîd*, "only child."

This observation offers an opportunity to compare the present account in other respects. The links and contrasts may be summarized in chart form as follows:

A Comparison of Abraham's and Jephthah's Sacrifices

Narrative Element	Genesis 22	Judges 11
Literary style	Deliberately detailed and slow-paced narrative, particularly the account of the sacrifice itself	Cursory and quick tele-scoped narrative, announcing the actual sacrifice in only five words
Literary content	Intentional climax of lengthy narrative[a]	Seemingly superfluous intrusion in the narrative
Purpose of sacrifice	Test the commitment of the sacrificer	Test the commitment of God
The role of God	Takes initiative in commanding human sacrifice; speaks directly to sacrificer	Silent in the initiation and performance of the sacrifice; sacrificer speaks directly to God
Identity of sacrificer	Father of the promise, called out from his home	Son of a harlot, cast out of his home

---

[113] Her coming out to meet him alone not only highlights her solitariness contextually, but also contrasts with the celebrations led by Miriam (Exod. 15:19–21) and the women (1 Sam 8:6–7) after Yahweh's victory at the Red Sea and David's victory over the Philistines respectively. For a study of the custom of skilled women participating in public festivities following military victories and ancient terra-cotta figurines of women hold frame drums from see C. L. Meyers, "Of Drums and Damsels: Women's Performance in Ancient Israel," *BA* 54 (1991): 16–27.

[114] Note the construction: וְרַק הִיא יְחִידָה אֵין־לוֹ מִמֶּנּוּ בֵּן אוֹ־בַת, "Now [there was] only she, an only [child]; he had no one else, neither son nor daughter." The construction of the first phrase recalls Job 1:15, לְבַדִּי רַק־אֲנִי, "Only I alone." On the apparently masculine suffix on מִמֶּנּוּ, referring to a feminine antecedent, see GKC §135o and n. 3.

A Comparison of Abraham's and Jephthah's Sacrifices

Narrative Element	Genesis 22	Judges 11
Character of sacrificer	Saintly patriarch Obedient to God Sacrificer agonizes over fate of his victim	Paganized deliverer-hero Independent of God Sacrificer grieves over his own loss
Identity of victim	Isaac, divinely named offspring of sacrificer	Nameless offspring of sacrificer
Relationship of victim to sacrificer	"One and only child" Loved deeply by the father Accompanied by father to the mountain of sacrifice	"One and only child" "Love" is absent Goes to the mountain alone, without the father
Gender of the sacrifice	Male victim	Female victim
Response of victim	Passive acceptance of fate	Energetic insistence on fate
Outcome of the sacrifice	Interrupted by voice of God	Fulfilled because of silence of God
Significance of the sacrifice	Confirmed the faith of the sacrificer Confirmed the faithfulness and presence of God Assured the future of the sacrificer and his victim	Confirmed the faithlessness of the sacrificer Confirmed the silence and withdrawal of God Signaled the end of the sacrificer and his victim

a. Note the introductory וַיְהִי אַחַר הַדְּבָרִים הָאֵלֶּה, "Now it happened after these things/events" (Gen 22:1).

11:35 Although the present story ends with the death of the young girl,[115] her father is the tragic figure, presenting a pathetic picture of stupidity, brutality, ambition, and self-centeredness. Ironically, the one who appeared to have become master of his own fate has become a victim of his own rash word. The strong man of Tob, the conquering hero, was a captive in his own house. There is no sign of divine empowerment or Spirit enduement as he seeks to extricate himself from his own foolish vow. Even in his response to the appearance of his daughter he could not get beyond his own personal welfare. He tore his clothes and exclaimed "Oh! [Hb. *'ăhāh*]" in grief, but despite his address of the girl as *bittî*, "My daughter," his grief was not for the death of this innocent maiden[116] but for himself. Far from dis-

---

[115] Though some, overlooking the plain meaning of עוֹלָה and overestimating Jephthah's spirituality, argue he presented her at the local shrine as a perpetual spiritual sacrifice. See, e.g., G. L. Archer, *Encyclopedia of Bible Difficulties* (Grand Rapids: Zondervan, 1982), 164–65.

[116] Contrast his hollow address of his daughter with Abraham's genuinely tender בְּנִי, "My son," in Gen 22:7,8.

playing any hint of tenderness toward his daughter, the tone in his double barrel reaction is accusatory: "You have indeed driven me to my knees![117] You are responsible for my ruin!" (author translation)[118] The irony of the scene is patent. The man who had tried to manipulate Yahweh to guarantee his "peace" *(šālôm)* is doomed by the one whose life he was willing to sacrifice for his own well-being. The last statement of v. 35 expresses tragic resignation. Jephthah had opened his mouth to God,[119] so he cannot retract his words. This man who sought so desperately to be head and ruler of Israel was a victim of his own vow and of his daughter.

11:36 The despicable behavior of this hero in Israel contrasts with the sensitivity and submissiveness of the child. Addressing him affectionately as "My father,"[120] her logic was simple and resigned: "You have opened your mouth to Yahweh. He has complied by avenging you of your enemies, the Ammonites. Now you must keep the commitment that issued from your own mouth" (author paraphrase). This comment is remarkable for two reasons. First, through the speech of this young girl the narrator offers a theological interpretation of the battle. The use of the verb *nāqam*, "to execute vengeance, just punishment," answers to Jephthah's declaration in v. 27, "Let the LORD, the Judge, decide this dispute this day between the Israelites and the Ammonites." Yahweh had indeed rendered judgment, which is expressed in the outcome of the battle.

11:37 Second, the young girl courageously and dutifully charged her father to do to her what he had vowed. Apparently this innocent child knew nothing of the Mosaic allowance for the annulment/transformation of vows involving human objects. She tried to soften the pain by requesting a concession for herself personally: that he leave her alone[121] for two months with her friends to the mountains so she may wander about[122] with her companions and

---

[117] The NIV's "You have made me miserable" hardly does justice to the emphatic causative construction of הִכְרַעְתָּנִי הַכְרֵעַ. In 7:5–6 the root כָּרַע, "to bow/kneel down," had described the posture of men drinking water from a brook.

[118] The choice of the root עָכַר reflects an intentional wordplay, reordering the consonants of the previous verb כָּרַע. The construction וְאַתְּ הָיִית בְּעֹכְרָי involves a *beth essentiae* (viz, "you act in the capacity/with the character of one who …") and an intensive plural, "who ruins me totally." Cf. *GBH* §133c and §136f.

[119] The word נֶדֶר, "vow," never surfaces in this conversation. Instead in vv. 35–36 both Jephthah and his daughter speak of him "opening his mouth to Yahweh" (פָּצָה־פֶּה אֶל־יְהוה) and even more generally of "what has proceeded from his mouth."

[120] This provides another link with Genesis 22. Cf. Isaac's address of his father Abraham in v. 7.

[121] NIV, "Give me." Hb. הַרְפֵּה מִמֶּנִּי, "refrain from me." Cf. Deut 9:14 for a similar construction.

[122] The MT's וְיָרַדְתִּי is pointed as if from יָרַד, "to go down," but a derivation from רוּד, "to wander," is generally accepted.

weep because she would never be fulfilled sexually.[123] She would indeed die a virgin, but this fact is expressed by the clause *lōʾ yādĕʿâ ʾîš*, literally "she did not know a man."[124] Why she should have asked for two months is unclear, and why she should have desired time alone with her companions rather than her family is unclear, but the image of her last days contrasts with the picture of the early Jephthah living in the hills of Gilead with his worthless companions (*ʾănāšîm rēqîm*, v. 3). In the end the nameless girl's friends wept with and for her, but Jephthah wept only for himself.

The narrator may also invite comparison to the sexual implications of these two scenes. Jephthah was expelled from home and sentenced to a life in the hills because he was the child of an illicit affair; this young girl chooses this sentence because she had had no children. This latter fact is critical. Not only would she die, never having conceived and borne a child, but because Jephthah had no other children, his seed would die with her. The general perspective of the Old Testament is that parents live on in their children. Accordingly, to die without progeny was considered a terrible fate.[125] With his vow Jephthah had tried to secure his present, but through it he ends up sacrificing his future.

11:38–39a Following this conversation the account moves quickly to its denouement. The narrator records Jephthah's verbal permission ("Go"), and then reports him sending her off for two months. Accompanied by her friends she spends the last days of her life in the mountains lamenting the fact that she will die a virgin, never having known the joy of sexual intimacy and, more importantly, failing to carry on the family line.[126] With her death the family

---

[123] By sexual fulfillment I do not mean "enjoy the experience of sexual intercourse" but realize the joy of motherhood, the natural longing of women, particularly in this ancient cultural context. Although בְּתוּלִים is often translated "virginity" (NASB, NRSV, REB, NAB, NJB), the word refers to the condition or state of being a בְּתוּלָה. The NIV's "because she would never marry" is better, but better still is the NJPV's "her maidenhood." On the form בְּתוּלִים, a plural of abstraction denoting a state or condition, see *GBH* §136h.

[124] The noun בְּתוּלָה does not mean "virgin" but "a female who had reached puberty and was therefore potentially fertile, but who had not yet given birth to her first child." Thus P. L. Day, "From the Child Is Born the Woman: The Story of Jephthah's Daughter," in *Gender and Difference in Ancient Israel*, ed. P. L. Day (Minneapolis: Fortress, 1989), 59. For further studies of the term see G. J. Wenham, "*Bĕtûlâ*, 'A Girl of Marriageable Age," *VT* 22 (1972): 326–48, and J. H. Walton, "בְּתוּלָה (*Bĕtûlâ*)," *NIDOTTE* 1.781–84. Walton defines the term as "an ostensibly reputable young girl who is past puberty and is, by default at least, still in the household of her father" (p. 782).

[125] Cp. article 66 of the curses in the vassal treaty of Esarhaddon: "Just as a mule has no offspring, may your name, offspring and descendants disappear from the land." *ANET*, 539.

[126] Contra K. H. Keukens ("Richter 11,37f.: Rite de passage und Übersetzungsprobleme," *BN* 19 [1982]: 41–42), who argues that the phrase בְּתוּלִים בָּכָה עַל denotes not bewailing the fact that she dies a virgin but that she performs the ritual appropriate to a בְּתוּלָה, and Day ("From the Child Is Born the Woman," 58–60), who interprets this as an etiological tale accounting for the annual ritual lament performed by young women at ceremonies marking the passage from childhood to physical maturity, the state of בְּתוּלִים.

dies. The narrator deliberately softens the horror of her end and spares the reader the horrific details. On the analogy of Gen 22:9b–10 we might have expected the following:

> Jephthah built an altar there and arranged the wood on it. He bound his daughter [name] and laid her on the altar on top of the wood. Then he reached out his hand and took the knife to slay his daughter.[127]

The details can be recounted in the earlier story because the actions demonstrate faith and have a positive outcome—Isaac is spared, and the commitment of the father is acknowledged by God. But here the narrator describes with five simple words in Hebrew the abhorrent and unspeakable notion that an Israelite sacrificed his child to Yahweh as a whole burnt offering: "and-he-did to-her his-vow which he-had-vowed." The contrast with the description of Abraham's sacrifice of Isaac could scarcely be starker. But there is more. Whereas Abraham's sacrifice of his son assured him of a hope and a future, Jephthah's sacrifice of his daughter robbed him of both. The conquering hero is reduced to nothing.

11:39b–40 The present narrative ends with a reflective comment and an aetiological note. Both elements reflect the irony of the event. First the narrator reminds the readers that despite her mourning over her virginity, Jephthah's daughter's condition did not change. Accordingly the fate of the man who tried so desperately to find security in life is sealed—he dies with his victim.[128] Second, the narrator notes the enduring luster of the young girl's reputation. No memorials were erected for Jephthah, but the memory of his daughter was immortalized in a festival celebrated in her honor. Nothing specific is known of this festival, except that it was observed four days each year by the women of Israel. It is doubtful this observance ever became a national event. The absence of any external attestation probably may be attributed to the fact that the events described to this point have all concerned only the Transjordanian tribes, whom their Cisjordanian countrymen tended to marginalize from the beginning.

Theological and Practical Implications

Some reflective comments are appropriate at this point before moving to the next episode in the recorded life of Jephthah.

First, scholars have long noted the thematic links between this short episode and several stories from ancient extrabiblical writings. A story from Crete has

---

[127] According to the NIV rendering of the Genesis text. Cf. the discussion by Bal, *Death and Dissymmetry*, 110–11.

[128] The narrator deliberately reminds the reader of Jephthah's origins (and prepares for the following episode) by identifying him as "Jephthah *the Gileadite*" in v. 40b.

the king of the island Idomenaeus caught in a shipwreck and making a vow to sacrifice to Neptune the first person to come out to meet him should he return safely.[129] Cited more often is the Greek legend of the daughter of Agamemnon, Iphegenia, which appears in many variations. Particularly tantalizing is one Euripidean version that has Agamemnon vowing to sacrifice to Artemis the most beautiful creature born that year within his kingdom. When that creature turns out to be his daughter, he wavers until the prophet Calchas declares to him that a fleet of ships that has been grounded for weeks in Aulis will be released by a favorable wind only if and when he complies. The speech of Calchas reads as follows:

> Agamemnon, Captain of Hellas, there can be no way of setting your ships free, till the offering you promised Artemis is given to her. You had vowed to render Her in sacrifice the loveliest thing each year should bear. You have owed long since the loveliness which Clytemnestra had borne to you, your daughter, Iphegenia. Summon your daughter now and keep your word.[130]

However, at the last moment Artemis provides a hind as a substitute and carries the young girl off to the region of the Taurians in the Crimea and makes her priestess.[131] Since the differences between the present Jephthah account and these Greek stories are much greater than the similarities, the links between them should not be pressed.[132] Perhaps the most that can be said is that the events described in this paragraph are realistic, especially if one recognizes the author's intent to describe a paganized Jephthah.

Second, it has often been noted that the narrator makes no evaluative comments on Jephthah's conduct in this event. Accordingly many continue to condone his actions, either by making his treatment of his daughter more spiritual than the text and context warrant (e.g., she was dedicated to Yahweh for a lifetime of celibate religious service) or by dismissing his vow as a rash act of folly. In any case, having made the vow and having witnessed Yahweh's fulfill-

---

[129] *Aenid* 11.264. Cf. 3:121.

[130] As translated by W. Bynner, "Iphegenia in Taurus," in *Euripides II*, ed. D. Greene and R. Lattimore (Chicago/London: University of Chicago Press, 1956), 117–87. Another Euripidean version (Iphegenia in Aulis) has Iphegenia rescued in the end, but this ending is suspect. See C. R. Walker, trans., "Iphegenia in Aulis," in *Euripides IV*, ed. D. Greene and R. Lattimore (Chicago/London: University of Chicago Press, 1958), 214. For a discussion of these and similar stories see Marcus, *Jephthah and His Vow*, 40–43; Burney, *Judges*, 332–33; Moore, *Judges*, 304–5.

[131] A. S. Way, *Euripides*, vol. 2 (London: William Heinemann, 1919), 287. This ending is also found in Apollodorus (J. G. Frazer, *Apollodorus: The Library*, vol. 2, Loeb Classical Library [New York: Putnam's, 1921], 191–93) and Hesiod's Cypria (H. G. Evelyn-White, *Hesiod: The Homeric Hymns and Homerica* (Cambridge: Harvard University Press, 1943).

[132] Drawing on these links, Day ("From the Child is Born the Woman, 58–74) concludes [speculates] that Israelite women recounted the story of Jephthah's daughter during rites of passage from adolescence to maturity.

ment of the eventuality demanded, Jephthah was faced with three options. First, assuming the irrevocability of a vow such as this, the valorous response would have been to sacrifice his own *šālôm* and leave the vow unfulfilled. To be sure, this would have brought the curse upon himself,[133] but it would have spared his daughter and in so doing secured his own future.

Second, he could have followed the Mosaic Torah and paid twenty shekels to the priest at the central shrine as compensation for the life of his daughter.[134] Leviticus 27:1–8 regulates cases in which one person vows another, that is, devotes a person to the sanctuary for sacred service[135] and then for reasons unspecified finds it impossible or impractical to fulfill the vow. Admittedly, the present case is different, inasmuch as Jephthah has vowed to sacrifice his daughter as a burnt offering, but one may argue on the rabbinic principle of *qal wāḥômer* (lit. "light and heavy") that a rule that applied in a lesser case would certainly apply in a more serious case involving the very life of a human being.

Third, Jephthah could have done as he in fact did; he fulfilled the vow to the letter. The text is silent on whether or not he contemplated a different option.[136] Given Jephthah's spiritual disposition his sacrifice of his daughter represented the ultimate expression of devotion and piety. But if the author found this act so abhorrent, why does he not express his revulsion at this outrage?[137] The answer is he does. On the one hand, as noted earlier, the superfluity of the vow is suggested by the way in which he includes it in an otherwise complete narrative. On the other hand, Jephthah's actions are implicitly denounced by the way in which the author makes certain statements. Not only does Jephthah's vow appear to have been deliberately cast to repress the notion of a child sacrificed to Yahweh,[138] but, even more telling, he describes Jephthah's fulfillment of the vow with a simple general statement: "He did to her as he had vowed" (v. 39). Although these features imply condemnation, the narrator's disposition is explicitly expressed by the locatiin of the Jephthah cycle within the "Book of Deliverers." In light of the editorial principle declared in

---

[133] Ironically this is what happened in any case.

[134] Lev 27:1–8 regulates the manner in which vows involving one person committing another to Yahweh were to be handled.

[135] By itself the text is ambiguous, not distinguishing between persons dedicated for religious service or for sacrifice, but in view of Yahwism's utter abhorrence of human sacrifice, the latter is excluded. On this text see Milgrom, *Leviticus*, 489; J. E. Hartley, *Leviticus*, WBC (Dallas: Word, 1992), 480–81.

[136] J. C. Exum overstates the case in claiming the vow is "irrevocable, irreversible and unalterable" ("On Judges 11," in *A Feminist Companion to Judges,* Feminist Companion to the Bible 4, ed. A. Brenner (Sheffield: Sheffield Academic Press, 1993], 131).

[137] According to Marcus (*Jephthah and His Vow,* 48), "Jephthah is not only *not* [italics his] condemned but referred to by the same Deuteronomist as a "savior of Israel," which is hardly an appellation to be applied to one guilty of such a crime."

[138] See above on v. 31b.

2:18–20 and following the Gideon story, which ended in the construction of the paganized ephod, Jephthah's conduct is to be interpreted as a further illustration of Israel's increasingly Canaanized character. The placement of the Jephthah cycle immediately after the story of Abimelech also invites a negative comparison with this man. Abimelech had sacrificed his Israelite half-brothers at the altar of his own ambition so he could rule over his Canaanite half-brothers. Jephthah did one better—he sacrificed his own daughter and with her himself that he might rule over a tribe of his Israelite half-brothers.[139]

Feminists have found in this text a store of ammunition to denounce any form of patriarchalism. In Jephthah's treatment of his daughter they recognize the inherently abusive character of traditional social structures, patriarchy in particular. Since the highest value in patriarchal societies is supposedly the maintenance of male dominance, in such contexts women have no value except as tools, chattel to be manipulated and disposed at will in the interests of and for the honor of men.[140]

In response it must be acknowledged without equivocation or qualification that Jephthah's sacrifice of his daughter represents the ultimate in abuse. He not only violated the human race by eliminating one of its members, an image of God with inherent dignity equal to his own, but he also violated his own flesh and blood. If homicidal crimes may be classified, pedicide must rank among the most heinous. This young woman, whose memory was celebrated in Israel for generations and whom we still honor by grieving over her death, was a victim of faithfulness to an unfaithful vow.[141] And in her fate she represents all the courageous daughters of abusive fathers.[142] But Jephthah does not represent normative patriarchy. It has been observed repeatedly that little in the Book of Judges is normal or normative. In fact, the farther one reads in the book the more aberrant and abhorrent the conduct of individuals (particularly men) becomes. Like many other males in the book, Jephthah represents patriarchy at its worst, where the focus is on the "archy," expressed in twisted and exploitative rule of the father.[143] Admittedly the narratives of the Old Testa-

---

[139] Cf. O'Connell, *Rhetoric of the Book of Judges*, 183.

[140] See the essays by Exum, "On Judges 11," esp. pp. 137–44; A. M. Tapp, "An Ideology of Expendability: Virgin Daughter Sacrifice," in *Anti-Covenant: Counter-Reading Women's Lives in the Hebrew Bible*, JSOTSup 81/Bible and Literature Series 22, ed. M. Bal (Sheffield: Almond Press, 1989), 171–72; E. Fuchs, "Marginalization, Ambiguity, Silencing: The Story of Jephthah's Daughter," *Journal of Feminist Studies of Religion* 5/1 (1989): 35–45.

[141] Thus P. Trible, *Texts of Terror: Literary-Feminist Readings of Biblical Theology*, Overtures to Biblical Theology (Philadelphia: Fortress, 1984), 102, in an updated version of an earlier essay, "A Meditation in Mourning: The Sacrifice of the Daughter of Jephthah," *USQR* 36 Supplementary (1981): 59–73.

[142] Ibid., 108.

[143] For a study of this issue see D. I. Block, "Crimes Unspeakable: The Abuse of Women in the Book of Judges," *SBJT* 2/3 (1998): 46–55.

ment all too often reflect a degenerate society in which those with power, whether kings, or judges, or elders, or fathers, use their office for their own personal ends and in the process abuse those over whom they have charge.

But this is not the normative biblical pattern, nor is the problem resolved by eliminating all hierarchical structures in society. The answer lies in the transformation of society so that those in authority, including fathers as heads of households, view themselves as servants of those under them and, like Christ, sacrifice all personal advantage for the well-being of others. This is true spiritual headship. Given the abuses that men have imposed upon women and children, it may be necessary to abandon the word "patriarchy," "the rule of the father," but this does not mean that the institution of fatherhood or the responsible headship of men in the homes should be abolished.

The inclusion of this episode in the Jephthah narrative heightens the tragic character of his life. Here was a man who overcame the abuses of his own past to become the foremost military general in his time and the ruler of the Transjordanian tribes. With the eventual support of his countryfolk and empowered by the Spirit of God, he possessed tremendous potential for greatness. Tragically and ironically the man whose basic gift was facility with words falls prey to his own foolish utterance. But the narrative also heightens our sympathy for his daughter. Her death was not her greatest tragedy. It was her death as a virgin. By Jephthah's vow she too is rendered childless. It is some consolation to learn that though we do not know her name, her companions did, and the daughters of Israel preserved her heroic memory in their annual ritual.

But where is Yahweh in all this? He remains strangely silent.[144]

(6) The Legacy of Jephthah (12:1–7)

[1]The men of Ephraim called out their forces, crossed over to Zaphon and said to Jephthah, "Why did you go to fight the Ammonites without calling us to go with you? We're going to burn down your house over your head."

[2]Jephthah answered, "I and my people were engaged in a great struggle with the Ammonites, and although I called, you didn't save me out of their hands. [3]When I saw that you wouldn't help, I took my life in my hands and crossed over to fight the Ammonites, and the LORD gave me the victory over them. Now why have you come up today to fight me?"

[4]Jephthah then called together the men of Gilead and fought against Ephraim.

---

[144] Some interpret this silence as acceptance of Jepthah's vow and complicity in the sacrifice of his daughter. Cf. J. C. Exum, "The Center Cannot Hold: Thematic and Textual Instabilities in Judges," *CBQ* 52 (1990): 422; Tapp, "Ideology of Expendability: Virgin Daughter Sacrifice," 169–70; C. Baker, "Pseudo-Philo and the Transformation of Jephthah's Daughter," 196–97. However, as Webb has demonstrated (*The Book of Judges*, 63), the victory is causally linked to the endowment of the Spirit but only incidentally linked to the vow. The structure of the narrative highlights the superfluity of the vow.

The Gileadites struck them down because the Ephraimites had said, "You Gileadites are renegades from Ephraim and Manasseh." ⁵The Gileadites captured the fords of the Jordan leading to Ephraim, and whenever a survivor of Ephraim said, "Let me cross over," the men of Gilead asked him, "Are you an Ephraimite?" If he replied, "No," ⁶they said, "All right, say 'Shibboleth.'" If he said, "Sibboleth," because he could not pronounce the word correctly, they seized him and killed him at the fords of the Jordan. Forty-two thousand Ephraimites were killed at that time.

⁷Jephthah led Israel six years. Then Jephthah the Gileadite died, and was buried in a town in Gilead.

JEPHTHAH'S CONFLICT WITH EPHRAIM (12:1–6). Jephthah may have survived the personal crisis of his own doing in 11:30–31,34–40, but his problems were not over. His victory over Ammon was further tarnished by the national crisis his achievements precipitated. The closing reference to "Jephthah the Gileadite" in the previous episode (11:40) is ominous. His military feats may have confirmed him as "ruler" *(qāṣîn)* and "head" *(rōʾš)* over the Transjordanian highlands, but not all in Israel accepted his leadership. As in the foregoing narratives, direct speech dominates the presentation of the new crisis that surfaces in chap. 12. But as with the Ammonites, this time Jephthah's skills as a negotiator were insufficient to resolve the problem. Again he must resort to arms, but now it would not be against a foreign enemy but against his own people! The final recorded episode of his life reflects the political disintegration within Israel that accompanied the spiritual declension. Jealousies drive east versus west, Gilead versus Ephraim.

12:1 The sad conclusion to the Jephthah story begins with the reappearance of the Ephraimites who are in a hostile mood. The narrator notes that they were summoned (to war).[145] In failing to identify the person who had called them, however, he shows that the disposition expressed is characteristic of the tribe as a whole, not simply of some disgruntled leader. As they had done to Gideon (8:1–3), the Ephraimites expressed resentment that they had not been invited to participate in the campaign against the Ammonites (cp. their comments in 8:1 and 12:1). But this time they were even more contentious and bellicose. With their armies ready for battle they appeared before Jephthah at Zaphon[146] and threatened to burn down his house for slighting them because he had dared to go into battle without them. Jephthah had already lost his household; now they announce their determination to burn down his physical house. Instead of congratulating Jephthah for his accomplishment and thanking him for delivering them from the Ammonite menace, in their jealousy and

---

[145] The use of the passive verb יִצָּעֵק raises the question whether this is an intentional divine passive.

[146] The site probably is to be identified with Tell es-Saʿdidiye, seventeen miles SSE of Beth Shan, just across the Jordan River. Cf. P. N. Franklin, "Zaphon," *ABD* 6.1040.

wounded sense of self-importance the Ephraimites determined to destroy the deliverer. Like the confrontation with Gideon, this event exposes a serious flaw in the Ephraimite character. They had no pride in greater Israel, let alone any respect for the Transjordanians.

12:2–3 True to form, Jephthah tried to talk his way out of another crisis. His carefully crafted disputation speech consists of five parts. First, he introduced himself. He had been involved in an intense controversy with his own people and with Ammon.[147] The NIV and most modern translations smooth out the odd construction of the first sentence by pitting Jephthah and his people against the Ammonites.[148] But in so doing an important nuance is lost. In the first part of the sentence Jephthah described himself (lit.): "I was a man of contention," that is, "a contentious man."[149] The narrator's choice of *rîb*, "contention," plus the addition of *mĕʾōd*, "very, much," intentionally places Jephthah in the same class as the Ephraimites (cf. 8:1b).[150] The loci of this Gileadite's stress are highlighted by the parenthetical addition "I, and my people, and the sons of Ammon."[151] He hereby reminded the Ephraimites that his entire public life has been characterized by contention, first with his own people (an allusion to 11:1–11), and then with the Ammonites (an allusion to 11:12–29,32–33). The Ephraimites may not have realized it, but in Jephthah they had finally met their match. At the same time, the narrative is reaching its climax. Jephthah's life of conflict has reached its fourth and final stage:

---

[147] By using the root רִיב, "to contend, contest," the narrator deliberately links this comment with his own evaluation of the Ephraimites in 8:1b.

[148] The NRSV (and many commentators, e.g., Boling, *Judges,* 212; Soggin, *Judges,* 220; Moore, *Judges,* 306–8) adds "who oppressed us" after "the Ammonites," assuming עֹנֵנִי has dropped out after עַמּוֹן by haplography. Support is found in the LXX, which adds ἐταπείνουν με after υἱοὶ Αμμών, "the sons of Ammon," and OL and Syr. Cf. O'Connell, *Rhetoric of the Book of Judges,* 471. But the shorter reading of the MT is preferred.

[149] The narrator hereby invites the reader to associate Jephthah with Gideon, whose real name, "Je-*rub*-baal," reflected his contentious character. Cf. Klein, *Triumph of Irony,* 97.

[150] The modifier is admittedly far from the antecedent, but the problem also exists for many translations (including the NIV), which read "great struggle." It may be that the text originally read אִישׁ רִיב הָיִיתִי מְאֹד, "I was an extremely contentious man," which answers to "and they contended with him vigorously" (בְּחָזְקָה, 'with strength') in 8:1. The intervening words in our text were added by the narrator to clarify the comment. Boling's translation of this sentence, "I was using diplomacy," interprets Jephthah's comment much too positively.

[151] Nothing about the Hb. אֲנִי וְעַמִּי וּבְנֵי־עַמּוֹן warrants the common pairing of "I" and "my people" against "Bene Ammon."

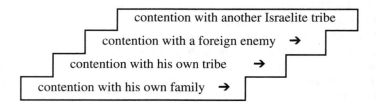

Second, Jephthah accused the Ephraimites of failing to respond to his call to arms. He claimed to have summoned them to rescue him from the Ammonites. Whether or not he had actually done so, we cannot tell. The narrator has not told us that he was ever in the clutches of the enemy, nor that he had summoned the Ephraimites. Knowing Jephthah this probably was a fabrication for the sake of the moment.

Third, he lauded himself for his own initiative and courage in the critical moment. Realizing that no help was forthcoming from the Ephraimites, he had risked his life and crossed over to the Ammonite camp. In 9:17 Jotham had used a similar idiom to laud the achievements of his father Gideon.[152] Again the comment invites comparison with Gideon's earlier response before the Ephraimites (8:2–3a). In the narratives, however, the roles are reversed. Whereas Gideon's self-deprecating comments are known to contradict his heroic actions, Jephthah's self-laudation flies in the face of the narrator's silence regarding any specific acts of heroism.

Fourth, employing the stereotypical committal formula, Jephthah acknowledged the role of Yahweh in the victory over the Ammonites. On the surface his declaration sounds as deferential as Gideon's comment in 8:3a, but this is undoubtedly nothing more than feigned piety intended to impress his challengers.

Fifth, he rebuked the Ephraimites for threatening him. The rhetorical question at the end of v. 3 appears to be seeking an explanation, but the sequel demonstrates that Jephthah really had no interest in waiting for an answer or negotiating a settlement. The question implies that it was foolish to be fighting him. How the Ephraimites should have responded to him is left unsaid. Did Jephthah expect them to acquiesce before him like his Gileadite compatriots had?

In examining Jephthah's speech as a whole, the alert reader cannot help but notice the change in his tone since his encounters with the Gileadites and Ammonites in chap. 11. Despite his reference to "my people" in v. 2 his use of first person singular pronouns throughout demonstrated that the Ephraimite

---

[152] The Hb. idiom וָאָשִׂימָה נַפְשִׁי בְכַפִּי translates lit., "I placed my life in my palms," is equivalent to וַיַּשְׁלֵךְ אֶת־נַפְשׁוֹ מִנֶּגֶד, "He thrust his life before him," in 9:17. The present expression occurs elsewhere in 1 Sam 19:5 and 28:21.

hostility was a personal matter to him. They had challenged his leadership. Jephthah's response lacks any moral interest, not to mention any concern for the solidarity of Israel. Unlike 11:27 there was not even an appeal to Yahweh as judge. Yahweh was brought in only to enhance Jephthah's own case.

12:4 Whereas Gideon's speech in 8:1–3 had effectively assuaged the wrath of the Ephraimites, Jephthah's address had the opposite effect. Instead of relaxing their spirits (cf. 8:3c), their hardened disposition toward him was expressed in a disparaging and taunting slur: he and his fellow Gileadites are nothing more than fugitives (NIV, "renegades") from Ephraim. The plural noun *pĕlîṭîm* should be interpreted in its normal sense, that is, as "fugitives, escapees," from some peril, especially battle.[153] The narrative provides no hint of a previous battle between Gilead and Ephraim, and one suspects the comment is a conscious and derogatory fabrication,[154] perhaps alluding to the Gileadite's occupation of land east of the Jordan, outside Israel's heartland.[155] At the same time, the use of the phrase "fugitives" is surely intended to touch a sore spot in Jephthah's own experience, generalizing his own painful personal experience as an outcast from his Gileadite countrymen (11:1–7) to the entire population. The meaning of the last phrase in v. 4, "in the midst of Ephraim and in the midst of Manasseh,"[156] is uncertain. It seems best to interpret this in a semignomic sense: "being in Ephraim is like being in Manasseh" (JPSV), that is, they would find no refuge in Manasseh, their homeland.

12:5–6 Jephthah responded to this personal insult by assembling all the troops of Gilead and attacking the Ephraimites who had crossed the Jordan to challenge him. In the meantime his men captured the fords of the Jordan to prevent any Ephraimite fugitives from escaping to their home territory. The repetition of the phrase, *pĕlîṭê ʾeprayim*, "fugitives of Ephraim," cleverly turns the Ephraimite taunt on their own heads, as the true fugitives of Ephraim are exposed. Whereas in v. 4b the phrase had referred to Gileadite fugitives fleeing from Ephraim, here it applies to Ephraimite fugitives fleeing from Gilead.

As in the case of Gideon in chap. 8, the Gileadite victory over the non-Isra-

---

[153] The NIV's "renegades" in v. 4b imposes an alien nuance on the term. The NASB's "fugitives" is preferable. Many commentators and some translations (REB, NEB) follow the LXX in deleting the comment of the Ephraimites, some arguing that the MT represents a partial dittography of v. 5. But the MT may be defended as the *lectio difficilior*—it is difficult to imagine why a later hand would have added this (the text makes good sense without it). The omission in the LXX looks like a haplographic error caused by homoioteleuton/homoioarcton, the scribe's eye having skipped from וַיַּכּוּ אַנְשֵׁי גִלְעָד אֶת־אֶפְרַיִם ("and the men of Gilead struck down Ephraim") in v. 4 to וַיִּלְכֹּד גִּלְעָד ("and Gilead captured ...") in v. 5. For more detailed discussion and proponents of the alternatives see O'Connell, *Rhetoric of the Book of Judges*, 471–72.

[154] Like Jephthah's own reference to Chemosh in 11:24.

[155] According to Numbers 32 and Joshua 22, Transjordania was settled by Gad, Reuben, and one-half of Manasseh, with the permission of Moses and Joshua.

[156] Reading בְּתוֹךְ אֶפְרַיִם וּבְתוֹךְ מְנַשֶּׁה: with many MSS and the versions.

elite enemies emboldened them to brutalize their own countrymen. Whenever an Ephraimite fugitive approached the Gileadites guarding the ford over the Jordan, the latter would inquire whether or not he was an Ephraimite. Understandably, to save their lives the Ephraimites would deny their tribal identity. The Gileadites, however, devised a clever way of exposing them. Suspicious persons were commanded to say *šibbōlet,* knowing full well that the Ephraimite pronunciation of the word sounded like *sibbōlet.* Although the origin of this *sh:s* contrast is not entirely clear, the issue seems to be phonetic rather than phonemic. This probably is not a case of divergent development of sibilants in Gileadite and Ephraimite dialects of Hebrew[157] but simply a case of differentiation in the pronunciation of the same sibilant in these regions.[158]

The results of this civil war were devastating, for there were some forty-two thousand Ephraimite casualties. If the figure is to be taken literally, the Ephraimites suffered almost as many losses as the Benjamites would later in 20:35,46, when they were virtually wiped out as a tribe.[159] The narrator seems to be satisfied that this is appropriate punishment for the Ephraimites' egomania. This event reflects and reinforces the Jordan River as a geographical and psychological barrier between eastern and western Israelites (cf. Joshua 22). It also reinforces the narrator's negative disposition toward the Ephraimites, whom he portrays as the principal instigators of civil strife in Israel. But, as after the final scene in chap. 11, in the face of this brutal slaughter Yahweh's silence is deafening. Israel has indeed become its own worst enemy, and God appears content to let the nation destroy itself.

EPILOGUE (12:7).   **12:7** Mirroring the spiritual and national disintegration within Israel, the narrative pattern established in the Othniel cycle shows

---

[157] Several explanations involving phonological merger have been proposed. (1) The Proto-Semitic spelling was *ṯblt; ṯ* became *š* in Ephraimite but is preserved as *ṯ* in Gileadite. Thus G. A. Rendsburg ("The Ammonite Phoneme /T/," *BASOR* 269 [1988]: 73–79; "More on Hebrew *šibbolet,*" *JSS* 33 [1988]: 255– 58); P. Swiggers ("The Word *Šibbōleṯ* in Jud. XII.6," *JSS* 26 [1981]: 205– 7); and A. Lemaire (L'Incident du sibbolet (Jg 12,6): Perspective historique," in *Mealanges, bibliques et orientaux en l'honneur de M. Mathias Delcor,* AOAT 215, ed. A. Caquot et al. (Neukirchen: Neukirchener Verlag, 1985], 275–81). (2) The Proto-Semitic spelling was *sblt; s* became *š* in Gileadite but is preserved in Ephraimite. Thus A. F. L. Beeston ("Hebrew *Šibbolet* and *Šobel,*" *JSS* 24 [1979]: 175–77). (3) The Proto-Semitic spelling was *šblt; š* becomes *s* in Ephraimite but is preserved in Gileadite. Thus J. Blau ("'Weak' Phonetic Change and the Hebrew *Śîn,*" *HAR* 1 [1977]: 67–119). (4) The Proto-Semitic spelling was *s1blt; s1* became *š* in Gileadite but is preserved in Ephraimite. Thus A. Faber ("Second Harvest: *šibbolet* Revisited [Yet Again]," *JSS* 37 [1992]: 1–10).

[158] So also J. A. Emerton, "Some Comments on the Shibboleth Incident (Judges XII 6)," in *Mélanges bibliques et orientaux en l'honneur de M. Mathias Delcor,* AOAT 215, ed. A. Caquot et al. (Neukirchen: Neukirchener Verlag, 1985], 150– 57, and more recently R. S. Hendel, "Sibilants and *šibbōlet* (Judges 12:6)," *BASOR* 301 (1996): 69–75.

[159] As elsewhere in the book (4:6; 7:3; 8:10; 20:35,46), the figure seems unrealistically high unless אֶלֶף is interpreted as "contingent" rather than "thousand." See above on 8:10.

increasing signs of disintegration. The Jephthah cycle ends without declaring that the Ammonite menace had been eliminated[160] or that the land was secure during his tenure,[161] let alone attributing this newfound security to Yahweh. In fact, as already noted, the ending bears a closer resemblance to the parenthetical notes concerning the secondary governors in 10:1–5 and 12:8–15 than the endings to most of the deliverer narratives.

In keeping with the pattern elsewhere, the narrator generalizes Jephthah's government *(šāpaṭ)* to Israel, but he reminds the reader of his tribal/regional context by identifying Jephthah as "the Gileadite" and noting that he was buried in one of the towns of Gilead.[162]

Theological and Practical Implications

The narrator's account of the Jephthah cycle underscores many of the lessons learned from previous episodes in the book. As in the accounts of Gideon before and Samson after, chaps. 11–12 paint an ambivalent picture of this "deliverer." Positively, the reader observes that although Jephthah began with several serious strikes against him he overcame all these deprivations and rose in power, eventually becoming the premier military and political figure in/from the Transjordan in Israelite history. Among the strikes against him we note: (1) he was an illegitimate child; (2) he was cast out by his family and tribe; (3) he gathered around him other social outcasts and lived a life of brigandry and banditry; (4) he was a Gileadite, which, from the Ephraimites' perspective in particular, is equivalent to living on the "wrong side of the tracks." Being strong and resourceful, however, Jephthah was able to overcome these odds and make a significant mark in history.

Negatively, Jephthah was an extremely tragic figure.[163] Overcoming mar-

---

[160] Cf. 3:30a; 4:23; 8:28.

[161] Cf. 3:11,30b; 5:31; 8:28b.

[162] Hb. plural בְּעָרֵי גִלְעָד, "in the cities of Gilead," is impossible unless, like the woman in chap. 19, his body was dismembered and the parts distributed to several sites. The LXX ἐν (τῇ) πόλει αὐτοῦ (ἐν) Γαλααδ may point to the original, בְּעִירוֹ בְגִלְעָד, "in his town in Gilead." Josephus (*Ant* 5.7.12) identifies Jephthah's city as Sebee (Σεβεη), which may reflect a Hebrew *Vorlage* בעירו בם[צפה גלעד, "in his city, in Mizpah of Gilead," the ם having been confused with ב and fallen out by haplography.

[163] See the study by J. C. Exum, "The Tragic Vision and Biblical Narrative: The Case of Jephthah," in *Signs and Wonders: Biblical Texts in Literary Focus*, ed. J. C. Exum (Decatur, Ga.: SBL, 1989), 59–84, and the cautious response by W. L. Humphreys, "The Story of Jephthah and the Tragic Vision: A Response to J. Cheryl Exum," ibid., 85–96. In a later essay Exum attributes the source of the tragic story of Jephthah to divine silence (not enmity as in Saul's case; "Jephthah: The Absence of God," in *Tragedy and Biblical Narrative: Arrows of the Almighty* [Cambridge: Cambridge University Press, 1992], 59), but this misses the point of the narrative. The ultimate source of the tragedy is Israel's rebellion/apostasy and the immediate source the flaws in Jephthah's own character.

ginalization by birth, family, clan, and geography and displaying a natural talent with words, the potential for true greatness was within his grasp. But in the end he became a victim of his own ambition and his tongue, dying without a descendant to carry on his name and his family. Though he rose as high as any man could, he operated as a man with inverted priorities, an eminent illustration of the adage "Everyone, including the 'deliverers,' did what was right in his own eyes."[164] He was Jephthah first, a Gileadite second, and an Israelite third. Accordingly, he displayed a willingness to sacrifice anything and anyone to satisfy his own ambition, which knew no bounds.[165] This egotistical man proves himself the consummate manipulator who opportunistically seizes power over his tribesmen, bargains with God, victimizes his daughter, and brutalizes fellow Israelites. The placement of this narrative within the book suggests that of all the 'deliverers' named to this point, Jephthah represents the ethical and spiritual low point. Perhaps most reprehensible of all his pagan or at least semipagan features, he stooped to the despicable act of offering his own daughter as a whole burnt offering to deity to achieve his goal. He may have been a governor, a head, a commander, and a leader in Israel, but he never cared about the people he governed nor about the God to whom they belong.

But the account of Jephthah also offers telling information on the state of the nation of which he is a citizen. As Jotham had so eloquently expressed in his fable (9:7–15), this people has received the leader they deserve. This son of a harlot embodies all that is wrong in spiritually harlotrous Israel. For him (and for Israel) sacrifice is not an expression of gratitude to God or a worshipful act of communion. Rather, it is a tool employed to manipulate God.[166] Leadership is a privilege to be received from God and the people and exercised for the glory of God and the well-being of the led. In the end Jephthah may have solved the Ammonite crisis, but he left his own nation in a worse state than he had found it (or it had found him). The people once united under Moses and Joshua were disintegrating under the cancer of jealousy, which exposed the raw nerves of linguistic, tribal, and spiritual division. Israel had become as fragmented as the Canaanite population they were commanded to expunge.

More particularly, this episode exposes the character of the Ephraimites. In the beginning they dismissed the Gileadites as good-for-nothing "survivors of Ephraim," but in the end they have themselves become the "survivors of Ephraim." Earlier in 8:1–3 the Ephraimites had been portrayed as an arrogant and independent tribe, easily offended when excluded from significant roles in military affairs. This episode has been rightly interpreted as a parody, a satiri-

---

[164] Cf. 17:6; 21:25.
[165] Cf. Webb, *Judges*, 75.
[166] Cf. Klein, *Triumph of Irony*, 91.

cal literary portrait, further exposing the same flaw.[167] In the narrator's eyes the high and mighty Ephraimites are an insufferable lot of bunglers, cowards, and dullards. They insult the Gileadites with demeaning epithets and presumptuously (and cowardly) threaten to burn down the house of the hero of the Ammonite battle, but they themselves are incompetent on the battlefield (they lose forty-two thousand men at the hands of these nobodies), fail to make good on their threat to Jephthah, stupidly try to cross the Jordan at fords controlled by the Gileadites, and cannot even speak proper Hebrew. The author's anti-Ephraimite disposition is obvious.

In the course of this national disintegration, we also witness the disintegration of the family and the evils of patricentric social structures run amok. Jephthah was a man without a father, the son of a woman who sold her body and a man who assumed no responsibility for his sexual conduct. Because Jephthah had no father, he had no past. Because he had no past, he eventually has no future. Jephthah lacked understanding of the theological origins of his nation and had no appreciation for Israel as a community—a community of blood, descended from one ancestor, and of faith, united in the worship of Yahweh their redeemer. Cut off from his own spiritual heritage, he had nothing to offer the nation but raw power. In this he highlights the problem not only of fatherlessness[168] but the loss of a biblical understanding of fatherhood. He appeared as an independent male, without father, brother, or son, lodged between two women—his mother and his daughter. Without godly role models and responsible peers he was left to carve out his own path. Unlike Samson, who follows, there is no record of his abuse of his sexual powers, but his image of masculinity is twisted out of shape. Male power was exercised for male ends; others—female and male—were exploited and abused in the interest of dominance.

But this narrative does not demonstrate that patricentrism is fundamentally evil and abusive. Jephthah does not represent the biblical model of fatherhood or male headship, which would have the leader sacrifice his own life for the sake of the led rather than vice versa.[169] Jephthah illustrates the problem of Canaanite forms of patriarchy, in which positions of responsibility are cut off from covenantal loyalty and spiritual devotion to God. The biblical norm views headship as responsibility, not privilege; as accountability, not power. Accordingly, one's personal *shalom* is brought about by promoting the *shalom* of those in one's charge.

Finally, in this account we witness the power of the spoken word, for ill or for good.[170] Jephthah, more gifted with words than any other character in the

---

[167] D. Marcus, "Ridiculing the Ephraimites: The Shibboleth Incident (Judg 12:6)," *MAARAV* 8 (1992): 95–105.

[168] A point well made by Klein, *Triumph of Irony*, 99.

[169] Cf. Isaiah 53; Eph 5:25–28; Phil 2:5–11.

[170] See Exum, "On Judges 11," 131–36.

book, trapped himself in his own speech. Even more tragically, he trapped his daughter as well. She courageously gave her life that he might be presented and preserved as a man of his word, but this does not transform his faithless vow into an act of piety. On the contrary, it renders him guilty of the blood of his own daughter. The young woman might have taken comfort in her female friends who commemorated her death annually or the fact that her memory was kept alive in the written word, but this cannot neutralize, let alone heal, the horrible grief Jephthah caused.

But how should we evaluate Yahweh's silence in this narrative? After Israel's sham repentance (10:10–16) he appears to have left the nation to its own resources. This seems to be confirmed by his silence in the rise of Jephthah as leader in Israel and in the wake of Jephthah's pedicidal outrage. And the brutal slaughter of the Ephraimites screams for an explanation. The narrator acknowledges, however, that in spite of Israel's false penitence and the defective qualities of her leaders, Yahweh does indeed give victory (11:32–33). But his responses to Israel are not based on merit or desert. His acts can only be characterized as gracious and merciful. He is more determined to save this Canaanized nation than they are to save themselves.

8. Parenthesis 3: The Governorships of Ibzan, Elon, and Abdon (12:8–15)

As noted earlier, these verses continue the list of secondary governors begun in 10:1–5, interrupted by the Jephthah narrative (10:6–12:6) and resumed by the concluding statement of the latter (12:7). These short notes provide the same basic details for three individuals as 10:1–5 had for the first two. The use of the temporal preposition "after" in each case invites the reader to interpret the list sequentially.

(1) Ibzan (12:8–10)

⁸After him, Ibzan of Bethlehem led Israel. ⁹He had thirty sons and thirty daughters. He gave his daughters away in marriage to those outside his clan, and for his sons he brought in thirty young women as wives from outside his clan. Ibzan led Israel seven years. ¹⁰Then Ibzan died, and was buried in Bethlehem.

12:8–10 Verses 8–10 summarize the tenure of Ibzan, the first of this triad. The name ʾibṣān, which occurs only here in the Old Testament, derives from a root meaning "swift." His place of residence is disputed since the Old Testament knows of two Bethlehems, one in Zebulun[171] and the other in Judah, the birthplace of David. Although most scholars favor the former identification,[172]

---

[171] Josh 19:15.
[172] Cf. Soggin, *Judges*, 223; Boling, *Judges*, 214; id., "Ibzan," *ABD* 3.356.

the omission of a tribal reference favors the better known Judean city.[173] Like Jair the Gileadite governor (10:4), Ibzan had the ideal family of thirty sons, for whom he secured thirty daughters-in-law, but he was doubly blessed with the addition of thirty daughters. In contrast to Jephthah, who sacrificed his only daughter, Ibzan capitalized on the political opportunity his family afforded him by having them all marry outside the clan. Reflective of the prevailing patricentric social order, he sent his own daughters away and brought *(hēbîʾ)* outside women in for his sons. In keeping with contemporary custom, these marriages probably cemented clan alliances and extended the scope of his political influence. At the same time, Ibzan's initiative in all of these marriages arises out of a concern to build a community with sound foundations.[174] The text fixes the tenure of Ibzan after Jephthah and reports that he governed for seven years before he died and was buried in his hometown of Bethlehem.

(2) Elon (12:11–12)

[11]After him, Elon the Zebulunite led Israel ten years. [12]Then Elon died, and was buried in Aijalon in the land of Zebulun.

12:11–12 Verses 11–12 provide only the barest of information on Elon, the second governor in this list. His name, *ʾêlôn,* means "oak, terebinth." Rooted in the tribe of Zebulun, it appears he was named after the eponymous ancestor of one of the major Zebulunite clans.[175] Elon is distinguished only by the fact that he governed Israel for ten years. When he died, he was buried in Aijalon, in the territory of Zebulun. Since the only Aijalon known elsewhere in the Old Testament lay in Danite land[176] and since the name is identical to

---

[173] The omission is possible because the location of Bethlehem may be taken for granted, especially if the author writes for a Judahite audience. But the omission is quite extraordinary if the book was composed primarily as a pro-Judahite polemic, as many contend. This lack occurs nowhere else.

[174] M. Tsevat ("Two Old Testament Stories and Their Hittite Analogues," in *Studies in Literature from the Ancient Near East: By Members of the American Oriental Society Dedicated to Samuel Noah Kramer,* ed. J. M. Sasson [New Haven: AOS, 1984], 35–42) draws attention to a parallel Hittite story in which the Queen of Kanish gives birth to thirty sons in a single year. Overwhelmed with this horde, she places them in baskets and sends them down the river to the land of Zalpuwa. The gods rescue them and raise them to adulthood. Later the queen gives birth to thirty daughters, but these she keeps. In time the sons return "driving a donkey"; except for divine intervention and quick thinking, they would have married their own sisters. For the story see H. A. Hoffner, "A Tale of Two Cities: Kanesh and Zalpa," in *Hittite Myths,* Writings from the Ancient World 2, ed. G. M. Beckman (Atlanta: Scholars Press, 1990), 62–63.

[175] Cf. Gen 46:14 and Num 26:26. Elsewhere the name identifies Esau's Hittite father-in-law (Gen 26:34; cf. 36:2).

[176] Cf. Judg 1:35. On this Aijalon see D. L. Peterson, "Aijalon," *ABD* 1.131.

Elon's in the consonantal script,[177] one may surmise that Elon gave his name to the town from which he governed.

(3) Abdon (12:13–15)

[13]**After him, Abdon son of Hillel, from Pirathon, led Israel. [14]He had forty sons and thirty grandsons, who rode on seventy donkeys. He led Israel eight years. [15]Then Abdon son of Hillel died, and was buried at Pirathon in Ephraim, in the hill country of the Amalekites.**

12:13–15 The last of this triad is identified by name, patronymic, hometown, and tribe. The name ʿAbdôn apparently means "service."[178] Abdon's father was a certain Hillel from Pirathon. No other Old Testament character bears the name Hillel, but the proper noun elsewhere names the home of Benaiah, one of David's thirty mighty men.[179] The town probably is to be identified with modern Farata, six miles west south west of Shechem.[180] The location of this town in Ephraim is problematic, since the brook Kanah several miles south of Pirathon formed the boundary between the territories allotted to Manasseh and Ephraim (Josh 17:7–9). Either the boundaries were not firmly fixed in these early days, or the term Ephraim is being used loosely for the hill country south of the Wadi Fariʿa. Verse 15 identifies Abdon's home territory also as the "hill of the Amalekite." How this region came to be associated with the Amalekites, a marauding desert band affiliated elsewhere with the Midianites (6:33; 7:12), we may only speculate. Perhaps they had left their mark on this region during the earlier period of oppression prior to Gideon's acts of deliverance.

Abdon's tenure is distinguished above all as a period of peace and prosperity. Like Gideon (8:30), Abdon had the ideal royal family consisting of seventy descendants. Forty of these were immediate sons, but the narrator looks to the future by noting that Abdon also had thirty grandsons. As in the days of Jair (10:4), the fact that each of these men rode on his own donkey is a sign of the tranquility of the times. But Abdon governed for only eight years before he died and was buried in Pirathon.[181]

The significance of this short list of secondary governors is twofold. First, it reminds the reader that the deliverer narratives do not provide an exhaustive

---

[177] Cf. LXX, which reads Αἰλών or Αἰλόν.

[178] The name was borne by three other men in the OT: a Benjamite son of Shashak (1 Chr 8:23), a person in Saul's ancestry (1 Chr 8:30; 9:36), and a son of Micah in the time of Josiah (2 Kgs 22:14).

[179] 2 Sam 23:30; 1 Chr 11:31; 27:14.

[180] R. W. Smith, "Pirathon," ADB 1.373, and E. A. Knauf, "Pireathon—Farʿatā," BN 51 (1990): 19–24, contra N. Naʾama,n who identifies Pirathon with Farkha ("Pirathon and Ophrah," BN 50 [1989]: 11–16).

[181] H. Jacobson suggests Abdon is remembered as Bedan in 1 Sam 12:11. See "The Judge Bedan (1 Samuel Xii 11)," VT 42 (1992): 123–24.

account of political realities during the period of settlement. The deliverer accounts have been selectively isolated and shaped to develop a particular theme. Second, it reminds the reader that the periods of oppression were interspersed with periods of prosperity and political independence for Israel. The tribes may be developing separately, but at least they seem to be at peace with each other and the world. But the account bears an air of unreality, and the calm is illusory. By now the reader knows both Israel and Yahweh too well to believe that the tranquility is deep-seated or that it will last.

9. The Philistine and Samson Cycle (13:1–16:31)

If the aesthetic value of a literary work is measured by the extent to which it "satisfies, surpasses, disappoints, or disproves the expectations of its first readers,"[182] then the Samson cycle of stories must rank as a masterpiece.[183] The narrator's skill in both meeting expectations and evoking surprise, if not consternation, begins with the structure of the story of Samson and the Philistines. Having begun in 3:7, to this point we have observed a gradual disintegration of the skeletal paradigm that determined the composition of the cycles of apostasy, oppression, appeals for relief, and deliverance. The paradigm is set forth with intentional simplicity in the story of Othniel (3:7–11). It is clearly visible in the accounts of Ehud (3:12–29) and Barak (4:1–5:31), though increasing detail in selected segments and the insertion of the Song of Deborah in the latter render it less obvious. All the elements are still evident in the Gideon account (6:1–9:57), but the basic structure is increasingly overshadowed by the narrator's interest in the personality of the deliverer. In the Jephthah cycle the structure itself begins to disintegrate. Missing in particular are any references to Yahweh raising up the agent of deliverance and in the end the land enjoying peace and/or security. This crumbling of the structure continues, indeed intensifies, in the Samson cycle.

First, battles of deliverance give way to a series of episodes in the deliverer's private life. The inexorable movement of apostasy → oppression → cry → deliverance is severely disturbed. The opening first two elements (the marks of Israel's Canaanization and God's agent of punishment) are merely announced (13:1), not described; a notice of Israel's response to the oppression is lacking altogether (though hinted at in 14:4 and 15:11); Yahweh's raising up a deliverer takes an entire chapter (13:1–14:4), but thereafter the deliverer never rallies the Israelite troops in battle against the oppressor, and there is no announcement of victory over the oppressor.[184]

---

[182] So H. R. Jauss, "Literary History as a Challenge to Literary Theory," *New Literary History* 2 (1970–71): 14.

[183] So also A. Reinhartz, "Samson's Mother: An Unnamed Protagonist," in *A Feminist Companion to Judges*, FCB 4, ed. A. Brenner (Sheffield: Sheffield Academic Press, 1993), 157.

[184] Samson's limited success is anticipated by the messenger of Yahweh in 13:6.

Second, the previous focus on national and tribal deliverance is almost completely eclipsed by the narrator's preoccupation with Samson's personal adventures. Repeatedly the focus is on Samson's deliverance from the difficult situations he brings upon himself with his private escapades.

Third, Israel's attitude toward the oppressors has changed. Far from crying out from under the burden of oppression, coexistence with the Philistines has become the norm. Accordingly, not only does the divinely raised deliverer fraternize freely with the enemy, but the Judahites also resist any actions that might upset the status quo. In fact, Yahweh must seek and create an occasion to disturb the relationship between oppressor and oppressed (14:4).

Fourth, the role of the šōpēṭ ("judge, governor, deliverer") has changed. The divine role in raising up the deliverer is indeed described more emphatically than in any previous cycle. More than any previous agent of deliverance, however, Samson demonstrates that the divinely chosen leaders were part of Israel's problem rather than a lasting solution. Although the narrator is obviously amused by some of Samson's antics and seems eager to share with his readers the humor and earthiness of his career, the issues are deadly serious. In fact, according to the preamble to the deliverer cycles (2:19), in Samson the crisis facing the nation reaches its climax and their spiritual condition its nadir. This man embodies/personifies all that is wrong in Israel.

Like Israel:

Samson is a *Wunderkind,* miraculously born by the will of God.
Samson is called to a high life of separation and devotion to Yahweh.
Samson has a rash, opportunistic, and immature personality.
Samson is inexorably drawn to foreign women, like Israel was drawn to
    foreign gods (both "play the harlot").
Samson experiences the bondage and oppression of the enemy.
Samson cries out to Yahweh from his oppression.
Samson is blinded (cf. 1 Sam 3:1–3).
Samson is abandoned by Yahweh and does not know it.

Fifth, in the Samson narrative the author is particularly sensitive to gender issues. Indeed, the interest in women, which had played a significant role in the Barak and Jephthah cycles and had surfaced in the story of Abimelech, now takes over completely. Women are principal actors in every episode of the Samson cycle. In chap. 13 his mother appears as a model of Israelite womanhood, pious, loyal, sensitive, logical, and theologically astute. But the female characters with whom the "hero" associates hereafter reflect Samson's downward ethical spiral. In chap. 14 he marries a woman, and it looks as though she will become his legal wife; but his motivation is quite wrong, and in any case she belongs to the enemy—she is a Philistine. In 16:1–3 Samson consorts with a Gazite (Philistine) prostitute, but the text is silent on her disposition toward him. In 16:4–20 he consorts with Delilah. The narrator does not identify her as a prostitute. In fact, the account suggests a more ongoing relationship. But in her disposition she is worse than a prostitute—she is an agent of the enemy who eventually brings about his downfall. His tragic personal story is marked by relationships with four women—mother, wife, prostitute, antagonist.

Structurally the Samson narrative is framed by accounts of his birth (13:1–24) and his death (16:28–31). Additionally, like Ophrah in the Gideon cycle, references to Zorah create a geographic inclusio (13:2; 16:31). Between these borders the account divides into three major parts, each of which is a short story in itself:[185]

1. The Birth Narrative (13:1–24). This section does not deal primarily with Samson but with his parents, providing background to the episodes that follow, specifically his prenatal calling.

2. Samson and the Timnite Woman (13:25–15:20). This section begins with an announcement of Yahweh's initiative in Samson's life (13:25) and ends with a formal notice of his tenure as judge (15:20).

3. Samson and the Gazite Women (16:1–31). This segment begins with Samson's voluntary trip to Gaza (16:1) and ends with his involuntary return to Zorah, the place where the Spirit of God had first begun to stir him (16:31; cf. 13:25).

The first two segments are both carefully constructed according to a balanced and symmetrical pattern, with the latter consisting of two phases (two women) described with a more or less common structure.[186]

(1) The Marks of Israel's Canaanization (13:1a)

[1]Again the Israelites did evil in the eyes of the LORD,

13:1a   The narrator summarizes the continued spiritual degeneration of Israel with one simple statement: "The Israelites continued to practice evil[187]

---

[185] This structure is also recognized by J. C. Exum ("The Theological Dimension of the Samson Saga," *VT* 33 [1983]: 30–45), who minimizes Samson's failure to fulfill his Nazirite status and maximizes the role of Yahweh in each of the three sections. For a detailed defense of the intentional coherence of the Samson narrative see J. Kim, *The Structure of the Samson Cycle* (Kampen: Kok Pharos, 1993).

[186] See the commentary below. V. H. Matthews ("Freedom and Entrapment in the Samson Narrative: A Literary Analysis," *Pers* 16 [1989]: 245–57) organizes the narrative around four traps: (1) "Theophany, Annunciation, Nazir" (13:1–25); (2) "The Timnite Woman" (14:1–15:20); (3) "Gazite Prostitute" (16:1–3); (4) "Delilah" (16:4–31). Cp. this with J. A. Freeman ("A Structural Reading of Judges 13–16," in *Literary Interpretations of Biblical Narratives*, vol. 2, ed. K. R. R. Gros Louis [Nashville: Abingdon, 1974], 145–60), who sees a repeated four-part structure (14:1–16:22) framed by two paradoxes: "birth from a barren wife" (chap. 13) and "death from a disabled warrior" (16:23–31).

[187] A better translation than the NIV "Again the Israelites did evil." "Again" requires an adverb עוֹד after וַיֹּסִפוּ. Cf. above on 11:14. For the present construction see above, 4:1 and 10:6.

in the eyes of the LORD." As in previous versions of this formula, the definite article on "evil" points to a specific kind of transgression—serving the Baals (and other gods) and abandoning Yahweh (2:10–13).

(2) God's Agent of Punishment (13:1b)

so the LORD delivered them into the hands of the Philistines for forty years.

13:1b Yahweh's response to Israel's rebellion is expressed in the milder version of the divine committal formula: "The LORD delivered/gave them into the hands of the Philistines" (cf. 2:14). This is the third time the Philistines have been identified as Israel's oppressors. Earlier the non-Israelite Shamgar had relieved the pressure by striking down six hundred Philistines with an ox-goad (3:31). Obviously this had been only a temporary solution, for in 10:7 we learn that while the Ammonites plagued the Transjordanian tribes in the east, the Philistines were applying pressure to the Cisjordanians on the west. These represented Yahweh's agents of punishment for having abandoned him in favor of these peoples' gods. Since 10:7 we have heard nothing of the Philistines, for the narrator has concentrated on the resolution of the Ammonite problem in the east. Now he picks up where that note had left off.

Although the origins of the Philistines[188] are still shrouded in mystery, most scholars agree that they came from the Aegean. They seem to have arrived in Canaan from two directions, some coming overland through Anatolia, the rest by sea via Crete[189] and Cyprus.[190] The former seem to have swept into the Levant from the north like Vikings, leaving a path of destruction in their wake throughout the once mighty Hittite empire, the region of Amurru, and the northern Levantine coastal city of Ugarit.[191] Allied with other Sea Peoples,[192] those who entered Canaan by sea originally had their sights on Egypt. Around 1190 B.C., however, they were defeated by Rameses III. Thereafter Rameses hired many of the defeated troops as mercenaries and stationed them in the coastal towns of Gaza, Ashkelon, and Ashdod.[193]

Given the timing of the Philistines' arrival in Canaan, a clash with the

---

[188] Referred to in Egyptian writings as *P-r-š-t-w* (= Hb. *pĕlištîm*).

[189] Caphtor in the Bible. Cf. Amos 9:7; Jer 47:4.

[190] Kittim in the Bible. Cf. Num 24:24, where "ships coming from the shores of Kittim" may refer to the first of several waves of new arrivals, generally referred to as the Sea Peoples.

[191] The most enduring contribution of the Philistines to the culture of the eastern Mediterranean was their name, from which is derived modern "Palestine."

[192] The Tjekker, Weshesh, Sherdan, Danuna, Sheklesh, and Tursha.

[193] Cf. Deut 2:23, where these are referred to as Caphtorites. The Egyptian connection is also reflected in Gen 10:13–14.

Israelites, who had recently arrived from the east across the Jordan, was almost inevitable. The Samson cycle reflects the tensions that existed between these two groups in the centuries leading up to the establishment of the monarchy in Israel. Indeed, 1 Samuel 8 suggests that their continued pressure was the catalyst that moved the Israelites to demand a king to lead them in battle. The moved failed, however, inasmuch as Saul and his son Jonathan fell in battle at the hands of the Philistines on Mount Gilboa (1 Samuel 31–2 Samuel 1). David served Achish the king of Philistine Gath as a vassal during his flight from Saul (1 Samuel 27; 29). But through a series of victories before (1 Samuel 17–18) and after (2 Sam 5:17–25) his assumption of the kingship, the son of Jesse solved the Philistine menace for good.[194]

(3) God's Agent of Deliverance (13:2–24)

Conspicuous for its absence in the Samson narrative is any reference to Israel crying out *(zāʿaq* or *ṣāʿaq)* to Yahweh for deliverance from the Philistine yoke (cf. 3:9,15; 6:6; 10:10). In the Gideon and Jephthah accounts this element had received detailed treatment, but here the pattern is broken. This is probably intentional. In this cycle the Israelites display little discomfort or evidence of even wanting to be delivered. Manoah and his family try simply to avoid the Philistines (14:3; 16:31); Samson fraternizes with them; Judah has lost its crusading spirit (cf. 1:1–2) and is content to maintain the status quo (15:9–13). It seems that for this reason Yahweh is driven to stir Samson (13:25) and to provoke discontent between Israel and the oppressor (14:4). On the other hand, the notion of crying out is not totally lost, but the motif is completely individualized. At two critical junctures Samson calls out to God for his own personal deliverance *(qārāʾ,* 15:1; 16:28).

Form critical scholars generally classify Judg 13:2–24 as a birth narrative. Ideally such accounts contain the following elements:

a. A pious but barren woman (who longs for a son) is introduced.

b. She receives a divine revelation/visitation announcing the conception of a special child and/or the special destiny of the child.

---

[194] Ironically, Gittite (from Gath) mercenaries and Cherethite and Pelethite bodyguards played a significant role in David's imperial achievements (2 Sam 8:18; 15:18; 20:7,23; 1 Kgs 1:38,44; 1 Chr 18:17). For further studies of the Philistines see K. A. Kitchen, "The Philistines," *POTT*, 53–78; D. M. Howard, Jr., "Philistines," in *Peoples of the Old Testament World*, A. J. Hoerth, ed. et al. (Grand Rapids: Baker, 1994), 231–50; D. T. Dothan and M. Dothan, *People of the Sea: The Search for the Philistines* (New York: Macmillan, 1992); T. Dothan, "Philistines," *ABD* 5.326–33.

c. The birth of the child is announced.

d. The child is named.[195]

The present concern for progeny provides an obvious link with the Jephthah narrative, in which the tragedy was not barrenness but virginity. Jephthah's daughter dies not having known a man.

Even if this segment contains several significant elements of birth narratives,[196] this is not its primary function in the context of the Samson cycle as a whole. In addition to failing to note explicitly Israel's response to the Philistine oppression, the omission of a formal announcement that "the LORD raised up a deliverer" is highly significant (cf. 2:16,18; 3:9,15). Like 4:4–10 and 6:11–24, however, vv. 2–24 appear precisely where such a notice would have occurred and function as an expansive substitution thereof. Although this passage contains no elements of a divine commission type-scene, like the aforementioned texts it functions primarily as a call narrative, with v. 5 representing the heart of the text.[197] To be sure, the call does not come directly to the person called. Instead, the announcement of Samson's vocation of divine service comes to his parents. Like the prophet Jeremiah, Samson was called to the role of deliverer before he was born. Indeed he was called prior to his conception—which raises interesting questions as we read through the successive episodes. Yahweh obviously knows that Samson has been called, Manoah and his wife know, the narrator knows, and the reader knows—but does Samson know? If he does, there is little evidence that he has any respect for his divine vocation. On the contrary, the narrator notes his repeated deliberate violation of the call (14:8,10; 16:17). In the context of the last reference he admits for the first time a consciousness of calling, but the very admission becomes his undoing. By uttering it (before the oppressors) he loses it (cf. 16:20).

From a literary perspective the account is framed by themes of problem and

---

[195] For other examples see the stories of Sarah (Gen 18:9–15), Rebekah (Gen 25:19–26), Rachel (Gen 30:1–24), Hannah (1 Sam 1:1–20), Elizabeth (Luke 1:5–25,57–80). Cf. also Isa 7:14. Many scholars also recognizes the links between this chapter and Gideon's call. Thus, e.g., Richter (*Traditionsgeschichtliche Untersuchungen*, 141), who finds here the employment of a series of conventional motifs: (a) a miraculous birth to a barren or old woman; (b) the promise of a son; (c) expressions of hospitality to the visiting deity; (d) recognition of the visitor; (e) expressions of fear at having seen deity/divine messenger. More recent scholarship prefers to speak of type scenes rather than birth narratives. O'Connell (*Rhetoric of the Book of Judges*, 217–18) recognizes an amalgamation of elements from two biblical type-scenes involving the angelic birth announcement (13:3–14) and the recognition of a theophany (13:3a,9,15–23). For a discussion of the former see R. Alter, "How Convention Helps Us Read: The Case of the Bible's Annunciation Type-Scene," *Prooftexts* 3 (1983): 115–30. The present text is discussed on pp. 123–24.

[196] O. Margalith ("More Samson Legends," *VT* 36 [1986]: 397–405) relates the narrative of Samson's birth to Greek mythology in which, among other elements, "divine paternity (and often maternity) of human heroes is taken as a matter of course" (p. 401).

[197] As correctly recognized by Richter, *Traditionsgeschichtliche Untersuchungen*, 141.

resolution, promise and fulfillment.[198] With respect to the former, v. 2 introduces a woman who is barren, that is, who had no children,[199] but in v. 24 she gives birth to a son. With respect to the latter, in v. 3 the messenger announces to the woman that she will bear a son, and in v. 24 his promise is fulfilled. Within this scheme the plot is complicated by the woman's husband. Ironically, Manoah, whose name sounds exactly like *mānôaḥ* (meaning "resting place") appears as a restless and insecure individual. The narrator casts him as a comical figure bound by ignorance and obtuseness.[200] In contrast to Manoah's restlessness, ignorance, and dim-wittedness, his wife is calm, collected, and knowledgeable concerning the significance of the events transpiring, not to mention their theological implications (cf. v. 23).[201] By thrusting this woman into the foreground the narrator has set the stage for the following episodes. If a woman is the key to Samson's birth, women will also be the key to his death.[202]

As in many other accounts in the book, this story is dominated by dialogue. The series of speeches is initiated by the messenger of the Lord who addresses Manoah's wife with a long speech announcing her imminent conception and the special role her son will play. While the contacts between the messenger and the woman are crucial to the story, significantly she never addresses the messenger. Instead she rushes home and reports to her husband what she has heard. Verses 8–18 are dominated by an almost comical series of interchanges between Manoah and the phantom (in his mind), as the former seeks to learn and thereby gain mastery over the situation and the latter displays reluctance to share any new information with Manoah. Although Manoah tries to control the dialogue, between him and his wife the latter has both the first and last word.

Indeed, as several have observed,[203] while the namelessness of Manoah's wife might suggest a marginalized character, Manoah is the one the narrator deliberately minimizes by (1) introducing him with the seemingly superfluous expression, "a certain man" *(ʾîš ʾeḥād)*[204] (13:2); (2) referring to his tribe, Dan, as a "clan" *(mišpāḥâ)* rather than a "tribe" *(šēbeṭ)*; (3) leaving his identi-

---

[198] This has been recognized and ably expounded by J. C. Exum, "Promise and Fulfillment: Narrative Art in Judges 13," *JBL* 99 (1980): 43–59.

[199] The redundancy is intentional and emphatic.

[200] Cf. Alter, "How Convention Helps Us Read," 124.

[201] Cf. E. Fuchs, "The Literary Characterization of Mothers and Sexual Politics in the Hebrew Bible," in *Feminist Perspectives in Biblical Scholarship*, ed. A. Y. Collins (Chico, Cal.: Scholars Press, 1985), 125; S. Niditch, "Samson as Culture Hero, Trickster, and Bandit: The Empowerment of the Weak," *CBQ* 52 (1990): 611.

[202] Cf. J. C. Exum, *Fragmented Women: Feminist (Sub)versions of Biblical Narratives*, JSOT-Sup 163 (Sheffield: JSOT Press, 1993), 63–68.

[203] E.g., Y. Amit, "Manoah Promptly Followed His Wife (Judges 13:11): On the Place of the Woman in Birth Narratives," in *Feminist Companion to Judges*, 147.

[204] On the use of אֶחָד to express indetermination see above on 9:53.

fication by name to the end of the note in 13:2; (4) noting that the divine messenger appears not once but twice to his wife, even after Manoah had summoned him; (5) characterizing Manoah as a skeptical person throughout, unlike his wife, who takes matters at face value; (6) keeping the focus on Manoah's wife and emphasizing particularly how *she,* the woman, is to act, even though Manoah seeks to control the actions and the conversations; (7) describing how, in the end, Manoah's reaction to the visitation is fear of death, while his wife reassures him with a reasoned explanation of what has transpired (v. 22); (8) noting that Manoah's wife, not Manoah, names Samson (v. 24). Meanwhile, as Manoah is being marginalized, the narrator skillfully enhances the image and importance of his wife.[205]

As one reads through the story, it is tempting to be taken in by the literary artistry of the narrator, his effective characterization, verbal interchanges, use of repetition, and other literary features for rhetorical effect but to miss the author's point.[206] As already indicated, the purpose of this chapter is to describe how Yahweh provided a deliverer from the Philistine oppression for the Israelites. The narrator's concern is not primarily the human characters (except to show their weaknesses) but on the divine force behind the events. The role of God is highlighted in many ways:

1. The choice of a barren woman as the agent through whom the deliverer will come to the nation, which recalls God's miraculous work in providing Sarah with a son.[207]

2. The initiative that Yahweh takes in providing a deliverer, despite Israel's lack of desire for deliverance (v. 2).

3. Yahweh's prescription of the lifestyle and conduct of Manoah's wife and her son (vv. 4–5,13–14) and her explicit recognition of this prescription (v. 7).

4. Although the messenger of Yahweh remains anonymous, the riddle of his identity keeps the reader focused on him throughout the chapter. Manoah's dim-wittedness serves as a foil for the messenger who retains control over the pace and direction of the narrative.[208]

---

[205] Cf. Amit, ibid., 150–56.

[206] For superb explorations of the literary artistry of the Samson narrative see Exum, "Promise and Fulfillment," 43–59, and J. A. Freeman, "A Structural Reading of Judges 13–16,"in *Literary Interpretations of Biblical Narratives*, vol. 2, ed. K. R. R. Gros Louis (Nashville: Abingdon, 1974), 145–60. Although the former's discussion of the Samson cycle's literary features is extremely insightful, she has been seduced with its literary artistry and misses the rhetorical point. The latter is more helpful in recognizing the theological implications of the account, particularly the relationship between Samson's apparently autonomous actions and Yahweh's sovereignty. Samson may exploit his gifts to satisfy narcissistic and selfish ends, but they were in fact given "for the greater glory of God" (p. 157).

[207] See further below.

[208] For a discussion of the narrator's characterization of the messenger see Reinhartz, "Samson's Mother," 160–62.

5. The narrator's recognition of the close relationship between Yahweh/God and the messenger/"man of God," who speaks for him, particularly in vv. 8–9.

6. The claim of the name "Wonder[worker]" by the heavenly visitor (v. 18).

7. Manoah's (and his wife's) growing awareness of the identity of the messenger, moving from "man of God" (vv. 6,8) to "Wonderful" (v. 18), to "messenger of God" (v. 21), to "God" (v. 22), as the source of these events.

8. The fulfillment of the promise in Samson's birth (v. 24a).

9. Yahweh's blessing of the child as he grows up (v. 24b).

If we interpret this primarily as a birth narrative, as many do, then we fall into the same trap as Samson, thinking that he is both the occasion for and the goal of the story. But this is to take the account out of context. This is a call narrative, unconventional to be sure, but its purpose is to describe how God provides Israel with a deliverer to deal with the Philistines, whom he has himself sent as agents to punish them for their spiritual infidelity. Both the messenger and the narrator, however, recognize that he will provide only a partial solution for the crisis (v. 5). The completion of the agenda will await another day and another man.

²A certain man of Zorah, named Manoah, from the clan of the Danites, had a wife who was sterile and remained childless. ³The angel of the LORD appeared to her and said, "You are sterile and childless, but you are going to conceive and have a son. ⁴Now see to it that you drink no wine or other fermented drink and that you do not eat anything unclean, ⁵because you will conceive and give birth to a son. No razor may be used on his head, because the boy is to be a Nazirite, set apart to God from birth, and he will begin the deliverance of Israel from the hands of the Philistines."

⁶Then the woman went to her husband and told him, "A man of God came to me. He looked like an angel of God, very awesome. I didn't ask him where he came from, and he didn't tell me his name. ⁷But he said to me, 'You will conceive and give birth to a son. Now then, drink no wine or other fermented drink and do not eat anything unclean, because the boy will be a Nazirite of God from birth until the day of his death.'"

THE PROMISE OF A DELIVERER (13:2–7).   **13:2**   The opening phrase, "There was a certain man" *(wayĕhî ʾîš ʾeḥād),* invites the reader to get ready for an entertaining story.[209] We are not disappointed. The narrator begins by introducing the cast of characters. The way in which the human cast is introduced is odd. The male character is introduced by genus ("a certain man"), geographic origin (from Zorah), tribal affiliation ("from a Danite clan"), and finally by name. The order is intentional, reflecting the fact that within the context of Samson's life as a whole his geographic setting and tribal identity were more important than the identity of his parents. Samson's father came from Zorah

---

[209] The episode initial וַיְהִי compares with 1 Sam 1:1.

(modern Sara), a small Israelite town on the north side of the fertile Sorek Valley, a few miles north of Beth Shemesh.[210] According to the tribal allotments described in the Book of Joshua, Zorah fell within the territories of both Judah (15:33) and Dan (19:41).[211] The construction, "a certain man from Zorah *(miṣṣorʿâ)*" rather than "a certain man of Zorah" may suggest that Manoah had moved out of the town and had settled in a more felicitous location up the valley toward Eshtaol.[212] The identification of the man as a Danite sets the stage not only for the coming conflicts between Samson and the Philistines to the west and the Judahites south and east of the Sorek but also the events in chaps. 17–18. According to 18:2,8,11, the region between Zorah and Eshtaol must have been the core area of Danite settlement prior to their migration north. Finally the "certain man" is identified by name as Manoah. The name is generally thought to mean "resting place," derived from the verb *nûaḥ*, "to rest," and related to the name Noah.[213] A derivation from a different root, *mānaḥ*, "to give," hence "gift" or "generosity," also is possible.[214]

A significant element in Manoah's identity is the fact that he had a barren wife. Ironically, although she turns out to be the most important human character in this chapter, she remains unnamed.[215] Throughout she is referred to simply as "the woman," or "Manoah's wife." The notice of her barrenness echoes Gen 11:30 both in its vocabulary and its redundancy,[216] not only inviting a comparison with the earlier birth narrative, but especially highlighting what happens in this chapter as a work of God. God is at work on Israel's behalf miraculously raising up a deliverer for his people.

The woman's barrenness should not be interpreted in light of modern day views of childbearing and family but against ancient Israelite values. In the

---

[210] In the Amarna Letters (EA 273) Zorah is named as one of the towns belonging to the king of Gezer being attacked by the ʿApiru. Cf. B. Halpern, *The Emergence of Israel in Canaan*, SBLMS 29 (Chico, Cal.: Scholars Press, 1983), 74.

[211] Presumably because the town was located on the wadi Sorek, which served as the boundary between Judah and Dan. Accordingly, territory associated with the town would have been located on both sides of the wadi. Cf. Josh 15:10–11; 19:40–48.

[212] Cf. v. 25, which describes the Spirit of Yahweh stirring up Samson in Mahaneh Dan, between Zorah and Eshtaol, and 16:31, which has Samson buried in the tomb of his father between Zorah and Eshtaol.

[213] Cf. Boling, *Judges*, 219.

[214] Cf. *HALOT*, 600. By this etymology the name is cognate to מִנְחָה, "gift, tribute [offering]."

[215] Though the rabbis give her a name, Zelalponit. See B. Bat. 91s; H. L. Ginsburg, *The Legends of the Jews* (Philadelphia: JPS, 1968), VI, 204–6, nn. 111–12. On the irony of her namelessness see further Reinhartz ("Samson's Mother," 158–70), who argues that the literary function of her anonymity is to highlight her relationship with the divine messenger. On pp. 162–70 Reinhartz presents an insightful analysis of the woman's character and her protagonistic role in the account.

[216] Cp. the construction:

Gen 11:30	וַתְּהִי שָׂרַי עֲקָרָה אֵין לָהּ וָלָד,	"And Sarah was barren; she had no child."
Judg 13:2	וְאִשְׁתּוֹ עֲקָרָה וְלֹא יָלָדָה,	"His wife was barren, and had no child."

ancient world barrenness was reckoned as punishment for an offense against the gods whose special domain was that of reproduction. In Israel children were a mark of the blessing of God, and barrenness was the sign of divine reproach, displeasure, his curse.[217] Furthermore, one's survival after one's death depended on progeny. Accordingly, if Jephthah's future is cut off at the back end because he sacrifices his daughter, Manoah's and his wife's futures are cut off at the front end because the woman was barren. This small note indicates that the oppression at the hands of foreign enemies was not the only covenant curse that was being fulfilled in Israel because of their apostasy.[218]

Unlike other birth narratives the present account offers no description of the woman's reaction to her barrenness[219] nor of her husband's disposition (cf. Isaac's prayer in Gen 25:21). Whether or not they had come to accept her infertility as a fact of life, their lives were unexpectedly interrupted by the visit of a divine messenger.[220] In keeping with the centrality of the (unnamed!) woman in the account, the envoy from the court of heaven comes to the woman, not Manoah.[221] Unlike Abraham, whose own role and faith are central to the patriarchal narratives, Manoah is introduced for other reasons.

13:3–5a The narrator provides no clues about the context of this first visit by the envoy,[222] preferring to focus on the divine message, which consists of three main elements. First, the messenger announces God's recognition of the woman's barrenness (v. 3b). The opening *hinnēh* ("behold") is intended to fasten the woman's attention on the whole speech, but especially to the first element. Obviously the announcement was no great revelation to her. She did not need to told that she was childless. The point is the woman's barrenness has not gone unnoticed with God. Unlike the story of Hannah in 1 Samuel 1, the narrative is silent on the woman's longing for a child, any appeals to God or her husband for a child, or even any notice of her piety in general. From the human perspective the angel appears to have come to her at random, reinforcing the fact that the raising up of this deliverer is a gracious work of God from beginning to end.[223]

Second, the messenger announces God's good news—she will conceive

---

[217] On children as a blessing see Deut 28:411; Pss 127; 128. On the lack of children as a curse see Deut 28:18.

[218] Ruth 1:1 notes that famine was also stalking the land.

[219] Cf. Sarah's offering of her maid to her husband (Gen 16:3); Rachel's complaint (Gen 30:1), offering her maid to her husband (Gen 30:3), and the use of aphrodisiacs (Gen 30:14–24); Hannah's prayer (1 Sam 1:11).

[220] As elsewhere in the book (2:1; 6:11), יְהוָה מַלְאַךְ, usually translated "angel of the LORD," refers to an authorized messenger from the court of God in heaven.

[221] Cf. Gen 18:9–15, where the messenger announces to Abraham that his wife will have a son, though he makes sure that Sarah is within earshot when he makes the announcement.

[222] Cf. v. 9, which notes that the second visit occurred while she was in the field.

[223] Subsequent elements in the story will raise serious questions about the piety of this couple. See below.

and bear a child (vv. 3c–5b).[224] This glorious promise for the woman subdivides into two main parts, each of which is introduced with news which, within that cultural context, will have been interpreted as doubly good—she will give birth to a son![225] With the privilege and joy of bearing a child for Yahweh will come some special obligations,[226] however, the seriousness of which is signalled by the opening line, *hiššāměrî nāʾ*, "Now guard yourself."[227] Hers is not to be a passive role. Thereafter the instructions divide into two parts, the first concerning her own lifestyle while she carries this child in her womb, the second concerning the lifestyle of the child himself. Because she will bear the one predestined to be the agent of divine grace, God retains the right to control both hers and the child's lives. Reflective of the biblical conviction that a child is a special creation of God from the moment of conception, the same standards that will govern his postnatal life will apply to his prenatal condition as well. Accordingly, she must watch her diet, abstaining from wine *(yayin)*, alcoholic drinks of any kind,[228] and food that Israelite laws forbade as defiled (ritually unclean) and defiling.[229] The movement from instructions pertaining to the woman herself and the prescriptions for her son is marked by another *hinnēh*, "Behold!" and a repetition of the announcement of the good news to the woman, this time declaring that she is already pregnant and the son is already on the way.[230] Thereupon

---

[224] When the promise is reiterated in v. 5, the messenger uses a different construction, הִנָּךְ הָרָה, "Behold you [are] pregnant," suggesting the conception has already occurred (thus Klein (*Triumph of Irony*, 111). Alternatively the adjective may function as a virtual participle, which would be expected after הִנֵּה, in which case imminent future action is intended.

[225] The form of the announcement is also echoed in Isa 7:14.

Judg 13:3b   הִנָּה־נָא ... וְהָרִית וְיָלַדְתְּ בֵּן, "Behold ... you will conceive and give birth to a son."
Isa 7:14   הִנֵּה הָעַלְמָה הָרָה וְיֹלֶדֶת בֵּן, "Behold a virgin will conceive and give birth to a son."
On the present use of the converted perfect (future) after a perfect (past) see *GBH* §119c.

[226] The shift from promise to instruction is signaled by עַתָּה, "Now, therefore."

[227] The niphal form of the verb שָׁמַר, "to guard [oneself]," occurs frequently in Deuteronomic injunctions to diligence in the observance of the divine will. Cf. Deut 2:4; 4:9,15; 6:12; 8:11; 12:13,19,30; 15:9; 24:8.

[228] שֵׁכָר is a general designation for any intoxicating drink, though Ibn Ezra excluded wine. The most common alcoholic drinks of the day were made of grains (beer), dates, or honey. See further J. Milgrom, *Leviticus 1–16: A New Translation with Introduction and Commentary*, AB 3 (New York: Doubleday, 1991), 611–12.

[229] Catalogs of these dietary laws and the types of food forbidden occur in Leviticus 11 and Deuteronomy 14. In general Israelites were permitted to eat the meat of animals that were sustained by plants and which did not prey on other animals or human beings. Such animals, however, had to be properly slaughtered according to Israelite law; otherwise their meat was also defiled and defiling. For detailed discussion see Milgrom, *Leviticus 1–16*, 642–742 and B. A. Levine, *Leviticus*, JPS Torah Commentary (Philadelphia: JPS, 1989), 63–72, 243–48.

[230] The NIV's use of the future in v. 5a is incorrect. Note the shift in the verbs from וְהָרִית וְיָלַדְתְּ בֵּן in v. 3b to כִּי הִנָּךְ הָרָה וְיֹלַדְתְּ בֵּן in v. 5a. וְיָלַדְתְּ is a hybrid form, giving the reader a choice between the participle (וְיֹלֶדֶת, as in Isa 7:14) and the converted perfect, וְיָלַדְתְּ). Cf. *GBH* §89j; GKC §80d, 94f.

she is informed that her son is never to have his hair cut.[231]

13:5b The divine messenger does not leave the woman to puzzle over the instructions or their rationale: from the moment of his conception[232] the boy is to be recognized and treated as a *nāzîr*, "Nazirite," of God. The noun *nāzîr* derives from a root meaning "to dedicate, consecrate [oneself in *niphal*]."[233] According to the Israelite Law of the Nazirite, preserved in Num 6:1–8, a person under the Nazirite committed himself to three abstentions: (1) from wine or any other intoxicating drink;[234] (2) from having his hair cut; (3) from contact with a corpse. According to this description a person would take the Nazirite vow voluntarily, simply as an act of dedication to God, for a specified and/or limited period of time. The present application of the law is extraordinary in four respects. First, it is divinely imposed rather than voluntary, which highlights Samson's role as a divinely appointed agent. He does not enter his office as *šōpēṭ* ("governor, judge") and *môšîaᶜ* ("savior, deliverer") voluntarily. Second, this vow takes effect from the moment of Samson's conception. Consequently it obligates his mother to observe the terms until he is born. Third, this vow is not temporary but remains in effect until his death (v. 7), which highlights the permanence of Samson's calling.[235] Fourth, to the three standard prohibitions this vow adds the proscription of any unclean food for the child's mother during her pregnancy. Actually all Israelites were subject to this law, but given the apostate condition of the nation as a whole, this law, like many others, appears to have been generally disregarded by the population. The fact that the woman needed to be reminded of this law may suggest that this household too had succumbed to the general spiritual malaise. By reiterating it in this context the divine messenger highlights the extraordinary scrupulosity with which the woman and her son are to conduct their lives.

Third, the messenger announces to the woman the divine calling of the son who has been conceived in her womb (v. 5c). According to the divine

---

[231] The charge is given obliquely: No razor (מוֹרָה) is ever to pass over his head.

[232] Contra the NIV's "from birth," which treats the preposition מִן in מִן־הַבֶּטֶן separately, the Nazirite clause provides the rationale for both the mother's dietary proscriptions and the taboo on haircuts for her son. מִן־הַבֶּטֶן, "from the womb," is shorthand for "from the time he is conceived in the womb." So also Milgrom, *Numbers*, JPS Torah Commentary (Philadelphia: JPS, 1990), 355.

[233] Cognate to נָדַר "to vow." Cf. 11:39. See *HALOT*, 674, 684. The word has nothing to do with the place name Nazareth, which derives from a root *נָצַר not נזר.

[234] The pair יַיִן וְשֵׁכָר (Num 6:3) is echoed in Judg 13:4.

[235] The only other person in the OT for whom the Nazirite status was imposed (rather than voluntary), in effect from conception (rather than from the moment the vow is taken) and permanent (rather than temporary), was Samuel, who was also the son of a previously barren woman and called to a life of special service for God. See 1 Sam 1:11,21. For further discussion of the Nazirite vow in Israel and the relationships of Samson's and Samuel's Nazirite status to the normative version see Milgrom, *Numbers*, 44–46, 355–58.

plan, Samson is to join the ranks of other saviors/deliverers and (lit.) "begin to save" Israel from the hand of the Philistines. The announcement is modest and realistic, reflecting what God in his omniscience knows will be the outcome of Samson's life. He will only "begin" the task. The narrator also is well aware of Samson's limited success (cf. 16:30), that the Philistines will remain a problem during the tenures of Samuel and Saul, and that the final solution will not be achieved until the reign of David (2 Sam 5:17–25).

13:6 The present account is modest in describing how the woman responded to the bearer of this news.[236] Instead of expressing amazement or humility before the divine messenger, the narrator describes her rushing to her husband to share the good news. The woman's report to Manoah divides into two parts. First, in v. 6 she describes the heavenly visitor to her husband; in so doing, with three significant expressions, she offers her own perception of his identity and role. First, she perceives him as "a man of God." Although the expression is used occasionally of prophets,[237] the following description she offers suggest she means "a divine man." The NIV's "He looked like an angel of God" is more literally, "his appearance was like the appearance of a messenger/angel [malʾāk] of God." The term malʾāk is the same as in 2:1 and 6:11. How she knew what a messenger/angel of God looked like we may only speculate. Whereas the narrator identifies him as "the messenger/angel of the LORD" (v. 3), however, she uses the generic designation for God. It seems the loss of the knowledge of the Lord referred to in the prologue to the deliverer stories (2:10) was a problem in this household as well. She further described him as "very awesome." The expressions used raise many questions in the reader's mind and apparently in hers too. But she responded with dutiful restraint and stifled her curiosity. Unlike Gideon she did not ask for a sign of the truthfulness and/or authenticity of his message. She asked no question about his origin or his identity (name). It will be left to Manoah to probe these issues.

13:7 In v. 7 Manoah's wife recounts the divine visitor's message for him. Although she had many questions about the heavenly visitor's nature and origin, she was crystal clear about his message. Indeed she claims to offer a verbatim report, complete with the second person of direct address (to her).

A comparison of her report and the original speech of the divine envoy is

---

[236] Cf. the birth narratives involving Hannah (1 Sam 1:18–2:10) and Mary (Luke 1:34–38, 46–55), which describe their humble response to the announcement and their effusive celebrations of the births of their respective sons.

[237] Josh 14:6; 1 Sam 2:27; 9:6–8; 1 Kgs 13:1; 17:18–24; etc.

facilitated by juxtaposing them phrase by phrase as in the following synopsis (using a more literal translation):[238]

Verses 3b–5	Verse 7
Behold,	Behold, you
You are barren and have not given birth,	
but you shall conceive and give birth to a son	have conceived and are about to bear a son.
And now	And now
guard yourself,	
and do not drink wine or intoxicating drink;	do not drink wine or intoxicating drink
and do not eat anything unclean,	and do not eat anything unclean,
for behold you have conceived	
and are about to bear a son.	
And no razor shall pass over his head,	
because the boy will be a Nazirite of God	because the boy will be a Nazirite of God
from the womb.	from the womb
	to the day of his death.
And he will begin to rescue Israel	
from the hand of the Philistines.	

The synopsis yields some interesting observations. First, the woman deletes the heavenly messenger's recognition of her barrenness, his injunction to guard herself, and the prohibition of a razor ever passing over her son's head. Second, the NIV rendering of the announcement of the woman's conception is not only incorrect in treating this as a future event but also obscures the fact that she is hereby clinging to the messenger's second version of the announcement (v. 5a) rather than the first (v. 3b). This raises the

---

[238] The following represents a synopsis of the Hb. texts:

הִנֵּה־נָא | הִנָּךְ
אַתְּ־עֲקָרָה וְלֹא יָלַדְתְּ |
וְהָרִית וְיָלַדְתְּ בֵּן: | הָרָה וְיָלַדְתְּ בֵּן
וְעַתָּה | וְעַתָּה
הִשָּׁמְרִי נָא |
וְאַל־תִּשְׁתִּי יַיִן וְשֵׁכָר | אַל־תִּשְׁתִּי יַיִן וְשֵׁכָר
וְאַל־תֹּאכְלִי כָּל־טָמֵא: | וְאַל־תֹּאכְלִי כָּל־טֻמְאָה
כִּי הִנָּךְ הָרָה וְיָלַדְתְּ בֵּן |
וּמוֹרָה לֹא־יַעֲלֶה עַל־רֹאשׁוֹ |
כִּי־נְזִיר אֱלֹהִים יִהְיֶה הַנַּעַר | כִּי־נְזִיר אֱלֹהִים יִהְיֶה הַנַּעַר
מִן־הַבָּטֶן | מִן־הַבָּטֶן
| עַד־יוֹם מוֹתוֹ:

וְהוּא יָחֵל לְהוֹשִׁיעַ אֶת־יִשְׂרָאֵל מִיַּד פְּלִשְׁתִּים:

question whether or not she realizes that she is already pregnant.[239] Third, to the messenger's declaration that the boy will be a Nazirite of God "from the womb" (NIV, "from birth"), she adds "until the day of his death." For the reader this addition, combined with the omission of the razor prohibition, has an ominous ring. In the end it is the violation of the latter that leads directly to Samson's death.

[8]Then Manoah prayed to the LORD: "O Lord, I beg you, let the man of God you sent to us come again to teach us how to bring up the boy who is to be born."
[9]God heard Manoah, and the angel of God came again to the woman while she was out in the field; but her husband Manoah was not with her. [10]The woman hurried to tell her husband, "He's here! The man who appeared to me the other day!"
[11]Manoah got up and followed his wife. When he came to the man, he said, "Are you the one who talked to my wife?"
"I am," he said.
[12]So Manoah asked him, "When your words are fulfilled, what is to be the rule for the boy's life and work?"
[13]The angel of the LORD answered, "Your wife must do all that I have told her. [14]She must not eat anything that comes from the grapevine, nor drink any wine or other fermented drink nor eat anything unclean. She must do everything I have commanded her."

THE REITERATION OF THE PROMISE OF A DELIVERER (13:8–14). Following v. 7 the plot should have moved quickly from the announcement of the woman's conception to an announcement of his birth in v. 24 (cf. 1 Sam 1:20). The bulk of the chapter (vv. 8–23), however, is taken up by a complication in the plot created by the woman's husband, Manoah. Apparently resentful that the heavenly messenger had appeared to his wife rather than to him,[240] like Barak in chap. 4 he goes to great lengths to try to take control of the situation, first by ensuring that he knows as much about the promise of the son as his wife does (vv. 8–14), and then by trying to assert his superiority over the divine envoy. He does so first by serving as his host at a meal and then by demanding his name (vv. 15–23). In both respects he is rebuffed. The first episode ends with him knowing no more than his wife had reported to him and that his wife, not he, is the focus of God's activity. The second ends with his wife lecturing him on the ways of God.[241]

---

[239] Klein (*Triumph of Irony*, 114) pushes the issue too far in associating her report that "a man of God came unto me" in v. 6 with the present use of the perfect to suggest a sexual encounter between the messenger of Yahweh and Manoah's wife. In her view this intentionally contributes the depiction of Manoah as a weak, "unmanly," and "unmanned" character.

[240] Josephus (*Ant.* 5.276–80) maintained that Manoah's jealousy was a major motif in the story.

[241] For an excellent treatment of the motifs of ignorance and knowing in this text see Polzin, *Moses and the Deuteronomist,* 181–87.

In the meantime Manoah seeks to extract information from the heavenly visitor with a series of entreaties, requests, and demands. It is remarkable that the divine envoy responds to him at all, but he teases Manoah with a series of cryptic and guarded responses. Although Manoah is frustrated because he is unable to determine the "man's" identity, his wife enters the plot at the beginning to announce to her husband the reappearance of the messenger of God and at the end to interpret for him the awesome events that have transpired in the meantime.

13:8 In v. 8 Manoah enters the story for the first time. Upon hearing his wife's report of the heavenly visitation, he goes on the offensive immediately, addressing God directly[242] and pleading[243] with him that he send the divine messenger back, ostensibly to "teach" him and his wife further on how they are to raise their son who is to be born.[244] But what more does he need? Is he ignorant of the Israelite law of the Nazirite? The repeated use of the pronoun "us" suggests that in the author's mind he was jealous because the messenger had approached his wife instead of him. If knowledge is power, then he is determined to recapture the power in this household.

13:9 Remarkably, but graciously, God[245] responds to Manoah's plea and dispatches his envoy back to earth. But neither Yahweh nor his emissary will be manipulated by the earthling. The time and place of his second visit are carefully planned. Instead of appearing to Manoah alone or even to both of them when they were together, as if to pour salt into the wounds of his pride the messenger comes to Manoah's wife while she is in the field alone.[246] The narrator does not tell us why the Lord teases Manoah this way, but it seems he is determined if not to keep the man in relative ignorance then certainly to ensure that the woman, who is the key to the plot, retains the advantage so far as knowledge of the work and ways of God are concerned. In any case, again Manoah must hear of the "man's" arrival second hand.

13:10–11 It appears from v. 10 that Manoah's wife has no interest in withholding information from her husband. Unlike Gideon, the woman declined to

---

[242] The vocative opening, אֲדוֹנִי בִּי, "Pardon me, Lord!" (cf. NIV's "O Lord, I beg you") echoes Gideon's response to the messenger of Yahweh's appearance to him in 6:13. On the interjection בִּי see *GBH* §105c.

[243] The verb עָתַר appears elsewhere in the *qal* stem only in Gen 25:21; Exod 8:26; 10:18; Job 33:26. Fundamentally the verb appears to mean "to plead with offerings," but in most contexts the sacrificial element is totally suppressed. See R. Albertz, *THAT* 2.385–86; *HALOT*, 905.

[244] On the *qal* passive form יֻלָּד see *GBH* §59b.

[245] The versions read "the LORD" instead of God in v. 9, but this is an unnecessary harmonization. The narrator's use of "God" (אֱלֹהִים) echoes the designations for God in the woman's speech (vv. 6–7).

[246] The narrator highlights the context with two carefully constructed circumstantial clauses. On the form of the first (וְהִיא יוֹשֶׁבֶת בַּשָּׂדֶה) see *GBH* §166i. On the use of אֵין, "there was not," with a determinate subject in the second (וּמָנוֹחַ אִישָׁהּ אֵין עִמָּהּ) see *GBH* §160i.

address the man.[247] Instead she ran to her husband and announced the reappearance of "the man" who had spoken to her previously. The couple returned quickly to the field, relieved to find that "the man" was still there.

The ensuing dialogue between Manoah and the heavenly visitor borders on the comical, as the former tries to extract from the latter all the information he can, but the latter refuses to satisfy him with long answers. His responses to Manoah's questions are polite but curt. Unwilling to let himself be manipulated by this man, the messenger of God says no more than necessary.

Manoah's first question (v. 11b) reflects his insecurity in this situation: "Are you the [same] one [lit., "man"] who talked to my wife [or "the woman"]?" The visitor's answer is short, consisting of a single word, ᵓānî, "I [am]."[248]

13:12 Hearing this, Manoah expresses both his desire (Was the promise to his son too good to be true?) and his uncertainty: "May your words be fulfilled![249] But what will become of the oracle concerning the boy and what will be his assignment?" (vv. 12–14). This translation of the question rests upon a reinterpretation of the two critical expressions: *mišpaṭ hannaᶜar* and *maᶜăśēhû*. The NIV's rendering of the former, "the rule for the boy's life" is forced and makes poor sense in the context. It is preferable to understand *mišpāṭ* along the lines of the use of the same word in 4:5, which notes that the people of Israel would come to Deborah for *mišpāṭ*, that is, for an oracular pronouncement concerning the crisis caused by the Canaanite oppression. Accordingly, *mišpaṭ hannaᶜar* refers to the oracle concerning the boy first announced in vv. 3b–5. Support for this interpretation is provided by a similar expression, *mišpaṭ hammelek*, "the oracle/pronouncement concerning the king" in 1 Sam 8:10–11, which identifies Samuel's response to a formal inquiry by the people before the prophet.[250] Interpreted this way our verse finds a remarkable parallel, indeed an almost exact counterpart, in a Ugaritic text (Ug. V 6.3–12). Although the fragmentary nature of the text inhibits a clear understanding of the entire passage, the reading of line 3 is quite secure:

> When he arrives at the lord of the great gods with a gift, he must ask for a decision *[mtpṭ]* about the child.

A few lines later the text reads:

---

[247] She was probably being faithful to an Israelite custom which frowned on women engaging male strangers in conversation.

[248] On the simple utterance of a single word as an affirmative answer to a question see *GBH* §161l.

[249] The NIV follows most English translations in interpreting this as a temporal clause, but the grammatical construction and the context favor a jussive sense, as in NJPV' "May your words soon come true!"

[250] This מִשְׁפָּט is not only identified as "the words of the LORD" (v. 10), but is also cast in formal oracular style, concluding with a warning that, should the people cry out (זָעַק) on account of the king's oppression, Yahweh would not answer (עָנָה) them.

And your messenger will arrive with a gift; he will receive a decision [mṭpṭ].[251]

The issue in this passage is clearly a divine determination concerning a child, perhaps at his birth or a time of illness. As Cazelles has observed, at Ugarit, as at Babylon, people's destinies (in this case a child's) were determined by the gods.[252] In a similar fashion, with his question Manoah is seeking to learn from the messenger of God the destiny of his son, whose birth has been so auspiciously announced.[253] Accordingly, the second expression in this context, ma‘ăśēhû, is also best interpreted vocationally (cf. NASB), that is, "What is the [divine] assignment/work for the boy?"[254]

13:13–14 If Manoah's first question was intended to authenticate the messenger, the second appears intended to authenticate the message. If the response of the envoy accords with the report his wife had given him after the first visit, then Manoah may have confidence that both the messenger and the message are trustworthy. The envoy's answer is still curt, but insofar as it reiterates what Manoah's wife had told him in v. 7, it passes the test of authentication. The "oracle concerning the boy," is actually an "oracle concerning the woman." The envoy offers Manoah little new information: his wife must abstain from wine or any other intoxicating drink and from any unclean food. The only significant addition is a tightening of the dietary restrictions by prohibiting the consumption of any grape products, not just wine.[255] This addition accords with the manner in which the envoy had framed the taboo. Perhaps because Manoah's wife had omitted the first line of the messenger's original instructions, "Now guard yourself" (hiššāmĕrî, v. 4), in her report of the message in v. 7, this time the messenger of Yahweh deliberately frames the dietary proscription with charges that the woman observe scrupulously all that she had been commanded. Accordingly, by repeating the charge in vv. 13b and 14b the messenger imposes upon Manoah responsibility for seeing to it that the child's Nazirite status is

---

[251] Ug. V 6.12, as translated by F. C. Fensham, "The Ugaritic Root špṭ," JNSL 12 (1984): 68. For another study of this text see H. Cazelles, "Mtpt a à Ugarit," Or 53 (1984): 177–82.

[252] Ibid., 77.

[253] For further discussion of this text and its relationship to the passages cited see D. I. Block, "Deborah Among the Judges: The Perspective of the Hebrew Historian," in Faith, Tradition, and History: Old Testament Historiography in Its Near Eastern Context, ed. A. R. Millard et al. (Winona Lake: Eisenbrauns, 1994), 241–43.

[254] Klein's interpretation, "How will the boy be judged, and how will his work be judged?" is unconvincing (Triumph of Irony, 124).

[255] But this is not a new element inasmuch as the original Law of the Nazirite prohibited one who took it from consuming any product of the vine, whether liquid or solid (Num 6:3–4).

carefully guarded from the beginning.[256]

From this conversation with the heavenly visitor Manoah has learned nothing new, but he has been assured that his wife's report in vv. 6–7 was not the delusion of a woman frustrated over her barren condition. He may indeed look forward to the birth of a special child and share with his wife the burden of preparing him for divine service.

[15]Manoah said to the angel of the LORD, "We would like you to stay until we prepare a young goat for you."

[16]The angel of the LORD replied, "Even though you detain me, I will not eat any of your food. But if you prepare a burnt offering, offer it to the LORD." (Manoah did not realize that it was the angel of the LORD.)

[17]Then Manoah inquired of the angel of the LORD, "What is your name, so that we may honor you when your word comes true?"

[18]He replied, "Why do you ask my name? It is beyond understanding." [19]Then Manoah took a young goat, together with the grain offering, and sacrificed it on a rock to the LORD. And the LORD did an amazing thing while Manoah and his wife watched: [20]As the flame blazed up from the altar toward heaven, the angel of the LORD ascended in the flame. Seeing this, Manoah and his wife fell with their faces to the ground. [21]When the angel of the LORD did not show himself again to Manoah and his wife, Manoah realized that it was the angel of the LORD.

[22]"We are doomed to die!" he said to his wife. "We have seen God!"

[23]But his wife answered, "If the LORD had meant to kill us, he would not have accepted a burnt offering and grain offering from our hands, nor shown us all these things or now told us this."

MANOAH'S RESPONSE TO THE MESSENGER OF DELIVERANCE (13:15–23). In the preceding commentary we have noted on several occasions the links between this chapter and the call of Gideon in chap. 6. In the description of Manoah's response to the announcement of the messenger of the Lord that his wife would give birth to a son, the connections between these two texts intensify and increase, as the accompanying synopsis illustrates. Although the circumstances of the events are not exactly parallel (the first concerns the call of an immediate deliverer, the second an announcement of the birth of a deliverer for the future), the broad structures of these accounts are similar. In both a heavenly visitor comes to a man with a divine message; the man responds with incredulity and uncertainty; in response to words of affirmation the man presents an offering of food to the visitor; the food is offered as a sacrifice to the Lord on a rock; it is consumed in flames; the divine envoy disappears; the observer expresses fright/awe at the sight

---

[256] Because the second masculine singular and third feminine plural forms of the imperfect are identical, both expressions are ambiguous: מִכֹּל אֲשֶׁר־אָמַרְתִּי אֶל־הָאִשָּׁה תִּשָּׁמֵר, "Of all that I have spoken to the woman she/you shall keep/guard/observe" (v. 13); כֹּל אֲשֶׁר־צִוִּיתִיהָ תִּשְׁמֹר, "All that I have commanded her she/you shall keep/guard/observe" (v. 14).

but then receives words of reassurance. The accounts also display significant differences, but the impressive list of parallels suggests that the narrator intends for vv. 17–23 to be interpreted in light of and in comparison/contrast to 6:17–24.

A Comparison of Gideon's and Manoah's Sacrifices to Yahweh:
Judg 6:17–24 and Judg 13:15–23

Element in Account	Judg 6:17–24	Judg 13:15–23
Context	Response to Gideon's call to deliver Israel	Response to Manoah's hearing the call of his son
Motivation	Desire for a sign of messenger's authenticity	Unstated. Desire to learn more
Intention	To present an offering *(minhah)* to the messenger	To present a meal to the messenger
Elements of Offering	A kid and unleavenen bread	A kid
Response of Messenger	Promised acceptance of offering	Rejection of offer for food; suggesion of alternative—present whole burnt offering to Yahweh
Elements of Offering	A kid and unleavened bread	A kid and a grain offering *(minhah)*
Place of offering	On the rock	On the rock
Response of Messenger to the Offering	Touched the sacrificial gifts with his staff and fire leaped from the rock and consumed the offering; messenger left.	He performed wonders. Flames leaped up from the rock to heaven; messenger returned to heaven.
Response of Offerer	Expression of woe; acknowledges he has seen messenger of Yahweh face to face	Prostration; recognizes he has seen messenger of Yahweh; expression of fear of death
Source of Reassurance	Yahweh tells him directly to be at peace; he will not die.	Wife tells him they will not die, for they have seen God, and he has accepted their offering and revealed his will to them.
Response of Offerer	Builds an altar to celebrate the peace of God	Unstated

13:15 Manoah responds to the good news of the conception of a son and the charge to prepare for the birth of this boy from the mouth of an extraordinary visitor by offering to host the envoy to a meal. In the case of Gideon, the proposal was motivated by the desire for a sign authenticating the messenger and his message that he, Gideon, had been favorably received and that he would defeat the Midianites as one man (6:16–18). Our text does not tell us why Manoah reacted to the messenger of God in a similar fashion. Is this simply an expression of typical Near Eastern hospitality—feeding strangers? (Cf. Judg 19:16–21.) Is it a spontaneous expression of gratitude—a way of saying thank-you for the good news that his barren wife would have a son? Is it curiosity—so he can get to know him better? Is it confidence—an expression of *shalom* often celebrated with a meal? Is it another test of the "man's" authenticity and the veracity of his words?[257]

Unlike Gideon, who hinted that he recognized the envoy as a divine figure by referring to the food he desired to present to the envoy as a *minḥâ*, "gift," to be "set before"[258] the envoy, Manoah's offer is quite secular. Manoah's words in v. 15 are constructed as a request (lit.), "Please let us detain[259] you and prepare a young goat[260] before you," but they function as a virtual question, "Will you eat with us?" The narrator's parenthetical comment at the end of v. 16 confirms that while Manoah obviously perceived the visitor as an extraordinary figure, perhaps even a prophet, he is merely a man. This probably accounts for the differences in the responses of the messenger of Yahweh in the two cases. In chap. 6 the envoy had accepted Gideon's offer of a *minḥâ* immediately, but here he rejects Manoah's offer of a meal.

13:16 Shedding some of his earlier reticence but employing the same verbs that Manoah had used, he says "No thanks." Even if he agrees to be detained, he will not eat Manoah's food. The narrator does not explain why he rejected the meal, but several reasons may be proposed. First, Manoah's offer reflects a defective view of his visitor. Manoah appears too dull to recognize the significance of his rejection, but the alternative suggested by the envoy presents a corrective to his flawed perception of what has been happening: if he is intent on preparing anything, let him prepare a whole burnt offering[261] for Yahweh and (lit.) "send it up" as a sacrifice. Manoah should have recognized in this

---

[257] On the significance of eating and drinking together and hosting a meal see A. W. Jenks, "Eating and Drinking in the Old Testament," *ABD* 2.250–54.

[258] The name Manoah (מָנוֹחַ) provides an effective play on both the noun מִנְחָה and the verb הֲנַחְתִּי, "to set down [before]," in 6:18.

[259] On עָצַר, "to detain, restrain, hold back," see *HALOT*, 870. The verb answers to מוּשׁ, "to withdraw, cease from," used by Gideon in 6:18.

[260] The expression גְּדִי עִזִּים, which refers to a specially selected young goat, is the same as that used by Gideon in 6:19.

[261] עוֹלָה is the same word Jephthah had used in 11:31.

answer a clue to the "man's" identity—he speaks directly for God. Second, since table fellowship assumes oneness, that is, *shalom* between the parties, by rejecting the invitation to a meal the visitor comments on the spiritual condition of the nation as a whole and this household in particular. The Israelites are in no state to fellowship this way with him, an envoy from the holy courts of heaven. Whole burnt offerings presented as sacrifices to Yahweh must come first.[262]

13:17 In vv. 17–18 the narrative takes a detour from the course set in chap. 6. Confused by the envoy's response but grateful for the good news he has brought to him and his wife, Manoah asks him, "What is your name?" The unusual form of the question (lit., "who is your name?")[263] suggests that he may have been flabbergasted by this rejection of his hospitality. But he gives his query a positive spin by suggesting that he needs to know whom to honor when the wonderful message they have received is fulfilled in nine months. He seems to accept that this "man of God" is a prophet whose words will be fulfilled in due course, but he is too obtuse to recognize that when a barren woman conceives it must be a miraculous work of God.

13:18 But the divine envoy maintains control of the conversation by answering a question with another question, which is evasive and essentially negative. "Why do you ask my name?" sounds like a rebuke for Manoah's obtuseness. He should have recognized his visitor by now, but like the rest of the Israelites this man has had no experience with God or his agents. Instead of acceding to Manoah's request and giving his name, the divine envoy describes it: his name is "beyond understanding" or better "extraordinary" *(pel'î)*[264] The word derives from a root *pālā'*, "to be extraordinary, marvelous."[265] The expression may have been chosen here because of its connections with the exodus[266] and the frequent use of the cognate noun *pele'* to identify God's miraculous acts of judgment and salvation.[267] Accordingly, by describing his own name as *pel'î* in this context, the messenger alludes to the saving acts God has placed on his agenda. On the other hand, it may be significant that the only other place in the Old Testament in which this adjective appears, Ps 139:6, the feminine form, *pĕlî'â*, describes the marvelous knowledge of God. Included in this hymn of praise is an expression of wonder at God's deliberate and skillful creation of a baby in the womb of its mother (vv. 13–16). If David did indeed

---

[262] Cp. the order of the whole burnt offerings and the peace *(šālôm)* offerings in Exod 24:5.

[263] The question מִי שְׁמֶךָ is a hybridized expression conflating elements of מִי אָתָּה, "Who are you?" and מַה־שְּׁמֶךָ, "What is your name?" Cf. *GBH* §144b. Boling (*Judges*, 222) characterizes the unusual form as "stuttering."

[264] וְהוּא־פֶלִאי is constructed as a circumstantial clause of classification.

[265] Cf. the Messianic title פֶּלֶא יוֹעֵץ, "Wonder of a Counsellor," in Isa 9:5 [Eng. 6].

[266] See especially Exod 15:11.

[267] Exod 15:11; Isa 25:1; Pss 77:12,15; 78:12; 88:11,13; 89:6.

write this psalm, as the superscription suggests,[268] then the author of the present narrative text will have recognized a special significance in the messenger's use of the word. If the conception and eventual birth of any baby is a miraculous work of God, how much more this child, conceived in the womb of a barren woman.[269] Even if the messenger were to give Manoah his name, he would not understand it or the incomprehensible work God is doing. This visitor, not to mention the ways of God, is a riddle, and he invites Manoah to try to figure out his identity and origin.

13:19 In the envoy's response to Manoah's invitation to dinner, the messenger tried to direct his attention away from himself, so the man might "watch/see" the work of the One who had sent him.[270] It seems to have worked, for immediately thereafter the narrator reports of Manoah offering the young goat to Yahweh as a whole burnt offering.[271] Like Gideon before him, he offered it on the sacrificial rock (*haṣṣûr*, cf. 6:19–21)[272] as a tribute, to secure the goodwill of the envoy. The NIV follows the pattern of most English translations in interpreting the following phrase as a designation for a second, supplementary grain offering. On the analogy of the use of the word in 6:18–20, however, where *minḥâ* had functioned as a general designation for a sacrificial offering that included the meat of a young goat, unleavened bread, and a broth libation, it is preferable to see here a clarifying comment, specifying the sense of the previous phrase.[273] The young goat represents a gift/tribute offering[274] to Yahweh who works wonders. Although the syntax of the last phrase is strange,[275] the terminology echoes the enthusiastic ascription of praise to Yahweh, the one "doing wonders" in Exod 15:11.[276]

---

[268] So also J. A. Motyer, "The Psalms," in *New Bible Commentary: 21st Century Edition*, ed. D. A. Carson et al. (Downers Grove: InterVarsity, 1994), 578.

[269] After a lengthy discussion of the word פֶּלִי, D. Grimm ("Der Name des Gottesboten in Richter 13," *Bib* 62 [1981]: 92–98) concludes that the birth of Samson is bound up with the beginning of Israel's deliverance from the Philistines, a feat only Yahweh can accomplish, hence a פֶּלִי—a wonder!

[270] The verb רָאָה occurs five times in vv. 19–23, functioning as the key word in this paragraph.

[271] The verb עָלָה, meaning "to send up," in *hiphil* is the same verb the envoy had used in v. 16 and cognate to עוֹלָה, "whole burnt offering."

[272] The article suggests sacrifices were customarily offered on this rock. In v. 20 it will be designated an "altar" (מִזְבֵּחַ).

[273] The *waw* on וְאֶת־הַמִּנְחָה functions epexegetically, on which see *IBHS* §39.2.4.

[274] The addition of מִנְחָה creates an effective assonantal play on the name מָנוֹחַ, which probably derives from the same root. See the etymology offered above on v. 2. Cf. Garsiel, *Biblical Names*, 217.

[275] The NIV's rendering is unlikely. Among numerous solutions suggested the best is to follow the lead of the LXX^A and Vg and to treat the initial *waw* as a mistake for *hē* and repoint the first word as הַמַּפְלִא. Cf. O'Connell, *Rhetoric of the Book of Judges*, 473, hence "the one who works wondrously."

[276] So also Webb, *Book of Judges*, 166.

13:20–21 It is difficult to know whether the narrator intends the title of "wonder worker" to apply to God's actions in the conception of the barren woman, his actions of deliverance, or the phenomena described in v. 20. In any case, while Manoah and his wife watched,[277] flames[278] leaped from the altar toward heaven, taking the messenger of Yahweh with them.[279] In comparison to 6:21, the narrator's account of what happened to the offering is sketched in the barest of terms. There is no reference to the divine envoy extending the staff in his hand and touching the offering with it or the fire consuming the offering. The twofold reference to the rock on which the offering was laid as "the altar" heightens the sacrificial nature of this event, but the activity is described in the simplest of terms.

For the first time in the account Manoah and his wife act in consort. When they see[280] the envoy and the flames go up to heaven, they fall down on their faces to the ground. This is an appropriate nonverbal gesture of prostration and submission in the presence of a superior or in response to the actions of a superior. The narrator notes in v. 21 that Manoah and his wife needed no further encounters with the envoy; these events had been sufficient to convince Manoah that this "man" was indeed a messenger of Yahweh.[281] When he stopped asking questions and offered the young goat to Yahweh, his questions concerning the divine visitor's identity were answered. Ironically, the presence of the envoy was a hindrance to Manoah's knowing. Only when he disappeared did he recognize him (cf. v. 8).

13:22–23 If the gesture of prostration represented an appropriate response to an encounter with God, so did Manoah's verbal utterance (lit.): "We will die for we have seen God!" (v. 22).[282] Theologically his statement was correct, for no one can see God and live,[283] but logically he is incorrect. His wife coolly and rationally allays his fears with three observations. First, Yahweh has accepted the whole burnt offering, that is, the tribute/gift *(minḥâ)* they have presented to him. The fire is the sign. Second, Yahweh has put on a visual display of all these things for them. "All these" would refer to everything they had

---

[277] וּמָנוֹחַ וְאִשְׁתּוֹ רֹאִים follows the classic construction of a circumstantial clause, describing a condition attendant to the main plot. Cf. GKC §156.

[278] This is the first reference in the Samson narrative to fire/flames, which will function as an important motif in the rest of the Samson cycle.

[279] The present text is more explicit in the manner of departure and destination of the envoy than the Gideon account had been. Judg 6:20 describes the envoy's departure in the blandest of terms: וּמַלְאַךְ יהוה הָלַךְ מֵעֵינָיו, "the messenger of the LORD went from his eyes."

[280] The construction of the circumstantial clause is identical to that found in v. 19, thus highlighting the motifs of "ignorance" and "perception."

[281] The fact that the problem of ignorance and obtuseness was Manoah's in particular is highlighted by dropping the reference to his wife in the second clause of v. 21.

[282] Cf. Gideon's response in 6:22.

[283] Exod 33:20; Isa 6:1–5; 1 Tim 6:16. Cf. Exod 24:11.

witnessed including the twofold appearance of the messenger and the fire that consumed the offering and took the messenger to heaven. Third, Yahweh has communicated orally[284] with them. "This" (lit., "like this") refers to "the oracle concerning the boy," inclusive of the promise of a son, the instructions for Manoah's wife, and the declared mission of the son (vv. 3–5,13–14). The addition of "now"[285] is highly significant, all the more so given the ambiguity of the expression. "Now," that is, the time of God's speaking, could refer either to the dark days of the Philistine oppression or in advance of the fulfillment of the oracle, that is, the birth of the son. With impeccable logic and according to the Israelite laws of evidence, Manoah's wife presents incontestable proof that they will not die. God has spoken cultically, visually, and orally, declaring to them the future, which obviously depends upon their continued living.[286]

24The woman gave birth to a boy and named him Samson. He grew and the LORD blessed him,

THE BIRTH OF THE DELIVERER (13:24).   **13:24**   The first phase of the Samson cycle is brought to a fitting conclusion with a birth announcement. Verse 24 consists of four simple statements: (1) The woman gave birth to a son. (2) The woman named her son Samson. (3) The boy grew. (4) Yahweh blessed him.

The first statement acknowledges the fulfillment of the promise announced in v. 3 and claimed by Manoah's wife in v. 7. The second deserves fuller comment. In ancient Israel children could be named by either parent, though the Old Testament reports mothers naming their children more often than fathers.[287] The narrator's ascription of this naming event to Manoah's wife serves to highlight the woman's role (and the feminine element in the Samson narrative as a whole) and also to marginalize Manoah even more.

Although names were chosen for a variety of reasons in biblical times,[288] it is not clear what we are to make of the name Samson. It consists of the Hebrew word for sun, *šemeš*, with the diminutive ending, *-ôn*, hence *Šimšôn*, "little sun" ["sunny-boy!"]. A variety of explanations for the name have been proposed. It is tempting to give the name a positive spin as a celebration of the ray

---

[284] הִשְׁמִיעָנוּ, literally "he has caused us to hear."

[285] On וְכָעֵת, "at about this time," meaning "now," see *HALOT*, 900.

[286] The verse actually begins with the conditional clause, on which see *GBH* 167k; *GKC* 106p.

[287] The picture is skewed somewhat by Genesis 30, which uses the naming of Jacob's children by his wives as an occasion to describe the tension in this household. Ruth 4:17 has Naomi's neighbors naming Ruth's and Boaz's son Obed. On naming in the OT see D. Stuart, "Names, Proper," *ISBE* (rev. ed.) 3.483–88.

[288] J. A. Motyer ("Name," *IBD* 2.1051–52) identifies the following categories of names: (1) status names, (2) occasion names, (3) event names, (4) circumstance names, (5) transformation/alteration names, (6) predictive/admonitory names, (7) precative/theophoric names.

of light the birth of this boy represented in the dark days of the judges. Some have suggested it was given in anticipation of his "sunlike" strength.[289] A more common view links the name with the solar cult, which provides the background for the Samson narratives. Strong support for this interpretation is found in the fact that Samson's name incorporates the same element as Beth-Shemesh (lit. "house of Shemesh"), the name of an important town just a few miles from Zorah and Eshtaol down the Sorek Valley,[290] once the focal point of sun worship.[291] The interpretation of the Samson narratives as a whole as an adaptation of a solar myth seems forced, but it still seems best to find in the name a memory of the sun god, Shemesh.[292] Theophoric names involving Shemesh/Shamash were common in the ancient Near East[293] and are exempli-

---

[289] Cf. 5:31; Ps 19:5–6[Eng. 4–5]. Thus D. R. Hildebrand, "Samson," *ISBE* (rev. ed.) 4.309. Samson's extraordinary strength has also led to comparisons with the Greek legends of Heracles/ Hercules. See, e.g., O. Margalith, "The Legends of Samson/Heracles," *VT* 37 (1987): 63–70; id., "The Legends of Samson/Heracles," *VT* 37 (1987): 63–70. Margalith proposes that the Israelites became familiar with the Greek legends through their contacts with the Philistines, whose roots are traced to the Aegean. But this interpretation was convincingly repudiated more than two decades ago by G. G. Cohen, "Samson and Hercules: A Comparison between the Feats of Samson and the Labours of Hercules," *EQ* 42 (1970): 131–41.

[290] According to Josh 19:41; 21:16, Ir/Beth Shemesh was allotted to the tribe of Dan. But Judg 1:34–36 reports the Danites were unable to conquer this territory. As noted at 1:35, the name הַר חֶרֶס, "Sun Mountain," which occurs only there in the OT, may be associated with Beth-Shemesh (cf. 1 Sam 6:9–15; 1 Kgs 4:9). Beth-Shemesh is identified with modern Tell er-Rumeilah, sixteen miles west of Jerusalem. See F. Brandfon, "Beth- Shemesh," *ABD* 1.696–98; S. Bunimovitz and Z. Lederman, "Beth-Shemesh," *NEAEHL* 1.249–53. Other supposed echoes of the solar cult preserved in the Samson narratives include the blinding of Samson, analogous to a solar eclipse, the similarity between the name Delilah and *laylâ*, the Hb. word for "night," the prominence of the fire motif in the narratives, and the involvement of foxes, which are reminiscent of a Roman ritual for the prevention of mildew. See further J. L. Crenshaw, "Samson," *ABD* 5.950; id., *Samson: A Secret Betrayed, a Vow Ignored* (Atlanta: John Knox, 1978), 15–16. This thesis is given full exposition in A. S. Palmer, *The Samson-Saga And Its Place in Comparative Religion* (1913; reprint, New York: Arno Press, 1977).

[291] J. Gray (*Joshua, Judges and Ruth*, 220) concludes that "the role of the hero with the sun-name as the upholder of God's order against the enemies of his people is reminiscent of the Sun as the protagonist of Cosmos against Chaos, in the Egyptian myth of the sun-god nightly menaced by Apophis, the serpent of darkness.

[292] This interpretation is rejected by Fowler, *Theophoric Names*, 167. On the divinity Shemesh (Shamash in Akk) see E. Lipiński, "Shemesh," *DDD,* 1445 52; K. van der Toorn, "Sun," *ABD* 6.237–39. It has often been noted that the name Dan derives from a root meaning "to judge," one of the principal functions of the sun god in antiquity.

[293] Attested Phoenician names of this type include אבשמש (*ʾbnšmš*), אדשמש (*ʾdnsms*), ברכשמש (*brkšmš*), עבדשמש (*ʿbdšmš*), שמשסלך (*šmšslk*), on which see F. L. Benz, *Personal Names in the Phoenician and Punic Inscriptions*, Studia Pohl Dissertationes Scientificae de Rebus Orientis Antiqui 8 (Rome: Pontifical Biblical Institute, 1972), 422. Attested Aramaic names include שמשדלה (*šmšdlh; KAI* 236, Rs 7) and שמשלטב (*šmšlṭb; KAI* 248:3). For Akk theophoric names involving Shamash see J. J. Stamm, *Die Akkadische Namengebung* (1939; reprint, Darmstadt: 1968), 349.

fied in the Old Testament by Shimshai in Ezra 4:8. The third and fourth statements represent a variation of 1 Sam 2:21, "The boy Samuel grew up in the presence of the LORD," and 1 Sam 3:19, "The LORD was with Samuel as he grew."[294] The narrator does not tell us how the blessing of Yahweh was experienced. In light of the accounts that follow it probably involved the gift of exceptional health and the development of an extraordinary strength, which may have been recognized early by his peers.[295]

Theological and Practical Implications

On the surface the narrative of Samson's conception and birth is a wonderful story of God intervening in human affairs by grace alone, without any merit on the people's part. At the level of human interest it is a beautiful story of promise and fulfillment, longing and realization. A woman, suffering the curse of barrenness, conceives and gives birth to a *Wunderkind.* In so doing she joins the ranks of other noble women of the Bible, like Sarah, Ruth, Hannah, and to an even greater degree Mary in the New Testament. Though nameless, the woman is portrayed as a beautiful person, unquestioning in her faith and logical in her thinking—a model of Israelite womanhood. She is a special woman, called by God to be the bearer of the deliverer of Israel.[296] Manoah, her husband, seems a curious person, eager to learn more and more about God and his ways and submissive to Yahweh. Together this couple appears to present a model home, a beacon of light in the dark days of the judges. They are a pair whose faith and piety are rewarded by the miraculous healing of the woman's barrenness and the birth of an extraordinary son. Unlike the earlier deliverers, most of whom began with serious disadvantages, this deliverer will start with the advantage of a godly heritage and the early hand of God upon him.

But the picture is not that clear, and the narrative contains numerous troubling features. First, why does it take so long for the couple, Manoah in particular, to catch on to who the heavenly visitor is? The woman seems to know what a "messenger of the LORD" looks like, but when one appears in their midst, they do not recognize him. Manoah's questions are not only curious but

---

[294] Cf. also Luke 2:52.

[295] According to *HALOT,* 160, with God as the subject בֵּרַךְ means fundamentally "to endue someone with special power." Cf. the definition given by T. G. Crawford: "Blessing consists of a wish for someone to receive the things considered good in life: land, numerous progeny, sufficient food, clothing, etc." (*Blessing and Curse in Syro-Palestinian Inscriptions of the Iron Age,* American University Studies 7/120 [New York: Peter Lang, 1992).

[296] Exum's conclusion (*Fragmented Women,* 67), that in failing/refusing to name this woman and in underscoring her role as mother the narrator has demeaned and fragmented her, is much too cynical and makes sense only in the contemporary Western cultural context, where the demeaning occurs in the depreciation of the honor of motherhood and the value of children.

also reveal a spiritual dim-wittedness and obtuseness. From the apparition and the oracle in vv. 3–5 he should have known who this person was. But because he, along with the rest of the Israelites, have had no experience with God, they are blind to his presence and his gracious actions on their behalf.

Second, why does the narrator portray Manoah as a jealous husband, who, like Barak in chap. 4, tries so desperately to reclaim the leadership in this household? The narrative is framed by two significant events, both highlighting the perspicacity and intelligence of the woman. In the beginning Manoah's wife is the recipient of direct divine revelation, which she accepts with simple faith. In the end she must lecture her husband on the ways of God and encourage him in his life of faith. By contrast, whenever Manoah opens his mouth, he proves both his own impotence and his ignorance. He seems to know nothing of the ways of God or the power of his grace.

Third, why is it that when Manoah and his wife speak of Yahweh, they refer to him only by Elohim, the generic designation for deity,[297] and they address him only as Adonay (the generic designation for "master" (v. 8)? As a symptom of the deep-seated nature of the problem, even the narrator gets taken in by the pattern (v. 9). Finally in v. 23, but only after a dramatic series of events, the reality sinks in. And the woman grasps it first.

Fourth, and most disturbing of all, how can this barren Israelite couple, who conceive and bear a child with the miraculous aid of the Lord, name their son Shimshon, "Little Sun" ("Sunny boy"!), which if not outrightly pagan is dangerously compromising?

These questions can be resolved only if and when we abandon our romantic and idealistic notions of this family and the Israelites in general. The reader must recognize that the Samson story represents the last of a series of cycles of apostasy-oppression-appeal-deliverance, in each of which, according to the narrator's own scheme, the depravity of the nation sank to a new low. Not only was this true of the nation in general, but it also applied to the men God raised up to provide deliverance from the enemy. Accordingly, of the cycles recounted so far, this and the following chapters must be interpreted as depicting the darkest period in the history of the judges. In the words of the author of 1 Sam 3:1– 3, the word of Yahweh was rare in those days, visions were infrequent, and the lamp of God was in danger of going out. It is no wonder that Manoah struggles so in this encounter with deity, and it is perhaps no wonder that his wife can name her son after the Canaanite sun god, even though Yahweh had miraculously enabled her to conceive. These folks do not know any better.

Although the account of the prenatal call of Samson poses some difficult questions, as the preamble to the Samson cycle it also raises the reader's expectations.[298] Not only is Samson's family background certainly superior to Jeph-

---

[297] Vv. 6 (bis), 7, 8, 22.
[298] A point made also by Freeman, "Samson's Dry Bones," 147.

thah's, but the divine oracle calls for a man who will be a Nazir from his birth. More than this, he is called prenatally by God to deliver Israel from the Philistines. And then when he is born, Yahweh's blessing is upon this lad. The questions that rise in the reader's mind are: "Will he succeed? Will the promise represented by his birth find fulfillment?" Only time will tell.

In this chapter the narrator intends not only to paint a realistic portrait of family life in Israel, but also to present the reader with a picture of God. In the days of the judges, when the light of genuine piety was in danger of being extinguished, and from the darkest tribe of Dan, where evidences of faith were rare, Yahweh raises a "sun." Israel may be moribund in its apostasy, but God is at work, graciously intervening, breaking in and preparing his agent of deliverance. The conception and birth of Samson declare emphatically God's refusal to let this nation die! Israel may be doing all in its power to destroy itself from within, but God must preserve this nation. The honor of his name and the cosmic mission of his grace are at stake.

(4) God's Gift of [Partial] Deliverance (13:25–16:31a)

Samson's story is filled with irony. No other deliverer in the Book of judges matches his potential. Called prenatally by Yahweh, stirred as a youth by the Spirit of Yahweh, empowered with extraordinary gifts by Yahweh, and granted exceptional opportunities for heroism by Yahweh, the narrator devotes more attention to Samson than to any other deliverer. Despite all these advantages and this special attention, Samson accomplishes less on behalf of his people than any of his predecessors. Perhaps herein lies his significance. The distinctive feature of chaps. 14–16 is the narrator's preoccupation with the man's personal exploits. Though Samson is impressive as an individual, he turns out to be anything but a military hero. He never leads Israel out in battle; he never engages the Philistines in martial combat; he never experiences a military victory. All his accomplishments are personal; all his victories, private.

Within the context of the book the literary picture the narrator paints in chap. 13 is a relatively pleasant one. A decent (if not overly devout) couple experiences the joy of the birth of a son, miraculously conceived by a barren woman and destined by God for a special place in history. One may assume from the fact that the blessing of Yahweh was upon Samson that his parents took great care to uphold the Nazirite vow divinely imposed upon his mother during her pregnancy and then upon the boy in his youth. In due course, when he had grown, the Spirit of Yahweh began to stir the young man. Verses 24–25 hold out such hope, such promise.

But how different is the dream from the reality! In chap. 14 the author paints a literary picture of a self-centered and rebellious child. Outwardly he appears respectful of his parents, but at heart he is utterly calloused and corrupted. Inwardly he looks spiritual (the Spirit of Yahweh stirs him), but in his actions he brazenly violates his Nazirite status[299] and fraternizes with the enemy. On the one hand, he is born and buried as a hero, but on the other he is a bandit, a trickster,[300] and one who frivolously fritters away his extraordinary calling and gifts.

The Samson stories proper consist of two principal parts, divided geographically into Samson's Timnite affairs (13:25–15:20) and Samson's Gazite affairs (16:1–31). Each of these sections makes sense on its own, for both conclude with a formulaic notice regarding Samson's tenure as governor of Israel (15:20; 16:31). In each of these halves Samson wins a dramatic personal victory over the Philistines, killing thousands of them, so that in the end the outcome of his life promised by the messenger of Yahweh in 13:5 is in fact realized. By the time he died Samson had indeed begun the process of delivering Israel from the Philistines.

SAMSON'S TIMNITE AFFAIRS (13:25–15:20).   Despite the chapter divisions in our Bibles, this lengthy section is held together by a single concluding verse (15:20) and an interdependence of the various elements in an extremely complex plot. Indeed an extraordinarily complicated series of events drives the plot forward inexorably, beginning with the promptings of the Spirit of Yahweh in Mahaneh Dan (13:25) and culminating in Samson's cry to Yahweh at En Hakkore (15:18–19). The complicated process whereby this end is achieved may be best grasped by telling the story backwards, in each episode moving from effect to cause. Sometimes it is difficult to determine who is responsible for which effect, but as a summary of the story in reverse we offer the following:

1. En Hakkore received its name because Samson was revived by the waters of Lehi (15:19b).
2. Samson was revived by the waters of Lehi because God opened up the hollow place and water came out of it (15:19a).
3. God opened up the hollow place because Samson cried out (15:18b).
4. Samson cried out because he was thirsty (15:18a).
5. Samson was thirsty because he had exhausted himself slaying a thousand Philistines (15:14b–17).
6. Samson slew a thousand Philistines because they had come to capture him (15:14a).
7. The Philistines came to take custody of Samson because Judah had handed him over (15:13).
8. Judah handed him over to the Philistines because he sought refuge from

---

[299] This interpretation is widely accepted by scholars, but for a recent dissenting view see H.-J. Stipp, "Samson, der Nasiräer," *VT* 45 (1995): 337–69. However, Stipp's interpretation depends on the removal of chap. 13 as a secondary addition without which one would not think of relating chaps. 14–15 to the Nazirite vow.

[300] Cf. S. Niditch, "Samson as Culture Hero, Trickster, and Bandit: The Empowerment of the Weak," *CBQ* 52 (1990): 608–24.

them in their territory (15:8b–12).

9. Samson sought refuge in Judah because the Philistines were after him (15:8–9).

10. The Philistines were after Samson because he had ruthlessly slaughtered many of their men (15:7–8a).

11. Samson slaughtered many of the Philistines because they had burned his wife and his father-in-law (15:6).

12. The Philistines burned Samson's wife and father-in-law because he had burned their crops (15:3–5).

13. Samson burned the Philistines' crops because his father-in-law had given his wife to someone else (15:1–2).

14. Samson's father-in-law gave his wife to someone else because Samson had returned home to his own father's house (14:20).

15. Samson returned to his father's house because the Ashkelonites were after him (14:19b).

16. The Ashkelonites were after Samson because he had killed thirty of their men (14:19a).

17. Samson killed thirty men of Ashkelon because the Philistines had solved his riddle (14:18)

18. The Philistines solved Samson's riddle because "they plowed with his heifer" (14:15b–17,18b).

19. The Philistines "plowed with Samson's heifer" because she was his wife (14:10–15).

20. She was Samson's wife because he wanted her (14:1–3).

21. Samson wanted the Timnite woman because ... Yahweh was seeking an occasion to confront the Philistines (14:4).

Judges 14:4 is not only shocking, but it is also the key to chaps. 14–15. Accordingly, although Yahweh is largely absent from the narrative, in one way or another his agenda is being achieved in Samson's life. At the same time, while Yahweh's agenda is being achieved, the course of Samson's life is all downhill, a fact reflected by the fivefold repetition of the verb *yārad,* "to go down" (14:1,5,7,19; 15:8).[301]

The Eclipse of the Divine Agenda (13:25–14:20). The first half of the account of Samson's Timnite affairs is framed by a skillful juxtapositioning of divine initiative and human decision. The story begins with Yahweh stirring Samson (13:25) and seeking an occasion against the Philistines (14:4) and ends with Yahweh empowering Samson by his Spirit and winning a great victory over the Philistines (14:19). But the divine agenda is completely eclipsed in the minds of the human characters. The story opens with Samson leaving his parents and heading for Timnah (14:1) and ends with him back in his parent's

---

[301] Cf. C. Exum, "Symmetry in the Samson Saga," 13; Webb, *Book of the Judges,* 169.

house (14:19). Reflective of his personality, in the beginning he sees a Timnite woman, burns with passion for her, and demands that his parents get her for him (14:1–3). In the end he burns with anger when he learns that this woman has been given to another man. But through it all he seems totally oblivious to what God is trying to accomplish through him.

²⁵and the Spirit of the LORD began to stir him while he was in Mahaneh Dan, between Zorah and Eshtaol.

¹Samson went down to Timnah and saw there a young Philistine woman. ²When he returned, he said to his father and mother, "I have seen a Philistine woman in Timnah; now get her for me as my wife."

³His father and mother replied, "Isn't there an acceptable woman among your relatives or among all our people? Must you go to the uncircumcised Philistines to get a wife?"

But Samson said to his father, "Get her for me. She's the right one for me." ⁴(His parents did not know that this was from the LORD, who was seeking an occasion to confront the Philistines; for at that time they were ruling over Israel.)

The Divine Initiative in Samson's Timnite Affairs (13:25–14:4). The opening episode in Samson's adventures with the Philistines is extraordinary especially for the way in which it portrays the interplay of divine and human motives in human experience. The notices of Yahweh's involvement in 13:25 and 14:4 create an effective inclusio around 14:1–3, in which Samson appears to be operating entirely on his own initiative and for his own reasons.

13:25 As if to reinforce the main point of chap. 13, that Samson is divinely chosen by God to deliver Israel from the Philistines, the Samson story proper opens with an announcement that the Spirit of Yahweh was the driving force in his adult life. While he was still at home with his parents in Mahaneh Dan,³⁰² between Zorah and Eshtaol,³⁰³ the Spirit of Yahweh began "stirring"

---

³⁰² The name, which means "the camp of Dan," suggests this may have been the site of the first camp of the Danite tribe after the Israelites had been dismissed by Joshua (Josh 24:28) and/or the headquarters from which the tribe set out later in their search for new territory (cf. Judg 18:2). Judg 18:12 suggests that the Danite warriors regrouped at another site several miles to the northeast, west of Kiriath Jearim shortly after they had set out. Considering it unlikely that there might have been two Mahaneh Dan's so close together, many delete the reference in 13:25 as a secondary gloss influenced by 18:12. See B. P. Irwin, "Mahaneh–Dan," *ABD* 4. 473–74; Gray, *Joshua, Judges and Ruth,* 347.

³⁰³ Eshtaol (like Eshtemoa, Josh 21:14) is analyzed as an archaic infinitive of the Gt stem (*ifteʿal*) from the root שׁאל, "to ask." Accordingly the name must mean something like "place of inquiry [before a deity]," presumably because in pre-Israelite times people came to this sanctuary site to ask for an oracle from the gods. On ancient Canaanite names of this type see C. F. Burney, "On Certain South Palestinian Place-names," *JTS* 13 (1912): 83–84; A. M. Honeyman, "Two Contributions on Canaanite Toponymy," *JTS* 50 (1949): 50; A. F. Rainey, "The Toponymics of Eretz-Israel," *BASOR* 231 (1978): 4–5 [1–17]; Layton, *Archaic Features,* 12.

him to action (13:25). Because this *(qal)* form of the verb "to stir, impel" *(pāʿam)* is unattested elsewhere, its meaning here is uncertain.[304] The significance of this verse becomes evident, however, if we disregard the chapter division and relate it to 14:4–7. From the following narratives one concludes that, left to himself, Samson would never have become involved in God's or even Israel's agenda; and, left to themselves, the Israelites would have been satisfied to continue to coexist with the Philistines. But Yahweh has other plans. He must preserve his people as a separate entity. Therefore, through his Spirit, God intervenes in Samson's life so that the agenda set for him in 13:5–7 may begin to be fulfilled. Accordingly, the narrator interprets Samson's trip to Timnah as an expression of divinely induced restlessness and the Timnite woman who catches his eye as an agent of Yahweh's grand design. This is verified by 14:4, in which the narrator writes that he [Yahweh] was seeking an opportunity to incite the Philistines and thereby disturb the comfortable status quo that existed between them and Israel.

14:1–2 Even though the narrator recognizes God's hand behind the coming confrontations between Samson and the Philistines, he describes Samson's antics as if they were entirely his own doing at his own initiative. This is highlighted by the way the events of the first episode are described (14:1–3): Samson goes down to Timnah, sees a woman, returns to his parents, demands they arrange for his marriage to her, and defends his demand on purely personal grounds—she meets his definition of "Miss Right."[305]

Timnah (modern Tell el-Batashi)[306] lay six miles straight west of Zorah. The description of Samson going down to Timnah is geographically accurate inasmuch as Timnah was located downstream from Zorah and Beth-Shemesh on the south side of the Wadi Sorek. According to Josh 19:43 Timnah was originally allotted to the tribe of Dan, though Josh 15:10 suggests it was located on Judah's northern border. At this time the town was obviously still in the hands of the Philistines, but because it was located in the border region between Israelite and Philistine populations, a clash was almost inevitable.

The image the narrator paints of Samson in the opening episode is anything but attractive. He is an insolent and independent young man, unafraid to venture into the pagan world of the Philistines and undaunted by potentially compromising situations. Seeing a young Philistine woman in Timnah, he returns home and commands his parents to get her for him because he

---

[304] It occurs in the *niphal,* "to be disturbed," in Gen 41:8; Ps 77:5; Dan 2:3, and in the *hithpael,* "to feel disturbed," in Dan 2:1.

[305] The verb יָשַׁר means fundamentally "to be straight," as opposed to twisted or crooked.

[306] See W. R. Kotter, "Timnah," *ABD* 6.557; A. Mazar and G. L. Kelm, "Batash, Tel (Timnah)," *NEAEHL* 1.152–57.

insists on marrying her.[307] The repetition of the verb "to see" in vv. 1–2 demonstrates that he is operating on appearance and for personal interest, not on principle or for the greater good.

14:3 The response of Samson's parents to his demand expresses pain and disappointment, as if his own tribes or countrywomen are not good enough for him. The reference to the woman as from "the uncircumcised Philistines" is intentionally pejorative. The Hebrews were just one of many Semitic peoples who practiced circumcision.[308] Ideally, in Israel circumcision was a religious rite, a mark of the covenant (Genesis 17), but there is no evidence in this text that Samson's parents have any interest whatsoever in covenantal issues. Their comment leaves the impression that they would have found a wife from the surrounding Canaanites acceptable. For Samson's parents his demand poses not only an ethnic problem but a cultural dilemma. Because the Philistines did not adhere to this practice, culturally they were considered at the bottom rung.[309] Within marriage this poses a special problem since sexual union brings an Israelite into direct physical contact with an uncircumcised heathen—a shocking thought. On the other hand, what Samson's parents do not say is as significant as the words they utter. They do not say, "Intermarriage with non-Israelites is forbidden by the LORD" (cf. Deut 7:1–5). Nor do they say, "The LORD has called you to special Nazirite status within Israel. This is one huge step lower even than compromising that call." They also do not say "The LORD's agenda is for you to deliver us from the Philistine oppression, not to marry them" (13:5). All this remains unsaid. To Samson's parents his proposition is simply a cultural and ethnic issue.

Samson's rejoinder is emphatic with the object coming first in the clause. The sense is "She is the one you must get for me!" His rationale is crass (lit.):

---

[307] Though parentally arranged marriages are nowhere mandated in the OT, this tended to be the practice, a fact reflected in expressions like "to give one's sons or daughters in marriage" (Deut 7:3). Cf. Gen 21:21 (Hagar arranges Ishmael's marriage); Genesis 24 (Abraham arranges Isaac's marriage); Judg 1:15 (Caleb arranges Achsah's marriage). Though practice and law were often quite different, the following clause from the Law of Eshnunna (ca. 2000 B.C.) declares that "If a man takes a(nother) man's daughter without asking the permission of her father and her mother and concludes no formal marriage contract with her father and her mother, even though she may live in his house for a year, she is not a housewife" (*ANET*, 162).

[308] On circumcision in the ancient Near East see J. M. Sasson, "Circumcision in the Ancient Near East," *JBL* 85 (1966): 473–76; T. Lewis and C. Armerding, "Circumcision," *ISBE* (rev. ed.) 1.700–702; R. G. Hall, "Circumcision," *ABD* 1.1025–27. For primary evidence see the illustrations in *ANEP* §629; the inscription dealing with the rite, *ANET*, 326; Herodotus, *Histories* 2.104; Josephus, *Antiquities* 8.10.3.

[309] In the OT the expression "uncircumcised NN" is used only of the Philistines. Cf. 15:18; 1 Sam 14:6; 17:26,36; 31:4 [1 Chr 10:4]; 2 Sam 1:20. According to Israelite perceptions of life after death, the uncircumcised are consigned to the farthest recesses and least desirable parts of the netherworld, together with the most undesirable residents of Sheol. See Block, "Beyond the Grave: Ezekiel's Vision of Life after Death," *BBR* 2 (1992): 122–29.

"Because she is right in my eyes." Far from being ethnically and culturally inferior, this woman is all that any Israelite is supposed to be.[310] Samson is insensitive and disrespectful toward his parents and their grief over the matter and totally calloused toward the theological implications of his demand, let alone the implications for his mission.

Like the rest of his compatriots, Samson, the typical Israelite, operates exclusively on the basis of his senses. This is not lost to the narrator, who will note later (17:6; 21:25) that in this period the Israelites generally did what was right in their own eyes. Most English translations place too much emphasis on Samson's visual sense. It is true that he "saw" this woman and liked what he saw, but the use of the variations of the same idiom in 17:6 and 21:25 demonstrates that the idiom (lit.), "she was right in the eyes of Samson" (vv. 3,7), should not be interpreted too literally. It means simply "she was right in his mind/opinion, according to his standards" rather than according to the standards of God. This "governor" is obviously part of the problem rather than a solution.

14:4 The narrator's interlude in v. 4 is the key to this episode and indeed the entire Samson account, for here he provides a theological explanation of Samson's escapades. The issues are much more momentous than simply a young man from an obscure Danite town arriving in a neighboring Philistine town, seeing a young woman there and desiring to marry her. The ignorance of Samson's parents is critical. Despite the young man's auspicious beginnings and their knowledge of his calling, they are as insensitive to the ways of Yahweh as they are of many other elements (cf. vv. 6,9,16). But the author is sensitive, which reminds the reader that God is at work. This marriage arises out of and reflects Israel's willingness to coexist peacefully with the Philistines. But Yahweh is determined to shatter the status quo. Samson is his tool chosen to rile up the Philistines, and this woman offers the opportunity to make it happen. Samson's sense of calling may have been eclipsed in the minds of the man and his parents, but with God it had not. The proverbial monkey wrench must be thrown into this comfortable relationship. If the Israelites do not have the heart to take action against the Philistines, God will cause the Philistines to take action against them.

But the way the account is written creates tension in the mind of the reader. Superficially we are fascinated by Samson's exploits, but at the deep level we must see the hand of God in these events. With brilliant irony the narrator describes a free spirit, a rebel driven by selfish interests, doing whatever he

---

[310] There probably is an intentional irony in the choice of verb יָשְׁרָה, "she is straight," which is cognate to יְשֻׁרוּן, "Jeshurun," God's honorific name for Israel in this early period. Cf. Deut 32:15; 33:5,26.

pleases without any respect for his parents and with no respect for the claims of God on his life, but in the process he ends up doing the will of God.

⁵Samson went down to Timnah together with his father and mother. As they approached the vineyards of Timnah, suddenly a young lion came roaring toward him. ⁶The Spirit of the LORD came upon him in power so that he tore the lion apart with his bare hands as he might have torn a young goat. But he told neither his father nor his mother what he had done. ⁷Then he went down and talked with the woman, and he liked her.

⁸Some time later, when he went back to marry her, he turned aside to look at the lion's carcass. In it was a swarm of bees and some honey, ⁹which he scooped out with his hands and ate as he went along. When he rejoined his parents, he gave them some, and they too ate it. But he did not tell them that he had taken the honey from the lion's carcass.

¹⁰Now his father went down to see the woman.

Preamble to Samson and the Timnite Woman's Wedding (14:5–10a). **14:5** Samson obviously succeeded in convincing his parents to arrange for a wedding with the Timnite woman, for the next scene finds them headed for the Philistine town to prepare for the event. Evidently some time before they reach their destination, Samson separated from his parents, for what happens next must occur without witnesses (cf. vv. 9,16). At first sight the following incident seems totally irrelevant to the plot. But a perceptive reader will recognize that the lion that jumps out of the vineyard and attacks Samson is another agent of Yahweh, who appears out of nowhere to complicate the plot.[311] Not only does this attack on Samson begin a chain of reactions that ultimately leads to 15:19; from here to v. 14 the narration will interweave two separate plots that converge in the riddle Samson puts to the wedding guests in v. 14. The plots, in which the motifs of knowledge and ignorance become increasingly important, may be summarized schematically as follows:[312]

---

[311] The narrator's observation that this event happened in a vineyard invites the reader to ask what this Nazirite is doing in a vineyard. The fruit of the vine was forbidden him. Did Yahweh bring him here to test him?

[312] Cf. the more complex interpretation of O'Connell, *Rhetoric of the Book of Judges*, 206–7.

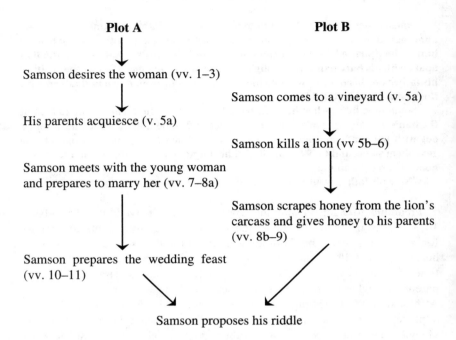

Plot A

↓

Samson desires the woman (vv. 1–3)

↓

His parents acquiesce (v. 5a)

Samson meets with the young woman
and prepares to marry her (vv. 7–8a)

↓

Samson prepares the wedding feast
(vv. 10–11)

Plot B

Samson comes to a vineyard (v. 5a)

↓

Samson kills a lion (vv 5b–6)

↓

Samson scrapes honey from the lion's
carcass and gives honey to his parents
(vv. 8b–9)

Samson proposes his riddle

14:6 Verse 6 makes two significant points. First, as if to highlight the role of the Lord in these events, the Spirit of the Lord "rushed" (rather than NIV "came") upon Samson.[313] The Spirit infuses him with superhuman strength, enabling him to tear to pieces the lion as a man might tear a kid. But the narrative leaves the reader wondering: Does Samson realize the source of his power?

Second, Samson does not tell his parents what has happened. His silence on the matter raises tantalizing questions regarding his motives. Is he intentionally keeping a secret to be used at a later date? If so, why? Or does he forget to tell them? But this is inconceivable since this is precisely the kind of feat about which one gloats. Like the unexpected appearance of the lion, Samson's silence probably is to be interpreted as another work of God.

14:7 In v. 7 the primary plot leading to Samson's marriage resumes.[314] The narrator notes for the first time that he has talked to the woman he is about to marry. Within that cultural context and in light of v. 1, which had only men-

---

[313] The strong form of the divine empowerment formula, with צָלַח, "to rush upon," rather than הָיָה, "to come upon," occurs also in v. 19. Cp. the milder form in 3:10; 6:34; 11:29; 15:14.

[314] Notice the key verb, יָרַד, "he went down."

tioned that he "saw" her, it is possible that this was indeed the first time he spoke with her. This conversation raises no red flags for the participants; on the contrary, it confirms that by his standards she is *yāšār*, "right." But the narrative leaves us wondering what she thinks of him.

14:8–10a As important as the primary plot is the subplot, which is picked up in v. 8. Some time later, presumably when his parents had completed the negotiations with the bride's parents, Samson returned to Timnah to get his wife. Apparently out of curiosity, just before he reached town he turned aside to see what had become of the carcass of the lion he had killed on his earlier trip. What he found caught him by surprise—[315] a carcass hosting a community of bees producing honey. This is not an irrelevant detail inserted secondarily in the text; the image is significant for at least three reasons.

First, for all whose eyes are open, this sight bears the signature of God. Bees do not normally inhabit cadavers; flies and maggots do. Apparently this carcass dehydrated quickly, bypassing putrification, and in no time at all provided a hospitable environment for bees not only to live but also to produce their honey. In the narrator's mind this is undoubtedly the work of God, teasing Samson and performing wonders for his own purpose.

Second, the image is patently ironic. In a world of decay and decomposition Samson discovers a "community" of bees not only existing but producing sweetness to the world around. The narrator's choice of *ʿēdâ*, "community," rather than *šereṣ*, the common word for "swarm" (as NIV translates) is deliberate. Except for Ps 68:30 [Hb. 31], elsewhere *ʿēdâ* always refers to a company of people, usually the Israelites as a faith community, called to be agents of grace and light in the decadent world. Third, like so many of the circumstances in Samson's life, this sight provided a test of Samson's character.

Empowered by the Spirit of Yahweh, Samson had passed the physical test posed by the lion. For a person who operates by his senses, these bees and their honey will test his spiritual mettle. Will he be true to his Nazirite calling and leave the honey alone? The answer is not long in coming—Samson scrapes some of the honey out of the cavity in the corpse with his hands and nonchalantly eats it as he resumes his walk to Timnah.[316] Like the Timnite woman in v. 1, the test has become a trap. In fact, Samson's response to this test is triply sinful. First, since contact with a corpse renders any object unclean, as an ordinary Israelite Samson should have left the honey alone (cf. Lev 11:24–25,39). Second, contact with a cadaver is particularly defiling for a Nazirite (Num 6:6). Third, Samson callously implicates his parents in the defilement, offering them some of the honey without telling them that he had scraped it out of the

---

[315] This is the sense of הִנֵּה, "Behold," which NIV ill-advisedly drops.

[316] The construction of וַיִּרְדֵּהוּ אֶל־כַּפָּיו וַיֵּלֶךְ הָלוֹךְ וְאָכֹל, "and he scooped it out to his palms and went on his way eating as he went," highlights the calloused nature of the act. On this use of the infinitive absolute see *GBH* §123m; Lambdin, *Introduction to Biblical Hebrew*, 158–59.

corpse[317] of a lion. Samson's perversity knows no bounds. His parents had sanctified him, but now he desecrates them. Unaware of his defilement, Samson's father continues the journey down to Timnah, presumably to finalize the wedding arrangements and to settle the business side of this "arranged" marriage.[318]

And Samson made a feast there, as was customary for bridegrooms. [11]**When he appeared, he was given thirty companions.**

[12]**"Let me tell you a riddle," Samson said to them. "If you can give me the answer within the seven days of the feast, I will give you thirty linen garments and thirty sets of clothes.** [13]**If you can't tell me the answer, you must give me thirty linen garments and thirty sets of clothes."**

"Tell us your riddle," they said. "Let's hear it."

[14]**He replied,**

"Out of the eater, something to eat;

out of the strong, something sweet."

For three days they could not give the answer.

[15]**On the fourth day, they said to Samson's wife, "Coax your husband into explaining the riddle for us, or we will burn you and your father's household to death. Did you invite us here to rob us?"**

[16]**Then Samson's wife threw herself on him, sobbing, "You hate me! You don't really love me. You've given my people a riddle, but you haven't told me the answer."**

"I haven't even explained it to my father or mother," he replied, "so why should I explain it to you?" [17]**She cried the whole seven days of the feast. So on the seventh day he finally told her, because she continued to press him. She in turn explained the riddle to her people.**

[18]**Before sunset on the seventh day the men of the town said to him,**

"What is sweeter than honey?

What is stronger than a lion?"

Samson said to them,

"If you had not plowed with my heifer,

you would not have solved my riddle."

[19]**Then the Spirit of the LORD came upon him in power. He went down to Ashkelon, struck down thirty of their men, stripped them of their belongings and gave their clothes to those who had explained the riddle. Burning with anger, he went up to his father's house.** [20]**And Samson's wife was given to the friend who had attended him at his wedding.**

---

[317] The noun גְּוִיָּה bears this sense elsewhere in 1 Sam 31:10–12; Nah 3:3; Ps 110:6.

[318] The present versification creates a significant textual problem in v. 10 by unexpectedly introducing Samson's father. *BHS* deletes אָבִיהוּ and treats Samson as the subject of the verb וַיֵּרֶד, "he went down." But the problem is resolved if the verse break is placed after this clause, linking it to the preceding.

Samson and the Timnite Woman's Wedding (14:10b–20).   **14:10b–11**   In
the remainder of the chapter, which revolves around Samson's wedding, the
two plots identified earlier coalesce. The context for the wedding is set in vv.
10b–11: Samson prepares a feast to celebrate his wedding to the Timnite
woman. The act seems innocent enough, until one realizes that the word for
feast, *mišteh,* in this context refers to a seven-day drinking bout at the home of
the bride's parents.[319] One more element of Samson's Nazirite vow is about to
be broken. The narrator notes that this stag party was a Philistine custom
involving the select young men of the town. The use of *bahûrîm,* "choice
[young men]" (rather than NIV "bridegrooms") seems deliberately ominous."
Elsewhere in the book the word refers to select warriors (20:15–16), which
hints that the narrator recognizes the military implications of this event.

When the young men[320] arrived at the feast and saw Samson, they conscripted thirty "companions" to stay with him. The meaning of v. 11 is unclear.
Traditionally the response of the Philistines has been interpreted as arising out
of a concern to maintain Philistine custom. Grooms did not host such feasts
without attendants.[321] By this understanding the narrator has created an effective ironical situation: the attention to custom given by these "uncivilized" Philistines stands in sharp contrast to Samson's own disregard for both Israelite
custom and the Nazirite vow.

This interpretation, however, is doubtful on several counts. First, the text
focuses on Samson, not on a Philistine custom: when they saw him they provided thirty companions. Second, the word used to identify these thirty men,
"companions," is quite ambiguous. On the surface the Philistines' action
appears to be a gesture of goodwill—they are providing companions for him.
Since Samson is a stranger in this town, however, and "friendship" implies a
measure of intimacy, it is doubtful the narrator looks upon these men as Samson's friends. Either the expression is used ironically or these thirty men are
"friends" of the Philistine guests. Third, the manner in which these thirty men
were engaged is odd. The Hebrew text does not say the men were "given"
(NIV) or "brought" (NASB) to Samson. They were "taken" *(lāqaḥ),* which
suggests they were conscripted or commandeered by the *bahûrîm* for this role.
Fourth, the text describes their assignment in the simplest of terms, "and they
were with him" (at the end of v. 11, not translated in the NIV), which may be
interpreted both positively (as his friends) or negatively (as his guards). Fifth,
if these men were to serve as Samson's personal attendants, why does he need

[319] The picture of drunken revelry is entirely realistic. Among the most common types of pottery found by archaeologists in Philistine settlements is the strainer-spout "beer jug," on which see
T. Dothan and M. Dothan, *People of the Sea: The Search for the Philistines* (New York: Macmillan,
1992), 90, 134.
[320] Hebrew does not specify the subject.
[321] Cf. Soggin, *Judges,* 241.

thirty escorts? Without any textual links with Philistine customs, it is preferable to interpret the number as a conventional figure for a body of public officers. Accordingly, David's thirty military men[322] provide a more likely analogue to this scene than modern peasant marriages in Syria.[323] Although we cannot tell how Samson received these thirty "companions," in view of all these factors it seems best to interpret the Philistines' response to Samson as a potentially hostile act. When they saw Samson, they were afraid of him. Not taking any chances, they surrounded him with bodyguards.[324] This interpretation accords well with earlier comments by the narrator that Yahweh was determined to create tension between Israel and the Philistines.

14:12–13 But the appointment of thirty Philistines to guard him does not seem to worry Samson. On the contrary, he makes sport of the situation and proposes a riddle[325] for his guards.[326] But before he presents the riddle, he must determine if the Philistines want to play with him. He wins their approval by proposing a contest that appears to be stacked overwhelmingly in their favor: If they can solve his riddle[327] within the seven days of the feast, he will provide each of them with a complete suit of clothes, consisting of long garments and shorter tunics.[328] If they fail, then they must provide him with thirty capes and thirty suits of clothing. Eager to play the game, the guards invite Samson to propound the riddle for them.[329]

14:14 Samson's riddle is short and cryptic, consisting of six words

---

[322] 2 Sam 23:13; 1 Chr 11:15.

[323] Contra Burney, *Judges*, 361. Cf. Boling, *Judges*, 231.

[324] This is certainly the interpretation of the LXX[A], which reads בְּיִרְאָתָם, "because they were afraid," instead of the MT's כִּרְאוֹתָם, "when they saw him." The divergent readings derive from two different roots יָרֵא and רָאָה, which are easily confused.

[325] The use of the cognate accusative after a verb (חוּד חִידָה, lit. "to riddle a riddle") is a common literary device in Hebrew. The present phrase occurs also in Ezek 17:2.

[326] The "guards," not the "guests," represent the antecedents for "them" in "Samson said to them" in v. 12.

[327] Here "solving a riddle" is described as "declaring, explaining" (הִגִּיד) it. In v. 18 the narrator uses מָצָא, "to find out." Ps 49:5 speaks of "opening" (פָּתַח) a riddle.

[328] Following the interpretation of סְדִינִים and חֲלִפֹת בְּגָדִים respectively by M. Görg, "Zu den Kleiderbezeichnungen in Ri 14,12f," *BN* 68 (1993): 5–9. The former is cognate to Akk. š/saddinu, which refers to an item of clothing (*AHw*, 1001b). The word appears elsewhere in the OT only in Isa 3:23, where it refers to an element of female festal attire, and Prov 31:24, where it identifies a garment made by a noble woman. In the Talmud and the NT (σινδών) the word denotes a sleeping wrap or shroud. Cf. Matt 27:59; Mark 14:51–52; 15:46; Luke 23:53. Traditionally the former has been understood as a luxurious cape and the latter as festal clothing, in contrast to everyday garments. Cf. Burney, *Judges*, 362.

[329] On riddles in the Bible and the ANE see J. L. Crenshaw, "Riddles," *ABD* 5.721–23. For detailed studies of this riddle see C. V. Camp and C. R. Fontaine, "The Words of the Wise and Their Riddles," in *Text and Tradition: The Hebrew Bible and Folklore*, ed. S. Niditch (Atlanta: Scholars Press, 1990), 127–59; P. Nel, "The Riddle of Samson (Judg 14,14.18)," *Bib* 65 (1985): 534–45. According to Nel the contrasting clues, "sweet" and "strong," point to the irrepressibility of love.

arranged in two parallel lines of three words each:
"From-the-eater   out-came   eat[s]
and-from-the-strong   out-came   sweet[s]."

In keeping with Hebrew riddles generally, this riddle plays on assonance,[330] repetition, and semantic ambiguity. The enigma consists of two paradoxes: a consumer produces food, and a strong person produces sweetness. The parallelism suggests an identification of the consumer with the strong and the food with the sweet, but without further data this is as far as one can go. The Philistines probably would have looked to the present context for the most likely clues to its solution. Accordingly, they could have guessed that the first line refers to the drunken revelers disgorging the food they had eaten, perhaps Samson in particular. The second is more difficult. The "strong" could be a flattering reference either to the *baḥûrîm*, or the guards, or to Samson himself, given the guests' response to him.[331] Either way the last word is the crux. The wedding context leads some scholars to conclude that this phrase refers to [Samson's] sperm.[332]

14:15 But Samson's guards are frustrated. For three days they pursue every possible lead, but they are stumped. The reader understands why. Of course they could not solve this riddle. They were not in the vineyard when Samson killed the lion or when he drew honey out of its body. Not even his parents could have solved this enigma. Realizing they cannot solve it on their own, on the fourth day[333] they blackmail Samson's wife[334] to extract[335] the answer from her husband. If she refuses or fails to do so, they will burn her and her father's family (lit. "house"). The threat sets the reader up for the ultimate irony: the woman draws the solution to the riddle out of Samson to prevent her and her family being burned, but in the end she succumbs to the very catastrophe she tried to avoid precisely because she got the answer from him (15:6). Not satisfied with the pressure of this blackmail, the men accuse the woman of complicity with Samson[336] in tricking them into this hopeless circumstance so

---

[330] The riddle contains four *mems* and four *alephs*.

[331] Given Samson's weakness for Philistine women, the "strong" could refer more specifically to his sex organ.

[332] Crenshaw argues that the riddle antedates its present context and that Samson has adapted it to his private experience (*ABD* 5.722; *Samson*, 112–17e).

[333] Reading הָרְבִעִי with the LXX[A] instead of the MT's הַשְּׁבִיעִי, "seventh," though the latter is supported by Tg and Vg. But this makes no sense in the context. See further O'Connell, *Rhetoric of the Book of Judges*, 473.

[334] In Hb. אִשָּׁה denotes both "woman" and "wife." If the Philistines followed the custom reflected in Gen 29:23,27, the marriage would not have been consummated until the seventh day of the feast, but the status of a betrothed woman was not sharply distinguished from that of a wife.

[335] Hb. פָּתָה in *piel* means "to persuade, entice." Cf. Judg 16:5; Hos 2:16; Prov 1:10. In Exod 22:15 it means "to seduce" (a virgin).

[336] Note the plural form of the verb, קְרָאתֶם, "you [pl.] called."

that they might be impoverished.[337] The narrator's use of the verb *yāraš*, "to possess, dispossess" (NIV, "rob"), suggests a veiled reference to the divine agenda. This is the most common expression for Israel's possession of the land of Canaan. Are the Philistines fearing an extension of the conquest to their territory?

14:16a Left with no choice the woman pleads with Samson for mercy. Her approach is entirely emotional. Weeping, she casts herself upon him, and for the first time in the narrative she speaks. From the beginning (v. 1) the reader has seen this love affair from only one side and has been left to wonder how Samson's soon-to-be wife feels about this relationship. When she finally opens her mouth, she goes straight to the heart of their relationship: Does Samson really love her? Employing the tactic of blackmail like her countrymen, she charges that since Samson does not share with her his deepest secrets he cannot love her. Surely if he is going to tease her countrymen with riddles, he must share his secrets with her.

14:16b Samson's response expresses a calloused disposition toward both her and his parents. First, he insists that love is not the issue. Pretending to love his parents, he asserts that not even those with whom he is most intimate know the answer to the riddle. This comment reminds the reader that Samson has had no change of heart since he defiled his parents by sharing the desecrated honey with them. Second, he lets his wife know that the apron strings have not been cut. Contrary to Gen 2:24, he sees no need to be more intimate with her than he is with his parents.

14:17 But she persists. For the rest of the seven days of the feast,[338] while the men are celebrating, she makes life miserable for Samson, weeping whenever she is in his presence. Her nagging[339] pays dividends. At the climactic "eleventh hour" on the seventh day, Samson melts under the heat. He gives his wife the solution to the riddle, and she passes the information on to her countrymen.

14:18a The Philistines time their approach to Samson for the most dramatic effect, just before sundown on the seventh day of the feast. It is not clear why the narrator should have employed the rare word *ḥeres* for "sun."[340] The word occurs elsewhere only in Job 9:7 and Isa 19:18, but it has appeared as part

---

[337] The vocalization of לְיָרְשֵׁנוּ is ambiguous. The form looks like a *qal* infinitive construct (thus GKC §69m,n) but probably should be interpreted as a *piel* (*HALOT*, 441). The NIV follows the suggested emendation in *BHS*, changing הֲלֹא, "Is it not [so]?" which is awkward, to הֲלֹם, "here."

[338] Contextually Hb. שִׁבְעַת הַיָּמִים (lit. "the seven days") must mean the remainder of the seven days of the feast.

[339] Hb. הֵצִיק, "to pressure, to constrain." The verb will recur in 16:16.

[340] *BHS* follows the old suggestion of Stade in proposing הֶחָרְסָה be emended to הַחַדְרָה, "the bride-chamber," which occurs in 15:1. Cf. Moore, *Judges*, 339. The ending *-ah* is best treated as an old locative case ending. Cf. GKC 90f.

of a place name earlier in 1:35. The word seems to have been chosen to highlight the timing of the Philistine's appearance before Samson and/or to send a
signal to the reader to listen carefully to the following lines:[341]

> What   is-sweeter   than-honey?
>
> And-what   is-stronger   than-a-lion?

Among other features, a phonic analysis of the Philistines' answer to Samson's riddle reveals a five[or six]fold repetition of the letter *mem*. Even more to
the point, these two lines constructed in poetic parallelism echo the two lines
of Samson's riddle in v. 14. The echo is heard also in the concentration on the
two key words: "honey," which is sweetness par excellence, and "lion,"[342]
which is strength par excellence.[343] Instead of answering Samson's riddle
forthrightly, by casting their response as two rhetorical questions the Philistines tease Samson with a riddle of their own. Samson recognizes immediately
that he has been caught, but the reader is left to ponder what these lines mean.
On contextual grounds this answer must be linked to a wedding, in which case
line 1 may be supposed to refer to love, which is incomparable in its sweetness;
and the second line, to Samson, who is incomparable in his strength. Ironically,
love proves to be the stronger, melting Samson like honey in a woman's hand.
From the narrator's perspective, despite Samson's great physical strength and
the force of his Nazirite vow, he is completely helpless when confronted with
the love of women.[344] From Yahweh's perspective (cf. v. 4) the amorous
desires of this man provide the occasions for the beginning of conflicts
between Samson and the Philistines.[345]

14:18b But Samson is totally insensitive to the theological implications of
his own riddle and the guards' response. He recognizes immediately that his
desecrating act has been exposed and that he has lost his wager. Furious, he
reacts to their riddle with another "two liner":

> If-you-had-not   plowed   with-my-heifer,
>
> Not   you-would-have-solved my-riddle."

In other words, "you cheated." But his reference to his wife as his "heifer"[346]

---

[341] Thus L. H. Silberman, "Listening to the Text," *JBL* 102 (1983): 15. Boling (*Judges*, 231–
32) suggests the word was preferred over שֶׁמֶשׁ to avoid confusion with the name of Samson.
Together with its echo in חֲרַשְׁתֶּם, "you plowed," in v. 18b, the narrator has produced an effective
inclusio around the riddle.

[342] Cf. vv. 5 and 8, which refer to the lion with אַרְיוֹת, כְּפִיר, and אַרְיֵה, respectively.

[343] Based on the fact that the word for lion is homonymous with an Arabic word for "honey"
(ʾary; cf. *HALOT*, 87), some see here an intentional word play. Accordingly the riddle could be
solved by discovering a pair of homonyms, which mean "sweet," and "strong," respectively. For
discussion see S. Segert, "Paranomasia in the Samson Narrative in Judges XIII–XVI," *VT* 34
(1984): 455–56.

[344] Cf. 16:1–3 and 4–22.

[345] Cf. Nel, "The Riddle of Samson," 544.

[346] עֶגְלָה, ʿeglâ, "heifer," recalls עֶגְלוֹן, "Eglon," in chap. 3.

is as disparaging in the Hebrew as it is in English.

14:19 Verses 19–20 are epilogic and anticlimactic as far as the account of Samson's wedding is concerned, but in the overall plot they represent the climax of this chapter. Yahweh's determination to stir up the relationship between Israel and the Philistines is bearing fruit. Accordingly, as in v. 6, with his agent facing a new physical challenge, Yahweh's Spirit rushes upon Samson, empowering him with superhuman strength. Hurrying down to the coastal city of Ashkelon,[347] Samson slaughters thirty of its male residents and seizes their arms[348] as booty. Carrying these items twenty miles back to Timnah, in a mocking gesture he presents them to the Philistine guards as their promised change of clothes.[349]

14:20 Still fuming, Samson returned up the Wadi Sorek to his father's house, presumably in Zorah (cf. 13:2). Meanwhile his father-in-law gave her to one of the "friends"[350] who had been guarding him.

Theological and Practical Implications

When we reflect on the significance of this chapter, we note first that from the perspective of literary style, this account shows the narrator at his best. With effective use of semantic ambiguity, wordplays, enigmatic speech, euphemisms, homonyms, synonyms, and assonance, the author draws the reader into the plot. Samson's riddle is a challenge not only for his Philistine guards but also for the reader. But the challenge to the reader's wit does not end with Samson's riddle. The guards' response is also intentionally enigmatic.

Second, this chapter presents a fascinating study in deceit, disingenuity, candor, and fairness. Since no one could have solved Samson's riddle without having been a witness to both his killing of the lion and his discovery of the honey, his challenge to his guards appears unreasonable if not downright unfair.[351] But this is his wedding, and he has the right to determine the games

---

[347] Ashkelon was located some twenty miles southwest of Timnah. Ashkelon, along with Ashdod, Ekron, Gaza, and Gath, constituted the Philistine pentapolis. This major port city is being currently excavated by archaeologists, on which see Dothan and Dothan, *People of the Sea*, 41–48; L. Stager, "The Philistines Ruled Ashkelon," *BAR* 17 (1991): 26–43; idem, "Ashkelon," *NEAEHL* 1.103–12. On the history of this city see D. L. Esse, "Ashkelon," *ABD* 1.487–90.

[348] Hb. חֲלִיצוֹת, which occurs elsewhere only in 2 Sam 2:21, denotes the equipment stripped from a slain man, particularly the belt from which weapons and tools were hung. See *HALOT*, 319.

[349] Note the narrator's impressive assonantal pairing of חֲלִיצוֹת, NIV "belongings," and חֲלִיפוֹת, "changes [of clothes]."

[350] Note the similarity to v. 11.

[351] Crenshaw (*Samson*, 114) recounts an analogous case of "The Princess Who Cannot Solve the Riddle." In the story a young man on the way to a riddle contest to see who could win the hand of the princess witnessed successively a horse die of poisoning, a raven devouring bits of its carcass, and twelve men die as a result of eating the raven. Devising a riddle out of this extraordinary series of events, the young man declared, "One killed none and yet killed twelve." Despite resorting to the mastery of dreams, the princess could not solve the riddle, and so she became the young man's wife.

that will be played. At the same time the reader observes that ancient Hebrew conventions of conversation differed greatly from modern western patterns of dialogue, which value economy, efficiency, forthrightness, and getting to the point. Strictly speaking, though we know Samson's riddle is solved, it is never explained. No one mentions the bees, let alone declares the relationship between the honey and the lion. But that is all right. Having identified the key elements, the Philistines leave it to Samson's and the narrator leaves it to the readers' imaginations to fill in the gaps. The real genius in the narrative is seen in the way one riddle follows another.

Third, this story is fascinating for the cultural information it bears. The account of this "courtship" and wedding undoubtedly reflects ancient customs, but whether these were Philistine or Israelite customs is not clear. It seems odd at first that this wedding feast should have been held in the home of the bride rather than the groom.

On the one hand, this may reflect a Philistine convention.[352] Some compare this event with the modern Arabic *ṣadīqa* marriage, which has the groom arranging the marriage directly with the family of the bride without involving the family of the groom or the bride herself. These were considered true marriages but without permanent cohabitation. The wife continued to live at home, and the husband would visit her at more or less regular intervals, bringing gifts. If this were the case, 15:1 takes on new meaning. Samson thinks he can return to his wife at any time.

On the other hand, one must be cautious about reading ancient documents in light of modern customs. Within the context of the Book of Judges we have come to expect the maverick, the irregular, the deviation from the norm. This is particularly true of Samson, who creates his own rules. Furthermore, it probably would have seemed incongruous for Samson's parents, who did not sanction this marriage, to have hosted the wedding. Accordingly, having decided to marry a Philistine and having to arrange this wedding with Philistine parents of the bride, the wedding itself may well have followed Philistine custom, which involved a seven-day festival of eating and drinking and games. In the event, the father of the bride has the last word in this marriage.

Fourth, this account is important for the picture it paints of Samson. Positively, the reader must be impressed by Samson's fidelity to his word. Having lost the contest, he does indeed keep his promise and provide each of his Philistine guards with a change of clothing. But apart from this one feature, the picture the author paints of this man is ugly. Samson is disrespectful of his parents, callous toward his Nazirite calling, without any loyalty to his own people, compromising in his ethic, rude to his wife, flippant with his tongue, and driven by lust, eroticism, and appetite. The only way in which good can come from

[352] Soggin, *Judges*, 240–41; de Vaux, *Ancient Israel*, 29.

this man is by Yahweh overpowering him with his Spirit and driving him to the task of delivering his people, something he is not naturally inclined to do.

Fifth, theologically the reader should recognize in this marriage a picture of Israel. In the narrator's eyes Samson represents the nation. This person— uniquely set apart, called, and gifted for divine service—not only fraternizes with the enemy, but he also seeks to live among them. But God is in control, and the story ends exactly where he wanted it. Yahweh is provoking tension between Israel and the Philistines. Unaware of their roles in divine providence the characters are creating the very situation Yahweh had planned. At the end of this chapter (1) the work against the Philistines has begun, (2) Samson is back in his father's house, and (3) the adventure in mixed marriage has collapsed. The woman has betrayed her husband, the husband is calling his wife disparaging names, and the father-in-law has given his daughter to another man. What was planned as an interracial marriage turns into war!

THE SUN STILL RISES (15:1–19).[353]　　The temporal note in 15:1 signals a break in the narrative, setting apart chap. 15 as a separate series of events. The chapter subdivides into four increasingly complex episodes, each of which transpires in a different location:

In Samson's father-in-law's house (15:1–3)

Out in the field (15:4–8)

In Judah (15:9–13)

At Lehi (15:14–19)

Verse 20 functions as a narrative epilogue. If the key word in chap. 14 was *yārad*, "to go down," the key word here is *ʿāśâ*, "to do," especially as an act of retaliation.[354] The episodes are all closely related and reach their climax with the Spirit of Yahweh "rushing upon" Samson. This is a story of action → reaction → reaction → reaction. ... The tempo of the narration picks up with the intensification of the action, so that in the end the reader feels the need to join Samson in crying for divine relief from exhaustion.

[1]Later on, at the time of wheat harvest, Samson took a young goat and went to visit his wife. He said, "I'm going to my wife's room." But her father would not let him go in.

[2]"I was so sure you thoroughly hated her," he said, "that I gave her to your friend. Isn't her younger sister more attractive? Take her instead."

[3]Samson said to them, "This time I have a right to get even with the Philistines; I will really harm them."

---

[353] The title plays on the name of Samson and on the motif of the sun setting in 14:18.

[354] Note: "I shall *do* [evil] to them" (v. 3); "Who has *done* this" (v. 6); "If you *do* this" (v. 7); "We have come to *do* to him as he has *done* to us" (v. 10); "What is this that you have *done* to us?" (v. 11); "As they have *done* to me, so I have *done* to them" (v. 11).

Samson's Return to His Wife (15:1–3). The previous chapter had provided no clear hints concerning the timing of the events described, though the motifs of romance and wedding may suggest early springtime. This accords well with the opening line of chap. 15, which notes that the events described in this chapter happened after some time, specifically at the time of the wheat harvest. The word used here for "wheat" is the most common Hebrew word for naked wheat of the durum variety.[355] Judging from its frequent occurrence in Ugaritic[356] and other Northwest Semitic texts from the first millennium B.C.,[357] this grain obviously was common throughout the ancient Near East.[358] According to the Gezer calendar, the wheat harvest occurred in May after the barley harvest.[359] The significance of this note will become apparent in the second episode (vv. 4–8).

15:1 The first episode in this chapter has Samson returning to Timnah at harvest time to reclaim his bride. His intention, expressed by the narrator through direct (internal) speech, is to "go in to her in the inner chamber."[360] But the statement is quite ambiguous. By "going in to her" does he intend simply to visit her or does he want to consummate the marriage with sexual intercourse? In either case he seeks to soften his wife's heart with a gift of a young goat.[361] Although Samson had left her home in a huff in the wake of the wedding fiasco (14:19–20), apparently he never meant to break off the marriage.

15:2 When Samson arrives at what he thought was his wife's house, she does not turn out to be the problem. Greeting him at the door, her father refuses to let him in. His explanation seems reasonable. Given Samson's reaction at the wedding, her father had concluded that Samson's love had given way to total rejection[362] and that he had abandoned her, with no intention of returning to claim her. Obviously this man had no greater affection for his son-in-law than Samson's parents had for their daughter-in-law. But as a dutiful father, he had found a felicitous solution for his daughter by giv-

[355] For discussion of *triticum durum* see Zohary, *Plants of the Bible*, 74.
[356] See *UT*, 397 (#881), for references.
[357] See *DNWSI*, 363, for Imperial Aramaic, Yaudic, and Palmyrene references.
[358] On the Akk. equivalent, *kibtu,* see *AHw*, 472; *CAD* 8.340–41.
[359] The ninth-century Gezer Calendar places the wheat harvest in the sixth agricultural season. See *ANET*, 320.
[360] Hb. חֶדֶר refers to an inner chamber. In 3:24 the same word had identified the cool room where Eglon's servants thought he was relieving himself. The verb חָדַר means "to penetrate deeply." Cf. *HALOT*, 292.
[361] Boling (*Judges*, 234) interprets the gift as the ancient counterpart to a box of chocolates.
[362] His evaluation, expressed emphatically with the infinitive absolute and finite verb (כִּי־שָׂנֹא שְׂנֵאתָהּ, "for you hated her thoroughly") may be interpreted as "you have surely divorced her." The root שָׂנֵא, "to hate," is the antonym of אָהֵב, "to love, to be covenantally committed to." Cf. M. S. Nicolo, "Vorderasiatisches Rechtsgut in der ägyptischen Eheverträgen der Perserzeit," *OLZ* 30 (1927): 218.

ing her to one of the men who had accompanied him at the wedding. But this action cannot be reversed. Taking a measure of responsibility for the way things had turned out, the man offers Samson what he thinks is a reasonable compromise—the hand of his second daughter. He attempts to put a positive spin on this turn of events by advising Samson that he should be pleased because his younger daughter is even more beautiful than the older one. The modern reader may be impressed by the man's efforts to placate Samson, but this is a Philistine way to treat one's daughter. Does she have no opinion on the matter?[363] For someone who operates according to "what seems right in his eyes," the offer should have been attractive. But Boling aptly observes that no one can tell Samson how to find a wife.[364] To him it was of little consequence that he had left the wedding in a rage. Apparently he expected to return to his wife and resume life as if nothing had happened.

15:3 Verse 3 describes Samson's reaction to the rebuff by the one who should have been his father-in-law. The words on his lips as he leaves are ominous (lit.): "This time I shall be absolved of all guilt[365] from the Philistines when I execute mischief [$r\bar{a}^c\hat{a}$] with them." For the moment the reader does not know what he has in mind. The word $r\bar{a}^c\hat{a}$ can mean "moral evil" or simply "disaster, harm." It may be significant that this is the same word that had characterized the Spirit of God in 9:23, sent to disturb the amicable relationship between Abimelech and the lords of Shechem. The author seems to be inviting the reader to interpret Samson's upcoming actions in a similar vein. Samson is about to fulfill Yahweh's design expressed in v. 4, rupturing the comfortable relationship then existing between the Israelites and the Philistines. Samson's words create an atmosphere of anticipation, and the reader wonders what this irascible character will do next. No doubt the narrator finds great amusement in telling the sequel.

⁴So he went out and caught three hundred foxes and tied them tail to tail in pairs. He then fastened a torch to every pair of tails, ⁵lit the torches and let the foxes loose in the standing grain of the Philistines. He burned up the shocks and standing grain, together with the vineyards and olive groves.

⁶When the Philistines asked, "Who did this?" they were told, "Samson, the Timnite's son-in-law, because his wife was given to his friend."

So the Philistines went up and burned her and her father to death. ⁷Samson said to them, "Since you've acted like this, I won't stop until I get my revenge on you." ⁸He attacked them viciously and slaughtered many of them. Then he went down and stayed in a cave in the rock of Etam.

---

[363] This is another of many instances in the book where a Canaanized society is expressed in abusive treatment of women.

[364] Boling, *Judges*, 235.

[365] The verb נָקָה means "to be free of blame," i.e., justified in one's action. Cf. Jer 2:35; Ps 19:14.

Torching the Fields (15:4–8).   **15:4–5**   These verses actually contain three episodes, three chain reactions, leading up to "then he went down" in v. 8. From his actions in vv. 4–5 the reader learns why the narrator had mentioned the time of Samson's return to Timnah in v. 1 as "the wheat harvest." Philistia was grain country, and with his actions Samson strikes at the heart of the Philistine economy.[366] The rapid succession of verbs in the description creates the impression that his actions took no effort at all.[367] Samson caught three hundred jackals,[368] tied their tails together, fastened torches to their tails, ignited the torches, sent them out, and burned not only the shocks of cut grain[369] but also the standing grain,[370] the vineyards, and the olive groves.[371] Why he should have sent the animals out as one hundred and fifty pairs rather than three hundred individuals is not clear. Presumably the animals' attempts to separate would force them to zig-zag up and down the fields and to stop periodically, long enough for the torches actually to light the crops, rather than hurrying off in straight lines and snuffing out the torches. How Samson accomplished this is a greater mystery.[372] But it fits into the picture of a man who kills a lion singlehandedly, kills thirty Philistines, breaks brand new ropes that bind him, slays a thousand Philistines with a jaw bone, and brings a house down over thousands of reveling Philistines. Samson's actions are all guerrilla tactics. All his achievements are personal, and all are provoked by his own [mis]behavior. Unlike the other deliverers, he never seeks to rid Israel of foreign oppressors, and he never calls out the Israelite troops. Samson is a man with a higher calling than any other deliverer in the book, but he spends his whole life "doing his own thing."

15:6   Samson's comment in v. 3 had hinted that his anger against his father-in-law would be generalized to the man's ethnic compatriots. By setting fire to the crops belonging to the Philistine population in general, he certainly

---

[366] In the narrator's mind the action may also contain a veiled polemic against idolatry, inasmuch as the primary god of the Philistines was Dagon, the god of grain *(dāgān)*. Cf. 16:23–24; 1 Sam 5:1–7.

[367] "Then he went [וַיֵּלֶךְ]… and caught [וַיִּלְכֹּד]… and took [וַיִּקַּח]… and turned [וַיֶּפֶן]… and put [וַיָּשֶׂם]… and set fire [וַיַּבְעֶר־אֵשׁ]… and sent out [וַיְשַׁלַּח]… and burned [וַיַּבְעֵר]."

[368] The Hb. word שׁוּעָלִים was used of both foxes and jackals. Since the latter were more common in Palestine and since foxes are solitary animals, Samson probably was dealing with jackals. Jackals are certainly intended in Ezek 13:4; Lam 5:18; and Ps 63:11, where the same word is used.

[369] Hb. גָּדִישׁ "heap of sheaves." Cf. Exod 22:5; Job 5:26.

[370] Hb. קָמָה, from קוּם, "to stand." Cf. Exod 22:5; Deut 16:9; 23:26; Isa 17:5.

[371] Note the chiastic construction and the double-duty role of the first preposition מִן: מִגָּדִישׁ וְעַד־קָמָה "From shock to standing [grain], וְעַד־כֶּרֶם זָיִת And to vineyard (from) olive (grove)." Cf. Boling, *Judges*, 235; D. N. Freedman, "A Note on Judges 15,5," *Bib* 52 (1971): 535.

[372] O. Margalith ("Samson's Foxes," VT 35 [1985]: 224–29) dismisses this as a fanciful aetiological tale based on the colloquial Greek word for fox, *lampouris,* "torch-tail," a name introduced by the Philistines, whose origin was in the Aegean.

stirred up the proverbial "hornet's nest." But the reaction of the Philistines is confusing. Their investigation of the source of the catastrophe uncovers Samson as the culprit, but they also learn that he was provoked by his father-in-law's action against Samson. By referring to him as "the son-in-law of the Timnite," they recognize Samson's status as the husband of the man's daughter and discredit his father-in-law's action in giving Samson's wife to the second man. Accordingly, they take it out on the Timnite by burning him and his daughter, presumably by torching their house (cf. 14:15).[373] Then, ironically, by a series of complex interrelated events, the very outcome Samson's wife tried to avoid occurs. People may act as though they are masters of their own fate, but the hidden providence of God is able to bring the schemes and conduct of human beings upon their own heads and thereby accomplish his own purposes. On the other hand, the Philistine rationalization sounds hollow. Needing a scapegoat, the Philistines may simply have concluded that it was easier to deal with the Timnite than with Samson.

15:7 In their response, however, the Philistines underestimated Samson's commitment to his wife, his preparedness to retaliate, and his physical strength. His justification for his action is classic, if ironic: "Since you've acted like this," (lit.) "I will get revenge on you and afterwards I will quit." The final phrase adds suspense to the story, but does Samson really think the vicious and escalating cycles of action and reaction violence can be broken with one more act of violence? Nevertheless, Samson always acts as if each destructive action will be the last, a disposition that is confirmed only when he destroys himself with his enemies (16:28–30).

15:8 The narrator describes Samson's response in the most cryptic terms. He (lit.) "struck them leg upon thigh with a great striking." The NIV's "viciously" offers a tolerable interpretation of the idiom, "leg upon thigh," presumably a wrestling idiom for total victory. Knowing this act had incited the ire of the Philistines as a whole, Samson flees to the territory of Judah and hides in a cave in a fissure in the rock at Etam. The location of Etam is uncertain and in any case may carry more meaning symbolically than geographically. He seeks refuge from his enemies like an animal hides from its predator.[374]

⁹The Philistines went up and camped in Judah, spreading out near Lehi. ¹⁰The men of Judah asked, "Why have you come to fight us?"

"We have come to take Samson prisoner," they answered, "to do to him as he did to us."

¹¹Then three thousand men from Judah went down to the cave in the rock of Etam and said to Samson, "Don't you realize that the Philistines are rulers over

---

[373] *BHS* follows the LXX^A and Syr in recommending the insertion of בֵּית, "house," before אָבִיהָ, "her father." See further O'Connell, *Rhetoric of the Book of Judges*, 474.

[374] Hb. עֵיטָם derives from the same root as עַיִט, "bird of prey." Cf. *HALOT*, 816–17.

us? What have you done to us?"

He answered, "I merely did to them what they did to me."

12They said to him, "We've come to tie you up and hand you over to the Philistines."

Samson said, "Swear to me that you won't kill me yourselves."

13"Agreed," they answered. "We will only tie you up and hand you over to them. We will not kill you." So they bound him with two new ropes and led him up from the rock.

The Capture of Samson (15:9–13). **15:9–10** Verses 9–13 break into two discreet parts, both dominated by dialogue involving the Philistines. In vv. 9–10 the Philistines confront the Judahites for harboring Samson, sending an army that set up camp and spread out in Judahite territory, near Lehi.[375] The use of the verbs *ḥānâ*, "to camp," and *nāṭaš*, "to spread out," provide the first hint in the Samson narratives of military activity and the first hint that Samson's adventures have more than personal significance. The Judahites are understandably alarmed and interpret the Philistine action as a declaration of war. Instead of calling on Samson to lead them in battle, however, as previous deliverers had done, they try to negotiate a peace. Their question, "Why have you come to fight us?" seems innocent enough. Little do they realize that the Philistine aggression is instigated by God to break the status quo between Israel and the enemy.

The Philistine answer is simple and to the point. They have come to bind Samson so they can do to him as he has done to them. This comment summarizes the Philistine ethic, the lowest level of morality, in a nutshell: "Do unto others as they have done unto you." What has he done to them but burned their crops, murdered their men, and toyed with them as a cat plays with a mouse? Ever since he arrived in Timnah, they have experienced one disaster after another. The time has come for them to inflict disaster (cf. *rāʿâ*, in v. 3) upon him.

Samson's flight to Judah has escalated his personal feud with the Philistines into an international crisis—which is precisely what God wants. But the Judahite response is disappointing. Instead of rallying their troops to defend their countryman (even if he is a Danite) and/or calling on Samson to lead the way, they acquiesce, creating for the reader one more case of frustrated expectations. The Judahites would rather deliver their countrymen into the hands of the enemy and live under that enemy's domination than fulfill the mandate Yahweh had given them to occupy the land and drive out the enemy.

15:11 Like dutiful subordinates to the Philistines the Judahites dispatch a host of men to get Samson from his hideout at Etam (vv. 11–13). Whether one interprets *šělōšet ʾělāpîm ʾîš* as "three thousand men" with the NIV or "three

---

375 The name לְחִי, "jawbone," anticipates the outcome of this crisis.

contingents of men,"[376] the image is both ironic and comical. Instead of sending an army against the Philistines, they send it against their own a countryman. Apparently they have come to fear Samson as much as the Philistines do.

The conversation between the Judahite delegation and Samson is critical for understanding the current state of affairs. First, Judah is determined to avoid confrontation with the Philistines at all cost. They are content to let the latter rule over them. In "Don't you realize [know] that the Philistines are rulers over us?" the reader may hear an echo of Gideon's comment in 8:23, "the LORD will rule over you." The Judahites are willing not only to substitute the rule of the Philistines for the rule of Yahweh, but also to sacrifice the divinely appointed leader to preserve the status quo. Samson has become a gadfly to Philistines and Israelites alike.

Second, Samson has adopted the Philistine ethic as his own. When asked to give an account of his behavior in stirring up this hornet's nest, Samson replies (lit.), "Just as they have done to me, so I have done to them."[377] When enemies with this kind of morality meet, there is no hope of resolution, only a final solution.

15:12a Third, having no stomach themselves to challenge existing political realities, the people of Judah are prepared to offer up their countryman because he represents a threat to national security and/or tranquility. Echoing the declared intention of the Philistines in v. 10, they do not even try to veil their treacherous purposes against their fellow Israelite: they have come to tie him up[378] and hand him over to the enemy. Judahites and Philistines are allied against Yahweh's chosen leader!

15:12b–13 Fourth, Samson fears that the Judahites will kill him. The connection is odd. The Judahites have just said they have come to get him to hand him over to the enemies. Apparently Samson does not believe them. But death at the hands of his own people would be more shameful and ignominious than death at the hands of a woman from the enemy's side (cf. 4:21; 9:54). It is better to be tortured and killed by the enemy! When the Judahites reiterate their intentions, Samson acquiesces, allows himself to be bound and handed over to the Philistines. The reference to "new ropes" heightens the tension and sets the stage for the following heroic scene.

[14]As he approached Lehi, the Philistines came toward him shouting. The Spirit of the LORD came upon him in power. The ropes on his arms became like charred

---

[376] On the large numbers in Judges see the commentary on 4:13–14; 7:3; and 12:6.

[377] The echo of v. 10 is intentional and obvious.

[378] But note the difference in verbs, reflecting the respective geographic positions of Judah and Philistia:

v. 10: "to bind Samson we have come up [עָלִינוּ]."

v. 12: "to bind you we have come down [יָרַדְנוּ]."

flax, and the bindings dropped from his hands. [15]Finding a fresh jawbone of a donkey, he grabbed it and struck down a thousand men.
[16]Then Samson said,

"With a donkey's jawbone
  I have made donkeys of them.
With a donkey's jawbone
  I have killed a thousand men."

[17]When he finished speaking, he threw away the jawbone; and the place was called Ramath Lehi.

[18]Because he was very thirsty, he cried out to the LORD, "You have given your servant this great victory. Must I now die of thirst and fall into the hands of the uncircumcised?" [19]Then God opened up the hollow place in Lehi, and water came out of it. When Samson drank, his strength returned and he revived. So the spring was called En Hakkore, and it is still there in Lehi.

Samson's Remarkable Victory (15:14–19). **15:14–15** With their captive in tow, the Judahites approach Lehi, where the enemy is camped. When the Philistines see Samson, they go out to meet him shouting like an army charging into battle.[379] But the sound of the Philistines also signals Yahweh to take over and intervene on behalf of his agent. Samson's work is not yet finished. As in 14:19 the Spirit of Yahweh rushes upon Samson, causing the flax ropes that bound him to disintegrate like burned flax and melt in his hands. Nothing is said yet about Samson's strength. The loosing of the man is entirely the work of Yahweh. But in v. 15 matters change as Samson goes on the offensive. Reminiscent of Shamgar's victory over the Philistines using an ox goad, Samson grabs a fresh jawbone lying nearby and slaughters one thousand men. The author's observation that the jawbone was fresh is significant for two reasons. First, this meant the bone was not yet dried out and hard, hence less useful as a weapon. But more importantly, being fresh it was still considered part of a corpse, in which case we witness another violation of the Nazirite vow.

15:16 With typical narcissistic flair Samson immortalizes his fabulous victory over the enemy with two responses. First, he composes a song to commemorate his accomplishment. The couplet consists of two lines constructed in impressive climactic parallelism (lit.):

With a donkey's jawbone, a heap, two heaps;
With a donkey's jawbone I have killed a thousand men.

The effectiveness of the verse depends not only on the poetic parallelism but also on effective wordplay. The Hebrew words for "donkey" and for "heap"

---

[379] The verb הָרִיעַ refers to a battle cry, which may sound a signal for war or march (Num 10:7,9; Hos 5:8; cf. Josh 1), an alarm of battle (Judg 7:21; Josh 6:10,16,20; 1 Sam 17:52; Isa 42:13), or a signal of triumph in battle (Jer 50:15; Ps 41:12; Zeph 3:14).

are spelled the same, *ḥămôr*.[380] Although the song is extremely effective poetically, it is quite perverse in substance. In contrast to the Song of Deborah in chap. 5, not a word is said about God. Samson claims all the credit for himself, which causes the reader to wonder if he is even aware of God's involvement in his life.

15:17 Second, Samson memorializes his achievement by renaming the place where it happened as Ramath-Lehi, "Jawbone Hill." Since military action frequently occurred on hilltops,[381] the reader might conclude that Samson is hereby naming the geographical site of the victory. That seems not to have been the issue here. "Jawbone Hill" apparently refers to the mound he had built with the corpses of the Philistines. Samson does not want to be forgotten!

15:18 Although Samson alludes to his victory in v. 18, and based on the analogy of 16:30, vv. 18–19 look like the climax of chaps. 14–15. Judges 15:18–19 is constructed as a separate episode, almost an afterthought. The reference to Samson's thirst in v. 18 is unexpected. Admittedly, his slaughter of one thousand Philistines with the jawbone of a donkey was an extraordinary achievement and may well have taken its toll on him physically. As in Samson's previous physical feats (14:6,19; 15:4,8), however, vv. 14–17 have left the reader with the impression that, empowered by the Spirit of Yahweh, his victory was effortless. But the narrator chooses his words carefully as he describes Samson calling out to God for the first time. Whereas in previous contexts of crying out the narrator had employed the more technical expression, *zāʿaq/ṣāʿaq*, here he employs *qārāʾ*, "to call out." In so doing he signals to the reader a fundamental difference between this crisis and the ones previously described. Here the issue is not a national emergency but a personal crisis—Samson is thirsty.

We may applaud Samson for finally recognizing his dependence upon God, and on first sight Samson's prayer to God seems pious. In fact, several features in his prayer suggest that he perceives himself as a second Moses. First, it is thirst that moves him to cry out to God. Second, he interprets his role as that of a savior, through whom Yahweh has given deliverance. Third, recalling the title ascribed to Moses in Josh 1:1, he refers to himself as Yahweh's "servant." Fourth, Yahweh responds to his cry in a manner reminiscent of Exod 17:6 and Num 20:10–13.

---

[380] Following the traditional interpretation reflected in the Masoretic pointing of חֲמוֹר חֲמֹרָתָיִם and the Septuagintal interpretation (ἐξαλείφων ἐξήλειψα αὐτούς, "a heap I heaped them"). This understanding also finds support in Exod 8:10 [Eng. 14], where חֳמָרִם חֳמָרִם means "heaps, heaps," i.e., "countless heaps." Cf. *HALOT*, 330. The rendering of the NIV assumes a repointing of חֲמֹרָתָיִם as חֲמֹרְתִּים and treats the word as a denominative verb from חֲמוֹר, "donkey." A more likely interpretation would derive חֲמֹרָתָיִם from another root, חָמַר, "to flay." Cf. *DCH* 3.258.

[381] Cf. 2 Sam 1:21. But see Judg 5:18.

As impressive as these links may be, the tone of Samson's prayer raises serious questions. To his credit he acknowledges the role of God in the deliverance, but his appeal sounds like an impudent harangue on Yahweh. In keeping with his self-centered approach to life in general and his adopted Philistine ethic, Samson's designation of himself as Yahweh's servant rings extremely hollow. Even his comment (lit.) "[It is] you [who] have given by the hand of your servant this great victory" is self-serving,[382] as if he deserves the credit. But more seriously, his prayer is as narcissistic as his manner of life. Far from displaying any concern about the fate of his people or the work that is yet to be done, let alone concern for the glory of God, his intention in this prayer is purely personal: to avert his own death and to avoid capture by the Philistines. What a shame it would be for him to fall into the hands of this uncircumcised people! This comment raises a serious question: Why this sudden concern about defilement and ritual issues? Where was this sensitivity to contamination when his parents had protested his desire to marry one of these uncircumcised (14:3)? Samson's motives are entirely selfish.

15:19 In reading this passage one is amazed not only by the fact that Yahweh answers Samson's prayer, but also by the miraculously way in which he does it. The narrator's switch from Yahweh to the generic designation for God, Elohim, in v. 19 suggests that even he was surprised.[383] With his thoroughly theocentric perspective, the author notes that "God opened up [*bāqaʿ,* "split open"] the hollow place *[maktēš]* in Lehi," causing the water to gush forth so Samson's spirit could be revived. The term *maktēš* occurs elsewhere only in Prov 27:22, where it denotes "mortar."[384] Here it seems to refer to a seam in the rock, which when struck opens up, releasing the water trapped between layers of limestone. Not one to miss an opportunity to leave his signature on the map, Samson named this spring near Lehi, En Hakkore, a name it still bore at the time this account was written. The name *ʿên haqqōrēʾ* is ambiguous. It may be interpreted either as "the spring of the caller" or "the spring of the namer." In either case it focuses on him and memorializes the power of this man to manipulate and move the hand of God rather than the gracious action of God on his behalf.[385]

---

[382] The expression נָתַן בְּיַד־PN תְּשׁוּעָה, "to give by the hand of X victory," occurs nowhere else in the OT. The NIV's rendering misses the point, interpreting this as an abstract version of the divine committal formula. But in such constructions the preposition בְּ‎ attached to יָד identifies the agent of an action, rather than the benefactor. On this use of בְּיַד־ see *DCH* 4:91.

[383] Cf. on 13:9 above.

[384] From כָּתַשׁ, "to pound, grind into powder." Cf. *HALOT,* 507, 583. The cognate also appears in extrabiblical Aramaic texts. Cf. *DNWSI,* 548–49.

[385] Cp. Gen 16:13–14, where Hagar (an Egyptian!) honors Yahweh for his kindness by calling him אֵל רֳאִי, "God [who] sees me," and renaming the well of water where God took note of her בְּאֵר לַחַי רֹאִי, "well of the living one who sees me."

20Samson led Israel for twenty years in the days of the Philistines.

EPILOGUE (15:20).   **15:20**   The narrative of Samson's Timnite affairs concludes with a note that Samson judged Israel twenty years. The form of the note recalls the conclusions to the entries in the secondary "governor" lists in 10:1–5 and 12:8–15, as well as the final note in the Jephthah narrative (12:7). Unlike earlier notes after the accounts of the deliverers, there is no reference to rest for the land (cf. 3:11,30; 5:31). On the contrary, the addition of "in the days of the Philistines" highlights the fact that this period bears the signature of the Philistines rather than the Israelites. The narrative leaves the reader wondering how this egotistical and self-centered man could have governed Israel for two decades. The fact that he did must be seen as a fulfillment of 14:4. Samson was Yahweh's agent, beginning the work of delivering the Israelites from the Philistines.

Theological and Practical Implications

Like chap. 14 this account is significant for the picture of Samson the narrator continues to paint. Even though the man is creative and energetic, there is nothing attractive in his personality. He is ruthless and self-centered. Nevertheless God continues to work. The tools available to him may be crude and imperfect, but he will deliver his people. As we have witnessed so many times before, contrary to the reader's expectations in this book God operates not on the basis of traditional orthodoxy, which teaches that obedience brings blessing; and disobedience, a curse. On the contrary, like the nation of Israel herself, Samson deserves no consideration from God. Yet Yahweh hears and delivers time and time again. His agenda for his people cannot fail, despite the people's seeming determination to commit national suicide.

SAMSON'S GAZITE AFFAIRS (16:1–31a).   The accounts of Samson's problems with women continue in chap. 16. The conclusion to chap. 15 (15:20) had teased the reader to expect a new cycle, with a new announcement of Israel's apostasy, a new notice of oppression, cry for relief, and description of deliverance. Judges 15:20 creates the impression that the Samson cycle had been completed. But the narrator has more evidence to present in his case against Israel as a whole and Samson in particular. Like the story of his Timnite adventures, the account of Samson's Gazite experiences divides into two parts, albeit quite uneven in length: 16:1–3 and 16:4–31. The common denominators in these stories are Samson's love affairs with Philistine women and the location of the events, the city of Gaza (16:1,21).

1One day Samson went to Gaza, where he saw a prostitute. He went in to spend the night with her. 2The people of Gaza were told, "Samson is here!" So they surrounded the place and lay in wait for him all night at the city gate. They made no

move during the night, saying, "At dawn we'll kill him."
³But Samson lay there only until the middle of the night. Then he got up and
took hold of the doors of the city gate, together with the two posts, and tore them
loose, bar and all. He lifted them to his shoulders and carried them to the top of
the hill that faces Hebron.

Samson and the Prostitute of Gaza (16:1–3). **16:1–3** The first cycle of
Samson's Gazite adventures is sketched in the briefest of terms. The plot is
simple and straightforward, consisting of three scenes: (1) Samson visits a
prostitute in Gaza (16:1); (2) the Gazites attempt to trap him in the city (16:2);
Samson escapes by picking up the gate of the city and carrying it off. Because
the plot is so simple, the account raises many questions.

First, why does the narrator fail to mention Yahweh in this episode?. The
story is totally secular in tone. The amazing physical feat of picking up the gate
and walking off with it is presented matter-of-factly, as if Samson's strength
may have been extraordinary, but it reflected his natural talent. Unlike the previous episodes and the story of Delilah to follow, there is no reference to the
Spirit of Yahweh coming upon him and energizing him supernaturally.

Second, why does the narrator refuse to interfere with the plot? There are no
editorial comments. The story is told with the greatest of economy.[386]

Third, why is the text itself so enigmatic? Who is this harlot? Like Samson's
mother and the Timnite woman in the previous chapter, she has no name. Furthermore, what is Samson doing forty-five miles from his home between Zorah
and Eshtaol, in Gaza, the southernmost city of the Philistine Pentapolis?[387]

Fourth, What is to be made of the sentence fragment at the beginning of
v. 2? The Hebrew text reads awkwardly, "To the Gazites saying."[388] The LXX
tries to fix the problem by adding two words which may presuppose an original
Hebrew *wayyuggad*, "and it was reported," or *wayyiwwādaʿ*, "and it was
made known."[389] The verb may have been dropped accidentally in transmission.[390] But even if the verb is reintroduced, how did Samson's reputation
spread this far south, and who reported to the Gazites that he was in town?

Fifth, what did the men of the city surround? The NIV's "The place" in v. 2
is missing in the Hebrew. Did they surround her house, or the city as a whole?
Or does the verb *sābab* ("surrounded") here mean simply "to gather"?[391]

Sixth, the last sentence of v. 2 reads literally "they kept silent all night, say-

---

[386] Note especially v. 3: Samson lay, got up, took hold of, tore, lifted, carried.

[387] On the city of Gaza in pre-Hellenistic times see H. J. Katzenstein, "Gaza," *ABD* 2.912–15.
On the archaeological exploration of the place see A. Ovadiah, *NEAEHL* 2.464–67.

[388] The NIV's smooth reading obscures the problem.

[389] The LXX adds καὶ ἀπηγγέλη. The other versions (Vg., Tg., Syr.) all reflect something
similar.

[390] See further O'Connell, *Rhetoric of the Book of Judges*, 474.

[391] Cf. Ps 118:12, where the verb describes the milling around/buzzing of bees.

ing, '… until the light of the morning, and we will kill him.' "[392] What were the men planning to do "until the light of the morning?" The NIV's "at dawn we'll kill him" obscures the difficulty of the Hebrew.

Seventh, how could Samson get past the men who lay in wait[393] at the city gate? This is rendered all the more unlikely given the nature of city gate structures in ancient Palestine, as illustrated by the following mock-up of a Canaanite/Israelite city gate:

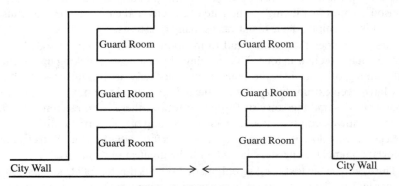

Swinging Double Gates

These elaborate gate houses were often two or three stories high with guard rooms flanking the tunnel-like opening. If the defensive gates of Gaza were like those of other cities of the time,[394] to get to the gate of the city Samson would have had to get past four or six groups of guards stationed in the guard rooms. Did the men posted here assume Samson would stay with the prostitute all night, or did they simply doze off? Surely Samson would have created considerable noise unlocking the gate, lifting the doors, and pulling the hinge posts out of their sockets. Is one to assume that Yahweh put the night sentries into a sleep so deep they did not wake up even from this racket?

Eighth, how could Samson pick up these huge gates and their bars, place them on his shoulder, and then carry them away? Based on previous incidents, the most likely answer is to be found in a special divine empowerment, as the Spirit of Yahweh rushes upon him. But why is the narrator silent on this?

---

[392] "Just before morning" offers a possible interpretation for עַד אוֹר הַבֹּקֶר. This exceptional [archaic?] usage of the preposition עַד, which usually means "unto," may find an analogue in Akk. *adi*, as in EA 96:21.

[393] On אָרַב, "to lie in wait/ambush," see above on 9:32–43 and below on 20:33,36,38; 21:20.

[394] The Philistine city of Ashdod is known to have had a four-room gate house in the eleventh century B.C. For discussion and illustrations of gate structures of this kind see Z. Herzog, "Fortifications (Levant)," *ABD* 2.844–52.

Ninth, why did Samson carry the gates to the top of a hill opposite Hebron? Was it because this was the territory of Caleb, deep in the heart of Israelite territory? Even more puzzling, how could he carry these gates forty miles (as the crow flies) uphill from the coastal town to the highland city? Was this feat made possible by another empowering rush of the Spirit of Yahweh?

The narrator does not answer any of these questions, which raises one more: What is the purpose of this text? The answer must be found in the context, not from explicit narratorial comment. Three explanations for the recounting of this event may be proposed. First, the narrator is concerned to reinforce the image of Samson the man that has emerged from chaps. 14–15. This segment reveals an Israelite inexorably drawn to the Philistines and continuing to be driven by his senses.[395] He has no scruples about fraternizing with the enemy. But this relationship is even more reprehensible than the one in chap. 14, since he does not bother to marry this woman. Furthermore, in going to Gaza to fraternize with a pagan woman he has gone as far as he could from his geographic and spiritual home. At the same time, while he appears to be a spiritual midget, physically Samson continues to cut an amazing figure. Without any reference to the Spirit of God the author forces the reader to contemplate whether or not Samson's strength was a natural talent.

Second, this brief episode adds to the picture being painted of the Philistines. Their ire against Samson is no longer limited to Timnah and environs. He has become a national target; there is a bounty on his head throughout the land.

Third, this narrative fragment introduces the reader to Gaza, which will serve as the venue for the most dramatic and climactic event in Samson's life. To continue the analogy, as concerts by world class artists are opened by colleagues of lesser importance, so this unnamed woman sets the stage for Delilah. At the same time this picture of Samson's extraordinary strength provides the background for what happens when his hair is shorn. Samson may be able to uproot the gates of a major city and carry them forty miles uphill, but he cannot withstand the wiles of a woman.

Samson and Delilah (16:4–22). The account of Samson and Delilah represents the longest story in the Samson cycle. The syntax and intentions of the plot are clear. With a deliberate combination of dialogue and repetition the narrator produces an aesthetically pleasing literary piece. Indeed, vv. 4–22 read like a self-contained short story. As we have witnessed so often in the Samson narrative, at the forefront of this story are the motifs of knowledge and ignorance, a fact reflected in the abundance of verbs of cognition and recounting: *rāʾâ*, "to see" (vv. 5,18); *higgîd*, "to tell, declare" (vv. 6,10,13,15,17,18a,18b); *yādaʿ*, "to know" (vv. 9,20); *dibbēr kĕzābîm*, "to declare falsehood," that is,

---

[395] He "saw" the woman in Gaza (cf. 14:1) and "went in to her," probably a euphemism for intercourse (cf. 15:1).

"to lead away from knowledge" (vv. 10,13); *tālal*, "to deceive" (vv. 10,13,15); and the question, *ʾêk tōʾmar*, "How can you say?" (v. 15). Samson has become a riddle to the Philistines.

But there is a powerful irony in the plot. The moment the Philistines discover the truth, Samson loses it (v. 20). At the same time, although Samson possesses important secret knowledge, he demonstrates himself the ultimate fool. He cannot learn from past events.[396] His experience with the woman of Timnah in chap. 14 does not alert him to the dangers that lurk in Delilah's world. More immediately, even as Delilah's efforts as an agent of the Philistines to destroy Samson intensify, he does not grasp the significance of what is transpiring around him. Infatuated with her and his own extraordinary talents, he is blinded to the reality she represents. In this man we witness a classic example of "all brawn and no brain."

The final episode in particular is impressive for its development of the "knowledge" motif, even though the words are never used. In v. 22 the narrator informs the reader that Samson's hair has begun to grow, raising a host of expectations. But did Samson realize this? If so, did it raise his expectations? Furthermore, what is the connection between vv. 22 and 28? Is Samson here testing God, experimenting with him to see if Yahweh had returned to him (cf. v. 20)?

In response to the last question, this chapter presents one of the supreme developments of the "testing" theme in the book.[397] First, the Philistine lords test Delilah: is she a Philistine, or is she Samson's lover?[398] Second, Delilah tests Samson: Does he love her, or is he just teasing her? Like the riddle in 14:14, for Samson this test becomes a trap. Third, Yahweh tests Samson: Will he remain true to his Nazirite vow (vv. 17,20)? Verses 15–17 contain the keys to the development of this motif as all three tests come together and Samson admits that the game is more than a test of love. Fourth, Yahweh tests Dagon: Can he stand up for himself and his people (vv. 23–30)? Fifth, Samson tests God: Will he intervene to defend his agent in the end (vv. 28–30)? Indeed in this section every speech is a test. As for Samson, the principal character, although he is able to shed the ropes and the web that bound his hair, he fails everyone's tests, ultimately being trapped in his own words.

---

[396] Cf. J. B. Vickery, "In Strange Ways: The Story of Samson," in *Images of God and Man: Old Testament Short Stories in Literary Focus*, ed. B. O. Long (Sheffield: Almond Press, 1981), 67.

[397] Cf. Polzin's treatment of the theme in *Moses and the Deuteronomist*, 191–93.

[398] Though some suggest that since the valley of Sorek bordered Danite territory, since the name Delilah is thoroughly Semitic, and since she is the only paramor of Samson who is named, she was an Israelite rather than a Philistine woman. Cf. J. M. Sasson, "Who Cut Samson's Hair? (And Other Trifling Issues Raised by Judges 16)," *Prooftexts 8* (1988): 334–35.

⁴Some time later, he fell in love with a woman in the Valley of Sorek whose name was Delilah. ⁵The rulers of the Philistines went to her and said, "See if you can lure him into showing you the secret of his great strength and how we can overpower him so we may tie him up and subdue him. Each one of us will give you eleven hundred shekels of silver."

Setting the Stage for Samson's Fall (16:4–5). **16:4** Verse 4 consists of only nine words in the Hebrew text, but it presents the reader with the basic information needed to understand the story that follows.

The time. "Some time later" (lit., "after this") links this episode chronologically with the preceding. This is reinforced by the narrator's omission of a specific subject for the following verb. In English translation the pronoun "he" provides the subject, but apart from vv. 1–3 this pronoun lacks an antecedent.

The problem. "He loved [ʾāhab] a woman." This has been Samson's problem from the beginning. Here the riddle of the Philistines in 14:18 finds its supreme answer. Samson's love of women is sweeter than honey and stronger than a lion. For the moment the woman remains unnamed because the primary issue at hand in this episode is Samson's disposition, not her identity. Unlike the references to his earlier affairs (cf. 14:1; 15:1), for the first time the text omits any reference to Samson "seeing." Whereas previously he had been driven by his senses, now womanizing has become a fundamental aspect of his character.

The place. "In the valley of Sorek." The problem with Samson was not simply that he loved a woman but the kind of woman he loved. In principal there is nothing wrong with a man loving a woman. After all, marriage, an institution sanctioned by God, depends upon the love of a man for his wife and the love of a woman for her husband. The issue here is the kind of person he loves. Rather than identifying her by ethnic or national affiliation, the narrator identifies the place where Samson expressed his love. As noted earlier, Sorek was the name of a wadi valley that ran from the hill country of Judah and Dan down to the Mediterranean coast, through the northern part of Philistia. Now the reader learns that the reference to the hilltop of Hebron referred to in v. 3 serves as a foil against which to read this event. It looked for a moment as though Samson had turned his back on the Philistines and set his sights on his own Israelite people. But the reader is disappointed. Rather than loving an Israelite woman from the high country of Hebron and orienting himself toward his people to the east, he attaches himself to a woman from the low country of Sorek, whose ethnic and communication links are all westward.

The woman. For the first time in the Samson narrative a woman is named. But like many other elements in the Samson narrative. the name Delilah is a riddle. Etymologically, the most likely explanation relates the name to Arabic *dalla,* "to flirt,"[399] but the name may be an artificial punning construct consisting of *d* + *lylh,* "of the night."[400] By this interpretation the name may offer an intentional allusion to Samson's blindness and fit in well with the motif of light and darkness that plays such an important role in the Samson narrative. Alternatively, the name may simply be a Philistine name whose meaning remains unknown.

16:5 If v. 4 sets the stage for the following account, v. 5 sets the agenda. When a Hebrew man falls in love with a Philistine woman, we may/should expect a clash of cultures. The story does not disappoint. When the Philistines discover that Samson has arrived in Gath, they take steps to capture him. Reports of his strength have preceded him, however, and the residents of Gath realize that mastering him physically will be a greater challenge than overcoming his love. So serious a menace is he that the governors of all the Pentapolitan cities, referred to by the non-Semitic term *sĕrānîm,*[401] unite to conspire to capture him. Like an ancient version of a spy movie, this plot involves a heroic male, a female agent, money, love, death, and ironic reversal.

The strategy of the governors of Pentapolitan Philistia involves engaging Delilah to entice Samson to reveal the secret of his strength. Just as the Timnites had tried to get Samson's wife to excavate the mind of the man for the solution to the riddle (14:15),[402] so now they hope to use Delilah to uncover the answer to the riddle of his person. Their objective is expressed in four verbs: "to discover/see" *(rāʾâ)* where his great strength resides; "to over-

---

[399] Boling (*Judges,* 248) defines the name as "flirtatious," analogous to Arabic *dallatum.* Other possibilities include derivation from דלל I, "to hang," perhaps an allusion to Delilah's hairstyle (cf. דַּלָּה, "hair," in *Cant.* 7:6; cf. Segert, "Paranomasia in the Samson Narrative," 460); derivation from דלל II, "to be submissive, low," but this seems unlikely in view of her connections with the Philistine nobility; association with Akk. *dalālum,* "to worship, honor, praise," as in the Akk. personal names, Dalīl-ᵈIshtar and Dalīlūša. On these names see J. J. Stamm, *Die akkadische Namengebung* (1939; reprint, Darmstadt: Wissenschaftliche Buchgesellschaft, 1968), 277. Related names have been recognized in Ug. Daḫli (√*dll,* *UT,* 385, #665) and Safaitic Daḫl (masculine) and Dalilat (feminine), on which see G. Ryckmans, *Les noms propres sud-sémitiques* (Leiden: Brill, 1934–35,) 1.66.

[400] Hb. דִּי/דְּ would be cognate to Northwest Semitic genitive particle דִּי, on which see *DNWSI* 1.310–18.

[401] Possible occurrences of the root have been recognized in twelfth century B.C. Ug. texts (*UT,* 452, #1797) and a fifth century B.C. Aramaic text from Elephantine (Donner & Röllig, *KAI* 271:B:4; cf. 2:324–252; but see the caution in *DNWSI* 2.803). In the OT the designation was applied to rulers in the Philistine Pentapolis prior to the time of David (cf. Josh 13:3; 1 Sam 21:10–15, where Achish is identified as the king [מֶלֶךְ] of Gath). While the etymology of the word remains a mystery, it is commonly associated with Neo-Hittite/Luwian *tarwanas* and/or Greek τυραννος, from which we get English "tyrant." This seems to have been an Indo-European expression brought with the Philistines to the Levant from the Aegean. Cf. Kitchen, "The Philistines," *POTT,* 67. Dothan and Dothan (*People of the Sea,* 5,7) understand these סְרָנִים as "warlords."

[402] The Hb. word פָּתָה (*piel*) is the same. In *qal* it means "to be open"; in *piel,* "to open up, expose."

power" *(nûkal)* him; "to bind" *(ʾāsar)* him; "to torture" *(ʿannâ)* him. Whereas in chap. 14 the Philistines had employed blackmail to engage Samson's wife in their plot against him, here they adopt a positive incentive, offering Delilah an exorbitant reward of 5,500 shekels of silver—1,100 shekels per governor. Although the value of a unit of silver fluctuated in biblical times, the significance of this figure can only be appreciated when this reward is compared with other transactions in Scripture. This is more than three times the weight of the gold retained by Gideon after the victory over the Midianite kings (Judg 8:26). With these figures we may also compare the four hundred shekels of silver paid by Abraham to purchase a burial plot for his wife (Gen 24:15,19), the fifty shekels David paid Araunah for his oxen and threshing floor (2 Sam 24:24), the seventeen shekels Jeremiah paid to purchase a field (Jer 32:9), and the thirty shekels set as a price for a slave in Exod 21:32. Viewing this figure as unreasonable, some have suggested deletion of *ʾelep,* "thousand," but even then the total of five hundred shekels is an exorbitant price. Without textual evidence to the contrary, however, the figure given should be accepted and placed alongside all the other extravagant elements of Samson's life. Everything in his life happens in the superlative degree.

[6]So Delilah said to Samson, "Tell me the secret of your great strength and how you can be tied up and subdued."

[7]Samson answered her, "If anyone ties me with seven fresh thongs that have not been dried, I'll become as weak as any other man."

[8]Then the rulers of the Philistines brought her seven fresh thongs that had not been dried, and she tied him with them. [9]With men hidden in the room, she called to him, "Samson, the Philistines are upon you!" But he snapped the thongs as easily as a piece of string snaps when it comes close to a flame. So the secret of his strength was not discovered.

[10]Then Delilah said to Samson, "You have made a fool of me; you lied to me. Come now, tell me how you can be tied."

[11]He said, "If anyone ties me securely with new ropes that have never been used, I'll become as weak as any other man."

[12]So Delilah took new ropes and tied him with them. Then, with men hidden in the room, she called to him, "Samson, the Philistines are upon you!" But he snapped the ropes off his arms as if they were threads.

[13]Delilah then said to Samson, "Until now, you have been making a fool of me and lying to me. Tell me how you can be tied."

He replied, "If you weave the seven braids of my head into the fabric [on the loom] and tighten it with the pin, I'll become as weak as any other man." So while he was sleeping, Delilah took the seven braids of his head, wove them into the fabric [14]and tightened it with the pin.

Again she called to him, "Samson, the Philistines are upon you!" He awoke from his sleep and pulled up the pin and the loom, with the fabric.

[15]Then she said to him, "How can you say, 'I love you,' when you won't confide

in me? This is the third time you have made a fool of me and haven't told me the secret of your great strength." [16]With such nagging she prodded him day after day until he was tired to death.

[17]So he told her everything. "No razor has ever been used on my head," he said, "because I have been a Nazirite set apart to God since birth. If my head were shaved, my strength would leave me, and I would become as weak as any other man."

[18]When Delilah saw that he had told her everything, she sent word to the rulers of the Philistines, "Come back once more; he has told me everything." So the rulers of the Philistines returned with the silver in their hands. [19]Having put him to sleep on her lap, she called a man to shave off the seven braids of his hair, and so began to subdue him. And his strength left him.

[20]Then she called, "Samson, the Philistines are upon you!"

The Implementation of the Plan (16:6–20). The process by which the plot is executed and the Philistines discover the answer to their riddle involves four discreet stages. The reports of each phase, particularly the first three, are constructed with a highly repetitious style, as the following table (based on the Hebrew)[403] illustrates:

Narrative Element	I	II	III	IV
	6–9	10–12	13–14	15–20
Delilah said to Samson/him	x	x	x	x
Look, you have deceived me		x	x	x
and you have told me lies		x	x	
Please tell me	x	x	x	x^a
where your great strength is	x			x
and how you may be bound	x	x	x	
to torture you	x			
[. . . . .]				x
So he [Samson] said to her	x	x	x	x
[. . . . .]				x
If	x	x	x	x
Then I shall become weak	x	x	x	x

Narrative Element	I	II	III	IV
	6–9	10–12	13–14	15–20
And become like another/any man	x	x	x	x
Then the Philistine governors . . .	x			
So she/Delilah	x	x	x	x
[. . . . .]				x
Then she said [to him]	x	x	x	x
The Philistines are upon you Samson	x	x	x	x
Then he	x	x	x	x

a. A variation, "But you have not told me."

The first and third episodes are held together by the number seven: seven fresh undried tendons (I) and seven locks of hair (III). But the tension increases from episode to episode as Samson teases Delilah, toys with her countrymen, and moves ever closer to the brink of disaster. The result is an artful building of suspense, which heightens the reader's impatience with this man who is both extraordinarily powerful and extraordinarily stupid.

The first attempt.   **16:6–9**   Motivated by the reward offered her and perhaps by a[n undeclared] sense of loyalty to her countrymen, Delilah agrees to cooperate with the Philistine lords in their plot to capture Samson and to torture him. When she questioned him concerning the secret of his remarkable strength, she may have been surprised at his willingness to answer her. Samson informs her that if the Philistine governors would bind him with seven tendons from an animal freshly slaughtered,[404] that is, which have not yet dried, then he would be reduced to the strength of any ordinary human being.[405] The answer seems ridiculous to the modern reader, and it probably was intended so by Samson. But it is not as innocent as either he or the reader might imagine. On the contrary, his specification of "fresh" and "undried" sinews means that once more he is trivializing his Nazirite vow. Like the fresh jawbone in 15:15, undried sinews would have been construed as still parts of a corpse. By inviting

---

[403] With vv. 13c–14a restored on the basis of the LXX. See below.

[404] The meaning of יְתָרִים is uncertain, but the word is used elsewhere of bowstrings (Ps 11:2; Job 30:11) and tent cords (Job 4:21).

[405] The use of אָדָם, ʾādām, rather than אִישׁ, "man," reflects Samson's own recognition of his superhuman strength.

Delilah to tie him up with these, Samson was asking for contact with an object that was unclean for him in particular. On the assumption that Samson was serious, Delilah procures the sinews through the governors and ties him up. But when she wakes him, announcing the arrival of the Philistines, the cords disintegrated like thread *(pĕtîl)* in a fire. The first attempt by the Philistines was a failure.

The second attempt.　**16:10–12**　Accusing him of lying, Delilah renews her appeals to Samson to reveal the secret of his strength, specifically how he may be bound. Having duped Delilah with an absurd answer the first time, Samson now offers a reasonable solution. If she will tie him tightly with new ropes *(ʿăbōtîm),*[406] he will become weak like any ordinary man. As in the previous case, when Delilah has tied him up and announced the arrival of the Philistines, he snaps these ropes like a thread.

The third attempt.　**16:13–14**　The Hebrew text of scene three is badly damaged and is generally restored on the basis of the Septuagintal reading.[407] Samson's instructions for Delilah in the third episode reflect his flair for hyperbole and the absurd. If she would take the seven locks[408] of his head and integrate them into the fabric being woven on a loom and then secure[409] them with a pin, he would be as vulnerable as any ordinary man. Now he is really playing with fire, since his hair represent the key to the riddle of Samson. The logistics of these instructions are hard to imagine. Presumably Samson would lie down on the floor next to the loom, near enough so Delilah could weave his long hair into the warp and tighten it with the weaver's pin. To her dismay, after she had followed his instructions, Samson had fallen asleep, and she had signaled the arrival of the Philistines, Samson simply pulled out the pin and was free.

The fourth attempt.　**16:15–16**　The narrative slows to a snail's pace as the climax of the drama approaches. After three failed attempts at discovering

---

[406] The word is the same as in 15:13–14.

[407] Though not all of the LXX text is accepted as authentic. εἰς τὸν τοῖκον, "to the wall," and καὶ ἐφυφανῆς ὡς ἐπὶ πῆκυν, "and weave [it] as upon a beam," seem to have been inserted by an overzealous translator who forgot for the moment that he was dealing with a part of a loom apparatus and not the loom itself. The error in the MT seems to have arisen because the scribe's eye having skipped from בַיָּתֵד וַתִּתְקַע, "and fasten it with a pin," in v. 13 to בַיָּתֵד וַתִּתְקַע, "So she fastened it with a pin." Cf. Tov, *Textual Criticism,* 239–40; O'Connell, *Rhetoric of the Book of Judges,* 474.

[408] Hb. מַחְלְפוֹת (NIV "braids") occurs only in this context (vv. 13–19) in the OT, but it is attested in an ancient Phoenician inscription (see *DNWSI* 2.612). For attempts to relate the connection between Samson's seven-locked hair and his extraordinary strength to ANE literature and sculptured portrayal of heroes, see R. Mayer-Opificius, "Simson, der sechslockige Held?" *UF* 14 (1982): 149–51; R. Wenning, "Der siebenlockige Held Simson. Literarische und ikonographische Beobachtungen zu Ri 13–16," *BN* 17 (1982): 43–55.

[409] The combination of verb וַתִּתְקַע, "to fasten, tighten," and object, יָתֵד, "peg, pin," links this account with 4:21, leading the reader to wonder if Delilah will use the pin as a weapon of murder. Cf. also 3:21, where וַתִּתְקַע had also described the penetration of a murder weapon.

the secrets of Samson's strength, Delilah adopts the blackmailing tactic of his Timnite wife in 14:16–17. She asserts that his love for her cannot be genuine if he is not fully committed to her[410] and then adds a double accusation of deception.[411] In all of these statements intimacy is the key. There is no love if there is no sharing of the innermost secrets of the heart. This had been the issue with regard to the riddle of the wedding, and this is the issue regarding the riddle of Samson's strength. Although the narrator omits any reference to Delilah's weeping,[412] like her Timnite predecessor Delilah nags[413] and torments[414] Samson "to death."[415] The reference to death is ominous.

16:17 Samson's will is finally broken. Verse 17a summarizes his capitulation to her incessant pressure. "He told her everything" (NIV) is literally "everything of his heart," that is, he "bared his soul." This expression answers directly to Delilah's accusation in v. 15 that his heart was not with her. Verse 17b summarizes his answer to Delilah's specific question: "Tell me the secret of your great strength?" For the first time Samson answers with candor and draws a direct link between his uncut hair and strength. He tells Delilah that if she cuts off his hair his strength will be gone. To the modern reader this connection sounds superstitious, but the Philistines immediately acted on it. But Samson is not content to leave it here. Like one who casts a pearl before a sow,[416] albeit in a veiled manner, he shares with this agent and representative of the uncircumcised Philistines the sacred truth that his strength comes from God: he has been a Nazirite of God from before his birth.

This confession is remarkable for two reasons. First, it declares to Delilah and the reader Samson's awareness of his high theological and spiritual calling. If Delilah the Philistine knew anything about the ascetic Nazirite vow, at this point she must have wondered how Samson could be so casual in his relations with not only foreign women but women of ill-repute like the prostitute of Gaza. More specifically, she must have wondered how he could allow himself to be defiled by contact with the fresh tendons that had been used to tie him up. But Samson's problem with his vow is not so much that he willfully violates it; he simply does not take it seriously. Like his strength, and the people around him, it is a toy to be played with, not a calling to be fulfilled.

Second, in a highly significant moment Samson refers to the deity by the

---

[410] Hb. אֵין אִתָּךְ לִבְּךָ, "Your heart/mind is not with me," means his commitment is elsewhere.

[411] By contrast, she has been perfectly open with him from the beginning. Cf. v. 6.

[412] Unlike the Timnite woman, her life does not appear to hang on the outcome of this case, only her fortune.

[413] The verb הֵצִיק, "to pressure," was encountered earlier in 14:17.

[414] Hb. אָלַץ (piel), "to importune," occurs only here in the OT.

[415] The English idiom captures the meaning of קְצָרָה נַפְשׁ לָמוּת, "the soul is depressed to the point of death," which means to be worn out by the importunity, to reach the limit of one's patience/endurance.

[416] Matt 7:6. Cf. the "heifer" metaphor in 14:18.

generic designation ʾĕlōhîm rather than the name of Yahweh. Accordingly, so far as Delilah is concerned, he could be an ascetic devotee of any god. At the same time, given the character and conduct of the man, the narrator probably was relieved to have Samson put it this way; it limited the damage he was causing for the reputation of the God of Israel.

16:18–20a The pace of the narrative continues to slow as the denouement of this four-act drama approaches. The narrator rivets the reader's attention on Delilah by his detailed attention to her actions. In the process we observe a dramatic shift of power from the strong man to his "lover" and the fulfillment of the riddle in 14:18: sweetness has won over strength. Samson has fallen. The real tragedy occurs not when Samson is overcome and tortured by the Philistine men (v. 21) but when he bares his soul to this pagan woman.

As already intimated, in vv. 18–20a the narrator intentionally thrusts the character of Delilah into the foreground by presenting her as the subject of all the significant verbs. (1) Delilah sees[417] that Samson has finally been open and truthful with her. What is unique about this episode is that she does not need to treat Samson's latest instruction as a hypothesis to be confirmed or disproved by experimentation. She has been burned three times by his lies; this time she recognizes the truthfulness of his statement. The firmness of her conviction is demonstrated by the narrator's deliberate echo of v. 15 in v. 18 and the fact that she calls the Philistine governors even before she starts to work on Samson. In fact, she is so confident and compelling that the Philistines are also convinced, so they arrive at her place with the reward jingling in their pockets. But the narrator leaves the reader to guess why this is so. (2) Delilah sends for the Philistine lords, dictating the message they are to hear. (3) Delilah gets Samson to sleep on her lap. (4) Delilah calls for a barber to come and snip off[418] his hair.[419] (5) She begins to torture Samson.[420] The verb "to afflict" is the same word Delilah had used in setting forth her agenda in v. 6. (6) Delilah announces, "The Philistines are upon you" (v. 20a) and with this announcement turns him over to them. Her assignment has been completed.

Delilah's success in neutralizing Samson's strength raises serious questions about the realism of this story, particularly the soundness of Samson's sleep in the last two episodes. When considering episode 3, we might have asked how

---

[417] The verb רָאָה, "to see" links v. 18 with v. 5. She has fulfilled the mission of the Philistine governors.

[418] The MT reads וַתְּגַלַּח, "and she shaved"; it probably should be revocalized וַתַּגְלַח, "and she caused [him] to be shaved" (cf. O'Connell, *Rhetoric of the Book of Judges*, 474), a sense reflected in numerous Hb. MSS that read וַיְגַלַּח, as well as the LXX.

[419] Sasson ("Who Cut Samson's Hair?" 336–38) argues that the man Delilah called is Samson, to test how soundly he is sleeping, and that the MT's feminine form, וַתְּגַלַּח, "and she shaved," should be retained.

[420] Thus the MT, וַתָּחֶל לְעַנּוֹתוֹ, in contrast to the LXX, which reflects וַיָּחֶל לְעָנוֹת, "and he began to weaken."

Samson could remain asleep while Delilah weaves his hair into the fabric on her loom and then fastens it with the weavers pin. But the issue had not been as serious there because when Samson is awakened he is able to extricate himself effortlessly from the contraption. In episode 4 the question is how Delilah could get him to sleep on her lap, call in the barber, and have him cut off his hair without him waking up. In response it should be noted that while this is remarkable, it is not new here. It has been anticipated in 16:1–3, where the Gazite guards had slept so soundly that Samson was able to remove the gates and carry them off. There we had concluded that this deep sleep must have been divinely induced. Now the tables seem to have turned. Instead of making Philistines oblivious to events transpiring around them, Yahweh puts his own agent to sleep. Samson can endure this so long as he retains his strength when he wakes up, but if he does not, he is lost. And this is precisely what happens during episode 4.

The timing of Yahweh's departure from Samson is not clear. The evaporation of his strength is associated most immediately with Delilah's torturous actions (v. 19b). This may have transpired earlier, however, either the moment he bared his soul to her and revealed the source of his strength, thereby announcing his special status with God, or as his hair was being cut. The narrator does not answer the question for us here or in the following description of Samson's rude awakening.

He awoke from his sleep and thought, "I'll go out as before and shake myself free." But he did not know that the LORD had left him. **21**Then the Philistines seized him, gouged out his eyes and took him down to Gaza. Binding him with bronze shackles, they set him to grinding in the prison. **22**But the hair on his head began to grow again after it had been shaved.

The Sun Has Set (16:20b–22). **16:20b** The climactic moment in this tragic account is rendered all the more powerful by the narrator's skillful use of direct speech. But how pathetic is the sound of "I'll go out as before and shake myself free."[421] This has been the story of his life. He has come and gone as he has pleased. No one has told him what he could or could not do—until now, that is. But the narrator reserves the most significant comments for himself. In v. 19 he had already observed that Samson's strength had left him. Now in v. 20 he announces the much more tragic theological reality: Samson did not know that Yahweh had left him.[422] The link between God and Samson's super-

---

[421] On the verb נָעַר (here *niphal*), see *HALOT*, 707. D. Wolfers ("The Verb *nᶜr* in the Bible," *DD* 18 [1989–1990]: 27–31) argues for a meaning "strip, expose" in all occurrences of the root. Here the word plays on the noun נַעַר, "young man," which Samson thought he was. Cp. this with נְעֹרֶת, "tow, string," used in v. 9 as a figure of weakness.

[422] Note how the final clause of v. 20 echoes the final clause of v. 19 (lit.): "and his strength turned from upon him" (v. 19) versus "Yahweh had turned from upon him" (v. 20).

natural strength had been hinted at in several earlier events where the rushing of the Spirit of Yahweh upon him had resulted in extraordinary physical feats. But to be abandoned by God is the worst fate anyone can experience. Now the divinely chosen agent of Yahweh has lost him. Samson's game is over. For a whole chapter he had been playing with his God-given talent; now he discovers that he has frittered it all away.

16:21 As the Samson saga reaches its denouement, the ironies in his life come to full fruition. Overnight this man is transformed from one whose life is governed by sight and whose actions are determined by what is right in his own eyes into a blind man with eyes gouged out. Overnight a life of coming and going as he pleases turns into a life of bondage and imprisonment. Overnight the person who had spent his life insulting and humiliating others becomes the object of their humiliation. Overnight a man with the highest conceivable calling, the divinely commissioned agent of deliverance for Israel, is cast down to the lowest position imaginable: grinding flour for others in prison.[423] Samson's sun has set!

Why Samson was transferred to Gaza and imprisoned there we may only speculate. Perhaps the Philistines feared the Israelites would try to rescue him, so they removed him as far away as possible. Perhaps they intended hereby to compensate the Gazites for their own humiliation in v. 13. Whatever the reason, Samson's experiences are paradigmatic for what happens to Israel when she fritters away her high calling, lives by what is right in her own eyes, and provokes Yahweh to abandon her. According to the covenant curses in Leviticus 26 and Deuteronomy 28, this is precisely the fate the nation should expect for persistent rebellion against the covenant Lord. Like Samson, the nation will be seized, blinded, exiled, imprisoned, and humiliated with forced labor. If our understanding of the circumstances and date of composition of this book are correct, the narrator may have been writing this against the background of the Northern Kingdom's fall to Assyria in 734–722 B.C. But this is not the only context for which the message of this chapter has special relevance, for Samson's experiences to a large extent represent the experiences of his people. In the dark days of the judges, because of her apostasy, Israel repeatedly found herself at the mercy of alien powers; and just as in Samson's case, the question of whether or not she would survive kept surfacing as a very real issue.

16:22 It is impossible to determine how much time the narrator has tele-

---

[423] In subjecting Samson to this kind of punishment, the Philistines were following a common ANE custom. In Mesopotamia defeated enemies were often blinded by gouging out their eyes and then humiliated by being forced to perform the most menial of tasks, those customarily assigned to slaves and women. For discussion see K. van der Toorn, "Judges XVI 21 in the Light of the Akkadian Sources," *VT* 36 (1986): 248–53. Beyond the commonness of the practice, from the perspective of the Philistines, there is ironic justice in Samson grinding grain, since he had destroyed so much of their crop.

scoped between vv. 21 and 22, but in the course of time, as is the case with any man, Samson's hair begins to grow back. Perhaps more than any other statement in the book, this simple but pregnant assertion elevates the narrator from the class of gifted writers to geniuses who in our day are rewarded for their literary skill with Nobel and Pulitzer prizes. In Crenshaw's words, "With a single stroke of the artist's brush the ominous skies give way to the promise of brilliant sunshine; all is not lost, for hair grows back."[424]

The key word is *wayyāḥel,* "it began." The word was encountered first in 10:18 and will appear later in 20:31,39,40, but it plays a special role in the story of Samson. In 13:5 the divine envoy had announced to Samson's mother that he would "begin" to deliver Israel from the Philistines. In 13:25 the narrator observed that at Mahaneh Dan the Spirit of Yahweh had "begun" to stir Samson. But in 16:19 Delilah's tormenting of Samson was only the "beginning" of his troubles. With this word the author manipulates the reader's emotions. Now, in the darkest pit of despair the word reappears (v. 22) to lift our hopes, raise our spirits, and create excitement at [re]new[ed] possibilities. The sight of Samson's seemingly hopeless lot in the prison grinding flour raises the question in the mind of the reader whether or not Samson can come back. Can he extricate himself from his irrevocably maimed condition? Can he still play a role in Yahweh's agenda? Can the life of this one born under such auspicious circumstances and with such [divine] promise still be salvaged? Hair grows back, and for one whose role is linked to hair, this growth offers hope.

The picture of Samson that is portrayed in this chapter is not a pleasant one. This man is indeed all brawn and no brain. He knows Delilah's motives from the beginning (v. 6), but instead of fleeing from disaster he plays with its agents. Stupidly he plays with his strength and lets others play with it as well. This is more than the seduction of a red-blooded male. It is the seduction of one who claims to be and in the mind of the narrator was called to be the servant of Yahweh. In the end his vitality is drained away, and he is left without strength, without sight, without freedom, without dignity, and without God! But like the fortunes predicted for Israel in Deuteronomy 28–30, for Samson there will be grace in the end. The phoenix will rise from the ashes to see another day.

23Now the rulers of the Philistines assembled to offer a great sacrifice to Dagon their god and to celebrate, saying, "Our god has delivered Samson, our enemy, into our hands."
24When the people saw him, they praised their god, saying,
"Our god has delivered our enemy
into our hands,
the one who laid waste our land
and multiplied our slain."

---

[424] Crenshaw, *Samson,* 501.

²⁵While they were in high spirits, they shouted, "Bring out Samson to entertain us." So they called Samson out of the prison, and he performed for them.

When they stood him among the pillars, ²⁶Samson said to the servant who held his hand, "Put me where I can feel the pillars that support the temple, so that I may lean against them." ²⁷Now the temple was crowded with men and women; all the rulers of the Philistines were there, and on the roof were about three thousand men and women watching Samson perform. ²⁸Then Samson prayed to the LORD, "O Sovereign LORD, remember me. O God, please strengthen me just once more, and let me with one blow get revenge on the Philistines for my two eyes." ²⁹Then Samson reached toward the two central pillars on which the temple stood. Bracing himself against them, his right hand on the one and his left hand on the other, ³⁰Samson said, "Let me die with the Philistines!" Then he pushed with all his might, and down came the temple on the rulers and all the people in it. Thus he killed many more when he died than while he lived.

³¹Then his brothers and his father's whole family went down to get him. They brought him back and buried him between Zorah and Eshtaol in the tomb of Manoah his father.

One More Sunrise—Then the Final Sunset (16:23–31a). The circumstantial clause in v. 23 signals the commencement of a new episode and a new day. The venue is new as well, and Delilah is out of the picture. Between vv. 21–22,23 the scene shifts from the prison house, where the broken Samson sits isolated and humiliated, to a Philistine palace, where the governors and the people are assembled for celebration. The celebration transpires in two parts, the first of which is dedicated to the praise of Dagon, the god of the Philistines (vv. 23–24); the second, to amusement at the expense of the captive (vv. 25–27). The description of the adoration of Dagon divides further into two parts, the first highlighting the roles of the governors (v. 23) and the second describing the activity of the people.

16:23 Verse 23a suggests that the celebration over the capture of Samson began with a gathering of the governors of the major Philistine cities. This is appropriate not only because they were the civil leaders but especially since they were the ones who had successfully conspired against Samson. The narrator notes two purposes for their gathering: to present a great sacrifice to Dagon and to rejoice. One may assume from the former that the festivities took place in the temple of Dagon, the patron deity of the Philistines.⁴²⁵

Although the Philistines were non-Semitic peoples, having originated in the Aegean,⁴²⁶ like the Israelites they appear to have adapted quickly to prevailing religious ideologies in Canaan. The name Dagon is related to the Hebrew (and Canaanite) word for grain, *dāgān,* which suggests he was pri-

---

⁴²⁵ Note the narrator's reference to "Dagon *their god*" and the Philistines own reference to him as "our god" (16:23–24).
⁴²⁶ See above on 13:5.

marily an agricultural divinity.[427] The antiquity of the veneration of this god in the ancient Near East is confirmed by third millennium B.C. texts from Ebla and the early second millennium documents from Mari. At Ugarit, which was destroyed by the Philistines, Dagon was recognized as the father of Baal, the weather deity, one of whose titles was *bn dgn,* "son of Dagon." In the Old Testament Dagon is always associated with the Philistines (cf. 1 Samuel 5), which demonstrates that the Israelites were not the only newcomers who were seduced by Canaanite religion.[428]

The direct quotation in v. 23b, which may have been chanted by the governors, captures the theme of the celebration. The declaration is significant in three respects. First, even though Dagon has been out of the picture in the preceding episodes and the narrator has presented the captivity of Samson as the result of human decision and machinations, the Philistines' version of the divine committal formula[429] credits the success of the mission to the divinity. Within the ancient religious context this is not unexpected since Near Easterners of the time generally viewed life from a theological perspective. To them the gods ultimately determine the fate and fortune of human beings. If one nation defeats another in battle, this reflects the superiority of the god of the victors over the god of the defeated.

Second, although Dagon was primarily associated with grain and harvest,[430] this chant portrays him in a military role, as the one giving the enemy into the Philistines' hands. This also is typically ancient Near Eastern. In many cases functional deities were adopted as patron divinities of specific localities, which means they bore the primary responsibility for the prosperity and security of the locale.

Third, the focus of Philistine concern is not Israel but Samson. He is the pest wreaking havoc on them wherever he goes. The narrator has recognized earlier that the Philistines have nothing to fear in the Israelite nation as a whole because they are content to live with the Philistines on the Philistines' terms.

16:24 It is obvious from v. 24 that the Philistine leaders were not alone in celebrating the capture of Samson. It seems that he was put on public display for all the people who were gathered. When they saw Samson, they broke out in spontaneous praise for their god.[431] Their song begins like the chant of the

---

[427] One tradition understands Dagon as the inventor of the plough. Cf. J. Black and A. Green, *Gods, Demons and Symbols of Ancient Mesopotamia: An Illustrated Dictionary* (London: British Museum Press, 1992), 56.

[428] On this deity see further J. F. Healey, "Dagon," *DDD,* 408–13O; L. K. Handy, "Dagon," *ABD* 2.1–3. Both articles provide further bibliography.

[429] On the formula, "*DN* [divine name] gave *X* [enemy name] into the hands of" see above, p 142f.

[430] It is appropriate that Samson be humiliated at the festival of the grain god, since he had earlier burned the crops of the Philistines. Cf. 15:4–5.

[431] The verb for praise, וַיְהַלְלוּ *(wayĕhalĕlû),* also underlies "hallelujah" (הַלְלוּיָהּ), the Israelite expression of praise to Yahweh so common in the psalms.

governors but adds an expository line. Together their utterance takes the form of poetic verse consisting of two roughly parallel lines (lit.):[432]

> Our god has given Samson our enemy into our hand;
> And the destroyer[433] of our land, who has multiplied our slain.

These quotations are important because they give the reader direct entrée into the minds of the Philistines, particularly what they think of Samson: he is "our enemy," "the devastator of our land," "the slayer of many of us." But like the Song of Deborah in chap. 5, this is an enthusiastic and lavish song of praise to Dagon that highlights the magnitude of their victory over their enemy. Ironically, the Philistines are singing the songs that should have been rolling off the lips of the Israelites.

16:25   But their celebration did not end with praise to their god. At the height of their merriment, when the celebrants were in high spirits,[434] they called for the trophy Dagon had delivered into their hands, Samson himself. When Samson was brought in from the dungeon, they placed him between the pillars at the center of the building so he could entertain[435] the crowd. Although no Philistine temple to Dagon has been discovered in Gaza, excavations at Tell Qasile have revealed a building in Stratum X that illuminates the impressions left by this text. The roof and upper story of this large temple were supported by two cedar pillars slightly less than three meters apart set on round stone bases.[436]

In v. 26 the attention shifts to the man who has been placed in the center of the crowd and of the building, the man who was the victim of Philistine torture and the butt of Philistine jokes. Verses 26–30 divide into four episodes, based on Samson's actions as reflected in four key verbs.

16:26   In the first episode (vv. 26–27) Samson requests a young boy standing nearby to guide his hands to the pillars supporting the structure, ostensibly so he could lean against them. The reference to this lad as a *naʿar* ("young boy") precludes a firm identification. The fact that he was holding Samson's hand suggests he may have been the attendant who brought him up from the dungeon.[437] The image is pathetic: this Israelite "hero" is blinded, imprisoned, ridiculed, and dependent on a young boy. He

---

[432] Boling's deletion (*Judges*, 251) of the relative pronoun and the sign of the accusative as secondary accretions is gratuitous and based on too rigid a definition of poetic parallelism.

[433] The *hiphil* form of the verb חָרַב means "to reduce to ruins."

[434] *Kethib* כִּי טוֹב לְבָּם, translates "because their hearts were good," but the NIV rightly follows *qere* in reading כְּטוֹב לְבָּם, "when their hearts were good."

[435] The summons and the report employ two variations of the same verb: יְשַׂחֶק and יְצַחֶק, "to make sport, entertain," from שָׂחַק and צָחַק, both of which mean "to laugh."

[436] See A. Mazar, "A Philistine Temple at Tell Qasile," *BA* 36 (1973): 43–48; id., *Archaeology of the Land of the Bible*, 319–23.

[437] On נַעַר as "attendant" see 7:10; 9:54; 1 Sam 31:4.

tells the lad he wants to touch[438] the pillar so he can lean on it, but he has much bigger plans.

16:27 Verse 27 is constructed as a circumstantial clause, adding important details that help the reader understand the following episodes and highlight the magnitude of Samson's final achievement. Whereas earlier (v. 24) the celebrants had been referred to vaguely as "the people," now the narrator notes that Samson's audience consisted of male and female revelers and all the pentapolitan governors (*sĕrānîm*). In addition to those in the main room with Samson, there were three thousand spectators on the roof being amused by Samson. The scene is difficult to visualize. Perhaps there was a balcony or terrace surrounding the central courtyard where Samson was standing. The figure three thousand seems inordinately high, but it should be interpreted along the lines of other high figures in the book.[439]

16:28 The second episode (vv. 28–29a) has Samson calling out to Yahweh for help one last time. On the surface the expression "Samson called out" (NIV, "prayed"), answers to the Philistines' summons to have him brought out of the dungeon (v. 25), but with this phrase the narrative reaches its climax. The author casts Samson's prayer as an impassioned plea for aid. He prefaces his plea by naming his addressee *ʾădōnāy yhwh*, "O sovereign LORD," which represents an advance over 15:18 and signals that Samson's attention is turned away from the image of the deity in whose house he finds himself. His request consists of two parts. First, he calls upon Yahweh to remember him. As elsewhere in the Old Testament, *zākar*, "remember," is not the opposite of "to forget," as if God has forgotten him. Rather, the verb means "to take note of, to act on behalf of."[440] Second, he asks Yahweh to strengthen him one last time. For what purpose he does not say.

Although Samson's prayer represents a last-ditch effort to secure divine aid, most readers will welcome the fact that he is finally acknowledging the role of Yahweh in his life. At last he cries for help, responding to his personal crisis like Israel as a whole should have been reacting to their national emergency. When all is lost, Samson knows to whom he must turn. In addressing Yahweh he calls for the last laugh; let the joke be on his hosts and tormentors. Indeed by beginning with *ʾădōnāy*, "Lord," he recognizes God's sovereignty over his own life.

An alert reader, however, will be troubled by several small but important details. First, Samson's requests are totally self-centered. In his plea for God to remember and strengthen him, he seems totally oblivious to the national emergency and unconcerned about the divine agenda he was raised up to fulfill. Sec-

---

[438] *Kethib* and *qere* are inconsistent in their understanding of the form. The former (וַיְהִימֵשֵׁנִי) is based on the root יָמֵשׁ, "to touch" (cf. *HALOT*, 416); the latter (וַהֲמֵשֵׁנִי), on a root מֹשׁשׁ (*HALOT*, 653). See further O'Connell, *Rhetoric of the Book of Judges*, 474.

[439] Cf. 7:3; 8:10; 12:6.

[440] Cf. Gen 8:1, "God remembered Noah."

ond, by asking for help "just once more" Samson betrays his shortsighted vision. For Samson, each action is intended as the last one (cf. 15:7). There is no thought for Yahweh's long-range plan for himself or his people.

If this reading seems overly negative, note the second half of the prayer. One troubling detail is the switch in addressee from *ʾădōnāy yhwh*, "O sovereign LORD," to *ʾĕlōhîm*, the same generic designation for "god" the Philistines had employed in vv. 23–24. Even more disconcerting is his expressly declared motive in v. 28b. The construction in Hebrew is difficult, but the NIV preserves a reasonable interpretation.[441] Deliberately contrasting "one vengeance" with "my two eyes," he expresses his hope that with a single blow he will be able to repay the Philistines for their cruelty in gouging out both his eyes. Although Samson is no longer driven by what he sees (14:1), his physical eyes continue to determine his actions. Unfortunately the account offers no hint of corresponding concern for spiritual perception/sensibilities. Again the reader is struck by a total lack of concern for the divine agenda or the fate of Samson's people. All he seeks is personal vengeance.

In looking back at the prayer as a whole, the reader must be struck by its ego-centricity. Although ostensibly addressed to Yahweh, God, in an utterance consisting of eighteen words, the first person pronoun occurs five times. In this respect it mirrors the Philistines' song, which consisted of fourteen words (not counting the sign of the direct object) but which contained eight first person pronouns.[442] But unlike the Philistines, Samson has no corporate sense. His preoccupation is expressed in "remember me," "strengthen me," "let me get revenge," "for my two eyes," and "let me die!" (v. 30). There is no thought for the nation he is supposed to be delivering, let alone for Yahweh whose name/reputation has been denigrated by this turn of events. Yahweh is the one who needs vindication. He is unconcerned that the victory song to the Philistines' god is a taunt against and a challenge to Yahweh. But Samson does not seem to care what is happening to Yahweh's reputation, even when the one on whose shoulders God has placed his trust languishes in prison, the victim of his own failures and, seemingly, Dagon's superiority.

16:29 The narrator interrupts Samson's verbal utterance with the third episode (v. 29). Having been led to the pillars by his attendant, Samson gets set for his final act. Bracing himself, Samson extends his arms so each of his hands could touch[443] one of the two pillars supporting the building.

---

[441] Hb. translates lit. "And let me take revenge with a singular vengeance—because of my two eyes—from the Philistines." For this interpretation of the *niphal* of נָקַם see *HALOT*, 721.

[442] "Our god," "our hand," "our enemies," "our god," "our hand," "our enemies," "our land," "our slain."

[443] Contra the NASB, לְפַת does not denote "to grasp" but "to touch" and is cognate to Akk. *lapātu*, "to smear, touch." Cf. *AHw*, 535; *HALOT*, 533. The latter is confirmed by the ca. three-meter distance between the main pillars of the Tell Qasile Temple referred to above.

With arms extended and hands resting on the pillars, Samson utters his last words, literally "Let my person die with the Philistines!" With this utterance Samson declares his total and final identification with the enemy. What a tragic inversion of the office to which he had been called! The Nazirite, set apart for the service of God, wants to die with the uncircumcised Philistines.[444]

As in previous episodes, the reader is left to puzzle over the silence of God in the face of Samson's prayer. What does this mean? Where is Yahweh in these final events? Is his presence evident in Samson's hair? The outcome of the drama, as described in the fourth episode (v. 29b), makes it difficult to believe that God did not answer Samson's prayer, but the narrator focuses entirely on the human actor. Demonstrating physical power greater than any witnessed in previous incidents and ever the entertainer, Samson literally brings the house down. He pushes simultaneously against the pillars, and they crumble, causing the roof to collapse on all the Philistine celebrants gathered inside.

In a concluding note the narrator acknowledges the significance of this act: in his death Samson killed more Philistines than he had slain in his life. In popular circles at least this statement is generally interpreted as a vindication of Samson. While he may have wasted his life, in the end he does indeed begin to deliver Israel from the Philistines. But the narrator's comment should not be interpreted as a compliment. This is a tragic note. This man, with his unprecedentedly high calling and with his extraordinary divine gifts, has wasted his life. Indeed, he accomplishes more for God dead than alive.

(5) Epilogue (16:31b)

He had led Israel twenty years.

16:31b The narrator's observation in v. 31a does double duty, for it concludes the Samson and Delilah story and brings the Samson cycle of narratives full circle. Whereas Samson had lived and died alone, his story ends not with his death but with his return to his family. His entire clan came down to Gaza, retrieved his body, took it up to their home, and buried it in the family grave in the tomb of his father Manoah, between Zorah and Eshtaol. He may have rejected his own people, but in the end they claimed him as their kinsman.

---

[444] This interpretation differs greatly from that of John Milton, who, in Samson Agonistes, has him emerging from his blindness and powerlessness enriched and ennobled, sacrificing his own life for the sake of the divine mission. For a discussion of related issues see E. Browne, "Samson: Riddle and Paradox," *TBT* 22 (1984): 161–67.

The chapter ends on a formal note, with a retrospective recognition that Samson had governed *(šāpaṭ)* Israel for two decades. The note is unexpected, inasmuch as the previous narrative has dealt exclusively with the man's private adventures and had left the impression that the events described succeeded one another in rapid succession. In fact, his relationships with the Philistine women imply he never really grew up. But the observation that he ruled for twenty years suggests he must have been almost forty years of age at the time of his death. Be that as it may, nothing outside of these narratives is known of his manner of rule. The narrator's selection of experiences for this cycle suggests Samson's style could hardly have been orthodox.

Theological and Practical Implications

First, this account exposes the kind of patriarchy in which men conduct their own lives, especially their relationships with women, in their own self-interest, without respect to the well-being or feelings of others. In so doing it offers a sad commentary on the ethical consequences of spiritual Canaanization, particularly its degenerative effects on male-female relations. In this Canaanized world if men do not view women merely as sex objects, they view them as persons to be controlled and exploited for personal and male ends. But when Samson operates according to "what is right in his own eyes" and when he demands women because "they seem right to him," he represents not only all of Israel but all unregenerate men who are driven by their sense and/or the need to control.[445] Never in the entire Samson narrative does he operate in anyone's interest but his own. He does not care about the divine agenda, the will of his parents, or the hearts of the lovers with whom he consorts. All are to be manipulated for his sake. Contrary to feminist rhetoric, however, this is not normative biblical patricentrism. Nor is this a picture of male-female relationships as God intended them to be experienced. If the divine order calls on men to function as heads of their homes and leaders in society, then these must be viewed primarily as positions of responsibility, not power. The normative biblical understanding of headship calls for servant leadership, in which the interests of those led take precedence over the interests of the leader.[446] Correspondingly, if men are the stronger gender physically and functionally, this

---

[445] Exum's characterization of Samson as "genuinely amoral" ("The Center Cannot Hold," 423), that is, without moral values, is too complimentary.

[446] Cf. Deut 12:14–20; Phil 2:1–11; 1 Peter 5:1–6.

strength is to be exercised in defense of and in the interest of those weaker than themselves.

Second, as a corollary, those called to the highest positions of leadership may be most tempted to operate on the basis of their senses rather than on the basis of principle. Samson was able to kill his enemies by the hundreds and thousands, but he was impotent in the face of women's charms. Whereas Barak was motivated by jealousy, Gideon by logic, Jephthah by ambition and pagan values, Samson was driven by lust. In a Canaanized society the exploitation of women may occur because men as a class view women fundamentally as dangerous and a threat to male power.[447] From a biblical perspective, however, it is more appropriately attributed to their depraved condition. In their fallen condition men often operate selfishly, either out of a desire to satisfy their lustful appetites or out of a degenerate need to control. But this is not because they are men. If the accounts in Judges take male oppression of women for granted, this is not because this is the accepted disposition. On the contrary, the exploitation and abuse of women by Samson is of a piece with the rest of the evidences of Israel's Canaanization catalogued by the narrator. Biblical norms of male conduct call for the highest respect for women, who also are created in the image of God and endowed with equal majesty and dignity. Biblical norms also regard sex and sexual activity as sacred, as something reserved for a man and woman within the context of marriage. Anything less is demeaning, exploitative, and perverse.

Third, those who are called into divine service must focus their energies on the divine agenda rather than getting sidetracked into personal adventures. Samson offers the reader of Scripture the clearest example of "Thy kingdom come" being supplanted and displaced by "My kingdom come." He also reminds us that the temptation may be the greatest to those who are most gifted. The extraordinary physical prowess and power of this man have become proverbial. Unfortunately, like many contemporary divinely called leaders, Samson wasted his life playing with the gifts God had given him and indulging in every sensual adventure he desired. Even in the aftermath of victory he thought only of his own thirst. There was no thought for the implications of his actions for Yahweh's agenda or the fortunes of Israel. It is not surprising then that he ends up one more example of fallen and failed leaders with whom the path of human history is strewn.

Fourth, as in the previous deliverer cycles, if anything positive comes of Samson's life, it is due to the gracious intervention of Yahweh. The man

---

[447] Cf. Exum, *Fragmented Women*, 86.

whose birth had promised so much is a disappointment. Nevertheless, ironically, by the free exercise of his own immoral will, Samson serves as an agent of the Lord's ethical will,[448] and by the narrator's own acknowledgment he accomplishes more dying than living. But God plays a critical role in each part of the account, sometimes behind the scenes, but explicitly in enabling a barren woman to conceive and give birth to the deliverer, empowering his deliverer through his spirit, and answering his deliverer's prayers. Life and death are in the hands of God.[449] And if Israel will eventually emerge as an identifiable entity from the dark period of the judges, this says nothing about the quality of her leaders. Yahweh is determined to build his people. Even if she becomes her own worst enemy and her human leaders fail her in the end, by the grace of God she will triumph.

---

[448] Cf. Klein, *Triumph of Irony*, 118.

[449] Cf. Exum, "The Theological Dimension of the Samson Saga," 30–45.

III. CLIMAX: THE DEPTHS OF THE CANAANIZATION OF ISRAEL
   (17:1–21:25)
   1. The Religious Degeneration of Israel (17:1–18:31)
      (1) The Corruption of an Israelite Household (17:1–6)
      (2) The Corruption of the Levitical Priesthood (17:7–13)
      (3) The Corruption of an Israelite Tribe (18:1–31)
         The Mission of the Danite Scouts (18:1–10)
         The Migration of the Danite Tribe (18:11–31)
            The Danite Trek to the Hill Country of Ephraim (18:11–13)
            The Encounter with the Levite (18:14–20)
            The Encounter with Micah (18:21–26)
            Mission Accomplished (18:27–31)
   2. The Moral Degeneration of Israel (19:1–21:25)
      (1) The Background to the Outrage at Gibeah (19:1–9)
      (2) The Nature of the Outrage at Gibeah (19:10–30)
         The Social Outrage (19:10–21)
            On the Road to Gibeah (19:10–15)
            In the Open Square (19:16–21)
         The Moral Outrage (19:22–28)
            In the Old Man's House (19:22–26)
            The Journey Home (19:27–28)
         The Call to Arms (19:29–30)
      (3) The Israelite Response to the Outrage (20:1–48)
         The Assembly of the Forces of Israel (20:1–17)
            The Assembly of the Tribes of Israel (20:1–3a)
            The Report of the Levite (20:3b–7)
            The Reaction of the Israelites (20:8–13)
            The Marshalling of the Troops (20:14–17)
         The [Three] Battles (20:18–48)
            The First Battle (20:18–21)
            The Second Battle (20:22–25)
            The Third Battle (20:26–48)
      (4) The National Crisis Created by the Outrage (21:1–24)
         The Israelites' Recognition of the Crisis (21:1–4)
         The Israelites' Responses to the Crisis (21:5–24)
            The Israelites' Initial Solution to the Crisis (21:5–14)
            The Israelites' Supplementary Solution to the Crisis
               (21:15–24)
      (5) Epilogue (21:25)

473

─── III. CLIMAX: THE DEPTHS OF THE CANAANIZATION ─── OF ISRAEL (17:1–21:25)

1. The Religious Degeneration of Israel (17:1–18:31)

The opening *wayĕhî ʾîš*, "Now there was a man" (NASB), in 17:1 announces the start of the third major section of the plot of the Book of Judges. With the report of Samson's death and burial the accounts of the lives of the governors have come to an end. Although they have all been raised up by Yahweh to deliver the Israelites from external control, the leaders of the nation have been increasingly found wanting, both morally and spiritually. More and more they have demonstrated fundamentally Canaanite dispositions. In the "Book of Deliverers" (2:6–16:31) the lives of ordinary Israelites has been of secondary interest. After opening each cycle with "The Israelites did evil in the sight of the LORD," the focus has consistently been on how God answers the increasing Canaanization by sending foreign powers to punish them, then raising a deliverer in response to the people's cries of pain and providing victory for Israel through the deliverer. The introductory "Now there was a man" hints at a new focus. In the following chapters the narrator will offer the reader a series of glimpses at how ordinary Israelites fared in the dark days of the "judges" (governors). The effect will be to confirm the picture of a pervasively and increasingly Canaanized society.

Structurally chaps. 17–21 divide into two parts. Even though the narrator will offer the reader a window into the private lives of Israelites in each part, the first segment describes the fate of the Danites in the period of the governors (17:1–18:31); the second, the fate of the Benjamites (19:1–21:25). The plots of these two segments go their own ways, but the narratives are linked by numerous common features.

1. Both tribes, Dan and Benjam, were assigned territory in Israel's heartland, between Judah and Ephraim, the tribes that would later lead the Southern and Northern Kingdoms respectively. By selecting episodes that concern these tribes the narrator cleverly emphasizes that the degenerating tendency in Israel was not simply a problem in the fringe territories. It had infected the very heart of the nation.

2. Both tribes found themselves in dire straights, though for different reasons. As announced in the prologue to the book (1:34–36), the tribe of Dan had been unable to occupy the territory allotted to it by Joshua and was forced to search for a homeland elsewhere. The tribe of Benjamin incurred the hostility of the rest of the nation and came frighteningly close to disappearing as a victim of Israel's "holy war."

3. In both accounts the crisis was precipitated by the actions of a nameless Levite.

4. In both accounts the Levite had a Bethlehem-Judah connection. The first Levite came from Bethlehem-Judah (17:7–8); the second traveled to Bethlehem-Judah (19:1–2).

5. Both Levites had connections with Mount Ephraim. The first Levite ended up in the household of Micah, who lived on Mount Ephraim (17:1); the second actually lived in this region (19:1).

6. Both accounts involved priestly characters inquiring of God concerning the outcome of a proposed plan of action (18:5–6; 20:27–28).

7. Both accounts conclude with a reference to Shiloh. Judges 18:31 notes that the Danites continued to use Micah's idols as long as the tabernacle was at Shiloh; in 21:19–24 the narrator describes an event that took place at Shiloh.

8. In both accounts military contingents consisting of six hundred men played a critical role (18:11,16–15,25; 20:47; 21:7,12,14,16–17,23).

9. Both accounts are punctuated by variations of the refrain "In those days Israel had no king" (17:6; 18:1; 19:1; 21:25). In the first the formula is inserted at critical junctures in the narrative and functions as an episode marker; in the second the formula frames the entire narrative, appearing at the beginning and the end. Twice, once in each section, the formula is augmented with, "Everyone did as he saw fit" (17:6; 21:25).

In general, scholars have interpreted the reference to the absence of a king, which is common to all four, as evidence of an idealized monarchicalist agenda in the final redaction of the Book of Judges as a whole.[1] But the repeated refrain need not imply a promonarchic, let alone a pro-Davidic, polemic.[2] It obviously dates the text after the establishment of the monarchy, but how soon thereafter is an open question.[3] The key to the significance of the refrain is found in the expanded versions in 17:6 and 21:25. Together these two create an inclusio, framing the entire work, that tells the reader how to interpret these events. The events described in chaps. 17–21 illustrate the democratization of Samson's problem:[4] Israel does not need a king to lead them in doing what is right in their own eyes—they will do exactly as they please without being led astray. Accordingly, this refrain functions as a posi-

---

[1] See most recently R. H. O'Connell, *The Rhetoric of the Book of Judges*, VTSup 63 (Leiden: Brill, 1996), 268–304. Further bibliography reflecting this perspective is provided on pp. 268–69.

[2] A point made thirty-five years ago by M. Noth, "The Background of Judges 17–18," in *Israel's Prophetic Heritage: Essays in Honor of James Muilenburg*, ed. B. W. Harrison and W. Harrelson (New York: Harper, 1962), 68–85. Note especially p. 81, where Noth declares that the view that the author of 17:6,18:1 can hardly have been an admirer of David, though for reasons different from our own.

[3] O'Connell, *Rhetoric of the Book of Judges* , 342, finds the rhetorical situation of the Book of Judges to be that described in 2 Samuel 1–4.

[4] The clause אִישׁ הַיָּשָׁר בְּעֵינָיו יַעֲשֶׂה, "Each did the right in his own eyes," in v. 6 echoes 14:3.

tive variation of the formula that occurs seven times in the "Book of Deliverers," "In those days [i.e., before there was a king in Israel] everyone did what was evil in the LORD's eyes [i.e., did what was right in his own eyes]." Far from evaluating the monarchy positively, the author's use of the formula deliberately extends to the citizenry in general the high-handed attitudes of later kings against the will of God.[5] The Israelites do not need either a governor (Samson) or a king to lead them into sin. They will do it on their own.

Most interpreters assume the reference in the formula is to a human king. It is possible, however, that the narrator is also thinking in terms of a divine king. The notion of Israel as the kingdom of Yahweh goes back at least to Exod 19:6, but it receives explicit expression in Deut 33:5, in a literary context widely acknowledged to be among the oldest compositions in the Scriptures:

> "He was king over Jeshurun
> when the leaders of the people assembled,
> along with the tribes of Israel.

Yahweh's kingship over Israel is assumed throughout the Book of Deuteronomy, which is structured on the paradigm of ancient Near Eastern suzerainty treaties.[6] With this fourfold repeated formula the author of Judges declares that despite Gideon's hollow assertion, the nation recognized no one, not even God, as king. Thus the episodes that follow are presented as evidence of Israel's complete repudiation of Yahweh's claims on their lives. Together these two accounts examine the general Canaanization of Israelite society from two perspectives: (1) Israel's religious and cultic Canaanization, illustrated by the Danites (17:1–18:31); (2) Israel's moral and ethical Canaanization, illustrated by the Benjamites (19:1–21:25).

The first unit intertwines three principal themes: the spiritual decline of the Levites in the period of the "judges" (governors), the Danite conquest of Laish, and the Israelite origins of the cult shrine at Dan. Structurally the account divides into three subunits whose boundaries are marked by the redactional formula at 17:6 and 18:1a. Although each section has its own focus, the cast of characters builds from 17:1–5 (Micah), to 17:7–13 (Micah and the Levite), to 18:1b–31 (Micah and the Levite and the Danites). The placement of the present account immediately after the Samson cycle seems

---

[5] In their use of this formula, the authors of Judges and 1,2 Kings betray their common Mosaic/Deuteronomic theological point of view.

[6] On which see J. A. Thompson, *Deuteronomy: Introduction and Commentary* , TOTC (Downers Grove: InterVarsity, 1974); id., *The Ancient Near Eastern Treaties and the Old Testament* (London: Tyndale, 1964); P. C. Craigie, *Deuteronomy*, NICOT (Grand Rapids: Eerdmans, 1976); M. Weinfeld, "Deuteronomy," *ABD* 2.168–71; E. H. Merrill, *Deuteronomy,* NAC (Nashville: Broadman & Holman, 1994).

deliberate. Not only do both involve the Danites, but the manner in which the plot of chaps. 17–18 is constructed also bears a remarkable similarity to chaps. 14–15. Just as Samson's attraction toward a Philistine woman, a totally private matter, served as a catalyst for a series of events that led eventually to the naming of a spring (En-hakkore) commemorating his victory over the Philistines, so Micah's seemingly inconsequential theft of silver from his mother led eventually to the Danite's naming of a city commemorating their domestication of a Canaanite cult site. The plot of the latter is complex,[7] but it is carefully composed so that the reader recognizes the links between the tribal apostasy officially instituted in 18:30–31 and the private apostasy of Micah in 17:5.[8]

(1) The Corruption of an Israelite Household (17:1–6)

[1]Now a man named Micah from the hill country of Ephraim [2]said to his mother, "The eleven hundred shekels of silver that were taken from you and about which I heard you utter a curse—I have that silver with me; I took it."

Then his mother said, "The LORD bless you, my son!"

[3]When he returned the eleven hundred shekels of silver to his mother, she said, "I solemnly consecrate my silver to the LORD for my son to make a carved image and a cast idol. I will give it back to you."

[4]So he returned the silver to his mother, and she took two hundred shekels of silver and gave them to a silversmith, who made them into the image and the idol. And they were put in Micah's house.

[5]Now this man Micah had a shrine, and he made an ephod and some idols and

---

[7] O'Connell (Rhetoric of the Book of Judges, 231–41) recognizes four plot levels in this narrative: (1) the execution of the curse upon the thief who stole Micah's mother's silver (17:1–2a[2b], 3a[3b],4a[4b–5,8b–13–18:13–17,22–26,30a,31]; (2) the Levite's [illegitimate] search for a place of employment (17:7–12,18:[2b–6,13–17]18–20, 30b); (3) the Danites' [illegitimate] quest for a tribal homeland (18:1–2a[2b–6],7–12[13–19],21[22–26],27–29); (4) the Danites' [illegitimate] adoption of a pagan cult (18:2b–6,13–20,22–26, 30a,31).

[8] Recognizing an open polemic against a kingless society, Y. Amit ("Hidden Polemic in the Conquest of Dan: Judges xvii–xviii," VT 40 [1990]: 4–20) contends that these two chapters contain an indirect/hidden polemic against the cult site at Beth-el. Evidence for this is found in (1) the reference to a region rather than a specific place (17:1,8b; 18:2b,13); (2) the use of אֶפְרַיִם הַר, "mountain of Ephraim," as a synonym for Beth-el (cf. Jer 4:15); (3) the reference to אֱלֹהִים בֵּית, "house of God," in 17:5, which links this passage with Gen 28:17,22; (4) the association of "Beth-el" and Dan (1 Kgs 12:26–33; cf. Amos 7:13); (5) the references to "carved image" (הַפֶּסֶל) and "cast idol" (הַמַּסֵּכָה, 18:14,17,18,31), which recall Jeroboam's golden calves (1 Kgs 12:28), which in turn were imitations of Aaron's "cast calf" (מַסֵּכָה עֵגֶל, Exod 32:4); (6) the linguistic links between the accounts of Micah's (17:5,12) and Jeroboam's appointments of priests (1 Kgs 12:26–13:34; cf. 13:33); (7) the expositional material of 17:1–5 and 17:7–13 with their attention to the hill country of Ephraim. These segments are not really necessary for the following chapter, but they prepare the way for the Bethel–Dan connection. Although Amit's main thesis is dubious, her conclusion that this story must have been written between 732 and 622 B.C. fits my own understanding of the date of authorship of the book.

installed one of his sons as his priest. **⁶In those days Israel had no king; everyone did as he saw fit.**

17:1–5 The picture of this otherwise insignificant Ephraimite family is ambivalent. They live in "the hill country of Ephraim"[9] which under normal circumstances would be inconsequential. But the author's earlier negative portrayal of Ephraimites raises suspicions in the mind of the reader, though these should not blind the reader to the positive elements in the narrative.

First, the main character bears an orthodox Yahwistic name. *mîkāyĕhû* (vv. 1,4) is the long form of the more common *mîkâ* used in the rest of the narrative (eighteen times in 17:5–18:31).[10] The name, consisting of the elements *mî* + *kā* + *yahu*, translates "Who is like Yahweh?" a rhetorical question anticipating the answer, "No one!" In the ancient world theophoric names (names with a reference to a god) of this type generally reflected the faith of the one who named the person. Accordingly one might surmise that the parent who named Micah was a devotèe of Yahweh and considered Yahweh to be in a class all his own, completely distinct from all the Canaanite gods.[11] But the use of the shortened form of the name after v. 4 may be intentional, reflecting the narrator's awareness of the incongruities in the story. Because this Yahwistic name is awkward in this context, the Yahwistic element *(yāhû)* is downplayed.

Second, Micah confesses his sin to his mother and returns the goods he had stolen from her (v. 2a).[12] The size of the theft is extraordinary—1,100 shekels of silver,[13] which is equal to the amount each of the Philistine governors had given Delilah as a reward for delivering Samson into their hands (16:5). Obviously his mother was a woman of considerable wealth. But the young man who robbed her eventually restores the silver.

Third, after Micah returns the stolen goods to his mother, she blesses him by Yahweh (v. 2). When Micah's mother learned that her precious silver objects were missing, in the hearing of her son she had pronounced a curse on the one who had committed the crime. The verb for "cursing," *ʾālâ*, is relatively rare,[14] and often serves as an abbreviated version of the

---

[9] On which see above on 3:27.

[10] Other variations include מִיכָיְה and מִיכָיְהוּ. The name is borne by the later Israelite prophets Micaiah ben Imlah (1 Kgs 22:8–28) and Micah of Moresheth (Mic 1:1). On the name see Fowler, *Theophoric Names*, 128–29 and 152.

[11] Cf. the play on the name in Mic 7:18. From other comparisons of Yahweh with other gods we learn that Yahweh is incomparable in his holiness (1 Sam 2:2), his creative power (Isa 40:18,25), the power/effectiveness of his word (Isa 46:5,9), and his grace toward sinners (Mic 7:18).

[12] Although he begins his confession gingerly (אִתִּי הַכֶּסֶף־הִנֵּה, "Behold the silver is with me"), the form of the last statement is emphatic: לְקַחְתִּיו אֲנִי, "I myself took it."

[13] As in 8:26; 9:4; 16:5, "shekels" is assumed in the phrase וּמֵאָה אֶלֶף הַכֶּסֶף, lit. "eleven hundred [of] silver."

[14] The *qal* form appears elsewhere only in Hos 4:2 and 10:4; the *hiphil* only in 1 Sam 14:24; 1 Kgs 8:31; 2 Chr 6:22.

curse formula that more often involves a verb plus the noun *ʾālâ*.[15] In general *ʾālâ* signifies a conditional curse, in this case some horrendous fate for committing a crime.[16] The blessing pronounced upon Micah by his mother is cast in typical form (lit.): "May my son be blessed by the LORD."[17] Utterances like this characteristically express the speaker's grateful response to a good deed done for him or her by the third party on whose behalf the blessing is invoked. But this utterance is more than an expression of thanksgiving because the woman has recovered her lost goods. It is also a plea to have the prior curse canceled by now commending the offender, her son, to Yahweh. The fact that she commends Micah to Yahweh rather than Baal or some other Canaanite deity, suggests she is devoted to the covenant God of Israel.

Fourth, Micah's mother "solemnly consecrates"[18] the money that has been recovered to Yahweh (v. 3), which leads the reader to expect a positive outcome to the story. Not only has the curse of the offender been canceled with a blessing; the tainted silver has also been consecrated for divine use.

Unfortunately, however, other features of vv. 1–5 demonstrate that the veneer of orthodox Yahwism is extremely thin. The four positive signals are more than neutralized by no fewer than eight troubling issues.

First, for all the piety expressed in his name, in the action to which he confesses guilt, Micah violates two fundamental principles of Yahweh's covenant with Israel: he steals (cf. Exod 20:15; Deut 5:19), and he displays contempt for his mother (cf. Exod 20:12; Deut 5:16).

Second, Micah's motive in returning the stolen goods is suspect. It is significant that he does not return it until he hears his mother pronounce a curse upon the criminal. Since there appears to have been no remorse, this act should not be interpreted as particularly pious. It was motivated by fear of the curse. Micah responded as any ancient Near Easterner would have, regardless

---

[15] (1) הָיְתָה אָלָה בֵּין, "to be a curse between," Gen 26:28; (2) נָתַן אָלָה עַל, "to put a curse on," Deut 30:7; (3) בְ אָלָה נָשָׂא, "to impose a curse upon," 1 Kgs 8:31; 2 Chr 6:22; (4) הֵבִיא בְּאָלָה, "to put under a curse," Ezek 17:13; (5) הֵבִיא עַל אָלָה, "to bring a curse upon," 2 Chr 34:24.

[16] J. Scharbert (*TDOT* 2.262) cites an analogue to the present case in contemporary Bedouin custom, according to which if a Bedouin loses something, he declares publicly, "I hold the person who finds this thing responsible for it. If he keeps it, may Allah cut him off from his property and his family." In such cases no one would dare keep the article one has found. Cf. Lev 5:1, which speaks of an audible curse (קוֹל אָלָה) shouted in the hearing of the people.

[17] Cf. Gen 14:19; 1 Sam 15:13; 23:21; 2 Sam 2:5; Ruth 2:20; 3:10; Ps 115:15. Cp. the form in two Hb. inscriptions:
Kuntillet ʿAjrud pithos: *brkt ʾtkm lyhwh šmrn wlʾšrth*, "May you be blessed by Yahweh of Samaria and by his Asherah"; Khirbet el-Qom: *brk ʾryhw lyhwh*, "May Uriyahu be blessed by Yahweh." On these inscriptions with further bibliography see J. Day, "Asherah," *ABD* 1.484–85.

[18] On the intensifying use of the infinitive absolute see *IBHS* 35.3.1c; *GBH* 123e.

of the god he or she served.

Third, as pious as the woman's dedication of the silver to Yahweh appears, she does not present it to the priests at Shiloh (cf. 18:31) but instead gives it back to her son. Additionally, it should be noted that the silver she dedicates is tainted (stolen) silver.

Fourth, although the woman emphatically dedicates the silver to Yahweh and announces that she is giving it back to her son to make a cult object, when it comes to engaging a silversmith, she only gives him two hundred shekels of silver. This would actually not have yielded a very impressive cult statue. Even if the image was carved of wood and then plated with silver rather than being made of solid silver, two hundred shekels amounts to only about eighty ounces or five pounds. This raises the question, What happened to the rest of the silver dedicated to Yahweh?

Fifth, the woman's intention in dedicating the silver flies in the face of the second principle of Yahweh's covenant with Israel: the prohibition of physical representations of deity (Exod 20:4–5; Deut 5:8–9). In flagrant violation of this prohibition she commissions her son to construct a cult image. The two words used to identify the object, *pesel* and *massēkâ*, reflect the manner in which idols were typically constructed.[19] The first, from *pāsal*, "to hew, cut," speaks of the carving activity of the craftsman as he sculpts a stone or piece of wood into the desired shape.[20] The second, from *nāsak*, "to pour," alludes to the melting down of precious metal with which the sculpture will then be overlaid. Although the cult object was clearly made in violation of the decalogic command, the narrator does not indicate what kind of image it was. Subsequent references to it associate this object with an ephod and teraphim (v. 5; 18:14,17,20). Micah's understanding of what he had made is clearly reflected in 18:24, where he laments the loss of "my gods [*ʾĕlōhîm*] which I have made." If this was not an explicitly Canaanite image, it was certainly syncretistic.

Sixth, Micah possesses a cult shrine (*bêt ʾĕlōhîm*, lit., "house of God") of his own (v. 5a), in obvious violation of Deuteronomy 12, which had explicitly declared that when the Israelites entered the land and had settled in it they

---

[19] The NIV's translation of פֶּסֶל וּמַסֵּכָה, "a carved image and a cast idol," creates the impression that she desired two objects. But the phrase, which translates literally "a sculpture and something poured," is a hendiadys, viz., "A carved image overlaid with molten metal." The compound phrase, which recurs in 17:4 and 18:14 (also Nah 1:14), derives from Deut 27:15. The two words appear as a parallel pair in Isa 30:22; 42:17.

[20] Cf. above on 3:18. See *HALOT*, 948–49. Cp. the satirical portrayal of the idol (פֶּסֶל) manufacturing process in Isa 44:9–17.

were to worship only at the place which Yahweh would authorize.[21] But like Gideon in 8:27, Micah established a cult center at the place of his own choosing.[22]

Seventh, Micah designed and manufactured his own cult accoutrements, which were specifically identified as an ephod and "some idols" (Hb. *tĕrāpîm;* v. 5b). As was noted above on 8:27 with reference to Gideon's ephod, the former object probably refers to the special garments draped over the cult image. Even though the use of teraphim seems to have been widespread in the ancient Near East,[23] the nature and function of teraphim in the ancient Near East remains unclear.[24] Based on Zech 10:2, which links *tĕrāpîm* with diviners *(qôsĕmîm)* who prophesy through visions *(ḥāzâ)* and dreams *(ḥălōmôt),* some form of divinatory object, comparable to oracular alabaster and hematite stones known from Akkadian sources,[25] may be involved. Contextually, this interpretation finds support in 18:5, where the

---

[21] See Deut 12:4–7,11,13–14,17–8,26–27. This chapter is usually interpreted as a call for the centralization of worship. But as S. Richter has recently demonstrated ("The Deuteronomistic Theology and the Place of the Name," paper read to the SBL, November 1996), Deuteronomy 12 has less to do with "name theology," centralizing worship at a place where Yahweh's name dwells, than with identifying a place authorized by him, with his name inscribed on it. Richter observes that in Mesopotamian and Canaanite Akk. (EA) usage *šakān,* "to establish, to set up, to deposit," in conjunction with *šumam,* "name," speaks of depositing, inscribing a name on a tablet, stele, or building, especially building inscriptions. The purpose of the inscriptions was to verify that the temple had not been built as a response to human motivation but initiated by divine decree and that this one was a replica of the original divinely revealed temple design. The site was hereby inscriptionally validated as chosen by the gods, therefore an efficacious place where the god could be invoked with confidence. Often such inscriptions contained a curse for tampering with the temple. Accordingly Deut 12:5 should be translated, "You will seek Yahweh at the place which Yahweh your God will choose out of all your tribes to set his name there, to establish/deposit/inscribe it, and there you shall come." Micah's cult center is an obvious violation of Deuteronomy 12.

[22] Rather than treating v. 5 as anticlimactic, as Boling does *(Judges,* 25), this verse represents the climax of the first phase of the plot of chaps. 17–18.

[23] In Gen. 31:30 the teraphim appear to have been miniature household gods. The word occurs also in 1 Sam 19:13; 2 Kgs 23:24; Ezek 21:21; Hos 3:4–5; Zech 10:2.

[24] No fewer than six different etymologies for the word have been proposed. Although O. Loretz ("Die Teraphim als 'Ahnen-Götter-Figur(in)en' im Lichte der Texte aus Nuzi, Emar, und Ugarit," *UF* 24 [1992]: 133–78) has recently made a strong case for treating םיפרת as a scribal invention substituting for an original םיאפר, "rephaim," which refers to divinized ancestors or their cult images, the most likely explanation recognizes in the expression a Hittite loanword from *tarpi(š),* which refers to "a spirit which can on some occasions be regarded as protective and on others as malevolent." See further H. A. Hoffner, "The Linguistic Origins of Teraphim," *BSac* 124 (1967): 230–38; id., "Hittite Tarrpiš and Hebrew Terāphîm," *JNES* 27 (1968): 61–68. For a discussion of the options and an examination of the significance of the word in the OT see T. J. Lewis, "Teraphim," *DDD,* 1588–1601.

[25] Identified as *gišnugallu* and *šadânu* respectively. On their relation to the Israelite Urim and Thummim see W. Horowitz and V. (A.) Hurowitz, "Urim and Thummim in Light of a Psephomancy Ritual from Assur (LKA 137)," *JANES* 21 (1992), 110–11.

Danite agents request an oracular word from Micah.[26] If this interpretation is correct, then the items crafted by Micah represent a direct challenge to the ephod of Israel's officially authorized priests (cf. Exodus 28)[27] and the Urim and Thummim which Yahweh had sanctioned for oracular purposes (Exod 28:30).[28]

Eighth, Micah installed one of his own sons as priest. In most instances involving the expression *millē' 'et-yād* (lit. "to fill the hands") in the Old Testament the consecration of priests is in view,[29] but in Ezek 43:26 the idiom applies to the dedication/initiation of the altar. The nature of the ceremony of dedication is unclear, but the occurrence in Akkadian of an exact cognate, *mulla qatâ*, "to fill the hands,"[30] suggests it involved the placement of some symbol of authority into the hands of the person being installed.[31] This action posed a direct challenge to the officially authorized Aaronic priesthood.

Looking back on vv. 1–5, the incongruities and ironies in the account produce a farcical tone in this paragraph. A woman, who, in her namelessness represents any female head of the household in Israel, openly confesses her devotion to Yahweh in blessing and dedication, but her actions run directly counter to that confession. Her son, who bears a thoroughly orthodox name, commits the ultimate crime, establishing a cult system in direct violation of Yahweh's incomparability, as expressed by the name, and Yahweh's explicit command not to worship any gods besides him nor to make any physical representations of deity. The tragedy is that the actors do not realize the incongrueity of their actions. Like Jephthah in 11:30–40, both Micah and his mother are deadly sincere in their religious expression but thoroughly pagan in action. After this episode Micah's mother disappears from the plot. Her function has been simply to provide a background to the character and actions of Micah. Given the syncretistic nature of this home, subsequent events in this and the next chapter are less surprising, if not actually to be anticipated. At the same time, several serious questions haunt the reader. Where is Micah's father, the woman's husband? What did the woman do with the nine hundred shekels of silver that she dedicated to Yahweh for the construction of an image but that were not delivered to the silversmith?

17:6 The negative assessment of the first episode is confirmed by the nar-

---

[26] The verb שָׁאַל, "to ask, inquire," is associated with teraphim in Ezek 21:21 (Hb. 28).

[27] In Israel the officially sanctioned ephod was worn by the priests, not the deity. After all, Yahweh could not be represented physically.

[28] On the use of the latter see Milgrom, *Numbers*, 484–86; E. Lipinski, "'Urîm and Thummîm," *VT* 20 (1970): 495–96; Horowitz and Hurowitz, "Urim and Thummim," 95–115.

[29] Exod 28:41; 29:9,29,35; 32:29; Lev 8:33; 16:32; 21:10; Num 3:3; 1 Kgs 13:33; 1 Chr 29:5; 2 Chr 13:9; 29:31.;

[30] Cf. *CAD* 9c, 187.

[31] So also Milgrom, *Numbers*, 300, and more fully id., *Leviticus 1–16*, 539.

rator himself, who inserts his own interpretive comment in v. 6. As noted earlier, this verse functions literarily as an episode marker, signaling a transition from v. 5 to v. 7.[32] Its theological importance, however, is even more important than its literary significance, for here the author betrays his own understanding of what has transpired.

First, he associates[33] these corrupt actions with the absence of a king. As noted earlier his is not a promonarchic comment[34] and does not mean that the author views the monarchy to be the solution to the present crises and that "things would be better under a king."[35] On the contrary, with the benefit of hindsight the narrator knows that the monarchy in Israel was largely responsible for the apostasy that led eventually to the demise of both Northern and Southern Kingdoms in the eighth and sixth centuries respectively. But the problems plagued the monarchy(ies) from the beginning from the tenth century B.C. In 1 Kings 11 Solomon, the second king in the Davidic dynasty, is cast as the antithesis of the Deuteronomic ideal spelled out in Deut 17:14–10 and is presented as the first royal sponsor of idolatry. According to 1 Kgs 12:25–33, Jeroboam, the first king of the North, established the paradigm for all subsequent rulers, "who did evil in the eyes of the LORD." This evil course reached its climax in Manasseh's reign of horror, the abominations of which even exceeded those of the Amorite and Canaanites (2 Kgs 21:1–18). Like Jeroboam, Micah (1) set up houses of worship at a place of his own choosing,[36] (2) erected images of worship, (3) referred to these images as gods,[37] and (4) installed his own priests at the shrines.[38] From the perspective of the Manassite abominations, the author of Judges observes that in the dark days of the "judges" (governors), Israel did not need kings to lead them into idolatry, since the people did it on their own.

Second, the narrator views the actions of Micah and his mother as typical of all Israel. Inasmuch as they did what was right in their own eyes, they illustrate the general disregard for Yahweh's covenant within the nation. The expression, "to do what is right in the eyes of the LORD," which is Mosaic in

---

[32] So also W. J. Dumbrell, " 'In Those Days There Was No King in Israel; Every Man Did What Was Right in His Own Eyes': The Purpose of the Book of Judges Reconsidered," *JSOT* 25 (1983): 23–24; Amit, "Hidden Polemic in the Conquest of Dan," 5–6.

[33] But contrary to prevailing scholarly opinion, he does not attribute them to the absence of a king.

[34] Contra Soggin, *Judges*, 265.

[35] Thus Howard, *Introduction*, 121, following Gerbrandt, *Kingship*, 123–40.

[36] The one at Dan had a direct link with Micah's image, which in the sequel ends up in Dan (18:29–31); 1 Kgs 12:33 emphasizes that Jeroboam's were of his own devising.

[37] Cp. 1 Kgs 12:28 with Judg 18:24.

[38] In 1 Kgs 13:33 the consecration is referred to with the same idiom, "he filled their hands."

origin,[39] represents the opposite of "doing what is right in one's own eyes."[40] "Everyone"[41] behaved just like later kings.[42] If "doing what is right in one's own eyes" is interpreted as equivalent to "doing what is evil in the LORD's eyes," the evidence is even more overwhelming. Variations of this phrase, which appears seven times in Judges, recur more than twenty times in Samuel-Kings, usually with reference to the conduct of kings.[43] The difference between the period of the governors and the monarchy/ies is not the presence or absence of idolatry or evil. Rather, it is the source from which the evil springs. During the monarchy kings led the way in abominable acts; in premonarchic times the people did it on their own.[44]

(2) The Corruption of the Levitical Priesthood (17:7–13)

[7]A young Levite from Bethlehem in Judah, who had been living within the clan of Judah, [8]left that town in search of some other place to stay. On his way he

---

[39] This phrase is Mosaic (Exod 15:26; Deut 6:18; 12:25,28; 13:19; 21:9), but it recurs with great frequency in the Deuteronomic History, especially in evaluations of and exhortations to the monarchies (see the following note) and in Jer 34:15.

[40] This expression is also Mosaic in origin, appearing in this form in Deut 12:8. The expression recurs with great frequency in the Deuteronomic History, esp. in evaluations of and exhortations to the monarchies (1 Kgs 11:33,38; 14:8; 15:5,11; 22:43; 2 Kgs 10:30; 12:2 [Hb. 3]; 14:3; 15:3,34; 16:2; 18:3; 22:2) and in Jeremiah 34:15.

[41] On the distributive use of שׁ֖יא see GKC §139b,c, DCH 1.222; GBH §155nf.

[42] Kings who are denounced for not doing what is right in the eyes of Yahweh, i.e., who did what was right in their own eyes, include Solomon (1 Kgs 14:8), Jehu (2 Kgs 10:30), and Ahaz (2 Kgs 16:2). Several others are commended for doing what was right but are still said to have fallen short of the ideal in failing to remove the high places: Asa (1 Kgs 15:11–14), Jehoshaphat (1 Kgs 22:43), Jehoash (2 Kgs 12:2–3 [Hb. 3–4]), Amaziah (2 Kgs 14:3–4), Azariah (2 Kgs 15:3–4), Jotham (2 Kgs 15:34–35). Only David (1 Kgs 22:2), Hezekiah (2 Kgs 18:3), and Josiah (2 Kgs 22:2) receive unqualified commendation in this regard. But even David, who is put forward as the model of doing what is right in the eyes of Yahweh (1 Kgs 11:33,38), is acknowledged to have fallen short of the ideal in his crime against Uriah the Hittite (1 Kgs 15:5).

[43] Of Saul (1 Sam 15:19), David (2 Sam 12:9, for the Bathsheba/Uriah affair), Nadab (1 Kgs 15:26), Baasha (15:34), Omri (16:25), Ahab (16:30), Ahaziah of Israel (22:53), Jehoram of Israel (2 Kgs 3:2), Jehoram of Judah (8:18), Ahaziah of Judah (8:27), Jehoahaz (13:2), Jehoash of Israel (13:11), Jeroboam II (14:24), Zechariah (15:9), Menahem (15:18), Pekahiah (15:24), Pekah (15:28), Hoshea (17:2), Manasseh (21:2), Amon (21:20), Jehoahaz of Judah (23:32), Jehoiakim (23:37), Jehoiachin (24:9), and Zedekiah (24:19). The only exceptions are found in 1 Sam 12:17, where Samuel accuses Israel for doing evil in the eyes of Yahweh by asking for a king, and 1 Kgs 14:22, where the narrator condemns Judah for provoking the "passion/jealousy" (קִנְאָה) of Yahweh with a series of abominable and idolatrous actions patterned after the conduct of the Canaanites.

[44] For a different and more common interpretation see F. E. Greenspahn ("An Egyptian Parallel to Judg 17:6 and 21:25," JBL 101 [1982]: 129–30), who argues that this statement implies that a king could and would ensure the people's doing what is right in God's eyes. But the later one dates the insertion of this editorial comment, the less sense it makes, inasmuch as the Deuteronomistic writers place responsibility for the ultimate demise of both Israel and Judah squarely on the shoulders of the kings. See esp. 2 Kgs 17:8,19–23; 21:10–22; 24:18–20.

came to Micah's house in the hill country of Ephraim.
⁹Micah asked him, "Where are you from?"
"I'm a Levite from Bethlehem in Judah," he said, "and I'm looking for a place
to stay."
¹⁰Then Micah said to him, "Live with me and be my father and priest, and I'll
give you ten shekels of silver a year, your clothes and your food." ¹¹So the Levite
agreed to live with him, and the young man was to him like one of his sons. ¹²Then
Micah installed the Levite, and the young man became his priest and lived in his
house. ¹³And Micah said, "Now I know that the LORD will be good to me, since
this Levite has become my priest."

17:7 The scene shifts in v. 7 with the introduction of a new character (lit.,
"now there was a young man from Bethlehem of Judah"),⁴⁵ about whom the
narrator provides some vital personal information.

First, he is labeled a youth *(naʿar)*.⁴⁶ The narrator's portrayal of the man as
a youth probably should be interpreted in light of the Mosaic prescription that
priestly service for descendants of Aaronite was to begin at age thirty.⁴⁷ His
relative youth compounds the irregularity of his later appointment as priest of
Micah.

Second, his geographic roots are traced to Bethlehem of Judah.⁴⁸ The
tribal reference intentionally distinguishes this site nine kilometers/five miles
south of Jerusalem, from a Zebulunite place of the same name near Nazareth
mentioned in Josh 19:15. The narrator's threefold repetition of the phrase
"from Bethlehem in Judah" in vv. 7–9 renders unlikely any interpretation that
treats the book primarily as a pro-Davidic/ anti-Saulide or pro-Judahite/anti-
Ephraimite polemic. By describing how this Judahite finds a home with
Micah, an Ephraimite, the narrator expresses his view that these two tribes,
Judah and Ephraim, are akin to one another, for both suffer from the same
spiritual disease. This character is an embarrassment to anyone who comes
from Bethlehem.

Third, he is from one of the clans of Judah. The NIV rendering, "who had
been living within the clan of Judah" is literally, "from a clan of Judah. Now
he was a Levite, and he was sojourning there." The expression *mimmišpaḥat
yĕhûdâ*, "from a clan of Judah," could be interpreted in one of two ways. For
legal purposes he could be considered a Judahite if he is the product of a Lev-
ite-Judahite intermarriage. In keeping with the compromising religious environment of the story, however, the narrator deliberately highlights his
Levitical heritage. On the other hand, he may have been a true Levite. Not

---

⁴⁵ The syntax of v. 7a is identical to v. 1, introducing a new character.
⁴⁶ On which see above on 16:26.
⁴⁷ Num 4:3,30. Num 8:24–26 prescribes a lower age limit of twenty-five years. The apparent
discrepancy (on which see Milgrom, *Numbers*, 65–66) does not affect the present argument.
⁴⁸ The identical phrase recurs in Ruth 1:1.

having been allotted territory like the rest of the Israelite tribes, the Levites were assigned forty-eight cities within the territories of the other tribes.[49] Since Bethlehem is not listed among these, it seems that some Levites had left their allotted cities and settled in unassigned towns and villages among their non-Levite countryfolk. Nevertheless, the narrator's circumstantial note that "he was sojourning there" suggests that this man's roots had not been firmly planted in Bethlehem.[50]

Fourth, with an added circumstantial clause the narrator observes that this young man was a Levite, the tribe that was given responsibility for the spiritual leadership of the nation by Moses. According to Exod 32:25–29, because the descendants of Levi had distinguished themselves by standing with Moses against the apostasy represented by the golden calf, they were rewarded for their faithfulness to Yahweh by receiving the divine blessing and being dedicated for priestly service.[51] The significance of this young man's Levitical status will not be lost to Micah in v. 13.

Fifth, the man was a sojourner in Bethlehem. As if to highlight his disposition, the narrator adds a second circumstantial clause to v. 7. The present statement, wĕhûʾ gār šām, "and he was sojourning there," echoes ʾăšer gār šām, "where he resides as an alien," in Deut 18:6, suggesting that the author is interpreting the present event as a parody of Moses' instructions regarding Levites in Deut 18:6–9. According to these verses, a Levite may leave his place of sojourn any time to go and live in the place Yahweh chooses, where he may offer cultic service in the name of Yahweh like his fellow Levites who stand before Yahweh and be rewarded with the same gifts as the resident Levites. As the present story progresses, however, this young man's conduct will violate those instructions in several vital respects. (1) His intended destination is not the central shrine of Yahweh but any place where he might find ...[52] (2) He does not join other Levites but displaces another unauthorized priest. (3)

---

[49] Cf. Num 35:1–8; Josh 21:1–42.

[50] The NIV's "who had been living within the clan of Judah" obscures the sense of גֵּר־שָׁ֖ם וְה֑וּא. The verb גּוּר means "to reside temporarily as an alien." In contrast to an אֶזְרָח, "one native born," a גֵּר, "sojourner," was a nonnative resident of a town or region, whose full acceptance as a citizen was resisted. As 19:16–30 indicates, sojourners were often viewed with suspicion and exploited by the local populace. On the status of resident aliens in ancient Israel see further D. I. Block, "Sojourner; Alien; Stranger," *ISBE* (rev. ed.) 4.561–63.

[51] Cf. the reference to the "covenant of Levi" in Mal 2:1–9. This is not the place to discuss the matter in detail, but critical scholarship has long distinguished between the Levitical and Aaronic priesthoods. For a survey and bibliography of the discussion see M. D. Rehm, "Levites and Priests," *ABD* 4.292–310. The present account shares the perspective of Deuteronomy, which uses the terms "Levites" and "priests" interchangeably and perceives the former as descendants from Levi (Deut 17:18; 21:5). On the Deuteronomic perspective see further Tigay, *Deuteronomy*, 169–70; Merrill, *Deuteronomy*, 267–69; J. G. McConville, *Law and Theology in Deuteronomy*, JSOT-Sup 33 (Sheffield: JSOT Press, 1984), 124–53.

[52] See further on v. 8 below.

He does not serve in the name of Yahweh but in the name of Micah. (4) He does not serve at the place of Yahweh's choosing but at a place chosen by a man. (5) He does not receive the honorarium prescribed in Deut 18:1–5 but room and board and garments agreed upon through negotiation.

The missing element in the description of the young man in v. 7 is his name, though the reader learns at the end of the next chapter (18:30) that his name was Jonathan ("The LORD has given") and that he was the son of Gershom and grandson of Moses. Ironically, while his employer Micah has a fine Yahwistic name, the reader is left to wonder who this character is. From the narrator's refusal to name him we may draw two conclusions. On the one hand, the author is embarrassed about his identity and tries to protect the memory of Moses.[53] On the other hand, by keeping the man anonymous the narrator invites the reader to generalize the present specific event to the Levite tribe as a whole. This man's behavior is typical of the group.

17:8 The man's character is revealed further by the actions attributed to him in v. 8. He departs from Bethlehem and sets out to sojourn any place he might find convenient. The purpose phrase *lāgûr baʾăšer yimṣāʾ*, "to sojourn wherever he could find" (NIV, "in search of some other place to stay") is quite ambiguous, leaving the reader to wonder for what he is searching: food? colleagues? a place to stay? a job? the place of Yahweh's choosing? Unlike Abraham, who also set out for an unknown destination but who went with a keen sense of the calling of God, this person is shiftless. He has no passion for God, no sense of divine calling, no burden of responsibility. He is a "laid back" professional minister following the path of least resistance and waiting for an opportunity to open up. And he just happens to arrive[54] at the house of Micah[55] in the hill country of Ephraim. But what a stroke of luck this turns out to be, for both him and Micah!

17:9 In the negotiations between the unnamed Levite and Micah we observe the narrator's literary flair at its best. The dialogue is deliberately cast to highlight the opportunism of both men. The conversation opens naturally enough with the host asking his newly arrived guest from where he has come. The reader already knows the answer, but as in the case of Micah's self-confessed thievery (v. 2), the narrator lets the characters speak for themselves. The man's answer is intentionally constructed to echo and confirm the narrator's own interpretation.[56] He begins not by answering Micah's question but

---

[53] Like the Massoretes. See on 18:30 below.

[54] The final expression in the verse, לַעֲשׂוֹת דַּרְכּוֹ, "making his way," is unusual.

[55] Most translations including the NIV see here simply a reference to Micah's house, but since Micah has established his place as a cult center, it could also be rendered Beth-Micah, in opposition to Beth-Yahweh, "the house of Yahweh," the place which Yahweh would choose.

[56] Literally, "I am a Levite from Bethlehem of Judah, and I am going to sojourn wherever I can find."

by declaring his tribal/professional class. Then he identifies his place of origin and the purpose[lessness] of his travels. Unashamedly he confesses his shiftlessness but also his openness to any opportunity that might come his way.

17:10 Never one to miss an opportunity himself, Micah immediately grasps the potential significance of this chance encounter. He offers the man a position as household priest, cleverly drafting a proposal for the unnamed visitor that appeals both to the man's ego and his ambition. His job description may be summarized with three simple propositions.

1. "Be my companion." His invitation, "Live with me," should be interpreted against the background of the Levite's previous sojourning. Micah hereby invites him to give up his unsettled life and find a true home here in his own household.

2. "Be my father." "Father" is a title of honor, analogous to the identification of Deborah as a "mother" in Israel in 5:7. During the monarchy "father" served as an honorific title for prophets (2 Kgs 6:21; 8:9; 13:14), but here, as in 18:19, it applies to a priest, who exercises spiritual authority and care. Micah's use of the title also suggests a willingness to subordinate himself to and be dependent upon the Levite. Micah may in fact have been fatherless,[57] and so he was relieved finally to have a father figure in his household. On the other hand, in the context the function of "father" may be intentionally ironic. The person who had been identified as a *naʿar*, "boy," in v. 7 is called upon to play a mature, fatherly role, another symptom of a topsy-turvy world (cf. Isa 3:12).

3. "Be my priest." Micah hereby invites the Levite to serve as his personal representative before God and to see to it that cultic activities are performed at his shrine on his behalf.

The insecurity of Micah in this proposition is obvious. Even though he has built his own shrine, installed his own shrine, arranged for the proper accoutrements, and dedicated his own son as his priest, he has been plagued by doubts. Instead of relying on a system of worship and cultic expression designed by God and guaranteed to be effective, his is a man-made religion. Such expressions of faith can never satisfy the doubts of the human soul. In the meantime Micah does not seem to have been troubled that with this proposition for the newcomer he has made his own son's role redundant (v. 5). On the contrary, to enhance the proposition for the Levite, Micah offers him a handsome salary of ten shekels[58] of silver annually,[59] a suit of clothes,[60] and a living allowance.[61]

---

[57] Vv. 1–5 had spoken only of his mother.

[58] As in vv. 3–4, a unit of weight, presumably the shekel, is assumed.

[59] Hb. לְיָמִים, lit. "with reference to days." On יָמִים meaning "years" see *GBH* 135dN, *HALOT*, 400–401. The present expression is equivalent to יָמִימָה מִיָּמִים in 11:40.

[60] Hb. בְּגָדִים עֵרֶךְ, lit. "arrangement of clothing," probably refers to the vestments worn while performing priestly duties.

[61] Hb. מִחְיָתֶךָ, "your sustenance." מִחְיָה, which appeared earlier in 6:4, derives from a root חָיָה, "to live."

Verse 10 and the episode conclude abruptly with "So the Levite went."[62] Whatever the significance of this clause, the deal is good for both Micah and the Levite.

17:11–12 Verses 11–12 emphasize that each of Micah's propositions is accepted, though not exactly as expected. First, the Levite agrees[63] to live with Micah.[64] Second, the Levite joins the family but with an ironic inversion. Micah hires the youth to be his father, but he treats him like one of his sons.[65] This relationship sets the stage for subsequent events. Third, the Levite allows himself to be ordained to the priesthood by Micah. As in v. 5 the idiom for ordination translates literally, "he filled his hands," which in this context may carry a double meaning. The narrator may also be referring to the silver wages with which Micah filled his hands. In any case he became Micah's private priest and settled down in his house.

17:13 As for Micah, he is thrilled by his stroke of luck. So long as he had his own son functioning as priest, doubts about the efficacy of his cultic provisions plagued his mind. But now his cult has legitimacy—he has a Levite for a priest.[66] But neither Micah nor the Levite seems aware of the incongruities in the situation. Aware of the tradition that gave the Levites a monopoly on the priesthood in Israel, Micah assumes that now that he has engaged a member of this clan he has automatic access to the resources of heaven. Surely Yahweh will be impressed by his adoption of a more orthodox approach to religious affairs. But he is totally oblivious to the fact that his approach, specifically his capitalization on the presence of a Levite to manipulate the deity, is fundamentally pagan. The Levite is nothing more than a good luck charm.

As for the Levite, instead of denouncing Micah for his aberrant cult and

---

[62] Most modern commentators and translations, including the NIV, simply drop the clause as spurious. *BHS* deletes the clause as a dittograph on the first two words of v. 11. Contextual requirements argue against translating it "And he departed" since v. 11 declares the opposite, unless the narrator hereby seeks to highlight the man's *Wanderlust*. It is possible he went restlessly on his way, looking for other opportunities but finally was convinced this was the most advantageous situation. Although the versions tend to support the MT, the most sensible solution may be to follow Peshitta in attaching these words to v. 11 and deleting one reference to the Levite (thus O'Connell, *Rhetoric of the Book of Judges*, 477). The text then reads לָשֶׁבֶת וַיּוֹאֶל הַלֵּוִי וַיֵּלֶךְ, "And the Levite went and agreed to stay …" Soggin (*Judges*, 266) follows G. R. Driver ("Problems in Judges Newly Discovered," *ALUOS* 4 [1962–63]: 18) in deriving וַיֵּלֶךְ from a root לָכַךְ, which in Arabic means "to hesitate."

[63] In *hiphil* Hb. יָאַל means "to be willing, keen," about something. The verb will return in 19:6.

[64] The statement echoes Exod 2:21, where Moses agrees to live with Jethro. Thus U. Cassuto, *Exodus*, trans. I Abrahams (Jerusalem: Magnes, 1967), 25–26.

[65] The syntax of מִבָּנָיו כְּאַחַד compares with מִמֶּנּוּ כְּאַחַד, "like one of us," in Gen 3:22. Cf. *GBH* 129o.

[66] M. D. Rehm ("Levites and Priests," *ABD* 4.301) notes correctly that from the beginning of the period of the Judges, Israelites perceived the Levites as Yahweh's authorized representatives and specialists in cultic affairs. Accordingly, Micah looked upon this Levite as a pledge of divine blessing upon his house.

warning him of the dangers of his course of action (cf. Deut 13:6–11), he capitalizes on this glorious opportunity. Micah has opened new doors for him by offering him meaningful employment and guaranteeing his well-being for the rest of his life. Blinded by his own ambition to the heterodoxy of the situation, the young Levite cannot resist the heady offer of "fatherhood" within the nation of Israel. The prospect of being looked to as a spiritual advisor and mentor of this rich man is intoxicating. No one in his "right mind" would turn it down. But in the mind of the narrator, the Levite's acceptance of the position represents one more symptom of the pervasive Canaanization of Israelite society. In the words of Malachi, the heirs of "the covenant of Levi" have corrupted their high calling. Instead of serving as an agent of life and peace, revering Yahweh and standing in awe of his name, offering truthful and righteous instruction, walking with Yahweh in peace and uprightness, turning Micah back from iniquity, preserving knowledge, and serving as a messenger of Yahweh of hosts, this Levite has himself apostasized. He has lent his support to the perversion of his countryman, failed to keep Yahweh's ways, and demonstrated partiality to this man with money (cf. Mal 2:1–9). The religious establishment in Israel has been thoroughly infected with the Canaanite disease.

(3) The Corruption of an Israelite Tribe (18:1–31)

The transition to a new phase in the plot of chaps. 17–18 is signaled in 18:1 with a shift from past action verbs to participle forms and an abbreviated version of the notice encountered earlier in 17:7: "In those days Israel had no king [lit., "there was no king in Israel"]." As an episode marker this formula invites the reader to look back and interpret the preceding events in light of the absence of a king. Whether the narrator has in mind the kingship of Yahweh or the reign of a human monarch, according to Deuteronomic law the entire nation should have risen up against Micah and stoned him for his idolatrous ways (Deut 13:6–11). Under later circumstances people should have been able to look to a king to ensure orthodoxy and orthopraxy in cultic affairs. Even if the narrator is looking forward to a human king, the comment reflects Israel's repudiation of Yahweh as sovereign. But Yahweh will not abdicate his rule simply because his people reject him. Although the Danite migration in chap. 18 is presented as a humanistic enterprise from beginning to end, in the providence of God the Danite treatment of Micah may be interpreted as the divine response to Micah for his abominable behavior.[67] With delightful irony the despised Danites serve as agents of judgment upon this representative of the high and mighty Ephraimites.

---

[67] So also Boling (*Judges*, 258–59), who notes astutely that the name Dan (דָן) means" judgment."

At the same time, "In those days Israel had no king" also represents the narrator's commentary on the following chapter. But what have the adventures of the Danites to do with the absence of a king? For those who interpret the Book of Judges as a promonarchic treatise, the connection is unsettling. According to 1 Samuel 4–8, particularly 8:20, a constitutional monarchy is perceived as the key to military success. But this chapter portrays a tribe venturing out independently of Yahweh and without the benefit of a king but achieving perfect success. The nation needs no king to lead them in battle or into apostasy. They will do both on their own.

Within the plot of chaps. 17–18, the corruption of the Danite tribe is obviously the narrator's primary concern. The primary function of chap. 17 has been to provide necessary background for the establishment of the aberrant cult site at Dan. But the placement of this narrative here is strategic, following the pattern of chap. 1, where the summary of the Danite fiasco vis-à-vis the Amorites in their allotted territory appears at the end. Furthermore, coming after the cycle of stories of Samson, a member of the Danite tribe but one who embodies all that is wrong with Israel, the reader anticipates evidence of a further downward spiral of Israel's spiritual condition.

From a literary perspective chap. 18 is a masterpiece, employing dialogue, characterization, plot, and point of view with great skill. Most impressive, however, is the narrator's use of irony, not only in the fine details but in the broader scheme as well. Many have recognized the links between this account and earlier descriptions of Israel's conquest of Palestine, particularly the sending of the twelve spies to scout the land, as recorded in Num 12:16–14:45 and Deut 1:19–46.[68] The points of contact among these three texts may be summarized as follows:

Narrative Element	Num 12:16–14:45	Deut 1:19–46	Judg 18:1–31
Landless situation of the participants	12:16	1:19–21	18:1
Selection of tribal representative to scout the land	13:4–16	1:23b	18:2a
Dispatch of scouts	13:17–20		18:2b
Arrival in the hill country	13:17(?)	1:24	18:2c

[68] See especially A. Malamat, "The Danite Migration and the Pan-Israelite Exodus-Conquest: A Biblical Narrative Pattern," *Bib* 51 (1970): 1–16; O'Connell, *Rhetoric of the Book of Judges*, 235–38.

Narrative Element	Num 12:16–14:45	Deut 1:19–46	Judg 18:1–31
Northern extremity of expedition	13:21		18:7
Return to base camp	13:23–26a	1:25a	18:8
Report about the land	13:26b–27 13:32a	1:25b	18:9
Report about the population	13:28–29 13:31,32b–33	1:28	18:10
Response of the people	14:1–4	1:26–33	18:11–13 18:27–31

Although the thematic links among these accounts are strong, verbal links are relatively rare. One may conclude, therefore, that this chapter offers an example of analogical narrative rather than echo narrative as we will find in the next chapter. In fact, the differences between this account and the previous reports are as striking as the similarities. Especially impressive is the present narrator's attribution of the Danite adventure entirely to human initiative and human effort. To be sure, they seek a divine oracle from Micah, but the response rings hollow, and in any case this is of a totally different order than Yahweh's charge to send out scouts in Num 13:1–3. Equally striking is the difference in the people's response to the report of the scouts. Whereas in the original event the people had refused to enter the land despite its attractiveness and the promise of divine presence, the Danites respond to the scouts' report with enthusiastic entry into the fray.

Based on these observations, one may conclude that this chapter is deliberately composed as a parody on the earlier spy mission traditions. Nothing in this chapter is normal; people's values and behavior are all topsy-turvy. Still the mission succeeds, on the surface at least. In the end the Danites have a territory they may claim as their home, but they have sold their souls to Canaanite values. Apart from differences in dialect perhaps, an outside observer visiting Laish before and after the conquest would hardly have noticed a difference. The Danites have discovered the enemy, and the enemy is themselves.

Structurally this chapter divides into two major parts, dealing respectively with the mission of the spies (vv. 1–10) and the migration of the tribe (vv. 11–31). The latter part subdivides further, but we will leave that for the commentary.

¹**In those days Israel had no king.**

And in those days the tribe of the Danites was seeking a place of their own where they might settle, because they had not yet come into an inheritance among

the tribes of Israel. ²So the Danites sent five warriors from Zorah and Eshtaol to spy out the land and explore it. These men represented all their clans. They told them, "Go, explore the land."

The men entered the hill country of Ephraim and came to the house of Micah, where they spent the night. ³When they were near Micah's house, they recognized the voice of the young Levite; so they turned in there and asked him, "Who brought you here? What are you doing in this place? Why are you here?"

⁴He told them what Micah had done for him, and said, "He has hired me and I am his priest."

⁵Then they said to him, "Please inquire of God to learn whether our journey will be successful."

⁶The priest answered them, "Go in peace. Your journey has the LORD's approval."

⁷So the five men left and came to Laish, where they saw that the people were living in safety, like the Sidonians, unsuspecting and secure. And since their land lacked nothing, they were prosperous. Also, they lived a long way from the Sidonians and had no relationship with anyone else.

⁸When they returned to Zorah and Eshtaol, their brothers asked them, "How did you find things?"

⁹They answered, "Come on, let's attack them! We have seen that the land is very good. Aren't you going to do something? Don't hesitate to go there and take it over. ¹⁰When you get there, you will find an unsuspecting people and a spacious land that God has put into your hands, a land that lacks nothing whatever."

THE MISSION OF THE DANITE SCOUTS (18:1–10).   **18:1**   Having fixed the context of the events of this chapter with "In those days Israel had no king," the narrator proceeds immediately to his primary focus of interest: the migration of the tribe of Dan. The crisis that precipitates the Danite migration is described in the last clause of v. 1, which translates literally "because until that day it had not fallen to them in the midst of the tribes of Israel as a grant." However, this text presents a dilemma. What is to be made of Josh 19:40–48, which explicitly recounts the allotment of a territory west of Benjamin to the Danites?[69] And what is to be made of vv. 2,8,11, not to mention 13:2,25, which have the Danites living in Zorah and Eshtaol? The problem is compounded by the absence of a subject for the verb. *What* had not fallen?

The translations answer the last question differently. Some assume that the subject is the lot, that is, at that time no land had been allotted the Danites as their inheritance.[70] But this interpretation is unlikely for several reasons. First, the full form of the idiom assumed by this reading never occurs in the

---

[69] Gray (*Joshua, Judges, and Ruth*, 366) maintains that Josh 19:40–48 is artificially constructed from the note of the second and fifth administrative districts of Judah found in Josh 15:33–36 and 45–46. These groupings supposedly all come from the period of the monarchy.

[70] Thus the NRSV, which reads, "for until then no territory among the tribes of Israel had been allotted to them." Similarly the NASB.

Old Testament.[71] Second, the account of the division of the land in Joshua 18–19 always uses different verbs in association with *gôrāl,* "lot."[72] Third, where lots are cast, using the idiom *hippîl gôral,* "to cast a lot," this always involves other rewards,[73] but never land. Fourth, because the verb *nāpĕlâ,* "it fell," is feminine, the masculine noun *gôrāl* is out of the question. Within this context the assumed subject must therefore be either *ʾereṣ,* "land," or *naḥălâ,* "grant," both of which are feminine. Indeed the closest analogue to the present reading is found in Ezek 47:14,18, where it is clearly the land, not the lot, that falls.[74] The narrator's point here is simply that the land allotted as the grant of the tribe of Dan in Josh 19:40–48 had not come into their possession. According to 1:34–36 the Danite efforts at taking the land had been ineffective because the Amorites had repulsed them and sent them into the hills.

Regarding the apparent Danite presence in Zorah and Eshtaol, it should be noted first that the references to only two sites suggests that the Danites as a tribe had not established firm and permanent residence in the region. Second, the generally east-to-west arrangement in the catalogue of cities allotted to the tribe of Dan in Josh 19:40–48 accords with a possible Danite presence in Zorah and Eshtaol. These two cities, near the western border of Benjamin, would have been the first ones encountered when the Danites separated from the rest of Israel and headed for their territory.[75] Indeed these cities probably served as base camps for their forays into their allotment.[76] Third, the Danite occupation of Zorah and Eshtaol is not excluded by 1:34–36. On the contrary, located in the hilly eastern part of their allotted territory, these cities would have provided a refuge for Danites repulsed from the lowlands by the Amorites. But the territory they occupied was too small, and the productive agricultural land in the valleys and the coastal plain was denied them. This accounts for the present crisis and explains the urgency with which the Danites pursue their migration northward. They need *Lebensraum* (living space).[77]

The Danites' response to the crisis is natural but humanistic. Instead of

---

[71] I.e., נָפַל גּוֹרָל בְּנַחֲלָה, "the lot fell as an inheritance." וְהוּא־הִפִּיל לָהֶן גּוֹרָל, "he allots their portions," does indeed occur in Isa 34:17, but the text is too vague to shed light on this text.

[72] יָרָה, "to throw," 18:6; הִשְׁלִיךְ, "to cast," 18:8,10; עָלָה, "to go up," 18:11; 19:10; יָצָא, "to go out," 16:1; 19:1,17,24,32,40; Num 33:54.

[73] People, Jonah 1:7; Neh 11:1; garments, Ps 22:19; supplies, Neh 10:34[Hb. 35]; money, Prov 1:14; people to serve, 1 Chr 24:31; 25;8; 26:13–14.

[74] So also Num 34:2.

[75] Josh 15:33 allocates these cities to Judah.

[76] Cf. the reference to מַחֲנֵה־דָן, "the camp of Dan" (Mahaneh Dan), in 13:25.

[77] Cp. the interpretation of F. A. Spina ("The Dan Story Historically Reconsidered," *JSOT* 2 [1977]: 60–71), who argues that the Danites were a disaffected ʿApiru-like group consisting of indigenous Palestinians ("the seven nations"), Sea People elements, and perhaps some recent fugitives from Egypt but united by their worship of Yahweh. These people were forced to migrate because of the aggression of others, not their own failure to take aggressive action.

confessing their sin of unbelief and appealing to Yahweh for aid, they do what is right in their own eyes. They seek a land they can claim as their grant and in which they can live. The narrator's use of the term *nahălâ* is patently ironic. Although the NIV ("inheritance") and most other English versions translate the word with inheritance terminology, this is a feudal expression, referring primarily to land given by a superior to his vassals as a reward for past services—fundamentally, military service is involved—and in anticipation of future service.[78] This designation is appropriate for the territory originally given to Israel by Yahweh and distributed by Joshua among the tribes by lot, but it does not suit territory seized by force, particularly when it is at another Israelite tribe's expense.[79] The latter may be designated a *yĕruššâ* or *ʾahuzzâ*, both of which mean "possession, property seized." Since *nahălâ* (NIV, "inheritance") expresses solidarity between a donor and recipient, however, this word is out of the question.

18:2 Perhaps mindful of an earlier generation, rather than moving the tribe en masse in search of a new homeland, the Danites appoint five men to find a suitable place. Theses men are referred to literally as "men, sons of strength/wealth," which should probably be translated "noble men."[80] The designation invites comparison with the divine envoy's address of Gideon as a *gibbôr hehayil*, "noble hero," in 6:12 (NIV, "mighty warrior") and the narrator's characterization of Jephthah in 11:1. The present designation would have suited Joshua and Caleb, the two trustworthy members of the original team of twelve Israelite scouts (Num 14:5–10), but here it is ironic. The Danites may be heroic figures physically and militarily, but they are spiritual pygmies.

The scouts' assignment is expressed with two purpose infinitives: *lĕraggel ʾet-haʾares ûlĕhoqrah*, "to scout [NIV, "spy out"] the land and to explore it." The former, a verb related to the noun *regel*, "foot," is not used in the account of the original spy mission in Numbers 13–14,[81] but it does occur in Num 21:32 and Deut 1:24.[82] The second, *haqar*, "to explore," is found elsewhere in prose texts in Deut 13:15; 2 Sam 10:3; 1 Chr 19:3 but is more common in poetry.[83] Although the meanings of the verbs are clear, the geographic goal of the scouts' mission is only vaguely referred to as "the land." But which land? Israelite territory? Ephraimite? foreign? The reader must wait for the answer.

---

[78] Cf. Block, *Gods of the Nations*, 76–79, for further discussion and bibliography.

[79] Although the northern boundary of Naphtali's allotment is not clearly spelled out in Josh 19:32–39, most biblical geographers include Laish/Dan within the territory of this tribe. See Rasmussen, *NIV Atlas*, 99; Beitzel, *Moody Atlas*, map 31.

[80] The NIV's "warriors" is too specific. The expression may also mean "men of wealth."

[81] Num 12:16–14:45 prefers תּוּר, "to spy out, explore." Cf. 13:2,16, etc.

[82] Cf. also Josh 6:25; 7:2; 14:7; 2 Sam 10:3; 1 Chr 19:3. The participle מְרַגְּלִים is used as a noun, "scouts," in Gen 42:9–34; Josh 2:1; 6:22–23; 1 Sam 6:24; 2 Sam 15:10.

[83] Cf. *HALOT* 1.347–48.

Despite the vagueness of the description of the mission, after quoting the orders to the scouts to go and explore the land, the narrator's report in v. 2c, particularly the phrase "to the house of Micah," creates the impression that they headed straight for Micah's place.[84] This assessment is reinforced by noting the similarities between v. 2 and Josh 2:1, as highlighted in the following synopsis:[85]

Joshua 2:1	Judges 18:2
And Joshua the son of Nun sent	And the sons of Dan sent
from Shittim	
two men	five men
	from their family,
	out of their whole number,
	noble men,
	from Zorah and Eshtaol
as scouts	to scout the land
secretly	and to explore it.
saying,	And they said to them,
"Go,	"Go,
view the land,	explore the land."
especially Jericho."	
And they went	
and they came	And they came
to the house of a prostitute,	to the hill country of Ephraim,
whose name was Rahab,	to the house of Micah,
and they lay down there.	and they lodged there.

The parallelism suggests that the narrator perceives "the house of Micah" to be equivalent to "the house of the prostitute" in the earlier account. This interpretation certainly suits the overall tenor of the book, especially in view of the narrator's earlier application of the language of prostitution ("playing the harlot") to Israel's idolatrous practices (2:17; 8:27; 8:33). This may explain also why Micah is out of the picture in vv. 2b–6. The scouts' primary interest is in the Levite, the facilitator of their spiritually harlotrous activity.

18:3 When the scouts arrived at Micah's house, they appear to have been greeted by the young man, the Levite. The narrator informs the reader that the Danites recognized the voice of the Levite immediately, but he does not explain how. One may speculate that in his shiftless sojournings the young man had spent some time in Danite territory. Since he arrived at Micah's house and

---

[84] So also Becker, *Richterzeit und Königtum*, 236.
[85] The underlined words represent equivalent expressions.

had been installed as his priest, the visitors would naturally not have recognized the Levite by his external appearance (he probably was wearing his vestments), but his voice was unmistakable. The reference to the voice is doubly significant, however, since the focus in the following scenes will be on his oral utterances. In the minds of the Danites his will be the voice of God.

Normally when people arrive at someone's place, the host initiates the conversation. But the Danites are so surprised at hearing the familiar voice of the Levite here in Micah's house they immediately begin interrogating him. Do they recognize the incongruity of the situation: a Levite living in the home of a known apostate? Whatever their motivation, the questions they ask are telling: (1) "Who brought you here?" (2) "What are you doing in this place?" (3) "Why are you here?"[86] If the Levite had been playing his rightful spiritual role, he would have turned the tables and asked these same questions of the scouts. If they were honest, they would have replied: (1) "The tribe of Dan has sent us." (2) "We have come to spend the night." (3) "We are scouting for a land where we can live and claim as our *naḥălâ* [NIV, "inheritance"]." Each answer deserves a stern priestly rebuke. (1) "You should be going where Yahweh sends you." (2) "You should not spend the night in the home of this apostate Micah; he should be stoned." (3) "You should not be scouting for territory; go back and claim the land Yahweh has granted you as your *naḥălâ.*"

18:4 As for the Levite, in his response to these questions he should have been able to say: (1) Yahweh has brought me here." (2) "I am instructing the people of this household in the way of Yahweh." (3) "I am faithfully fulfilling my charge as a Levite." Instead he answers: (1) "Micah has done all kinds of things for me."[87] Although the narrator allows the reader to fill in the details from 17:10–11, the Levite gives Micah full credit for his present position. (2) "He has hired me [for wages]." This comment not only demonstrates that his motives are totally self-serving, but they also open the possibility of being employed by someone else who might pay more. (3) "I have become [NIV, "I am"] his priest." His answer echoes the last clause of 17:5. The Levite is as humanistic as the Danites. His primary obligation is to a man, not a deity, let alone the God of Israel.

18:5 Like Micah in 7:10–13, the Danites immediately recognize their good fortune in this surprise encounter. Just as Micah's cult had lacked credibility and authority until the Levite arrived, so the mission of these scouts lacks authority without an oracular authentication from deity. But what a

---

[86] On the use of a triplet of rhetorical questions as an intentional literary device see Boling, *Judges,* 75, 263.

[87] The NIV obscures the direct quotation ("He told them what Micah had done for him"). The idiom וָכָֽזֶה זֹה כָּ, lit., "like this and like that," which occurs elsewhere only in 2 Sam 11:25 and 1 Kgs 14:4, is casual and flippant.

stroke of luck! This stopover will provide them with much more than rest for the journey. Opportunistically, but without challenging the man's credentials, the Danite scouts present their solicitation to the Levite. Their request is cast in the standard form of an oracular inquiry: "Please inquire of God ..."[88] The reference to the deity by the generic designation Elohim rather than Yahweh, the covenant name of the God of Israel, is telling. Although the scouts assume that any Levitical priest has access to the mind of God, the narrator does not explain how they expect the Levite to extract an oracle from the deity. Presumably he would use the teraphim or ephod mentioned in 17:5.

18:6 The question on the Danites' mind is, Will their present course of action[89] be a complete success?[90] Although the scouts obviously welcomed the Levite's response, the reader will find it intriguing in several respects. First, the Levite's answer is extremely glib, both in its immediacy and in its content. The narrator's placement of the oracular declaration immediately after the request raises questions about whether or not the Levite even bothered to consult the deity. He seems to know instinctively that their mission will prove successful. With respect to content, he begins his answer with a standard formula, "Go in peace." This kind of pronouncement requires no effort at all. Second, like the Delphic oracles and others recorded in Scripture, the Levite's answer is extremely vague.[91] Contrary to the NIV and many modern translations, he does not declare outrightly that the mission will succeed, only that, literally, "The course on which you are going is before the LORD." This could mean that it has the approval of Yahweh's watchful eye, but it could also mean the opposite,[92] that is, the conduct of the scouts and the Danites as a tribe is under critical scrutiny by Yahweh. In any case, the scouts interpret it positively; the Levite has uttered the words they wanted to hear. Third, the Levite piously camouflages the irregularity of the proceedings by invoking the name of Yahweh. The Danites had asked for a word from God (Elohim); he replies with a message supposedly from Yahweh. But the reader can see through this charade. Yahweh would never sanction such a faithless mission. Later the "oracle" will be used to rationalize the slaughter of the Laishites (v. 10).

18:7 The reader is left to fill in the gaps between vv. 6 and 7. Refreshed after a night at Micah's house and armed with a word from Yahweh, the scouts

---

[88] Cf. 1:1; 20:23; 1 Sam 14:37; 22:13,15. For discussion see G. Gerleman, *THAT* 2.843–45.

[89] The construction, with דַּרְכֵּנוּ, "our way," as the subject rather than the scouts focuses the attention on the mission rather than the men.

[90] On the elative use of the *hiphil* (הַצְלִיחַ) see *IBHS,* 27 n.16.

[91] Cf. the thrice repeated oracle in 1 Kgs 22:6,12,15. On the vagueness of this oracle see Block, "Empowered by the Spirit: The Spirit of Yahweh in the Historiographic Writings," *SBTJ* 1 (1997): 48–50.

[92] Cf. Amos 9:4. "To be before the LORD" could be the obverse of "the LORD has set his face against," as in Lev 17:10; 20:3,5; Jer 21:10; 44:11.

continued on their journey, which eventually took them to Laish, at the northern extremity of the promised land.[93] Identified as Leshem in Josh 19:47,[94] Laish ("lion") had a long history even before the arrival of the Israelites.[95] With its pleasant climate and watered by copious springs that feed into the Jordan River, this site at the foot of Mount Hermon was the most productive region of the country. Its political power in the region in the second millennium was exceeded only by Hazor, eighteen miles to the south down the Huleh Valley.

The scouts' impression of the population of Laish is summarized in two words: beṭaḥ and šōqēṭ. Since both expressions are quite ambiguous, however, it is difficult to know exactly what they thought. Since the former derives from a root that means fundamentally "to trust," it could denote either "confident" or "carefree, unsuspecting."[96] The latter, coming from a root meaning "to rest," could denote either "peaceful, tranquil" or "relaxed, idle."[97] This raises the question of whether the people of Laish were careful or careless, confident or lax.[98] Perhaps the narrator intends both. In any case he effectively transfers the reader's sympathies from the Israelite Danites to the Canaanite residents of this town.

But why did the Laishites feel so secure? The text offers five clues, to which we may add one more extratextual consideration. First, they lived "according to the custom of the Sidonians" (NIV, "like the Sidonians"). Again a firm understanding of the sense is precluded by the vagueness of the expression, in this case kĕmišpaṭ ṣidōnîm, which could mean either "according to the rule of the Sidonians" or "according to the custom of the Sidonians." In the latter interpretation, the Laishites would have adopted Sidonian standards of sociopolitical order.[99] But the former interpretation is more likely, in which

---

[93] The northern and southern extremities of the land are defined in the formula "from Dan to Beersheba," which occurs in 20:1; 1 Sam 3:20; 2 Sam 3:10; 17:11; 24:2,15; 1 Kgs 5:5; reverse order, 1 Chr 21:2; 2 Chr 30:5. The names appears as a stereotypical word pair in Amos 8:14.

[94] This verse functions as a footnote describing the migration of the tribe and the renaming of Laish as Dan.

[95] The name appears in the nineteenth century Execration Texts from Egypt (*ANET*, 329) and in the early fifteenth century list of Asiatic cities conquered by Thutmose III (*ANET*, 242), as well as the eighteenth century Mari texts from Mesopotamia (*La-yi-iš*; also in association with Hazor). On the last named see A. Malamat, "Northern Canaan and the Mari Texts," in *Near Eastern Archaeology in the Twentieth Century, N. Glueck Festschrift*, ed. J. A. Sanders (Garden City: Doubleday, 1970), 164–77. On the excavation and pre-Danite history of the site see A. Biran, *Biblical Dan* (Jerusalem: Israel Exploration Society, 1994), 27–58; id., "Dan," *ABD* 2.12–14. Further bibliography is provided.

[96] Cf. *HALOT* 1.120. Cp. Ezekiel's use of the phrase *yāšab lābeṭaḥ* in 28:26 and developed more fully in 34:25–31. Cf. also 38:8,11,14; 39:26.

[97] NIV, "secure." Cf. BDB, 1053.

[98] On Laishite life and culture in the Late Bronze Age see Biran, *Biblical Dan*, 105–23.

[99] Soggin (*Judges*, 272) suggests Laish was a place where Phoenician customs were followed, including the Phoenician disinterest in war.

case the Laishites lived under the umbrella of the Sidonians. The idiom *kĕmišpāṭ*, "according to the custom of," bears the sense that Laish "is located within the sphere of influence of the coastal city of Sidon."[100] This would accord with what we know of Sidon's status at the end of the second millennium B.C. Although Sidon existed in the shadow of Tyre from the time of Solomon, prior to this she had been the premier Phoenician city.[101]

Second, there was no one to humiliate the people of the region in any way (NIV, "and since their land lacked nothing").[102] The participle *maklîm*, "putting to shame," probably refers to the effects of military defeat at the hands of external enemies.[103]

Third, no one exercised oppressive rule over the citizens (NIV, "they were prosperous). The phrase *yôrēš ʿeṣer*, which translates literally "seizing restraint," refers to exploitative internal rulers brutalizing the people.[104] The story of Abimelech graphically illustrates a problem that was common in the ancient world.

Fourth, they were far from the Sidonians. Separated from Laish by the Lebanon mountains and preoccupied with their maritime interests, the Sidonians had no time or interest in exerting political control in the interior. The expression "they were [NIV "lived"] a long way from the Sidonians" is more than a geographic idiom. The language belongs to the category of international relations, speaking of regression in legal obligations caused by distance.[105]

---

[100] Thus A. Malamat, "'... After the Manner of the Sidonians ... and How They Were Far from the Sidonians," *EI* 23 (A. Biran volumel, 1992): 194–94 [Hb.; Eng. summary p. 153*]. Cf. the Akk. expression, *kima paras Halab.*

[101] The Table of Nations, which omits Tyre all together, lists Sidon as the firstborn of Canaan (Gen 10:15). In the OT the gentilic "Sidonians" stands for "the Phoenicians" (Deut 3:9; Josh 13:4,6; Judg 3:3; 10:12; 18:7; 1 Kgs 5:20; 11:5; 16:31; 2 Kgs 23:13; Ezek 32:30; Ezra 3:7; 1 Chr 22:4). In Homer, "Sidonian" and "Phoenician" are interchanged, suggesting that the Greeks considered this city to be representative of the entire region. Cf. *Iliad* 6.290, 291; 23.743–44; *Odyssey* 4.83–85, 618; 13.270ff.; 14.288–91; 15.118, 415–17, 473. See further J. D. Muhly, "Homer and the Phoenicians," *Berytus* 19 (1970): 27; H. J. Katzenstein, *The History of Tyre* (Jerusalem: Magnes, 1973), 62–63.

[102] The addition of דָּבָר at the end of the clause is awkward, but it probably functions adverbially, "in any matter." A. A. Macintosh ("The Meaning of *mklym* in Judges xviii 7," *VT* 35 [1985]: 76) treats the word as an accusative of respect. Soggin (*Judges*, 272) and *HALOT*, 212, apparently followed by the NIV, read מַחְסוֹר כָּל־דָּבָר וְאֵין, "there was no lack of anything," after v. 10. *BHS* emends the entire phrase to read בָּאָרֶץ מַדְבֵּר מֶלֶךְ וְאֵין, "there was no king who ruled over the land," based on the Syriac and Arabic meanings of *dbr*. See the full discussion by Macintosh, *VT* 35 (1985): 68–69. For a defense of the MT see O'Connell, *Rhetoric of the Book of Judges,* 477–80.

[103] For examples of the root כלם, "to be humiliated," used in contexts of military defeat see Isa 45:17; 50:7; 54:4; Prov 25:8; Ps 44:10.

[104] The MT's עֶצֶר יוֹרֵשׁ is difficult, and many solutions to the problem have been offered. See O'Connell, *Rhetoric of the Book of Judges*, 479–80.

[105] Cf. Malamat, "'... After the Manner of the Sidonians,'" 195 [Hb.; Eng. summary, 153*].

Fifth, the Laishites lived in splendid isolation from the Aramaeans (Hb. *ʾārām*).[106] The NIV follows the MT in reading "[they] had no relationship with anyone else" (lit., "and a matter there was not to them with man *[ʾādām]*"). But this reading seems to be the result of a scribal misreading of Hebrew *d* for *r* in *ʾādām*.[107] By the late second millennium B.C., Aramean tribal groups had begun infiltrating Palestine from the north and east. If this interpretation is correct, the Laishites' isolation from the Arameans across the Anti-Lebanon mountain range to the east answers to their isolation from the Sidonians in the west.

Recent archaeological excavations of Dan may have unearthed one more reason for the Laishite smugness: massive defensive ramparts. Unlike most Canaanite cities of the time, Laish was not defended by stone walls but by huge ramparts consisting of alternating layers of soil from the surrounding region and debris from previous settlements.[108] The catalogue of descriptive phrases and clauses in v. 7 reflects the Danite scouts' excitement over the potential they saw in this city for their own people. Not only would the carefree and smug people of Laish be easy pickings for their own tribe, but the idyllic life of the residents of this part of the world offered a splendid answer for the restlessness and frustration of their countrymen back in Zorah and Eshtaol.

18:8 The narrative is further telescoped in v. 8, announcing the return of the scouts to the Danite base at Zorah and then moving quickly to their report, cast in the form of direct speech. Their tribespeople initiate the conversation with a sentence fragment *mâ ʾattem,* "What do you …?" (NIV, "How did you find things?").[109] Either they are so anxious to hear the report or the scouts are so eager to give it that they cut off the questioners. The narrator assumes the reader will supply an ending like "… have to report?" or "… recommend we do?"

18:9–10 The scouts' enthusiasm for the prospects now before the tribe stands in starkest contrast to the report of the original twelve scouts sent out by Moses (Num 13:25–14:10). The earlier scouts had described the land of Canaan in the most glowing of terms but then discouraged the people from taking up the challenge. The present narrator captures the Danite scouts'

---

[106] Following the LXX, Old Latin, and Syr. in reading אֲרָם, *Aram,* in place of the MT's אָדָם. So many modern translations (NRSV, REB, NJB) and commentators (e.g., Soggin, *Judges,* 273; Boling, *Judges,* 263).

[107] These characters were often confused. Cf. Gen 10:3, which reads Riphath for Diphath (cf. 1 Chr 1:6), and 10:4, which exhibits the reverse error, read Dodanim for Rodanim (cf. 1 Chr 1:7).

[108] For further discussion see A. Biran, "Tell Dan, Five Years Later," *BA* 43 (1980): 169–72; id., *Biblical Dan,* 59–75.

[109] Soggin (*Judges,* 273, and *BHS*) recommend emendation to אַתֶּם מִי after Ruth 3:16, but this expression is no clearer.

excitement about what they have seen by opening the speech with a call to the Danites to get going. The account of the report is obviously abbreviated. Not only does the pronoun in "let's attack them" require an antecedent, but the article on "the land" also assumes the people know which specific territory they are talking about. They draw the people into their report of the land with their enthusiastic report (lit.): "We have seen the land, and behold! It is very good!"[110] Then they proceed to laud its utopian qualities with four irresistible qualifiers: (1) the land is very good/beautiful; (2) the people are secure/unsuspecting;[111] (3) the land has plenty of room for them all;[112] and (4) the land has absolutely no deficiency of resources.[113]

These descriptors are intentionally framed to ignite the enthusiasm of the Danites—each one presenting a stark contrast to their present situation in a region that lacks beauty/goodness—offers no living space, is occupied by hostile Amorites, and offers few resources to the tribe. After an opening exhortation in v. 9, the scouts seem impatient with their audience. They accuse them of stalling[114] and call on them to stop hesitating[115] (lit.) "to go, to enter, to possess the land." As if this triad of verbs is not enough to recall the original entry into Canaan,[116] the scouts add a note of piety with the committal formula, assuring their audience that God has given the land into their hands.[117] Much time has passed. Do not blame them for their ancestors' mistake. But the orthodoxy of their conviction is thrown into question by the substitution of the divine name, Yahweh, with Elohim, the generic designation for God. In the mind of the narrator, the divine name would have been

---

[110] "Behold" (הִנֵּה) is missing in the NIV. With the combination of רָאִינוּ and הִנֵּה, "We have seen … and behold …" they are trying to recreate their own experience in the minds of the audience. On הִנֵּה as an emotional rhetorical marker see *IBHS* 40.2.1b. Contra D. J. McCarthy ("The Uses of *wĕhinnēh* in Biblical Hebrew," *Bib* 61 [1980]: 333–34), who treats this as a causal particle equivalent to כִּי, "for, because."

[111] If one interprets עַם בֹּטֵחַ, "a secure people," the men are imagining what their lot would be like if they lived there, in contrast to their present lot, harassed by the Amorites. If one interprets the phrase, "an unsuspective people," the men are emphasizing how easy it will be to capture the city of Laish.

[112] Hb. רַחֲבַת יָדַיִם, lit. "breadth of hands,"

[113] Note the emphatic statement at the end of v. 10 (lit.): "a place where there is no lack of a thing which is in the land."

[114] The participle מַחְשִׁים derives from a root, חָשָׁה, "to be silent." The *hiphil* form, meaning "to hesitate, to do nothing," occurs elsewhere in 1 Kgs 22:3 and 2 Kgs 7:9. See further *DCH* 3.330.

[115] The verb עָצֵל, "to vacillate, hesitate," occurs only here *(niphal)*. The cognate adjective עָצֵל means "slow, idle."

[116] Cf. Deut 4:1,5; etc. On the Deuteronomic combinations of בּוֹא/יָרַשׁ and הֵבִיא/הוֹרִישׁ, see Weinfeld, *Deuteronomy and the Deuteronomic School*, 342.

[117] On the divine committal formula see above, p. 147f. and on 3:8. This form of the formula appears more than twenty times in the book. Cf. 1:2; 2:14a,23; 3:10,28; 4:7,14; 6:1; 7:7,9,15; 8:3,7; 9:29; 11:30,32; 12:3; 13:1; 15:12; 20:28.

incongruous in this compromising context.

THE MIGRATION OF THE DANITE TRIBE (18:11–31). In v. 11 the focus shifts from the scouts sent out by the tribe of Dan to the tribe as a group. The plot is complex, but its boundaries are set by the verbs *wayyisⁱû*, "and they set out," in v. 11 and *wayyāśîmû*, "and they set up," in v. 31 (NIV, "they continued to use"). In the narrator's mind this story is obviously not only about land, or the plot would have moved directly from vv. 11–13a (omitting the reference to Micah) to v. 27b–29 (again omitting the reference to Micah and his cultic property). What concerns the author more than land is the erection of the pagan image at Dan. The account breaks down into three discreet parts, each with its own geographic provenance: on the road to the hills of Ephraim (vv. 11–13); at the house of Micah (vv. 14–26, which bifurcates further into the Danite encounter with the Levite, vv. 14–20, and their encounter with Micah, vv. 21–26); at Laish (vv. 27–31). The narrator's special interest in religious rather than territorial issues is reflected in the amount of space devoted to the visit to Micah's house and the concluding two verses, which report the establishment of the pagan cult site at Dan.

¹¹Then six hundred men from the clan of the Danites, armed for battle, set out from Zorah and Eshtaol. ¹²On their way they set up camp near Kiriath Jearim in Judah. This is why the place west of Kiriath Jearim is called Mahaneh Dan to this day. ¹³From there they went on to the hill country of Ephraim and came to Micah's house.

The Danite Trek to the Hill Country of Ephraim (18:11–13). **18:11** The narrator does not divulge how many Danites responded to the challenge of the scouts to go and claim Laish as their own, but he seems intentionally to minimize their number. First, he notes that [only] six hundred men armed for battle set out from Zorah and Eshtaol. The number seems small,[118] especially when compared with other military figures in the book: the ten thousand men from Zebulun and Naphtali that Barak leads against Sisera (4:14) and the thirty-two thousand Gideon recruits from Asher, Zebulun, Naphtali, and Manasseh (7:3).[119] This number is also the same as the figure given for the remnant of the decimated tribe of Benjamin in 20:47. Although the present figure appears more normal than these large numbers, against the backdrop of those responses to calls to war it suggests limited response. Second, although the preposition "from" *(min)* in "from Zorah and Eshtaol" is a preposition of source, in "from the clan of the Danites" the preposition is best interpreted as designating a portion/segment of the clan of the Danites. Third, whereas in v.

---

[118] To this number probably should be added an equal number of women and perhaps double this number of children, making for a total population count of 2,400. Cf. v. 21.

[119] Cf. 6:35.

1 the narrator had spoken of the "tribe" *(šēbeṭ)* of Dan, here he uses the more limited expression *mišpāḥâ,* "clan."[120] Based on these three observations, it seems the scouts had reason to be critical and impatient with their tribesmen in vv. 9–10. Having been commissioned by the tribe as a whole, only a small fraction accepted their report. The rest of the Danites disappeared from history all together.

This conclusion is of great significance within the broader context of the story and heightens the irony of its outcome. The Danites as a tribe were unable to claim their relatively small territory in which no city was larger than Laish.[121] But this small band managed to march all the way to Laish and apparently take the city without any difficulty. They needed no divinely called governor, nor a king, as a later generation would demand.

18:12–13 By noting that the Danite force numbered six hundred men (lit.) "armed with weapons of war"[122] the narrator emphasizes that this is a military force from the outset, not a peaceful migration (v. 11). Having set out, their first stop was at Kiriath-jearim in Judah.[123] The parenthetical note added at the end of v. 12 observes that their campsite was actually located "behind" Kiriath-jearim.[124] This temporary stop seems to have been without incident, but it was significant enough for the event to be memorialized in the [re]naming of the site as Mahaneh-dan, "the camp of Dan."[125] From here the group moved on to the hill country of Ephraim, to the home of Micah. The addition of the last phrase creates the impression that this was an intentional intermediate destination from the outset and heightens the readers' anticipation. What will happen there this time? And will Micah enter the picture again? The narrative does not disappoint. In fact, two extremely significant encounters transpire here.

[14]Then the five men who had spied out the land of Laish said to their brothers, "Do you know that one of these houses has an ephod, other household gods, a carved image and a cast idol? Now you know what to do." [15]So they turned in there and went to the house of the young Levite at Micah's place and greeted him. [16]The

---

[120] On the difference see the introduction, p. 32f. This literary explanation is preferable to that of Becker *(Richterzeit und Königtum,* 236).

[121] The size of the tell at Ekron (Tell Miqne), including the acropolis, matched the size of the tell at Dan (formerly Tell el Qadi); both cover fifty acres. None of the remaining Danite cities named in Josh 19:40–48 was larger than this.

[122] On the absolute passive participle connected with an adverbial accusative in the construct state see GKC 116k; *GBH* 121o; *IBHS* 37.3b. These would have consisted of offensive armaments (spears, swords, bows and arrows) and defensive gear (shields, armor, helmets).

[123] Modern Tell el-Achar, eight miles north of Jerusalem.

[124] Most translate "behind" to mean "west of" (NASB, RSV, NRSV, REB, JPSV, NIV); Soggin *(Judges,* 273) reads "east of."

[125] Cf. the reference to another site by the same name in 13:25.

six hundred Danites, armed for battle, stood at the entrance to the gate. [17]The five men who had spied out the land went inside and took the carved image, the ephod, the other household gods and the cast idol while the priest and the six hundred armed men stood at the entrance to the gate.

[18]When these men went into Micah's house and took the carved image, the ephod, the other household gods and the cast idol, the priest said to them, "What are you doing?"

[19]They answered him, "Be quiet! Don't say a word. Come with us, and be our father and priest. Isn't it better that you serve a tribe and clan in Israel as priest rather than just one man's household?" [20]Then the priest was glad. He took the ephod, the other household gods and the carved image and went along with the people.

The Encounter with the Levite (18:14–20). **18:14** The narrator's amusement with the story is evident in the way he crafts the next episode.[126] When the Danites arrive at Micah's place, the scouts add a detail that had been missing in their previous report of their reconnaissance mission. But their disclosure of new information is craftily cast as a rhetorical question to their kinfolks: Are they aware that in Micah's compound[127] is a complete set of religious and cultic appurtenances—ephod, teraphim, and idol?[128] The scouts no doubt have an idea what should be done about these, but they put it to their confederates in the form of a proposition, "Now you know what to do."[129]

18:15–19 The narrator does not give their verbal answer. Instead, he lets the Danites' actions speak for themselves. Their strategy appears deliberate. First, they turn aside and head straight for the young Levite's house on the Micah compound (v. 15a).[130] The scouts' addendum to their report in v. 14 had said nothing about the Levite, but one may assume this is an abbreviation of a fuller version that calls attention to the cult objects. Second, they greet the Levite warmly, no doubt to curry his favor (v. 15b).[131] Third, the Dan-

---

[126] The integrity of this paragraph is questioned by many. H. Schmoldt ("Der Überfall auf Michas Haus (Jdc 18,13–18)," *ZAW* 105 [1993]: 92–98) reduces the original [emended] text to [13]"From there they went on to the hill country of Ephraim and came to Micah's house. [17]And the five men who had spied out the land 'answered' 'Go inside and take the carved image,' while the priest stood at the entrance to the gate." The remainder is deleted as secondary. But this method is based on extremely subjective standards of literary consistency.

[127] Note the plural בַּבָּתִּים הָאֵלֶּה, "in these houses."

[128] As in 17:4, פֶּסֶל וּמַסֵּכָה is a hendiadys, "molten sculpture."

[129] "You know" is the imperative דְּעוּ, "know," which can be understood with the sense, "Make up your minds."

[130] Hb. בֵּית מִיכָה, "house of Micah," may be understood as a name for the site as a whole, i.e., Beth-Micah.

[131] Hb. וַיִּשְׁאֲלוּ־לוֹ לְשָׁלוֹם, "and they asked concerning his well-being," is the standard Israelite greeting (1 Sam 10:4; 17:22; 25:5; 30:21; 2 Sam 8:10; Jer 15:5; 1 Chr 18:10). Cf. the interrogative forms in 1 Sam 17:56; Jer 18:13; 30:6. Cp. the form of the farewell in v. 6, לְכוּ לְשָׁלוֹם, "Go with reference to well-being."

ites[132] employ blackmail (v. 16). By stationing their six hundred men armed with their weapons of war at the gate of the compound,[133] they leave the Levite with few, if any, options but to comply with whatever the Danites demand. Fourth, the five scouts, who are familiar with the compound, go and seize the cultic objects (v. 17a). The repetition of cultic elements from vv. 14 and 17 is intentional, highlighting the narrator's primary focus.[134] Fifth, they stifle the priest. In v. 17b the Levite (now referred to by the narrator as "priest") is described as standing (helplessly) by at the entrance of the gate surrounded by the six hundred armed men.[135] All he can do is offer a verbal protest, "What are you doing?" (v. 18). To which the armed men respond (lit.): "Be quiet! Put your hand over your mouth." They did not want Micah to know what they were doing. Sixth, they bribe the Levite to abandon his employer and join their migration. The fact that the young man has been hired by Micah has not been lost on the Danites. Now, with classic appeal to ambition and opportunism, they offer him the status of "pope"[136] to an entire tribe/clan.[137] They cast their offer in the form of a rhetorical question, whose answer is obvious.[138]

18:20 The effectiveness of the Danites' strategy is described with impressive simplicity in v. 20. The narrator's focus on the priest, who is the subject of all the verbs, is deliberate. Not only was he happy to accept the offer,[139] but he took the ephod and the image and joined the Danites. In so doing, these acts are cast as grand larceny and treachery as well. The man has betrayed his patron and employer.

[21]Putting their little children, their livestock and their possessions in front of them, they turned away and left. **[22]**When they had gone some distance from Micah's house, the men who lived near Micah were called together and overtook the Danites. **[23]**As they shouted after them, the Danites turned and said to Micah, "What's the matter with you

---

[132] The expression בְּנֵי־דָן, "sons of Dan," which compares with the "tribe" of Dan in v. 1 and the "clan" of Dan in v. 11. These expressions (along with אֲחֵיהֶם, "their brothers, kinsmen," in v. 14) reflect a perception of ethnic cohesiveness based on descent from a common ancestor.

[133] The expression פֶּתַח הַשָּׁעַר, "opening of the gate," contributes the impression of a walled compound.

[134] The order in which the elements are listed (פֶּסֶל, אֵפוֹד, תְּרָפִים, מַסֵּכָה) is different from v. 14. The hendiadys פֶּסֶל וּמַסֵּכָה has been split up to frame the entire list and to focus attention on the image.

[135] Note the redundancy of "six hundred men armed with weapons of war." Cf. vv. 11,16.

[136] The word derives from Gk. παππας, which is equivalent to Hb. אָב.

[137] Note the contrast between בֵּית אִישׁ, "house of a man," and שֵׁבֶט, "tribe," and מִשְׁפָּחָה, "clan."

[138] In quoting the question the narrator also asks the same of the reader.

[139] וַיִּטַב לֵב הַכֹּהֵן, "and the heart of the priest was good/glad," occurs elsewhere in 19:6–9; 1 Kgs 21:7; 2 Kgs 25:24; Ruth 3:7; Eccl 7:3. In these contexts the idiom may also be interpreted "to be in high spirits."

that you called out your men to fight?"
²⁴He replied, "You took the gods I made, and my priest, and went away. What else do I have? How can you ask, 'What's the matter with you?'"
²⁵The Danites answered, "Don't argue with us, or some hot-tempered men will attack you, and you and your family will lose your lives." ²⁶So the Danites went their way, and Micah, seeing that they were too strong for him, turned around and went back home.

The Encounter with Micah (18:21–26). Since Micah's triumphant declaration in 17:13 he has been out of the picture. The Danites' contacts have all been with his priest, the Levite, and the reader is left wondering what has become of this person who figured so prominently in the opening episodes (17:1–6). Was he unaware of the scouts' first visit to his compound (18:3–6)? Did he not hear the commotion of the Danites as they burglarized his shrine and negotiated with his priest? Did he not hear sounds of the Danites' children[140] and their livestock? Has he been bound and gagged? Only after the raiding party has left does he reappear in the narrative, but by now it is too late.

18:21–22 On the surface vv. 21–22a seem to describe the Danites breaking camp in a matter-of-fact manner,[141] but the horde's order of departure from Beth-Micah (see n. 64, p. 505) was carefully planned. Ahead of the armed troops they sent their children, livestock, and treasured belongings,[142] which now included the precious cultic articles. This arrangement was designed to force the infuriated Micah to deal with the warriors first, should he pursue the robbers and try to reclaim his stolen property. The narrator does not report how long it took for Micah to react to his loss. By the time he could rally[143] his neighbors[144] to help him, however, the Danites had put some distance between themselves and their victim. Not being slowed by children and livestock, Micah was able to overtake them. Approaching the Danite vandals, Micah's people shouted after them, but they were rebuffed with threats of brutality not only against them but their families as well.

18:23 The conversation reported in vv. 23b–24 is classic. The Danites' pseudoinnocent/ignorant question is intentionally insulting, "What's the matter with you that you have called out your men to fight?" The verb, *zāʿaq*, which the NIV translates expansively as "called out your men to fight," means

---

[140] The reference to the children as טַף echoes Num 14:3,31, the original pan-Israelite scout narrative.

[141] Note the sequence of verbs, וַיִּפְנוּ וַיֵּלְכוּ וַיָּשִׂימוּ, "They turned and went and put ..."

[142] כְּבוּדָה, "heavy/glorious/valuable possessions," occurs only here. Ezek 23:41 and Ps 45:14 are textually uncertain.

[143] Here and in v. 23 the narrator employs a rare *niphal* form of זָעַק, "to cry out" (cf. 6:34–35; elsewhere only in Josh 8:16 and 1 Sam 14:20), in a military sense, "to muster. The *niphal* of the by-form, צָעַק, is also employed with the present sense of "to be mustered, called together," as in 7:23–24; 10:17; 12:1; 1 Sam 13:4; 2 Kgs 3:21.

[144] Lit. "the men who were in the houses with the house of Micah."

"to call for help, to summon (the militia), to raise a battle cry."[145] The choice of this verb seems deliberate, linking the present cry of Micah to previous cries of the Israelites to Yahweh because of their oppression.[146] Ironically, this time the oppressors are not foreign enemies sent in by Yahweh to punish Israel for her apostasy; they are fellow apostate Israelites.

18:24 Micah's answer is cast in a series of passionate utterances. He opens with a cry of desperation (lit.): "My gods which I have made, you have taken away, and the priest, and you have left!" The narrator forces the reader's focus on the stolen objects by thrusting it to the beginning of the sentence ahead of the verb. As noted repeatedly already, the use of the term *ʾĕlōhîm*, "god," reveals Micah's own understanding of his earlier actions. Although the term "god/gods" may refer collectively to the ephod, teraphim, and sculptured image, his [and the narrator's] primary interest is in the image. But the irony in the modifying clause, "which I have made," is patent, feeding into the narrator's anti-idolatry polemic.[147] The gods made with human hands cannot defend either themselves (cf. 6:28–32) or their makers! The man who had installed a god in his own house finds his house plundered. The impression of his distress is intensified by the ungrammatical addition of "and the priest!" But this addendum must be interpreted in light of 17:13. Micah had thought that now that he had a Levite for a priest Yahweh would guarantee his well-being. But now he discovers that the very reason the priest had agreed to serve him is also the reason he cannot hold him. The "young man" who had become his father, but whom he had treated like his son, has become a traitor. There is no integrity in any of the characters in the account. Having lost his gods and his priest, it is no wonder that Micah cries out, "What else do I have?" (or "What is there left for me?" lit., "What to me still?"). Not only has he been robbed and betrayed, but without divine or priestly support he feels naked, completely vulnerable to the forces of evil and disaster. And the Danites have the gall to ask, "What's the matter with you?"!

18:25 The depravity and brutality of the Danites is exposed in their rejoinder to the victim of their crimes, whose tone is captured by translating "Shut up[148] if you don't want savages to attack you and if you and your family members don't want to lose their lives!" Although the speakers intend the expression *ʾănāšîm mārê nepeš*, "men bitter of disposition/soul,"[149] to intim-

---

[145] *HALOT*, 1.277.

[146] 3:91–5; 6:9–10; 10:10–14. Cf. the use of the by-form, צָעַק, in Judg 4:3 and 10:12.

[147] Cf. 6:31–32.

[148] Though the NIV offers a tolerable verbal rendering of אַל־תַּשְׁמַע קוֹלְךָ עִמָּנוּ, lit., "Do not make your voice heard in our midst," but "Don't argue with us" hardly catches the emotion of the speaker.

[149] The NIV translates "hot-tempered men," but the NASB's "fierce men" seems more likely. L. Kutler ("A 'Strong' Case for Hebrew *mar*," *UF* 16 [1984]: 112–13) argues that the word *mar* here means "strong" rather than "bitter."

idate Micah into immediate retreat, it represents an apt characterization of the Danites. These men are brutes before whom any right-thinking person will step aside. By threatening to take the lives of Micah's household as well as his own life, they escalate the threat and also confirm their own inhumanity.

18:26 Verse 26 summarizes the observable result. Knowing his forces are no match for the criminal Danites, Micah retreats to his home. The narrator's omission of a verbal response leaves the reader to imagine what might have been going on in his mind. Will he be as theological in interpreting this event as he was in the chance arrival of the Levite at his house? Will he recognize the divine hand of judgment upon him for his apostate ways? Micah's fate is filled with irony. The young man who had first entered the picture as a thief finds himself the victim of grand larceny. The reader should note the intrinsic unity of these events. The object the Danites stole from Micah is made of the very substance he had stolen from his mother. The silver had been melted down and used to fashion this very idol, which makes a comparison with the prophetic satire on idolatry in Isa 40:18–20; 44:9–20 all the more apt.

But the polemic is not limited to idolatry itself. Even as he convinces the reader of the folly of idolatry, the narrator toys with the reader's disposition toward the characters involved. The narrative began with a sympathetic portrayal of Micah's mother, but before the first episode is over, we have changed our minds about her. The narrative began with an unfavorable portrayal of Micah, and this perspective continues through chap. 17. But in the end, one feels like Habakkuk in the opening chapter of the prophetic book. We know Micah has behaved wickedly, but how can Yahweh use the more wicked Danites to punish someone relatively less wicked? This man, whose ethical (and spiritual) values were clearly pagan, finds himself the victim of his own Canaanized countrymen. The final scene casts Micah as one of the most pathetic characters in all of Scripture. But the reader must not allow his sympathies to obscure his crime, for by Deuteronomic standards his idolatry called for the death penalty. The Danites threatened to kill him and in so doing could have inadvertently served as the divine agents of judgment.[150] But since they are pragmatists, not driven by any theological convictions, when the threat has achieved its purpose, they go on their way.

²⁷Then they took what Micah had made, and his priest, and went on to Laish, against a peaceful and unsuspecting people. They attacked them with the sword and burned down their city. ²⁸There was no one to rescue them because they lived a long way from Sidon and had no relationship with anyone else. The city was in a valley near Beth Rehob.

---

[150] Boling (*Judges*, 265) finds a link between the Danites' involvement in the judgment of Micah and the Testament of Jacob in Gen 49:16–18: "Dan will provide justice [יָדִין] for his people as one of the tribes of Israel" (v. 16).

The Danites rebuilt the city and settled there. ²⁹They named it Dan after their forefather Dan, who was born to Israel—though the city used to be called Laish. ³⁰There the Danites set up for themselves the idols, and Jonathan son of Gershom, the son of Moses, and his sons were priests for the tribe of Dan until the time of the captivity of the land. ³¹They continued to use the idols Micah had made, all the time the house of God was in Shiloh.

Mission Accomplished (18:27–31). If the narrator has created ambivalent feelings toward Micah and his mother, his consistently negative portrayal of the Levite and the Danites reaches its literary climax (but its spiritual nadir) in the final episode. Ironically, in the process the reader's sympathies are transferred to the Canaanite inhabitants, who as a class embody all that is abominable and should have been targets of Israel's *herem* (extermination) policy (cf. Deut 7:1–5). Unlike the preceding episodes, this phase of the account is totally devoid of conversation. Opening with an episode initial circumstantial clause, the author simply offers a narrative summary of events at Laish/Dan. These events may be outlined as follows.

18:27–28a First, the Danites arrived at Laish with the religious items Micah had manufactured and the priest he had claimed as his own. The narrator refuses to dignify the former, the cultic artifacts, with any label. They are simply the product of Micah's hands. He also refuses to dignify the latter with the label of Levite. He is merely the priest who belonged to Micah.

Second, they attacked the city of Laish, slaughtering the population and torching the city. The narrator keeps the reader's sympathies with these Canaanites, even though the Danites are technically applying the law of *herem* to the place. He reminds the reader that the population of Laish was defenseless/unsuspecting, far from Sidon, and had no dealings with the Arameans.[151] To concretize the comment the narrator adds a circumstantial clause in v. 28 (lit.), "Now it [Laish] was in the valley belonging to Beth Rehob."

The surprise reference to Beth-Rehob highlights the northern location of Laish and represents one more link with the account of the pan-Israelite scouting mission in Num 13:21. The exact location of the site remains unknown, but the phrase there, "Rehob near the entrance of Hamath" (see NIV note), suggests a site at the northern extremity of the officially recognized promised land. An Aramean composition of the population is suggested by 2 Sam 8:3–8, which notes that David defeated the Aramean king of Zobah, identified as Hadadezer, "the son of Rehob."[152] The territory claimed by Beth-Rehob may be understood broadly as the Beka‘ Valley. Although Beth-Rehob Arameans claimed control of the entire valley, apparently their jurisdiction was effective primarily in the

---

[151] As in v. 7, preferring to read אָדָם with the LXX (Συρια) rather than the MT's אֲרָם, as reflected in the NIV's "they had no relationship with anyone else."

[152] Most accept "Rehob" in 2 Sam 8:3,12 as an abbreviation of Beth-Rehob.

part drained by the northward flowing Litani River. Living beyond the height of land that separated the Litani drainage basin from the southward sloping Huleh basin, the Canaanite population of Laish managed to live independently of the Arameans. But like Micah in chap. 17, the Danites are characterized as opportunists. They are not driven by any divine mandate but solely by their need for living space and their own notions of where and how that need should be satisfied. Thus their conquest of Laish is described as a human achievement without any sense of reliance upon God.

18:28b–29 Third, they rebuilt and renamed the conquered city after their eponymous ancestor, Dan, the son of Jacob/Israel. But the reader may recognize another significance in the name. Even though the Danites seem to have been completely unaware of their role and since *dān* derives from a root meaning "to judge," in the providence of God the name also commemorates Yahweh's judgment upon this Canaanite town.[153]

18:30a Fourth, they established Dan as a primary cult center. Without any concern for "the place which the LORD would choose" (cf. Deuteronomy 12) and in overt violation of the ban on images (Deut 27:15), this event also is presented as a purely human affair—human in its origin, design, and intention. This action involved the erection "for themselves" of the image they had stolen from Micah[154] and the installation of the Levite who had come with them as their own priest.

To the complete surprise of the reader, at the end of the account the Levite who first appeared in 17:7 is finally named. Instead of referring to the priest generically as "the Levite," the narrator identifies him by name, patronymic, and descent: "Jonathan son of Gershom, the son of Moses." Although this is the first occurrence in the Old Testament of the personal name Jonathan, hereafter it becomes one of the more common biblical names, being borne by twenty different persons.[155] As a thoroughly orthodox name, Jonathan ("Yahweh has given") supposedly reflects the faith of the man's parents.[156] If that is so, this

---

[153] Formerly identified as Tell el Qadi, the tell has been recently confirmed archaeologically as the ancient city of Laish/Dan by the discovery of a bilingual inscription (Aramaic and Greek) that translates "to the god who is at Dan." For discussion of this inscription see A. Biran, "To the God Who Is in Dan," in *Temples and High Places in Biblical Times* (Jerusalem: Magnes, 1981), 142–51; id., *Biblical Dan*, 221–24. On the archaeological evidence for the Danite takeover of Laish see Biran, *Biblical Dan*, 125–46; "Dan," *NEAEHL* 1.323–31. On archaeological evidence for the later history of the city and the cult site see ibid., 255–78; id., "High Places at the Gates of Dan?" *EI* 24 (A. Malamat volume; 1993): 55–58 (Hb.); V. Tzaferis, "The 'God Who Is in Dan' and the Cult of Pan at Banias in the Hellenistic and Roman Periods," *EI* 23 (A. Biran Volume; 1992), 128*–35*, esp. pp. 128–31.

[154] The NIV wrongly interprets פֶּסֶל as plural ("idols"). The reference is primarily to the sculptured image.

[155] See J. M. Berridge, "Jonathan," *ABD* 3.942–44.

[156] On the name see Fowler, *Theophoric Names*, 91–92, 352.

man obviously did not share the spiritual commitment expressed in his name. Jonathan is described as the son of Gershom, but the term *ben* may also be understood more generally as "grandson, descendant." The Gershom referred to is the eldest son of Moses and Zipporah (Exod 2:22). But it is the reference to Moses that catches the reader off guard. Indeed the rabbinic scribes found the present association of Moses' name with such abominable idolatrous behavior so objectionable they refused to accept the statement and inserted a super-scripted *nun* between the first two consonants, transforming unpointed *mšh,* "Moses," into *mⁿšh,* "Manasseh."[157]

Scholars have argued that, unlike the previous narrative, this closer identi-fication of the person lacks any pejorative connotations, and they conclude that this must be a later editorial insertion.[158] But to remove the Yahwistic name Jonathan and the names of Moses and his son robs this text of its pro-phetic punch. Previously the narrator has intentionally referred to this young man generically as a Levite so the reader would generalize the present symp-toms of spiritual Canaanization to the priestly class/tribe as a whole. To con-cretize the issue he shocks the reader by associating the abominations committed in this chapter with Moses, the most venerable character in Israel-ite history. The problem of religious syncretism is so deeply rooted it has infected the most sacred institutions and the most revered household. Fur-thermore, this note suggests a time frame for the present apostate activity of the Danites. If *ben* means "son" rather than "grandson" or "descendant," then these events must have happened within a hundred years of the arrival of the Israelites. The earlier note in 2:6–10 that the Israelites abandoned Yahweh as soon as the generation that had witnessed the exodus and the conquest under Joshua had died is hereby confirmed concretely.

18:30b–31 Verses 30b–31 offer the reader a synchronized summary, making two critical chronological observations, both of which are critical for dating the authorship of the book. First, Jonathan and his descendants served as priests of the tribe of Dan at this cult site until the day the land went into captivity. The word for captivity, *gĕlôt,* refers to the common ancient Near Eastern practice of deporting the populations of conquered territories. But the present reference to the exile of a *land* is exceptional.[159] Accordingly,

---

[157] See Tov, *Textual Criticism,* 57. Both variations in reading are reflected in editions of the LXX. The Vg reads "Moses"; Tg reads "Manasseh." The insertion of the *nun* not only resolves a difficult theological issue but also links this account specifically with the name of a person who, more than any other, sponsored and promoted apostasy in Israel/Judah (cf. 2 Kgs 21:1–18).

[158] Becker, *Richterzeit und Königtum,* 244.

[159] O'Connell (*Rhetoric of the Book of Judges,* 481) rightly observes that place and national names (Judah, Israel, Jerusalem, Gilgal) are spoken of metonymously (for their inhabitants) as being exiled, but this never applies to a land without further specification (cf. 2 Kgs 17:23; 25:21; Jer 1:3; 52:27; Amos 5:5).

some emend the consonantal text (without manuscript support) to read "until the exile of the ark."[160] In that case, the present reference is to the Philistine capture of the ark as described in 1 Samuel 4–6. But this reading is too speculative, too dependent on arguments from silence,[161] and too driven by the need to interpret Judges as a pro-Davidic and anti-Saulide tractate.[162] It is best, therefore, to maintain the traditional interpretation and to recognize here a reference to the deportation of the population of Dan by Tiglath Pileser III to Assyria in 734 B.C. (2 Kgs 15:29). If the book was written from the perspective of the Manassite apostasy, as we have argued above, this comment makes perfect sense. The narrator is hereby warning his readers by citing the eventual fate of the Danites. Because of their persistent apostasy the covenant curses cited in Leviticus 26 and Deuteronomy 28 were finally imposed upon the northern tribes. If the policies of Manasseh continue, the same fate will await the nation of Judah.

Second, the narrator highlights the horror of the apostasy by linking it with the location of the residence of God at Shiloh. This is the first reference to Shiloh in the book.[163] Located midway between Bethel and Shechem in the Ephraimite heartland, Shiloh (modern Seilun) offered an appropriate place in the middle of the land of Israel to house the ark prior to the construction of the temple. Although the nature of the sanctuary at Shiloh is unknown, many scholars accept that by the time the Philistines captured the ark a more permanent structure than the tabernacle used in the desert wanderings had been erected.[164] This may find support in the fact that here, for the first time in the Old Testa-

---

[160] עַד גְּלוֹת הָאָרוֹן. The assumption is that a carelessly written *waw* and final *nun* may have been misread as a *ṣadeh* in the archaic cursive script.

[161] Regarding the lack of exact parallel to the exile of a land, two cautions should be noted. First, absence of evidence is not evidence of absence. Second, we must be hesitant to deny/eliminate the evidence of a single witness. On the problem of arguing from silence see Hackett, *Historians' Fallacies*, 47–48.

[162] As is the case with O'Connell, *Rhetoric of the Book of Judges*, 481–83, though he cites other proponents of this operation who do not necessarily agree with him in the last respect.

[163] Cf. 21:12–21; Josh 19:51; 1 Samuel 1–4; 14:3; 2 Kgs 2:27. Also Jer 7:12–14; 26:6–9; Ps 78:60.

[164] For a contrary opinion see D. G. Schley (*Shiloh: A Biblical City in Tradition and History*, JSOTSup 63 (Sheffield: JSOT Press, 1989], 129–31), who argues that the chronological notes at the ends of vv. 30 and 31, refer to the same time period. If that is the case, then either the structures defined by archaeologists as the cult site at Shiloh have been misidentified or the site was rebuilt and continued to function as a northern place of worship after the division of the kingdom. But archaeological excavations at Seilun demonstrate that the fortunes of Shiloh reached their peak in the eleventh century B.C. and that the ruins dated to the middle of that century are to be associated with the Philistine victory reported in 1 Sam 4:10. See I. Finkelstein, "Excavations at Shiloh," *TA* 12 (1985): 123–80. For an entirely different approach see Ahlström (*History of Ancient Palestine*, 366–69), who argues that Shiloh was in fact a Canaanite cult site and that its associations with Yahweh cult were later inventions of Israelite historians. For the archaeological history of Shiloh see A. Kempinski, "Shiloh," *NEAEHL* 4.1364–66.

ment, the residence of Yahweh in Israel is referred to as *bĕt hā'ĕlōhîm,* "the house of God."[165] If the narrator had had in mind the tabernacle used by the Israelites in the desert, he should have identified this structure as the *'ōhel mô'ēd,* "tent of meeting," or the *miškan yhwh,* "tabernacle of Yahweh."[166] The narratives of 1 Samuel 1–4 seem to assume an actual temple at Shiloh.[167] The narrator's point is that throughout the period of the judges the cult site at Dan functioned as an apostate challenge to the true worship of Yahweh. The final note reiterates that this center was of human design from start to finish. Micah had made the image, and the Danites had set it up for themselves.

Theological and Practical Implications

Literarily and historically this account serves the aetiological function of explaining the origins of the cult center at Dan. The role of this shrine in the history of the nation can scarcely be overestimated. In fact, together with the shrine at Bethel it served as an icon of northern Israelite spiritual and national identity after Jeroboam assumed control over the northern ten tribes toward the end of the tenth century (1 Kgs 12:25–33). His golden calves represented one more expression of the nation's propensity to syncretistic religious expression. As a symbol of persistent northern apostasy Dan became a favorite target of prophetic denunciations.[168]

But the significance of this chapter within the plot of the Book of Judges should not be overlooked. In keeping with earlier presentations of the nation and its governors as increasingly Canaanized, this chapter portrays individual Israelites and an entire tribe as faithless and opportunistic. There is not an admirable character in these chapters. No one displays any devotion to Yahweh; no one demonstrates any concern for national well-being; no one behaves with any integrity. The Israelites have become as shameless in their religious expression and ethical conduct as they need to be to get their way.

In this portrayal of the events the narrator provides another challenge to the traditional scholarly understanding of Deuteronomism, which insists that sin brings on the curse, but blessing follows obedience. Here sin succeeds! Ironically, and perhaps tragically, the agendas people set for themselves are sometimes achieved—which sends a solemn warning to the church at the close of the twentieth century. Success is not necessarily a sign of righteousness or an

---

[165] Though *bêt yhwh,* "house of the LORD," is known from Exod 23:19; 34:26; Deut 23:19; Josh 6:24. In Gen 28:17,22 "the house of God" is used more generally.

[166] Cf. Exod 33:7–11; Josh 22:9–34. Cf. Ps 78:60–72, which speaks of the *miškan šîlōh,* "tabernacle of Shiloh," and the *'ōhel yôsēp,* "tent of Joseph."

[167] So also Schley, *Shiloh,* 129.

[168] Cf. 2 Kgs 10:29; Amos 8:14; Jer 4:15. 1 Kgs 13:1–10 concerns only Bethel. For descriptions of the Jeroboamic installation see Biran, "Dan," *ABD* 2.14–15; id., *Biblical Dan,* 165–83; on the cult site in later history see ibid, 184–234.

indication that we must be doing something right. It may in fact be the opposite. God does not stifle every corrupt thought and scheme of the human heart. Finally, this series of episodes illustrates the extent to which the religious perspectives and institutions of Israel have been Canaanized. Now the problem has become overt. Individuals design and construct their own shrines in defiance of divine prohibitions; the professional priests have been thoroughly corrupted, selling their service to the highest bidder; and entire tribes have become sponsors of paganism. The people do not need a king to lead them down this path. They are quite capable of sinning on their own. After chap. 18 the population in Canaan and Laish may be new, and the names of the occupants may be different, but at heart nothing has changed. Like the native Canaanites the Israelites are observed reducing divinity to physical images, manipulating God for private ends, appropriating pagan cult installations, and brutalizing each other in the process. Even the Levites, including the descendants of Moses, have been corrupted! The cult is syncretistic, the priesthood is mercenary, and the devotees are evil. Instead of calling people to repentance the professional spiritual leaders capitalize on the degeneracy of the times. Similarly, the "spiritual service" of many current pastors is motivated not by the call of God but by the opportunities for personal gain. The question the Danites posed to him is asked every day by pastoral search committees: "Which is better, to be the pastor of a small family or to be the pastor of a megachurch?" The contemporary problem of ambition and opportunism in the ministry has at least a three-thousand-year history.

2. The Moral Degeneration of Israel (19:1–21:25)

The boundaries of the final compositional unit are fixed by the formula, "In those days Israel had no king" in 19:1 and 21:25. The narrator expands the latter with his final verdict on the spiritual condition of the nation of Israel in the premonarchic period (lit.): "Everyone did what was right in his own eyes." With its 103 verses this subcomposition is exceeded in length within the book only by the Gideon cycle (inclusive of the Abimelech debacle, chap. 9). Even more than in the previous unit (17–18) and the story of Samson, particularly chaps. 14–15, what looks at first like nothing more than a personal crisis in a private household escalates into a citywide problem, then becomes a crisis for an entire tribe and ultimately jeopardizes the integrity of the entire nation of Israel itself. The plot is so complex that by the time a reader reaches the end of the book, the roots of the problem may have been forgotten.[169] As with

---

[169] O'Connell (*Rhetoric of the Book of Judges*, 242–58) recognizes three plot levels in this narrative: (1) The Levite's recovery of his concubine (19:1b–9,10aβ); (2) the execution of justice upon Gibeah/Benjamin for the outrage against the Levite and his concubine (19:10aγ–20:48); (3) the recovery of wives for the remnant of Benjamin (21:1–25).

chaps. 14–15, therefore, it is possible to get a picture of the significance of individual episodes by reading the story backward, paying particular attention to the links between cause and effect within and across the episodes.

1. Two hundred Benjamite men capture two hundred female dancers at Shiloh and take them as their wives because the elders of Israel gave them permission to do so (21:23–24).
2. The elders of Israel gave the two hundred men permission to capture the two hundred young women because Jabesh-Gilead could not provide enough wives for the six hundred men, all that remained of the tribe of Benjamin (21:13–22).
3. Jabesh-Gilead could provide only four hundred wives for the Benjamites because that is all the virgins the Israelites found for the remnant of six hundred Benjamin men among the inhabitants of Jabesh-Gilead (21:8–12).
4. The Israelites went to Jabesh-Gilead to get wives for the Benjamites because they felt sorry for them (21:1–7).
5. The Israelites felt sorry for the Benjamites because they had reduced this tribe to six hundred men in a series of fierce battles (20:14–48).
6. The Israelites had engaged Benjamin in battle because they had refused to deliver into their hands the inhabitants of Gibeah (20:12–13).
7. The Israelites had demanded the deliverance of Gibeah into their hands because of the Levite's testimony concerning their conduct (20:4–11).
8. The Israelites had demanded an explanation after they had gathered in response to receiving fragments of a woman's body (19:29–20:3).
9. The Levite had cut up the woman because she had been gang-raped and left for dead at his doorstep (19:25a–29).
10. The woman had been gang-raped because the man had given her to the men of Gibeah (19:25a).
11. The man had given his concubine to the men of Gibeah because his host felt obligated to protect him (19:22–24).
12. The Levite's host felt obligated to protect the man because he found him in the open square of Gibeah (19:16–21).
13. The Levite was in Gibeah to spend the night because he was on a journey and could not make it home by nightfall (19:10–15).
14. The Levite was on a journey because he had gone to get his concubine (19:3–9).
15. The Levite needed to get his concubine because she had left him (19:2b).
16. The woman had left him because she was angry with him (19:2a).
17. She was angry with him because … everyone was doing what was good in his own eyes (21:25).

But there is another striking feature about this account. In previous narratives minor figures were often named,[170] even when a knowledge of their identity is not crucial to the story. In this, the longest coherent account in the book, the only person named is a minor figure, the priest who officiates at Bethel (20:28). The main figures are all anonymous: the Levite, who has a geographic home but no genealogy;[171] his concubine, whose death is central to the entire plot;[172] the concubine's father, whose effusive hospitality provides a foil for the inhospitality of the people of Gibeah; the old man from Ephraim, living in Gibeah, who tries to protect these visitors. And when, in 20:8, the plot involving personal experiences and fates gives way to tribal and national concerns, the individual identities are swallowed up in collective action and reaction. When an individual is finally named in 20:28, it catches the reader by surprise and has a shocking rhetorical effect. Phinehas the priest is the grandson of Aaron, which means that the events transpiring in this chapter occurred within one hundred years of the death of Moses and probably within decades after the death of Joshua.

D. M. Hudson has rightly recognized a twofold significance to the namelessness of the principal characters in this account.[173] First, their anonymity expresses what is declared editorially in the refrain at the end (lit.): "In those days ... everyone did what was right in his own eyes." This means that the Levite represents every Levite; the concubine, every woman; the father-in-law, every host; the old man residing in Bethel, every outsider in a Benjamite town. Because everyone did as he saw fit, every host was capable of committing the atrocities of the Benjamites; every guest could be mistreated; and every woman was a potential victim of rape, murder, and dismemberment.

---

[170] Like Sheshai, Ahiman, and Talmai in 1:10; Achsah in 1:11–15; Jabin in 4:2,24; Heber the Kenite in 4:11,17,21; Purah, Gideon's servant, in 7:10; Oreb and Zeeb the Midianite leaders in 7:25; 8:3; Gideon's son Jether in 8:20; Jephthah's father in 11:1–2. Several minor figures remain unnamed, as we would expect (the youth of Succoth, 8:14; Abimelech's mother, 8:29–9:3; the Philistine prostitute, 16:1–2; the boy who held Samson's hand in the Philistine temple, 16:26). But this is not to say that every significant character is named. The reader is surprised at the anonymity of others who play significant roles in the plot: the Canaanite spy who betrayed his own people in 1:22–26, to keep the focus on geographical issues; Yahweh's messengers in 2:1–5 and 6:11–24 and his prophet in 6:7–10, undoubtedly to keep the focus on Yahweh; the woman who dropped the millstone on Abimelech's head, to quicken an already overly long plot; Jephthah's daughter in 11:34–40, Manoah's wife in chap. 13, Samson's wife in 14:1–15:8, and Micah's mother 17:1–6, in each instance to provide ironic female foils against which to evaluate the men; the king of Ammon in 11:12–28, to keep the focus on Jephthah; Samson's Philistine father-in-law in 15:1–8, to keep the focus on Samson and marginalize the Philistines.

[171] Contrast this with Elkanah, another Levite from the hill country of Ephraim, in 1 Sam 1:1.

[172] Contrast this with Peninnah, Elkanah's second-ranked wife in 1 Sam 1:2–4, whose primary function in the narrative is to serve as a foil for Hannah.

[173] "Living in a Land of Epithets: Anonymity in Judges 19–21," *JSOT* 62 (1994): 49–66, esp. 59–65.

Ironically, just as the Levite would dismember his concubine, so the nation would gather "as one man" (20:11) to dismember itself. Anonymity is a deliberate literary device adopted to reflect the universality of Israel's Canaanization.

Second, the namelessness of the characters reflects the dehumanization of the individual in a Canaanized world. To have a name is to be somebody, to have identity, and since names are given and used by others, to have a name is to have significance within the community. Even Micah's Levitical priest in the previous chapters has a name. To be sure, his identity is withheld until the very end (18:30), when he is officially installed as priest of what became an important Israelite shrine; but this is Jonathan, the son of Gershom, the son of Moses. But the Levite in these chapters has no name. To the men of Gibeah he is nothing more than a sex object. What happens to his concubine is even more striking. In contrast to the strength and freedom of Achsah and Deborah and Jael, the Levite's concubine is reduced to human flesh whom the rapacious men of Gibeah may devour and whom even her own "husband" may cut up like the carcass of an animal.[174] Anonymity not only expresses corporate qualities, but it also deconstructs significance and identity. It reflects not only the disintegration of individual value, but also the failure of the community to speak up—to name the characters. It denies individuality and humanity to both criminals and victims. This nameless woman remains a poignant reminder of what happens to anonymous victims of crimes committed by anonymous perpetrators of crimes against humanity. Ironically in a world in which the individual makes himself the measure of all things ("each man did what was right in his own eyes," 21:25), the individual eventually counts for nothing. The exceptional identification of Phinehas by name and genealogy in 20:28 asserts to the reader how quickly this had happened in Israel. He represents the generation that rose after the death of Joshua that knew not Yahweh nor all the things he had done on their behalf (2:10), that do what is evil in the sight of Yahweh (2:11) but what is right in their own eyes until it was too late (cf. 19:20). By means of anonymity the narrator has depicted a sinister world of alienation, denigration, and deconstruction.[175]

Just as in chaps. 17–18 the Danite problem had been the primary concern of the author, so here the Benjamite crisis is uppermost in his mind. The epi-

---

[174] His actions in 19:29 compare with Saul's dismemberment of his oxen in 1 Sam 11:7, on which see further below.

[175] Cf. P. Trible's opening volley in her discussion of this chapter: "The betrayal, rape, torture, murder, and dismemberment of an unnamed woman is a story we want to forget but are commanded to speak. It depicts the horrors of male power, brutality, and triumphalism; of female helplessness, abuse, and annihilation. To hear this story is to inhabit a world of unrelenting terror that refuses to let us pass by on the other side" (*Texts of Terror: Literary-Feminist Readings of Biblical Narratives*, OBT [Philadelphia: Fortress, 1984], 65).

sodes at Gibeah and the personal experiences of the Levite serve as background, demonstrating how individualized and deep-seated is the Canaanite rot in Israel, as well as the communal implications of personal actions.[176] With the formulaic inclusio (19:1; 21:25) this long literary unit looks like a self-contained, independent short story, with its own plot and points of tension. Its significance, however, is determined by its place in the structure of the book. As will be borne out by the exposition, this episode represents the climactic and supreme demonstration of the Canaanization of Israel.

Structurally the unit divides into four subsections as follows:
1. The Background to the Outrage at Gibeah (19:1–10a)
2. The Nature of the Outrage at Gibeah (19:10b–30)
3. The Israelite Response to the Outrage at Gibeah (20:1–48)
4. The National Crisis Precipitated by the Outrage at Gibeah (21:1–25)

From a theological point of view the composition is remarkably secular. God never enters the picture in (1) and (2), either by his name Yahweh or by the generic designation of Elohim. In (3) Israel assembles "before the LORD" at Mizpah (20:1) as the "people of God" (20:2), and when they consult him at Bethel he responds (20:18,23,27–28). In (4) the Israelites weep before Yahweh at Bethel (21:1) and let his name drop freely from their lips (21:3,5,7–8). Otherwise people are making decisions—often ridiculously—on their own. God is strangely silent, allowing them to pursue their foolish courses and even permitting them to succeed. The key to the narrator's understanding of these events is found in 21:15: "The LORD had made a gap in the tribes of Israel." Just as Samson's fascination with the Philistine woman of Timnah had its roots in the divine determination to disrupt the status quo (14:4), so the author hereby calls upon the reader to recognize the hand of God. As the commander in chief of the nation, in the "holy war" against Benjamin he had delivered the enemy into Israel's hand (cf. 20:28). In this final composition Israel discovers her greatest enemy, and the enemy is in her very own midst.

Within this larger complex chap. 19 has a character and agenda of its own. S. Niditch has argued convincingly that 19:10–30 in particular is an integral part of a larger, beautifully crafted story (encompassing chaps. 19–21) that deals with lofty notions of community, family, caring, and responsibility.[177]

---

[176] In Hos 9:8–9; 10:9 Hosea generalizes the problem of Gibeah, not [merely] to the tribe of Benjamin but to Ephraim, his preferred appellation for the Northern Kingdom of Israel in the eighth century B.C. For a study of Hosea's treatment of Gibeah see P. M. Arnold, "Hosea and the Sin of Gibeah," *CBQ* 51 (1989): 447–60. Arnold understands the core narrative to have arisen in northern Israelite circles as a literary piece to absolve Ephraim of responsibility for an ancient massacre of Benjamin (p. 451). He discusses recent literary approaches to chaps. 19–20 more fully in *Gibeah: The Search for a Biblical City in History and Tradition*, JSOTSup 79 (Sheffield: JSOT Press, 1990), 61–86.

[177] S. Niditch, "The 'Sodomite' Theme in Judges 19–20: Family, Community, and Social Disintegration," *CBQ* 44 (1982): 365–78.

But in the development of these themes this chapter by itself presents a remarkable parallel to Genesis 19.[178] The following represent the most obvious links:

1. A small group of travelers arrives in the city in the evening.
2. A person who is himself an alien observes the presence of this company.
3. The travelers have a mind to spend the night in the open square *(rāḥôb)*.
4. At the insistence of the host, the travelers agree to spend the night in his house.
5. The host washes the guests' feet (implied in Gen 19:3 after the offer of v. 2).
6. The host and guest share a meal.
7. Depraved men of the city surround the house.
8. They demand that the host deliver his male guests to them so they may commit homosexual gang rape.
9. The host protests this display of wickedness.
10. When the protests prove futile, a substitute female is offered or handed over.

But the connections extend beyond common motifs. The chapters also share a common vocabulary, particularly verbs: "to spend the night,"[179] "to turn aside,"[180] "to rise early and go on one's way,"[181] "to dilly-dally,"[182] "to wash the feet,"[183] and they ate."[184] The substantives also correlate, as in "at evening"[185] and "house."[186] As we will see, the parallels intensify as the narratives proceed and reach their climax in Gen 19:4–8 and Judg 19:22–24 respectively.[187] The significance of these links will be explored below.

The deliberate casting of this account after the analogy of Genesis 19 plays a vital role in the narrator's negative portrayal of Benjamite spirituality. Although the text is remarkably free of the narrator's own evaluative comments, the negative picture of Israel is fleshed out with the author's skillful portrayal of the characters. By these and other literary means the reader is

---

[178] For a detailed study see D. I. Block, "Echo Narrative Technique in Hebrew Literature: A Study in Judges 19," *WTJ* 52 (1990): 325–41. Cp. the analyses of O'Connell, *Rhetoric of the Book of Judges*, 250–52, and Arnold, *Gibeah*, 72–74.

[179] Hb. לִין, Gen 19:2; eleven times in Judges 19, functioning as a Leitmotif that ties vv. 1–9 to the events that transpire in Gibeah.

[180] Hb. סוּר; Judg 19:11–12,15.

[181] Hb. וְהִשְׁכַּמְתֶּם וַהֲלַכְתֶּם לְדַרְכְּכֶם, Gen 19:2; Judg 19:9.

[182] Hb. וַיִּתְמַהְמָהּ Gen 19:16; Judg 19:8.

[183] Hb. וְרַחֲצוּ רַגְלֵיכֶם, Gen 19:2; Judg 19:21.

[184] Hb. וַיֹּאכֵלוּ, Gen 19:3; Judg 19:21. Cf. also, "And he prepared a banquet" (וַיַּעַשׂ מִשְׁתֶּה, Gen 19:3) and "and they drank" (וַיִּשְׁתּוּ, Judg 19:21).

[185] Hb. בָּעֶרֶב, Gen 19:1; Judg 19:16.

[186] Hb. בַּיִת, Gen 19:2–4,11; Judg 19:18,21–23.

[187] See my synopsis of these texts, "Echo Narrative Technique," 328–21. See also below.

drawn into one of the darkest pictures of Israelite life in the entire Old Testament.[188] But the narrator leaves it to the reader to draw the implications from the conversations and the events themselves.

(1) The Background to the Outrage at Gibeah (19:1–9)

[1]In those days Israel had no king.

Now a Levite who lived in a remote area in the hill country of Ephraim took a concubine from Bethlehem in Judah. [2]But she was unfaithful to him. She left him and went back to her father's house in Bethlehem, Judah. After she had been there four months, [3]her husband went to her to persuade her to return. He had with him his servant and two donkeys. She took him into her father's house, and when her father saw him, he gladly welcomed him. [4]His father-in-law, the girl's father, prevailed upon him to stay; so he remained with him three days, eating and drinking, and sleeping there.

[5]On the fourth day they got up early and he prepared to leave, but the girl's father said to his son-in-law, "Refresh yourself with something to eat; then you can go." [6]So the two of them sat down to eat and drink together. Afterward the girl's father said, "Please stay tonight and enjoy yourself." [7]And when the man got up to go, his father-in-law persuaded him, so he stayed there that night. [8]On the morning of the fifth day, when he rose to go, the girl's father said, "Refresh yourself. Wait till afternoon!" So the two of them ate together.

[9]Then when the man, with his concubine and his servant, got up to leave, his father-in-law, the girl's father, said, "Now look, it's almost evening. Spend the night here; the day is nearly over. Stay and enjoy yourself. Early tomorrow morning you can get up and be on your way home."

19:1 The climactic phase in the plot of Judges is signaled by an ominous formulaic notice of the absence of a king in Israel. Because Israel refuses to acknowledge Yahweh as king, the nation lacks a theological reason for not sinking to the ethical level of the Canaanites at the personal, tribal, and national levels. At the same time the Israelites do not need to wait for a human monarch to lead them in perfidious and treacherous ways. Although this people claims to be the people of Yahweh, their conduct and their consequent fate contradict this claim.[189]

Following the formulaic introduction to the literary unit as a whole, the narrative proper begins by introducing the main characters—another Levite and his concubine. The way the narrator presents the man suggests this person is to be viewed as a variation of the kind of personality encountered in the preceding

---

[188]Cf. M. Bal's evaluation of this account as "the most horrible story of the Hebrew Bible." "A Body of Writing: Judges 19," in *A Feminist Companion to Judges*, ed. A. Brenner (Sheffield: Sheffield Academic Press, 1993), 209.

[189]Unlike the success of the Danites in the previous unit, which is achieved despite the tribe's blatant covenant disloyalty.

two chapters: (a) The main character is classified as a Levite, that is, of the tribe charged with the spiritual leadership of the nation. (b) Like everyone else in the narrative (except Phinehas, 20:28), this Levite has no name. The author hereby invites the reader to treat the problem reflected in the following verses as a general problem; the identity of personalities is subordinate to the issues they represent. (c) He was a sojourner, a temporary resident, with no fixed abode, no sense of mission, no sense of home.[190] (d) He was sojourning in the hill country of Ephraim, the very region where the Levite in the previous unit had found a home.[191] (e) He is associated with Bethlehem of Judah, though the nature of that relationship is reversed from chap. 17. In 17:8 the Levite travels from Bethlehem of Judah to the hill country of Ephraim. This Levite travels from the hill country of Ephraim to Bethlehem of Judah (19:1–2). (f) Hospitality is a key issue in both episodes, though the forms of hospitality expressed are quite different. In 17:10–12 the hospitality is professional. There Micah invites the Levite to live with him permanently and serve as his priest. In this text the hospitality is familial. (g) Both texts involve intergenerational relationships. In 17:10–11 Micah gives the Levite the honorific title of "father" but treats him as his own son. Here the Levite is the son-in-law of the second character.

Like the Levite, the second character in the story also remains nameless. But the narrator presents the woman as a significant figure by offering three vital pieces of information about her. First, she is identified by role: she is the Levite's concubine. Having encountered *pîlegeš,* "concubine," earlier in 8:31, the moment we see this word we expect trouble. The fact that she is introduced as a second-class wife of this Levite raises the question of whether or not he has other wives. If not, why is she not treated as a normal wife? Second, she is repeatedly referred to as *hannaʿărâ,* "the young woman" (vv. 3, 4,5,6,8,9), which fits the picture of her running back to her father's house.

19:2   Third, she leaves her husband and returns to her paternal home. But the Hebrew rendering of her motive (v. 2) is problematic. On the surface *wattizneh* means "she played the part of a prostitute." The first impulse is to see in her a picture of Israel, whom the narrator portrays repeatedly as "playing" the harlot after other gods (2:17; 8:27,33). However, arguing against this metaphorical interpretation is the narrator's identification of her as a "concubine," a secondary wife, which is never used of Israel's relationship to Yahweh. Accordingly, if the Hebrew text is to be taken at face value, she seems simply to have abandoned her husband, perhaps because she was tired of being treated as a secondary wife, and returned to her father's home. Since Israelite law never mentions a woman divorcing a man, for a woman to divorce a man,

---

[190] Cp. the use of the verb גּוּר, "to sojourn," in v. 1 with the threefold occurrence of the same verb in 17:7–9.

[191] The Hb. verb יָשַׁב, which appears twice in 17:10–11, appears three times in 19:4,6,7, though with a slightly different sense.

she may have been designated a prostitute simply because she walked out on her husband.[192] On the other hand, these are strange and evil times; and we should not be surprised if, when she returned home, her father sent her out to work as a prostitute to contribute to the family economy.[193] Perhaps this explains his reluctance to let her go. By this interpretation we witness a reversal of roles from the Samson affairs, in which the man, the last of the deliverers, is portrayed as an unscrupulous womanizer, who felt quite at home with prostitutes.[194]

This interpretation, however, is not as obvious at it first appears. Logically, it is odd that she is said to play the prostitute and then go home to her father. The actions should have been reversed. Furthermore, the expression zānâ ʿal, "to commit prostitution against," is peculiar, appearing nowhere else and perhaps signalling to the reader a special sense. A more likely interpretation is suggested by the ancient versions. The LXX^A reads ōrgisthē autō, "she was angry with him,"[195] and Targum wbsrt ʿlwhy, "she despised him," both of which make perfect sense in the context. Accordingly, against the NIV's bland "she was unfaithful," it seems best either to see in Hebrew wtznh as a scribal error for wtznḥ, from a root zānaḥ, which means "to reject, detest,"[196] or, more likely, to retain the Hebrew and recognize a second root, zānâ, "to be angry, to quarrel."[197]

The text does not explicitly blame either the man or the woman for this falling out. But in light of the Levite's later conduct and the narrator's portrayal of men in the book as a whole, his sympathies seem to lie with the concubine, though this is not apparent at the outset. In any case, her father accepts her back home. At the same time it should be noted that the quarrel was not so intense that a full reconciliation was precluded. On the contrary, when the Levite arrives at his father-in-law's house, both the young girl and her father receive him gladly.

19:3 Nevertheless, apparently embittered over some marital crisis, the concubine had left her husband's house and headed south, back to her father's house in Bethlehem of Judah. The man seems to have waited patiently for her to return,[198] but he waited in vain. Finally, after four months

---

[192] Cf. Boling, *Judges*, 275.

[193] Cf. the prohibition on fathers doing this in Lev 19:29.

[194] The word זָנָה in 16:1 derives from the same root as the present verb.

[195] ὠργίσθη αὐτω. The LXX^B ἐπορεύθη ἀπ᾽ αὐτοῦ, "she deserted him," interprets rather than translates the Hebrew.

[196] Thus *BHS*. Cf. *HALOT* 1.276; *DCH* 3.124.

[197] This word finds a cognate in Akk. zenû, "to be angry." Cf. *AHw*, 1519; *HALOT* 1.275; *DCH* 3.123.

[198] Some argue that the Levite's effort to get his wife back was motivated by his desire to defend male honor, correcting the impression that as a husband he had not been able to control his wife. Cf. K. Stone, "Gender and Homosexuality in Judges 19: Subject-Honor, Object-Shame," *JSOT* 67 (1995): 91, 94–103. But this view does not accord well with his four-month wait before initiating action to get her back.

he takes the initiative and heads for Bethlehem himself to fetch her. In the account of the encounter with his father-in-law and the reconciliation, every one of the characters is painted in a positive light. Taking with him a servant and a pair of donkeys, the Levite's aim is to persuade[199] his concubine to return with him.[200] The former do not figure in the narrative until later, but their presence must have impressed the father-in-law and the young women with the Levite's seriousness. The man's concubine appears to welcome the Levite warmly, for when he arrives, she immediately invites him into her father's house.

19:4 As for the Levite's father-in-law, he too rejoices at the arrival of his son-in-law. Why he was so happy we may only speculate. Was he tired of having his daughter back and anxious to recover his "empty nest" status? Or was he simply overjoyed at the reconciliation between his daughter and her husband. In any case, by the end of v. 4 the reconciliation seems complete. The tension expressed in vv. 1–2 has been resolved, and the story seems to have arrived at a happy conclusion. All that remains is for the Levite and his concubine to return home.

19:5–9 The plot is complicated by the father-in-law's actions in vv. 5–9. At this point the narrative becomes almost comical, as the overly gracious host for some unknown reason tries to detain his guest and the guest becomes increasingly desperate to extricate himself.[201] The tension increases as the narrator recounts the efforts of both men in repetitive style as the following synopsis illustrates.[202]

Judges 19:4–7   **Judges 19:8–10a**

⁴And his father-in-law,
the girl's father,
detained him,
and he remained with him
for three days.

---

[199] The Hb. idiom לְדַבֵּר עַל־לִבָּהּ, "to speak on her heart," is commonly interpreted as "to speak tenderly/lovingly to," but the NIV's "to try to persuade her" captures the required sense. The idiom occurs elsewhere in Gen 34:3; 50:21; 2 Sam 19:7[Hb. 8]; Isa 40:2; Hos 2:16; Ruth 2:13; 1 Chr 30:22; 32:6. For a discussion of its significance here and elsewhere see G. Fischer, "Die Redewendung דבר על־לב im AT —Ein Beitrag zum Verständnis von Jes 40,2," *Bib* 65 (1984): 244–50, esp. pp. 247–48 on this text.

[200] While the effect is the same, *kethib* להשיבו, "to cause it [her heart] to [re]turn," and *qere* להשיבה, "to cause her to [re]turn," offer an interesting literary play. Cf. B. Costacurta, "Implicazioni semantiche in alcuni casi di *Qere-Ketib,*" *Bib* 71 (1990): 226–39, esp. pp. 236–37 on this text.

[201] Is this an intentional parody of Jacob's efforts to extricate himself from Laban in Genesis 31?

[202] For purposes of comparison the translation given must of necessity be more literal than that offered by the NIV.

So they ate and drank,
and they spent the night there.

⁵And on the fourth day
they rose early in the morning.
He got up to go,
but the father of the girl said,
to his son-in-law,
"Refresh your heart
with a bit of food
and afterward you may go."
⁶So they remained
and the two of them ate together
and they drank.

Then the father of the girl
said to the man,
"Please be willing,

and spend the night,

and let your heart be merry."

⁷Then the man arose to go,
but his father-in-law pressured him.
So he remained
and spent the night there.

⁸And he arose early in the
morning on the fifth day
to go.
Then the father of the girl said

"Please refresh your heart

and tarry until midday.

So the two of them ate.

⁹Then the man arose to go,
along with his concubine
and his servant.
Then his father-in-law,
the father of the girl,
said to him,
"Look now,
the day has turned into evening.
Please spend the night here,

so your heart may be merry.
Then you may rise early tomorrow
for your journey
and you may go to your tent.
¹⁰But the man was not willing
to spend the night.
So he arose
and went.

The repeated time references (cf. vv. 4–5a,b,c,8a,b,c,9a,b,c,d) in vv. 5–10 set the stage for what follows, when timing will become a critical factor. The issue is intensified by the motifs of "remaining,"[203] "tarrying,"[204] "spending the night."[205] The last of these will appear in following episodes (cf. vv.

---

[203] Hb. יָשַׁב, vv. 4,6– 7.

[204] Hb. הִתְמַהְמֵהוּ, v. 8. The form is a *hithpalpel* of מהה. The verb has appeared earlier in 3:26, but it sends an early signal of a link between this event and the destruction of Sodom and Gomorrah in Genesis 19, where the verb also appears (v. 16).

[205] Hb. לִין appears in vv. 4,6,7,9a,9b,10a.

11,13,15,20); but the pressure the host puts on[206] his son-in-law and his insistence on stopping the clock contrasts sharply with the Levite's impatience, reflected in the repeated "rising early"[207] and "getting up"[208] "to go."[209] The clash of wills is expressed overtly in the host's plea (lit.), "Please be willing and spend the night" in v. 6 and the guest's final refusal, "the man was not willing," in v. 10a.[210] References to eating and drinking (vv. 4,6,8), "refreshing your heart,"[211] and "letting the heart be merry [lit. 'good']"[212] highlight the hospitality motif, though this is an issue only for the father-in-law, whose intensity is reflected in the emphatic forms of the imperatives he uses.[213] Even more than Abraham in Genesis 18, the girl's father is determined to transform an occasion for expressing normal oriental hospitality into a celebration with plenty of food and drink and lasting for days.

Nowhere does the narrator reveal why the girl's father is so intent on celebrating, but his efforts create increasing tension and frustration in the mind of the Levite, who has no interest in merriment. He just wants to take his concubine and leave. As an oriental guest and as a dutiful son-in-law, however, the Levite must honor prevailing mores of hospitality, so he spends three days with the man and then concedes to a fourth. But by the fifth day his patience has run out, and toward evening he finally leaves, though not before the host has made one more impassioned appeal for him to stay. The Levite recognizes the lateness of the day with two rare expressions in v. 9. The NIV's "It's almost evening" is not a translation but an interpretation of *rāpâ hayyôm la'ărōb*, which translates literally "the day had withered/collapsed to setting."[214] Similarly, the NIV's "the day is nearly over" is an interpretive rendering of *ḥănôt hayyôm*, "the decline of the day," which occurs only here.

---

[206] Expressed by two different words, הֶחֱזִיק, lit., "to make strong" (NIV "prevail") in v. 4, and פָּצַר, "to coerce," in v. 7. Then later provides another link with the Sodom and Gomorrah account (cf. Gen 19:3,9.)

[207] Hb. שָׁכַם, vv. 5,8–9.

[208] Hb. קוּם, vv. 5,7,9.

[209] Hb. הָלַךְ, vv. 5,7–9,10a.

[210] Two different verbs are used: הוֹאִיל (√יאל), "to be prepared, be keen on" in v. 6; אָבָה, "to be willing" in v. 10.

[211] Vv. 5,8. Although סָעַד means fundamentally "to support, sustain," i.e., help individuals in distress, as in Gen 18:5, here it refers to the refreshment that derives from food and drink. Cf. *HALOT*, 761. On the vocalization with *qamets* rather than *ḥōlem* as theme vowel see *GBH* §48a; GKC §64c. This word sends another signal of a link with the Sodom and Gomorrah narrative in Genesis 18–19.

[212] Vv. 6, 9. The idiom has been encountered earlier in 18:20.

[213] V. 6, הוֹאֶל־נָא, "Please be prepared"; v. 8, סְעָד־נָא, "Please refresh …"; v. 9, הִנֵּה־נָא, "Behold please"; v. 9, לִינוּ־נָא, "Please spend the night."

[214] The verb עָרַב, "to turn into evening," which occurs elsewhere in *qal* only in Prov 7:9 and Isa 24:11 and in *hiphil* in 1 Sam 17:16, is cognate to the noun עֶרֶב, "evening." The Akk. cognate *erēbu*, "to go in, go down," is used of the setting of the sun. Cf. *AHW*, 234–35.

Although the expressions seem redundant, they are critical for setting the stage for the events to follow. Had the Levite left in the morning rather than so late in the day, he would never have arrived in Gibeah at night. In this chapter timing is everything, and it is the unfortunate timing of the Levite's departure from his father-in-law's house that precipitates the crisis that follows.

But the events in this house bear a significance far beyond simply setting the chronological context for subsequent events, for they also set the social context. The father-in-law's effusive and persistent expression of hospitality presents a foil against which to interpret the experience of this small company of Levite, concubine, and servant in the town of Gibeah. The man's hospitality is not excessive.[215] To be sure, the reader's sympathies are drawn toward the Levite, who is trying to put his family together again and would like to extricate himself from his father-in-law. But nowhere does the narrator criticize him for it, nor do subsequent events see him reaping negative consequences for his actions. On the contrary, once this scene is over, the Levite's father-in-law disappears from the scene. Far from being cast as a negative character, the man is portrayed as a model of hospitality,[216] exceeding even the oriental standards honored by Abraham in Genesis 18.

(2) The Nature of the Outrage at Gibeah (19:10–30)

With this effective portrayal of normal oriental hospitality the stage is set for a series of events in which Israel's ethical conduct sinks to its lowest point in the Book of Judges, if not the entire Old Testament. The text divides into two equal parts,[217] the first of which depicts the social outrage of the residents of Gibeah (vv. 10b–21); the second, their moral outrage (vv. 22–30). Each half divides further into two parts, which are best considered separately.

THE SOCIAL OUTRAGE (19:10–21). Through the narrator's skillful employment of dialogue and characterization, the Bethlehemite father-in-law and Levite son-in-law come alive as real persons, but the questions about the female character raised by the account go beyond her reason for running away from her husband. Although she seems to welcome her husband warmly when he arrives at her father's house, is she sincere? Does she really want to return with the Levite? Has she nothing to say about the festivities

---

[215] Contra S. Lasine, "Guest and Host in Judges 19: Lot's Hospitality in an Inverted World," *JSOT* 29 (1984): 56–57, n. 34.

[216] So also Niditch ("The Sodomite Theme in Judges 19–20," 366–67), who traces a pattern of community breakdown that grows from a problem between one man and a woman to a full-scale civil war.

[217] By word count (excluding the sign of the definite article) the first consists of 181 words and the second of 177 words.

and/or the delay in their departure? Does she not recognize when they finally leave in the evening of the fifth day that the timing is unwise? Though none of the characters in the account is named, she is the most faceless of all. The only events in which she is an active participant are her abandonment of her husband (v. 2) and her welcoming him at her father's house (v. 3). In the former the narrator portrays her in a negative light, but in the latter she appears to be completely rehabilitated. But unlike Achsah in 1:14–15, who importunes her father on behalf of her husband, after v. 3 she seems a completely passive actant rather than actor. She plays no part in her father's expressions of hospitality, and she has no say in when the group departs from the house. In fact, the text says nothing about her disposition toward leaving her father's house. But in portraying her this way the narrator prepares the reader for her role in subsequent events. In this androcentric world she passively accepts the role expected of her, and in the end she dies, a victim of men who have no thought whatsoever for the dignity and feelings of this woman.

[10]But, unwilling to stay another night, the man left and went toward Jebus (that is, Jerusalem), with his two saddled donkeys and his concubine.
[11]When they were near Jebus and the day was almost gone, the servant said to his master, "Come, let's stop at this city of the Jebusites and spend the night."
[12]His master replied, "No. We won't go into an alien city, whose people are not Israelites. We will go on to Gibeah." [13]He added, "Come, let's try to reach Gibeah or Ramah and spend the night in one of those places." [14]So they went on, and the sun set as they neared Gibeah in Benjamin. [15]There they stopped to spend the night. They went and sat in the city square, but no one took them into his home for the night.

On the Road to Gibeah (19:10b–15). **19:10b** Verse 10a is transitional. For the first time the Levite asserts himself.[218] Refusing to stay at his father-in-law's house any longer, he loads his donkeys[219] and sets out for home, accompanied by his servant and his concubine. Having departed in the afternoon (cf. v. 8), this company had only traveled nine or ten kilometers (six miles), the distance from Bethlehem to Jebus, that is, Jerusalem,[220] when they realized they would need to look for a place to spend the night. The author departs from convention and applies the ethnic name of the inhabit-

---

[218] His determination is reflected in the rapid succession of verbs: "He was not willing (לֹא אָבָה), "he rose" (וַיָּקָם), "he went" (וַיֵּלֶךְ), "he came as far as" (וַיָּבֹא).
[219] The donkeys will figure again in vv. 19–21,28.
[220] As noted earlier, the name Jerusalem antedates the arrival of the Israelites by many centuries, appearing not only in the fourteenth century B.C. Amarna Correspondence as URU-*salim* and in the nineteenth century B.C. Egyptian Execration Texts as *Rusalimum*. See P. J. King, "Jerusalem," *ABD* 3.761.

ants of the region to the city.[221] The gentilic "Jebusites" appears twenty-two times in the twenty-seven occurrences of lists of pre-Israelite inhabitants of Canaan. Although the relationship of the Jebusites to the other Canaanite nations is not clear, most agree that, like the Hittites and Hivites, the Jebusites were a non-Semitic people.[222] In employing Jebus as a place name here, the author draws attention to the ethnic ramifications of what is about to transpire.

19:11–13 As the company approaches the city of Jebus, the Levite and his servant discuss their options. The latter makes a logical suggestion: Why not turn in here and spend the night in the city? Although the Levite rejects the proposal, both the servant's suggestion and the reasons for its rejection are critical elements in the plot. The Levite's answer to his servant is logical. He correctly recognizes Jebus as a "foreign city" and its inhabitants as ethnically distinct from the Israelites. But his response leaves the reader wondering why, when the Israelites generally had been living comfortably among the Canaanites, this little band could not spend the night in a Canaanite city. Significantly, not a word is said about the divine prohibition on any communication with Canaanites or the mandate to conquer them. Israel had given up on the holy war long ago, and in many places their only achievement was the provocation of the natives. Here the issue is simply one of hospitality. The Levite recognizes that the group cannot expect to be safe in the Jebusite town, so they will go on another nine or ten kilometers to Gibeah or Ramah, both Benjamite cities north of Jerusalem.[223]

19:14–15 As is to be expected, the will of the master prevails, and the little band of travelers continues on its way. In typical Hebrew narrative style the events of the journey are telescoped into a couple of verses. Although vv. 11–13 have the appearance of a single conversation, the comments of v. 13 were obviously made some hours after v. 12. But not a word is said about the trip from Jebus/Jerusalem to Gibeah. No sooner have these travelers discussed whether or not they should stop in Jebus than they have arrived at

---

[221] Jebus occurs as a place name only four times in the OT: Judg 19:10,11; 1 Chr 11:4,5. In both contexts the narrative is careful to equate Jebus with Jerusalem. So also Josh 15:8, where the gentilic form, יְבוּסִי, functions as a toponym. Some have argued that the place name is primary and that the gentilic "Jebusite" derives from this toponym. J. M. Miller ("Jebus and Jerusalem: A Case of Mistaken Identity," *ZDPV* 90 [1974]: 115–27) argued that Jebus identified the northern suburb of Jerusalem, modern *Šaʿfat*.

[222] Cf. H. A. Hoffner, "The Hittites and Hurrians," *POTT*, 225.

[223] Gibeah of Benjamin probably is to be identified with modern Jabaʿ (P. M. Arnold, "Gibeah," *ABD* 2.1007–9), though some continue to equate the site with Tell El- Fûl (N. L. Lapp, " Fûl, Tell El-," *NEAEHL* 2.445–48). Gibeah (not to be confused with Gibeon, modern el-Jib, ten kilometers west) will play an important role in the Saul narratives in 1 Samuel 9–14. For a detailed study of Gibeah in history and tradition see Arnold, "Gibeah." Ramah (modern er-Ram) is located seven kilometers north of Jerusalem. Cf. Arnold, "Ramah," *ABD* 5.613–14.

Gibeah. Having passed by Jebus because they would not be received there, they enter the city of Gibeah, expecting, in good oriental custom, to be taken in by someone.[224] But they would be disappointed. In contrast to the lavish hospitality the Levite had experienced at Bethlehem in the home of his father-in-law, no one invites them in.

Finally they return to the city square, just inside the gate, where they could not be missed. Surely the townsfolk coming in from their work in the fields would notice them. But this was not to be. It makes no difference that this was not a "foreign city" and that the inhabitants were "from the descendants of Israel" like the travelers. The last clause in v. 15 would have been shocking anywhere in the ancient Near East. But it is especially shocking in Israel. The social disintegration has infected the very heart of the community. People refuse to open their doors to strangers passing through. It makes no difference that these travelers are their own countrymen.

[16]**That evening an old man from the hill country of Ephraim, who was living in Gibeah (the men of the place were Benjamites), came in from his work in the fields. [17]When he looked and saw the traveler in the city square, the old man asked, "Where are you going? Where did you come from?"**

[18]**He answered, "We are on our way from Bethlehem in Judah to a remote area in the hill country of Ephraim where I live. I have been to Bethlehem in Judah and now I am going to the house of the LORD. No one has taken me into his house. [19]We have both straw and fodder for our donkeys and bread and wine for ourselves your servants—me, your maidservant, and the young man with us. We don't need anything."**

[20]**"You are welcome at my house," the old man said. "Let me supply whatever you need. Only don't spend the night in the square." [21]So he took him into his house and fed his donkeys. After they had washed their feet, they had something to eat and drink.**

In the Open Square (19:16–21). **19:16–17** This scene consists largely of dialogue (vv. 17b–20) framed by a narrative introduction (vv. 16–17a) and conclusion (v. 21). The opening statements draw the reader's attention away from the small company huddled in the open square to a new character, returning home from his work in the fields.[225] The pace of the story slows as the narrator pauses to describe this person, who on first sight appears to be a very pleasant figure. In keeping with the narrator's pattern, the man is not identified by name. He is simply presented as any old man, who, like the Lev-

---

[224] Whereas the Levite has identified the preferred destination simply as Gibeah in v. 12, the narrator sets the stage for events to follow by noting in v. 14 that Gibeah belongs to Benjamin. This fact seems unimportant for the moment, but it will have gigantic and tragic consequences in the next chapters.

[225] Note the attention-grabbing construction (lit.): "Behold, an old man coming from his work in the field in the evening."

ite and his company, is an outsider in this place. Indeed, like the Levite, this man is from the hill country of Ephraim (cf. v. 1), but he has taken up temporary residence[226] in this Benjamite town. Although he has not been integrated into the community, in vv. 22–23 he is identified as (lit.) "the man, the owner of the house, the old one."

19:18–19 When the old man comes through the gate, he notices the traveler in the square and strikes up a conversation. He asks the newcomer where he is headed, then from where he has come. Answering the questions in the order they were framed, the Levite states the facts: they are traveling from Bethlehem to the hill country of Ephraim. The latter is where he lives, but he has taken a trip to Bethlehem of Judah and is now returning home.[227] Whereas the old man has not acknowledged the Levite's concubine or servant in either his opening question (v. 17b) or his concluding invitation (v. 20), the Levite's response with plural forms includes his companions in the answer. But he offers no explanation for the trip. In the narrator's presentation the problem with the concubine has provided necessary background for the events that are about to transpire, but it has ceased to be an issue in the plot.

After complaining in v. 18b that no one in Gibeah will offer lodging for the night, the Levite expands on the seriousness of Gibeah's social dysfunction. He and his party are asking only for a bed. Since they have brought food and wine for themselves and fodder for their donkeys, they are not even expecting an evening meal. Ironically, they had by-passed Canaanite Jebus, knowing they would find no welcome there, but now they have been rebuffed by their own countrymen. With his comment the Levite verbalizes the social malignancy in Israel. The mores of the nation have been infected at the most fundamental level—the people of one tribe sense no obligation to the members of another. There is no sense of community.

19:20–21 The old man's reaction in v. 20 represents the voice of experience. Politely and warmly he greets the visitors with "Peace to you" (*šālôm lāk*, NIV, "you are welcome at my house") and then puts himself and his resources at their disposal. He insists that whatever they do, these travelers must not spend the night in the city square. The old man does not say why.

---

[226] The expression וְהוּא־גָר בַּגִּבְעָה, "Now he was sojourning in Gibeah" (19:16), recalls both v. 1, which describes the Levite as a sojourner in the hill country of Ephraim, and 17:7, which had another Levite sojourning in Bethlehem.

[227] The NIV's "house of the LORD" follows the MT's בֵּית יְהוָה, along with Tg, Syr, and Vg, even though this makes no sense in the context. The LXX's καὶ εἰς τὸν οἶκόν μου, "and to my house," suits the context better. So most modern translations (NASB, RSV, NRSV, NEB, REB, GNB, JPSV). It is conceivable the Levite's itinerary would have involved a visit to the central shrine at Shiloh, but in this book this place is called the "house of God" (בֵּית אֱלֹהִים, 18:31). Presumably the MT, which provides the base for most ancient versions, mistook consonantal בֵּיתִי, "my house," for an abbreviation of בֵּית יְהוָה. For a discussion see E. Tov, *Textual Criticism*, 256–57; O'Connell, *Rhetoric of the Book of Judges*, 483.

Since this is a walled city, they should be safe from outsiders, but as a resident alien he has learned that the problem is inside. He knows the ways of the citizens of Gibeah all too well. As a dutiful host, he takes the visitors to his own house and lavishes on them his hospitality. He feeds the donkeys, has the Levite and his companions wash their feet, and then serves them a meal of food and wine. But the continued marginalization of the concubine is reflected in the text with the shift from "No one took them into his home" in v. 15b to "he took him into his house" in v. 21. Men may find hospitality and protection in each others' homes, but the woman will find neither.

In contrast to the reality that is Israel, the old man's response illustrates the ideal. Through this conversation the narrator exposes the state of Israelite society. He does not declare outrightly that the social fabric of the nation has rotted. Instead he tells a story to illustrate the point. This conversation turns out to be a self-analysis—an Israelite is telling a story about Israelites.

22While they were enjoying themselves, some of the wicked men of the city surrounded the house. Pounding on the door, they shouted to the old man who owned the house, "Bring out the man who came to your house so we can have sex with him."

23The owner of the house went outside and said to them, "No, my friends, don't be so vile. Since this man is my guest, don't do this disgraceful thing. 24Look, here is my virgin daughter, and his concubine. I will bring them out to you now, and you can use them and do to them whatever you wish. But to this man, don't do such a disgraceful thing."

25But the men would not listen to him. So the man took his concubine and sent her outside to them, and they raped her and abused her throughout the night, and at dawn they let her go. 26At daybreak the woman went back to the house where her master was staying, fell down at the door and lay there until daylight.

THE MORAL OUTRAGE (19:22–28). *In the Old Man's House (19:22–26).* The scene described in vv. 22–26 is among the most grotesque and sickening in the book, if not in the entire Scripture. Anyone familiar with the narratives of Genesis will hear in this account remarkable echoes of the depravity at Sodom and Gomorrah in Genesis 19.[228] These echoes may be highlighted by placing woodenly literal translations of the texts in parallel columns as follows:

Key: <u>Underline</u>: Verbatim quotations in the Hebrew (with grammatical adjustments)
Bold Italics: Necessary contextual alterations
Bold: Paraphrastic alterations
Normal Font: Unique features

---

[228] Contra Niditch ("The 'Sodomite' Theme in Judges 19–20," 365–78), who argues for the chronological priority of Judges 19.

Genesis 19:4–8	Judges 19:22–24
[4]**Before they lay down**	[22]**While they were making merry,** behold,
the men of the city	the men of the city
the men of Sodom	men of **the sons of belial**
surrounded	surrounded
with reference to the house	the house
	pounding on the door.
both young and old	
all the men totally.	
[5]And they **called**	and they **said**
to Lot,	**to the old man,**
	the owner of the house,
and they said to him,	**saying,**
"Where are	Bring out
the men	the man
who have come	who has come
to **you**?	to your house,
Bring **them** out	
to us,	
that we may 'know' them."	that we may 'know' him."
[6]And **Lot**	[23]And **the man**
	the owner of the house
went out	went out
to them	to them.
at the doorway	
and shut the door	
behind him.	
[7]And he said,	And he said
	to them,
"Please,	
do not, my brothers,	"Do not, **my brothers,**
act wickedly.	**do not** act wickedly
	please.
	Because
	this man has come
	to my house,
	do not commit this folly.
[8]Please,	[24]
behold	Behold
I have two daughters	*my daughter*

who have never 'known' a man.	*a virgin*
	and his concubine.
Please,	Please,
let me bring them out	let me bring them out.
	Ravish them.
to you.	
Do to them	Do to them
according to what is good	what is good
in your eyes.	in your eyes.
Only to these men	**But** to this man
do not commit	do not commit
	this foolish
an act,	act.
because	
this man	
	under the shelter of my roof.
to my house,	
do not commit	
this folly.	

Of the words found in Genesis almost one-fourth (sixteen) occur in the same form in Judges. An additional twenty-four expressions from Genesis find a close counterpart in Judges, the variations being grammatical, stylistic, or such as are required by the context. Occasionally, as in the opening lines, Genesis 19 statements are recast and/or paraphrased. "Before they lay down" in Gen 19:4 is roughly equivalent to "While they are making merry" in Judg 19:22, inasmuch as both identify the temporal context for the events that follow. What appears as a question and a command in Gen 19:5 is conflated into a single command in Judg 19:22. The causal clause at the end of Gen 19:8 is recast and brought forward to precede the first warning not to commit the evil deed in Judg 19:23. "I have two daughters" in Gen 19:8 is answered with "my daughter and his concubine" in Judg 19:24, preserving the involvement of two female victims. "Who have not known a man" in Gen 19:8 is replaced by a single word, *bĕtûlâ*, "young woman," in Judg 19:24. But the correspondence between these texts extends beyond the echoes of detail, to the overall lengths of the texts. In Hebrew the number of words in each is identical—sixty-nine.[229] In view of these extraordinary parallels, there can be little doubt that the narrator was composing this text with Genesis 19 in mind and doing so intentionally that a reader might experience a sense of déjà vu. Indeed, the

---

[229] Treating the *nota accusative* and the following substantive as a lexical unit. A count of accentual units yields similar conclusions.

opening *hinnēh*, "Behold,"[230] calls readers to sit up and pay careful attention to what follows.

19:22 The pleasant scene of the host and his guests "enjoying themselves"[231] is rudely interrupted by a loud pounding on the door. The men of the city have finally arrived, but it is definitely not to extend their hospitality to these visitors. Whereas in 11:3 the narrator had described the good-fornothings who had gathered around Jephthah as "worthless men" (*ʾănāšîm rêqîm*), here they are characterized as *ʾanšê bĕnê bĕliyyaʿal*, "men of the sons of Belial."[232] Although the origin of this strange expression remains uncertain,[233] the most likely explanation finds in *bĕliyyaʿal* a combination of the negative particle *bĕlî*, "nothingness, not, without,"[234] and the noun *yaʿal*, "worth, profit, benefit," from a root meaning "to be worthy,"[235] hence "sons of worthlessness, men without worth/honor." Variations of the present expression occurs sixteen times in the Old Testament.[236] The moral/ethical sense of the idiom may be recognized by noting the parallel expressions with which it is associated[237] but also the kinds of people who are so characterized: murderers, rapists, false witnesses, corrupt priests, drunks, boors, ungrateful and selfish folk, rebels, those who lead others into idolatry and who do not know Yahweh. Following several Old Testament texts that associate *bĕliyyaʿal* with Sheol and death,[238] in the pseudepigraphic and Qumran literature Belial/ Beliar serves as the name for the angel of wickedness, the ruler of this world, the devil who heads all the forces of darkness. This usage is picked up in the New Testament (2 Cor 6:15), where *Beliar* (NIV, "Belial") serves as a virtual synonym for "Satan." In our context the narrator's juxtaposing of the "sons of

---

[230] Following the temporal clause that set the stage. The particle is omitted in the NIV.

[231] The NIV's rendering of אֶת־לִבָּם מֵיטִיבִים הֵמָּה, "they were making good their hearts."

[232] The NIV "wicked men." The LXX and the Vg omit אַנְשֵׁי, "men of." Many Hb. MSS, Syr omit בְּנֵי, "sons of." Cf. 20:13, הָאֲנָשִׁים בְּנֵי־בְלִיַּעַל, "the men, the sons of belial."

[233] For possibilities see S. D. Sperling, "Belial," *DDD,* 322–27; T. J. Lewis, "Belial," *ABD* 1.654–656.

[234] Cf. *HALOT* 1.133; *DCH* 1.177–78.

[235] Cf. *HALOT* 1.420.

[236] אִשׁ הַבְּלִיַּעַל, "man of belial," 1 Sam 25:25; 2 Sam 16:7; 20:1; Prov 16:27. אַנְשֵׁי הַבְּלִיַּעַל, "men of belial," 1 Kgs 21:13. בֶּן־בְּלִיַּעַל, "son of belial," 1 Sam 25:17; Nah 2:1. בְּנֵי־בְלִיַּעַל, "sons of belial," Deut 13:13 [Hb. 14]; Judg 19:22; 20:13; 1 Sam 2:12; 10:27; 1 Kgs 21:10,13; 2 Chr 13:7. בַּת־בְּלִיַּעַל, "daughter of belial," 1 Sam 1:16.

[237] אָוֶן אִישׁ, "man of iniquity," Prov 6:12; רָע אִישׁ, "evil man," 1 Sam 30:22; הַדָּמִים אִישׁ, "man of blood/murderer," 2 Sam 16:7 (cf. 2 Sam 12:5); רְשָׁעִים, "the wicked," Prov 19:28.

[238] Ps 18:4–5 [Hb. 5–6] (= 2 Sam 22:5–6); 41:8 [Hb. 9]. This usage may call for a different etymology, perhaps יַעַל בַּל, "[the land from which] one does not come up," or the verb בָּלַע, "to swallow." According to J. Tigay (*Deuteronomy*, 134), the two meanings of בְּלִיַּעַל (*bĕliyyaʿal*) may be unrelated homonyms. But it is conceivable that the term originally meant "the netherworld" and that בְּנֵי־בְלִיַּעַל meant "denizens of the netherworld," or "demons," and then "evildoers, scoundrels."

belial" with "the old man" pits the new morality, the new Canaanite ethic, against the old normative Israelite ethic.

By characterizing the "men of the city" as "sons of Belial," the author has generalized the depravity of Gibeah to the entire male population, whose ravenous lust is demonstrated in their pounding on the door[239] and their demand to the host to hand the Levite over to them so they may have sexual relations with him. The narrator follows Gen 19:5,8 in deliberately using an ambiguous term *yādaᶜ*, "to know." Under normal circumstances, where the proper standards of hospitality would be operative, the expression could reflect a positive desire to get to know a new person in town, to establish social relations with the person. But here as elsewhere the verb serves euphemistically for "to engage in sex."[240] Although they later concede to receive a woman, the fact that they ask for the man betrays their homosexual orientation. Accordingly, their demand represents a violation of three fundamental social/ moral laws: the law of hospitality, the proscription on intercourse outside of marriage, and proscription on heterosexual intercourse.

19:23–24 Verses 23–24 describe the response of the host. Although he is an outsider, like Lot in Gen 19:7, he politely expresses solidarity with the men of the town by addressing them as "my brothers" (NIV, "my friends"). But he rebukes them sharply for their inhospitality, characterizing their intended actions as "vile" and "disgraceful." The words he uses are critical for interpreting the crimes perpetrated in this event. The first verb, *rāᶜâ*, "to do evil," deliberately links the Gibeahites' behavior with the general spiritual and ethical malaise of the nation during the days of the judges: "The Israelites did what is evil [*ᶜāśâ hāraᶜ*] in the sight of the LORD,"[241] which is the obverse of "Each person did what was right (*ᶜāśâ hayyāšār*) in his own eyes" (17:6; 21:25) The second expression, *hannĕbālâ hazzōʾt*, translates literally "this foolishness." *nĕbālâ* denotes emptiness, vanity, without moral, spiritual, or reasonable restraint, hence intellectual stupidity and/or moral turpitude. Here and in 20:6 the latter is obviously intended.

There are actually two dimensions to the crime intended by the men of Gibeah. First, their action is *nĕbālâ* because it violates sexual norms.[242] These men have come to commit a perverse homosexual act.[243] Second, their

---

[239] Hb. מִתְדַּפְּקִים עַל־הַדָּלֶת. The verb appears elsewhere only in Gen 33:13 (of hard/excessive driving of cattle) and Song 5:2 (of urgent knocking on a door).

[240] Cf. Gen 4:1; 19:5,8; Num 31:17; 1 Kgs 1:4.

[241] Cf. 2:11; 3:7,12; 4:1; 6:1; 10:6; 13:1.

[242] The word is applied to deviant sexual acts elsewhere in Gen 34:7 (the rape of Dinah); Deut 22:21 (a woman committing harlotrous acts); 2 Sam 13:12–13 (Ammon's sexual violation of his sister Tamar); and Jer 29:23 (adultery with a neighbor's wife).

[243] The disposition of the Torah toward male homosexual acts is explicitly declared in Lev 18:22; 20:13. In the sight of God this is a capital crime to be punished by execution.

action is *něbālâ* because it violates customary norms of hospitality.[244] Although the Old Testament offers no specific legislation on how guests are to be treated, in keeping with oriental custom to this day hosts are responsible for the welfare of their guests. By demanding to lie with the Levite, the men are violating this custom. Having rebuked the townsmen, the host proposes and authorizes an alternative. Now doing what is right in his own eyes, he offers to bring out his young daughter and the Levite's concubine. The mob could humiliate and abuse them[245] by doing to them whatever "is good in their own eyes."[246]

The ethical issues involved here are complex, involving homosexuality (the men of Gibeah demanded the male guest), the rape of a woman (they took the man's concubine and abused her all night), and adultery (the woman was another man's wife). Recent interpretations have tended to examine the actions described from sociological and anthropological perspectives, paying particular attention to its implications for gender relations and male honor and shame. With respect to the former, consistent with the patricentrism the host had expressed earlier (vv. 17,20), he now declares a sense of responsibility only for the Levite. From his perspective, and also that of the townsmen, the man's servant and concubine are irrelevant. But not for long. In a heartless and outrageous caricature of normative androcentrism, he offers the young women in the house as substitutes for the Levite. Unlike the case with Lot, his guest is not a divine person, who can protect the visitors by smiting the criminals with blindness. This outsider finds himself between a rock and a hard place. In the end his sense of duty to a male guest supersedes his obligation to his own daughter, not to mention the man's concubine.[247] A host's honor is at stake—not justice or morality. That is why to him heterosexual rape is preferable to homosexual rape. The host cannot betray his obligation to his male guest.

But is it only the host's honor that is at stake? The response of the men of Gibeah raises several important issues. First, the intended object of their immoral acts is the Levite in particular. They are not interested in the host

---

[244] Cf. the application of the word to the violation of the customs of holy war (Josh 7:15) and to paying tribute (1 Sam 25:25).

[245] The verb עָנָה is capable of a wide range of meanings: "to humiliate, afflict, do violence to." Here and in 20:5 it functions as a technical term for rape. Cf. Gen 34:2; Deut 22:24; 2 Sam 13:12,14,22,32; Lam 5:11. The NIV's "you can use them" understates the crime.

[246] The NIV's "whatever you wish" obscures the link between this statement and the refrain in 17:6 and particularly 21:25. The present preference for הַטּוֹב, "that which is good," over הַיָּשָׁר, "that which is right," is stylistic.

[247] Note the emphatic construction of the Hb., which places the prepositional phrase first in the clause: וְלָאִישׁ הַזֶּה לֹא תַעֲשׂוּ דְּבַר הַנְּבָלָה הַזֹּאת, "To this man do not do this disgraceful thing."

or the Levite's servant, let alone his concubine. The Levite is their target.[248]

The narrator's own ignoble estimation of the spiritual state of the Levites is evident from this chapter and the previous account of Micah's Levite (chaps. 17–18). As representatives of Israel, these men of Gibeah demonstrate that they have no respect for Levites at all. Although there is no indication that they are even aware that he is a Levite,[249] their actions represent a violation not only of the host's honor but also Levitical honor. Those who had been set apart and ordained for divine service[250] are desecrated by vile acts.

19:25–26 As in Gen 19:8, the host's counterproposal in v. 25 offers the criminals two helpless women in place of the male guest. First, like Jephthah he offers his most precious treasure, his own virgin daughter, as a sacrifice, but this time it is not to fulfill a stupid vow. He may be demonstrating proper respect for a Levite,[251] but concern for his own and his male guest's honor demands that he give a nameless traveler, who just happens to be passing through, preference to his own flesh and blood. Second, he offers another man's wife to protect his own honor as host. His presentation of the concubine marks the first time he acknowledges her in this account. But in his mind she has significance only as a potential sacrifice in defense of his own reputation. He invites the men of Gibeah to rape[252] these women and do whatever else they want with them, but do not touch his primary male guest. To ravish the Levite would not only be disgraceful; it would violate his honor.

By noting the open-ended invitation, "Do to them what is good in your eyes," the narrator invites the reader to interpret this episode as an illustration of the principle explicitly declared in 17:7 and 21:25: "Everyone (lit. "a man") did what was right in his own eyes."[253] Israel does not need a king to lead them into these depths of depravity. The inhabitants of Gibeah

---

[248] This focus contrasts with Gen 19:5, according to which the men of Sodom demanded "them," i.e., both of Lot's visitors.

[249] He is identified as a Levite only at the beginning (v. 1) and at the end (20:4). Between these texts he is identified as "her husband" (אִישָׁהּ, v. 2), "his master" (אֲדֹנָיו, vv. 11–12), "her master" (אֲדוֹנֶיהָ, vv. 26–27) but most often simply as "the man" (הָאִישׁ, vv. 7,9,10,25). When he introduces himself to his host (v. 18), he makes no mention of his Levitical status. When the men of Gibeah demand him from their host, they identify their target simply as "the man who came into your house" (v. 22), and the host refers to him as "this man" (v. 24).

[250] Cf. Exod 32:25–29; Num 8:10–18; Deut 18:1–8.

[251] Though the text is silent on whether or not the host was aware that he was a Levite.

[252] Here and in 20:5, Hb. עָנָה, "to humiliate, do violence to," functions as a technical term for rape. Cf. Gen 34:2; 2 Sam 13:12,14,22,32; Lam 5:11. The NIV's "you can use them" understates the crime.

[253] The substitution of הַיָּשָׁר, "what is right," with הַטּוֹב, "what is good," is stylistic.

are determined to sink this low on their own.

But the men of Gibeah reject the host's compromising offer.[254] Sensing their refusal to negotiate, finally "the man" seizes his concubine and thrusts her out like one tosses a scrap of meat to dogs. But the statement raises several questions. First, who delivered the concubine to the men of Gibeah? The Hebrew text is quite ambiguous. Since "the old man" has been the main character in the previous verses, one's first impulse is to identify this "man" as the host, fulfilling one half of his offer. But this raises a second question. Where is his virgin daughter? Because the primary character in the broader narrative is the Levite, however, it is preferable to recognize here the actions of the Levite, who stands up in defense of his host and in so doing also defends masculine honor. Having gone to so much effort to bring back his concubine, he now willingly offers her up to these dogs. By the time she is thrust upon them, the men surrounding the house are uncontrollably aroused. What was "good in their eyes" turns out to be a stupid *(něbālâ)* and monstrous series of actions that are summarized in three short clauses: they "knew" *(yādaʿ)* her,[255] they "abused" *(hitʿallēl)*[256] her all night until morning, and at dawn they "discarded" *(šillēaḥ)* her. Sunrise[257] finds her dragging herself back to the house of the old man, where her master[258] was staying, but she collapses on the threshold, outside the door.[259]

As intimated earlier, the narrator places great emphasis on the timing of events in this chapter. The stage for this tragic sequence of incidents was set in v. 10, when the Levite had finally extricated himself from his father-in-law. But

---

[254] The expression וְלֹא אָבוּ, "they were not willing," echoes the Levite's own response to his previous host (v. 10).

[255] The verb יָדַע, "to know," in this context means "rape."

[256] Hb. הִתְעַלֵּל בְּ, "to abuse, deal wantonly with," occurs elsewhere in Exod 10:2; Num 22:29; 1 Sam 6:6; 31:4; Jer 38:19; 1 Chr 10:5.

[257] The odd expression לִפְנוֹת הַבֹּקֶר, lit. "at the turn of the morning," occurs elsewhere only in Exod 14:27 and Ps 46:5 [Hb. 6].

[258] The narrator's choice of אֲדֹנֶיהָ, "her lord," rather than אִישָׁהּ, "her husband," may be intentional, reflecting the subversion of what should have been normal marital affiliation into a master-slave relationship.

[259] Readers have often puzzled over the men of Gibeah's acceptance of the Levite's concubine as a substitute for the Levite himself, on the one hand, and the complete absence of any reference to the host's young daughter after v. 24 on the other. If the scoundrels' intent was simply sexual release or to violate male honor in general, either woman or the host would have been acceptable as a sexual object. Although they would not listen to the host's rebuke (v. 25a), they do accept the Levite's concubine when he thrusts her out of the house to them. The best explanation is to be found in the Gibeahite's specific intention to violate the Levite. If they cannot do so by attacking him personally (Stone has noted that the men of Gibeah do not speak to the Levite directly; they speak to his host, who controls access to the man's sexuality ["Gender and Homosexuality in Judges 19," 99]), they will do so indirectly by desecrating his concubine. Women are acceptable not only as objects of rape, but also as objects through which male honor may be attacked.

he had no idea how dark the coming night would be. The narrator keeps the reader's attention on the timing of episodes with repeated chronological references that beat ominously throughout the narrative. (1) When "the day had withered/collapses to setting" and at "the decline of the day," the Levite decides to leave (v. 9).[260] (2) "When the day had gone down," he was faced with the reality that he would not make it home, hence the need to find a place to spend the night (v. 11). (3) Refusing to seek the hospitality of the Jebusites, "as the sun was setting" the Levite and his companions arrive at the outskirts of Gibeah, which should provide a safe haven (v. 14). (4) "At evening" the old man who would be his host arrives and invites them to his house (v. 16). (5) The plot reaches its nadir when the wicked men of the city rape and torture the Levite's concubine "all night" (v. 25).[261] (6) The addition of "until the morning" in v. 25b invites the reader to await a new day, but this is a ruse. The horrors have not yet ceased. (7) "At dawn" *(haššāḥar)* the mob discards her (v. 25c). (8) "At the turn of the morning" the pitiful victim collapses on the doorstep of the host's house (v. 26a).[262] (9) There she remains "until the light" (v. 26b).

With these chronological notes the narrator has given his verdict on the spiritual and moral state of Israel. The light of the knowledge of Yahweh[263] and "doing what is right in his [Yahweh's] eyes" have been eclipsed by the depravity of the human soul expressed in "doing what is good in one's own eyes."

[27]When her master got up in the morning and opened the door of the house and stepped out to continue on his way, there lay his concubine, fallen in the doorway of the house, with her hands on the threshold. [28]He said to her, "Get up; let's go." But there was no answer. Then the man put her on his donkey and set out for home.

The Journey Home (19:27–28).   **19:27–28** The narrator commences his account of the final episode in this dreadful series of events from the victim's perspective by continuing the identification of the subject as "her master." Although this rhetorical ploy keeps the reader's sympathies with the woman, the tone of vv. 27–28 is cold and calculated to fit the Levite's attitude. Morning finds the Levite emerging from his host's house, ready to resume his journey. The sequence of verbs reflects his indifference to his concubine's fate: "He arose in the morning," "he opened the door of the house," "he went out." If these verbs sound nonchalant, the motive clause is shocking. Instead of going out to look for his concubine, the man intends "to continue on his way." To his surprise, however,[264] when he steps outside, he trips over the woman,

---

[260] On these odd expressions see above on v. 9.

[261] Hb. כָּל־הַלַּיְלָה. The term "night" appears for the first time in v. 25. The Eng. phrase "spend the night" translates a different expression, לִין, "to lodge."

[262] For the first time since the beginning of the story the concubine is the subject of active verbs.

[263] Cf. 1 Sam 3:1–3.

[264] The NIV omits the particle, הִנֵּה, "Behold," which expresses surprise.

lying at the doorway with her hands on the threshold. The image is concretized by the reference to the hands. Reaching out for the door, reaching for the protection of her husband, reaching for the security of their host's house, reaching—but all she could grasp was death. Obviously she had been too weak to open the door or even to knock.

As if nothing unusual had occurred, he commands her, "Get up; let's go!" The narrator's report of her response is deafening: *wĕʿên ʿôneh,* "But no one answered."[265] Apparently with no expression of emotion the man picks up the woman, places her on his donkey, arises, and goes home. Verses 27–28 portray the Levite as incredibly calloused.

These last episodes raise a host of troubling questions. (1) How could the host offer his own virgin daughter and the guest's concubine to this mob? How could the laws of fatherhood be suspended, and did the laws of hospitality not apply to women? (2) After going to such effort to recover his concubine, how could the Levite thrust her out to these brutes? (3) Why did the men of the town accept the concubine as a substitute for the Levite? (4) Where was the host's virgin daughter in all this? (5) Where was the Levite while the men of the town were abusing his concubine? Could he really have continued his merriment or gone to bed and slept? (6) Why is there no apparent remorse when he discovers her? (7) Perhaps most torturous of all, was the woman dead when the Levite found her? The LXX (and the Vg) answers the question, "but she was dead,"[266] which renders the mob guilty of murder, as well as gang rape. It is not clear from the sequel (vv. 29–30), however, whether the Levite simply dismembers a corpse or whether he himself murders his concubine in a fit of rage. In his testimony in 20:5–6 he will exonerate himself, but by this time the reader is no longer sure he can be trusted. The narrator's identification of the Levite in this episode as "her master" rather than "her husband" (cf. v. 2), does not enhance his reputation. And the fact that he describes the concubine's fate with "And she died" (20:5) rather than "And they killed her" leaves open the possibility that he, rather than the rapists, was responsible for her death. In any case his speech is entirely self-serving, expressing no pain or grief whatsoever at the death of the woman. The narrator tantalizes the reader by leaving all the options open. If she was not dead when he found her, then the Levite is guilty of murder. If she was dead, he desacralizes her body, treating her as if it were an animal carcass.[267]

---

[265] The LXX neutralizes the rhetorical effect by personalizing the clause, "But she did not answer him."

[266] ἀλλ᾽ ἐτεθνήκει, which, according to Boling (*Judges,* 276) preserves an original כִּי מֵתָה, which may have been lost through haplography due to homoioteleuton. Cf. 20:5.

[267] M. Bal ("Body of Writing," 218) overstates the case when she says in so doing he transgresses the laws of his own status as priest. According to Leviticus 21 the laws of priestly purity, particularly with respect to the dead, applied specifically to Aaron and his descendants, apparently not to Levites in general. The same is true in Ezek 44:25, which apples this rule to the Zadokites.

In reality the unnamed woman's death started much earlier and unfolded in a series of painful stages: (1) when the host offered her as a substitute sacrifice for his male guest; (2) when her husband, the Levite, thrust her out to the mad dogs of Gibeah; (3) when the Gibeahites exposed and raped her; (4) when they left her for dead at the threshold of the host's house; (5) when the Levite cut up her body and distributed the pieces among all the tribes. From start to finish it is indeed one of the most horrible deaths imaginable. In the evening the Levite had opened the door to sexual violence; in the morning he opens it to death.

Theological and Practical Implications

On the surface this story is about hospitality. Initially it appears that the primary defect of the people of Gibeah is their inhospitality. Although the old man's warning to the party of travelers not to spend the night in the open square has an ominous ring for those who know the outcome of the story, the reader is led not to expect anything more serious. In fact, this impression is reinforced by the author's careful attention to detail when the actions of the Levite's father-in-law and the old man of Gibeah are described. Although the latter and the travelers are enjoying each other's company, evil crashes in on them.

Ethically, this story is about unrestrained animal lust and human depravity. Initially the men of Gibeah demand a homosexual expression of this depraved instinct. But when this drive is frustrated, a woman suffers rape, abuse, and murder. As already observed, the silence of the concubine in v. 28 is deafening. But her voice has been stifled throughout this account. To be sure, she does assert herself in v. 3, and some would find in her ultimate fate the punishment for her abandonment of her husband. But it is striking that after the stage has been set, she has been a passive actant rather than an actor. The fact that she is a woman in a man's world need not be a problem by definition. But in a world of depraved men, women have no protection, especially not against male exploitation and violence. In this world hosts need not protect women as they protect men, husbands may seize their wives and throw them out to the mob, and men may rape, abuse, and discard women without restraint. The rules of hospitality and family order protect only males, and where the wills of males conflict, it is quite acceptable to offer females as sacrifices in defence of male honor. D. N. Fewell is correct.

> Stories like the rape and dismemberment of the Levite's concubine in Judges 19 and the sacrifice of Jephthah's daughter in Judges 11 show the darkest side of patriarchy yet—the torture and murder of the most vulnerable and innocent for the sake of male honor and pompous religiosity.[268]

---

[268] D. N. Fewell, "Feminist Reading of the Hebrew Bible: Affirmation, Resistance, and Transformation," *JSOT* 39 (1987): 86. For another discussion of this text from the woman's perspective see Trible, *Texts of Terror*, 64–91.

It is easy to overlook the fact that most of what transpires in the Book of Judges is not intended to be interpreted as normal or normative. Whereas responsible headship would find men expressing their love for women sacrificing themselves in their [the women's] interests,[269] this is a portrait of patriarchy gone mad. The narrator here describes a social system in which men rule over women in the worst sense of the phrase and sacrifice them for their own interests rather than providing responsible leadership and sacrificing themselves for the best interests of women.[270] This is cancerous patriarchy expressed according to Canaanite standards. The Levite had preferred Gibeah over Jebus to avoid the dangers of Canaanism, only to discover that Canaan had invaded his own world.

It is tempting to interpret this passage only or primarily as a commentary on the abusive violation of male power and honor,[271] but there is much more to the story. From it one might conclude simplistically that in a patriarchal system it is generally preferable for men to rape women rather than to rape men. Specifically, the rape of women is acceptable if male honor is thereby served. But this is to misconstrue the broader goal of the book: to chronicle the increasing Canaanization of Israelite society. As noted earlier, here Canaanization involves at least four heinous crimes: homosexuality, rape, adultery, and murder. The first two require comment.

Contemporary feminist approaches tend to see in this account evidences for the fundamental injustice of patriarchy. But this is to miss the point. Instead of asking why heterosexual rape is preferable to homosexual rape (as if it is good in any sense at all), we should be asking, "What is it about homosexual rape that makes it worse even than heterosexual rape?" In no way does this episode reflect acceptable treatment of women by men in any context. The Scriptures are unequivocal in their denunciation of sexual crimes by men against women. Male violations of female sexuality are characterized elsewhere as $n\check{e}b\bar{a}l\hat{a}$[272] and a violation of the clearly and unequivocally revealed will of Yahweh in the Torah.[273] Whatever one makes of the social structures of ancient Israel, by the nation's normative standards both rape and adultery were heinous crimes. They are never acceptable forms of behavior by men or women.

But what is it about homosexual acts that makes them even worse, as the

---

[269] Jesus Christ is the supreme example of sacrificial love for the church. See Eph 5:23–25 and Phil 2:5–8.

[270] The problem will accelerate and intensify in chaps. 20–21, where the daughters of Jabesh Gilead and Shiloh will be captured, betrayed, raped, scattered, and delivered into the hands of these same Benjamites.

[271] On the latter see especially Stone, "Gender and Homosexuality in Judges 19," 87–107.

[272] See Gen 34:7 (Shechem's rape of Dinah); 2 Sam 13:12–13 (Ammon's rape of his sister Tamar); Jer 29:23 (adultery with a neighbor's wife).

[273] See Exod 20:14; Lev 18:24–25; 20:10–21; Deut 22:22–30; Jer 9:1; Mal 3:5; Job 24:14–15.

host in our passage suggests? The question may best be answered by examining the biblical perspective on human sexuality as a whole. The issue is extremely complex, but one must begin by affirming that, as with animals, the primary function of human sexual activity is procreation, a means whereby human beings fulfill the mandate and promise of God to be fruitful. Although some organisms are hermaphroditic[274] and/or androgynous,[275] this is not true of humans. Heterosexual copulation is "natural" (*phusikos,* Rom 1:26–27) and necessary for reproduction. Since reproduction is both impossible by and irrelevant to homosexual activity, it is "against nature" (*para phusin,* Rom 1:26–27). From the biblical perspective the "image of God" is complete when a "man" (*ʾîš*) "clings to" (*dābaq*) "his wife" (*ʾiššâ*) and they become "one flesh" (*bāśār ʾeḥād,* Gen 2:24). But this "clinging" is not simply to procreate; within the context of the Old Testament, since one lives on in one's progeny, sexual activity takes on added significance in securing one's future. Homosexual activity thinks only of the present.

A second function of sexual activity is to express intimacy and marital commitment. Beginning with Gen 1:27–28, the Scriptures are consistent in affirming only heterosexual marriage. The intimacy described in Gen 2:24–25 is natural, good, and holy, and it remains so even after the fall. Within the context of marriage, through sexual activity a husband and wife express physical intimacy to complement their emotional and spiritual union. Although this form of intimacy is celebrated in Scripture as beautiful and good, according to Lev 18:22 and 20:13, the same kind of intimacy between two males is condemned in the sharpest of terms as *tôʿēbâ,* "an abomination," as on a par with adultery and incest, as a capital crime. Accordingly, homosexual activity is not only "against nature"; it is a crime "against God," another expression of "doing what is right in one's own eyes."[276]

The echo of Genesis 19 in this text is intentional. By patterning this account after the earlier story, the narrator serves notice that, whereas these travelers had thought they had come home, finding safety with their own countrymen, they have actually arrived in Sodom. The nation has come full circle. The Canaanization of Israel is complete. When the Israelites look in the mirror, what they see is a nation that may be ethnically distinct from the natives but which is indistinguishable from them with regard to morality, ethics, and social values. They have sunk to the level of those nations whom they were commanded to destroy and on whom the judgment of God hung. And in the words of Moses in Deut 8:19–20, when Israelites act like Canaanites, they may expect the same fate.

---

[274] An organism that combines characteristics of male and female sexes.

[275] Having both male and female sexual organs.

[276] For an excellent summary of the biblical perspective on homosexuality see J. G. Taylor, "The Bible and Homosexuality," *Themelios* 21/1 (1995): 4–9.

The account raises many more questions. How does the narrator really feel about the concubine? the Levite? his father-in-law? the old man of Gibeah? The only group about which his impressions are transparent are the men of Gibeah. For these Benjamites there are no boundaries to "doing what is right in their own eyes." And their depravity has forced the outsiders to make seemingly impossible choices. Ironically, although their intentions have been to preserve male honor, in the end all the men in this account turn out to be dishonorable characters.

By verse count the narrator devotes almost one-half (50/103) of this final story to Israel's response to the horrendous events of chap. 19. On the first sight this alone should encourage the reader to read on to the end. Surely the nation will deal justly with the people of Gibeah and be rewarded for defending Yahweh's definition of what is right *(hayyāšār)* and good.[277] But the story disappoints. Despite the nation's initial noble intentions, Israel's actions raise more questions than they answer, and Yahweh is strangely silent. The events of 19:29–20:48 bear the marks of a holy war, but like a literary cartoon the campaign is caricatured and almost contorted beyond recognition. Israel has found her enemy, and the real enemy is herself. The account of the holy war divides into three primary parts: (1) the call to arms (19:29–30); (2) the assembly of the forces of Israel (20:1–17); (3) the [three] battles (20:18–48). As we will see, the second and third sections subdivide further.

[29]When he reached home, he took a knife and cut up his concubine, limb by limb, into twelve parts and sent them into all the areas of Israel. [30]Everyone who saw it said, "Such a thing has never been seen or done, not since the day the Israelites came up out of Egypt. Think about it! Consider it! Tell us what to do!"

THE CALL TO ARMS (19:29–30).   On the way home the Levite had a lot of time to reflect on what had happened and what course of action he should take. When he arrived at his house, he performed an act of unspeakable gruesomeness. He took a knife,[278] seized[279] his concubine, cut her into twelve

---

[277] R. R. Wilson ("Israel's Judicial System in the Preexilic Period," *JQR* 74 [1983]: 238–39) interprets this account sociojuristically, finding here an illustration of how disputes involving individuals from different tribes and clans were to be adjudicated. Operating at a tribal (rather than the town) level, the tribal elders assemble, the Levite testifies, and the assembly decides to punish the criminals. When the latter's clansmen refuse to hand them over, the Israelites enforce the court decision with military action. Miffed by the Benjamites' refusal to cooperate but lacking confidence in their decision to solve the problem militarily, the Israelites present the case to God for a divine determination. Shocked by the catastrophic consequences of their decisions and actions, the Israelites resort to further legal decisions to undo the damage that has been done. Wilson finds these events illustrative of the weaknesses in premonarchic social structures: there is no central authority (king) capable of adjudicating disputes and executing decisions.

[278] The word מַאֲכֶלֶת, "eating utensil," occurs elsewhere only in Gen 22:6,10 and Prov 30:14.

[279] Note the use of the same verb (חָזַק) as in v. 25.

pieces,[280] and sent the fragments to each of the tribal territories of Israel. The narrator does not interpret the actions for the reader, but its significance may be recognized at several levels. First, whatever else may be said about this Levite, he is still aware of the nation's geographic and ethnic cohesiveness. The nation occupies its own territory and consists of twelve tribes. Second, even in death there is no respect for this woman. Seized for the second time, she becomes a sacrificial victim to male violence. By sending the fragments of her body throughout the nation, the Levite provides all his countrymen with shockingly concrete evidence of the inhospitality, brutality, and degeneracy of their own society. He and his small company had avoided a Canaanite city in favor of one of their own, only to discover that the worst of Canaanite values ruled in Gibeah.

Third, on the basis of extrabiblical and inner biblical analogues, and on contextual grounds, this action must be interpreted as a call to arms. While the reader may puzzle over where the man got this horrible idea, a remarkable parallel may be found in a Mari document from several centuries earlier. In a letter to his king Zimri-Lim, Baḫhdi-Lim writes:

> To my lord, speak. Baḫhdi-Lim your servant [speaks] as follows: For five full days I have waited for the Hanaeans but the people do not gather. The Hanaeans have arrived from the steppe and established themselves among the settlements. Once, twice, I have sent [word] to the settlements and the appeal has been made. But they have not gathered together, and for the third day they have not gathered. Now, if I had my way, a prisoner in jail should be killed, his body dismembered, and transported to the area between the villages as far as Hudnim and Appan in order that the people would fear and gather quickly, and I could make an attempt in accordance with the command which my lord has given, to carry out the campaign quickly.[281]

The purpose of such actions was clear: to mobilize the troops by creating shock and evoking fear.

This conclusion is confirmed by 1 Sam 11:1–11. The parallels between these two texts, particularly Judg 19:29–30 and 1 Sam 11:7, may be highlighted by juxtaposing literal translations as follows:

Judges 19:29–30:1	1 Samuel 11:7
Then he took a knife	Then he took a team of oxen
and he seized the concubine	
and he cut up her bones	and he cut them up

---

[280] Hb. לְעֲצָמֶיהָ, lit. "according to her bones."

[281] ARM 2.48. For the Akk. text, German translation and commentary see G. Wallis, "Eine Parallele zu Richter 19 29ff. und 1 Sam. 11 51ff. aus dem Briefarchiv von Mari," *ZAW* 64 (1952): 57–61.

into twelve cuts
<u>and he sent</u> them
<u>throughout the territory of Israel</u>.

<u>and he sent</u>
<u>throughout the territory of Israel</u>
by the hand of messengers.
saying,
"Anyone who does not go out
after Saul and after Samuel,
thus it shall be done to his oxen."

And it happened that
all who saw said,
"Nothing has ever happened
and nothing has ever been seen
like this
since the day
the sons of Israel came up
from the land of Egypt
unto this day."

Then the dread of the Lord
fell on the people,

. . . .
And all the sons of Israel went out
and the congregation was assembled
<u>as one man</u> . . . .

<u>and</u> they <u>went out</u>

<u>as one man</u>.

The similarities between these accounts are obvious.[282] In both cases a man cuts up a carcass and sends its pieces throughout the nation; then the people respond emotionally and gather "as one man." On the other hand, the differences are equally significant. The Saul narrative is much more transparent with respect to divine involvement (the Spirit of God rushed mightily upon Saul, and the dread of Yahweh fell on the people), the primary character's emotion (Saul was driven by intense rage[283]), the means by which the pieces

---

[282] Noting the linguistic, thematic, and ideological links between Judges 19 and Genesis 22, J. Unterman ("The Literary Influence of 'The Binding of Isaac (Genesis 22) on The Outrage at Gibeah' (Judges 19)," *HAR* 4 [1980]: 161–66) argues that the author of this text borrowed not only from Genesis 19, but also from Genesis 22, but to present a contrastive case. Whereas God had intervened to stop Abraham from sacrificing his son at a pagan location, he did not intervene to save the innocent at Gibeah. According to Unterman, this lack of divine intervention at Gibeah is used to discredit Saul as an unworthy king in contrast to David, who hails from Bethlehem (like the Levite) and reigns in Jerusalem. The conviction that the present Judges account is based on the story from the life of Saul is a critical element in O'Connell's thesis that the Book of Judges was written as a pro-Davidic tractate (*Rhetoric of the Book of Judges*, 299–304). But it is more likely that the influence was in the reverse direction. The author of the Saul narrative seems to have deliberately cast his account to show that the reign of Saul was an extension of the dysfunctional period of the governors.

[283] 1 Sam 11:6, מְאֹד אַפּוֹ וַיִּחַר, "and his nose burned greatly."

were distributed ("by the hand of messengers"), the purpose of the action (to mobilize the troops), and the emotion (fear) the action evoked in the people. But other differences also are apparent. Our text is more specific in noting that the body was cut into twelve pieces, but it makes no reference to the involvement of Yahweh or his prophet. The people recognize openly that such a horrific act is unprecedented since the descendants of Israel came up out of Egypt. Together with the reference to twelve pieces, this comment acknowledges the common descent of all twelve tribes from the eponymous ancestor, Israel/Jacob, as well as the birth of the nation in the exodus from Egypt.[284] With reference to the latter, however, the eclipse of the nation's theological traditions is reflected in the fact that the exodus is perceived as a purely human event. This declaration derives from the confession of faith, but a spiritually alert people would have said, "Nothing like this has happened or been seen since Yahweh brought the sons of Israel up from the land of Egypt"[285] rather than "... since the sons of Israel came up ..."

Verse 30 ends awkwardly with a public appeal, "Think about her![286] Consider it! Speak up!" The NIV and most other translations punctuate the final exclamation in v. 30 as if it came from the lips of the people,[287] as in 20:7, but in its present form it has the appearance of the narrator's own call to his immediate readers. Despite the classification of Joshua-Kings as [former] prophetic literature, such forthright appeals in Hebrew narrative are admittedly rare. Alternatively one may follow the Septuagint, which offers a much more natural reading by expanding the end of the verse as follows:

> And he charged the men whom he sent, saying, "Thus you shall say to every man of Israel: 'Has anything like this happened since the day the sons of Israel came up from the land of Egypt until this day? Consider it, take counsel, and speak up!'"[288]

If the NIV is to be followed, the verbs at the beginning of the verse should be

---

[284] M. J. Haunan ("The Background and Meaning of Amos 5:17b," *HTR* 79 [1986]: 341–43) interprets the Levite's (and Saul's) actions covenantally. The threat of judgment by a cutting act is related to the cutting of an animal in a treaty ceremony; and the passage of the covenant participants between the pieces, as a ritual self-curse enacting the fate of would-be transgressors.

[285] A perspective acknowledged even by the apostate Jeroboam in 1 Kgs 12:28.

[286] Hb. שִׂימוּ לָכֶם, "Set for yourselves," is an abbreviation for שִׂימוּ לְבַבְכֶם, "Set your hearts," a common idiom for "pay attention." The NIV and most translations obscure the focus on the woman by translating עָלֶיהָ, "about it." The form is better rendered "about her."

[287] Cf. also NASB, NRSV, JPSV, REB, NJB, and many commentators.

[288] For the Hb. underlying the LXX see *BHS*. By this interpretation "until this day" originally occurred twice in the verse, but the scribe's eye skipped from the first to the second occurrence, omitting the intervening material. While preferring the longer reading of the LXX, Soggin (*Judges*, 289) suggests that this expanded version originally stood at the beginning of the verse. But see O'Connell, *Rhetoric of the Book of Judges*, 483–84, who defends the LXX order on syntactical grounds.

understood as frequentative, "Everyone who would see it would say ..." How low the nation has sunk from the domestic tranquility of 1:11–15 to the utter degradation of 10:22–30!

(3) The Israelite Response to the Outrage (20:1–48)

THE ASSEMBLY OF THE FORCES OF ISRAEL (20:1–17). The account slows to a crawl as the narrator recounts the Israelite reaction to the call to arms. Intent on exposing the character of the Levite, the Israelites, and the Benjamites, he describes in detail the preparations for the coming battle. The account breaks down into four episodes, as reflected in the following commentary.

¹Then all the Israelites from Dan to Beersheba and from the land of Gilead came out as one man and assembled before the LORD in Mizpah. ²The leaders of all the people of the tribes of Israel took their places in the assembly of the people of God, four hundred thousand soldiers armed with swords. ³(The Benjamites heard that the Israelites had gone up to Mizpah.)

The Assembly of the Tribes of Israel (20:1–3a). **20:1–3a** The reader may be encouraged by the description of the Israelite response to the Levite's dismemberment of his concubine for several reasons. First, the narrator highlights the scope and unanimity of those who "came out" with a series of impressive expressions. (1) "All the sons of Israel" occurs elsewhere in the book only in 2:4.[289] Since the following episodes present the Benjamites as antagonists, the collective refers to the other eleven tribes.[290] (2) This is the first occurrence of "from Dan to Beersheba," a merismic geographic definition of the nation in the Old Testament. This stereotypical phrase reflects the perspective of the narrator's own time, when Dan was well established as the major northern outpost of Israelite settlement. The biblical historians' perspective on the definition of "Israel" is reflected in the fact that the phrase never appears after the division of the kingdom[291] except in 2 Chr 30:5, which describes Hezekiah's attempt to recapture pan-Israelite jurisdiction in his religious reforms.[292] (3) "And from the land of Gilead" is a significant comment, especially in light of Gilead's sense of isolation in the Jephthah

---

[289] But note "all Israel" in 8:27.

[290] As if to emphasize that the Benjamites were not to be considered less Israelite, the narrator deliberately draws attention to their kinship with the rest of Israel in vv. 13,23.

[291] Cf. 1 Sam 3:20; 2 Sam 3:10; 17:11; 24:2,15; 1 Kgs 5:5; 1 Chr 21:2.

[292] Cf. Amos 8:14, which names Dan and Beersheba as a parallel pair. M. Sæbø ("Grenzbeschreibung und Landideal im Alten Testament mit besonderer Berücksichtigung der *min-ʿad* Formel," *ZDPV* 90 [1974]: 21–22) observes that the expression concerns above all else the people and land of Israel as a whole and a unity.

cycle (10:17–12:7); however, 21:1–9 notes that at least one Gileadite town was excepted. (4) "As one man" occurs three times in vv. 1,8,11. (5) "All the tribes of Israel" (vv. 2,10; 21:5) highlights the collective participation of the tribal groups that have previously displayed such pronounced centrifugal tendencies. This emphasis will continue in the following paragraphs with references to "all the people" (v. 8) and "all the men of Israel" (v. 11).

Obviously not every Israelite was there. The narrator qualifies the assembly by noting that "the leaders[293] of all the people" took their places at the meeting. But this is no casual gathering. It is a military camp, whose size is highlighted by the reference to "four hundred thousand men, soldiers[294] armed with swords" (v. 2). Although the figure accords with other numbers in the book, four hundred thousand seems a large figure, which, if taken literally, could mean the total population of Israel was more than two million. Perhaps *ʾelep* should be interpreted as "contingent,"[295] in which case the number could be reduced to as low as forty thousand. Whatever the significance of the number, it should be interpreted like the totals for the censuses of the Israelites who came out of Egypt in Numbers 1 and 26. Accordingly, if the narrator's emphasis on the unanimity of the response means that all the fighting forces of Israel came assembled at Mizpah, it appears that the population of the nation has fallen by one-third since they left Egypt. Any explanation for this decrease in the population is speculative, but a reduced birth rate in this time of stress may have been another curse imposed upon the nation for their persistent apostasy (cf. Deut 28:18).

Viewed within the context of the book as a whole, it is truly remarkable that this nameless Levite from an obscure place in Ephraim was able to accomplish what none of the divinely called and empowered deliverers had been able to do. Not even Deborah and Barak had been able to galvanize support and mobilize the military resources of the nation to this extent.

In addition to highlighting the unanimity and comprehensiveness of the Israelites' response to the outrage in Israel, the narrator heightens the reader's expectations by drawing attention to the spiritual nature of this gathering. First, he refers to it as an "assembling" of the people (v. 1). The verb is related to the noun *qāhāl*, "assembly," and also occurs in 21:5,8. Although both noun and verb forms of the root often carry military nuances,[296] the phrase *qĕhal yhwh*, "the assembly of the LORD," identifies the nation as a body "called

---

[293] Hb. פִּנּוֹת, lit. "corners," an abbreviated designation for "corner stones" or "corner towers," is used as a metaphorical technical term for chieftains elsewhere only in 1 Sam 14:38; Isa 19:13; Zeph 3:6.

[294] Hb. אִישׁ רַגְלִי, "foot men," denoting foot soldiers elsewhere in 2 Sam 8:4; 1 Chr 18:4; 19:18.

[295] Cf. above on 3:29; 4:10; 5:8; 7:3; 12:6.

[296] Gen 49:6; 2 Sam 20:14; 1 Kgs 12:21.

out" by Yahweh to engage in holy war.[297] Indeed, in the Torah *qāhāl* was one of the favorite designations for the religious community of Israel gathered to worship Yahweh.[298]

Second, the narrator identifies the assembled group as *hāʿēdâ,* "the congregation."[299] Deriving from the same root as *ʿēd,* "witness," and *ʿûd,* "to testify," *ʿēdâ* is a legal term that denotes Israel as a vassal community covenantally committed to Yahweh.[300] The present description is reminiscent of Josh 22:12, which states that (lit.) "the whole congregation of the sons of Israel gathered together at Shiloh to go up against them in battle" because they thought the altar constructed by the Transjordanian Israelites represented a gross violation of the covenant. Whereas Phinehas, the son of Eleazar the priest, is said to have played a leading role in the earlier assembly (22:13–34), no individual convener or leader is named here.[301] The narrator's choice of expression is intentional, highlighting Israel as a spiritual community.

Third, lest any reader miss the point, the narrator adds that they assembled "before the LORD in/at Mizpah." This Mizpah is not to be confused with the Transjordanian site where Jephthah had sealed his pact with the Gileadites in 11:11. The present site is generally identified with modern Tell an-Nasbeh, twelve kilometers north of Jerusalem and four to five and one-half kilometers northwest of Gibeah, on the boundary between Benjamin and Ephraim.[302] The phrase" before the LORD" indicates this place was recognized as a sanctuary where the community could meet with their divine Lord.[303] It is unknown whether the tabernacle was ever located here. According to 21:19–21, at this time the tabernacle was located at Shiloh, though v. 27b suggests the ark of the covenant was at Bethel.

Fourth, in v. 2 the gathering is called "the assembly of the people of God."[304]

---

[297] Cf. expressions like קְהַל יְהוָה, "the assembly of the LORD" (Num 16:3; 20:4; Deut 23:2–4,9; Mic 2:5) and קְהַל הָאֱלֹהִים, "the assembly of God," in Neh 13:1. See further H.-P. Muuller, *THAT* 2.611–12.

[298] See ibid., 615–18.

[299] This is the subject of the verb "assembled" in v. 1, but is not translated by the NIV.

[300] Cf. the cognate עֵדוּת, "covenant [stipulations]," and the cognate Akk. term *adû/adê,* which denotes "contractual obligations, loyalty oath, treaty." On the latter see S. Parpola and K. Watanabe, *Neo-Assyrian Treaties and Loyalty Oaths,* SAA 2 (Helsinki: Helsinki University Press, 1988), xv–xxv.

[301] Cf. Num 1:18, which has Moses and Aaron assembling the entire congregation. In Num 16:19 Korah seems to have presided over the assembly at the tent of meeting.

[302] Cf. Josh 18:13–20. See further P. M. Arnold, "Mizpah," *ABD* 4.879–81; J. R. Zorn, "Naṣbeh, Tell en-," *NEAEHL* 3.1098–1102.

[303] A short time later, after the Ark of the Covenant had been recovered from the Philistines and brought back to Kiriath-jearim by the Philistines, Samuel assembled the Israelites at Mizpah for prayer and spiritual renewal (1 Sam 7:5–6). Mizpah also served as one of Samuel's regular bases for ministering in Israel (1 Sam 7:15–17), and here Saul was presented as king to Israel (1 Sam 10:17).

[304] This expression occurs only here in the OT.

All these features seem promising. Perhaps the Israelites have finally matured, and perhaps they have finally acknowledged Yahweh as their covenant Lord. Unfortunately this is not a gathering for worship; this is an assembly for war against their own kinsmen! Even so it is unclear whether the Israelites knew the precise reason for their gathering. The report of the Levite's summons makes no mention of the cause of his own outrage. It seems the sight of the fragments of his concubine's body alone was enough to galvanize his countrymen. Not until v. 3a do we learn that one tribe failed to come. By means of a circumstantial clause the narrator notes that the Benjamites had not responded. On the contrary, they are presented as outsiders to the summons who hear about the gathering of the rest of the tribes secondhand. Why the Benjamites did not appear before Yahweh at Mizpah is not stated. Have they already decided to stand with their tribesmen from Gibeah against their countrymen [and against Yahweh]?

Then the Israelites said, "Tell us how this awful thing happened."
[4]So the Levite, the husband of the murdered woman, said, "I and my concubine came to Gibeah in Benjamin to spend the night. [5]During the night the men of Gibeah came after me and surrounded the house, intending to kill me. They raped my concubine, and she died. [6]I took my concubine, cut her into pieces and sent one piece to each region of Israel's inheritance, because they committed this lewd and disgraceful act in Israel. [7]Now, all you Israelites, speak up and give your verdict."

The Report of the Levite (20:3b–7). **20:3b–4a** In 19:25–27 the narrator reported what happened in Gibeah, but that account left many questions unanswered. Now, by means of direct speech, the same narrator invites consideration of the same event through the eyes of the Levite himself. From the direct quotation of v. 3b one thing is clear: the assembled Israelites are wondering how "this wickedness [NIV, "awful thing"]" had happened. But once again the question is quite ambiguous. First, to whom is it addressed? To anyone in general who might be able to shed light on the issue? or to the Levite? Second, to what wickedness are they referring? the dismemberment of the Levite's concubine? Or are they aware of what has provoked this drastic action by the Levite?

Whether or not the question was addressed to him, the Levite is the first to speak. But note how carefully the speaker is introduced: he is (lit.) "the man, the Levite, the husband of the murdered woman." The first expression simply reflects the fact that he is a man among men, gathered at Mizpah. The second is ironic. As a Levite, a member of the tribe charged with spiritual oversight in Israel, he should have taken the responsibility to lead, especially at an assembly before Yahweh; but as his speech will demonstrate, spiritual leadership is the farthest thing from his mind. As the husband of the murdered woman he is presented as an aggrieved party. And it is as an aggrieved party that he will speak.

Even so the description of the true victim, the concubine, as "the murdered woman" rather than "the dead woman" is troubling. Although the verb *rāṣâ* can denote an accidental act of homicide,[305] it refers primarily to premeditated murder,[306] and this seems to be the narrator's interpretation of the concubine's death. But the choice of words compounds our unease over the way her final fate was described in 19:27–29. Was not the intention of the men of Gibeah to rape her and abuse her all night, and then to let her go (19:25)? If her death was a secondary effect of their violence, would it be called murder? On the other hand, 19:27 leaves open the question whether she was even dead when the Levite found her. If not, then the person who answers the Israelites' questions is no longer an aggrieved party but the criminal.

20:4b–7 These suspicions regarding the Levite are not allayed by the man's speech in vv. 4b–7. In direct response to the question raised by the Israelites, the Levite describes what had happened on that fateful night. Cast in the form of a first person report, the tragic sequence of happenings is reduced to four episodes:

1. The Levite and his concubine came to Gibeah of Benjamin to spend the night.
2. The men of the city rose against him and surrounded the house, intent on killing him.
3. But they raped and abused his concubine, resulting in her death.
4. Enraged by this lewd and disgraceful act, he took hold of his concubine, cut her in pieces, and sent the bits throughout the land of Israel.

Having completed his report, he calls on the Israelites to speak up and give their recommendation.[307]

On the surface the speech is impressive. The Levite has been graphic in his description, and in his deliberate choice of words he has claimed for himself the high moral ground. First, he sarcastically refers to the criminals as "the lords [*baʿălê*] of Gibeah," which recalls Abimelech's identification of the aristocracy of Shechem in 9:2. Second, he characterizes their actions as "lewd" *(zimmâ)* and "disgraceful" *(nĕbālâ)*. The former is a technical expression for shameful behavior, especially fornication and incest[308] and murder (Hos 6:9). The latter, which the Levite had heard his host use in 19:23–24, denotes stupid and senseless acts and willful sin. Third, he generalizes the

---

[305] As in the descriptions of the cities of refuge in Numbers 35, Deuteronomy 19, and Joshua 20:3–6.

[306] As in the Decalogue, Exod 20:13; Deut 5:17.

[307] His comment, הָבוּ לָכֶם דָּבָר וְעֵצָה הֲלֹם, "now give your word and advice," answers to the exclamatory sentence ending 19:30.

[308] Lev 18:17; 19:29; 20:14; Ezek 16:27,43,58; 22:9,11; 23:21,27,29,35,44; 24:13; Jer 13:27.

problem by identifying the site of the crime as (lit.) "Gibeah which belongs to Benjamin." Fourth, with his reference to the land of Israel as "the region of Israel's inheritance" he sounds as though he is defending the sanctity of the land.

Upon closer examination, however, certain features of the speech are extremely troubling. The Levite expresses no concern whatsoever for his concubine. On the contrary, he diminishes her role at the outset by opening with a first person singular verb (v. 4b). In fact, he transforms an explanation of the events into a self-centered apologia. The Levite makes it sound as though Gibeah was his destination,[309] saying nothing of his domestic troubles or how he had been proved wrong for recommending to his servant and concubine that they spend the night in Gibeah rather than Jebus. He blatantly twists the facts by claiming that he was the primary target of the men of the city. They had risen against him, surrounded the house because of him, and sought to kill him. For some (undeclared) reason, their attention had been deflected to the concubine, whom they raped and violated, though he does explicitly link the woman's death to the actions of the men of the city. His addition of "and she died" at the end of v. 5 does not preclude the possibility that he may himself have had a hand in her death. Finally, although his vocabulary sounds pious, he makes no reference to Yahweh, let alone appeal to him to act in defense of the covenant and/or the sanctity of the land.

Regardless of the Levite's motives and despite his self-interest, the effect of his speech is overwhelming. Because of his nonverbal declaration (the distribution of his concubine's body parts) the Israelites have gathered "as one man" (v. 1). Because of his verbal performance the assembled forces will rise and mobilize against Gibeah "as one man" (vv. 9,11). Remarkably, having completed his speech the Levite exits from the stage and is never heard from again. As in the story of Micah and his mother in 17:1–6, for the narrator this man's significance lies more in the events his actions precipitate than in the events of which he is a part.

But this depiction of the man also demonstrates the narrator's artful command of irony. He has him introduced as a Levite and a victim of a series of unfortunate circumstances, and even though he does not lead the nation in battle, he is caricatured as a deliverer figure,[310] like the ones in chaps. 3–16. But this man is different in several respects. In galvanizing the entire nation to concerted military action, he achieves what none of them had been able to do. But he does so without any reference to divine involvement in his life or in the life of Israel as a whole. In fact, these last three

---

[309] "I came to spend the night in Gibeah."

[310] Boling (*Judges*, 277) observes in this account "a calculated inversion of elements in the story of Lot, of whom the locals complained, "This fellow came to sojourn, and he would play the judge" (Gen 19:9).

chapters may be interpreted as a foil to these earlier chapters that force the reader to go back and reread and reinterpret the earlier oppression and deliverer accounts. Contrary to prevailing scholarly opinion, the deuteronomic formula is not operative here. Despite people's ignoring of Yahweh, their plans succeed. Or so it seems.

⁸All the people rose as one man, saying, "None of us will go home. No, not one of us will return to his house. ⁹But now this is what we'll do to Gibeah: We'll go up against it as the lot directs. ¹⁰We'll take ten men out of every hundred from all the tribes of Israel, and a hundred from a thousand, and a thousand from ten thousand, to get provisions for the army. Then, when the army arrives at Gibeah in Benjamin, it can give them what they deserve for all this vileness done in Israel." ¹¹So all the men of Israel got together and united as one man against the city.

¹²The tribes of Israel sent men throughout the tribe of Benjamin, saying, "What about this awful crime that was committed among you? ¹³Now surrender those wicked men of Gibeah so that we may put them to death and purge the evil from Israel."

The Reaction of the Israelites (20:8–13). Obviously impressed by the Levite's speech, the assembled forces of Israel take immediate action, first against the city of Gibeah, the scene of the crime (vv. 8–11), and then against Benjamin, the tribe to which the city belongs (vv. 12–13). Apart from a brief narrative frame around each part, the report of their response is cast in direct speech that expresses the resolve of the assembled troops.

20:8–9 First, regarding the city of Gibeah, the troops of Israel agree unanimously that none of their number is to return home to his tent or his house (v. 8).[311] Then they resolve to attack Gibeah (vv. 9–10).[312] The first hint of something amiss surfaces in the method used to determine which contingent should lead the charge. Unlike chap. 1, where the tribes had inquired of Yahweh directly to see who was to lead the attack against the Canaanites, here there is no reference to Yahweh, only a statement of how they intend to discern his will—by lot.[313]

---

[311] The parallel pair, "tent" and "house," highlights the unanimity of the action but also reflects the transitional nature of Israelite society at the time. Although some were settling down in permanent houses, others were still living in tents.

[312] The NIV correctly assumes הגבעה, "to Gibeah," is intended by לגבע, "to Gebaᶜ."

[313] Appealing to the analogy of Num 31:3–6, Z. Weisman ("The Nature and Background of *bāḥûr* in the Old Testament," *VT* 41 [1981]: 445–46) argues that the selection applied to the fighting forces rather than the quartermasters, an interpretation he sees supported by the reference to ten thousand choice men (אִישׁ בָּחוּר) in v. 34. Added support might be drawn from the verb "we will take" (לָקַח), which comes naturally after a reference to the lot (גּוֹרָל) in v. 10 (cf. Josh 7:14–18; 1 Sam 10:20–24; 14:41–42). The use of the lot is required in the absence of a leader, who would normally have chosen his troops. Cf. Gideon in 7:1–8. But the reference to the lot in v. 9 should be linked with v. 18, in which case it was used to determine tribal order in the attack.

556

20:10–11 The Israelites seem to have anticipated a difficult and protracted campaign, however, for before they launch the attack, they set apart 10 percent of their troops to maintain the supply lines for the fighting forces.[314] Presumably they would be sent out to forage for food in the Benjamite countryside while the troops were on the campaign.[315] Their military goals are spelled out at the end of v. 10: to defend the covenant standards of justice by dealing with Benjamites of Gibeah in accordance with their disgraceful act in Israel. Support for the resolution is unanimous. Finally the tribes of Israel are allied in a common military exercise. But tragically, instead of taking aim at the Canaanites, in keeping with the divine mandate they have set their sights on one of their own cities.

20:12–13 Before the Israelites launch the attack against Gibeah, they send delegates throughout the entire tribe[316] of Benjamin, demanding an accounting of the crime that has been committed in their midst. They demand further that the Benjamites hand over the criminals[317] of Gibeah so they may execute them and thereby excise this "wickedness" *(rāᶜâ)* from Israel. The Benjamites refuse the demand of their kinsmen, the rest of the tribes of Israel, however, declaring their solidarity with the rapists rather than "the assembly of God" thus setting the stage for a direct military confrontation.

But the Benjamites would not listen to their fellow Israelites. **14**From their towns they came together at Gibeah to fight against the Israelites. **15**At once the Benjamites mobilized twenty-six thousand swordsmen from their towns, in addition to seven hundred chosen men from those living in Gibeah. **16**Among all these soldiers there were seven hundred chosen men who were left-handed, each of whom could sling a stone at a hair and not miss.

17Israel, apart from Benjamin, mustered four hundred thousand swordsmen, all of them fighting men.

The Marshalling of the Troops (20:14–17). **20:14–16** The belligerence of the Benjamites is evident from their hostile response to the Israelite overture. Determined to defend the evildoers, they prepare for battle by

---

[314] The NIV offers a paraphrastic rendering of the MT's awkward triad of infinitives absolute in v. 10b: לְבוֹאָם ... לַעֲשׂוֹת ... לָקַחַת. Perhaps the latter two, "to do for/with reference to their going," should be transposed and repointed, לַבָּאִים לַעֲשׂוֹת, "to those who go to do …," with the LXX.

[315] Although all the numbers in the present account seem inflated, the present proportion of one tenth of the force being assigned supply duty finds a close parallel in a report from Mari in which a force of twelve thousand troops one thousand were appointed to transport food. Cf. *ARM* 6, 27:16, also cited by Boling, *Judges*, 284.

[316] The NIV reads singular with the LXX and the Vg against the MT. If the MT is to stand, שֵׁבֶט must function as a synonym for מִשְׁפָּחָה, "clan."

[317] On בְּנֵי־בְלִיַּעַל see above on 19:22.

summoning the troops from all the towns of Benjamin. The results of the call-up are tabulated in v. 15: twenty-six thousand[318] swordsmen, to go with the seven hundred "chosen" warriors from Gibeah.[319] As if to explain the amazing effectiveness of the Benjamites against the vastly superior forces of Israel in the following battles, the narrator adds a note in v. 16 describing the extraordinary talent of one group of Benjamites. Whereas the twenty-six thousand men appear to have been ordinary soldiers, the Benjamites could send into the battle a special contingent of seven hundred soldiers. These men were unique because they were all left-handed, like their fellow Benjamite, Ehud, in 3:15.[320] Alone a left-handed person was considered handicapped and in a contingent of right-handed troops an actual liability, but if enough left-handed men could be assembled to make up an entire contingent, a disadvantage would be transformed into a distinct advantage, physically and psychologically.[321] Second, these left-handed Benjamites were extraordinary marksmen, whose sling shots never missed even their smallest targets.[322] Remarkably their left-handedness is never mentioned again.

20:17 The narrator reiterates the size of the Israelite forces: four hundred thousand swordsmen, everyone a trained soldier.[323] The insertion of the verb "they were mustered/mobilized" renders this notice more official than v. 2 but also demonstrates that all the men had complied with the order issued in v. 8.

THE [THREE] BATTLES (20:18–48). The amount of space devoted to the battles between the Israelites and the Benjamite forces is remarkable. But so is the rhythmic and repetitive nature of the account. The threefold division of the narrative reflects the three battles in which these antagonists engage. Although the account of the last battle is greatly expanded, the structure of the narrative is clear and deliberate, each using the same cycle, as the following schemata illustrates:

---

[318] On the large number see above on v. 2. The decline of Benjamin's military force since the Exodus (cf. Num 1:37 [35,400]; 26:41 [45,600]) is proportionate to the drop in Israel as a whole.

[319] On the meaning of בָּחוּר אִישׁ, "choice men," see Weisman, "Nature and Background," 441–50. See also v. 34.

[320] The identical expression is used: אִטֵּר יַד־יְמִינוֹ, "constrained in the right hand." The LXX again reads "ambidextrous."

[321] Students who read this text in Hb. will not miss the ironic fact that the Benjamites, whose name means "son of the right hand," should have been the ones to produce so many left-handers. This left-handed dexterity was preserved within the genes of the six hundred that survived the battle (chap. 21) and transmitted to the next generation, as evidenced by Saul's ambidextrous kinsmen in the list of David's band of troops (1 Chr 12:2).

[322] Hb. יַחֲטִא לֹא וְלֹא, "and he did not miss."

[323] Lit. "every one of these a man of war."

The First Battle (20:18–21)

Inquiry ("Who shall go up first?")
⟹   Answer ("Judah")
⟹   Attack
⟹ Defeat

The Second Battle (20:22–25)

Inquiry (Shall we go up again?")
⟹   Answer ("Yes")
⟹   Attack
⟹ Defeat

The Third Battle (20:26–48)

Inquiry ("Shall we go up again or not?")
⟹   Answer (Yes, the victory is yours")
⟹   Attack
⟹   Victory [at last!]

In the course of these three cycles the anxiety of the Israelites (and the reader) grows.

[18]The Israelites went up to Bethel and inquired of God. They said, "Who of us shall go first to fight against the Benjamites?"

The LORD replied, "Judah shall go first."

[19]The next morning the Israelites got up and pitched camp near Gibeah. [20]The men of Israel went out to fight the Benjamites and took up battle positions against them at Gibeah. [21]The Benjamites came out of Gibeah and cut down twenty-two thousand Israelites on the battlefield that day.

The First Battle (20:18–21).   **20:18**   The first cycle of battle narratives opens hopefully, with the Israelites at Bethel inquiring of God which tribe should lead the charge against the Benjamites. The name of the site where the inquiry is made is given as *bêt ʾēl*, which may be interpreted either as "the house of God," that is, the sanctuary, or as a proper name, Bethel. Since El is never used as the name for God in the book, and, more importantly, since the same form clearly refers to the town Bethel, the latter is preferable.[324] Bethel had a long-standing history as a sacred site in Israelite tradition,[325] and its place in Israel's cultic life was secured by Jeroboam at the time of the split of the kingdoms in 932 B.C. (1 Kgs 12:25–33).

---

[324] So also Soggin (*Judges*, 292) and Gray (*Joshua, Judges, and Ruth*, 384), contra Boling (*Judges*, 285), who maintains the sanctuary in question here and in v. 23 was located at Mizpah (cf. v. 3). The Vg locates the sanctuary at Shiloh, in keeping with vv. 27–28. On the location of Bethel see above on 1:22–23.

[325] As witnessed by Jacob's encounter with God in Genesis 28.

On the surface the fact that the Israelites approach God for guidance in the conduct of the war appears hopeful. But the manner in which the narrator casts the inquiry raises several concerns. First, the Israelites do not ask, "Shall we go up against our brother?" but "Who shall go up first?" Their decision seems to have been made without reference to God. Second, in contrast to 1:1, which otherwise employs the same formula for oracular inquiry, here the narrator refers to deity by the generic designation "God," *Elohim*, rather than by the personal covenant name, Yahweh. In noting this, the narrator reveals his own disposition toward these events.

Remarkably, Yahweh answers:[326] "Judah shall go up first." This response is appropriate because the victims were from Bethlehem in Judah. The Judahites had a personal reason for demanding justice in the land. Furthermore, the tribe of Judah had played this role earlier and had demonstrated its effectiveness in battle (1:1–10). Indeed one may recognize in the narrator's crafting of this account a deliberate echo of 1:1–2, suggesting that in his mind Israel was now engaged in a similar kind of holy war. Tragically, however, now the enemy is a tribe of fellow Israelites, who by their conduct have demonstrated themselves functionally and spiritually Canaanites.

20:19–21   The course of the battle is recounted in vv. 19–21. Despite the eagerness of the Israelites for the attack (they rose early), the results proved disastrous. The vastly outnumbered Benjamites struck down twenty-two thousand Israelite soldiers—almost one for every Benjamite that went out into the field. Curiously the narrator says nothing about Benjamite casualties or the method by which the Benjamites achieved the remarkable rout.

[22]But the men of Israel encouraged one another and again took up their positions where they had stationed themselves the first day. [23]The Israelites went up and wept before the LORD until evening, and they inquired of the LORD. They said, "Shall we go up again to battle against the Benjamites, our brothers?"

The LORD answered, "Go up against them."

[24]Then the Israelites drew near to Benjamin the second day. [25]This time, when the Benjamites came out from Gibeah to oppose them, they cut down another eighteen thousand Israelites, all of them armed with swords.

The Second Battle (20:22–25).   **20:22–25**   The results of the first engagement with the Benjamites did not seem to demoralize the Israelites. Taking courage,[327] they prepared for a second battle on the same spot as the earlier fiasco. But this time they did not rush into battle. Before they attacked, they went up to the sanctuary (presumably at Bethel) to weep[328]

---

[326] Note the narrator's use of the divine name in v. 18b.

[327] Hb. וַיִּתְחַזֵּק הָעָם אִישׁ יִשְׂרָאֵל, "And the people, the men of Israel, strengthened themselves."

[328] A cultic lamentation is involved.

before Yahweh until evening and to seek a new word from God.[329] Since the events of the previous day had cast their agenda as a whole into question, this time they come to Yahweh with the fundamental question: Should they attack Benjamin, their own kinsman? The answer they receive is an unequivocal yes. Armed with this reassurance of the divine will, the next day the Israelites launched a new attack on the Benjamites. But the results were not much better than on the first encounter. The victims this time numbered eighteen thousand Israelite swordsmen. Again not a word is said about Benjamite casualties.

The Third Battle (20:26–48). Every element found in the previous cycles is expanded in the third and decisive account.

26Then the Israelites, all the people, went up to Bethel, and there they sat weeping before the LORD. They fasted that day until evening and presented burnt offerings and fellowship offerings to the LORD.

The Preparation (20:26). **20:26** The narrator had described the Israelites' grief over their first rout at the hands of the Benjamites in simple terms (lit.): "then all the sons of Israel, even all the people, went up and came to Bethel and wept and sat there before the LORD and fasted on that day until the evening." He captures the deepening crisis in the Israelite camp in the wake of the second defeat by intensifying each aspect of the earlier statement. Now the subject is not simply "the sons of Israel" but "all the sons of Israel, even all the people." Now the verb of translocation is not simply "they went up" but "they went up and came." Now their destination is not simply "before the LORD" but "to Bethel," where "they sat before the LORD." Now they express their grief not simply by "weeping until evening" but by "weeping and fasting until the evening." They also "offered whole burnt and peace offerings to the LORD." The reference to offerings is especially telling, suggesting the Israelites may have finally come to realize that their covenant relationship with Yahweh is in doubt.[330]

27And the Israelites inquired of the LORD. (In those days the ark of the covenant of God was there, 28with Phinehas son of Eleazar, the son of Aaron, ministering before it.) They asked, "Shall we go up again to battle with Benjamin our brother, or not?"

The LORD responded, "Go, for tomorrow I will give them into your hands."

The Inquiry (20:27–28). **20:27** On the surface the nature of the inquiry itself seems to differ little from v. 23. But the redundant construction (lit.), "Shall I do yet again to go up?" and the addition of (lit.) "or shall I desist?" at

---

[329] Note the reversion to the divine name. They dare not treat the battle so casually.
[330] Cf. Exod 24:5.

the end reflect Israel's growing doubts. Even more significant are the additions of detail around the inquiry, particularly the parenthetical note in vv. 27b–28a, which yields important information for our understanding of Israelite religion in the premonarchic period.

First, the Ark of the Covenant of God was at Bethel at the time. Under normal circumstances the ark was supposed to be in the inner sanctum, the holy of holies of the tabernacle, where it functioned as the throne for the invisible God. The phrase "ark of the covenant,"[331] however, places the emphasis on this cultic object as the receptacle of the tablets on which the ten principles of covenant relationship were inscribed.[332] It seems the Israelites had brought the ark to Bethel from Shiloh, presumably to function as a palladium,[333] a symbol of God's presence and "good luck charm" in the battle against the Benjamites. They might have claimed precedents for this manipulation of the ark in the Israelites' crossing of the Jordan (Joshua 3) and the circling of Jericho (Joshua 6),[334] except that in those instances they had clear and explicit instructions from Yahweh, the nation's Commander in Chief. A more likely analogue is found in 1 Samuel 4, where the ark is brought up to secure victory for the Israelites after a disastrous defeat at the hands of the Philistines.[335] By this interpretation "in those days" probably refers to the days of the first two battles described in vv. 18–25. If this interpretation is correct, then the strategy had obviously failed.

20:28   Second, at that time Phinehas, the son of Eleazar and grandson of Aaron, was presiding (ʿâmad, lit. "standing") before Yahweh. The name Phinehas is Egyptian in origin, being derived from pʾ-nḥśy, "the dark-skinned, the Negro." The present genealogy agrees with other accounts,[336] which present Phinehas as an energetic and sometimes violent defender of Yahwism.[337] Unless this genealogy is telescoped,[338] this note suggests that the events described in this text transpired relatively early in the postcon-

---

[331] As in v. 18, the narrator's critical disposition toward this "magical" use of the ark may be reflected in his substitution of the generic designation of deity, הָאֱלֹהִים, "God," in the formula "the ark of the covenant of God." The present phrase occurs elsewhere only three times: 1 Sam 4:4; 2 Sam 15:24; 1 Chr 6:6.

[332] Cf. Deut 10:1–5. The phrase "ark of the covenant of the LORD" is generally considered "deuteronomic." See Gray, *Joshua, Judges, and Ruth*, 386; C. L. Seow, "Ark of the Covenant," *ABD* 1.387. But it occurs in at least two nondeuteronomic texts: Num 10:33–36; 14:42–44.

[333] The word derives from the image of the goddess Pallas, located in the citadel of Troy, on which the security of the city was thought to depend.

[334] And other battles in the desert. Cf. Num 14:44.

[335] On the use of the ark as a palladium and ANE analogues see Milgrom, *Numbers*, 373–75.

[336] Exod 6:25; Num 25:7–11; 1 Chr 6:4,50 [Hb. 5:30; 6:35]; Ezra 7:5. This Phinehas is not to be confused with the ungodly son of Eli and brother of Hophni in 1 Samuel 1–2.

[337] In addition to the references in the previous note see also Numbers 31 and Josh 22:11–20.

[338] Boling (*Judges*, 286) follows E. Meyers (*IB* 2.819) in identifying him as Phinehas II, the predecessor of Eli.

quest period, probably within a century of the death of Joshua. Here Phinehas apparently was presiding over the cultic ritual by which an oracle was procured from Yahweh, presumably by means of the Urim and Thummim. According to v. 28b, the effort was successful; for in response to the question whether or not the Israelites should attack Benjamin again, an affirmative word comes back from the Lord, complete with the committal formula promising deliverance of the Benjamites into the hands of the Israelites on the morrow.

[29]Then Israel set an ambush around Gibeah. [30]They went up against the Benjamites on the third day and took up positions against Gibeah as they had done before. [31]The Benjamites came out to meet them and were drawn away from the city. They began to inflict casualties on the Israelites as before, so that about thirty men fell in the open field and on the roads—the one leading to Bethel and the other to Gibeah.

[32]While the Benjamites were saying, "We are defeating them as before," the Israelites were saying, "Let's retreat and draw them away from the city to the roads."

[33]All the men of Israel moved from their places and took up positions at Baal Tamar, and the Israelite ambush charged out of its place on the west of Gibeah. [34]Then ten thousand of Israel's finest men made a frontal attack on Gibeah. The fighting was so heavy that the Benjamites did not realize how near disaster was. [35]The LORD defeated Benjamin before Israel, and on that day the Israelites struck down 25,100 Benjamites, all armed with swords. [36]Then the Benjamites saw that they were beaten.

Now the men of Israel had given way before Benjamin, because they relied on the ambush they had set near Gibeah. [37]The men who had been in ambush made a sudden dash into Gibeah, spread out and put the whole city to the sword. [38]The men of Israel had arranged with the ambush that they should send up a great cloud of smoke from the city, [39]and then the men of Israel would turn in the battle. The Benjamites had begun to inflict casualties on the men of Israel (about thirty), and they said, "We are defeating them as in the first battle." [40]But when the column of smoke began to rise from the city, the Benjamites turned and saw the smoke of the whole city going up into the sky. [41]Then the men of Israel turned on them, and the men of Benjamin were terrified, because they realized that disaster had come upon them. [42]So they fled before the Israelites in the direction of the desert, but they could not escape the battle. And the men of Israel who came out of the towns cut them down there. [43]They surrounded the Benjamites, chased them and easily overran them in the vicinity of Gibeah on the east. [44]Eighteen thousand Benjamites fell, all of them valiant fighters. [45]As they turned and fled toward the desert to the rock of Rimmon, the Israelites cut down five thousand men along the roads. They kept pressing after the Benjamites as far as Gidom and struck down two thousand more.

[46]On that day twenty-five thousand Benjamite swordsmen fell, all of them valiant fighters. [47]But six hundred men turned and fled into the desert to the rock of

Rimmon, where they stayed four months. [48]The men of Israel went back to Benjamin and put all the towns to the sword, including the animals and everything else they found. All the towns they came across they set on fire.

The Result (20:29–48). Certain aspects of the Israelites' final battle with the Benjamites are not entirely clear, particularly the relationship between the specific campaigns against Gibeah and the broader campaign against the tribe of Benjamin. Until recently scholars have commonly held that the account is composite and that the editor has included two narrations of the same event.[339] Recent studies have recognized the text's intentional rhetorical features, however, including the skillful use of resumptive repetition. E. J. Revell, for example, has demonstrated that the narrator has carefully traced the activities of three separate groups: the main Israelite army, the Israelite ambush, and the Benjamite forces.[340] P. E. Satterthwaite has carried Revell's work farther by showing how the three-staged battle between Benjamites and Israelites reaches a climax in this the third phase. Not only is the account of the third battle three times as long as the accounts of the first two combined, but the author also builds his case with the skillful employment of "quasi-cinematic shifts" between Israelite and Benjamite points of view. He focuses particularly on the emotions of the Benjamites at the moment they realize they are about to be annihilated. This moment of realization is the high point of the chapter.[341]

This phase of the account subdivides into three segments roughly similar in length: vv. 29–34 [ninety-three words in Hb.]; 35–41 ([110 words]; 42–48 [105 words].[342] The narrator's own insights into the Benjamite disposition toward the course of the battle, strategically placed in vv. 34 and 41, function as transitional markers as well as plot signals tracing Benjamin's growing awareness of their own doom (lit.): "But they did not know that the disaster was about to strike them" (v. 34); "For he [Benjamin] saw that the disaster had struck him" (v. 41). One might have expected a similar comment at the end of v. 48, except that there is no one left to respond. The minuscule remnant of Benjamin that had escaped the slaughter fled far away to the desert.

---

[339] Gray (*Joshua, Judges, and Ruth*, 379–81) argues for a Mizpah (vv. 29,33a,34b,36b–48) and a Bethel (vv. 30–32,35,33b–34a,35) account. Soggin (*Judges*, 294) rejects this breakdown as simplistic, preferring a division into sources as follows: A = vv. 29,36b–37a,38–42a,45,46; B = vv. 30–36a,37b,42b,47.

[340] "The Battle with Benjamin (Judges xx 29–48) and Hebrew Narrative Techniques," *VT* 35 (1985): 417–33. On resumptive repetition as a rhetorical technique see S. Talmon, "The Presentation of Synchroneity and Simultaneity in Biblical Narrative," in *Studies in Hebrew Narrative Art Through the Ages*, ed. J. Heinemann and S. Werses, *ScrHier* 27 (Jerusalem: Magnes, 1978): 9–26.

[341] P. E. Satterthwaite, "Narrative Artistry in the Composition of Judges xx 29ff.," *VT* 42 (1992): 80–89.

[342] The NIV's paragraphing obscures this plot-structure.

All that is left for the narrator to do is to summarize the outcome of the battle. The reader should not be surprised if this account of the most tragic civil war in Israel's history does not present all the details of the battle in strict chronological sequence. The author's interest is rhetorical. By skillful juxtaposing of words and phrases, careful repetition, and effective shifts in points of view he exposes the folly of the Benjamites in taking their stand on the side of evil. In the process he also explores how justice may be administered in a nation that has all but abandoned its covenantal commitments.

20:29–34 Verses 29–34 describe the first phase of the Benjamites' dawning awareness of their doom. Verses 18–28 have described the battles between the Israelites and Benjamites entirely from the perspective of the Israelites. Two overwhelming routs and the loss of forty thousand soldiers left the nation demoralized and wondering where God was in their defense of justice. The narrator's silence on the reaction of the Benjamites, who have trounced the remaining eleven-tribe alliance despite being vastly out-manned, has left the reader wondering about their emotional state. One may imagine a growing sense of confidence, if not invincibility, in their camp. But little did they know what lay ahead.

By English standards of logic, vv. 29,30 should be reversed, except that the narrator is setting the stage for the reader. Central to the Israelites' new strategy is the placement of an ambush[343] around the town of Gibeah. But vv. 30–32a deliberately describe the ensuing events in such a way that the reader, like the Benjamites, is lulled into anticipating a result similar to the previous encounters. First, the Israelite mobilization follows the same pattern as in the previous engagements.[344] Second, the Benjamite military reaction and the initial stages of the battle follow the course of previous encounters.[345] The Benjamites responded to the Israelites' action by going out to meet them and experiencing immediate success wherever they went.[346] The ratio of casualties in the preliminary skirmishes suggested another rout-in-the-making for the Benjamites. Third, the Benjamites' emotional response expresses confidence in an outcome similar to the earlier battles.[347] Clearly they believe things are going exactly as they had before.

Superficially, even as the battle seems to be going well for the Benjamites, to the reader and the Israelites it looks like the results of this

---

[343] The word אֹרְבִים has been encountered earlier in 16:9,12.

[344] The idiomatic phrase כְּפַעַם בְּפַעַם, "as on previous occasions," which also echoes 16:20, is the key.

[345] Note the repetition of כְּפַעַם בְּפַעַם

[346] This seems to be the sense of "on the highways, one going up to Bethel and one to Gibeah, and in the open field."

[347] Note the addition of כְּבָרִאשֹׁנָה, "as at first." Does the use of the passive הֵם נִגָּפִים, "they are struck down," in v. 32 suggest divine causation?

engagement will be as disastrous for the latter as the previous ones had been. The narrator, however, has provided a hint of his own point of view in the key phrase, "they were drawn/lured away from the city," in v. 31.[348] The repetition of the verb *nātaq*, "to lure away," on their own lips in v. 32b suggests that the Israelites looked upon their loss of thirty men as a minor setback. In fact, drawing the Benjamites out of Gibeah on the highways has been a deliberate part of their strategy. Once the Benjamites had been lured away far enough from the safety of their own walls, the Israelites arose from their posts and quickly moved into formation at Baal Tamar,[349] and the men in the ambush at Maareh-geba[350] came out of their hiding places. The critical moment in the ensuing battle occurred when a contingent of ten thousand hand-picked troops encountered a company of soldiers from Gibeah.[351] But the Benjamites were unaware of the trap they had been lured into and were oblivious to the catastrophe that was about to break in on them.

20:35–41 The second phase of the account opens with a summary of the actions described in detail in vv. 36–41. But the narrator introduces this section with his own theological interpretation of the outcome of the battle: as in the days of the conquest under Joshua, the credit for this victory must go to Yahweh who struck[352] the Benjamite forces ahead of the Israelites. This divine intervention accounts for the rout of the Benjamites.

Resuming the Israelites' point of view in v. 35b, the author notes that by the end of the day the tables had turned completely, a fact given concrete expression by the corpses of 25,100 skilled Benjamite swordsmen that littered the battlefield. Only then did the Benjamites realize they had been defeated (v. 36a).[353]

In v. 36b the narrator resumes his detailed account of the battle from the Israelites' perspective. Relying on the strength of their forces set in ambush, the main Israelite force had intentionally given ground to the Benjamites to draw them out of Gibeah. Once they were out, the troops who lay in wait in the ambush rushed into the city, slaughtered the entire population in a ruth-

---

[348] The *hophal* form of פָּתַק occurs only here. Most other contexts prefer the *niphal* as the passive form.

[349] The site was obviously near Gibeah, but its precise location is unknown.

[350] The meaning of מִמַּעֲרֵה־גָבַע is uncertain. The versions (LXX, Syr, Vg) read מִמַּעֲרָב־גָּבַע, "west of Gibeah." The names Geba, Gibeah, and Gibeon are easily confused.

[351] Contra Weisman ("Nature and Background," 445–446), like the Benjamites in vv. 15–16, to whom the same epithet (בָּחוּר אִישׁ, "choice men") was applied, these men were presumably picked for their skill rather than by the lot referred to in v. 9b.

[352] The same verb (נָגַף) is used of the plagues with which Yahweh struck Egypt (Exod 7:27; 12:23,27; Josh 24:5).

[353] Observe the shift back to the Benjamite point of view. The verb נָגַף, "to strike down," is the same as in v. 35, where Yahweh was the subject.

less manner, and torched the place. Earlier the Israelite forces had agreed with the men in the main[354] ambush that the sight of smoke rising from the city would be the signal for all the Israelite troops that the ambush had succeeded.

In v. 39 the narrator shifts back to the Benjamite point of view. So long as they were pursuing the Israelites, they could not see what was happening behind them. Not recognizing the significance of the Israelites' about-face, they welcomed another opportunity to engage them in combat. In fact, the initial results were encouraging: thirty more Israelite casualties; no Benjamites slain. The latter's heightened certainty is expressed verbally in words that echo but also intensify the declaration in v. 31.

The narrator intentionally places this most emphatic expression of confidence immediately prior to the point at which they realize their doom. Bolstered by their initial success, the Benjamites do not realize that the Israelites' actions have been a ruse. Nor do they realize what is happening behind them—until they turn around and observe the city of Gibeah going up in flames. Logically this detail belongs before v. 38, but the narrator has intentionally withheld it until the moment the Benjamites could see it in order for the reader to observe this reversal of fortune through their eyes.[355]

The narrator's skillful manipulation of perspective continues in v. 41. For the Israelites the sight of smoke rising from the city served as a signal to wheel around and go on the offensive. But for the Benjamites it was a dreadfully portentous sign. Terrified by the image of the column of smoke, they finally realize they are doomed.

20:42–43 The narrative gains momentum and the battle rushes to its denouement. Realizing that all hope is lost, the Benjamite forces abandon the combat and flee eastward toward the desert. But the battle would not let them go![356] Meanwhile the ambush forces who had sacked Gibeah abandoned the city[357] and joined the rout of the fleeing Benjamites. The Israelites spread a huge "net" around them to prevent their escape,[358] pursued[359] them relent-

---

[354] Repointing the MT's inscrutable הֶרֶב as הָרָב, "the great, numerous." The NIV has the adjective modifying "cloud." The LXX reads חֶרֶב, "sword," which is impossible in this context.

[355] So also Satterthwaite, "Narrative Artistry," 86, who notes further that Deut 13:16[Hb. 17] prescribes this kind of incineration as a whole burnt offering for any city that turns to idolatry.

[356] The striking construction of וְהַמִּלְחָמָה הִדְבִּיקָתְהוּ, "and the battle clung to them [lit. it]," is obscured by the NIV's "but they could not escape the battle."

[357] The MT's מֵהֶעָרִים, "from the cities," is awkward. The final *mem* is probably a dittograph of the first letter of the next word, and the *'ayin* and *yodh* seem to have been transposed.

[358] The verb כָּתְרוּ, "to surround," occurs elsewhere in *piel* only in Ps 22:13; the *hiphil* occurs in Hab 1:4 and Ps 142:8. Many (e.g., Soggin, *Judges*, 295) read כָּרְתוּ, "they cut them down," with the LXX.

[359] The *hiphil* of רָדַף, "to pursue," occurs only here, as an internal *hiphil*, i.e., "they had him pursued." Cf. *IBHS* §27.2f.

lessly,[360] and caught up with them[361] opposite Gibeah to the east.

20:44–47 Verses 44–47 provide a statistical summary of the Benjamite casualties in this battle. First, eighteen thousand men fell on the battlefields around Gibeah. The narrator highlights the loss to Israel by characterizing these all as "noble/valiant men." Second, five thousand fugitives were "picked off" (NIV, "cut down")[362] as they fled down the highways for the Rock of Rimmon ["pomegranate"] in the desert. More precisely, they probably were heading for the el-Jaia cave in the Wadi es-Swenit two kilometers east of Gibeah (modern Jabaᶜ). This thirty-meter-high cave, pitted on the inside with hundreds of smaller caves and holes, not only resembled a split pomegranate but also offered an ideal refuge for beleaguered warriors.[363] Third, two thousand escaped this first slaughter, but the Israelites "hung in there,"[364] pursuing them as far as Gidom,[365] where they struck them down. Verse 46 totals the losses in terms of quantity (twenty-five thousand swordsmen) and quality (all valiant/noble men). Fourth, six hundred men had turned and headed for the Rock of Rimmon, where they were holed up for four months—a pathetic remnant of the proud Benjamite army.

20:48 Meanwhile, the Israelite forces turned their attention to the mopping-up operations, which involved the *herem*-style slaughter of the entire population of Benjamin—human and animal alike—and the torching of all the cities they could find. The tribe of Benjamin was very nearly literally wiped off the map.

Theological and Practical Implications

First, positively this chapter portrays the nation of Israel finally wholeheartedly involved in the holy war against evil. All the key elements of Israel's holy war traditions are found in this chapter: (1) The people assemble as one man before Yahweh. (2) The priest leads the people in seeking the will of Yahweh. (3) Yahweh gives directions about the order of march into battle. (4) Yahweh goes before Israel as the divine Warrior striking the enemy. (5)

---

[360] Hb. מְנוּחָה, "resting place," is difficult. The LXX ἀπὸ Νουα, "from Nohah," understood this as a place name. In 1 Chr 8:2 Nohah is named as the fourth son of Benjamin. The most likely explanation of the MT would treat the prefixed *mem* as a partitive *min*, i.e., "without rest." Cf. *HALOT*, 680.

[361] On Hb. הִדְרִיכֻהוּ, "to catch up, overtake" (NIV "overtake") see *HALOT*, 231. Like the previous הִרְדִּיפֻ֫ו this is an internal *hiphil*. The pairing of asyndetic *hiphils* suggests vigorous and violent pursuit.

[362] Hb. עֹלֵל, "to glean." Cf. עֹלֵלוֹת, "gleanings" [of grape harvest] in 8:2. Here the term is obviously used metaphorically.

[363] See further P. M. Arnold, "Rimmon," *ABD* 5.773–74.

[364] Hb. וַיַּדְבִּיקֻו, "and they stuck closely" (NIV, "kept pressing"), another internal *hiphil*.

[365] The site is unknown.

The people apply the law of holy war.

Some of the links between this chapter and chap. 1 have been noted in the commentary, but this account also echoes several significant features of the description of Joshua's defeat of Ai in Joshua 7–8. In both accounts the final victory comes only after serious initial failure. In both, the first battles are described in the briefest of terms, the elaboration of detail being reserved for the last engagement. Both portray the protagonists following similar strategies: (1) setting up ambush forces; (2) feigning defeat and luring the enemy out; (3) attacking and burning the city; (4) the enemy noticing the fire and fleeing in panic; (5) the slaughter of the enemy forces.

However, there are negative elements in the present event as well. Although the Israelites are finally galvanized into concerted action against Canaanites, the enemy is in fact one of their own. The extent to which people will stand up to defend evil and evildoers is a measure of how deeply rooted is the Canaanizing rot in a culture.

Second, this account presents an interesting portrait of Yahweh. The chapter opens with him as the passive witness to the assembly of his people at Mizpah (vv. 1–2), then as the respondent to oracular inquiry concerning battle strategy (vv. 18,23,28), and finally as an active divine Warrior on the side of Israel. In the latter he clearly acts in judgment, for he punishes the Benjamites for defending the perpetrators of gross violence in Israel. Indeed, this account provides the clearest example of deuteronomistic theology in the book. Here disobedience finally brings divine curse. For once Yahweh has not operated in mercy. Justice is brutally exercised, but the criminals and their defenders are not the only ones who experience the loss. All Israel suffers for the sin of one city, for with the annihilation of Benjamin they lose a brother and one-tenth of their own male population (over forty thousand soldiers from their own ranks).

Third, from a literary perspective, although the final outcome represents the outworking of well-established ethical and spiritual principles, this is one of the most effective examples of ironic narrative in the Old Testament. A nation increasingly Canaanized appears before Yahweh as the covenant community of God (vv. 1–3). Where divinely called and empowered judges had failed to mobilize the nation into concerted action, a nameless Levite of questionable character and with questionable methods is able to rally all the troops "as one man." The tribe that embodies right-handedness (Benjamin, "son of the right hand") not only demonstrates its left-handedness metaphorically by being completely out of step with orthodox theological and ethical standards, but also, ironically, is able to field an entire contingent of first class left-handed warriors. A little army of twenty-six thousand, seven hundred of whom are "handicapped with respect to the right hand," is able to put to rout an army more than fifteen times its size, not once but twice. In the process they slaughter forty thousand Israelite soldiers, without a single stated casualty of their own. Perhaps most ironic of all, this chapter portrays the nation of Israel engaged in a holy war against their own kinsmen[366] with all the passion they should have displayed in their war against the Canaanites. Israel has discovered who her greatest foe is: she is her own worst enemy.

(4) The National Crisis Created by the Outrage (21:1–24)

The last chapter of the Book of Judges is the strangest of all. Chapter 20 closes with the tribe of Benjamin wiped out—except for a frightened group of six hundred fugitives huddled in Pomegranate Rock. The account of the Israelite response to what had transpired is somewhere between comical and grotesque, as the victors scramble to find a solution to the problem they have created by amputating one member of the twelve-tribe confederacy.

¹**The men of Israel had taken an oath at Mizpah: "Not one of us will give his daughter in marriage to a Benjamite."**
²**The people went to Bethel, where they sat before God until evening, raising their voices and weeping bitterly.** ³**"O LORD, the God of Israel," they cried, "why has this happened to Israel? Why should one tribe be missing from Israel today?"**
⁴**Early the next day the people built an altar and presented burnt offerings and fellowship offerings.**

THE ISRAELITES' RECOGNITION OF THE CRISIS (21:1–4). **21:1** The circumstantial clause opening chap. 21 serves as an episode marker. In fact, v. 1 offers a flashback to an unexpected element in the earlier meeting at Mizpah. Now we find that when the "people of God" who had assembled at Mizpah had learned of the crime that precipitated the Levite's call to arms, they had not only resolved to join forces in punishing the men of Gibeah; they had all also pledged on oath that none of them would ever give his daughter to a Benjamite man in marriage. Originally this pact may have been intended to secure league security and loyalty, but after chap. 20 it looks like another aspect of the holy war. Ironically, whereas earlier in the Book the Israelites had displayed few scruples in intermarriage with Canaanites, evidently they had pledged not to intermarry with their own countrymen. The men of Israel do not realize the significance of their action, but in the mind of the narrator this grotesque application of Yahweh's prohibition on intermarriage with Canaanites (Deut 7:1–5) to their own kinfolks serves as a final acknowledgment of the Canaanization of Israel.

But now, after the battle is over and the victors have had some time to reflect, they reconsider the wisdom of the decision taken in the heat of the cri-

---

[366] Note the emphasis on Benjamin as the brother (אָח) of the other tribes in vv. 13,23,28.

sis and under passion for revenge. Now the ties of brotherhood resurface. The six hundred men in Pomegranate Rock are Benjamites to be sure, but they are also Israelites, and they represent all that is left of one of their tribes. But the damage has been done. The women of Benjamin have all been slaughtered, and these six hundred men are doomed to a life of celibacy, unless of course they marry outside Israel. In either case there is no future for Benjamin. Jacob's fears concerning his youngest son expressed centuries ago have come true: in bizarre fashion Joseph's brothers have taken Benjamin (Gen 42:36).

21:2 The Israelites' reaction to the new crisis is described in vv. 2–3. First, they reassembled at Bethel, sat down before God, and wept until evening.[367] Their weeping with loud voices[368] is the wail of a funeral dirge, not only over the death of an individual but the death of an entire tribe. The reader wishes the weeping were over the sins of Israel. But if in 20:26 their weeping had more to do with wounded pride at having been humiliated by vastly outnumbered Benjamites on the battlefield, here their grief is rooted in a sentimental loss (vv. 6,15). There still appears to be no concern for their spiritual well-being.

21:3 Second, they express bitterness. In v. 3 the narrator adds poignancy to the Israelites' reaction to the crisis by using direct speech, in this case a question addressed to God. To them the significance of what has transpired is clear: in a roll call of the tribes of Israel assembled before Yahweh today (at Mizpah), one tribe is missing.[369] The statement sounds pious, but if the Israelites are really this concerned about concerted military action, why had they been unable or unwilling to join forces earlier in the battles against foreigners? Doubts about their motives are also raised by the prior question: "O LORD, the God of Israel, why has this happened in Israel?" This too sounds pious, especially the manner in which they address God: "Yahweh, the God of Israel." The Israelites may feign spirituality by addressing Yahweh by his covenant name, but the narrator's preference for the generic designation God, *ʾĕlōhîm,* in v. 2 shows that he recognizes their insincerity.

The peoples' question may be interpreted several different ways. Interpreted most positively, it represents a request for information, specifically Yahweh's perspective on the causes of the present crisis. But they should have been able to discern this themselves. Examined simply on the level of

---

[367] On sitting as a posture of grief and lamentation cp. Ps 132:1. See also Judg 20:26.

[368] The construction of וַיִּשְׂאוּ קוֹלָם וַיִּבְכּוּ echoes 2:4, but the addition of בְּכִי גָדוֹל, "a great weeping," expresses even more intense lamentation.

[369] The *niphal* form of the verb פָּקַד, with the sense "to be missing," occurs elsewhere in Num 31:49; 1 Sam 20:18, 2 Sam 2:30; 1 Kgs 30:39; Jer 2:4. As the first of these references indicates, the verb has to do fundamentally with the mustering of men for military service, taking a census of men eligible for war or counting those who have been summoned. In contexts like this the preposition מִן on מִיִּשְׂרָאֵל is partitive, hence "to be counted out of Israel."

human experience, the chain of events leading up to this catastrophe began with a concubine abandoning her husband (19:1–2). More to the point of the book, however, the question the narrator asks of the reader, and which the people should have been asking themselves, is, "How did we get to this point?" It is doubtful the Israelites would have accepted Yahweh's answer to the question even if he had responded. Why is one tribe missing in Israel? Because Israel, as Yahweh defines it, has ceased to exist. The problem is not restricted to Gibeah (which is as Canaanite as Jebus and Sodom) or the Benjamites. It is characteristic of the nation as a whole, and unless the Israelites wake up, what has happened to their youngest brother could happen to all. But reading between the lines, the question is not only about the causes of the crisis. Like the previous inquiries before Yahweh in 20:18,23,28, this request surely reflects a desire by the men of Israel to know where they should go from here. What is Yahweh's solution to the dilemma in which they find themselves?

On the other hand, this question sounds more like a cry of protest than an honest query. Indeed the tone is accusatory. The Israelites are blaming God, as if Yahweh has failed to fulfill his role as divine patron protecting his people. Their query seems to represent an attempt to evade the requirements of covenant justice and to find a scapegoat.[370] Whatever the Israelites' motive, the silence of God is deafening! In contrast to chap. 20, where the issue was still retribution for gross violation of covenantal standards, this time Yahweh will not be drawn in. He will not accept responsibility for what has happened in Israel.[371]

21:4 Verse 4 seems to express the peoples' desperation over God's silence. Rising early the next morning, they try to arrest God's attention by ritual observance. They construct an altar,[372] and then they offer their whole burnt and peace offerings (as in 20:26) as if nothing has changed since Exodus 24[373] and as if God is obligated to those who perform perfunctory religious and cultic service. But God does not answer, and the people are thrown back on their resources. The results would be comical if they were not so tragic.

THE ISRAELITES' RESPONSES TO THE CRISIS (21:5–24). The following narrative raises many questions, particularly about the Lord's intentions toward the tribe of Benjamin. Is it his will that Benjamin be preserved? The issue is highlighted by the narrator's twofold reference to the Israelites' sor-

[370] O'Connell, *Rhetoric of the Book of Judges*, 255.

[371] Webb (*Book of Judges*, 195) comments aptly, "In the previous episode he chastised them by speaking; in this one he chastised them by remaining silent. He will not be used by them."

[372] Why do they not present their offerings on the one they had used earlier (20:26)?

[373] Cp. Gideon's altars in 6:24 (erected to celebrate the peace of God) and 6:25–27 (erected and offered at the command of God).

row over the loss of Benjamin (vv. 6,15), which divides the account into two parts consisting of vv. 5–14 and 15–24 respectively.[374]

5Then the Israelites asked, "Who from all the tribes of Israel has failed to assemble before the LORD?" For they had taken a solemn oath that anyone who failed to assemble before the LORD at Mizpah should certainly be put to death. **6Now the Israelites grieved for their brothers, the Benjamites. "Today one tribe is cut off from Israel," they said. 7"How can we provide wives for those who are left, since we have taken an oath by the LORD not to give them any of our daughters in marriage?" 8Then they asked, "Which one of the tribes of Israel failed to assemble before the LORD at Mizpah?" They discovered that no one from Jabesh Gilead had come to the camp for the assembly. 9For when they counted the people, they found that none of the people of Jabesh Gilead were there.**

10So the assembly sent twelve thousand fighting men with instructions to go to Jabesh Gilead and put to the sword those living there, including the women and children. 11"This is what you are to do," they said. "Kill every male and every woman who is not a virgin." 12They found among the people living in Jabesh Gilead four hundred young women who had never slept with a man, and they took them to the camp at Shiloh in Canaan.

13Then the whole assembly sent an offer of peace to the Benjamites at the rock of Rimmon. 14So the Benjamites returned at that time and were given the women of Jabesh Gilead who had been spared. But there were not enough for all of them.

The Israelites' Initial Solution to the Crisis (21:5–14). With the disjointed style of the beginning of this paragraph the narrator has captured the Israelites' frustration at the silence of God in the face of their inquiry. The insertion of v. 6 in the middle of the speech (vv. 5,7) seems disruptive but should be interpreted as an intentional rhetorical ploy by the narrator to remind the reader of the central issues in the plot. What happens around this verse represents the people's own attempt to solve the crisis, made all the more necessary by Yahweh's silence on its causes and its solution.

21:5–9 In v. 6 the Israelites' sorrow over the loss of their brother Benjamin is expressed with a direct quotation (lit.): "Today one tribe has been hacked off from Israel." Although the name of Gideon, "Hacker," derives from the same root, this is the only occurrence of the verb *gādaʿ* in the book. This is a violent expression employed elsewhere of cutting off limbs of trees (Isa 10:33), arms of humans (1 Sam 2:31), horns of animals (Lam 2:3) and altars (Amos 3:14), and pegs (Isa 22:25).

The use of the passive verb in v. 6 leaves open the question of who the Israelites thought was accountable for the amputation of Benjamin from the

---

[374] V. 25 functions as the conclusion to the broader narrative (19:1–21:24) and the book as a whole.

nation. But the question is closed by the narrator in v. 15. This verse is constructed as a circumstantial clause that functions as an episode marker. In this statement the narrator places responsibility for the loss of Benjamin squarely on the shoulders of Yahweh: The Israelites felt sorry for Benjamin because Yahweh had created a breach in Israel. The noun *pereṣ* in v. 15 is used elsewhere of a "breach/gap" in a wall (1 Kgs 11:27; Isa 58:12), which may result from gradual deterioration or violent action by an enemy army, as well as a break in a dike that allows the water to burst out (2 Sam 5:20). With the verb *ʿāśâ*, "to make, cause," here the image is created of a willful divinely caused rupture.[375] But the text is not clear whether the ascription of responsibility to Yahweh represents the people's complaint or the narrator's own theological (hence normative) interpretation of the preceding events. By the former understanding this verse reinforces the peoples' comment in v. 6 and closes the question of the passive verb. By the latter interpretation this statement compares with the one in 14:4. The ambiguity seems intentional.

Feeling sorry for their youngest brother but rejected by God, the Israelites take matters into their own hands and begin to explore their previous decisions and actions for any loopholes. Their reflection yields several possibilities. First, they recognize that rather than perceiving the six hundred Benjamite soldiers hiding in Pomegranate Rock as a hopeless remnant of the once-proud though degenerate tribe, they may indeed hold the key to resurrecting the tribe and reattaching the amputated member to the larger body. If they would provide these Benjamites with wives, the tribe could be revived.

But the issue is complicated by the Israelites' own previous decisions. When they had assembled at Mizpah to determine the fate of Benjamin, they had agreed that "the great oath" should be imposed upon anyone who had failed to appear before Yahweh at this assembly. Although the sentence of death[376] is explicitly pronounced on all who stayed away, the precise nature of "the great oath" is unclear.[377] If the definite article is taken seriously, it could refer to some recognized body of adjuration that involved the death penalty. The most likely candidates would be the Twelve Adjurations codified in Deut 27:15–26, each of which imposes a curse on the offender, and Lev 20:9–21, which calls for the sentence of death for sexual crimes. On the other hand, the expression may be interpreted less technically. Its

[375] With support from 2 Sam 6:8, Soggin (*Judges,* 299) interprets the word as "catastrophe."

[376] The construction of יוּמָת מוֹת, "He shall surely be put to death," is patterned after formal sentences of death in the casuistic laws. Examples are found in Lev 20:9–27, which includes among other laws proscriptions on all sorts of sexual crimes and their capital consequences. In contrast to the ambiguous formula "He shall be cut off," this formula means execution by human hands. On these and related formulae see K.-J. Illman, *Old Testament Formulas about Death,* Meddelanden Fran Stiftelsens for abo Akademi Forskningsinstitut 48 (Abo, 1979).

[377] The NIV's "solemn oath" translates Hb. הַשְּׁבוּעָה הַגְּדוֹלָה, lit. "the big oath."

use here could simply mean that at the assembly of Mizpah the Israelites had extended the curse of *ḥerem* beyond the Benjamites (as applied in 20:48) to all who failed to take their stand against them. Failure to appear at the assembly in Mizpah would be considered a sign of the latter.

So now the question for the Israelites became, Did any tribe or clan[378] fail to attend the gathering at Mizpah? When they review the roll of those who had appeared "before the LORD" and placed themselves under obligation to the great oath, by a perverse stroke of luck they are relieved to discover one such clan. For whatever reason, the people of Jabesh-Gilead were not represented at the assembly. Consequently they are not bound by the oath to give their daughters to the Benjamites.

This is the first mention of Jabesh-Gilead in the Old Testament. Although the name, which means "well-drained soil of Gilead," is preserved in modern Wadi el-Yabis, one of the main east-west tributaries of the Jordan cutting through the hills of Gilead, the precise location of the town along this wadi is uncertain. The most likely candidate is Tell Maqlub seven miles east of the Jordan and thirteen miles southeast of Beth-Shan. According to 1 Sam 11:1–11, some time later Saul is said to have rescued the town from the oppression of the Ammonites, for which they remained grateful until Saul's death.[379] When Saul died, David recognized their kindness to him and tried to persuade them to switch allegiance to him (2 Sam 2:4–7). The narrator does not disclose the reason the men of Jabesh-Gilead did not appear in Mizpah (whether ignorance, neglect, or defiance), but the account elicits sympathy for this city. Suddenly, from out of nowhere, their own fellow Israelites will storm the town, slaughtering men, women, and children. Unlike the Benjamites in 21:12–13, they appear not to have been afforded an opportunity to give an account for their absence.

21:10–11 But with the decision to attack Jabesh-Gilead one dilemma coalesces with a second. How can the Israelites keep "the great oath" by applying the law of *ḥerem* (the ban; e.g., Num 21:2–3) to those who refused to take action against Benjamin and still claim their women as brides for the Benjamite soldiers? The answer, as outlined in vv. 10–11, would involve the launching of a second holy war, this time against an unsuspecting town far removed from the heart of the problem in the hills of Gilead. An army of valiant warriors twelve thousand (or twelve contingents) strong is dispatched by the congregation with orders to annihilate the entire population, men, women, and children, with one notable exception: all the virgin women of marriageable age were to be spared.

How the men of Israel arrived at this solution we may only surmise. By sheer

---

[378] V. 5 had asked if anyone from any of the tribes of Israel had not been present at the assembly in Mizpah.

[379] Being a descendant of one of the six hundred Benjamites, Saul's interest in Jabesh-Gilead was based upon his sense of kinship with the people of this region.

casuistry they may have reasoned that their oath at Mizpah (vv. 1,7), literally interpreted, proscribed only giving their own daughters as wives to Benjamites. It said nothing about giving someone else's daughters. Nor could it be said that the fathers of Jabesh-Gilead had given their daughters to the Benjamites if they are slain. Consequently, if the Israelites give the virgin daughters of Jabesh-Gilead to the Benjamite warriors, they have not violated the oath of Mizpah. But this still leaves the second oath, "the great oath," to apply the law of *herem* to the town. But again by casuistry, although the sparing of the virgin women of Jabesh-Gilead falls short of the full application of the law of *herem* to the entire population, the Israelites might have pointed to a Mosaic precedent for their decision as recorded in Num 31:13–20. After the Midianite women had seduced the Israelites into sin at Baal-Peor (Num 25:1–18), at the command of Yahweh Moses declared holy war against the Midianites (31:1–12). When his troops returned from battle with a crowd of captive women and children,[380] however, Moses commanded them to kill all the male children and all the women "who had never known a man by lying with a male."[381] In the present case the Israelite decision appears arbitrary and opportunistic. The men offer no legal or theological rationale for the exclusion from the law of *herem*. Nevertheless, from a human perspective this is a clever strategy, exploiting one oath to circumvent another by the selective application of the law of *herem*. This operation has the appearance of legality, the strict letter of the law, but it violates its spirit and is certainly morally questionable.

21:12–14 The results of the Israelites' decision are described in vv. 12–14. Because the significance of the attack on Jabesh-Gilead for the present context lies exclusively in resolving the current crisis, the narrator is able to telescope the account. Omitting any reference to the actual attack on the eastern town, he announces simply the result. In their campaign the troops had discovered four hundred women who met the criteria stated in v. 11. Indeed, as if to highlight the scrupulosity with which the soldiers had searched Jabesh-Gilead, the narrator refines the definition of those that were spared (lit.): "a young woman, a virgin who has not known a man according to the bed of a male."[382]

---

[380] The term ףַט, "children," provides a lexical link between these texts (cf. Judg 21:10). The word usually means "children," but it may include girls past puberty, as in Num 14:31, where it refers to anyone under twenty years of age.

[381] The clause (lit.), "and every woman knowing the bed of a male," in Judg 21:11 echoes Num 31:17, "and every woman knowing a man according to the bed of a male." Cf. also v. 18, "and every child among the women who has not known a bed of a male." Further echoes are found in 21:12.

[382] The text does not describe how virgins were distinguished from nonvirgins. A rabbinic midrash (*Tg. Jon., Yev.* 60b) offers a lie detector test: "Every female child you shall stand before the holy crown (the gold frontlet of the High Priest) and cross-examine her. And whoever has slept with a man, her face will pale; and whoever has not slept with a man, her face will blush like a fire, and you shall spare." As rendered by Milgrom, *Numbers*, 259.

The troops brought the virgins across the Jordan to the camp at Shiloh (lit.), "which is in the land of Canaan."[383] The reference to Shiloh is unexpected. Why not to Bethel or Mizpah? But the decision seems wise for several reasons. Psychologically the preference for Shiloh expresses sensitivity to the Benjamite warriors. Because both Mizpah and Bethel had served as military camps during this war, the Benjamite warriors would have been reluctant to come to either camp to get their wives. Shiloh was nearby, but it was neutral militarily. Religiously, since Shiloh was the location of the tabernacle and principal cult center, the Israelites may have felt that they could sanctify their decisions by bringing the women here and presenting them to the Benjamites before the priest.

Scholars have long puzzled over the explanatory clause, "Which is in the land of Canaan." Unlike other names, like Mizpah, which identified sites on both sides of the Jordan, no Transjordanian Shiloh is known. In the past this clause has been interpreted as a redactional gloss, perhaps to set the stage for the next phase of the Deuteronomic history as presented in 1 Samuel 1–4.[384] This not only links the two books too tightly literarily, however, but also overlooks the rhetorical significance of the reference. Since the occupants of the land the Israelites entered under Joshua were Canaanites,[385] biblical writers naturally referred to the Promised Land as "the land of Canaan," especially in narratives dealing with the preconquest and conquest periods.[386] But this is the only place in the entire Old Testament where the designation "land of Canaan" applies to the postconquest period. Minimally the expression suggests that the material in these last chapters derives from the nation's earliest history within the land. But the strange insertion is better interpreted as an intentional rhetorical device. The narrator has already deliberately portrayed the inhabitants of Gibeah as neo-Sodomites/Canaanites by casting the Levite's overnight sojourn in the town and the rape of his concubine (19:16–26) as an echo of Genesis 19. By defending the men of Gibeah the Benjamites have placed themselves in the same category. Now the narrator makes the shocking suggestion that Shiloh is fundamentally a Canaanite site. Since this is the most sacred Israelite shrine, he invites the reader to generalize the characterization to the entire land and to evaluate all the activities that transpire at Shiloh in this chapter as essentially Canaanite in character and intent. Accordingly, far from sanctifying the transfer of the women of Jabesh-Gilead and the invitation to the Benjamites to come to Shiloh to get them, these gestures are

---

[383] On the location and significance of Shiloh see above on 18:31.

[384] Cf. Gray, *Joshua, Judges, and Ruth*, 393.

[385] The author of Judges identifies them as such seventeen times in 1:1–3:6 alone. He also refers to "king/s of Canaan." Cf. 4:2; 5:19.

[386] E.g., Gen 11:31; Exod 6:4; Lev 14:34; Num 13:17; Deut 32:49; Josh 5:12; 24:3; 1 Chr 16:18; Ps 105:11.

spiritually felonious. They reflect the same Canaanized disposition as the other actions and attitudes that caused Yahweh to refuse to answer the Israelites' overtures earlier in this chapter.

To return to the narrative, having transferred the women to Shiloh, the entire congregation[387] of Israel commissioned messengers[388] to announce a formal declaration of peace to the Benjamites in Pomegranate Rock. The NIV rendering is paraphrastic: "[they] sent an offer of peace." The verse in Hebrew, however, contains three verbs and may be rendered (lit.), "They sent ... and they spoke ... and they called out *[qārā^ʾ]* to them 'Peace' *[šālôm]*." This last expression is generally interpreted as indirect speech, as in the NRSV rendering, "proclaimed peace to them." For grammatical,[389] topographical,[390] psychological,[391] and analogical[392] reasons, however, these three words are best interpreted as describing the nature of the communication ("They cried/called out"), the identity of the audience ("to them," that is, the six hundred men), and the content of the declaration, "Peace!" Nevertheless, the sense is essentially the same.

Having nothing to lose and everything to gain, the Benjamites accepted the offer and returned with the Israelite delegation. The Israelites then gave them the women they had spared in the massacre of Jabesh-Gilead. For the first time, at the end of v. 14, the narrator notes what the reader has already concluded from v. 12: the soldiers responsible for bringing the women from the Transjordanian town had not been able to find enough virgins for all the

---

[387] As in v. 10 the reference to Israel as הָעֵדָה, "the congregation," is ironic. The qualifier כָּל, "all," implicates the entire nation in the actions that follow.

[388] By custom and on the analogy of v. 10, the implied object after the verb וַיִּשְׁלְחוּ, "and they sent," is "messengers." The plural (rather than "a messenger") is suggested by the following verb וַיְדַבְּרוּ, "and they spoke." The NIV obscures these details.

[389] Note the sequence of verbs: "Then the whole congregation sent (וַיִּשְׁלְחוּ) [messengers] and they spoke (וַיְדַבְּרוּ) to the sons of Benjamin who were in Pomegranate Rock and they cried out (וַיִּקְרְאוּ) to them, 'Peace.'" Note also the placement of שָׁלוֹם, "peace," after the prepositional phrase לָהֶם, "to them," suggesting a quoted direct object of a speech verb.

[390] Since the Benjamites were hiding in the caves of Pomegranate Rock, the messengers would logically have called out to them from the entrance.

[391] Since the Benjamites were understandably afraid of their Israelite countrymen after the slaughter at Gibeah, the messengers would have approached them carefully, calling out to them as soon as they were within earshot.

[392] The verb קָרָא, "to call," is frequently followed by the content of the proclamation. Within this book: Judg 7:20, "A sword of the LORD and of Gideon!" Elsewhere: Gen 41:43, "Attention!"; Exod 34:6, "The LORD! The LORD! Compassionate and gracious God ..."; Lev. 13:45, "Unclean! Unclean!"; cf. Lam 4:15, "Depart! Unclean!"; Jer 31:6, "Arise! Let us go up to Zion! To the LORD our God!" The present construction is to be distinguished from וְקָרָאתָ אֵלֶיהָ לְשָׁלוֹם, "and you will offer it terms of peace," i.e., terms of surrender, in Deut 20:10, on which see Tigay, *Deuteronomy*, 188. Mic 3:5 offers a similar construction (without the prepositional phrase), with שָׁלוֹם being the content of the proclamation (קָרָא). For an analogous case of קָרָא + לְ meaning "to call out" see Jer 35:17.

Benjamite men.[393] But this observation performs an important transitional function, reminding the reader that it will take the shrewdest of human scheming to solve the increasingly complex Benjamite problem.

15The people grieved for Benjamin, because the LORD had made a gap in the tribes of Israel. **16**And the elders of the assembly said, "With the women of Benjamin destroyed, how shall we provide wives for the men who are left? **17**The Benjamite survivors must have heirs," they said, "so that a tribe of Israel will not be wiped out. **18**We can't give them our daughters as wives, since we Israelites have taken this oath: 'Cursed be anyone who gives a wife to a Benjamite.' **19**But look, there is the annual festival of the LORD in Shiloh, to the north of Bethel, and east of the road that goes from Bethel to Shechem, and to the south of Lebonah."

20So they instructed the Benjamites, saying, "Go and hide in the vineyards **21**and watch. When the girls of Shiloh come out to join in the dancing, then rush from the vineyards and each of you seize a wife from the girls of Shiloh and go to the land of Benjamin. **22**When their fathers or brothers complain to us, we will say to them, 'Do us a kindness by helping them, because we did not get wives for them during the war, and you are innocent, since you did not give your daughters to them.'"

23So that is what the Benjamites did. While the girls were dancing, each man caught one and carried her off to be his wife. Then they returned to their inheritance and rebuilt the towns and settled in them.

24At that time the Israelites left that place and went home to their tribes and clans, each to his own inheritance.

The Israelites' Supplementary Solution to the Crisis (21:15–24).
21:15–16   The narrator's presentation of the problem in vv. 15–18 recalls vv. 6–7. For the second time he observes that the Israelites felt sorry for Benjamin, though, as noted earlier, now Yahweh is held responsible for the crisis facing the tribe and the nation. The issue is raised formally by the elders of the congregation, who, in the absence of a centralized monarchy, had ultimate responsibility for the government of the nation. In its reflection on the current problem, this body presents itself in the best light by assuming responsibility for the Benjamites' welfare ("What shall we do ...?"), but their use of the passive, "because the women of Benjamin are destroyed," obscures the Israelite's role in creating the predicament.

21:17   The Hebrew of v. 17 is difficult. It would be rendered literally, "a possession for the survivors of Benjamin and a tribe must not be blotted

---

[393] The NIV's "there were not enough for all of them" obscures the fact that the sack of Jabesh-Gilead was motivated primarily by the search for wives for the Benjamites. The verb מָצָא, "to find," links this verse with the beginning of v. 12.

out from Israel."[394] But the awkward construction captures the vexed emotional state of the elders. They seem to be concerned about two separate but
related issues. First, since the word *yĕruššâ*, "possession," usually refers to
the land allotted to the nation of Israel or one of its tribes,[395] the elders
seem to be worried about how this small group of survivors will retain possession of the tribe of Benjamin's territorial allotment.[396] Second, rephras-
ing the notion expressed in v. 6, they express concern that the four hundred
Benjamites who have been provided with wives will not be able to maintain
the tribe's independent existence within the twelve-tribe confederacy. To
prevent the tribe from being blotted out they must find wives for all the
Benjamites who survived the battle. The shift in verbs from *gādaʿ*, "to hack
off," in v. 6 to *māḥâ*, "to blot out, wipe out," heightens the crisis since in
the majority of cases in the Old Testament the latter describes the disappearance of the name or the memory of a person or group.[397] Not only is
this the worst fate one could experience, but it would leave the nation with a
permanent blank in its roster of tribes.

21:18 But the elders acknowledge again that their own daughters are off
limits for the remaining Benjamites, since they have invoked a curse upon
themselves if they should give their daughters to the Benjamites (v. 18).[398] If
they cannot offer their own daughters, how will they find two hundred more
young women for the Benjamites?

21:19 Verse 19 describes the elders' reasoning as they attempt to evade
the consequences of their oath and still achieve their goals. They need to find
a way for the two hundred remaining Benjamites to take someone else's
daughters by force. But this raises the question, In what circumstance are two
hundred eligible young virgins most likely to congregate? Portrayed as thinking aloud, the elders remember the annual festival of Yahweh at Shiloh. Their
self-conscious shrewdness is signaled by the opening *hinnēh*, "Look!" It is
unclear which specific festival they had in mind. The term *ḥag* is a generic
term for any periodic pilgrimage festival. According to Deut 16:1–17[399] three
times a year all Israelite males were required to appear before Yahweh in the

---

[394] Many add תִּשָּׁאֵר אֵיךְ to the first phrase on the basis of some LXX MSS, which begin the
sentence with πῶς ἔσται, reading, "How shall an inheritance remain for the Benjamin survivors
…?" Thus Boling, *Judges*, 290. Soggin (*Judges*, 298–99) claims to follow the LXX, but he leaves
יְרֻשַּׁת unaccounted for.

[395] This observation renders unlikely the NIV's and the NRSV's "heirs." The only exception is
2 Chr 20:11, which treats Judah as Yahweh's. Cf Deut 2:5,9,19; 3:20: Josh 1:15; Jer 32:8; Ps 61:6.
See further Block, *Gods of the Nations*, 80–81.

[396] In which case יְרֻשַּׁת פְּלֵיטָה לְבִנְיָמִן could be translated something like "It is a [territorial]
possession of a survivor belonging to Benjamin."

[397] See *HALOT* 2.567 for references.

[398] The form of the curse recalls Deut 27:15–16.

[399] Cf. also Exod 23:14–17; 34:18–23; Num 28:26.

place Yahweh would approve and establish as his authorized cult site.[400] According to Deut 16:16 and Exod 23:17 only adult males were obligated to attend these festivals, though it is evident from Deut 16:11,14 that women and children were welcome.

The elders identify this feast simply as "the annual festival of the LORD." A positive interpretation of this expression would see it as a general designation for one of the three obligatory feasts (the narrator saw no need to be specific). On the other hand, this vague expression creates the impression that they do not really know what they are talking of. In keeping with the narrator's earlier comments that this generation does not know Yahweh or the things Yahweh has done for Israel (2:10), these festivals seem either to have been neglected for a long time or to have been transformed/debased beyond recognition. The former finds support in the elders' struggle to fix the location of Shiloh in v. 19b: to the north of Bethel, east of the highway that goes from Bethel up to Shechem, to the south of Lebonah.[401] The latter finds support in the character of the festival as reflected in v. 21. Although the three festivals prescribed in Exodus 23 and Deuteronomy 16 oblige all males to appear, this celebration is known as a festival of dancing women. The elders again try to sanctify their strategy by calling this event a "festival of the LORD." But the narrator's refusal to specify which festival is in mind suggests that in his view this is another symptom of the Canaanization of Israel.[402]

21:20–22 After reporting the elders' announcement of "the annual festival of the LORD in Shiloh," the reader expects the narrator either to describe the festival or to outline the elders' plan whereby the two hundred maidens are to be procured for the Benjamites. But he telescopes the account in vv. 20–22, breaking off his report of the elders' deliberation and moving directly to their charge to the Benjamite men who still lack wives. The strategy is simple, though the tinkering with legality [not to mention morality] continues.

The elders order the two hundred Benjamites to lie in wait in the vineyards, and when the girls come out to dance,[403] each of them is to abduct one of the women and then return to his own land. Several elements in the directions call for comment.

---

[400] On this interpretation of the idiom שָׁם שְׁמוֹ לְשַׁכֵּן, "to establish/deposit his name there" (which appears in vv. 2,6,11) see most recently S. Richter, "The Deuteronomistic Theology and the Place of the Name," paper presented at the SBL, New Orleans, November 1976. The three obligatory festivals are the Feast of Passover and Unleavened Bread, the Feast of Weeks (also known as the Feast of Harvest), and the Day of the Firstfruits (Exod 23:16; 34:22; Num 28:26).

[401] The location of Lebonah is uncertain. El-Lubban and Lubban Sherqujeh have been proposed. Many interpret the topographical note as a late editorial addition for the benefit of readers who might not have been familiar with the premonarchic geography of the land. Cf. Soggin, *Judges*, 299, and Gray, *Joshua, Judges, and Ruth*, 395.

[402] Cf. the comment above on v. 12.

[403] The same verb is used in 11:34.

First, the narrator captures the anxiety in the disposition of the elders by employing a forceful verb to describe their communication with the Benjamites. Unlike v. 13, which has the Israelites proclaiming a message ["Peace!"], here they are commanded what to do.

Second, no one, neither elders nor narrator, explains the significance of the girls' dancing. Interpreted positively this may be simply a cultic dance in joyful celebration of Yahweh's favor, especially if this feast is one of the three festivals obligatory for all males. On the other hand, the emphasis on the vineyards as the hiding place for the Benjamites may be intended as more than a topographical note. It may also provide a clue to the time of this festival—the grape harvest, which would be characterized by revelry, music, and dance. In the context of what the narrator perceives as an increasingly Canaanized society, this interpretation would certainly fit. It may also explain the unusual identification of the dancers as (lit.) "daughters of Shiloh." If these were ordinary young girls accompanying their parents at the annual festival, the elders would have referred to them as "daughters of Israel." But "daughters of Shiloh" sounds like a special professional class of female dancers associated with the cult of Shiloh. The inspiration for such cultic personnel and such cultic activity may well have come from Canaanite religious customs.[404]

Third, in keeping with the characteristically abusive manner in which men treat women in the Book of Judges, the elders of Israel sanction violence against their own daughters. The verb that describes the authorized action of the Benjamites, *ḥāṭap,* appears in only one other place in the Old Testament. In Ps 10:9 the verb appears twice, comparing the forceful seizure of an innocent person by a wicked and violent man to that of a lion pouncing upon its prey to devour it.[405] Although the elders may claim a stroke of genius in their solution to the problem of the Benjamites, viewed from the perspective of the young virgins what they have sanctioned is an unspeakable crime. In the midst of joyful celebration these young women are suddenly to be abducted and dragged away from home. It does not seem to matter to the elders that these same Benjamites have only recently defended their fellow tribesmen after they had gang-raped a young woman.

The final speech act in this "comedy of legality" is recorded in v. 22. Expecting a protest from the natural protectors of the victims of this despicable scheme, in advance the elders devise a defense for the Benjamites. If

---

[404] The reference to girls dancing at a festival raises another question: How could such festivals go on in the wake of the horrible tragedy that has befallen Israel? While men are weeping at Bethel (v. 2), women are dancing at Shiloh (vv. 19–21)!

[405] The identification of the victim in Ps 10:8–9 as נָקִי, "innocent," חֵלְכָה, "unfortunate," and עָנִי, "needy," offers a telling commentary on the young maidens' condition.

the fathers or brothers of the abducted girls lodge a protest[406] to the elders, they have prepared a standardized response. Unfortunately, the meaning of their prepared statement is obscure.

The problems begin with the first expression, *honnûnû ʾôtām*, which is best translated with the JPSV, "Be gracious to them [the Benjamites] for our sake."[407] Although the elders accept responsibility for the fate of the girls, this answer is clearly crafted to serve their own and the Benjamites' interests. But in the clarifying comment, the elders admit that in the war (i.e., the attack on Jabesh-Gilead) they had been unable to provide wives for the two hundred men. The last clause in v. 22 is intended to reassure the fathers of the victims that they will not be in violation of the oath since they have not given their daughters to the Benjamites. Although it transgresses every standard of morality and decency, this rationalization satisfies the letter of the law. No Israelite will have given his daughter in marriage to the Benjamites. At the same time, the rationalization puts the protesting fathers and brothers in a bad light for putting personal and family interests ahead of the interests of the tribe and the nation.

21:23–24 The description of the implementation of this scheme is presented as an objective third person report. The narrator introduces the report with a comprehensive statement: "So that is what the Benjamites did." Then he matter-of-factly describes their specific actions with four verbs: (1) they "seized" (NIV, "caught")[408] the number of dancers they needed to fill the quota;[409] (2) they "carried" them off; (3) they "returned" to their patrimonial territories; (4) they "rebuilt" their cities; (5) and they "lived" (NIV, "settled") in them. To the reader it sounds so casual and inconsequential, but this report must be interpreted in light of Deut 13:13–19, which describes how cities and regions that have been subjected to the law of holy war are to be dealt with: they are to remain a ruin in perpetuity, and they must never be rebuilt (v. 16) as a warning of the grave consequences of abandoning the standards of covenant commitment and life.[410] Through Moses Yahweh had warned that if the Israelites stoop to behaving like Canaanites, then they can expect

---

[406] Read לְרִיב with *qere* rather *kethib*'s לָרוּב. The verb רִיב is a legal term, meaning fundamentally "to contest, to make a case." Cf. above on the renaming of Gideon (6:31–32) and Jephthah's negotiations with the Ammonites (11:25–28).

[407] Following the LXX, Syr, and Vg, which presuppose חָנֵּנוּ, in which case the final נוּ- on חָנּוּנוּ functions as an adverbial accusative. Cf. *HALOT*, 334. The NIV's reading, which reverses the pronouns, is equivalent to "Be gracious to us for their sakes."

[408] The violence of the action is reflected in the choice of גָּזַל, which in 9:25 has been used of highway robbery. Elsewhere the word is used of tearing off skin (Mic 3:2); seizing wells (Gen 21:25), fields (Mic 2:2), and houses (Job 20:19); and robbing property (Lev 19:13, etc.). The present usage of the forceful taking of women recalls Gen 31:31.

[409] Hb. לְמִסְפָּרָם, "according to their number."

[410] Cf. Deut 13:11; 17:13; 19:20; 21:21.

the same fate (Deut 8:19–20). The narrator never declares so outrightly, but the present account, coming as it does at the end of the book affirms the total Canaanization of the tribe of Benjamin and the Israelites' falsely based sympathy for their brothers. Having taken what they deemed appropriate steps to revive the fallen tribe, the Israelites broke camp and set out for their respective tribes and families and their own patrimonial holdings as if everything was in order (v. 24).

(5) Epilogue (21:25)

25In those days Israel had no king; everyone did as he saw fit.

21:25 Lest the reader fail to grasp the point of the final narrative and the Book of Judges as whole, the narrator concludes with the refrain heard earlier in 17:6. This refrain must be interpreted as a commentary on the events of this chapter. Nothing about the foregoing events is right in Yahweh's eyes. These are apostate Israelites acknowledging no king, neither divine nor human. But then there is no need for a king in the estimation of the narrator. Wickedness is democratized; everyone does what is right in his own eyes, and the results are disastrous.[411]

Theological and Practical Implications

With the rehabilitation of the Benjamites and the concluding statement the narrator has brought his essay on the Canaanization of Israel to a fitting conclusion. But this final episode makes its own contribution to the book's main theme.

First, socially this chapter illustrates the continuation and intensification of cancerous Canaanite expressions of patriarchy. The account invites the reader to view this final chapter through the eyes of the women. The women of Jabesh-Gilead lose their families, are dragged out of their homes, and are forced to live with cursed Benjamites. Would the fate of the rest of their townspeople not have been preferable? Then in the midst of an exuberant celebration the "daughters of Shiloh" are ambushed, violently captured, removed from their families, and also forced to live with the cursed Benjamites. No one considers their feelings about this fate. On the contrary, all voices of protest are stifled. The rape of an individual has multiplied into the rape of four hundred victims of war and two hundred innocent merry maidens. Indeed by now

---

[411] Contra prevailing opinion (e.g., H.-W. Jüngling, "Propaganda für das Königtum. Die Tendenzgeschichte in Richter 19," *Bibel und Kirche* 2 [1983]: 64–65), it is difficult to see how an exilic or postexilic redactor would have looked favorably upon kingship, since in the eyes of the deuteronomists, Israel's and Judah's monarchs were primarily to blame for the nations' ruin at the hands of the Assyrians and the Babylonians respectively.

the Israelite landscape is strewn with the victims of violence: the Levite's concubine (19:29–30), the women of Benjamin (20:48), the virgins of Jabesh-Gilead (21:14), and the dancers of Shiloh (21:23). In the words of one commentator, "Israelite males have dismembered the corporate bodies of Israelite females. Inasmuch as they have done it to one of the least of women, they have done it unto many."[412]

The reader is cautioned, however, against generalizing the problems reflected in these final chapters to all androcentric social structures, as if the system itself is fundamentally flawed. What happens here is not expressive of normal androcentrism any more than the altar in Joash's backyard, Gideon's ephod, Jephthah's vow, and Micah's image reflect normative Yahwism. The entire book portrays a nation rotting at the core. Nothing is normal, least of all the Canaanite version of patriarchy. Normative biblical patricentrism perceives male headship not as a position of power but one of responsibility, in which the leader sacrifices himself for the well-being of the led. In the Book of Judges this pattern is reversed. Repeatedly women and children are sacrificed for males.

Second, historically, because of the actions of the elders of Israel the tribe of Benjamin is rescued, and the full complement of twelve tribes is thereby preserved. Whether or not this was the divine intention is never explicitly asserted, but the manner in which the narrator tells the final stories certainly raises doubts about the wisdom of the remaining tribes. They were more concerned to save each appendage of the organism that is physical Israel than preserving the covenant, the very heart of Israel. Hereafter Benjamin, sandwiched between Judah and Ephraim, will struggle to find a role in national life. But in the providence of God, this tribe would yield some important historical figures, most notably Saul, the experimental king,[413] and a thousand years later his namesake Saul/Paul, the apostle to the Gentiles (Rom 11:1). Like the stories of Tamar and Rahab and even Ruth, this account serves as a witness to God's ability to turn around the wrath of human beings and make it praise him.

Third, theologically, the events of this chapter call for a response from God. But his silence leaves the reader with all kinds of unanswered and unanswerable questions. What did Yahweh think of these actions? Did he really want Benjamin eliminated (cf. 21:15) as if this were an eighth Canaanite tribe (20:35; cf. Deut 7:1–5)? Was Israel's first mistake sparing the six hundred? The narrator devotes this entire chapter to a description of human schemes and machinations, human efforts to preserve a spiritual entity whose

---

[412] Trible, *Texts of Terror*, 83–84.

[413] From the narratives of 1 Samuel 8–16, however, it seems that in giving the Israelites the Benjamite Saul as king in response to the people's ill-motivated and ill-timed demand Yahweh imposed upon the nation the harvest of the people's own sinful deeds.

heart has long since been lost. In the broader context of chaps. 19–21 it is remarkable that Yahweh intervenes on Israel's behalf so long as they are waging holy war, even if that war is against one of their own tribes. As soon as human sentimentality interferes, however, he withdraws. To a people that claims to be his but behaves in every respect like a Canaanite people, he is absolved of all obligation.

Perhaps this is why the nation must strain so hard in the final chapter to preserve the Israelite ideal, employing reasoning and strategies that appear to fulfill the letter of the law but at every turn violate its spirit. The future of Benjamin depends on finding loopholes in the law. The final rationalization (lit.), "Be gracious to them for our sakes" (v. 22) exposes the ultimate irony of the ancient event. But in so doing it also captures the perversion of our modern world in which sympathy for the criminal so often eclipses compassion for the victims and commitment to righteousness. To the modern ear the statement sounds so human, so sensitive, so caring; but these people are blinded to the reality that in lavishing grace on neo-Canaanite Benjamites they have oppressed society's innocent and weak. There is indeed no king in Israel. Every man does what is right in his own eyes. The entire nation becomes an accomplice in the defense of Canaanism. What Benjamin did for Gibeah the nation does for Benjamin.

Through this final episode, as through the Book of Judges as a whole, the reader witnesses the amazing grace of God. Yahweh does indeed permit the Israelites to pursue their foolish rationalizations, but despite their persistent expressions of Canaanite social and religious degeneracy he does not destroy them. Because of his grace the nation of Israel does indeed emerge more or less intact from the dark days of the governors/judges. Looking to the future Yahweh cannot allow his people to succumb totally to the Canaanite world. But the reader must know that his work continues here and generally in human history in spite of, rather than because of, his people. And the nation's propensity to capitulate to Canaanite ways and attitudes will not end here. It persists throughout her history, until in 722 and 586 B.C., after more than half a millennium, Yahweh has finally had enough.

If the reader will read on to the beginning of the next book of the Hebrew canon (1 Samuel), however, he or she will discover that while the darkness continues, the grace of Yahweh will begin to penetrate that darkness. He will remove those who embody Canaanite values (Eli and his sons, Saul) and replace them with agents of light and grace (Samuel, David). This book and the history of the nation that follows serve as eternal testimony to the grim reality that God's people are often their own worst enemy. It is not the enemies outside who threaten the soul but the Canaanite within. At the same time this book and the ones that follow declare in most emphatic terms that God's work will get done! His kingdom is eternal; his covenant with this people is eternal; his promises are eternal.

Human heroes in the Book of Judges are few and far between.[414] The same is true in the history of the church and especially in the contemporary American evangelical church. No book in the Old Testament offers the modern church as telling a mirror as this book. From the jealousies of the Ephraimites to the religious pragmatism of the Danites, from the paganism of Gideon to the self-centeredness of Samson, and from the unmanliness of Barak to the violence against women by the men of Gibeah, all of the marks of Canaanite degeneracy are evident in the church and its leaders today. This book is a wake-up call for a church moribund in its own selfish pursuits. Instead of heeding the call of truly godly leaders and letting Jesus Christ be Lord of the church, everywhere congregations and their leaders do what is right in their own eyes.

In the meantime Yahweh, the Lord of history and the Lord of the church, remains unchanged in character and intent. Because of his bountiful grace he continues to hear the cry of the oppressed and to deliver those who call upon him. In his grace he reaches out to those who claim to be his own, pleading for them to return to him, to abandon their Canaanite ways, and to recommit themselves to joyful obedience to his will. May the Lord of the church continue to lavish his mercy upon an undeserving people.

---

[414] Othniel and Deborah are the only unsullied heroes.

Ruth

1. Title of the Book and Its Place in the Canon

The biblical Book of Ruth derives its name from one of its three main characters, the Moabite daughter-in-law of Naomi and eventual wife of Boaz. The traditional derivation of the name from *rĕ'ût*, "friendship," is tempting but wishful thinking,[1] so the etymology of the name remains a mystery. Ruth is

---

[1] The dropping of the 'ayin is difficult to explain. Cf. J. M. Sasson, *Ruth: A New Translation with a Philological Commentary and a Formalist-Folklorist Interpretation*, 2d ed. (Sheffield: Academic Press, 1989), 20–21; E. F. Campbell, *Ruth: A New Translation with Introduction, Notes, and Commentary*, AB 7 (Garden City: Doubleday, 1975), 56.

named twelve times in the book but elsewhere in the Bible only in Matthew's genealogy of Jesus in Matt 1:5. That the book should be named after Ruth is truly remarkable for several reasons. First, Ruth was not even an Israelite. She was a Moabite, a fact the narrator and Boaz emphasize by their combined fivefold reference to her as "Ruth the Moabitess."[2] This is the only book in the Old Testament canon named after a non-Israelite.[3] Second, Ruth is not the main character of the book. The story opens by describing the crisis in Naomi's family, highlighting her own emptiness, and concludes with the resolution of the crisis and the declaration of her fullness in the birth of Obed. Indeed in the conclusion (4:13–17) the narrator appears intent on drawing the reader's attention away from Ruth. This impression of the secondary role of Ruth is reinforced by the manner in which the characters relate in the book. Scholars have recognized the importance of direct speech in this book. No fewer than fifty-five of the eighty-five verses contain dialogue. To be even more precise, of the 1,294 words in the book,[4] 678 (52.4 percent) occur on the lips of the characters. Of the three main actors in the drama, however, Ruth speaks least often, and her speeches are the shortest.[5] Based on the plot, the book is more appropriately titled "The Book of Naomi"; and on the dialogue, "The Book of Boaz." On the other hand, given the concluding episode and genealogy, as well as the purpose of the book, it might even have been called "The Book of Obed." No doubt the present title reflects the narrator's and reader's fascination with and special admiration for the character of Ruth.

The canonical status of the Book of Ruth seems to have been recognized from the beginning.[6] The four fragments of the book found in the caves of Qumran attest to its importance in this community. The placement of the Book of Ruth after Judges in our English Bibles follows the arrangement of the Septuagint. This position seems to have been recognized by Josephus, whose tally of twenty-two books for the Old Testament suggests that Ruth was attached to Judges, just as Lamentations was combined with Jeremiah.[7] With this arrangement of the canon, after the Book of Judges the Book of Ruth offers the reader welcome relief. Whereas Judges had developed the theme of Israel's increasing

---

[2] 1:22; 2:2,21; 4:5,10; cf. also 2:6.

[3] Cf. the Gospel of Luke, the only NT book attributed to a Gentile.

[4] The figure provided by E. Jenni and C. Westermann, *Theologisches Handwörterbuch zum Alten Testament*, 2 vols. (Munich/Zurich: Chr. Kaiser Verlag/Theologischer Verlag, 1979), II:540.

[5] Ruth speaks a total of 120 words in ten speeches (twelve words per speech); Naomi speaks 225 words in twelve speeches (almost nineteen words per speech); Boaz speaks 281 words in fourteen speeches (twenty words per speech).

[6] The slightest hint of debate may be found in the Babylonian Talmud, where *t. Meg* 7a observes that Ruth, like Esther and the Song of Songs, does indeed "make the hands unclean" (the talmudic expression for the canonical books).

[7] *Against Apion* 1.7–8. For further discussion see R. Beckwith, *The Old Testament Canon of the New Testament Church* (Grand Rapids: Eerdmans, 1985), 253–54.

spiritual infidelity in the premonarchic period, this book highlights the presence and nature of genuine spirituality during this same period. In contrast to Canaanized characters like Gideon, Jephthah, and Samson, all of the personalities in Ruth display authentic faith and true covenant faithfulness. The Book of Ruth demonstrates that the lights of God's grace and human integrity still shone in the small rural community of Bethlehem.

On the other hand, although the Christian canonical tradition associates Ruth with the historiographic writings (former prophets in the Jewish canon), in the vast majority of Hebrew manuscripts and published editions Ruth appears as the first of five *Megilloth*, the five scrolls regularly read at annual Jewish festivals.[8] In the Ben Asher family of manuscripts,[9] this group as a whole appears after Proverbs. This arrangement is propitious, for it places the story of Ruth immediately after the alphabetic celebration of wifely nobility in Prov 31:10–31. Did the Massoretes view Ruth and/or Naomi as exemplars of the type of woman there described? The arrangement in the majority of Hebrew manuscripts, however, contradicts the order of books in several Talmudic lists, most notably *Baba Batra* 14b, which places Ruth ahead of Psalms at the beginning of the Writings.[10]

It is difficult to determine which arrangement is original. Although they derive from the fifth-sixth centuries A.D., it seems most likely that the Talmudic lists, with Ruth placed before the Psalms, reflect the earliest order, and that Josephus's version, with Ruth appended to Judges, represents a later accommodation to the twenty-two letters of the alphabet. The secondary placement of Ruth after Judges is certainly more easily explained than the placement of the book ahead of Psalms. The tradition reflected in the Septuagint takes the process one step further by separating Ruth from Judges. The prevailing Hebrew manuscript arrangement with Ruth as the first of five *Megilloth* derives from a desire to group the small scrolls associated with the major Jewish festivals.[11]

2. Text

Compared with many other Old Testament books, the textual integrity of Ruth is remarkable. The best recent commentators have agreed that, while a

---

[8] The Song of Songs at Passover (Nisan), Ruth at *Shabuʿoth* (Feast of Weeks, fifty days after Passover); Lamentations at the commemoration of the fall of Jerusalem in 596 (9th of Ab); Ecclesiastes at the Feast of Booths/Tabernacles (Tishri); Esther at the Feast of Purim (Adar).

[9] Represented by the modern standard *BHK* and *BHS* editions, which are based on *Codex Leningradensis,* the earliest complete edition of the Hebrew Bible available.

[10] For the text and discussion see Beckwith, *Canon*, 121–22.

[11] For further discussion see Beckwith, *Canon*, 158–59, 252–56; Campbell, *Ruth*, 32–36; F. W. Bush, *Ruth, Esther*, WBC 9 (Dallas: Word, 1996), 5–9.

handful of readings in the MT may be improved on the basis of the ancient versions and *qere* [versus *kethib*] readings in the Hebrew manuscripts, only the last line of 2:7 defies solution.[12] The NIV is based largely on *Codex Leningradensis*, an early eleventh century A.D. manuscript in the Ben Asher tradition. Four fragments of Ruth have been found in the caves of Qumran.[13] In general these readings support the MT. The only significant variant is found in 3:14, where the Qumran scroll reads *mrgltyw*, "place of his feet," rather than the MT's *mrgltw*, "place of his foot."

3. Date and Authorship

Although the Talmud attributed the authorship of both Judges and Ruth to Samuel,[14] like the rest of the books in the Old Testament and most literary texts from the ancient Near East in general,[15] the book offers no hint of interest in the identity of its author. We can only speculate about who might have written the Book of Ruth, and its provenance and date must be deduced from the internal evidence—language and style, historical allusions, and themes. However, the evidence is frustratingly inconsistent and has led to a wide range of dates, from the time of David to the postexilic period.

For most of the past century, since the time of Julius Wellhausen, critical scholars have tended to date Ruth in the postexilic period. This conclusion is based on five principal arguments: (1) the language of the book, particularly its alleged Aramaisms[16] and late Hebrew forms;[17] (2) the legal customs reflected, specifically the explanation of the ceremony of the shoe in 4:7, which presupposes a time when the practice was no longer understood; (3) the interest in genealogies expressed in 4:18–22, which recalls the "priestly" genealogies in the Pentateuch and Chronicles, especially 1 Chr 2:3–15; (4) the extremely favorable portrayal of Ruth the Moabitess, which, along with a

---

[12] Cf. Bush, *Ruth*, 9–10; R. Hubbard, *The Book of Ruth*, NICOT (Grand Rapids: Eerdmans, 1989), 2–5; Sasson, *Ruth*, 8–11.

[13] Two have been published by M. Baillet, J. T. Milik, and R. de Vaux, *Les 'petites grotees' de Qumrân*, DJD 3 (Oxford: Clarendon, 1962), 71–75; and two remain unpublished, though they are discussed by Campbell, *Ruth*, 40–41.

[14] According to *B. Bat* 14b–15a, "Samuel wrote the book which bears his name and the Book of Judges and Ruth."

[15] The extant literary texts from ancient Mesopotamia that identify their historical authors number no more than four or four. On the anonymity of ancient writers see W. Hallo, "New Viewpoints on Cuneiform Literature," *IEJ* 12 (1962): 13–26; W. G. Lambert, "A Catalogue of Texts and Authors," *JCS* 16 (1962): 59–81; id., "Ancestors, Authors, and Canonicity," *JCS* 11 (1957): 1–9.

[16] נָשָׂא נָשִׁים, "to take wives" (1:4); לָהֵן, "therefore" (1:13); עָגַן, *niphal*, "to be chained" (1:13); שָׂבַר, *piel*, "to wait" (1:13); קוּם, *piel*, "to confirm" (4:7).

[17] מַרְגְּלֹת, "place of feet" (3:4,7,8,14); עָשָׂה, "to work" (2:19); נָעַל שָׁלַף, "to remove a sandal" (4:7–8).

book like Jonah, balances the narrow ethno-centrism of Ezra and Nehemiah (Ezra 10; Neh 13:23–27);[18] (5) the allusions to the allegedly postexilic "deuteronomic" work of Judges, especially 1:1;[19] (6) the canonical placement of Ruth, not with the former prophets but among the Writings (Hagiographa), on the assumption that these texts were gathered after the prophetic collection had been closed.[20]

At first sight the cumulative force of this list of arguments seems impressive.[21] Taken individually, however, none is as convincing as it seems, and several are simply too subjective to be helpful. F. W. Bush has attempted to place the discussion of the date and provenance of the Book of Ruth on a more objective footing.[22] Recognizing that languages grow and develop over time, and taking advantage of the work of several recent diachronic analyses of biblical texts,[23] Bush observes that the author employed a series of features that are characteristic of standard biblical Hebrew (SBH), which is preexilic by definition: (1) the preference of *ʾānōkî* over *ʾănî* for the first person singular pronoun; (2) the prevalence of the *waw*-consecutive; (3) the introduction of temporal clauses with *wayěhî/wěhāyâ b/k* instead of *b/k* plus infinitive or substantive; (4) the use of *kî* rather than *ʾăšer* to introduce a noun clause object of a verb; (5) the object-subject rather than subject-object word order in verbless clauses following *kî* or *ʾăšer;* (6) the complete absence of *l* rather than *ʾet* to mark the direct object of a verb; (7) the plene spelling of the name David, *dwyd,* rather than the defectively written *dwd;* (8) the use of the prep-

---

[18] See N. K. Gottwald, *A Light to the Nations: An Introduction to the Old Testament* (New York: Harper & Brothers, 1959), 519–20. However, in keeping with recent shifts in understanding, in a later work (*The Hebrew Bible—A Socioliterary Introduction* [Philadelphia: Fortress, 1985], 552), Gottwald offers a more nuanced appraisal, even suggesting the book "need be no later than the united monarchy."

[19] See R. H. Pfeiffer, *Introduction to the Old Testament* (New York: Harper & Row, 1948), 718. For my own interpretation of the date of the Book of Judges see above.

[20] Cf. P. T. Nash, "Ruth: An Exercise in Israelite Political Correctness or a Call to Proper Conversion?" in *The Pitcher Is Broken: Memorial Essays for Gösta W. Ahlström*, ed. S. W. Holloway and L. K. Handy, JSOTSup 190 (Sheffield: JSOT Press, 1995), 350–51.

[21] Some current scholars still argue for a postexilic date. See Bush, *Ruth*, 16–30; A. Lacocque, "Date et milieu du livre de Ruth," *RHPR* 59 (1975): 583–93; C. Frevel, *Das Buch Ruth*, Neuer Stuttgarter Kommentar: Altes Testament (Stuttgart: Theologisher Verlag, 1992), 34; E. Zenger, *Das Buch Ruth*, Zürcher Bibelkommentar, Altes Testament 8 (Zurich: Theologisher Verlag, 1986), 28. Zenger dates the book to the second century B.C. in the time of the Hasmoneans.

[22] Bush, *Ruth*, 16–30.

[23] R. Polzin, *Late Biblical Hebrew: Toward an Historical Typology of Biblical Hebrew Prose* (Missoula: Scholars Press, 1976); A. Hurvitz, *A Linguistic Study of the Relationship between the Priestly Source and the Book of Ezekiel* (Paris: Gabalda, 1982); id., "On 'Drawing the Sandal' in the Book of Ruth," *Shnaton* 1 (1975): 45–59 [Hebrew]; A. Guenther, "A Diachronic Study of Biblical Hebrew Prose Syntax: An Analysis of the Verbal Clause in Jeremiah 37–45 and Esther 1–10," Dissertation, University of Toronto, 1977; M. Rooker, *Biblical Hebrew in Transition: The Language of the Book of Ezekiel*, JSOTSup 90 (Sheffield: JSOT Press, 1990).

ositions *bên* ... *ûbên* ..., literally "between ... and between ...," instead of the late biblical Hebrew (LBH) *bên* ... *l* ...; (9) the occasional failure of the final *nun* of the preposition *min*, "from," to assimilate before an inarticulate noun; (10) the sevenfold occurrence of second or third person dual morphemes of common gender,[24] a feature that never occurs in LBH.[25]

Based on these ten features, it looks as though Ruth is an SBH composition, and one is tempted to accept Campbell's assertion that "no linguistic datum points unerringly toward a later date."[26] But this does not mean that scholars are agreed on how early prior to the exile the book was written. On the contrary, the dates ascribed to the Book of Ruth vary four hundred years, from the tenth to the sixth centuries.

Some date the writing of Ruth to within a few generations of the events described in the book. M. D. Gow, for example, contends that the book was composed during David's lifetime as an apology for his kingship. We know from the books of Samuel that resistance to David's rule persisted throughout his reign. Such opposition came most naturally from the Saulide party, particularly Benjamites and others from the northern tribes who resented the favoritism with which they perceived David to be treating Judah.[27] One can imagine the opposition demeaning David by pointing to his lowly origins in Bethlehem[28] and the contemptuous Moabite connection in his genealogy. Against this backdrop the author intentionally highlights Bethlehem as an oasis of tranquility and honor in the troubled period of the judges and Ruth, David's Moabite ancestress, as a paragon of virtue. Noting the narrator's rare literary talent, sensitive disposition toward women, access to the family traditions, devout Yahwistic faith, and the literary integrity of the book (it is not simply cheap propaganda), Gow speculates that Nathan may have been the author.[29]

Recent scholarship has been more prepared to date the composition of Ruth in the reign of Solomon.[30] It is possible that during his reign some of his subjects questioned his character and his right to rule, since he achieved the

---

[24] Apparently second or third person masculine pronominal suffixes referring to women occur in 1:8 (עִמָּכֶם, "with you"); 1:9,11 (לָכֶם, "to you"); 1:13 (מִכֶּם, "more than you"); 1:19 and 4:11 (שְׁתֵּיהֶם, "the two of them"). Cf. also the verb עֲשִׂיתֶם, "you have done," in 1:8.

[25] See Bush's detailed discussion of these features in *Ruth*, 22–24. He also lists eight features of LBH in Ruth that lead him to an early postexilic date for the book. See further below.

[26] Campbell, *Ruth*, 26.

[27] Cf. 2 Sam 19:40–20:2.

[28] Cf. Mic 5:2[Hb. 5:1].

[29] M. D. Gow, *The Book of Ruth: Its Structure, Theme and Purpose* (Leicester: Apollos, 1992), 207–10.

[30] Thus Hubbard, *Ruth*, 46. Cf. p. 30, n. 43, for a listing of others who favor this view. Campbell (*Ruth*, 28) imagines the origins of the book to lie in the period of Solomon, though its fixed writing may have occurred in the ninth century.

throne through intrigue and violent elimination of other contenders (1 Kings
1–2). The opposition against his rule certainly increased toward the end of his
reign (1 Kings 12).[31] On the other hand, the long and relatively peaceful reign
of Solomon provided an ideal context for the flourishing of culture. The biblical literary arts may find their fullest bloom in the Book of Ruth. In defense of
this view scholars have opined repeatedly that literarily the Book of Ruth
bears a closer resemblance to the so-called Yahwist narratives of Genesis and
the stories in Samuel than to the accounts in Chronicles and the Book of
Esther (though additional linguistic considerations raised by Bush undermine
such arguments). Recognizing that the book tells a woman's story, A. J. Bledstein argues that the book is the work of a female author. Specifically, she suggests the author might have been Tamar, the daughter of David, and great-
great-granddaughter of Ruth, who had herself experienced the tragedies that
befell even royal women in a patriarchal culture. With her portrayal of Boaz
she offered a radical redefinition of "a mighty man of valor" (ʔîš gibbôr
ḥayil) and presented an ironic if idealistic female view of life within the Covenant.[32]

M. Weinfeld argues that the linguistic evidence of the book points to a
composition in Northern Israel during the time of Elisha.[33] He cites a long
series of clichés and phrases that have affinities with early Israelite literature
but are not found after the period of Elisha. He interprets the alleged Aramaisms and apparently late biblical Hebrew features (see below) as evidences of
a Northern Hebrew dialect. Weinfeld recognizes that the book aims to present
an idyllic account of the origin of the great king David. But he does not

---

[31] For a discussion of the pro-Davidic polemic in defense of David's family's claim to the
throne of Israel see K. Nielsen, *Ruth: A Commentary,* OTL (Louisville: Westminster/John Knox,
1997), 21–29.

[32] A. J. Bledstein, "Female Companionships: If the Book of Ruth Were Written by a Woman
…," in *A Feminist Companion to Ruth,* ed. A. Brenner (Sheffield: Academic Press, 1993), 116–35.
To Bledstein's credit the story of Naomi and Ruth does indeed present women's experiences from
a sympathetic female point of view, but this does not mean the book could not have been written
by a man. On the contrary, the opening paragraph and the concluding episode and genealogy (4:9–
22) obviously represent traditional male perspectives. Cf. R. Bauckham, "The Book of Ruth and
the Possibility of a Feminist Canonical Hermeneutic," *Biblical Interpretation* 5 (1997): 29–45.
While the possibility of a woman author of the book cannot be ruled out *a priori,* given the paucity
of evidence for female literary activity in Israel and in the world around, the theory smacks of wishful and fanciful feminist thinking. The unlikelihood of a female author is recognized by C. Meyers,
who comments ("Returning Home: Ruth 1.8 and the Gendering of the Book of Ruth," in *A Feminist
Companion,* 89): "Even if the existence of female authors for certain biblical verses, chapters or
even books can be accepted, the idea of female authorship seems problematic in the light of the fact
that the literary context of Scripture, in the redactional and recording stages even if not in all its
compositional ones, was that of male scribal activity." Accordingly Meyers recognizes that it is
more appropriate to focus on the gender perspective of the book than the gender of its author.

[33] M. Weinfeld, "Ruth, Book of," *EncJud* 5.518–22.

explain why this would have been an issue for a Northern author a century after the Northern Kingdom had split off from the Davidic house. One may speculate that the book was written to convince Northerners to abandon their own kings, whom the author considers illegitimate, and to reunite with Judah under the house of David. The composition, however, lacks any hint of polemics against the kings of Northern Israel.

The renaissance of the Davidic house under Hezekiah (716–687 B.C.) could also have inspired the Book of Ruth. In the opening thesis statement of the account of Hezekiah's reign, the historian observes that Hezekiah did right in the sight of the LORD according to all that his ancestor David had done (2 Kgs 18:3) and that the LORD was with him (v. 7), which recalls two similar comments concerning David in 1 Sam 16:18 and 18:14. Even the note that Hezekiah defeated the Philistines (v. 8) may be intended to link him with David (cf. 2 Sam 5:17–25).

Earlier we noted the linguistic elements that the book shares with standard biblical Hebrew (SBH), which seemed to suggest that the book derives from preexilic times. The situation is complicated, however, by a series of linguistic features that push it in the direction of late biblical Hebrew (LBH). Bush has recognized as clearly characteristic of LBH the following: (1) the overwhelming preference for attaching the pronominal object directly to the verb (ten times) rather than the direct object marker *'et/'ôt* (zero times); (2) specifically, the direct attachment of the third feminine suffix to a plural verb ending in -*û* (*taklîmûhā* 2:15) in contrast to SBH, which regularly attaches masculine pronominal suffixes with such verb forms to the direct object marker and displays a distinct preference for the same with feminine suffixes; (3) the general preference for the preposition *l* rather than *'el* before the indirect object following the verb *'āmar*, "to say" (also the phrase *qārôb lānû*, "near to us" in 2:20); (4) the use of the idiom *nāśā' 'iššâ* in 1:4 rather than *lāqaḥ 'iššâ* for "to take a wife, marry"; (5) the *piel* form *lĕqayyēm*, "to confirm, establish," in 4:7, probably under Aramaic influence, which contrasts with SBH's preference for the *hiphil* form; (6) the form *wĕnātan* in 4:7, reflecting the decreasing use of *waw*-consecutive tenses in LBH; (7) the use of the idiom *šālap naʿal*, "to draw off a sandal," in 4:7, probably a neologism created by the author under Aramaic influence; (8) the use of the *piel* verb *śibbēr* in 1:13 for SBH *qiwwâ* and *yiḥēl*, "to hope."[34]

Based on these considerations Bush concludes that the author of the Book of Ruth cannot have lived earlier than Ezekiel, whose work reflects the linguistic transition between SBH and LBH. He contends that the work could have been composed at the earliest in the late preexilic or early exilic period. If 4:7 is indeed original to the composition, however, the cluster of late and

---

[34] See Bush's detailed discussion of these features in *Ruth*, 24–30.

Aramaic features suggests an early postexilic date, which must mean shortly after 538 B.C. Recognizing that languages do indeed evolve from generation to generation, he has attempted to put the dating of the Book of Ruth on more objective grounds than the subjective ideological or thematic bases that have been appealed to in earlier studies. Contrary to some, who treat the book as a fictional piece, the author obviously did not originate the story. The faithful in Israel, particularly those associated with the Davidic house and perhaps women in general, will have delighted in this story of a resourceful Naomi and her courageous foreign-born daughter-in-law and passed it on from generation to generation by word of mouth. In fact, although the language of narrative (in contrast to poetry) tends to be updated with the retelling in each generation, some of the archaic features may represent linguistic fossils from earlier times.

Bush interprets the Book of Ruth as an edifying short story, whose primary goal is to reveal its characters. He argues that the author's aim is to present Naomi, Ruth, and Boaz as models of *ḥesed* for his readers to emulate. But the narrator was also driven by several secondary aims. On the one hand he was concerned to affirm God's absolute control over the affairs of this world and his providential involvement in the lives of individuals. On the other, the link with David in the dénouement and conclusion/coda (4:17–22) elevates both the story and David by focusing the reader's attention on development beyond the events of the account and by reflecting David's worth "through the quality of life of his forbears."[35] Although a previous generation of scholars dismissed 4:17–22 (exclusive of 4:17c) as a postexilic "priestly" addition to the story, in an otherwise excellent discussion of the nature and function of the genealogy in the overall plot of the book, Bush highlights its role as the capstone of the book.

One wonders, however, how the concluding genealogy can be viewed as the capstone of the plot on the one hand and play so minor a role in the intention of the book as a whole on the other. Because he relegates the Davidic agenda to a tertiary role, he fails to consider seriously the social and political conditions that called for this kind of composition. It seems, however, that what Bush identifies as a tertiary goal, the elevation of David, is in fact the primary reason for writing the book. As I will note in greater detail later, the author's aim is to explain how, in the providence of God, the divinely chosen King David could emerge from the dark period of the judges. Gow and Nielsen are correct in interpreting the book as an apology for the Davidic monarchy, but they err in their conclusions regarding the context in which this apology was written.

But the question remains: what was that context? On the surface Bush

---

[35] Bush, *Ruth*, 53. For his detailed discussion of these verses see pp. 30–53.

appears to have adduced strong arguments for a late exilic provenance. On the other hand, it must be admitted that the entire Old Testament represents but a linguistic fragment of the full Hebrew language spoken in ancient Israel,[36] and we do well to hold loosely to our reconstructions of the history of language. Weinfeld may be correct in arguing that the Aramaisms and supposedly late features are in fact evidences of a dialect removed by some distance from Jerusalem/Judah, which provided the linguistic grid through which Old Testament texts were filtered before achieving their final form. If the Book of Ruth derives from late exilic or early postexilic times, it is remarkable how hard scholars must strain to find eight late features in a composition of 1,294 words.[37] Furthermore, Bush does not explain satisfactorily why the late exilic or early postexilic period should have called for this edifying story presenting its characters as models of *ḥesed* for his readers to emulate. On the other hand but for the same linguistic reason, Weinfeld's dating of this book to the ninth century may be too early. Although the book shares some linguistic features with compositions that appear to be attested at the latest only in the prophetic circles of Elisha, this may be an argument from silence. The truth is it shares many other features with books much later than the time of Elisha.

In our estimation, any dating of Ruth should take into consideration three critical factors. First, the reference to "the days when judges governed" in the opening verse suggests that the author was familiar with the premonarchic period as a distinct era and that this idyllic account may have been deliberately composed against the darkness of the period as it is portrayed in the Book of Judges. The ignoble qualities of most of the characters in the Book of Judges cast into even sharper relief the nobility and integrity of the characters in this book. To be more specific, if the Book of Judges was composed to alert what remained of the nation of Israel to the people's spiritual declension during the reign of wicked Manasseh, as we have suggested, it is unlikely that the Book of Ruth was written before the latter half of the seventh century B.C.

Second, the book's interest in the Davidic house is best interpreted against the backdrop of the renaissance of the dynasty. If the book was written after Manasseh, only the reign of Josiah (540–609 B.C.) qualifies as a chronological candidate for the origin of Ruth.[38] Indeed the link between the book and Josiah may be observed at several levels. (1) The historian is even more explicit in his comparison of Josiah with David (2 Kgs 22:2) than he had been with respect to Hezekiah. In fact, in his estimation spiritually Josiah exceeded

---

[36] The expression "linguistic fragment" derives from E. Ullendorff, who offers healthy caution on what can be known of ancient Hebrew in "Is Biblical Hebrew a Language?" *Bulletin of the School of Oriental and African Studies* 34 (1971): 241–55.

[37] The figure provided by Jenni and Westermann in *THAT* 2.540; id. *TLOT* 3.1445.

[38] Thus Sasson, *Ruth,* 250–52, who argues, however, that Ruth is a fictional folktale composed for the glorification of David.

his illustrious ancestor (2 Kgs 23:25). (2) With his extension of the religious
reforms to the territory of the former Northern Kingdom of Israel (2 Kgs
23:15–20), Josiah appears to have claimed jurisdiction over the entire Israelite's heartland ruled by David and Solomon prior to the division of the kingdom in 931 B.C. (3) Even the Moabite connection surfaces in the Josiah
narrative. In 2 Kgs 23:13 the historian notes that among Josiah's purging measures was the removal of the high place in Jerusalem that Solomon had built
for Chemosh, "the abomination of Moab." By highlighting the personal and
spiritual integrity of Ruth, the Moabitess, the author of this book may have
tried to diffuse the charges of Josiah's detractors that blood of the despicable
Moabites flowed through the veins of the king. (4) This date respects the cultural and chronological distance between the composition of 4:7 and the
events described in this chapter. Apparently the author's audience was no
longer familiar with the custom of the sandal.

Third, a Northern provenance fits both the political and linguistic realities
of Josiah's reign. Concerning the former, according to 2 Kgs 23:19 Josiah
extended his reforms into the heartland of what once had been the Northern
Kingdom. Concerning the latter, these political developments opened the door
to northern intersections with Judean culture. Although Bush himself opts for
an early postexilic period for the Book of Ruth, he acknowledges the possibility of a date in the late preexilic period.[39] If this possibility is combined with
Weinfeld's dialect argument, the linguistic anomalies are accounted for.

The Book of Ruth may have been written by a resident of the formerly
Northern Kingdom, an Israelite whose family had survived the Assyrian conquest and deportation a century earlier. But this raises the question of why a
resident of the North would have composed a literary piece like this involving
a Judahite family from Bethlehem from half a century earlier. The answer
may be nearer than we think. No doubt there were many in the North who
objected to Josiah's political ambitions. In response to his detractors who may
have pointed to the ethnic blemish in the royal family, our author demonstrates that nobility is more than an issue of blood; it is a matter of character.
There may indeed have been Moabite blood in Josiah's veins, but Ruth represents all that is noble in Israel and outside the nation. No doubt the rabbinic
tradition that Ruth was a daughter of Eglon the king of Moab (Judg 3:12–
17)[40] was based more on wishful thinking than on fact. But in the eyes of
Boaz (3:10–11) and the author of the book, Ruth's nobility was demonstrated
not by her genealogy but by her character. The Moabite blood flowing in
Josiah's veins represented all that was virtuous and authentically pious

---

[39] Bush, *Ruth,* 30.
[40] Cf. *Ruth Rabbah* to Ruth 1:4 in *Ruth Rabbah: An Analytical Translation,* by J. Neusner,
Brown Judaic Studies 183 (Atlanta: Scholars Press, 1989), 60.

(ḥesed) in Israel's own covenantal tradition.

Even more important than silencing Josiah's detractors, by writing the Book of Ruth the author celebrated the return of his own region to the only legitimate dynasty the Israelites had ever known. The narrator was undoubtedly drawing on traditions based in Bethlehem, but the story of the rise of the house of David from the ashes of the premonarchic period must have been told and retold throughout the nation's history. The linguistic features that link the work with early biblical Hebrew may represent echoes of earlier versions of the story, but in retelling the story for his own generation the author sought to inspire his fellow Northerners to cast their lots with the revived Davidic house. Indeed he may have found in the story grounds for hope for his own time. Just as Yahweh had preserved the lineage of David through the dark days of the judges, so he had preserved the residents of the North through the night of Assyrian domination. In Josiah the hope is renewed for the entire nation of Israel. Just as a person like David had emerged from the dark days of the judges, so, in the providence of God, Josiah had been raised up in these dark days to bring light to all Israel. The Book of Ruth is a testimony to the blessing that comes to those who will live in faithful covenant relationship with God *(ḥesed)* and to God's providential hand upon the house of David. In claiming Ruth as an ancestress, the Davidic dynasty has nothing to be ashamed of. On the contrary, she symbolizes the universal scope of the Davidic covenant implied by the enigmatic but profound affirmation in 2 Sam 7:19: "This is the instruction/revelation for humanity" (*zōʾt tôrat hāʾādām,* author translation).

But for the author and his fellow Northerners the significance of the book extends beyond its royal dimensions. As a resident of the Assyrian province the narrator was surrounded by many non-Israelites, the descendants of the alien populations that had been brought into the province of Samaria in the wake of the Assyrian conquest of the land in the eighth century (2 Kgs 17:24–41). For the mixed population one hundred years later the book carries a special poignancy. Not only does Ruth's Moabite status not disqualify her descendants from the throne of Israel, but she also represents another way. In fact, more than any Israelite in the Book of Judges (save perhaps Deborah) and more than many of the Judeans of the author's day, she, a foreigner, embodies true covenant faithfulness. With her immortal declaration in Ruth 1:16–17, this Moabite serves as a model for all ethnic non-Israelites: if they will cast their lot in with the people of Israel and commit themselves to Yahweh their God, they too may find a home in the covenant community. Naomi and Boaz for their parts embody true *ḥesed* in responding to Ruth with compassion and acceptance. But all of this happens on God's terms, not the terms of compromising Israelites, let alone the terms of the foreigners.

4. Genre and Intention

Generically the Book of Ruth divides into two unequal parts: a complex narrative account constructed with a typical plot leading from problem/crisis (1:1–5; cf. v. 21) to resolution (4:13–17)[41] and a short genealogy (4:18–22). We begin by considering the latter first because the issues are simpler.

Structurally the genealogy consists of a formal heading, *wĕ'ēlleh tôlĕdôt pāreṣ*, "Now these are the generations of Perez," followed by nine entries constructed after the pattern "*A* generated *B*,"[42] yielding a total of ten names/ generations. The form of the title is familiar from Genesis, where it occurs nine times,[43] and Num 3:1, where (except perhaps for Gen 2:4) it typically precedes the lists of generations. The linear (as opposed to segmented) form and the pattern of the entries, with ten generations (cf. Gen 5; 11:10–26), climaxing in the seventh generation (Boaz; cf. Enoch in Gen 10:21–24), are also familiar. When this document is compared with the official record preserved in 1 Chr 2:1–15, one observes three striking modifications. First, this genealogy is linear rather than segmented, listing only the names of those in the direct line of descent from Perez to David. By-lines (brothers and sisters) are omitted. Second, this genealogy is not as deep, omitting Judah, the tribal ancestor at the beginning, and the sons of David's sisters at the end. Third, this genealogy is stylistically consistent, each generation being cited with exactly the same formula. Although biblical genealogies represent a form of historiography, the aim of linear lineages is not necessarily to offer a complete account of the line. Their function is rather to legitimate the claims of the last person named to certain rights, privileges, roles, and power that come with membership in this direct line.[44] Accordingly, by attaching this genealogy to the story of Naomi and Ruth the narrator emphasizes that the significance of Obed's birth goes far beyond satisfying Ruth's maternal instincts or filling the emptiness Naomi had experienced at the beginning. The birth of Obed represents a critical link in the sequence of historical events that will climax in the divine election of David as king over Israel. While the experiences of Ruth

---

[41] Cf. the discussion of T. Longman, *Literary Approaches to Biblical Interpretation* (Grand Rapids: Zondervan, 1987), 93.

[42] We have rendered the *hiphil* verb הוֹלִיד as "generated" (lit. "fathered, caused to give birth") to reflect its cognate relationship to תּוֹלְדוֹת, "generations."

[43] 2:4; 6:9; 10:1; 11:10,27; 25:19; 36:1,9; 37:2. Cf. 5:1 and 1 Chr 1:29.

[44] Cf. Matthew's presentation of Jesus' Messianic claims in Matthew 1. For a detailed study of the nature and function of biblical genealogies see R. R. Wilson, *Genealogy and History in the Biblical World*, Yale Near Eastern Researches 7 (New Haven: Yale University Press, 1977); id., "The Old Testament Genealogies in Recent Research," *JBL* 94 (1975): 169–89; M. Johnson, *The Purposes of the Biblical Genealogies with Special Reference to the Setting of the Genealogies of Jesus* (Cambridge: Cambridge University Press, 1969). See also K. A. Mathews, *Genesis 1–11:26*, NAC (Nashville: Broadman and Holman, 1996), 296–99.

and Naomi and Boaz are of great interest to the reader, and in their responses they serve as models of *ḥesed* for all who claim membership in the covenant community, the lives of these women have primary significance for the part they play in the eventual emergence of David.

Identifying the genre of the preceding narrative is a more difficult task. Discussions of the genre of the Book of Ruth generally begin by considering the work of H. Gunkel, who argued that in general biblical narratives, especially the stories in Genesis circulated in poetic form as oral folklore. The Book of Ruth he characterized as an "idyllic" narrative, "a poetic popular sage."[45] In a related vein J. M. Myers has also argued that the original story was transmitted in poetic form, something like an ancient nursery tale.[46] Not only do such theories leave one wondering why it was committed to writing in prose rather than poetic form, but his analysis also relies on a simplistic distinction between poetry and prose that is no longer accepted.[47]

One of the more interesting recent analyses of the genre of Ruth is provided by J. M. Sasson. Applying the conclusions of the folklorist V. Propp regarding the characteristics of personae found in Russian fairy tales,[48] he concluded that Ruth has the form of a folktale. His methodology is extremely problematic, however, especially in light of Propp's own caution that his approach was valid only for the kinds of folktales he analyzed. It is always dangerous to transfer the conclusions derived from the literature of one culture to that of another, all the more so since Sasson is imposing categories derived from Russian stories from the second millennium A.D. upon a Near Eastern text from two thousand years earlier.[49] Following an evaluation of Sasson's work, A. Brenner contends that the present account is a combination of two distinct orally transmitted tales, "a Naomi story and a Ruth story; that each of the two strands originally belonged to a separate, although parallel, folktale or novella; and that the seams which combine them are still discernible."[50] Both tales supposedly develop a common

---

[45] H. Gunkel, "Ruth," in *Reden und Aufsätze* (Göttingen: Vandenhoeck & Ruprecht, 1913), 84; id., "Ruth," *RGG* (1930): 4.2180–82.

[46] J. M. Myers, *The Linguistic and Literary Form of the Book of Ruth* (Leiden: Brill, 1955).

[47] See J. Kugel, *The Idea of Biblical Poetry: Parallelism and Its History* (New Haven: Yale University Press, 1981), 59–95; A. Berlin, *The Dynamics of Biblical Parallelism* (Bloomington: Indiana University Press, 1985), 1–7.

[48] V. Propp, *Morphology of the Folktale,* 2d ed., ed. L. A. Wagner (Austin: University of Texas Press, 1968). Propp's list of typical figures includes (a) a villain; (b) a donor/provider; (c) a helper; (d) a sought-for person or a father; (e) a dispatcher; (f) a hero (seeker or victim); (g) a false hero. Cf. Sasson *Ruth*, 200–215. According to Sasson, Ruth is the hero/heroine; Naomi, the dispatcher; Boaz functions in the dual role of donor (chap. 2) and hero's helper (chap. 4); Mr. So-and-So (4:1–2) is the false hero; the *goel* is the sought-for person.

[49] For a critique of Sasson see P. Milne, "Folktales and Fairy Tales: An Evaluation of Two Proppian Analyses of Biblical Narratives," *JSOT* 34 (1986): 35–60.

[50] A. Brenner, "Naomi and Ruth," *Feminist Companion to Ruth*, 70. She summarizes the two stories on pp. 77–81.

theme, one that is familiar from the patriarchal stories of Genesis: the reversal of feminine fortune. Specifically, a barren/destitute woman becomes the mother of an important person/a hero.[51] However, not only are Brenner's bases for dividing the strands extremely subjective, but her solution leaves gaps and inconsistencies in both accounts.[52]

More recent commentators tend to apply three literary terms to the Book of Ruth: tale, novella, short story. Because biblical scholars sometimes use expressions like this slightly differently from students of other literary traditions and because the meanings of these terms overlap, we will need to be as precise as possible in our definitions.

A **tale** may be defined as a short narrative written or spoken in prose or verse. Typically the plot of a tale is simple, moving quickly from problem to resolution without complication or subplots. Presentation of the event is more important than developing the characters of the principal participants.[53] In common literary usage a **novella** is "a fictional narrative of indeterminate length (a few pages to two or three hundred), restricted to a single event, situation, or conflict, which produces an element of suspense and leads to an unexpected turning point so that the conclusion surprises even while it is logically consistent."[54] Typically the novella describes not only the evolution of an event (plot) but also the evolution of the characters.[55] The definition of the **short story** is most elusive. How long is short? For Cuddon the difference between a novella and a short story is one of length. If a novella is viewed as a middle-distance race, then the short story is a one hundred- or two-hundred-meter sprint.[56] According to Humphreys, length and complexity of plot represent the most obvious differences between a novella and a short story, with the short story typically having a simpler plot and fewer characters. He also notes another extremely important difference: whereas a novella develops its characters, a short story reveals them. In the latter the issue is not how characters evolve with changing circumstances but how different events and situations reveal the true characters of the participants. Following James Joyce, Humphreys refers to this as the "epiphany quality" of the short story.[57]

---

[51] Ibid., 77.

[52] Cf. the critique of Bush, *Ruth*, 11–12.

[53] For a brief description of the common literary use of the term see J. A. Cuddon, *A Dictionary of Literary Terms and Literary Theory*, 3d ed. (Oxford: Basil Blackwood, 1991), 954–55. For a discussion of the use of the term in biblical scholarship see G. W. Coats, "Tale," in *Saga, Legend, Tale, Novella, Fable: Narrative Forms in Old Testament Literature*, ed. G. W. Coats, JSOTSup 35 (Sheffield: JSOT Press, 1985), 63–70.

[54] Thus Cuddon, *Dictionary*, 641–42.

[55] Cf. the excellent discussion and application of this conception by W. Humphreys, "Novella," in *Narrative Forms in Old Testament Literature*, 82–96.

[56] Cuddon, *Dictionary*, 866–65.

[57] Humphreys, "Novella," 84–85.

Given these definitions, it is easier to classify the Book of Ruth. Bush[58] is correct that with respect to length and complexity, the book falls between the tale and the novella, that is, within the range of the short story. This classification is confirmed by the manner in which the characters are treated: although one may detect some development in the character of Naomi, the author's primary purpose with respect to characterization is to expose the characters of Naomi, Ruth, and Boaz. As we will see, with great literary skill he describes a series of scenes, all of which contribute to the revelation of their *hesed*, their genuine goodness and loyalty that expresses itself in "loving their neighbors more than they love themselves."

There is another reason for classifying the book as a short story rather than a tale or a novella, namely, its historical character. As a short story the book evidences a high and entertaining literary style on the one hand and communicates a lofty moral and spiritual ideal on the other. Unlike the tale and the novella, the short story also is open to a historical interpretation. Although many scholars treat the Book of Ruth as ideological fiction, this approach seems unwarranted for several reasons. First, the story is explicitly and deliberately rooted in a specific historical period: "the days when judges judged Israel" (1:1).[59] Second, the story is linked by the genealogy at the end to a particular family, whose existence and family history are confirmed elsewhere (1 Chr 2:1–17). It is commonly acknowledged that the genealogies in Chronicles derive from official court records (cf. 1 Chr 9:1). Third, the narrative contains no literary or linguistic features that push it in the direction of fiction. Although generic literary categories are rare in the Old Testament, the narrator makes no plea to interpret this account as a *māšāl*, "proverb, figure of speech, parable," or a *šîr*, "song, poem."[60] Fourth, since the book records no miracles, no supernatural visits, no revelations of extrahistorical and extraterrestrial realities, it cannot be dismissed by critics as legendary or imaginary. On the contrary, the picture of the lives of the characters is entirely realistic and in keeping with what is known of life in Palestine in the late second millennium B.C.: the famine and consequent migration of Elimelech and his family (1:1); the allusions to methods of burial (1:17); the geographic portrayal of Bethlehem as a walled town with gates and the location of the threshing floor outside the town; the scenes of workers harvesting the grain (chap. 2); emotions of the characters in the face of grief, anxiety, joy; the nature of the social relationships between mother-in-law and daughter-in-law, landowner and workers, citizen and the citizenry, husband and wife, grandmother and grandson; the legal process (4:1–12). On the last point the narrator is so concerned

---

[58] Bush, *Ruth*, 41–42.

[59] Contra Berlin, *Poetics and Interpretation*, 102.

[60] Cf. Ezekiel's classification of oracles as "laments" (קִינוֹת, 19:1), "riddles" (חִידוֹת, 17:2), and "parables" (מְשָׁלִים, 17:2).

that his audience understand the historical and cultural context of the story that he adds a parenthetical explanation for their benefit. Fifth, as Hubbard correctly notes,[61] it is highly unlikely that an author of a story whose aim was to honor David would have invented a plot in which the great-grandmother of Israel's greatest king was a despised Moabite. Sixth, the witness of the New Testament confirms the historicity of the story. Matthew obviously viewed the record this way, for in his genealogy of Jesus in Matt 1:1–17, whose aim was to affirm Jesus' right to the Messianic title, he deliberately includes Ruth's name (along with Tamar, Rahab, and the wife of Uriah [Bathsheba]), even though her name was missing from the genealogy at the end of Ruth and her presence here does nothing to enhance Jesus' royal claims. Matthew must have gotten the name from the book, since it appears nowhere else in the Old Testament. Like the Book of Judges, the Book of Ruth should be interpreted as a historiographic document. It describes real experiences of real people in real times at real places. The storyteller does indeed exhibit great literary skill and promote a particular ideology, but to relegate the book to the shelf of fiction is to miss the primary point of the book—honoring David by remembering the noble characters in his family history.[62] Accordingly, the Book of Ruth is best classified as an independent historiographic short story. One might point to the story of Joseph in Genesis 37–50 or the Gideon cycle in Judges 6–9 as analogues, except that these have been adapted and integrated into larger compositions. The Book of Ruth stands alone, unattached to other Hebrew historiographic writings.[63]

5. Themes and Purpose

The Book of Ruth is one of the most delightful literary compositions of the ancient world. The narrator is a master at painting word pictures. He skillfully employs the techniques of dialogue, characterization, repetition, reticence, ambiguity, suspense, wordplays, inclusios, et cetera to produce this moving work of art. But what is it about this picture that moves the reader? And what are the points he seeks to get across? Although Ruth is a short book, it is complex in its plot and subtle in its development of themes (of which there are several).

From a literary perspective we recognize in the book a beautiful development of the theme of "from emptiness to fullness." At the outset Naomi is

---

[61] Hubbard, *Ruth*, 48.

[62] On the historiographic significance of biblical narrative texts see S. Lasine, "Fiction, Falsehood, and Reality in Hebrew Scripture," *HS* 25 (1984): 24–40.

[63] Although the Book of Ruth is classified technically as a short story, the preponderance of dialogue affords the composition a dramatic flavor. For the sake of convenience our commentary below will interpret the book as a drama in four acts, followed by a short epilogue. See p. 619ff.

emptied of all her resources (food, home, male support). But in the end she experiences complete filling/fulfillment through a daughter-in-law declared by the women of the town to be more valuable than seven sons. This theme is elevated to the theological level at the beginning by Naomi, who blames God (Shadday/Yahweh) for emptying her life and making her bitter (1:20–21), and at the end by the narrator, who in an exceptional overt recognition of divine involvement declares that Yahweh gave Ruth conception (4:13).[64]

The narrator may have had one primary goal in mind—the exaltation of David by telling the beautiful story of his roots—but in the process of developing that goal he plays with several themes. People who read the book tend to focus on one of these themes as if it were primary or the only one that mattered, but we must resist that temptation. This composition bears several different meanings. But to say this is not to free the reader to make any sense of the text whatever. As in the reading of any document, ancient or modern, we must pay careful attention to the literary conventions employed by an author to get the points across. This is particularly true of the Scriptures, for the only authoritative meanings they bear are those the divine and human authors intended in the composition.

But biblical *narratives* pose special challenges for those who seek the authoritative meaning. Whereas in didactic (e.g., "You shall love the LORD your God with all your heart") and many forms of lyrical texts ("The heavens are telling the glory of God") the intended message is declared explicitly, in narrative the permanent lesson is often, if not generally, implicit in the telling. With respect to short stories like the Book of Ruth, which are at the same time historiographic in nature, the biblical narrator's aim is never merely to recreate or reconstruct past events. And we have not fulfilled the demands of the text even when we, in our minds, have come to recognize exactly what has happened. In the Scriptures historiographic compositions are primarily ideological in purpose. The authoritative meaning of the author is not found in the event described but in the author's interpretation of the event, that is, his understanding of their causes, nature, and consequences. But that interpretation must be deduced from the telling. How is this achieved? By asking the right questions of the text: (1) What does this account tell us about God? (2) What does it tell us about the human condition? (3) What does it tell us of the world? (4) What does it tell us of the people of God—their collective relationship with him? (5) What does it tell us of the individual believer's life of faith? These questions may be answered by careful attention to the words employed and the syntax exploited to tell the story. But they also require a cautious and

---

[64] J. A. Loader ("Job's Sister: Undermining an Unnatural Religiosity," *OTE* 6 [1993]: 312–29): observes astutely that, like the Book of Job, a satisfactory ending to the story is made possible by Naomi's bitterness at the beginning. She argues that the book undermines unnatural religiosity that makes no allowance for bitterness toward God.

disciplined reading between the lines, for what is left unstated also reflects an ideological perspective. Having described the problem and set the agenda, we may proceed to answer the questions raised.

(1) Theology: What Does the Book of Ruth Teach Us about God?

We are indebted to R. Hals for drawing attention to the profound theological message of the book.[65] In exploring its lessons on theology proper the reader will notice immediately that most explicit references to God come from the lips of the characters in the story. It is instructive to observe what the characters have to say about God.

Naomi refers explicitly to God five times. In three of these she expresses her identification with the community of faith by using the covenant name for Israel's God, "Yahweh" (*yhwh;* 1:8,21; 2:20). Twice she identifies him as "Shadday" (1:20–21, "Almighty" in NIV). This is an abbreviation of El Shadday, an ancient title of God. The etymology of the name is obscure.[66] A clue to its significance, however, if not its meaning, may be found in the early seventh century B.C. Balaam texts from *Deir ʿAllah.* Observing that plural *šdyn* is used interchangeably with *ʾlhn,* "gods," to denote a group of gods that make up the heavenly council, J. A. Hackett proposes that *šadday* represents an epithet of El, as chief of the council.[67] The association of the group with mountains occurred naturally since the council normally met on top of the sacred mountain. In the Old Testament it is as Shadday that God creates and rules the world and supervises the moral order, punishing evil and rewarding good.[68]

In Naomi's first speech (1:8) we are introduced to the key theological term in the book and one of Yahweh's most treasured characteristics: *ḥesed. Ḥesed* is one of those Hebrew words whose meaning cannot be captured in one English word. This is a strong relational term that wraps up in itself an entire cluster of concepts, all the positive attributes of God—love, mercy, grace, kindness, goodness, benevolence, loyalty, covenant faithfulness; in short, that quality that moves a person to act for the benefit of another without respect to the advantage it might bring to the one who expresses it.[69] Naomi's use of

---

[65] R. Hals, *The Theology of the Book of Ruth* (Philadelphia: Fortress, 1969).

[66] It is commonly derived from a root *ṯdw/y,* which in Ugaritic meant "mountain," hence "one of the mountain." On the etymology of *šdy* see F. M. Cross, *Canaanite Myth and Hebrew Epic: Essays in the History and Religion of Israel* (Cambridge: Harvard University Press, 1973), 52–60; E. A. Knauf, "Shadday," *DDD,* 1416–23.

[67] J. A. Hackett, *The Balaam Text from Deir ʿAllah,* HSM 31 (Chico, CA: Scholars Press, 1989), 87.

[68] Cf. R. H. Hubbard, "Ruth: Theology of," *NIDOTTE* 5.1155.

[69] For studies of the word see N. Glueck, *Hesed in the Bible,* 2d ed., trans. A. Gottschalk (Cincinnati: Hebrew Union College, 1967); K. Sakenfeld, *The Meaning of Hesed in the Hebrew Bible: A New Inquiry,* HSM 17 (Missoula: Scholars Press, 1978); id., *Faithfulness in Action: Loyalty in Biblical Perspective* (1985); D. A. Baer and R. P. Gordon, "חֶסֶד" *NIDOTTE* 2.211–18.

ḥesed as the direct object of the verb ʿāśâ, "to do, act, demonstrate," reflects the fact that this quality is expressed fundamentally in action rather than word or emotion.[70] This is confirmed in v. 7, where she requests that Yahweh might grant (nātan) rest (mĕnûḥâ), that is, security, in the house of her husband. This active sense of ḥesed is reinforced in Naomi's second use of the word in 2:20, where she recognizes Yahweh's ḥesed in Ruth's return from Boaz with an abundant supply of food. In response she prays that Yahweh would reward the generous benefactor with a blessing of his own. The fact that Naomi uses the word in a prayer in the first instance and an expression of gratitude in the second demonstrates the freedom of God to demonstrate or refrain from expressing ḥesed. The first also expresses a confidence that Yahweh will show kindness even to outsiders to the covenant community. After all, Ruth and Orpah are Moabites.

On the other hand, Naomi also recognizes Yahweh's freedom to act in judgment against a person. In 1:13 she expresses this notion generally as "the LORD's hand has gone out against me" (yāṣĕʾâ bî yad yhwh) and the effects as "extreme bitterness" (mar mĕʾōd). When she returns to Bethlehem, her accusation against God is even more bitter. In 1:20–21 she complains that Shadday has made her life very bitter; Yahweh has brought her back empty; Shadday has brought her misfortune (hēraʿ).

It is not clear, however, that Naomi is a confessional monotheist. Her comment in 1:15, that Orpah has gone back to her people and her gods, suggests that hers was a compromised theology. She recognized that Yahweh was the God of Israel; but like Ruth, Jephthah (Judg 11:24), and undoubtedly many other Israelites of the time, she may have believed that each nation had its own particular patron deity. This observation will influence how we interpret the move of this family to the land of Moab in the commentary below.

Only in her opening speech (1:16–17) does Ruth explicitly express a theological awareness, but her declarations here represent one of the most significant statements in the entire book. The reader is not surprised by Naomi's expressions of her view of God, but Ruth's declaration of faith is truly remarkable. To be sure, initially she does refer to God by his generic title, ʾĕlōhîm, "Deity" (1:16), which one expects from the lips of a non-Israelite. Later in this same speech, however, she recognizes that she is subject to Yahweh, whom she invokes to visit her with a curse should she fail in her commitment to her mother-in-law. But this is a natural consequence of her earlier declaration: "Your people shall be my people, and your God my God." In keeping with prevailing ancient Near Eastern perceptions, she recognized that

---

[70] The same combination of verb and object is found in 3:10 and Judg 1:24; 8:35, though with humans as subjects. For the numerous other occurrences of the phrase עָשָׂה חֶסֶד, "to demonstrate ḥesed," see DCH 3.278–79. In Ruth 2:20 the opposite of "demonstrating ḥesed" is expressed with עָזַב חֶסֶד, "to abandon ḥesed."

when one transferred ethnic and national allegiance, one placed oneself under the authority of the god of the adopted people.[71]

Boaz refers to God six times, five times by covenant name (Yahweh), and once by his relationship to Israel ("God of Israel"). The first four occurrences appear in blessings (2:4,12a,12b; 3:10), which reflect Boaz's recognition of Yahweh as a gracious God who dwells with his people ("The LORD be with you!" 2:4) and who rewards people for their acts of devotion and kindness (2:11–12). The addition of "the God of Israel" in 2:12 is significant, especially since he is talking to a Moabite. With the final clause, "under whose wings you have come to take refuge," he recognizes another important characteristic of Yahweh that is the obverse of Ruth's own declaration in 1:16; as patron of the nation Yahweh offers protection to all who will identify with his people. Like Naomi in 2:20, in 3:10 Boaz perceives Yahweh as the source of all blessing. The oath "as the LORD lives" (3:13) is formulaic, but it expresses Boaz's recognition of Yahweh as the living God, in contrast, for example, to the gods of Moab. The prophets denounce these as mere figments of a depraved imagination, and in any case they are represented by lifeless images of wood and stone.

The speeches of the secondary characters of the book also reflect particular views of God. With their greeting to Boaz in 2:4 the field workers recognized his dependence upon Yahweh as the source of blessing. The same is true of the people of the court and the elders in 4:11, when they pray that Yahweh might exalt Ruth to the status of Rachel and Leah and when they express confidence that he will give Boaz offspring through this woman. They hereby acknowledge that children are a gift from God (Ps 127:3). In 4:14 the women of the community credit Yahweh with providing Naomi with a *goʾel.*

Despite the fundamentally theological perspective of the characters in the book, commentators have often recognized the relative secularity of the narrator himself. Yahweh's name is on the lips of his characters at every turn, but the narrator acknowledges the involvement of God only twice, in 1:6 and 4:13. And the first of these is indirect, inasmuch as he states that Naomi recognized Yahweh's intervention on behalf of his people by giving them food, and the reader must infer that this is also the author's viewpoint. The last statement, however, is explicit: Yahweh enabled Ruth to conceive. Like the members of the court and the elders (4:12), the narrator recognizes the hand of God in the conception and birth of children. By framing the story with these two references, the narrator highlights his conviction that in the end the book is more about the providence of God than the deeds of human beings.

Apart from these two statements the narrator never refers directly to God,

---

[71] For a full development of this notion see D. I. Block, *The Gods of the Nations: Studies in Ancient Near Eastern National Theology,* 2d ed. (Grand Rapids: Baker, 1999).

leading some to suggest that the book is devoid of any theology at all.[72] However, others have rightly spoken of "the hidden hand of God."[73] The narrator may not speak directly of God's involvement, but reading between the lines we may recognize his hand in at least four ways.

First, God's hand is present in apparently natural events. The book opens on an ominous note: there was a famine in the land. The clause seems insignificant and irrelevant to this discussion. Given the state of modern technology our professional meteorologists would tend to attribute the drought to the failure of low pressure systems to develop in the Mediterranean or the fact that cold fronts kept passing by north or south of the region of Bethlehem. But for any Israelite familiar with Yahweh's covenant with Israel or Moses' final address to the people on the plains of Moab, the crisis derives from an entirely different cause. In the "blessings and curses" attached to Yahweh's covenant with Israel, he had warned that he would certainly turn off the rains if his people would persist in rebellious and pagan behavior. This covenant threat is described metaphorically in Lev 26:19–20 (lit.):

> I will punish you for your sins seven times over. I will break down your stubborn pride and make the sky above you like iron and the ground beneath you like bronze. Your strength will be spent in vain, because your soil will not yield its crops, nor will the trees of the land yield their fruit.

Using slightly different language, Moses declares in his final sermon in Deut 28:23–24 (lit.):

> The sky over your head will be bronze, the ground beneath you iron. The LORD will turn the rain of the country into dust and powder; it will come down from the skies until you are destroyed.[74]

In the Book of Judges, when God sends in the enemy to punish the Israelites for their rebellion against him, he does so in fulfillment of his covenant curse in Lev 26:17 and Deut 28:32–33 (cf. 49–52). Now we learn that foreign

---

[72] Cf. Sasson, *Ruth*, 249.

[73] See especially Hals, *Theology of the Book of Ruth*; id., "Ruth, Book of," *IDBS*, 758–59.

[74] This covenant curse compares with several that appear in ANE treaties. One of the curses in the treaty of Ashur-nirari V with Mati'-ilu, king of Arpad reads: "May they [Mati'-ilu and his magnates] be deprived of Adad's thunder so that rain becomes forbidden to them. May dust be their food, pitch their ointment, donkey's urine their drink, papyrus their clothing, and may their sleeping place be in the dung heap." Thus the translation of S. Parpola and K. Watanabe, *Neo-Assyrian Treaties and Loyalty Oaths,* SAA 2 (Helsinki: Helsinki University Press, 1988), 11 (cf. *ANET*, 533). Even more like the biblical curse is a clause in Esarhaddon's Succession Treaty: "May they make your ground like iron (so that) nothing can sprout from it. Just as rain does not fall from a brazen [copper] heaven, so may rain and dew not come upon your fields and your meadows; instead of dew may burning coals rain on your head" (Parpola and Watanabe, 51 [§§ 63–64]; cf. *ANET*, 539). For a discussion of these and other texts see D. Hillers, *Treaty-Curses and the Old Testament Prophets*, BibOr 16 (Rome: Pontifical Biblical Institute, 1964).

oppression was not the only punishment for the rebellion of Israel as described in the Book of Judges. Yahweh had also sent this famine. Although the text does not state that the departure of Elimelech and his family for Moab was a symptom of the general lack of faith in Israel, one may surmise that in the narrator's mind the deaths of Elimelech, Chilion, and Mahlon in Moab were further consequences of the spiritual crisis in the land. Naomi certainly recognizes the hand of God behind her personal misery (1:20–21).[75]

Second, God's hand is present in seemingly chance events. In 2:3 *wayyiqer miqrehâ*, "Her encounter encountered," is an odd but deliberately constructed clause that in context must mean "her chance chanced upon" or in colloquial English, "Her luck brought her to."[76] The statement is ironic. The narrator deliberately employs an expression that forces the reader to sit up and ask, How was it that Ruth "happened" to land in the field of a man who was not only gracious but also a potential *gōʾēl?* If for the true believer even the way dice fall in the lap is determined by God (Prov 16:33), how much more the movements of this woman, who at the moment has no idea what destiny awaits her and her progeny. But from the perspective of the author, Ruth's arrival at Boaz's field was one more evidence of the providential hand of God, who is directing the personal affairs of the characters toward the goal announced in 4:17c.[77]

Third, God's hand is present in the delicate and daring schemes of humans. Regardless of the meaning of *margĕlôt* in 3:4,7,8,14 (NIV "feet"), the scheme to provide security *(mānôaḥ)* for Ruth concocted by Naomi and implemented by her daughter is suspicious from the standpoint of custom and morality and fraught with danger.[78] Ruth's preparations and the choice of location for the encounter suggest the actions of a prostitute. Under normal circumstances, if a self-respecting and morally noble man like Boaz, sleeping at the threshing floor, should wake up in the middle of the night and discover a woman beside him, he would surely have shooed her off, protesting that he had nothing to do with women like her. But if Ruth's actions are questionable ethically, her demand that Boaz marry her are highly irregular from the perspective of custom: a for-

---

[75] Note the expressions she uses in 1:21. First, "Yahweh has answered against me." Here עָנָה בִי carries a quasi-legal sense, "responded against," presumably for violation of a legal contract (the covenant) and in keeping with the covenant curses. This construction occurs elsewhere in legal contexts in Gen 30:33; Exod 20:13; Num 35:30; Deut 5:17; 19:16,18; 1 Sam 12:3. Second, "Shaddai has caused evil for me/done me harm." For examples of the *hiphil* of רָעַע with Yahweh as the subject to express the consequences of covenantal infidelity see Josh 24:20; Jer 25:6,29; Zech 8:14.

[76] The meaning of the word קָרָה in this context is suggested by 1 Sam 6:9, where in the minds of the Philistines it clearly means "chance." Similarly 1 Sam 6:9.

[77] The same could be said for the appearance of *the gōʾēl* just as Boaz sat down at the gate in 4:1–2.

[78] See the commentary below.

eigner propositioning an Israelite; a woman propositioning a man; a young person propositioning an older person; a destitute field worker propositioning the landowner. But instead of taking offense at Ruth's forwardness, Boaz blesses her, praises her for her *ḥesed,* calls her "my daughter," reassures her by telling her not to fear, promises to do whatever she asks, and pronounces her a noble woman *(ʾēšet ḥayil).* This extraordinary reaction is best attributed to the hand of God controlling his heart and his tongue when he awakes.

Fourth, God's hand is present in the legal process. Having heard Ruth's request that he marry her and having told her he will do so if the nearer relative permits him, Boaz arranges for the legal resolution of the issue (4:1–12). By now the reader knows that nothing happens by chance, and when Mr. So-and-So (NIV "my friend," 4:1) happens to pass by the gate where Boaz had sat down, this too is attributable to the hand of God. If Ruth was present for the proceedings, one may only imagine her emotions as the case proceeded. Her heart must have sunk as the man with first rights to Elimelech's land said he would take it. However, when he declined because Boaz reminded him that Ruth goes with the land, her hope will have risen. But how does one account for this change of mind on the man's part? Ostensibly the answer is found in v. 6, but the excuse he gives is garbled and feeble sounding. But it is enough for Boaz, whose speech of acceptance of the verdict is a model of clarity and logic. The case could easily have gone the other way, but it appears that in the mind of the narrator the outcome was determined by God from the beginning.

Despite the relative secularity of the book as a whole, it must be interpreted as a glorious account of divine providence. Underlying every episode is God's determination to produce David the king from the depressing and chaotic Israelite environment during the days of the judges. Unlike the Book of Judges, however, here his hand is not driving the movers and shakers in Israel. David does not emerge because of divine manipulation of the ruling class. On the contrary, the seeds of the great dynasty that would arise in the future are being sown in this private family of Bethlehem. This family consists of the most unlikely candidates for divine service: a widow left without husband or sons, an alien in a similar state, and a bachelor from the humble town of Bethlehem.

(2) Ecclesiology: What Does the Book of Ruth Teach Us about the People of God?

Although the main characters in the story are Judahites from Bethlehem, the narrator obviously has the entire nation of Israel in mind. The name "Israel" appears five times in the book, first in 2:12 and then four times in the last chapter. According to v. 7, where the name appears twice, "Israel" refers to a distinct national and cultural entity. This is obviously also the view of outsiders, for when Naomi advises her daughters-in-law to return to their own mothers' houses and expresses the hope that they might find security in

the houses of their respective husbands, these Moabites express their determination to go with her to "your people" (ʿammēk, 1:10). Ruth expresses this
view even more emphatically when she announces in 1:16 her total identification with Naomi's people. Boaz also recognizes his own nation as a distinct people, when in 2:11 he commends Ruth for leaving her father and
mother and her native land (ʾereṣ môladtēk) and coming to a people previously unknown to her. It is in the midst of this new people that Ruth learns
about the Israelites' unique theology of land and the customs of the gōʾēl.

If all the characters in the book recognize Israel as a distinct cultural and
ethnic entity, it is apparent that its Israelite characters are also aware of their
particular national history. The witnesses to the legal scene, by which Boaz
wins the right to marry Ruth, acknowledge Rachel and Leah as the matriarchs
of long ago who built the house of Israel (4:11). The priority of Rachel suggests they also remembered that she was Jacob's favorite wife, and the
absence of the names of the handmaids Zilpah and Bilhah indicates an awareness of their secondary role in the original family. They also express awareness of the origins of the tribe of Judah (4:12), particularly the Judahite line of
Perez, whom Tamar bore to this son of Jacob. However, though the account in
Genesis 38 casts doubts on the morality of both Judah and Tamar, here Tamar
is upheld as a model for Ruth to duplicate.

Although the narrator and his characters are all keenly aware of Israel's
distinct ethnic entity and history, they also recognize the nation's unique spiritual identity. They are a people Yahweh has claimed as his own and for whom
he exercises providential care (1:6). Conversely, through the lips of Boaz,
Yahweh is also recognized as "the God of Israel" (2:12). The Moabite Ruth
also acknowledges this reality. Indeed she knows that if she would return with
Naomi to the land of Israel, she must transfer her allegiance to the God of this
land and this people. Boaz applauds her for casting herself on the care of Yahweh, the God of Israel.

The book is most eloquent in portraying the practical ethical implications
of membership in the Israelite community of faith. In stark contrast to the
Book of Judges, where many of the major characters are spiritually compromising at best and pagan in outlook and conduct at worst, every person in this
story is a decent person;[79] they are presented as authentic people of faith.
Although ḥesed is only attributed explicitly to Ruth (3:10), the kindness,
goodness, loyalty, and faithfulness that are characteristic of God are true of
his people. Indeed, ranking just below the narrator's concern to essay God's
providential care and direction of history is his goal of describing what ḥesed

---

[79] Some would argue that the unnamed primary gōʾēl in chap. 4 is portrayed negatively. In my
view the narrator is neutral toward him at worst. In any case he is nothing like Gideon or Jephthah
or Samson or Micah or the Levites in chaps. 17–18 and 19–20.

looks like in the context of personal, family, and communal life. But unlike the emphasis of some today, the symptoms and effects of the life of faith are totally unspectacular. No one in the book demands of God that he meet his/her needs, and no one demands specific miraculous divine intervention on his/her own behalf. On the contrary, true covenant faith is expressed by concern for the welfare of others. In the story this concern is expressed by loving actions that promote the next person's well-being and by verbal expressions of prayer for the next person. Below we will survey the actions of the characters individually, but it may be helpful to examine the prayers in the book as a group, for they offer a window into the hearts of the people.

When we examine the speeches in the book, we are impressed by how naturally and spontaneously the characters give verbal expression to their faith.[80] These expressions of faith appear in the forms of accusations (1:13,20–21), an oath (3:13), and especially in blessings (1:8–9; 2:4a,b,12,19 [without naming Yahweh]; 2:20; 3:10; 4:11–12,14a,b–15).[81] In general a blessing may be defined as an expressed wish for someone to receive what is considered good in life, such as land, progeny, protection, food, clothing, health. The blessings in Ruth may be grouped into two categories: those that explicitly employ the root *brk* and those that do not. Both occur five times, the former in 2:4b,19,20; 3:10; 4:14a; the latter in 1:8–9; 2:4a,12; 4:11–12,14b–15. The blessings that use *brk* may be further divided into two groups: those that appeal to God to bless his people by conferring good upon them (2:4b,19,20; 3:10)[82] and one that blesses God, in effect by praising the good in him (4:14a).[83] None of the former specify what that good might be. The blessings that omit the verb *brk* generally express a wish that a specific benefaction be conferred on another person: divine *ḥesed*, specifically rest in the house of a husband (1:8–9); divine presence (2:4a); reward for work, full wages from God (2:12); progeny (4:11–12); fame in Israel (4:14b);[84] life and security in old age (4:15). At the same time, it is striking that no one in the book prays for a resolution of his

---

[80] M. E. Thompson notes that the book's intertwining of divine and human activity is especially emphasized through the prayers of intercession and thanksgiving uttered by the characters ("New Life Amid Alien Corn: The Book of Ruth," *EvQ* 65 [1993]: 197–210).

[81] For a discussion of blessing in recent literature see T. G. Crawford, *Blessing and Curse in Syro-Palestinian Inscriptions of the Iron Age*, American University Studies, series VII, vol. 120 (New York: Peter Lang, 1992), 7–34; M. L. Brown, "בָּרַךְ," *NIDOTTE* 1.757–67.

[82] Structurally these blessings are of three types: (1) the jussive form of בָּרַךְ with pronominal suffix + *yhwh* (as subject): יְבָרֶכְךָ יְהוָה (2:4b); (2) the jussive form of הָיָה ("to be") + passive participle of בָּרַךְ: יְהִי בָּרוּךְ (2:19); (3) passive participle of בָּרַךְ + personal pronoun + *lamed* with *yhwh*: בָּרוּךְ הוּא לַיהוָה (2:20); בָּרוּכָה אַתְּ לַיהוָה (3:10).

[83] The form is passive participle + *yhwh* as object (בָּרוּךְ יְהוָה). When God is the object of the verb, בָּרַךְ functions within the semantic range of "praise." Cf. Brown, "בָּרַךְ," 764, and the commentary on 4:14 below.

[84] The statement is ambiguous—the antecedent could be Yahweh. See the commentary.

own crisis. In each case a person prays that Yahweh would bless someone else. This is a mark of *ḥesed*.

But the characters also express *ḥesed* in practical, more tangible ways. As already intimated, the opening scene raises questions concerning the faith of Elimelech and Naomi. Like Abraham's excursion to Egypt in Gen 12:10–20, the family's move to Moab to escape the famine looks like a lapse of spiritual commitment. Instead of dealing with root causes, they reacted to symptoms. Instead of recognizing the famine to be punishment for the nation's sin and repenting of their spiritual infidelity, they left their people and their land for the "unclean" land of Moab. It seems, however, that once the men in this family had been removed through further acts of judgment and all her economic props had been removed, Naomi came to her senses. Hearing that Yahweh had intervened *(pāqad)* on behalf of his people by ending the famine, in faith she returned to Bethlehem.[85] After this she expresses *ḥesed* practically in many ways: she addresses her Moabite daughters-in-law tenderly as "my daughters" (1:11–13; 2:2,22; 3:1,16,18); she tries to spare them her own distress by inviting them to return to their mother's homes (1:8–14); she allows Ruth to convince her to let her go with her back to Bethlehem (1:15–8); she permits Ruth to take the initiative in finding food (2:2); she blesses the person who had been so generous to her daughter-in-law (2:19–20); she expresses concern for Ruth's welfare when she goes out to glean (2:22); she recognizes her responsibility for Ruth and creatively devises a way to provide for her security (3:1–4); she gently advises Ruth on further steps (3:16–18); she claims Ruth's child as her own. All this is despite Israel's fundamentally hostile disposition toward Moabites.

Ruth's practical demonstration of *ḥesed* is equally impressive. She casts her lot with her widowed mother-in-law (1:15–18);[86] she takes the initiative in providing food (2:2); she expresses deep and humble appreciation for the kindness of Boaz (2:10,13); she works hard in Boaz's field (2:17–18,23); she follows her mother-in-law's counsel in approaching Boaz (3:6–13); she sensitively listens to Boaz's concerns and patiently waits for a legal resolution (3:14–18); she apparently lets her mother-in-law adopt her son as her own (4:16).

The narrator's admiration for Boaz is evident from the opening introduction; he introduces him as a *gibbôr ḥayil* (2:1). Although generally interpreted as "a man of wealth, standing," the expression also connotes nobility

---

[85] The verb שׁוּב, "to turn, return," which elsewhere denotes "repent," functions as a key word in chap. 1, occurring eight times (vv. 6,7,8,10,15a,15b,16,22).

[86] Cp. Boaz's glowing testimony in 2:11–12 and 3:10 and his recognition of Ruth as a noble woman in 3:11.

and honor, a man of sterling character.[87] The quality of the man is recognized by his workers, who, unlike the situation in many modern workplaces today, bless him when he appears at the field (2:4a). He responds with a blessing of his own for them (2:4b). But the narrator highlights the man's moral character by noting how sensitive he is toward Ruth and how effusive in his generosity, even though she is a Moabite (2:8–16). He addresses Ruth tenderly as "my daughter" (2:8), invites her to work with his female workers (2:8–9), protects her from potential abuse from his male workers (2:9,15), invites her to drink from the same source as his regular harvesters (2:9), praises her publicly and blesses her (2:11–12), invites her to eat with him and his workers, serves her himself, giving her more than she can eat (2:14), and commands his men to drop grain that they have cut deliberately so she can pick it up more easily (2:15–16). Later, when Ruth risks her honor and indeed her welfare, if not her life, at the threshing floor, he blesses her, praises her again for her sterling character, and promises on oath to redeem her as a *gōʾēl*, protects her from potential abuse by sending her home before dawn, and then sends her home with as much food as she can carry (3:6–16). In the final scene he demonstrates *ḥesed* by permitting the primary kinsman to claim Naomi's land and Ruth, guaranteeing the proper legal resolution of the issue of redemption, publicly and self-effacingly declaring his determination to raise up the name of his deceased relative and to preserve the land in his name (4:1–10). Despite traditional Israelite hatred of Moabites and despite Ruth's destitute state, he receives her first as a worker, then as a night guest, and finally as his wife. Never does he or the narrator hide her ethnic identity.

The minor characters in this story also display covenantal *ḥesed*. Boaz's workers bless their boss and receive his blessing (2:4). But even before Boaz had arrived, they apparently had approved of Ruth's presence in the field. At least they did not send her away. After Boaz has won the legal right to marry Ruth, the citizens of Bethlehem express incredible magnanimity by blessing her effusively, praying that Yahweh would elevate this Moabite woman to the status of their venerated ancestresses, Rachel, Leah, and Tamar (4:11–12). The women of the town get into the act after the birth of Obed by blessing Yahweh for what he has done for Naomi and encouraging her with a blessing for the child. Even their naming the child may be interpreted as an expression of community and covenant loyalty.

In contrast to the Book of Judges, where the nation of Israel as a whole and most of the characters are portrayed as thoroughly Canaanized in heart and mind and deed, this story describes an oasis in an ethical wasteland. Although

---

[87] The application of the expression to Boaz invites comparison with Jephthah in Judg 11:1. The contrast in personality and character could hardly be greater. Cf. the characterization of Ruth as a "noble woman" in 3:11; also Prov 31:10.

the narrator deliberately hides the hand of God, by a combination of natural forces, apparently chance events, human scheming, and customary and legal procedures the will of God is accomplished. In the account we witness the sincere piety of the human characters expressed in the sensitivity of Naomi, the devotion *(ḥesed)* of Ruth, the kindness and tenderness of Boaz, the openness of the first candidate for the rights to Ruth, and the whole-hearted acceptance of Ruth by the townsfolk. Ironically, in the story no one prays or implores God for guidance. Still the events are carefully controlled by the divine hand so that Ruth happens to stumble upon Boaz, Boaz responds positively to Ruth's brash proposition, and the first candidate concedes to Boaz the rights of the *gōʾēl*.

In retelling the story of these long-ago people from Bethlehem, the narrator describes for the modern reader what the life of faith should look like. The measure of a people's or a person's faith is not found in the miracles that one can wrest from the hand of God nor in one's personal health and prosperity, but in demonstrating ethical character. If the words of James are true [and they are], that "faith without works is dead (Jas 2:17), then this book paints a picture of a lofty theology and an inspiringly vibrant faith. In this respect it speaks to readers of every age. To tie together the loose thematic strands, we may summarize the practical and theological lessons as follows:

1. God will not let his promises to Israel and Judah and David die.

2. God works in a mysterious way his wonders to perform and his goals to achieve.

3. In all things God works for the good of those who love him and are called according to his purpose (Rom 8:28).

4. Genuine piety is expressed primarily in devotion, sensitivity, grace, and kindness toward others and openness to the working of God.

5. God's grace knows no boundaries. Even a despised Moabitess is incorporated into the nation of Israel. In fact, the royal [and Messianic!] line has Moabite blood in its veins.

Nevertheless, although the inspiring spiritual quality of the characters represents a major theme of the Book of Ruth, this was not the author's primary purpose in writing. His goal was broader on the one hand and more specific on the other. He may have focused on the lives of one particular family in Bethlehem, but their experiences had significance for the readership primarily because of the link they provide between the Canaanized period of the judges and the hopeful reign of David. Writing in the aftermath of the fall of Samaria and the resurgence of the house of David under Josiah, the narrator tells his readers that the same LORD who raised up the house of David in these most unlikely circumstances has preserved it all these years in fulfillment of his promise to David in 2 Samuel 7. But Yahweh still seeks people of *ḥesed* through whom to effect his plans. In the providence and grace of God, five hundred years later the New Testament opens with an announcement of the fulfillment of this promise to another young woman who displayed all the marks of *ḥesed* and had found favor with God (Luke 1:26–38). Mary would be most blessed among women, for she too would bear a son. But this son would be greater than Ruth's child and even greater than her grandchild. His name would be Jesus, he would be called the Son of the Most High (*hupsistos* in the LXX = *ʿelyôn* in Hb.), and the LORD (= Yahweh) would give him the throne of his father David. This greatest son of Boaz and Ruth would rule over Jacob forever in a reign that knows no bounds.

6. Structure and Design

We have already noted that from a literary perspective the Book of Ruth is one of the most delightful pieces ever produced in the history of literature. The narrator is a master at painting word pictures; skillfully employing the techniques of suspense, dialogue, characterization, repetition, reticence, ambiguity, wordplays, and inclusios; and creatively adapting ancient traditions[88] to produce this moving work of art. But it is the tightly knit and carefully controlled plot of this composition that is especially impressive.[89] Although we have classified the account generically as a *short story*, it provides a classic example of the plot of a *tale* as outlined by G. W. Coats.[90] Its structure may be portrayed graphically as in the diagram below.

The Plot Structure of the Book of Ruth

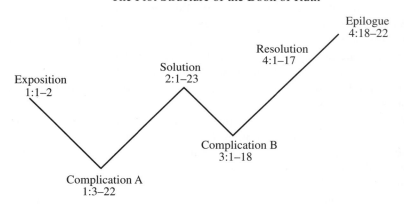

Epilogue
4:18–22

Resolution
4:1–17

Solution
2:1–23

Exposition
1:1–2

Complication B
3:1–18

Complication A
1:3–22

---

[88] On the relationship between the Book of Ruth and Genesis 38, esp. the portrayal of Ruth as a second Tamar, see Nielsen, *Ruth*, 11–17 and more fully, E. Van Wolde, "Texts in Dialogue With Texts: Intertextuality in the Ruth and Tamar Narratives," *Biblical Interpretation* 5 (1997): 1–28.

[89] For a superb discussion of the book from a literary perspective see A. Berlin, *Poetics and Interpretation of Biblical Narrative* (Sheffield: Almond, 1983), 83–110.

[90] Coats, "Tale," in *Saga, Legend, Tale, Novella, Fable*, 64–67.

(1) The Exposition (1:1-2)

By exposition we do not mean an interpretation of a text or verbal statement. In literary discussions an exposition typically defines the circumstances of the story, introducing the principal characters and the situation and events that hold them together. In our case the main characters are Elimelech, his wife Naomi, and their two sons Mahlon and Chilion. Because of a famine in their hometown of Bethlehem in Judah, they move to Moab to sojourn *(gûr)*, but they end up living there for quite some time *(wayĕhî šām)*. This sets the stage. Anyone who is aware of the significance of famine in Israelite experience and theology and of the relationship of Israel with Moab will immediately wonder how things will turn out.

(2) The First Complication (1:3-22)

The second element typically introduces a complication in the relationships, often by announcing a problem, describing a crisis, or introducing conflict. This segment of our text is framed by a narrative description of the causes of the crisis (the deaths of the three men, Elimelech, Mahlon, and Chilion) at the beginning (vv. 3-5) and Naomi's theological interpretation of the crisis (vv. 19-21). Naomi's comment that she went away full and has come back empty is incorrect if by fullness we mean having food and enjoying life, for the family had moved to save their lives. But she is correct if by "fullness" we mean family. She had left with a husband and two sons; she returns a widow without progeny. Between these verses the narrator introduces Ruth, the second principal character in the plot, and describes the responses of Naomi and Ruth to the crisis. Naomi heard that God had again provided food in Bethlehem, so she returned in the hope of finding bread. Her conversation with her daughters, however, particularly her despairing note that she is too old to remarry and bear sons, makes it look as though the second emptiness will never be resolved. This creates the real crisis: the line of Elimelech is in danger of dying out. Unless one has read the book to the end, this may not seem of great consequence beyond Naomi's personal grief, but for the narrator this introduces the key issue in the book: How can the line be rescued so that Yahweh's chosen king David may appear in due course? Verse 22 is transitional, summarizing Naomi's response and setting the stage for the next phase.

(3) The Solution (2:1-23)

According to Coats, in a tale the third element is characteristically short and to the point, breaking the tension and pointing the way to the conclusion. In this account, however, the path to the resolution is complex, and the solution is only indirectly suggested. Like the "Complication" above, this section has a clear framework, being bounded by an expositional introduction of the third principal, Boaz (2:1), and Naomi's interpretation of the intervening events, particularly the contact with Boaz (2:20–22). Between this framework the narrator summarizes the events that led to this interpretation. Boaz and Ruth are not only linked in an economic relationship, but they are introduced to one another in ways that reveal the finest aspects of both characters. Naomi's concluding statement heightens the reader's interest and expectation of a quick resolution of the crisis. Also similar to the "Complication," this section ends with a transitional comment summarizing the previous happenings and preparing the way for chap. 3.

(4) A Second Complication (3:1–18)

To a large extent chap. 2 had resolved the problem of the physical emptiness of Naomi and Ruth. They had found food for the moment in the field of Boaz, and because of his generosity this problem seems to have been resolved for the future as well. Naomi's speech in 2:20 had also raised the prospect of an early resolution of the second form of emptiness, Naomi's lack of progeny and Ruth's lack of security in the house of a husband. Chapter 3, which is framed by two speeches of Naomi (vv. 1–4,18), opens by raising this very issue. Feeling obligated to provide a husband, that is, rest and security for her daughter-in-law,[91] Naomi hatches a plan to make it happen. The chapter concludes with her encouraging Ruth to wait with confidence, for Boaz will not relax (*šqṭ*) until the problem has been solved. However, the narrative between beginning and ending has introduced a second complication. Faithfully following her mother-in-law's instructions and brazenly calling upon Boaz to marry her, Ruth discovers that Boaz is not in a position to do so. According to Israelite custom, the privilege and rights of the *gōʾēl* are strictly governed by primogeniture. Because Boaz is not the first in line to claim Elimelech's property and with it the widowed Ruth, he must decline her proposition. But he reassures her that all is not lost; there is still the possibility that the other person will defer to Boaz, in which case Boaz would marry her.

(5) The Resolution (4:1–17)

Neither Ruth nor the reader waits long for the resolution of the crisis. The final act in the drama commences with Boaz taking the initiative to resolve the legal question and concludes with the narrator's announcement that the son that is born to Naomi is the grandfather of David. Between these borders three groups comment on what has happened and in so doing provide important

---

[91] The word מְנוּחָה, "rest, security," in 3:1 echoes מְנוּחָה "rest, security," in 1:9.

clues to the significance of these events: (1) Having won the right to Elimelech's land and Ruth's hand, Boaz declares his intention of preserving the name of the deceased (Mahlon and Elimelech).[92] (2) The men of Bethlehem pronounce a blessing upon Ruth, praying that she may join the ranks of Rachel and Leah and Tamar, who built the house of Israel/Judah.[93] (3) The women of Bethlehem announce Naomi's complete fulfillment in her daughter-in-law and her grandson and pray that the son's name may become famous in Israel. In the meantime, recognizing the divine involvement in everything, the narrator declares Yahweh's auspicious role in the birth of the boy (v. 13). With the narrator's final statement (v. 17c) he declares the fulfillment of all the pronouncements in vv. 10–17a and announces the significance of the story as a whole.

(6) Genealogical Epilogue (4:18–22)

To concretize the significance of the story of Naomi, Ruth, and Boaz and to assure that the reader does not simply read this book for entertainment or for its human interest value, the narrator draws on official records to remind the reader of David's genealogical history. The story he has just told is more than an inspiring tale of genuinely good people; it describes the critical role played by the seventh link in this chain. This story is to the genealogy leading from Perez to David what Enoch is to the family line that leads from Adam to Noah in Gen 5:22a,24. In both cases the seventh generation is distinguished for its spirituality. Whereas the author of Genesis states the case with a sentence ("Enoch walked with God"), our author develops the theme with a story. Righteous Boaz shows us what it means to walk with God. In the process the narrator offers another dimension of David's right to the throne. Far from being disqualified because Moabite blood flows in his veins, it is precisely the Moabite connection that raises this genealogy above the ordinary.

7. Outline of the Contents of the Book

Although the Book of Ruth is constructed as a tightly knit piece that must be read or heard at one sitting,[94] the preponderance of dialogue also encourages one to interpret the composition as a drama in four main acts, followed

---

[92] Little does he realize that in so doing he is laying the foundation for the rise of the name of David.

[93] Like Boaz, they realize that in so doing they were laying the foundation for the rise of the house of David.

[94] So also Nielsen, *Ruth*, 4.

by a genealogical postlude.[95] Each act is set in its own time and place, but together they contribute to the artful presentation of the narrator's central theme—the providential hand of God in the preservation of Israel's royal line during the dark days of the judges. As a four-act drama, the book may be outlined as follows:

Act 1: The Crisis for the Royal Line (1:1–21). The expository opening to Act I (vv. 1–5) provides the hearer/reader with necessary background for the story: the time, the place, the characters, and the issue. Chronologically the events are set in Israel's premonarchic period. Although the crisis has its roots in the land of Israel, the narrator telescopes a series of events inviting the hearer/reader to move with the characters from the town of Bethlehem in Judah to the fields of Moab, where the principal action transpires. The heart of the first act is taken up with the dialogue between Naomi and her daughters (vv. 6–18), climaxing in Ruth's speech in vv. 16–17. The act concludes with a dialogue between Naomi and the women of Bethlehem through which the reader/hearer comes to feel Naomi's pain. The first act is dominated by the tenfold occurrence of the *Leitwort šûb*, "to turn, return," skillfully employed to trace Naomi's travels. When the act ends, she has come full circle—from Bethlehem to Moab to Bethlehem.

Act 2: The Ray of Hope for the Royal Line (1:22–2:23). Ruth 1:22 is transitional, reminding the hearer/reader of what has transpired in Act I and setting the chronological and geographical context for Act II: at the beginning of the barley harvest in the region of Moab. Ruth 2:1 completes the introduction to the new act by introducing a new character. Through the skillful use of dialogue the narrator will show how the grace of God is expressed through the grace of a man (vv. 2–16), which raises Naomi's (and the hearer/reader's) hope of a possible resolution to the crisis. Verse 23 summarizes the effects of the preceding events.

Act 3: The Complication for the Royal Line (3:1–18). The tension mounts in Act III as Naomi proposes and Ruth carries out a potentially dangerous scheme for bringing the crisis to a resolution. Again through impressive use of conversation the narrator draws the hearer/reader into the lives of the characters and the issues they confront. The introduction of another person, the nearer relative, who must be eliminated, sets the stage for the final Act.

Act 4: The Rescue of the Line (4:1–17). The final act describes the legal proceedings by which Ruth and Boaz are finally united in marriage and Naomi's emptiness is resolved by the birth of a son. In this Act, Ruth never speaks. She is a catalyst of resolution rather than an actor. With the hearer/

---

[95] Cf. E. Zenger, *Das Buch Ruth*, ZBKAT 8 (Zurich: Theologischer Verlag, 1986), 15–18. Cf. R. Grant ("Literary Structure in the Book of Ruth," *BSac* 148 [1991]: 424–41), who sees the plot structure as moving from tragedy through antiromance and then through comedy to romance.

reader she observes the legal proceedings from the sidelines (vv. 1–12) and is the recipient of other's actions (v. 13).

Epilogue (4:18–22). The concluding genealogy functions as a historical summary of the royal line of David, highlighting Boaz as the seventh link in the chain.

As noted earlier, the narrator displays great literary skill in the composition of this drama. This skill is evident not only in the use of dialogue, characterization, et cetera but also in the proportion invested in the drama. The symmetry and balance of the four acts may be highlighted by portraying the plot diagrammatically as follows:[96]

THE STRUCTURE OF RUTH
The Preservation of Israel's Royal Line[97]

Act 1:	The Crisis for the Line	1:1–21
	1. The Setting for the Crisis	1:1–2
	2. The Nature of the Crisis	1:3–5
	3. The Response to the Crisis	1:6–18
	4. The Interpretation of the Crisis	1:19–21
Act 2:	The Ray of Hope for the Line	1:22–2:23
	1. The New Setting	1:22–2:1
	2. The Initiative of Ruth	2:2–3
	3. The Grace of Boaz	2:4–16
	4. The Results	2:17–23
Act 3:	The Complication for the Line	3:1–18
	1. The Scheme	3:1–5
	2. The Implementation of the Scheme	3:6–15
	3. The Results of the Scheme	3:16–18
Act 4:	The Rescue of the Line	4:1–17
	1. The Legal Resolution	4:1–12
	2. The Genealogical Resolution	4:13–17
Epilogue:	The Royal Genealogy	4:18–22

---

[96] The space allotted to each section is based on the number of verses of which it is composed.

[97] The term "preservation" may seem anachronistic, but it reflects the later perspective of the author.

I. ACT 1: THE CRISIS FOR THE ROYAL LINE (1:1–21)
  1. Scene 1: The Setting for the Crisis (1:1–2)
  2. Scene 2: The Nature of the Crisis (1:3–5)
  3. Scene 3: The Response to the Crisis (1:6–18)
    (1) The First Interchange (1:6–10)
    (2) The Second Interchange (1:11–14)
      Naomi's First Argument (1:11)
      Naomi's Second Argument (1:12–13a)
      Naomi's Third Argument (1:13b–14)
    (3) The Third Interchange (1:15–18)
  4. Scene 4: The Interpretation of the Crisis (1:19–21)

———— I. ACT 1: THE CRISIS FOR THE ROYAL LINE (1:1–21)————

Act 1 of the Book of Ruth begins and ends in Bethlehem. Meanwhile the narrator takes the reader through a series of tragic scenes that climax in Naomi's woeful declaration to the women of Bethlehem.

1. Scene 1: The Setting for the Crisis (1:1–2)

[1]In the days when the judges ruled, there was a famine in the land, and a man from Bethlehem in Judah, together with his wife and two sons, went to live for a while in the country of Moab. [2]The man's name was Elimelech, his wife's name Naomi, and the names of his two sons were Mahlon and Kilion. They were Eph‑rathites from Bethlehem, Judah. And they went to Moab and lived there.

1:1–2 The author sets the stage for the story of Naomi, Ruth, and Boaz by describing the context in which the events will occur. *Chronologically* the time is described as "in the days when the judges ruled."[1] Usually in the Old

---

[1] Hebrew narratives often begin with an introductory וַיְהִי, "and it happened," followed by a temporal clause or phrase. Cf. Josh 1:1; Judg 1:1; 1 Sam 1:1; 2 Sam 1:1; Neh 1:1; Jonah 1:1. See further GKC §111g. Contra A. Berlin (*Poetics and Interpretation of Biblical Narrative* [Sheffield: Almond, 1983], 102), this company of occurrences suggests the author regarded the events in Ruth as historical in his past. Cf. J. M. Sasson, *Ruth: A New Translation with a Philological Commentary and a Formalist-Folklorist Interpretation,* 2d ed. (Sheffield: Academic Press, 1989), 14. The temporal phrase involves a construct chain with three links, בִּימֵי שְׁפֹט הַשֹּׁפְטִים lit. "in the days of the judging of the judges."

Testament the word *šp̄ṭ* relates to internal administration, that is, the maintenance of internal harmony by settling disputes. However, the author betrays
his familiarity with the Book of Judges by using the expression in its relatively rare (in Hb.) but original sense, "to govern." The "judges," namely,
"governors," were local chieftains called up by Yahweh to deliver the people
from foreign oppressors.[2] The opening line reflects the narrator's determination to place the events of the book in a truly historical context. The use of the
phrase "in the days when judges ruled" indicates the premonarchic period was
recognized as a clearly identifiable phase in Israel's history, between the death
of Joshua and the crowning of Saul as the nation's first king. Any attempt to
narrow the particular time of the events recorded in this book is speculative.[3]

Historically, the events of the book are precipitated by a famine that struck
the land, apparently the entire land of Israel.[4] The cause of the famine is not
indicated. From a natural meteorological perspective it seems that the rains,
so critical for the growing season in the land of Israel, had failed to fall, presumably for several successive years. From a theological perspective, however, this famine may be explained as a judgmental act of God. According to
the covenant curses outlined in Leviticus 26 and Deuteronomy 28, if Yahweh's people would go after other gods and persist in rebelling against their
covenant LORD, he would respond not only by sending in enemies to destroy
their crops and occupy the land (as in the Book of Judges), but also by cutting
off the rains and sending famine. This consequence is specifically predicted in
Lev 26:18–20 and Deut 28:23–24.

Geographically, the story begins in Bethlehem of Judah. The irony of crisis is apparent. Bethlehem, which means "house, granary of bread," has no
food for this family. The qualifier "of Judah" distinguishes this Bethlehem
from the Zebulunite town where Ibzan lived and was buried according to Judg
12:8–10. However, it links this story geographically with the account in Judg
17:7–8 of the wandering Levite who ends up in the apostate Micah's home. In
the premonarchic period Bethlehem was an insignificant town located five
miles south of Jerusalem (cf. Mic 5:2[Hb. 5:1]).

Personally, the story involves a certain man from Bethlehem, his wife,
and their two sons. The narrator's temporary withholding of their names
invites the reader for the moment to generalize the problem of the famine to
the rest of the population. But not for long, for the author interrupts the narrative in v. 2a to identify the characters by name: Elimelech, Naomi, Mahlon,
and Chilion (*kilyōn*; pronounced in Hb. *machlōn*). Although the narrator
makes no attempt to play on the men's names, they do sound ominous if not

---

[2] Judg 2:16; 3:10.
[3] See R. Hubbard, *The Book of Ruth,* NICOT (Grand Rapids: Eerdmans, 1988), 84, for some
suggestions.
[4] So Sasson, *Ruth,* 18.

portentous. Elimelech appears to be a sentence name meaning either "My God is king" or "El is Milku,"[5] expressing the faith of the one who gave and/ or bore the name. Elimelech's departure for Moab may reflect his own doubts about the truth his name declared. Naomi is mentioned secondarily to her husband, but she will turn out to be the key character in this chapter. As the explanation in vv. 20–21 suggests, her name derives from a root, n°m, "to be pleasant." This may be an abbreviated name, missing the theophoric element and thereby suppressing the role of God.[6] The meaning of Mahlon is uncertain. If it is related to Mahlat or Mahalat, the names of Esau's and Rehoboam's wives respectively,[7] a connection with ḥālî or ḥelyâ, "jewelry, adornment," is possible.[8] It seems more likely to be derived from ḥālă. "to be sick," in which case it is related semantically to Chilion. Chilion is constructed from the root kālâ, "to be finished, come to an end," hence "frailty, mortality." Each of these names functions as a *nomen omen* ("ominous name"),[9] implicitly pointing to the intensification of the crisis about to strike Naomi. The entire family is identified ethnically as "Ephrathites." Unlike Judg 12:15 (as well as 1 Sam 1:1 and 1 Kgs 11:26), where the singular gentilic denotes membership in the tribe of Ephraim, here the term derives from a place name, Ephrathah, which seems to have represented the region around Bethlehem.[10]

In the first two verses Elimelech is clearly the focus of attention. He is the one who leaves (hālak min, lit. "to go from") Bethlehem of Judah to live for a while (gûr, "to sojourn") in the field of Moab, and he is the one who comes to (bô°, "to enter") the field of Moab and lives (hāyâ, "to be") there. The syntax of these two verses suggests that the initiative for the trip to Moab was Elimelech's and the participation of his wife and sons a secondary issue. The

---

[5] Cf. K. A. Mathews, "Elimelech," *ABD* 2.469. This is the only person in the OT with this name, but it is found in the El-Amarna letters. One letter from a king of Jerusalem dated 1365 B.C. names a ruler *i-li-mil-ku* (EA 286:36). See W. L. Moran, ed. and trans., *The Amarna Letters* (Baltimore: Johns Hopkins University Press, 1987), 326–27. It also occurs in a ninth-century inscription from Hazor (*SSI* 1.18–19). The name also resembles Abimelech, "My father is king," on which see above.

[6] Cf. Abinoam, "My [divine] father is pleasant" (e.g., Judg 4:6); Elnaam, "God is pleasant" (1 Chr 11:46), on which see J. Fowler, *Theophoric Personal Names in Ancient Hebrew: A Comparative Study*, JSOTSup 49 (Sheffield: Academic Press, 1988), 81, 351.

[7] See Gen 28:9 and 2 Chr 11:18 respectively.

[8] Cf. S. Layton, *Archaic Features of Canaanite Personal Names in the Hebrew Bible*, HSM 47 (Atlanta: Scholars Press), 215.

[9] Ibid., 216.

[10] In 4:11 Ephrathah functions as an alternate name for Bethlehem. Gen 35:16–19; 48:7 relate that Rachel died some distance from Ephrathah, i.e., Bethlehem; Mic 5:2[Hb. 5:2] identifies the town as Bethlehem Ephrathah. Ephrathah could represent a specific subarea of Bethlehem and that the term Ephrathites identifies the clan (מֶפְרָשֵׁתַה) of this area. Cf. N. Gottwald, *The Tribes of Yahweh* (Maryknoll: Orbis, 1979), 269; F. W. Bush, *Ruth, Esther*, WBC 9 (Dallas: Word, 1996), 65.

thematic links with the story of Abraham, particularly Gen 12:10,[11] reinforce this interpretation, leading the reader to expect an Abraham-like character. Naomi and the sons are presented as tagalongs.

Whereas Abraham sought relief from the famine in Egypt, Elimelech headed for Moab. His destination is identified specifically twice as *śĕdê mô'āb*, "the field of Moab."[12] Since national territory is usually referred to as the *'ereṣ*, "land," of a nation, one would have expected Elimelech to head for *'ereṣ mô'āb*, "the land of Moab," a form found elsewhere in the Old Testament.[13] Fundamentally *śādeh* refers to land as a field that has been wrested from an original wild state and brought under human occupation and cultivation. Specifically it may refer to unoccupied territory, in contrast to *môšab*, "inhabited land"; the region surrounding a city, in contrast to *'ir*, "walled town"; or a field, in contrast to *bayit*, "house."[14] Although elsewhere *śādeh* only rarely denotes a tribal or national territory,[15] in at least five instances[16] *śĕdēh mô'āb* functions as an alternate to *'ereṣ mô'āb*, "land of Moab."[17] The present author's preference for the former may have arisen from the book's focus on the fields to be harvested and Boaz's efforts to redeem the "field" of Naomi (4:3,5).[18]

The fact that Elimelech headed across the Jordan to Moab east of the Dead Sea suggests the famine was localized in the land of Israel. The narrator does not tell us how to interpret the move. Was it an act of faith or unbelief? The parallels with the account of Abraham's sojourn in Egypt in Genesis 12 suggest the latter. According to the Book of Deuteronomy, if the

---

[11] Note the identical announcements of the famine (וַיְהִי רָעָב בָּאָרֶץ), the references to departure (וַיֵּלֶךְ, "and he went," in Ruth 1:1; וַיֵּרֶד, "and he went down," in Gen 12:19), and the identical notice of the purpose in going (לָגוּר, "to sojourn"). The pattern of famine and migration occurs also in the lives of Isaac (Gen 26:1) and Jacob (Gen 41:54). For a discussion of the links see Nielsen, *Ruth: A Commentary*, OTL (Louisville: Westminster/John Knox, 1997), 40–41.

[12] The orthography of the first word is strange. Although the form recurs in vv. 6,22, it contrasts with the normal spelling, שְׂדֵה, found elsewhere in the book (2:6; 4:3). Scholarly opinions differ on the significance of this alternation, but it seems best to interpret the present form either as a dialectical variation or as an archaic variant spelling of the word. Hubbard (*Ruth*, 87) treats the form as a plural construct, based on the Ug plural form *śdm*. But this is unlikely because geographic terms are normally feminine, and the absolute form is attested in Exod 8:9; 1 Sam 22:7; etc.

[13] Deut 1:5; 28:69; Judg 11:15,18; Jer 48:24,33.

[14] For a full discussion of the term see D. I. Block, *The Foundations of National Identity: A Study in Ancient Northwest Semitic Perceptions* (Ann Arbor: University Microfilms, 1983), 327–33.

[15] "Field of Aram" (Hos 12:13), "field of Edom" (Gen 32:4; Judg 5:4), "field of the Philistines" (1 Sam 6:1; 27:7,11; cf. "land of the Philistines" in v. 1), "field of the Amalekites" (Gen 14:7). Cf. also שְׂדֵה נַחֲלַת יִשְׂרָאֵל, "field of the possession of Israel" (Judg 20:6).

[16] Gen 36:35 (= 1 Chr 1:46); Num 21:20; Deut 34:6; 1 Chr 8:8.

[17] This expression occurs in Deut 1:5; 28:69; Judg 11:15,18a,18b; Jer 48:24,33. For further discussion see Block, *Foundations*, 333–39.

[18] Thus M. A. Grisanti, "שׂד/שׂדה," *NIDOTTE* 3.1218.

people would repent,[19] Yahweh would withdraw his anger and lift the famine.[20] It seems, however, that Elimelech designed his own solution instead of calling on God for mercy and repenting of the sins that plagued the nation during the dark days of the judges. The narrator's choice of verb, *gûr*, "to sojourn," suggests that he intended to wait out the famine in the land of Moab and to return to Bethlehem when it was over. Not that this was an easy choice. The move to Moab must be interpreted in light of the general Israelite disposition toward the Moabites. That disposition seems to have been colored by five factors in their history: (1) the Moabites' contemptible origins in the incestuous relationship of Lot and his daughter (Gen 19:30–38); (2) the Moabites' resistance to Israelite passage through their territory when they came from Egypt (Numbers 22–24); (3) the Moabite women's seduction of the Israelites and the latter's subsequent punishment (Num 25:1–9); (4) Israel's constitutional exclusion of Moab from the assembly of the LORD (Deut 23:3–6); and (5) the recent oppression of the Israelites by Eglon the king of Moab (Judg 3:15–30). This combination of factors may explain the impression created by the narrator that of the Bethlehemites only Elimelech's family sought refuge from the famine in Moab.[21] They also render even more remarkable the whole-hearted acceptance of Ruth successively by Naomi, Boaz, and the people of Bethlehem.

2. Scene 2: The Nature of the Crisis (1:3–5)

³Now Elimelech, Naomi's husband, died, and she was left with her two sons. ⁴They married Moabite women, one named Orpah and the other Ruth. After they had lived there about ten years, ⁵both Mahlon and Kilion also died, and Naomi was left without her two sons and her husband.

1:3–5 How different from the dream were the experiences of this Israelite family in Moab! Figuratively speaking, having escaped *Rāʿāb,* the divine agent of famine, they walked right into the clutches of *Môt,* the even more fearful agent of death.[22] Soon after arriving in Moab, Elimelech died, leaving Naomi a widow and her sons fatherless. The narrator adds poignancy to the statement by the choice of the verb, *šāʾar (niphal),* "to be left over, to remain," which often speaks of bereavement at the death of another[23] and

---

[19] The Hb. word for repent is שׁוּב, "to turn, return," which will occur a dozen times in this chapter but never with this theological meaning.

[20] Deut 30:1–3,8–10.

[21] On the surface David's sojourning among the enemy Philistines in 1 Samuel 27 seems similar, but unlike Elimelech, David was fleeing from Saul, who sought his life.

[22] Cf. Amos 5:19. In pagan Canaanite thought *Rāʿāb* and *Môt* were viewed as divinities. Of course in the OT these notions are demythologized.

[23] Gen 7:23; 14:10; 42:38; Exod 14:28; etc. Cf. Hubbard, *Ruth,* 92.

often refers to those who have survived the wrath and judgment of God.[24] Furthermore, to be buried in an unclean foreign land was considered the ultimate punishment (Amos 7:17). Naomi's new position as the head of this household is reflected in the reversal of roles in the text; she is no longer Elimelech's wife (v. 2); he is her husband (v. 3). And the sons are no longer Elimelech's children but hers. From here on she will be the center of attention, and contrary to the expectations raised by vv. 1–2, Elimelech is out of the picture. But all is not lost. The line may still be saved, for the marriage of both sons raises the hopes of all for progeny through whom Elimelech and Naomi will live on.

The meanings of the names of the women Naomi's sons marry are unclear. Orpah is often associated with ʿōrep, "neck," from which is derived the Jewish midrashic explanation that she turned her neck/nape on her mother-in-law.[25] Today the name is commonly treated as fictitious, created to suit her role in the story.[26] Ruth (rût) is the most obscure name in the book. Syriac renders it rĕʿût, "female companion," as if from rēaʿ, "friend," but the assumed disappearance of the middle consonant (ʿayin) is unlikely. A derivation from a root rwh, "to soak, irrigate, refresh," hence "refreshment, satiation," is more likely.[27] Although it is not clear at the moment which of the sons married which woman, in 4:10 we will learn that Ruth was the wife of Mahlon.[28]

How is this marriage to Moabites to be evaluated? The narrator does not declare his own opinion, but several features of the account may be telling. First, he employs an unusual expression to announce their marriages, nāśāʾ ʾiššâ, literally "to lift/carry a woman," instead of lāqaḥ ʾiššâ, "to take a woman," the more common idiom for "to marry." Although lexicons tend to treat these expressions as virtually synonymous, closer examination of the latter reveals a phrase loaded with negative connotations. The present idiom occurs only nine times in the Old Testament.[29] As we have seen, in Judg 21:23 it speaks of marriage by abduction: with the consent of the rest of the Israelites, the Benjamites forcibly seized the dancers at Shiloh and took them

---

[24] Lev 26:36,39; Deut 4:27; 28:62; 2 Chr 34:21; Ezek 6:12; 9:8; Zech 11:9.

[25] Cf. E. F. Campbell, *Ruth: A New Translation with Introduction, Notes, and Commentary*, AB 7 (Garden City: Doubleday, 1975), 55; Sasson, *Ruth*, 20. For fuller discussion of the possibilities see Hubbard, *Ruth*, 94.

[26] Cf. M. Bal, "Heroism and Proper Names, or the Fruits of Analogy," in *Feminist Companion to Ruth*, 49–50.

[27] So also Hubbard, *Ruth*, 94, following H. Bruppacher, "Die Bedeutung des Names Ruth," *TZ* 22 (1966): 12–18. E. A. Knauf ("Ruth la Moabite," *VT* 44 [1944]: 547–48) suggests a link with the Moabite toponym *yārūt*, a *yqtl* formation of the root *rwt*, comparable to Moabite *ryt*, "offering."

[28] Later Jewish tradition thought Orpah and Ruth to be sisters. See Sasson, *Ruth*, 21.

[29] Judg 21:23; Ruth 1:4; 2 Chr 11:21; 13:21; 24:3; Ezra 9:2,12; 10:44; Neh 13:25. Cf. *HALOT*, 2.726.

as wives. It appears that because most marriages by abduction would be exogamous (outside the clan), in later usage this idiom came to be used mainly of illegitimate marriages, especially with non-Israelites, whether by kings[30] or laymen.[31] The present usage fits the latter class.[32] Second, these marriages must be interpreted in light of Mosaic prohibitions against marriage with pagans, particularly Deut 7:3–4. The Moabites are not listed with these Canaanite nations, but since they were the people of Chemosh, a foreign God, the spirit of the law would have them included. As the new head of this household, Naomi should have forestalled these marriages. Third, like Elimelech's movement to Moab in the first place, according to the covenant curses, marriage to foreigners in the land of exile was considered the judgment of God (Deut 28:32).[33] Fourth, Naomi's sons lived in their married state for ten years but without fathering any children. The barrenness of Ruth and Orpah too must be interpreted as evidence of the punitive though hidden hand of God (Deut 28:18). Indeed later it would take an act of God to enable Ruth, who had been barren, to conceive and bear a son for Boaz (4:13). Fifth, the climactic blow is struck when both Mahlon and Chilion die (1:5), leaving Naomi with no male remnant, neither husband nor children. The poignancy of the situation is highlighted by the construction of v. 5 (lit. "and even their two died—Mahlon and Chilion") and the designation of the sons as *yĕlādîm*, "children," rather than the conventional *bānîm*, "sons" (vv. 1–3,11–12). The choice of this word here creates an inclusio with *hayyeled* in 4:16 and highlights the issue of progeny as a key theme in the book.[34]

3. Scene 3: The Response to the Crisis (1:6–18)

Scene 3 describes the response of Naomi and her daughters-in-law to the intensified crisis they now face: a present without men and a future without hope. The conversation that follows demonstrates how tightly related these two issues are. The amount of space devoted to describing the response of the

---

[30] The idiom occurs three times in 2 Chronicles, twice of building of harems by a king (Rehoboam, 2 Chr 11:21; Abijah, 2 Chr 13:21) and once of the priest Jehoiadah's bigamous marriage (24:3). Since harems tended to involve foreign contract marriages, exogamy probably was involved in the first two. Whether or not this was the case with Johoiadah cannot be determined. If exogamy was not involved, however, in all three instances the men operated from positions of power, and abduction may have been involved.

[31] Ezra 9:2,12; 10:44; Neh 13:25.

[32] Bush (*Ruth*, 26) interprets this as a mark of linguistic lateness, but the evidence is not as clear as he suggests. For a detailed study of the idiom see M. D. Gow, *The Book of Ruth: Its Structure, Theme, and Purpose* (Leicester: Apollos, 1992), 186–93.

[33] So also C. P. Baylis, "Naomi Through Covenant Glasses: Concerned Mother-in-Law or Ignorant Obstacle?" (paper read to the Evangelical Theological Society, November 20, 1997): 10.

[34] So also Hubbard, *Ruth*, 96.

women to the deaths of their husbands reflects the importance of the questions raised in the narrator's mind. In contrast to the previous scene, which had been devoid of dialogue altogether, direct speech dominates here. Based on the structure of the conversation, the scene subdivides into three discreet parts, each with its own character and purpose. Of special interest are Ruth's emergence as a character of incredible courage and nobility in her own right and Naomi's growing acceptance of her daughter-in-law as a permanent part of her life. The three verbal interchanges reflect both of these themes. The first exchange (vv. 6–10) involves two parties, Naomi on the one side and Orpah and Ruth in concert on the other; in the second (vv. 11–13) the alliance of Orpah and Ruth is ended; in the third (vv. 14–18) a new alliance is created between Naomi and Ruth, and Orpah is marginalized. The shift in relationships may be illustrated as follows:

Exchange 1: Naomi + (Ruth and Orpah)

Exchange 2: Naomi + Ruth + Orpah

Exchange 3: (Naomi + Ruth) + Orpah

(7) The First Interchange (1:6–10)

⁶When she heard in Moab that the LORD had come to the aid of his people by providing food for them, Naomi and her daughters-in-law prepared to return home from there. ⁷With her two daughters-in-law she left the place where she had been living and set out on the road that would take them back to the land of Judah.

⁸Then Naomi said to her two daughters-in-law, "Go back, each of you, to your mother's home. May the LORD show kindness to you, as you have shown to your dead and to me. ⁹May the LORD grant that each of you will find rest in the home of another husband."

Then she kissed them and they wept aloud ¹⁰and said to her, "We will go back with you to your people."

1:6–10 The stage for the scene as a whole and the first conversation in particular is set by the first two verses (vv. 6–7). Although Yahweh's action is decisive in the sequence of events (v. 6b), the narrator deliberately forefronts Naomi by making her the subject of the principal clauses in vv. 6a and 7[35] and by including her daughters-in-law with explanatory additions.[36] Only at the end of v. 7 does an inclusive feminine plural verb appear (*wattēlaknâ*, "and they went").

---

[35] All the main verbs are feminine singular: "she arose," "she returned," "she heard," "she went out." The NIV's rendering of these verses totally obscures the focus of the original.

[36] After the first verb in v. 6, וַתָּקָם, "and she arose," he adds, הִיא וְכַלֹּתֶיהָ, "she and her daughters-in-law." After the first verb in v. 7, וַתֵּצֵא:, "and she went out," he adds, וּשְׁתֵּי כַלֹּתֶיהָ עִמָּהּ, "and her two daughters-in-law with her."

Even though Yahweh's action is described in a single subordinate causal clause (better rendered "for she had heard in the land of Moab that Yahweh had come to the aid of his people by giving them bread"), it is chronologically primary and breaks the clouds in Naomi's dark world. Four elements in this statement combine to paint a picture of divine grace. First, it was a gift from God that in the midst of her grief and pain Naomi was able to hear good news. Second, Naomi heard Yahweh had intervened on behalf of his people. The critical word in this clause is *pāqad*, which bears a wide range of meanings. It occurs most often in military contexts, where it means "to assemble, count, and muster" men for battle.[37] But it is also common in theological contexts, with God as the subject. In such cases it means generally "to attend to, to visit," but this visitation may be either favorable or unfavorable. In negative contexts (usually expressed by *pāqad ʿal*) it denotes "to intervene against," that is, "to punish,"[38] though always in keeping with the covenant stipulations. In positive contexts (expressed by *pāqad ʾet*, as in our text), the word means "to intervene on behalf of, to come to the aid of." The latter is certainly the case here.[39] Third, the object of the divine favor is identified as *ʿammô*, "his people," the nation of Israel. The term expresses the normal covenant relationship between deity and people.[40] The return of the rains was a signal that God had not forgotten or rejected them. Fourth, Yahweh had given his people bread.[41] The reader of Hebrew will recognize the play on the name Bethlehem. The "house of bread" is being restocked.

The narrator's eyes of faith undoubtedly recognized in this gift of food the grace of God. He does not explicitly speak about divine grace, but the absence of any hint of repentance on the part of Israel as a whole or Naomi in particular suggests that the motivation behind the lifting of the famine and the provision of food lies elsewhere. The reader will recognize here the providential hand of God, guiding natural and historical events for the fulfillment of his purpose and setting the stage for the ultimate emergence of David's ancestor.

Naomi's response to the report of good news from the homeland is decisive, expressed in three simple verbs: with her daughters-in-law[42] she *arose*,

---

[37] See above on Judg 20:15,17.

[38] E.g., Exod 20:5; 34:7; Num 14:18; Deut 5:9–10. This usage is especially common in the prophets.

[39] For a survey of the range of meanings of פָּקַד see T. F. Williams, "פָּקַד," *NIDOTTE* 3.657–63.

[40] See further Block, *Gods of the Nations*, 29–30.

[41] Note the alliteration of לָתֵת לָהֶם לָחֶם, "by giving them bread."

[42] The word for "daughter(s)-in-law," כַּלָּה/כַלֹּת, which occurs seven times in the book (1:6,7,8,22; 2:20,22; 4:15), is used elsewhere for "bride" (e.g., Cant 4:8–12; 5:1) and means something like "veiled one" (*HALOT*, 477–78). For a discussion of the word see R. Wakely, "כלה," *NIDOTTE* 2.644–52.

632

she *returned* from the territory of Moab, and she *went out* from the place
where she was staying.[43] The end of v. 7 observes the trio of women on the
road headed back to the land of Judah. The key word in the chapter as a
whole, *šûb,* "to return," occurs twice in these verses. Since Orpah and Ruth
are both Moabites, strictly speaking only Naomi is returning home. The narrator is obviously looking at these events through the eyes of the Israelite
woman. She is the one who is leaving Moab and heading home for Judah.

Having come to Moab as an alien herself, Naomi undoubtedly recognized
from the outset the problems her daughters-in-law would face if they would
accompany her back to Bethlehem. Intending to spare them her grief, at
some point along the way Naomi finally broke the silence, initiating a conversation that continues to the end of this scene. Her first speech offers a
beautiful illustration of "tough love," combining firmness with tenderness.
Conveying a sense of urgency, she begins with a double command, "Go,
return." Since they were well on the way to Judah, now the application of the
verb *šûb,* "return," to Orpah and Ruth makes sense. But she is even more
specific, encouraging her daughters-in-law to reverse their personal histories
and go back to the houses of their mothers from which her own sons had
"carried/lifted" them in the first place. In view of the common androcentric
identification of a home or a family in the Bible as a *bêt ʾāb,* "house of a
father" and the customary return of widows to the security of their "father's
house,"[44] the expression *bêt ʾēm,* "house of a mother," is striking.[45]

The phrase *bêt ʾēm* occurs elsewhere only three times. In Song 3:4; 8:2 it
refers to the bedroom of a person's mother, where lovers might find privacy.
In Gen 24:28 Rebekah is said to have run home to her mother's house to
report her conversation with Abraham's servant, who was sent to find a wife
for Isaac. In each instance the phrase "house of a mother" is found in a context involving love and marriage. Accordingly, by sending each of her daughters-in-law home to her "mother's house" Naomi is releasing them to
remarry.[46] Support for this interpretation may be found in v. 9, where Naomi

---

[43] The clause אֲשֶׁר הָיְתָה־שָּׁמָּה, "where she was staying" (NIV "where she had been living"),
points back to וַיִּהְיוּ־שָׁם, "and they stayed there" (NIV "and lived there") in v. 2.

[44] Cf. Gen 38:11; Lev 22:12; Num 30:17; Deut 22:21; Judg 19:2,3.

[45] The Alexandrinus recension of the LXX harmonizes the reading with the customary form by
reading πατρος, "father."

[46] Note that Isaac consummates his marriage in his mother's tent (Gen 24:67) and that Solomon
was supposedly crowned by his mother on his wedding day (Song 3:11). For a study of these texts
see C. M. Meyers, "Returning Home: Ruth 1.8 and the Gendering of the Book of Ruth," in *Feminist
Companion to Ruth,* 99–114. She observes that in each case (1) a woman's story is being told; (2)
a wisdom association is present; (3) women function as agents of their own destiny; (4) the agency
of women affects others; (5) the setting is domestic; and (6) marriage is involved.

prays that both of them would find security in the "house of her husband."[47]

The firmness of Naomi's double command to Orpah and Ruth to return to their mother's homes is matched by the tenderness toward them she expressed in a double blessing. She begins by praying that Yahweh would demonstrate[48] the same *hesed* toward them[49] that they have demonstrated toward her (v. 8b). This statement is remarkable for three reasons. First, she invokes the name of Yahweh when she addresses her Moabite daughters-in-law, apparently assuming that the authority of the God of Israel extended beyond the nation's borders into foreign territory, in this instance the territory of Chemosh. On the surface the prayer appears to express deep faith in Yahweh. This impression is compromised later in v. 15, where she gives tacit recognition to the gods of Moab.

Second, the blessing assumes that Yahweh is interested in the affairs of this family and can be invoked to deal favorably with these Moabites. In so doing Naomi introduces one of the key theological terms in the book. As we have noted earlier, *hesed* (NIV "kindness") cannot be translated with one English word. It is a covenant term, wrapping up in itself all the positive attributes of God: love, covenant faithfulness, mercy, grace, kindness, loyalty. In short, it refers to acts of devotion and lovingkindness that go beyond

---

[47] Like many other features of the Book of Ruth the use of בֵּית אֵם rather than בֵּית אָב reflects the gynocentricity of this chapter, if not the story as a whole. But this does not mean that the author of the book was female. Rather, as a skillful and sensitive literary artist he was able to look at and describe women's experiences from the perspective of the female characters. For excellent discussions of this issue in general and the phrase in particular see Meyers, "Returning Home," 85–114; R. Bauckham, "The Book of Ruth and the Possibility of a Feminist Canonical Hermeneutic," *Biblical Interpretation* 5 (1997): 28–45.

[48] The LXX and the Vg follow *qere* in reading a shortened form of the jussive, יַעַשׂ, in place of the MT's יַעֲשֶׂה. Cf. Gen 22:12. But of the six jussive verbs in the Aaronic blessing in Num 6:24–26 only two are shortened forms. The Massoretes recognized the anomaly of the *kethib* reading and left out the final vowel.

[49] This verse contains the first two of six apparently masculine plural forms in this chapter (עִמָּכֶם, "with you"; עֲשִׂיתֶם, "you have done") in place of expected feminine plurals. The others are לָכֶם, "to you" (1:9,11); מִכֶּם, "more than you" (1:13); שְׁתֵּיהֶם, "the two of them" (1:19), which also occurs in 4:11. Several explanations of this phenomenon are possible. (1) This represents a weakening of gender distinctions (GKC §135*o*). (2) This represents a phase in the history of Hebrew when the generic had not yet been restricted to the masculine and the separate pronoun had not yet taken full hold. (3) These forms represent relics of an earlier feminine dual suffix *-m*, resembling the masculine plural consonantally but distinguished vocalically. (4) These forms represent dialectical idiosyncrasies. The narrator's scrupulous observance of gender issues elsewhere argues against any cavalier interpretation. (Thus Campbell, *Ruth*, 65, following F. I. Andersen.) The last explanation is the most likely, though it must be recognized that the plural feminine is used for two women four times in the book: לָהֶן, "[she kissed] them" (1:9b); בֹּאֲנָה, "their coming" (1:19a,19b); עֲלֵיהֶן, "over them" (1:19).

the requirements of duty.[50] Divine acts of *ḥesed* would bring the opposite of the pain and grief these women have all been experiencing for more than a decade. Specifically it could involve the application of the covenant blessings specified in Lev 26:3–13 and Deut 28:1–14.[51]

Third, Naomi recognizes the acts of *ḥesed* that Orpah and Ruth have performed on behalf of the dead and herself in the past. With "your dead and ... me" she means her deceased husband and her two sons and herself, that is, all the Israelites in this family. Indeed in her effusive praise of her daughters-in-law she presents these Moabite women as models of grace for Yahweh himself.[52] She holds out the possibility that human kindness may be answered in kind by divine action, based of course on the assumption that Yahweh, the God of Israel, actually cares about these Moabite women. Inasmuch as they have shown kindness to the least of the Israelites, so may Yahweh show kindness to them.

Naomi's second blessing represents a corollary to the first: she invokes Yahweh to grant *(nātan)* them both security, each in the house of her own husband.[53] Like the cognate expression *mānôaḥ* in 3:1, the word for security, *mĕnûḥâ*, derives from a root *nûaḥ*, "to rest." Naomi hereby expresses concern that her daughters-in-law be spared a life of restlessness and wandering and that they find a home in which they enjoy peace, permanence, and the satisfaction of having their daily needs met. If the expression *bêt ʾēm*, "house of one's mother," in the previous verse leads the reader to expect a subversion of patricentric structures, the present reference to "the house of her man" *(bêt ʾiššāh)* reigns in any such temptation. Naomi acknowledges that in the world in which they all live security and well-being were directly dependent upon a link with some male. The death of a husband meant the loss of one's economic support base and the severing of connections to the kinship structures. Widowhood often meant inevitable alienation and destitution. Naomi knows that if she leaves, no links between her daughters-in-law and their former husbands will remain. Therefore they are advised to return to their homes and to find new husbands.[54]

With this utterance Naomi kisses her daughters-in-law farewell and all three

---

[50] Cf. K. D. Sakenfeld, *Faithfulness in Action: Loyalty in Biblical Perspective* (Philadelphia: Fortress, 1985).

[51] The link of חֶסֶד with covenant is made explicit in the hendiadic expression הַבְּרִית וְהַחֶסֶד, "the covenant and the lovingkindness," viz., "the gracious covenant," in Deut 7:9,12; 1 Kgs 8:23 = 2 Chr 6:14; Neh 1:5; 9:32; Dan 9:4.

[52] Cf. P. Trible, *God and the Rhetoric of Sexuality* (Philadelphia: Fortress, 1978), 169–70.

[53] The syntax of the petition is awkward: יִתֵּן יְהוָה לָכֶם וּמְצֶאןָ מְנוּחָה (lit.), "May Yahweh give to you and may you find security." See also a variant form of the idiom in Judg 9:29.

[54] On the state of the widow in the ancient biblical world see P. S. Hiebert, "'Whence Shall Help Come to Me?': The Biblical Widow," in *Gender and Difference in Ancient Israel*, P. L. Day, ed. (Minneapolis: Fortress, 1989), 125–41.

of them give vent to their emotions with loud cries and wailing.[55] But Naomi's daughters-in-law are not easily persuaded. On the contrary, in v. 10 they declare their determination to "return" with Naomi to her people. The statement is truly remarkable, for it demonstrates that after all the grief these two young women have shared with their mother-in-law, they are more attached to her than to their own people. They will not "return" to their mothers' houses.

(8) The Second Interchange (1:11–14)

[11]But Naomi said, "Return home, my daughters. Why would you come with me? Am I going to have any more sons, who could become your husbands? [12]Return home, my daughters; I am too old to have another husband. Even if I thought there was still hope for me—even if I had a husband tonight and then gave birth to sons— [13]would you wait until they grew up? Would you remain unmarried for them? No, my daughters. It is more bitter for me than for you, because the LORD's hand has gone out against me!"

[14]At this they wept again. Then Orpah kissed her mother-in-law good-by, but Ruth clung to her.

The second interchange involves another speech by Naomi (vv. 11–13) followed by a brief description of Ruth's and Orpah's nonverbal reaction (v. 14). This is Naomi's longest speech in the book. It divides into three parts, each introduced by an emphatic word, followed by a tender direct address of Orpah and Ruth: (1) "Return, my daughters," *šōbnā běnōtay* (v. 11); (2) "Return, my daughters," *šōbnā běnōtay* (v. 12); (3) "No, my daughters," *ʾal běnōtay* (v. 13b). Her purpose is to convince her daughters-in-law that their personal interests are best served by remaining in Moab.

NAOMI'S FIRST ARGUMENT (1:11).   **1:11**   In the first speech Naomi challenges Ruth and Orpah's perception of reality by asking two rhetorical questions. On the surface the first, "Why would you come with me?" looks as though Naomi is asking them to recite the advantages for them of casting their lot with her. But it is much more—it is actually a rebuke, which may be rephrased indicatively as "It is foolish for you to come with me; you will be much better off in your home country."[56] The second question is even more pointed (lit.): "Do I have any more sons in my 'guts' that they could become your husbands?" Some curtness is reflected in her reference to her womb by *mēʿîm*, which elsewhere refers to either a man's or a woman's intestines[57]

---

[55]וַתִּשֶּׂאנָה קוֹלָן וַתִּבְכֶּינָה, (lit.) "and they raised their voice and wept," is a hendiadic expression for "and they wept loudly." To this day loud wailing is a common feature of Near Eastern expressions of grief.

[56]On the purpose of this kind of question see R. T. Hyman, "Questions and Changing Identity in the Book of Ruth," *USQR* 39 (1984): 190.

[57]The word often denotes the male source of procreation: Gen 15:4; 2 Sam 7:12; 16:11; Isa 48:19; 2 Chr 32:21.

rather than "womb," *reḥem*, or "belly," *beṭen*. The question actually sounds silly for several reasons. First, it assumes that Naomi is capable of bearing a child even though she has been a widow for more than a decade and presently has expressed no interest in remarrying. Second, it assumes that she is the only source from which her widowed daughters-in-law might find second husbands and that if they return with her they will not socialize with other Bethlehemites. Third, it imagines that they might wait around for twenty years until the child was old enough to marry, but by which time Orpah and Ruth would be past child-bearing age. The question may sound silly, but it is deadly serious. Naomi assumes rightly that uppermost in her daughters-in-law's minds is remarriage. Their chances of satisfaction in this respect are much better if they remain at home.

But Naomi's comment raises the question of why Orpah and Ruth might even think about marrying another one of her sons. Would they do so because they are at home in this family and have confidence in the men Naomi has produced? Or does Naomi have in her mind the Israelite custom of the levirate marriage, by which the nearest unmarried relative of a man who died without progeny would marry his widow and preserve the family by fathering a child on his behalf?[58] But she expresses no interest in the preservation of the family and probably had given up on this prospect. Her declared concern is for the welfare of the two younger widows.

NAOMI'S SECOND ARGUMENT (1:12–13a). **1:12–13a** In the second phase of this speech Naomi answers her own rhetorical question. First she calls upon Orpah and Ruth to be realistic. She is too old to remarry.[59] If she was married at fifteen years of age and had her sons by twenty, and they in turn were twenty when they married, and this event occurs at least ten years later, she would now be at least fifty years of age, a senior citizen in that context and certainly past menopause. Second, in a flight of fancy she imagines[60] a more hopeful situation.[61] Even if she could marry and could bear

---

[58] The word "levirate" derives from the Latin *levir*, "brother-in-law." It has nothing to do with Levi or Levitical. See C. T. Lewis, trans., *A Latin Dictionary* (Oxford: Clarendon, 1879), 1054. For fuller discussion of the levirate marriage see below on 2:20.

[59] On the absolute comparative sense of לְאִ֔ישׁ מִהְי֣וֹת זָקַ֙נְתִּי֙, "I am too old to belong to a man," see GKC §133c.

[60] כִּ֤י אָמַ֙רְתִּי֙, "If I say" (NIV "even if I thought"), introduces a hypothetical situation. Cf. P. P. Joüon, *Ruth: Commentaire philologique et exégetique* (Rome: Pontifical Biblical Institute, 1953), 39.

[61] On תִקְוָ֔ה as an expression of "hope, positive expectation," see D. Schibler, "קוה," *NIDOTTE* 3.892–96.

sons, would her daughters-in-law wait[62] for those lads[63] to grow up and marry them? Would they, in the meantime, restrain[64] their own impulses and remain single until the boys had grown up, refusing to give themselves to a man?

NAOMI'S THIRD ARGUMENT (1:13b–14). **1:13b** In the last phase of this speech Naomi begins by answering her own question with an emphatic "No!"[65] In the following sentence she gives the reason for her rejection of this possibility. The sentence is introduced by the causal *kî* (usually "for), but the construction is awkward: *kî mar lî mĕʾōd mikken*. Literally it translates "for bitter to me much from you," which is idiomatic for either "I am much too bitter for you"[66] or "My bitterness is greater than yours." In either case, together with her last statement, "because the LORD's hand has gone out against me!" Naomi's disposition toward her lot in life is exposed. Naomi is a bitter old woman who blames God for her crisis. Naomi feels that she is the target of God's overwhelming power and wrath. The divine hand that had struck Egypt with plagues (Exod 9:3), destroyed a generation of Israelites in the desert (Deut 2:15), and punished the apostasizing nation of Israel in the land of Canaan (Judg 2:15) was now stretched out against her. The reader may not have recognized the earlier famine in Bethlehem, her family's exile in Moab, the deaths of her husband and sons, and the barrenness of her daughters-in-law as evidences of the hand of God, but Naomi is clear about the cause of her troubles.

Many readers of biblical narrative tend to idealize and idolize the human characters, but in the context Naomi's comment is troubling. The same person who had earlier implored Yahweh to be as gracious to her daughters-in-law as they had been to her and to provide them with security in the house of a husband turns around and accuses God of making her life bitter. Her comments offer no hint of human causation behind her tragedies. Instead of repenting of her own and her people's sin *(šûb)*, she accuses God of injustice toward her. Hubbard gives her the benefit of the doubt, noting that she did indeed acknowledge Yahweh's participation in her life and, since he is involved,

---

[62] The verb שָׂבַר, "to wait for," always in the *piel* stem, occurs elsewhere in Isa 38:38; Pss 104:27; 119:166; 145:15; Est 9:1. Cf. derived noun forms in Pss 119:116; 146:5. Whereas Campbell (*Ruth*, 69) argues that this is an archaic Hb. word, Bush (*Ruth*, 29) insists this is a word that entered Hebrew late under the influence of Aramaic.

[63] The first word in v. 13, הֲלָהֵן, looks like the interrogative particle attached to the suffixed preposition. But the feminine suffix is difficult, and the word probably should be read masculine. See Hubbard, *Ruth*, 111.

[64] The verb תֵּעָגֵנָה (NIV "remain unmarried") is a hapax in the OT derived from a root עגן, defectively vocalized for תֵּעָגֵנָה. In Mishnaic Hebrew and late Aramaic it means "to lock up, hinder a woman from entering into a new marriage" (*HALOT*, 785).

[65] On the negative particle אַל with a jussive verb יְהִי, "let it be," see *GBH* §160j.

[66] Cf. *GBH* §141i.

things are not out of control. He interprets this as "bitter complaint cloaked firm faith."[67] But this may be too optimistic. Except that she accuses Yahweh by name, her comments are no different from one would have expected from any ancient Near Easterner under similar circumstances. Her faith is apparently not as mature or orthodox as some would think. This conclusion is confirmed by the next verse.[68]

1:14 From the first sentence of v. 14 it seems that Naomi's speech has had no effect on anyone. The scene described in v. 9 is repeated: again the trio of women raise their voices in loud wailing. But this phase of the interchange climaxes in the second half of v. 14. Apparently impressed by Naomi's arguments, Orpah kissed her mother-in-law[69] good-bye; but Ruth remained firm and clung[70] to her. The narrator's aim in the second interchange has been achieved: Orpah and Ruth, who began as coequal daughters-in-law of Naomi, have now been distinguished. Orpah pursues the natural course; Ruth is determined to swim upstream. We can only imagine what happened to Orpah and whether Naomi's prayers for her were answered. Significantly the narrator does not criticize her. She is not presented as a negative example of unbelief; the narrator interprets her role in the narrative as a foil for Ruth. Her actions also highlight the incredible fortitude and faith of this other Moabite, qualities that will become even more evident in the final interchange.

(9) The Third Interchange (1:15–18)

[15]"Look," said Naomi, "your sister-in-law is going back to her people and her gods. Go back with her."

[16]But Ruth replied, "Don't urge me to leave you or to turn back from you. Where you go I will go, and where you stay I will stay. Your people will be my people and your God my God. [17]Where you die I will die, and there I will be buried. May the LORD deal with me, be it ever so severely, if anything but death separates you and me." [18]When Naomi realized that Ruth was determined to go with her, she stopped urging her.

1:15–18 In the third interchange the tables are turned. Naomi opens with a short statement, but it is Ruth's speech that dominates. In her statement

---

[67] Hubbard, *Ruth*, 113. Jeremiah and Job also complain that God has treated them harshly, but the contexts of their comments never contemplate the existence of any other gods, as Naomi seems to do.

[68] Cf. the ironic ambivalence in Naomi's speeches recognized by Trible, *God and the Rhetoric of Sexuality*, 170.

[69] The word for "mother-in-law," חֲמוֹתָהּ, "husband's mother," occurs nine times in the book (1:14; 2:11,18,19,23; 3:1,6[2x],17). The masculine counterpart, חָם, "father-in-law," appears twice in the story of Tamar and Judah, which also involves the fulfillment of levirate responsibilities (Gen 38:13,25). See R. H. O'Connell, "חָם," *NIDOTTE* 2.165–66.

[70] The verb דָּבַק, "to cling to," is used in Gen 2:24 of a man clinging to his wife.

Naomi draws Ruth's attention to[71] Orpah headed down the road back to Moab and encourages her to follow her sister-in-law.[72] But her interpretation of Orpah's action is remarkable. The first part is understandable, inasmuch as going home involves not only a return to the land of Moab but also to her kinfolks.[73] Her acknowledgment that Orpah has gone back to her gods does not suit an orthodox Yahwist perspective, but it makes perfect sense within the context of ancient Near Eastern perceptions of national identity. In the biblical world nations tended to be distinguishable on the bases of ethnicity (hence "her people"), territory (hence "land of Moab"), kingship (hence "Eglon king of Moab" in Judg 3:12–17), language (Moabite, Hebrew, etc.), and theology. The last element is involved here. Just as the Israelites were known as "the people of Yahweh" (cf. *'ammô*, "His people" in v. 6 above), so the Ammonites were known as the "people *['am]* of Malkam" (Jer 49:1) and the Moabites as the "people *['am]* of Chemosh" (Num 21:29; Jer 48:46). This does not mean that the Moabites, for example, worshiped only one god, Chemosh—they actually worshiped many gods. But being henotheists rather than monotheists, they venerated one god in particular because he was considered their divine patron. He was the god to whom they looked for protection, prosperity, and internal order. Since the Old Testament uses the plural form *'ĕlōhîm* for both singular deity and a plurality of gods,[74] it is impossible to know whether Naomi perceived Orpah to have returned to Chemosh or the gods of Moab in general.[75] In either case her comment is troubling. Her theological perceptions at this point seem no more orthodox than those of many characters in the Book of Judges. If she represents the highest level of faith in Israel, it is no wonder Yahweh had sent a famine on the land.

Hearing Naomi's command to return to Moab for the fourth time and watching her sister-in-law head down the road, Ruth stood between a rock and a hard place. Would she choose her own people the Moabites and their god

---

[71] This is the intention of the particle הִנֵּה, "behold," on which see A. Berlin, *Poetics and Interpretation of Biblcial Narrative* (Sheffield: Almond, 1983), 91–95.

[72] The technical word for "sister-in-law," יְבָמָה, occurs elsewhere only in the Mosaic prescription regarding levirate marriage in Deut 25:5–9, where it denotes the widow of one's deceased brother. In Gen 38:8 and Deut 25:5,7 the *piel* form of the verb from the same root, יָבַם, denotes "to perform the duty of a deceased brother-in-law of a widow by marrying her." But Gen 38:8–9 identifies the widow simply as אֵשֶׁת אָח, "wife of a brother." The Akk. cognate *yabamum*, "brother-in-law," is attested in a seventeenth century B.C. West Semitic text. Cf. Sasson, *Ruth*, 29.

[73] In contrast to the fundamentally political term גּוֹי, "nation," עַם, "people" is a warm relational term. The word derives from a root עָמַם, "relative on my father's side." For analyses of the word see Block, *Foundations of National Identity*, 12–83; id., "Nations/Nationality," *NIDOTTE* 4.966–72; id., "Nations," *ISBE*, rev. ed., 3.492–96.

[74] Except for the change in suffix, the form used by Naomi is the same as that used by Ruth in the next verse when she declares her commitment to Yahweh. On Chemosh the divine patron of Moab see the commentary above on Judg 11:24.

[75] Cf. the discussion by A. G. Hunter, "How Many Gods Had Ruth?" *SJT* 34 (1981): 427–36.

Chemosh with whom she was no doubt familiar, or would she cast her lot with her mother-in-law and her alien kinsmen, and their God Yahweh, whom she knew only through the grid of Naomi's imperfect faith? The first act reaches its climax as she declares her answer in vv. 16–17.

The first words we hear from Ruth's lips alone[76] are among the most memorable in all of Scripture. Few utterances in the Bible match her speech for sheer poetic beauty, and the extraordinary courage and spirituality it expresses. Broadly speaking the speech breaks down into three major parts: a plea [in the imperative] for Naomi not to try to change Ruth's mind, a threefold declaration of commitment to Naomi, and a final oath, invoking Yahweh as a witness to this pledge. Many commentators have admired the rhythm and symmetry of Ruth's immortal words.[77] Structurally the speech breaks down into five two-line couplets whose flow and form may be illustrated as follows:

A *al-tipgĕʿî-bî lĕʿozbēk*   Do not pressure me to leave you,
   lāšûb mēʾahǎrāyik   To turn back from behind you.

B *kî ʾel-ʾǎšer tēlĕkî ʾēlēk*   For where you go I will go,
   ûbaʾǎšer tālînî ʾālîn   And where you lodge I will lodge.

C *ʿammēk ʿammî*   Your people my people,
   wēʾlōhayik ʾĕlōhāy   Your God my God.

B′ *baʾǎšer tāmûtî ʾāmût*   Where you die I will die,
   wĕšām ʾeqqābēr   And there I shall be buried.

A′ *kōh yaʿǎśeh yhwh lî wĕkōh yōsîp*   Thus may Yahweh do to me and
                                        thus may he add,
   kî hammāwet yaprîd bênî ûbênēk   Surely nothing but death will
                                        separate me and you.

The three central pairs of lines are framed by A, an introductory command (imperative) to the rhetorical audience (Naomi) and A′, a concluding challenge (optative) to the [divine] witness (the LORD) to this statement. The second and fourth pairs of lines (B and B′) correspond in content (note their locative emphasis) and form (verbal sentences in contrast to the nominal sentences in C). Together B and B′ constitute a merism, a pair of opposites (life and death) brought together to declare, "Everywhere you will be I will be." Based on the location and the cryptic staccato style of the nominal statements

---

[76] She had spoken earlier in v. 10, but her utterance was in unison with Orpah.

[77] See P. Humbert, "Art et leçon de l'histoire de Ruth," *RTP* 26 (1938): 257–86; W. Prinsloo, "The Function of Ruth in the Book of Ruth," *OTWSA* 21 (1978): 114–15; Bush, *Ruth*, 74; J. de Waard and E. A. Nida, *A Translator's Handbook on the Book of Ruth*, 2d ed. (New York: United Bible Societies, 1992), 17.

in the middle, these obviously represent the fulcrum on which the rest of the speech balances.

Just as Naomi's speeches increase in intensity, so Ruth's first statement intensifies her joint response to Naomi with Orpah in v. 10. Her disposition is more hurt than resentful as she begs her mother-in-law to stop pressuring[78] her to leave Naomi. To return to her own land, people, and gods might be her most natural response, but it would mean abandoning her mother-in-law. The use of the strong verb ʿāzab, "to forsake, abandon," suggests that even at this early stage Ruth felt obligated for Naomi's sake to accompany her.

Whereas the first couplet had been cast in the form of a negative imperative, the second and fourth are cast as positive declarations. Far from abandoning Naomi, Ruth is determined to accompany her for the rest of her life and beyond. With the merismic pair of expressions, "where you go I will go," and "where you lodge I will lodge" (NIV, "where you stay I will stay"),[79] she emphasizes that just as she had shared Naomi's grief in the past, so she will share her every experience in the future. Even in death she will accompany her. The reference to burial with Naomi indicates she considers herself a part of Naomi's family and is determined to be buried in the same family tomb.

But the center couplet is the most impressive of all. Using a mere four words she answers Naomi's final plea to join Orpah in returning to the people and the god of Moab. With radical self-sacrifice she abandons every base of security that any person, let alone a poor widow, in that cultural context would have clung to: her native homeland, her own people, even her own gods. Like any Near Easterner of her time, she realized that if she would commit herself to Naomi and go home with her, she must also commit herself to Naomi's people (Israel) and to Naomi's God (Yahweh). Although some would interpret Ruth's declaration as a sign of conversion, it is better viewed as an affirmation of a transfer of membership from the people of Moab to Israel and of allegiance from Chemosh to Yahweh. How much she knew about the implications of claiming Yahweh as one's God we do not know. She had indeed been observing Naomi for more than a decade, but from what we have seen of her in this chapter she hardly qualified to be a missionary of orthodox Yahwistic faith and theology.[80] But this is a start, a noble beginning.[81] The observer may only pray that when she arrives in Bethlehem she will find individuals who

---

[78] Usually the verb פָּגַע means "to confront, assault, touch." The present sense of "put pressure on" (confront with words) occurs elsewhere in Jer 7:16; 27:18; Job 21:15.

[79] The verb לִין, translated by the NIV here as "stay," means "to spend the night."

[80] Similarly W. Rudolph, *Das Buch Ruth, Das Hohe Lied, Die Klagelieder*, KT 17 (Gütersloh: Gerd Mohn, 1962), 43.

[81] Ruth's responses in subsequent chapters will give clear evidence that she has been wholeheartedly converted to Yahweh, but it is premature to conclude this from her comments here. At issue is her commitment to Naomi.

will model true Yahwistic piety more perfectly.

Ruth's concluding oath gives this entire speech the flavor of a formal pledge of commitment. The form of this asseveration is typical of Israelite self-imprecatory oaths, with the statement of effect preceding a conditional statement of cause.[82] Variations of the oath appear elsewhere in the Old Testament twelve times.[83] As in Ruth's statement, in these oaths the verb of imprecation ("may X do") tends to be in the indicative, even though the oath carries an optative sense.[84] Furthermore, in none is the invoked calamity actually named. Presumably the kōh, "Thus," in kōh ya‘ăśeh yhwh lî, "Thus may Yahweh do ..." stood for the widely acknowledged series of disasters (death, plague, fire, famine, sword) that Yahweh could inflict on any and all who would renege on their commitments. Perhaps an individualized version of the covenant curses found in Leviticus 26 and Deuteronomy 28 was involved. Alternatively, "Thus may Yahweh do to me" may have been accompanied by a nonverbal gesture such as the speaker passing his/her hand across the throat, or in our context, pointing our index finger to our temple.[85] In any case, Ruth expresses the common ancient Near Eastern conviction that divine witnesses function as guarantors of promises and pledges human beings make under oath. She also shares the common conviction that if she is to move with Naomi to Israel, where Yahweh is the divine patron, it is the deity of the land to whom she must appeal to guarantee her fidelity to this pledge.

The addition of wĕkōh yōsîp, literally "and may he add," (NIV "be it ever so severely") is also typical of oaths. The idiom strengthens the force of the oath by invoking the deity to impose any curse the deity may choose (presumably beyond the standard list of calamities) if the speaker should renege on the commitment declared in the pledge.

The last line of the oath consists of a conditional clause introduced by the conjunction kî, "if." Although the rendering of the NIV accords with prevailing understanding of the following statement,[86] based on a comparison with other occurrences of the oath formula and the syntax of the present statement, the REB's "Nothing but death will part me from you" represents a more likely

---

[82] The order is the reverse of most casuistic laws that begin with a conditional clause and end with a statement of the consequences: "If ... then ..." For numerous examples see Exodus 21–23.

[83] Cf. GKC §149d; *GBH* §165a.

[84] See also the discussion of the maledictive use of the jussive in *IBHS* §334.3.c.

[85] Cf. *GBH* §165jN.

[86] Note the slight variations in the standard translations:

NIV   If anything but death separates you and me.
NASB   If *anything but* death parts you and me.
NRSV   If even death parts me from you.
NJB   If anything but death should part me from you.
JPSV   If anything but death parts me from you.
NLT   If I allow anything but death to separate us.

interpretation. The Old Testament attests three ways of introducing the apodasis (following conditional clause) of an oath formula: (1) with *ʾim* for negative statements;[87] (2) with *ʾim lōʾ* for positive statements;[88] (3) with *kî*, meaning "Surely, indeed," before positive statements.[89] Since our text clearly follows this last pattern, it should be interpreted accordingly, "Death [alone] will separate[90] me from you."[91] The interpretation "nothing but death" is driven by the context, specifically the emphatic position of *hammawet*, "the death," before the verb.[92] On first blush this interpretation seems to contradict Ruth's earlier statement that she will die and be buried with Naomi, but the emphasis in that pledge is her lifelong commitment to her mother-in-law.

As noted earlier, Ruth's pledge of devotion to Naomi ranks among the loftiest expressions of commitment in Scripture and in our own time frequently provides the basis for wedding meditations. But this application of the passage is odd, especially when it is recognized that this pledge is made by one woman to another, specifically a daughter-in-law to her mother-in-law. Accordingly, one might justify using this text for weddings if one adopted the biblical understanding of marriage as a union of families and, placing the words in the mouths of both bride and groom, extended Ruth's statement to include the commitment of each to the entire family of in-laws. But given the modern individualistic approach to marriage (the commitment of two individuals independent of and in isolation from their families of origin), this application of the text is not to be expected. This text could be legitimately used in marital situations if one assumes that Ruth's speech follows a standardized pattern of pledges of commitment. This pledge involves four significant elements: (1) an appeal to resist all pressures to break the relationship; (2) a commitment to the other person for life; (3) the adoption of the other person's family and faith as one's own and the abandonment of prior allegiances; and (4) an awareness that God is a witness to all the promises we make. Since every one of these elements should be a part of any Christian marriage, this speech does indeed illustrate the nature and depth of total commitment.

Ruth's eloquent declaration of devotion to Naomi leaves the older woman speechless. No doubt she was impressed by Ruth's rhetoric, but it was the

---

[87] E.g., 2 Kgs 6:31, עָלָיו ... רֹאשׁ יַעֲמֹד אִם, "If his head remains … on him" (i.e., surely it will not remain). Similarly 1 Sam 3:17; 25:22; 1 Kgs 20:10; 2 Kgs 6:31.

[88] E.g., 2 Sam 19:13[Hb. 14] לְפָנַי תִהְיֶה צָבָא שַׂר־לֹא אִם, "If you will not be commander of the army before me" (i.e., you will certainly be).

[89] E.g., 1 Sam 14:44, תָּמוּת מוֹת כִּי, "You shall surely die!" Similarly 1 Sam 20:13; 2 Sam 3:9; 1 Kgs 2:23; 19:2.

[90] This use of the *hiphil* of פָּרַד occurs also in Deut 32:8; 2 Kgs 2:11; Prov 16:28; 17:9.

[91] So also Bush, *Ruth*, 83, contra Hubbard, *Ruth*, 119–20.

[92] Cf. Rudolph, *Das Buch Ruth*, 41; Joüon, *Ruth*, 42.

firmness of her resolve and the determination[93] in her voice that convinced the older woman to back off and to stop trying to convince her[94] to return to Moab. Subsequent episodes will prove that she really meant what she said; Ruth was casting her lot with her mother-in-law "till death do them part."[95]

4. Scene 4: The Interpretation of the Crisis (1:19–21)

[19]So the two women went on until they came to Bethlehem. When they arrived in Bethlehem, the whole town was stirred because of them, and the women exclaimed, "Can this be Naomi?"

[20]"Don't call me Naomi," she told them. "Call me Mara, because the Almighty has made my life very bitter. [21]I went away full, but the LORD has brought me back empty. Why call me Naomi? The LORD has afflicted me; the Almighty has brought misfortune upon me."

1:19–21 The narrator has left no clues where the foregoing interchange between Naomi and her daughters-in-law had occurred, whether east or west of the Jordan. Wherever it happened, the remainder of the journey to Bethlehem is summarized in one short statement in v. 19a, and the reader's attention is quickly drawn to a new scene at a new location with new characters. Like the previous episode, this scene is cast primarily as dialogue, initiated by the townsfolk at the sight of Naomi but dominated by Naomi, who claims the final word in Act 1. From a dramatic and literary perspective, the women function as a chorus that appears near the ends of the first and last acts (cf. 4:14–15).

One wonders if either Ruth or Naomi was prepared for the reception they would receive when they arrived in Bethlehem. The narrator observes that it caused a stir throughout the whole town *(kol hāʿîr)*. The nature of the response is captured effectively with a single word, *wattēhōm,*[96] rendered by the NIV "was stirred." The interpretation of the word is complicated by uncertainty regarding its root. The problem arises from the fact that Hebrew con-

---

[93] מִתְאַמֶּצֶת appears elsewhere only in 1 Kgs 12:18 (= 2 Chr 10:18) and 2 Chr 13:7. Because these contexts call for a different understanding, we are left to interpret the word solely on the basis of contextual needs. The NIV's "she was determined" suits the present context, though it loses something of the force of the participle, which expresses duration, persistence.

[94] וַתֶּחְדַּל לְדַבֵּר אֵלֶיהָ, lit., "she ceased to speak to her."

[95] Some interpret Naomi's silence "as resentment, irritation, frustration, unease. Ruth the Moabite is to her an inconvenience, a menace even." Thus D. N. Fewell and D. M. Gunn, "'A Son Is Born to Naomi!': Literary Allusions and Interpretation in the Book of Ruth," *JSOT* 40 (1988): 104. Elsewhere these same authors write, "With sinking feeling and sudden weariness, Naomi knew that she would be stuck with her"; id., *Compromising Redemption: Relating Characters in the Book of Ruth* (Louisville: Westminster/John Knox, 1990), 28.

[96] The feminine verb is required by Hb.'s regular treatment of geographical and topographical entities as feminine.

tains several different roots that, like English "murmur," are onomatopoetic derivations from *hm: hāmâ, hāmam, hôm/hûm, niham.* These words bear a wide range of meanings, "to hum, groan, be agitated, panic, be in an uproar, make a noise."[97] In 1 Sam 4:5 and 1 Kgs 1:45 the same form describes the excited noise with which the arrival of the ark and the coronation of Solomon respectively were greeted. In this context one may translate "hummed," or "buzzed." No doubt Naomi's relatives had heard of the grief she had experienced since she and her husband had left the town and headed for Moab more than a decade ago. So one can imagine their excitement when she suddenly shows up unannounced.

The surprise and incredulity of the townspeople at the "appearance" of Naomi is reflected in the question the women[98] ask each other when they see her: "Is this Naomi?" Our use of the ambivalent word "appearance" is deliberate. On the one hand, the fact of her epiphany, that she should show up at all, was remarkable enough. On the other hand, the years of grief and deprivation have surely taken their toll on Naomi's form and visage. This one who had left Bethlehem as *Naomi,* "the pleasant one," a robust woman in her prime, had returned as a haggard and destitute old woman.

This fact is not lost to Naomi. Overhearing the question that is circulating among the women, she interrupts the "buzz" with a pointed retort. Giving public vent to her years of frustration and pain, she demands a new name. She may have left Bethlehem as *Naomi,* but she has returned as a different person; from now on they must call her *Mārā².* With a final *aleph* the form of the name is unusual,[99] but its derivation from *mārar,* "to be bitter,"[100] is not to be doubted. The depth of Naomi's bitterness is reflected in her outburst in vv. 20b–21. The exclamation involves four accusations leveled against God, who is referred to by title or name four times according to the following A B B A pattern: Shadday, Yahweh, Yahweh, Shadday.

Shadday is not a name but a title for God (he has only one name, Yahweh!), an abbreviation of ancient appellation, El Shadday. The expression is commonly derived from *ṯdw/y,* which in Ugaritic meant "mountain," hence,

---

[97] See A. Baumann, "הָמָה *hāmâ,* " *TDOT* 3.414–18; H.-P. Müller, "הָמַם, *hmm,*" ibid., 419–22; H. van Rooy, "הוּם," *NIDOTTE* 3.1018–20; W. R. Domeris, "הָמָה," ibid., 1041–43; O'Connell, "הָמַם," ibid., 1046–48. The present form is pointed either as a *qal waw* consecutive imperfect from הוּם or a *niphal* of הָמַם. Cf. GKC §67t.

[98] Unlike the verb "buzzed," no subject for וַתֹּאמַרְנָה, "and they said," is specified. The NIV's insertion of "women" is appropriate in light of the feminine plural form of the verb and the analogy of 4:14, which specifies "women" (נָשִׁים) as the subject of the same verb.

[99] The final *aleph* reflects the influence of Aramaic, which commonly used this letter (rather than *hē* as in Hb.) to denote a final long *a* sound. Cf. *GBH* §89k. Sasson's association of the name with מָרָא, "to fatten," or מָרַר, "to strengthen," (*Ruth,* 32–33) is gratuitous.

[100] On which see G. V. Smith, "מרר," *NIDOTTE* 2.1110–12.

"the one of the mountain."[101] Admittedly, however, its etymology remains obscure. A clue to the significance if not the meaning of *šdy* may be found in the early seventh century B.C. Balaam texts from *Deir ʿAllā*. Observing that *šdyn* is used interchangeably with *ʾlhyn*, "gods," to denote the group of gods that make up the heavenly council, J. A. Hackett proposes that *šadday* represents an epithet of El, as chief of the heavenly council. The association of the group with mountains is a natural development since the council normally met on top of a mountain.[102] As overseer of the heavenly council, Shadday commands all the angelic hosts through whom his providential care and disciplinary judgment of humans is exercised. Whether or not Naomi's perceptions of God were this sophisticated, in her mind it is by his title Shadday that Yahweh has made her the target of his arrows of misfortune.

The treatment that Shadday has dealt Naomi is described with two expressions. First, he has made her life extremely bitter: *hēmar lî mĕʾōd*. The verb *hēmar*, "to cause bitterness," is a causative *(hiphil)* form of *mārar*, from which is derived the adjective *mar*, "bitter" (v. 13), and the name *Mārāʾ*, which Naomi claimed in the previous sentence. Second, at the end of v. 21 she accuses Shadday of afflicting her. The verb *hēraʿ*, "to inflict calamity/disaster," derives from a root *rʿ*, "to be evil, bad."[103] The cognate noun *rāʿâ*, "calamity, disaster," is often used of calamities sent by God in fulfillment of the covenant curses.[104] Accordingly, Naomi does not hereby ascribe moral evil to God but the disastrous, grievous misfortune that she has experienced.

Between these two accusations against Shadday, Naomi inserts a double volley against Yahweh. The first charge is constructed in chiastic contrastive parallelism:

ʾănî	*mĕlēʾâ*	*hālaktî*	I	full	went away
wĕrêqām	*hĕšîbanî*	*yhwh*	but empty	brought me back	Yahweh

By having the subjects of the sentences occupy the extremities, Naomi pits herself against Yahweh. But she also highlights the fullness-emptiness contrast by placing these words before the verbs in each case. The careful reader will notice that both statements are double-edged. On the one hand, if "fulness" is

---

[101] Ugarit is modern Ras Shamra on the Syrian coast. On the etymology of *šdy* see F. M. Cross, *Canaanite Myth and Hebrew Epic: Essays in the History and Religion of Israel* (Cambridge: Harvard University Press, 1973), 52–60. Cf. M. Weippert, *THAT* 2.873–81. E. A. Knauf ("Shadday," *DDD*, 1416–23) prefers "god of the wilderness."

[102] J. A. Hackett, *The Balaam Text from Deir ʿAllā*, HSM 31 (Chico, Cal.: Scholars Press), 87. The NIV's "Almighty" derives from the Septuagintal rendering of the name as παντοκράτωρ via the Vg *omnipotens*.

[103] The same root is involved in "the calamitous spirit" referred to in Judg 9:23. On the root see D. W. Baker, "רעע," *NIDOTTE* 3.1154–58.

[104] E.g., Ezek 6:10; 7:5; 14:22.

understood in terms of food and satisfied stomachs, the first statement is patently false. Otherwise, why had they left the land of Israel in the first place? On the other hand, if "fulness" is understood in terms of family and progeny, the statement is true. When she left, she was secure in her husband, and her future was secured by her two sons. But now she has neither, and this is what evokes the second statement.

The second statement may also be interpreted two ways. The NIV offers a plausible translation, but the way the sentence is constructed sounds like the LORD is responsible for emptying her life and then bringing her back. But line 2 does not actually accuse the LORD of emptying her life. Strictly interpreted, Naomi says simply "empty the LORD brought her back." Accordingly, and if viewed in isolation from v. 20b, divine intervention is limited to her return, which, in light of v. 6, may even be interpreted positively.

Even if the reader may be inclined to give Naomi the benefit of the doubt, v. 21a dashes a positive interpretation. Repeating the question why the townsfolk should continue to call her Naomi, "Pleasantness," she places the blame for her present destitution squarely on Yahweh: he has testified against her. By itself ʿānâ is a neutral term meaning "to answer," but followed by the preposition bĕ it bears a pronounced juridical sense.[105] As Job laments, when a mere mortal is confronted by God in a court of law, a person is at his mercy. This had been Naomi's experience. For whatever reason, Yahweh had called her to account and declared her guilty. However, when it comes to describing the implementation of the sentence, the covenant name for God is replaced by the numinous title Shadday.[106]

With this final outburst by Naomi the curtain falls on Act 1. The narrative leaves the reader with ambivalent feelings toward the woman. On the one hand, she had responded to the report of Yahweh's favor upon Bethlehem by setting out for home (v. 6), and then wishing upon her daughters-in-law the blessing of Yahweh the God of Israel (vv. 8–9). On the other hand, she seems to have conceded to pagan worldviews by acknowledging that Orpah had returned to her gods (v. 15). Naomi may have come back home in faith, but hers is a flawed faith. Unable to see human causation in Israel's famine and in her own trials, the woman the neighbors greet is a bitter old woman. She does indeed ascribe sovereignty to God, but this is a sovereignty without grace, an omnipotent power without compassion, a judicial will without mercy. In a patricentric world where a woman's security is found in her husband and her

---

[105] See Exod 20:16; Num 35:30; Deut 5:20. C. J. Collins ("Ambiguity and Theology in Ruth 1:21 and 2:20," *Presbyterion* 19 [1993]: 97–102) interprets "he has testified against me" as "he has brought some secret sin to light."

[106] Cf. the description of Shadday in Ezek 1:22–25 and Ezekiel's reaction to the vision in v. 28. The name appears more than thirty times in the Book of Job, in which Job, like Naomi, feels unjustly afflicted by Shadday. See, e.g., 5:17; 6:4.

future is determined by her sons, she stands alone—except, of course, for this Moabite who has chosen to cast her lot with her.

When the curtain falls, Naomi's bitter outburst in vv. 20–21 overwhelms and overshadows the eloquent pledge of commitment to Naomi by Ruth (vv. 16–18). Viewed side by side, there is no doubt that the young foreign woman cuts a more impressively noble figure. In the end the reader/observer is repulsed by Naomi but drawn to her Moabite daughter-in-law. But if the final scene leaves questions in the reader's mind about the older woman, it does the same regarding Ruth. The plural verbs in v. 19 still include her in the action, but once the conversation with the women of Bethlehem begins, she is out of the picture. So one is left wondering what Ruth must have made of the towns-folks' reception of Naomi and Naomi's final impassioned accusation of the God to whom she had just declared allegiance. One also wonders if Naomi's emptiness can be filled and if Ruth might still have a role to play. Surely the dramatist/narrator would not have introduced her in such glowing terms only to have her drop out of the play.

II. ACT 2: THE RAY OF HOPE FOR THE ROYAL LINE (1:22–2:23)
   1. Scene 1: The New Setting (1:22–2:1)
   2. Scene 2: The Initiative of Ruth (2:2–3)
   3. Scene 3: The Grace of Boaz (2:4–16)
      (1) The First Interchange (2:4–7)
      (2) The Second Interchange (2:8–14)
         Boaz's First Speech (2:8–9)
         Ruth's First Response (2:10)
         Boaz's Second Speech (2:11–12)
         Ruth's Second Response (2:13)
         Boaz's Third Speech (2:14)
      (3) The Third Interchange (2:15–16)
   4. Scene 4: The Results (2:17–23)

II. ACT 2: THE RAY OF HOPE FOR THE ROYAL LINE (1:22–2:23)

In the overall plot of the Book of Ruth, 1:22 is transitional. Most commentators treat the verse as the conclusion to the first major segment of the book. If one reads the story as a drama, however, it is more appropriately recognized as a summary flashback, preparing the reader/audience for the second Act. Together with 2:1 this verse helps set the stage for Act 2. After the brief introduction this act consists of three scenes, arranged in an A B A pattern with dialogue involving Naomi and Ruth at home (A) sandwiching a series of interchanges out in the field (B).

1. Scene I: The New Setting (1:22–2:1)

²²So Naomi returned from Moab accompanied by Ruth the Moabitess, her daughter-in-law, arriving in Bethlehem as the barley harvest was beginning.

¹Now Naomi had a relative on her husband's side, from the clan of Elimelech, a man of standing, whose name was Boaz.

1:22–2:1 The last verse of chap. 1 sets the stage for the second act by summarizing the critical information. The way the verse opens, one is led to believe that Naomi will continue to be the principal character; she is the one who returned (*šûb*, singular). As in 1:7, Ruth is named as a tagalong (lit.):

649

"and Ruth ... with her" *(wĕrût ... immāh)*. This impression is reinforced by the beginning of 2:1, which declares Boaz's significance by virtue of his relationship to her. After 2:2 she will disappear from the scene for the major portion of chap. 2, resurfacing only at the end to have the last word.

The syntax of v. 22a suggests that Ruth will remain a secondary character, but for readers/hearers who have missed or forgotten the first Act, the narrator hints at her coming prominence by offering three critical pieces of information about her. First, she is a Moabite woman. This alien status underlies much of the tension that will surface in chap. 2. As a Moabite in an Israelite world she has little reason to expect acceptance with the townsfolk.[1] Second, she is Naomi's daughter-in-law.[2] Third, she accompanied Naomi, who returned from Moab. By associating her first appearance with a "return,"the narrator piques the reader's interest and creates anticipation for the coming scenes. Literally Naomi is the one who has returned [empty], but Ruth will be the one whose life is filled first in every case (with food, a husband, a son).

The narrator also reminds the reader of the place and the time of Act 2: in Bethlehem at the beginning of the barley harvest. The timing is critical and providential, for it means that Naomi and Ruth arrive in "the house of bread" just when the grain for bread is ready to be cut,[3] that is, in late April or early March by our calendars. Since barley was the first crop to be harvested each year, the timing of their arrival meant that Naomi and Ruth could get settled at a time when food would be relatively plentiful and that they were around to lay up stores of each crop for the dry season.

In 2:1 the narrator introduces a new character. The circumstantial clause[4] by which he is presented provides four important details about him.[5] First, he is a "relative" of Naomi's husband. The meaning of the word *môda*[6] is clarified by its only occurrence elsewhere, Prov 7:4, where it appears opposite *ʾāḥôt*, "sister." The familial interpretation of the expression is con-

---

[1] On the Moabite problem see above.

[2] On this word (כַּלָּה) see comments on 1:6.

[3] Hb. קְצִיר שְׂעֹרִים. The identical expression [minus the vowel letters], קְצֹר שְׂעָרִם, occurs in the tenth century B.C. "Gezer Calendar," which lists the months of the year according to agricultural activity: (1) vintage and olive harvest; (2) sowing; (3) spring pasture; (4) flax pulling; (5) barley harvest; (6) wheat harvest and measuring; (7) pruning; (8) summer fruit. See J. C. L. Gibson, *Syrian Semitic Inscriptions,* Vol. I, Hebrew and Moabite Inscriptions (Oxford: Clarendon, 1971), 1.1–2 [hereafter *SSI*]; *ANET,* 320.

[4] On the *waw*-initial signaling a shift in scene or referring to new participants see *IBHS* § 39.2.3c.

[5] The details are presented in the reverse of logical order. Under normal circumstances we would have learned successively his name, his family, his status, and his significance for the story.

[6] Reading מוֹדַע with *qere* rather than *kethib,* מֹידָע . If *kethib* is to be followed, it should be vocalized as a *pual* participle from יָדַע, "to know, hence "a close acquaintance, friend." Cf. 2 Kgs 10:11; Pss 31:12; 55:14; 88:9,19; Job 19:14.

firmed by the way in which Boaz's relationship to Naomi is described elsewhere. In 2:20 he is *qārôb lānû*, "our relative." Three times he is referred to as a *gōʾēl*, "kinsman redeemer," to Naomi and Ruth (2:20; 3:9,12).[7] The NIV rightly recognizes that the narrator's point is not that he is an acquaintance of Naomi but a relative of her husband. This small detail raises the interest and hopes of the readers, especially those who are familiar with Israelite family law and custom.

Second, this character is an *ʾîš gibbôr ḥayil*. This expression is quite ambiguous and capable of a wide range of interpretations. By using this phrase, the author invites the reader to compare Boaz with Gideon, who is characterized similarly in Judg 6:12. In that context it means "mighty man of valor, noble warrior, military hero."[8] But the reader will discover that Boaz is nothing like Gideon. He never fights in a battle or leads an army; he never performs any heroic feats. In this context the phrase may bear two other meanings. In its simplest sense the expression means "man of substance, wealth," hence a man of standing in the community. Boaz is no ordinary, run-of-the-mill Israelite.[9] This will be confirmed in the following episode, where he is presented as a man with land and servants. On the other hand, as in Prov 31:10, which employs the feminine equivalent, the name can also mean "noble with respect to character," a genuine *Mensch*. In this respect in the end his actions must be deemed heroic, for he rescues a family and a name from the curse of oblivion. By this interpretation the narrator offers a proleptic impression of the man.

Third, he was from the clan of Elimelech. This phrase clarifies the first, "a relative on her husband's side." The word for "clan," *mišpāḥâ*, denotes a subdivision of a tribe.[10]

Fourth, his name was Boaz.[11] The root *bʿz* occurs nowhere else in the Old Testament. Some have proposed a link with Arabic *baġz*, "to be vigorous, strong of spirit,"[12] but this has been largely rejected. The Septuagint's transliteration of the name as *Booz* may suggest a hypocoristic (abbreviated) version of *bĕʾōz yhwh*, "in the strength of Yahweh [I will rejoice/trust]." The meaning

---

[7] On the meaning of this expression see below on 2:20.

[8] Cf. also Josh 6:2–3; 2 Sam 17:8; 2 Kgs 24:16; etc.

[9] Thus J. M. Sasson, *Ruth: A New Translation with a Philological Commentary and a Formalist-Folklorist Interpretation*, 2d ed. (Sheffield: Academic Press, 1989), 40.

[10] Perceived as an ethnic unity, a large extended family, Israel's social structure broke down as follows: people, descendants of one ancestor, Israel (עַם, בְּנֵי יִשְׂרָאֵל), tribe (שֵׁבֶט/מַטֶּה), clan (מִשְׁפָּחָה), family, "father's house" (אָב בֵּית). For further discussion see the introduction to Judges.

[11] The circumstantial construction, וּשְׁמוֹ בֹּעַז, "and his name was Boaz," introduces his name almost as an afterthought.

[12] W. Rudolph, *Das Buch Ruth, Das Hohe Lied, Die Klagelieder*, KT 17 (Gutersloh: Gerd Hohn, 1962), 48.

of the name remains obscure, and since it plays no part in the narrative, we may drop the matter.[13]

2. Scene 2: The Initiative of Ruth (2:2–3)

2And Ruth the Moabitess said to Naomi, "Let me go to the fields and pick up the leftover grain behind anyone in whose eyes I find favor."
Naomi said to her, "Go ahead, my daughter." 3So she went out and began to glean in the fields behind the harvesters. As it turned out, she found herself working in a field belonging to Boaz, who was from the clan of Elimelech.

2:2–3 In this short scene the roles reverse. For the first time Ruth is portrayed as the primary actor, and Naomi's role is that of "reactor." The scene consists of two phases, the first transpiring in the house where Naomi and Ruth are staying and the second on the way to the field. As in previous episodes, the former phase is taken up almost entirely with dialogue. But this time Ruth seizes the initiative. The narrator's identification of her again as "the Moabitess" reflects the extraordinary nature of her action. She, an alien in a foreign land, is determined to make something of her life.

Ruth approaches her mother-in-law and requests permission to go out and get some food for them by gleaning in the fields. Although recent commentators have tended to understand the construction *ʾēkĕlâ-nāʾ*, "Let me go," as an expression of firm resolve,[14] the NIV and most other translations rightly interpret her speech as a polite request. Her intended actions are defined by the verb *liqqēṭ (piel)*, "to glean, to gather scraps." This activity is to be distinguished from ordinary harvesting (*qāṣar*, cf. *qāṣîr* in 1:22), inasmuch as it involves picking up ears (*šibbŏlîm*) of grain that the harvesters have inadvertently dropped or left standing. The Mosaic law displayed particular compassion for the alien, the orphan, and the widow by prescribing that harvesters deliberately leave the grain in the corners of their fields for these economically vulnerable classes and not go back to gather (*liqqēṭ*) ears of grain they might have dropped (Lev 19:9,10; 23:22; Deut 24:19). As a Moabite and a widow Ruth qualified to glean on two counts. But for these same two reasons she could not count on the goodwill of the locals, hence her concern to glean behind someone who would look upon her with favor.

The expression "find favor in the eyes of" (*māṣāʾ ḥēn bĕʿênayim*) is at home in the court, where a subject would acknowledge his/her dependence upon and need for mercy at the hands of the king. The favor of a superior can-

---

[13] For further discussion see Sasson, *Ruth*, 41; Campbell, *Ruth*, 90–91.

[14] Thus JPSV, T. O. Lambdin, *Introduction to Biblical Hebrew* (New York: Scribners, 1971), 170–71; *IBHS* §34.5.1. But then the narrator should have used the imperfect rather than cohortative, which implies subordination.

not be taken for granted. Whether Ruth is thinking of the harvesters or the owner of the land is not clear. In either case she seems to be aware that the right to glean was frequently denied to the destitute; she was dependent upon the mercy *(hēn)* of the men in the field. This word provides the key to interpreting the next scene.

Naomi's affirmative response is described in two short but tender words, "Go ahead, my daughter." The bitterness of her tone at the end of Act 1 seems to have subsided by now, and v. 3a finds her daughter-in-law headed for the fields to glean. The reader wonders if Ruth will find a gracious harvest host. Before the narrator describes how the issue will be resolved, however, in v. 3b he adds one of the most significant interpretive comments in the book (lit.): "and her chance chanced upon the allotted portion of the field of Boaz" *(wayyiqer miqrehā ḥelqat haśśādeh lĕbōʿāz).*[15] The meaning of *qārâ* (a variant form of *qārāʾ*, "to meet, encounter") is illuminated by 1 Sam 6:9, where it expresses the Philistine notion of chance: if the cows do not carry the Ark of the Covenant to Beth-Shemesh, they will know that their calamities are not attributable to the hand of God; they have happened by chance.[16] In this context the narrator draws attention to Ruth's chance arrival at a field of Boaz even more pointedly with the redundant phrase "her chance chanced upon," which in modern idiom would be rendered "by a stroke of luck."

Though many will balk at this interpretation, this must be recognized as one of the key statements in the book. Now it is true that to the orthodox Israelite there was no such thing as chance. An Israelite proverb declares: "The lot is cast into the lap, but its every decision is from the LORD" (Prov 16:33). If the Lord even determines how the dice falls, how can the narrator speak so explicitly of chance? Perhaps he is looking at the event through Ruth's eyes. As one who has only recently transferred her spiritual allegiance to the God of Israel, like the Philistines in 1 Sam 6:9 she may well have retained pagan perspectives concerning fate and fortune. This is better interpreted, however, as a deliberate rhetorical device on the part of the narrator. By excessively attributing Ruth's good fortune to chance, he forces the reader to sit up and take notice, to ask questions concerning the significance of everything that is transpiring. The statement is ironical; its purpose is to undermine purely rational explanations for human experiences and to refine the reader's understanding of providence.[17] In reality he is screaming, "See the hand of God at work here!" The same hand that had sent the famine (1:1) and later provided food

[15] Nowhere else in the OT does the word מִקְרֶהָ, "her chance," have a suffix. On the use of the *waw*-consecutive construction to denote concomitant time see *GBH* §118k.

[16] Cf. also 1 Sam 20:26. The present expression, קָרָה מִקְרֶה קָרָה, occurs elsewhere only in Eccl 2:14–15, where it means "fate befalls/happens."

[17] On the nature and purpose of irony in literature see J. A. Cuddon, *A Dictionary of Literary Terms and Literary Theory*, 3d ed. (Oxford: Blackwell, 1991), 457–62.

(1:6) is the hand that had brought Naomi and Ruth to Bethlehem precisely at the beginning of the harvest (1:22) and has now guided Ruth to that portion of the field belonging specifically to Boaz.[18]

Ruth's "chance" arrival at the field of Boaz is providential on two accounts. First, as the following episode will demonstrate, Boaz was a gracious man in whose eyes Ruth would find favor (v. 10). Second, he was from the same clan as Ruth's deceased father-in-law Elimelech. In order for the divine agenda to be fulfilled, both elements had to be present. In long-range terms the royal line of David would not be (pre)served if the man at whose field Ruth arrived was gracious but from outside the clan; he could not have functioned as a "kinsman redeemer," preserving the name and family of the deceased. Conversely, the line would not have been served if Ruth had indeed found the field of her deceased husband's (and father-in-law's) kinsman, but he turned out to be a rogue, shooing off aliens, orphans, and widows. In the providence of God, the man she meets is indeed a gracious near kinsman.

3. Scene 3: The Grace of Boaz (2:4–16)

The major portion of this act takes place in the field of the gracious man to whom the hand of God had led Ruth. Like the heart of Act 1 (1:6–18), this scene is dominated by dialogue. The conversations break down into three episodes, again arranged in an A B A pattern.

A Boaz and the harvesters (vv. 4–7)
  B Boaz and Ruth (vv. 8–14)
A′ Boaz and the harvesters (vv. 15–16)

(1) The First Interchange (2:4–7)

4Just then Boaz arrived from Bethlehem and greeted the harvesters, "The LORD be with you!"

"The LORD bless you!" they called back.

5Boaz asked the foreman of his harvesters, "Whose young woman is that?"

6The foreman replied, "She is the Moabitess who came back from Moab with Naomi. 7She said, 'Please let me glean and gather among the sheaves behind the harvesters.' She went into the field and has worked steadily from morning till now, except for a short rest in the shelter."

2:4–7 The opening *hinnēh*, "Behold," of v. 4 not only shifts the reader's attention from Ruth to Boaz, who has arrived at the field where Ruth is, but

---

[18] This is the sense of חֶלְקַת הַשָּׂדֶה לְבֹעַז, "the portion of the field, the one belonging to Boaz." The word חֵלֶק, "portion," harps back to the apportionment of the land of Israel under Joshua, and highlights the land as Yahweh's property, which he has "rented out" to Israel.

also expresses wonder at his arrival and its timing.[19] In the providence of God Ruth got there on time for Boaz. The first words we hear at the field are pleasant and cheerful words of greeting. Appropriately, Boaz, the landowner, initiates the conversation, but he does so with two simple but profound words, *yhwh ʿimmākem,* "May the LORD be with you!"[20] From the outset we sense that Boaz has provided a positive work environment for his people. In this regard he serves as a model of true covenant *ḥesed* for all who supervise others in their work; his speech from beginning to end is characterized by grace. And with a boss like this it is no wonder that Boaz's workers respond with a blessing of their own: *yĕbārekĕkā yhwh,* "May the LORD bless you!" Unlike Boaz's greeting, this blessing follows the traditional pattern (cf. Num 6:24).

It seems not to have taken Boaz long to notice a stranger in his field, for he turns to (lit.) "his young man" to find out what he can about her. The narrator's use of *naʿar,* "young man," rather than *ʿebed,* the normal designation for "servant," may be intentional to reflect the difference in age between Boaz and the man (cf. 3:10). Qualified with *hanniṣṣāb ʿal haqqôṣĕrîm,* "who was stationed over the harvesters," he was obviously "the foreman" or supervisor.[21]

On first sight the question Boaz poses to his attendant seems odd. Instead of an expected "Who is this young woman?" he asks (lit.), "To whom does this woman belong?" *(lĕmî hanna ʿărâ hazzōʾt).* He assumes that Ruth, obviously a stranger, would not be independent; she must belong to someone or be engaged to some landowner like himself, though not necessarily as a slave. But the question could also mean "Whose daughter or wife is she?" or "To which clan or tribe does she belong?"[22] In any case he knows she is out of place among his workers and in his field. For the reader, however, there is more. The question refocuses the attention on Ruth and indirectly draws attention to the line of Elimelech, which gives her identity in this context. For the first time Ruth is a spectacle among Israelites. Again Boaz's recognition

---

[19] Cf. Bush's rendering (*Ruth,* 113), "Wouldn't you know it!" or "Of course!" It is unclear how much time separated Ruth's and Boaz's arrivals. Sasson (*Ruth,* 46) thinks they arrived "within seconds of each other." J. de Waard and E. A. Nida (*A Translator's Handbook on the Book of Ruth,* 2d ed. [New York: UBS, 1992], 27) suggest Boaz came several hours later.

[20] Unlike Judg 6:12, the context requires this nominal clause be interpreted optatively rather than indicatively. Here the idiom functions as both a greeting and a blessing.

[21] Although the word נַעַר "young man," originally referred primarily to a person's age, here and in the following narrative it bears the sense of "servant." A similar use of the word is found in Gen 18:7; 22:3,5,9; and the feminine equivalent, in Exod 22:5 (the princess of Egypt's attendants). In the Ugaritic texts from a century or two before the events of this book *nʿr* denotes (1) an overseer or supervisor; (2) a class of palace personnel; (3) military personnel. For a discussion of the word see J. McDonald, "The Status and Role of the *naʿar* in Israelite Society," *JNES* 35 (1976): 147–70; V. Hamilton, "נַעַר," *NIDOTTE* 3.124–27.

[22] Cf. Sasson, *Ruth,* 46, "Where does she fit in?"

of her as "the young woman" suggests she is considerably younger than he. It also raises expectations in the mind of the reader.

The servant's answer to Boaz's question repeats information the narrator had offered at the beginning of this act (1:22): she is a Moabite woman, the one who "returned/came back" *(šûb)* from the land of Moab with Naomi. Although the supervisor obviously knows who Naomi is, he provides no hint that he knows Ruth's name. But he has answered Boaz's question: she belongs to Naomi. His addition of "young woman" again raises the reader's hopes (lit., "a young woman, a Moabitess, is she").[23]

Then the supervisor reports an earlier conversation he had had with Ruth. She had asked him whether she could glean[24] among the sheaves behind the harvesters. As the NIV and most other versions translate the text, the question is extraordinary if not a contradiction in terms. If *liqqēṭ* means "to glean," why would Ruth request permission to glean behind the harvesters among the *ʿŏmārîm*, which some interpret as "small heaps of grain."[25] Normally a "gleaner" gathered the "gleanings" *(leqeṭ)*, that is, the remnants of harvest, either uncut corners of the field or stalks of grain inadvertently dropped by the harvesters (Lev 19:9; 23:22). By the NIV's interpretation she is brashly asking either to pick up grain among the harvesters in the midst of the field, perhaps even taking ears of grain from the heaps of cut grain, or to take her place among them as a harvester. On the other hand, if the preposition before *ʿŏmārîm* is interpreted as "in" or "into" instead of "among," and noun is understood as "bundles,"[26] the request makes perfect sense. Then the clause *wĕʾāsaptî boʿŏmārîm* serves to define *liqqēṭ*: "to glean" means "to gather in bundles" behind the harvesters the *leqeṭ* they have missed.

But what then is to be made of the next line, literally "and she came and stood from then the morning and until now" *(wattābôʾ wattaʿămôd mēʾāz habbōqer wĕʿad-ʿattâ)?*[27] The first verb is easy, but what is the meaning of *wattaʿămôd?* Usually the verb means "to stand," but this creates a contradiction: Why would she ask permission to come in[to the field] and then simply stand around. Many maintain that the supervisor hesitated to give her permission either because he was offended by her request or he lacked

---

[23] The construction of this verbless clause of classification, הִיא מוֹאֲבִיָּה נַעֲרָה, compares with אָנֹכִי מִצְרִי נַעַר, "I am a young Egyptian," in 1 Sam 30:13.

[24] Again the cohortative form should be interpreted as a polite request. Cf. v. 2.

[25] *HALOT*, 849. The word occurs elsewhere in v. 15; Lev 23:10–12,15; Deut 24:19; Job 24:10. A *piel* denominative verb meaning "to cut ears of corn" is found in Ps 129:7. The container used to measure the volume of dry cereal, the omer (עֹמֶר), one-tenth of an ephah, derives from the same root. See Exod 16:16–36.

[26] Roughly equivalent to צְבָתִים, "handfuls" (NIV "bundles") in v. 16.

[27] D. Lys ("Résidence ou repos? Notule sur Ruth ii 7," *VT* 21 [1971]: 497–99) summarizes nineteen different ways in which the sentence had been interpreted by 1971!

the authority to do so.[28] The NIV offers a "persistive" sense to the word: Ruth has been on her feet [working] without stopping to rest,"[29] but this interpretation of *ʿāmad* is rightfully criticized by many as odd. A better solution is to recognize that this verb, which normally means "to stand," is capable of meaning "to remain, stay."[30] In Exod 9:28 it means the opposite of *šālaḥ*, "to send away"; in Deut 5:31 and 2 Kgs 15:20 it serves as the opposite of *šûb*, "to return."[31] Accordingly in this context the supervisor means to tell Boaz that he did not send Ruth away; nor did she "turn back" to find another field or to return to Naomi. "She came and she has remained here" is his way of indicating that he gave her permission to glean and she accepted his invitation.[32] In fact she has been working from the moment he approved *(mēʾāz,* "from then" or more loosely "since"), that is, early morning *(habbōqer)* until now, that is the arrival of Boaz.[33]

But the interpretive problems continue in the rest of the verse. There is no consensus on the meaning of the last clause *(zeh šibtāh habbayit mēʿāṭ)*, unquestionably the most difficult line in the book. The line translates literally as "This (masculine)[34] her sitting/dwelling the house a little," but this makes no sense. Indeed the text is so difficult that Campbell does not even translate it.[35] Given the NIV's rendering of the previous line, "except for a short rest in the shelter" makes sense in English,[36] but it is far removed from the Hebrew. This reading of *šibtāh*, "her sitting," is based on the LXX, "she has not rested in the field,"[37] which assumes a root *šābat*, "to stop," that is, "to rest." Hub-

---

[28] Sasson (*Ruth*, 48) comments: "Ruth had come with a request that could not be fulfilled by a mere overseer. All that he could do was to ask her to step aside and wait until the 'boss' arrived. In this way Ruth was assured of meeting Boaz, since the latter could hardly fail to notice her as she stood by." Cf. Campbell, *Ruth*, 95–96; Hubbard, *Ruth*, 149–50.

[29] Similarly JPSV, "She has been on her feet ever since she came this morning." Also REB, NRSV, Rudolph, *Ruth*, 45–46.

[30] Thus JB; Bush, *Ruth*, 118; E. A. Martens, "עמד," *NIDOTTE* 3.432.

[31] Cf. also Deut 10:10; 2 Kgs 6:31; Est 7:7; Dan 10:17. The word is also capable of meaning "to abide, to continue." For references see BDB, 764, 3c; *HALOT*, 841, 3c.

[32] Similarly Bush, *Ruth*, 118.

[33] But note the opposite interpretation by M. Carasik, "Ruth 2,7: Why the Overseer Was Embarrassed," *ZAW* 107 (1995): 493–94. Based on Boaz's response to Ruth (rather than to the overseer) in the succeeding verses, Carasik argues that Ruth was actually leaving the field when Boaz arrived. Rather than politely granting her permission to glean, Ruth is the victim of sexual harassment, and the supervisor is embarrassed before Boaz about it. Accordingly, the present sequence of words represents "a deliberate device to depict confused and apologetic speech because of an incident of sexual harassment." These words represent some lame explanation like "This fellow ... she's just going home for a bit."

[34] The antecedent must be "the field."

[35] Campbell opines "that a hundred conjectures about a badly disrupted text are all more likely to be wrong than any one of them absolutely right!" (*Ruth*, 96).

[36] Similarly NRSV, REB, JB. Cf. JPSV, "She has rested but little in the hut."

[37] οὐ κατέπαυσεν ἐν τῷ ἀγρῷ

bard's "this field has been her residence" for the first part is not much better, though "the house [in town] has meant little to her"[38] is a gallant attempt at the last phrase. Bush's "she has stopped only a moment" follows the LXX in reading *šābĕtâ* for *šibtāh* and dropping *habbayit,* "the house." In our estimation the text defies explanation, and we are left with admitting that any explanation, including the NIV's reading, is a guess.[39]

(2) The Second Interchange (2:8–14)

⁸So Boaz said to Ruth, "My daughter, listen to me. Don't go and glean in another field and don't go away from here. Stay here with my servant girls. ⁹Watch the field where the men are harvesting, and follow along after the girls. I have told the men not to touch you. And whenever you are thirsty, go and get a drink from the water jars the men have filled."

¹⁰At this, she bowed down with her face to the ground. She exclaimed, "Why have I found such favor in your eyes that you notice me—a foreigner?"

¹¹Boaz replied, "I've been told all about what you have done for your mother-in-law since the death of your husband—how you left your father and mother and your homeland and came to live with a people you did not know before. ¹²May the LORD repay you for what you have done. May you be richly rewarded by the LORD, the God of Israel, under whose wings you have come to take refuge."

¹³"May I continue to find favor in your eyes, my lord," she said. "You have given me comfort and have spoken kindly to your servant—though I do not have the standing of one of your servant girls."

¹⁴At mealtime Boaz said to her, "Come over here. Have some bread and dip it in the wine vinegar."

When she sat down with the harvesters, he offered her some roasted grain. She ate all she wanted and had some left over.

The bulk of this scene is taken up with the dialogue between Boaz and Ruth. However, this is not one continuous conversation. The reference to "mealtime" in v. 14 suggests a temporal break between vv. 13 and 14. Presumably after the initial encounter (vv. 8–13) Ruth had gone back out to glean, and when it was time to eat he called her in from the field (v. 14). In the first part the speakers alternate: Boaz, Ruth, Boaz, Ruth, Boaz. In the second only Boaz speaks. The reader will also recognize a pattern in the lengths of the respective speeches. In keeping with their social positions, Boaz takes the initiative, and his first two speeches are rather lengthy discourses. On the other hand, as an alien, a young woman, and a field worker, Ruth's responses are short and to the point. The function of these two con-

---

[38] Hubbard, *Ruth,* 151.

[39] J. A. Loader suggests the last four words contain two nominal sentences, both of which had זֹאת, "This," as the subject: "This is where she stays; this is her home in a sense" ("Ruth 2:7—An Old Crux," *Journal for Semitics* 4 [1992]: 151–59).

versations in the overall flow of the book is to give the reader a clear view of the character of Boaz, and to recount the first stage in his relationship with Ruth. From the first time Boaz opens his mouth until the last words he utters (4:9–10), his tone exudes compassion, grace, and generosity. In the man who speaks to this Moabite field worker biblical *ḥesed* becomes flesh and dwells among humankind.

BOAZ'S FIRST SPEECH (2:8–9). **2:8–9** Whatever the meaning of the field supervisor's comment in v. 7, when he had said his piece Boaz turned his attention to Ruth. He breaks the ice by addressing her directly (lit.), "Have you not heard, my daughter" *(hălô³ šāmaʿat bittî)*, which in effect means "Listen carefully, my daughter.[40] His address of Ruth as "my daughter" is remarkable not only because it is reminiscent of how Naomi perceived Ruth (1:11,12; 2:2), but also because of Boaz's intention to break down the barriers that naturally separate her from him. The expression is not patronizing but reflects the age difference between these two persons, and it arises out of the genuine sense of responsibility that Boaz feels for Ruth. Despite the fact that she is a Moabite, and he knows it, like a loving father he will offer this foreigner his protection and his resources.

The formal part of the speech consists of four basic statements. First, Ruth is not to go and glean in any other field; she has no need to leave at all (v. 8b).[41] Second, Ruth is to attach herself to Boaz's regular female servants.[42] Like the previous piece of advice, this point is made repetitiously. The NIV's rendering of the phrase *dābaq ʿim*, "to stick with," in v. 8c (and vv. 21,23) as "to stay with" is too weak. The verb is the same as had been used earlier in 1:14 of Ruth "clinging" to Naomi. In v. 10a Boaz explains specifically what he means. Ruth is to keep her eyes on[43] which fields Boaz's people are harvesting,[44] and she is to follow them. Third, Ruth is not to worry about harassment from the male workers *(nĕʿārîm)* because Boaz is commanding them not to bother her. Normally the verb *nāgaʿ* means "to touch," but in this case it functions more generally for "to strike,

---

[40] Thus the NIV and virtually all English translations. On the use of the negative to express strong affirmation see GKC *§150e* and Hubbard, *Ruth*, 154.

[41] The statement is emphatically redundant. The phrase מִזֶּה תַעֲבוּרִי לֹא וְגַם, "and also do not pass over from here," means "do not cross the boundaries into another field."

[42] The NIV rightly renders נַעֲרוֹת, lit. "young girls," as "servant girls." This is the feminine plural of the masculine singular form used for the field supervisor in v. 6 and the masculine plural (נְעָרִים) in v. 9. In v. 4 קֹצְרִים had been used of all the "harvesters" without respect to gender.

[43] בַּשָּׂדֶה עֵינַיִךְ, "let your eyes be on the field," is a subject-predicate verbless clause constructed just like עִמָּכֶם יהוה, "May the LORD be with you," in v. 4.

[44] The masculine form of the verb יִקְצֹרוּן assumes all the harvesters, without respect to gender.

harass, take advantage of, mistreat."[45] Contemporary readers will be struck by how modern this comment sounds. Boaz is hereby instituting the first anti-sexual-harassment policy in the workplace recorded in the Bible. Fourth, Ruth may drink freely of the water that is provided for Boaz's regular field workers. Presumably at the beginning of each day, as the servants *(hanně'ārîm)* left town for the fields they would stop to "draw" *(šā'ab)* water from a well or cistern, perhaps by the gate of Bethlehem (2 Sam 23:16), and carry it with them in containers *(kēlîm)* to the plot where they were harvesting. In a cultural context in which normally foreigners would draw for Israelites, and women would draw for men (Gen 24:10–20), Boaz's authorization of Ruth to drink from water his men had drawn is indeed extraordinary.

RUTH'S FIRST RESPONSE (2:10). **2:10** Overwhelmed by Boaz's generosity, Ruth (lit.) "fell on her face and worshiped him" (the NIV reverses the two clauses and translates the second as a prepositional phrase, "she bowed down with her face to the ground"). This verse illustrates the biblical understanding of worship. The Hebrew word for worship, *hištaḥăwâ*, occurs only here in the Book of Ruth.[46] As the first clause, "and she fell on her face" *(wattippōl 'al-pānêhā)* explains, fundamentally *hištaḥăwâ* denotes the physical gesture of prostration, that is, falling to one's knees and bowing with face/nose to the ground[47] before royalty or deity. But the gesture was also performed in less significant contexts as a secular greeting, mark of respect, or expression of gratitude. Unless the gesture was hypocritical, in every case the socially inferior would bow down before the superior (not vice versa), in recognition of the latter's authority and honor and as an external sign of the inner spirit.

Ruth's physical gesture of submission and gratitude was accompanied by a verbal expression of amazement that Boaz should have been so gracious

---

[45] On the surface אֵת־הַנְּעָרִים לְבִלְתִּי נָגְעֵךְ צִוִּיתִי הֲלוֹא looks like a negative question, "Have I not commanded the young men not to touch you?" But the first word should be interpreted as an emphatic particle, hence, "Surely I am commanding ..." On this use of הֲלוֹא see M. L. Brown, "Is It Not? Or Indeed!: *HL* in Northwest Semitic," *Maarav* 4 (1987): 201–19. The NIV and most English translations render the perfect verb צִוִּיתִי literally in the past tense, but this is an example of the perfect "used for an action which in fact belongs to the future, but which is represented as being performed at the very moment of utterance." Thus *BHS* §112g.

[46] The LXX uses προσκυνέω, "to fall down and worship, to do reverence to, etc." (Gen 18:2; 27:29, etc.). חוה occurs four times in Judges: 2:12,17,19; 7:15. For further discussion on the form and meaning of the word see the commentary on Judg 2:12. In addition to the bibliography cited there see M. Gruber, *Aspects of Nonverbal Communication in the Ancient Near East* (Rome: Pontifical Biblical Institute, 1980), 187–99, 303–10; T. E. Fretheim, "חוה, *NIDOTTE* 2.42–44; H. D. Preuss, " חוהhwh; השתחוה, *hishtachăvāh,*" *TDOT* 4.248–56.

[47] See Gen 19:1; 1 Sam 25:23,41; cf. 1 Kgs 18:42.

to her and even taken notice of her (*lĕhakkîrēnî*, "to notice me").[48] After all, she is a foreigner! The addition of the circumstantial verbless clause (lit.), "Now I am a foreigner" *(wĕʾānōkî nokriyyâ),* creates an effective wordplay after *lĕhakkîrēnî.* Both words, *lĕhakkîrēnî* and *nokriyyâ,* derive from the root *nkr,* which must have meant "to be strange, unknown."[49] By a strange quirk of linguistic development, another form of the verb (the *hiphil* stem) means the virtual opposite, "to investigate [what is unknown], to recognize, to take note of."[50] Here the last-cited definition applies. Even though we do not know whether Boaz even knew Ruth's name at this point,[51] he acknowledged her. But there is more than one form of acknowledgment. The foreman had noticed her, and it was taken for granted that other men in the fields would take notice of her, as a potential victim of abuse—hence Boaz's proscription on touching her. But Boaz had dignified this destitute widow from a foreign land and treated her as a significant person, on par socially with his hired and presumably Israelite field workers. Ruth, who is obviously extremely self-conscious about her alien status, cannot believe Boaz's indifference to the fact that she is a Moabite.

BOAZ'S SECOND SPEECH (2:11–12). **2:11–12** Boaz continues to dignify Ruth in his answer to her question. He begins by explaining why he has shown her such favor: he has heard all about her.[52] Although his foreman had not identified Ruth by name, as soon as he had identified her by status (a Moabitess) and affiliation (the daughter-in-law of Naomi) the lights went on. So this is the woman everyone in Bethlehem was talking about! The reports that he has heard have emphasized two details about her in particular: her extraordinary kindness to her mother-in-law and her extraordinary courage in accompanying her back. Her kindness is referred to simply as (lit.) "all that you have done for your mother-in-law" *(kol ʾăšer ʿāśît ʾet-hămôtĕkā).* Later these actions will be characterized as *ḥesed*

---

[48] The *lamedh* + infinitive construction לְהַכִּירֵנִי, "to notice me," is to be interpreted consequentially or modally, i.e., Ruth is noticed as a result of finding favor with Boaz, *or* Ruth's being noticed is the expression of finding favor. The assumed subject for the infinitive is provided by the suffix of בְּעֵינֶיךָ, "in *your* eyes."

[49] The root נכר, which is unattested in the *qal,* is widely attested in the Semitic languages, appearing as נכרא in Old Aramaic (*DNWSI,* 732) and *nakrum,* "enemy" (*AHw,* 723). Cf. the Akk verb *nakāru,* "to be indifferent, hostile" (*Ahw* 718). Cf. *HALOT,* 699. R. Martin-Achard ("נכר *nēkār* Fremde,' *THAT* 2.66–68) suggests the *niphal* "to disguise oneself" and *piel* "to deface, make strange" are denominative verbs derived from the noun נֵכָרִי.

[50] Cf. Martin-Achard, ibid., 67. On the possibility of two separate roots see B. Lang, "נכר *nkr,*" *TWAT* 5.454–63.

[51] Neither the field supervisor nor Boaz ever mention her name in this chapter.

[52] Note the emphatic expression of scope by means of the *hophal* infinitive absolute and perfect of the same root in הֻגֵּד הֻגַּד לִי. The clause translates literally as "being reported it was reported to me" but idiomatically as "it has been fully reported to me." On this emphatic construction see *IBHS* §35.3.1–2.

(3:1), but for the moment no designation is given.

Boaz goes on to explain that what has particularly impressed him in the reports is her treatment of Naomi after the death of her husband. With her declarations in 1:8–9 and 12–13 Naomi had released both Ruth and Orpah of all legal and moral obligation toward her. Orpah's response was natural and rational. She accepted the release Naomi offered and returned to that which was familiar and secure: her own land, her own people, and her own gods. By contrast, Ruth's response was radical and irrational. Preferring the unknown world of her mother-in-law, like Abraham centuries before (Gen 12:1–4), she abandoned (ʿāzab, NIV, "left") her own father and mother[53] and her native land[54] and cast her lot with a people (ʾam) whom she had not previously known. As the daughter-in-law of Naomi, she had learned to know one specific Israelite and will certainly have heard about Naomi's people, but the expression here means "to have firsthand experience with." Like Abraham, she had left the security of the familiar (family and land) and committed herself to the unknown. Nothing is said here of leaving her gods and committing herself to Yahweh, the God of Israel (cf. 1:16).

From this answer Boaz leads Ruth to believe that his generosity was simply his response to her acts of kindness toward her mother-in-law. He leaves her no hint that this was such an important issue to him because Naomi was his relative or that he is repaying her for her kindness to a member of his family. Although Boaz's explanation makes perfect sense, the reader suspects that this is an incomplete answer to Ruth's question: "Why have I found favor in your eyes?" Indeed several additional answers could be given. First, Boaz has been kind to Ruth because he is fundamentally a good man. The narrator had introduced him as a noble character in 2:1. As a genuine member of the community of faith, one who embodies the standards of covenant faithfulness, he spontaneously utters words of encouragement and naturally performs deeds of kindness (ḥesed) and would have treated any destitute gleaner this way. Second, in Boaz's response the reader must recognize the providence of God. In v. 2 Ruth had expressed the wish to Naomi that she might glean behind someone in whose eyes she might find favor. Although it was not expressed as a prayer, Yahweh had heard her wish. Boaz is kind to Ruth because Yahweh has prepared his heart for her!

Evidence of both Boaz's nobility and the work of God in his heart is provided by v. 12. Not satisfied with answering Ruth's question or content with

---

[53] The expression "to abandon father and mother" occurs elsewhere only in Gen 2:24. The verb עָזַב, "to abandon, forsake," is the opposite of דָּבַק, "to cling to."

[54] The choice of מוֹלֶדֶת, "place of birth/relatives," is significant on two counts. First, being derived from יָלַד, "to give birth," it raises issues of genealogy and progeny (to be answered later). Second, as an abbreviation of אֶרֶץ מוֹלֶדֶת, "land of one's birth/relatives," the word provides a specific link between Ruth's and Abraham's migrations (cf. Gen 11:28; 24:7; 31:13).

his own generosity, he invokes Yahweh to intervene on her behalf as well. The blessing breaks down into three parts, First, he prays that Yahweh would repay Ruth for her actions. The verb for "repay," *šillēm*, is derived from the same root as *šālôm*, "peace, wholeness." This use of the word is based on the assumption of a universe governed by order. For every action there must be an equal reciprocal action. In legal and economic contexts the verb form used here (the *piel*) means "to compensate, replace with an equivalent, repay." But the idiom is also used in theological situations, recognizing that in principle Yahweh maintains order by repaying people according to their deeds.[55] In general this involves punishment for sin,[56] but for Israel it involved specifically retribution for violating the covenant standards.[57] Yet biblical writers also know of Yahweh repaying people for good deeds.[58] The present case illustrates the principle enunciated in Prov 19:17: "He who is kind to the poor lends to the LORD, and he will reward him for what he has done." By her acts of kindness to Naomi, Ruth has indebted not only her mother-in-law but also Yahweh. Thus Boaz prays that Yahweh will repay her for her work.[59]

The second clause of this blessing concretizes the image by focusing on the wages (lit., "and may your wages be full ...") and specifying that the deity who has been indebted by Ruth's kindness is indeed the God of Israel. The word for wages, *maśkōret*, occurs elsewhere only in Gen 29:15 and 31:7,41, where it refers to the wages Laban owed Jacob. Here the word is modified by *šēlēmâ*, "complete, full." The nearer identification of Yahweh as "the God of Israel" is extremely significant in this instance. Ruth is a Moabite. Because of her deeds of kindness to Naomi, an Israelite, she, an outsider, had obligated the God of Israel to repayment. As the last line of v. 12 indicates, however, by transferring her spiritual allegiance from the gods of Moab to Yahweh the God of Israel, Ruth was also claiming Yahweh as her divine patron and protector.

To express this notion Boaz introduces one of the most beautiful pictures of divine care in all of Scripture. He imagines Yahweh as a mother bird who offers her wings *(kānāp)* for the protection of her defenseless young.[60] In perceiving God as a bird Boaz draws on an image that was common throughout the ancient Near East.[61] He speaks of Ruth's experience as "coming to seek

---

[55] In general, 2 Sam 3:39; Job 34:11; Pss 28:4; 31:24; 62:12; Jer 25:14; cf. Prov 24:12; Jer 17:10.

[56] Isa 59;18; 66:6; Jer 16:18; 50:29; 51:24,56; Ps 94:2.

[57] Deut 7:10; 23:21[Hb. 22] (vow); 32:41; Isa 65:6

[58] 1 Sam 24:20; Prov 13:21; 25:22.

[59] פֹּעַל, "action, effort," is a poetic synonym for מַעֲשֶׂה, "work."

[60] Cf. Deut 32:11; Isa 31:5; Matt 23:37.

[61] Cf. O. Keel, *The Symbolism of the Biblical World*, trans. T. Hallett (New York: Seabury, 1978), 190–92, etc.

refuge/asylum under his wings."[62] Although Boaz is probably thinking primarily of the day when Ruth transferred her allegiance from Chemosh, the god of the Moabites, to Yahweh, the God of Israel, her actions this morning represent a specific application of her general looking to him for protection. Inasmuch as she had come to Boaz and he had offered her his protection, he was personally functioning as the wings of God. But in so doing he was not only offering her asylum but also honoring God, for in the words of the Israelite proverb: "He who oppresses the poor shows contempt for their Maker, but whoever is kind to the needy honors God" (Prov 14:31; cf. 17:5). With this final statement Boaz raises the question of the link between reward and protection. Only time will tell how both will be experienced by Ruth.

RUTH'S SECOND RESPONSE (2:13). **2:13** After Boaz's first speech Ruth had responded with a physical act of obeisance and an interrogative expression of incredulity. It is unclear how her second response is to be interpreted. The idiom itself is clear, having been encountered twice already in this chapter (vv. 2,10). But a problem is created by her use of the imperfect, which under normal circumstances would be translated declaratively, "I shall find grace in your eyes, my lord." However, this makes little sense in the context, especially if the following clause is interpreted causally, "because I have been comforted." If anything, the cause-effect relationship should be reversed, "I have been comforted because I have found grace in your eyes." The NASB overrides the imperfect and finds here a reference to past action, "I have found favor in your sight," but this rendering of the verb is cavalier. More likely is the common treatment of the imperfect as a virtual cohortative, in which case Ruth expresses her wish that his grace would continue.[63] But such a response is odd after v. 10 and even less suited to the following causal clauses. Better still is the interpretation that turns the idiom around and treats its occurrence here as an expression of gratitude, which is exactly what one expects in this context. Modern English rarely uses the biblical idiom "I have found favor with you," preferring "You have been gracious to me." Accordingly, here the imperfect "I am finding favor with you" may be rendered "You are kind to me."[64] Support for this interpretation is found in several other texts where the same idiom serves as an expression of thanks.[65]

---

[62] The use of חָסָה for "to take refuge, seek asylum" is common in the OT, but in all but three instances (Judg 9:15; Isa 30:2; Prov 14:22) the verb is used of finding protection with God. For references see *HALOT,* 337.

[63] Thus NIV. Cf. NRSV, "May I continue to find favor in your sight"; also REB; JB; Hubbard, *Ruth,* 168. NAB suggests "May I prove worthy of your kindness."

[64] Thus RSV; JPSV; *HALOT,* 332; Bush, *Ruth,* 123–24; R. Alter, *The Art of Biblical Narrative* (New York: Basic, 1981), 85; Rudolph, *Ruth,* 47; L. Morris, *Ruth: An Introduction and Commentary,* TOTC (Downers Grove: InterVarsity, 1968), 277.

[65] Cf. JPSV rendering of Gen 47:25, "We are grateful, my lord"; 1 Sam 1:18, "You are most kind to your handmaid"; 2 Sam 16:4, "Your Majesty is most gracious to me."

In the remainder of the verse Ruth gives two reasons for her gratitude. First, she expresses thanksgiving to Boaz for calming her emotionally: "You have given me comfort." The root *nhm* in this verb form *(piel)* is capable of a wide range of meanings: to comfort, to console, to bring relief. The word appears to be related to Arabic *nḥm*, "to breathe deeply," a sense that is still recognizable in the Old Testament.[66] In contexts like this it conveys the sense of relieving tensions, easing the mind. Ruth hereby tells Boaz that his kindness has brought her great relief. Like a young chick frightened by the pouring rain, she has come out of her fears and found comfort and security under the wings of God. Those wings are embodied in the person of Boaz.

Second, she expresses gratitude for his kind words ("You ... have spoken kindly"). The idiom *dibbēr ʿal-lēb*, "to speak on the heart," carries a considerable range of meanings, but in this context it means "to speak compassionately and sympathetically.[67] In v. 10 Ruth's expression of amazement at Boaz's kindness was based on racial considerations; he had paid attention to her even though she was a foreigner. Now the issue is class: he has spoken kindly to her his *šiphâ* (NIV "servant"), even though she was not like his *šiphôt* (NIV "servant girls"). Hebrew employs several different words for female subordinates: *naʿărâ*, "young servant girl" (v. 5); *šiphâ*, "servant"; *ʾāmâ*, "maidservant" (3:9).[68] Even though the words are often used interchangeably, their differing etymological roots invite a consideration of possible variations in meaning. Fundamentally *naʿărâ* reflects the young age of the woman without specifying her placement in the rank of servants. *šiphâ* is cognate to *mišpāḥâ*, "clan, family" (cf. v. 2), but this is of little help. According to Sasson *ʾāmâ* seems to have represented women who could advance to the status of wives or concubines. He plausibly considers a *šiphâ* a female servant of the lowest rank. She could be given as a gift to accompany a bride and, if her mistress proved barren, could bear a child on her behalf for the husband, although this would not change her status.[69] By claiming the status of *šiphâ*, Ruth views herself as occupying the lowest rung on the ladder. But by insisting that she will never be (i.e., futuristic rather than the NIV present) like Boaz's *šiphôt*,[70] she places herself even lower. Ruth is totally amazed

---

[66] J. Scharbert (*Der Schmerz im Alten Testament*, BBB8 [Bonn: P. Hanstein, 1955], 62–63) cites Gen 5:29; Isa 12:1; Pss 23:4; 86:17; Job 7:13 (all *piel*); Ezek 14:22; 31:16; 32:31 (all *niphal*); Gen 27:42; Ps 119:51; Isa 1:24; Ezek 5:13 (all *hithpael*).

[67] For a study of the word see G. Fischer, "Die Redewendung דבר על־לב im AT –Ein Beitrag zum Verständnis von Jes 40,2," *Bib* 65 (1984): 244–50.

[68] Significantly, Hb. lacks a feminine form of the most common term for male servant, עֶבֶד, and the cognate verb never appears with a female subject.

[69] Sasson, *Ruth*, 53. On the position of slaves in Israel see R. de Vaux, *Ancient Israel* (New York: McGraw-Hill, 1961), 82–90; M. A. Dandamayev, "Slavery," *ABD* 6.62–65.

[70] וְאָנֹכִי לֹא אֶהְיֶה כְּאַחַת שִׁפְחֹתֶיךָ should be translated "though I shall never be like [i.e., be equal to] your servants."

that differences of race or class could not stifle Boaz's compassion toward her.
BOAZ'S THIRD SPEECH (2:14). **2:14** The phrase "at mealtime" in the
Hebrew text follows "Boaz said to her." Assuming the originality of the MT,
this phrase (lit., "at the time of eating," *lĕʿet hāʾōkel*, i.e., at the time of the
noon meal) signals a chronological separation between vv. 13 and 14.[71] With
Boaz's previous speech and Ruth's response still in mind, the reader now discovers that Boaz has not yet exhausted his compassion toward Ruth; he would
invite her to dine with him.

In the ancient Near East people did not eat only to satisfy hungry stomachs; eating together also had great symbolic significance. Meals were put on
by hosts as an expression of hospitality (Gen 18:1–8) and to celebrate special
occasions (Ps 23:5; Matt 22:1–14; Luke 12:36; 14:8; 15:22–23; John 2:1–11);
treaty partners climaxed agreements with a covenant meal (Gen 31:54; Exod
24:11; Luke 22:14–20); social realities were expressed at mealtime (Gen
43:33–34; Luke 14:7–11; 16:21); religious groups met over meals (Exod
32:5–6; 1 Cor 10:21; 11:20,33);[72] and people ate and drank together just for a
good time (Isa 21:5; Amos 6:7).

The present meal begins innocently enough, as Boaz and his workers pause
at noon to refresh themselves after a morning of hard work. The fact that Boaz
ate with his harvesters says something about the man, but his actions at this
meal must have caught everyone by surprise. First, he invites Ruth, an outsider and a Moabite, to join him and his workers. The choice of verb, *nāgaš*,
"to come near, approach" (NIV, "come over"), suggests that as a stranger
Ruth had deliberately and appropriately (according to custom) kept her distance.

Second, he encourages her to share the food prepared for his workers. The
narrator does not tell us whether or not she had brought her own lunch, but it
seems unlikely given her economic condition and the uncertainty with which
she had left Naomi in the morning. In any case Boaz invites her to (lit.) "eat
from the bread." The definite article on *hallehem* ("the bread") suggests this
food had been prepared and brought for his workers.

Third, Boaz beckons Ruth to "dip it [your morsel] in the wine vinegar."
The word for "morsel," *pat* (omitted in the NIV), is an abbreviation for the
fuller expression *pat lehem*, "morsel of bread."[73] The meaning of *ḥōmeṣ*,
NIV's "wine vinegar," is less certain. Numbers 6:3 prohibits Nazirites from
drinking *ḥōmeṣ*, which suggests the word could denote an alcoholic beverage,

---

[71] The LXX assumes the phrase לְעֵת הָאֹכֶל is part of Boaz's speech, in which case this speech
probably was given soon after the preceding conversation.

[72] Cf. Josephus, *Jewish Wars* 2.8.5; IQS 6:1–6; IQSa 2;11–22; Pliny, *Ep.* 10.96, on which see
further D. E. Smith, "Greco-Roman Meal Customs," *ABD* 4.650–53.

[73] The full phrase occurs in Gen 18:5; Judg 19:5; 1 Sam 2:36; 28:22; 1 Kgs 17:11; Prov 28:21.
פַּת alone is found in 2 Sam 12:3; Job 31:17; Prov 23:8. Cf. פַּת חֲרֵבָה, "a dry crust," in Prov 17:1.

made either from wine or *šēkār*, any other intoxicant. According to Prov 10:22 *hōmeṣ* is unpalatable to the taste.[74] The association of *hōmeṣ* with poison in Ps 69:21[Hb. 22] suggests that Boaz was not offering her a beverage in which to soak her bread. Here *hōmeṣ* is best understood as a sour sauce or condiment used to moisten and spice up dry bread. Boaz could not allow her to eat dry bread while he enjoyed more pleasant food.

Fourth, when Ruth had taken her seat beside Boaz's harvesters, he served her roasted grain himself. The narrator deliberately highlights this extraordinary action by using a word that occurs only here in the Old Testament. In mishnaic Hebrew *ṣābaṭ* denotes "to grasp, seize,"[75] a sense found also in Akkadian *ṣabātum* and Arabic *dabaṭa*.[76] Our word is undoubtedly based on the same root, but by a curious lexical development an expression that originally meant "to seize with the hand" has come to mean "to hand," that is, "to give with the hand." The food handed to Ruth is identified as *qālî*, from a root *qālâ*, "to roast."[77] From 1 Sam 17:17; 25:18; and 2 Sam 17:28, it is apparent that *qāli*, "roasted grain," was a staple of Israel's diet, as it was in the broader ancient Near Eastern world.[78]

Fifth, Boaz gives her food enough to satisfy her and to have some left over. This last observation is added to emphasize Boaz's generosity.

Obviously this verse is not simply about feeding the hungry. The narrator hereby shows how Boaz took an ordinary occasion and transformed it into a glorious demonstration of compassion, generosity, and acceptance—in short, the biblical understanding of *hesed*. The text offers no hint of any romantic attraction between Boaz and Ruth. Given the racial and social barriers that separated them, the thought would not have crossed Ruth's mind, and she could not have known that he was a kinsman of her deceased husband. As for Boaz, he was simply a good man, "sent" by God to show favor to this woman. The wings of God are not only comforting to Israelites; they offer protection even for despised Moabites.

---

[74] Actually "to the teeth." The meaning of this vague statement may be suggested by Ezek 18:2 and Jer 31:29, which describe the effects of sour grapes on the teeth with *qāhâ*, traditionally rendered "to set the teeth on edge." The expression describes the puckery, styptic sensation in the mouth when unripe fruit is eaten. Cf. Block, *Ezekiel 1–24*, 558.

[75] M. Jastrow, *A Dictionary of the Targumim, the Talmud Babli and Yerushalmi, and the Midrashic Literature* (New York: Judaica Press, 1985), 1258. Probably guessing about the meaning of the word, the LXX interpreted this hapax by creating one of its own, ἐβούνισεν, "to pile up," from βουνός, "hill, mound," here and in v. 16 for הַצְּבָתִים.

[76] A cognate noun, *mṣbṭm*, "tongs," exists in Ug. Cf. *HALOT*, 997.

[77] The *qal* form of the verb occurs in Lev 2:14; Josh 5:11 (both of grain); Jer 29:22 (of people, as punishment).

[78] P. P. Joüon (*Ruth: Commentaire philologique et exegetique* [Rome: Pontifical Biblical Institute, 1953], 59–60) cites an 1838 report by E. Robinson that roasted grain was commonly sold in the marketplaces of Palestine.

(3) The Third Interchange (2:15–16)

[15]As she got up to glean, Boaz gave orders to his men, "Even if she gathers among the sheaves, don't embarrass her. [16]Rather, pull out some stalks for her from the bundles and leave them for her to pick up, and don't rebuke her."

2:15–16 This scene ends with a final interchange between Boaz and his workers. As Ruth was getting up to return to her gleaning, he gave his regular harvesters one final reminder. His speech in vv. 15–16 is constructed with an A B A B order, the A elements relating to permission for Ruth to glean, and the B elements to how the other workers are to treat her.

The A elements represent Boaz's specific answer to Ruth's request to the foreman in v. 7: to glean behind the harvesters among the stacks of grain. As noted earlier, we are not sure what the field supervisor told her. But now all of Ruth's and our own questions are answered. The owner of the field commands his workers emphatically[79] to permit Ruth to glean among the sheaves.[80] In fact, they must intentionally pull[81] some of the stalks from the bundles and leave them lying for her to pick without effort. But the interpretation of the first sentence in v. 17 is complicated by the narrator's use of two special words. The verb rendered "pull" by the NIV is apparently derived from a root *šll*, but the sense required by this context occurs nowhere else. Elsewhere *šālal* always means something like "to plunder, to take spoil/booty."[82] The word probably is derived from a different homonymic root, cognate to Arabic *šll*, "to draw [a sword],"[83] or Akkadian *šalālu*, "to slide, slither [like a snake]."[84] The object of the verb is unspecified (stalks of grain no doubt), but the items from which they are to be pulled are identified by a word occurring only here, *ṣ̌ebātîm*, of uncertain derivation. The most likely Semitic connection is found in Arabic *dabtat*, "handful, sheaf."[85] In fact, commentators tend to follow Dalman in interpreting the word as "handfuls," that is, "the ears of the sheaf which are grasped in the left hand while being cut with [a sickle in] the right."[86] By this interpretation Ruth does not even need to cut or pull out the grain she is gleaning. As the harvesters cut the standing barley, they were to pull out some of the stalks and leave (*ʿāzab*) them lying on the stubble for her.

---

[79] Note the introductory particle גַם, "Even, indeed, in fact," and the unusual adverb-verb word order of בֵּין הָעֳמָרִים תְּלַקֵּט, "between/among the sheaves she may glean."

[80] On עֳמָרִים, "sheaves, stacks of grain," see above on v. 7.

[81] Note the emphatic combination of infinitive absolute and imperfect.

[82] Cf. BDB, 1021.

[83] Thus Campbell, *Ruth*, 104; Bush, *Ruth*, 126; Hubbard, *Ruth*, 177.

[84] See *AHw*, 1142.

[85] Cf. P. Humbert, "En marge du dictionnaire hébräique," *ZAW* 62 (1949–50): 206–7. Cf. *HALOT*, 1000, for other possible cognates.

[86] Thus *HALOT*, 1000, following G. Dalman, *Arbeit und Sitte in Palästina* (1933; reprint, Hildesheim: Georg Olms, 1964), 3.42. Cf. the LXX βεβουνισμένων, "piled up items."

The B elements in Boaz's speech prescribe the disposition of his harvesters toward Ruth. They are not to humiliate (v. 15) or insult (v. 16) her. The first word, *haklîm* (NIV "embarrass"), derives from a root, *kālâ*, "to be humiliated, shamed, disgraced."[87] The second, *gāʿar* (NIV "rebuke"), means "to insult, to rebuke." Together these words reiterate and extend the protection Boaz had offered in v. 9, when he commanded his servants not to touch her. One can well imagine the abuse that persons like Ruth, who arrive at the field uninvited or unengaged, might receive from those "upstanding" citizens who have been properly hired by the land owner to harvest the crops. Now Boaz lets his workers know that they are to have no part in such action toward Ruth. They will not threaten her physically or shame her psychologically with snide comments about her alien status or the low class she represents just because she is forced to go begging for fields in which she might glean. This final interchange contributes to the image of a compassionate and kindly Boaz.

4. Scene 4: The Results (2:17–23)

[17]So Ruth gleaned in the field until evening. Then she threshed the barley she had gathered, and it amounted to about an ephah. [18]She carried it back to town, and her mother-in-law saw how much she had gathered. Ruth also brought out and gave her what she had left over after she had eaten enough.

[19]Her mother-in-law asked her, "Where did you glean today? Where did you work? Blessed be the man who took notice of you!"

Then Ruth told her mother-in-law about the one at whose place she had been working. "The name of the man I worked with today is Boaz," she said.

[20]"The LORD bless him!" Naomi said to her daughter-in-law. "He has not stopped showing his kindness to the living and the dead." She added, "That man is our close relative; he is one of our kinsman-redeemers."

[21]Then Ruth the Moabitess said, "He even said to me, 'Stay with my workers until they finish harvesting all my grain.'"

[22]Naomi said to Ruth her daughter-in-law, "It will be good for you, my daughter, to go with his girls, because in someone else's field you might be harmed."

[23]So Ruth stayed close to the servant girls of Boaz to glean until the barley and wheat harvests were finished. And she lived with her mother-in-law.

2:17–23 Like the previous field scene, the final episode of the chapter is dominated by dialogue. The first two verses (vv. 17–18) are in narrative prose, but thereafter dialogue takes over, as Naomi and Ruth discuss the results and the implications of the events of the day (vv. 19–22). A summary statement concludes the chapter (v. 23).

---

[87] *HALOT*, 480. Considering this too strong for the context, some prefer to explain תַכְלִימוּהָ as derivative from כָּלָא, "to restrain." Cf. Joüon, *Ruth*, 60. Others simply soften the sense in the present context by translating "to rebuke, reprove." See Hubbard, *Ruth*, 126–27.

The detail with which the conversations at the field are recounted contrasts with the cursory description of Ruth's activity in the field. Obviously the narrator is more concerned to portray Boaz's generosity and grace than Ruth's industry. Not that the latter is to be underestimated. According to v. 17 Ruth scavenged for grain in the field until evening. Then, presumably with a flail or a stick, she "beat out" the grain from the heads of barley. Where she did this is not indicated. In Judg 6:11, where the same verb, *ḥābaṭ*, was used, Gideon had used a winepress to hide from marauding Midianites. Given Boaz's generosity in the previous scene, one may imagine that Boaz had invited her to use his threshing floor.

The results of a day's work in the field are nothing short of amazing. When Ruth measured the grain that she had threshed, it amounted to one ephah.[88] Hebrew *ʾēpâ*, a loanword from Egyptian *ypt*, denotes the unit of measurement used for dry goods, especially grain and flour. According to Ezek 45:11 it was equivalent to the *bath*, used in the measurement of liquids, and one-tenth of a *ḥōmer*,[89] the amount of grain a donkey *(ḥāmôr)* could carry. Scholars are not agreed on the size of an ephah. Containers marked *bt* found at Tell Beit Mirsim and Lachish averaged twenty-two liters (5.8 U.S. gallons). Other calculations are more generous. According to Josephus (*Ant* 3.8.3 §197), the *bath* (= ephah) was thirty-six liters. The differences may reflect competing standards within biblical Israel.[90] By either standard, to thresh an ephah of grain from one day's labor is an extraordinary feat, not to mention Ruth's having to carry it home! Depending upon the quality of the grain and which standard one uses, an ephah of barley could have weighed from thirty to fifty pounds. The harvesters obviously followed Boaz's instructions and allowed Ruth to scavenge liberally.[91]

Verse 18 has Ruth picking up the fruits of the day's labor and heading for the city. After she had showed[92] her mother-in-law what she had gleaned,

---

[88] The NIV renders the *kaph* prefixed to אֵיפָה, "ephah," as "about." This is a common use, but in some cases the prefixed *kaph* actually serves not as a mark of approximation but exactitude, a *kaph veritatis*, as in Neh 7:2, "He is an honest man precisely." This usage is attested in the seventh century B.C. Yabneh Yam Ostracon in which a harvester argues to his master that he has delivered the exact amount of grain requested (Gibson, *SSI* 1.26–30). For discussion see S. Talmon, "The New Hebrew Letter from the Seventh Century B.C. in Historical Perspective," *BASOR* 176 (1964): 33. For other examples of the *kaph veritatis* in extrabiblical inscriptions see *DNWSI*, 482–83.

[89] Not to be confused with the *ʿōmer*, which is one-tenth of an ephah (Exod 16:36).

[90] For recent discussion and bibliography see R. Fuller, "אֵיפָה," *NIDOTTE* 1.382–88.

[91] According to 1 Sam 17:17, an ephah of grain could feed fifty fighting men. According to Old Babylonian records from Mari (nineteenth century B.C.), the ration of threshed grain demanded of a male harvester rarely was more than one or two pounds. Cf. Sasson, *Ruth,* 57. The text is published by J. Bottéro, *Textes économiques et administratifs,* ARMT 7 (Paris: 1958), 272.

[92] The MT *wattēreʾ* reads "when her mother-in-law saw." A few MSS, the LXX, and the Vg read *wattarʾ*, "and she showed." In the absence of the sign of the definite direct object, אֵת, the former is preferred. So also Bush, *Ruth,* 133, who cites supporters of both readings. The meaning is the same either way.

Ruth measured out as much as she needed and gave Naomi the rest.[93]

Not surprisingly, the grain that Ruth brought home sparked conversation between her and her mother-in-law. Naomi's incredulity at the sight of so much grain evokes a response whose sense is as much exclamation as question: "Where[94] in the world did you glean today, and where did you work?"[95] By our standards the verbs are illogically sequenced, but the order and the redundancy combine to reflect her utter amazement at Ruth's productivity. But she is not really interested in the geographical location of the field. Before Ruth can answer, Naomi breaks out in a spontaneous utterance of blessing upon the man who had taken notice of her daughter-in-law.

Naomi's excitement is also reflected in the form of the blessing (lit.): "May he who took notice of you be blessed!" *(yĕhî makkîrēk bārûk).* This structure[96] occurs elsewhere only in 1 Kgs 10:9 (= 2 Chr 9:8), in an expression of praise to Yahweh, and Prov 5:18, in a metaphor using "fountain" in place of "wife."[97] In this instance the word order highlights the person "who paid attention to" Ruth.[98]

In Ruth's response to Naomi's question she seems to be just as excited as her mother-in-law. Her emotional state is reflected in the redundancy of v. 19b. First, the narrator notes that Ruth reported *(higgîd)* to Naomi with whom she had worked; then he quotes her speech, using some of the same words: "the one with whom she/I worked" *(ʾăšer ʿāśĕtâ/ ʿāśîtî ʿimmô).* The repetition has the additional effects of slowing down the narrative,[99] setting the stage for the climactic announcement of Boaz's name, and drawing the reader's attention to the blessing that follows.[100] Ruth's statement, "The name of the man ... is Boaz," does not answer Naomi's question precisely. She had asked "where" Ruth had worked; Ruth answers "with whom" she has worked. This intentional switch draws the reader's attention to the person who has been the focus of the narrator's interest throughout this chapter. Since Boaz's name was never mentioned in the preceding dialogue, we may assume that Ruth had heard it repeatedly in his conversations with his workers.

Realizing the significance of Ruth's "chance" encounter with Boaz,

---

[93] Note the reversal of verbs from v. 14, which has וַתִּשְׂבַּע וַתֹּתַר, "And she was satisfied and had some left over." Here it is הוֹתִרָה מִשָּׂבְעָהּ, "she had left over from her satisfaction/being satisfied."

[94] The particle אֵיפֹה *(ʾêpōh),* "where," plays on אֵיפָה *(êpâ),* the word for measurement.

[95] The context suggests a note of incredulity.

[96] Involving the jussive of *hāyâ* + object + passive participle of *brk.* Cp. the form in v. 4. The root בָּרַךְ occurs in the *qal* stem only in the passive participle form. Cf. *HALOT,* 159–60.

[97] The more common form occurs in v. 14.

[98] מַכִּרֵךְ involves the same root as לְהַכִּירֵנִי in v. 10.

[99] Notice also the wordiness of Ruth's answer, particularly the addition of a seemingly unnecessary הַיּוֹם, "today."

[100] Cf. Hubbard, *Ruth,* 184.

Naomi spontaneously erupts with a second blessing for him. The opening line follows the conventional pattern of Israelite blessings:[101] *bārûk* + subject + *lamedh* attached to the name *yhwh*.[102] Scholars are not agreed on the meaning of this blessing. Assuming that the passive form represents a modification of the active construction, "I bless him to Yahweh," some treat *bārûk* as a virtual synonym for "praise." Accordingly, Naomi's utterance is an exclamation of praise to Boaz and a commendation of him to Yahweh.[103] But despite the 235 occurrences of this form *(piel)* of the verb in the Old Testament,[104] this use is lacking entirely. It is preferable, therefore, to interpret the *lē* (otherwise "to") attached to *yhwh* as introducing the actor/agent behind a passive verb, who becomes the subject when changed into the active (as in NIV).[105]

As already intimated, how one interprets the *lē* prefix has an important bearing on one's understanding of the following clause (in the Hb. text "Naomi said to her daughter-in-law" comes first in the verse). As it stands, the clause is quite ambiguous for two reasons. First, it begins with an introductory particle *ʾăšer*, which may be treated either as a relative pronoun (viz., "who has not abandoned his *ḥesed*") or a subordinate conjunction introducing a causal clause (viz., "because he has not abandoned his *ḥesed*").[106] Second, to whom does *ʾăšer* refer if the word is treated as a relative pronoun, or who is the subject of the verb *ʿāzab*, "to abandon" (NIV "stopped") if one treats the particle as a causal conjunction? If one treats

---

[101] Cf. the unconventional form in the previous verse.

[102] For other biblical examples see Ruth 3:10; Gen 14:19; Judg 17:2; 1 Sam 15:13; 23:21; 2 Sam 2:5; Ps 115:15. The form is also common in extrabiblical inscriptions. Note especially: (1) Kuntillet ʿAjrud Pithos 5: "Belonging to Obadyahu son of ʿAdnah, may he be blessed by Yahweh." (2) Khirbet el-Qôm Tomb Inscription: "Uriyahu the rich wrote it: Blessed be Urihau by Yahweh, for from his enemies by his Asherah he has saved him. By Oniyahu and by his Asherah." A slight variation uses the *piel* finite verb, as in Kuntillet Ajrud Pithos 3: "I bless you by Yahweh of Samaria and his Asherah." For a discussion of these blessings see T. G. Crawford, *Blessing and Curse in Syro-Palestinian Inscriptions of the Iron Age,* American University Studies, Series VII, 120 (New York: Peter Lang, 1992), 46–53. For further discussion of the form see J. Scharbert, "בּרך *brk*," *TDOT* 2.279–308, esp. 284–88.

[103] Thus Waltke and O'Connor (*IBHS* §11.2.10.d), "May he be pronounced blessed to Yahweh." Similarly Hubbard, *Ruth*, 185.

[104] The *piel* form followed by לַיהוָה does indeed occur once in the OT, in 1 Chr 29:20, but here the *lamedh* introduces the direct object. Cf. GKC 117*n*; *BHS* §125*k*, note. Possible examples may be found in Arad Ostracon 16:2–3 (בֵּרַכְתִּךָ לַיהוָה, "I bless you to Yahweh") and perhaps 21:2 and 40:3, though the inscriptions on these are incompletely preserved. So also *BHS* §132f, note. Crawford (*Blessing and Curse*, 35–40) is inconsistent, interpreting these texts this way but a similar construction in Kuntillet ʿAjrud Pithos 3 as "by Yahweh." P.47. The *lamedh* in the Arad texts should be interpreted similarly. Thus *DCH* 1.270.

[105] On which see *HALOT,* 510; *BHS* §132f; GKC §121f.

[106] Thus Sasson, *Ruth,* 60. On the causal use of *ʾăšer see* GKC §158*b*; *BHS* §170*e*; *DCH* 1.432–33. Most of the examples cited here involve a perfect verb, as in our text.

the blessing as a commendation of Boaz to Yahweh, then the answer to both questions must be Boaz, in which case the clause introduced by *ᵃšer* expresses the reason Boaz is to be commended: he has not abandoned his *ḥesed*. That is, he has fulfilled the covenant people's highest ideals.[107] But this interpretation is doubtful, first because *yhwh* is the nearer antecedent. Second, and more importantly, by this interpretation it is difficult to explain Naomi's specification of the nearer relative as *hā'îš*, "the man." One would have expected the simple pronoun *hû'*, "he," as at the end of the verse. On the other hand, if Yahweh is the one who has faithfully demonstrated *ḥesed*, then the reference to "the man" is necessary to distinguish the subject of the last two clauses of the verse from the subject of the preceding clause. Finally, an analogue to this text by this interpretation is provided by Gen 24:27. After Abraham's servant has discovered Rebekah as a potential wife for Isaac, he declares, "Blessed be the LORD ... who has not abandoned his *ḥesed* and his truth toward my master."[108]

But what does Naomi mean when she says that Yahweh has not abandoned his *ḥesed* toward the living and the dead? First, *haḥayyîm*, "the living," in this context must refer to Naomi and Ruth, who survive of this family, and *hammētîm*, "the dead," to the deceased Elimelech, Mahlon, and Chilion.[109] Together this pair of antonyms functions as a figure *(merism)* referring to the family as a whole. Second, the word *ḥesed* bears a much fuller sense than "kindness" as rendered by the NIV. This is the second time we have heard it from the lips of Naomi (cf. 1:8). As noted in the introduction, this is one of the key theological expressions in the book. It wraps up in itself an entire cluster of concepts—love, mercy, grace, kindness, goodness, benevolence, loyalty, and covenant faithfulness. As the following clauses indicate, here it involves Yahweh's covenant grace to this family. This speech represents a total turnaround from her despairing and accusatory words in 1:20–21. The expression she uses, *ᶜāzab ḥesed*, "to abandon *ḥesed*," occurs elsewhere in Gen 24:27 and Jonah 2:9[110] and represents the

---

[107] Thus Hubbard, *Ruth*, 186.

[108] Note the similarities of construction:

Gen 24:27 בָּרוּךְ יְהוָה אֱלֹהֵי אֲדֹנִי אַבְרָהָם אֲשֶׁר לֹא־עָזַב חַסְדּוֹ וַאֲמִתּוֹ מֵעִם אֲדֹנִי

Ruth 2:10 בָּרוּךְ הוּא לַיהוָה אֲשֶׁר לֹא־עָזַב חַסְדּוֹ אֶת־הַחַיִּים

Campbell (*Ruth*, 106) rightly observes that the shift in prepositions from מֵעִם to אֶת is inconsequential.

[109] Cf. 1:8, where the Naomi juxtaposes the dead with herself.

[110] This is one of several expressions available in Hb. for not keeping a covenant promise or not demonstrating grace. Cf. כָּחַד חֶסֶד, "to hide *ḥesed*" (Ps 40:11); מָאַס חֶסֶד, "to reject *ḥesed* " (Job 6:14); אָסַף חֶסֶד, "to take away *ḥesed* " (Jer 16:5); הֵסִיר חֶסֶד, "to remove *ḥesed*" (Pss 66:20; 89:34[MSS]; 1 Chr 17:13); הֵפִיר חֶסֶד, "to violate *ḥesed*" (Ps 89:34); מָחָה חֶסֶד "to wipe out *ḥesed*" (Neh 13:14).

opposite of *ʿāśâ ḥesed*, "to demonstrate *ḥesed*," in 1:5.[111]

Specifically, in Naomi's eyes Ruth's coming upon the field of Boaz was a demonstration of God's grace and favor. In 1:8–9 she had prayed that Yahweh would match Ruth's *ḥesed* to her family by granting her rest in the house of her own husband. There she had in mind a Moabite husband, but now, in remarkable fulfillment of that prayer, she is struck by the potential of Ruth's encounter with Boaz. Her amazement at what has transpired is expressed in two emphatically redundant descriptions of the man. First, (lit.) "The man is our near [relative]" *(qārôb lānû hāʾîš)*.[112] The expression represents a stylistic variant of *môdaʿ*, "relative," in 2:1. Second, "He is one of our kinsman-redeemers" *(miggōʾălēnû hû)*.

With this comment Naomi has raised another one of the most important notions in the book. Hebrew has two words commonly translated "to redeem." The first, *pādâ*, is used with reference to "redeeming" the firstborn (Exod 13:13–15) with a sheep or money (Num 18:15–17) or cultic offerings that could be "redeemed" with money (Leviticus 27). In such cases the object is always a human or an animal and is the work of a near male relative, usually the father. By contrast, the second, *gāʾal*, may have an inanimate object. In contexts like this, *gōʾēl*, a participle form of the verb, functions as a technical legal term, related specifically to Israelite family law.[113] As a kinship term it denotes the near relative who is responsible for the economic well-being of a relative, and he comes into play especially when the relative is in distress and cannot get himself/herself out of the crisis. The Scriptures note five aspects of a *gōʾēl*'s redemptive role: (1) to ensure that the hereditary property of the clan never passes out of the clan (Lev 25:25–30); (2) to maintain the freedom of individuals within the clan by buying back those who have sold themselves into slavery because of poverty (Lev 27:47–55); (3) to track down and execute murderers of near relatives (Num 35:12,19–27);[114] (4) to receive restitution money on behalf of a deceased victim of a crime (Num 5:8); and (5) to ensure that justice is served in a lawsuit involving a relative (Job 19:25; Ps 119:154; Jer 50:34). The Israelite provision for the *gōʾēl* is based upon an assumption of corporate solidarity and the sanctity of the family/clan: to offend a relative is to

---

[111] Other antonymic expressions are מָשַׁךְ חֶסֶד, "to extend *ḥesed*" (Jer 31:3; Pss 36:11; 109:12; Gen 39:21; Ezra 7:28; 9:9); שָׁמַר חֶסֶד, "to keep *ḥesed*" (Deut 7:9,12; 1 Kgs 8:23 = 2 Chr 6:14; Hos 12:7; Ps 89:29; Dan 9:4; Neh 1:5; 9:32 [often with בְּרִית, "covenant"]); זָקַר חֶסֶד, "to remember *ḥesed*" (Jer 2:2; Pss 25:6 [+ רַחֲמִים, "compassion"]; 98:3 [+ אֱמוּנָה, "faithfulness"]; 1 Chr 17:13).

[112] The expression לְקָרוֹב, "near to," as an expression of near kinship is found also in Neh 13:4. Cf. אֶל קָרוֹב, "near to," in Lev 21:2–3; 25:25; Num 27:11; 2 Sam 19:42[Hb. 43].

[113] More than half of its occurrences are found in four texts involving Israelite family matters: Leviticus 25; 27; Numbers 35; Deuteronomy 19.

[114] Note the expression גֹּאֵל הַדָּם, "avenger of blood" in vv. 19,21,25,27.

offend oneself. The custom of redemption was designed to maintain the wholeness and health of family relationships, even after the person has died.[115]

Remarkably, in none of the texts clarifying the role of the *gōʾēl* is there any reference to marrying the widow of a deceased person. Still it is commonly assumed that in addition to these functions of the *gōʾēl* the kinsman-redeemer also came into play in the case of a widow whose husband had died without leaving progeny. This view is based largely on the use of the word *gōʾēl* in the Book of Ruth and the relationship between the customs reflected here and Deut 25:5–10, the defining text regarding the custom of levirate marriage in Israel.

As noted earlier on 1:11–13, by definition a levirate marriage represents a legally sanctioned union between a *yĕbāmâ,* a widow whose husband has died without having fathered any offspring, and the *yābām,* the brother of the deceased. Variations of this type of marriage are attested in second millennium B.C. Ugaritic,[116] Hittite,[117] and Middle Assyrian[118] sources. According to the Israelite custom as recorded in Deut 25:5–10, the unmarried brother-in-law was obligated to "perform the duties of the *yābām*" by marrying the widow. To prevent the name and family of the deceased from dying out, the first child born of this union should assume the name of the deceased. If a *yābām* chose to forego his responsibility, in the presence of the elders the widow should remove his sandal and humiliate him publicly by spitting in his face.

Because of differences in language between the Book of Ruth and the Deuteronomic prescription, specifically because the marriage in the Book of Ruth does not involve a brother *(ʾāḥ)* but a more distant relative, and because Ruth expresses no concern to fulfill her part in the levirate,[119] some have argued that a levirate marriage is not involved in this book.[120] However, this conclu-

---

[115] See further the studies of the word by R. L. Hubbard, "The *gōʾēl* in Ancient Israel: The Theology of an Israelite Institution," *BBR* 1 (1991): 3–19; id., "גאל," *NIDOTTE* 1.789–94.

[116] In an Akk. text from Ugarit a certain Arhalba writes, "After my death, whoever takes (in marriage) my wife, Kubaba daughter of Takan (?), from my brother—may Baal crush him." *PRU* 3: 16.144.

[117] Hittite Law §193 reads: "If a man has a wife, and the man dies, his brother shall take his widow as wife. (If the brother dies,) his father shall take her. When afterwards his father dies, his (i.e., the father's) brother shall take the woman whom he had." As translated by H. A. Hoffner, Jr., in *Law Collections from Mesopotamia and Asia Minor,* 2d ed., M. T. Roth, ed.; SBL Writings from the Ancient World Series 6 (Atlanta: Scholars Press, 1997), 236.

[118] MAL §33 reads: "If a woman is residing in her own father's house, her husband is dead, and she has sons [...], or [if he so pleases], he shall give her into the protection of the household of her father-in-law. If her husband and her father-in-law are both dead, and she has no son, she is indeed a widow; she shall go wherever she pleases." As translated by Roth, ibid., 165.

[119] Cf. Tamar's sense of compulsion in Gen 38:24.

[120] See, e.g., A. A. Anderson, "The Marriage of Ruth," *JSS* 23 (1978): 171–83.

sion derives from an invalid demand for conformity between narrative accounts and formal statements on the one hand and a misreading of Deut 25:5–10 as a legal code rather than an individual decision incorporated in a larger literary document on the other.[121] Although the story of Boaz and Ruth does not follow the letter of the law of the *levir*, it certainly captures its spirit.

When Naomi learns that Ruth has met up with Boaz, the sun rises again in her life. Yahweh has been gracious to her deceased husband and her sons by sending a potential "redeemer-kinsman" into their lives. Here the use of the plural (Boaz is *"our* near relative," he is *"our* kinsman-redeemer)" suggests the wheels are turning in her mind, a conclusion that is confirmed in the next chapter.

Having heard this, Ruth adds[122] another small but significant comment. But before we comment on her statement, we note the oddness of the addition of "the Moabitess" after her name. Bush suggests plausibly that, like "Uriah the Hittite" in 2 Samuel 11, in this alien context "Ruth the Moabitess" functioned as her full name.[123] One may surmise that this was how the citizens of Bethlehem distinguished her from other women in town who had the same name. On the other hand, the narrator may hereby be deliberately reflecting a clash of cultures. Naomi's reference to Boaz as a *gōʾēl* makes sense only within the context of Israel's unique theology of family and land.[124] As a Moabite, Ruth may not have grasped the significance of Naomi's statement. Not being on Naomi's train of thought, the latter's use of the word *qārôb,* "one near by," may have triggered Ruth's apparent quotation of Boaz's words inviting/advising her "to cling to"[125] or stay nearby his servants until his entire harvest has been taken in. Her continued amazement is expressed by placing the prepositional phrase before the verb.[126] The previous scene contains no report of Boaz telling Ruth that she could

---

[121] Cf. the analysis of R. Westbrook, "The Law of the Biblical Levirate," in *Revue Internationale des Droits de l'Antiquité,* 3d Series 24 (1977): 65–87, especially his critique of those who reject the levirate in Ruth on p. 67. This article is republished in *Property and the Family in Biblical Law,* JSOTSup 193 (Sheffield: Sheffield Academic Press, 1991), 69–89. For additional studies of the levirate law in Israel see D. Daube, "Consortium in Roman and Hebrew Law," *JR* 62 (1950): 71–91; D. Leggett, *The Levirate and Goel Institutions in the Old Testament with Special Attention to the Book of Ruth* (Cherry Hill, N.J.: Mack, 1974); V. P. Hamilton, "Marriage: Old Testament and Ancient Near East," *ABD* 4.567–68; F. R. Ames, "Levirate Marriage," *NIDOTTE* 5.902–5; Gow, *Book of Ruth,* 143–82.

[122] The emphatic tone of אֵלַי כִּי־אָמַר גַּם may be captured with "And guess what else he said to me!" or "There is one other thing he said to me." This expression occurs ten times in the OT. Cf. *DCH* 1, 361. On the emphatic sense of כִּי גַּם see *HALOT,* 195.

[123] Bush, *Ruth,* 138.

[124] Cf. Jezebel's failure to comprehend Naboth's refusal to sell Ahab his field in 1 Kgs 21:3.

[125] Her use of the word דָּבַק links this comment with v. 8. The NIV's "stay with" is much too mild for דָּבַק, better rendered "to cling to."

[126] The Hb. order translates, "With the servants who belong to me stick."

work in his field until the harvest was completed, but it makes sense that he would have said this (the reported speech does not contain the entire conversation), On the other hand, Ruth may be drawing logical implications from what he has said and putting the words in his mouth.

In her final comment (v. 22) Naomi approves of Boaz's offer, but not because of the food this guarantees Ruth and her. Concerned about her welfare, she changes Boaz's *nĕ'ārîm*, "servants" (the masculine stands for all harvesters, irrespective of gender), to *na'ărôt*, "female servants." Apparently Naomi had been worried about Ruth as she sent her out of the house in the morning and she would have been relieved to see her return safe and sound. The danger she fears, presumably from male workers in the field, is expressed with *pāga'*. Elsewhere the verb means "to meet, encounter, attack." In 1:16 it had been used of "to pressure, compel." But coming after the conversations in vv. 8–16, the reader may interpret it as a catchall for *nāga'*, "to touch, harass," in v. 9, *hiklîm*, "to shame, embarrass," in v. 15, and *gā'ar*, "to rebuke, insult," in v. 16.

The chapter ends with a summary of the results of all that transpired in this chapter. Ruth clung to *(dābaq)* Boaz's female servants *(na'ărôt*, as per Naomi's advice), intending to scavenge (NIV "glean")[127] in Boaz's field not only to the end of the barley harvest but until the end of the wheat harvest as well. Obviously she was comfortable with Boaz's generosity and the crew of women workers he had in the field. Based on the information provided by the Gezer agricultural calendar alluded to earlier,[128] Ruth must have been out in the fields for six to seven weeks, from late April till early June by our designations of the months. The narrator does not indicate whether there were any further contacts between her and Boaz. Meanwhile, in fulfillment of her oath of commitment in 1:16–17, Ruth settled down *(yāšab)* with her mother-in-law. The note not only brings the chapter full circle (cf. 1:22) but also creates the impression that they had settled into a regular routine. We are left to wonder what has happened to Naomi's dream (v. 20). Boaz has been introduced as an extremely kind and gracious man and as one who qualifies to rescue the line of Elimelech. But the dream seems to have died an early death; Boaz has helped Naomi and Ruth economically, but he is doing nothing about the real crisis in the family created by the deaths of all the male members. Only time will tell if this situation will be resolved.

---

[127] Note the purpose infinitive construction, לְלַקֵּט, "in order to scavenge."
[128] See above p. 650, n. 3.

III. ACT 3: THE COMPLICATION FOR THE ROYAL LINE (3:1–18)
1. Scene 1: The Scheme (3:1–5)
   (1) The Problem (3:1)
   (2) The Summary of the Facts (3:2)
   (3) Prescriptions of the Procedure (3:3–5)
2. Scene 2: The Implementation of the Scheme (3:6–15)
   (1) Phase 1: The Night Encounter (3:6–13)
   Ruth's Action (3:6–7)
   Boaz's Reaction (3:8)
   Ruth's Answer (3:9)
   Boaz's Reply (3:10–13)
   (2) Phase 2: The Morning Send-off (3:14–15)
3. Scene 3: The Results of the Scheme (3:16–18)

III. ACT 3: THE COMPLICATION FOR THE ROYAL LINE (3:1–18)

The ending to chap. 2 leaves the reader wondering what would come of Naomi's dream and what would happen to Ruth, the alien, settling down in Naomi's house. It seems that several weeks had elapsed between the end of chap. 2 and the beginning of chap. 3. The events of this chapter occur at barley winnowing time, which probably happened after both the barley and the wheat had been cut and gathered at the threshing floor. Except for the absence of a preliminary setting of the stage (cf. 1:22–2:1) based on locale and characters, the broad structure of Act 3 duplicates that of Act 2, with relatively short scenes at the home of Naomi and Ruth framing events in the field that take up the major portion of the text, as the following comparison illustrates:

Domestic Scene	2:2–3	3:1–5
Field Scene	2:4–16	3:6–15
Domestic Scene	2:17–23	3:16–18

679

The central scenes display further similarity inasmuch as both break into two unequal subunits, the division being marked by temporal notes:
Chapter 2   2:4–13 ... "at mealtime" ... 2:14–16
Chapter 3   3:6–13 ... "until morning" ... 3:14–15[1]

1. Scene 1: The Scheme (3:1–5)

Except for six words, four at the beginning of v. 1 and two at the beginning of v. 5, the first scene of Act 3 consists entirely of direct speech. As in chap. 1, the senior partner dominates the dialogue. The fifty-five words that make up Naomi's first speech present a sharp speech contrast to the four words in Ruth's response.

In light of the closing verses of chap. 2, one may speculate that Naomi hoped Boaz would take the initiative in establishing a relationship with Ruth that was more personal than that of native landowner and alien scavenger and that would eventually lead to marriage. Perhaps he was being sensitive toward Ruth as a widow, not wishing to impose himself upon her until she was emotionally healed and ready to contemplate remarriage. Obviously he was not making any moves; so as Ruth's mother-in-law, Naomi took it upon herself to overcome his inertia.[2] Her speech to Ruth breaks down into three parts: (1) a statement of the problem (v. 1), (2) a summary of the facts (v. 2), and (3) a detailed prescription of the procedure (vv. 3–4).

(1) The Problem (3:1)

[1]One day Naomi her mother-in-law said to her, "My daughter, should I not try to find a home for you, where you will be well provided for?

3:1 Naomi broaches the subject of finding a husband for her daughter-in-law gently, with an affectionate address of Ruth as "My daughter." This is only one word in Hebrew, but it is highly significant, expressing the relationship between these two women from Naomi's perspective and laying the foundation for the daring scheme she will propose. She then poses a rhetorical question: Is it not up to her to secure Ruth's future?[3] The question actually has

---

[1] Based on temporal shifts M. D. Gow (*The Book of Ruth: Its Structure, Theme and Purpose* [Leicester: Apollos, 1992], 63–74) divides the chapter differently into evening (vv. 1–7), midnight (vv. 8–14a), and dawn (vv. 14b–18) parts, but these do not accord with thematic, geographic, or dialogic features.

[2] D. N. Fewell and D. M. Gunn argue that Boaz was trapped by patriarchy and privilege as much as Naomi was by dependence ("Boaz, Pillar of Society: Measures of Worth in the Book of Ruth," *JSOT* 45 [1989]: 45–59).

[3] Even if הֲלֹא (NIV "should I not") is interpreted as an emphatic particle, "Surely" (cf. M. L. Brown, "Is It Not? Or Indeed!: *HL* in Northwest Semitic," *Maarav* 4 [1987]: 201–19), the sense is the same, since the rhetorical question expects a strongly affirmative response, "Of course!"

two parts. First, as her mother-in-law, Naomi asks if she should not provide[4] "rest" (NIV "home") for her daughter-in-law. The word *mānôaḥ*, "place of rest," derives from the same root as *mĕnûḥâ* in 1:9 and speaks of the security and tranquility that a woman in Israel longed for and expected to find in the home of a loving husband. The verbal link invites the reader to consider whether subsequent events are to be viewed not only as the consequences of Naomi's scheming, but also the results of her prayer in 1:8–9. Furthermore, to pick up the imagery of 2:12, a responsible husband functions as the wings of God offering protection and security for all who dwell in his house. Second, she defines the purpose of her quest for *mānôaḥ* for Ruth: that it may go well for her (contra NIV, "where you will be well provided for").[5] This is a general statement by which she means the removal of the reproach of her widowhood and the solution of her destitution by securing the economic necessities of life (food, shelter, clothing) and the calming of her anxieties concerning the future. As she declares it, Naomi's sole motivation in proposing the following scheme is the welfare of her daughter-in-law. Not a word is said about her personal anxieties about the future. Nor is their any hint of a concern to provide an heir for her own husband Elimelech or her son Mahlon by a levirate marriage. She expresses no interest whatsoever in what will be high in Boaz's mind as he marries Ruth: to secure the place of Mahlon's family in Israel by raising up his name on his patrimonial estate and in the court of Bethlehem (4:10). It seems that in this patricentric environment, concerns involving inheritance and the place and reputation of the family within the family history were primarily male concerns. Women in general and widows in particular were more anxious about life for the living in the present.[6]

In that cultural context Ruth certainly would have answered Naomi's rhetorical question of v. 1 in the affirmative. Yes, it is the duty of a widowed mother-in-law to see to the welfare and security of her widowed daughter-in-law. This applies all the more in this case since Ruth committed herself on oath to Naomi till death do them part. As in any healthy covenant relationship, these are two people who have committed themselves to the other's good above their own.

(2) Summary of the Facts (3:2)

[2]Is not Boaz, with whose servant girls you have been, a kinsman of ours? Tonight he will be winnowing barley on the threshing floor.

---

[4] The verb בקשׁ means "to seek, pursue, provide for." Cf. the expression לְבַקֵּשׁ טוֹבָה לְ, "to seek the good/welfare for," in Neh 2:10.

[5] The NIV interprets the conjunction אֲשֶׁר as a subordinating conjunction, but it is preferable to interpret it telically, expressing purpose or result. Cf. GKC § 165*b*.

[6] Cf. the comments by P. Trible, *God and the Rhetoric of Sexuality* (Philadelphia: Fortress, 1978), 192–93.

3:2   Again drawing Ruth into her thinking by using another rhetorical question, Naomi begins by setting forth the facts.[7] First, Boaz is the two women's near relative. The order of the sentence, subject-predicate, is not merely emphatic; it establishes this as a verbless clause of identification, which suggests that in Naomi's mind Boaz is not simply a relative but *the* near kinsman who must fulfill the role she has in mind.[8] Whereas in 2:20 she had identified him as a *qārôb* and a *gōʾēl*, now she refers to him as *mōdaʿtānû*, "our acquaintance, relative," using a stylistic variant of *mōdaʿ*, which the narrator had used in 2:1.[9] Again the use of the plural suffix "our" draws Ruth in, highlighting the solidarity of the mother-in-law with her Moabite daughter-in-law in what is essentially an Israelite custom. But the narrator does not tell us whether at this time or on any previous occasion Naomi had lectured Ruth on Israelite family theology and custom. Ruth's awareness seems assumed.

Second, calling Ruth to special attention with *hinnēh*, "Behold" (missing in NIV), Naomi reminds her that tonight Boaz will be winnowing barley at the threshing floor.[10] Barley was typically threshed at the onset of the dry season (late May-June), after all the grain, both barley and wheat, was cut and gathered. The best threshing floors involved rock outcrops on hilltops. The hard surface was needed to keep the grain free of dirt and to facilitate sweeping up the grains at the end of the day. The hilltop location was required to take advantage of the wind that would blow away the chaff when the threshed grain was tossed in the air with a fork, allowing the separated heavier kernels of grain to fall to the floor. This threshing floor probably was located in or near the field where Ruth had been gleaning, some distance from the town of Bethlehem (cf. v. 15). Boaz chose to do his winnowing at night,[11] presumably because the night breezes were more desirable than the gusty winds of the daytime.

(3) Prescription of the Procedure (3:3–5)

[3]Wash and perfume yourself, and put on your best clothes. Then go down to the threshing floor, but don't let him know you are there until he has finished eating and drinking. [4]When he lies down, note the place where he is lying. Then go

---

[7] The opening וְעַתָּה, "and now," serves a double function, introducing the logical conclusion to the preceding and signaling the beginning of a new phase in the drama.

[8] The NIV's rendering should therefore be changed to "Is not Boaz *the* kinsman of ours?"

[9] Like קֹהֶלֶת (*qōhelet*), מֹדַעַת is a formal feminine variant.

[10] הִנֵּה־הוּא זֹרֶה אֶת־גֹּרֶן הַשְּׂעֹרִים הַלָּיְלָה, "behold he winnows the threshing floor of barley tonight," involves a metonymic figure of speech whereby "threshing floor" stands for the products one gets from the threshing floor.

[11] As in Josh 2:2 הַלַּיְלָה, "tonight," means "this evening." Interestingly, the word הָעֶרֶב is never found in the MT meaning "this evening." 2 Sam 11:2 is the closest. Otherwise it is only used in "until the evening" or "in the evening."

and uncover his feet and lie down. He will tell you what to do."
⁵"I will do whatever you say," Ruth answered. ⁶So she went down to the
threshing floor and did everything her mother-in-law told her to do.

3:3–5 Without telling Ruth specifically that she has her marriage to Boaz
in mind, Naomi gives her daughter-in-law detailed instructions on how to take
advantage of the situation.[12] Of course all of these actions are designed to
make Ruth as attractive to Boaz as possible and to break down resistance. The
steps may be summarized briefly.

First, Ruth is to take a bath (*rāḥaṣ*, "to wash), a normal first step in preparation for a sexual encounter and/or marriage.[13]

Second, she is to apply perfume. The verb *sûk* means "to anoint." Here it
refers to the application of perfumed olive oil. The need for perfume was
heightened by the hot climate and the lack of modern style deodorants to
combat body odors.

Third, Ruth is to put on her dress. The word used for "dress" is *śimlâ*,
which normally refers to the outer garment that covered virtually the entire
body except the head. The word designated garments worn by both men and
women, though Deut 22:5 suggests they were distinguished. In no case,
including the present, does the word require the meaning "best clothes," as
rendered by the NIV. This interpretation seems to be based on the parallel
between this text and Ezek 16:8–12.[14] Both texts contain the sequence of
bathing, applying perfume, and putting on garments in preparation for an
encounter with a male. It is therefore commonly assumed that Naomi would
have Ruth follow a bride's normal preparation for marriage. But such a brazen
act would have repulsed rather than attracted Boaz.[15] On the other hand, some
see Naomi simply advising Ruth to dress up to attract a man.[16] But this text
bears no resemblance at all to accounts of seductive dress, as in Isa 5:1–3 and
Jdt 10:4. On the contrary, there seems little point in dressing up to go out in
the dark. Nor would Naomi have used the generic word for an outer garment,
śimlâ. According to Exod 22:25–26, poor people used this garment for a blanket at night. Since Ruth was a poor person going out to spend the night in the
field, she will have needed this blanket to keep warm.[17]

---

[12] Contra Nielsen (*Ruth*, 67) it is unnecessarily speculative to associate Ruth's visit to the
threshing floor with a religious festival.

[13] Cf. Ezek 16:9; *Sus* 17.

[14] On which see Block, *Ezekiel 1–24*, 477–86.

[15] So also Bush, *Ruth*, 150.

[16] Nielsen (*Ruth*, 68) comments, " 'The instructions to Ruth to wash and perfume herself are
naturally to make her irresistible." Cf. Hubbard, *Ruth*, 201; G. Gerleman, *Ruth,* BKAT 18/1 (Neukirchen: Neukirchener Verlag, 1960), 31.

[17] The root is common Semitic for "mantle, cloak." On שִׂמְלָה in the OT see further *HALOT,*
1337–34.

On the analogy of 2 Sam 12:20, it appears that Naomi is hereby advising Ruth to end her period of mourning over her widowhood and get on with normal life. According to the Samuel text, when David had been informed of the death of his son, he washed himself, applied perfumed oil, put on his *śimlâ,* and then went to the temple to worship, after which he came back home and ate and drank. To David's puzzled contemporaries this signaled the end of his period of mourning for his son. It may well be that until this time Ruth had always worn the garments of widowhood, even when she was working out in the field. Perhaps this was the reason for Boaz's inertia. As an upright man, he would not violate a woman's right to grieve the loss of her husband nor impose himself upon her until she was ready. We know too little about how long widows would customarily wear their mourning clothes, but it may be that Naomi is now telling Ruth the time has come to doff her "garments of widowhood" (Gen 38:14,19) and let Boaz know that she is ready to return to normal life, including marriage, if that should become possible.[18] Naomi may have had all this in mind already in 2:20, but if she did, she kept these notions to herself until such a time as she deemed Ruth ready for the move.

Fourth, Ruth is to go down to the threshing floor where Boaz is working and where he will spend the night. In Hebrew a town *(ʿîr)* is by definition a walled settlement. For defensive purposes they were usually situated on top of a hill, natural or man-made. Therefore Naomi's use of the verb *yārad* makes perfect sense from a topographical point of view. To some it may seem odd that Boaz should have stayed out in the field for the night. It is true that normally landowners and field workers would go out to the fields in the morning and return at dusk to the security of the walled village for the night. It seems that at winnowing time, however, an exception was made, and the men would sleep at the threshing floors to guard the fruits of their hard labor against thieves or marauding animals. But Naomi adds a rider to this command. Ruth is not to let Boaz know she has come until he has finished eating and drinking and lain down for the night. According to v. 7, after a long day of hard work, "eating and drinking" would put him in a relaxed mood, and he would quickly drop off to sleep.

The reference to eating and drinking prior to an encounter reminds the reader of Gen 19:30–38, according to which Lot's daughters deliberately got their father drunk so they could have intercourse with him. Although Boaz's "drinking" probably included an alcoholic beverage, our passage makes no mention whatsoever of him getting drunk or of engaging in actions that he would not have done sober. Ruth the Moabitess is indeed descended from Lot

---

[18] For a similar interpretation see Bush, *Ruth,* 152, following B. Green, "The Plot of the Biblical Story of Ruth," *JSOT* 23 (1982): 61.

by his eldest daughter, but the narrator is careful to present her as the antithesis of the stereotypical Moabite. In fact she is deliberately portrayed throughout as embodying the Israelite standards of *ḥesed*.

Fifth, lurking incognito near the threshing floor, Ruth is to observe carefully where Boaz finally lies down.[19]

Sixth, Ruth is to uncover his "lower limbs" and go and lie down herself. Few texts in the book have generated as much discussion as this command. There is a line of interpretation that treats it as a command to engage in risque and seductive behavior. It seems that in this cultural context, at winnowing time the threshing floor often became a place of illicit sexual behavior. Realizing that the men would spend the night in the fields next to the piles of grain, prostitutes would go out to them and offer their services. As a Moabite Ruth might not have had scruples about feigning the role of a prostitute to secure a sexual favor from a "near relative" any more than Tamar did in Genesis 38.

This interpretation is rendered all the more attractive by the fact that each of the three Hebrew words that make up this sentence is capable of more than one meaning, and each is capable of bearing an overtly sexual meaning. First, the root *glh*, "to uncover," is often used in sexual contexts of "uncovering someone's nakedness" (a euphemism for exposing the genitals[20]) or of "uncovering someone's skirt."[21] Second, the final verb, *šākab*, "to lie," is often used to denote sexual relations.[22] Third, the noun between these verbs, *margĕlôt*, derives from *regel*, "foot," the dual and plural of which may be used euphemistically for the genitalia.[23] Not surprisingly, therefore, some interpret Naomi's scheme as delicate and dangerous, charged with sexual overtones.[24]

The ambiguities in the words and the circumstances chosen by Naomi are

---

[19] The sequence of *waw* conjunctive + jussive in וִיהִי֑...וְיָדַעַתְּ is odd, but not unprecedented. Cf. 1 Sam 10:5; 2 Sam 5:24; 1 Kgs 14:5. This probably is intended as an emphatic form of command before the following converted perfect: "Let it be when he lies down that you shall know/note the place." On the use of the *waw* conjunction + jussive where a perfect with *waw* consecutive or imperfect with simple *waw* is expected, see GKC § 109k and § 112z.

[20] גָּלָה עֶרְוַת אִב/אֵם, Lev 18:6–19; 20:11,17–21; Ezek 22:10.

[21] גָּלָה כְּנַף אָב, Deut 22:30[Hb. 23:1]; 27:20. Nielsen (*Ruth*, 66–70) interprets the verb to mean "undress [herself]," the object being implicit. But this is impossible since the *piel* form of the verb always has a specified direct object, and when the reflexive sense is intended, Hb. uses the *niphal* (Exod 20:26; 2 Sam 6:20) or the *hithpael* stem (Gen 9:21).

[22] Except for Gen 30:15–16 and 2 Sam 11:11, the relations are always illicit (incest, homosexuality, bestiality, rape, seduction): Gen 19:32–33; Lev 20:11–13,18,20; Deut 22:25; 27:20–23; 35:22. Cf. W. Williams, "שׁכב," *NIDOTTE* 4.100.

[23] Exod 4:25; Judg 3:24; 1 Sam 24:3[4]; Isa 7:20 (all male); Deut 28:57; Ezek 16:25 (both female); Isa 6:2 (heavenly creatures). Occasionally urine is called "water of the feet" (2 Kgs 18:27 = Isa 36:12).

[24] Cf. Trible, *God and the Rhetoric of Sexuality*, 182, and 198, n. 23.

indeed provocative.[25] What is one to think of a woman who bathes, puts on perfume, and then in the dark of night goes out to the field where the man is sleeping and uncovers his legs? Under ordinary circumstances these look like the actions of a prostitute. On the other hand, this overtly sexual interpretation of Naomi's directions seems to read far more into the text than is intended. Each of the three words probably is misinterpreted. First, there is no suggestion in Naomi's tone or intention that either verb is to be interpreted sexually. The verb *gillâ* need not be interpreted along the lines of "uncovering someone's nakedness," and it is unlikely that Naomi would have encouraged her daughter-in-law to immoral action by using *šākab* sexually. Although Naomi may show signs of compromising theologically, especially at the beginning, unlike Lot's daughters, who do use *šākab*, after chap. 1 the picture the narrator paints of Naomi is consistently virtuous.

Second, Naomi may have deliberately used the word *margĕlôt* to exclude the genital interpretation that is occasionally intended with *regel/raglayim*. On the analogy of *mĕraʾăšôt*, "place of the head, head support," in Gen 28:11,18, some interpret *margĕlôt* as "place of the feet, footing."[26] However, a better clue to its meaning is found in Dan 10:6, the only place outside this context (here it occurs four times: vv. 4,7,8,14) where the word appears. There, juxtaposed with *zĕrōʿôt*, "arms," the word means "lower limbs," inclusive of feet, legs, and thighs. Accordingly, it seems Naomi is advising Ruth to uncover Boaz's lower limbs, probably exclusive of his genitals, and then go and lie down herself. Naomi says nothing about lying next to him or even lying at his feet. She is simply to lie down and watch what happens. Although the action is suggestive, by either of these last two interpretations the choice of *margĕlôt* actually draws the reader's attention away from the genitals and diffuses it over the limbs as a whole.

Third, rather than noting the restraint and care with which Naomi chooses her words, the overtly sexual interpretation exaggerates the significance of Naomi's previous instructions[27] and runs roughshod over the narrator's characterization of both her and Ruth in the story. How could Boaz, also a virtuous person, bless Ruth for her action (v. 10) and characterize her as a supremely noble woman (v. 11) if she was seeking sexual favors from him? Neither Naomi nor Ruth seems interested in sex or progeny at this point. Naomi is driven throughout by a concern to provide more security for Ruth than she, as mother-in-law, can provide. Ruth needs long-range protection and

---

[25] H. J. Harm ("The Function of Double Entendre in Ruth Three," *JOTT* 7 [1995]: 19–27) observes a series of double entendres in the chapter: יָדַע ,שָׁכַב ,בּוֹא ,גָּלָה ,מִגְלַת ,לְבוֹ ,וַיִּטַב ,אָחַר הָלַךְ. The author leads the reader to expect a sexual affair but then goes on to show that the godly are above their culture.

[26] Thus *HALOT*, 631; Hubbard, *Ruth*, 203; V. P. Hamilton, "רגל," *NIDOTTE* 3.1048–49.

[27] Trible, *God and the Rhetoric of Sexuality*, 182, has Ruth dressing in her finest clothes.

support such as only a husband can provide.

Seventh, Ruth is to wait for further instructions from Boaz. With this comment Naomi expresses remarkable confidence in Boaz to take the matter from here. Or is she at this point placing her faith in God to guide Boaz in making the appropriate response? In either case she was letting Boaz have the last say in Ruth's fate.

The delicacy of the scheme is obvious, and the potential for disaster is extreme. From a human perspective Naomi seems to be taking a huge gamble that Boaz may not interpret this series of nonverbal gestures in accordance with the meaning she intends.[28] Obviously when Boaz awakes and discovers his feet uncovered and a woman lying nearby, the nonverbal communication is sufficiently ambiguous to be interpreted in any one of several ways. First, in that cultural and spiritual context, Boaz could wake up in the middle of the night and willingly accept Ruth's overtures, in his grogginess interpreting her actions to be those of a common prostitute. After all, the events described occur in the dark days of the judges. Second, Boaz could wake up and interpret Ruth's actions as those of a prostitute but as a noble and genuinely virtuous Israelite shoo her off as an immoral woman with whom he will have nothing to do. Third, Boaz could wake up and recognize immediately the true meaning of Ruth's actions and respond favorably to her.

Naomi's scheme is obviously a gamble. The effectiveness of her plan is measured by the extent to which Boaz's interpretation when he awakes conforms to the meaning she has intended in Ruth's actions. Either of the first two responses would have defeated Naomi's purpose; and far from securing Ruth's welfare, this poor Moabite woman would have returned home broken in body and bruised in spirit. From a natural perspective the desired response was actually the least likely to occur. What are the chances that Boaz will wake up and in his groggy state notice that Ruth has covered herself with a *śimlâ* rather than the seductive garb of a prostitute, that he will understand when she introduces herself, that he will respond favorably toward her, overlooking the irregularities of the situation (a woman proposing to a man, a younger person proposing to an older, a field worker proposing to the field owner, an alien proposing to a native), and that, in fulfillment of Naomi's words, he will give Ruth rational

---

[28] This episode offers a classic illustration of the pitfalls of an audience-response hermeneutic. This proposal also provides the student of communication theory with a classic illustration of the power of ambiguity in rhetoric. Communication always involves three elements: a speaker, a message, and an audience. Understood traditionally, communication is the process whereby the message is transferred from speaker to audience. It used to be assumed that true communication has not occurred unless the audience has arrived at the speaker's understanding of an issue. The source of a communication was the final authority over its meaning, and it was the duty of the audience to determine that intended sense. In our postmodern culture this entire scheme has been turned on its head. According to audience-response theory communication has potential meaning, but the hearer is the active agent in determining the meaning. Authorial intent has become irrelevant.

instructions concerning how to proceed? But by this time Naomi's faith is strong. She has confidence in Boaz's integrity and apparently in the hidden hand of God to govern his reactions when he awakes.

Remarkably Ruth's faith appears to be equal to that of her mother-in-law, for she gives herself wholly to carrying out Naomi's scheme in full. Meanwhile the narrator challenges the reader to trust God the way these women do. The first scene closes, leaving us to wonder if this delicate and dangerous plan will work.

2. Scene 2: The Implementation of the Scheme (3:6–15)

Scene 2 of Act 3 is framed by two topographical notes: "She went down to the threshing floor" (v. 6a) and "He went into the town" (v. 15c; NIV "he went back to town"). As noted earlier, this scene divides into two unequal parts. The first (vv. 6–13), which transpires between evening and midnight, describes Ruth's implementation of Naomi's scheme and Boaz's immediate response; the second (vv. 14–15), which occurs from midnight to morning, describes a subsequent scene at the threshing floor and sees this party back into town. The first part subdivides further as the focus of attention shifts back and forth between Ruth and Boaz.

(1) Phase 1: The Night Encounter (3:6–13)

6So she went down to the threshing floor and did everything her mother-in-law told her to do.

7When Boaz had finished eating and drinking and was in good spirits, he went over to lie down at the far end of the grain pile. Ruth approached quietly, uncovered his feet and lay down. 8In the middle of the night something startled the man, and he turned and discovered a woman lying at his feet.

9"Who are you?" he asked.

"I am your servant Ruth," she said. "Spread the corner of your garment over me, since you are a kinsman-redeemer."

10"The LORD bless you, my daughter," he replied. "This kindness is greater than that which you showed earlier: You have not run after the younger men, whether rich or poor. 11And now, my daughter, don't be afraid. I will do for you all you ask. All my fellow townsmen know that you are a woman of noble character. 12Although it is true that I am near of kin, there is a kinsman-redeemer nearer than I. 13Stay here for the night, and in the morning if he wants to redeem, good; let him redeem. But if he is not willing, as surely as the LORD lives I will do it. Lie here until morning."

RUTH'S ACTIONS (3:6–7). **3:6–7** This scene opens with a transitional expository note that Ruth made good on her promise to Naomi (v. 6). She went down to the threshing floor and carried out all of Naomi's commands.[29] Ruth's unquestioning obedience to her mother-in-law represents one more sign of the *ḥesed* that Boaz will talk about in v. 10. In v. 7 the narrator describes what Ruth observed at the threshing floor. First, she watched Boaz eat and drink until he "was in good spirits." The idiom *yāṭab lēb,* literally "a heart is good," describes a sense of euphoria and well-being.[30] No doubt Boaz was satisfied with the work that was accomplished this day, but he probably also was feeling the effects of the wine. But unlike Lot in Genesis 19, there is no reason to interpret this as a drunken stupor. The narrator paints an image of a contented man at peace within himself and in harmonious step with a world that is yielding its fruit as a result of Yahweh's blessing (1:6) and his hard work.

Second, she watched him leave the supper and go and lie down at the far end of the heap of threshed grain. *ʿărēmâ,* "pile," which derives from a root *ʿāram,* "to pile up, store," refers to the pile of grain that had accumulated from days of threshing and winnowing and was waiting to be transported into the city. Normally the pile would have been at the edge of the winnowing floor. Describing the scene from Ruth's perspective, the preposition *qāṣeh,* "end," suggests that Boaz lay down on the opposite end of the pile.

BOAZ'S REACTION (3:8). How much time elapsed between these observations and Ruth's next action is not clear. From what follows it seems that Boaz must have fallen asleep before Ruth made her move, or he would have noticed immediately when she uncovered his legs. Once he had fallen asleep, she sneaked up[31] to him and uncovered his legs, and then lay down herself.[32] Satisfied with the accomplishments of the day and relaxed after a good meal, Boaz had drifted off into a deep sleep, so that in the warm late spring evening he was oblivious to her exposing his legs. At midnight, however,[33] he shivered (*ḥārad;* NIV "something startled the man"), probably because of the chilling

---

[29] Note the use of the stronger verb, צָוָה, "to command," here, in contrast to אָמַר, "to say," in v. 5.

[30] The expression occurs elsewhere in Judg 18:20; 19:6,9; 1 Kgs 21:7; 2 Kgs 25:24; Eccl 7:3. Note also the related expression לֵב טוֹב, "a good heart," which describes the contented state of those who have eaten and drunk well (1 Sam 25:26; 2 Sam 13:8; Esth 1:10). The Aramaic Tg. adds interpretively, "He blessed the Lord who had accepted his prayers and removed the famine from the land of Israel."

[31] וַתָּבֹא בַלָּט, "and she came with stealth, in secret." In Judg 4:21 the same word, לָט, describes Jael's surreptitious approach to Sisera. Cf. also 1 Sam 18:22 and 24:5.

[32] The precise repetition of the wording in v. 4 highlights how carefully she was following Naomi's plan. Contra Berlin (*Poetics of Biblical Narrative,* 91), who insists that Naomi had intended Ruth to approach Boaz as soon as he had lain down, before he went to sleep, when his spirits were still high and he was in a receptive mood. In her view Ruth misunderstood Naomi's romantic mission as a secret legal business.

[33] בַּחֲצִי הַלַּיְלָה, lit., "at the half of the night."

of the night air,[34] and, groping for his covers,[35] he was surprised (Hb. *hinnēh,* "behold," left untranslated by NIV) to find someone lying by his legs *(margĕlôt).* The narrative is telescoped at this point, not telling the reader how he recognized her as a woman.[36]

Given the spiritual climate in the period of the judges, an average Israelite might have welcomed the night visit of a woman, interpreting her presence as an offer of sexual favors, but not so Boaz.[37]

RUTH'S ANSWER (3:9). **3:9** Not recognizing who she was in the dark of night but curious about her identity, Boaz asked the natural question, "Who are you?" This question is an advance over his first encounter with her, when he had asked, "To whom does she belong?" (2:5).

Ruth answers the question forthrightly, "I am your servant Ruth." Unlike the field supervisor, she does not introduce herself as "the Moabitess," nor as "the one who returned with Naomi from the land of Moab" (2:6). Nor does she introduce herself as Ruth, the widow of the deceased Mahlon. Though conscious of her own identity, she is keenly aware of her place in the social structure, deferentially identifying herself further as "your servant" (*ʾămātĕkā*). The choice of *ʾāmâ,* "handmaid," rather than *šipḥâ* as in 2:13, and the twofold repetition of the word in her answer reflect Ruth's growing self-confidence and the requirements of the context. After all, she is about to propose marriage to her superior, which would have been ruled out for a *šipḥâ.*

There is nothing unusual about the first part of Ruth's answer, either in

---

[34] חָרַד means "to tremble," usually with fright, but the notion of fear is not inherent in the word. Cf. Exod 19:16; 1 Sam 14:15; Isa 32:11. The NIV's unlikely "something startled the man" follows the versions. The Tg. reads "and he was afraid, and his flesh became soft like turnip from fear." Cf. the discussion by D. R. G. Beattie, *The Targum of Ruth,* Aramaic Targum 19 (Collegeville, Minn.: Liturgical Press, 1994), 26, n. 5. Any effort to attribute the "startling" to a dream or a midnight apparition or a visit by a night demon (*Lilith*) is unnecessarily speculative. See the discussion by Bush, *Ruth,* 162. The immediate context still offers the best clue.

[35] The NIV's "and he turned" associates the word לְפָת with Arabic *lapata,* "to turn, twist," but this misunderstands the situation. The Arabic cognate may help to explain Job 6:18, which uses the *niphal* to describe the winding paths of caravans. But nearer to the point of our text is the only other occurrence of the verb in the OT, Judg 16:29, where the *qal* describes Samson's "taking hold of" the pillars of the temple of Dagon. This interpretation finds support in the Akk cognate *lapātu,* "to touch, grope, feel" (*AHw,* 534; cf. the discussion by O. Loretz, "Das hebr *LPT*," in *Studies Presented to A. Leo Oppenheim* [Chicago: University of Chicago Press, 1964], 155–58).

[36] It is not clear that he recognized her as a woman immediately. The use of the feminine for "someone" is determined by the reader's awareness that this was a woman. The impersonal use of the normal *ʾîš,* which is masculine, would have been incongruous to the reader. Cf. Berlin, *Poetics of Biblical Narrative,* 152, n. 6.

[37] Note the expansion by the Tg.: "But he restrained his desire and did not approach her, just as Joseph the righteous did, who refused to approach the Egyptian woman, the wife of his master, just as Paltiel bar Laish the Pious did, who placed a sword between himself and Michal daughter of Saul, wife of David, whom he refused to reproach" (Beattie, *Targum of Ruth,* 26–27).

form[38] or content. But the second part is extraordinary for several reasons. First, she seizes the initiative and turns the attention away from herself and onto Boaz. This is extraordinary, for as she has just described herself she is a lowly servant, and he is the master; she is an uninvited visitor on his turf; she is a woman, and he is a man; she is a foreigner, and he is a native.

Second, the addition contributes nothing to the question Boaz has asked. On the contrary, it raises the question, "Who is Boaz?"

Third, out of the blue and without equivocation, Ruth requests that Boaz marry her. The idiom she used may be puzzling to the modern reader, but there was no question about its meaning in the Israelite context in which it was given. Literally *pāraś ānāp ʿal* translates "to spread one's wing over." One recognizes immediately a play on 2:12, where *kěnāpîm,* "wings," had served as a metaphor for the refuge that Yahweh, the God of Israel provides. Accordingly, one's first impulse is to interpret this statement similarly. Ruth is hereby requesting (even demanding) that Boaz take her under his wing and assume responsibility for her security. But there is more to the demand than this. The word *kānāp* is gloriously ambiguous, referring not only to the wings of a bird but also to a skirt, the corners of one's flowing garments (hence NIV). Literally then this statement could be interpreted as a request by Ruth to Boaz to cover her and protect her from the chill of the night. He is not the only one shivering. But there is still more to the demand, for in common Hebrew usage "to spread one's wings over someone" was a euphemistic idiom for marriage.[39] The gesture of a man covering a woman with his garment was a symbolic act, which according to Near Eastern custom signified "the establishment of a new relationship and the symbolic declaration of the husband to provide for the sustenance of the future wife."[40] This is what Naomi had in mind when she proposed this scheme as a way of providing *mānôaḥ,* "rest, security," for Ruth in 3:2. In essence she challenges Boaz to be the answer to his own invocation of blessing upon her in 2:12. Remarkably, Boaz interpreted this immediately not as a demand for sex but as a proposition for marriage, a conclusion supported by his response in vv. 10–13.

Fourth, the grounds Ruth gives for her demands are also extraordinary: *kî gōʾēl ʾattâ,* "since you are a kinsman redeemer." She puts the issue to him as if she, a Moabite, is fully aware and fully at home with the Israelite custom. Obviously Ruth and Naomi had discussed the subject fully. But a careful

---

[38] The form of her answer is identical to the common divine self-identification formula, "I am Yahweh your God."

[39] See esp. Deut 22:30[Hb. 23:1]; 27:20; Mal 2:16; Ezek 16:8. On the last named reference see Block, *Ezekiel 1–24,* 482.

[40] Thus P. A. Kruger, "The Hem of the Garment in Marriage: The Meaning of the Symbolic Gesture in Ruth 3:9 and Ezek 16:8," *JNSL* 12 (1984): 86.

reader will notice a significant syntactical shift from Naomi's first identification of Boaz as the kinsman redeemer in v. 2. The orders of the two statements may be compared by juxtaposing them as follows:

3:2   Surely Boaz is our kinsman *(hălō' bō'āz mōda 'tānu).*
3:9   Because a kinsman-redeemer are you *(kî gō'ēl 'attâ).*

Whereas Naomi's subject-predicate order *identifies* Boaz as *the* kinsman obligated to perform redemption duties for a widow, Ruth's predicate-subject order merely *classifies* him as one qualified to fulfill the role. As it turns out, she is correct, for there is one who has first rights/obligations as kinsman-redeemer.

Ruth's speech may be short, but it is extraordinary. Naomi had ended her instructions for her daughter-in-law (vv. 2–4) by telling her to do whatever Boaz would say she should do. Now she turns around and lectures Boaz on his obligations to her! The reader stands back in awe, wondering what has possessed her. Here is a servant demanding that the boss marry her, a Moabite making the demand of an Israelite, a woman making the demand of a man, a poor person making the demand of a rich man. Was this an act of foreigner naïveté, or a daughter-in-law's devotion to her mother-in-law,[41] or another sign of the hidden hand of God? From a natural perspective the scheme was doomed from the beginning as a hopeless gamble, and the responsibility Naomi placed on Ruth was quite unreasonable. But it worked!

BOAZ'S REPLY (3:10–13). **3:10–13** Boaz's response to Ruth's actions and to her proposition is as remarkable as her deeds and words. His speech breaks down into four parts: (1) a blessing for and eulogy of Ruth (v. 10), (2) a promise (v. 11), (3) a revelation of a complication (v. 12), and (4) words of reassurance (v. 13). We will comment on each in turn.

In Boaz's remarkable opening remarks, first, instead of cursing her and shooing her off as some immoral whore, he blesses her. Like Naomi in v. 1, he expresses his respect for and sense of obligation to Ruth by addressing her with *bittî*, "my daughter." The form of the blessing he pronounces is identical to that which Naomi had pronounced upon him in 2:20 in response to his kindness to Ruth. These opening words are extremely important, for they break the tension in the drama. Now the reader as witness to the drama may relax, knowing that Ruth's brazen acts and extraordinary proposition have received a sympathetic response. But this raises the question of why he responds this way. How is it that, being awakened at midnight in a most unusual and compromising situation, he knows exactly what Ruth has meant by her veiled speech, and he commends her for it? These are hardly the flippant words of one who has been seduced by a woman of the night. Again the reader is inclined to see the hidden hand of God guiding not only the actions

---

[41] Thus Hubbard, *Ruth,* 213.

of individuals but their reactions and their dispositions so that in the end Yahweh's agenda is fulfilled. Boaz's words have the ring of divine inspiration.

Second, Boaz praises Ruth for her remarkable demonstration of *ḥesed*. He says, literally, "Your act of *ḥesed* [display of family loyalty and devotion] is better than the first." What Boaz has in mind by Ruth's last *ḥesed* is obviously her daring appearance at the threshing floor to ask him to marry her. For the *ḥesed* against which he evaluates this act we must go back to his previous eulogy of this woman in 2:11: Ruth's radical abandonment of her own past in order to cast her lot with Naomi and her people.[42] Although the *ḥesed* character of her previous actions is clear, it is not so obvious how Boaz could interpret the events of this night as an act of even greater kindness and grace.

But Boaz answers this question in part himself by lauding Ruth for not going after other more desirable men. The expression "to go after" *(hālak ʾaḥărê)* is more commonly used in a religious sense of devoting oneself to other gods and following them in cultic procession, but it also describes the efforts one person makes to establish sexual relations with another (Prov 7:22; Hos 2:5[Hb. 7]). Boaz qualifies the kinds of men Ruth might more naturally have pursued as "the young men" *(habbĕḥûrîm)* and "whether poor or rich" *(ʾim dal wĕʾim ʿāšîr).*[43] Derived from a root *bāhar,* "to choose," "young men" refers to choice young men, men in the prime of their strength and virility.[44] In Amos 8:13 the word is paired with "the virgins" *(habbĕtûlôt).* The last expression, "whether poor or rich," functions as a merism for "anyone at all." Viewed as a whole, this sentence is remarkably deferential. Boaz is obviously not a withered old man (he is still able to put in a full day's work in the fields with his young workers and then stay at the threshing floor all night), and he is obviously not a poor man (he is characterized as a "man of standing" in 2:1, and he owns land and servants). He recognizes, however, that if Ruth would have married for status ("young man") or love ("poor") or money ("rich"), she could have gone elsewhere. Boaz himself may qualify on these counts, but he intentionally deflects the attention from the object of this "search"[45] to the seeker.

But this still does not explain how Ruth's preference for Boaz is to be understood as an act of *ḥesed,* loyalty, and kindness. Although the men of integrity in Bethlehem would have hesitated to overstep the rights of the near relative(s) and sought the widow Ruth's hand in marriage, Boaz's comment suggests she was a "free agent" who could have pursued anyone she wanted.

---

[42] Additional support for a link between these chapters is found in Ruth's reference to "wings" in 2:12.

[43] The NIV reverses the order.

[44] The frequent use of the word for the "selected soldiers." For brief discussion of the word see the commentary on Judg 20:15–16,34. See also E. Nicole, "בחר," *NIDOTTE* 1.638–69.

[45] Cf. Naomi's use of the verb בָּקַשׁ, "to seek," in v. 1.

But instead she chose him. The issue revolves around Ruth's use of the word *gōʾēl*, "kinsman-redeemer." Ruth's primary demand is simply that he marry her, but Boaz knows as soon as she utters this word that the stakes are higher, and this is what triggers his interpretation of her words as an act of *ḥesed;* they represent kindness and grace for the benefit of someone else.

The opening word of v. 11, *wěʿattâ*, "and now," signals a shift in focus from Boaz's interpretation of Ruth's actions to the consequences of those actions. Continuing his warm and tender tone, Boaz addresses Ruth once more as *bittî*, "my daughter," and he calms her fears with the traditional word of comfort, *ʾal tîrěʾî*, "do not be afraid." Shifting his own attention from the past to the future, Boaz reassures Ruth further by promising to do for her everything that she asks. This remarkable declaration completes the reversal of roles that we had begun to see in Ruth's speech in v. 9. In v. 4 Naomi had advised Ruth that she should do everything that Boaz would tell her to do, assuming that he would respond favorably and that she was under his authority. Ruth acknowledges this social order in v. 9 (she is Boaz's servant), but then proceeds immediately to subvert it by lecturing him on his obligations. Now Boaz declares that he is the servant of Ruth, the destitute Moabite widow!

But Boaz adds his rationale for submitting to Ruth: all the citizens of Bethlehem know that she is indeed a noble woman. In his reference to the citizens Boaz employs a special idiom, *kol šaʿar ʿammî*. This expression translates literally "all the gate of my people,"[46] but it means "all of my people who gather at the gate," that is, the full citizens of the town. Some of these will appear in formal session in the next act (4:1–12). The formal construction of his statement, "you are a woman of noble character," suggests Boaz may be reporting the consensus of the court. By quoting it Boaz elevates Ruth to the same status the narrator had ascribed to him in 2:1 *(gibbôr ḥayil)*. The phrase *ʾēšet ḥayil*, "woman of worth," or "woman of strength," occurs elsewhere only in Prov 12:4 and 31:10.[47] But what an amazing turn of events this declaration signifies! Ruth had arrived in Bethlehem a few short weeks ago as a destitute widow, a foreigner at the mercy of the locals. And Act 2 had demonstrated that this was how she perceived herself. She was the lowest of the low, with no recourse but to scavenge in the fields behind the servants of the landowners. But because of her devotion to her mother-in-law and her willingness to abandon all for her, the townspeople knew her true character. But she did not gain this reputation by trying to be somebody, by associating with the important people. On the contrary, it was her self-effacing embodiment of

---

[46] For the literal use of the same expression, "the gate of my people," see Mic 1:9 and Obad 13.

[47] The placement of the Book of Ruth after Proverbs in some canonical traditions suggests that in some circles Ruth was considered the supreme illustration of feminine nobility. See the comments in the introduction (p. 589).

Israel's lofty covenant standards, her *ḥesed*, her kindness and loyalty to the family of her deceased husband, especially her mother-in-law, that has won her the praise of all. Boaz could have treated her as Moabite trash, scavenging in the garbage cans of Israel, and then corrupting the people with her whorish behavior; but with true *ḥesed* of his own, he sees her as a woman equal in status and character to himself.

Ruth's heart must have skipped more than one beat as she listened to Boaz's warm response to her overtures. But a second *wĕʿattâ*, "But now," in v. 12 signals a disturbing development, and the disclosure that follows will have caused her heart to stop. Boaz is forced by his own integrity to report that he is indeed *a* kinsman-redeemer, but not *the* kinsman redeemer. His own frustration over this reality is reflected in the convoluted and redundant syntax of the first part of the sentence: "But now look! It is certainly true that I am a kinsman-redeemer"[48] (*wĕʿattâ kî ʾim gōʾēl ʾānōkî*[49]). But the second sentence declares the troubling truth: there is a kinsman-redeemer who is a closer relative than he.[50]

In v. 13 Boaz tries to pacify Ruth with some immediate counsel: he advises her to spend the night there ("here" is implied but is not in the text). To guard against any sexual misinterpretation, however, he avoids the word *šākab*, preferring to speak of lodging or spending the night *(lîn)*. He uses the same word that Ruth had used in 1:16 when she committed herself to lodging wherever Naomi would lodge. By his speech as a whole and his choice of words in particular, Boaz maintains the same kind of integrity that he had displayed in chap. 2. He will not take advantage of Ruth.

Boaz is not only committed to keeping the ethical and moral norms of the people of Yahweh; he is also determined and resigned to abide by the nation's legal and social customs. As much as he respects Ruth and as much as he would like to marry her, he willingly defers to the primary *gōʾēl*. But he is not oblivious to the implications of his decision for Ruth. The NIV obscures the fact that three times in this verse she is the object of the verb *gāʾal* (which itself appears four times): "If he will *redeem* you, fine; but if he does not desire to *redeem* you, then I will *redeem* you." His eagerness is expressed by

---

[48] The NIV renders the statement as a concessive clause, "Although it is true that I am near of kin," but this seems too mild.

[49] *Kethib* reads אָנֹכִי גֹאֵל אִם כִּי אֲמָנָם כִּי וְעַתָּה. The problem is created by the fact that no fewer than six of these words and/or combinations thereof can function as asseverative or emphatic particles: (1) וְעַתָּה (*HALOT*, 3.d., 902); (2) כִּי by itself (*HALOT*, 1.a,b, 470); (3) כִּי אִם (*HALOT*, B.1.b, 471); (4) אֲמָנָם by itself (*HALOT*, 65); (5) כִּי אֲמָנָם (Job 12:1); (6) כִּי אֻמְנָם (Job 36:4). The best solution is to drop אִם with *qere* as a dittographic error and to link the first כִּי to וְעַתָּה as a separative particle between the adverbial expression וְעַתָּה and the rest of the sentence. See the fine discussion by Bush, *Ruth*, 174.

[50] Note the comparative construction, מִמֶּנִּי קָרוֹב גֹאֵל יֵשׁ, "There is a redeemer nearer than I." The word קָרוֹב recalls Naomi's use of the same expression in 2:20.

his determination to settle the matter in the morning.

Boaz's determination to redeem Ruth if she becomes available to him is expressed even more emphatically by the oath at the end, *ḥay yhwh,* rendered "as the LORD lives." This oath occurs after the assertion to which it applies only here and in 1 Sam 20:21. The standard order has the oath first and then a declaration of the intended action. Whereas the NIV follows the traditional rendering, the oath is better interpreted "by the life of the LORD."[51] Sasson observes that the oath controls two promises: a promise to marry Ruth, which relates to the issue of security for her, and a promise to redeem her if he has the opportunity. These two differ in respect to content (marriage vs. redemption), time (now vs. tomorrow), beneficiary (Ruth vs. Naomi), and potential for success (Boaz's will pitted against the will of "Mr. So and So."[52] But he wisely tells Ruth to lie down until morning.

Before moving on to the next episode, we may reflect further on the nature of the marriage envisioned by Boaz and Ruth. It is important to note that nowhere in the dialogue between Naomi and Ruth or between Boaz and Ruth is there a hint of concern for progeny, that is, the preservation of the family *a la* the prescriptions regarding levirate marriages in Deut 25:5–10. If Ruth asks for "redemption" and if Boaz is determined to "redeem" her, the aim is not primarily the preservation of Mahlon's family name.[53] Naomi's aim in devising the scheme was to end the destitution and disgrace of Ruth's widowhood and to provide greater security than she can offer to her in the house of her own husband. Since the Torah contains no specific prescription concerning situations like this, Naomi's scheme rests not on a legal obligation but on confidence in Boaz's sense of moral obligation to the family. In this matter she will not be disappointed. The lives of genuinely good people are not governed by laws but character and a moral sense of right and wrong. For Boaz Yahweh's covenant with Israel provides sufficient guidance for him to know what to do in this case.

(2) Phase 2: The Morning Send-off (3:14–15)

[14]So she lay at his feet until morning, but got up before anyone could be recognized; and he said, "Don't let it be known that a woman came to the threshing floor."

[15]He also said, "Bring me the shawl you are wearing and hold it out." When she did so, he poured into it six measures of barley and put it on her. Then he went back to town.

---

[51] For a discussion of the oath formula see M. Greenberg, "The Hebrew Oath Particle *ḥay/ḥē,*" *JBL* 76 (1957): 34–39. See also Block, *Ezekiel 1–24,* 207–8.

[52] Sasson, *Ruth,* 92–93.

[53] But this will become an important issue in the following chapter. See esp. 4:10.

3:14–15 Heeding both Naomi's (3:4) and Boaz's advice, Ruth lay back down at his feet *(margĕlôt)* for the remainder of the night. In the wake of their midnight conversation neither Ruth nor Boaz probably slept much that night. Boaz's mind probably was preoccupied with plans for resolving the case in the morning and anxieties over whether he would be able to gain the right to Ruth's hand. No doubt these issues were also on Ruth's mind, but she had the added concern of getting away unnoticed in the morning. In order to preserve her reputation (note Boaz's concern expressed in v. 11) she would need to be gone before anyone could recognize[54] her. To prevent suspicions about her activities at night on the threshing floor where Boaz slept, before dawn broke she got up and prepared to leave.

By now Boaz was awake as well, and under the dark sky he initiated a second conversation. He supported her efforts to get away without being noticed, for he had a reputation to preserve as well. He could not afford to have Ruth discovered and recognized by the rest of the workers. However, maintaining his lavish generosity and demonstrating his good faith (or to make it look as though she had gone to get the grain, rather than spending the night with him), he sent her off with another substantial gift of food.

The narrator concretized the image by reporting their conversation. He quotes Boaz requesting a garment from Ruth to be used as a container for grain, and then holds it so he can fill it. The verb for "bring," from a root, *yāhab*, "to give," is rare in the Old Testament but common in Aramaic as the equivalent of Hebrew *nātan*.[55] Most of the occurrences of *yāhab* in the Old Testament are in the imperative, and all are in quoted speech. In a few instances the word is used as an interjection, "Come!" (i.e., "Come on!"),[56] but usually it bears the sense it has here, "Give, hand over."[57] The word for the garment requested, *miṭpaḥat* (rendered "shawl" in NIV), is found elsewhere only in Isa 3:22, in the context of a list of jewelry and clothing worn by women. It cannot refer to Ruth's primary garment, nor should it be equated with the "outer garment" *(śimlâ)* referred to in v. 3. But since it was obviously a piece of outer clothing (it is "on" Ruth) and had to be large and strong enough to use as a sack for grain, "cape," "scarf," or "shawl" are all reasonable interpretations.

Ruth held the garment like a sack while Boaz poured in the grain, six "measures" of barley. Because the unit of measurement is omitted in the text, it is difficult to calculate the amount of grain Boaz sent home with Ruth. This

---

[54] The verb היכר, "to notice, recognize," was encountered earlier in 2:10,19.
[55] On *yhb* in Aramaic see *DNWSI*, 442–48; in other Semitic languages see *HALOT*, 236.
[56] Gen 11:3–4,7; 38:16; Exod 1:10; perhaps also 2 Sam 11:15.
[57] See above on Judg 1:15. Also Gen 29:21; 30:1; 47:15; 1 Sam 14:41; etc. On the word in Hb. see further GKC § 69*o*.

kind of omission is common in Hebrew,[58] but it is especially frustrating here. If we assume the ephah, the measuring instrument used in 2:17, she would have carried home on her shoulder 180 or 300 pounds, depending on which size ephah is used as the basis of calculation![59] This is certainly too much for a woman to carry from the field and then up the hill to town. A more reasonable unit of measurement is the omer (ʿōmer), which was one-tenth the size of an ephah (Exod 16:36). By this standard he gave her eighteen or thirty pounds, which is far less than she had gleaned the first day (2:17) but which she would have been able to carry home. A third option is the seah, a capacity measure of approximately one third of an ephah,[60] yielding a weight of sixty or one hundred pounds of grain for Ruth to carry. Even if a strong young woman could have carried this amount, it is doubtful whether a cape could hold that much barley. Perhaps the best solution is to assume that the numeral "six" refers simply to "six scoops," either with both hands cupped or with some other handy utensil used at the threshing floor.

This scene closes on a confusing note. According to the Masoretic text, the last sentence in v. 15 has Boaz going back to the town. This is unexpected, not only because Ruth is the one who has just been preparing to leave the threshing floor, but also because Boaz has more work to do there. Recognizing this problem, the Syriac and Vulgate versions have changed the masculine verb form (wayyābōʾ) into a feminine form (wattābōʾ), a reading followed by most modern translations.[61] The NIV (also NRSV) is surely right in preserving the masculine, however, not only on the principle of lectio difficilior (the more difficult reading is preferred), but also as the narrator's way of highlighting Boaz's eagerness to resolve the issue that has been raised overnight. The narrator assumes the audience/reader knows that Ruth will have left after Boaz had poured the grain on the cape and placed it on her shoulder. But without a statement concerning Boaz, there is no transition from his location at the field in chap. 3 to his presence in town in chap. 4.

3. Scene 3: The Results of the Scheme (3:16–18)

[16]When Ruth came to her mother-in-law, Naomi asked, "How did it go, my daughter?"

Then she told her everything Boaz had done for her [17]and added, "He gave me

---

[58] Cf. GKC § 234n; IBHS § 15.2.2b; GBH § 142n.; J. C. L. Gibson, *Davidson's Introductory Hebrew Grammar: Syntax*, (Edinburgh: T & T Clark, 1994), § 47.

[59] See the commentary on 2:15.

[60] The size of the seah (סְאָה) seems to have doubled from six to twelve liters after the exile. On the seah see R. Fuller, "אֵיפָה," *NIDOTTE* 1.382–84.

[61] NASB, JB, JPSV, RSV, GNB, REB.

these six measures of barley, saying, 'Don't go back to your mother-in-law empty-handed.'"
18Then Naomi said, "Wait, my daughter, until you find out what happens. For the man will not rest until the matter is settled today."

3:16–18 If Ruth and Boaz had been deprived of sleep that night, no doubt the same was true of Naomi. The one who had concocted this scheme probably lay awake all night wondering how her daughter-in-law was faring. But the question with which Naomi greets Ruth when she returns catches us all by surprise. Instead of "Who is there/here?" *(mî šām/pōh)*, or "What did he do?" *(meh ʿāśâ)*, or "How are you?" *(mah lāk)*, she asks *mî ʾatt bittî*, which translates literally, "Who are you my daughter?" Obviously she knows who Ruth is, or she would not have added "my daughter." This question illustrates the fluidity of Hebrew interrogative particles. Here *mî* probably should be interpreted as an accusative of condition, that is, "In what condition or state are you?" which is equivalent to "How are you"[62] or "How did it go for you?"

This is certainly how Ruth interpreted the question, for she proceeds to report to Naomi everything the man had done for her. The reference to Boaz as "the man" rather than by name is curious. A similar pattern in 2:19–20 and 3:18 suggests this was a deferential way for these women to speak about an absent male who was socially their superior. It prevents the impression of presumptive familiarity. The narrator summarizes Ruth's story of the momentous events of the night in one short sentence (v. 16b), but when he reaches the climax, the account slows down and breaks into direct speech (v. 17). The structure of the sentence, with the front loading of the direct object and the addition of the demonstrative pronoun, *ʾēlleh, "These* six barleys he gave to me ...," suggests that both women were continuing to wonder at the load Ruth had brought home.

But Ruth's quotation of Boaz's explanation of the gift is as amazing as the amount of the gift itself. Earlier we had speculated that Boaz may have given Ruth the grain as one more expression of his lavish generosity, or as a measure of his good faith, or even as a ruse to make it look as though she had gone to get the grain rather than spending the night with him. Now from Boaz's own words we finally get a clue about its true significance. It seems that when Boaz requested Ruth's cape and poured out the barley for her, she had expressed some puzzlement over his actions and may even have asked him why he was doing this. He answered Ruth's verbal or nonverbal question by explaining that it would be inappropriate for her to return to her mother-in-law empty. Presumably he meant "empty-handed" (thus NIV), that is,

---

[62] Cf. *IBHS* § 18.2.d. The interrogative particle מָה, "What?" bears a similar sense in Judg 18:8.

"without a gift,"[63] although the use of the word here represents an effective play on its occurrence in Naomi's bitter accusation of God in 1:21. But why should Boaz be interested in Ruth's mother-in-law at this point? Several answers may be proposed.

First, his interest in Naomi may derive from his understanding of the custom of the *gōʾēl*. Boaz's kinship obligations are based on his relationship with Naomi rather than Ruth. Not only is Ruth a Moabite woman; in 2:1 the narrator had specifically noted that Boaz was related to Elimelech, who is Naomi's deceased husband, rather than Mahlon, Ruth's husband. This interpretation will be reinforced in chap. 4, where the issue before the court is primarily the disposition of land that belongs "to our brother Elimelech" (4:3). Only at the end does Boaz bring Mahlon into the picture (4:9–10). Furthermore, from a literary point of view, this scene will be the last in which Ruth is portrayed as a primary character. Once she has gotten Boaz to agree to fulfill his kinship-redeemer obligations, her role in the plot is finished.

Second, Boaz may have sent this gift as an expression of appreciation for Naomi's initiative in proposing the scheme that has gotten them to this point. She was the one who had encouraged Ruth to end her mourning and put on normal garments as a signal of her readiness to resume normal life, including making herself available for marriage. She was the one who had devised the scheme to bring Boaz and Ruth together and to have Ruth put the issue of his kinship obligations directly before Boaz. In short she was the mastermind behind the entire plot.

Third, Boaz may have sent this gift to Naomi as a sign of good faith, his determination to carry through with his promise to try to gain the right to Ruth, and if he could not, to see that the primary kinsman-redeemer would marry her. In fact, since Naomi was Ruth's legal guardian (2:1), he may even have intended the grain as a down payment of the *mōhar*, the bride price paid at the time of betrothal. The *mōhar* was often given by the groom at the time of betrothal, not as a purchase price (women were not commodities to be bought and sold) but as a promise to prepare for the wedding in good faith and a pledge for the good behavior of the groom toward the bride in the meantime.[64]

Naomi's response in v. 18 indicates that this is how she accepted it. She advises Ruth to relax and wait to see how the matter will turn out. The verb that the NIV renders "Wait" is *yāšab*, which normally means "to sit, to

---

[63] The adverb רִיקָם is very common after verbs of motion: בּוֹא, "to come" (Ruth 3:17); הָלַךְ, "to go" (Exod 3:21); רָאָה (niphal), "appear before" (Exod 23:15; 34:20; Deut 16:16); שָׁלַח (piel), "to send" (Gen 31:42; Deut 15:13; 1 Sam 6:3; Job 22:9). רִיקָם also means "without success," especially with the verb שׁוּב, "to return" (2 Sam 1:22; Isa 55:11; Jer 14:3; 50:9).

[64] On the nature and function of the *mōhar* in Israel see R. Wakely, "מֹהַר," NIDOTTE 2.859–63. Further bibliography is provided.

dwell," but in this context in our idiom it means "to sit tight." Naomi's advice here is the opposite of what she had said at the beginning of the chapter. There she had called Ruth to action: to wash, anoint herself with perfume, put on her clothes, go down to the threshing floor, watch where Boaz lies down, approach him and uncover his legs, and then listen to what he tells her to do. Now that Ruth has done her part, she may sit down and wait to see what will happen next. The expression *ʾēk yippōl dābār,* literally "how the matter will fall," is an idiomatic expression for "how things will turn out." Again this is not a resignation to chance or fate in the abstract. In the statement we recognize a note of confidence in the hidden hand of God, who will direct affairs to the proper conclusion. But Naomi hereby also expresses great confidence in Boaz. Ruth may sit back and relax, but she knows Boaz will not. Indeed he will not rest *(šāqaṭ)*[65] unless[66] the matter is brought to a conclusion, today![67]

With this statement the curtain falls on Act 3. All the characters have played their roles perfectly. Naomi has taken the initiative and gotten the ball rolling, Ruth has carried out her delicate and daring scheme, and Boaz has responded right on cue. The reader as witness to the drama waits with Ruth to see "how the matter will fall."

---

[65] In Judges the same word had been used several times to describe the land at peace, i.e., unmolested by outside enemies or internal strife (3:11,30; 5:31; 8:28 [all of Israel]; 8:7,27 [of the Canaanite population of Laish]). The pairing of the participle of שֹׁקֵט, "resting, undisturbed," with בֹּטֵחַ, "trusting," in the last two references is especially instructive for the understanding of the word in this context.

[66] כִּי אִם is used to introduce exceptive clauses (GKC § 163; GBH § 173*b*), not temporal clauses as the NIV reads it.

[67] כָּלָה, in *qal* means "to be finished." The *piel* used here is factitive: "to bring to an end, to finish." The word prepares the reader and the characters for the quick resolution of the complication in the plot.

IV. ACT 4: THE RESCUE OF THE ROYAL LINE (4:1–17)
1. Scene 1:   The Legal Resolution (4:1–12)
   (1) Boaz's Preparation for Court Action (4:1–2)
   (2) The Report of the Court Proceedings (4:3–8)
       Boaz's First Speech (4:3–4c)
       The *Gōʾēl's* First Speech (4:4d)
       Boaz's Second Speech (4:5)
       The *Gōʾēl's* Second Speech (4:6)
       The *Gōʾēl's* Nonverbal Speech (4:7–8)
   (3) Boaz's Response to the Outcome of the Court Proceedings
       (4:9–10)
   (4) The Public's Reaction to the Outcome of the Court Proceedings
       (4:11–12)
2. Scene 2: The Genealogical Resolution (4:13–17)
   (1) The Narrative Report of the Birth of a Boy (4:13)
   (2) The Women's Reaction to the Birth of the Boy (4:14–15)
       The Women's Blessing for Yahweh (4:14a)
       The Women's Prayer for the Child (4:14b)
   (3) The Narrative Report of Naomi's Adoption of the Boy (4:16)
   (4) The Women's Naming of the Child (4:17a–b)
   (5) The Narrator's Conclusion (4:17c)

—— **IV. ACT 4: THE RESCUE OF THE ROYAL LINE (4:1–17)** ——

The final act brings the drama of Naomi, Ruth, and Boaz to a remarkable conclusion. This act consists of two scenes, the first transpiring in the gate of Bethlehem, that is, in the legal setting of a court; the second occurs at least nine months later, presumably in the home of Boaz and Ruth.

1. Scene 1: The Legal Resolution (4:1–12)

The first scene divides stylistically and logically into four readily identifiable segments: (1) Boaz's preparation for court action (vv. 1–2), (2) the transcript of the court proceedings (vv. 3–8), (3) Boaz's response to the outcome of the court proceedings (vv. 9–10), and (4) the public reaction to the outcome of the court proceedings (vv. 11–12). We will examine each in turn.

(1) Boaz's Preparation for Court Action (4:1–2)

¹**Meanwhile Boaz went up to the town gate and sat there. When the kinsman-redeemer he had mentioned came along, Boaz said, "Come over here, my friend, and sit down." So he went over and sat down.**
²**Boaz took ten of the elders of the town and said, "Sit here," and they did so.**

4:1–2 The atypical placement of the subject before the verb in the opening line of the final act is deliberate and literarily significant for two reasons. First, by avoiding the usual sequential narrative verb form (*waw*-consecutive imperfect) the narrator breaks the temporal sequence of episodes and signals the beginning of a new act rather than another scene within the preceding act.¹ But in so doing he does not intend to drive a major chronological wedge between chaps. 3 and 4. On the contrary, in view of Boaz's midnight promise to take action on behalf of Ruth "in the morning" (3:13) and Naomi's expression of confidence that Boaz will not rest unless he settles the matter "today" (3:18), this episode must be understood to have transpired that very day.

Second, by front-loading Boaz, the reader's attention is drawn to this character. Admittedly Ruth's fate will be a key issue in the court proceedings, but the narrator hereby forces the reader to focus on Boaz. This first impression is confirmed by the way in which each of the segments of this scene are constructed. In this first episode he is the one who takes the initiative in calling the court into session: he goes up to the gate and sits down; he notices the nearer kinsman and calls him over; he summons ten of the elders to session. The other characters merely respond to his initiatives. In the second stage (vv. 3–8) Boaz presents the issue to the nearer redeemer with a thirty-six-word speech, to which the man replies positively with two words. Then Boaz introduces the complicating factor in the case, and the man declares his change of mind. In the end the audience's and the reader's attention is shifted to Boaz by the transfer of the nearer kinsman's sandal. The third episode (vv. 9–10) is taken up entirely with Boaz's speech, as he explains the significance of his actions this day. In the final segment (vv. 11–12) Boaz is silent to be sure, but he is the focus of the court witnesses' blessing.

Boaz's first action in this scene is to go up to the gate. The verb ʿālâ, "to go up," reflects the relatively higher position of the town vis-à-vis the surrounding countryside and answers to Ruth's movement from town "down" (yārad) to the threshing floor in 3:3,6. But since to "go up to the gate" is also idiomatic for "to go to court," this sentence introduces a secondary function of city gates in this context. City gates in Palestine in the early iron age were complex structures with lookout towers at the outside and a series of rooms on either side of the gateway where defenders of the town would be stationed.

---

¹ Cf. the use of the *waw*-consecutive to begin a new scene in v. 13.

But these gateways also served a secondary purpose, as a gathering place for the citizens of the town.[2] This was where the official administrative and judicial business of the community was conducted. Verse 13 of chap. 3 had left Ruth and the reader wondering how Boaz would overcome the obstacle to their desire to marry. Now we learn that Boaz has decided to put the case to a court of law.

Normally when individuals would come in from the fields and go up to the town, they would pass right through the gate and go straight to their homes. But Boaz seems to have had no time to go home. Having arrived at the gate, he "sat there." The citizens would recognize this as an official act; he had arrived for legal business. No sooner had he sat down than the *gōʾēl* "just happened" to pass by. The word *hinnēh*, "Behold," which begins the second sentence of v. 1 (not reflected in the NIV), serves two functions: expressing Boaz's surprise at his appearance and turning the reader's attention to a new character in the drama. With a superficial reading of the book the timing of the kinsman-redeemer's arrival may seem coincidental, but a deeper reading will recognize again the hidden hand of God. In 3:13, when Boaz had suggested to Ruth that he would take action in the morning, he had invoked the name of Yahweh in an oath as a sign of his determination to resolve the issue quickly. Now Yahweh ensures the quick resolution of the matter by sending him by the gate just as Boaz was sitting down. Presumably the *gōʾēl* was on his way out of town to work in his fields.

Addressing the man directly, Boaz invited the *gōʾēl* to turn aside and sit down. But the way in which he addressed the man is curious. The expression *pělōnî ʾalmōnî*, rendered "my friend" in the NIV, has caused difficulty since Talmudic times.[3] Although most modern versions render the word "My friend,"[4] the REB and the NAB follow the Latin Vulgate in reading variations of "He called to him by name." But this seems to be precisely what he did not do. The NJPS has "So-and so."

The rhyming of these words creates the impression of an artificial creation, a kind of wordplay known as *farrago*, in which unrelated and perhaps even

---

[2] The tenth century B.C. gates at Gezer illustrate this legal function well. The gate structure consisted of a middle passageway slightly more than thirteen feet wide, with three chambers on each side. The side chambers measured slightly more than seven feet wide and fourteen feet deep. Running around the three walls of each side chamber were plastered benches. This feature was deemed so essential that with each reconstruction of the gate the bench was rebuilt and replastered. For photographs, a mock-up, and discussion see W. G. Dever, "Gezer," *NEAEHL* 2.503–4; id., "Gezer," *ABD* 2.1001–2. For a full discussion of gate fortifications in ancient Israel see Z. Herzog, "Fortifications (Levant)," *ABD* 2.848–52. The gate at Bethlehem probably was more modest than these but of a similar pattern.

[3] The Tg. seems to have given up on its meaning long ago and, like the NIV, simply put in what they think worked: גְּבַר הַצְּנִעֻו, "O modest man!"

[4] Thus NIV, NASB, NRSV, JB.

meaningless rhyming words are combined to produce a new idiom. English equivalents might be "hodge-podge," "helter-skelter,"[5] "heebie-jeebies," and "hocus-pocus." In such wordplays the meaning of the phrase is much greater than the sum of its parts. In fact, it may be unrelated to the meaning of the parts. The meanings of *pĕlōnî* and *ʾalmōnî* individually are difficult to establish. The first could be derived from *pālâ*, "to be different, distinct,"[6] but this scarcely advances the discussion. More helpful are the occurrences of related words in the cognate Semitic languages, specifically *plny/pila-nu*, "a certain one," in Aramaic,[7] *fulān* in Arabic (the origin of Spanish *fulano*, "John Doe"), and *fellān* in Tigre, on the basis of which *pĕlōnî* may be defined as "so and so," "someone known." Apparently the word is used "when the proper name cannot or should not be used."[8] The second element, in this idiom *ʾalmōnî*, is equally enigmatic. Some find the origin of this word in *ʾal-mōneh*, "not counted, not named,"[9] but a derivation from *ʾālam*, "to be silent, dumb," hence "quiet one," is more likely. Whatever Boaz's motivation in using this designation for the *gōʾēl*, in the present literary context *ʾalmōnî* seems to play on *ʾalmānâ*, the Hebrew word for "widow." Remarkably, the latter expression never occurs in this book, even though three of the characters (Naomi, Ruth, Orpah) are widows. This chapter specifically deals with a legal resolution of the problem of widowhood for two of these.

A clue to the meaning of the idiom here may be found in its two other occurrences in the Old Testament. In 1 Sam 21:2[Hb. 3] and 2 Kgs 6:8 the same expression is applied to places whose names are withheld, hence "such and such a place." The idiom seems to be archaic, its real meaning having been lost; but it continues to be used merely as an indicator of an indefinite person or place. The rendering "Mr. So-and-so," found in the NJPS, certainly captures the sense better than the NIV's "my friend," but our "Hey you" also works in the present context.[10]

---

[5] Sasson, *Ruth*, 106; id., *IDBSup*, 969.

[6] Cf. E. A. Martens, "פלה," *NIDOTTE* 3.620; Rudolph, *Ruth*, 59. The LXX κύριε, "O hidden one," or "one [whose name is] hidden," seems to have derived the word from פֶּלֶא, "to be wonderful, unusual, difficult." So also וַתִּקְמִיר כְּסִי, "hidden and concealed," the Tg.'s rendering of the present idiom in 1 Sam 21:3 and 2 Kgs 6:8. Commenting on the latter, M. Cogan and H. Tadmor (*II Kings*, AB [Garden City: Doubleday, 1988], 72) explain it as "an indefinite pronoun of uncertain derivation."

[7] The first in official Aramaic inscriptions; the second in a cuneiform text from Uruk. See *NWDSI*, 916 for references. Cf. פלן/פלון in later Christian Aramaic.

[8] *HALOT*, 934. See also the discussions by Sasson, *Ruth*, 105–107; Campbell, *Ruth*, 141–42; Hubbard, *Ruth*, 233–34; Rudolph, *Ruth*, 59.

[9] H. Bauer and P. Leander, Historische Grammatik des hebräischen Sprache des Alten Testaments (Halle: Niemeyer; reprinted Hildesheim: Olms, 1962), § 34a. Rudolph (*Ruth*, 59) rightly notes that in this case the preceding negative should be לֹא rather than אַל.

[10] Some LXX MSS read ὁ δεῖνα, "such a one" (cf. Matt 26:18), which is an improvement over κύριε in the better MSS. Cf. Old Latin *quicumque es*, "Whoever you are."

But this raises an important question: Why would the narrator, who is otherwise so careful with names, keep this character anonymous?[11] Whatever the motivation, the effect is to diminish our respect for him. To be sure, nothing overtly negative is said about him, but like Orpah, who serves as a foil for Ruth in chap. 1, this man presents a contrast to Boaz. He may be the *gōʾēl*, but he will shortly be dismissed as irrelevant to the central theme of the book: the preservation of the royal line of David.

Whatever the meaning of Boaz's expression for the *gōʾēl*, it communicated, and the man came and sat down with Boaz. With the principals in this court case present, it remained for Boaz to gather a quorum of witnesses. The verb *lāqaḥ*, "to take, procure," suggests that, unlike the *gōʾēl*, who happened to be passing by just then, Boaz had to go and round up enough men to constitute a legal assembly. Obviously the men were all full citizens of Bethlehem; being identified as elders they were responsible for the administration of the town. The fact that they left their work and followed Boaz reflects his stature in the community. As noted earlier, the side chambers of town gates in ancient Israel were designed so that the town's business could be done here, complete with plastered benches around the walls for the men to sit. If the gate at Bethlehem was the size of the tenth century B.C. Gezer gate (slightly more than seven by fourteen feet,[12] there would have been room for all twelve men, but it would have been crowded; and observers would have had to look on from the passageway outside the chamber. Since Bethlehem was always a less significant center than Gezer, the gateway might have been smaller, in which case the proceedings probably transpired in the plaza just inside the gate.

(2) The Report of the Court Proceedings (4:3–8)

[3]Then he said to the kinsman-redeemer, "Naomi, who has come back from Moab, is selling the piece of land that belonged to our brother Elimelech. [4]I thought I should bring the matter to your attention and suggest that you buy it in the presence of these seated here and in the presence of the elders of my people. If you will redeem it, do so. But if you will not, tell me, so I will know. For no one has the right to do it except you, and I am next in line."

"I will redeem it," he said.

[5]Then Boaz said, "On the day you buy the land from Naomi and from Ruth the Moabitess, you acquire the dead man's widow, in order to maintain the name of the dead with his property."

[6]At this, the kinsman-redeemer said, "Then I cannot redeem it because I might endanger my own estate. You redeem it yourself. I cannot do it."

[7](Now in earlier times in Israel, for the redemption and transfer of property to

---

[11] Assuming of course the פְּלֹנִי אַלְמֹנִי is not a personal name, Ploni Almoni, as it was treated by some rabbinic writers. Cf. *b. B.Bat.* 91a; *Ruth Rab.* 7:7 (midrash).

[12] See above, p. 650.

become final, one party took off his sandal and gave it to the other. This was the method of legalizing transactions in Israel.)
8So the kinsman-redeemer said to Boaz, "Buy it yourself." And he removed his sandal.

These verses represent an ancient equivalent to modern transcripts of court proceedings. The report flows smoothly except for the insertion of v. 7, which is an explanatory comment for a readership unfamiliar with the legal custom reflected in v. 6. Excepting this verse, the account is dominated by dialogue, with Boaz and the *gōʾēl* exchanging speeches. Boaz's primary role in the proceedings and in the mind of the narrator is reflected by the amount of space devoted to his comments. In three speeches he utters ninety-three words, while his counterpart speaks only nineteen.

Unfortunately, however, the interpretation of these speeches is fraught with problems, primarily because of our chronological and cultural distance from the events recorded here. Whereas the author knew exactly what he was writing about and was in fact extremely concerned that his readers understand (note the addition of v. 7), modern readers have inadequate grasp of the language of the book, and above all of ancient Israelite customs regarding widowhood, inheritance, redemption, and so forth.

BOAZ'S FIRST SPEECH (4:3–4c). **4:3–4c** It seems Boaz wasted no time in getting to the heart of the matter. The NIV obscures the emphatic construction of the Hebrew, which places the object in front (lit.): "the portion of field belonging to our brother Elimelech Naomi, who returned from the field of Moab, is selling." As in 2:3 the identification of the property in question as Elimelech's portion *(ḥelqâ;* cf. Deut 33:21; Josh 24:32; 2 Kgs 9:21,25) is rooted in the apportionment of the land among the tribes and clans of Israel under Joshua. According to Mosaic law this land was never to leave the family, and the institution of the *gōʾēl* was one of the nation's customs designed to prevent this from happening (Lev 25:25–30). Boaz reminds the man of a small but significant detail: the owner of the land was "our brother," that is, a relative to both of them. How closely related they were we may only speculate. As recounted in Deut 25:5–10, the legal levirate obligation applied to the immediate brothers of a deceased man (so also Genesis 38). While we have no textual documentation, it is possible, perhaps even likely, that according to Israelite custom (not law), in cases where there was no unmarried brother, the principle of levirate obligation was extended in accordance with the "pecking order" in inheritance law. According to Num 27:9–11, if a man died without a progeny (either son or daughter), his property would pass to his brothers; if he had no progeny or brothers, it would pass to his paternal uncles (father's brothers); if he had no progeny, brothers, or paternal uncles, the property would pass to his nearest relative from his own clan. The text does not indicate how far down this order Boaz and the *gōʾēl* were. In 2:1, however, the narrator does note that Boaz was from the clan of Elimelech. If the *gōʾēl* was a closer relative than Boaz (3:12), he must have been ahead in the pecking order.

According to Boaz's opening line in v. 3, the need for the present court case was precipitated by a decision of Naomi, who had recently returned from the land of Moab. But the nature of that decision is disputed. According to the NIV, Naomi was *selling* the land that belonged to Elimelech. This looks like an appropriate rendering of the verb *mākĕrâ*, the feminine perfect of *mākar*, which normally means "to sell." However, this interpretation flies in the face of ancient Israelite customs regarding land ownership, according to which Naomi, a widow, was in no position to sell the land. The regulations concerning the transfer of real estate in Numbers 27 cited above have the land of a deceased man passing to the son or daughter(!), or brother, or uncle, or another near relative; but there is no hint of a widow being allowed to claim the land.[13] This explains why a widow's lot in Israel was so precarious. With the death of her husband, she lost her base of support.[14] It also explains why Mosaic law was so concerned to protect the widow, along with the orphan and the alien, from oppression and exploitation.[15] The precarious economic position of widows has been assumed in the previous chapters; why else would Ruth need to experience the humiliation of scavenging after harvesters, and why was she at the mercy of some gracious landowner (2:2)?

If Naomi was not selling the land, then what was she doing? The answer lies in part in a more nuanced understanding of the verb *mākar*. It is true that in most cases in the Old Testament the word denotes an economic transaction involving transfer or sale of property, movable or real estate, from one owner to another. By no means, however, does it always involve a sale. In the Book of Judges we observed the figurative use of the verbs in the formula, "the LORD 'sold' Israel into the hand of [the enemy]" (Judg 3:8; 4:2–3; 10:7–8). Here *mākar* serves as a stronger alternative to *nāten*, "to give." None of these cases involved a purchase or money. At the personal economic level a person

---

[13] That a widow might have owned land is hinted at in Prov 15:25, but this may be intended as a metaphor declaring that God defends the rights of the widow in general.

[14] Note the frequent association of widows with orphans, aliens, and Levites (Job 29:13; 31:16; Jer 22:3; Zech 7:10) and the parallel conjoining of widows with divorced women (Lev 21:14; 22:13; Num 30:9[Hb. 10]; Ezek 44:22).

[15] Exod 22:21–24[Hb. 20–23]; Deut 10:18; 14:28–29; 24:19–21; 26:12–13; 27:19. But note the prophetic railing against those who violate these standards: Isa 1:17,23; Isa 9:17[Hb. 16]; 10:2; Jer 7:6; 22:3; Ezek 22:7,25; Zech 7:10; Mal 3:5; cf. also the complaint in Job 24:3,21. Note also the references in the Psalms to Yahweh as the defender of widows: Pss 68:5[Hb. 6]; 94:4–7; 146:9 (cf. also Prov 15:25) and Job's claims (contra his detractors, 22:9) to have done the same (Job 29:12–13; 31:16–17). On the status of the widow in ancient Israel see Hiebert, "The Biblical Widow," 125–41; F. C. Fensham, "Widow, Orphan and the Poor in Ancient Near Eastern Legal and Wisdom Literature," *JNES* 21 (1962): 129–39; de Vaux, *Ancient Israel*, 39–40.

in debt may "hand himself over" or "be handed over" *(yimmākēr)* to a creditor for six years (Deut 15:12; Jer 34:14) or until the next Year of Jubilee (Lev 25:39–54),[16] or a piece of patrimonial land may be "handed over" *(timmākēr)* to another person until the next Year of Jubilee (Lev 25:23–28; 27:20–24), but neither case constitutes a true sale. This interpretation is confirmed in the regulations concerning the use of patrimonial lands in Lev 25:13–16 and houses in 25:29–31. At issue is not the transfer of ownership of property but "the acquisition of the right of holding in usufruct someone else's property until the next Jubilee Year."[17] Accordingly, Naomi's action was not to sell the land that belonged to her deceased husband Elimelech; it was not hers to sell because by law ownership of the land would be transferred to the nearest relative (Num 27:8–11). What she had done was authorize the court to give it in usufruct to the *gōʾēl*.

What had happened to Elimelech's land since he had taken his family to Moab and since he had died we can only speculate. It seems most reasonable that moving to Moab had been a last resort for Elimelech. Before he would embark on such a drastic (and shameful) course of action, he would have attempted every other alternative, including selling the land to an outsider (cf. Lev 25:25–30). Obviously the poverty continued; and after the money from the sale was used up, he seems to have been faced with two choices: sell himself into slavery (cf. Lev 25:47–55) or move to a place where food was available. In moving to Moab he chose the lesser of two evils.

Meanwhile ten years had elapsed. During that time Elimelech and his two heirs had died in the land of Moab, and back in Bethlehem it appears the land had fallen into the hands of someone outside the family. When Naomi returned with Ruth, she could not automatically reclaim the land and begin making her own living from it. Consequently she and Ruth are left with no options but to scavenge for food. It seems, however, that because of Boaz's generosity Naomi and Ruth had been assured of sufficient food for the near future, enabling the senior widow to turn her attention to the legal issues relating to the patrimonial holdings of her husband.

Boaz's use of the perfect, *mākĕrâ*, is best interpreted as "a perfective of resolve," that is, "she has decided to give up the right of usufruct."[18] But Boaz was now initiating efforts to get the land back into the family. Nowhere does

---

[16] See the NJPS rendering of Lev 25:39.

[17] Thus E. Lipinski, "מכר, *mkr*," *TDOT* 8.292. "Usufruct" is defined as "the right of using the property of another and of drawing the profits it produces without wasting its substance" (*The New International Webster's Comprehensive Dictionary of the English Language* [Naples: Trident Press, 1996], 1382).

[18] On the "perfect of resolve" see *IBHS* § 30.5.1.d. For a much more detailed discussion of the problems posed by this verse and the variety of solutions that have been proposed see Bush, *Ruth*, 199–204 and his Excursus, pp. 211–15.

the text suggest that Naomi had contacted Boaz to arrange for the legal transfer of the rights. Nevertheless he seems to have concluded from the events of
the previous night that he must do something about the land; it is not right for
it to remain in an outsider's hands. Even though his conversation with Ruth at
the threshing floor had not mentioned land at all, he knew that gaining the
rights to the use of Naomi's property was the key to winning the right to
Ruth's hand.

Having announced the occasion for calling the court to session in v. 3, that
is, Naomi's decision to dispose of her deceased husband's land in v. 4, Boaz
explained his own involvement in this case. Not presuming upon a favorable
reception from the *gōʾēl*, he began cautiously and apologetically (more literally): "As for me, I thought,[19] I will open your ears by saying, …" The idiom
"to open the ears" has its origin in a nonverbal gesture to be sure, but to suggest that it has its background in a legal context where one party exposes the
ear of the other by pushing the hair back[20] is unnecessarily speculative and
precise. This idiom occurs thirteen times in the Old Testament and is usually
interpreted by the NIV and most others to mean "to inform." But the present
form, with a following *lēʾmōr* (lit. "to say"), occurs elsewhere only in 1 Sam
9:15 and 2 Sam 7:27. Since these two cases have *lēʾmōr* followed by declara-
tive sentences describing the information communicated, to translate the
idiom as "to inform" might be justified.[21] It hardly suits the present situation,
however, which has an imperative (*qĕnēh*, "acquire," rendered by the NIV,
"and suggest that you buy it"), not information for the *gōʾēl*, following the
idiom. In this context "to open the ears" is best interpreted as "to get someone's attention," that is, to make a person receptive to communication.[22] The
following *lēʾmōr*, which should be rendered "by saying"[23] introduces the
quoted statement.

Having won the *gōʾēl's* attention, Boaz challenged him to acquire the

---

[19] The verb אָמַר, "to speak," is often used of internal speech, "to say to oneself, to think." Here
אָמַרְתִּי, lit. "I said," functions as an abbreviation for אָמַרְתִּי בְלִבִּי, "I said in my mind." For
examples of the latter construction see Gen 17:17; 27:41; 1 Kgs 12:26; Isa 47:10; Obad 3; Zech
12:5; Pss 10:6,11,13; 14:1; 35:25; 53:2; 74:8; Eccl 2:1,15; 3:17,18; Esth 6:6. For discussion see J.
A. Lund, "אמר," *NIDOTTE* 1.444; S. Wagner, "אמר *ʾāmar*, *TDOT* 1.332. Here the following
clause, "I will open your ears by saying," declares the content of the thought. Some (Hubbard, *Ruth*,
239; Sasson, *Ruth*, 115) interpret the perfect form in a more legal sense: "I hereby declare," but this
is rendered unlikely by the following clause and would require the content of the declaration to follow immediately, i.e., the command to the *gōʾēl* to acquire the rights to the land.

[20] Thus Sasson, *Ruth*, 116, followed by Hubbard, *Ruth*, 240.

[21] In these cases לֵאמֹר functions in place of quotation marks.

[22] That the idiom does not automatically mean "to inform" is confirmed by Job 36:10, according to which God opens people's ears for/to instruction (וַיִּגֶל אָזְנָם לַמּוּסָר) and commands that
they turn from evil.

[23] On this use of the infinitive construct with *lamedh* see *GBH* § 124o.

rights to Elimelech's land in the presence of the gathered witnesses. Just as *mākar* in v. 3 does not mean "to sell," so here *qānâ* does not mean "to buy" but to accept Naomi's offer and "acquire the rights of usufruct." The witnesses are identified as those sitting in the gate, that is, the officially summoned ten, along with the elders of his people. It is possible that "the elders of my people" represents a nearer definition of the quorum of sitting witnesses, but it seems more likely that by now others have gathered in the passageway to observe the spectacle. Boaz's ultimatum is simple: if the *gōʾēl* wishes to perform the duty or exercise the rights of a *gōʾēl*, then let him act; but if he prefers not to do so, then he should let Boaz know.

The prescriptive texts concerning the role of the *gōʾēl* mentioned earlier had not covered the present case, that is, the rights of usufruct. This application of the laws suggests that the prescriptions in Leviticus and Deuteronomy were viewed neither as exhaustive nor restrictive to the situations described. Not every circumstance in which the principle could or should be applied is covered in that text. The present application arises from Israel's distinctive theology of land (which is a gift of God and must remain within the family) and family (which must remain intact in order for the life of the ancestors to continue).

Boaz concluded his first speech by asserting his need to know[24] and giving the reason for presenting the demand to the *gōʾēl:* he has first rights to acquire the land,[25] and he, Boaz, is next in line. As recorded, he did not declare that he would like to acquire the rights, but the implication would have been clear to everyone.

THE *Gōʾēl*'s FIRST SPEECH (4:4d). **4:4d** The *gōʾēl* answered Boaz with a mere two words, *ʾānōkî ʾegʾāl*, "I will redeem it." If Ruth was watching, her heart must have sunk. Boaz had expressed resignation to the will of the *gōʾēl* earlier (3:13), but in Ruth's mind this was probably not an acceptable option. Meanwhile the reader wonders why Boaz has not mentioned her in the transaction.

BOAZ'S SECOND SPEECH (4:5).   **4:5** In v. 5 Boaz introduces Ruth as a complication to the present case.[26] But the verse raises some of the most difficult problems in the book. The first part of the temporal clause is clear, anticipating a time (lit. "on the day") when the *gōʾēl* would acquire the rights to Elimelech's field from the hand of Naomi, that is, the transfer of

---

[24] Reading וְאֵֽדְעָה with *qere*. The cohorative ending suggests a legal sense, "that I may have it confirmed for the purpose of taking legal action."

[25] Literally כִּי אֵין זוּלָתְךָ לִגְאוֹל translates "because there is no one except you to redeem." זוּלָה with the preposition *lamedh* always denotes the only exception. אֵין is in the construct state but separated from the genitive by זוּלָתְךָ. According to GKC § 152*o*, the form אֵין became so fixed that its state was forgotten, and it was often separated from its genitive by shorter words.

[26] Answering to the complication the *gōʾēl* had represented in chap. 3.

the rights of usufruct. But what is to be made of the following clause, rendered, "and from Ruth the Moabitess, you acquire the dead man's widow …"? Limitations of space prevent a discussion of all the options and force us to get to the point as quickly as possible.[27] The NIV's "and from Ruth" represents a fairly literal reading of *ûmēʾēt*, "*and from with* Ruth," creating the impression that Ruth also had some legal interest in the land.[28] But this is highly improbable. Because the verb *qānîtā*, "you acquire," lacks a direct object according to the preserved Hebrew text *(kethib)*, Hubbard follows *BHS* in emending consonantal *wmʾt* ("and from") to *wgm ʾt* ("and also") and understands Ruth to be the direct object.[29] The same effect can be achieved, however, without the textual surgery by assuming that consonantal *wmʾt* consists of the conjunction *waw*, an enclitic *mem* and the sign of the direct object.[30]

The second major problem involves the form of the verb. the traditional Hebrew consonantal text reads *qnyty*, which normally would mean "I have acquired."[31] However, the Massoretes recognized the improbability of this spelling by vocalizing the word *qānîtāy* and suggesting an alternate reading *qnyth*. Vocalized *qānîtāh*, the latter means "you have acquired her." This is the preferred reading, with the feminine suffix referring to Ruth, the direct object named at the beginning of the clause.

Combining these solutions to the problems of this clause yields a sensible sentence that balances the previous, as the following juxtapositioning illustrates:

On the day you buy the field from the hand of Naomi,
And Ruth the Moabite, the wife of the deceased, you acquire.

Boaz hereby reminded the *gōʾēl* that this transaction is more complex than merely acquiring usufruct rights to Elimelech's field. Elimelech had a son whose death has left a second widow in the picture. This woman is implicated in any action that he as a *gōʾēl* might take. The manner in which

---

[27] For detailed discussions of the options see Gow, *Book of Ruth*, 150–65; Bush, *Ruth*, 215–29; Hubbard, *Ruth*, 237, 243–44; Sasson, *Ruth*, 121–31; Campbell, *Ruth*, 146–47.

[28] So also Gow, *Book of Ruth*, 164.

[29] Hubbard, *Ruth*, 247. The echo of this phrase in v. 10, where םגו replaces the present תאמו, may support this emendation.

[30] So also Bush, *Ruth*, 217; Campbell, *Ruth*, 146. On the enclitic *mem* see F. I. Andersen, *The Hebrew Verbless Clause in the Pentateuch*, JBLMS 14 (Nashville: Abingdon, 1970), 48, 124, n. 13; G. Rendsburg, "Eblaite *ô-MA* and Hebrew *WM* and Hebrew *WM-*," in *Eblaitica: Essays on the Ebla Archives and Eblaite Languages*, vol. I, ed. C. H. Gordon, G. Rendsburg, and N. Winter (Winona Lake: Eisenbrauns, 1987), 33–34.

[31] Thus REB, "I take over the widow, Ruth, the Moabite." Some understand קָנִיתִי as a legal perfect that may be understood as a present, "I am acquiring." Thus REB, "I take over the widow, Ruth, the Moabite."

Boaz introduced Ruth is significant. First, he introduced Ruth by her full name, "Ruth the Moabitess." This more precise identification seems intended to cast doubts about the wisdom of acquiring the rights to Elimelech's land in the mind of the *gōʾēl*. For Boaz, who has had direct contact with the woman, this is no problem, but he may have been counting on a measure of anti-Moabite sentiment on the part of his kinsman, rendering him less inclined to accept Naomi's offer. Second, he introduced her as "the wife of the deceased," though which deceased he does not specify. The *gōʾēl* obviously knew about the death of Naomi's husband. In view of Boaz's comment in 3:11, he must also have known about Ruth, but at this point he withholds the name of her husband. We will not know until v. 9 whether Ruth's deceased husband was Mahlon or Chilion.

To this point in Boaz's efforts to resolve the issue of Elimelech's land, he seems to have sought an application of the Israelite custom of the *gōʾēl*, according to which a close relative was responsible for ensuring that the patrimonial land stayed within the family (Lev 25:25–30). With the final purpose clause, however, Boaz introduced a new notion. If the *gōʾēl* would acquire the usufruct rights to Elimelech's land, he must also assume responsibility for rescuing the line of Elimelech. Presently the line is hanging on by two fragile threads: Naomi, Elimelech's elderly widow, who is past child-rearing age, and Ruth, Elimelech's Moabite daughter-in-law. But realistically the latter represented the only hope for the line. Accordingly Boaz added that if the *gōʾēl* would acquire rights to the land, he must also acquire Ruth with the specific purpose of marrying her and fathering a child through her on behalf of Elimelech and his son. Since the clause (lit.) "to establish the name of the deceased on his patrimonial land" borrows heavily from Deut 25:7, we observe here for the first time in the book an explicit reference to the levirate law.[32]

The word *šēm*, "name," does not mean simply the label by which one is identified. Boaz was not asking the *gōʾēl* to recover the name "Elimelech" (or "Mahlon") by giving it to someone. Rather, he used the name in its dynamic sense as a designation for the memory of a person's deeds and achievements, ones' reputation and honor, as well as a metonymic expression for one's descendants, who give one a sort of posthumous existence.[33] In the ancient world one of the most fearful curses one person could invoke on another was

---

[32] In Deut 25:9 "to raise/establish the name of his brother," is replaced with "build the house of his brother" (יִבְנֶה אֶת־בֵּית אָחִיו). Cf. Judah's command to his son Onan "to raise up seed for your brother" (Gen 38:8).

[33] For a study of the word see A. S. van der Woude, "שֵׁם *šēm* Name." *THAT* 2.935–63, esp. 948.

"May your seed perish and your name die out."[34]

Technically there is nothing in the prescription concerning the levirate marriage in Deut 25:5–10 that obligated either Boaz or the *gōʾēl* to marry Ruth and establish the name of Elimelech or Mahlon. The Mosaic prescription had the immediate brothers of the deceased in mind, and this is assumed in the application of the custom in Genesis 38 and 2 Sam 14:7. Accordingly, when Boaz challenged the *gōʾēl* to "establish the name of the deceased," he was not appealing to the letter of the law but its spirit.[35] Neither man was legally bound by Deut 25:5–10, but this does not eliminate a moral obligation. Boaz was prepared to operate on these grounds. The question is, Was the *gōʾēl*?

With the purpose clause in v. 5 the reader observes the convergence of two distinctly Israelite customs: the preservation of a genealogical line, through the levirate law, and the maintenance of the patrimonial estate through the law of the *gōʾēl*. But Boaz's motivation in summoning the court and his concern for Ruth are of interest for a second reason. In the previous chapter Naomi's scheme to have Ruth and Boaz marry was grounded in her concern for Ruth's security, and this was obviously part of Boaz's motivation as well (3:10–13). The reference to a *gōʾēl* introduces a second incentive, however, which is in fact uppermost in the narrator's mind. His concern is for the line of Elimelech, not his land nor the welfare of Ruth. Because the personal story of these characters must lead inexorably and ultimately to David, this sentence is one of the most significant in the book.

THE *Gōʾēl's* SECOND SPEECH (4:6). **4:6** Whatever enthusiasm the *gōʾēl* may have had after Boaz's first speech for acquiring the rights of usufruct to Elimelech's land was completely dampened by his second speech.

---

[34] Cf. Saul's demand that David not cut off his descendants and destroy his name "from the house of my father" (אָבִי מִבֵּית) in 1 Sam 24:21[Hb. 22]. In 2 Sam 14:7 a widow complains that her townspeople would execute her only son for murdering his brother, and in so doing "they would put out the only burning coal I have left, leaving my husband neither name nor descendant on the face of the earth." Because Absalom had no children to proclaim (הַזְכִּיר) his name after his death, he set up a memorial for himself (2 Sam 18:18). Total annihilation of a person, family, group, or nation means the blotting out of the name. Different verbs are used for the annihilation: הַכְרִית, "to cut off" (Josh 7:9; Isa 14:22; Zech 1:4; Ruth 4:10 *[niphal]*); נִגְרַע, "to be withdrawn" (Num 27:4); אָבַד, *qal*, "to perish" (Ps 41:6); *piel*, "to obliterate" (Deut 12:3); *hiphil*, "to destroy" (Deut 7:24); מָחָה, "To blot out" (Deut 9:14; 2 Kgs 14:27); שָׁמַד, "To destroy," *niphal* (Isa 48:19); *hiphil* (1 Sam 24:22); הֵסִיר, "to remove" (Hos 2:19). For extrabiblical references to the same notion see in particular *VTE (Vassal Treaty of Eshaddon)*, where the curse of "blotting out the name/memory" of the enemy occurs repeatedly: 140, 161, 255, 315, 435, 524, 537, 663 (*ANET*, 534–41). As in Hb. "name" (*šumu*, cf. Hb. *šēm*) is closely linked with "seed" (*zarʾu*, cf. Hb. *zeraʿ*).

[35] J. A. Loader argues the author's intent was to show that *ḥesed* represents living by the spirit of the law ("Of Barley, Bulls, Land, and Levirate," in *Studies in Deuteronomy in Honour of S. J. Labuschagne on the Occasion of His Sixty-fifth Birthday*, VTSup 53 [New York/Leiden: Brill, 1994], 123–38).

Having received this added information, that Ruth came with the transfer, he declared that he could not "redeem," that is, perform the obligation of a *gōʾēl*, for himself. No object for the verb *gāʾal* is specified. Ruth would be the nearer antecedent, but the "land" is apparently the primary object. The addition of *lî*, "for myself," in the Hebrew text heightens the contrast between this man and Boaz, who appears throughout to be operating in the interests of others.

After Boaz's second speech the *gōʾēl* found himself on the horns of a dilemma. Actually he was faced with four options:[36] First, while not legally bound, he could accept moral responsibility for Elimelech's estate, redeem the field, marry Ruth, and ensure the well-being of Naomi, the senior widow. This would have been an honorable course of action. Second, he could redeem the field and pledge to marry Ruth but then renege on the pledge after the transaction was complete. By doing this, however, he would have jeopardized his own reputation and standing in the community. Third, he could reject the offer, thereby ceding the rights to the land and the responsibility of raising up the name of the deceased to Boaz. This move would not necessarily have been irresponsible. After all, Boaz intimated his interest in assuming the role of *gōʾēl* by declaring that he was next in line (v. 4). Fourth, he could accept the responsibility of a *gōʾēl* and redeem the field but reject the responsibility of a *levir* and cede to Boaz the moral obligation and/or right to marry Ruth. This would doubtless have cost him considerably in terms of respect and honor in the community in the short range and in long-range terms could have proved economically precarious. If Boaz would raise up the name of Elimelech by producing an heir through Ruth, this heir could eventually claim the original patrimony of Elimelech.

Faced with this economic and ethical dilemma, the *gōʾēl* chose the third option. The negative purpose clause explaining his rationale suggests he seriously considered only the first two options. The clause itself is not difficult to translate: *pen-ʾaḥšît ʾet-naḥălātî*, means "lest I destroy/jeopardize my patrimonial estate." However, it is not so clear how this statement is to be interpreted. How could the addition of Ruth into the equation jeopardize his own hereditary holdings, which presumably referred to the land that he had inherited from his own ancestors? Two factors need to be considered. First, when he added up the cost of redeeming the property, plus the cost of maintaining the widow Naomi, plus the cost of marrying Ruth, he may have concluded that this was not a fiscally sound move. Rather than enhancing his assets, the newly acquired responsibilities would drain resources from the holdings he had inherited from his own ancestors. Second, he probably also considered the implications of raising up the name of the deceased,

---

[36] These are succinctly summarized by Bush, *Ruth*, 232.

that is, producing an heir for Elimelech. Given his own age and the age of Ruth, he may have thought that she might bear him no more than one child. Since this child would be legally considered the heir and descendant of Elimelech, upon the death of the *gōʾēl* he would inherit the property that had come into his hands through this present transaction as well as the *gōʾēl's* inherited holdings. Furthermore, since the name of Elimelech had been established/raised up through the child, the *gōʾēl's* entire estate would fall into the line of Elimelech, and his own name would disappear. Third, in view of Boaz's introduction of Ruth as "the Moabitess," he may have have pondered the ethnic implication of the transaction, concluding that his patrimonial estate would not be jeopardized by falling into the hands of one with Moabite blood in his veins.

Having reflected on the implications, the *gōʾēl* announced his decision. In unequivocal and emphatic terms he declared (lit.), "Redeem for yourself, you,[37] my redemption right [*gĕʾullâ*]." The noun *gĕʾullâ*, from the same root as *gāʾal*, is a technical term for the rights, privileges, and obligations of *gōʾēl* status.[38]

THE *Gōʾēl's* NONVERBAL SPEECH (4:7–8). **4:7–8** In v. 7 the narrator interrupts the report of the court proceedings with a parenthetical comment concerning an ancient legal custom. By modern standards of composition the clarification would have been more appropriate after v. 8, but its present location creates the impression of a pause in the proceedings and a shift from verbal to nonverbal legal communication. In any case, having said his piece in v. 6, the *gōʾēl* removed his sandal and handed it to Boaz. This was a symbolic act declaring his abdication of his own rights as *the gōʾēl* and their transfer to the next in line. The gesture was accompanied by another verbal declaration (v. 8), *qĕnēh lāk*, "Acquire for yourself." The utterance represents a two-word recapitulation of his statement in v. 6. The use of the verb *qānâ* in place of *gāʾal*, "to redeem," confirms our earlier interpretation of this verb as "to acquire" (see comments on v. 4).

The narrator's insertion of the parenthetical comment in v. 7 suggests that this custom was no longer understood at the time of the writing of the book. For the sake of the modern reader we add some additional explanatory comments. Sandals *(naʿal)* were the most common form of footwear in the ancient world, generally being made of leather and fastened with straps or laces.[39] The act involved in this transaction is described as "taking off"[40] the sandal and hand-

---

[37] On emphatic use of the independent personal pronoun אַתָּה after לְךָ see GKC §§ 135*d*–*g*.

[38] See R. L. Hubbard, "גָאַל," *NIDOTTE* 1.789–94.

[39] For illustrations see *ANEP*, 2–3, 120–22, 190–91.

[40] The verb שָׁלַף is used elsewhere of drawing a sword from its sheath (Judg 8:20). The present verb is used in place of נָשַׁל (Exod 3:5; Josh 5:15) and חָלַץ (Deut 25:9–10: Isa 20:2).

ing it to the person to whom rights are ceded.[41] The narrator notes that the *gōʾēl's* action follows an ancient practice[42] in Israel.[43] This nonverbal gesture was performed particularly in legal contexts involving[44] "redemption" *(haggĕʾûllâ)* and "transfer of property" *(hattĕmûrâ)*. The meaning of the former expression is clear by now; but the latter calls for further comment. The noun *tĕmûrâ* occurs elsewhere only five times, twice in Leviticus and three times in Job. Derived from a root *mûr*, which in the causative stem *(hiphil)* means "to change, exchange," in Lev 27:10,33 the word denotes a "substitute" sacrificial animal. Job 28:17 declares that no vessels of gold can equal or substitute for wisdom. Job 15:31 employs the expression in the sense of "reward, recompense" and in 20:18 as the act of bartering, trading. In contexts like the present it has to do with legal attestation of a transfer of goods or rights.

The purpose of this legal gesture is defined with two expressions. The first is in the form of a purpose infinitive phrase (lit.), "to put any matter into effect," that is, to make it legally binding (NIV "to become final"). Boaz used the same verb in v. 5 of "establishing" the name of the deceased.[45] The second expression of purpose functions as a summarizing verbless clause (lit.), "Now this is/was the form of attestation/legalization in Israel." The noun *tĕʿûdâ*, "form of attestation/legalization," occurs elsewhere only in Isa 8:16,20. It derives from a root *ʿûd*, which in the causative stem *(hiphil)* carries two senses, "to warn, admonish" and "to call to witness." The latter is obviously intended here, a conclusion confirmed by Boaz's declaration of the role of the observers in v. 9: they are *ʿēdîm*, "witnesses," which derives from the same root.

(3) Boaz's Response to the Outcome of the Court Proceedings (4:9–10)

⁹Then Boaz announced to the elders and all the people, "Today you are witnesses that I have bought from Naomi all the property of Elimelech, Kilion and Mahlon. ¹⁰I have also acquired Ruth the Moabitess, Mahlon's widow, as my wife,

---

[41] Here referred to as רֵעֵהוּ, "his neighbor." The present use of the *waw*-conjunction plus perfect in place of the expected *waw*-consecutive plus imperfect is seen by some as a mark of late Hebrew. Cf. Bush, *Ruth,* 27. But since this is a customary rather than narrative statement, the construction may simply serve to highlight the explanatory nature of the verse. Cf. Exod 34:34–35.

[42] The LXX recognizes the cryptic nature of וְזֹאת לְפָנִים בְּיִשְׂרָאֵל, "and this formerly in Israel," by adding a predicate noun, τὸ δικαίωμα, "the judgment," which fills in for an assumed הַמִּשְׁפָּט. But the feminine form of זֹאת calls for a more abstract understanding, perhaps "This is how things were done formerly in Israel."

[43] On the use of the *waw* to initiate a circumstantial parenthetical clause, see *IBHS* § 39.2.3.c. On the temporal use of the adverb לְפָנִים, "formerly, in earlier times," see *HALOT,* 942. The parenthetical v. 7 is actually framed by two formally similar sentences: וְזֹאת לְפָנִים בְּיִשְׂרָאֵל, "and this formerly in Israel," and וְזֹאת הַתְּעוּדָה בְּיִשְׂרָאֵל, "and this is the attestation in Israel."

[44] On עַל meaning "with regard to, concerning," see *HALOT,* 826.

[45] לְקַיֵּם involves an Aramaized *piel* form of קוּם. Cf. Bush, *Ruth,* 27.

in order to maintain the name of the dead with his property, so that his name will not disappear from among his family or from the town records. Today you are witnesses!"

4:9–10 With the transfer of the sandal as the final legal gesture, the official court proceedings were complete. The rights and responsibilities of redemption vis-à-vis Elimelech's estate had been officially transferred to Boaz, and he was legally recognized as the *gōʾēl*. Boaz's legal standing had been advanced, but now the "peloni almoni" (v. 1) may disappear from the scene. In relinquishing his rights in the present context his name also disappears from history. In keeping with ancient legal proceedings, Boaz then turned to the witnesses and presented an impassioned closing speech, offering his interpretation of the significance of the scene they have observed.[46] As in v. 4 the narrator refers to two groups of observers, though they are identified slightly differently: "those sitting" and "the elders of my people" are replaced by "the elders" *(hazzĕqēnîm)* and "all the people." The former expression probably refers to the ten whom Boaz had formally summoned (v. 2); and the latter, to all who had in the meantime been passing through the gate on the way to work but who had stopped to watch what was happening in one of the chambers.

Boaz's speech is framed by identical clauses at the beginning and at the end. With this declaration he adds a second form of attestation to go along with the passing of the sandal he now has in his possession. In the future if his claims to the rights to Elimelech's land or his claim to Ruth are ever questioned, not only will he be able to produce the sandal, but he also will appeal to this host of witnesses that has observed him gain this right through legal process. Within this framework Boaz's speech divides into two parts: a summary of his own role and the legal transaction on the one hand and an explanation of his motivation in seeking the status of *gōʾēl* with respect to the estate of Elimelech on the other. From the narrator's perspective the twofold reference to "today" highlights Boaz's promptness in fulfilling his promise to Ruth in 3:13 and in the fulfillment of Naomi's words in 3:18.

Boaz's summary of his actions consists of two parts. The first (v. 9b) focuses on the estate of Elimelech, and the second focuses on the person of Ruth (v. 10a). With respect to the former, Boaz refers to the estate as "all that belongs to Elimelech, Chilion and Mahlon." The addition of the names of Elimelech's sons raises the inheritance implications. Boaz reverses the narrator's order of the two names in 1:2,5, presumably because he will name Mahlon again in v. 10. The NIV's rendering of v. 9 creates the impression that Boaz actually bought the estate of Elimelech, but this is wrong on several counts. First, as noted earlier, the estate was not Naomi's to sell. She had

---

[46] This is the last time Boaz speaks in the book.

merely relinquished the right to hold it in trust and transferred that right to the *gōʾēl*. Second, the court proceedings were not about redeeming land but transferring the right to redeem it.[47] Through this action Boaz's status is changed from being a *gōʾēl* to being the *gōʾēl (haggōʾēl)*. Third, the actual redemption of the land still lay in the future and would involve negotiations between Boaz and the person who currently held Elimelech's estate.

In the second portion of his summary Boaz declared that he had also acquired the rights to Ruth. He mentioned the estate of Elimelech first because his right to Ruth was contingent upon gaining the right to the property. It is obvious from the construction of the sentence, however, that Ruth was his primary goal (lit.): "And also Ruth, the Moabitess, the wife of Mahlon, I have acquired for myself."[48] The use of the full name "Ruth the Moabitess" may be required by the legal context, but it is evident that Ruth's Moabite status is no barrier for Boaz. On the contrary, perhaps because of her public reputation but especially because of his personal contacts with her, he seems to relish the prospect of marriage to this foreigner. His identification of Ruth specifically as the wife of Mahlon is also illuminating. We had known since the beginning that both she and Orpah were married to the sons of Elimelech and Naomi, but now for the first time we learn which woman had been married to which man.

The remainder of v. 10 is devoted to explaining Boaz's motivation in the preceding legal proceedings. Again it is obvious that his primary interest is Ruth and not the estate. In v. 9 he had not bothered to explain why he desired the status of *haggōʾēl*, "the kinsman-redeemer," vis-à-vis Elimelech's property, but now he offers his reasons for wanting Ruth. The addition of "for a wife" (NIV "as my wife") creates the initial impression that his motives are purely personal. But not for long. In Boaz's explanation of his motivation in the foregoing legal efforts he used three significant expressions. His first goal was to establish the name of the deceased on his own patrimonial holding. The infinitive phrase translated "in order to maintain the name of the dead with his property" is identical to the challenge he had put to the *gōʾēl* in v. 5. Boaz's second goal was to prevent the name of the deceased from being (lit.) "cut off from his brothers." The expression "cut off the name" represents one of several expressions for annihilating one's honor and reputation and preventing one's posthumous existence.[49] Boaz's third goal is to prevent his name from being cut off from (lit.) "the gate of his place." "His place" is a designation for the town, that is, Bethlehem, but the NIV's interpretation of *šaʿar*, "gate," as "records" is mis-

---

[47] As in v. 4, in vv. 9 and 10 the verb קָנָה does not mean "to buy" but "to acquire." See above.

[48] Note the opening וְגַם, "and also," the front-loading of the direct object, and the double modification. The way Boaz identifies Ruth here echoes his introduction of her in v. 5, except for the opening particle and the fact that "the deceased" (הַמֵּת) is now named.

[49] The present idiom occurs elsewhere in Josh 7:9; Isa 14:22; and Zech 1:4. For other expressions for annihilation of one's reputation and the cutting off of the family see n. 34 above.

leading. Here "gate" functions metonymically for "the assembly" that meets at the gate. This decision by Boaz is intended to guarantee Elimelech/Mahlon the right to representation in the gathering of the town council. In the end Mr. So-and-So will disappear without a name, but the security of Mahlon's and Elimelech's names is hereby guarded.

(4) The Public Reaction to the Outcome of the Court Proceedings (4:11–12)

[11]Then the elders and all those at the gate said, "We are witnesses. May the LORD make the woman who is coming into your home like Rachel and Leah, who together built up the house of Israel. May you have standing in Ephrathah and be famous in Bethlehem. [12]Through the offspring the LORD gives you by this young woman, may your family be like that of Perez, whom Tamar bore to Judah."

4:11–12 The response to Boaz's appeal by (lit.) "all the people who were in the gate" and "the elders" (the NIV reverses the order of the two groups) was positive in the extreme.[50] First, they answer Boaz's twofold challenge at the beginning and end of his speech and accept their official role in the legal proceedings. Since biblical Hebrew has no word for "Yes,"[51] they declare their response by repeating Boaz's last word and affirming unanimously, *ʿēdîm*, "Witnesses!"[52] With this speech-act they have indeed fulfilled their present legal obligations, but this does not mean they are finished. On the contrary, they break out in an effusive pronouncement of blessing upon Boaz.

The benediction consists of three parts. Although the people's attention was focused primarily on Boaz, they expressed their concern for him with a prayer for Ruth's fertility. They did not mention her by name but referred to her as "the woman who is coming into your house." The expression "who is coming/about to come[53] to your home" derives from the ancient customary practice of the wedding party proceeding to the home of the groom after the marriage ceremony and him formally ushering the bride into his house.[54] The witnesses' request concerning Ruth is extraordinary inasmuch as they pray that Yahweh would grant[55] this foreign woman a place among the

---

[50] The order of subjects is reversed from v. 9, but this is an insignificant stylistic variation. The LXX has "all the people in the gate" declaring "We are witnesses" and the elders pronouncing the blessing that follows. On the LXX reading see A. Rof, *Text, Temples, and Tradition: A Tribute to Menahem Haran* (Winona Lake: Eisenbrauns, 1996), 119–24 [Hb.].

[51] Several particles are occasionally translated "Yes" (cf. כִּי in Josh 2:4; and גַּם in Gen 20:6; 2 Kgs 2:3), but strictly speaking, neither term is equivalent to Eng. "yes."

[52] On the elision of the subject see GKC § 150n. A parallel text occurs in Josh 24:22.

[53] The participle expresses present or imminent action. Cf. *GBH* § 121i.

[54] Cf. Gen 24:67; Deut 20:7.

[55] The verb יִתֵּן is a jussive of נָתַן, "to give, grant," but in this instance it means "appoint a place/role."

matriarchs of Israel along with Rachel and Leah. As is well known, Rachel and Leah were the daughters of Laban the Aramean, whom Jacob married and who became the ancestresses of the twelve tribes of Israel.[56] The order of the names, with Rachel before Leah, is striking not only because Leah was the senior and dominant wife but especially because Bethlehem belonged to the tribe of Judah, whose eponymous ancestor was one of Leah's sons. But just as the order of Chilion and Mahlon in v. 9 prepares for the reference to the latter in the following verse, so this order sets the stage for the attention given to Judah in v. 12. By invoking the intervention of Yahweh on Ruth's behalf, the townsfolk are thinking specifically of the matriarchs' fertility. Just as Rachel and Leah had built up the house of Israel, so, they pray, may Ruth build up the house of Boaz. The idiom "to build a house," which means "to have progeny, descendants, to establish a family," derives from the Mosaic Torah concerning the levirate marriage (Deut 25:9),[57] adding further evidence that Boaz's marriage to Ruth is intended as such. But the people's invocation of Yahweh to make this possible is in keeping with the psalmist's notion that "unless the LORD builds a house, they labor in vain who build it" (Ps 127:1).[58]

The second part of the blessing was directed to Boaz and is constructed of

---

[56] Technically there were four ancestresses, but since Zilpah and Bilhah were Leah's and Rachel's handmaidens respectively, the sons they bore to Jacob were considered the children of their father's wives. See Genesis 30.

[57] On this use of the idiom see also 1 Sam 2:35; 2 Sam 7:27=1 Chr 17:25; 1 Kgs 1:38; 1 Chr 17:10.

[58] Cf. Sarah's human effort to build a house for Abraham by giving him her handmaid, Hagar, in Gen 16:3. The present pronouncement of blessing upon Boaz by invoking divine granting of fertility to his bride is reminiscent of the blessing pronounced upon Kirta in a twelfth century B.C. text from Ugarit:

ᵓIlu blessed [noble] Kirta,
[Pronounced the benediction] upon the goodly lad of ᵓIlu:
The woman you take, Kirta,
   the woman you take to enter your house,
   the girl who enters your courts,
She shall bear you seven sons,
   even eight shall she produce for you.
. . . .
Greatly uplifted is Kirta,
   amongst the Shades of the earth,
   in the gathering of the assembly of Ditānu.

As translated by D. Pardee in *The Context of Scripture*, vol. I, *Canonical Compositions from the Biblical World*, ed. W. W. Hallo and K. L. Younger (Leiden/New York: Brill, 1997), 337–38. Note the conjunction of notions of fertility for the wife and guaranteeing the man's place in the assembly. But in this case his place in the afterlife will be with the deified Ditānu, the eponymous ancestor of the tribe to which Kirta belonged. On the relationship between this text and the blessing of Boaz see S. Parker, "The Marriage Blessing in Israel and Ugaritic Literature," *JBL* 95 (1976): 23–30.

two parallel lines:

May you prosper (lit. make wealth) in Ephrathah *(waʿăśēh ḥayil bĕʾeprātâ),*[59]
And may a name be called in Bethlehem   *(ûqĕrāʾ-šēm bĕbêt lāḥem).*

Because of the wide range of meanings that may be ascribed to *ḥayil,* the meaning of the first line is difficult to pin down. *ʿāśâ ḥayil* could mean "to act valiantly," "to perform honorably," or "to show great strength," but "to make wealth," that is, "to prosper," seems most appropriate in the context of a blessing associated with marriage.[60]

Typical of Hebrew parallelism, the second line builds on the first. The idiom *qārāʾ šēm,* "to call a name," is normally used of naming a person, the phrase being followed immediately by the name given or introduced by a preposition.[61] The present construction with "in" + geographic name occurs only here.[62] To call/mention a person's name in a place after his death means more than "to keep the name [that is, the reputation] alive" (REB); it also perceives the person as living on in his descendants in the place named. The ancients believed that when a person's name is never mentioned after his death, he ceases to exist (Isa 14:20).[63]

In the third element of their blessing (v. 12) the witnesses prayed that Boaz's house would become like the house of Perez, whom Tamar bore to Judah. This reference to Tamar, Judah, and Perez reinforces the impression that the narrator has been writing the story of Boaz and Ruth with Genesis 38 in the back of his mind.[64] This most celebrated narrative of levirate obligation and betrayal also involved a widow whose husband, Er, had died without producing an heir. Failing to get Er's brother, Onan, to fulfill his levirate obligation and despairing of waiting for Shelah, another younger

---

[59] On Ephrathah see the commentary above on 1:2.

[60] Cf. Psalm 128. C. J. Labuschagne's interpretation of חַיִל as "procreative power" ("The Crux in Ruth 4:12," *ZAW* 79 [1967]: 364–67) is to be rejected, not only because this expression is never used this way elsewhere but also because concern for male virility is rarely if ever expressed in the OT. Sterility was perceived as primarily a female problem.

[61] Followed by the name in the accusative (Gen 3:20; 4:25–26; 5:2–3,29; etc.); followed by the preposition לְ or אֶל (Gen 2:20; 26:18; Ruth 4:17; Ps 147:4; Isa 65:15). Sometimes שֵׁם is dropped (Gen 1:5,8,10; 2:19; 33:20; etc.).

[62] While many emend to a more natural *niphal* form and add a suffix to "name," וְנִקְרָא שִׁמְךָ, "and may your name be called," the text as it stands makes good sense if the *qal* is interpreted impersonally, "and one will call a name," which is equivalent to "and a name will be called."

[63] Cf. L. Yonker, "קרא," *NIDOTTE* 3.973. The present idiom is related to a similar construction with the preposition בְּ but with a reference to descendants instead of the place name. When Jacob blesses his two grandsons, he prays that his name, and the name of Abraham and Isaac, will live on in them (Gen 48:16).

[64] See especially Nielsen (*Ruth,* 12–17) and E. van Wolde ("Texts in Dialogue with Texts: Intertextuality in the Ruth and Tamar Narratives," *Biblical Interpretation* 5 [1997]: 1–27) for a discussion of the connection between these accounts.

brother, to grow up, Tamar pretended to be a prostitute and tricked Judah, her own father-in-law, into having sexual intercourse with her. As unlikely as it may seem, she conceived and eventually bore twin sons, Perez and Zerah. Together with Shelah these two sons become the ancestors of the tribe of Judah (Gen 46:12; Num 26:20; etc.) Of these three, Perez's descendants seem to have played the most significant role in Israel's history, but Perez is mentioned here because he was the ancestor of Boaz's clan living in Bethlehem. The point of comparison between Ruth and Tamar is neither their characters nor the manner in which they conceived (Tamar's was the result of incestuous deception)[65] but the common levirate nature of their unions. Through Tamar, whose husband had died childless, Judah had fathered Perez,[66] who became the ancestor of a host of clans, including the clan (*mišpāḥâ;* cf. 2:1) of Boaz. Now the witnesses prayed that through this widow, Ruth, Boaz may father a son and live on through his numerous progeny,[67] even as Judah lives on in his descendants. There is no mention of the men's characters either. However, considering the rabbinic hermeneutical principle of "from greater to lesser," the reader cannot help but think that if Yahweh had given immoral Judah a double blessing in the birth of twins and if Judah flourished through Perez, how much brighter are the prospects for Boaz and Ruth. These two have been presented from beginning to end as persons with the highest ethical standards; they embody covenant *ḥesed.* But the witnesses did not appeal to their characters. Recognizing Yahweh as the source of blessing and family, they assumed that Boaz's having offspring through Ruth depended on the divine gift.

Little did those who uttered these words realize how prophetic the words would be. Ten of them were witnesses to this event because they had been summoned; the rest had simply gathered out of curiosity over what was happening in the gate. Now, inspired by the Spirit of God, they joined in a spontaneous and unanimous pronouncement of blessing upon Boaz. They had come to witness, but they left prophesying. Had they been around long enough to see the fulfillment of their prayer, they would have observed the establishment of a name and a house far greater than Perez, the house of King David, a name commemorated to this day in the flag of the state of Israel.

---

[65] Tamar's case represented the female counterpart to Lev 18:17, which forbids an Israelite man from having sexual relations with a woman and her daughter.

[66] The phrase "whom Tamar bore to Judah" reflects the common ancient notion that women bore children for their husbands. Cf. Ezek. 16:15ff.

[67] The choice of זֶרַע *(zeraʿ),* "seed," may represent an intentional play on Zerah (זֶרַח), the name of Perez's twin brother.

2. Scene 2: The Genealogical Resolution (4:13–17)

The story of Boaz, Ruth, and Naomi concludes with a glorious resolution of a fundamental issue in the book: the filling of Naomi's emptiness and the birth of a son through whom the royal line of David will eventually appear. Unlike the formal court scene in the gate, the climax of the story occurs in the home of Boaz and Ruth at least nine months later. The account divides into five parts: (1) a narrative report (v. 13), (2) a speech by the women of Bethlehem (vv. 14–15), (3) a narrative report (v. 16), (4) a speech by the women of Bethlehem (v. 17a,b), and (5) a narrative conclusion (v. 17c).

(1) The Narrative Report of the Birth of a Boy (4:13)

¹³So Boaz took Ruth and she became his wife. Then he went to her, and the LORD enabled her to conceive, and she gave birth to a son.

4:13 Verse 13 telescopes nine months of personal history. The first half focuses on Boaz's actions after the court scene of the previous chapter. Following the spontaneous pronouncement of the blessing upon Boaz, without emotion the narrator announces the basic facts of any Israelite marriage, noting the roles of each of the participants in the event.

First, Boaz married Ruth. According to the Hebrew idiom he took her and she became his wife. The expression is typically ancient Near Eastern and biblical, inasmuch as the responsibility for the establishment and maintenance of the household rested on the man's shoulders. The idiom also reflects the specific custom of the man taking *(lāqaḥ)* his wife to his house as part of the marriage ritual (Deut 20:7). In "becoming his wife" Ruth's social progression is completed. She had graduated from the status of *nokriyyâ*, "foreigner" (2:10), to *šiphâ*, "lowest servant" (2:13), to *ʾāmâ*, "maidservant" (3:9), and now to *ʾiššâ*, "wife." Having married Ruth, Boaz "went to" Ruth. This is the common Hebrew expression for the consummation of a marriage through sexual intercourse. The idiom is popularly thought to derive from the male act of penetration, but this would have been expressed with *bôʾ bĕ*, "to enter,"[68] rather than *bôʾ ʾel*, "to go to." The idiom actually reflects the entrance of a man into the tent or bride chamber of his wife for the purpose of intercourse.[69]

Second, "the LORD gave her [Ruth] conception" (literal rendering). This is only the second time in the book where the narrator has God as a subject of a verb (cf. 1:6), but how significant is this statement! The expression *hērāyôn*,

---

[68] Num 5:24,27 records the only place where this idiom is used with a woman as the object, but here the reference is to water entering through the mouth.

[69] E.g., Gen 30:3–4; 39:14,17; Judg 15:1; 2 Sam 12:24; 17:25; Prov 2:19. For further references see *DCH* 1.113.

"conception, pregnancy," occurs in only two other Old Testament texts: Gen 3:16 and Hos 9:11. But the present idiom, "to grant/give conception," is unique. This statement must be interpreted against the backdrop of Ruth's apparently ten-year marriage with Mahlon, for whom she seems to have been unable to conceive. Now, in fulfillment of the prayer of the witnesses in the gate (vv. 11–12), Yahweh graciously grants Ruth pregnancy as a gift. This is the narrator's modest way of identifying a miracle; she who had been unable to bear a child for Mahlon has conceived for Boaz.

Third, Ruth "gave birth to a son." She did her part as well, carrying the child to full term, and then delivering a son.[70]

The reader marvels at the narrator's skill in portraying his characters and in his theological perception. Ultimately the royal line is preserved because two pious human beings and Yahweh act in consort for the achievement of his purpose.

(2) The Women's Reaction to the Birth of the Boy (4:14–15)

[14]The women said to Naomi: "Praise be to the LORD, who this day has not left you without a kinsman-redeemer. May he become famous throughout Israel! [15]He will renew your life and sustain you in your old age. For your daughter-in-law, who loves you and who is better to you than seven sons, has given him birth."

The second episode of the final scene involves the women of Bethlehem, who, as in 1:19, function as a chorus in the drama. Their speech divides into three parts: (1) a blessing for Yahweh (v. 14a), (2) a prayer for the child (v. 14b), and (3) a declaration of confidence for Naomi (v. 15).

THE WOMEN'S BLESSING FOR YAHWEH (4:14a).   **4:14a**   When the women of Bethlehem hear of the birth of the son to Boaz and Ruth, they respond with a spontaneous outburst of praise to Yahweh for his kindness to Naomi and a prayer for the young lad and his grandmother. This blessing must be interpreted against the backdrop of Naomi's painful and bitter complaint about God in 1:20–21 for the grief she perceived him to have caused her. There is a recognition now that she whose life had been emptied by God has now experienced his filling.

The form of the blessing uttered by the women differs from those encountered earlier, consisting simply of the passive verb *bārûk* followed by the name of Yahweh. In such contexts the word "blessed" functions as a virtual synonym for "praise."[71] In the Old Testament blessings represent expressions of a positive relationship. Yahweh blesses his people on the basis of relation-

---

[70] The verb יָלַד is used in the *qal* stem when a woman is the subject; the *hiphil* is used if a man is the subject. Cf. the following genealogy.

[71] The NIV usually renders בָּרוּךְ in such contexts with "praise."

ship by conferring good on them; humans bless God by praising the good that is in him and that he expresses in conveying benefactions.

The present construction follows the pattern typical for this kind of blessing by introducing the grounds of the blessing with the conjunction *ʾăšer*, "who ..."[72] Here the women bless Yahweh because this day he has provided Naomi with a redeemer. The present negative form of the declaration translates literally "he has not stopped for you a *gōʾēl*," that is, he has not prevented Naomi from having her *gōʾēl*.[73] Although some scholars insist that Boaz is the *gōʾēl* the women have in mind,[74] the adverb *hayyôm*, "this day," and the reference to the child's birth in v. 15 make it clear that the women look upon the child as Naomi's *gōʾēl*. It is evident from the following invocation on behalf of the child, however, that they are not using the term *gōʾēl* in the technical legal sense employed earlier in the chapter.[75] On the contrary, the birth of the child is not viewed as a solution to a long-standing legal problem but from a practical women's perspective as the solution to Naomi's insecurity. Although they do not use the word, they envision this lad providing for her the "rest/security" *(mānôah/měnûha)* that she had tried to procure for her daughter-in-law (cf. 1:9; 3:1). The women are not concerned about the restoration of hereditary land to the clan of Elimelech or raising up a name for Mahlon. They are interested only in the well-being of this widow.

THE WOMEN'S PRAYER FOR THE CHILD (4:14b). **4:14b** The thought of the *gōʾēl* as Yahweh's provision for Naomi's well-being inspires a spontaneous blessing for the boy: literally, "And may his name be called in Israel!" But what does it mean to have someone's name called in Israel? Since the locative designation "in Israel" occupies the place normally held by a personal name when the formula is used in a naming context, and since the actual naming will be recounted later (v. 17), this cannot refer to the naming of the lad (or Yahweh for that matter). How the idiom is interpreted depends upon whose name the women are referring to. Grammatically the antecedent of "his name" could be either Yahweh, who is the subject of the previous clause, or the *gōʾēl* two words prior. If one understands the refer-

---

[72] See Gen 14:20; 24:27; Exod 18:10; 1 Sam 25:32,39; 2 Sam 18:28; 1 Kgs 1:48; 5:21; 8:15 (= 2 Chr 6:4); 1 Kgs 8:56; 10:9 (= 2 Chr 9:8); Ps 66:20; Ezra 7:27; 2 Chr 2:11. Alternatively the clause may be introduced with -שֶׁ (Ps 124:6); or כִּי (Pss 28:6; 31:22). Cf. C. A. Keller, "בָּרַךְ *brk* pi. segnen," *THAT* 1.357; K. H. Richards, "Bless/Blessing," *ABD*, 1.754; M. L. Brown, "בָּרַךְ," *NIDOTTE* 1.766.

[73] Derived from the intransitive verb שָׁבַת, "to stop," unmodified by a prepositional phrase the *hiphil* stem denotes "to cause to cease, put an end to," or even "cause to fail." See BDB, 992.

[74] See Bush, *Ruth,* 254, for discussion.

[75] Earlier in the chapter we witnessed Boaz gain the legal right to function as *gōʾēl*. In court he had gained the privilege and obligation to redeem the estate of Elimelech and to rescue the name of Mahlon from annihilation.

ence to be to Yahweh's name, then the idiom calls for the naming of Yahweh in celebration or supplication.[76] Accordingly, the birth of this lad is seen as a demonstration that Yahweh is God in Israel. On the other hand, since the *gōʾēl* is the nearer antecedent, it is preferable to interpret this utterance as applying to the boy, in which case this declaration represents a passive version of the very same construction in v. 11.[77] As we noted there, to call/mention a person's name in a place means to "to keep the name/fame alive," even after his death, and to perceive the person as living on in his descendants in the place named. In the previous context the men at the gate had applied the prayer to Boaz, with the desire that his name would live on in Bethlehem. But these women expand the scope of the *gōʾēl's* fame beyond the walls of their town to the nation of Israel as a whole.

THE WOMEN'S DECLARATION OF CONFIDENCE FOR NAOMI (4:15). **4:15** In v. 15 the women's attention returns to the implications for Naomi of the birth of the *gōʾēl*. They recognize the boy's significance for Naomi's disposition in the present and her well-being in the future. The first expression, literally, "And he will become for you a restorer of life," presents a stark contrast to the bitter comments the women had heard from Naomi's lips when she first arrived back from Moab.[78] They hereby express confidence that with the birth of this lad Naomi will find new hope for life—all is not lost—and her spirit will revive. The second expression looks into the more distant future: literally "and to sustain your grey hair."[79] Here the word *šēbâ*, "grey hair," is a euphemism for old age. The perceptiveness of the women to recognize in the birth of this child the guarantee of Naomi's future well-being is remarkable! She who had been so concerned about the security of her daughter-in-law is now rewarded in kind.

But the women's last statement is the most remarkable of all. In the beginning Naomi had bitterly accused God of emptying her life by robbing her of

---

[76] In which case the passive *(niphal)* form is roughly equivalent to the active *(qal)* קָרָא שֵׁם יְהוָה, "to call on the name of the LORD," or קָרָא לַיהוָה and קָרָא אֶל־יהוה, "to call out to the LORD." Cf. L. Jonker, "קרא," *NIDOTTE* 3.972.

[77] Except for the addition of the suffix after שֵׁם, viz., "his name," in this verse. Note the parallel structures:

v. 11   וּקְרָא־שֵׁם   בְּבֵית לָחֶם׃   "And may one call a name in Bethlehem."
v. 14   וְיִקָּרֵא־שְׁמוֹ   בְּיִשְׂרָאֵל   "And may his name be called in Israel."

[78] The *hiphil* participle מֵשִׁיב, "one who brings back," answers to the use of the same stem (הֵשִׁיב) in Naomi's accusation that Yahweh had brought her back empty (1:21). This form also plays more generally on שׁוּב, "to return, to come back," the key word in chap. 1. The sense of הֵשִׁיב נֶפֶשׁ, "to bring back/restore life," is illustrated in Job 33:30 and Prov 25:13. Cf. the *qal* form of the same idiom, יָשׁוּב נֶפֶשׁ, "life returns," in 1 Kgs 17:21–22.

[79] The combination of participle followed by לְ + infinitive construct occurs elsewhere only in Jer 44:19. Joüon (*Ruth*, 93) notes that the לְ goes with the finite verb הָיָה, "to be." According to GKC §114, the verb + לְ + infinitive construct sequence conveys urgency and purpose. כִּלְכֵּל is a *pilpel* form of כּוּל, "to comprehend, to take hold of." Cf. *HALOT*, 463.

her husband and her two sons. But now the women console her: she may have lost her sons, but she has gained a daughter-in-law. And what a daughter-in-law Ruth is! First, Ruth loves Naomi. In fact, in her action we observe one of the most dramatic demonstrations of the meaning of the Hebrew word for "love," ʾāhēb. Whereas modern definitions of love tend to view the word as an emotional term, in the Old Testament love is fundamentally an expression of covenant commitment, the kind of devotion to which Ruth had given such eloquent verbal expression in 1:16–17.[80] But "love" is not demonstrated primarily in words; it is expressed in acts of ḥesed, placing the welfare of the other ahead of oneself. In fact, more than anyone else in the history of Israel, Ruth embodies the fundamental principle of the nation's ethic: "You shall love your God with all your heart" (Deut 6:5) "and your neighbor as yourself" (Lev 19:18). In Lev 19:34 Moses instructs the Israelites to love the stranger as they love themselves. Ironically, it is this stranger from Moab who shows the Israelites what this means.[81]

Second, Ruth has given birth to the gōʾēl. On the surface this may not seem so remarkable, but when one considers that she had been married to Mahlon for ten years but had borne no children for him, the significance of the statement becomes evident. The barren womb has been opened.

Third, Ruth is better for Naomi than seven sons. The reference to "seven sons" is conventional, reflecting the ancient Israelite view that the ideal family consisted of seven sons.[82] This is an amazing affirmation of the character of Ruth. All Bethlehem knew she was a noble woman (3:11), but these women place her value above seven sons; what extraordinary compensation for the two sons Naomi had lost!

(3) The Narrative Report of Naomi's Adoption of the Boy (4:16)

[16]Then Naomi took the child, laid him in her lap and cared for him.

4:16 Naomi's response to the birth of Boaz's son and to the blessing of

---

[80] On אָהֵב as an expression of "covenant commitment" see W. L. Moran, "The Ancient Near Eastern Background of the Love of God in Deuteronomy," *CBQ* 25 (1963): 77–87, esp. 78–81.

[81] The meaning of the saying "You shall love your neighbor as yourself" is eloquently explained by A. Malamat, "'You Shall Love Your Neighbor as Yourself': A Case of Misinterpretation?" in *Die Hebräische Bibel und ihre Nachgeschichte*, Rendtorff Festschrift, ed. E. Blum, et al. (Neukirchen: Neukirchener Verlag, 1990), 111–15. Appealing to the pairing of עָזַר and אָהֵב in texts like 2 Chr 19:2, Malamat argues convincingly that the latter is an active and concrete, rather than abstract, expression. Here the verb means "to be helpful to, to assist, to serve," hence to love is "to be helpful to someone."

[82] Cf. 1 Sam 2:5; Job 1:2; 42:13; 2 *Macc* 7; Acts 19:14–17. The present grammatical form is identical to 1 Sam 1:8 as the following comparison reveals:

| Ruth 4:15 | הִיא טוֹבָה לָךְ מִשִּׁבְעָה בָּנִים | She is better than seven sons. |
| 1 Sam 1:8 | אָנֹכִי טוֹב לָךְ מֵעֲשָׂרָה בָּנִים | I am better than ten sons. |

the women is described in three simple verbs: She took *(lāqaḥ)* the child, placed *(šît)* him in her bosom *(ḥêq)*, and became his nanny *(hāyâ lô lĕʾōmenet)*. The choice of noun, *yeled,* "child," rather than *bēn,* "boy," may be influenced by the use of the root *yld,* "to give birth," which serves as the key word in these last paragraphs.[83] In a world previously characterized by famine, barrenness, and death, there is birth, new life.

But the words *ḥêq* and *ʾōmenet* are the keys to determining the significance of Naomi's actions. *ḥêq* denotes the bosom, the front of one's body where one holds a child (Num 11:12) or embraces a loved one. The word is applied to both males (Deut 13:7; 28:54; 1 Kgs 1:2; Jer 32:18; Mic 7:5; Eccl 7:9; etc.) and females (Deut 28:56; Prov 5:2; Lam 2:12) and is never used of the breast at which a child nurses; it should not be interpreted more precisely here.[84] The word *ʾōmenet* derives from a root *ʾmn,* "to be firm." Here the expression denotes a guardian, "nanny" in the true sense.[85] The present action obviously has nothing to do with wet-nursing; nor should it be viewed as some sort of adoption ritual.[86] Not only would there be no need for a grandmother to adopt a child legally, but it is not clear that women in the ancient world were in a position to adopt children. Within this family context these are not legal actions but the loving, natural actions of a grandmother, gratefully accepting her new status and tenderly receiving the baby. Within the context of the book, however, the action is much more significant. The image of this woman taking the child in her arms must also be seen against the backdrop of her previous experience. She had not only had her bread basket emptied by famine; in the deaths of her husband and sons her bosom had also been emptied of her men.[87]

(4) The Women's Naming of the Child (4:17a–b)

[17]**The women living there said, "Naomi has a son." And they named him Obed.**

4:17a–b The story of Boaz, Ruth, and Naomi comes to a fitting conclusion in the naming of the son born to Ruth. But this last statement is also extraordinary for several reasons. First, this is the only place in the Old Testament where females (other than the mother) are said to be present at the naming event. A more literal rendering of v. 17a–b makes this more clear:

---

[83] Cf. יָלַד, "to give birth, gender" *(qal),* in vv. 13,15; תּוֹלְדֹת, "generations [birthings!]" in v. 18; הוֹלִיד, "to father, engender, cause birth" *(hiphil),* nine times in vv. 1–22.

[84] The NIV "lap" is fine in Prov 16:33, but here it unnecessarily creates an image of a seated Naomi. The phrase שִׂית בְּ-, "to place in," is equivalent to "to take, receive in."

[85] Assuming "nanny" to be an affectionate diminutive expression for Grandmother/Grandma.

[86] Contra Gerleman, *Ruth,* 37–38; L. Köhler, "Die Adoptionsform von Ruth 4,16," *ZAW* 29 (1909): 312–14.

[87] Cf. the expression אִישׁ חֵיק קָהּ, "husband of her bosom," in Deut 28:56.

"And the neighbors [i.e., women] called for him a name saying, 'A son has been born to Naomi,' and they called his name Obed." The narrator personalizes the event somewhat by designating these women *šĕkēnôt*, "neighbors" (NIV "the women living there"), rather than using a more generic expression like *hannāšîm*, "the women," in v. 14.[88] His comment does not mean that neither Ruth nor Boaz had a say in the naming of the child—such a notion would be ludicrous. This event must have involved the women affirming the name given to the child by his mother or father, but the narrator appropriately casts it in a literary form that has the "female chorus," as representatives of the community, celebrating his birth and declaring its significance.[89]

Second, the text is redundant. Twice the narrator notes that the neighbors "named" the boy.[90] The verse begins with "and they called for him ... a name saying," but then four words later reads "and they called his name Obed." Stylistically the formulas differ slightly ("for him a name" versus "his name"), but as it stands the literary effect is to invite the reader to associate the utterance following the first ("A son has been born to Naomi!") with the name "Obed." Even so the order of explanation + name reverses the normal biblical sequence of name + explanation. In keeping with the pattern elsewhere, one would have expected a much simpler "And they called his name Obed, saying, 'A son has been born to Naomi.' "[91] But the redundancy seems to signal a climactic moment in the narrative.

Third, the declaration, "A son has been born[92] to Naomi," has the conventional form of an ancient Near Eastern birth announcement. Biblical analogues are found in Isa 9:6[Hb. 5] and Jer 20:15, and an extrabiblical version appears in the *Aqhat* text from Ugarit.[93] In each case the announcement consists of a third masculine singular of the verb *yld*, "to give birth," in the passive stem, followed by *bn*, "a son," as the subject and introducing the benefactor with a preposition (*lĕ*, "to"): "A son has been born to X!" The form of the announcement has its origin in the familiar context of a father waiting outside a delivery room for word from the midwife of the safe arrival of a child. Because of this family's need for a *gōʾēl*, the fact that

---

[88] שְׁכֵנוֹת derives from שָׁכֵן, "to dwell," and refers to those who lived near Naomi.

[89] Contra Hubbard (*Ruth*, 11–12, 269) there is no need to ascribe some ad hoc meaning to the first form like "they proclaimed his significance." Others delete the first שֵׁם, resulting in "And they cried out." Cf. Rudolph, *Ruth*, 70.

[90] This is totally obscured by the NIV.

[91] Cf. Gen 3:20; 4:25; 29:32; Exod 2:10; etc.

[92] The verb *yullad* is pointed as a *pual* (or *hophal*) but carries the sense of a passive *qal*. Cf. GKC §53u; GBH §58a–c.

[93] *KTU* 1.17,I I.14–15 reads *kyld bn ly*. Cf. Parker, *Ugaritic Narrative Poetry*, 56; Hallo and Younger, eds., *Canonical Compositions*, 344.

this child is a boy will have heightened the excitement of the women and Naomi.[94]

Fourth, as already intimated, unlike other naming events, the name Obed is left unexplained. Any reader of Hebrew knows the name is a participle form of ʿābad, "to serve." Obed, "one who serves," is a hypocoristic (abbreviated version)[95] of "Obadiah," servant of Yahweh," a name held by no fewer than a dozen men in the Old Testament[96] and attested in numerous Hebrew seals,[97] or Abdiel, "servant of God."[98] By dropping the appellation for God, however, this name is rendered ambiguous. Is the boy viewed as a servant of God or as a servant of Naomi? If the former applies, then he represents an agent of God born to Naomi to take away the bitterness she accuses God of having imposed on her in 1:20–21 and to redeem the estate of her husband. If the latter applies, then his service to Naomi must be more direct. This son is her redeemer, the one who has come to serve her by restoring her life and offering her security in her old age.

(5) The Narrator's Conclusion (4:17c)

He was the father of Jesse, the father of David.

The story of Ruth ends on a surprising but climactic interpretive note. In the mind of the narrator, the historical significance of the birth of Obed does not lie in the resolution he brings to the personal crises of the characters in this book. Nor does he derive his significance from valorous deeds either of mercy or power. Neither the present narrator nor any other Old Testament author writes any stories about him. On the contrary, the birth of Obed has historical significance because he lives on and achieves his significance through the lives of his son Jesse and particularly his grandson David. Through David the blessing of the male witnesses to the court proceedings (4:11) is fulfilled; Boaz's name is "called out" in Bethlehem. And through David the prayer of the female witnesses to the birth of Obed is fulfilled; Obed's name is "called out" in Israel. Indeed, to this day their names and the names of Naomi and Ruth are "called out" all over the world as their story is read. In the providence of God the genuine piety of all the major characters is rewarded, and the divine plan for Israel and her kings is fulfilled.

---

[94] For excellent discussions of the form and function of these birth announcements see R. L. Hubbard, "Ruth IV:17: A New Solution," *VT* 38 (1988): 293–301; S. Parker, "The Birth Announcement," in *Ascribe to the Lord*, P. C. Craigie Festschrift, ed. L. Eslinger and G. Taylor, JSOTSup 67 (Sheffield: JSOT Press, 1988), 133–49.

[95] Five other characters in the OT bear this name. See K. A. Mathews, "Obed," *ABD* 5.5.

[96] See J. M. Kennedy, "Obadiah," *ABD* 5.1–2.

[97] See Fowler, *Theophoric Names,* 116, 353.

[98] 1 Chr 5:15. Names of this type involving the root ʿbd + divine name are common in other Semitic languages as well. See Layton, *Archaic Features of Canaanite Personal Names,* 130–31.

IV. EPILOGUE: THE GENEALOGY OF THE ROYAL LINE (4:18–22)

The Book of Ruth closes with a genealogical epilogue, some form of which probably existed independent of the story. In the ancient world genealogies represented an efficient and economical way of writing history. They tended to be of two types: (1) segmented genealogies that display ethnic relationships among families, clans, tribes, and even nations by showing descent from a common ancestor;[1] (2) linear genealogies that trace the line of descent from the first name entered to the last entry. The latter are usually intended to legitimate, that is, to establish the claims of the last person named to fulfill an official function.[2] The present genealogy obviously falls into the latter category.

[18]This, then, is the family line of Perez:
Perez was the father of Hezron,
[19]Hezron the father of Ram,
Ram the father of Amminadab,
[20]Amminadab the father of Nahshon,
Nahshon the father of Salmon,
[21]Salmon the father of Boaz,
Boaz the father of Obed,
[22]Obed the father of Jesse,
and Jesse the father of David.

4:18–22 The present genealogy is introduced formally with (more literally), "Now these are the generations of Perez." The formula is familiar from the Book of Genesis, where variations occur eleven times.[3] The material found in this linear genealogy is also found in 1 Chronicles 2 but in slightly different form and in the context of a segmented genealogy. Although these

---

[1] E.g., the Table of Nations in Genesis 10, on which see D. I. Block, "Table of Nations," *ISBE* (rev. ed.): 4.707-13.
[2] The genealogies in Ezra and Nehemiah are intended to answer the questions: Who is of royal descent? Who may serve as priest? Who is a true Israelite? For a superb survey of the issue and comparison of biblical and extrabiblical genealogies from the ANE see P. E. Satterthwaite, "Genealogy in the Old Testament," *NIDOTTE* 4.654-63.
[3] Gen 2:4; 5:1; 6:9; 10:1; 11:10,27; 25:12,19; 36:1,9; 37:2. Cf. also Num 3:1; 1 Chr 1:29.

two records agree both in the number and names of the specific links in the chain between Perez and David, the Chronicler's version is inconsistent in the formulas used to identify each generation. It is impossible to decide which author was original and whose record was derivative. They may indeed represent two separate adaptations of the same royal archival source.

The title of this list of names identifies the genre of the document: it is a *tôlĕdôt*. Derived from the verb *yālad*, "to give birth, beget," *tôlĕdôt* ("generations"; NIV "family line") is a plural noun that can also be rendered "genealogy." Read [in English] from left to right this genealogy traces the line of descent from Perez to David;[4] read from right to left it traces a line of ancestry from David back to Perez.[5] This genealogy identifies ten generations, each linked to the next by the identical formula: *A hôlîd B, B hôlîd C, C hôlîd D*, etc. Like *tôlĕdôt*, the verb *hôlîd*, "to father," derives from the verb *yālad*. The causative *(hiphil)* stem is used here, meaning "to cause to give birth, to engender."[6]

The individual entries need not detain us for long. The Old Testament contains no information (other than genealogical) on most of them. We have already commented on Perez, the head of this line of descent. However, in light of texts like Gen 49:8–10, which gives ancestral legitimacy to Judah's right to hold the scepter in Israel, it is remarkable that the author began with Perez rather than Judah, whom he knows to be the father of Perez (v. 12). The present point of reference may have been determined by the need to restrict this genealogy to ten generations[7] or the narrator's recognition of the levirate links between this story, which climaxes in the birth of Obed, and Genesis 38, which climaxes in the birth of Perez [and Zerah].

The name Hezron (Hb. *ḥeṣrôn*) is related to *ḥāṣēr*, "court, yard." The spelling *Hesrōm* (NIV, Hezron) in both Matt 1:3 and Luke 3:33 corrects the Greek Septuagint *(Esrōn)* in the direction of the Hebrew.[8] Ram, "exalted," is spelled *Arran* in the LXX and *Aram* in Matt 1:3-4 but *Arni* in Luke 3:33. Amminadab, "my father's brother is generous," is spelled *Aminadab* in Matt 1:4 and Luke 3:33, following the LXX. According to Exod 6:23, Amminadab was the father of Nahshon and Elisheba, Aaron's wife. Nahshon, "little snake," spelled *Naasson* in Matt 1:4 and Luke 3:32, after the LXX, was the brother-in-law of Aaron and a leading Judahite during the desert wanderings.[9] Salmon, "mantle?" is spelled *Salmah* and *Salma*ᵓ in 1 Chr 2:10-11.

---

[4] This is how Matthew presents the genealogy of Jesus in Matthew 1.

[5] This is how Luke presents the genealogy of Jesus in Luke 3.

[6] The NIV's stative rendering "A was the father of B" misses this nuance.

[7] Cf. Genesis 5,11.

[8] The interchange of *m* and *n* is evident in several other names as well: Gershom/Gershon; Zeytam/Zeytan.

[9] Num 1:7; 2:3; 7:12,17; 10:14.

Boaz and Obed have already been discussed. The meaning of Jesse *(yišay* in Hb.) is unknown. The name is spelled *Iessai* in the LXX and in the Gospels. The Old Testament narratives tell us little about Jesse, except for his role as the father of David (1 Sam 16:1-13). Some suggest that David, from a root meaning "paternal uncle" or "beloved," is a royal title, a throne name, rather than a personal name.[10] With the possible exception of Moses, David is without doubt the most important character in the Old Testament. He was the first legitimate king of Israel (from God's perspective) and preoccupies the authors of 1 and 2 Samuel, 1 and 2 Kings,[11] and 1 and 2 Chronicles, and was the composer of many psalms and the subject of many prophetic utterances. In fact, all the Messianic hopes of Israel are grounded in David and go back to Nathan's oracle, announcing the Davidic covenant, in 2 Samuel 7.[12] He represents the pinnacle of Old Testament history and the climax of Perez's genealogy.

All of this raises the question of the purpose of this genealogy in this context. The analogies presented by other linear genealogies in the Bible and from the ancient Near Eastern world suggest that since this is a linear genealogy, its function must be to legitimize the claims of the last member named to the rights and privileges of power he presently holds. This is a logical first response, except that elsewhere the claim is based on a genealogical link with the first entry in the list, who represents the founder of a critical position or office.[13] But as far as we know, Perez, with whom this genealogy begins, plays no significant role as a founder of any authoritative line, priestly or royal. Even more telling, if this had been the narrator's intention, his aims would have been better served by beginning with Judah, the father of Perez, to whom, under the inspiration of God, Jacob actually assigned the right to the throne in Israel (Gen 49:8-10).

On the other hand, the limits of this genealogy may have been determined by the previous references to Perez in v. 12 and to David in v. 17. By tracing the descent from Perez to David, the narrator may have intended this as a historical summary, filling in the gap between these two names and answering the reader's question, How did we get from there to here? But even if this genealogy provides a partial explanation of how the "house of Perez" was built, this is a minor issue.

---

[10] Remarkably, unlike many other royal names, no one else in the OT bears the name David. On David see D. M. Howard, Jr., "David," *ABD* 2.41-49.

[11] Forty-two of the 102 chapters (41 percent) of Samuel-Kings is devoted to the forty years of David's rule (9 percent of Israel's history).

[12] On David in history, tradition, and prophecy see R. P. Gordon, "David," *NIDOTTE* 4.505-12.

[13] The role of David as the founder of a significant royal lineage is reflected not only in the genealogy of Matthew 1 but also the repeated references to Jesus as "Son of David" in Matthew and elsewhere: Matt 1:1 (cf. v.20); 9:27; 12:23; 15:22; 20:30–31; 21:9,15; 22:45; etc.

The key to the purpose of the genealogy is found in the narrative to which it is attached. We have already noted that literarily the epilogue forms an expository conclusion answering to the expository opening in 1:1–5. But there is more to it than this. Throughout the book the narrator has deliberately cast the characters as stellar models of *ḥesed,* of deep and sincere devotion to God and to one another, expressed in self-sacrificial acts of kindness toward one another. Into the plot he has also carefully woven markings of the providential hand of God, rewarding who rewards authentic piety with his fullness and care. The birth of Obed symbolizes the convergence of these two themes: piety and providence. But the narrator is aware that in the providence of God the implications of a person's covenantal fidelity often extend far beyond the immediate story. In fact, the story of Naomi, Ruth, and Boaz does not end with the birth of Obed. It simply signals a significant turn in the history of this family and the history of Israel, down a course that leads directly to King David. The place of Boaz, who like Enoch in Genesis 5 represented the seventh of ten generations, may be portrayed diagrammatically as in the graph below. Significantly, although Boaz's role in the story is to redeem the line of Mahlon and to raise a son to carry on his name, Obed enters this line as a son of Boaz, not the son of Mahlon. Authentic lines of blood have won out over legal fiction.

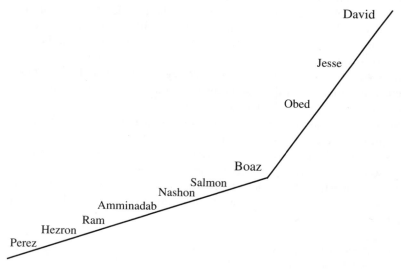

This book and this genealogy demonstrate that in the dark days of the judges the chosen line is preserved not by heroic exploits by deliverers or kings but by the good hand of God, who rewards good people with a fulness beyond all imagination. These characters could not know what long-range

fruit their compassionate and loyal conduct toward each other would bear.
But the narrator knows. With this genealogy he declares the faithfulness of
God in preserving the family that would bear the royal seed in troubled times
and in rewarding the genuine godliness of his people.[14] If only the rest of the
nation had demonstrated such covenant faithfulness at the same time! In this
genealogy the names of Boaz and Obed are indeed proclaimed far beyond
Bethlehem and Israel, to the ends of the earth.

But the narrator could not know what implications the piety of these characters would have on generations of his own people that would come after
him. If only he could have known that in the glorious providence of God the
hesed of Boaz, Ruth, and Naomi would have laid the groundwork for the history of salvation that extends far beyond his own time and place. For as the
genealogy of Matthew 1 indicates, one greater than David comes from the
loins of Boaz. In the dark days of the judges the foundation is laid for the
line that would produce the Savior, the Messiah, the Redeemer of a lost and
destitute humanity.

---

[14] Cf. J. A. Loader ("David and the Matriarch in the Book of Ruth," *In de Skriflig* 28 [1994]:
25-35) notes especially the motif of the matriarch as part of a royal theme. Israel's royal house is
not founded on "pure" descent but on solidarity and love.

Selected Bibliography

Bibliography for the Book of Judges

Commentaries

Auld, A. G. *Joshua, Judges, and Ruth*. DSB. Philadelphia: Westminster, 1984.

Boling, R. G. *Judges: A New Translation with Introduction and Commentary*. AB. Garden City: Doubleday, 1975.

Burney, C. F. *The Book of Judges with Introduction and Notes*. London: Rivingtons, 1918. Reprinted with Introduction by W. F. Albright, New York: Ktav, 1970.

Cundall, A. E., and L. Morris. *Judges and Ruth: An Introduction and Commentary*. TOTC Downers Grove: InterVarsity, 1968.

Goslinga, C. J. *Joshua, Judges, Ruth*. Trans. R. Togtman. BSC. Grand Rapids: Zondervan, 1986.

Gray, J. Joshua, *Judges and Ruth*. NCB. London: Thomas Nelson, 1967.

Hamlin, E. J. *At Risk in the Promised Land: A Commentary on the Book of Judges*. International Theological Commentary. Grand Rapids: Eerdmans, 1990.

Hertzberg, H. W. *Die Bucher Josua, Richter, Ruth*. ATD 9. Göttingen: Vandenhoeck & Ruprecht, 1969.

Wolf, H. "Judges." In The Expositor's Bible Commentary. F. E. Gaebelein, ed. Grand Rapids: Zondervan, 1992. 3.375–508.

Lindars, B. Judges 1–5: *A New Translation and Commentary*. A. D. H. Mayes, ed. Edinburgh: T. & T. Clark, 1995.

Moore, G. F. *A Critical and Exegetical Commentary on Judges*. 2nd ed. ICC. Edinburgh: T. & T. Clark, 1908.

Soggin, J. A. *Judges: A Commentary*. Trans. J. S. Bowden. OTL. Philadelphia: Westminster, 1981.

Webb, B. G. "Judges." *New Bible Commentary*. 21st Century ed. G. J. Wenham, et al, eds. Downers Grove: InterVarsity, 1994, 261–86.

Wilcock, M. *The Message of Judges*. BST. Downers Grove: InterVarsity, 1992.

Special Studies

Ahlström, G. W. *The History of Ancient Palestine from the Paleolithic Period to Alexander's Conquest*. JSOTSup 146. Sheffield: Sheffield Academic Press, 1993.

Albertz, R. *The History of Israelite Religion in the Old Testament Period*. 2 vols. Trans. J. Bowden Louisville: Westminster/John Knox, 1994.

Alt, A. "The Settlement of the Israelites in Palestine." In *Essays on Old Testament History and Religion*. Trans. R. A. Wilson. Garden City: Doubleday, 1968, 173–221.

Alter, R. *The Art of Biblical Narrative*. New York: Basic Books, 1981.

Amit, Y. "The Art of Composition in the Book of Judges." Ph.D. dissertation, Tel Aviv University, 1984.

Arnold, P. M. *Gibeah: The Search for a Biblical City in History and Tradition*. JSOT-

Sup 79. Sheffield: JSOT Press, 1990.

Bal, M. *Death & Dissymmetry: The Politics of Coherence in the Book of Judges.* Chicago Studies in the History of Judaism. Chicago: University of Chicago Press, 1988.

————, ed. *Anti-Covenant: Counter Reading Women's Lives in the Hebrew Bible.* JSOTSup 81/Bible and Literature Series 22. Sheffield: Almond, 1989.

————. *Murder and Difference: Gender, Genre, and Scholarship on Sisera's Death.* Indiana Studies in Biblical Literature. Trans. M. Gumpert Bloomington, IN: Indiana University Press, 1988.

Barrera, J. T. "Textual Variants in 4QJudga and the Textual and Editorial History of the Book of Judges 1." *RevQ* 14 (1989): 229–45.

Bartelmus, R. "Forschung am Richterbuch seit Martin Noth." *TRu* 56 (1991): 221–59.

Becker, U. *Richterzeit und Königtum: Redaktionsgeschichtliche Studien zum Richterbuch.* BZAW 192. Berlin/New York: de Gruyter, 1990.

Berlin, A. *Poetics and Interpretation of Biblical Narrative.* Bible and Literature Series 9. Sheffield: Almond Press, 1983.

Beyerlin, W. "Gattung und Herkunft des Rahmens im Richterbuch." *Tradition und Situation: Studien zur alttestamentlichen Prophetie. Festschrift A. Weiser.* E. Wurthwein and O. Kaiser, eds. Göttingen: Vandenhoeck & Ruprecht, 1963.

Block, D. I. *The Book of Ezekiel 1–24.* NICOT. Grand Rapids: Eerdmans, 1997.

————. *The Book of Ezekiel 25–48.* NICOT. Grand Rapids: Eerdmans, 1998.

————. *Foundations of National Identity: A Study in Ancient Northwest Semitic Perspectives.* Ann Arbor: University Microfilms, 1983.

————. "Deborah among the Judges: The Perspective of the Hebrew Historian." *Faith, Tradition, and History: Old Testament Historiography in Its Near Eastern Context.* A. R. Millard, et al, eds. Winona Lake: Eisenbrauns, 1994, 229–53.

————. "Echo Narrative Technique in Hebrew Literature: A Study in Judges 19." *WTJ* 52 (1990): 325–41.

————. "Empowered by the Spirit of God: The Holy Spirit in the Historiographic Writings of the Old Testament." *SBJT* 1 (1997): 42–61.

————. *The Gods of the Nations: Studies in Ancient Near Eastern National Theology.* ETSMS 2. Winona Lake: Eisenbrauns, 1988.

————. "'Israel'–'Sons of Israel': A Study in Hebrew Eponymic Usage." *Studies in Religion* 13 (1984): 301–26.

————. "The Period of the Judges: Religious Disintegration Under Tribal Rule." In *Israel's Apostasy and Restoration: Essays in Honor of Roland K. Harrison.* A. Gileadi, ed. Grand Rapids: Baker, 1988, 39–58.

————. "The Prophet of the Spirit: The Use of *rwh* in the Book of Ezekiel." *JETS* 32 (1989): 33–34.

————. "Will the Real Gideon Please Stand Up? Narrative Style and Intention in Judges 6–9." *JETS* 40 (1997): 359–60.

Bodine, W. R. *The Greek Text of Judges: Recensional Developments.* HSM 23. Chico: Scholars Press, 1980.

Brenner, A. ed. *A Feminist Companion to Judges.* FCB 4. Sheffield: JSOT Press, 1993.

Brettler, M. "The Book of Judges: Literature as Politics." *JBL* 108 (1989): 395–418.

Chalcraft, D. F. "Deviance and Legitimate Action in the Book of Judges." *The Bible in Three Dimensions: Essays in Celebration of Forty Years of Biblical Studies in the*

University of Sheffield. D. J. A. Clines, et al, eds. JSOTSup 87. Sheffield: Academic Press, 1990, 177–201.

Clark, R. E. D. "The Large Numbers of the Old Testament." *JTVI* 87 (1955): 82–90.

Crenshaw, J. L. *Samson: A Secret Betrayed, a Vow Ignored.* Atlanta: John Knox, 1978.

Cundall, A. E. "Judges—An Apology for the Monarchy?" *ExpTim* 81 (1970): 178–81.

Dietrich, W. *Prophetie und Geschichte: eine redaktionsgeschichtliche Untersuchung zum deuteronomistischen Geschichtswerk.* FRLANT 108. Göttingen: Vandenhoeck & Ruprecht, 1977.

Dumbrell, W. J. "'In those days there was no king in Israel; every man did that which was right in his own eyes.' The Purpose of the Book of Judges Reconsidered." *JSOT* 25 (1983): 23–33.

Exum, J. C. "The Centre Cannot Hold: Thematic and Textual Instabilities in the Book of Judges." *CBQ* 52 (1990): 410–31.

Fleming, D. E. "The Etymological Origins of the Hebrew *nabîʾ* : The One Who Invokes God." *CBQ* 55 (1993): 217–24.

Fouts, D. M. "A Defense of the Hyperbolic Interpretation of Large Numbers in the Old Testament." *JETS* 40 (1997): 377–88.

Garsiel, B. *Biblical Names: A Literary Study of Midrashic Derivations and Puns.* Trans. P. Hackett. Ramat-Gan: Bar-Ilan University, 1991.

Gerbrandt, G. E. *Kingship According to the Deuteronomistic History.* SBLDS 87 Atlanta: Scholars Press, 1986.

Gottwald, N. K. *The Tribes of Yahweh: A Sociology of the Religion of Liberated Israel, 1250–1050 B.C.E.* Maryknoll: Orbis, 1979.

Gros Louis, K. R. R. "The Book of Judges." *Literary Interpretations of Biblical Narratives.* Edited by K. R. R. Gros Louis et al. Nashville: Abingdon, 1974, 141–62.

Halpern, B. *The Emergence of Israel in Canaan.* SBLMS 29. Chico: Scholars Press, 1983.

———. *The First Historians: The Hebrew Bible and History.* San Francisco: Harper & Row, 1988.

Hauser, A. J. "The 'Minor Judges'—A Re-Evaluation." *JBL* 94 (1975): 190–200.

Hertzberg, H. W. "Die Kleinen Richter." *TLZ* 79 (1954): 285–90 (= *Beitrage zur Traditionsgeschichte and Theologie des Alten Testaments.* Göttingen: Vandenhoeck & Ruprecht, 1962, 118–25.

Howard, D. M. Jr. *An Introduction to the Old Testament Historical Books.* Chicago: Moody, 1993.

Kaufmann, Y. *The Biblical Account of the Conquest of Canaan.* 2nd ed. With preface by M. Greenberg. Jerusalem: Magnes, 1985.

Keel, O. and C. Uehlinger, *Gods, Goddesses and Images of God in Ancient Israel.* Trans. T. Trapp. Minneapolis: Fortress, 1998.

Klein, L. R. "The Book of Judges: Paradigm and Deviation in Images of Women." In *A Feminist Companion to Judges.* FCB 4. A. Brenner, ed. Sheffield: Academic Press, 1993, 55–60.

———. "A Spectrum of Female Characters in the Book of Judges." In *A Feminist Companion to Judges.* FCB 4. A. Brenner, ed. Sheffield: Academic Press, 1993, 24–33.

———. *The Triumph of Irony in the Book of Judges.* JSOTSup 68. Sheffield: Almond

Press, 1987.

Lemche, N. P. *Early Israel: Anthropological and Historical Studies on the Israelite Society Before the Monarchy.* VTSup 37. Leiden: E. J. Brill, 1985.

———. *The Canaanites and Their Land: The Tradition of the Canaanites.* JSOTSup 110. Sheffield: JSOT Press, 1991.

Lilley, J. P. U. "A Literary Appreciation of the Book of Judges." *TynBul* 18 (1976): 94–102.

Malamat, A. "Charismatic Leadership in the Book of Judges." *Magnalia Dei: The Mighty Acts of God: Essays on the Bible and Archaeology in Memory of G. Ernest Wright.* Edited by F. M. Cross et al. Garden City: Doubleday, 1976, 152–68.

Malamat, A. "The Egyptian Decline in Canaan and the Sea Peoples." In *Judges.* Vol. 3 of *The World History of the Jewish People.* Edited by B. Mazar. Tel-Aviv: Massada, 1971.

Malamat, A. "The Period of the Judges." In *A History of the Jewish People.* Edited by H. H. Ben-Sasson. Cambridge, Mass.: Harvard University Press, 67–87.

———. "Judges." In *Judges.* Vol. 3 of *The World History of the Jewish People.* Edited by B. Mazar. Tel-Aviv: Massada, 1971.

Mazar, B., ed. *Judges.* Vol. 3 of *The World History of the Jewish People.* Tel-Aviv: Massada, 1971.

McKenzie, S. L. and M. P. Graham, eds. *The History of Israel's Traditions: The Heritage of Martin Noth.* JSOTSup 182. Sheffield: JSOT Press, 1994.

Mendenhall, G. "The Hebrew Conquest of Canaan." *Biblical Archaeologist Reader 3.* Edited by E. F. Campbell, Jr., and D. N. Freedman. Garden City: Doubleday, 1970, 100–120.

Merrill, E. G. *Kingdom of Priests: A History of Old Testament Israel.* Grand Rapids: Baker, 1987.

Millard, A. R. "Story, History, and Theology." In *Faith, Tradition, and History: Old Testament Historiography in Its Near Eastern Context.* Edited by A. R. Millard et al. Winona Lake: Eisenbrauns, 1994, 37–64.

Mullen, E. T. "The 'Minor Judges': Some Literary and Historical Considerations." *CBQ* 44 (1982): 185–201.

Nelson, R. D. *The Double Redaction of the Deuteronomistic History.* JSOTSup 18. Sheffield: JSOT Press, 1981.

Noth, M. *The Deuteronomistic History.* Translated by D. Orton. JSOTSup 15. Sheffield: JSOT Press, 1981, 43–52. Translation of Überlieferungsgeschichtliche Studien, 2d ed. Tübingen: Max Niemeyer, 1957.

O'Brien, M. A. "Judges and the Deuteronomistic History." In *The History of Israel's Traditions: The Heritage of Martin Noth.* JSOTSup 182. Sheffield: JSOT Press, 1994, 235–59;

O'Connell, R. H. *The Rhetoric of the Book of Judges.* VTSup 63. Leiden: Brill, 1996.

Polzin, R. *Moses and the Deuteronomist: A Literary Study of the Deuteronomic History. Part I, Deuteronomy, Joshua, Judges.* New York: Seabury, 1980.

Radday, Y. T., G. Leb, D. Wickmann, and S. Talmon. "The Book of Judges Examined by Statistical Linguistics." *Bib* 58 (1977): 469–99.

Richter, W. *Die Bearbeitungen des "Retterbuches" in der deuteronomischen Epoche.* BBB 21. Bonn: P. Hanstein, 1964.

———. *Traditionsgeschichtliche Untersuchungen zum Richterbuch.* BBB 18. Bonn:

P. Hanstein, 1966.

Rosel, H. N. "Die 'Richter Israels.' Rückblich und neuer Ansatz." *BZ* 25 (1981): 180–203.

Saldarini, A. J. *Targum Jonathan of the Former Prophets: Introduction, Translation and Notes.* The Aramaic Bible 10. Wilmington: Michael Glazier, 1987.

Schley, D. G. *Shiloh: A Biblical City in Tradition and History.* JSOTSup 63. Sheffield: JSOT Press, 1989.

Simpson, C. A. *The Composition of the Book of Judges.* Oxford: Basil Blackwell, 1957.

Smend, R. "Das Gesetz und die Völker: Ein Beitrag zur deuteronomistischen Redaktionsgeschichte." *Probleme biblischer Theologie: Gerhard von Rad zum 70. Geburtstag.* H. W. Wolff, ed. Munchen: Chr. Kaiser, 1971, 494–509.

Soggin, J. A. "Das Amt der 'Kleinen Richter' in Israel." *VT* 30 (1980): 245–48.

Sternberg, M. *The Poetics of Biblical Narrative: Ideological Literature and the Drama of Reading.* Bloomington: Indiana University Press, 1985.

Toorn, K. van der, et al, eds. *Dictionary of Deities and Demons in the Bible.* Leiden: Brill, 1995.

———. *Family Religion in Babylonia, Syria and Israel: Continuity and Change in the Forms of Religious Life.* SHCANE 7. Leiden: Brill, 1996.

Trible, P. *Texts of Terror: Literary-Feminist Readings of Biblical Narratives.* OBT. Philadelphia: Fortress, 1984.

Vaux, R. de. *The Early History of Israel.* Translated by D. Smith. Philadelphia: Westminster, 1978.

Veijola, T. *Das Königtum in der Beurteilung der deuteronomistischen Historiographie: Eine redaktionsgeschichtliche Untersuchung.* AASF Series B 193. Helsinki: Suomalainen Tiedeakatemia, 1977.

Washburn, D. L. "The Chronology of Judges: Another Look." *BibSac* 147 (1990): 414–25.

Webb, B. G. *The Book of Judges: An Integrated Reading.* JSOTSup 46. Sheffield: JSOT Press, 1987.

Weber, M. *Gesammelte Aufsätze zur Religionstheologie. Vol. III, Das antike Judentum.* Tübingen: Mohr, 1921.

Wenham, J. W. "Large Numbers in the Old Testament." *TynBul* 18 (1967): 19–53.

Williams, J. G. "The Structure of Judges 2:6–16:31." *JSOT* 49 (1991): 77–85.

Wood, L. J. *Distressing Days of the Judges.* Grand Rapids: Zondervan, 1975.

Yee, G., ed. *Judges and Method: New Approaches in Biblical Studies.* Minneapolis: Fortress, 1995.

Bibliography for the Book of Ruth

Commentaries

Atkinson, D. *The Message of Ruth.* The Bible Speaks Today. Downers Grove: InterVarsity, 1985.

Baldwin, J. "Ruth." New Bible Commentary. 4th ed. Downers Grove: InterVarsity, 1994, pp. 287–95.

Bertholet, A. *Das Buch Ruth.* KHAT 17. Tübingen: Mohr, 1989.

Bush, F. W. *Ruth, Esther.* WBC 9. Dallas: Word, 1996.

Campbell, E. F. *Ruth: A New Translation with Introduction, Notes, and Commentary.*

AB 7. Garden City: Doubleday, 1975.

Frevel, C. *Das Buch Ruth*. Neuer Stuttgarter Kommentar: Altes Testament. Stuttgart: 1992.

Gerleman, G. *Ruth: Das Hohelied*. BKAT 18. Neukirchen-Vluyn: Neukirchener, 1965.

Goslinga, C. J. *Joshua, Judges, Ruth*. BSC. Grand Rapids: Zondervan, 1986.

Gray, J. *Joshua, Judges, and Ruth*. NCBC. Grand Rapids: Eerdmans, 1986.

Hertzberg, H. W. *Die Bücher Josua, Richter, Ruth*. ATD 9. 2d ed. Göttingen: Vandenhoeck & Ruprecht, 1959.

Hubbard, R. L. *The Book of Ruth*. NICOT. Grand Rapids: Eerdmans, 1988.

Joüon, P. P. *Ruth: Commentaire philologique et exegetique*. 1924. Reprint, Rome: Pontifical Biblical Institute, 1953.

Keil, C. F. *Joshua, Judges, Ruth: Biblical Commentary on the Old Testament*. Translated by J. Martin. Grand Rapids: Eerdmans, 1950.

Morris, L. *Ruth: An Introduction and Commentary*. TOTC. Downers Grove: InterVarsity, 1968.

Nielsen, K. *Ruth: A Commentary*. OTL. Louisville: Westminster/John Knox, 1997.

Rudolph, W. *Das Buch Ruth, Das Hohe Lied, Die Klegelieder*. KT 17. Gütersloh: Gerd Mohn, 1962.

Sasson, J. M. *Ruth: A New Translation with a Philological Commentary and a Formalist-Folklorist Interpretation*. 2d ed. Sheffield: Academic Press, 1989.

Zenger, E. *Das Buch Ruth*. Zürcher Bibelkommentar, Altes Testament 8. Zurich: Theologischer Verlag, 1986.

Special Studies

Anderson, A. A. "The Marriage of Ruth." *JSS* 23 (1978): 171–83.

Bal, M. "Heroism and Proper Names, or the Fruits of Analogy." In *A Feminist Companion to Ruth*. Edited by A. Brenner. Sheffield: Academic Press, 1993, pp. 42–69.

Bauckman, R. "The Book of Ruth and the Possibility of a Canonical Hermeneutic." *Biblical Interpretation* 5 (1997): 29–45.

Beattie, D. R. G. *The Targum of Ruth*. Aramaic Targum 19. Collegeville, Minn.: Liturgical Press, 1994.

Berlin, A. *Poetics and Interpretation of Biblical Narrative*. Sheffield: Almond, 1983.

Bledstein, A. J. "Female Companionships: If the Book of Ruth Were Written by a Woman ..." In *A Feminist Companion to Ruth*. Edited by A. Brenner. Sheffield: Academic Press, 1993, pp. 116–35.

———. "Naomi and Ruth: Further Reflections." In *A Feminist Companion to Ruth*. Edited by A. Brenner. Sheffield: Academic Press, 1993, pp. 140–45.

Block, D. I. *Ezekiel 1–24*. NICOT. Grand Rapids: Eerdmans, 1997.

———. *Ezekiel 25–48*. NICOT. Grand Rapids: Eerdmans, 1998.

———. *The Foundations of National Identity: A Study in Ancient Northwest Semitic Perceptions*. Ann Arbor: University Microfilms, 1983.

———. *The Gods of the Nations: Studies in Ancient Near Eastern National Theology*. 2d ed. Grand Rapids: Baker, 1999.

Brenner, A. ed. *A Feminist Companion to Ruth*. Sheffield: Academic Press, 1993.

———. "Naomi and Ruth." In *A Feminist Companion to Ruth*. Sheffield: Academic Press, 1993.

————. "Naomi and Ruth: Further Reflections." In *A Feminist Companion to Ruth*. Sheffield: Academic Press, 1993.

Bruppacher, H. "Die Bedeutung des Names Ruth." *TZ* 22 (1966): 12–18.

Carasik, M. "Ruth 2, 7: Why the Overseer Was Embarrassed." *ZAW* 107 (1995): 493–94.

Collins, C. J. "Ambiguity and Theology in Ruth 1:21 and 2:20." *Presbyterion* 10 (1993): 97–102.

Feely-Harnik, G. "Naomi and Ruth: Building Up the House of David." In *Text and Tradition: The Hebrew Bible and Folklore*. Edited by S. Niditch. Atlanta: Scholars Press, 1990, pp. 163–84.

Fensham, F. C. "Widow, Orphan and the Poor in Ancient Near Eastern Legal and Wisdom Literature." *JNES* 21 (1962): 129–39.

Fewell, D. N. and D. M. Gunn. *Compromising Redemption: Relating Characters in the Book of Ruth*. Louisville: Westminster/John Knox, 1990.

————. "'A Son Is Born to Naomi!:' Literary Allusions and Interpretation in the Book of Ruth." *JSOT* 40 (1988): 99–108.

Glueck, N. *Hesed in the Bible*. 2d ed. Translated by A. Gottschalk. Cincinnati: Hebrew Union College, 1967.

Gow, M. D. *The Book of Ruth: Its Structure, Theme and Purpose*. Leicester: Apollos, 1992.

Grant, R. "Literary Structure in the Book of Ruth." *BibSac* 148 (1991): 424–41.

Green, B. "The Plot of the Biblical Story of Ruth." *JSOT* 23 (1982): 55–68.

Gunkel, H. "Ruth." In *Reden und Aufsätze*. Göttingen: Vandenhoeck & Ruprecht, 1913, pp. 69–92.

Hals, R. *The Theology of the Book of Ruth*. Philadelphia: Fortress, 1969.

Hiebert, P. S. "'Whence Shall Help Come to Me?' The Biblical Widow." In *Gender and Difference in Ancient Israel*. Edited by P. L. Day. Minneapolis: Fortress, 1989, pp. 125–41.

Hubbard, R. L. "The gōʾēl of Ancient Israel: The Theology of an Israelite Institution." *BBR* 1 (1991): 3–19.

————. "Ruth IV:17: A New Solution." *VT* 38 (1988): 293–301.

Humbert, P. "Art et leçon de l'histoire de Ruth." *RTP* 26 (1938): 257–86.

————. "En marge du dictionnaire hébraïque." *ZAW* 62 (1949–50): 199–207.

Hunter, A. G. "How Many Gods Had Ruth?" *SJT* 34 (1981): 427–36.

Hurvitz, A. "On 'Drawing the Sandal' in the Book of Ruth." *Shnaton* 1 (1975): 45–59 [Hebrew].

Hyman, R. T. "Questions and Changing Identity in the Book of Ruth." *USQR* 39 (1984): 189–201.

Knauf, E. A. "Ruth la Moabite." *VT* 44 (1994): 547–48.

Köhler, L. "Die Adoptionsform von Ruth 4,16." *ZAW* 29 (1909): 312–14.

Kruger, P. A. "The Hem of the Garment in Marriage: The Meaning of the Symbolic Gesture in Ruth 3:9 and Ezek 16:8." *JNWSL* 12 (1984): 79–86.

Labuschagne, C. J. "The Crux in Ruth 4:12." *ZAW* 79 (1967): 364–67.

Lacocque, A. "Date et milieu du livre de Ruth." *RHPR* 59 (1975): 583–93.

Leggett, D. *The Levirate and Goel Institutions in the Old Testament with Special Attention to the Book of Ruth*. Cherry Hill: Mack, 1974.

Loader, J. A. "David and the Matriarch in the Book of Ruth." In *de Skriflig* 28 (1994): 25–35.

————. "Job's Sister: Undermining an Unnatural Religiosity." *OTE* 6 (1993): 312-29.

————. "Ruth 2:7—An Old Crux." *Journal for Semitics* 4 (1992): 151–59.

————. "Of Barley, Bulls, Land, and Levirate." In *Studies in Deuteronomy in Ho nour of S. J. Labuschagne on the Occasion of His 65th Birthday*. VTSup 53. Nev York/Leiden: Brill, 1994, pp. 123–38.

Lys, D. "Résidence ou repos? Notule sur Ruth ii7." *VT* 21 (1971): 497–99.

Merrill, E. H. "The Book of Ruth: Narration and Shared Themes." *BSac* 142 (1985) 130–41.

Meyers, C. "Returning Home: Ruth 1.8 and the Gendering of the Book of Ruth." In *Feminist Companion to Ruth*. Edited by A. Brenner. Sheffield: Academic Press 1993, pp. 85–114.

Milne, P. "Folktales and Fairy Tales: An Evaluation of Two Proppian Analyses c Biblical Narratives." *JSOT* 34 (1986): 35–60.

Myers, J. M. *The Linguistic and Literary Form of the Book of Ruth*. Leiden: Brill 1955.

Nash, P. T. "Ruth: An Exercise in Israelite Political Correctness or a Call to Prope Conversion?" In *The Pitcher Is Broken: Memorial Essays for Gösta W. Ahlström* Edited by S. W. Holloway and L. K. Handy. JSOTSup 190. Sheffield: JSO Press, 1995, pp. 347–54.

Neusner, J. *Ruth Rabbah: An Analytical Translation*. Brown Judaic Studies 183. At lanta: Scholars Press, 1989.

Parker, S. "The Marriage Blessing in Israel and Ugaritic Literature." *JBL* 95 (1976) 23–30.

Prinsloo, W. "The Function of Ruth in the Book of Ruth." *OTWSA* 21 (1978): 114-15.

Rauber, D. F. "Literary Values in the Bible: The Book of Ruth." *JBL* 89 (1970): 27-37.

Rofé, A. "Ruth 4:11 LXX: A Midrashic Dramatization." In *Text, Temples, and Tradi tion: A Tribute to Menahem Haran*. Winona Lake: Eisenbrauns, 1996, pp. 119-24 (Hebrew).

Sakenfeld, K. *The Meaning of* Hesed *in the Hebrew Bible: A New Inquiry*. HSM 17 Missoula: Scholars Press, 1978.

————. *Faithfulness in Action: Loyalty in Biblical Perspective*. Philadelphia: For tress, 1985.

Thompson, M. E. "New Life Amid Alien Corn: The Book of Ruth." *EvQ* (1993) 197–210.

Trible, P. *God and the Rhetoric of Sexuality*. Philadelphia: Fortress, 1978.

de Waard, J. and E. A. Nida. *A Translator's Handbook on the Book of Ruth*. 2d ed New York: United Bible Societies, 1992.

Westbrook, R. "The Law of the Biblical Levirate." *Revue Internationale des Droit de l'Antiquité*. 3d Series 24 (1977): 65–87.

————. *Property and the Family in Biblical Law*. JSOTSup 193. Sheffield: Academ ic Press, 1991.

Wolde, E. Van. "Texts in Dialogue with Texts: Intertextuality in the Ruth and Tama Narratives." *Biblical Interpretation* 5 (1997): 1–28.

Selected Subject Index

Person Index

Selected Scripture Index

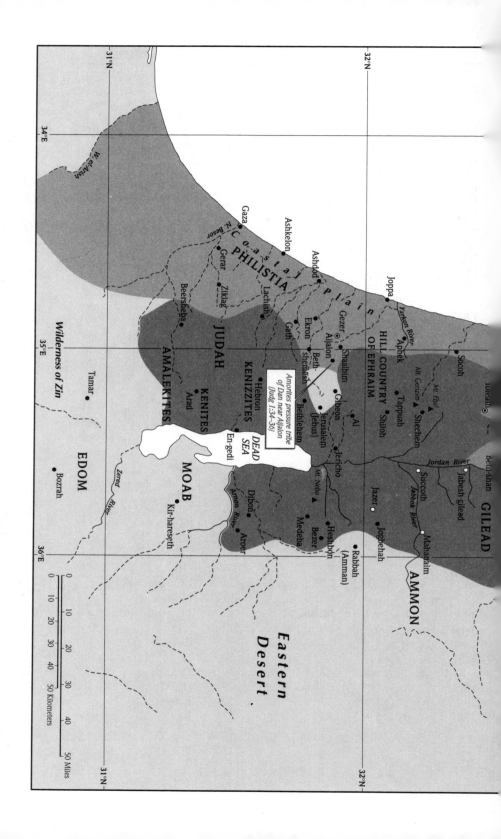

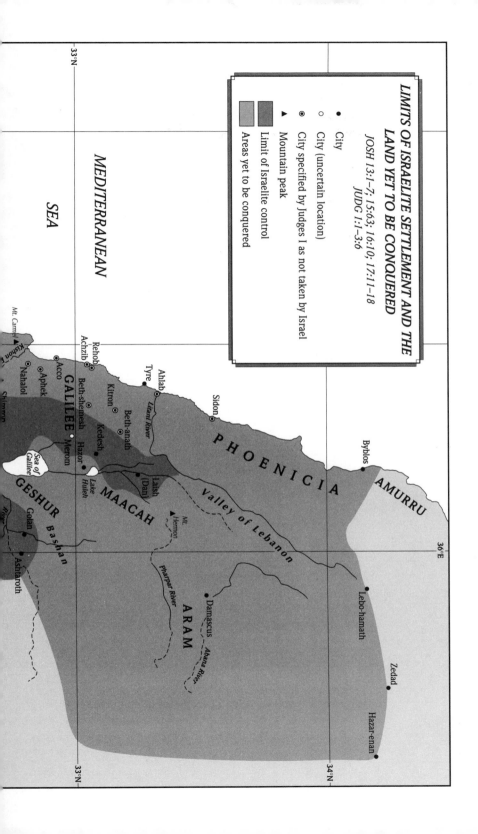

LIMITS OF ISRAELITE SETTLEMENT AND THE LAND YET TO BE CONQUERED

JOSH 13:1–7; 15:63; 16:10; 17:11–18
JUDG 1:1–3:6

- ● City
- ○ City (uncertain location)
- ◉ City specified by Judges 1 as not taken by Israel
- ▲ Mountain peak
- Limit of Israelite control
- Areas yet to be conquered